FAMILY LAW

FAMILY LAW

Third Edition

LESLIE JOAN HARRIS
Dorothy Kliks Fones Professor of Law
University of Oregon

LEE E. TEITELBAUM
the late Hugh B. Brown Professor of Law
University of Utah

JUNE CARBONE
Presidential Professor of Ethics and the
Common Good and Professor of Law
Santa Clara University

ASPEN

PUBLISHERS

111 Eighth Avenue, New York, NY 10011
www.aspenpublishers.com

© 2005 Aspen Publishers, Inc.
A Wolters Kluwer Company
www.aspenpublishers.com

Printed in the United States of America.

3 4 5 6 7 8 9 0

ISBN 0-7355-4029-2

Library of Congress Cataloging-in-Publication Data

Harris, Leslie J., 1952-
  Family law / [Leslie J. Harris, June Carbone, Hugh Brown].—3rd ed.
    p. cm.
  ISBN 0-7355-4029-2   (alk. paper)
  1. Domestic relations—United States—Cases.   I. Carbone, June.
II. Brown, Hugh, 1941-   III. Title.

KF504.H33 2005
346.7301'5—dc22

2005002547

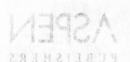

About Aspen Publishers

Aspen Publishers, headquartered in New York City, is a leading information provider for attorneys, business professionals, and law students. Written by preeminent authorities, our products consist of analytical and practical information covering both U.S. and international topics. We publish in the full range of formats, including updated manuals, books, periodicals, CDs, and online products.

Our proprietary content is complemented by 2,500 legal databases, containing over 11 million documents, available through our Loislaw division. Aspen Publishers also offers a wide range of topical legal and business databases linked to Loislaw's primary material. Our mission is to provide accurate, timely, and authoritative content in easily accessible formats, supported by unmatched customer care.

To order any Aspen Publishers title, go to *www.aspenpublishers.com* or call 1-800-638-8437.

To reinstate your manual update service, call 1-800-638-8437.

For more information on Loislaw products, go to *www.loislaw.com* or call 1-800-364-2512.

For Customer Care issues, e-mail *CustomerCare@aspenpublishers.com*; call 1-800-234-1660; or fax 1-800-901-9075.

Aspen Publishers
A Wolters Kluwer Company

For Lee

L.J.H. and J.C.

Summary of Contents

Contents		*xi*
Preface		*xxix*
Acknowledgments		*xxxi*

I MARRIAGE AND ITS ALTERNATIVES

Chapter 1.	When Are Adult Partners a Family?	3
Chapter 2.	The Importance of Being a Family	31
Chapter 3.	Entering Ceremonial Marriage	155
Chapter 4.	Alternatives to Ceremonial Marriage	229

II FAMILY DISSOLUTION

Chapter 5.	Divorce Grounds and Procedures	287
Chapter 6.	Property Division and Spousal Support	387
Chapter 7.	Parent-Child Support Duties	501
Chapter 8.	Modification, Termination, Enforcement, and Tax and Bankruptcy Treatment of Orders	549
Chapter 9.	Child Custody	621
Chapter 10.	Family Contracts	725
Chapter 11.	Jurisdiction	769

III CHILDREN, PARENTS, AND THE STATE

Chapter 12.	Determining Legal Parenthood: Marriage, Biology, and Function	839
Chapter 13.	Adoption and Alternative Reproductive Technologies	943

Table of Cases		*1011*
Index		*1021*

Contents

Preface   *xxix*
Acknowledgments   *xxxi*

I MARRIAGE AND ITS ALTERNATIVES

Chapter 1. When Are Adult Partners a Family?   3
    Regan, Calibrated Commitment: The Legal
      Treatment of Marriage and Cohabitation   3
    Fineman, Why Marriage?   6
    Wardle, The Bonds of Matrimony and
      the Bonds of Constitutional Democracy   7
    Foster, The Family Paradigm of
      Inheritance Law   10
    Hewitt v. Hewitt   10
    NOTES AND QUESTIONS   12
    Braschi v. Stahl Associates Company   13
    NOTES AND QUESTIONS   17
    City of Ladue v. Horn   18
    NOTES AND QUESTIONS   22
    Borough of Glassboro v. Vallorosi   25
    NOTES AND QUESTIONS   30
Chapter 2. The Importance of Being a Family   31
  A. Introduction   31
  B. Marital Property   34
    1. Ownership and Control of Wealth   35
      a. The Common Law Tradition   35
        PROBLEM   39
        Murdoch v. Murdoch   40
        NOTES AND QUESTIONS   42
        PROBLEMS   43
      b. The Estate by the Entirety   44
        NOTES AND QUESTIONS   46
        PROBLEMS   47
      c. Community Property   47
        Oldham, Management of the Community
        Estate During an Intact Marriage   50

2. "New" Property   51
   Boggs v. Boggs   53
   NOTES AND QUESTIONS   59
   PROBLEM   63
3. The Daily Management and Control of
   Marital Wealth   63
   McGuire v. McGuire   63
   *Glendon, Power and Authority in the
     Family: New Legal Patterns as Reflections
     of Changing Ideologies*   67
   Teitelbaum, Family History and Family Law   68
   Hafen, The Family as an Entity   70
   *Teitelbaum, The Family as a System:
     A Preliminary Sketch*   70
   Galbraith, Economics and the Public Purpose   74
   *Oldham, Management of the Community
     Estate During an Intact Marriage*   76
   Sharpe Furniture, Inc. v. Buckstaff   77
   NOTES AND QUESTIONS   81
   Note: "Necessaries" and "New
     Property"   82
   NOTES AND QUESTIONS   85
4. Constitutional Limits on Gender-Based
   Classifications   85
   PROBLEM   85
   a. Relevant Statutes   86
   b. Materials Regarding Domicile   87
   c. Additional Materials Concerning
       Liability for Necessaries   87
   d. Empirical Data   89
   e. Constitutional Decisions   89
5. Spousal Contracts During Marriage   98
   Borelli v. Brusseau   98
   NOTES AND QUESTIONS   103
   PROBLEMS   106
   Pacelli v. Pacelli   107
   NOTES AND QUESTIONS   112
C. Violence Between Spouses   113
1. Crimes Between Spouses   114
   People v. Liberta   114
   NOTES AND QUESTIONS   117
2. Police Response to Domestic Violence
   Calls   118
   PROBLEM   118
   a. Constitutional Decisions   119
   b. Fourth Amendment Limits   122
   c. Historical and Social Background   123

		Pleck, Domestic Tyranny: The Making of Social Policy Against Family Violence from Colonial Times to the Present	123
		Fagan & Browne, Violence Between Spouses and Intimates: Physical Aggression Between Women and Men in Intimate Relationships	124
		Gelles & Straus, Intimate Violence	126
		Fagan & Browne, Violence Between Spouses and Intimates: Physical Aggression Between Women and Men in Intimate Relationships	128
		Maxwell, Garner & Fagan, The Effects of Arrest on Intimate Partner Violence: New Evidence from the Spouse Assault Replication Program	130
	3.	Legal Alternatives: Criminal Prosecution and Protective Orders	131
		Note: Federal Legislation	136
	4.	Spousal Tort Liability	137
		Burns v. Burns	137
		Hill v. Hill	138
		NOTES AND QUESTIONS	139
		PROBLEMS	140
D.	Reproductive Choice Within the Family		140
	1.	Reproductive Rights and Interests	140
	2.	Reproductive Choice Within the Family	143
		Planned Parenthood of Central Missouri v. Danforth	143
		NOTES AND QUESTIONS	145
		Planned Parenthood of Southeastern Pennsylvania v. Casey	145
		NOTES AND QUESTIONS	147
		PROBLEM	148
E.	Medical Decision Making About Family Members		149
		Cruzan v. Director, Missouri Department of Health	149
		NOTES AND QUESTIONS	153
Chapter 3.	Entering Ceremonial Marriage		155
A.	Introduction		155
B.	Formalities		156
		Uniform Marriage and Divorce Act	156
		NOTES AND QUESTIONS	156
		Note: "Void" and "Voidable" Marriages	157
C.	The Agreement to Marry		158
	1.	The Content of the Agreement	158
		Lutwak v. United States	158

            NOTES AND QUESTIONS   162
            PROBLEMS   164
     2.   Capacity to Agree   165
            Edmunds v. Edwards   165
            NOTES AND QUESTIONS   168
     3.   Fraud and Duress   171
            Wolfe v. Wolfe   171
            NOTES AND QUESTIONS   173
            PROBLEMS   174
            Note: Names   175
  D. Substantive Restrictions on Marrying   176
     1.   The Constitutional Framework   176
            Zablocki v. Redhail   176
            NOTES AND QUESTIONS   182
            PROBLEMS   184
     2.   Particular Restrictions   184
        a. Monogamy   184
            Potter v. Murray City   184
            NOTES AND QUESTIONS   186
        b. Relationship   191
            State v. Sharon H.   191
            NOTES AND QUESTIONS   192
            PROBLEMS   194
        c. Different Sexes   195
            Goodridge v. Department of Public Health   195
            Opinions of the Justices to the Senate   205
            NOTES AND QUESTIONS   206
            Note: International Developments
              in Same-Sex Marriage   211
            Note: Developments in Transsexual
              Marriage   214
        d. Age   215
            In re Barbara Haven   215
            NOTES AND QUESTIONS   217
  E. Conflict of Laws   218
            In re May's Estate   218
            NOTES AND QUESTIONS   220
            The Defense of Marriage Act   223
            *Kramer, Same-Sex Marriage, Conflict
              of Laws, and the Unconstitutional
              Public Policy Exception*   223
            NOTES AND QUESTIONS   225
            PROBLEM   227
Chapter 4. Alternatives to Ceremonial Marriage   229
  A. Introduction   229
            *Forste, Prelude to Marriage or
              Alternative to Marriage?*   229

Glendon, *Marriage and the State:*
The Withering Away of Marriage 230
B. Common Law Marriage, Presumptions
of Marriage, and Putative Spouses 231
1. Common Law Marriage 232
Grossberg, *Governing the Hearth* 232
In re Marriage of Winegard 233
NOTES AND QUESTIONS 237
PROBLEMS 240
2. Presumptions of Marriage and Putative
Spouses 241
Spearman v. Spearman 241
NOTES AND QUESTIONS 243
PROBLEMS 245
C. Legal Alternatives to Marriage 246
Estin, *Ordinary Cohabitation* 246
Forste, *Prelude to Marriage*
or Alternative to Marriage? 248
1. Judicially Created Solutions 249
Marvin v. Marvin 249
NOTES AND QUESTIONS 251
In the Matter of the Estate of Roccamonte 253
NOTES AND QUESTIONS 258
Connell v. Francisco 260
NOTES AND QUESTIONS 263
Wardle, *Deconstructing Family:*
A Critique of the American Law Institute's
"Domestic Partners" Proposal 265
PROBLEMS 266
2. Statutory Solutions: Domestic Partnerships,
Civil Unions, Reciprocal Beneficiary
Relationships, and More 267
Hawaii H.B. 118 (1997) 268
Vermont Legislature, Act No. 91 (H. 847)
(1999) 269
Cal. Stats. 2003, C. 421 (A.B. 205) 270
New Jersey Domestic Partnership Act (2004) 272
NOTES AND QUESTIONS 276
PROBLEM 279
3. Nonmarital Cohabitation in Other
Western Countries 280

II FAMILY DISSOLUTION

Chapter 5. Divorce Grounds and Procedures 287
A. Introduction 287

Schneider, *Moral Discourse and
the Transformation of Family Law*   291
B.   The Traditional Divorce System   293
1.   Grounds for Divorce   293
*New Hampshire Public Statutes
Chapter 175, §5 (1901)*   294
Kucera v. Kucera   295
Simpson v. Simpson   297
NOTES AND QUESTIONS   301
PROBLEMS   305
2.   Divorce Procedure   306
C.   The Adoption of No-Fault Divorce   309
Friedman, *Rights of Passage: Divorce
Law in Historical Perspective*   309
1.   Grounds for Divorce   311
Uniform Marriage and Divorce Act   311
Desrochers v. Desrochers   312
NOTES AND QUESTIONS   314
2.   No-Default Divorce Procedure   316
Boddie v. Connecticut   316
NOTES AND QUESTIONS   318
Manion v. Manion   319
NOTES AND QUESTIONS   320
*California Family Code—Summary
Dissolution*   322
D.   Evaluating Divorce Reform   323
DeWitt, *Breaking Up Is Hard to Do*   324
Glenn, *Is the Current Concern About
American Marriage Warranted?*   324
Ellman, *The Misguided Movement to
Revive Fault Divorce, and Why
Reformers Should Look Instead to the
American Law Institute*   327
Weisbrod, *On the Expressive Functions
of Family Law*   328
NOTES AND QUESTIONS   329
Shiono & Quinn, *Epidemiology of Divorce*   330
Spaht, *Louisiana's Covenant Marriage:
Social Analysis and Legal Implications*   332
Nock, Sanchez, Wilson & Wright, *Covenant
Marriage Turns Five Years Old*   333
Scott, *Divorce, Children's Welfare, and
the Culture Wars*   335
Cahn, *The Moral Complexities of Family Law*   339
NOTES AND QUESTIONS   340
E.   Lawyers and the Divorce Process   345
1.   Creating the Lawyer-Client Relationship   345

	Klemm v. Klemm	*345*
	NOTES AND QUESTIONS	349
	PROBLEMS	352
	Note: Fee Arrangements	352
	PROBLEMS	355
2.	Counseling and Client Relations	356
	Elkins, A Counseling Model for Lawyering in Divorce Cases	*358*
	Sarat & Felstiner, Law and Strategy in the Divorce Lawyer's Office	*359*
	NOTES AND QUESTIONS	363
	PROBLEMS	366
3.	Alternative Dispute Resolution	366
	Pearson & Thoennes, Mediating and Litigating Custody Disputes: A Longitudinal Evaluation	*366*
	Carbonneau, Alternative Dispute Resolution: Melting the Lances and Dismounting the Steeds	*367*
a.	Negotiation	368
	Melli, Erlanger & Chambliss, The Process of Negotiation: An Exploratory Investigation in the Context of No-Fault Divorce	*368*
	NOTES AND QUESTIONS	370
	PROBLEMS	374
b.	Arbitration	374
	Koritzinsky, Welch & Schlissel, The Benefits of Arbitration	*375*
	Flaherty v. Flaherty	*376*
	NOTES AND QUESTIONS	378
	PROBLEM	379
c.	Mediation	379
	Pearson & Thoennes, Mediating and Litigating Custody Disputes: A Longitudinal Evaluation	*379*
	NOTES AND QUESTIONS	380
	Fineman, Dominant Discourse, Professional Language, and Legal Change in Child Custody Decisionmaking	*384*
	PROBLEMS	385
Chapter 6.	Property Division and Spousal Support	387
A.	Overview	387
1.	Historical Justifications of and Criteria for Economic Awards	388
2.	Economic Orders in the No-Fault Era	389
3.	Criticism of No-Fault Economics	390

B. Property Division at Divorce   398
        Uniform Marriage and Divorce Act §307   399
        NOTES AND QUESTIONS   400
        PROBLEM   402
    1. The Meaning of "Equitable Distribution"   402
        In the Matter of the Marriage of Pierson   402
        NOTES AND QUESTIONS   405
        PROBLEMS   411
    2. Characterization of Property as Separate
        or Marital   412
        O'Brien v. O'Brien   412
        NOTES AND QUESTIONS   418
        PROBLEMS   423
    3. Choice-of-Law Issues   424
    4. Dividing Debts   425
        Geldmeier v. Geldmeier   425
        NOTES AND QUESTIONS   428
        PROBLEM   429
    5. The Marital Home   429
C. Spousal Support at Divorce   430
        Vernier & Hurlbut, The Historical
        Background of Alimony Law and Its
        Present Structure   430
        Peele, Social and Psychological Effects of the
        Availability and the Granting of Alimony
        on the Spouses   432
    1. Changing Attitudes Toward Spousal
        Support in the No-Fault Era   433
        Kay, Equality and Difference:
        A Perspective on No-Fault Divorce
        and Its Aftermath   435
        England & Farkas, Households,
        Employment and Gender   435
        Ellman, The Theory of Alimony   437
        Oldham, Putting Asunder in the 1990s   437
        Williams, Is Coverture Dead? Beyond
        a New Theory of Alimony   438
    2. Applying the Changing Views   439
        Uniform Marriage and Divorce Act §308   439
        NOTES AND QUESTIONS   439
        PROBLEM   440
        Turner v. Turner   440
        In re Marriage of Larocque   443
        Rogerson, Spousal Support After Moge   448
        NOTES AND QUESTIONS   450
        Carbone, The Futility of Coherence:
        The ALI's Principles of the Law

	of Family Dissolution, Compensatory Spousal Payments	453
	NOTES AND QUESTIONS	455
	PROBLEMS	456
3.	Spousal Support for the Caregiving Parent?	457
	PROBLEM	457
	Empirical Data on Working Parents	457
	The General State of the Law	457
	The Politics and Social Value of Caregiving	458
D.	Divorce and New Property	459
1.	Introduction	459
	Note: Valuing Streams of Payments	460
2.	Pensions and Other Employment-Related Benefits	461
	Laing v. Laing	463
	NOTES AND QUESTIONS	466
	PROBLEMS	470
	Note: Social Security, Military, and Other Pensions	470
	Note: Assigning Present Values to and Dividing Pensions	473
	NOTES AND QUESTIONS	474
	Note: Qualified Domestic Relations Orders	474
3.	Personal Injury Awards, Disability Pay, and Similar Interests	476
	NOTES AND QUESTIONS	477
	PROBLEMS	478
4.	Professional Practices and Other Closely Held Businesses	479
	May v. May	479
	NOTES AND QUESTIONS	489
	PROBLEMS	491
5.	Degrees, Licenses, Jobs, and Earning Capacity	492
	PROBLEM	492
	Case Law and Statutes	493
	Mahoney v. Mahoney	493
	O'Brien v. O'Brien	495
	NOTES AND QUESTIONS	497
	California Family Code §2641	498
	Public Opinion	499
	Empirical Information	500
Chapter 7.	Parent-Child Support Duties	501
	Harris, Waldrop & Waldrop, Making and Breaking Connections Between	

Parents' Duty to Support and Right
to Control Their Children 501
A. The Prevailing Child Support Model 504
Williams, Guidelines for Setting Levels
of Child Support Orders 505
NOTES AND QUESTIONS 508
Thoennes et al., The Impact of Child
Support Guidelines on Award Adequacy,
Award Variability and Case Processing
Efficiency 510
B. Challenges to the Prevailing Model 511
Harris, The Proposed ALI Child Support
Principles 511
Beld & Biernat, Federal Intent for State
Child Support Guidelines: Income
Shares, Cost Shares, and the Realities
of Shared Parenting 515
NOTES AND QUESTIONS 517
C. Particular Issues in Applying Child
Support Formulas 519
Peterson v. Peterson 519
NOTES AND QUESTIONS 522
Note: Children's Medical Expenses 524
PROBLEMS 525
Melli, Guideline Review: Child Support
and Time Sharing by Parents 526
Colonna v. Colonna 528
NOTES AND QUESTIONS 531
Note: Child Support Obligations of
Low-Income Parents 532
D. Support for Older Children 533
Harris, Waldrop & Waldrop, Making
and Breaking Connections Between
Parents' Duty to Support and Right
to Control Their Children 533
Childers v. Childers 534
Wallerstein & Blakeslee, Second Chances:
Men, Women & Children a Decade
After Divorce 537
Fabricius, Braver & Deneau, Divorced
Parents' Financial Support of Their
Children's College Expenses 538
NOTES AND QUESTIONS 539
PROBLEMS 541
E. Support for Parents 542
American Healthcare Center v. Randall 543
Swoap v. Superior Court 545
NOTES AND QUESTIONS 547

Chapter 8. Modification, Termination, Enforcement, and
            Tax and Bankruptcy Treatment of Orders   549
            A. Introduction   549
            B. Modification and Termination of Support   549
                1. "Foreseeable" Changes in Circumstances   550
                2. "Voluntary" Versus "Involuntary" Decreases
                    in the Payor's Income   551
                    Deegan v. Deegan   *551*
                    NOTES AND QUESTIONS   554
                    PROBLEMS   556
                3. New Families—Spousal Support, Remarriage,
                    and Cohabitation   557
                    Peterson v. Peterson   *557*
                    NOTES AND QUESTIONS   559
                    PROBLEMS   561
                    In re Marriage of Dwyer   *561*
                    NOTES AND QUESTIONS   562
                    PROBLEM   565
                4. New Families—Child Support   566
                    Ainsworth v. Ainsworth   *566*
                    NOTES AND QUESTIONS   571
                    PROBLEMS   575
                5. A Comparison: Child Support Duties When
                    the Family Receives Public Assistance   576
                    PROBLEMS   577
            C. Enforcement   578
                    *Grall, Custodial Mothers and Fathers
                    and Their Child Support: 2001*   *578*
                1. Private Enforcement Mechanisms—Liens,
                    Trusts, and Insurance   581
                2. Jailing "Deadbeat" Parents   582
                    Moss v. Superior Court   *582*
                    NOTES AND QUESTIONS   589
                    Note: Civil or Criminal Contempt?   592
                    PROBLEMS   594
                3. The State-Federal Child Support
                    Enforcement Program   594
                    *DHHS, Office of Child Support Enforcement,
                    Child Support Enforcement FY 2003
                    Preliminary Data Report*   *596*
                4. The Continuing Challenge of Childhood
                    Poverty   600
                    *U.S. Commission on Interstate Child
                    Support, Supporting Our Children:
                    A Blueprint for Reform*   *600*
            D. Taxes   602
                1. Taxation of the Ongoing Family   602
                2. Taxation of the Family After Divorce   605

		a.	Property Division—IRC §1041	605
		b.	Spousal Support—IRC §§71 and 215	607
		c.	Child Support	609
		d.	Dependency Exemptions, Child Tax Credits, Child Care Credits, Earned Income Credits, and Children's Medical Expenses	610
			PROBLEMS	610
	E.	Bankruptcy		611
			In re Huckfeldt	612
			NOTES AND QUESTIONS	614
			Sylvester v. Sylvester	616
			NOTES AND QUESTIONS	618

Chapter 9. Child Custody — 621

	A.	Introduction		621
			Grossberg, Governing the Hearth: Law and the Family in Nineteenth Century America	621
	B.	Standards for Custody Determination		622
		1.	An Introduction to the "Best Interests" Standard	622
			Painter v. Bannister	623
			Freud, Painter v. Bannister: Postscript by a Psychoanalyst	627
			NOTES AND QUESTIONS	631
			Wexler, Rethinking the Modification of Child Custody Decrees	632
		2.	The Primary Caretaker	634
			Burchard v. Garay	635
			NOTES AND QUESTIONS	638
			American Law Institute, Principles of the Law of Family Dissolution §2.08 (2002)	640
			NOTES AND QUESTIONS	641
			PROBLEMS	642
		3.	Joint Custody	643
			Taylor v. Taylor	644
			NOTES AND QUESTIONS	649
			Fineman, Dominant Discourse, Professional Language, and Legal Change in Child Custody Decisionmaking	653
			Principles of the Law of Family Dissolution §2.05 (2002)	655
			NOTES AND QUESTIONS	656
			Lombardo v. Lombardo	657
			NOTES AND QUESTIONS	659
			PROBLEMS	660

4. Judging Parenthood: What Makes
   Parents Unfit?												660
   Fineman, The Illusion of Equality:
   The Rhetoric and Reality of
   Divorce Reform												661
   a. Sexual Activity											661
   Taylor v. Taylor											661
   NOTES AND QUESTIONS									665
   b. Race													669
   Palmore v. Sidoti										669
   NOTES AND QUESTIONS									671
   PROBLEMS												672
   c. Religion												672
   Shelley v. Westbrooke									673
   In re Marriage of Hadeen								673
   NOTES AND QUESTIONS									676
   Wizner & Berkman, Being a Lawyer
   for a Child Too Young to Be a
   Client: A Clinical Study									679
   PROBLEMS												680
   d. Spouse Abuse											681
   Opinion of the Justices to the Senate					681
   NOTES AND QUESTIONS									684
   PROBLEMS												686
   e. Unfriendly Co-parenting								687
   Renaud v. Renaud										687
   NOTES AND QUESTIONS									690
   Carbone, From Partners to Parents: The
   Second Revolution in Family Law						694
   C. Visitation and Its Enforcement							695
   Morgan v. Foretich										695
   NOTES AND QUESTIONS									697
   Burgess v. Burgess										700
   NOTES AND QUESTIONS									706
   PROBLEMS												711
   Bersani v. Bersani										711
   NOTES AND QUESTIONS									714
   PROBLEMS												715
   D. Modification of Custody and Visitation Orders			715
   State ex rel. Johnson v. Bail							715
   NOTES AND QUESTIONS									719
   PROBLEMS												722
Chapter 10. Family Contracts										725
   A. Introduction: Status and Contract Revisited			725
   B. Premarital Agreements									728
   Sanders v. Sanders										728
   NOTES AND QUESTIONS									732
   Simeone v. Simeone										732

                              NOTES AND QUESTIONS   738
                              Brod, Premarital Agreements and Gender
                                 Justice   741
                              Weisbrod, Practical Polyphony: Theories of
                                 the State and Feminist Jurisprudence   742
                              Bix, Bargaining in the Shadow of Love:
                                 The Enforcement of Premarital
                                 Agreements and How We Think
                                 About Marriage   742
                              Uniform Premarital Agreements Act   745
                              NOTES AND QUESTIONS   746
                              Principles of the Law of Family Dissolution   749
                              Younger, A Minnesota Comparative
                                 Family Law Symposium: Antenuptial
                                 Agreements   750
                              NOTES AND QUESTIONS   751
                              PROBLEMS   752
                     C.   Separation Agreements   754
                          1.   The Permissible Scope of the Agreement   754
                              Sharp, Fairness Standards and Separation
                                 Agreements: A Word of Caution on
                                 Contractual Freedom   754
                              Uniform Marriage and Divorce Act §306   755
                              ALI Principles of the Law of Family
                                 Dissolution §7.09   756
                              Mnookin & Kornhauser, Bargaining in the
                                 Shadow of the Law: The Case of
                                 Divorce   756
                              NOTES AND QUESTIONS   757
                          2.   Post-Decree Attacks on Agreements
                               and Decrees Based on Them   758
                              Hresko v. Hresko   758
                              NOTES AND QUESTIONS   761
                              PROBLEMS   761
                          3.   Modification of Agreements   762
                              In re Estate of Hereford   762
                              NOTES AND QUESTIONS   766
                              PROBLEM   767
        Chapter 11. Jurisdiction   769
                     A.   Introduction   769
                     B.   Divorce Jurisdiction   770
                              Sherrer v. Sherrer   774
                              NOTES AND QUESTIONS   776
                              PROBLEMS   778
                     C.   Divisible Divorce   778
                              Vanderbilt v. Vanderbilt   779
                              NOTES AND QUESTIONS   780

Note: Property Division—Jurisdiction
and Full Faith and Credit   781
    PROBLEMS   781
D. Jurisdiction and Full Faith and Credit for
Support Duties   782
  1. Long-Arm Jurisdiction in Support Cases   783
    Kulko v. Superior Court   *783*
    NOTES AND QUESTIONS   786
    PROBLEMS   787
  2. Interstate Modification and Enforcement
of Support   787
    Philipp v. Stahl   *789*
    NOTES AND QUESTIONS   796
    PROBLEMS   799
    Note: International Support
Enforcement   799
E. Child Custody Jurisdiction   801
  1. Initial Jurisdiction   803
    In re McCoy   *803*
    NOTES AND QUESTIONS   807
  2. Interstate Enforcement and Modification
Jurisdiction   809
    In re Forlenza   *810*
    NOTES AND QUESTIONS   814
    Note: Domestic Violence Cases
and the UCCJEA   818
    PROBLEMS   819
  3. Adoption Jurisdiction   820
  4. International Enforcement of Custodial
Rights   822
    Friedrich v. Friedrich   *822*
    NOTES AND QUESTIONS   826
F. Federal Court Jurisdiction over Domestic
Relations   831
    Ankenbrandt v. Richards   *831*
    Resnik, "Naturally" Without Gender:
Women, Jurisdiction, and
the Federal Courts   *834*
    NOTES AND QUESTIONS   836

III CHILDREN, PARENTS, AND THE STATE

Chapter 12. Determining Legal Parenthood: Marriage,
Biology, and Function   839
A. Introduction   839
  1. The Constitutional Rights of Parents   841

		Troxel v. Granville	841
		NOTES AND QUESTIONS	848
		PROBLEMS	850
	2.	The Relationship Between Parenthood and Marriage	850
		Blackstone, Commentaries on the Laws of England	850
		Michael H. v. Gerald D.	852
		NOTES AND QUESTIONS	861
	3.	Children's Emotional Needs	864
		Bartlett, Rethinking Parenthood as an Exclusive Status: The Need for Legal Alternatives When the Premise of the Nuclear Family Has Failed	864
	4.	The Possibility of Multiple Parenthood	866
		PROBLEMS	866
B.	Unmarried Fathers		867
	1.	Child Support, Inheritance, and Public Benefits	868
		Matter of L. Pamela P. v. Frank S.	869
		NOTES AND QUESTIONS	870
		Carbone, From Partners to Parents: The Second Revolution in Family Law	871
		PROBLEMS	871
		Bennemon v. Sullivan	872
		NOTES AND QUESTIONS	875
		PROBLEMS	877
	2.	Unmarried Fathers' Custodial Rights	877
		Lehr v. Robertson	878
		NOTES AND QUESTIONS	885
		PROBLEMS	888
		Adoption of Michael H.	888
		NOTES AND QUESTIONS	897
		PROBLEMS	898
	3.	Establishing Paternity	899
		Plemel v. Walter	900
		NOTES AND QUESTIONS	907
		PROBLEMS	910
C.	Legal Recognition of Functional Families		911
	1.	Stepparenthood	911
		Chambers, Stepparents, Biologic Parents, and the Law's Perceptions of "Family" After Divorce	911
		M. H. B. v. H. T. B.	914
		NOTES AND QUESTIONS	918
		PROBLEM	921
		In re Nelson	921
		NOTES AND QUESTIONS	925
		PROBLEMS	927

2.   Second-Parent Adoption?   927
        Sharon S. v. Superior Court   927
            NOTES AND QUESTIONS   940
            PROBLEM   941
Chapter 13. Adoption and Alternative Reproductive Technologies   943
    A.   Adoption   943
            Sokoloff, Antecedents of American Adoption   943
        1.   Terminating the First Parent-Child
             Relationship   946
                In re Petition of S. O.   947
                    NOTES AND QUESTIONS   951
                Note: Parental Consent to Adoption   952
                Note: Grounds for Dispensing with
                    Parental Consent   953
                Note: Open Adoption and Open Records   953
                PROBLEMS   956
        2.   Establishing the New Parent-Child
             Relationship—Independent vs.
             Agency Adoption and Adoption
             of Special-Needs Children   957
        3.   Child Placement, Race, and Religion   961
                *Mississippi Band of Choctaw Indians
                    v. Holyfield*   962
                    NOTES AND QUESTIONS   969
                Note: Transracial Placement   972
                *Perry, Transracial and International
                    Adoption: Mothers, Hierarchy,
                    Race and Feminist Legal Theory*   974
                *Bartholet, International Adoption: Propriety,
                    Prospects and Pragmatics*   976
                    NOTES AND QUESTIONS   978
                Note: Religious Matching   979
                PROBLEM   980
    B.   Alternative Reproductive Technologies   981
        1.   Artificial Insemination and In Vitro
             Fertilization   981
                Uniform Parentage Act (2002)   981
                    NOTES AND QUESTIONS   982
                    PROBLEMS   983
        2.   Surrogate Motherhood   984
                Johnson v. Calvert   984
                    NOTES AND QUESTIONS   995
                    PROBLEMS   997
                J.F. v. D.B.   997
                    NOTES AND QUESTIONS   1008

Table of Cases   1011
Index   1021

Preface

This casebook is intended for a basic course in family law. It is a large book, in part because it covers a broad area and in part because of the characteristics of the fields it addresses.

One of those characteristics is enormous dynamism, amounting almost to revolution, in doctrines concerning families, parents and children, spouses, and domestic partners. Long-settled principles and practices regarding marriage, divorce, marital property, spousal support, and custody, to mention only a few areas, have been abandoned or substantially modified over the last few decades. Even the kinds of relationships relevant in family law have changed. Far more important than before, they now include unmarried cohabitants, same-sex couples, and single-parent families.

These and other issues are in flux. The questions they present can be considered from a number of perspectives. We have attempted a sympathetic and balanced presentation that addresses immediate issues while retaining a wider focus on family and the state, the role of internal groups and mediating institutions, and the efficacy of law and particular methods of enforcing the law. We have also sought to present many different voices and accounts without, we hope, privileging any particular account as representing that of the book as a whole. Perspectives in this book shift regularly, through the notes and questions and also through the Teacher's Manual, which continues conversations opened in the notes and questions.

In addition to exploring the difficult social and theoretical issues in family law, this casebook has another, equally important purpose: to prepare students for practice in the field. At many law schools, including our own, family law is an immediately practical course. Many students at these schools will practice domestic relations shortly after graduation, and a family law course must introduce them to doctrine, literature, and techniques as they appear in law offices and courts.

This is a far more complex enterprise than is the case for many other fields. In other areas, introduction to a body of statutory and judicial doctrine in the field will serve that purpose. Family law, however, draws on doctrines in a number of other areas, such as property, contracts, torts, criminal law, conflict of laws, and constitutional law, whose principles must be reviewed or, in some cases, introduced.

This is, if anything, more true now than ever before, because the range of issues falling within "family law" is understood to be more broad than before. The poor and the elderly deal with issues that are, in essence, family law questions as they seek support, medical care, and other forms of assistance. And for all domestic groups, the sources of practical wealth are likely to be found in "new property"—interests and benefits associated with private and public employment and with some aspects of public assistance—as much as in houses and cars. Accordingly, students are introduced to the bodies of law dealing with pensions, bankruptcy, and health care, among others.

In addition, family law is—even more than most other areas—not only permissibly but of necessity cross-disciplinary, and students must learn the importance of becoming intelligent consumers of "non-legal" disciplines. To take only a few examples, some notion of financial principles (such as the time value of money) is essential to valuation of property at divorce. Some notion of genetics and statistics is essential to paternity matters (among other issues); some understanding of the method of clinical psychology is regularly necessary in custody disputes. Social history is important to understanding the context in which the law has developed and to the interpretation of current bodies of doctrine. And discussions of legal and policy responses to domestic violence should draw on social scientific evidence regarding the incidence, distribution, and causes of such violence.

Moreover, family law cannot be effectively taught without some attention to process. The course should incorporate some exposure to principles of interviewing, counseling, negotiation, and ethics.

The casebook seeks to carry out this agenda in several ways. It includes broad doctrinal coverage. Materials from a number of law fields and non-legal disciplines have been chosen not only to provide a basis for evaluating doctrine but as matter to be employed in creating legal arguments within family law doctrine. They are often, although not always, associated with problem sets for which such data is necessary to the construction of arguments. Social scientific and historical information regarding the incidence of domestic violence, for example, is presented in the context of a problem requiring evaluation of the prospects for a successful class action for failure to arrest and, as well, the efficacy of nonlitigative approaches to domestic assault. In constructing these materials and problems, we have sought to show that the gap between theory and practice is largely fictitious.

One further aspect of a family law course, and this book, should be mentioned. Many students take the course because the subject is on a state bar examination or will be part of a general practice, rather than because of particular interest in the field. Indeed, some students may bring a bias against the field because it does not enjoy the prestige of, say, antitrust law—although the total number of antitrust cases in one year amounts to a good day's work in an urban domestic relations court. The final purpose of the basic family law course, then—and perhaps the only consistent subtext of this casebook—is to convey the importance, the legal and human complexity, and the sophistication of family relations and family law.

Leslie J. Harris
June Carbone

February 2005

Editors' note: Throughout the book, footnotes to the text and to opinions and other quoted materials are numbered consecutively from the beginning of each chapter. Some footnotes in opinions and secondary authorities are omitted. Editor's footnotes added to quoted materials are indicated by the abbreviation: —Ed.

Acknowledgments

Professor and former dean Lee Teitelbaum of the University of Utah was a principal author of the first two editions of this book, upon which this edition draws heavily. His deep understanding of the subject and how to teach it, his voice, and his humor pervade the book. He had begun work on this edition before his death in 2004, and he is rightfully recognized as an author of it.

We also owe special debts to colleagues, friends, and research assistants who provided substantive assistance in the preparation of this work. Leslie Harris thanks her colleagues Merle Weiner, Caroline Forell, Margie Paris, Ib Gassama, Keith Aoki, and Michael Moffitt, as well as her student research assistants Emily Schoonmaker and Melissa Hurley. June Carbone thanks her research assistants Alexander Weddle and Jennie Winter. Professor Carol A. Weisbrod was a co-author of the first edition of this book, and we gratefully acknowledge the continuing value of her contributions.

We also thank Debby Warren at the University of Oregon and Christina Johnson at Santa Clara University for assistance in manuscript preparation. Institutional debts are owed to our law schools and their administrations for their support, endurance, and tolerance.

Finally, we all wish to thank Melody Davies, Betsy Kenny, Ruth Kwon, and others at Aspen for their assistance in many ways over many years.

American Academy of Matrimonial Lawyers, Bounds of Advocacy, Comments to Standard 2.12 (1991). Reprinted by permission of the American Academy of Matrimonial Lawyers.

American Law Institute, Principles of the Law of Family Dissolution, Sections 2.05, 2.08, 7.04, 7.05, and 7.09 (2002). Copyright 2002 by the American Law Institute. Reproduced with permission. All rights reserved. The complete publication, *Principles of the Law of Family Dissolution: Analysis and Recommendations*, is available in hardcover or softcover through the American Law Institute at www.ALI.org or 1-800-253-6397.

Bartholet, Elizabeth, International Adoption: Propriety, Prospects and Pragmatics, 13 J. Am. Acad. Matrimonial L. 181 (1996). Reprinted by permission.

Bartlett, Katherine, Rethinking Parenthood as an Exclusive Status: The Need for Legal Alternatives When the Premise of the Nuclear Family Has Failed, 70 U. Va. L. Rev. 879 (1984). Copyright © by the University of Virginia Law Review Association. Reprinted by permission of the Virginia Law Review Association and Fred B. Rothman & Co.

Becker, Gary, A Treatise on Family 327-329. Cambridge, Mass.: Harvard University Press, Copyright © 1981, 1991 by the President and Fellows of Harvard College. Reprinted by permission.

Fagan, Jeffrey & Angela Browne, Violence Between Spouses and Intimates: Physical Aggression Between Women and Men in Intimate Relationships, 3 Understanding and Preventing Violence 115-121, 225-239 (Albert J. Reiss, Jr. & Jeffrey A. Roth eds., 1994). Reprinted by permission.

Fineman, Martha A., Why Marriage?, 9 Va. J. Soc. Pol'y & L. 239 (2001). Reprinted by permission of Professor Fineman and Virgina Journal of Social Policy and the Law.

————, Dominant Discourse, Professional Language and Legal Change, 101 Harv. L. Rev. 727 (1988). Copyright © 1988 by the Harvard Law Review Association. Reprinted by permission of Professor Fineman and the Harvard Law Review Association.

Forste, Renata, Prelude to Marriage or Alternative to Marriage?, 4 J. L. & Fam. Stud. 91 (2002). Reprinted by permission.

Foster, Frances H., The Family Paradigm of Inheritance Law, 80 N.C. L. Rev. 199 (2001). Reprinted by permission.

Freud, Anna, Painter v. Bannister, 7 The Writings of Anna Freud 247-255 (1966-1970). Reprinted by permission of International Universities Press.

Friedman, Lawrence, Rights of Passage: Divorce in Historical Perspective, 63 Or. L. Rev. 649. Copyright © 1984 by University of Oregon. Reprinted by permission of the Oregon Law Review and of Professor Friedman.

Galbraith, John Kenneth, Economics and the Public Purpose 31-37. Copyright © 1973 by John Kenneth Galbraith. Reprinted by permission of Houghton Mifflin Company. All rights reserved.

Garrison, Marsha, The Economic Consequences of Divorce, 32 Fam. & Conciliation Cts. Rev. 10 (1994). Copyright © 1994 by Sage Publications, Inc. Reprinted by permission of Sage Publications, Inc.

Gelles, Richard & Murray A. Straus, Intimate Violence 130-136, 250-251. Copyright © 1988 Lescher & Lescher Ltd. Reprinted by permission.

Ginzburg, Rebecca, Note, Altering "Family": Another Look at the Supreme Court's Narrow Protection of Families in Belle Terre, 83 B.U. L. Rev. 875 (2003). Reprinted by permission.

Glendon, Mary Ann, Marriage and the State: The Withering Away of Marriage, 62 Va. L. Rev. 663 (1976). Copyright © the Virginia Law Review Association. Reprinted by permission of the Virginia Law Review Association and Fred B. Rothman & Co.

————, Power and Authority in the Family: New Legal Patterns as Reflections of Changing Ideologies, 23 Am. J. Comp. Law 1 (1975). Copyright © by the Regents of the University of California, Berkeley. Reprinted by permission of Professor Glendon.

————, The New Family and the New Property. Copyright © 1980, Lexis Publishing. Reprinted with permission from Lexis Publishing, Charlottesville, VA (800) 446-3410.

Glenn, Norval D., Is the Current Concern About American Marriage Warranted?, 9 Va. Soc. Policy & L. 5 (2001). Reprinted by permission.

Griffiths, John, What Do Dutch Lawyers Actually Do in Divorce Courts?, 20 Law & Soc'y Rev. 135 (1986). Copyright © 1986, State University of New York. Reprinted by permission.

Grossberg, Michael, Governing the Hearth. Reprinted from Governing the Hearth: Law and the Family in Nineteenth-Century America, by Michael Grossberg. Copyright © 1988 by the University of North Carolina Press. Used by permission of the publisher and Professor Grossberg.

Harris, Leslie, The New ALI Child Support Proposal, 35 Willamette L. Rev. 473 (1999). Reprinted by permission.

Harris, Leslie, Dennis Waldrop & Lori Waldrop, Making and Breaking Connections Between Parents' Duty to Support and Right to Control Their Children, 69 Or. L. Rev. 689 (1990). Copyright © 1990 University of Oregon. Reprinted by permission.

Kay, Herma Hill, Equality and Difference: A Perspective on No-Fault Divorce and Its Aftermath, 56 U. Cin. L. Rev. 1 (1987). Copyright © University of Cincinnati. Reprinted by permission.

Koritzinsky, Allan, Robert Welch & Stephen Schlissel, The Benefits of Arbitration 14(4) Fam. Adv. 45. Copyright © 1992 Family Advocate. Reprinted by permission of the American Bar Association.

Kramer, Larry, Same-Sex Marriage, Conflict of Laws, and the Unconstitutional Public Policy Exception, 106 Yale L.J. 1965 (1997). Copyright © The Yale Law Journal Company. Reprinted by permission of The Yale Law Journal Company and William J. Hein Company from the Yale Law Journal, Vol. 106, pages 1965-2008 and by permission of Professor Kramer.

McDermott, Mark T., Agency Versus Independent Adoption: The Case for Independent Adoption, 3(1) The Future of Children: Adoption 146 (1993). A publication of the Center for the Future of Children. Copyright © The Center for the Future of Children, The David and Lucile Packard Foundation.

Melli, Marygold S., Constructing a Social Problem, Am. B. Found. Res. J. 759 (1986). Copyright © 1986 The University of Chicago Press. Published by the University of Chicago Press. Reprinted by permission of Professor Melli and the publisher.

Melli, Marygold S., Howard S. Erlanger & Elizabeth Chambliss, The Process of Negotiation: An Exploratory Investigation in the Context of No-Fault Divorce, 40 Rutgers L. Rev. 1133 (1988). Copyright © 1988 by Rutgers University. Reprinted by permission of Professors Melli, Erlanger, and Chambliss.

Menolascino, Frank J. & Michael L. Egger, Medical Dimensions of Mental Retardation xx-xxii (1978), published by the University of Nebraska Press. Reprinted by permission.

Mnookin, Robert H. & Lewis Kornhauser, Bargaining in the Shadow of the Law: The Case of Divorce, 88 Yale L.J. 950 (1979). Copyright © The Yale Law Journal Company. Reprinted by permission of The Yale Law Journal Company and Fred B. Rothman & Company from the Yale Law Journal and by permission of Professor Mnookin.

Nock, Steven L., Laura Sanchez, Julia Wilson & James D. Wright, Covenant Marriage Turns 5 Years Old, 10 Mich. J. Gender & L. 169 (2003). Reprinted by permission.

————, Moral Discourse and the Transformation of Family Law, 83 Mich. L. Rev. 1803 (1985). Copyright © Michigan Law Review. Reprinted by permission of Michigan Law Review Association.

Scott, Elizabeth S., Divorce, Children's Welfare, and the Culture Wars, 9 Va. J. Soc. Pol'y & L. 95 (2001). Reprinted by permission.

Sharp, Sally Burnet, Fairness Standards and Separation Agreements: A Word of Caution of Contractual Freedom, 132 U. Pa. L. Rev. 1399 (1984). Copyright © University of Pennsylvania Law Review and Fred B. Rothman and Company. Reprinted by permission.

Shiono, Patricia H. & Linda Sandman Quinn, Epidemiology of Divorce, 4(1) The Future of Children: Children and Divorce 15 (Spring 1994). Reprinted by permission. A publication of the Center for the Future of Children. Copyright © The Center for the Future of Children, The David and Lucile Packard Foundation.

Sokoloff, Burton Z., Antecedents of American Adoption, 3(1) The Future of Children: Adoption 17 (1993). A publication of the Center for the Future of Children. Copyright © The Center for the Future of Children, The David and Lucile Packard Foundation.

Spaht, Katherine Shaw, Louisiana's Covenant Marriage: Social Analysis and Legal Implications, 59 La. L. Rev. 63 (1998). Reprinted by permission.

Steele, Jr., Walter W., Deceptive Negotiating & High-Toned Morality, 39 Vand. L. Rev. 1387 (1986). Reprinted by permission.

Teitelbaum, Lee E., Family History and Family Law, 1985 Wis. L. Rev. 1135. Copyright © 1985 by The Board of Regents of the University of Wisconsin System; Reprinted by permission of the Wisconsin Law Review.

————, The Family as a System: A Preliminary Sketch, 1996 Utah L. Rev. 537. Reprinted by permission.

Uniform State Laws: The following have been reproduced in whole or in part: Uniform Adoption Act, Uniform Child Custody Jurisdiction and Enforcement Act, Uniform Interstate Family Support Act, Uniform Marital Property Act, Uniform Marriage and Divorce Act, Uniform Parentage Act, Uniform Premarital Agreements Act, Copyright © The National Conference of Commissioners on Uniform State Laws. Reprinted by permission of the National Conference of Commissioners on Uniform State Laws.

Utset, Manuel, A Theory of Self Control Problems and Incomplete Contracting: The Case of Shareholder Contracts, 2003 Utah L. Rev. 1329 (2003). Reprinted by permission.

Vernier, Chester G. & John B. Hurlbut, The Historical Background of Alimony Law and Its Present Structure, 6 Law & Contemp. Probs. 197 (1939). Copyright © 1939 Journal of Law and Contemporary Problems. Reprinted by permission.

Wallerstein, Judith & Sandra Blakeslee, Second Chances: Men, Women and Children a Decade After Divorce, 157-160. Copyright © 1989 by Judith Wallerstein and Sandra Blakeslee. Reprinted by permission of Ticknor & Fields/Houghton Mifflin Co. All rights reserved.

Wardle, Lynn E., Deconstructing Family: A Critique of the ALI's "Domestic Partners" Proposal, 2001 BYU L. Rev. 1190 (2001). Reprinted by permission.

———, The Bonds of Matrimony and the Bonds of Constitutional Democracy, 32 Hofstra L. Rev. 349 (2003). Reprinted with permission from Hofstra Law Review Association.

Weisbrod, Carol, On the Expressive Functions of Family, U.C. Davis L. Rev. 991 (1989). Copyright © 1989 by The Regents of the University of California. Reprinted by permission.

———, Practical Polyphony: Theories of the State and Feminist Jurisprudence. This article was originally published at 24 Ga. L. Rev. 985 (1990) and is reprinted with permission.

Wexler, Joan G., Rethinking the Modification of Child Custody Decrees. Copyright © 1985. Reprinted by permission of The Yale Law Journal Company and Fred B. Rothman & Company, vol. 94, pp. 757-820. Reprinted by permission of Dean Wexler.

Williams, Joan, Is Coverture Dead: Beyond a New Theory of Alimony, 82 Geo. L.J. 2227 (1994). Copyright © by Joan Williams. Reprinted by permission of Professor Williams.

Williams, Robert G., Guidelines for Setting Levels of Child Support Orders, 21 Fam. L.Q. 281 (1987). Copyright © Robert G. Williams. Reprinted by permission of Robert G. Williams, President, Policy Studies, Inc.

Wizner, Stephen & Miriam Berkman, Being a Lawyer for a Child Too Young to Be a Client: A Clinical Study. 68 Neb. L. Rev. 330. Copyright © 1989 Nebraska Law Review. Reprinted by permission.

MARRIAGE AND ITS ALTERNATIVES

I

1

MARRIAGE AND ITS
ALTERNATIVES

When Are Adult Partners a Family?

A generation or two ago, *family* had a fairly clear connotation, although many people even then did not live in families that fit the standard image. Today, however, the meaning of *family* is contested in many realms of life, including the law. This chapter introduces some of the recurring themes in the legal debates:

- Should the law make distinctions among people based on their family status at all?
- When family membership matters, how should it be determined? On the basis of formal markers such as blood relationship or legal ceremony, or on the basis of function?
- If family is defined by function, what kinds of behavior indicate that people belong to a family?
- What are the roles of legislatures and judges in making these decisions?

These issues will continue to arise throughout the following three chapters in this section. Chapter 2 explores in some detail the myriad ways in which the law does treat adults differently if they are considered "married" or the equivalent thereof. Chapter 3 examines the law of formal marriage, and Chapter 4 deals with informal domestic arrangements among adults. Chapter 7 returns to some of these issues in the context of the parent-child relationship.

MILTON C. REGAN, JR., *CALIBRATED COMMITMENT: THE LEGAL TREATMENT OF MARRIAGE AND COHABITATION*

76 Notre Dame L. Rev. 1435, 1435-1438, 1442, 1445 (2001)

The rate of cohabitation without marriage has increased dramatically in Western countries over the past few decades. Moreover, research suggests that cohabitation has become less of an "engagement" that serves as a prelude to marriage and more of an intimate arrangement that may serve as an alternative to it. In other words, it is less accurate than before to describe those who cohabit as simply involved in a "trial" marriage. Many cohabitors instead regard living together as a way to have an intimate relationship that may or may not result in a decision to marry. This is reflected, for instance, in the declining percentage of cohabitors who eventually marry and in the fact that a portion of the declining rate of marriage is due to the increasing rate of cohabitation. In addition, the percentage of cohabitors who have been together for three years or more has increased, as well as the percentage of cohabiting households in which children reside.

These trends raise the question whether American law should more explicitly "institutionalize" cohabitation by ending the different treatment of marital and non-marital relationships, thereby making available to cohabitors a host of benefits currently available only to those who are married. . . .

On one view, full institutionalization is warranted because cohabitation and marriage involve substantially the same attitudes and orientation. The claim is that they differ only in the willingness of the couple to go through the formality of marriage, which is an insufficient basis for distinguishing between them. From this perspective, cohabitation has become a more important relationship for persons who desire intimate commitment but reject the need for formal legal recognition of this commitment. For these couples, "real" marriage is a frame of mind, not the possession of a marriage certificate. . . .

An alternative argument for institutionalization is that respect for individual privacy and autonomy mandates that the state not favor any particular form of intimate relationship above others. If marriage is losing favor because it meets the needs of fewer people, then the state should not try artificially to prop it up by creating incentives for partners to enter into an arrangement that they otherwise would not choose. On this view, the rise in cohabitation reflects the fact that many partners now desire more individual independence, and less commitment, as a part of their intimate relationships. Rather than take the whole package of benefits and burdens that marriage provides, couples prefer to tailor the terms of their relationships so they reflect their own unique preferences. Cohabitation, thus, can accommodate the wide range of wishes about how people want to arrange their personal lives better than marriage. Its growth reflects the greater prominence of the ideals of individual autonomy and privacy in intimate matters.

Are these arguments persuasive? Should legal trends continue so that cohabitation and marriage ultimately receive virtually identical legal recognition? On balance, I think that the answer is no. First, I am skeptical that cohabitors are married in substance but simply not in form. Research indicates that cohabiting relationships are less stable than marriages and that they generally reflect less commitment by partners to one another. Second, law need not be agnostic among types of intimate relationships. There are good reasons for law to promote marriage, because there are good reasons to promote intimate commitment. Blurring the line between married and unmarried couples would undermine the ability to express this preference.

* * *

. . . [S]ociety has a legitimate interest in promoting intimate commitment between adults, regardless of whether the relationship also involves children. . . .

I begin with a powerful fundamental value of modern liberal society: individual authenticity. Three concepts cluster around this value. The first is what we might call self-fidelity: "to thine own self be true," in Polonius's words. Each of us has a unique identity and potential that we should strive to attain. The second concept is autonomy, the idea that human beings can be self-governing. I am true to myself when my life is shaped by my own wishes and values rather than by the unreflective acceptance of others.

Finally, individual authenticity involves integrity. This requires that a person remain true to her principles or commitments in the face of temptation to do otherwise. Integrity thus involves consistency. An individual needs to harmonize her values so that she can live life without being constantly pulled in different directions. Further, she needs to be willing to act in accordance with those values. Integrity is complementary to self-fidelity and autonomy. A person who tries to be true to herself values integrity, because it helps her resist acting in a way that does not reflect her deep sense of self. An autonomous person seeks to live with integrity, because it helps to harmonize her values into principles of self-governance.

Authenticity and the set of ideals that cluster around it require a sense of the continuity and stability of the self over time. Self-fidelity requires a coherent self to whom one can be true. The aspiration to autonomy assumes a self who can establish standards to govern her behavior in a variety of circumstances, rather than one who is "radically situated" and moved only by immediate impulse. Finally, the harmonization of values and of beliefs and behavior that characterizes integrity implies a self that establishes limits on what she will do on the ground that some conduct is inconsistent with who she is. Without this stability, as Lynne McFall puts it, "there would be nothing to fear the loss of, not because we are safe but because we have nothing to lose." Self-fidelity, autonomy, and integrity thus contribute to a sense of individual stability and are predicated upon its existence.

The ability to make and keep commitments is critical to the unity of the self over time. Commitment reflects the intention to restrict future possible courses of action for the sake of values that one regards as especially important. It means that one is not receptive in an undifferentiated fashion to all possibilities available in all circumstances, but is responsive to experience in terms of its significance for what we care about. Indeed, commitments help bestow that significance, making possible the understanding of oneself as a unique protagonist in a coherent narrative that gives meaning to what otherwise would be a series of discrete random events. Commitments thus are what Lynne McFall calls "identity-conferring." As she puts it, "they reflect what we take to be most important and so determine, to a large extent, our [moral] identities." In this way, the foreclosure of possibility that commitment represents is the precondition of agency. The adoption of constraints on action ironically makes possible a sense of individual freedom.

Among our most profound commitments, of course, are those to other people. In particular, romantic intimacy, at least in Western contemporary society, is regarded as a relationship that engages identity in an especially deep way. The relationship between identity and intimacy is expressed by Anthony Giddens, who notes the strong hold of the idea of romantic love as "an odyssey, in which self-identity awaits its validation from the discovery of the other." Because of this role of intimacy in fostering authenticity, intimate commitment enjoys a privileged status among the various kinds of commitments that we may make. In sum, there is a powerful claim that society should promote commitment as a valuable good, because it is essential to realization of the deeply rooted aspiration that individuals lead lives that they can call their own.

Even if we accept a role for law in promoting intimate commitment, are we justified in privileging marriage as the form that such commitment should take? One may argue that what gives meaning to intimate allegiances is not the assumption of a formal legal status, but the personal choice to commit to another. If that is so, then law should ratify the intimate choices that people make, married or unmarried, rather than holding up one particular form of commitment as the ideal.

Choice per se does not bestow value upon alternatives, however, nor does it play any role in constructing an authentic identity. The sense that the choices one makes have significance—that they matter—depends on the existence of a social background that designates what is of value. These values are diverse and sometimes incommensurable. A person's choices among them have implications for her identity, because they reflect her own distinctive evaluation, ordering, and attempted reconciliation of values that she regards as having independent value. Making difficult choices is character-forming, because it represents confrontation with the pull of obligations whose force we cannot control solely by ourselves. By contrast, a person for whom things assume value simply by virtue of her own fiat could always dissolve any dilemma merely by proclaiming that one of the alternatives no longer possesses any significance.

For intimate commitment to be constitutive of identity thus requires that it be seen as something that derives its value from a source outside the self's choice to engage in it. It requires, in other words, social validation. The legal institution of marriage plays an especially significant role in providing such validation for the value of commitment. It bestows a legal status on partners that is the basis for impersonal rights and obligations. Those who marry participate in a public ritual that marks entry into a social institution that is intended to embody the value of intimate commitment. That institution transcends any specific couple who may be a part of it and has a history that dwarfs any couple's particular experience. Marriage is not static; understandings of the proper role of wives, for instance, have shifted dramatically over the past generation and are still the focus of contention. Nonetheless, marriage offers a reasonably coherent set of expectations and traditions about commitment that aids in the construction of a narrative identity both for each partner and for the couple together. Indeed, this role of marriage is reflected in the fact that many gay and lesbian critics argue that denying same-sex couples the right to marry is injurious, precisely because it deprives such couples of this social acknowledgment of the value of their intimate commitments.

MARTHA ALBERTSON FINEMAN, *WHY MARRIAGE?*

9 Va. J. Soc. Pol'y & L. 239, 245-246 (2001)

. . . I argue that for all relevant and appropriate societal purposes we do not need marriage, per se, at all. To state that we do not need marriage to accomplish many societal objectives is not the same thing as saying that we do not need a family to do so for some. However, family as a social category should not be dependent on having marriage as its core relationship. Nor is family synonymous with marriage. Although both of these things might historically have been true, things have changed substantially in the past several decades. Marriage does not have the same relevance as a societal institution as it did even fifty years ago, when it was the primary means of protecting and providing for the legal and structurally devised dependency of wives.

The pressing problems today do not revolve around the marriage connection, but the caretaker-dependent relationship. In a world in which wives are equal partners and participants in the market sphere, and in which the consensus is that bad marriages should end, women do not need the special protection of legal marriage. Rather than marriage, we should view the parent-child relationship as the quintessential or core family connection, and focus on how policy can strengthen this tie. Thus, in a responsive society, one could have a marriage [or other long-term sexual affiliation] without necessarily constituting a "family" entitled to special protection and benefits under law. Correspondingly, one might have dependents, thereby creating a family and gaining protection and benefits, without having a marriage.

If this suggestion seems extreme and radical, it only serves to demonstrate the extent to which marriage continues to be uncritically central to our thinking about the family. What is bizarre is that it remains central in spite of the fact that the traditional marital family has become a statistical minority of family units in our society. The tenacity of marriage as a concept explains the relatively unsophisticated and uninformed policy debates. Marriage, as the preferred societal solution, has become the problem. The very existence of this institution eclipses discussion and debate about the problems of dependency and allows us to avoid confronting the difficulty of making the transformations necessary to address these problems.

LYNN E. WARDLE, *THE BONDS OF MATRIMONY AND THE BONDS OF CONSTITUTIONAL DEMOCRACY*

32 Hofstra L. Rev. 349, 371-373, 375-377 (2003)

I suggest that society has an interest in promoting individual happiness, and in encouraging social stability, and in fostering good citizenship, and in preventing the explosion of social problems, and that these interests gives it a direct interest in fostering secure, happy, marriage-based families. Marriage is the best, most promising foundation for lasting, growing, individual, and family happiness and security. It also is "the very seedbed of democracy. Home is the place where we get our first ideas about ourself [sic], our attitudes toward other people, and our habits of approaching and solving problems." It is in the home that spouses as well as children learn lessons about cooperation and commitment, sharing and sacrifice, and obedience to the unenforceable that form the foundation for self-government. It is from their marriages that husbands and wives learn how to make the best of shortages, how to care for others, how to be happy, to love liberty, to fulfill one's duty, and the critical citizenship skills of mutual respect and cooperation. It is in marriage and in raising children that most adults relearn the importance of and refine the techniques of sacrificing for others, how to really care for the next generation, to look beyond the present, to nurture the basics of life and community. The interconnectedness of our lives, the first lesson of all government, especially self-government, is learned first (as children) and most thoroughly (as spouses and parents) in the home. The home is the first and the most important schoolhouse in a democracy. Husband and wife, as well as parents and children, learn the most important lessons of happy, successful living as they work together, play together, plan together, cooperate together, laugh together, weep together, prosper together, and share each other's pains and sorrows. It is in the home that trust in others and in the future is nurtured — or hindered — and that is the indispensable prerequisite for democracy. Marriage-based families are best for children, providing the potentially optimal environment in which children may be conceived, raised, and taught the lessons of responsible living.

The normative nature and structure of marriage and family are closely tied to the model of state authority. "[The family has a] critical role in raising good citizens. . . . The localist theory of family law affirms the vital role that families play in preserving the fundamental liberal values underlying the constitutional structure." This is true not just in Western societies. In Japan, for example, the structure of the family and the cultural values inculcated by the family affect the successful use of informal dispute resolution procedures in courts. And after World War II, the Allies insisted on the dismantling of the traditional Ie family structure in Japan because they believed that there was a direct link between that potentially autocratic family form and the social, political, and militaristic values of the nation.

Marriage structures that underscore public commitment are an important foundation for self-government because such marriages are as much for the community as for the individuals. Couples say their vows for the community who gather to witness them pledge their troth to each other. Their marriage reaffirms a community value, the identity of the community and of the couple.

* * *

Marriage is of such profound importance to society that there is great danger if its meaning and definition become ambiguous. It could be said that changing the meanings of marriage would be like moving the furniture in the house of a person who is blind.

* * *

No government could be established on the same principle as that of the United States, with a different code of morals. The American Constitution is remarkable for its simplicity; but it can only suffice a people habitually correct in their actions, and would be utterly inadequate to the wants of a different nation. Change the domestic habits of the Americans, their religious devotion, and their high respect for morality, and it will not be necessary to change a single letter in the Constitution in order to vary the whole form of their government. Proposals to abolish marriage (per Professor Fineman) or legalize same-sex marriage would radically "change the domestic habits of the Americans" [and] inevitably would lead to a radical variation of our constitutional government.

Society can accommodate some "free riders" living in alternative, nonmarital relationships. Our democratic society can carry on adequately despite some family form deviation, some domestic failure, some breakdown of family integrity, but when the quantity of those problems become significant, they burden the entire society and undermine society and its institutions.

[Society] requires a critical mass of married, two-parent families, both to raise their own children well and to serve as models for those who are being reared outside of the "conventional" family. The great tragedy today is that there are communities—especially low-income communities—where we have already lost that critical mass.

The price of devaluing marriage is being paid already by many in our society who have suffering, broken, and dysfunctional families, who have experienced sorrow, pain, and regret. It is paid by society in general in heightened incidence and rates of premarital sexual exploitation and pregnancy, nonmarital childrearing, single parenting, juvenile crime, lowered academic achievement, increased physical and mental health problems, drug use and alcohol abuse, increased poverty, and reduced productivity. If we embrace the legalization of alternative family forms as equivalent to marriage, the toll will be even higher.

Society has an interest in fostering family structures that produce these kinds of positive and socially beneficial results, results that avoid lost productivity, reduce tax expenditures for medicines, health services, social security, and prevent to some degree the social costs of broken homes. Thus, society has a direct and measurable interest in fostering good, happy marriages, and stable, loving families.

Once the institution of marriage slips off its foundation, it is very difficult to restore. The family demographer William Goode suggested that after marriage is weakened in a society it is nearly impossible to revitalize it without perhaps some traumatic and dramatic external pressure such as military conquest, economic collapse, or natural disaster of widespread proportions. One wonders whether even those external disasters are not a natural consequence of radical alteration of the foundation of a society.

Conferring the label and legal status of "marriage" on same-sex unions and other noncapital relationships will not magically transform them into the kind of socially valuable units historically called marriage. The defect of that classic Kelsenian (positivist) flaw was exposed by Abraham Lincoln when he asked how many legs a dog would have if you counted a tail as a leg. To the response "five legs," Lincoln said, "No; calling a tail a leg doesn't make it a leg."

Viewed from almost any credible theoretical framework, including civic republicanism, liberalism, utilitarianism, and pragmatism, it can be shown that marriage is the seedbed of government. The bonds of marriage are reflected in the bonds of citizenship, and the bonds that tie us to support and preserve our constitutional government imitate the bonds of responsible marriage-based families. Our Constitution was founded on a particular vision of marriage. An abolition or radical redefinition of marriage will have extreme consequences for our government, probably within a generation.

FRANCES H. FOSTER, *THE FAMILY PARADIGM OF INHERITANCE LAW*

80 N.C. L. Rev. 199, 245-248 (2001)

The family paradigm "transmits a culture through property" that is alien to many Americans. It declares "unnatural" the very relationships that many people, but most frequently ethnic and cultural minorities, often experience as "natural"—caring relationships with extended family members, nonmarital partners, close friends, and nonrelated caregivers.

"Extended care systems," support networks beyond the immediate family circle, have long been a fundamental feature of African-American, Asian-American, Latino, and Native-American culture. They remain so today. In the past decade alone, ethnic minority communities have witnessed an extraordinary increase in so-called "kinship caregiving" to the point that hundreds of thousands of American children are now raised by extended family members and nonrelatives rather than their "legal" parents. Similarly, for many African-American, Mexican-American, and Native-American communities, nonmarital cohabitation is both a cultural tradition and common practice. The family paradigm disregards these ethnic differences. It places family status above any "cultural values of care and support."

The family paradigm is not only ethnically biased, however. It also excludes cultural minorities—that is, individuals whose lifestyles, values, or beliefs diverge from those of the majority. In particular, the family paradigm excludes individuals who are unable or unwilling to enter into formal "legal" family relationships. It denies inheritance rights to same-sex partners based on their sexual orientation alone. The family paradigm, even in its most expansive version, also fails to accommodate those who reject "family" classification on ideological or personal grounds. It requires such individuals to accept a family label they find repugnant in order to devise or inherit.

For those excluded from the family paradigm, the effects can be emotionally as well as financially devastating. Decedents are unable to die secure in the knowledge that they have provided for dependent loved ones. Survivors find themselves "treat[ed] . . . as if they were strangers" to the individuals with whom they shared years of affection, intimacy, and companionship. But the family paradigm cuts even more deeply. Its discriminatory rules do not just affect inheritance. They also send a message to society that only some human relationships and losses matter.

HEWITT V. HEWITT

77 Ill. 2d 49, 394 N.E.2d 1204 (1979)

UNDERWOOD, J. The issue in this case is whether plaintiff Victoria Hewitt, whose complaint alleges she lived with defendant Robert Hewitt from 1960 to 1975 in an unmarried, family-like relationship to which three children have been born, may recover from him "an equal share of the profits and properties accumulated by the parties" during that period.

Plaintiff initially filed a complaint for divorce, but at a hearing on defendant's motion to dismiss, admitted that no marriage ceremony had taken place and that the parties have never obtained a marriage license. . . .

Plaintiff thereafter filed an amended complaint alleging the following bases for her claim: (1) that because defendant promised he would "share his life, his future, his earnings and his property" with her and all of defendant's property resulted from the parties' joint endeavors, plaintiff is entitled in equity to a one-half share; (2) that the conduct of the parties evinced an implied contract entitling plaintiff to one-half the property accumulated during their "family relationship"; (3) that because defendant fraudulently assured plaintiff she was his wife in order to secure her services, although he knew they were not legally married, defendant's property should be impressed with a trust for plaintiff's benefit; (4) that because plaintiff has relied to her detriment on defendant's promises and devoted her entire life to him, defendant has been unjustly enriched.

The factual background alleged or testified to is that in June 1960, when she and defendant were students at Grinnell College in Iowa, plaintiff became pregnant; that defendant thereafter told her that they were husband and wife and would live as such, no formal ceremony being necessary, and that he would "share his life, his future, his earnings and his property" with her; that the parties immediately announced to their respective parents that they were married and thereafter held themselves out as husband and wife; that in reliance on defendant's promises she devoted her efforts to his professional education and his establishment in the practice of pedodontia, obtaining financial assistance from her parents for this purpose; that she assisted defendant in his career with her own special skills and although she was given payroll checks for these services she placed them in a common fund; that defendant, who was without funds at the time of the marriage, as a result of her efforts now earns over $80,000 a year and has accumulated large amounts of property, owned either jointly with her or separately; that she has given him every assistance a wife and mother could give, including social activities designed to enhance his social and professional reputation.

The amended complaint was also dismissed, the trial court finding that Illinois law and public policy require such claims to be based on a valid marriage. The appellate court reversed, stating that because the parties had outwardly lived a conventional married life, plaintiff's conduct had not "so affronted public policy that she should be denied any and all relief," and that plaintiff's complaint stated a cause of action on an express oral contract. We granted leave to appeal. Defendant apparently does not contest his obligation to support the children, and that question is not before us. . . .

* * *

. . . The issue of unmarried cohabitants' mutual property rights, however, as we earlier noted, cannot appropriately be characterized solely in terms of contract law, nor is it limited to considerations of equity or fairness as between the parties to such relationships. There are major public policy questions involved in determining whether, under what circumstances, and to what extent it is desirable to accord some type of legal status to claims arising from such relationships. Of substantially greater importance than the rights of the immediate parties is the impact of such recognition upon our society and the institution of marriage. Will the fact that legal rights closely resembling those arising from conventional marriages can be acquired by those who deliberately choose to enter into what have heretofore been commonly referred to as "illicit" or "meretricious" relationships encourage formation of such relationships and weaken marriage as the foundation of our family-based society? In the event of death shall the survivor have the status of a surviving spouse for purposes of inheritance, wrongful death actions, workmen's compensation, etc.? And still more importantly: what of the children born of such relationships? What are their support and inheritance rights and by what standards are custody questions resolved? What of the sociological and psychological effects upon them of that type of environment? Does not the recognition of legally enforceable property and custody rights emanating from nonmarital cohabitation in practical effect equate with the legalization of common law marriage at least in the circumstances of this case? And, in summary, have the increasing numbers of unmarried cohabitants and changing mores of our society reached the point at which the general welfare of the citizens of this State is best served by a return to something resembling the judicially created common law marriage our legislature outlawed in 1905? . . .

* * *

. . . We cannot confidently say that judicial recognition of property rights between unmarried cohabitants will not make that alternative to marriage more attractive by allowing the parties to engage in such relationships with greater security. As one commentator has noted, it may make this alternative especially attractive to persons who seek a property arrangement that the law does not permit to marital partners. This court, for example, has held void agreements releasing husbands from their obligation to support their wives. In thus potentially enhancing the attractiveness of a private arrangement over marriage, we believe that the appellate court decision in this case contravenes the [Illinois Marriage and Dissolution of Marriage] Act's policy of strengthening and preserving the integrity of marriage.

* * *

We accordingly hold that plaintiff's claims are unenforceable for the reason that they contravene the public policy, implicit in the statutory scheme of the Illinois Marriage and Dissolution of Marriage Act, disfavoring the grant of mutually enforceable property rights to knowingly unmarried cohabitants. The judgment of the appellate court is reversed and the judgment of the circuit court of Champaign County is affirmed.

Appellate court reversed; circuit court affirmed.

NOTES AND QUESTIONS

1. Since Victoria Hewitt was not married and was prevented from asserting claims against Robert based on contract or equity principles, their relationship

was essentially that of long-term roommates. Each owned the property in his or her name, and neither had any economic claim against the other. Why would Victoria have agreed to live in a relationship that left her so economically vulnerable? Does the reason that she agreed matter now that she is seeking legal relief? Professor Fineman proposes that the law provide no special protection to adults who live together on the basis of that relationship alone, and that instead family rights should be based on the existence of caretaking relationships. Her proposal, as fully developed, would include legal protection for an adult who is the caretaker for dependent children (or adults). Martha Albertson Fineman, The Neutered Mother, the Sexual Family and Other Twentieth Century Tragedies (1995). She would, therefore, provide a remedy for Victoria, the mother and caretaker of three children. However, if Victoria and Robert had not had children but still lived a role-divided life in which Victoria maintained the home and Robert worked as a children's dentist, Victoria would not have a claim under Fineman's proposal. Would you agree with this result?

2. The Illinois court was concerned that allowing Victoria to make a claim against Robert would undermine marriage. In what ways would allowing her to make a claim make living together more desirable than marriage? Are there ways in which marriage would still be more desirable to the individuals involved?

3. Professor Regan argues against equating cohabitation with marriage (though in a later part of the article he makes clear that cohabitants should have some rights vis-à-vis one another) on the basis that, in general, cohabitation arrangements are less stable than marriages. Does this matter in a day when half of all marriages end in divorce? Why or why not? Professor Regan also argues that treating marriage as special promotes commitment among adults. Why is commitment important? How does treating marriage differently from cohabitation promote commitment?

4. As we will see in Chapter 4, in most states in the United States today Victoria would be able to state a claim against Robert for common law marriage or, where common law marriage is not permitted, based upon the contract or equity theories that the Illinois court in *Hewitt* rejected.

BRASCHI V. STAHL ASSOCIATES COMPANY

74 N.Y.2d 201, 543 N.E.2d 49, 544 N.Y.S.2d 784 (1989)

TITONE, J. Appellant, Miguel Braschi, was living with Leslie Blanchard in a rent-controlled apartment located at 405 East 54th Street from the summer of 1975 until Blanchard's death in September of 1986. In November of 1986, respondent, Stahl Associates Company, the owner of the apartment building, served a notice to cure on appellant contending that he was a mere licensee with no right to occupy the apartment since only Blanchard was the tenant of record. In December of 1986 respondent served appellant with a notice to terminate informing appellant that he had one month to vacate the apartment and that, if the apartment was not vacated, respondent would commence summary proceedings to evict him.

Appellant then initiated an action seeking a permanent injunction and a declaration of entitlement to occupy the apartment. By order to show cause appellant then moved for a preliminary injunction, pendente lite, enjoining respondent from evicting him until a court could determine whether he was a member of Blanchard's family within the meaning of 9 NYCRR 2204.6(d). After examining the nature of the relationship between the two men, Supreme Court concluded that appellant was a "family member" within the meaning of the regulation and, accordingly, that a preliminary injunction should be issued. . . .

The Appellate Division reversed, concluding that section 2204.6(d) provides noneviction protection only to "family members within traditional, legally recognized familial relationships." . . . We now reverse.

The present dispute arises because the term "family" is not defined in the rent-control code and the legislative history is devoid of any specific reference to the noneviction provision. All that is known is the legislative purpose underlying the enactment of the rent-control laws as a whole. Rent control was enacted to address a "serious public emergency" created by "an acute shortage in dwellings," which resulted in "speculative, unwarranted and abnormal increases in rents." These measures were designed to regulate and control the housing market so as to "prevent exactions of unjust, unreasonable and oppressive rents and rental agreements and to forestall profiteering, speculation and other disruptive practices tending to produce threats to the public health . . . [and] to prevent uncertainty, hardship and dislocation." . . .

To accomplish its goals, the Legislature recognized that not only would rents have to be controlled, but that evictions would have to be regulated and controlled as well. Hence, section 2204.6 of the New York City Rent and Eviction Regulations (9 NYCRR 2204.6), which authorizes the issuance of a certificate for the eviction of persons occupying a rent-controlled apartment after the death of the named tenant, provides, in subdivision (d), noneviction protection to those occupants who are either the "surviving spouse of the deceased tenant or some other member of the deceased tenant's family who has been living with the tenant [of record]." The manifest intent of this section is to restrict the landowners' ability to evict a narrow class of occupants other than the tenant of record. The question presented here concerns the scope of the protections provided. Juxtaposed against this intent favoring the protection of tenants is the over-all objective of a gradual "transition from regulation to a normal market of free bargaining between landlord and tenant." One way in which this goal is to be achieved is "vacancy decontrol," which automatically makes rent-control units subject to the less rigorous provisions of rent stabilization upon the termination of the rent-control tenancy.

Emphasizing the latter objective, respondent argues that the term "family member" as used in 9 NYCRR 2204.6(d) should be construed, consistent with this State's intestacy laws, to mean relationships of blood, consanguinity and adoption in order to effectuate the over-all goal of orderly succession to real property. Under this interpretation, only those entitled to inherit under the laws of intestacy would be afforded noneviction protection. . . .

* * *

Contrary to all of these arguments, we conclude that the term "family," as used in 9 NYCRR 2204.6(d), should not be rigidly restricted to those people who have formalized their relationship by obtaining, for instance, a marriage certificate or an adoption order. The intended protection against sudden eviction should not rest on fictitious legal distinctions or genetic history, but instead should find its foundation in the reality of family life. In the context of eviction, a more realistic, and certainly equally valid, view of a family includes two adult lifetime partners whose relationship is long term and characterized by an emotional and financial commitment and interdependence. This view comports both with our society's traditional concept of "family" and with the expectations of individuals who live in such nuclear units. In fact, Webster's Dictionary defines "family" first as "a group of people united by certain convictions or common affiliation." Hence, it is reasonable to conclude that, in using the term "family," the Legislature intended to extend protection to those who reside in households having all of the normal familial characteristics. Appellant Braschi should therefore be afforded the opportunity to prove that he and Blanchard had such a household.

This definition of "family" is consistent with both of the competing purposes of the rent-control laws: the protection of individuals from sudden dislocation and the gradual transition to a free market system. Family members, whether or not related by blood or law, who have always treated the apartment as their family home will be protected against the hardship of eviction following the death of the named tenant, thereby furthering the Legislature's goals of preventing dislocation and preserving family units which might otherwise be broken apart upon eviction. This approach will foster the transition from rent control to rent stabilization by drawing a distinction between those individuals who are, in fact, genuine family members, and those who are mere roommates or newly discovered relatives hoping to inherit the rent-controlled apartment after the existing tenant's death.

The determination as to whether an individual is entitled to noneviction protection should be based upon an objective examination of the relationship of the parties. In making this assessment, the lower courts of this State have looked to a number of factors, including the exclusivity and longevity of the relationship, the level of emotional and financial commitment, the manner in which the parties have conducted their everyday lives and held themselves out to society, and the reliance placed upon one another for daily family services. These factors are most helpful, although it should be emphasized that the presence or absence of one or more of them is not dispositive since it is the totality of the relationship as evidenced by the dedication, caring and self-sacrifice of the parties which should, in the final analysis, control. Appellant's situation provides an example of how the rule should be applied.

Appellant and Blanchard lived together as permanent life partners for more than 10 years. They regarded one another, and were regarded by friends and family, as spouses. The two men's families were aware of the nature of the relationship, and they regularly visited each other's families and attended family functions together, as a couple. Even today, appellant continues to maintain a relationship with Blanchard's niece, who considers him an uncle. In addition to their interwoven social lives, appellant clearly considered the apartment his home. He lists the apartment as his address on his driver's license and passport, and receives all his mail at the apartment address. Moreover, appellant's tenancy was known to the building's superintendent and doormen, who viewed the two men as a couple. Financially, the two men shared all obligations including a household budget. The two were authorized signatories of three safe-deposit boxes, they maintained joint checking and savings accounts, and joint credit cards. In fact, rent was often paid with a check from their joint checking account. Additionally, Blanchard executed a power of attorney in appellant's favor so that appellant could make necessary decisions — financial, medical and personal — for him during his illness. Finally, appellant was the named beneficiary of Blanchard's life insurance policy, as well as the primary legatee and coexecutor of Blanchard's estate. Hence, a court examining these facts could reasonably conclude that these men were much more than mere roommates.

. . . Accordingly, the order of the Appellate Division should be reversed and the case remitted to that court for a consideration of undetermined questions. The certified question should be answered in the negative.

SIMONS, J. (dissenting). I would affirm. The plurality has adopted a definition of family which extends the language of the regulation well beyond the implication of the words used in it. In doing so, it has expanded the class indefinitely to include anyone who can satisfy an administrator that he or she had an emotional and financial "commitment" to the statutory tenant. Its interpretation is inconsistent with the legislative scheme underlying rent regulation, goes well beyond the intended purposes of 9 NYCRR 2204.6(d), and produces an unworkable test that is subject to abuse. . . .

* * *

. . . [T]here are serious practical problems in adopting the plurality's interpretation of the statute. Any determination of rights under it would require first a determination of whether protection should be accorded the relationship (i.e., unmarrieds, nonadopted occupants, etc.) and then a subjective determination in each case of whether the relationship was genuine, and entitled to the protection of the law, or expedient, and an attempt to take advantage of the law. Plaintiff maintains that the machinery for such decisions is in place and that appropriate guidelines can be constructed. He refers particularly to a formulation outlined by the court in 2-4 Realty Assocs. v. Pittman, 137 Misc. 2d 898, 902, 523 N.Y.S.2d 7, which sets forth six factors to be weighed. The plurality has essentially adopted his formulation. The enumeration of such factors, and the determination that they are controlling, is a matter best left to Legislatures because it involves the type of policy making the courts should avoid, but even if these considerations are appropriate and exclusive, the application of them cannot be made objectively and creates serious difficulties in determining who is entitled to the statutory benefit. Anyone is potentially eligible to succeed to the tenant's premises and thus, in each case, the agency will be required to make a determination of eligibility based solely on subjective factors such as the "level of emotional and financial commitment" and "the manner in which the parties have conducted their everyday lives and held themselves out to society."

(The concurring opinion of Bellacosa, J., is omitted.)

NOTES AND QUESTIONS

1. The governing statute in this case provides protections to members of a decedent's "family." Upon what theory does the majority find that Miguel Braschi and Leslie Blanchard were a family? Do you think that the court would have found that Victoria and Robert Hewitt, who could have married but did not, were a family?

2. How does the majority determine whether a relationship constitutes a family? How would the dissent determine this question? What role do stereotypes and cultural norms play in these definitions? If Miguel and Leslie had been a married heterosexual couple who lived apart for half the year, maintained separate finances, and kept their marriage secret from family and friends, would Miguel have been a surviving family member for purposes of the statute as interpreted by the majority? The dissent?

3. What values are promoted by the majority's test for "family"-ness? By the dissent's? The dissent says that this value choice should be made by the legislature, not the court. Do you agree? Why or why not? On facts such as this, is it possible for a court not to make a value choice?

4. In Fitzpatrick v. Sterling Housing Association, [1999] 4 All ER 705, involving legislation governing tenants' rights, the English House of Lords interpreted the term *family* similarly to how *Braschi* did. The decision is available at *http://www.parliament.the-stationery-office.co.uk/pa/ld199899/ldjudgmt/jd991028/fitz01.htm*.

5. *Braschi* has not been broadly applied by the New York courts. For example, the Court of Appeals refused to apply *Braschi*'s analytical approach to a custody dispute between a biological mother and her former mate, even though the two women had agreed to have the child and had functioned as parents together for the first two years of the child's life. Alison D. v. Virginia M., 572 N.E.2d 27 (N.Y. 1991).

6. Whether cohabitants are entitled to public benefits dependent on family relationships has arisen in a number of other situations, with mixed results. *See, e.g.*, MacGregor v. Unemployment Insurance Appeals Board, 689 P.2d 453 (Cal. 1984) (allowing unemployment compensation benefits to a woman who quit work to follow fiance); Norman v. Unemployment Insurance Appeals Board, 663 P.2d 904 (Cal. 1983) (denying unemployment benefits to a woman who quit work to follow cohabitant because this was not "good cause"). Some jurisdictions have statutes that provide relief in specific instances. *See, e.g.*, Or. Rev. Stat. §656.226:

> In case an unmarried man and an unmarried woman have cohabited in this state as husband and wife for over one year prior to the date of an accidental injury received by one or the other as a subject worker, and children are living as a result of that relation, the surviving cohabitant and the children are entitled to compensation under this chapter [workers' compensation] the same as if the man and woman had been legally married.

7. Rutgers Council of AAUP Chapters v. Rutgers University, 689 A.2d 828 (N.J. Super. App. Div. 1997), held that limitation of benefits to employees' spouses does not violate the New Jersey Law Against Discrimination or the

New Jersey Constitution, but University of Alaska v. Tumeo, 933 P.2d 1147 (Alaska 1997), held that denial of health benefits to university employees' same-sex partners violates the Alaska Human Rights Act barring discrimination in employment on the basis of marital status. As the *Tumeo* court noted, however, while the case was pending the Human Rights Act was amended to allow employers to offer coverage only to spouses of employees.

Oregon Health Sciences University v. Tanner, 971 P.2d 435 (Or. App. 1998), construed the state's employment statutes as allowing public employers to offer benefits only to employees' spouses, but the court then ruled that denying benefits to the same-sex domestic partners of employees constituted sex-based discrimination in violation of the state constitution.

CITY OF LADUE V. HORN

720 S.W.2d 745 (Mo. App. E.D. 1986)

CRANDALL, Judge. Defendants, Joan Horn and E. Terrence Jones, appeal from the judgment of the trial court in favor of plaintiff, City of Ladue (Ladue), which enjoined defendants from occupying their home in violation of Ladue's zoning ordinance and which dismissed defendants' counterclaim. We affirm.

The case was submitted to the trial court on stipulated facts. Ladue's Zoning Ordinance No. 1175 was in effect at all times pertinent to the present action. Certain zones were designated as one-family residential. The zoning ordinance defined family as: "One or more persons related by blood, marriage or adoption, occupying a dwelling unit as an individual housekeeping organization." The only authorized accessory use in residential districts was for "[a]ccommodations for domestic persons employed and living on the premises and home occupations." The purpose of Ladue's zoning ordinance was broadly stated as to promote "the health, safety, morals and general welfare" of Ladue.

In July, 1981, defendants purchased a seven-bedroom, four-bathroom house which was located in a single-family residential zone in Ladue. Residing in defendants' home were Horn's two children (aged 16 and 19) and Jones's one child (age 18). The two older children attended out-of-state universities and lived in the house only on a part-time basis. Although defendants were not married, they shared a common bedroom, maintained a joint checking account for the household expenses, ate their meals together, entertained together, and disciplined each other's children. Ladue made demands upon defendants to vacate their home because their household did not comprise a family, as defined by Ladue's zoning ordinance, and therefore they could not live in an area zoned for single-family dwellings. When defendants refused to vacate, Ladue sought to enjoin defendants' continued violation of the zoning ordinance. Defendants counterclaimed, seeking a declaration that the zoning ordinance was constitutionally void. They also sought attorneys' fees and costs. The trial court entered a permanent injunction in favor of Ladue and dismissed defendants' counterclaim. Enforcement of the injunction was stayed pending this appeal.

* * *

. . . Defendants allege that the United States and Missouri Constitutions grant each of them the right to share his or her residence with whomever he or she chooses. They assert that Ladue has not demonstrated a compelling, much less rational, justification for the overly proscriptive blood or legal relationship requirement in its zoning ordinance.

Defendants posit that the term "family" is susceptible to several meanings. They contend that, since their household is the "functional and factual equivalent of a natural family," the ordinance may not preclude them from living in a single-family residential Ladue neighborhood. Defendants argue in their brief as follows:

> The record amply demonstrates that the private, intimate interests of Horn and Jones are substantial. Horn, Jones, and their respective children have historically lived together as a single family unit. They use and occupy their home for the identical purposes and in the identical manners as families which are biologically or maritally related.

To bolster this contention, defendants elaborate on their shared duties, as set forth earlier in this opinion. Defendants acknowledge the importance of viewing themselves as a family unit, albeit a "conceptual family" as opposed to a "true non-family," in order to prevent the application of the ordinance.

The fallacy in defendants' syllogism is that the stipulated facts do not compel the conclusion that defendants are living as a family. A man and woman living together, sharing pleasures and certain responsibilities, does not *per se* constitute a family in even the conceptual sense. To approximate a family relationship, there must exist a commitment to a permanent relationship and a perceived reciprocal obligation to support and to care for each other. Only when these characteristics are present can the conceptual family, perhaps, equate with the traditional family. In a traditional family, certain of its inherent attributes arise from the legal relationship of the family members. In a non-traditional family, those same qualities arise in fact, either by explicit agreement or by tacit understanding among the parties.

While the stipulated facts could arguably support an inference by the trial court that defendants and their children comprised a non-traditional family, they do not compel that inference. Absent findings of fact and conclusions of law, we cannot assume that the trial court's perception of defendants' familial status comported with defendants' characterization of themselves as a conceptual family. In fact, if a finding by the trial court that defendants' living arrangement constituted a conceptual family is critical to a determination in defendants' favor, we can assume that the court's finding was adverse to defendants' position. Ordinarily, given our deference to the decision of the trial court, that would dispose of this appeal. We decline, however, to restrict our ruling to such a narrow basis. We therefore consider the broader issues presented by the parties. We assume, *arguendo*, that the sole basis for the judgment entered by the trial court was that defendants were not related by blood, marriage or adoption, as required by Ladue's ordinance.

We first consider whether the ordinance violates any federally protected rights of the defendants. Generally, federal court decisions hold that a zoning classification based upon a biological or a legal relationship among household members is justifiable under constitutional police powers to protect the public health, safety, morals or welfare of the community.

More specifically, the United States Supreme Court has developed a two-tiered approach by which to examine legislation challenged as violative of the equal protection clause. If the personal interest affected by the ordinance is fundamental, "strict scrutiny" is applied and the ordinance is sustained only upon a showing that the burden imposed is necessary to protect a compelling governmental interest. If the ordinance does not contain a suspect class or impinge upon a fundamental interest, the more relaxed "rational basis" test is applied and the classification imposed by the ordinance is upheld if any facts can reasonably justify it. Defendants urge this court to recognize that their interest in choosing their own living arrangement inexorably involves their fundamental rights of freedom of association and of privacy.

* * *

In the *Village of Belle Terre v. Boraas*, 416 U.S. 1 (1974), the court addressed a zoning regulation of the type at issue in this case. The court held that the Village of Belle Terre ordinance involved no fundamental right, but was typical of economic and social legislation which is upheld if it is reasonably related to a permissible governmental objective. The challenged zoning ordinance of the Village of Belle Terre defined family as:

> One or more persons related by blood, adoption or marriage, living and cooking together as a single housekeeping unit [or] a number of persons but not exceeding two (2) living and cooking together as a single housekeeping unit though not related by blood, adoption, or marriage. . . .

The court upheld the ordinance, reasoning that the ordinance constituted valid land use legislation reasonably designed to maintain traditional family values and patterns.

The importance of the family was reaffirmed in *Moore v. City of East Cleveland*, 431 U.S. 494 (1977), wherein the United States Supreme Court was confronted with a housing ordinance which defined a "family" as only certain closely related individuals. Consequently, a grandmother who lived with her son and two grandsons was convicted of violating the ordinance because her two grandsons were first cousins rather than brothers. The United States Supreme Court struck down the East Cleveland ordinance for violating the freedom of personal choice in matters of marriage and family life. The court distinguished *Belle Terre* by stating that the ordinance in that case allowed all individuals related by blood, marriage or adoption to live together; whereas East Cleveland, by restricting the number of related persons who could live together, sought "to regulate the occupancy of its housing by slicing deeply into the family itself." The court pointed out that the institution of the family is protected by the Constitution precisely because it is so deeply rooted in the American tradition and that "[o]urs is by no means a tradition limited to respect for the bonds uniting the members of the nuclear family."

Here, because we are dealing with economic and social legislation and not with a fundamental interest or a suspect classification, the test of constitutionality is whether the ordinance is reasonable and not arbitrary and bears a rational relationship to a permissible state objective.

Ladue has a legitimate concern with laying out guidelines for land use addressed to family needs. "It is ample to lay out zones where family values, youth values, and the blessings of quiet seclusion and clean air make the area a sanctuary for people." The question of whether Ladue could have chosen more precise means to effectuate its legislative goals is immaterial. Ladue's zoning ordinance is rationally related to its expressed purposes and violates no provisions of the Constitution of the United States. Further, defendants' assertion that they have a constitutional right to share their residence with whomever they please amounts to the same argument that was made and found unpersuasive by the court in *Belle Terre*.

* * *

For purposes of its zoning code, Ladue has in precise language defined the term "family." It chose the definition which comports with the historical and traditional notions of family; namely, those people related by blood, marriage or adoption. That definition of family has been upheld in numerous Missouri decisions. *See, e.g., London v. Handicapped Facilities Board of St. Charles County*, 637 S.W.2d 212 (Mo. App. 1982) (group home not a "family" as used in restrictive covenant); *Feely v. Birenbaum*, 554 S.W.2d 432 (Mo. App. 1977) (two unrelated males not a "family" as used in restrictive covenant); *Cash v. Catholic Diocese*, 414 S.W.2d 346 (Mo. App. 1967) (nuns not a "family" as used in a restrictive covenant).

Decisions from other state jurisdictions have addressed identical constitutional challenges to zoning ordinances similar to the ordinance in the instant case. The reviewing courts have upheld their respective ordinances on the ground that maintenance of a traditional family environment constitutes a reasonable basis for excluding uses that may impair the stability of that environment and erode the values associated with traditional family life.[1]

---

1. *See, e.g., City of White Plains v. Ferraioli*, 34 N.Y.2d 300, 357 N.Y.S.2d 449, 313 N.E.2d 756 (1974) (married couple, their two children and 10 foster children not a family under city's ordinance); *Rademan v. City and County of Denver*, 186 Colo. 250, 526 P.2d 1325 (1974) (two married couples living as a "communal family" not a family); *Town of Durham v. White Enterprises, Inc.*, 115 N.H. 645, 348 A.2d 706 (1975) (student renters not a family); *Prospect Gardens Convalescent Home, Inc. v. City of Norwalk*, 32 Conn. Supp. 214, 347 A.2d 637 (1975) (nursing home employees living together not a family). *See generally* Annot., 12 A.L.R. 4th 238 (1985). A number of jurisdictions have found restrictive zoning ordinances invalid. *See, e.g., City of Des Plaines v. Trottner*, 34 Ill. 2d 432, 216 N.E.2d 116 (1970) (ordinance with restrictive definition of family violates authority delegated by state legislature in the enabling statute); *City of Santa Barbara v. Adamson*, 27 Cal. 3d 123, 164 Cal. Rptr. 539, 610 P.2d 436 (1982) (zoning ordinance limiting the number of unrelated persons who could live together, but not related persons, did not further legislative goals); *Charter Township of Delta v. Dinolfo*, 419 Mich. 253, 351 N.W.2d 831 (1984) (restrictive definition of family not rationally related to achieving township's goals).

The handwritten note in the left margin reads: *Government interest in marriage*

The essence of zoning is selection; and, if it is not invidious or discriminatory against those not selected, it is proper. There is no doubt that there is a governmental interest in marriage and in preserving the integrity of the biological or legal family. There is no concomitant governmental interest in keeping together a group of unrelated persons, no matter how closely they simulate a family. Further, there is no state policy which commands that groups of people may live under the same roof in any section of a municipality they choose.

The stated purpose of Ladue's zoning ordinance is the promotion of the health, safety, morals and general welfare in the city. Whether Ladue could have adopted less restrictive means to achieve these same goals is not a controlling factor in considering the constitutionality of the zoning ordinance. Rather, our focus is on whether there exists some reasonable basis for the means actually employed. In making such a determination, if any state of facts either known or which could reasonably be assumed is presented in support of the ordinance, we must defer to the legislative judgment. We find that Ladue has not acted arbitrarily in enacting its zoning ordinance which defines family as those related by blood, marriage or adoption. Given the fact that Ladue has so defined family, we defer to its legislative judgment.

The judgment of the trial court is affirmed.

NOTES AND QUESTIONS

1. Why did the City of Ladue limit buildings in this part of town to "single family dwellings"? How does the Ladue zoning ordinance define "single family"? What assumptions about the meaning of "family" does this definition make? Is this definition of "family" consistent with the goal of the ordinance? If Horn and Jones had married, they would have fit squarely within the ordinance's definition of "family"; how would the fact that they were married have made them more suitable residents of this neighborhood? Could the court have interpreted the ordinance in a manner similar to that in *Braschi*, or did the statutory language prevent this? Consider the following comment.

> Zoning urban, suburban, and rural areas has proven a useful tool for local and state governments to control population, traffic, pollution, and other social problems. Unfortunately, zoning has also been used to control the identity of the population, and with some success. The ordinance at issue in *Belle Terre* was a common instance of this kind of control; it limited the number of unrelated people that could live in a home, but put no such limit on the number of related people that may live together. Using this type of zoning ordinance, many municipalities have successfully kept out or forced out unrelated people living communally and other non-traditional families. This sort of discrimination, although purportedly for the lawful purpose of protecting traditional family values, effectively imposes the municipality's social preferences on the individuals in the community. Not only does this seem contrary to the most basic and often quoted American themes of plurality and individuality, it summarily dismisses the value of the voluntary family.

* * *

The 1960s and 1970s were a period of great social and political upheaval. Along with the era's more familiar symbols of protest and civil unrest—anti-war demonstrations, civil rights demonstrations, and the "hippie" movement—many Americans expressed their discontent with mainstream culture by moving into cooperative-living communities, such as communes.

Communes, however, were nothing new to the United States in the 1960s and 1970s. That period of communal development was the fourth such period in the nineteenth and twentieth centuries; the previous periods took place between 1842 and 1848, between 1894 and 1900, and during the 1930s. Like the movement of the 1960s and 1970s, the others "coincided with [periods] of millennial anticipation" and with fifty to fifty-five year waves, known as Kondratiev cycles, that corresponded to economic fluctuations. Motivation for the movement of the 1960s and 1970s differed from the others, however. Communes in existence through 1845 often formed as a result of religious issues; economic and political issues were the impetus behind many developed between 1820 and 1930; and psychosocial issues provoked the establishment of communes between the Second World War and the 1970s. Interestingly, a study of some of the 1960s communards demonstrated that they came predominantly from nuclear families that they described as "loving and intimate," and from homes in which their parents had nurtured and loved them unconditionally. The study seems to suggest, then, that the communards of the 1960s and 1970s were not seeking a better family, as they left perfectly good ones behind. Instead, they were moved by a sense of alienation, by ideological, relational, and personal reasons, and for convenience. Many hoped to find utopia or experiment with a new way of life.

* * *

. . . By contrast, many of today's communards are seeking a place to settle down with some measure of efficiency and community. New communards "tend not to reject the values of society, but select what they like from mainstream society and supplement their lives with those aspects of communal living which enhance and strengthen their sense of self." If trends continue as some sociologists expect, communal arrangements of the twenty-first century "will focus more and more on issues related to health, the environment, stress reduction, personal morality, and building community," rather than a vision of utopia.

Communards today also represent a wider cross-section of Americans. Many communards of the past were individuals who either became ideologically disillusioned by the socio-political state of affairs in the "outside world" or decided to venture out on a spiritual journey; more importantly, they were people who had the time and resources to take this step. Today, communal living draws people wishing to share resources and community, including a large number of single parents and elderly people struggling to live independently on inadequate social security payments.

Co-housing groups are comprised of a group of households "looking for a way to share some of the responsibilities of day-to-day living—preparing and sharing meals, providing child care, maintaining a garden and even sharing cars." Co-housing communities attempt to strike a balance between privacy and cooperation, while also coming together as a community. Within a typical co-housing development, some space is shared by the whole group, but there are also self-sufficient residences. Individuals, couples, or related groups might have their own "apartment" and share a common play area, a common dining area, or a common work space. In this way, members can enjoy peace and quiet or company as they wish, an arguably less all-encompassing and intrusive arrangement than in a traditional family's home.

* * *

No doubt the law-abiding citizens of Belle Terre believed that the Supreme Court had saved their neighborhood. After all, if those students were allowed to live there, others could follow, until the streets were lined with traffic and empty beer bottles. Once the "weirdos" got in, they might never be able to get rid of them, and the quiet of their waterfront enclave would be forever lost.

Those students were not the weirdos the villagers thought, however. In fact, they were probably making better use of the six-bedroom house than anyone else had ever made of it. They shared responsibilities and intellectual conversations, and lived as efficiently as they could on their limited means. During the summer, they, like everyone else in town, looked forward to relaxing on the beach with their family. This family was simply a little bit different in character than the others: there were no noisy children and no wedding rings. Instead there was friendship, camaraderie, and a well-run household.

Rebecca Ginzburg, Note, Altering "Family": Another Look at The Supreme Court's Narrow Protection of Families in Belle Terre, 83 B.U. L. Rev. 875, 877, 878-879, 888-890 (2003).

2. Horn and Jones argued that the zoning ordinance should be subject to strict scrutiny under the equal protection clause because it adversely affects their fundamental rights of freedom of association and of privacy. To succeed, they would have had to distinguish their situation from that in Belle Terre v. Boraas and analogize it to the situation in Moore v. City of East Cleveland. If you had represented them, how would you have made this argument? If you represented the City of Ladue, how would you have responded?

3. No state or federal statute prohibiting discrimination in housing explicitly prohibits discrimination against unmarried couples. Matthew J. Smith, The Wages of Living in Sin: Discrimination in Housing Against Unmarried Couples, 25 U.C. Davis L. Rev. 1055, 1071-1091 (1992) (discussing the Fair Housing Act of 1968, 42 U.S.C. §§3601-3619, 3631, and fair housing statutes in 47 states and the District of Columbia). The state courts are divided about whether statutory provisions prohibiting housing discrimination on the basis of marital status protect unmarried couples.

4. The California Supreme Court has rejected the argument that a landlord may be exempted for religious reasons from complying with a fair housing law prohibiting discrimination on the basis of marital status. In Smith v. Fair Employment and Housing Commission, 913 P.2d 909 (Cal. 1996), the court concluded that the landlord's religious exemption claim fails under Employment Division v. Smith, 494 U.S. 872 (1990), which held that enforcement of a generally applicable law that is neutral toward religion does not violate the First Amendment even if it burdens religious practice. Contra Minnesota v. French, 460 N.W.2d 2 (Minn. 1990). See also McCready v. Hoffius, 593 N.W.2d 545 (Mich. 1999), holding that landlords who refuse to rent to unmarried couples violate the state's statutory ban on discrimination on the basis of marital status

and remanding for consideration of the landlords' claim that applying the statute to them violates their religious freedom.

BOROUGH OF GLASSBORO V. VALLOROSI

117 N.J. 421, 568 A.2d 888 (1990)

PER CURIAM. . . . In July 1986, the Borough [of Glassboro] amended its zoning ordinance, apparently in response to a rowdy weekend celebration by Glassboro State College students. The amendment applied to the Borough's residential districts and limited the use and occupancy of "detached dwellings" and structures with "two dwelling units" to "families" only. The ordinance defined a "family" as

> one or more persons occupying a dwelling unit as a single non-profit housekeeping unit, who are living together as a stable and permanent living unit, being a traditional family unit or the functional equivalency [sic] thereof.

The amendment included a statement of purpose that plainly reflected the Borough's intention to confine college students either to the dormitories provided by Glassboro State College or to the other zoning districts that permit apartments and townhouses:

purpose of amendment

> The preservation of "family style living" and the preservation of the character of residential neighborhoods as such are legitimate zoning goals. The Borough of Glassboro is concerned with maintaining the stability and permanence generally associated with single family occupancy throughout its residential neighborhoods. A municipality may endeavor, by legitimate means, to secure and maintain the blessings of quiet seclusion and to make available to its inhabitants the refreshment of repose and the tranquility of solitude. The Borough of Glassboro possesses these goals and, by the regulation herein contained, implements them in a manner which bears a reasonable relationship to the problem sought to be ameliorated. That problem is the use and occupancy of single family and two family dwellings, interspersed among the residential neighborhoods of the community, by groups of individuals whose living arrangements, although temporarily in the same dwelling unit, are transient in nature and do not possess the elements of stability and permanency which have long been associated with single family occupancy. Such living arrangements are not compatible with the family style living sought to be preserved. Such occupancies are in the nature of rooming houses, boarding homes, hotels, motels, and the like. Such uses do not meet the definition of family as contained in this ordinance and are prohibited in detached dwellings and structures with two dwelling units in all residential zones. This ordinance provides zoning classifications which allow for ample apartment and townhouse uses, and there are presently many such uses in existence throughout the Borough. Likewise, Glassboro State College maintains substantial dormitory and apartment facilities for students and faculty members. Therefore, ample housing exists within the Borough for college students and others who choose to live under arrangements which do not meet the definition of family as provided in this ordinance.

In June 1986, defendants purchased a home located in the restricted residential zone. The purchase was intended to provide a college home for Peter Vallorosi, the brother of defendant Diane Vallorosi and the son of two partners in S & V Associates, a real-estate investment partnership. (Under the partnership agreement, S & V Associates acquired equitable title to the premises when defendants purchased the home.) It was contemplated that nine of Peter's friends would share the house with him while the group attended Glassboro State College. Seven of the ten students renting the house were sophomores at the time their lease took effect. They were all between the ages of eighteen and twenty. All ten students entered into separate, renewable leases for a semester-long period of four months. At the end of each semester, a student could renew the lease for another term "if the house is found to be in order at [the] end of [the preceding] term."

The students moved into their new home in early September 1986. The house had one large kitchen, which was shared by all ten students. The students often ate meals together in small groups, cooked for each other, and generally shared the household chores, grocery shopping, and yard work. A common checking account paid for food and other bills. They shared the use of a telephone. Although uncertain of living arrangements after graduation, the students intended to remain tenants as long as they were enrolled at Glassboro State College.

The Borough commenced this action in September 1986, seeking an injunction against the use and occupancy of the house by the students. The complaint alleged that the occupants did not constitute a "family" as defined in the Borough's ordinance. . . . [D]efendants argued that the communal nature of the students' occupancy, coupled with their intention to live there together throughout their college careers, satisfied the ordinance's requirement that any occupancy be functionally equivalent to "a traditional family unit."

The Chancery Division . . . focused on whether the specific circumstances of the students' occupancy satisfied the ordinance's requirements:

> The testimony that was most helpful to the Court in determining if a group of young men living together exhibited the "generic character" of a family was that of the students themselves. They stated that they do not just rent a room, but that they rent the whole house. The common areas are shared by all with free access; there is one kitchen that is used by the students and meals are either eaten together or in small groups. There is a common checkbook from which the bills of running the house are paid. Although their leases are for a short period of time, they intend to stay in Glassboro so long as they attend the college.

Based on this testimony, the court concluded that the relationship among the students "shows stability, permanancy and can be described as the functional equivalent of a family." The Appellate Division affirmed on the basis of the trial court's analysis.

We granted the Borough's petition for certification. . . .

During the pendency of this appeal, the Court was notified that Peter Vallorosi withdrew from Glassboro State College and that the use of the home by the students ended effective September 1, 1988. Nevertheless, we render a decision on the merits because of the important issues presented.

II.

The legal principles determinative of this appeal are clear and well-settled. The courts of this state have consistently invalidated zoning ordinances intended "to cure or prevent . . . anti-social conduct in dwelling situations." *Kirsch Holding Co. v. Borough of Manasquan*, 59 N.J. 241, 253-54, 281 A.2d 513 (1971). We have insisted that the municipal power to adopt zoning regulations

> be reasonably exercised; they may be neither unreasonable, arbitrary nor capricious. The means chosen must have a real and substantial relation to the end sought to be achieved. Moreover, the regulation must be reasonably designed to resolve the problem without imposing unnecessary and excessive restrictions on the use of private property.

In *Kirsch Holding Co. v. Borough of Manasquan, supra*, 59 N.J. 241, 281 A.2d 513, we invalidated ordinances in two shore communities that restrictively defined "family" and prohibited seasonal rentals by unrelated persons. We held that the challenged ordinances "preclude so many harmless dwelling uses. . . . that they must be held to be so sweepingly excessive, and therefore legally unreasonable, that they must fall in their entirety." . . .

In *Berger v. State, supra*, 71 N.J. 206, 364 A.2d 993, we expressed our agreement with the principle that "[t]he concept of a one family dwelling is based upon its character as a single housekeeping unit." A significant issue in *Berger* was the validity of a restrictive zoning ordinance limiting the definition of family to "persons related by blood, marriage or adoption." . . . The challenged use was a group home for eight to twelve multi-handicapped, pre-school children who would reside in a twelve-room ocean-front house with a married couple experienced as foster parents. Staff hired by the New Jersey Department of Institutions and Agencies would provide support services but would not reside on the premises. We concluded that the State's proposed use of the premises was reasonable and thus immune from regulation by the local zoning ordinance. . . . Finally, we held that an ordinance limiting the term "family" to persons related by blood, marriage, or adoption cannot "satisfy the demands of due process." Such an ordinance

> so narrowly delimits the persons who may occupy a single family dwelling as to prohibit numerous potential occupants who pose no threat to the style of family living sought to be preserved.

Accordingly, we expressed our clear preference for zoning provisions that equated the term "single family" with a "single housekeeping unit."

In *State v. Baker*, 81 N.J. 99, 405 A.2d 368 (1979), we invalidated the City of Plainfield's zoning ordinance that defined "family" in terms of a "single non-profit housekeeping unit" but limited to four the number of persons unrelated by blood, marriage, or adoption that would constitute a "family." Defendant was convicted of violating the ordinance when he and his wife, their three children, and Mrs. Conata and her three children lived in his home. Defendant, an ordained Presbyterian minister, testified that the Bakers and Conatas had common religious beliefs and lived together as an extended family, sharing common areas and household expenses. Recognizing that the municipality's goal of preserving stable, single-family residential areas was entirely proper, we nevertheless held that the ordinance was violative of our state constitution because "the means chosen [did] not bear a substantial relationship to the effectuation of that goal." . . .

We noted that municipalities could appropriately deal with overcrowding or congestion by ordinance provisions that limit occupancy *"in reasonable relation to available sleeping and bathroom facilities or requiring a minimum amount of habitable floor area per occupant."* Declining to follow the United States Supreme Court's decision in *Village of Belle Terre v. Boraas,* 416 U.S. 1 (1974), which upheld a comparable ordinance, we concluded that "[r]estrictions based upon legal or biological relationships such as Plainfield's impact only remotely upon [overcrowding and congestion] and hence cannot withstand judicial scrutiny."

Several of our reported cases involve municipalities whose zoning ordinances defined "family" in terms of a "single housekeeping unit" as suggested by *Berger v. State, supra.* In *Township of Washington v. Central Bergen Community Mental Health Center, Inc.,* 383 A.2d 1194 (Law Div. 1978), the municipality challenged the occupancy of a residential dwelling used as a transitional residence for five former mental patients who shared rent, expenses, and housekeeping chores under the supervision of a community mental-health center. . . . The Law Division held that the challenged occupancy qualified as a single housekeeping unit, observing that "the residents present a picture very much akin to that of a traditional family and their lifestyle is not of a transient or temporary nature. . . ."

In *Township of Pemberton v. State,* 429 A.2d 360 (App. Div. 1981), the township challenged the use of residential property as a group home for six to eight boys, ages eight to thirteen, who had been committed to the State Training School for Boys but were considered suitable for diversion from that institution to a residential setting that approximated a normal family environment. The boys would be supervised by a married couple with appropriate professional training. They would attend local schools, be encouraged to participate in scouting and Little League, and otherwise be expected to integrate with the community. The arrangement contemplated a residency period of approximately six months. . . . Reversing a Law Division decision enjoining the proposed use, the Appellate Division concluded that the use was permitted by the ordinance, noting that our case law afforded "protection for groups of unrelated persons which have been formed for the purpose of permitting traditionally institutional functions to be performed in the more salutary and constructive context of a 'reproduced' single-family setting." *Accord Holy Name Hosp. v. Montroy,* 153 N.J. Super. 181, 188-89, 379 A.2d 299 (Law Div. 1977) (invalidating local zoning ordinance limiting occupancy by more than three unrelated persons, upholding ordinance only as limiting occupancy by single housekeeping unit, and holding that three residences occupied by groups of nuns constituted single housekeeping units).

By contrast, in *Open Door Alcoholism Program, Inc. v. Board of Adjustment of New Brunswick,* 200 N.J. Super. 191, 491 A.2d 17 (App. Div. 1985), the court held that a halfway house for ten recovering alcoholics did not constitute a single-family dwelling, on the basis that the occupants lacked the "generic characteristics of a single family." The residents of the halfway house were referred there after having satisfactorily completed treatment for alcoholism. The average occupancy was for six months, although an occupant was free to leave at any time. The residents shared cooking and household chores and took meals together. A resident manager administered the facility. . . . The court concluded that the halfway house occupants did not constitute a single housekeeping unit:

> It is thus evident that in order for a group of unrelated persons living together as a single housekeeping unit to constitute a single family in terms of a zoning regulation, they must exhibit a kind of stability, permanency and functional lifestyle which is equivalent to that of the traditional family unit. In our view, the residents of plaintiff's proposed halfway house, although comprising a single housekeeping unit, would not bear these generic characteristics of a single family. While the residents would share in the household responsibilities and dine together, their affiliation with one another would be no different than if they were fellow residents of a boarding house. Clearly, their living arrangements would not be the functional equivalent of a family unit. The individual lifestyles of the residents and the transient nature of their residencies would not permit the group to possess the elements of stability and permanency which have long been associated with single-family occupancy.

Thus, our cases preclude municipalities from adopting zoning regulations that unreasonably distinguish between residential occupancy by unrelated persons in comparison with occupancy by individuals related by blood, marriage, or adoption. Our decisions permit zoning regulations to restrict uses in certain residential zones to single housekeeping units. But the standard for determining whether a use qualifies as a single housekeeping unit must be functional, and hence capable of being met by either related or unrelated persons.

III.

The Glassboro ordinance at issue here defines "family" by a standard consistent with our decisional law. . . . It provides a functional description of a single housekeeping unit, in terms of "persons . . . living together as a stable and permanent living unit, being a traditional family unit or the functional equivalency [sic] thereof." The ordinance's statement of purpose clearly reflects Glassboro's assumption that the occupancy of residential dwellings by college students would not satisfy the ordinance's standard, but the ordinance makes no impermissible distinction between college students and any other group of unrelated individuals.

. . . The narrow issue before us is whether there is sufficient credible evidence in this record to sustain the trial court's factual finding that the occupancy of defendants' dwelling by these ten college students constituted a single housekeeping unit as defined by the Glassboro ordinance.

In view of the unusual circumstances of this case, we find adequate evidence to uphold the Law Division's ruling. The uncontradicted testimony reflects a plan by ten sophomore college students to live together for three years under conditions that correspond substantially to the ordinance's requirement of a "stable and permanent living unit." To facilitate the plan, the house had been purchased by relatives of one of the students. The students ate together, shared household chores, and paid expenses from a common fund. Although the students signed four-month leases, the leases were renewable if the house was "in order" at the end of the term. Moreover, the students testified to their intention to remain in the house throughout college, and there was no significant evidence of defections up to the time of trial. As noted above, the students' occupancy ended in September 1988 because of Peter Vallorosi's post-trial withdrawal from college.

It is a matter of common experience that the costs of college and the variables characteristic of college life and student relationships do not readily lead to the formation of a household as stable and potentially durable as the one described in this record. On these facts, however, we cannot quarrel with the Law Division's conclusion that the occupancy at issue here "shows stability, permanency and can be described as the functional equivalent of a family."

It also bears repetition that noise and other socially disruptive behavior are best regulated outside the framework of municipal zoning. . . .

NOTES AND QUESTIONS

1. The Borough of Glassboro enacted its "single family" zoning ordinance after the New Jersey Supreme Court, parting ways with the U.S. Supreme Court in *Belle Terre*, held that zoning ordinances based on traditional definitions of "family" violated the state constitution. How does the analysis of the two courts differ?

2. Consider the definition of family in the Glassboro ordinance. What is the "functional equivalent" of a "traditional family unit"? What is a "single non-profit housekeeping unit"? Do the cases discussed in *Vallorosi* make the meaning clear? Under these definitions, what is the role of the court in defining "family"?

3. Does the "single housekeeping unit" test suggested by the New Jersey court adequately protect a community's interests in restricting some areas to "single family dwellings"? What does the breakup of the group of college students in *Vallorosi* suggest about the utility of this definition? On the other hand, would there be any question that a married couple who divorced after a few months were still, while they were married, a "single family"?

4. Most lower courts have upheld restrictive applications of single-family zoning laws, applying *Belle Terre*. State court decisions interpreting state constitutions as providing greater protection to nontraditional families, in addition to those in New Jersey, include Baer v. Town of Brookhaven, 537 N.E.2d 619 (N.Y. 1989) (four former mental patients who lived with a family were the functional equivalent of a family for purposes of zoning laws; zoning laws violated state constitution because they limited cohabitation of unrelated persons while not limiting the number of related people who could live together); City of Santa Barbara v. Adamson, 610 P.2d 436 (Cal. 1980); and Charter Township of Delta v. Dinolfo, 351 N.W.2d 831 (Mich. 1984).

The Importance of Being a Family 2

A. INTRODUCTION

The historian Arthur Lovejoy once said that every age is dominated by a set of "implicit or incompletely explicit *assumptions*, or more or less *unconscious mental habits*," which predisposes us "to think in terms of certain categories or of particular types of imagery." Arthur O. Lovejoy, The Great Chain of Being: A Study of the History of an Idea 7 (1960). This predisposition also may be applied to social institutions. One image that has been employed in legal and social thought about the family is the "family unit" or "family entity." This image is ubiquitous in modern legal discourse; it is not practicable to collect even the relatively recent references by judges and lawyers to the "family unit."[1] The notion of the family unit has been put to various uses. Descriptively, it identifies and summarizes the characteristics of the family as a sociolegal institution. Normatively, it provides a basis for establishing how members of such an institution should conduct themselves and how society should deal with that institution.

Although the metaphor of the family unit occurs routinely in modern legal discourse, its ancient roots are also familiar. The Book of Genesis (Genesis 2:24) declares that a husband must leave the home of his parents to be joined to his wife, "and they shall become one flesh," a declaration Paul repeats in his Epistle to the Ephesians (Ephesians 5:31). This notion made its way through medieval Normandy and became a staple of English legal discourse in the form now typically called the fiction of marital unity. Bracton, writing in the thirteenth century, said that husband and wife "are *quasi* one person, for they are one flesh and one

---

1. The authority for this conclusion is Linda Stephenson, reference librarian at the University of Utah College of Law, who sought to make such a collection. LEXIS informed her, you may think rudely, that the number of references was too great to permit a listing of cases and articles employing this single phrase.

31

blood." 4 Bracton on the Laws and Customs of England 335 (Samuel E. Thorne trans., 1977). Blackstone explained, to some degree, the significance of the marital unity doctrine in observing that "[b]y marriage, the husband and wife are one person in law: that is, the very being or legal existence of the woman is suspended during the marriage, or at least incorporated and consolidated into that of the husband." William Blackstone, Commentaries on the Laws of England *442 (W. Lewis ed., 1897). The first American treatise on Husband and Wife noted the common law identity of spouses, but saw this doctrine as a fiction designed to protect wives from coercion. Tapping Reeve, The Law of Baron and Femme: of Parent and Child, of Guardian and Ward, of Master and Servant, and of the Powers of Courts of Chancery 98 (1816).

Careful scholars of family law, including Reeve, observed that, however frequently it is invoked, the myth of marital unity has never been employed as its logic would fully imply and that it does not provide a satisfactory analytical basis even for early family law doctrine. Pollock and Maitland, for example, observed:

> If we look for any one thought which governs the whole of this province, we shall hardly find it. In particular we must be on our guard against the common belief that the ruling principle is that which sees an 'unity of person' between husband and wife. This is a principle which suggests itself from time to time; it has the warrant of holy writ; it will serve to round a paragraph; and may now and again lead us out of or into a difficulty; but a consistently operative principle it can not be. We do not treat the wife as a thing or as somewhat that is neither thing nor person; we treat her as a person. Thus Bracton tells us that if either the husband without the wife, or the wife without the husband, brings an action for the wife's land, the defendant can take exception to this 'for they are *quasi* one person, for they are one flesh and one blood.' But this impracticable proposition is followed by a real working principle: — 'for the thing is the wife's own and the husband is guardian as being the head of the wife.' The husband is the wife's guardian: — that we believe to be the fundamental principle; and it explains a great deal, when we remember that guardianship is a profitable right.

2 Frederick Pollock & Frederic W. Maitland, The History of English Law 405-406 (2d ed. 1968).

It is nonetheless clear that the myth of marital unity has substantially influenced the ways in which family law has been and is conceptualized as well as the development of specific doctrines. It has been invoked, at least superficially, to explain a number of rules that will appear in the course of this chapter, including rules assigning control of marital property and choice of domicile to the husband and prohibitions against suits by one spouse against another. These notions may be insufficient and inaccurate guides to the law of domestic relations, but their popularity has been sufficiently great that they must be dealt with consciously when considering both the traditional and the modern meanings of marriage.

The notion of the family unit is, however, broader than the myth of marital unity. Specific doctrines that were once justified by reference to the doctrine of marital unity have survived the enactment of Married Women's Property Acts recognizing separate ownership interests by married women. The important point suggested by Pollock and Maitland may well be not the crudity of the myth but the existence of powerfully held, if poorly articulated, sentiments about how the family should conduct itself and how the law should deal with the family.

As we will see, the idea of the "family unit" remains with us. It is often invoked by cases throughout this chapter to explain doctrines once justified more simply by reference to the doctrine of spousal unity. More generally, the picture of a family unit is seemingly central to the emphasis on "family privacy" and "family autonomy" that characterizes much discussion of the relationship between state and family. In this chapter and later, courts will frequently advert to these principles (privacy and autonomy) when they decline to intervene to resolve intrafamilial disputes and when they say, even more strongly, that legislatures and courts may not properly regulate certain aspects of family behavior. The most familiar illustration of the first category is the reluctance of courts to order the financial and personal arrangements of spouses where the marriage is "intact." See, for example, McGuire v. McGuire and the materials at page 63, below. Use of the notion of family autonomy as a matter of right rather than prudence is often found in discussions of the sphere of parental control over child rearing. Here and in other settings, the family seems often to be conceived as an entity having claims separate from those of both the state and its members individually.

It has nonetheless occasionally been suggested that the notion of the family as a "unit" or "entity" is itself subject to question and that use of such language tends both to make legal treatment of the family seem inevitable or "natural" and to obscure the effects of that treatment on family members. See Lee E. Teitelbaum, Family History and Family Law, 1985 Wis. L. Rev. 1135. Whether there is anything to this argument, or whether it matters, is something you may want to consider. In any event, the image of the family unit has considerable power and wide implications. It suggests that the family stands independent of the state or, as is sometimes said, that it is itself a vehicle for governance with claims to "sovereignty." At the least, regard for the family unit suggests that governmental agencies—whether courts, legislatures, or others—should carefully consider the extent to which and the ways in which their rules affect relations within the family.

The materials in this chapter provide an opportunity to consider the meaning of a couple being legally regarded as a family and the tension between a traditional view of the family as a unit and a more recent tendency to view the family as an association of independent actors. Most of the cases involve couples who are formally married, but the same issues may arise for other couples who are regarded as being a family. Section B, dealing with family property, introduces the common law and community property systems. The section explores the doctrines that allocate ownership and management of wealth between adult partners and that determine the availability of family wealth to third parties who make claims against a family member. Notions of family privacy and family protection will compete with the interests of individual family members in making decisions about how wealth is used.

Section C, which addresses the legal treatment of violence between adult family members, presents the same tension as courts and legislatures consider whether notions of family privacy or other concerns should prevent criminal or civil prosecution of one spouse for assault of another, and the recognition of tort liability between spouses.

The next section considers reproductive rights and interests, focusing first on the rights of family members to decide themselves whether to beget and bear children and then on the allocation of procreative authority between spouses. The last part, Section E, examines another area presenting similar issues, those surrounding medical decision making. Here again we will be concerned both with claims of public interest in controlling choices about medical care by family members and with responsibility for medical decision making as between the partners themselves.

B. MARITAL PROPERTY

This section provides an overview of the significance of marriage for ownership, management, control, and distribution of property or, more generally, wealth. More particularly, the first part deals with doctrines relating to the ownership of real and personal property, including what is often called "new property"—public and private entitlements related to employment. The next part concerns the power of spouses to manage and control family wealth with respect to each other and with respect to creditors. The third subpart deals with spousal contracts during marriage.

The concepts and doctrines discussed here are, of course, relevant when the parties' relationship is dissolved and, accordingly, this section provides a background for the extensive treatments of property distribution upon dissolution of a marriage or cohabiting relationship that appear later in this book. However, the subject of family property is important not only at dissolution. Management and control of wealth during the relationship may be highly significant for the partners themselves. While we expect and hope that family members arrange their financial affairs by mutual agreement, whether articulated or not, questions of right and power may nonetheless arise overtly for couples who do not intend to separate. Moreover, for each case where questions arise overtly, there are many more relationships where the fact or appearance of lawful control defines how each person understands the allocation of decisional authority within the family. If, for example, husbands possess the legal authority to manage available family wealth (as has been true until only recently in common law and community property jurisdictions alike), wives may accept—perhaps without even conscious thought about it—their husbands' ultimate responsibility for determining where and how they will live, who will work at what and how much, and the myriad other matters that involve decisions about the acquisition and expenditure of wealth.

The location and character of property ownership may also substantially affect the position of third parties who deal with a married person. Creditors, for example, may find themselves situated differently with respect to property owned by a single person or the "nonmarital" wealth of a spouse than they are with respect to property characterized as "marital."

Finally, consideration of family property, broadly understood, includes kinds of wealth that are not distributable at dissolution and may or may not be available to a surviving spouse upon the other's death. This aspect of marital property incorporates public, and some private, benefit schemes that are as important to the economic condition of beneficiary families as are farms and bonds to the middle and upper socioeconomic groups.

1. Ownership and Control of Wealth

Generally speaking, the marital property systems of Western nations today are divided into two types: "those in which husband and wife own all property separately except those items that they have expressly agreed to hold jointly (in a nontechnical sense) and those in which husband and wife own a substantial portion or even all of their property jointly unless they have expressly agreed to hold it separately." Charles Donahue, Jr., What Causes Fundamental Legal Ideas? Marital Property in England and France in the Thirteenth Century, 78 Mich. L. Rev. 59 (1979). The scheme of separate property ownership is the common law system, which operates or has operated in some fashion in most Anglo-American jurisdictions. The system of joint property is found, in some fashion, in many countries of Western Europe and in nine American states.[2]

These labels—"common law property" and "community property"— capture certain substantial differences in the ways the two systems treat wealth acquired during the marriage. However, there are important aspects in which both regimes in their traditional forms treat the property of married persons alike, particularly with respect to the management of wealth generated during the marriage.

a. The Common Law Tradition[3]

While the common law system was originally a scheme of separate property, this characteristic was more important for purposes of claims by others, including heirs, than for the spouses themselves. Indeed, one of the most frequently discussed features of the common law system is the extent to which during the time of the marriage it concentrated effective control of the wealth of married persons in one pair of hands. In the traditional common law scheme, marriage had a significant effect on the management and control of property. While she was single, a woman's position in matters of contract and property was much the same as a man's. Generally, a

---

2. The nine states are Arizona, California, Idaho, Louisiana, Nevada, New Mexico, Texas, Washington, and (by recent legislation) Wisconsin. Puerto Rico has also adopted community property.

3. To talk of the "common law tradition," however conventional, risks two kinds of errors. One is to suggest that the common law treatment of marital property was static, that is, that marital property was treated alike over a lengthy period and that this treatment was the province of courts rather than legislation. The other is to suggest that the common law at a single point in time treated all forms of property alike. Both of these are untrue. English law developed significantly in this as in other respects over time, and by statute as well as by judicial decision. See, e.g., Charles Donahue, Jr., What Causes Fundamental Legal Ideas? Marital Property in England and France in the Thirteenth Century, 78 Mich. L. Rev. 59 (1979), on early developments of marital property doctrine.

woman could hold and manage real and personal property, contract with other persons, sue and be sued. Upon marriage, however, her position changed dramatically. The main effects of marriage, or coverture, can be summarized briefly.

(1) **Real Property**   Upon marriage, the husband was entitled to the use of his wife's land for the period of the marriage and, if a child were born, for the period of the husband's life. This was not merely a right to enjoy the property. The husband had a recognized legal right of his own in the property, which he could, for example, sell to another. With regard to the rents that the land might generate, the husband had absolute discretion. The result might be something like this: Ralph married Elizabeth, who had already inherited a piece of land. Before her marriage, Elizabeth could have conveyed the land to another, or she would have been entitled to any rents or profits the land produced to keep and use as she liked. Upon her marriage to Ralph, however, Ralph acquired an estate that gave him authority to manage the land and to use the rents it produced, at the very least during Elizabeth's lifetime. If Ralph wished to devote lands to hunting that had previously been used for pasturage, he was legally free to do so; if he wished to direct the profits from the land to a crusade, or to a mistress, he could also do so. Elizabeth, on the other hand, lost the power to convey the property she brought to, or was given after, her marriage.

One effect of the common law scheme was therefore to transfer administration of the wife's realty to her husband *during their joint lives*, that is, for the duration of the marriage (divorce being extremely rare). The "myth of marital unity" — the notion that, upon marriage, husband and wife became one person — is often invoked either to explain or to describe this body of doctrine.

The situation changed, however, when one of the spouses died. A wife who survived her husband recaptured her rights with respect to the property she brought into the marriage. Equally important, her husband could not, during his life, alienate that property without her active participation. Moreover, as in the above example, Elizabeth acquired through her marriage an inchoate life interest in some part of the land that Ralph had owned and possessed (of which he was "seised") during the time of their marriage. This dower right came typically to mean one-third of Ralph's property if there were children and one-half if there were not. In character, this interest closely resembled Ralph's interest in the wife's real property during the marriage. It was a life estate (or in some places a life estate unless she remarried) in the dower lands, including the right to rents and profits generated by those lands. Elizabeth's interest was jealously protected against alienation by Ralph, and under general English practice, Ralph could not sell his land free of that interest unless Elizabeth consented. Moreover, her consent was valid only if given in a judicial proceeding (a "fine"), during which she would be examined privately to ensure that her consent was voluntary.[4]

---

4. Although the procedure of the fine was not followed in the American colonies generally, the requirement of a private examination concerning the wife's volition in joining a conveyance of land in which she held an interest was often recognized, although with varying degrees of strength. *See* Marylynn Salmon, Women and the Law of Property in Early America 17-37 (1986).

Even if Ralph survived Elizabeth, he did not acquire her property by the fact of that survivorship. If the marriage ended without children, her property passed immediately to her heirs, free of all claims by Ralph. If they had children, however, Ralph's rights in the property extended throughout the rest of his life (whether he remarried or not).

(2) Personal Property The husband's rights in the wife's personal property were even more extensive than those concerning her realty. Except for certain personal items (such as clothing, jewelry, and the like), Ralph owned and could do as he wished with Elizabeth's personal wealth. Concomitantly, Ralph married not only Elizabeth and her assets, but her liabilities. During coverture, he was responsible, with all of his property, for any debts incurred or civil wrongs done by his wife before or during the marriage. In an American setting, it followed that a man could spend his wife's money and sell her stocks and slaves as well as make all managerial decisions concerning her lands and tenements.

The treatment of personal property, like that of real property, can be regarded as a transfer of administration. It may also be thought to serve commercial and social interests by making one family member responsible for all family wrongs. And if, indeed, a husband is to be personally responsible for all liabilities incurred by him and his wife, it has sometimes been said to follow that the administration of assets most readily used to satisfy personal liabilities — personal property — should rest in his hands.

(3) Modifications in the Common Law Scheme During the seventeenth and eighteenth centuries, courts of equity devised principles that in certain situations preserved the wife's use of property given to her before or during marriage. If a grantor of property clearly specified that the property transferred was for the exclusive use of the wife, the transferor's limitation would be given effect in equity. The legal device used for this purpose was a form of trust. For example, if Elizabeth's father wanted to give Elizabeth a parcel of land and feared that she would marry somebody like Ralph, whose intellect and character appeared deficient, he would grant the land "to Elizabeth and her heirs, for Elizabeth's separate and peculiar use exclusive of her husband." When Elizabeth married Ralph, the common law would say that he acquired an estate by marital right to the land that included the right to the rents and profits it produced. A court of equity would say, however, that Ralph's legal interest in the land existed but was held for the benefit of Elizabeth. The ultimate effect was to ensure that Elizabeth received the benefit of the land, if not necessarily full control over it.

The separate estate in equity was frequently used in some early American settings, particularly for the situation described above. Agnes, the daughter of Petersburg, Virginia, businessman Edward Ruffin, married Dr. T. Stanley Beckwith, whom Ruffin considered (with some warrant) a "spendthrift," "lazy and heedless of the future," indeed "despicable." When Mr. Ruffin retired and wished to distribute his wealth among his children, he deeded her part to Agnes's brother Julian in trust, to manage for her benefit as he saw fit. Suzanne Lebsock, The Free Women of Petersburg: Status and Culture in a Southern Town, 1784-1860 61-62 (1984). Equitable devices were also created in other ways and for other purposes.

They sometimes arose from premarital agreements between engaged couples, where the wife had money she wished to protect or continue to manage. At least in some areas, equitable estates also often arose after marriage and in response to the economic surges and falls characteristic of that period. According to Lebsock's study of the status of women in early nineteenth-century Virginia:

> The prototypical sequence ran like this. The man and woman were married without any kind of equitable settlement; to demand a separate estate at the outset was to insult the groom and deprive him of working capital. . . . It was only after the husband had demonstrated his inability to stay out of debt that a separate estate was created: better to settle property on the wife than to see it sold off to pay the husband's creditors. The wife would not be granted much discretion over her new estate, for if she had active power over it, she, too, might lose it in paying off debts of her own contracting.

Id. at 61. Indeed, it appears that after the panics of the late 1830s, the most prominent businessmen in this town adopted the practice of sheltering "themselves and their families from . . . 'the casualties and hazards of trade' by granting separate property to their wives." And, of course, so did the town's most devious businessmen. *Id.* at 66.

The woman's separate estate in equity had substantial limitations, however. Except when a third party was the grantor, the husband ordinarily had to agree to the creation of such an estate. Moreover, there were often complications with trustees, not to mention the need for fees to pay them. In some cases, a late-arising agreement might be set aside as a fraud on creditors. By about 1840, American legislatures, not satisfied with the married woman's separate estate in equity, began to enact statutes that had the effect of reducing or eliminating the more obvious disabilities associated with marriage. With some exceptions, these laws, generally called Married Women's Property Acts, were noncontroversial, perhaps because they were perceived as achieving the same results as the separate estate in equity rather than as declarations of equality between the sexes. *See* Lebsock, above at 85-86. Their general thrust was to give married women the same legal capacity to deal with their property that single women had. The 1861 Illinois Married Women's Act, for example, provided as follows:

> Section 1. *Be it enacted* . . . That all property, both real and personal, belonging to any married woman, as her sole and separate property, or which any woman hereafter married owns at the time of her marriage, or which any married woman, during coverture, acquires, in good faith, from any person, other than her husband, by descent, devise or otherwise, together with all the rents, issues, increase and profits thereof, shall, notwithstanding her marriage, be and remain, during coverture, her sole and separate property, under her sole control, and be held, owned, possessed and enjoyed by her the same as though she was sole and unmarried; and shall be exempt from execution or attachment for the debts of her husband.

1861 Ill. Laws 1433. It is important to recognize that these acts, which are still in effect generally, address only a married woman's *separate* property—that is, property she acquired before marriage or by her efforts or gift during marriage. They do not create any interest in the wife in her husband's separate property. Accordingly, this legislation did not affect the wife's position in the common situation where she did not bring wealth into the marriage, inherit wealth, or work in the paid economy during marriage.

PROBLEM

George and Martha were married in 1970. At that time, Martha owned a small portfolio of stocks (worth approximately $25,000) given her by her parents; George owned nothing. During their marriage, Martha acted as a homemaker, while George was first an employee and then a partner in a real estate group. Fifteen years after their marriage, George and Martha decided to evaluate their financial arrangements, both as a matter of curiosity and because George is concerned about a potential liability as a result of some recent unsuccessful investments on his part. Assuming that the stocks remain titled in Martha's name, that the current value of the real estate partnership is approximately $100,000, and that George has over the years purchased a house and made investments in his own name that amount to approximately $250,000, advise them on the following questions. Under a Married Women's Property Act like that quoted above, who owns what property? To what extent can George's creditors reach their wealth?

As we have seen, both the woman's separate estate in equity and Married Women's Property Acts addressed only property given to or earned by women; they generally had no effect on property titled in the husband but to which both spouses had in some way contributed. In this latter situation, spouses (particularly wives) sometimes sought relief through generally applicable equitable remedies,[5] particularly resulting and constructive trusts.

_____

5. The terms *equity* and *equitable* appear in a number of property contexts. Their meanings within each are specific, and the meaning within one context cannot safely be employed in another. Sometimes these terms refer to remedies created by courts of equity, such as the wife's separate estate in equity (based, as we have seen, on an express trust), or the resulting and constructive trust remedies described immediately below, which are extensions, with some modification, of generally applicable doctrines recognizing ownership interests that are not reflected in the legal title. Such equitable interests in specific items of wealth may be recognized at any time.

These uses should be distinguished from "equitable distribution," which is *not* intended to reflect ownership interests in particular items of property but deals only with the distribution of all family property at divorce. Equitable distribution is discussed in detail in Chapter 6.

MURDOCH V. MURDOCH

[1975] 1 S.C.R. 423 (S.C.C.)

MARTLAND, J. [Appeal from a dismissal of the wife's claim to a one-half interest in a ranch property including land and other ranch assets held in the name of the husband alone. The evidence indicated that the wife worked doing chores on several ranches, which were bought and sold prior to purchase of the ranch in question, and that she did "[h]aying, raking, swathing, moving, driving trucks and tractors and teams, quietening horses, taking cattle back and forth to the reserve, dehorning, vaccinating, branding, anything that was to be done" on all of these ranches, especially during the five months a year that her husband was working for the Stock Association in the Forestry Service. The husband agreed that his wife engaged in those activities, which were "just about what the ordinary rancher's wife does." It also appears that the wife's earnings were used in part to make the down payment on the initial ranch property, whose proceeds were reinvested in later properties, and that she had bought all the household furniture and appliances except a stove.]

        . . . It has already been noted that the *Pettitt* decision disposed of the idea that [the Married Women's Property Act] gave a discretionary jurisdiction to pass proprietary interests from one spouse to the other. . . . [I]t may be possible, on the evidence, to establish the existence of a resulting trust in favour of one spouse as against the other, who has the legal title to the matrimonial home. . . .

        . . . I would point out that there is no evidence, on the findings of fact made by the trial Judge in this case, that the appellant did contribute towards the purchase of the property in issue, and, further, that the property in which she claims an interest is not restricted to the marital home.

        I am in agreement with the view expressed by Lord Diplock . . . as to what is necessary to be established in order to prove the existence of a resulting trust:

        "Any claim to a beneficial interest in land by a person, whether spouse or stranger, in whom the legal estate in land is not vested must be based on the proposition that the person in whom the legal estate is vested holds it as trustee on trust to give effect to the beneficial interest of the claimant as cestui que trust. . . . Where the trust is expressly declared in the instrument by which the legal estate is transferred to the trustee or by a written declaration of trust by the trustee, the court must give effect to it. But to constitute a valid declaration of trust by way of gift of a beneficial interest in land to a cestui que trust the declaration is required . . . to be in writing. If it is not in writing it can only take effect as a resulting, implied or constructive trust. . . .

        "A resulting, implied or constructive trust — and it is unnecessary for present purposes to distinguish between these three classes of trust — is created by a transaction between the trustee and the cestui que trust in connection with the acquisition by the trustee of a legal estate in land, whenever the trustee has so conducted himself that it would be inequitable to allow him to deny to the cestui que trust a beneficial interest in the land acquired. And he will be held so to have conducted himself if by his words or conduct he has induced the cestui que trust to act to his own detriment in the reasonable belief that by so acting he was acquiring a beneficial interest in the land. . . .

" . . . [B]eneficial interest[s] in a matrimonial home where the legal estate is vested solely in the other spouse, only arise where the court is satisfied by the words or conduct of the parties that it was their common intention that the beneficial interest was not to belong solely to the spouse in whom the legal estate was vested but was to be shared between them in some proportion or another."

In my opinion . . . it cannot be said that there was any common intention that the beneficial interest in the property in issue was not to belong solely to the respondent, in whom the legal estate was vested.

LASKIN, C.J. (dissenting). The legal proposition upon which the respondent husband rests is that his wife's work earned her nothing in a share of the assets in his name when it had not been recognized by him in a way that would demand an apportionment, that is by proof of an agreement or at least of a common intention that she should share in the acquisitions. In my view, this is to state too narrowly the law that should apply to the present case.

The case is one where the spouses over a period of some 15 years improved their lot in life through progressively larger acquisitions of ranch property to which the wife contributed necessary labour in seeing that the ranches were productive. There is no reason to treat this contribution as any less significant than a direct financial contribution, which to a much lesser degree she also made. . . .

. . . We are nearing a century . . . since married women's property legislation was enacted in England and in Canada. It offered merely mute testimony to the legal personality and capacity of the wife. As was said in a recent piece of periodical literature on the subject (*see* Foster Freed, Marital Property Reform: Partnership of Co Equals? (1973), 169 New York L.J.):

" . . . It is relatively meaningless for a wife to acquire legal capacity to own property if she does not have any, or to become entitled to keep her own wages if she is forced to stay at home and raise children, or employment opportunities are limited. . . ."

A court with equitable jurisdiction is on solid ground in translating into money's worth a contribution of labour by one spouse to the acquisition of property taken in the name of the other, especially when such labour is not simply housekeeping, which might be said to be merely a reflection of the marriage bond. . . .

On one point, a starting point, there can be no dispute. The fact that legal title is vested in a person does not necessarily exclude beneficial interests in others. Evidence of a common intention before or at the time of acquisition, qualifying the formal legal title, is generally admissible. A long-established presumption of a resulting trust operates in equity in favour of a purchaser who takes title in another's name, and this presumption, a rebuttable one, is equally operable in favour of one who contributes some but not all of the purchase money. This is as true in the relations of husband and wife as it is in the relations of strangers.

The appropriate mechanism to give relief to a wife who cannot prove a common intention or to a wife whose contribution to the acquisition of property is physical labor rather than purchase money is the constructive trust which does not depend on evidence of intention. Perhaps the resulting trust should be as readily available in the case of a contribution of physical labour as in the cases of a financial contribution, but the historical roots of the inference that is raised in the latter case do not exist in the former. It is unnecessary to bend or adapt them to the desired end because the constructive trust more easily serves the purpose. As is pointed out by Scott, Law of Trusts, 3rd ed., 1967, vol. 5, p.3215:

"... a constructive trust is imposed when a person holding title to property is subject to an equitable duty to convey it to another on the ground that he would be unjustly enriched if he were permitted to retain it. ... The basis of the constructive trust is the unjust enrichment which would result if the person having the property were permitted to retain it. Ordinarily, a constructive trust arises without regard to the intention of the person who transferred the property.". . .

. . . [T]he wife has, in my view, established a right to an interest which it would be inequitable to deny and which, if denied, would result in the unjust enrichment of her husband. Denial would equate her strenuous labours with mere housekeeping chores which, an English Court has held, will not per se support a constructive trust. . . ."

NOTES AND QUESTIONS

1. Although *Murdoch* is a Canadian case, the principles on which it relies — and the differences between the majority and dissenting views — regularly appear in American common law states. Five years after *Murdoch* was decided, the Canadian Supreme Court overruled it, adopting the position of Chief Justice Laskin. Rathwell v. Rathwell, [1978] 2 S.C.R. 436 (S.C.C.). The Canadian Supreme Court has expanded the availability of the constructive trust remedy in subsequent cases, and legislation in all the Canadian provinces now provides for sharing of family assets when the parties break up, though not during the relationship. Lorna Fox, Reforming Family Property — Comparison, Compromises and Common Dimensions, 15 Child & Fam. L.Q. 1, 6-8 (2003).

2. The majority and dissent in *Murdoch* agree that if property is titled in the name of one spouse but the evidence indicates that the other spouse contributed to the acquisition of the property and that the parties intended that both spouses have an interest in the property, a resulting trust will be invoked to recognize the equitable interest of the spouse whose name is not on the title. The resulting trust is an equitable remedy that is generally available whenever the evidence proves that a person who gives consideration for property and titles it in the name of another does not intend to make a gift but rather intends to keep some or all of the beneficial interest. In many circumstances, then, determining whether to impose a resulting trust requires determining whether the person who provided the consideration intended to make a gift or not.

If two unrelated persons purchase property and title it in the name of only one, the presumption will be that the person whose name was not on the title did not intend to make a gift; in other words, the presumption will be in favor of a resulting trust. In *Murdoch*, the wife made some financial contribution to the acquisition of the property. Why does the majority not impose a trust on the property? Does something about family relationships make it sensible for courts not to find a resulting trust from the use of the nontitled person's money in purchasing property where they might do so absent the relationship?

3. At common law, a distinct body of law developed in connection with gifts between spouses. Transfers from husband to wife, such as when the husband purchased property from wealth he controlled and placed title in the wife's name alone or in joint ownership, were generally presumed to be gifts to her or to the marital estate. *See* Maxwell v. Maxwell, 109 Ill. 588 (1884) (gift presumed although both parties treated property as husband's); Brown v. Brown, 507 A.2d 1223 (Pa. Super. Ct. 1986) (titling property jointly is strong evidence of intent of donor to make gift to marital estate). Where, however, the wife transferred wealth to her husband, courts often treated the transfer as a loan or as a bailment for safekeeping and would impose a constructive trust for her benefit on that property. *See* Comment, Transfers from Wife to Husband: A Reexamination of Presumptions in Illinois, 53 Nw. U. L. Rev. 781 (1959). Modern equal protection doctrine and, where applicable, equal rights amendments have cast doubt on inconsistent treatment of transfers by spouses. *See* Butler v. Butler, 347 A.2d 477 (Pa. 1975).

In what direction should the presumption concerning gifts run, assuming that a common presumption will apply to transfers by husbands and wives?

4. Neither the majority nor Chief Justice Laskin treats Mrs. Murdoch's contribution of labor or services as a sufficient contribution toward the acquisition of the property to justify the resulting trust remedy. This is consistent with the generally applicable law of resulting trusts. Chief Justice Laskin would, however, recognize such contributions on a different theory: a constructive trust. Some courts view the constructive trust relatively narrowly as a device for the rectification of fraud, duress, undue influence, or the breach of a confidential relationship. Other courts apply it more broadly any time they find it necessary to prevent "unjust enrichment." Under each view would Mrs. Murdoch have been entitled to a constructive trust? Which is the preferable view?

5. Why does Justice Laskin distinguish between service on a ranch and "mere housekeeping chores"? If one did not draw that distinction, would the republic — or at least the common law property system — survive?

PROBLEMS

1. For many years, Mr. and Ms. Wirth worked and pooled their earnings. After some time, however, the husband started a "crash" savings program for, as he told his wife, "our latter days." From then on, the wife's earnings were used for family expenses and the husband's earnings were invested, entirely in his name. The family house was also in the husband's name, having been purchased with a down payment of $6500 supplied by his mother. Does the wife have any interest in these properties? What arguments would be made for her position?

2. William and Mary were married in 1957. Shortly afterward, William, together with a partner, established a business. William's initial investment came from savings the couple had accumulated over the first few years of their marriage. During the early years of the business, the wife helped out as a business

advisor and bookkeeper. After the birth of their children, she still assisted with the bookkeeping. She has been paid a salary by the company for these services. In conversations with his wife, William often referred to the business as "our company" and its profits as "our security blanket." However, Mary never owned any of the stock in this closely held corporation, nor did she hold any management office in it. The business is now worth approximately one-half million dollars. Assuming that all of the stock in the company is held in the husband's name, does the wife have any legal or equitable interest in the company?

3. Stephanie inherited $170,000 from her aunt before her marriage, which she used to purchase a home for herself and her boyfriend, Daniel. The home was titled solely in the name of Daniel, who later became her husband. Stephanie said that she put sole title in Daniel because she feared that if her name were on the title, her former husband's creditors would try to attach the home. Daniel said that he was unaware of this concern and that instead Stephanie had insisted that the home be titled in his name alone because she wanted to make a gift to him and for him to be head of the household. At divorce Daniel claimed the house was his separate property; Stephanie sought imposition of a constructive trust. What arguments should the parties make?

b. The Estate by the Entirety

Joint ownership with a right of survivorship has become an extremely popular form of home ownership among married couples. A study conducted in a county in Pennsylvania found that, in 1890, less than 1 percent of married testators had taken title to a house jointly with his spouse. By 1920, the percentage of joint ownership had risen to 20 percent and, by 1960, to 80 percent. Carole Shammas, Marylynn Salmon & Michel Dahlin, Inheritance in America: From Colonial Times to the Present 172 (1987). The survivorship feature of joint ownership provides a way of avoiding probate. "Half of the estates of middle class, married persons pass through one or more informal, no-lawyer-needed devices. As much as two-thirds of residential real estate is purchased in [joint ownership with right of survivorship]. More than half the wealth in the country passes outside the probate process." Thomas L. Shaffer, Death, Property and Ideals, in Death, Taxes, and Family Property 26, 38 (Edward C. Halbach, Jr. ed., 1977).

The common law recognized a distinct form of ownership reserved for married couples: tenancy by the entirety (or entireties). In its traditional form, tenancy by the entirety reflected several of the principles of common law marital property and also suggested points of similarity between common law and community property regimes. As is true of community property (discussed in the next section), husband and wife possessed equal ownership interests in the tenancy. During the marriage, however, the wife's interest was essentially inchoate. The husband's interest, by contrast, was active: He was not only entitled to manage and control the property (and its profits) but could convey or mortgage the estate, subject to the possibility that the wife might become entitled to the whole estate on his death.

Approximately 20 states have retained some form of tenancy by the entirety. In those that have not, husbands and wives often hold property in joint tenancy, which closely resembles tenancy by the entirety as long as the joint tenancy is intact. Joint tenants, like tenants by the entirety, constitute a "fictitious personality" in the sense that all the tenants are regarded as one tenant having an undivided interest in the whole of the property during the tenancy and through survivorship. *See* Herbert T. Tiffany, Real Property §§418-430 (1939).

These methods of holding land differ, however, in the ways in which they can be severed. Apart from statutory modifications, tenancy by the entirety could be severed only by death, divorce, or annulment; its survivorship aspect could not be frustrated by a conveyance (or mortgage) by one tenant to a stranger. By contrast, joint tenancy can be terminated by the act of one owner. One tenant may convey his or her proportionate interest to a third party (in which case the stranger becomes a tenant in common with the remaining joint tenant). Moreover, the individual interest of a joint tenant can be mortgaged and is subject to execution.

Although a number of jurisdictions preserve the estate by the entirety, its characteristics now often differ in various respects from the traditional common law form. The Supreme Court of Hawaii describes the modern alternatives as it considers the position it should take on the characteristics of this tenancy:

> In the Group I states . . . the estate is unaffected by the Married Women's Property Acts. . . . In all three states, as at common law, the *husband* may convey the entire estate subject only to the possibility that the wife may become entitled to the whole estate upon surviving him. As at common law, the obverse as to the wife does not hold true. Only in Massachusetts, however, is the estate in its entirety subject to levy by the husband's creditors (during the marriage for the separate debts of either spouse).
>
> In the Group II states . . . the interest of the debtor spouse in the estate may be sold or levied upon for his or her separate debts, subject to the other spouse's contingent right of survivorship. . . .
>
> In the Group III jurisdictions . . . an attempted conveyance by either spouse is wholly void, and the estate may not be subjected to the separate debts of one spouse only.
>
> In Group IV, . . . the contingent right of survivorship appertaining to either spouse is separately alienable by him and attachable by his creditors during the marriage. The use and profits, however, may neither be alienated nor attached during coverture.

Sawada v. Endo, 561 P.2d 1291, 1294-1295 (Haw. 1977). In *Sawada*, the plaintiffs were struck and injured in November 1968 by a car driven by Kokichi Endo. Several months later, the Sawadas filed separate tort actions against Endo alleging that his negligent driving caused the accident. Between the dates of the two filings, Kokichi Endo and his wife, Ume, conveyed a house they owned as tenants by the entirety to their two sons. The senior Endos continued to live in the house. The complaints in the negligence action were not served until after the date of the conveyance. The case went to trial in 1971, and the Sawadas received judgments totaling slightly more than $25,000. Frustrated in their efforts to recover, the Sawadas brought suit to set aside the Endos' conveyance of their house. The trial court refused to do so, and the Hawaii Supreme Court affirmed.

NOTES AND QUESTIONS

1. If the family home had not been conveyed, what remedy would have been available to the Sawadas?

2. The *Sawada* court took as the central issue before it whether the interest of one spouse in property held in tenancy by the entirety is subject to levy and execution by his individual creditors. Why is that the determinative issue?

3. Assuming that is the determinative issue, which of the positions now taken by the various states should be adopted? Consider the way in which the *Sawada* majority resolved this question:

In Fairclaw v. Forrest [130 F.2d 829 (1942)], the court makes this observation: "The interest in family solidarity retains some influence upon the institution [of tenancy by the entirety]. It is available only to husband and wife. It is a convenient mode of protecting a surviving spouse from inconvenient administration of the decedent's estate and from the other's improvident debts. It is in that protection that the estate finds its peculiar and justifiable function.". . . When a family can afford to own real property, it becomes their single most important asset. Encumbered as it usually is by a first mortgage, the fact remains that so long as it remains whole during the joint lives of the spouses, it is always available in its entirety for the benefit and uses of the entire family. Loans for education and other emergency expenses, for example, may be obtained on the security of the marital estate. This would not be possible where a third party has become a tenant in common or a joint tenant with one of the spouses.

561 P.2d at 1297.

4. Is it likely that the Endos took title as tenants by the entirety when they purchased the house because of the debt protection benefits associated with that estate? If they anticipated any legal benefit from the form of ownership, what was it? At what point does it seem likely that the Endos knew that tenancy by the entirety might protect their house from attachment?

5. In United States v. Craft, 535 U.S. 274 (2002), the Court held that tenancy by the entireties property could be reached to satisfy the husband's federal tax debt. Justice O'Connor recognized that, under state law, a tenant by the entireties has no individual interest in that property and cannot alienate or encumber the property by his act alone. However, while state law determines the rights a taxpayer has in the property the government seeks to reach, federal law determines whether the taxpayer's state-delineated rights qualify as "property" or "rights to property" within the meaning of federal tax legislation. The Court held that the tax law meant to reach anything that might be understood to qualify as property, and a tenant by the entirety was given by Michigan law some of the essentials of property—the rights to use the property, receive income from it, and exclude others from the property. The husband also possessed the right to alienate or otherwise encumber the property with the consent of his wife. Justice Thomas, joined by Justice Scalia, dissented. He argued that Mr. Craft did not have any "rights to property," since he had nothing that he could sell, encumber, or transfer alone. Justice Scalia noted that a traditional function of this form of tenancy was to protect the stay-at-home spouse or mother from just this kind of threat to her source of support.

6. Tenancy by the entirety is not the only form of protection for marital property. Homestead statutes in many states protect a specified (but usually small) amount of the value of the family home from the claims of creditors. The homestead is exempt from judicial liens, execution, or levy except for tax assessments, purchase money security interests on the property, and judicial liens derived from child support obligations; e.g., Utah Code §78-23-3(1). In addition, homestead statutes commonly restrict the legal title holder's power to convey or encumber the property without spousal consent; e.g., Utah Code §78-23-4(4).

PROBLEMS

1. Pearlman, who was injured in an automobile accident by Dennis and suffered permanent injuries, received a $500,000 judgment for medical bills and disability. Pearlman seeks to enforce the judgment. Dennis and his wife own the following property as tenants by the entirety: a home that is valued at approximately $100,000, a late-model Lexus (valued at $45,000), and a one-half interest in the Hideaway Motel, valued at $3,500,000. On what property can Pearlman seek to enforce his judgment?

2. Would and should it make any difference if Pearlman's judgment were based on a breach of contract by Dennis? On Dennis's failure to repay a loan?

3. Suppose that Dennis lived in a jurisdiction recognizing joint tenancy, not tenancy by the entirety? What would be the result?

4. Joyce and Bert had a traditional, role-divided relationship, though they were not married. She was a homemaker, and he worked as an attorney. Over the years he purchased with his earnings a home, which he had titled in the names of himself and Joyce as joint tenants. He also purchased a portfolio of stocks and bonds, also held as joint tenants. We know that if Bert predeceases Joyce, she will take the home and the securities as the surviving joint tenant. What, though, if they break up? Are Joyce and Bert equal owners of the home and the securities? Or does Bert own the entire beneficial interest in the property on resulting trust because he paid for all of it?

c. Community Property

Community property principles were once largely neglected, other than by passing comparison to the common law system, except in books especially directed to lawyers in community property states. The subject no longer suffers that marginality. As the materials in Chapter 6 reveal, the principle of "equitable distribution" of property at divorce, which plainly draws on the theory of community property, has achieved wide acceptance. Community property principles have also influenced other aspects of marital property law, such as restrictions on wealth transfers by one spouse that affect the size of the estate available to the other spouse upon the transferor's death.

The community property approach, which is often traced to Visigothic Spain, generally recognizes that both spouses own wealth acquired by the labor of either of them during the marriage. As with common law property, the notion of community property has been understood and applied differently at different times and in different places. Community property jurisdictions differ in their treatment of debts and of property owned prior to or inherited during marriage. In one scheme (the Roman-Dutch), all property becomes community property upon marriage; in the Spanish form commonly followed in U.S. community property states and in South America, premarital wealth is regarded as separate property, and its ownership is not affected by marriage. And there are, as one would expect, intermediate schemes as well as differences with respect to the treatment of the income produced by premarital (separate) assets.

Despite these variations, community property interests seem very different from those in a separate property system, where, even under Married Women's Property Acts, each spouse *owns* only what he or she has been given or earns during the marriage. Moreover, community and common law property schemes differ substantially in their treatment of wealth *not* earned during the marriage but brought into the marriage as separate property. Whereas a married woman lost her right to manage her real and personal property during marriage at common law, that was never the case under community property principles. Except for her dowry, a wife has always enjoyed the exclusive rights to control, manage, and dispose of her separate property and can, without her husband's consent, convey her separate property.[6] Similarly, she has had the right to deal with the rents and profits of her separate property in jurisdictions where such rents and profits are separate rather than community property.

Lest one believe, however, that the wife under community property principles stood entirely equal to her husband, it should be added that she occupied much the same position as her sisters in common law jurisdictions before Married Women's Property Acts with respect to management of wealth generated *during* the marriage. While she held an ownership interest in that wealth that wives in common law states did not possess, her interest was passive as long as her husband was alive; the husband possessed full power to manage all of the

---

6. The Spanish law recognized three kinds of property at the time of marriage: dowry, paraphernalia, and other separate property. The dowry was, of course, the consideration, or part of the consideration, paid the husband for marrying his wife. Accordingly, the right of management and control was placed in his hands. However, as with the wife's realty at common law, neither the husband nor his heirs (assuming they were not also hers) had any interest in dower property after dissolution of the marriage.

Paraphernalia included personal property brought by the wife into the marriage, but for her separate use. She retained all rights of control in this property unless she placed the management in her husband's hands by an express writing. *Other separate property* included wealth owned by the wife but not brought by her into the marriage for common use. Here again, the husband had no right of management.

If the wife received property by gift or inheritance, this was treated as other separate property, and the donee wife retained the power of management and distribution. *See* William Q. de Funiak & Michael J. Vaughan, Principles of Community Property 270-273 (2d ed. 1971).

community property, absent an agreement to the contrary. This state of the law resulted, according to the leading commentators on community property principles, "from the consideration of the husband as head of the family,[7] as the one who due to economic and biological factors has been the member of the marital partnership more practiced and experienced in the acquisition and management of property." W. deFuniak & M. Vaughan, at 276.

Sole management power in the husband disappeared during the 1970s as legislatures, either on principle or in anticipation of equal protection challenges, revised their statutes to provide that each spouse or both spouses could manage community wealth. In Kirchberg v. Feenstra, 450 U.S. 455 (1981), the U.S. Supreme Court upheld a Fifth Circuit decision holding the Louisiana "head-and-master" rule unconstitutional.

> By granting the husband exclusive control over the disposition of property, Art. 2404 clearly embodies the type of express gender-based discrimination that we have found unconstitutional absent a showing that the classification is tailored to further an important governmental interest. . . . [Appellant's claim that wives may choose to avoid the impact of Art. 2404] overlooks the critical question: Whether Art. 2404 substantially furthers an important government interest. As we have previously noted, the "absence of an insurmountable barrier" will not redeem an otherwise unconstitutionally discriminatory law. Instead the burden remains on the party seeking to uphold the statute that expressly discriminates on the basis of sex to advance an "exceedingly persuasive justification" for the challenged classification. Because appellant has failed to offer such a justification . . . we affirm the judgment of the Court of Appeals invalidating Art. 2404.

Id. at 459-461.

Statutory formulations now commonly allow "each" or "either" spouse the power to manage and control community property. *E.g.*, Ariz. Rev. Stat. §25-214 (1991) ("each"); Cal. Fam. Code §1100 (West 1994) ("either"); N.M. Stat. Ann. §40-3-14 (Michie 1994) ("either"). However, equalization of authority over community wealth has not been easy to accomplish in practice. After the demise of sole male authority, three different systems have been used to allocate management authority. A "joint management" system requires spouses to make joint decisions regarding community wealth. "Sole management" allocates to one spouse the sole power to manage particular community assets; for example, a spouse may have sole authority to manage his or her earnings. An "equal management" approach authorizes *either* spouse, acting alone, to manage the community property. Professor Thomas Oldham provides the following review of these schemes.

---

7. Without reference to a doctrine of marital unity, Spanish law — quite as clearly as English law — declared that "the husband was head of the family, with the duty to provide for its wants and the right to choose its place of residence." de Funiak & Vaughan, *supra* at 270.

J. Thomas Oldham, *Management of the Community Estate During an Intact Marriage*

56 L. & Contemp. Probs. 99, 106-107 (1993)

Each system has its drawbacks. Joint management ensures that both owners will have the opportunity to participate in management of the community, but this requirement could place a substantial burden upon commerce, particularly if it were applied to all transactions involving any amount of community property. Furthermore, some spouses might not want to manage; the joint management system would burden them, unless some way of opting out were created. Also, what should occur under such a system if only one spouse purports to transfer community property? . . .

The sole management system clearly specifies who will have management power over each item of community property. However, if each spouse does not accumulate (or in some states have record ownership of) the same amount of property during marriage, this system would grant one spouse power over more than half of the community estate, even though both spouses possess a present, vested fifty percent interest. If one spouse works outside the home and the other does not, in many instances the spouse working in the home would manage little or no community property.

The equal management system, like the joint management system, reflects a general norm of equality; it does present a problem, however, if the spouses disagree, and especially if they give contradictory instructions to a third party. In addition, even though either spouse in theory may exercise management power, one might argue that the system facilitates the usurpation of management of the community by the dominant spouse. Also, equal and sole management both permit one spouse to affect the property interests of the other without giving that spouse notice.

No state has accepted one of these management systems for all transactions involving community property. Each has adopted a combination of management rules, in which some transactions are governed by one set of rules, and others by another set.

Similar problems arise with regard to the authority of married persons in community property states to make gifts of community assets. Community property states differ greatly in their responses. California law requires the written consent of the other spouse to make a gift of community personal property, and both spouses generally must join in gifts of real property. Cal. Fam. Code §§1100(b) (personal property), 1102(a) (real property). Texas, by contrast, allows the managing spouse to make "moderate gifts for just causes outside the community," but the managing spouse bears the burden of proving fairness to the other spouse. *See* Mazique v. Mazique, 742 S.W.2d 805 (Tex. App. 1987). Wisconsin, on the third hand, allows unilateral gifts to third persons up to an amount of $1,000 per donee. Wis. Stat. Ann. §766.53.

Consider, as well, the operation of these approaches when one spouse becomes a guarantor without consideration for a third person's debt. Will a general understanding that one spouse will manage the family wealth authorize such an act? Will inaction after knowledge of the transaction constitute a ratification by the nondonor spouse? If there is neither authorization nor ratification, will the donor's part of the community property be reachable by the creditor, or only against his or her separate property? For an extensive analysis of these and the many other problems of management, *see* Oldham, above. The same kinds of issues arise at divorce and are considered at pages 398-430, below.

The Uniform Marital Property Act, drafted by the National Conference of Commissioners on Uniform State Laws, embraces community property principles. Approved by the American Bar Association in 1984, the act has been adopted only in Wisconsin. Section 4, dealing with classification of property, provides as follows:

Section 4. Classification of Property of Spouses
(a) All property is marital property except that which is classified otherwise by this [Act].
(b) All property of spouses is presumed to be marital property.
(c) Each spouse has an undivided one-half interest in marital property.
(d) Income earned or accrued by a spouse or attributable to property of a spouse during marriage and after the determination date [of the Act] is marital property.
(g) [Treats as nonmarital property received: by gift to one but not both spouses; in exchange for individual property; by decree or agreement designating property as individual; some recoveries for damage to individual property; and personal injury awards except to the extent they are reimbursements for expenses paid from marital property.]
(h) Except as provided otherwise in this [Act] the enactment of this [Act] does not alter the classification and ownership rights of property acquired before the determination date.

Section 5 deals with management and control of property. It creates a title-based system in which each spouse acting alone may manage his own individual property, any marital property held in that spouse's name alone (or not held in the name of either spouse), and marital property held in the names of both spouses in the alternative (commonly, as "Mr. Ralph or Mrs. Louise Jones"). Property held jointly (and not in the alternative) can be managed only by joint action. As with classification, the provisions concerning management do not apply to property acquired before the effective date of the Act.

On the history of the Uniform Marital Property Act, *see* William P. Cantwell, The Uniform Marital Property Act: Origin and Intent, 68 Marq. L. Rev. 383 (1985).

2. *"New" Property*

To this point, we have largely been concerned with traditional forms of property: houses, ranches, bank accounts, and the like. A great deal of wealth, however, takes a different form: what is sometimes called "the new property." That phrase is most strongly associated with a series of writings by Charles Reich, including The New Property, 73 Yale L.J. 733 (1964); Individual Rights and Social Welfare: The Emerging Legal Issues, 74 Yale L.J. 1245 (1965); and The Greening of America (1970). He observed in the first of these that "today more and more of our wealth takes the form of rights or status rather than of tangible goods. An individual's profession or occupation is a prime example. To many others, a job with a particular employer is the principal form of wealth." 73 Yale L.J. at 738.

The importance of this new form of wealth was suggested 25 years ago by Peter Drucker, who characterized the modern American economy as "pension socialism":

> If "socialism" is defined as "ownership of the means of production by the workers"—and this is the most orthodox definition—then the United States is the most "socialist" country in the world. . . .
>
> [T]he largest employee pension funds . . . own a controlling interest in practically every single one of the "command positions" in the economy. . . . Indeed, a larger sector of the American economy (outside of farming) today is owned by the American worker—through his investment agent, the pension fund—than Allende in Chile proposed to bring under government ownership to make Chile a "socialist country. . . ."

Peter Drucker, Pension Fund "Socialism," in The Public Interest 3-6 (Winter 1976). Whether this is indeed socialism or rather a way for capitalism to assert control over labor's financial resources even after workers cease their labor is an interesting question. See William Graebner, A History of Retirement: The Meaning and Function of an American Institution: 1885-1978 220-221 (1980).

The importance of this form of property for its holders as well as for the economy has grown enormously. Professor Glendon observed:

> [F]or the majority in modern welfare states, old property (in the sense of traditional assets of real and personal property) is less important than individual earning power and public and private benefits based on such labor. To the extent that there are savings apart from home equity in a middle-aged middle-income family, they tend less to be represented by bank accounts or tangible assets than by employment-related pension plans, profit-sharing plans, insurance or other benefits. . . .

Mary Ann Glendon, The New Family and the New Property 93-94 (1981).

An enormous amount of personal wealth rests in pension funds, and far more so recently than earlier. Private and public pension funds held $4.6 trillion in assets in 1993, more than three times the asset level ten years earlier. Pension plans covered 55 percent of nonagricultural workers in 1991, or if marginal workers (part-time workers, younger workers, short-term employees, and self-employed persons) are excluded, 70 percent of all nonfarm workers. Pension coverage is more common for higher-earning workers than for lower-earning workers, for older rather than younger workers, and for public- rather than private-sector employees. Data concerning coverage are summarized in John H. Langbein & Bruce A. Wolk, Pension and Employee Benefit Law 24-29 (2nd ed. 1995). More recently, pension coverage has declined. In 2002, 46 percent of nonagricultural wage and salary workers in the private sector aged 25-74 participated in a pension plan. Over a lifetime, coverage increases. For households of persons aged 59-69, approximately 60 percent had some sort of pension coverage in 2000. For high-income households the rate of coverage was 77 percent; in the bottom quintile coverage was 25 percent. Alicia H. Munnell, Jamie Lee & Kevin Meme, An Update on Employer-Sponsored Pensions (2004).

In addition, government programs directed to employment security, social insurance benefits, and a variety of other aspects of income maintenance and protection of health and welfare constitute significant forms of wealth in a modern welfare society. These benefits substantially increased during the 1970s from earlier levels, as did the level of wages subject to Social Security tax.

Statutory and judicial decisions have increasingly come to accept Reich's understanding of the importance of "new property." The Employee Retirement Income Security Act of 1974 (ERISA), 29 U.S.C. §1001 et seq., sets forth a comprehensive scheme for the regulation of private pension plans to protect their participants and beneficiaries. Government pension plans are not covered, although they may include provisions similar to those found in the federal statute.

The relationship between ERISA, as modified by the Retirement Equity Act (REAct) of 1984, and state laws generally governing the ownership of wealth by family members is of great importance. In general, state laws define the treatment of wealth earned or held by one or more members of a family and the extent to which family members may dispose of that wealth. ERISA, however, incorporates a critical principle that affects the power of pension plan participants to deal with their pension funds and, concomitantly, the power of others—particularly spouses and creditors—to reach or use those funds. ERISA §206(d)(1) requires that "[e]ach pension plan shall provide that benefits provided under the plan may not be assigned or alienated." The relationship between that principle and other aspects of ERISA to state laws governing marital property (and especially community property) is explored in the following case.

BOGGS V. BOGGS

520 U.S. 833 (1997)

KENNEDY, J., delivered the opinion of the Court, in which STEVENS, SCALIA, SOUTER and THOMAS, JJ., joined, and in which REHNQUIST, C.J., and GINSBURG, J., joined as to Part III. BREYER, J., filed a dissenting opinion, in which O'CONNOR, J. joined, and in which REHNQUIST, C.J., and GINSBURG, J., joined except as to Part II-B-3.

* * *

Isaac Boggs worked for South Central Bell from 1949 until his retirement in 1985. Isaac and Dorothy, his first wife, were married when he began working for the company, and they remained husband and wife until Dorothy's death in 1979. They had three sons. Within a year of Dorothy's death, Isaac married Sandra, and they remained married until his death in 1989.

Upon retirement, Isaac received various benefits from his employer's retirement plans. One was a lump-sum distribution from the Bell System Savings Plan for Salaried Employees (Savings Plan) of $151,628.94, which he rolled over into an Individual Retirement Account (IRA). He made no withdrawals and the account was worth $180,778.05 when he died. He also received 96 shares of AT&T stock from the Bell South Employee Stock Ownership Plan (ESOP). In addition, Isaac enjoyed a monthly annuity payment during his retirement of $1,777.67 from the Bell South Service Retirement Program.

The instant dispute over ownership of the benefits is between Sandra (the surviving wife) and the sons of the first marriage. The sons' claim to a portion of the benefits is based on Dorothy's will. Dorothy bequeathed to Isaac one-third of her estate, and a lifetime usufruct in the remaining two-thirds. A lifetime usufruct is the rough equivalent of a common-law life estate. She bequeathed to her sons the naked ownership in the remaining two-thirds, subject to Isaac's usufruct. All agree that, absent pre-emption, Louisiana law controls and that under it Dorothy's will would dispose of her community property interest in Isaac's undistributed pension plan benefits. A Louisiana state court, in a 1980 order entitled "Judgment of Possession," ascribed to Dorothy's estate a community property interest in Isaac's Savings Plan account valued at the time at $21,194.29.

Sandra contests the validity of Dorothy's 1980 testamentary transfer, basing her claim to those benefits on her interest under Isaac's will and 29 U.S.C. §1055. Isaac bequeathed to Sandra outright certain real property including the family home. His will also gave Sandra a lifetime usufruct in the remainder of his estate, with the naked ownership interest being held by the sons. Sandra argues that the sons' competing claim, since it is based on Dorothy's 1980 purported testamentary transfer of her community property interest in undistributed pension plan benefits, is pre-empted by ERISA. The Bell South Service Retirement Program monthly annuity is now paid to Sandra as the surviving spouse.

After Isaac's death, two of the sons filed an action in state court requesting the appointment of an expert to compute the percentage of the retirement benefits they would be entitled to as a result of Dorothy's attempted testamentary transfer. They further sought a judgment awarding them a portion of: the IRA; the ESOP shares of AT&T stock; the monthly annuity payments received by Isaac during his retirement; and Sandra's survivor annuity payments, both received and payable.

In response, Sandra Boggs filed a complaint in the United States District Court for the Eastern District of Louisiana, seeking a declaratory judgment that ERISA pre-empts the application of Louisiana's community property and succession laws to the extent they recognize the sons' claim to an interest in the disputed retirement benefits. The District Court granted summary judgment against Sandra Boggs. It found that, under Louisiana community property law, Dorothy had an ownership interest in her husband's pension plan benefits built up during their marriage. The creation of this interest, the court explained, does not violate 29 U.S.C. §1056(d)(1), which prohibits pension plan benefits from being "assigned" or "alienated," since Congress did not intend to alter traditional familial and support obligations. In the court's view, there was no assignment or alienation because Dorothy's rights in the benefits were acquired by operation of community property law and not by transfer from Isaac. Turning to Dorothy's testamentary transfer, the court found it effective because

"[ERISA] does not display any particular interest in preserving maximum benefits to any particular beneficiary."

A divided panel of the Fifth Circuit affirmed. . . .

* * *

. . . In large part the number of ERISA pre-emption cases reflects the comprehensive nature of the statute, the centrality of pension and welfare plans in the national economy, and their importance to the financial security of the Nation's work force. ERISA is designed to ensure the proper administration of pension and welfare plans, both during the years of the employee's active service and in his or her retirement years.

This case lies at the intersection of ERISA pension law and state community property law. None can dispute the central role community property laws play in the nine community property States. It is more than a property regime. It is a commitment to the equality of husband and wife and reflects the real partnership inherent in the marital relationship. State community property laws, many of ancient lineage, "must have continued to exist through such lengths of time because of their manifold excellences and are not lightly to be abrogated or tossed aside." 1 W. de Funiak, Principles of Community Property 11 (1943). . . .

The nine community property States have some 80 million residents, with perhaps $1 trillion in retirement plans. This case involves a community property claim, but our ruling will affect as well the right to make claims or assert interests based on the law of any State, whether or not it recognizes community property. Our ruling must be consistent with the congressional scheme to assure the security of plan participants and their families in every State. In enacting ERISA, Congress noted the importance of pension plans in its findings and declaration of policy, explaining:

> [T]he growth in size, scope, and numbers of employee benefit plans in recent years has been rapid and substantial; . . . the continued well-being and security of millions of employees and their dependents are directly affected by these plans; . . . they are affected with a national public interest [and] they have become an important factor affecting the stability of employment and the successful development of industrial relations. . . . 29 U.S.C. §1001(a).

ERISA is an intricate, comprehensive statute. Its federal regulatory scheme governs employee benefit plans, which include both pension and welfare plans. All employee benefit plans must conform to various reporting, disclosure and fiduciary requirements, while pension plans must also comply with participation, vesting, and funding requirements. The surviving spouse annuity and QDRO provisions, central to the dispute here, are part of the statute's mandatory participation and vesting requirements. These provisions provide detailed protections to spouses of plan participants which, in some cases, exceed what their rights would be were community property law the sole measure.

ERISA's express pre-emption clause states that the Act "shall supersede any and all State laws insofar as they may now or hereafter relate to any employee benefit plan. . . ." §1144(a). We can begin, and in this case end, the analysis by simply asking if state law conflicts with the provisions of ERISA or operates to frustrate its objects. We hold that there is a conflict, which suffices to resolve the case. . . .

III

Sandra Boggs, as we have observed, asserts that federal law pre-empts and supersedes state law and requires the surviving spouse annuity to be paid to her as the sole beneficiary. We agree.

The annuity at issue is a qualified joint and survivor annuity mandated by ERISA. . . . ERISA requires that every qualified joint and survivor annuity include an annuity payable to a nonparticipant surviving spouse. The survivor's annuity may not be less than 50% of the amount of the annuity which is payable during the joint lives of the participant and spouse. Provision of the survivor's annuity may not be waived by the participant, absent certain limited circumstances, unless the spouse consents in writing to the designation of another beneficiary, which designation also cannot be changed without further spousal consent, witnessed by a plan representative or notary public. Sandra Boggs, as the surviving spouse, is entitled to a survivor's annuity under these provisions. She has not waived her right to the survivor's annuity, let alone consented to having the sons designated as the beneficiaries.

Respondents say their state-law claims are consistent with these provisions. Their claims, they argue, affect only the disposition of plan proceeds after they have been disbursed by the Bell South Service Retirement Program, and thus nothing is required of the plan. . . .

We disagree. The statutory object of the qualified joint and survivor annuity provisions . . . is to ensure a stream of income to surviving spouses. . . .

ERISA's solicitude for the economic security of surviving spouses would be undermined by allowing a predeceasing spouse's heirs and legatees to have a community property interest in the survivor's annuity. Even a plan participant cannot defeat a nonparticipant surviving spouse's statutory entitlement to an annuity. It would be odd, to say the least, if Congress permitted a predeceasing nonparticipant spouse to do so. Nothing in the language of ERISA supports concluding that Congress made such an inexplicable decision. . . .

Louisiana law, to the extent it provides the sons with a right to a portion of Sandra Boggs' §1055 survivor's annuity, is pre-empted.

IV

Beyond seeking a portion of the survivor's annuity, respondents claim a percentage of: the monthly annuity payments made to Isaac Boggs during his retirement; the IRA; and the ESOP shares of AT&T stock. As before, the claim is based on Dorothy Boggs' attempted testamentary transfer to the sons of her community interest in Isaac's undistributed pension plan benefits. Respondents argue further—and somewhat inconsistently—that their claim again concerns only what a plan participant or beneficiary may do once plan funds are distributed, without imposing any obligations on the plan itself. Both parties agree that the ERISA benefits at issue here were paid after Dorothy's death, and thus this case does not present the question whether ERISA would permit a nonparticipant spouse to obtain a devisable community property interest in benefits paid out during the existence of the community between the participant and that spouse.

The principal object of the statute is to protect plan participants and beneficiaries. . . .

ERISA confers beneficiary status on a nonparticipant spouse or dependent in only narrow circumstances delineated by its provisions. For example, as we have discussed, §1055(a) requires provision of a surviving spouse annuity in covered pension plans, and, as a consequence the spouse is a beneficiary to this extent. Section 1056's QDRO provisions likewise recognize certain pension plan community property interests of nonparticipant spouses and dependents. A QDRO is a type of domestic relations order which creates or recognizes an alternate payee's right to, or assigns to an alternate payee the right to, a portion of the benefits payable with respect to a participant under a plan. . . . A domestic relations order must meet certain requirements to qualify as a QDRO. QDRO's, unlike domestic relations orders in general, are exempt from both the pension plan anti-alienation provision, and ERISA's general pre-emption clause. . . . These provisions are essential to one of REA's central purposes, which is to give enhanced protection to the spouse and dependent children in the event of divorce or separation, and in the event of death the surviving spouse. Apart from these detailed provisions, ERISA does not confer beneficiary status on nonparticipants by reason of their marital or dependent status. . . .

The surviving spouse annuity and QDRO provisions, which acknowledge and protect specific pension plan community property interests, give rise to the strong implication that other community property claims are not consistent with the statutory scheme. ERISA's silence with respect to the right of a nonparticipant spouse to control pension plan benefits by testamentary transfer provides powerful support for the conclusion that the right does not exist. . . .

We conclude the sons have no claim under ERISA to a share of the retirement benefits. To begin with, the sons are neither participants nor beneficiaries. A "participant" is defined as an "employee or former employee of an employer, or any member or former member of an employee organization, who is or may become eligible to receive a benefit." A "beneficiary" is a "person designated by a participant, or by the terms of an employee benefit plan, who is or may become entitled to a benefit thereunder." §1002(8). Respondents' claims are based on Dorothy Boggs' attempted testamentary transfer, not on a designation by Isaac Boggs or under the terms of the retirement plans. . . .

The conclusion that Congress intended to pre-empt respondents' nonbeneficiary, nonparticipant interests in the retirement plans is given specific and powerful reinforcement by the pension plan anti-alienation provision. Section 1056(d)(1) provides that "[e]ach pension plan shall provide that benefits provided under the plan may not be assigned or alienated." Statutory anti-alienation provisions are potent mechanisms to prevent the dissipation of funds. . . . The anti-alienation provision can "be seen to bespeak a pension law protective policy of special intensity: Retirement funds shall remain inviolate until retirement."

Dorothy's 1980 testamentary transfer, which is the source of respondents' claimed ownership interest, is a prohibited "assignment or alienation." An "assignment or alienation" has been defined by regulation, with certain exceptions not at issue here, as "[a]ny direct or indirect arrangement whereby a party acquires from a participant or beneficiary" an interest enforceable against a plan to "all or any part of a plan benefit payment which is, or may become, payable to the participant or beneficiary." Those requirements are met. Under Louisiana law community property interests are enforceable against a plan. If respondents' claims were allowed to succeed they would have acquired, as of 1980, an interest in Isaac's pension plan at the expense of plan participants and beneficiaries.

As was true with survivors' annuities, it would be inimical to ERISA's purposes to permit testamentary recipients to acquire a competing interest in undistributed pension benefits, which are intended to provide a stream of income to participants and their beneficiaries. Pension benefits support participants and beneficiaries in their retirement years, and ERISA's pension plan safeguards are designed to further this end. . . . Under respondents' approach, retirees could find their retirement benefits reduced by substantial sums because they have been diverted to testamentary recipients. Retirement benefits and the income stream provided for by ERISA-regulated plans would be disrupted in the name of protecting a nonparticipant spouse's successors over plan participants and beneficiaries. Respondents' logic would even permit a spouse to transfer an interest in a pension plan to creditors, a result incompatible with a spendthrift provision such as §1056(d)(1). . . .

The axis around which ERISA's protections revolve is the concepts of participant and beneficiary. When Congress has chosen to depart from this framework, it has done so in a careful and limited manner. Respondents' claims, if allowed to succeed, would depart from this framework, upsetting the deliberate balance central to ERISA. It does not matter that respondents have sought to enforce their rights only after the retirement benefits have been distributed since their asserted rights are based on the theory that they had an interest in the undistributed pension plan benefits. Their state-law claims are pre-empted. The judgment of the Fifth Circuit is

Reversed.

Justice BREYER, with whom Justice O'CONNOR joins, and with whom THE CHIEF JUSTICE and Justice GINSBURG join except as to Part II-B-3, dissenting. The question in this case is whether the Employee Retirement Income Security Act of 1974 (ERISA), 29 U.S.C. §1001, et seq., "pre-empts," and thereby nullifies, state community property law. The state law in question would permit a wife to leave to her children her share of the pension assets that her husband has earned (or, to put the matter in "community property" terms, that she and her husband together have earned) during their marriage. From the perspective of property law, the issue is unusually important, for, we are told, the answer potentially affects nine community property States, with more than 80 million residents, and over $1 trillion in ERISA-qualified pension plans — plans that are often a couple's most important lifetime assets. In my view, Congress did not intend ERISA to pre-empt this testamentary aspect of community property law — at least not in the circumstances present here, where a first wife's bequest need not prevent a second wife from obtaining precisely those benefits that ERISA specifically sets aside for her. See §1055(a). The Fifth Circuit's determination is consistent with this view. I would therefore affirm its judgment. . . .

The state law in question concerns the ownership of benefits. I concede that a primary concern of ERISA is the proper financial management of pension and welfare benefit funds themselves, and that payment of benefits (which amounts to the writing of checks from those funds) is closely "connected with" that management. . . . But, even so, I cannot say that the state law at issue here concerns a subject that Congress wished to place outside the State's legal reach.

My reason in part lies in the fact that the state law in question involves family, property, and probate — all areas of traditional, and important, state concern. When this Court considers pre-emption, it works "on the 'assumption that the historic police powers of the States were not to be superseded by the Federal Act unless that was the clear and manifest purpose of Congress.' "

I can find no reasonably defined relevant category of state law that Congress would have intended to displace. Obviously, Congress did not intend to pre-empt all state laws that govern property ownership. After all, someone must own an interest in ERISA plan benefits. Nor, for similar reasons, can one believe that Congress intended to pre-empt state laws concerning testamentary bequests. . . . The question, "who owns the property?" needs an answer. Ordinarily, where federal law does not provide a specific answer, state law will have to do so.

Nor can I find some appropriately defined forbidden category by looking to the congressional purpose of establishing uniform laws to regulate the administration of pension funds. This case does not involve a lawsuit against a fund. I agree with the majority that ERISA would likely pre-empt state law that permitted such a suit. But this is not such a case; nor is there reason to believe Louisiana law would produce such a case. . . .

NOTES AND QUESTIONS

1. The Supremacy Clause of the United States Constitution states that the "laws of the United States . . . shall be the supreme law of the Land." Accordingly, state laws inconsistent with federal law are void. Federal legislation may preempt state law in two ways. It may undertake to provide the sole body of law in a field, either by express statutory provision or by implication. Even if Congress has not expressly or implicitly undertaken to occupy the entire field, state law is preempted to the extent of any conflict with a federal statute. Such a "conflict" preemption arises when a private party cannot comply with both federal and state law or when compliance with the challenged state law will frustrate accomplishment of important federal purposes embodied in Congressional legislation.

The preemption issue in *Boggs* arose because ERISA regulates pension plans for the benefit of individual beneficiaries and specified others, while community property law treats pension plan wealth as property owned by both the employee and his or her then-current spouse at the time the pension is earned. A similar issue can arise when any federal law addresses what a state may regard as community property. In Rodrigue v. Rodrigue, 218 F.3d 432 (5th Cir. 2000), *cert. denied*, 121 S. Ct. 1227 (2001), another case originating in Louisiana, the question was whether the wife of a highly successful artist was entitled to rights in the husband's copyrighted works. The husband argued that the Copyright Act of 1976 provided that ownership of a copyright "vests initially in the author" at the time of the creation of the work. From this, the husband contended, it follows that the community property principle that property acquired during marriage is owned equally by the spouses had been preempted by federal law assigning full ownership solely in the author, and thus his copyrighted works were separate property not subject to division at divorce.

While §301 of the Copyright Act provides that the Act governs "all legal or equitable rights that are equivalent to any of the exclusive rights with the general scope of copyright," the Fifth Circuit concluded that this language did not amount to a preemption of the entire field of marital property. Rather, it held that the Act protects five exclusive rights: reproduction, adaptation, publication, performance, and display of protected works. The Act does not treat enjoyment of the economic benefits of copyrighted materials as an exclusive right of the author, and the Act does not preempt the entire field of copyright ownership.

Accordingly, the question was whether the operation of Louisiana community property law conflicted with the purposes of particular provisions of the Act. The strongest argument for finding a conflict—an argument adopted by the district court—was that Louisiana state law would give the nonauthor spouse equal management rights to copyrighted works, which was functionally inconsistent with Copyright Act's grant to authors of exclusive rights related to management. The Fifth Circuit agreed that dividing these management rights, as opposed to the right to enjoy income or other economic benefits from copyrighted works, would conflict with the federal scheme. However, the court held that the conflict was not ineluctable and that Louisiana community property law was not preempted to the extent that it allowed a nonauthor spouse the right to share in the economic benefits created by copyrighted works during the existence of the marriage.

This decision is reviewed favorably in Neely S. Griffith, Comment, When Civilian Principles Clash with the Federal Law: An Examination of the Interplay Between Louisiana's Family Law and Federal Statutory and Constitutional Law, 76 Tul. L. Rev. 519 (2001), and Garth R. Backe, Note, Community Property and the Copyright Act: Rodrigue's Recognition of a Community Interest in Economic Benefits, 61 La. L. Rev. 655 (2001). *Rodrigue* is sharply criticized as "egregiously wrong" in its interpretation of the Copyright Act and in its "dismemberment" of copyright ownership by Dane S. Ciolino, How Copyrights Became Community Property (Sort of): Through the Rodrigue v. Rodrigue Looking Glass, 47 Loy. L. Rev. 631 (2001) (Professor Ciolino acknowledges participation as counsel in connection with this litigation). For analysis of the broader issues *see* Ann Bartow, Intellectual Property and Domestic Relations: Issues to Consider When There Is an Artist, Author, Inventor, or Celebrity in the Family, 35 Fam. L.Q. 383 (2001).

2. A number of both common law and community property states have adopted "automatic redesignation" statutes. These statutes address the frequent

failure of holders of insurance policies and pension plans to change the designated beneficiary of their plan or policy after divorce. The Washington statute provided that the designation of a spouse as the beneficiary of a nonprobate asset is revoked automatically upon divorce. In Egelhoff v. Egelhoff, 532 U.S. 141 (2001), the Supreme Court held that the operation of the redesignation statute was preempted as it applied to ERISA benefit plans.

Mr. Egelhoff was employed by the Boeing Company, which provided him with a life insurance policy and a pension plan, both covered by ERISA. Mr. Egelhoff designated his then-wife as beneficiary under both. Mr. and Mrs. Egelhoff divorced and, two months later, Mr. Egelhoff died. He had not changed the beneficiary on either the life insurance policy or the pension plan, and the life insurance proceeds were paid to Ms. Egelhoff as the named beneficiary. Respondent's children by a prior marriage, who were entitled to his estate as his heirs, claimed that the life insurance proceeds and pension benefits were part of his estate, relying on the state redesignation statute.

The Supreme Court held that the Washington statute was preempted by ERISA. The majority noted that the state law here involved both family law and probate law, areas of traditional state regulation and therefore entitled to a presumption against preemption. However, the Court said, that presumption could be and was here overcome by the clear Congressional intent to preempt. The preemption clause of ERISA supersedes all state laws insofar as they "relate to" any employee benefit plan covered by ERISA, a term that has been interpreted to cover any state law that "has a connection with" such a plan. The Court said that the Washington statute had an impermissible connection with the insurance and pension plan because it bound ERISA administrators to a particular choice of rules for determining beneficiary status (that is, according to state law rather than the plan documents), which would affect the payment of benefits, a central ERISA concern. The Court also found that state law interfered with a nationally uniform plan of administration insofar as it required the plan administrator to determine the law of each state and administer the benefit award according to that law.

Justice Breyer dissented in Egelhoff. The principal thrust of his dissent is the Court's failure here, as in Boggs, to limit preemption to direct conflicts between federal and state statutes in areas such as family law and family property, where there is a presumption against preemption.

Professors Samuel and Spaht have criticized the adverse impact of Boggs and Egelhoff on community property schemes and discuss how ERISA could be amended to restore the primacy of the state law property scheme. Cynthia A. Samuels & Katherine S. Spaht, Fixing What's Broke: Amending ERISA to Allow Community Property to Apply upon the Death of a Participant's Spouse, 35 Fam. L.Q. 425 (2001).

3. In addition to preemption, the opinion in Boggs also discusses the anti-alienation provision of ERISA, which precludes any person, including the plan participant, from using pension benefit funds prior to retirement. In that respect, it resembles a spendthrift trust, where the corpus and expected future income cannot be transferred by the beneficiary or attached by the beneficiary's creditors. This result reflects deference to the interests of the grantor and a recognition that the creditor has no special right to rely on the availability of those assets.

The purpose of the spendthrift trust is to protect the beneficiary from his or her own improvidence. As John Langbein and Bruce Wolk point out, however, ERISA's alienation rule is an even more dramatic protective strategy than its private trust analogue. For one thing, in most states the spendthrift trust is exceptional, usually employed only when the settlor has some special reason to mistrust the beneficiary's judgment. ERISA makes the protective feature universal. For another, spendthrift clauses do not prevent creditors who have supplied necessaries to the beneficiary from collecting from the trust; creditors are not exempt from the ban on alienation imposed by ERISA. John H. Langbein & Bruce A. Wolk, above, at 546.

Finally, if a settlor creates a spendthrift trust for his or her own benefit, he or she cannot voluntarily alienate an interest in the trust assets, but his or her creditors can still reach them. Restatement of Trusts (Second) §156(1) (1959). If we viewed pension benefits as deferred compensation and the pension plan as having been created by the employee, it would seem that ERISA allows a person to shelter assets from his or her own creditors. Is this comparison between the settlor of a trust and an employee apt?

4. ERISA covers only benefit plans established by (1) employers who are engaged in or affect interstate commerce or (2) employee organizations representing employees engaged in or affecting commerce, or both. While many of its provisions apply to all benefit plans, including welfare benefit plans such as health insurance or vacation plans, the anti-alienation provision applies only to pension benefit plans. Mackey v. Lanier Collection Agency & Service, Inc., 486 U.S. 825 (1988). As the Court notes in *Boggs*, however, benefits other than annuity payments — there, employee stock option benefits and profit sharing plans — may qualify as "pension benefits" and therefore come under the anti-alienation provisions of ERISA. For discussion of the requirements for qualification as a pension plan, *see* 1 Ronald J. Cooke, ERISA Practice and Procedure §2.4 (2nd ed. 1998).

5. In addition to the private pension benefits governed by ERISA, government benefit programs directed to employment security, social insurance benefits, and a variety of other aspects of income now constitute significant forms of wealth. Federal legislation extends immunity from execution for debt to a considerable array of benefits associated with retirement or disability. Exemptions have been enacted for Social Security payments (42 U.S.C. §407 (1988)), Civil Service retirement benefits (5 U.S.C. §8346(a) (1988)), Railroad Retirement Act benefits (45 U.S.C. §231(m)(a) (1988)), and veterans' benefits (38 U.S.C. §3101(a) (1988)), among others. These exemptions are typically based on policy judgments about the importance of preserving these benefits to avoid impoverishment (and the need for public support) of debtors.

State legislatures have created exemptions for analogous entitlements. Public assistance and unemployment benefits typically are immunized from forcible collection; *e.g.*, Cal. Civ. Proc. Code §704.120 (unemployment) (West 1987). Workers' compensation benefits are also largely exempted from execution by state law. To varying extents, the same treatment is given to accident and disability insurance proceeds, but less often to tort judgments for personal injuries. Theodore Eisenberg, Debtor-Creditor Law 37-03[B].

PROBLEM

While Harry and Fran were married, he earned substantial benefits in a pension covered by ERISA. When they divorced 14 years ago, Fran expressly waived any interest in Harry's pension in exchange for other property as part of their divorce agreement. Two years later Harry married Sally. Harry recently died without changing the original designation of Fran as beneficiary of his pension plan. As a matter of state law, Fran's waiver is valid, and Sally argues that it should be enforced, which will have the effect of making the pension benefits payable to Harry's estate, of which Sally is the primary beneficiary. Fran argues that the state law is preempted by ERISA, relying on *Egelhoff*, and that she is therefore entitled to the money as the designated beneficiary. All states permit spouses to waive rights to property and support by contract incident to divorce, and the legal principles governing the validity of these waivers are similar. How should the court rule, and why?

3. The Daily Management and Control of Marital Wealth

McGuire v. McGuire

59 N.W.2d 336 (Neb. 1953)

MESSMORE, J. The plaintiff, Lydia McGuire, brought this action in equity in the district court for Wayne County against Charles W. McGuire, her husband, as defendant, to recover suitable maintenance and support money, and for costs and attorney's fees. Trial was had to the court and a decree was rendered in favor of the plaintiff.

The district court decreed that the plaintiff was legally entitled to use the credit of the defendant and obligate him to pay for certain items in the nature of improvements and repairs, furniture, and appliances for the household in the amount of several thousand dollars; required the defendant to purchase a new automobile with an effective heater within 30 days; ordered him to pay travel expenses of the plaintiff for a visit to each of her daughters at least once a year; that the plaintiff be entitled in the future to pledge the credit of the defendant for what may constitute necessaries of life; awarded a personal allowance to the plaintiff in the sum of $50 a month; awarded $800 for services for the plaintiff's attorney; and as an alternative to part of the award so made, defendant was permitted, in agreement with plaintiff, to purchase a modern home elsewhere. . . .

The record shows that the plaintiff and defendant were married in Wayne, Nebraska, on August 11, 1919. At the time of the marriage the defendant was a bachelor 46 or 47 years of age and had a reputation for more than ordinary frugality, of which the plaintiff was aware. She had visited in his home and had known him for about 3 years prior to the marriage. After the marriage the couple went to live on a farm of 160 acres located in Leslie precinct, Wayne County, owned by the defendant and upon which he had lived and farmed since 1905. The parties have lived on this place ever since. The plaintiff had been previously married.

1st husband died & 2 daughters 64

Her first husband died in October 1914, leaving surviving him the plaintiff and two daughters. . . .

At the time of trial plaintiff was 66 years of age and the defendant nearly 80 years of age. No children were born to these parties. The defendant had no dependents except the plaintiff.

The plaintiff testified that she was a dutiful and obedient wife, worked and saved, and cohabited with the defendant until the last 2 or 3 years. She worked in the fields, did outside chores, cooked, and attended to her household duties such as cleaning the house and doing the washing. For a number of years she raised as high as 300 chickens, sold poultry and eggs, and used the money to buy clothing, things she wanted, and for groceries. She further testified that the defendant was the boss of the house and his word was law; that he would not tolerate any charge accounts and would not inform her as to his finances or business; and that he was a poor companion. The defendant did not complain of her work, but left the impression to her that she had not done enough. On several occasions the plaintiff asked the defendant for money. He would give her very small amounts, and for the last 3 or 4 years he had not given her any money nor provided her with clothing, except a coat about 4 years previous. The defendant had purchased the groceries the last 3 or 4 years, and permitted her to buy groceries, but he paid for them by check. There is apparently no complaint about the groceries the defendant furnished. The defendant had not taken her to a motion picture show during the past 12 years. They did not belong to any organizations or charitable institutions, nor did he give her money to make contributions to any charitable institutions. The defendant belongs to the Pleasant Valley Church, which occupies about 2 acres of his farm land. At the time of trial there was no minister for this church, so there were no services. For the past 4 years or more, the defendant had not given the plaintiff money to purchase furniture or other household necessities. Three years ago he did purchase an electric, wood-and-cob combination stove which was installed in the kitchen, also linoleum floor covering for the kitchen. The plaintiff further testified that the house is not equipped with a bathroom, bathing facilities, or inside toilet. The kitchen is not modern. She does not have a kitchen sink. Hard and soft water is obtained from a well and cistern. She has a mechanical Servel refrigerator, and the house is equipped with electricity. There is a pipeless furnace, which she testified had not been in good working order for 5 or 6 years, and she testified she was tired of scooping coal and ashes. She had requested a new furnace, but the defendant believed the one they had to be satisfactory. She related that the furniture was old and she would like to replenish it, at least to be comparable with some of her neighbors; that her silverware and dishes were old and were primarily gifts, outside of what she purchased; that one of her daughters was good about furnishing her clothing, at least a dress a year, or sometimes two; that the defendant owns a 1929 Ford coupe equipped with a heater which is not efficient, and on the average of every 2 weeks he drives the plaintiff to Wayne to visit her mother; and that he also owns a 1927 Chevrolet pickup which is used for different purposes on the farm. The plaintiff was privileged to use all of the rent money she wanted to from the 80-acre farm, and when she goes to see her daughters, which is not frequent, she uses part of the rent money for that purpose, the defendant providing no funds for such use. . . . At the present time the plaintiff is not able to raise chickens and sell eggs. She has about 25 chickens. The plaintiff has had three abdominal operations for which the defendant has paid. She selected her own doctor, and there were no restrictions placed in that respect. When she has requested various things for the home or personal effects, defendant has informed her on many occasions that he did not have the money to pay for the same. She would like to have a new car. She visited one daughter in Spokane, Washington, in March 1951 for 3 or 4 weeks, and visited the other daughter living in Fort Worth, Texas, on three occasions for 2 to 4 weeks at a time. She had visited one of her daughters when she was living in Sioux City some weekends. The plaintiff further testified that she had very little funds, possibly $1,500 in the bank, which was chicken money and money which her father furnished her, he having departed this life a few years ago; and that use of the telephone was restricted, indicating that defendant did not desire that she make long distance calls; otherwise she had free access to the telephone.

It appears that the defendant owns 398 acres of land with 2 acres deeded to a church, the land being of the value of $83,960; that he has bank deposits in the sum of $12,786.81 and government bonds in the amount of $104,500; and that his income, including interest on the bonds and rental for his real estate, is $8,000 or $9,000 a year. There are apparently some Series E United States Savings Bonds listed and registered in the names of Charles W. McGuire or Lydia M. McGuire purchased in 1943, 1944, and 1945, in the amount of $2,500. Other bonds seem to be in the name of Charles W. McGuire, without a beneficiary or co-owner designated. The plaintiff has a bank account of $5,960.22. This account includes deposits of some $200 and $100, which the court required the defendant to pay his wife as temporary allowance during the pendency of these proceedings. One hundred dollars was withdrawn on the date of each deposit.

The facts are not in dispute.

The defendant assigns as error that the decree is not supported by sufficient evidence; that the decree is contrary to law; [and] that the decree is an unwarranted usurpation and invasion of defendant's fundamental and constitutional rights. . . .

The plaintiff relies upon the following cases from this jurisdiction, which are clearly distinguishable from the facts in the instant case, as will become apparent.

In the case of Earle v. Earle, the plaintiff's petition alleged . . . that the defendant sent his wife away from him, did not permit her to return, contributed to her support and maintenance separate and apart from him, and later refused and ceased to provide for her support and the support of his child. The wife instituted a suit in equity against her husband for maintenance and support without a prayer for divorce or from bed and board. The question presented was whether or not the wife should be compelled to resort to a proceeding for a divorce, which she did not desire to do, or from bed and board. On this question, in this state the statutes are substantially silent and at the present time there is no statute governing this matter. The court stated that it was a well-established rule of law that it is the duty of the husband to provide his family with support and means of living—the style of support, requisite lodging, food, clothing, etc., to be such as fit his means, position, and station in life—and for this purpose the wife has generally the right to use his credit for the purchase of necessaries. The court held that if a wife is abandoned by her husband, without means of support, a bill in equity will lie to compel the husband to support the wife without asking for a decree of divorce. . . .

In the instant case the marital relation has continued for more than 33 years, and the wife has been supported in the same manner during this time without complaint on her part. The parties have not been separated or living apart from each other at any time. In the light of the cited cases it is clear, especially so in this jurisdiction, that to maintain an action such as the one at bar, the parties must be separated or living apart from each other.

The living standards of a family are a matter of concern to the household, and not for the courts to determine, even though the husband's attitude toward his wife, according to his wealth and circumstances, leaves little to be said in his behalf. As long as the home is maintained and the parties are living as husband and wife it may be said that the husband is legally supporting his wife and the purpose of the marriage relation is being carried out. Public policy requires such a holding. It appears that the plaintiff is not devoid of money in her own right. She has a fair-sized bank account and is entitled to use the rent from the 80 acres of land left by her first husband, if she so chooses. . . .

For the reasons given in this opinion, the judgment rendered by the district court is reversed and the cause remanded with directions to dismiss the cause.

Reversed and remanded with directions to dismiss.

YEAGER, J. (dissenting). I respectfully dissent. . . .

From the beginning of the married life of the parties the defendant supplied only the barest necessities and there was no change thereafter. He did not even buy groceries until the last 3 or 4 years before the trial, and neither did he buy clothes for the plaintiff. . . .

There is and can be no doubt that, independent of statutes relating to divorce, alimony, and separate maintenance, if this plaintiff were living apart from the defendant she could in equity and on the facts as outlined in the record be awarded appropriate relief.

The principle supporting the right of a wife to maintain an action in equity, independent of statute, for maintenance was first announced in this jurisdiction in Earle v. Earle, 27 Neb. 277, 43 N.W. 118, 119, 20 Am. St. Rep. 667. In the opinion it was said: "While the statute books of this and other states amply provide for the granting of divorces in meritorious cases, yet we do not apprehend that it is the purpose of the law to compel a wife, when the aggrieved party, to resort to this proceeding, and thus liberate her husband from all obligations to her, in order that the rights which the law gives her, by reason of her marital relations with her husband, may be enforced. Such a conclusion would not generally strike the conscience of a court of equity as being entirely equitable." . . .

If relief is to be denied to plaintiff under this principle it must be denied because of the fact that she is not living separate and apart from the defendant and is not seeking separation.

In the light of what the decisions declare to be the basis of the right to maintain an action for support, is there any less reason for extending the right to a wife who is denied the right to maintenance in a home occupied with her husband than to one who has chosen to occupy a separate abode?

The *McGuire* case raises central questions about the relationship of government, particularly courts, to family governance. These questions, and the case itself, have been the subjects of wide comment and some disagreement. The following materials explore some aspects of that debate, including the importance, utility, and implications of treating the family as an economic and social unit.

MARY ANN GLENDON, *POWER AND AUTHORITY IN THE FAMILY: NEW LEGAL PATTERNS AS REFLECTIONS OF CHANGING IDEOLOGIES*

23 Am. J. Comp. L. 1, 5-10 (1975)

The impossibility of providing a definitive answer to the question whether one spouse should predominate in the family decision-making process has not impeded heroic efforts to settle the matter once and for all by legislative edict or executive decree. . . .

French and German law traditionally dealt elaborately with the allocation of powers of decision in matters of family life between husband and wife. From 1804 until 1938 Art. 213 of the French Civil Code read: "The husband owes protection to his wife, the wife obedience to her husband." . . . Little by little up to 1970 the husband's actual powers as head of the family were eroded, but his symbolic title ["head of the family"] remained. . . .

In the law of 4 June 1970 the historical principle "The husband is head of the family" was eliminated from Art. 213 of the Civil code and the following statement was substituted: "The spouses together assure the moral and material direction of the family." . . . The hierarchical principle which at one time had organized French family law was casually swept away and Art. 215 was amended to include what may be the new organizing principle: "The spouses are mutually bound to a community of life." . . .

In the Anglo-American system spouses have by and large been left to work out their roles, to make their decisions and to divide their labor by themselves so long as the marriage is functioning. This attitude is illustrated by the well-known case of McGuire v. McGuire. . . .

Judicial handling of recent cases brought by husbands asserting a right to participate in the decision whether or not to have an abortion has been consistent with traditional American reluctance to intervene in marital decisionmaking. The Massachusetts Supreme Judicial Court, declining to recognize such a right in the husband, said: "Except in cases involving divorce or separation, our law has not in general undertaken to resolve the many delicate questions inherent in the marriage relationship. . . . Some things must be left to private agreement." While the legislatures of a few states have not been so reticent and have enacted statutes requiring the husband's consent under some circumstances, such statutes have so far been struck down by the courts as unconstitutional.[8]

LEE E. TEITELBAUM, *FAMILY HISTORY AND FAMILY LAW*

1985 Wis. L. Rev. 1135, 1144-1145, 1174-1178

[The social history of the nineteenth- and twentieth-century American family] is developmental, moving from an hierarchically ordered household closely integrated with the community towards an egalitarian, companionate family sharply separated from the public world. The trend is not so much toward a nuclear as an enucleated family. . . .

. . . "[P]rivacy" for the household is often given an objective meaning. . . . The meaning given to privacy . . . is the familiar one of autonomy or freedom from governmental control. A clear statement of this association has been provided by Judith Stiehm:

> In this country, intrafamily relations are a private rather than a governmental concern. The state does establish a legal basis for the family's existence, but this defining function is exercised principally when families are either being founded, as in marriage or adoption, or dissolved, as in divorce or death. Even then, the state's role is minimal unless property is involved. The government is only too happy to avoid having either to forbid or to require particular interpersonal behavior.

Judith Stiehm, Government and the Family: Justice and Acceptance, in Changing Images of the Family 361, 362 (V. Tufte & B. Myerhoff eds., 1979).

Both the notion of family privacy and its meaning of autonomy or freedom from governmental concern are used in legal discussions as well. . . . Generally, the notion of family privacy includes two situations: those in which courts decline to intervene to resolve intra-familial disputes for prudential reasons and those in which they say that law may not properly regulate certain aspects of family relationships. The most familiar illustration of the first situation is the reluctance of courts to order the financial and personal arrangements of spouses. Where the marriage is "intact," meaning that proceedings for separation or divorce have not been instituted, courts traditionally have refused to enter support decrees unless gross and dangerous neglect is proved. . . .

. . . When courts refuse to resolve intra-spousal financial disputes, that decision is founded on the principle of family autonomy. . . . However, the practical consequence of many, if not all, of these decisions is to confer or ratify the power of one family member over others. While Professor Glendon sees cases like McGuire v. McGuire as leaving spouses free to work out their own roles within

---

8. Professor Glendon's article was written before the Supreme Court's decision in Planned Parenthood of Central Missouri v. Danforth, 428 U.S. 52 (1976), holding that a husband could not be given a veto over his wife's decision to terminate her pregnancy.

the family, one wonders in what sense the family as an entity was made free. Certainly Mrs. McGuire was not "free to work out her own role" in the marriage if Mr. McGuire had all the money. She could not get the new cloth coat she wanted, or new linoleum for the kitchen, or a warm heater for their old car. Her only choice lay without the marriage, in seeking a judicial separation or divorce. When the majority in McGuire say that "the living standards of the family are a matter of concern to the household," they mean only that they propose to leave the parties where they are. The "household" does not make decisions about living standards, unless that is informally agreed. Otherwise, the husband will make those decisions. . . .

[Analysis that assumes that the state does not intervene in the family unit] depends on a particular conceptualization of law. We mean by intervention public activity through proscriptive and prescriptive rules: "Thou shalt not steal" or "Thou shalt support thy wife." Commands of these kinds are sharply distinguished from facilitative rules and from silence or abstention, which are considered instances of nonregulation. A rule that says "Fathers must leave at least one-third of their wealth to their children at death" is considered different in kind from one that says "Any testamentary provision made in a certain form will be enforced." Similarly, a rule reciting that "Husbands shall adequately support their wives" is different, not only in its content but in its nature, from one that says, "The state will not resolve financial disputes between spouses." The first of these pairs of rules would be considered an instance of intervention because each manifestly limits individual choice; the second of these pairs would ordinarily be regarded as facilitating or conveying autonomy. . . .

The entity approach . . . hides decisions about family relationships that are worth examining. Although only prescriptive and proscriptive rules are taken as cases of intervention, it is surely true that all forms of societal behavior — including facilitative rules and silence — involve policy choices. Moreover, the choice of strategies is not simply between domination (intervention) and freedom (non-intervention), but between two kinds of authority. When government acts by commands, it thereby authorizes an exercise of public authority. . . .

Facilitative rules and silence, by contrast, leave people to their own strengths and thereby authorize personal authority. If bargains will always be enforced, the making of that bargain reflects only the power, skill, and knowledge of the parties. When the parties are in fact unequal in these characteristics, the weaker party is subject to the domination of the stronger. That domination is personal rather than public; law only ratifies the naturally existing or socially created inequalities which have led to the victory of one over the other.

By regarding the family as an entity which is left free by governmental silence, the effects of a policy permitting personal domination are obscured. When . . . Mrs. McGuire is left to her own resources in dealing with her husband, she is subject to his personal authority in seeking a car or a coat. No rules require that he treat her as other husbands treat their wives, or as he treated a former wife, had he married previously. It does not in principle matter that her neighbors have bought cars, coats, or an electric range for their wives. . . . Because we focus on "the family" rather than on Mrs. McGuire, however, her condition becomes invisible.

BRUCE C. HAFEN, *THE FAMILY AS AN ENTITY*

22 U.C. Davis L. Rev. 865, 909, 912 (1989)

We might help to restore a more familistic perspective on family relationships by regarding the family as a structurally significant and legally meaningful entity that affects both individual and social interests. . . .

This notion of entity is nothing more mysterious than what most Americans still assume (even if partly as myth) is "the dominant American ideal"—namely, relationships based upon marriage and kinship in which legal, biological, and social expectations convey long-term, normative, familistic assumptions. Those who accept membership in such an entity implicitly accept in a general—even if, in many ways, unenforceable—sense the familistic model's characteristics. . . .

Emphasizing the family's "internal" institutional autonomy may leave some deserving individuals without legal recourse for unequal treatment or other wrongs (short of actual abuse) that they may suffer within the sphere of family privacy. However, unless we to some degree assume that risk, constant legal intervention (or the threat of it) will destroy the continuity that is critically necessary for meaningful, ongoing relationships and developmental nurturing. Even the "direct, prolonged conflict" that may characterize some family continuity may play a significant role in "forging communal bonds." . . .

Moreover, when we increase state intervention in an ongoing family to protect the autonomy of some family members against others, we may be simply exchanging one threat to autonomy for another. We must then ask which threat is worse—the state or other family members? In cases of serious spousal or child abuse, the threat from within the family is obviously worse. Over the long run, however, liberal thought has usually, and accurately, perceived the state as a more frightening enemy of personal liberty.

LEE E. TEITELBAUM, *THE FAMILY AS A SYSTEM: A PRELIMINARY SKETCH*

1996 Utah L. Rev. 537

In view of the extent to which family life and function are thought to have changed, it is not surprising to find differing efforts to understand family life. Two of these understandings have dominated legal, social, and popular discourse for many years. Both have continuing currency and support, but they differ greatly in what they emphasize about the nature and function of the family. They are important not merely as descriptions of family organization and behavior but normatively, as they reflect and reproduce ideas of how families should be organized and behave, and about the relation of families to society.

The earlier understanding talks in terms of the family as a "unit" or "entity." . . .

I have, on other occasions, expressed reservations about the adequacy of understanding the family as a unit or entity. . . .

. . . I would suggest that [the alternative] view of the family only as a collection of individuals who come together in a contractarian arrangement for so long and for such purposes as they choose is also deeply unsatisfying. . . . [A]n emphasis upon contract and individualism seems especially unsuited to the discourse about families. The individualism that marks "classical" contract law supposes a world populated by freestanding, abstracted, anonymous persons. After the demise of feudalism, legal relations came to depend on the personhood of a legal actor and not on his or her social position, religion, or nationality. The removal of ascriptive or status elements left each person standing alone.

At the same time, the demands of an increasingly national and even international commerce required some capacity for abstract calculability—that commercial actors be able to make business judgments with security that they know the conventions and expectations that would govern their transactions in a society which has become large and differentiated. . . .

It is, however, hard to reconcile an approach based on formal rationality and formally calculable chances with the circumstances of families. At the most obvious level, such an assumption seems inconsistent with the current view that families serve principally affective rather than economic functions in modern society.

It is also impossible to discuss the spousal positions in this situation by reference to formally calculable chances. Unlike most contracts, the marriage relationship is formally and often actually conceived in life-long terms. Consequently, the variety of circumstances that may intervene is infinite. No spouse or spouse to be can anticipate all of the things that may affect her relationship with her mate, or even predict the significance of changed circumstances.

If abstract calculation tells us little about families, so does the assumption of anonymity that founds contract law. . . . Now that marriages result from close familiarity and affection, anonymity is a peculiar characteristic to attribute to family relations. Anonymity and calculation are also normatively inconsistent with family life. Indeed, the significance of family life is thought to lie just in its lack of anonymity: in the sharing of hopes, dreams, or frustrations within the home. To deal with a spouse as one deals with a stranger would universally be understood as an occasion for professional intervention. . . .

Neither the notion of the family unit nor reconceptualization of the family as a collection of individuals united by contract provides a satisfying approach to understanding the family. What is needed is an understanding of "the family" that does two things. For one, it should take better account of how families actually function than does either of the current modes: the family imagined as an island or refuge, which takes account of neither systems in the "public sphere" (except in opposition to the family) or of individual choice, and the family as a collection of individuals, which takes little account of the intimacy and interrelatedness of family life. . . .

I would propose a sketch, and only that, of another approach. Thinking of the family as a "system" may not only accommodate but help define the relation of individual choice and public power to the family. I do not mean to place too much weight on the term "system." Indeed, the term "community" is in some ways better, at least by reminding us that the family provides the paradigm case for "communitarian" values. . . .

However, the term "community" may not as fully capture the importance of relations between families and external agencies and rules as does "system." And the concept of a system surely incorporates a number of aspects of family life. In general, a system is understood as a network that integrates parts into a whole. This understanding incorporates both the sense of an identifiable, special relationship and the sense of membership by individuals that seem characteristic of families. The concept of a "system" may also be understood as referring not only to the internal ordering of parts, but in terms of its interaction with and response to the environment in which it is situated. This aspect, too, is important in modern family life, having regard to the frequency and significance of the relationship between families and intermediate social systems. . . . .

Although it is often said that the modern family has lost all but an affective function, that view seems extreme and inaccurate. Families still serve in significant ways as economic systems, moral systems, and educational systems; they remain important agencies for the distribution of goods in our society. . . . .

This variety of functions itself distinguishes families from specialized or "functions" systems, such as business organizations or government agencies. In addition, however, the family is a special system in the sense that it not only performs all of these functions but performs all of them at the same time. Whereas specialized or functional social systems, such as business organizations and public schools, typically are created to serve particularized purposes and determine their actions by primary reference to those purposes in a more or less formally rational way, the family must accommodate a broad set of purposes, often without a single primary reference. . . .

[For example,] educational decisions likewise may be driven by religious values . . . or by social and political values. Some parents may refuse to send their daughter to college because, in their view, her role is to be a wife and mother. Others may choose not to send a son to a private college for which he is well qualified because they resent its "elitist" attitude or the political tendencies of its faculty. Yet others may elect to send a child to such a college just because the social values they hold make doing so seem inevitable. And in doing so, such parents may thereby choose to invest what, if only economic rationality were considered, seems a "disproportionate" amount of their earnings in securing "the best" educational opportunity for their children. At least within an intact family, social and legal norms seem to grant families this latitude. . . . One other special aspect of the family system must be mentioned: its dynamism and mutability, both internally and with respect to external authority. The most familiar aspect of the dynamic character of family life is, of course, the parent-child relation. Spousal relations, however, are also dynamic and mutable, and perhaps more so now than previously. . . .

An understanding of the complexity and dynamism of the family system may help us deal with one of the problems presented by "entity" or contractarian theories of the family: that of reconciling unity with choice. As we have seen, the notion of the family unit in its "entity" or anthropomorphic form leaves little space for recognizing individual claims — the interests that arise from a wide range of individualized decisions and arrangements — within a family. Respect for the "privacy" of the family unit seemingly requires ignoring other, possibly competing, bearers of rights — the individual family members. So Mr. and Mrs. McGuire are merged into the McGuires, an association whose internal relations are opaque to legal scrutiny. However, a theory of the family as the sum of agreements made by separate individual wills leaves little room for the sense of commitment experienced by and valued in family life.

But if we think of the family as a dynamic system . . . family relations can be seen as a series of choices by which various goals, values, and material conditions are accommodated. Because of their number, interrelatedness, and imbeddedness in everyday life, these choices are made as a matter of course, often without much discussion or even recognition that they are being made. Nonetheless, the success of family arrangements supposes that all parties in the system accept, on some basis, that arrangement.

At the same time, thinking of the family as an interactive system does not require ignoring the collective character of family life. We can suppose that choices are made, without believing that each is a simple expression of individual will. Rather, these choices can be understood in the context of a system that does not expect formal election and negotiation, and in which family members at some point cease to think of their wills and choices as radically independent of those of others. Decisions are made as part of a carrying out of collective life, and reflect not only individual preference but love, sympathy, and common enterprise. The wishes of each family member are partly defined by the complex histories and relations that characterize the family system, which cannot be reconstructed on an exigently individualistic or rationalistic basis. . . .

Let us return for a moment to the *McGuire* case. That situation presents what seems to be an insoluble dilemma. On the one hand it seems quite wrong to leave Mrs. McGuire without the capacity to buy things — linoleum, a new stove, and a new cloth coat — that are surely appropriate to a woman of her age and the extent of family wealth. To follow the traditional view of the "family unit" appears to deny her any individual role in the marriage. While she may in principle be able to pledge her husband's credit to purchase necessaries, that remedy is practically uncertain and ethically doubtful. Practically, the availability of credit is up to the seller, and in a small Nebraska town, many merchants may be unwilling to antagonize Mr. McGuire or to risk a lawsuit in order to collect. Ethically, it seems wrong to treat Mrs. McGuire as if she had, during the course of their marriage, earned nothing and had no call on family resources for expenses associated with family life. The formal equality provided by Married Women's Property Acts is, of course, useless to the many families where, like the McGuires, husbands and wives follow traditional role allocations. On the other hand, the remedy Mrs. McGuire sought — which seems appropriate if we emphasize a strong notion of individual choice — has real disadvantages. As we have already seen, families may make any number of financial decisions, and these decisions reflect highly contextualized (localized) calculations. For courts to decide whether savings should be spent on vacation or preserved for retirement and whether earnings should be spent to purchase home-making services or saved through the labor of one spouse, seems both inappropriate and unwise — not only for the obvious reasons but because, in many such cases, courts are asked implicitly to decide whether one or both spouses should work. They may also be asked to reform the consequences of decisions made, expressly or not, by both parties during the course of the marriage by giving effect to a single preference. In short, the doctrinal basis of the *McGuire* decision seems defensible.

If, however, the family is regarded as a group that defines and redefines its own values over time, the problem in *McGuire* may be open to a different analysis. The dilemma we have observed is created by the legal and social background against which this particular aspect of the marital relationship is set. The legal background in question is, of course, a marital property system that regards wealth as earned solely by the spouse in the paid economy. The social background is a cultural understanding that women need not, and even should not, work in the paid economy.

Attention to these background rules may provide a solution that neither denies Mrs. McGuire any access to "family" wealth nor involves the court in routine supervision of family finances. One possible modification is to define the expectations for wives in a way that takes advantage of Married Women's Property Acts and relieves the need for courts to allocate domestic finances. Wives, it may be said, must behave as if they were unmarried in the economic sphere. They should maintain their own employment throughout marriage, and allow their careers to develop as their husbands' careers develop. Such a solution does not seem, however, to solve the problem of fairness within the family; it rather seeks to avoid the problem by reducing the choices available to women and men. An alternate approach, which recognizes rather than rejects the choices of married couples, is to say that each spouse does not choose his or her own career individually. An interpretive approach would regard the employment, child care, and other decisions within the household as a joint undertaking. Unlike the decisions of formal organizations, whether business or clubs, these decisions would inevitably be multivalent. Unlike contracting parties, these decisions might never be the subject of discussion and agreement, and some might never be recognized or articulated in the course of the family's life. They would be made, often enough, *en passant*, without any specification of the time at which minds met or their exact terms. The decisions may also have altered over the course of the marriage, without any conversation that began, "Let's change our agreement regarding employment."

On this approach, the problem in *McGuire* lies in the relationship of background rules to family decisionmaking. Rules regarding ownership and control of marital wealth should not suppose that married persons will formally decide about paid employment, nor should it require them to make some particular choice. Rather, those rules should reflect the collective quality of domestic relations and assume that economic decisions are part of the broad range of decisions within a family which will be reached and carried out by both parties. This is, of course, a marital or community property system with joint management of family wealth. Unlike Mr. and Mrs. McGuire, family members within a community property system can work out their relationship under conditions of financial equality, and in a setting where "working things out" does not mean implicit deference to the wishes of the spouse who works in the paid economy.

JOHN KENNETH GALBRAITH, *ECONOMICS AND THE PUBLIC PURPOSE*

31-37 (1973)

In preindustrial societies women were accorded virtue, their procreative capacities apart, for their efficiency in agricultural labor or cottage manufacture or, in the higher strata of society, for their intellectual, decorative, sexual or other entertainment value. Industrialization eliminated the need for women in such cottage employments as spinning, weaving or the manufacture of apparel. . . . Meanwhile rising standards of popular consumption, combined with the disappearance of the menial personal servant, created an urgent need for labor to administer and otherwise manage consumption. In consequence a new social virtue came to attach to household management—to intelligent shopping for goods, their preparation, use and maintenance and the care and maintenance of the dwelling and other possessions. The virtuous woman became the good housekeeper or, more comprehensively, the good homemaker. . . .

The conversion of women into a crypto-servant class was an economic accomplishment of the first importance. . . . The value of services of housewives has been calculated, somewhat impressionistically, at roughly one fourth of total Gross National Product. . . . If it were not for this service, all forms of household consumption would be limited by the time required to manage such consumption—to select, transport, prepare, repair, maintain, clean, service, store, protect and otherwise perform the tasks that are associated with the consumption of goods. . . .

As just noted, the labor of women to facilitate consumption is not valued in national income or product. This is of some importance for its disguise; what is not counted is often not noticed. The neoclassical model has, however, a much more sophisticated disguise for the role of women. That is the household. . . .

. . . Though a household includes several individuals—husband, wife, offspring, sometimes relatives or parents—with differing needs, tastes and preferences, all neoclassical theory holds it to be the same as an individual. Individual and household choices are, for all practical purposes, interchangeable.

The household having been made identical with the individual, it then distributes its income to various uses so that satisfactions are roughly equal at the margin. This, as observed, is the optimal state of enjoyment, the neoclassical consumer equilibrium. An obvious problem arises as to whose satisfactions are equated at the margin—those of the husband, the wife, the children with some allowance for age or the resident relatives, if any. But on this all accepted theory is silent. Between husband and wife there is evidently a compromise which accords with the more idyllic conception of the sound marriage. . . .

In fact, the modern household does not allow expression of individual personality and preference. It requires extensive subordination of preference by one member or another. The notion that economic society requires something approaching half of its adult members to accept subordinate status is not easily . . . reconciled with a system of social thought which not only esteems the individual but acclaims his or her power. So neoclassical economics resolves the problem by burying the subordination of the individual within the household, the inner relationships of which it ignores. Then it recreates the household as an individual consumer. There the matter remains. The economist does not invade the privacy of the household.

The common reality is that the modern household involves a simple but highly important division of labor. With the receipt of the income, in the usual case, goes the *basic* authority over its use. This usually lies with the male. Some of this authority is taken for granted. The place where the family lives depends over-whelmingly on the convenience or necessity of the member who makes the income. And both the level and nature or style of expenditure are also extensively influenced by its source — by whether the recipient is a business executive, lawyer, artist, accountant, civil servant, artisan, assembly-line worker or professor. More important, in a society which sets store by pecuniary achievement, a natural authority resides with the person who earns the money. This entitles him to be called the *head* of the family.

The administration of the consumption resides with the woman. This involves much choice as to purchases. . . . The conventional wisdom celebrates this power; it is women who hold the purse strings. In fact this is normally the power to implement decisions, not to make them. Action, within the larger strate-gic framework, is established by the man, who provides the money. The house-hold, in the established economics, is essentially a disguise for the exercise of male authority.

J. THOMAS OLDHAM, *MANAGEMENT OF THE COMMUNITY ESTATE DURING AN INTACT MARRIAGE*

56 L. & Contemp. Probs. (Spring 1993) 99, 101-104

Factors other than legal rules affect how spouses make decisions about the expenditure of marital funds. For example, a study of management decisions con-ducted two decades ago in England (a common law jurisdiction where, at least according to the law, a spouse has no vested property right in the other's accumu-lations during marriage) found that more than fifty percent of all couples took title to their houses jointly. About forty percent of the couples had joint bank accounts.

A 1983 English study by Jan Pahl of management decisions by spouses found that fifty-six percent of the couples studied pooled their funds. [J. Pahl, Money and Marriage (1989).] Additionally, in fourteen percent of the marriages, the wife had by spousal agreement sole management over marital funds, while in none of the marriages did the spouses agree that the husband alone should make all man-agement decisions regarding marital funds. So, although the husbands in the sam-ple generally made much more money than their spouses, and were therefore the legal owners and managers of that money, by private agreement the wife could manage funds earned by the husband in seventy percent of the marriages.

These two studies suggest that factors other than legal rules have a signifi-cant effect upon how spouses manage their money. . . .

Even if one accepts that a number of factors other than legal rules affect how spouses manage marital funds, this does not render legal rules irrelevant. . . . Pahl attempted to learn more about how the couples made management decisions. She discovered that the manner in which the spouses said they managed their money did not accurately depict who really controlled important decisions. She found that in all marriages studied, even in those where the spouses pooled resources, one spouse controlled financial decisions. She therefore categorized the spouses into four types: marital resources controlled by the wife alone; marital resources controlled by the husband alone; pooled resources controlled by the wife; and pooled resources controlled by the husband.

. . . [W]hen a wife earned less than thirty percent of what her husband earned, she controlled the household's finances thirty-one percent of the time. When she earned over thirty percent of what her husband earned, however, she had financial control sixty-four percent of the time. This strongly suggests that if the wife works and contributes a significant amount to the household budget, it is much more likely that she will have financial control.

The study does not establish what causes this increased level of control by the working wives. It could be attributed to Britain's legal rule that each wife "owns" those wages that she contributes to the household. Alternatively, the employment could raise her self-esteem so that she feels more able or entitled to participate in management of household funds. Also, women who make a substantial wage might be members of a group who are generally more assertive than others. It is reasonable to conclude from Pahl's study that, although legal rules may have some effect upon the manner in which spouses manage marital funds, it is likely that management patterns selected by spouses for their marriages can be substantially affected by considerations unrelated to legal rules.

— Common Law
Doctrine of
necessities

SHARPE FURNITURE, INC. V. BUCKSTAFF

299 N.W.2d 219 (Wis. 1980)

purchase of
sofa

BEILFUSS, C.J. This controversy centers around the purchase of a sofa from Sharpe Furniture, Inc. (Sharpe). The purchase was made by Karen Buckstaff on August 15, 1973. On that date, Mrs. Buckstaff signed in her own name a special order for a "Henredon 6800 Sofa." Under the terms of the order she was to pay $621.50 within 60 days after the item was received from the factory. Interest at a rate of 1.5 percent per month was charged on the unpaid balance after that 60-day period. No representations were made to Sharpe at the time of the purchase that Mrs. Buckstaff was acting on behalf of her husband in purchasing the furniture. Indeed, John Buckstaff had previously written to the local credit bureau service to advise that office that he would not be responsible for any credit extended to his wife.

The Henredon sofa was received from the factory and delivered to the residence of the defendants on February 8, 1974. This piece of furniture has been a part of the Buckstaff home ever since its delivery. Despite this fact, neither John Buckstaff nor his wife have tendered payment for the sofa.

On November 20, 1975, Sharpe commenced this action against both Buckstaffs. The parties agreed to allow the trial court to decide the dispute on the basis of the undisputed facts as they appeared in the trial memoranda submitted by counsel. In addition to the facts already stated above, the informal stipulation of the parties reveals that John Buckstaff, Jr., is the president of Buckstaff Company of Oshkosh, Wisconsin. Mrs. Buckstaff is a housewife. Mr. Buckstaff earns a substantial income and the Buckstaff family is one of social and economic prominence in the Oshkosh area. It was further set forth that Mr. Buckstaff has always provided his wife with the necessaries of life and has never failed or refused to provide his wife with items which could be considered necessaries.

On the basis of these facts, the trial court found that Karen Buckstaff was liable on her contract and that John Buckstaff was also liable for the amount due on the sofa under the common law doctrine of necessaries. . . .

There are two issues which we must consider in reviewing the decision of the court of appeals:

1. Whether, under the common law doctrine of necessaries and in the absence of any contractual obligation on his part, a husband may be held liable for sums due as payment for necessary items purchased on credit by his wife.

2. Whether, in an action for recovery of the value of necessaries supplied on credit to a wife, it is essential for the plaintiff-creditor to prove either that the husband has failed, refused or neglected to provide the items which have been supplied by the plaintiff-creditor or that the items supplied were reasonably needed by the wife or the family.

Before proceeding to a discussion of the merits of this case, we examine the substance of the doctrine of necessaries.

The Wisconsin Supreme Court restated the common law rule of necessaries early on in the history of the jurisprudence of this state. In 1871, in the case of Warner and Ryan v. Heiden, 28 Wis. 517, 519 (1871), the court wrote:

> The husband is under legal obligations to support his wife, and nothing but wrongful conduct on her part can free him from such obligation. If he fails to provide her with suitable and proper necessaries, any third person who does provide her therewith, may maintain an action against him for the same. 1 Bishop on Mar. and Div., sec. 553. The same learned author, in the next section (sec. 554), thus defines what are necessaries which the husband is bound to furnish to his wife: "And, in general, we may say, that necessaries are such articles of food, or apparel, or medicine, or such medical attendance and nursing, or such provided means of locomotion, or provided habitation and furniture, *or such provision for her protection in society*, and the like, as the husband, considering his ability and standing, ought to furnish to his wife for her sustenance, and the preservation of her health and comfort."

This doctrine traditionally required the creditor to show that he supplied to the wife an item that was, in fact, a necessary and that the defendant had previously failed or refused to provide his wife with this item. . . . When such a showing was made, the creditor was entitled to recovery as against the husband despite the fact that the husband had not contractually bound himself by his own act or by the act of an agent. The doctrine of necessaries is not imposed by the law of agency. This duty is placed upon a husband by virtue of the legal relationship of marriage. It arises as an obligation placed on him as a matter of public policy.

The appellant challenges the continued vitality of this common law rule. Mr. Buckstaff charges that the necessaries doctrine conflicts with contemporary trends toward equality of the sexes and a sex neutral society. . . .

It is true that the necessaries rule has been justified in the past on the basis of a social view of the married woman as a person without legal capacity. However, the nature of the woman's obligations under the necessary rule in relation to the obligation of her husband is not at issue here. That question has been treated in our decision in Estate of Stromsted, —Wis. 2d—, 299 N.W.2d 226 (1980), wherein we concluded the husband was primarily liable for necessities and the

wife secondarily liable. The question presented in this case involves a consideration of the nature of the husband's obligation. We must decide whether such a liability imposed upon the husband furthers a proper purpose in contemporary
society.

We are of the opinion that the doctrine of necessaries serves a legitimate and
proper purpose in our system of common law. The heart of this common law rule
is a concern for the support and the sustenance of the family and the individual
members thereof. The sustenance of the family unit is accorded a high order of
importance in the scheme of Wisconsin law. . . . The necessaries rule encourages
the extension of credit to those who in an individual capacity may not have the
ability to make these basic purchases. In this manner it facilitates the support of
the family unit and its function is in harmony with the purposes behind the support laws of this state. The rule retains a viable role in modern society. . . .

We conclude that when an item or service is obtained for the benefit of the
family which is necessary and no payment for that item or service has been made,
the elements of an action for an implied-in-law contract exist and the husband is
primarily liable. . . .

Mr. Buckstaff's second argument is that, as a matter of law, he is not liable
for the necessaries purchased by his wife because Sharpe did not plead or prove
that he as a husband failed, refused or neglected to provide a sofa for his wife. It
is also argued that liability cannot be found in the face of the parties' stipulation
which states that Mr. Buckstaff has always provided his wife with the necessaries
of life and has never failed or refused to provide her with items which would constitute necessaries. . . .

In the case of Eder v. Grifka, 149 Wis. 606, 136 N.W. 154 (1912), it was held
that, besides demonstrating that necessaries were furnished by the creditor to the
defendant's spouse, a plaintiff-creditor must also plead and prove that the defendant wilfully refused to provide the necessaries for his wife. . . .

The merchant's burden of proof was modified by the decision in Simpson
Garment Co. v. Schultz, 182 Wis. 506, 196 N.W. 783 (1924). . . .

The *Simpson Garment Company* rule required only that the creditor show
that the item was "reasonably needed" by the wife or family, and not that the husband wilfully refused to provide his wife with the necessary item as suggested by
Eder v. Grifka, supra. . . .

Buckstaff's first argument, that the court's judgment of liability is invalid in
the absence of a finding of refusal or neglect by a husband, must be rejected.
Under *Simpson Garment Company*, the refusal or neglect of the husband is not an
element essential to recovery by the creditor. Mr. Buckstaff's second contention is
that the sofa should not be considered a necessary in view of the stipulation that
he as a husband provided his wife with all necessaries. Whether or not, as a general matter, a man provides his wife with necessaries is irrelevant to a determination of whether a particular item is reasonably needed under the *Simpson Garment
Company* rule. . . .

We have reviewed the stipulation of the parties in this matter and we are satisfied that ample evidence supported the trial court's conclusion that the
Henredon sofa was a legally necessary item. The Buckstaffs are a prominent family and their socio-economic standing justifies a finding that the sofa at issue here

was a suitable and proper item for their household. With reference to the element of reasonable need, we note that the sofa has been in use in the Buckstaff home since its delivery. Such continued use gives rise to an inference of reasonable need. This inference is not rebutted by the stipulation stating that Mr. Buckstaff provided his wife with "all necessaries.". . . .

The decision of the court of appeals is affirmed.

ABRAHAMSON, J. (concurring). I join the court in retaining the doctrine of necessaries and imposing liability on Mr. Buckstaff for the cost of the sofa. I do not agree, however, with that portion of the opinion in which the court adopts a rule placing primary liability on the husband to the creditor for necessaries supplied to the family. . . .

. . . [I]f the common law doctrine of necessaries is to survive as a rule of law it must be modified in accordance with the developing laws recognizing equal rights and responsibilities of both marital partners and the changes in the economic and social conditions of society. The common law doctrine of necessaries was premised on the legal disability of the married woman and on the husband's duty to support. Today, the married woman is free to contract, and the duty of support rests not on the husband alone but on both the husband and wife. While these changes in the law will require an alteration of the doctrine of necessaries, I would leave that alteration to a case in which the application of the common law doctrine conflicts with the married women statutes and the support statutes. This is not the case.

I believe the court has erred in adopting a flat, general rule which places primary liability on the husband to the creditor who supplies necessaries to the family. In my opinion, the rule suffers from two infirmities. First, the rule is not in harmony with the legislatively established public policy of this state, which is to impose the obligation to support on both the husband and wife on the basis of their respective economic resources and not on one spouse or the other on the basis of gender. Second, the rule discriminates against men and thus contravenes the state and federal constitutional guarantees of equal protection of law. . . .

I am persuaded that the majority rule which effects an unequal distribution of economic benefits and burdens on the basis of gender cannot pass muster under the federal and Wisconsin constitutions. Craig v. Boren, 429 U.S. 190 (1977); Weinberger v. Wiesenfeld, 420 U.S. 636 (1975).

The New Jersey Supreme Court similarly concluded that a rule imposing liability for necessaries solely on the husband was unconstitutional under the federal and state constitutions, reasoning as follows:

> Under the [common law] rule, even a husband who is economically dependent on his wife would be liable for the necessary expenses of both spouses, while the wife would not be liable for either. In perpetuating additional benefits for a wife when the benefits may not be needed, the rule runs afoul of the equal protection clause. Orr, supra, 440 U.S. at 282-283.
>
> We recognize that in many instances the present rule correctly operates to favor a needy wife. Even wives who have entered the work force generally earn substantially less than their husbands. . . . However, that is an insufficient reason to retain

a gender based classification that denigrates the efforts of women who contribute to the finances of their families and denies equal protection to husbands. Weinberger v. Weisenfield, supra, 420 U.S. at 645.

NOTES AND QUESTIONS

1. Discussions of McGuire v. McGuire frequently observe that Mrs. McGuire could have pledged her husband's credit to purchase necessaries; *e.g.*, Bruce C. Hafen, The Family as an Entity, 22 U.C. Davis L. Rev. 865 (1989). How useful is the power to pledge a husband's credit for the wife who does not possess independent means? Consider the situation from the creditor's point of view. If the husband did not pay, what would the creditor have to prove to recover from him: (1) the validity of the marriage, (2) the level of the parties' "station in life," (3) the failure of the husband to supply the allegedly necessary item? Cases dealing with the merchant's burden of proof are collected in Annotation, Necessity, in Action Against Husband for Necessaries Furnished Wife, of Proving Husband's Failure to Provide Necessaries, 19 A.L.R. 4th 432 (1983). Consider also that it was traditionally a defense to an action for necessaries that the wife had forfeited her right to support by adultery or abandonment of her husband. *See* Homer H. Clark, Jr., The Law of Domestic Relations in the United States 252-257 (2d ed. 1988).

2. The husband's responsibility for necessaries is explained in *Buckstaff* and most other cases as a device for enforcing his duty of support. Why is the wife privileged to undertake piecemeal steps to ensure her level of support but not to bring a support action to secure that right through a single, overall remedy? Is one or the other strategy more respectful of "family autonomy"?

3. The obligation to supply necessaries is sometimes said to rest on a theory that the wife acts as the husband's agent for the purchase of such items. That theory has the appeal of preserving a notion of family unity. Is *Buckstaff* consistent with such a theory? If the Buckstaffs had discussed the purchase of the sofa, had disagreed, and Mr. Buckstaff had then told Sharpe Furniture not to sell the sofa to his wife, would he be liable if the store nonetheless sold the sofa to Mrs. Buckstaff?

The court describes the furniture as a "suitable and proper item for their household." Did the Buckstaff "household" make this purchase? Is the "household" sued for the price in this case? Does the "household" now own the sofa? Is a "household" a legal entity for any purpose?

4. The Henredon sofa cost Mr. Buckstaff $621.50. On what basis does the court decide that this, rather than a less expensive piece of furniture, is a suitable and proper item for their household? Could a fur coat be a "necessary"? *See* Gimbel Bros., Inc. v. Pinto, 145 A.2d 865 (Pa. Super. 1958). On the other hand, would Mr. McGuire likely be required to pay for a $621.50 sofa if Mrs. McGuire charged it?

After reading *McGuire*, how would one describe the level of support to which a married woman who works only in the home is entitled? What level does *Buckstaff* suppose? How does one explain the difference?

5. A number of cases say that the married woman was entitled to support even when she had earnings or property of her own—as Mrs. McGuire certainly did. *See* Pezas v. Pezas, 201 A.2d 192 (Conn. 1964); Ewell v. State, 114 A.2d 66 (Md. 1955). Nor, according to some authority, would it matter if Mrs. McGuire's children were supporting her. Ulrich v. State, 59 A.2d 460 (Del. 1948).

6. There are at least four schemes of ordering the liability of spouses for "necessaries" purchased by one of them. At common law, of course, the husband was liable for both his own debts and those incurred by his wife: a perhaps inevitable result having regard to his virtually plenary control over the wife's wealth during the marriage. A second approach is that developed in Estate of Stromsted, 299 N.W.2d 226 (Wis. 1980), and employed in *Buckstaff*. The husband is primarily liable for necessaries and the wife only secondarily responsible. Accordingly, a creditor must first seek satisfaction from the husband and can go against the wife only if the husband's assets are inadequate. A third possibility is to impose joint and several liability, allowing the creditor to choose either or both spouses as the target(s) for collection. *See* Cooke v. Adams, 183 So. 2d 925 (Miss. 1966). The fourth is to hold that the creditor should seek to recover first against the spouse incurring the obligation, making the other secondarily liable. This is the result reached in Jersey Shore Medical Center v. Baum, 417 A.2d 1003 (N.J. 1980), discussed by Justice Abrahamson.

NOTE: "NECESSARIES" AND "NEW PROPERTY"

The obligation to provide necessaries is not always invoked only in the comfortable middle-class setting of *Buckstaff* or even in the less comfortable setting of *McGuire*. It can also arise in connection with the "new property."

Consider, for example, the situation of a person needing nursing home care. Medicare, a federal program available to everyone 65 or older who is eligible for Social Security benefits (and to certain others on Social Security disability), is regarded as an insurance program on which one may draw as a matter of right. Medicare coverage does not, however, cover the costs of custodial care for a disabled person. *See* Joseph L. Matthews, Social Security, Medicare and Pensions 6:20 (5th ed. 1990).

A person without enough money to pay for needed nursing home care may turn to Medicaid, a joint federal and state program that provides medical assistance to the poor. Because Medicaid is a welfare program for the poor, persons with property or income above certain levels do not qualify. For those who do qualify, most of their income must be used to pay for care, and Medicaid picks up the remaining cost. Determining the income of a married applicant brings into play spousal support issues.

If the institutionalized spouse is the primary income producer, federal law provides that the community spouse is entitled to a portion of that income for his or her living expenses. The amount of the community spouse's living allowance is determined by a standardized formula that is updated annually, and all the rest of the institutionalized spouse's income goes toward his or her care. The amount of the community spouse's allowance is low enough that the spouse's standard of living may decline significantly when his or her mate goes into the nursing home. Generally, however, states exempt from the eligibility calculation portions of the institutionalized spouse's income that must be paid to support dependents pursuant to a court order. This rule clearly applies to court orders that preexist the application for Medicaid. What is not so clear is whether the community spouse can circumvent the income rules discussed above by getting a court order for a higher level of support than the rules allow.

In Septuagenarian v. Septuagenarian, 483 N.Y.S.2d 932 (Fam. Ct. 1984), the court allowed such an order. Mr. Septuagenarian lived in a nursing home and received Medicaid, and Mrs. Septuagenarian, the recipient's wife of 50 years, sought a court order for support in the amount of $1125, based on New York law, which requires a spouse to pay fair and reasonable spousal support. Her suit did not reflect any estrangement—on the contrary, she remained devoted to her husband, whom she visited and cared for in the hospital—but rather was to gain access to her husband's pension and Social Security benefits, on which they had lived prior to his confinement. The Commissioner of Social Services opposed the petition, arguing that the exemption should apply only to orders of support already issued at the time the Medicaid recipient became eligible for assistance.

The court recognized that to grant the petition would increase the public cost and would place the petitioner in a somewhat better position than spouses of other public assistance recipients. Under Medicaid rules, if her income fell below the public assistance level, she would be entitled to an amount equal to the difference between her income and that level. If she received support under the Family Court Act, however, it would be measured by her prior lifestyle rather than by public assistance guidelines, and the net effect would be that the public would pay for both her husband's care and her support at that higher level. Nonetheless, the court granted the petition:

> To deprive women, and particularly women of petitioner's generation who, in many cases, were denied an equal opportunity to fulfill their potential in the employment market and are, therefore, dependent on their husbands for support, access to their husbands' pension and assets in their later years effectively sentences many of them to tremendous hardship and a complete disruption of their lives at a time when they are extremely vulnerable.
>
> We must note that an overwhelming majority of married women are younger than their husbands. In addition, actuarial tables tell us that women live longer than men. . . . (For example, a woman of 70 will outlive her 75 year old husband by more than eleven years.) From those facts, together with the common knowledge that medical costs for many illnesses of old age are beyond the financial means of most American families, we can reasonably draw the conclusion that husbands are more likely to require care which will deplete the marital assets than their wives, who are likely to be the economically weaker spouse. So in cases such as this, where the petitioner is 72 years old and infirm, women will be forced from their homes, deprived of even their modest life styles and relegated to a life of grinding poverty.

We must presume that the legislature considered both of these issues [the effect on wives and the effect on public assistance costs] when it enacted the statute. We must presume as well that it considered the question of a spouse's interest in his or her spouse's pension.

. . . [O]ur appellate courts have held spouses to have a proprietary interest in their spouse's pension in matrimonial actions. The law in this state was clearly summarized by Justice Mollen in Damiano v. Damiano, 94 A.D.2d 132 (2nd Dept. 1983), at p.137, when he wrote:

A pension fund is properly considered to be an asset of the marriage since it represents in essence a form of deferred compensation derived from a spouse's employment and contemplated to be enjoyed by both spouses at a future date. . . .

[Social Security Income] Recently, the Appellate Division considered the question of whether basic Social Security benefits were public assistance or insurance and found them to be "akin to an annuity" and "not a form of public assistance." Matter of Kummer, 93 A.D.2d 135, 461 N.Y.S.2d 845 (2nd Dept. 1983). . . . No other conclusion can be reached in this case and all of Mr. Septuagenarian's income will be treated as pension proceeds. Were Social Security benefits public assistance, the petitioner would not be able to consider them as a potential source for her support. . . .

. . . Accordingly, petitioner is awarded support in the sum of $1,125 a month, retroactive to the date that she filed her petition.

However, in In the Matter of Gomprecht, 652 N.E.2d 936 (N.Y. 1995), the New York Court of Appeals reached the opposite conclusion. An institutionalized husband had income of $5721.31 per month. His wife, who had two residences assessed at more than $430,000, was entitled to a standard community spouse allowance of only $306.71 from her husband's income. She sought an increase in order to maintain her standard of living before her husband was institutionalized. The trial and intermediate appellate courts held that Family Court was not limited by the guidelines of the Social Services law and awarded her an increased allowance of $3339.26. The Court of Appeals reversed, saying that the purpose of the federal provisions for the community spouse is to "end the pauperization of the community spouse by assuring that the community spouse has a sufficient—but not excessive—amount of income and resources available." On the facts of the case, the court concluded that allowing the wife such a large portion of her husband's income was inconsistent with the purposes of the federal act.

Now consider the situation in which the community spouse has most of the income. To what extent is he or she obligated to contribute that income to pay for nursing home care of the institutionalized spouse? Since 1988, federal law has said that the community spouse has no obligation; only the institutionalized spouse's income is considered in determining Medicaid eligibility. However, this is a special rule applicable only to nursing home cases. In other situations, if one spouse applies for Medicaid, the income of the other is deemed to be available to the applicant, and eligibility is determined on the basis of the combined income of the spouses. In Schweiker v. Gray Panthers, 453 U.S. 34 (1981), the Supreme Court upheld spousal income, deeming rules as consistent with the statutory language and with legislative history indicating a congressional intent to hold spouses responsible for each other's support.

NOTES AND QUESTIONS

1. It is possible to view *Septuagenarian* and *Gomprecht* as standard cases of the spousal support obligation. To do so, however, it is necessary for the court in *Septuagenarian* to view Social Security benefits as a form of property or wealth belonging to the husband. Is there any inconsistency between that approach and the view taken in *Gomprecht?*

2. What is the theory behind "deeming"? Is it simply an application of the general rule that a creditor may recover against one spouse for the necessaries supplied to the other? Are the positions of the creditor and the Social Security Administration alike?

3. Federal and state statutes also allow for setting aside a portion of an institutionalized person's income to support the person's or the person's spouse's minor child, dependent child, dependent parent, or dependent sibling if more than half of the needs of the child, parent, or sibling have been provided by the institutionalized person or the person's spouse. 42 U.S.C. §1396r-5(d)(1)(C). In another New York case, In the Matter of Schachner, 648 N.E.2d 1321 (N.Y. 1995), a community spouse claimed an increase in his allowance from his institutionalized wife's income to pay for their daughter's education in a private high school and in college. The Court of Appeals concluded that under the governing statutes a community spouse is entitled to an increased allowance only for true financial hardships caused by circumstances over which the spouse has no control, and that voluntary support of a child in private school does not fall into this category.

4. *Constitutional Limits on Gender-Based Classifications*

PROBLEM

It has been clear even in these introductory materials dealing with marital property that traditional approaches incorporate certain assumptions about the roles of family members and the relative capacities of husbands and wives. We have also seen that these assumptions have been subjected to constitutional examination, typically on equal protection grounds. Because the status of laws that treat husbands and wives differently is relevant not only to marital property law but also to the law of marital relations generally, it is useful to examine further the constitutional and other aspects of equality of spouses, within and outside the "household."

Assume that your office represents Dr. Willa Sanchez, an oral surgeon. She has recently treated Ms. Alicia Duran, whom she has also known socially for some time. Dr. Sanchez has billed Ms. Duran $2300 for this surgery but would prefer to collect from Ms. Duran's husband, Roberto, both because she would like to accommodate Ms. Duran's desire that she do so and because she thinks Mr. Duran ought to pay the bill.

Interviews with Dr. Sanchez and Ms. Duran, who is cooperative, reveal the following facts. Ms. Duran has been married to Roberto for five years. Before and during her marriage, Ms. Duran has been employed as a caseworker in the state Department of Human Services, an occupation she enjoys and thinks worthwhile, and in which she has had considerable success. She is well on her way to achieving a Master's of Social Work degree, which is the standard professional credential for personnel occupying supervisory positions in the department. Reviews of her performance to this point suggest that she will achieve a promotion when or soon after she receives this degree.

Mr. Duran is a contractor and a native of Florida. The construction business has been in decline in your state for the last several years, and no substantial improvement is in sight. Mr. Duran has essentially given up — in his own words, "no more" — and decided to return to Florida, where construction continues to boom. Ms. Duran has repeatedly urged him to remain here and equally often declares that she had no desire to leave her job and go to Florida.

Three months ago, Mr. Duran took the car and most of their liquid assets with him to Fort Lauderdale. His departure followed an argument during which he insisted that Alicia go with him and her refusal to do so. Ms. Duran has, since her husband's departure, been able to manage on her salary except for the expenses associated with oral surgery.

She notified Mr. Duran of this bill, and he has refused to pay it while repeating his insistence that she join him in Florida. He has also consulted a lawyer in Florida — not for purposes of divorce, which is for religious reasons unacceptable to both him and Ms. Duran — but in order to cut off any financial obligations he may have as long as she remains away from him.

Your research has disclosed the statutory provisions set out immediately below. Please prepare a memorandum analyzing the legal possibility of collecting the debt from Mr. Duran, assuming that he will (as seems likely) return to the state at least temporarily. Your analysis should incorporate the materials considered to this point, as well as the following materials.

a. Relevant Statutes

Section 1. Both wives and husbands have the duty to support each other during marriage. However, when either party to a marriage incurs a debt for purchase of an item or service that is reasonably necessary to maintenance of the household, the husband shall be primarily liable for that debt and the wife shall be secondarily liable for that debt.

Section 2. Notwithstanding the provisions of Section 1, there shall be no liability for debts incurred by a spouse if the spouse incurring the debt has been given adequate resources to purchase the item or service, nor shall a husband be liable for the debts incurred by his wife if she has abandoned the marital home.

b. Materials Regarding Domicile

The theory of marital unity has been said to account for the common law rule that the husband may choose the marital residence. Madden's hornbook on Domestic Relations explains matters as they stood in 1931 in the following way:

> The general rule is that on marriage the domicile of the wife merges in that of the husband and changes with his during coverture. He has the power to establish the family domicile, and it is the duty of the wife to follow him, and her refusal to do so without sufficient excuse amounts to desertion.

J. Madden, Domestic Relations 46 (1931). The Ohio Revised Code in 1973, for example, provided that "[t]he husband is the head of the family. He may choose any reasonable place or mode of living and the wife must conform thereto." Ohio Rev. Code Ann. §3103.02 (Baldwin, 1973). The same principle has existed in civil law jurisdictions and in community property states, as we have seen in both the materials dealing with estates by the entirety and, particularly, Kirchberg v. Feenstra, above, page 49.

It followed that a wife who resided away from her husband without his consent or fault forfeited her right to support. *See* Richardson v. Stuesser, 103 N.W.261 (Wis. 1905); Notes, 10 Minn. L. Rev. 171 (1925); 11 Cornell L.Q. 213 (1925). If, however, the husband abandoned his wife, either actually or constructively, the wife could acquire a separate residence, at least for purposes of divorce. Nor did the wife's duty require her to follow her husband when the new residence would be manifestly unsuitable to her health, safety, or physical comfort.

In the common enough situation where the spouses live apart for some time by agreement, it appears that the wife's obligation to accept her husband's decision could be revived if the latter clearly has indicated his wish that she return to him. Although it most frequently arises in connection with divorce actions, the rule regarding choice of residence may arise in other settings where domicile is important, such as liability for state taxes, voting, deciding whether a spouse who is a student is treated as a resident or nonresident for tuition purposes, and the like.

It is quite clear that a woman may possess a domicile other than that of her husband for divorce purposes. As we will see in Chapter 10, jurisdiction for divorce may now be founded on the domicile of *either* spouse, and it clearly follows that a wife must be able to claim an independent domicile for that jurisdictional scheme to be intelligible.

c. Additional Materials Concerning Liability for Necessaries

Marshfield Clinic v. Discher, 314 N.W.2d 326, 329-331 (Wis. 1982): While the necessaries doctrine remains important in modern society, it is clear from *Stromsted* that the old common law rule, whereby the husband was solely responsible for his family's necessaries, is out of touch with the changing role of women. Thus, *Stromsted* held that wives share with their husbands the legal duty of support of the family. But it is also inappropriate to impose this obligation in the form of joint and several liability on the husband and the wife. Although many more married women are now working than were in the past, they still contribute less to the typical family income than do their husbands.

We do not view [the *Stromsted*] rule as one which "denigrates the efforts of women who contribute to the finances of their families." Nor do we feel that it is paternalistic or based on an "archaic and overbroad generalization." Schlesinger v. Ballard, 419 U.S. 498, 508 (1975). Rather, we feel that this rule accurately reflects the position of married women in contemporary society. . . . [D]espite great progress, married women still lag far behind their husbands in earning power. This may be due to any number of reasons, such as: discrimination that still exists in the job market; a socialized tendency for women to choose lower paying jobs; the fact that many married women still do not work outside the home, or at least work only part time. For the purposes of this case, these reasons are irrelevant. What is relevant is the verifiable fact that wives are still far from equal with their husbands in economic resources.

The United States Supreme Court has not upheld classifications based on gender when the classifications ". . . command dissimilar treatment for men and women who are . . . similarly situated." Schlesinger v. Ballard. But when the classification reflects a demonstrable fact that men and women are not similarly situated in a certain respect, then the classification has been upheld.

NORTH OTTOWA COMMUNITY HOSPITAL V. KIEFT, 578 N.W.2d 267 (Mich. 1998): The Michigan Supreme Court struck down the common law necessaries doctrine on equal protection grounds in *Kieft*. The suit was brought by plaintiff hospital against Ms. Kieft for medical services rendered to Mr. Kieft prior to his death. The state Married Women's Property Act (MWPA) found in both statutory and state constitutional provisions declared that a married woman's property was not liable for debts of any other person, including those of her husband. The court concluded that these provisions made it impossible for Michigan courts to extend the common law necessaries doctrine, which imposed liability only on husbands, to make wives liable as well. And if a wife could not be liable for her husband's debts, the common law obligation on husbands was a gender-based classification that could not be justified in modern times and thus offended the Equal Protection Clause:

> [T]he common-law necessaries doctrine imposing the support burden only on a husband could be justified in the past because it was substantially related to the important governmental objective of providing necessary support to dependent wives. However, the contemporary reality of women owning property, working outside the home, and otherwise contributing to their own economic support calls for abrogation of this sex-discriminatory doctrine from early common law.

The court also noted that the legislature might choose to modify the statutory and constitutional provisions of the Michigan MWPA so as to permit enforcement of obligations for necessaries supplied to husbands against the property of wives and to extend the necessaries doctrine to both spouses.

d. Empirical Data

MEDIAN INCOME OF PERSONS (1992)*
YEAR-ROUND, FULL-TIME WORKERS

	Males	*Females*
All	$31,012	$22,167
Age		
15-24 years	$15,769	$14,698
35-44 years	$34,945	$24,189
55-64 years	$35,351	$22,623
Occupational group		
Executive, admin.	$42,509	$27,495
Professional	$44,015	$31,261
Sales	$31,346	$17,924
Clerical	$27,186	$20,321
Service	$20,606	$12,931
Educational attainment (25 years or older)		
Less than 9th grade	$17,445	$13,000
High school graduate	$27,357	$19,462
Bachelor's degree	$41,406	$30,394

*United States Department of Commerce, Bureau of the Census, Money Income of Households, Families, and Persons in the United States: 1992 94-95.

e. Constitutional Decisions

BRADWELL V. ILLINOIS, 83 U.S. (16 Wall.) 130, 141 (1873): [Petitioner, Myra Bradwell, was denied admission to the bar of Illinois because she was a woman. The Supreme Court upheld the denial without substantial discussion. Justice Bradley concurred, offering this basis:] [T]he civil law, as well as nature herself, has always recognized a wide difference in the respective spheres and destinies of man and woman. Man is, or should be, woman's protector and defender. The natural and proper timidity and delicacy which belongs to the female sex evidently unfits it for many of the occupations of civil life. The constitution of the family organization, which is founded in the divine ordinance, as well as in the nature of things, indicates the domestic sphere as that which properly belongs to the domain and functions of womanhood. The harmony, not to say identity, of interests and views which belong, or should belong, to the family institution is repugnant to the idea of a woman adopting a distinct and independent career from that of her husband.

GOESART V. CLEARY, 335 U.S. 464, 465-466 (1948): [Michigan law provided that no woman could obtain a bartender's license unless she was the wife or daughter of the male owner of a licensed liquor establishment. Justice Frankfurter stated:] Michigan could, beyond question, forbid all women from working behind a bar. This is so despite the vast changes in the social and legal position of women. The fact that women may now have achieved the virtues that men have long claimed as their prerogatives and now indulge in vices that men have long practiced, does not preclude the States from drawing a sharp line between the sexes, certainly in such matters as the regulation of the liquor traffic. . . . The Constitution does not require legislatures to reflect sociological insight, or shifting social standards, any more than it requires them to keep abreast of the latest scientific standards. . . . Since bartending by women may, in the allowable legislative judgment, give rise to moral and social problems against which it may devise preventive measures, the legislature need not go to the full length of the prohibition if it believes that as to a defined group of females other factors are operating which either eliminate or reduce the moral and social problems otherwise calling for prohibition. Michigan evidently believes that the oversight assured through ownership of a bar by a barmaid's husband or father minimizes hazards that may confront a barmaid without such protecting oversight. The Court is certainly not in a position to gainsay such belief by the Michigan legislature.

CRAIG V. BOREN, 429 U.S. 190, 197-200 (1976): [Oklahoma law prohibited the sale of 3.2 percent beer to males under the age of 21 and to females under the age of 18.] To withstand constitutional challenge, previous cases establish that classifications by gender must serve important governmental objectives and must be substantially related to achievement of those objectives. Thus, in [Reed v. Reed, 404 U.S. 71 (1971)[9]] the objectives of "reducing the workload on probate courts" and "avoiding intrafamily controversy" were deemed of insufficient importance to sustain use of an overt gender criterion in the appointment of administrators of intestate decedents' estates. Decisions following *Reed* similarly have rejected administrative ease and convenience as sufficiently important objectives to justify gender-based classifications. *See, e.g.,* . . . Frontiero v. Richardson [411 U.S. 677 (1973)][10]; *cf.* Schlesinger v. Ballard [419 U.S. 498

---

9. Idaho law provided a preference for men over women in the appointment of administrators of estates. The preference was justified by the need for an easy method of deciding upon administrators and by the assumption that men were more likely than women to possess the business experience called for by the activity in question. The Court held this preference violated equal protection and that use of gender classification to reduce the workload of courts was "the very kind of arbitrary legislative choice forbidden by the Equal Protection Clause."

10. *Frontiero* struck down on equal protection grounds a federal law permitting male armed forces personnel an automatic dependency allowance for their wives but requiring service women to prove that their husbands were dependent. A plurality employed strict

(1975)].[11] And only two terms ago, Stanton v. Stanton expressly stating that Reed v. Reed was "controlling," held that Reed required invalidation of a Utah differential age-of-majority statute, notwithstanding the statute's coincidence with and furtherance of the State's purpose of fostering "old notions" of role typing and preparing boys for their expected performance in the economic and political worlds.

Reed v. Reed has also provided the underpinning for decisions that have invalidated statutes employing gender as an inaccurate proxy for other, more germane bases of classification. Hence, "archaic and overbroad" generalizations, Schlesinger v. Ballard, supra, concerning the financial position of servicewomen, Frontiero v. Richardson, supra, and working women, Weinberger v. Wiesenfeld [420 U.S. 636 (1975)],[12] could not justify use of a gender line in determining eligibility for certain governmental entitlements. Similarly, increasingly outdated misconceptions concerning the role of females in the home rather than in the "marketplace and world of ideas" were rejected as loose-fitting characterizations incapable of supporting state statutory schemes that were premised upon their accuracy. . . .

We turn then to the question whether, under *Reed*, the difference between males and females with respect to the purchase of 3.2% beer warrants the differential in age drawn by the Oklahoma statute. We conclude that it does not. . . .

We accept for purposes of discussion the District Court's identification of the objective underlying [the statute] as the enhancement of traffic safety. Clearly, the protection of public health and safety represents an important function of state and local governments. However, appellees' statistics in our view cannot support the conclusion that the gender-based distinction closely serves to achieve that objective and therefore the distinction cannot under *Reed* withstand equal protection challenge. . . .

The most focused and relevant of the statistical surveys, arrests of 18-20-year-olds for alcohol-related driving offenses, exemplifies the ultimate unpersuasiveness

---

scrutiny, rejecting the government's reliance on "administrative convenience" and, particularly, the proposition that wives are more likely to be dependent on their husbands than husbands on their wives. This was not regarded as a sufficient ground for the gender-based distinction. The minority observed that even under ordinary review, *Reed* required a finding that the statute was unconstitutional.

11. The Court sustained a federal statute granting female naval personnel a longer period to achieve mandatory promotion than men. The Court distinguished *Reed* and *Frontiero* on the ground that the statutory distinction was based not on "archaic and overbroad generalizations" but rather on the "demonstrable fact that male and female line officers in the Navy are *not* similarly situated with respect to opportunities for professional service."

12. The Court struck down a Social Security Act provision entitling a widowed mother, but not a widowed father, to benefits based on the earnings of the deceased spouse. The Court characterized *Frontiero* as making plain that gender classifications founded on "archaic and overbroad [generalizations]" were unconstitutional. The distinction drawn by the Act violated this principle in its assumption that male workers' earnings are essential to support of the family while those of female workers are not essential to family support.

of this evidentiary record. Viewed in terms of the correlation between sex and the actual activity that Oklahoma seeks to regulate . . . the statistics establish that .18% of females and 2% of males in that age group were arrested for that offense. While such a disparity is not trivial in a statistical sense, it hardly can form the basis for employment of a gender line as a classifying device. Certainly if maleness is to serve as a proxy for drinking and driving, a correlation of 2% must be considered an unduly tenuous "fit." Indeed, prior cases have consistently rejected the use of sex as a decisionmaking factor even though the statutes in question certainly rested on far more predictive empirical relationships than this.

CALIFANO V. GOLDFARB, 430 U.S. 199 (1977): [The Federal Old-Age, Survivors, and Disability Insurance Benefits program (OASDI) provides survivors' benefits to widows generally, but to widowers only where the widower was receiving at least one-half of his support from his deceased wife. Hannah Goldfarb had worked as a secretary for the New York City public school system for almost 25 years before her death. Her husband was denied a widower's benefit because he could not show that he had been receiving half his support from his wife when she died. The majority of the Court declared that requirement unconstitutional.]

Brennan, J. [with Justices White, Marshall, and Powell]: The gender-based distinction drawn by [OASDI] — burdening a widower but not a widow with the task of proving dependency upon the deceased spouse — presents an equal protection question indistinguishable from that decided in Weinberger v. Wiesenfeld. That decision and the decision in Frontiero v. Richardson plainly require affirmance of the judgment of the District Court.

[Wiesenfeld] condemns the gender-based distinction . . . in this case. For that distinction too operates "to deprive women of protection for their families which men receive as a result of their employment": social security taxes were deducted from Hannah Goldfarb's salary during the quarter century she worked as a secretary, yet, in consequence of [the statutory scheme], she also "not only failed to receive for her [husband] the same protection which a similarly situated male worker would have received but she also was deprived of a portion of her own earnings in order to contribute to the fund out of which benefits would be paid to others." Wiesenfeld thus inescapably compels the conclusion reached by the District Court that the gender-based differentiation created by [the statute] — that results in the efforts of female workers required to pay social security taxes producing less protection for their spouses than is produced by the efforts of men — is forbidden by the Constitution, at least when supported by no more substantial justification than "archaic and overbroad generalizations," or 'old notions,' such as "assumptions as to dependency," that are more consistent with the roletyping society has long imposed, than with contemporary reality. . . .

The gist of the [appellant's] argument is that, analyzed from the perspective of the widower, the denial of benefits reflected the congressional judgment that aged widowers as a class were sufficiently likely not to be dependent upon their wives that it was appropriate to deny them benefits unless they were in fact dependent.

. . . But Weinberger v. Wiesenfeld rejected the virtually identical argument when appellant's predecessor argued that the statutory classification there attacked should be regarded from the perspective of the prospective beneficiary and not from that of the covered wage earner.

Appellant next argues that *Frontiero* and *Wiesenfeld* should be distinguished as involving statutes with different objective from [OASDI]. Rather than merely enacting presumptions designed to save the expense and trouble of determining which spouses are really dependent . . . Congress may reasonably have presumed that nondependent widows, who receive benefits, are needier than nondependent widowers, who do not, because of job discrimination against women (particularly older women), *see* Kahn v. Shevin [416 U.S. 351 (1974)],[13] and because they are more likely to have been more dependent on their spouses.

But "inquiry into the actual purposes" of the discrimination proves the contrary. First, [OASDI] is phrased in terms of *dependency*, not *need*. Congress chose to award benefits, not to widowers who could prove that they are needy, but to those who could prove that they had been dependent on their wives for more than one-half of their support.

We conclude, therefore, that the differential treatment of nondependent widows and widowers results . . . from an intention to aid the dependent spouses of deceased wage earners, coupled with a presumption that wives are usually dependent. . . . [S]uch assumptions do not suffice to justify a gender-based discrimination in the distribution of employment-related benefits.

[Justice Rehnquist, dissenting, joined by Chief Justice Burger and Justices Stewart and Blackmun]: The effect of the statutory scheme is to make it easier for widows to obtain benefits than it is for widowers, since the former qualify automatically while the latter must show proof of need. Such a requirement in no way perpetuates or exacerbates the economic disadvantage which has led the Court to conclude that gender-based discriminations must meet a different test from other types of classifications. . . .

[A] legislative judgment implicit in the widow's and widower's provisions is that widows, as a practical matter, are much more likely to be without adequate means of support than are widowers. The plurality opinion makes much of establishing this point, that the absence of any dependency prerequisite to the award of widow's benefits reflects a judgment, resting on "administrative convenience," that dependence among aged widows is frequent enough to justify waiving the requirement entirely. I differ not with the recognition of this administrative convenience purpose but with the conclusion that such a purpose *necessarily* invalidates the resulting classification. Our decisions dealing with social welfare legislation indicate that our inquiry must go further. For rational classification aimed at distributing funds to beneficiaries under social insurance legislation weigh a good deal more heavily on the governmental interest side of the equal protection balance than they may in other legislative contexts [because of the millions of beneficiaries involved in social insurance programs].

---

13. The Court sustained a Florida statute giving a property tax exemption for widows but not widowers. Differential treatment in this case was justified by the relatively greater financial difficulties facing a woman upon widowhood, and particularly by the circumstance that "the job market is inhospitable to the woman seeking any but the lowest paid jobs."

CALIFANO V. WEBSTER, 430 U.S. 313 (1977): [The Court unanimously sustained a provision of the Social Security Act, which had the effect of granting retired female workers higher monthly old-age benefits than those awarded similarly situated retired male workers. This distinction resulted from a statutory formula allowing women to exclude more lower-earning years from the average on which compensation was based than men could exclude. The Court found:] "Reduction of the disparity in economic condition between men and women caused by the long history of discrimination against women has been recognized as such an important governmental objective" (citing Ballard v. Schlesinger and Kahn v. Shevin) and that the more favorable treatment of female wage earners embodied in the Act did not result from "archaic or overbroad generalizations" about women or from role-typing assumptions, but from current economic realities. "The challenged statute operated directly to compensate women for past economic discrimination. Retirement benefits under the Act are based on past earnings. But as we have recognized": 'Whether from overt discrimination or from the socialization process of a male-dominated culture, the job market is inhospitable to the woman seeking any but the lowest paid jobs.' Thus, allowing women, who as such have been unfairly hindered from earning as much as men, to eliminate additional low-earning years from the calculation of their retirement benefits works directly to remedy some part of the effects of past discrimination.

ORR V. ORR, 440 U.S. 268 (1979): Brennan, J. The question presented is the constitutionality of Alabama alimony statutes which provide that husbands, but not wives, may be required to pay alimony upon divorce. . . .

In authorizing the imposition of alimony obligations on husbands, but not on wives, the Alabama statutory scheme "provides that different treatment be accorded . . . on the basis of . . . sex. [Reed v. Reed.] The fact that the classification expressly discriminates against men rather than women does not protect it from scrutiny. Craig v. Boren, 429 U.S. 190 (1976). To withstand scrutiny under the Equal Protection Clause, "classifications by gender must serve important governmental objectives and must be substantially related to achievement of those objectives." Califano v. Webster, 430 U.S. 313, 316-17 (1977). We shall, therefore, examine the three governmental objectives that might arguably be served by Alabama's statutory scheme.

Appellant views the Alabama alimony statutes as effectively announcing the State's preference for an allocation of family responsibilities under which the wife plays a dependent role, and as seeking for their objective the reinforcement of that model among the State's citizens. . . . We agree, as he urges, that prior cases settle that this purpose cannot sustain the statutes. Stanton v. Stanton, 421 U.S. 7, 10 (1975), held that the "old notion" that "generally it is the man's primary responsibility to provide a home and its essentials," can no longer justify a statute that discriminates on the basis of gender. "No longer is the female destined solely for the home and the rearing of the family, and only the male for the marketplace and the world of ideas. . . ."

The opinion of the Alabama Court of Civil Appeals suggests other purposes that the statute may serve. . . . One is a legislative purpose to provide help for needy spouses, using sex as a proxy for need. The other is a goal of compensating women for past discrimination during marriage, which assertedly has left them unprepared to fend for themselves in the working world following divorce. We concede, of course, that assisting needy spouses is a legitimate and important governmental objective. We have also recognized "[r]eduction of the disparity in economic condition between men and women caused by the long history of discrimination against women . . . as . . . an important governmental objective," Califano v. Webster, 430 U.S., at 317. It only remains, therefore, to determine whether the classification at issue here is "substantially related to achievement of those objectives."

Ordinarily, we would begin the analysis of the "needy spouse" objective by considering whether sex is a sufficiently "accurate proxy," Craig v. Boren, 429 U.S. at 204, for dependency to establish that the gender classification rests "upon some ground of difference having a fair and substantial relation to the object of the legislation. . . . Similarly, we would initially approach the 'compensation' rationale by asking whether women had in fact been significantly discriminated against in the sphere to which the statute applied a sex-based classification, leaving the sexes *not* similarly situated with respect to opportunities in that sphere." Schlesinger v. Ballard, 419 U.S. 498, 508 (1975).

But in this case, even if sex were a reliable proxy for need, and even if the institution of marriage did discriminate against women, these factors still would "not adequately justify the salient features of" Alabama's statutory scheme, Craig v. Boren, 429 U.S., at 202. Under the statute, individualized hearings at which the parties' relative financial circumstances are considered *already* occur. There is no reason, therefor, to use sex as a proxy for need. . . . In such circumstances, not even an administrative convenience rationale exists to justify operating by generalization or by proxy. Similarly, since individualized hearings can determine which were in fact discriminated against vis-à-vis their husbands, as well as which family units defied the stereotype and left the husband dependent on the wife, Alabama's alleged compensatory purpose may be effectuated without placing burdens solely on husbands. . . . "Thus, the gender-based distinction is gratuitous. . . ."

Legislative classifications which distribute benefits and burdens on the basis of gender carry the inherent risk of reinforcing stereotypes about the "proper place" of women and their need for special protection. Thus, even statutes purportedly designed to compensate for and ameliorate the effects of past discrimination must be carefully tailored. Where, as here, the State's compensatory and ameliorative purposes are as well served by a gender-neutral classification as one that gender classifies and therefore carries with it the baggage of sexual stereotypes, the State cannot be permitted to classify on the basis of sex.

KIRCHBERG V. FEENSTRA, 450 U.S. 455 (1981): See above, page 49.

MICHAEL M. V. SUPERIOR COURT OF SONOMA COUNTY, 450 U.S. 464 (1981): [Petitioner, a 17½-year-old male, was convicted of statutory rape for having intercourse with a 16½-year-old female. Under California law, this offense is committed when an accused has intercourse with a female under the age of 18 years.

Petitioner claimed that the act, because it made only men liable for this offense, violated equal protection.]

Rehnquist, J. [joined by Chief Justice Burger and Justices Stewart and Powell]: As is evident from our opinions, the Court has had some difficulty in agreeing upon the proper approach and analysis in cases involving challenges to gender-based classifications. . . .

[We] have not held that gender-based classifications are "inherently suspect" and thus we do not apply "strict scrutiny" to those classifications. Our cases have held, however, that the traditional minimum rationality test takes on a somewhat "sharper focus" when gender-based classifications are challenged. In Reed v. Reed, for example, the Court stated that a gender-based classification will be upheld if it bears a "fair and substantial relationship" to legitimate state ends, while in Craig v. Boren, the Court restated the test to require the classification to bear a "substantial relationship" to "important governmental objectives."

Underlying these decisions is the principle that a legislature may not "make overbroad generalizations based on sex which are entirely unrelated to any differences between men and women or which demean the ability or social status of the affected class." But because the Equal Protection Clause does not "demand that a statute necessarily apply equally to all persons" or require "things which are different in fact . . . to be treated in law as though they were the same" . . . this Court has consistently upheld statutes where the gender classification is not invidious, but rather realistically reflects the fact that the sexes are not similarly situated in certain circumstances. . . .

The justification for the statute offered by the State, and accepted by the Supreme Court of California, is that the legislature sought to prevent illegitimate teenage pregnancies. . . .

We need not be medical doctors to discern that young men and young women are not similarly situated with respect to the problems and the risks of sexual intercourse. Only women may become pregnant, and they suffer disproportionately the profound physical, emotional, and psychological consequences of sexual activity. The statute at issue here protects women from sexual intercourse at an age when those consequences are particularly severe. . . .

Because virtually all of the significant harmful and inescapably identifiable consequences of teenage pregnancy fall on the young female, a legislature acts well within its authority when it elects to punish only the participant who, by nature, suffers few of the consequences of his conduct. It is hardly unreasonable for a legislature acting to protect minor females to exclude them from punishment. Moreover, the risk of pregnancy itself constitutes a substantial deterrence to young females. No similar natural sanctions deter males. A criminal sanction imposed solely on males thus serves to roughly "equalize" the deterrents on the sexes. . . .

Brennan, J. [with Justices White and Marshall], dissenting: [California had failed to show that because the statutory rape law punishes males but not females, it more effectively deterred minor females from sexual intercourse. The bare assertion of such an effect was not sufficient where a gender-based classification is used. Moreover, the dissent noted that the claimed legislative purpose had only recently been suggested; historically such laws were premised on the belief that young women, unlike young men, were incapable of consenting to an act of sexual intercourse and were especially in need of the state's protection. This is the kind of stereotyping that prior decisions have prohibited.]

ROTSKER V. GOLDBERG, 453 U.S. 57 (1981): [Respondents challenged the constitutionality of congressional legislation requiring men, but not women, to register for the draft. A three-judge district court held the classification unconstitutional; the Supreme Court, in an opinion by Justice Rehnquist, reversed. Congress determined that the draft itself would result from a need for combat troops and women as a group, unlike men as a group, are not eligible for combat. Accordingly,] Men and women, because of the combat restrictions on women, are simply not similarly situated for purposes of a draft or registration for a draft. [The] Constitution requires that Congress treat similarly situated persons similarly, not that it engage in gestures of superficial equality. . . . With respect to the need for some 80,000 women inductees (in noncombat roles), Congress concluded that the need could be met by volunteers and that "staffing non-combat positions with women during a mobilization would be detrimental to the important goal of military flexibility."

J. E. B. V. ALABAMA EX REL. T. B., 511 U.S. 515 (1994): [At a paternity and child support trial, respondent State used nine of its ten peremptory challenges to remove male jurors. The court empaneled an all-female jury. The Supreme Court, in an opinion by Justice Blackmun, reversed, holding that gender-based juror challenges could not survive the heightened equal protection scrutiny used for distinctions based on gender. The State's argument that women and men may differ in receptivity to arguments of the children's mother is based on the very stereotypes the law condemns.]

UNITED STATES V. VIRGINIA, 518 U.S. 515 (U.S. 1996): The United States sued Virginia Military Academy (VMI) and the state of Virginia, claiming that VMI's exclusively male admissions policy violated the Equal Protection Clause. After the Fourth Circuit reversed a trial court decision in VMI's favor, the state proposed establishment of a parallel program for women. The district court found that this proposal satisfied the equal protection requirement and the Fourth Circuit affirmed, although it recognized that the new school would lack the historical benefit and prestige of VMI.

The United States Supreme Court reversed, in an opinion by Justice Ginsburg joined by Justices Stevens, O'Connor, Kennedy, Souter, and Breyer. Any gender-based government action must rest on an "exceedingly persuasive justification." To meet this burden, a state must demonstrate "at least that the classification serves 'important governmental objectives' and that the discriminatory means employed are 'substantially related to the achievement of those objectives.'" The justification must be genuine and not merely pretextual or post hoc, and must not rely on overbroad generalizations about the different talents, abilities, or preferences of men and women. The majority also observed that, under its decisions, sex classifications may be used to compensate women for particular economic disabilities they have suffered, to promote equality of employment opportunity, but not to create or perpetuate the legal, social, and economic inferiority of women.

The categorical exclusion of women from VMI did not meet this test. The state's claim that VMI's "adversative" method of training to instill physical and mental discipline could neither be made available to women nor modified sufficiently without great compromise to VMI's program was not proved and thus rested on overbroad notions concerning the roles and abilities of males and females. The Supreme Court also held that the creation of a separate program for women did not cure the constitutional violation. The violation was the categorical exclusion of women, without regard for their individual capacities, from an educational opportunity provided to men. The proposed alternative institution was different in kind and unequal in tangible and intangible resources, and thus did not provide substantial equality in educational opportunities.

5. *Spousal Contracts During Marriage*

In McGuire v. McGuire, the wife sought to enforce a set of expectations associated with marriage. The court refused to grant relief, leaving it to the parties to "work out" their relationship. The following materials explore the extent to which married persons can, and should be able to, work out their relationship themselves.

BORELLI V. BRUSSEAU

16 Cal. Rptr. 2d 16 (Cal. App. 1993)

PERLEY, J. . . . On April 24, 1980, appellant and decedent entered into an antenuptial contract. On April 25, 1980, they were married. Appellant remained married to decedent until the death of the latter on January 25, 1989.

In March 1983, February 1984, and January 1987, decedent was admitted to a hospital due to heart problems. As a result, "decedent became concerned and frightened about his health and longevity." He discussed these fears and concerns with appellant and told her that he intended to "leave" the following property to her.

1. "An interest" in a lot in Sacramento, California.
2. A life estate for the use of a condominium in Hawaii.
3. A 25 percent interest in Borelli Meat Co.
4. All cash remaining in all existing bank accounts at the time of his death.
5. The costs of educating decedent's stepdaughter, Monique Lee.
6. Decedent's entire interest in a residence in Kensington, California.
7. All furniture located in the residence.
8. Decedent's interest in a partnership.
9. Health insurance for appellant and Monique Lee.

In August 1988, decedent suffered a stroke while in the hospital. "Throughout the decedent's August, 1988 hospital stay and subsequent treatment at a rehabilitation center, he repeatedly told [appellant] that he was uncomfortable in the hospital and that he disliked being away from home. The decedent repeatedly told [appellant] that he did not want to be admitted to a nursing home, even though it meant he would need round-the-clock care, and rehabilitative modifications to the house, in order for him to live at home."

"In or about October, 1988, [appellant] and the decedent entered an oral agreement whereby the decedent promised to leave to [appellant] the property listed [above]. . . . In exchange for the decedent's promise to leave her the property . . . [appellant] agreed to care for the decedent in his home, for the duration of his illness, thereby avoiding the need for him to move to a rest home or convalescent hospital as his doctors recommended. . . .

Appellant performed her promise but the decedent did not perform his. Instead his will bequeathed her the sum of $100,000 and his interest in the residence they owned as joint tenants. The bulk of decedent's estate passed to respondent, who is decedent's daughter.

DISCUSSION

"It is fundamental that a marriage contract differs from other contractual relations in that there exists a definite and vital public interest in reference to the marriage relation. . . ."

"The laws relating to marriage and divorce have been enacted because of the profound concern of our organized society for the dignity and stability of the marriage relationship. This concern relates primarily to the status of the parties as husband and wife. The concern of society as to the property rights of the parties is secondary and incidental to its concern as to their status." . . .

In accordance with these concerns the following pertinent legislation has been enacted: Civil Code section 242 — "Every individual shall support his or her spouse. . . ." Civil Code section 4802 — "[A] husband and wife cannot, by any contract with each other, alter their legal relations, except as to property. . . ." Civil Code section 5100 — "Husband and wife contract toward each other obligations of mutual respect, fidelity, and support." Civil Code section 5103 — "[E]ither husband or wife may enter into any transaction with the other . . . respecting property, which either might if unmarried." Civil Code section 5132 — "[A] married person shall support the person's spouse while they are living together."

The courts have stringently enforced and explained the statutory language. "Although most of the cases, both in California and elsewhere, deal with a wife's right to support from the husband, in this state a wife also has certain obligations to support the husband."

"Indeed, husband and wife assume mutual obligations of support upon marriage. These obligations are not conditioned on the existence of community property or income." "In entering the marital state, by which a contract is created, it must be assumed that the parties voluntarily entered therein with knowledge that they have the moral and legal obligation to support the other."

Moreover, interspousal mutual obligations have been broadly defined. "[Husband's] duties and obligations to [wife] included more than mere cohabitation with her. It was his duty to offer [wife] his sympathy, confidence [citation], and fidelity." When necessary, spouses must "provide uncompensated protective supervision services for" each other.

Estate of Sonnicksen (1937) 23 Cal. App. 2d 475, 479 [73 P.2d 643] and Brooks v. Brooks (1941) 48 Cal. App. 2d 347, 349-350 [119 P.2d 970], each hold that under the above statutes and in accordance with the above policy a wife is obligated by the marriage contract to provide nursing-type care to an ill husband. Therefore, contracts whereby the wife is to receive compensation for providing such services are void as against public policy; and there is no consideration for the husband's promise.

Appellant argues that *Sonnicksen* and *Brooks* are no longer valid precedents because they are based on outdated views of the role of women and marriage. She further argues that the rule of those cases denies her equal protection because husbands only have a financial obligation toward their wives, while wives have to provide actual nursing services for free. We disagree. The rule and policy of *Sonnicksen* and *Brooks* have been applied to both spouses in several recent cases arising in different areas of the law. . . .

Vincent v. State of California (1971) 22 Cal. App. 3d 566 [99 Cal. Rptr. 410], held that for purposes of benefit payments spouses caring for each other must be treated identically under similar assistance programs. In reaching such conclusion the court held: "Appellants suggest that one reason justifying denial of payment for services rendered by ATD attendants who reside with their recipient spouses is that, by virtue of the marriage contract, one spouse is obligated to care for the other without remuneration.

Such preexisting duty provides a constitutionally sound basis for a classification which denies compensation for care rendered by a husband or wife to his spouse who is receiving welfare assistance. . . . But insofar as one spouse has a duty created by the marriage contract to care for the other without compensation when they are living together, recipients of aid to the aged, aid to the blind and aid to the disabled are similarly situated."

These cases indicate that the marital duty of support under Civil Code sections 242, 5100, and 5132 includes caring for a spouse who is ill. They also establish that support in a marriage means more than the physical care someone could be hired to provide. Such support also encompasses sympathy, comfort, love, companionship and affection. Thus, the duty of support can no more be "delegated" to a third party than the statutory duties of fidelity and mutual respect. Marital duties are owed by the spouses personally. This is implicit in the definition of marriage as "a personal relation arising out of a civil contract between a man and a woman." (Civ. Code, sec. 4100.)

We therefore adhere to the long-standing rule that a spouse is not entitled to compensation for support, apart from rights to community property and the like that arise from the marital relation itself. Personal performance of a personal duty created by the contract of marriage does not constitute a new consideration supporting the indebtedness, alleged in this case. . . .

Speculating that appellant might have left her husband but for the agreement she alleges, the dissent suggests that marriages will break up if such agreements are not enforced. While we do not believe that marriages would be fostered by a rule that encouraged sickbed bargaining, the question is not whether such negotiations may be more useful than unseemly. The issue is whether such negotiations are antithetical to the institution of marriage as the Legislature has defined it. We believe that they are.

The dissent maintains that mores have changed to the point that spouses can be treated just like any other parties haggling at arm's length. Whether or not the modern marriage has become like a business, and regardless of whatever else it may have become, it continues to be defined by statute as a personal relationship of mutual support. Thus, even if few things are left that cannot command a price, marital support remains one of them. . . .

POCHE, J., dissenting. A very ill person wishes to be cared for at home personally by his spouse rather than by nurses at a health care facility. The ill person offers to pay his spouse for such personal care by transferring property to her. The offer is accepted, the services are rendered and the ill spouse dies. Affirming a judgment of dismissal rendered after a general demurrer was sustained, this court holds that the contract was not enforceable because — as a matter of law — the spouse who rendered services gave no consideration. Apparently, in the majority's view she had a preexisting or precontract nondelegable duty to clean the bedpans herself. Because I do not believe she did, I respectfully dissent.

The majority correctly read Estate of Sonnicksen (1937) 23 Cal. App. 2d 475 [73 P.2d 643] and Brooks v. Brooks (1941) 48 Cal. App. 2d 347 [119 P.2d 970] as holding that a wife cannot enter into a binding contract with her husband to provide "nursing-type care" for compensation. . . . It reasons that the wife, by reason of the marital relationship, already has a duty to provide such care, thus she offers no new consideration to support an independent contract to the same effect. The logic of these decisions is ripe for reexamination.

Sonnicksen and *Brooks* are the California Court of Appeal versions of a national theme. Excerpts from several of these decisions reveal the ethos and mores of the era which produced them.

"It would operate disastrously upon domestic life and breed discord and mischief if the wife could contract with her husband for the payment of services to be rendered for him in his home; if she could exact compensation for services, disagreeable or otherwise, rendered to members of his family; if she could sue him upon such contracts and establish them upon the disputed and conflicting testimony of the members of the household. To allow such contracts would degrade the wife by making her a menial and a servant in the home where she should discharge marital duties in loving and devoted ministrations, and frauds upon creditors would be greatly facilitated, as the wife could frequently absorb all her husband's property in the payment of her services, rendered under such secret, unknown contracts." (Brooks v. Brooks, supra, 48 Cal. App. 2d 347 at p. 3500.

"A man cannot be entitled to the services of his wife for nothing, by virtue of a uniform and unchangeable marriage contract, and at the same time be under obligation to pay her for those services. . . . She cannot be his wife and his hired servant at the same time. . . . That would be inconsistent with the marriage relation, and disturb the reciprocal duties of the parties." . . .

Statements in two of these cases to the effect that a husband has an entitlement to his wife's "services" smack of the common law doctrine of coverture which treated a wife as scarcely more than an appendage to her husband. . . . One of the characteristics of coverture was that it deemed the wife economically helpless and governed by an implicit exchange: "The husband, as head of the family, is charged with its support and maintenance in return for which he is entitled to the wife's services in all those domestic affairs which pertain to the comfort, care, and well-being of the family. Her labors are her contribution to the family support and care." But coverture has been discarded in California, where both husband and wife owe each other the duty of support.

Not only has this doctrinal base for the authority underpinning the majority opinion been discarded long ago, but modern attitudes toward marriage have changed almost as rapidly as the economic realities of modern society. The assumption that only the rare wife can make a financial contribution to her family has become badly outdated in this age in which many married women have paying employment outside the home. A two-income family can no longer be dismissed as a statistically insignificant aberration. Moreover today husbands are increasingly involved in the domestic chores that make a house a home. Insofar as marital duties and property rights are not governed by positive law, they may be the result of informal accommodation or formal agreement. If spouses cannot work things out, there is always the no longer infrequently used option of divorce. For better or worse, we have to a great extent left behind the comfortable and familiar gender-based roles evoked by Norman Rockwell paintings. No longer can the marital relationship be regarded as "uniform and unchangeable." . . .

No one doubts that spouses owe each other a duty of support or that this encompasses "the obligation to provide medical care." There is nothing found in *Sonnicksen* and *Brooks*, or cited by the majority, which requires that this obligation be *personally* discharged by a spouse except the decisions themselves. However, at the time *Sonnicksen* and *Brooks* were decided — before World War II — it made sense for those courts to say that a wife could perform her duty of care only by doing so personally. That was an accurate reflection of the real world for women years before the exigency of war produced substantial employment opportunities for them. . . .

However the real world has changed in the 56 years since *Sonnicksen* was decided. Just a few years later with the advent of World War II Rosie the Riveter became not only a war jingle but a salute to hundreds of thousands of women working on the war effort outside the home. We know what happened thereafter. Presumably, in the present day husbands and wives who work outside the home have alternative methods of meeting this duty of care to an ill spouse. Among the choices would be: (1) paying for professional help; (2) paying for nonprofessional assistance; (3) seeking help from relatives or friends; and (4) quitting one's job and doing the work personally.

A fair reading of the complaint indicates that Mrs. Borelli initially chose the first of these options, and that this was not acceptable to Mr. Borelli, who then offered compensation if Mrs. Borelli would agree to personally care for him at home. To contend in 1993 that such a contract is without consideration means that if Mrs. Clinton becomes ill, President Clinton must drop everything and personally care for her.

According to the majority, Mrs. Borelli had nothing to bargain with so long as she remained in the marriage. This assumes that an intrinsic component of the marital relationship is the *personal* services of the spouse, an obligation that cannot be delegated or performed by others. The preceding discussion has attempted to demonstrate many ways in which what the majority terms "nursing-type care" can be provided without either husband or wife being required to empty a single bedpan. It follows that, because Mrs. Borelli agreed to supply this personal involvement, she was providing something over and above what would fully satisfy her duty of support. That personal something—precisely because it was something she was not required to do—qualifies as valid consideration sufficient to make enforceable Mr. Borelli's reciprocal promise to convey certain of his separate property.

Not only does the majority's position substantially impinge upon couples' freedom to come to a working arrangement of marital responsibilities, it may also foster the very opposite result of that intended. For example, nothing compelled Mr. Borelli and plaintiff to continue living together after his physical afflictions became known. Moral considerations notwithstanding, no legal force could have stopped plaintiff from leaving her husband in his hour of need. Had she done so, and had Mr. Borelli promised to give her some of his separate property should she come back, a valid contract would have arisen upon her return. Deeming them contracts promoting reconciliation and the resumption of marital relations, California courts have long enforced such agreements as supported by consideration. Here so far as we can tell from the face of the complaint, Mr. Borelli and plaintiff reached largely the same result without having to endure a separation. There is no sound reason why their contract, which clearly facilitated continuation of their marriage, should be any less valid. . . .

NOTES AND QUESTIONS

1. Contracts by married women were generally unenforceable at common law, although—as the opinions in *Borelli* indicate—the basis for that view has been placed on several grounds. For Blackstone, the myth of marital unity was a sufficient bar to recognition of agreements between spouses. "A man cannot grant any thing to his wife, or enter into covenant with her: for the grant would be to suppose her separate existence; and to covenant with her, would be only to covenant with himself." 1 William Blackstone, Commentaries on the Laws of England *430. The author of the first treatise on marital relations in the United States took a more sophisticated view: "The law considers the wife to be in the power of the husband; it would not, therefore, be reasonable that she should be bound by any contract she makes during the coverture. . . ." Moreover, execution upon contracts included arrest and confinement in prison; these remedies imposed upon a wife would deprive the husband of her household and other services. Tapping Reeve, Baron and Femme 98 (1970). Marylynn Salmon provides a third explanation:

In one way or another, everything women owned before marriage became their husbands' afterwards. A significant result of this social policy was the inability of femes coverts to contract. No agreement a woman made could be enforced against her because she owned nothing the court could seize to meet a judgment. Even a woman's contract to provide services was unenforceable. According to common law rules, a woman's services belonged to her husband. They could not be given to another unless he consented.

Marylynn Salmon, Women and the Law of Property in Early America 41 (1986).

A fourth, perhaps more modern, rationale for the refusal of courts to enforce spousal agreements is found in the classic case of Balfour v. Balfour, L.R. 2 K.B. 571 (C.A. 1919). Plaintiff wife sued her husband for money she claimed to be due from an agreed allowance of £30 a month. The agreement was entered on the occasion of their visit to England from their home in Ceylon. The wife was unable for medical reasons to return with her husband and, she testified, Mr. Balfour agreed to send her £30 per month until she returned. Subsequently, she decided not to return, and her husband said he would send her £30 a month for maintenance until he returned. Mrs. Balfour later pursued a divorce action. On appeal from a judgment in favor of the wife, the Court of Appeals reversed.

The defence to this action on the alleged contract is that the defendant, the husband, entered into no contract with his wife, and for the determination of that it is necessary to remember that there are agreements between parties which do not result in contracts within the meaning of that term in our law. The ordinary example is when two people agree to take a walk together. . . . [O]ne of the most usual forms of agreement which does not constitute a contract appears to me to be the arrangements which are made between husband and wife. It is quite common, and it is the natural and inevitable result of the relationship of husband and wife, that the two spouses should make arrangements between themselves—agreements such as are in dispute in this action—agreements for allowances, by which the husband agrees that he will pay to his wife a certain sum of money per week, or per month, or per year, to cover either her own expenses or the necessary expenses of the household and of the children of the marriage. . . . To my mind, these agreements, or many of them, do not result in contracts at all, and they do not result in contracts even though there may be what as between other parties would constitute consideration for the agreement. . . .

To my mind it would be the worst possible example to hold that agreements such as this resulted in legal obligations which could be enforced in the Courts. . . . All I can say is that the small Courts of this country would have to be multiplied one hundredfold if these arrangements were held to result in legal obligations. They are not sued upon, not because the parties are reluctant to enforce their legal rights when the agreement is broken, but because the parties, in the inception of their arrangement, never intended that they should be sued upon. . . . The terms may be repudiated, varied or renewed as performance proceeds or as disagreements develop, and the principles of the common law as to exoneration and discharge and accord and satisfaction are such as find no place in the domestic code. The parties themselves are advocates, judges, Courts, sheriff's officer and reporter. In respect of these promises each house is a domain into which the King's writ does not seek to run, and to which his officers do not seek to be admitted.

The appellate court then decided that the burden was on the plaintiff to establish that the promise was intended to carry legal consequences and she failed to do so.

2. It might seem that Ms. Brousseau would have had a greater chance of success in enforcing her contract if she had not been married to Mr. Borelli and thus not subject to the assumption that her services were already due because of her marriage. However, American courts have generally regarded with suspicion contractual efforts to induce or acknowledge support by non–family members. They may impose heightened evidentiary standards for enforcement, such as the requirement of writing for any recovery beyond quantum meruit. *See, e.g.,* Uniform Probate Code §2-514 (requiring written evidence of contract to devise) and comment; Frances H. Foster, The Family Paradigm of Inheritance Law, 80 N.C. L. Rev. 199, 215-216 (2001). Even if evidentiary requirements for proving the contract are met, contractual caregiving provisions may be challenged by "natural" objects of a decedent's bounty on grounds of fraud, duress, and undue influence. If nonmarital sexual relations with the caregiver were also involved, courts may occasionally invalidate the contract on the ground that it rests on "illegal consideration." *See* Foster, *supra* at 217.

3. Although the court refused to enforce the promise involved in *Borelli,* some agreements by persons entering marriage will be enforced. As the materials in Chapter 10 on antenuptial contracts reveal, premarital agreements regarding the treatment of property are now widely recognized, assuming certain requirements of disclosure and fairness are satisfied. In common law states, they may agree to create a community property scheme. *See, e.g.,* Alaska Stat. §34.75.010 et seq. (1997), setting forth a comprehensive scheme for creating community property agreements and trusts. Partners in community property states (particularly if they are entering late or second marriages) may be allowed to contract an ownership arrangement in which each retains ownership and control of their own earnings and the profits from property acquired prior to the marriage. *See, e.g.,* In re Marriage of Dawley, 551 P.2d 323 (Cal. App. 1976).

One obvious issue in enforcing certain kinds of agreements concerns the ability of courts to enforce their orders. As you know, courts of equity generally will not require specific performance where doing so presents insuperable practical difficulties and extensive judicial supervision. *See* John D. Calamari & Joseph D. Perillo, Contracts 672 (3d ed. 1987).

4. Gregg Temple, Freedom of Contract and Intimate Relationships, 8 Harv. J.L. & Pub. Pol'y 121, 150-152 (1985), deals primarily with antenuptial agreements. However, his arguments may also have something to say about agreements within marriage.

> The very purpose of marriage and the family has changed over the last several decades. . . .
>
> Whereas marriage once served a variety of institutional functions, the current marriage is viewed as a vehicle for personal happiness and fulfillment. One of the most important changes is the lessening of social and economic importance of marriage and the family. Family members no longer rely on the family for economic security and social position to the extent they once did. . . . As these institutional functions

lost importance, the purpose of marriage became more and more one of personal ful-fillment; modern marriage is often described as "companionate marriage."

If marriage has lost many of the economic and social functions that defined the traditional marriage terms, it follows that the state's interest in regulating marriage has lessened. Since the new function of marriage is happiness and fulfillment of the individuals, it also follows that personal preferences as to the substance of the mar-riage should be honored. Our society is based on diversity and tolerance of that diversity. If marriage has truly become a personal rather than a social institution, we should defer to personal, private ordering of the relationship. . . .

There have been other social developments which support a private ordering of intimate relationships. The successes of the equality movement support the notion of marriage as the mutually satisfying relationship of two independent autonomous individuals. The goal of many modern married couples is an egalitarian relationship with equal sharing of responsibility for decision making. The increase in the number of women who work outside the home, either through choice or through necessity, also supports the idea of marriage of independent equals.

5. With Temple, *compare* Carl E. Schneider, who notes a major transforma-tion in American family law over the last two decades: a transformation character-ized by a diminution of "moral discourse" relating to the family and a transfer of responsibility "from the law to the people the law once regulated." One of the causes for this transformation is the immanent appearance of "psychologic man," who takes as life's goal "the search for personal well-being, adjustment, and con-tentment. . . ." In other words, psychological man cannot come to rest in any rela-tionship, or any community, or any creed; he must keep asking whether they are working for him. Personal and family relationships, in this view, become "arrangement[s] of convenience designed to advance the personal satisfaction and self-fulfillment of [their] members." Carl Schneider, Moral Discourse and the Transformation of American Family Law, 83 Mich. L. Rev. 1803, 1847-1849 (1985).

Would it be right to regard Temple's view as expressing psychologic man? Is Ms. Borelli seeking to advance her personal fulfillment at the cost of moral responsibility? Is it desirable that spouses, rather than social institutions, define the expectations associated with marriage?

PROBLEMS

1. Two of your friends, Tristan and Isolde, are marrying, and have been encouraged to draft a marriage contract. He is a first-year medical student; she had hopes of a career as a writer. They have known each other for several years but have only fallen in love within the last several months. Tristan is intelligent but poor, and Isolde will have to work to support them while he is in medical school. She is willing to do that and, for that matter, to forgo her career as a writer, believing that she can be happy as the wife of a successful doctor. She wants, however, to be sure of their arrangement.

Tristan came across a book by the sociologist Lenore Weitzman, *The Marriage Contract* (1981). The book contains several examples of contracts into which people who are marrying might enter. One, at pages 340-344, seems to fit their situations well, and Isolde has chosen several clauses from that to include in the agreements she wishes to have drafted. With some adaptation, those provisions are:

1. Isolde agrees to give up her career aspirations and to support Tristan through medical school. She also realizes that, while he is in medical school, Tristan's studies will be time-consuming and he will be less than an ideal companion. In return, she expects financial security, the assurance of a comfortable life, and an interest in Tristan's career.

2. All property and income of the parties, however acquired, will be jointly owned as community property.

3. After graduation from medical school, Tristan will accept the highest-paying job available. Isolde will not work outside the home after Tristan's career has commenced.

4. The location of the family residence will be chosen by Tristan.

5. Tristan agrees to schedule at least two two-week vacations each year, with one to be spent in Europe at a place of Isolde's choosing.

6. Children will be postponed until Tristan's education is complete. If Isolde should become pregnant prior to that time, she will secure an abortion.

How would you advise Tristan and Isolde?

2. Tom and Margaret also wish to marry. She is a law student, he an accountant. Neither wishes to give up his or her occupation or lifestyle. A different kind of contract seems to suit their needs. Among the clauses they agree to are the following:

1. Tom and Margaret intend to marry for as long as their relationship is rich and rewarding. Both intend to continue their professional activities. All of the property and income of each shall be owned and managed separately.

2. Tom and Margaret agree that they will share household duties equally, including shopping, cooking, and house cleaning. They will establish a schedule of weekly responsibilities, and failure by either to carry out assigned responsibilities will result in a fine of $100, to be paid the other.

3. Tom and Margaret hope to have children at such time as they both agree to do so. Both will use birth control until they mutually agree to have a child.

4. If a child or children are born, child care responsibilities, after the child is weaned, will be shared equally.

How would you advise Tom and Margaret?

PACELLI V. PACELLI

725 A.2d 56 (N.J. Super. Ct. App. Div. 1999)

D'ANNUNZIO, J.A.D. . . .

The parties were married in June 1975. The husband, plaintiff Antonio Pacelli, was forty-four years of age at that time; defendant [Francesca Pacelli] was twenty. Defendant had been born in Italy, but migrated to the United States when she was fourteen. Plaintiff was a builder and a real estate developer. He also owned a restaurant at the time of the marriage. Plaintiff testified that he was worth three million dollars when the parties married, but he presented no documents to support that statement.

Two children were born of the marriage. Tony was born in 1976 and Franco was born in 1977. The family lived in a very substantial home in Passaic County and enjoyed a high standard of living. Their income tax returns showed a gross income of $540,000 in 1984 and $476,000 in 1985. Defendant contributed no income to the family.

In mid-1985, plaintiff informed defendant that he would divorce her unless she agreed to certain terms regarding their economic relationship. To punctuate his demand, plaintiff moved out of the marital bedroom and into an apartment above their garage.

At or about the time he made this demand on defendant, plaintiff sought the advice of matrimonial counsel Barry Croland. Croland testified that he advised plaintiff of his economic exposure for equitable distribution and alimony. According to Croland, plaintiff admitted to a net worth of $4.7 million in 1985, $1.7 million more than he had when he married defendant. Croland informed plaintiff that any agreement between plaintiff and defendant, to be enforceable, had to be fair and made only after full disclosure of relevant information regarding the parties' assets. Croland also informed plaintiff that defendant should be represented by counsel.

The record establishes that defendant did not want a divorce. Upon being informed of plaintiff's demand and suggestion that she should retain counsel, defendant consulted matrimonial lawyer, Gary Skoloff, in July 1985. Skoloff advised defendant of her rights in the event of a divorce.

Defendant's next contact with Skoloff was in the fall of 1985. At that time, she informed Skoloff that plaintiff was going to pay her $500,000 in the event of a future divorce, as full satisfaction of plaintiff's equitable distribution and alimony obligations. Skoloff advised her not to sign such an agreement and that if she divorced plaintiff in 1985, a judge would award her much more than $500,000 in equitable distribution and alimony. Defendant did not take Skoloff's advice. Defendant informed Skoloff that she wanted to preserve the marriage and did not want her children to grow up in a broken family. Skoloff testified that defendant told him that she would sign anything in an effort to preserve the marriage.

Thereafter, Skoloff received a form of agreement drafted by Croland and the family's tax returns for four years, through 1984. Croland also provided Skoloff with financial statements. Skoloff testified that the agreement was not negotiable and it was presented as an agreement to be signed as is, otherwise there would be a divorce.

Defendant signed the agreement in February 1986 and plaintiff signed it in March 1986. The parties resumed their marriage until 1994, when plaintiff filed a complaint for divorce. In 1994, plaintiff's assets totaled $14,291,500. He had a net worth of $11,241,500.

The issues are: whether the agreement was the result of coercion or duress and, therefore, unenforceable; and whether the agreement was unfair and, therefore, unenforceable. Regarding the fairness issue, a subsidiary issue is whether the agreement should be measured for fairness as the facts were in 1985 or as the facts were in 1994 when plaintiff filed his divorce complaint. . . .

Pre-nuptial agreements made in contemplation of marriage are enforceable if they are fair and just. Agreements made at the end of a marriage in contemplation of a divorce and to fix each party's economic rights on entry of a divorce judgment are enforceable if "fair and equitable."

* * *

We are persuaded that the mid-marriage agreement in the present case differs from pre-nuptial agreements and property settlement agreements made at a marriage's termination. It was entered into before the marriage lost all of its vitality and when at least one of the parties, without reservation, wanted the marriage to survive. Plaintiff also wanted to continue the marriage, but only on his terms.

Here, unlike the pre-nuptial bride, Francesca Pacelli had entered into the legal relationship of marriage when her husband presented her with his ultimatum. Moreover, the marriage had produced two children. Thus, defendant faced a more difficult choice than the bride who is presented with a demand for a pre-nuptial agreement. The cost to Francesca would have been the destruction of a family and the stigma of a failed marriage. She testified on several occasions that she signed the agreement to preserve the family and to make sure that her sons were raised in an intact family.

The mid-marriage agreement in this case also differs from a property settlement agreement made when the marriage has died. In that case, as Judge Lesemann perceptively observed in *Marschall*, each party, recognizing that the marriage is over, can look to his or her economic rights; the relationship is adversarial.

Our point is that the context in which plaintiff made his demand was inherently coercive. Defendant's access to eminent counsel is of little relevance because her decision was dictated not by a consideration of her legal rights, but by her desire to preserve the family.

We have found no decision in New Jersey or other jurisdictions addressing the enforceability of this type of agreement. Courts have addressed "reconciliation" agreements, however.

Nicholson v. Nicholson, 199 N.J. Super. 525, 489 A.2d 1247 (App. Div. 1985), involved a reconciliation agreement made after the couple had separated due to the husband's second episode of infidelity. As consideration for resumption of the marriage, the wife demanded and received a conveyance of the marital home from the husband. Previously, the couple had held title as tenants by the entirety. Twelve years later, the couple divorced and the trial court determined that the home was not subject to equitable distribution, thereby enforcing the reconciliation agreement.

On appeal, we observed that "[i]n some circumstances a reconciliation agreement will be enforced if it is fair and equitable." A prerequisite to enforcement is a requirement that "the marital relationship has deteriorated at least to the brink of an indefinite separation or a suit for divorce." Under such circumstances a "promise that induces a reconciliation will be enforced if it is fair and equitable." We summarized additional factors that must be considered by the trial court in evaluating such an agreement:

> Before a reconciliation agreement will be enforced, the court must determine that the promise to resume marital relations was made when the marital rift was substantial. If the agreement was oral and enforcement is sought of a promise to convey real estate, there must also be compliance with the statute of frauds. The court may have to resolve disputes over the terms of the agreement. The court must consider whether the circumstances under which the agreement was entered into were fair to the party charged. Changed circumstances must not have rendered literal enforcement inequitable.

We remanded to the trial court for further consideration.

Two of our observations in *Nicholson* are particularly relevant in the present case. In *Nicholson*, we required a showing that the marital relationship had genuinely deteriorated "to the brink of an indefinite separation or a suit for divorce."

Here, the testimony of plaintiff and his lawyer establish that plaintiff's primary interest was financial. Plaintiff wanted an agreement that would limit his exposure to his wife's economic demands. Plaintiff testified on direct that . . .

> Well, I just wasn't comfortable, you know, knowing that the marriage is always on a — sort of on the rocks. And I wanted to put everything in its [perspective]. I wanted to know that if I was going to go into a deal, I could not worry about, you know, getting involved in all kinds of legal stuff. . . .

Plaintiff's lawyer, Croland, testified that plaintiff's purpose "was to stay married, that's what he wanted." But he wanted to understand his financial exposure in the event of a divorce. Croland also testified that during their initial conference Pacelli stated that he had "new deals coming his way," and he was concerned that his wife "not share beyond a certain point."

The evidence, therefore, supports an inference that the marital "crisis" was artificial, created by plaintiff to take advantage of his wife's dedication to the marriage and her family.

The second relevant standard in *Nicholson* is that the agreement must be fair and equitable when made and when it is sought to be enforced. We will allude to this standard later in this opinion.

The majority view in other jurisdictions is that "[a]n agreement the object of which is to restore marital relations after a separation has taken place will generally be upheld." 17 C.J.S. Contracts, §236 (1963). According to Annotation, Validity and enforceability of agreement designed to prevent divorce, or avoid or end separation, 11 A.L.R. 277 (1921), a "contract between a husband and wife, made when the spouses are separated for legal cause, and providing for the payment of a consideration for their reunion, is, by weight of authority, enforceable by either spouse." The annotation offers the policy reasons for the majority and minority views:

> In most jurisdictions, an agreement of that character is held not only to be unobjectionable in this respect, but to promote the stability of the relation, as it purports to do. On

the other hand, several courts have considered such an agreement as mischievous, because it offers an inducement for domestic discord to persons who are willing to occupy this vantage ground for the purpose of obtaining pecuniary or other concessions.

* * *

Mid-marriage agreements closely resemble so-called reconciliation agreements. We must be aware, however, that such circumstances are pregnant with the opportunity for one party to use the threat of dissolution "to bargain themselves into positions of advantage."

We need not decide whether such agreements are so inherently and unduly coercive that they should not be enforced, though we conclude that, at the very least, they must be closely scrutinized and carefully evaluated. In the present case, we conclude that the terms were not fair and just.

Defendant contends that the fairness of the agreement must be measured as of 1994 when plaintiff sought to enforce it. At that time, plaintiff's net worth was approximately $11,000,000. Defendant's argument relies in part on the Uniform Premarital Agreement Act, N.J.S.A. 37:2-31 to -41. It provides that an agreement is not enforceable if it was "unconscionable at the time enforcement was sought." The Act, however, only applies to premarital agreements and, consequently, it does not control the present case.

Defendant limits her attack on the agreement's fairness to the circumstances existing in 1994. We conclude, however, that the agreement was unfair in 1986, when it was signed. The trial court determined that the agreement was fair and equitable when it was made because the agreement gave the wife "approximately 32% of the husband's net worth subject to equitable distribution in 1985." The agreement promised defendant $500,000 in the event of a divorce. Additionally, it called for immediate payment on execution in the amount of $40,000. Thus, $540,000 of the presumed marital estate of $1,700,000 is 32%.

But, the court's numbers are wrong, the court and counsel having been misled by plaintiff's creative accounting. Plaintiff introduced into evidence a financial statement showing a "net worth" of $4,786,800 in 1985, or $1,786,000 more than he claimed to be worth in 1975 when he married defendant.

The financial statement listed assets worth $7,696,200. Liabilities totaled $1,643,300. Plaintiff's net worth, therefore, was $6,053,100. Plaintiff and his accountant reached the net worth figure of $4,786,800 by deducting $1,266,100 in potential income taxes due upon a hypothetical sale of those of plaintiff's assets whose value exceeded their basis. We know of no authority to justify that deduction in determining net worth in a matrimonial context or in the circumstances in this case. . . .

We conclude that in 1985 the marital estate was $3,000,000, not $1,700,000. Thus, the $540,000 provided in the agreement was 18% of the marital estate. Plaintiff's lawyer, Croland, testified that he had advised plaintiff that he could expect "the probable range of equitable distribution could be somewhere around . . . one-third. Could be less, it could be more. . . ." Thus, the $500,000 buy out was approximately half of a potential equitable distribution award, using the low end of the range.

The $500,000 also purchased defendant's waiver of alimony. An alimony award in 1985 would have been substantial, perhaps approaching six figures. Plaintiff's annual income in 1984 and 1985 averaged $500,000. The parties lived well. They lived in an expensive home, drove luxury automobiles and vacationed at some of the most desirable destinations. Plaintiff estimated that defendant spent $20,000 to $30,000 per year on clothing from stores such as Bergdorf Goodman. . . .

Defendant argues that the agreement should be measured for fairness in 1994, when plaintiff sought to enforce it. In *Nicholson, supra*, we observed that in evaluating a reconciliation agreement "[c]hanged circumstances must not have rendered literal enforcement inequitable." We are persuaded that the close scrutiny and careful evaluation of mid-marriage agreements also requires consideration of the agreement's impact when enforced. This is so for at least two reasons. A marriage may survive for many years after such an agreement, as in this case. During that time, the family may continue to prosper, due in part to the contribution of a spouse, such as defendant, in her capacity as mother, homemaker and helpmate. It may be inequitable to preclude her participation in post-agreement wealth.

Moreover, post-agreement prosperity may elude the parties. A family's assets may be worth less at the time of enforcement than when the agreement was executed. In that case, enforcement of the agreement may be inequitable to the obligor.

It is apparent that the agreement is also unfair when measured in 1994. . . . In light of the inherently coercive circumstances leading to the agreement, the result is unfair, inequitable and unenforceable. The trial court, on remand, must make determinations regarding equitable distribution and alimony, and other ancillary economic issues, if any.

NOTES AND QUESTIONS

1. Both *Borelli* and *Pacelli* suggest that agreements by persons entering marriage and by spouses ending their marriage will be enforced and, indeed, are favored. How is an agreement intended to procure continuation of a marriage more coercive than an agreement intended to procure entrance into a marriage, or than an agreement intended to permit exit from a marriage?

2. In Borelli v. Brusseau, the court found no consideration for the wife's agreement to provide personal care for her ill husband. Does the consideration in *Pacelli* differ?

3. In what ways was Ms. Pacelli coerced into signing the agreement? Why wasn't advice of eminent counsel sufficient to provide freedom from coercion? Did Ms. Pacelli have no choice, or did she have no choice that met her actual preferences? Does the lack of the latter kind of choice amount to a coercive situation?

C. VIOLENCE BETWEEN SPOUSES

Examination of legal and social issues relating to family violence is peculiarly difficult. The topic presents hard questions of law, history, and social science. For example, a recent discussion of family violence observes that "[n]o doubt, acts of violence and willful neglect within families have been occurring as long as there have been human families," and at the same time recognizes that family violence as a subject of social science research dates only to the early 1960s. Lloyd Ohlin & Michael Tonry, Family Violence in Perspective, Family Violence 1 (Lloyd Ohlin & Michael Tonry eds., 1989).

The definition of domestic violence itself is sharply contested. Ohlin and Tonry's statement that acts of violence and neglect have occurred as long as there have been families seems on its face both obvious and unexceptionable. Does that mean, however, that there are kinds of conduct that everyone has always regarded as "violence" and "neglect" (and therefore wrongful), or does it mean that kinds of conduct we now regard as violent and neglectful have always occurred but previously have been largely tolerated? What does one say of the classical Roman family, which accorded a father life-and-death power over his sons and, in Maine's phrase, "constitutes one of the strangest problems in legal history," Henry Sumner Maine, Ancient Law 133 (3d ed. 1888), or of the Anglo-Saxon family, in which, it seems, the father could sell into slavery a child younger than seven and perhaps could lawfully kill a child "who had not yet tasted food"? Frederick Pollock & Frederic W. Maitland, History of English Law 436-437 (2d ed. 1909).

There are also problems of what one counts as a "legal response" to conduct within families. The historian Elizabeth Pleck reports that the "first law against wife abuse anywhere in the Western World was written into a new criminal code of the Massachusetts Bay Colony [during the middle of the seventeenth century]." Elizabeth Pleck, Criminal Approaches to Family Violence: 1640-1980, in Family Violence, above, at 19, 22. However, ecclesiastical courts had long allowed a spouse who had been seriously physically abused relief from the marital obligation of cohabitation with the offender through judicial separations (divorces a mensa et thoro), which provided support while allowing the victim to live apart from her or his abuser.

It is tempting to regard the lack of clarity associated with the definition of family violence as itself an indication of lack of social concern with conduct of this kind. While this conclusion has appeal, it assumes that deviant conduct is a natural phenomenon, like an earthquake or hurricane, that has universal meaning. In this respect, it overlooks a variety of contingencies in our understanding of crime or wrongdoing.

Some of these contingencies are associated with the meanings of legal terms. Killing is an act; murder is not. To call a homicide murder requires judgments about the subjective mental state of the actor, the existence of such provocation as would lead an ordinary person to kill, the degree of dangerousness involved in the activity leading to death, and a variety of other circumstances. Plainly, crucial elements (such as the "reasonableness" of a risk resulting in death) may vary from place to place and time to time.

However, the meaning given by courts is not the only area of contingency in the definition and treatment of deviance. An event occurring in real life must first be discovered, and the observer or victim must decide to bring the matter to official attention. It has been observed in connection with conduct by minors that "the moral standards of the citizenry have more to do with the definition of juvenile deviance than do the standards of policemen on patrol." Donald Black & Albert Reiss, Police Control of Juveniles, 35 Am. Soc. Rev. 63, 66 (1970). For domestic conduct, which rarely occurs on the street, official notice depends even more heavily on whether the victims so identify themselves, how seriously they regard the conduct they encounter, and whether they wish to become involved in the formal processing of a complaint. Thus, the definition of domestic deviance is largely in the control of wives and husbands.

There are intermediate systems as well between conduct that might be considered domestic violence and the definitions employed by courts. Police officers, lawyers, social workers, and judges all have something to do with the fact and the form of response to those complaints that are made. How they respond will be influenced by both institutional and personal views of the gravity of the behavior, the perceived utility of various kinds of response, and interpretations of the outcomes that will likely be associated with judicial processing of the complaint.

In considering the following materials, it may be useful to consider not only the doctrinal issues that arise in connection with family violence but the associated problems of defining and responding to conduct between spouses at various levels of practical responsibility.

1. Crimes Between Spouses

PEOPLE V. LIBERTA

474 N.E.2d 567 (N.Y. 1984)

WACHTLER, J. . . . Defendant Mario Liberta and Denise Liberta were married in 1978. Shortly after the birth of their son, in October of that year, Mario began to beat Denise. In early 1980 Denise brought a proceeding in the Family Court in Erie County seeking protection from the defendant. On April 30, 1980 a temporary order of protection was issued to her by the Family Court. Under this order, the defendant was to move out and remain away from the family home, and stay away from Denise. The order provided that the defendant could visit with his son once each weekend.

On the weekend of March 21, 1981, Mario, who was then living in a motel, did not visit his son. On Tuesday, March 24, 1981 he called Denise to ask if he could visit his son on that day. Denise would not allow the defendant to come to her house, but she did agree to allow him to pick up their son and her and take them both back to his motel after being assured that a friend of his would be with them at all times. The defendant and his friend picked up Denise and their son and the four of them drove to defendant's motel.

When they arrived at the motel the friend left. As soon as only Mario, Denise, and their son were alone in the motel room, Mario attacked Denise, threatened to kill her, and forced her to perform fellatio on him and to engage in sexual intercourse with him. The son was in the room during the entire episode, and the defendant forced Denise to tell their son to watch what the defendant was doing to her.

The defendant allowed Denise and their son to leave shortly after the incident. Denise, after going to her parents' home, went to a hospital to be treated for scratches on her neck and bruises on her head and back, all inflicted by her husband. She also went to the police station, and on the next day she swore out a felony complaint against the defendant. On July 15, 1981 the defendant was indicted for rape in the first degree and sodomy in the first degree.

Section 130.35 of the Penal Law provides in relevant part that "A male is guilty of rape in the first degree when he engages in sexual intercourse with a female . . . by forcible compulsion." "Female," for purposes of the rape statute, is defined as "any female person who is not married to the actor" (Penal Law, §130.00, subd. 4). . . . [D]ue to the "not married" language in the definitions of "female" and "deviate sexual intercourse," there is a "marital exemption" for both forcible rape and forcible sodomy. The marital exemption itself, however, has certain exceptions. For purposes of the rape and sodomy statutes, a husband and wife are considered to be "not married" if at the time of the sexual assault they "are living apart . . . pursuant to a valid and effective: (i) order issued by a court of competent jurisdiction which by its terms or in its effect requires such living apart."

We first address the defendant's argument that, despite the order of protection, he was within the "marital exemption" to rape and sodomy and thus could not be prosecuted for either crime. . . . We agree with the Appellate Division that the order of protection in the present case falls squarely within the first of these situations. . . .

[The defendant then argued that the New York law violated equal protection by punishing rape by "unmarried" men but not by married men with respect to their wives.]

As noted above, under the Penal Law a married man ordinarily cannot be convicted of forcibly raping or sodomizing his wife. This is the so-called marital exemption for rape. . . . The assumption, even before the marital exemption was codified, that a man could not be guilty of raping his wife, is traceable to a statement made by the 17th century English jurist Lord Hale, who wrote: "[T]he husband cannot be guilty of a rape committed by himself upon his lawful wife, for by their mutual matrimonial consent and contract the wife hath given up herself in this kind unto her husband, which she cannot retract" (1 Hale, History of Pleas of the Crown, p.629). Although Hale cited no authority for his statement it was relied on by State Legislatures which enacted rape statutes with a marital exemption and by courts which established a common-law exemption for husbands.

* * *

Presently, over 40 States still retain some form of marital exemption for rape. While the marital exemption is subject to an equal protection challenge, because it classifies unmarried men differently than married men, the equal protection clause does not prohibit a State from making classifications, provided the statute does not arbitrarily burden a particular group of individuals (Reed v. Reed, 404 U.S. 71). Where a statute draws a distinction based upon marital status, the classification must be reasonable and must be based upon "some ground of difference that rationally explains the different treatment."

We find that there is no rational basis for distinguishing between marital rape and nonmarital rape. The various rationales which have been asserted in defense of the exemption are either based upon archaic notions about the consent and property rights incident to marriage or are simply unable to withstand even the slightest scrutiny. We therefore declare the marital exemption for rape in the New York statute to be unconstitutional.

Lord Hale's notion of an irrevocable implied consent by a married woman to sexual intercourse has been cited most frequently in support of the marital exemption. Any argument based on a supposed consent, however, is untenable. Rape is not simply a sexual act to which one party does not consent. Rather, it is a degrading, violent act which violates the bodily integrity of the victim and frequently causes severe, long-lasting physical and psychic harm. To ever imply consent to such an act is irrational and absurd. Other than in the context of rape statutes, marriage has never been viewed as giving a husband the right to coerced intercourse on demand. Certainly, then, a marriage license should not be viewed as a license for a husband to forcibly rape his wife with impunity. A married woman has the same right to control her own body as does an unmarried woman. If a husband feels "aggrieved" by his wife's refusal to engage in sexual intercourse, he should seek relief in the courts governing domestic relations, not in "violent or forceful self-help."

The other traditional justifications for the marital exemption were the common-law doctrines that a woman was the property of her husband and that the legal existence of the woman was "incorporated and consolidated into that of the husband" (1 Blackstone's Commentaries [1966 ed.], p.430). Both these doctrines, of course, have long been rejected in this State. Indeed, "[n]owhere in the common-law world — [or] in any modern society — is a woman regarded as chattel or demeaned by denial of a separate legal identity and the dignity associated with recognition as a whole human being."

Because the traditional justifications for the marital exemption no longer have any validity, other arguments have been advanced in its defense. The first of these recent rationales, which is stressed by the People in this case, is that the marital exemption protects against governmental intrusion into marital privacy and promotes reconciliation of the spouses, and thus that elimination of the exemption would be disruptive to marriages. While protecting marital privacy and encouraging reconciliation are legitimate State interests, there is no rational relation between allowing a husband to forcibly rape his wife and these interests. The marital exemption simply does not further marital privacy because this right of privacy protects consensual acts, not violent sexual assaults. Just as a husband cannot invoke a right of marital privacy to escape liability for beating his wife, he cannot justifiably rape his wife under the guise of a right to privacy.

Similarly, it is not tenable to argue that elimination of the marital exemption would disrupt marriages because it would discourage reconciliation. Clearly, it is the violent act of rape and not the subsequent attempt of the wife to seek protection through the criminal justice system which "disrupts" a marriage. Moreover, if the marriage has already reached the point where intercourse is accomplished by violent assault it is doubtful that there is anything left to reconcile. This, of course, is particularly true if the wife is willing to bring criminal charges against her husband which could result in a lengthy jail sentence.

Another rationale sometimes advanced in support of the marital exemption is that marital rape would be a difficult crime to prove. A related argument is that allowing such prosecutions could lead to fabricated complaints by "vindictive" wives. The difficulty of proof argument is based on the problem of showing lack of consent. Proving lack of consent, however, is often the most difficult part of any rape prosecution, particularly where the rapist and the victim had a prior relationship. Similarly, the possibility that married women will fabricate complaints would seem to be no greater than the possibility of unmarried women doing so. . . .

The final argument in defense of the marital exemption is that marital rape is not as serious an offense as other rape and is thus adequately dealt with by the possibility of prosecution under criminal statutes, such as assault statutes, which provide for less severe punishment. The fact that rape statutes exist, however, is a recognition that the harm caused by a forcible rape is different, and more severe, than the harm caused by an ordinary assault. . . .

Moreover, there is no evidence to support the argument that marital rape has less severe consequences than other rape. On the contrary, numerous studies have shown that marital rape is frequently quite violent and generally has *more* severe, traumatic effects on the victim than other rape. . . .

. . . Justice Holmes wrote: "It is revolting to have no better reason for a rule of law than that so it was laid down in the time of Henry IV. It is still more revolting if the grounds upon which it was laid down have vanished long since, and the rule simply persists from blind imitation of the past" (Holmes, The Path of the Law, 10 Harv. L. Rev. 457, 469). This statement is an apt characterization of the marital exemption; it lacks a rational basis, and therefore violates the equal protection clauses of both the Federal and State Constitutions.

NOTES AND QUESTIONS

1. A number of legislatures and courts have abandoned the traditional view that a wife cannot be raped by her husband, often sharing the view of Professor Clark that "any criminal code which is not barbaric should find no room for the so-called marital exemption to the offense of rape, and the contemporary trend seems headed in this direction." 1 Homer H. Clark, Jr., The Law of Domestic Relations in the United States 523 (2d ed. 1987). On the elimination of a marital exemption for all sexual offenses, see Note, *Liberta* Revisited: A Call to Repeal the Marital Exemption for All Offenses in New York's Penal Law, 23 Fordham Urb. L.J. 857 (1996).

It has been suggested that a majority of the states still retain some form of the exception; they may criminalize a narrower range of offenses if committed within marriage, subject a marital rape to less serious sanctions than nonmarital rape, and/or create special procedural requirements for prosecutions of marital rape. Jill Elaine Hasday, A Legal History of Marital Rape, 88 Cal. L. Rev. 1373, 1375 (2000). This article examines at length the history of the marital rape exemption.

2. The common law has been accused of allowing husbands to inflict not only undesired sexual relations but other forms of battery on their wives. While the former was true, the latter is less so. While it is true that an English case in

1783 announced a "rule of thumb"—permitting a husband to beat his wife with a stick no thicker than his thumb—and a few nineteenth–century American cases seem to follow suit, the current view is that these cases were exceptional and generally contrary to prevailing legal opinion. *See* Elizabeth Pleck, Criminal Approaches to Family Violence, 1640-1980, in Family Violence 19, 32-33 (Lloyd Ohlin & Michael Tonry eds., 1989).

2. *Police Response to Domestic Violence Calls*

Domestic violence has become a matter of profound national concern. As the issue has become more central in public discussion, a variety of legal strategies have been suggested or adopted, and some have been adopted and then modified or abandoned. The following problem and materials examine the history of social treatment of domestic violence, what is known about it, and various responses through the lens of the following problem.

PROBLEM

You are the city attorney for the City of Morristown. The chairman of the city council has come to your office for advice concerning the legal liability of the city, and the posture it should adopt, with respect to what appears to be an increased incidence of domestic violence.

The immediate cause for the chairman's concern is a group calling itself the Society for Protection of Battered Wives. This group is convinced that the police department in Morristown has systematically refused to provide appropriate protection to victims of spouse abuse. The Society recently visited the chairman's office with what it believes is the basis for a cause celebre: the beating of one of its members, Ms. Rachel Allen, by her husband after the police had refused to intervene effectively.

The chairman wants your advice on three questions:

1. Will the city be liable if Ms. Allen brings a lawsuit against it for violation of her constitutional rights through nonperformance by the police of its duties? This threat is not idle, because the society has said that it is prepared to support Ms. Allen financially in such a suit. The chairman has thoughtfully provided you a copy of Ms. Allen's statement.

2. Should the city adopt an ordinance requiring the arrest of any person accused of spousal abuse when there are reasonable grounds to believe the accusation is true?

3. Should the city, notwithstanding a budgetary crisis that has prevented it from giving police officers and firemen a raise for three years, nonetheless establish one or more shelters for battered wives? What resources do such shelters imply?

After the chairman left, you examined the statement by Ms. Allen concerning her situation. Ms. Allen and her husband, Willis, have experienced severe marital difficulties for a number of months. On two previous occasions, Ms. Allen had called for police protection and asked that her husband be arrested and removed from the house. These requests had not been carried out. On this occasion, she told Officer Krauss that her husband had struck her with his fist and that she was afraid that he would hurt her badly. Officer Krauss asked her what had caused the quarrel, and Mr. Allen claimed that his wife had "begun things" by attacking him verbally and slapping him because he came home drunk. The officer told both Ms. Allen and her husband that these quarrels had to be resolved peacefully and that, if Mr. Allen had trouble with that, maybe they should see a counselor. He then asked Mr. Allen if he was through for the night. He said that he was and that he felt badly about hitting his wife. The former, at least, was untrue; Mr. Allen beat his wife with his fist after the officer left, breaking her nose and arm and causing cuts to her scalp and face.

A telephone call to the police legal advisor (an attorney who serves as staff to the city police department) confirmed that Officer Krauss did not arrest Mr. Allen despite his wife's request that he do so and that its police manual specifies that arrest is generally to be avoided when domestic disputes are involved. The manual incorporates the policy stated in training materials published by the International Association of Chiefs of Police through the early 1970s, which the Morristown Police Department still believes to be the proper approach. The police legal advisor further stated that police are currently instructed to follow that policy and that arrests have not been made in any instance where the victim did not appear to have suffered "serious" physical injury at the time the officer visited the home.

Your research indicates that law enforcement officers and the city may be held liable under 42 U.S.C. §1983 for performance or failure to perform their duties in a way that denies a person equal protection of the laws. *See* Smith v. Ross, 482 F.2d 33, 36-37 (6th Cir. 1973). A federal district court case also holds that facts somewhat like those in the present situation state a cause of action under §1983. Thurman v. City of Torrington, 595 F. Supp. 1521 (D. Conn. 1984).

Write a memorandum analyzing the city's motion to dismiss. In doing so, take the following materials into account.

a. Constitutional Decisions

In addition to the cases on gender-based discrimination at pages 89-98, above, consider the following:

WASHINGTON V. DAVIS, 426 U.S. 229 (1976): [Respondents, unsuccessful black applicants for positions on the District of Columbia police force, claimed that a test measuring verbal ability, reading comprehension, and vocabulary resulted in a higher percentage of blacks failing the test and therefore unconstitutionally discriminated against them. There was no claim that use of the test was an intentional or purposeful act of discrimination.]

The central purpose of the Equal Protection Clause of the Fourteenth Amendment is the prevention of official misconduct discriminating on the basis of race. [However,] our cases have not embraced the proposition that a law or other official act, without regard to whether it reflects a racially discriminatory purpose, is unconstitutional *solely* because it has a racially disproportionate impact. . . .

This is not to say that the necessary discriminatory racial purpose must be express or appear on the face of the statute, or that a law's disproportionate impact is irrelevant in cases involving Constitution-based claims of racial discrimination. A statute, otherwise neutral on its face, must not be applied so as invidiously to discriminate on the basis of race. . . .

Necessarily, an invidious discriminatory purpose may often be inferred from the totality of the relevant facts, including the fact, if it is true, that the law bears more heavily on one race than another. Nevertheless, we have not held that a law, neutral on its face and serving ends otherwise within the power of government to pursue, is invalid under the Equal Protection Clause simply because it may affect a greater proportion of one race than of another. Disproportionate impact is not irrelevant, but it is not the sole touchstone of an invidious racial discrimination forbidden by the Constitution. Standing alone, it does not trigger the rule, that racial classifications are to be subjected to the strictest scrutiny and are justifiable only by the weightiest of considerations. . . .

. . . [We] have difficulty understanding how a law establishing a racially neutral qualification for employment is nevertheless racially discriminatory . . . simply because a greater proportion of Negroes fail to qualify than members of other racial or ethnic groups. . . . [The test] is administered generally to prospective Government employees, concededly seeks to ascertain whether those who take it have acquired a particular level of verbal skill; and it is untenable that the Constitution prevents the Government from seeking modestly to upgrade the communicative abilities of its employees rather than to be satisfied with some lower level of competence, particularly where the job requires special ability to communicate orally and in writing.

VILLAGE OF ARLINGTON HEIGHTS V. METROPOLITAN HOUSING DEVELOPMENT CORP., 429 U.S. 252 (1977): [Respondent sought rezoning of a parcel in Arlington Heights in order to build low- and moderate-income housing. Denial of the request was challenged as racially discriminatory.] Determining whether invidious discriminatory purpose was a motivating factor demands a sensitive inquiry into such circumstantial and direct evidence of intent as may be available. The impact of the official action [may] provide an important starting point. Sometimes a clear pattern, unexplainable on grounds other than race, emerges from the effect of the state action even when the governing legislation appears neutral on its face. The evidentiary inquiry is then relatively easy. But such cases are rare. . . . [I]mpact alone is not determinative, and the Court must look to other evidence.

The historical background of the decision is one evidentiary source, particularly if it reveals a series of official actions taken for invidious purposes. The specific sequence of events leading up to the challenged decision also may shed some light on the decisionmaker's purposes. [Deviations] from the normal procedural sequence also might afford evidence that improper purposes are playing a role. . . .

[In this case, respondents] simply failed to carry their burden of proving that discriminatory purpose was a motivating factor in the Village's decision.

PERSONNEL ADMINISTRATOR V. FEENEY, 442 U.S. 256 (1979): Stewart, J. This case presents a challenge to the constitutionality of the Massachusetts veterans' preference statute on the ground that it discriminates against women in violation of the Equal Protection Clause of the Fourteenth Amendment. Under [the statute], all veterans who qualify for state civil service positions must be considered for appointment ahead of any qualifying nonveterans. The preference operates overwhelmingly to the advantage of males. . . .

If the impact of this statute could not be plausibly explained on a neutral ground, impact itself would signal that the real classification made by the law was in fact not neutral. But there can be but one answer to the question whether this veteran preference excludes significant numbers of women from preferred state jobs because they are women or because they are nonveterans. Apart from the facts that the definition of "veterans" in the statute has always been neutral as to gender and that Massachusetts has consistently defined veteran status in a way that has been inclusive of women who have served in the military, this is not a law that can plausibly be explained only as a gender-based classification. Indeed, it is not a law that can rationally be explained on that ground. Veteran status is not uniquely male. Although few women benefit from the preference, the nonveteran statute is not substantially all female. . . .

The appellee's ultimate argument rests upon the presumption, common to the criminal and civil law, that a person intends the natural and foreseeable consequences of his voluntary actions. . . .

. . . [It] cannot seriously be argued that the Legislature of Massachusetts could have been unaware that most veterans are men. . . . It would thus be disingenuous to say that the adverse consequences of this legislation for women were unintended, in the sense that they were not volitional or in the sense that they were not foreseeable.

"Discriminatory purpose," however, implies more than intent as volition or intent as awareness of consequences. It implies that the decisionmaker [chose] or reaffirmed a particular course of action at least in part "because of," not merely "in spite of," its adverse effects upon an identifiable group. Yet nothing in the record demonstrates that this preference for veterans was originally devised or subsequently reenacted because it would accomplish the collateral goal of keeping women in a stereotypic and predefined place in the Massachusetts Civil Service.

Veterans' hiring preferences represent an awkward — and, many argue, unfair — exception to the widely shared view that merit and merit alone should prevail in the employment practices of government. [The] edge granted to veterans . . . may reflect unwise policy. The appellee, however, has simply failed to demonstrate that the law in any way reflects a purpose to discriminate on the basis of sex.

See also Comment, Gender Based Discrimination in Police Reluctance to Respond to Domestic Assault Complaints, 75 Geo. L.J. 667 (1986); Recent Development, Mandatory Arrest for Domestic Violence, 11 Harv. Women's L.J. 213 (1988); Eppler, Battered Women and the Equal Protection Clause: Will the Constitution Help Them When the Police Won't?, 95 Yale L.J. 788 (1986).

b.   Fourth Amendment Limits

In Schieber v. City of Philadelphia, 156 F. Supp. 2d 451 (E.D. Pa. 2001), the victim cried out for help as she was attacked in her apartment. A neighbor called the police for assistance. In response to the neighbor's "Priority 1" emergency call, two police officers arrived at the apartment building, where the neighbor stood ready to assist. The officers knocked on Schieber's door. Receiving no answer, they made no further inquiry and did not attempt to enter Schieber's apartment. They did not call for assistance to break down the door. Neighbors, including the original 911 caller, were assured by the officers that Schieber was not home and therefore took no further action that they may have otherwise taken. The following afternoon, Schieber's brother found her raped and dead on the floor of her apartment.

On the motion for summary judgment in *Schieber*, the Eastern District of Pennsylvania held that there was sufficient showing to state a claim that the police had an affirmative duty to protect Schieber because the officers' conduct had increased Schieber's vulnerability to harm. The court refused to credit the officers' contention that they lacked probable cause to enter Schieber's home and dismissed the argument that invasion of the home would have implicated Fourth Amendment protections.

Fourth Amendment aspects of entry into the home under a domestic violence statute were also considered in Henderson v. City of Simi Valley, 305 F.3d 1052 (9th Cir. 2002). The police were seeking to implement a court order, obtained by the plaintiff's former husband, giving their daughter the right to possess certain personal belongings. They did not have a search warrant. The mother refused to comply and sought to release two Rottweilers on the officers. She was taken into custody and later filed an action under 42 U.S.C. 1983 claiming an invasion of her Fourth Amendment rights by the police.

The Ninth Circuit upheld a district court decision rejecting the Fourth Amendment claim. While recognizing that invasion of a person's home is the chief concern addressed by that amendment, the court held that the facts here fell within an exception to the warrant requirement when "special needs, beyond the normal need for law enforcement, make the warrant and probable-cause requirement impracticable," previously applied in, for example, school searches.

The special need asserted in this case parallels the aims of California's Domestic Violence Prevention Act. . . . Like drug use and violent crime in the schools, domestic violence has become a "major social problem." . . .

[T]he officers were engaged outside the ordinary needs of law enforcement. Keeping the peace while a minor child exercises her rights pursuant to a court order is not akin to typical law enforcement functions. Rather, the officers were serving as neutral third parties acting to protect all parties. The officers did not enter the house to obtain evidence of criminal wrongdoing. . . .

Requiring the officers to get a warrant in this situation would not only be impracticable, but superfluous. The officers already had a court order in their possession detailing the relevant restraints imposed and property rights protected. . . . Moreover, the delay inherent in obtaining a warrant would make it more difficult for officers to respond quickly to potentially violent violations of the court order, an eventuality the court order was designed to prevent. . . .

c.   Historical and Social Background

ELIZABETH PLECK, *DOMESTIC TYRANNY: THE MAKING OF SOCIAL POLICY AGAINST FAMILY VIOLENCE FROM COLONIAL TIMES TO THE PRESENT*

7-9 (1987)

The history of reform against family violence . . . , although similar in some respects to many [other social movements in the United States], has had one aspect that necessarily limited it and made it more controversial.

The single most consistent barrier to reform against domestic violence has been the Family Ideal — that is, [related] but nonetheless distinct ideas about family privacy, conjugal and parental rights, and family instability. In this ideal with origins possibly extending into antiquity, the "family" consists of a two-parent household with minor children. Other constellations, such as a mother and her two children, were seen not as a family but as a deviation from it.

One crucial element of the Family Ideal was belief in domestic privacy. . . . By the 1830s the private sphere came to acquire a deeply emotional texture; it became a refuge from the hard, calculating dealings of the business world. . . . Even more than before, intervention in the family was viewed as problematic, a violation of family intimacy. Although there have been many periods of American history since the 1830s when family privacy has declined in importance, belief in it has persisted to the present day. Modern defenders are likely to argue that the family has a constitutional right to privacy or insist that the home is the only setting where intimacy can flourish, providing meaning, coherence, and stability in personal life.

A second element of the Family Ideal is a belief in conjugal and parental rights. In ancient times, the head of the household had the power to compel obedience from his wife, children, and servants and maintain domestic harmony. . . .

The Romans had the most extensive legal definition of these traditional rights. A Roman wife remained under the guardianship of her husband, who possessed *patria potestas*, including the power to sell his wife and children into slavery or put them to death. Since Roman times, the husband's power has been gradually restricted, and the rights of women and children have correspondingly increased. Yet in many areas of law a stranger is entitled to more legal protection than a family member. In most states, a wife does not have the right to charge her husband with rape, nor in many can a family member sue a relative for damages arising from assault. . . .

A third element of the Family Ideal is belief in the preservation of the family. Marriage was supposed to be life long, for religious reasons and for the responsibility of raising children. Conservatives of the nineteenth century argued that women were dependent on the family for their happiness. They were tethered to it because of their children and in order to make the home a place of affection. . . .

. . . [R]eform against family violence is an implicit critique of each element of the Family Ideal. It inevitably asserts that family violence is a public matter, not a private issue. Public policy against domestic violence offers state intervention in the family as a major remedy for abuse, challenges the view that marriage and family should be preserved at all costs, and asserts that children and women are individuals whose liberties must be protected.

JEFFREY FAGAN & ANGELA BROWNE, *VIOLENCE BETWEEN SPOUSES AND INTIMATES: PHYSICAL AGGRESSION BETWEEN WOMEN AND MEN IN INTIMATE RELATIONSHIPS*

3 Understanding and Preventing Violence 115-211 (Albert J. Reiss, Jr. & Jeffrey A. Roth eds., 1994)

In this paper, the discussion of research and policy on violence between intimate adult partners includes physical assault, sexual assault, and homicide, committed, threatened, or attempted by spouses, ex-spouses, common-law spouses, or cohabitants toward their partners. We also note other harmful behaviors that occur as part of the natural history of marital violence: psychological abuse, economic deprivation, threats to others in the family, and threats as a method of coercion. These behaviors co-occur with physical assault, and although we do not focus on them specifically, they are part of the "ecology of aggression" that characterizes marital violence. They may also constitute antecedents of physical aggression, part of the maintenance of a pattern of marital violence, or displacements of aggression when assaults desist.

Marital violence is intrinsic to many cultures. Levinson (1988) using cross-cultural data on family violence from the Human Relations Area Files (HRAF) data base identified eight varieties of martial violence in 330 societies. Levinson (1988, 1989) estimated the prevalence of wife beating in a representative sample of 90 societies from the 330 cultural groups in the HRAF data base. Wife beating occurred in 84.5 percent of the 90 cultures. It occurred "at least occasionally" in all or nearly all households in 18.8 percent of the societies and in a majority (but not all) in 29.9 percent. Husband beating was reported in 6 percent of all societies; it was rare or unheard of in 73.1 percent and occurred in a minority of households in 20.2 percent. Other studies (cited in Levinson, 1989) report comparable data: Wife beating occurs in 71 to 92 percent of the societies studied.

Motivations for wife beating in these societies included sexual jealousy or infidelity (45.5%), insubordination or disobedience by the wife (25.5%), and the wife's failure to meet "household responsibilities" (23.3%). Societal responses to wife beating varied extensively. In 91.2 percent of the societies, intervention by outsiders occurred. These interventions included help or intercession by kin or neighbors (17.6%), shelter for the wife (14.7%), legal intervention (17.6%), marital violence as grounds for divorce (11.8%), and supernatural sanctions (e.g., casting a spell) in an unspecified proportion. In 29.4 percent of the societies, interventions are limited to beatings that exceed societal norms for the "physical discipline" of wives. Interventions were reportedly unavailable in 8.8 percent of the societies. The study gave no indication of the legal status of wife or husband assaults in the societies studied. . . .

The first general population study of family violence in the United States was the 1975 National Family Violence Survey (NFVS), based on interviews with a probability sample of 2,143 intact couples in households. Straus (1978) and Straus et al. (1980) reported that 16 percent of all marital couples experienced physical aggression during the year before the survey; 28 percent had experienced physical aggression at some point in their relationship. Among those reporting at least one act of violence in the past year, more than one in three involved acts such as punching, kicking, hitting with an object, beating up, and assaults with a gun or knife. These items formed the "severe violence" scale (or what Straus initially termed "wife beating"). Straus and his colleagues reported that 3.8 percent of female respondents and 4.6 percent of males were victims of at least one of these acts of "severe violence."

The NFVS used the Conflict Tactics Scales (Straus, 1978, 1979)—items that operationalized tactics used by couples to settle conflicts into specific acts. Rational, verbal, and physically aggressive acts were included in the scale. Aggressive acts included eight items, ranging in severity from throwing objects to using a gun or knife. An additional item on "choking" was included in the 1985 survey and two later waves with the 1985 panel. Threats of violence were considered nonviolent acts. Respondents reported whether and how often they had engaged in each of the CTS behaviors during the past year. They also reported whether each behavior had ever happened during their lifetime. Straus et al. (1980) reported "violence participation" rates for both members of the couple. . . . [The following table summarizes national interview sample studies.]

Although there may be circumstances in which men and women share equal proclivities for aggressive behavior, Maccoby and Jacklin (1974:274) concluded that "there is a sex-linked differential readiness to respond in aggressive ways to the relevant experiences. Eron and Huesmann (1989:65) concluded that male aggression is more prevalent and serious, more stable over time, and attributable to different socialization experiences in our society. Outside the home, it is widely accepted that men are more likely to commit robberies or assaults. . . ."

Table 1
PAST YEAR PREVALENCE RATES OF VIOLENCE AMONG INTIMATES
(PER 1,000 POPULATION)

Study	Sample (n)	Any Violence by	
		Husband or Male Partner	Wife or Female Partner
National probability samples			
Straus and Gelles (1990)	6,002	116	124
Straus et al. (1980)	2,143 couples	121	116
Straus and Gelles (1986)	3,520 couples	110	120
Elliot et al. (1985)	1,725 (ages 18-24)	368	471

However, there is a lively and contentious debate on gender differences between men and women in physical assaults between spouses or partners. Depending on the data source and the dimension of marital violence, gender differences may point to greater injury risk for women or, conversely, higher "violence" rates for women. The two perspectives are not easily reconciled, and the disparity goes to the heart of definitional and philosophical debates in the study of family violence. Moreover, perceptions of the relative violence rates for men and women may reflect different parameters of criminal careers that are used to weight the evidence.

Both victimization data and intervention reports suggest that more women are victimized than men. NCS data suggest that women are victimized more often by male spouses or ex-spouses than strangers, and also by the broader group of "intimates." NCS data also show that injuries sustained by women from marital violence were more frequent, more serious, and more often required medical care. Stets and Straus (1990) showed that more women than men are injured from marital assault in the home and are also injured more often. Homicide data shows that more women than men are victims of marital homicide. From the earliest origins of family violence intervention programs, women victims sought services and protection more often than men. However, these programs often directed their outreach to women, were staffed by women, oriented their services toward women, and in residential programs, could only accommodate women.

However, self-reports reveal a different and more complex pattern. Gender specific participation rates for marital violence are 10 percent in both the 1975 NFVS data and the 1985 resurvey. The participation rates of reported wife-to-husband assaults were slightly higher than husband-to-wife assault rates when data were aggregated over the two surveys, but the prevalence of severe assaults was slightly higher for males. . . . Adjusting the rates for assaults that produced injuries showed marked gender differences; however, males inflicted injury-assaults at a rate of 3.5 per 1,000, compared to 0.6 per 1,000 for women. . . .

Although published research from the NFVS data has emphasized the "equality" of violence participation rates for women and men, Straus et al. (1980) list five reasons to interpret issues of gender equality in marital violence cautiously: (1) the perpetration of "severely" violent acts is greater for men than women; (2) violence by husbands does more damage due to their greater size and physical strength; (3) the offending rate for men is higher than for women — that is, the number of times that men hit women is greater; (4) men often hit women when they are pregnant, posing dangers of miscarriage and infertility; and (5) women remain in marriages and thus at risk for injury more often than men, primarily due to their economic circumstances.

RICHARD J. GELLES & MURRAY A. STRAUS, *INTIMATE VIOLENCE*

250-251, 130-136 (1988)

The physical consequences of wife battering are often obvious—blackened eyes, bruises, and fractures. Many battered women try to hide these physical scars with dark glasses, makeup, or by staying out of sight until the bruises and scars fade. Psychic scars are not visible. They are hidden deep within the battered spirit of the victims of domestic assault.

The actual physical assaults are only one cause of the psychic damage experienced by women. Many battered women explain that waiting and wondering what will set off the next incident is even more damaging than being hit. . . .

The psychologist Lenore Walker explains that women are neither constantly abused nor is abuse inflicted at totally random times. She describes her theory as a "Cycle of Violence." The first stage is the "tension building stage." Verbal abuse, threats, and minor battering incidents occur at this time. Women attempt to calm the batterer during this phase. They may become nurturant or compliant. They try to anticipate every need, wish, and whim. Their goal is to keep the minor incidents from escalating. Yet the battering does escalate at stage two, "the acute battering incident." Walker describes this stage as characterized by the "uncontrollable discharge of tension." Uncontrolled battering is usually brief and followed by the third stage of "kindness and contrite loving behavior." The abusive husband knows he has gone too far and tries to compensate by being kind and loving to his victim. Eventually, the calm is followed by a slow buildup of tension. . . .

It is the full cycle of violence and not just the battering incidents that inflict the psychic and physical damage on battered wives.

Clinicians who have worked with and studied battered women report consistent patterns among their patients and clients. Battered women are generally reported as having poor self-concepts. Battering leaves them feeling worthless, powerless, helpless, and humiliated. Shame and self-blame are two of the most common feelings expressed by battered wives. Many of the women we interviewed in small towns explained that they were so ashamed of being beaten that they would not even call the police for help. . . .

Our Second National Family Violence Survey offered us the unique opportunity to ask a large national sample questions about physical/mental health and emotional conditions. Here, for the first time, we could compare women who lived in violence-free homes with women who endured a wide range of violence at the hands of their partners or mates.

Sadly, the results of our national survey confirmed what we had already expected. The pain and suffering endured by battered women are substantial. Our statistical data bear out the expectation that women who live amidst violence are compromised in nearly every area of their physical and mental health. Moreover, the greater the severity of violence, the greater the chances that a woman's well-being will suffer.

A study by the National Institute of Justice and the Centers for Disease Control and Prevention reports that 22 percent of surveyed women reported that they were victims of rape and/or physical assault by a spouse, cohabiting partner, or date at some time in their lives. *See* Patricia Tjaden & Nancy Thoennes, Full Report of the Prevalence, Incidence, and Consequences of Violence Against

Women: Findings from the National Violence Against Women Survey 2, 12 (1998). Of all women murdered, 30 percent, a number that has remained constant since 1976, are killed by intimate partners. U.S. Dept. of Justice, Bureau of Justice Statistics, Intimate Partner Violence 1 (2000). *See generally* Kapila Juthani, Police Treatment of Domestic Violence and Sexual Abuse: Affirmative Duty to Protect vs. Fourth Amendment Privacy, 59 N.Y.U. Ann. Surv. Am. L. 51 (2003).

As the data from Fagan and Browne indicate, the incidence of violence by women against men is substantial — indeed, approximately equal in rates (if not effects). Studies on this subject are summarized in Linda Kelly, Disabusing the Definition of Domestic Abuse: How Woman Batter Men and the Role of the Feminist State, 30 Fla. St. U. L. Rev. 791 (2003). Professor Kelly notes that studies on the effects of arrest on domestic violence have excluded female offenders, that police are unlikely to arrest women offenders or ask them to leave the home after a domestic violence incident, and that treatment programs are likely to presume that the offender is male. In State v. Wright, 563 S.E.2d 311 (S.C. 2002), the defendant was convicted of aggravated criminal domestic violence. One of the aggravating factors was the difference in the sexes of the victim (a woman) and the defendant (a man). The defendant argued that the "difference in sexes" provision violated equal protection. The South Carolina Supreme Court upheld the conviction, finding that "the differences in gender aggravator is legitimately based upon realistic physiological size and strength differences in men and women." Does that outcome seem consistent with the equal protection decisions above?

JEFFREY FAGAN & ANGELA BROWNE, *VIOLENCE BETWEEN SPOUSES AND INTIMATES: PHYSICAL AGGRESSION BETWEEN WOMEN AND MEN IN INTIMATE RELATIONSHIPS*

3 Understanding and Preventing Violence 115, 225-239 (Albert J. Reiss, Jr. & Jeffrey A. Roth, eds. 1994)

Both research and litigation have led to mandatory arrest policies in some jurisdictions for incidents in which there is probable cause of wife assault. . . .

The premise is that strict and swift application of criminal sanctions in wife assault cases will better protect victims and reduce the likelihood of repeat violence. The empirical basis for these policies derives both from accumulated evidence of the ineffectiveness of nonarrest or informal police dispositions of family violence calls and from experimental evidence of the deterrent effects of arrest compared to nonarrest dispositions.

The Minneapolis Domestic Violence experiment has been the most influential study in the development of policies to increase the likelihood of arrest in misdemeanor wife assault cases. It was designed as a test of the specific deterrent effects of arrest on the recurrence of wife assault and was intended to provide a critical test of the effectiveness of legal sanctions compared to nonlegal, informal police responses. Sherman and Berk (1984) used an experimental design in two Minneapolis police precincts to randomly assign violent family disputes to one of three police responses: arrest, separation of victim and assailant, and advice/mediation. The study was limited to situations in which the assailant was present when the police arrived. During the six-month follow-up, biweekly interviews with victims and reviews of official reports of family violence were collected. Despite the repeated measures on subsequent violence, dichotomous measures of recidivism were used. Neither the severity, the incidence, nor the time to recurrence was reported.

Sherman and Berk (1984) concluded that arrest was more effective in reducing subsequent violence in misdemeanor wife assault cases than other police responses. Those arrested had the lowest recidivism rate based on official (10%) and victim (19%) reports. There was no evidence of differential effects across conditions based on offender characteristics, although within-group differences were found. This led to their recommendation that "police adopt arrest as the favored response to domestic assault on the basis [in the original] of its deterrence power." A subsequent reanalysis offered more qualified support for the deterrent effects of arrest. Findings from the Minneapolis experiment, together with results of nonexperimental studies comparing arrest with other police dispositions of spouse assault cases provided evidence that influenced police policy and legislation nationwide. Thus, for several years, the Minneapolis study provided critical, determining evidence in criminal justice policy development for wife assault.

However, several reviews have cited internal and external validity problems in the Minneapolis experiment that, together with contradictory results from replications in Omaha and Charlotte, North Carolina raise serious questions about the deterrent effects of arrest on repeat spouse assault. In both the Omaha and the Charlotte replications, there were no significant differences in recidivism for any type of police response (advice, warning, citation, arrest) for several measures of recidivism. Moreover, the incidence of recidivism in Charlotte was *highest* for the arrest group, which directly contradicted the results in Minneapolis.

Results of additional replication experiments are available for . . . Colorado Springs, Dade County, and Milwaukee. Only Dade County reported results similar to the original Minneapolis experiment: a reduction in the prevalence of recidivism for arrested suspects in both official records and interviews. Even here, the reduction reported in official records was not statistically significant. In the Charlotte, Colorado Springs, Milwaukee, and Omaha experiments, analysis of official records showed that arrest was associated with higher rates of reoffending; but results based on interview data showed that arrest was associated with lower rates of reoffending. Except for the Colorado Springs experiment, none of the results approached traditional levels of statistical significance.

Reviewing the five replications, together with the original Minneapolis experiment, Sherman (1992) reported that three experiments found that rates of spouse assault escalated among male arrestees who were unemployed or unmarried. The results suggest that arrest has variable effects on different types of people and also people in different types of neighborhoods. Sherman (1992) claims that escalation of spouse assault following arrest was evident in neighborhoods in Milwaukee and Omaha where there were concentrations of poverty and social disorganization, but escalation was not evidence in economically stable areas where unemployment was lower and poverty less acute.

CHRISTOPHER D. MAXWELL, JOEL H. GARNER & JEFFREY A. FAGAN,
*THE EFFECTS OF ARREST ON INTIMATE PARTNER VIOLENCE: NEW
EVIDENCE FROM THE SPOUSE ASSAULT REPLICATION PROGRAM*

National Institute of Justice, July 2001

. . . We studied the deterrent effect of arrest, using an approach that addressed many problems faced by prior efforts to synthesize the results from SARP. . . . [T]he project pooled incidents from the five replication experiments, computed comparable independent and outcome measures from common data intentionally embedded in each experiment, and standardized the experimental designs and statistical models. Using the increased power of the pooled data, this study provides a more consistent, more precise, and less ambiguous estimation of the impact of arrest on intimate partner violence. . . .

Our multisite pooled analysis of the five replication experiments found good evidence of a consistent and direct, though modest, deterrent effect of arrest on aggression by males against their female intimate partners. The victim interviews indicate that the arrest of the suspect and any subsequent confinement, when compared with the alternative interventions collectively, significantly reduced the expected frequency of subsequent aggression by 30 percent. Similarly, arrest may have reduced by a smaller amount the number of times the police responded to subsequent domestic violence incidents involving the same victim and suspect and may have extended the time between the initial incident and the first subsequent incident. . . .

The findings of this research have several implications for policy. First, our findings provide systematic evidence supporting the argument that arresting male batterers may, independent of other criminal justice sanctions and individual processes, reduce subsequent intimate partner violence. The size and statistical significance of the effect of arrest varied depending on whether the subsequent aggression was measured by victim interviews or police records; even so, in all measures (prevalence, frequency, rate, and time-to-failure), arrest was associated with fewer incidents of subsequent intimate partner aggression. This finding exists during the first several days after the experimental incident regardless of the period of detention, as well as beyond 1 year. The arrested suspects were detained an average of 9 days, but the reduction in aggression associated with arrest did not vary by the length of the suspect's detention. Thus, our research finds no empirical support for the argument that arrest may eventually increase the risk for violence against women.

Second, our research showed that a minority of suspects continued to commit intimate partner violence, regardless of the intervention they received. While arrest reduced the proportion of suspects who reoffended and the frequency with which they reoffended, arrest did not prevent all batterers from continuing their violence against their intimate partners. In fact, we found a small number of victims who have chronically aggressive intimate partners. Future research needs to build on preliminary efforts to accurately predict high-rate repeat offenders and to find methods of helping their victims before they are victimized further.

Third, our research showed that a majority of suspects discontinued their aggressive behaviors even without an arrest. This suggests that policies requiring arrest for all suspects may unnecessarily take a community's resources away from identifying and responding to the worst offenders and victims most at risk. Our research has documented the size of the specific deterrent effects of arrest, which, although consistent across sites and time, appeared modest compared with the overall percentage of suspects desisting from intimate partner violence. Although there may be other benefits from policies requiring arrest that this research has not measured (including general deterrence), there are also likely costs of using arrests every time the police respond to an incident of intimate partner violence.

3. Legal Alternatives: Criminal Prosecution and Protective Orders

A person who commits assault or battery on a domestic partner may, of course, be prosecuted for that offense, and in some states the fact that the victim is a family member makes the crime more serious. In addition, stalking is an offense in all 50 states, the District of Columbia, and federally, although definitions and penalties vary greatly. While all laws sometimes treat stalking as a felony, in 13 states and the District of Columbia a first stalking offense is always a misdemeanor, though subsequent acts are felonies. Neal Miller, Stalking Laws and Implementation Practices: A National Review for Policymakers and Practitioners 35 (2001) (visited Aug. 23, 2004) *http://www.vaw.umn.edu/ documents/ilj_stalk/iljfinalrpt.html*. This article contains an extensive review of data and issues related to stalking.

Stalking occurs among all populations; however, battered women who have separated from their batterer are especially subject to being stalked. One study reported that, depending on the definition of stalking used, between 13 and 29 percent of a sample of 144 battered women claimed to have been stalked in the six months immediately following separation. Mindy B. Mechanic, Terri L. Weaver & Patricia A. Resick, Intimate Partner Violence and Stalking Behavior: Exploration of Patterns and Correlates of Acutely Battered Women, 15 Violence & Victims 55 (2000). Another study put the rate of domestic violence calls that involved allegations of stalking at 16.5 percent. The National Violence Against Women Survey found that slightly more than half (54 percent) of all stalking is done by current or former intimates or dating partners, with about 60 percent of the victims being women. Patricia Tjaden & Nancy Thoennes, Stalking in America: Findings from the National Violence Against Women Survey, National Institute of Justice/Centers for Disease Control and Prevention: Research in Brief 6, 9 (April 1998).

Not surprisingly, official statistics do not match these self-reported data; they are far lower. Most states do not, in fact, report stalking cases at all, but even when they do, the rates are greatly smaller than self-reported data would suggest. Florida typically reports the most stalking criminal cases, and it reported a total of 704 such offenses in 1999 (down from 920 in 1998). Neal Miller, above at 18.

A recurring problem for prosecutors is the unwillingness of victims of domestic violence to pursue charges against their assailants both here and in other countries. On efforts to secure their cooperation, *see* Thomas L. Kirsch II, Problems in Domestic Violence: Should Victims Be Forced to Participate in the Prosecution of their Abusers?, 7 Wm. & Mary J. Women & L. 383 (2001) (examining reasons why domestic abuse victims decline to pursue prosecution, tactics of prosecutors in Lake County, Indiana, to secure cooperation, and costs and benefits of forcing participation by victims). *See also* Heather Fleniken Cochran, Improving Prosecution of Battering Partners: Some Innovations in the Law of Evidence, 7 Tex. J. Women & L. 89, 107-08 (1997); Brooks Holland, Using Excited Utterances to Prosecute Domestic Violence in New York: The Door Opens Wide, or Just a Crack?, 8 Cardozo Women's L.J. 171 (2002); Louise Ellison, Prosecuting Domestic Violence without Victim Participation, 65 Mod. L. Rev. 834 (2002).

Perhaps the most widely used judicial response to domestic violence is the protective order. Protective orders are civil orders restraining the offender from conduct that endangers the person seeking the order. Such orders are available in every, or virtually every, state for threats to the safety of a domestic partner, and "domestic partner" and "family" are often defined broadly. The possible breadth of coverage is illustrated by the California Domestic Violence Prevention Act, §6200 et seq., which defines "domestic violence" as abuse against a spouse, former spouse, cohabitant, former cohabitant, a person with whom the respondent is having or has had a dating or engagement relationship, a person with whom the respondent has had a child or presumed child, or any other person related by consanguinity or affinity within the second degree. Cal. Fam. Code §6211. Other statutes may not reach quite so far, but most reach cohabitant or former cohabitant relationships as well as parties to marriage and divorce. For a comprehensive review of state and territorial laws governing protective orders, *see* Catherine F. Klein & Leslye E. Orloff, Providing Legal Protection for Battered Women: An Analysis of State Statutes and Case Law, 21 Hofstra L. Rev. 801 (1993).

While their application to married persons is now largely uncontroversial, the availability of protective orders to cohabitants varies. Many statutes speak in terms of "residing together" or "living together as spouses," opening the question of the extent of coresidence required. Among the pertinent factors are the duration of the relationship, frequency of contact, financial interdependence, the existence of common children, and household arrangements. The Wisconsin statute uses the term *household*; the Wisconsin Court of Appeals held that this term did not reach an unmarried couple who stayed together only during summer vacations. Petrowsky v. Krause, 588 N.W.2d 318 (Wis. App. 1998). The court noted that the domestic violence statute also uses the word *reside* to define the actions of a household member and found that, both as a matter of the plain (dictionary) meaning and in legal use, the term *reside* implies a continuous living arrangement, which did not apply in this case. *See* Yankoskie v. Lenker, 526 A.2d 185 (N.J. Super. App. Div. 1990). Protection for same-sex coresidents was provided in 34 states, Puerto Rico, and the District of Columbia as of 1993. By contrast, only a dozen jurisdictions extend protection to persons in a dating relationship, as California does. Klein & Orloff, 21 Hofstra L. Rev. at 835.

Emergency protective orders can ordinarily be issued ex parte in cases of immediate danger of domestic violence and may include provisions excluding the respondent from entering the petitioner's home and any other appropriate relief. *See* Utah Code Ann. §30-6-4.2 (1998):

(2) A court may grant the following relief without notice in an order for protection or a modification issued ex parte:
(a) enjoin the respondent from threatening to commit or committing domestic violence or abuse against the petitioner and any designated family or household member;
(b) prohibit the respondent from harassing, telephoning, contacting, or otherwise communicating with the petitioner, directly or indirectly;
(c) order that the respondent is excluded from the petitioner's residence and its premises, and order the respondent to stay away from the residence, school, or place or employment of the petitioner . . . ;
(d) upon a finding that the respondent's use or possession of a weapon may pose a serious threat of harm to the petitioner, prohibit the respondent from purchasing, using, or possessing a firearm or other weapon . . . ;
(e) order possession and use of an automobile and other essential effects . . . ;
(f) grant temporary custody of any minor child to the petitioner;
(g) order any further relief . . . necessary to provide for the safety and welfare of the petitioner and any designated family or household member. . . .

See also Cal. Fam. Code §§6321-6322 (1994). More than one-half of the states (29) authorize civil protection orders against stalking, in addition to laws in all states providing for orders against domestic violence. Violation of a stalking protective order is a crime in 24 of those states and may be criminal contempt in others. Neal Miller, above at 38.

When an emergency order is entered, a hearing must be held within some reasonably brief time period (usually five to ten days). The Utah Code provides that a court may order any of the forms of relief appropriate to an ex parte order, but further requires that the order include separate sections for violations that will be criminal offenses (those listed in subsections (a) through (e) above) and those that will be civil offenses (only (f) and (g) of those set out). Violation of a criminal provision is defined as a class A misdemeanor; the civil portion is enforceable through contempt. Utah Code Ann. §30-6-4.2(5) (1998).

The ex parte procedure for issuing protective orders was challenged unsuccessfully on procedural due process grounds in Kampf v. Kampf, 603 N.W.2d 295 (Mich. App. 1999). The court analyzed the issue as follows:

There is no procedural due process defect in obtaining an emergency order of protection without notice to a respondent when the petition for the emergency protection order is supported by affidavits that demonstrate exigent circumstances justifying entry of an emergency order without prior notice, see, e.g., Mitchell v. WT Grant, 416 U.S. 600 (1974), and where there are appropriate provisions for notice and an opportunity to be heard after the order is issued. Here, subsection 12 permits a court to issue an *ex parte* order only if it clearly appears from specific facts shown by verified complaint, written motion, or affidavit that *immediate and irreparable injury, loss, or damage will result from the delay required to effectuate notice or that the notice will itself precipitate adverse action before a personal protection order can be issued* [emphasis added].

Further, [the statute] gives a respondent the right to bring a motion to rescind a PPO within fourteen days of being served with notice or receiving actual notice of the PPO, and requires the court to schedule a hearing on the motion within five or fourteen days, depending on whether the PPO enjoins the respondent from purchasing and possessing a firearm. Clearly, the procedural safeguards employed under the statute are sufficient to meet respondent's due process challenge.

603 N.W.2d at 299.

Gonzalez v. City of Castle Rock, 366 F.3d 1093 (10th Cir. 2004), presents the question of whether a refusal by police to enforce a protective order creates a cause of action under 42 U.S.C. §1983 when the protected person is harmed by the party against whom the order is entered. In 1999 Ms. Gonzales obtained a restraining order limiting her husband's ability to have contact with her and their daughters, aged ten, nine and seven. Shortly after the issuance of the permanent restraining order, the children disappeared from the front of the Gonzalez home. Ms. Gonzalez suspected (correctly) that her husband had taken the children, and called the Castle Rock Police Department. Two officers came to the home, where she showed them a copy of the restraining order and asked that it be enforced and her children returned to her immediately. The Officers "stated that there was nothing they could do about the TRO and suggested that Plaintiff call the Police Department again if the children did not return home by 10:00 p.m." Subsequently, Ms. Gonzalez heard from her husband that he was at an amusement park with the children. She called the police, who told her to wait until 8 p.m. At 8 p.m. she was told to wait until 10 p.m., a pattern which continued all evening. At approximately 3:20 a.m., Mr. Gonzales arrived at the Castle Rock police station in his truck. He got out and opened fire on the station with a semi-automatic handgun he had purchased soon after abducting his daughters. He was shot dead at the scene. The police found the bodies of the three girls, who had been murdered by their father earlier that evening, in the cab of the truck.

Ms. Gonzalez brought a 1983 action on behalf of herself and her deceased daughters against the City of Castle Rock, Colorado, and three Castle Rock police officers. She claimed her due process rights were violated by the officers' failure to enforce the restraining order against her husband. She also alleged the city maintained a custom and policy of failing to respond properly to complaints of domestic restraining order violations and tolerated the nonenforcement of such protective orders by police officers, resulting in the reckless disregard of a person's right to police protection granted by such orders.

The district court dismissed the case, holding that there was no violation of either substantive or procedural due process. On appeal, a panel of the Tenth Circuit affirmed the district court's dismissal of Ms. Gonzales's substantive due process claim and held that the restraining order, coupled with the Colorado statute mandating the enforcement of such orders, established a protected property interest in the enforcement of the restraining order which could not be taken away by the government without procedural due process. The Tenth Circuit, en banc, affirmed the panel's decision regarding the procedural due process claim.

For the purposes of this decision, the en banc court assumed that the issue was not whether Ms. Gonzalez had a substantive right under the Constitution to receive government protection. While Ms. Gonzalez had argued that she and her daughters had an inherent constitutional right to police protection against harm from her husband, the Tenth Circuit panel opinion noted that the Supreme Court had held in DeShaney v. Winnebago County Dep't of Soc. Servs., 489 U.S. 189 (1989), that the Constitution itself does not require a state to protect its citizens from third-party harm, and Ms. Gonzales's case does not fall within the narrow "danger creation" exception arising out of *DeShaney*. The critical issue was whether the state of Colorado created in Ms. Gonzales an entitlement that cannot be taken away from her without procedural due process, and if so, whether the officers' arbitrary denial of that entitlement was procedurally unfair.

The majority concluded that the Colorado restraining order statute did create an cognizable entitlement.

> In order for an entitlement to exist, the underlying state law or order must contain particularized standards or criteria [guiding] the State's decision makers. *If the decision maker* is not required to base its decisions on objective and defined criteria, but instead *can deny the requested relief for any constitutionally permissible reason or for no reason at all, the State has not created a constitutionally protected interest.*
>
> Conversely, "the use of explicitly mandatory language, in connection with the establishment of specified substantive predicates to limit discretion, forces a conclusion that the state has created a [protected] interest."

366 F.3d at 1102. The Colorado statute used explicit mandatory language, and the majority concluded that that, contrary to the defendants' claim, did not vest discretion in officers to decide whether to enforce an existing order but rather mandated arrest or issuance of an arrest warrant for a restrained party when there was probable cause to believe the party had violated or was attempting to violate any provision of the restraining order.

Accordingly, the majority recognized a specific government benefit provided by state law in the enforcement of the objective terms of the court order protecting her and her children against her abusive husband, noting that such an entitlement fits within the other types of entitlements acknowledged by the Supreme Court and is properly deemed a property interest such as a free education, continued utility service, and welfare or disability benefits.

The next question was whether Ms. Gonzalez was denied an appropriate hearing with respect to her property interest in enforcement of the restraining order. The majority held that she was:

> A meaningful hearing protects an individual's use and possession of property from arbitrary encroachment [and] minimize[s] substantively unfair or mistaken deprivations of property. . . . So viewed, the prohibition against the deprivation of property without due process of law reflects the high value, embedded in our constitutional and political history, that we place on a person's right to enjoy what is his, free of governmental interference.
>
> Based on the allegations in Ms. Gonzales' complaint, she did not receive any process whatsoever prior to the deprivation of her interest in enforcement of the restraining order. Instead, the officers repeatedly ignored and refused her requests for enforcement.

366 F.3d at 1111. The majority also held that the individual police officers were entitled to qualified immunity, and that the city was not entitled to qualified immunity.

NOTE: FEDERAL LEGISLATION

Although not directed specifically at domestic violence, the Violence Against Women Act of 1994 (VAWA), Pub. L. No. 103-322, codified as amended in various sections of 8, 18, and 42 U.S.C. (1994), provides federal civil and criminal remedies for victims of violence motivated by gender-based animus. The Act creates a federal crime for physical injury to a "spouse or intimate partner" while in interstate travel, which was upheld against constitutional attack in United States v. Bailey, 112 F.3d 758 (4th Cir. 1997). VAWA also authorized the creation of a hotline for domestic violence victims and authorized grants for battered women's shelters.

The broadest provision of VAWA, 42 U.S.C. §13981, declares that all persons have "the right to be free of crimes of violence motivated by gender" and creates a federal cause of action, including compensatory and punitive damages, for victims of such offenses. Federal authority for this legislation rested on the Commerce Clause and §5 of the Fourteenth Amendment. The question whether there was a sufficient nexus between gender-based violence and effect on interstate commerce to satisfy the requirements of United States v. Lopez, 514 U.S. 549 (1995), and justify congressional authority was quickly raised.

In United States v. Morrison, 529 U.S. 598 (2000), the Supreme Court held that Congress lacked authority under the commerce clause or otherwise to enact the civil rights remedy. The Court expressed concern about the extent to which the assumption of congressional authority over domestic violence impaired state authority over family law issues. Those challenging the statute argued that upholding VAWA would allow Congress to assert authority generally over domestic relations issues, as VAWA itself had already done by overriding spousal tort immunity and marital rape exemptions recognized by state law. Justice O'Connor's questioning during oral argument explored whether upholding VAWA under the Commerce Clause would entail congressional power to legislate a comprehensive federal domestic relations code dealing with marriage, divorce, alimony, and child support. Those supporting the statute, on the other hand, noted that VAWA itself expressly disclaimed any federal authority over marriage and divorce.

For a discussion of Morrison and its implications for VAWA, on the one hand, and state authority over family law matters, on the other, see Sally F. Goldfarb, "No Civilized System of Justice": The Fate of the Violence Against Women Act, 102 W. Va. L. Rev. 499 (2000).

On VAWA generally, see Sally Goldfarb, The Civil Rights Remedy of the Violence Against Women Act: Legislative History, Policy Implications and Litigation Strategy, 4 J.L. & Pol'y 391 (1996); Jenny Rivera, The Violence Against Women Act and the Construction of Multiple Consciousness in the Civil Rights and Feminist Movements, 4 J.L. & Pol'y 463 (1996); Reva B. Siegel, "The Rule of Love": Wife Beating as Prerogative and Privacy, 105 Yale L.J. 2117 (1996).

State and federal laws have also increasingly addressed the availability of firearms to domestic violence offenders. The Federal Gun Control Act of 1994, 18 U.S.C.A. §922(g)(8) (West Supp. 1996), adopts a number of provisions related to firearms for persons subject to state protective orders, including receipt of any firearm shipped in interstate or foreign commerce. However, the statute does not cover relationships where the parties have never resided together. See 18 U.S.C. §921(a)(32), defining "intimate partner" (the class to be protected) in terms of spouse, former spouse, parent, or "an individual who cohabitates or has cohabitated. . . ." A number of states have enacted statutes prohibiting persons subject to a protective order from owning or possessing a firearm as long as the order is in effect. *E.g.*, Cal. Fam. Code §6389(a) (West 1996); Haw. Rev. Stat. §124-7(f) (1995). Some codes direct law enforcement agencies to enforce prohibitions on weapons ownership either through denying applications to purchase firearms or seizure of firearms. Fla. Stat. Ann. §790.065(2)(c) (West 1996) (applications); Utah Code Ann. §53-5-704(f) (1995) (concealed weapons permits); Haw. Rev. Stat. §134-7(f) (1995). A review of the relationship between domestic violence fatality and the availability of guns, together with questions concerning the effectiveness of enforcement of federal legislation are raised in Sharon L. Gold, Note, Why Are Victims of Domestic Violence Still Dying at the Hands of Their Abusers? Filling the Gap in State Domestic Violence Gun Laws, 91 Ky. L.J. 935 (2002-2003).

A different approach is found in federal welfare reform and the Personal Responsibility and Work Opportunity Reconciliation Act of 1996 (PRWORA), Pub. L. No. 104-193, which gives states the option of granting Temporary Assistance to Needy Families (TANF) benefits to victims of domestic violence while exempting them from some of the Act's requirements. PRWORA allows states to screen applicants for TANF for domestic violence, make appropriate referrals, and, as appropriate, grant individuals good cause waivers for as long as necessary from the two-year time limit before work is required, the five-year lifetime limit on benefits, residency requirements, and child support cooperation requirements.

4. *Spousal Tort Liability*

BURNS V. BURNS

518 So. 2d 1205 (Miss. 1988)

PRATHER, J. At issue in this appeal is the question of continuance of the judicially imposed rule of interspousal immunity in Mississippi. The Circuit Court of Alcorn, on a motion for judgment on the pleadings, dismissed a complaint filed by Betty Burns, against her husband, Erit Lamar Burns, for an alleged assault and battery. The court ruled that the complaint was barred by the doctrine of interspousal immunity. This Court reverses the dismissal of that complaint.

The only facts before the Court are that on August 1, 1984, Erit Burns allegedly assaulted and battered his wife Betty Burns. . . .

Interspousal tort immunity is an ancient common law doctrine founded on the theoretical unity of husband and wife. 1 W. Blackstone, Commentaries 433.

* * *

A survey of all states and the District of Columbia reveals that at present 31 states have fully abrogated the doctrine of interspousal immunity. Eight states have abrogated the rule for vehicular torts; four states have abrogated the rule for intentional torts; one state for all personal injury actions; and one state where death of either spouse intervenes between tortuous [sic] acts and commencement of suit. One state has immunity imposed by statute while five states plus the District of Columbia continue to acknowledge and sustain the doctrine. One state has a cause of action but no remedy to enforce it.

The forty-four states abrogating the doctrine recognize that reasons for the common law rule no longer exist. Three reasons traditionally assigned as justification for the doctrine of interspousal immunity are: (A) the legal unity of the husband and wife recognized at common law; (B) the promotion of peace and harmony in the home; and (C) the avoidance of fraudulent or collusive claims. The common law unity concept which prohibited suits between spouses for any claim is no longer viable [after passage of the constitutional and statutory provisions referred to above].

. . . When the Constitution and Legislature emancipated women from the disability of coverture, they necessarily made her a legal person, and made her sui juris, capable of attending to her own affairs to the same extent that she could if she had never been married at all. . . . Every person who is sui juris has the right under the law to a redress for a personal injury. [This legislation] does not merely place the wife on an equality with her husband, but it places her on an equality with a single woman, and gives her all the rights that she would have had under the same facts if she were single instead of married. . . .

The ideal that maintenance of interspousal immunity will promote the public interest in domestic tranquility is wholly illusory. If one spouse commits against the other an act which, but for the immunity, would constitute a tort, the desired state of matrimonial tranquility is necessarily destroyed. But common sense suggests the peace is destroyed by the act of the offending spouse, not the lawsuit filed by the other. Beyond that, maintenance of the immunity surely cannot prevent injured spouses from harboring ill will and anger. . . .

The third argument espoused in support of the doctrine is that to allow such suits would encourage fraud and collusion. The Supreme Court of California, in abrogating the interspousal immunity rule reasoned:

> It would be a sad commentary on the law if we were to admit that the judicial processes are so ineffective that we must deny relief to a person otherwise entitled simply because in some future case a litigant may be guilty of fraud or collusion. Once that concept were accepted, then all causes of action should be abolished. Our legal system is not that ineffective.

Klein v. Klein, 58 Cal. 2d 692, 26 Cal. Rptr. 102, 376 P.2d 70 (1962).

HILL V. HILL

415 So. 2d 20 (Fla. 1982)

OVERTON, J. . . . We hold that the protection of the family unit and its resources requires us to . . . reject a change in the interspousal immunity doctrine at this time. In doing so, however, we emphasize that the trial judge in a dissolution proceeding has authority to require an abusive spouse to pay necessary medical expenses and the authority to consider any permanent injury or disfigurement or loss of earning capacity from such abuse when setting alimony.

Interspousal tort immunity is a judicial doctrine established to protect the family unit. Historically, under Biblical, Roman, and English common law, the "family" has had certain responsibilities, obligations, and special protections. . . . For example, we acknowledge the obligations of spouses for child support, alimony, and, in the event of marriage dissolution, the fair division of property acquired during marriage. We also protect homestead property from creditors, prohibit garnishment of head of family wages, and safeguard the interest of surviving family members in a decedent spouse's estate.

The family continues to be an unofficial sociological governmental structure necessary and vital to our free, independent society. . . . Protection of the family unit is a significant public policy and we are greatly concerned by any intrusion that adversely affects the family relationship or the family resources. That is the reason we rejected abolition of the interspousal immunity doctrine. . . . We emphasize, however, that the purpose of the doctrine is to protect family harmony and resources, not to shield the wrongful acts of a spouse . . . and not to protect insurance companies. . . .

Our concern is in what manner the abolition of this common law doctrine will affect the family unit, including children and the family resources. We conclude that the abolition would be detrimental to the family as a whole.

We choose not to place lawyers, judges, litigation costs, and the full trappings of an adversary tort system into a family dispute while the parties remain married. The ramifications of that type of action are not in any way conducive to reconciliation.

NOTES AND QUESTIONS

1. The history and demise of interspousal tort immunity in this country are reviewed and analyzed in Carl Tobias, Interspousal Tort Immunity in America, 23 Ga. L. Rev. 359 (1989). The seminal article on this topic is William E. McCurdy, Torts Between Persons in Domestic Relation, 43 Harv. L. Rev. 1030 (1930).

2. *Hill*, which recognized and rejected the general trend, was considered a case of great importance. Appearances were made by the counsel for the Academy of Florida Trial Lawyers, Legal Services of Greater Miami, the National Organization of Women and Florida Now, the Florida Association of Women Lawyers, the Florida Women's Political Caucus, the American Civil Liberties Union, and the University of Miami School of Law, as well as for the parties. What makes the issue so important?

3. In McGuire v. McGuire, above, page 63, the court relied on a principle of family privacy to explain its refusal to order a husband to provide his wife with a certain measure of financial support. Does that principle also support the conclusion reached in *Hill*?

4. Does it follow from abolition of tort immunity that the standards for intentional or negligent tortious conduct will be the same for spouses as for

strangers? In S. A. V. v. K. G. V., 708 S.W.2d 651 (Mo. 1986), the court indicated that abolition did not lead to liability in every "unwanted kiss and rolling pin" case. *See also* Merenoff v. Merenoff, 388 A.2d 951 (N.J. 1978); Lewis v. Lewis, 351 N.E.2d 526 (Mass. 1976). Why should it not?

5. The Mississippi and Florida courts disagree sharply concerning the desirability and adequacy of relying on divorce proceedings to provide a remedy for spousal torts. This issue, and its procedural implications, will be considered in Chapter 6.

PROBLEMS

1. Joan Arguello is injured when her husband, Ruben, loses control of an electric hedge trimmer he is using to trim bushes. She sues Ruben for the rather serious injuries suffered. Ruben owns their home and carries umbrella insurance for negligently caused injuries. Will Joan's suit be barred by interspousal tort immunity? Should it be?

2. Linda Schwartz has been trying to get her husband, Ralph, to trim the hedges for a year and a half. In a fit of anger caused by his unwillingness to help around the house, Linda throws a rock at Ralph as he sits on the deck with a beer. Unfortunately, the rock strikes Ralph in the eye, causing loss of vision in that eye. Ralph sues Linda for the injury. What arguments might Ralph make if state law has to this point continued to recognized interspousal immunity?

D. REPRODUCTIVE CHOICE WITHIN THE FAMILY

The following materials deal with reproductive decision making within the family. The first section summarizes Supreme Court doctrine announcing an interest in privacy with respect to procreative choice and defining the extent to which the state can limit that liberty interest. Here, the question is allocation of authority between the state and the mother (whose interests are usually assumed to be identical to those of the father). The second section addresses the question of who has the authority to make reproductive decisions within the family—that is, between the mother and the father. These materials raise once again difficult problems in conceptualizing the family and in defining its internal relations and its relations with the state.

1. Reproductive Rights and Interests

The body of doctrine with which we are concerned here begins with Griswold v. Connecticut, 381 U.S. 479 (1965), and the Supreme Court's recognition of a constitutionally protected interest in privacy. Appellant Griswold, the executive director of Planned Parenthood of Connecticut, sought to have declared unconstitutional a Connecticut statute making it an offense to use, or assist another in using, "any drug, medicinal article, or instrument for the purpose of preventing conception." It is impossible to capture the flavor of this case briefly, but for our purpose it is enough to say that a majority of the Court held the law unconstitutional. Justice Douglas, writing for the Court, concluded that specific constitutional guarantees generated "penumbras," which, although not mentioned in specific terms by the Constitution, nonetheless were entitled to constitutional protection. With respect to this case, Justice Douglas found that a number of specific guarantees—including the First Amendment's protection of speech and belief; the Third Amendment's prohibition against the quartering during peacetime of soldiers in any house; the Fourth Amendment's protection of persons, houses, and property against unreasonable search and seizure; and the Fifth Amendment privilege against self-incrimination—created zones of privacy that are entitled to constitutional protection. This right to privacy, Justice Douglas concluded, reached the law forbidding the *use* of contraceptives.

Such a law cannot stand in light of the familiar principle, so often applied by this Court, that a "governmental purpose to control or prevent activities constitutionally subject to state regulation may not be achieved by means which sweep unnecessarily broadly and thereby invade the area of protected freedoms." NAACP v. Alabama, 377 U.S. 288, 307. Would we allow the police to search the sacred precincts of marital bedrooms for telltale signs of the use of contraceptives? The very idea is repulsive to the notions of privacy surrounding the marriage relationship.

We deal with a right of privacy older than the Bill of Rights—older than our political parties, older than our school system. Marriage is a coming together for better or for worse, hopefully enduring, and intimate to the degree of being sacred. It is an association that promotes a way of life, not causes; a harmony in living, not political faiths; a bilateral loyalty, not commercial or social projects. Yet it is an association for as noble a purpose as any involved in our prior decisions.

Justice Goldberg, joined by Chief Justice Warren and Justice Brennan, concurred. They agreed that the concept of liberty in the Fourteenth Amendment due process clause was not confined to the specific terms of the Bill of Rights and, moreover, that it "embraced the right of marital privacy."

Roe v. Wade, 410 U.S. 113 (1973), presented the Court a further opportunity to define the scope of, and state power with respect to, the privacy right. The appellant was a single woman residing in Texas who sought a declaratory judgment that the Texas criminal abortion statutes were unconstitutional on their face. She alleged that she was unmarried, pregnant, indigent, and could not secure a legal abortion because her life was not threatened by her pregnancy.

Justice Blackmun's opinion for the Court has generated perhaps more comment than any other Supreme Court decision. His argument includes the following elements: The right to privacy is broad enough to encompass a woman's decision whether or not to terminate her pregnancy; that right is a "fundamental right" that can be restricted by the state only when it can show a "compelling interest" and when its regulations are "narrowly drawn to express only the legitimate state interests at stake."

Justice Blackmun then applied this analytical framework to the Texas statute. The state had argued that a fetus is a "person" and therefore its protection under the Fourteenth Amendment was a compelling state interest. Justice Blackmun found no consensus in either state laws or other sources for the proposition that the "unborn" are persons in the whole sense and held that Texas could not, by adopting one of the various theories of life, generally override the rights of the pregnant woman.

He did find that the state had two valid interests. One lay in protecting potential human life and the other in preserving the mother's health. Either of these might become compelling at various points in the pregnancy. Justice Blackmun's opinion indicates that a state interest in protecting human life is compelling at viability: the point at which a fetus could be expected to live outside the mother's womb. Consequently, the state could, if it chose, prohibit abortions after viability (which was placed at the beginning of the third trimester) except when termination was necessary to preserve the life or health of the mother. With respect to governmental concern for maternal health, the "compelling point" was placed at the end of the first trimester, based on evidence that until that point, mortality in abortion may be less than mortality in normal childbirth. However, any state regulation predicated on maternal health must be closely related to that goal and cannot sweep more broadly than that purpose justifies.

Justice Rehnquist dissented. He could not agree that the right of privacy recognized in earlier cases included a right to terminate a pregnancy, nor that any liberty interest the mother might have in consensual transactions was entitled to the high level of protection accorded fundamental rights.

Entirely predictably, Roe v. Wade was followed by a wide variety of state, and some federal, statutes seeking to define (or limit) the conditions under which women could obtain abortions. Throughout the opinions addressing the permutations of abortion legislation, the continued viability of Roe v. Wade itself was a recurring theme. The much-anticipated, or much-feared, overruling of *Roe* did not, however, occur. In Planned Parenthood of Southeastern Pennsylvania v. Casey, 505 U.S. 833 (1992), Justice O'Connor announced the judgment of the Court and concluded, after lengthy consideration of the policy embodied in *stare decisis*, that *Roe* should not be entirely abandoned. More particularly, Justice O'Connor concluded that *Roe* has not proved unworkable and that subsequent decisions had not implicitly or explicitly left *Roe*'s doctrine a "mere survivor of obsolete constitutional thinking." On the contrary, she observed, *Roe* can be seen as an exemplar not only of the liberty interest recognized in *Griswold* but as consistent with principles of personal autonomy and bodily integrity reflected in recent decisions limiting governmental power to mandate medical treatment.

Justice O'Connor's opinion holds that the basic decision in *Roe*—that is, recognizing a constitutional liberty to some freedom in deciding whether to terminate a pregnancy—will not be repudiated. In addition, the opinion reaffirms the proposition that, before viability, a woman has the right to choose to terminate her pregnancy. However, the opinion does reconsider some parts of the trimester test employed in Roe v. Wade.

We reject the trimester framework, which we do not consider to be part of the essential holding of *Roe*. . . . The trimester framework suffers from these basic flaws: in its formulation it misconceives the nature of the pregnant woman's interest; and in practice it undervalues the State's interest in potential life, as recognized in *Roe*.

As our jurisprudence relating to all liberties save perhaps abortion has recognized, not every law which makes a right more difficult to exercise is, ipso facto, an infringement of that right. . . . The fact that a law which serves a valid purpose, one not designed to strike at the right itself, has the incidental effect of making it more difficult or more expensive to procure an abortion cannot be enough to invalidate it. Only where state regulation imposes an undue burden on a woman's ability to make this decision does the power of the State reach into the heart of the liberty protected by the Due Process Clause. . . .

A finding of an undue burden is a shorthand for the conclusion that a state regulation has the purpose or effect of placing a substantial obstacle in the path of a woman seeking an abortion of a nonviable fetus. A statute with this purpose is invalid because the means chosen by the State to further the interest in potential life must be calculated to inform the woman's free choice, not hinder it. And a statute which, while furthering the interest in potential life or some other valid state interest, has the effect of placing a substantial obstacle in the path of a woman's choice cannot be considered a permissible means of serving its legitimate ends. To the extent that the opinions of the Court or of individual Justices use the undue burden standard in a manner that is inconsistent with this analysis, we set out what in our view should be the controlling standard. Understood another way, we answer the question, left open in previous opinions discussing the undue burden formulation, whether a law designed to further the State's interest in fetal life which imposes an undue burden on the woman's decision before fetal viability could be constitutional. The answer is no.

Some guiding principles should emerge. What is at stake is the woman's right to make the ultimate decision, not a right to be insulated from all others in doing so. Regulations which do no more than create a structural mechanism by which the State, or the parent or guardian of a minor, may express profound respect for the life of the unborn are permitted, if they are not a substantial obstacle to the woman's exercise of the right to choose. Unless it has that effect on her right of choice, a state measure designed to persuade her to choose childbirth over abortion will be upheld if reasonably related to that goal. Regulations designed to foster the health of a woman seeking an abortion are valid if they do not constitute an undue burden.

2.   *Reproductive Choice Within the Family*

PLANNED PARENTHOOD OF CENTRAL MISSOURI V. DANFORTH

428 U.S. 52 (1976)

BLACKMUN, J. This case is a logical and anticipated corollary to Roe v. Wade, 410 U.S. 113 (1973), and Doe v. Bolton, 410 U.S. 179 (1973), for it raises issues secondary to those that were then before the Court. Indeed, some of the questions now presented were forecast and reserved in *Roe* and *Doe*. . . .

The spouse's consent. Section 3(3) requires the prior written consent of the spouse of the woman seeking an abortion during the first 12 weeks of pregnancy, unless "the abortion is certified by a licensed physician to be necessary in order to preserve the life of the mother."

The appellees defend §3(3) on the ground that it was enacted in the light of the General Assembly's "perception of marriage as an institution," and that any major change in family status is a decision to be made jointly by the marriage partners. Reference is made to an abortion's possible effect on the woman's childbearing potential. . . . Reference is made to adultery and bigamy as criminal offenses; to Missouri's general requirement that for an adoption of a child born in wedlock the consent of both parents is necessary; to similar joint-consent requirements imposed by a number of States with respect to artificial insemination and the legitimacy of children so conceived; to the laws of two States requiring spousal consent for voluntary sterilization; and to the long-established requirement of spousal consent for the effective disposition of an interest in real property. It is argued that "(r)ecognizing that the consent of both parties is generally necessary . . . to begin a family, the legislature has determined that a change in the family structure set in motion by mutual consent should be terminated only by mutual consent," and that what the legislature did was to exercise its inherent policymaking power "for what was believed to be in the best interests of all the people of Missouri."

The appellants on the other hand, contend that §3(3) obviously is designed to afford the husband the right unilaterally to prevent or veto an abortion, whether or not he is the father of the fetus, and that this not only violates *Roe* and *Doe* but is also in conflict with other decided cases. They also refer to the situation where the husband's consent cannot be obtained because he cannot be located. And they assert that §3(3) is vague and overbroad.

In *Roe* and *Doe* we specifically reserved decision on the question whether a requirement for consent by the father of the fetus, by the spouse, or by the parents, or a parent, of an unmarried minor, may be constitutionally imposed. We now hold that the State may not constitutionally require the consent of the spouse, as is specified under §3(3) of the Missouri Act, as a condition for abortion during the first 12 weeks of pregnancy. We thus agree with the dissenting judge in the present case, and with the courts whose decisions are cited above, that the State cannot "delegate to a spouse a veto power which the state itself is absolutely and totally prohibited from exercising during the first trimester of pregnancy." Clearly, since the State cannot regulate or proscribe abortion during the first stage, when the physician and his patient make that decision, the State cannot delegate authority to any particular person, even the spouse, to prevent abortion during that same period.

We are not unaware of the deep and proper concern and interest that a devoted and protective husband has in his wife's pregnancy and in the growth and development of the fetus she is carrying. Neither has this Court failed to appreciate the importance of the marital relationship in our society. *See*, e.g., Griswold v. Connecticut, 381 U.S. 479, 486 (1965); Maynard v. Hill, 125 U.S., 190, 211 (1888). Moreover, we recognize that the decision whether to undergo or to forgo an abortion may have profound effects on the future of any marriage, effects that are both physical and mental, and possibly deleterious. Notwithstanding these factors, we cannot hold that the State has the constitutional authority to give the spouse unilaterally the ability to prohibit the wife from terminating her pregnancy, when the State itself lacks that right.

It seems manifest that, ideally, the decision to terminate a pregnancy should be one concurred in by both the wife and her husband. No marriage may be viewed as harmonious or successful if the marriage partners are fundamentally divided on so important and vital an issue. But it is difficult to believe that the goal of fostering mutuality and trust in a marriage, and of strengthening the marital relationship and the marriage institution, will be achieved by giving the husband a veto power exercisable for any reason whatsoever or for no reason at all. Even if the State had the ability to delegate to the husband a power it itself could not exercise, it is not at all likely that such action would further, as the District Court majority phrased it, the "interest of the state in protecting the mutuality of decisions vital to the marriage relationship."

We recognize, of course, that when a woman, with the approval of her physician but without the approval of her husband, decides to terminate her pregnancy, it could be said that she is acting unilaterally. The obvious fact is that when the wife and the husband disagree on this decision, the view of only one of the two marriage partners can prevail. Inasmuch as it is the woman who physically bears the child and who is the more directly and immediately affected by the pregnancy, as between the two, the balance weighs in her favor.

We conclude that §3(3) of the Missouri Act is inconsistent with the standards enunciated in Roe v. Wade, and is unconstitutional. It is therefore unnecessary for us to consider the appellants' additional challenges to §3(3) based on vagueness and overbreadth.

NOTES AND QUESTIONS

1. Could the Court have left *Roe* standing without invalidating the spousal consent provision in *Danforth*? Could, for example, the Court have said that *Roe* involved only the claim of a single woman and could not, therefore, have considered the claims of her husband?

2. The majority understands the issue in terms of a zero-sum game involving the husband and wife. Is there no intermediate ground? Suppose that the husband brought an action to enjoin his wife from having an abortion. Suppose he conceded that the marriage might not survive his action, but announced a readiness to take sole custody of the child upon delivery, if the mother so desired. Does *Danforth* control the result of that proceeding?

PLANNED PARENTHOOD OF SOUTHEASTERN PENNSYLVANIA V. CASEY

505 U.S. 833 (1992)

[Other portions of this opinion are discussed at pages 142-143, above.]

Section 3209 of Pennsylvania's abortion law provides, except in cases of medical emergency, that no physician shall perform an abortion on a married woman without receiving a signed statement from the woman that she has notified her spouse that she is about to undergo an abortion. The woman has the option of providing an alternative signed statement certifying that her husband is not the man who impregnated her; that her husband could not be located; that the pregnancy is the result of spousal sexual assault which she has reported; or that the woman believes that notifying her husband will cause him or someone else to inflict bodily injury upon her. A physician who performs an abortion on a married woman without receiving the appropriate signed statement will have his or her license revoked, and is liable to the husband for damages.

The District Court heard the testimony of numerous expert witnesses, and made detailed findings of fact regarding the effect of this statute. These included:

273. The vast majority of women consult their husbands prior to deciding to terminate their pregnancy. . . .

281. Studies reveal that family violence occurs in two million families in the United States. This figure, however, is a conservative one. . . . In fact, researchers estimate that one of every two women will be battered at some time in their life. . . .

298. Because of the nature of the battering relationship, battered women are unlikely to avail themselves of the exceptions to section 3209 of the Act, regardless of whether the section applies to them.

These findings are supported by studies of domestic violence.

The American Medical Association (AMA) has published a summary of the recent research in this field, which indicates that in an average 12-month period in this country, approximately two million women are the victims of severe assaults by their male partners. In a 1985 survey, women reported that nearly one of every eight husbands had assaulted their wives during the past year. The AMA views these figures as "marked underestimates," because the nature of these incidents discourages women from reporting them, and because surveys typically exclude the very poor, those who do not speak English well, and women who are homeless or in institutions or hospitals when the survey is conducted. According to the AMA, "[r]esearchers on family violence agree that the true incidence of partner violence is probably double the above estimates; or four million severely assaulted women per year. Studies suggest that from one-fifth to one-third of all women will be physically assaulted by a partner or ex-partner during their lifetime." AMA Council on Scientific Affairs, Violence Against Women 7 (1991). Thus on an average day in the United States, nearly 11,000 women are severely assaulted by their male partners. Many of these incidents involve sexual assault. . . .

The limited research that has been conducted with respect to notifying one's husband about an abortion, although involving samples too small to be representative, also supports the District Court's findings of fact. The vast majority of women notify their male partners of their decision to obtain an abortion. In many cases in which married women do not notify their husbands, the pregnancy is the result of an extramarital affair. Where the husband is the father, the primary reason women do not notify their husbands is that the husband and wife are experiencing marital difficulties, often accompanied by incidents of violence. . . .

The spousal notification requirement is thus likely to prevent a significant number of women from obtaining an abortion. It does not merely make abortions a little more difficult or expensive to obtain; for many women, it will impose a substantial obstacle. . . .

We recognize that a husband has a "deep and proper concern and interest . . . in his wife's pregnancy and in the growth and development of the fetus she is carrying." *Danforth*, supra. With regard to the children he has fathered and raised, the Court has recognized his "cognizable and substantial" interest in their custody. Stanley v. Illinois, 405 U.S. 645, 651-52 (1972). . . . If this case concerned a State's ability to require the mother to notify the father before taking some action with respect to a living child raised by both, therefore, it would be reasonable to conclude as a general matter that the father's interest in the welfare of the child and the mother's interest are equal.

Before birth, however, the issue takes on a very different cast. It is an inescapable biological fact that state regulation with respect to the child a woman is carrying will have a far greater impact on the mother's liberty than on the father's. . . . The Court has held that "when the wife and the husband disagree on this decision, the view of only one of the two marriage partners can prevail. Inasmuch as it is the woman who physically bears the child and who is the more directly affected by the pregnancy, as between the two, the balance weighs in her favor." *Danforth*. This conclusion rests upon the basic nature of marriage and the nature of our Constitution: "[T]he marital couple is not an independent entity with a mind and heart of its own, but an association of two individuals each with a separate intellectual and emotional makeup. If the right of privacy means anything, it is the right of the *individual*, married or single, to be free from unwarranted governmental intrusion into matters so fundamentally affecting a person as the decision whether to bear or beget a child.". . .

The principles that guided *Danforth* should be our guides today. For the great many women who are victims of abuse inflicted by their husbands, or whose children are the victims of such abuse, a spousal notice requirement enables the husband to wield an effective veto over his wife's decision. Whether the prospect of notification itself deters such women from seeking abortions, or whether the husband, through physical force or psychological pressure or economic coercion, prevents his wife from obtaining an abortion until it is too late, the notice requirement will be tantamount to the veto found unconstitutional in *Danforth*. . . .

NOTES AND QUESTIONS

1. *Casey* held unconstitutional the Pennsylvania requirement that a married woman seeking an abortion inform her husband of her intent and produce a signed statement that she has done so. However, it upheld a parental notification provision in the same statute. The opinion indicates that "[r]egulations which do no more than create a structural mechanism by which the State, or the parent or guardian of a minor, may express profound respect for the life of the unborn are permitted, if they are not a substantial obstacle to the woman's exercise of a right to choose." Why is a regulation that creates a structural mechanism allowing the husband to express his respect for the life of the unborn not permissible?

2. Does the husband of a pregnant woman have any constitutionally cognizable interest deciding whether a fetus will be terminated? If not, on what basis can responsibility after birth be predicated?

3. The access of a woman of limited means to abortion, with or without spousal support, may also be affected by the availability of abortion services. At the federal level, the Hyde Amendment continues to ban abortion coverage under Medicaid, unless a woman's life is endangered or the pregnancy results from incest or rape. Pub. L. No. 94-439, §209, 90 Stat. 1418 (1976). Similar limitations apply to a range of other federal departments and programs, and military health care coverage does not include abortion except where the mother's life is at risk.

Most states have followed suit. Thirty-two states pay for abortions for indigent women whose lives are endangered by the pregnancy, as well as in cases of rape or incest, as mandated by federal law. A few of these states also pay in cases of fetal impairment or when the pregnancy threatens "severe" health problems, but none provides reimbursement for all medically necessary abortions for indigent women. Currently, only 17 states fund abortions for indigent women on the same terms as other pregnancy-related and general health services. Three of these states provide funding voluntarily (Hawaii, New York, and Washington); in 14 states, courts have interpreted their state constitutions to give broader protection for reproductive choice than the United States Constitution and have ordered nondiscriminatory public funding of abortions (Alaska, Arizona, California, Connecticut, Illinois, Indiana, Massachusetts, Minnesota, Montana, New Jersey, New Mexico, Oregon, Vermont, and West Virginia). *See* Sara G. Gordon, Note: A Woman' s Life, A Woman' s Health: Equalizing Medicaid Abortion Funding in Simat Corp. v. Arizona Health Care Cost Containment System, 45 Ariz. L. Rev. 1127, 1129 & n.18 (2003).

PROBLEM

You are a law clerk to Justice Groat of your state supreme court. The court has taken an appeal in a case arising under a recently adopted state statute, and he would like you to analyze the issues presented.

The facts of the case can be stated relatively simply. Ms. End, the appellant in this case, was pregnant (by her husband) when a long history of marital trouble led to divorce. By the time the divorce action was heard, a child (Ellen) had been born. Mr. End objected to the imposition of any child support obligation for Ellen, citing State Stat. §400, adopted last year. That statute now provides as follows:

> In cases of divorce, the court shall enter a support order consistent with the [state child support guidelines], unless to do so would be unjust in the circumstances of the case. *It shall be presumed to be unjust to require child support where the mother has intentionally borne a child over the reasonable objection of the father, the father has reasonably sought to avoid conception or birth, and the mother is capable of adequately supporting the child.*

Mr. End testified at the hearing that he did not want to have a child, particularly when it was evident (as it had been for some time) that the marriage was likely to fail. He also testified that his wife had purported to agree and assured him that she was continuing to take birth control pills. Finally, Mr. End testified that, when his wife became pregnant, he immediately and repeatedly asked her to terminate the pregnancy, which she refused to do.

Mr. End called the family physician who delivered Ellen to testify that Ms. End was in good health and that performance of an abortion would not have presented any danger. She further testified that the statistical chances of harm to the mother are greater when bearing the child to term than with an abortion during the first trimester.

Ms. End, testifying as a hostile witness, confirmed Mr. End's testimony. She conceded that she had not used the pill or any other birth control device around the time she became pregnant, explaining that she "wanted to have a child now, whatever happened to the marriage." Ms. End also stated that this desire explained her refusal to seek an abortion, against which she has neither religious nor social objections in general. She further testified that she is currently employed as an insurance adjustor, earns an income of $30,000 per year (which is equal to that of Mr. End), and plans to continue working.

On this evidence, the trial judge noted that she ordinarily would be compelled to follow the state child support guidelines, which would have required Mr. End to pay 24 percent of his gross monthly earnings for the support of Ellen. However, she felt that her decision was governed by the italicized portion of §400, and that no rebuttal evidence had been offered.

Ms. End appeals the trial court decision, arguing that its enforcement is unconstitutional. Please prepare the requested memorandum, analyzing arguments for and against the validity of the italicized portion of the statute.

E. MEDICAL DECISION MAKING ABOUT FAMILY MEMBERS

Despite the constitutional doctrine explored in the previous section, decisions about bringing children into the world are usually considered "family matters" to be made by husbands and wives. We often think the same of decisions about medical care. You will want to consider whether constitutional and other legal doctrines concerning medical decision making capture this sense of family activity.

CRUZAN V. DIRECTOR, MISSOURI DEPARTMENT OF HEALTH

497 U.S. 261 (1990)

REHNQUIST, C.J. [As the result of injuries suffered in an automobile accident, Nancy Beth Cruzan, who was twenty-five years old, was hospitalized in a persistent vegetative state: a condition in which the patient exhibits motor reflexes but no significant cognitive function. When it became clear that Nancy had virtually no chance of regaining her mental faculties, her parents asked hospital employees to terminate artificial nutrition and hydration procedures. Because that act would cause her death, hospital employees refused to honor this request without court approval. Although the trial court granted the request, finding that Nancy's informal conversation with a friend indicated that she would not wish to continue living in her current condition, the Missouri Supreme Court reversed. The court did recognize a common law doctrine of informed consent but not a broader constitutional right of privacy to refuse medical treatment. It concluded that the Missouri Living Will statute embodied a state policy favoring the preservation of life except where the wish to die was established by clear and convincing evidence, and that Nancy's statements were not sufficiently probative on that issue. The Missouri court also rejected the argument that Nancy's parents were entitled to order termination of treatment on behalf of their daughter.

The U.S. Supreme Court granted certiorari to consider whether Cruzan has a right under the U.S. Constitution that would require the hospital to withdraw life-sustaining treatment from her under these circumstances. Chief Justice Rehnquist held that there is a well-established common law right to decide whether to accept or refuse treatment, and then turned to the federal constitutional issue presented.]

The Fourteenth Amendment provides that no State shall "deprive any person of life, liberty, or property, without due process of law." The principle that a competent person has a constitutionally protected liberty interest in refusing unwanted medical treatment may be inferred from our prior decisions. In Jacobson v. Massachusetts, 197 U.S. 11, 24-30 (1905), for instance, the Court balanced an individual's liberty interest in declining an unwanted smallpox vaccine against the State's interest in preventing disease. Decisions prior to the incorporation of the Fourth Amendment into the Fourteenth Amendment analyzed searches and seizures involving the body under the Due Process Clause and were thought to implicate substantial liberty interests.

But determining that a person has a "liberty interest" under the Due Process Clause does not end the inquiry; "whether respondent's constitutional rights have been violated must be determined by balancing his liberty interests against the relevant state interests."

Petitioners insist that under the general holdings of our cases, the forced administration of life-sustaining medical treatment, and even of artificially delivered food and water essential to life, would implicate a competent person's liberty interest. . . . For purposes of this case, we assume that the United States Constitution would grant a competent person a constitutionally protected right to refuse lifesaving hydration and nutrition.

Petitioners go on to assert that an incompetent person should possess the same right in this respect as is possessed by a competent person. . . . The difficulty with petitioners' claim is that in a sense it begs the question: an incompetent person is not able to make an informed and voluntary choice to exercise a hypothetical right to refuse treatment or any other right. Such a "right" must be exercised for her, if at all, by some sort of surrogate. Here, Missouri has in effect recognized that under certain circumstances a surrogate may act for the patient in electing to have hydration and nutrition withdrawn in such a way as to cause death, but it has established a procedural safeguard to assure that the action of the surrogate conforms as best it may to the wishes expressed by the patient while competent. Missouri requires that evidence of the incompetent's wishes as to the withdrawal of treatment be proved by clear and convincing evidence. The question, then, is whether the United States Constitution forbids the establishment of this procedural requirement by the State. We hold that it does not.

Whether or not Missouri's clear and convincing evidence requirement comports with the United States Constitution depends in part on what interests the State may properly seek to protect in this situation. Missouri relies on its interest in the protection and preservation of human life, and there can be no gainsaying this interest. . . .

. . . The choice between life and death is a deeply personal decision of obvious and overwhelming finality. We believe Missouri may legitimately seek to safeguard the personal element of this choice through the imposition of heightened evidentiary requirements. It cannot be disputed that the Due Process Clause protects an interest in life as well as an interest in refusing life-sustaining medical treatment. Not all incompetent patients will have loved ones available to serve as surrogate decision-makers. And even where family members are present, "[t]here will, of course, be some unfortunate situations in which family members will not act to protect a patient." A State is entitled to guard against potential abuses in such situations. Similarly, a State is entitled to consider that a judicial proceeding to make a determination regarding an incompetent's wishes may very well not be an adversarial one, with the added guarantee of accurate factfinding that the adversary process brings with it. Finally, we think a State may properly decline to make judgments about the "quality" of life that a particular individual may enjoy, and simply assert an unqualified interest in the preservation of human life to be weighed against the constitutionally protected interests of the individual.

In our view, Missouri has permissibly sought to advance these interests through the adoption of a "clear and convincing" standard of proof to govern such proceedings. . . . "This Court has mandated an intermediate standard of proof — 'clear and convincing evidence' — when the individual interests at stake in a state proceeding are both 'particularly important' and 'more substantial than mere loss of money.'" . . .

We think it self-evident that the interests at stake in the instant proceedings are more substantial, both on an individual and societal level, than those involved in a run-of-the-mine civil dispute. But not only does the standard of proof reflect the importance of a particular adjudication, it also serves as "a societal judgment about how the risk of error should be distributed between the litigants." The more stringent the burden of proof a party must bear, the more that party bears the risk of an erroneous decision. We believe that Missouri may permissibly place an increased risk of an erroneous decision on those seeking to terminate an incompetent individual's life-sustaining treatment. . . .

Petitioners alternatively contend that Missouri must accept the "substituted judgment" of close family members even in the absence of substantial proof that their views reflect the views of the patient. . . .

No doubt is engendered by anything in this record but that Nancy Cruzan's mother and father are loving and caring parents. If the State were required by the

United States Constitution to repose a right of "substituted judgment" with any-one, the Cruzans would surely qualify. But we do not think the Due Process Clause requires the State to repose judgment on these matters with anyone but the patient herself. Close family members may have a strong feeling — a feeling not at all ignoble or unworthy, but not entirely disinterested, either — that they do not wish to witness the continuation of the life of a loved one which they regard as hopeless, meaningless, and even degrading. But there is no automatic assurance that the view of close family members will necessarily be the same as the patient's would have been had she been confronted with the prospect of her situation while competent. All of the reasons previously discussed for allowing Missouri to require clear and convincing evidence of the patient's wishes lead us to conclude that the State may choose to defer only to those wishes rather than confide the decision to close family members. . . .

O'CONNOR, J. concurring. I . . . write separately to emphasize that the Court does not today decide the issue whether a State must also give effect to the decisions of a surrogate decisionmaker. In my view, such a duty may well be constitutionally required to protect the patient's liberty interest in refusing medical treatment. . . .

STEVENS, J., dissenting. . . . Ultimate questions that might once have been dealt with in intimacy by a family and its physician have now become the concern of institutions. When the institution is a state hospital, as it is in this case, the gov-ernment itself becomes involved. Dying nonetheless remains a part of "the life which characteristically has its place in the home." The "integrity of that life is something so fundamental that it has been found to draw to its protection the principles of more than one explicitly granted Constitutional right," and our deci-sions have demarcated a "private realm of family life which the state cannot enter." The physical boundaries of the home, of course, remain crucial guarantors of the life within it. Nevertheless, this Court has long recognized that the liberty to make the decisions and choices constitutive of private life is so fundamental to our "concept of ordered liberty," that those choices must occasionally be afforded more direct protection. . . .

   . . . Nancy Cruzan's interest in life, no less than that of any other person, includes an interest in how she will be thought of after her death by those whose opinions mattered to her. There can be no doubt that her life made her dear to her family, and to others. How she dies will affect how that life is remembered. The trial court's order authorizing Nancy's parents to cease their daughter's treat-ment would have permitted the family that cares for Nancy to bring to a close her tragedy and her death. Missouri's objection to that order subordinates Nancy's body, her family, and the lasting significance of her life to the State's own inter-ests. The decision we review thereby interferes with constitutional interests of the highest order. . . .

   In this case, as is no doubt true in many others, the predicament confronted by the healthy members of the Cruzan family merely adds emphasis to the best interests finding made by the trial judge. Each of us has an interest in the kind of memories that will survive after death. To that end, individual decisions are often motivated by their impact on others. A member of the kind of family identified in the trial court's findings in this case would likely have not only a normal interest in minimizing the burden that her own illness imposes on others, but also an interest in having their memories of her filled predominantly with thoughts about her past vitality rather than her current condition. The meaning and completion of her life should be controlled by persons who have her best interests at heart — not by a state legislature concerned only with the "preservation of human life."

NOTES AND QUESTIONS

1. The *Cruzan* case happens to involve decisions by parents regarding the continuing treatment of their daughter. The daughter was an adult at the time of her injury, and the Court's analysis would seem to apply to decisions regarding the treatment of spouses as well as of children.

2. What role or roles do the various opinions contemplate for the family of a comatose or otherwise incompetent patient? How are they justified?

3. What assumptions do the opinions make about the attitudes, interests, and relationships of families facing the situation in *Cruzan*? For discussion of varying "pictures" of families in judicial discourse, *see* Martha Minow, The Role of Families in Medical Decisions, 1991 Utah L. Rev. 1.

4. What is the relationship between the approach in *Cruzan* and the approaches in *Danforth* and *Casey* regarding "family" decision making? Are the situations distinguishable?

5. Most states (including New York) now have adopted "living will" statutes, which, in general, relieve physicians and other health care providers of liability if the statutory requirements are followed and the desires expressed are followed. These statutes differ in a number of details, such as duration and scope of applicability. The 1994 Uniform Health Care Decisions Act provides a definition of capacity to make such decisions and incorporates flexible procedures for implementing them.

An alternative strategy for persons who want to influence their medical care is the durable power of attorney for health care. Most states have adopted statutes that authorize durable powers of attorney for this purpose. *See generally* Barry R. Furrow, Sandra H. Johnson, Timothy S. Jost & Robert L. Schwartz, Bioethics: Health Care Law and Ethics 262-279 (1991).

Entering Ceremonial Marriage 3

A. INTRODUCTION

To state the requirements for getting married seems simplicity itself. The parties must agree to marry; they must be generally eligible ("competent") to marry; they must be eligible to marry each other; and they must go through whatever forms are required for marriage in the state where they intend to marry. As we examine the law in this area, what seems simple will come to seem less so. States differ regarding the nature of the requisite agreement. The weight given to compliance with statutory forms for marriage also differs. Laws regarding eligibility to marry differ from state to state and are potentially qualified by constitutional doctrines concerning the power of the state to limit entrance into marriage. Moreover, people in this society tend not to stay put, creating circumstances in which a court in one jurisdiction must pass on the effect to be given marriages contracted in another state or nation.

Finally, whether any given marriage is valid may vary from time to time and from purpose to purpose. As we will see in the course of this chapter, marriage can be—and perhaps ordinarily is—viewed in terms of the social and economic rights and duties of husband and wife for domestic relations purposes. However, that relationship also is as important for determining the various rights, incidents, and benefits that depend on marital or family relationships as it is for its own sake. A variety of social institutions employ familial terms to express the relationships and obligations with which these institutions are concerned; for example, immigration law accords to "spouses of American citizens" a special position, and "spouses" of decedents have an established priority for inheritance purposes and for possible entitlements of workers' compensation and Social Security benefits. To some considerable extent, "one can accurately imagine the family as a hub around which [various intermediate social systems] turn . . . in [their] reliance . . . on family relationships." Lee E. Teitelbaum, Placing the Family in Context, 22 U.C. Davis L. Rev. 801, 818

(1989). Because the various institutional interests that draw on family relationships have their own purposes, however, it is not surprising to find that a marriage may be considered valid for one purpose but not for another.

B. FORMALITIES

UNIFORM MARRIAGE AND DIVORCE ACT

Section 203. When a marriage application has been completed and signed by both parties to a prospective marriage and at least one party has appeared before the [marriage license] clerk and paid the marriage license fee of [_____], the [marriage license] clerk shall issue a license to marry and a marriage certificate form upon being furnished:

(1) satisfactory proof [of age]; and
(2) satisfactory proof that the marriage is not prohibited;
[(3) a certificate of the results of any medical examination required by the laws of this State].

Section 206. (a) A marriage may be solemnized by a judge of a court of record, by a public official whose powers include solemnization of marriages, or in accordance with any mode of solemnization recognized by any religious denomination, Indian Nation or Tribe. . . .

(b) If a party to a marriage is unable to be present at the solemnization, he may authorize in writing a third person to act as his proxy. . . .

(d) The solemnization of the marriage is not invalidated by the fact that the person solemnizing the marriage was not legally qualified to solemnize it, if either party to the marriage believed him to be so qualified.

NOTES AND QUESTIONS

1. The formal requirements for marriage vary somewhat from state to state. Ordinarily, the parties must secure a license. Both may be required to appear, or, as under the Uniform Marriage and Divorce Act (UMDA), only one may be required to do so. Many states impose a minimum waiting period between the issuance of a license and the marriage celebration, but this can often be waived under certain circumstances, such as the pregnancy of the bride-to-be.

Requirements for medical examinations, where they exist, typically have been limited to blood tests for venereal disease. However, the widespread appearance of acquired immunodeficiency syndrome (AIDS) led some states to include HIV testing to identify persons who may develop AIDS. At one time the Illinois Marriage and Dissolution Act § 204 (1987) required all parties to be tested by the ELISA test and, if either party tested positive, by the Western blot assay or a more reliable test. Notice of a positive result was to be given both parties, but a marriage license could be issued. This statute was repealed in 1989 after criticism directed at the cost and relative inefficiency of AIDS testing. The Utah legislature went further, prohibiting marriage by a person afflicted with AIDS. That statute was held invalid because of inconsistency with the Americans with Disabilities Act, 42 U.S.C. §§ 1201 et seq. in T. E. P. v. Leavitt, 840 F. Supp. 110 (D. Utah 1993).

A ceremony is also generally required in all states that do not recognize common law marriage (and, even in those states, for marriages that do not meet the requirements of common law wedlock). However, the form of ceremony is rarely specified and is usually left to the parties and the solemnizing official. A marriage in which the parties read the Kama Sutra to each other is valid as long as it has been solemnized by some appropriate person who is willing to put up with this behavior.

2. A wide variety of nontraditional marriage ceremonies have been upheld against challenge. Marriages have been recognized when a husband proved that a French marriage had been performed by an unauthorized person, Amsellem v. Amsellem, 730 N.Y.S.2d 212 (N.Y. Sup. 2001), and when the parties failed to secure a license for their Hindu marriage or prayer ceremony, Persad v. Balram, 724 N.Y.S.2d 560 (N.Y. Sup. 2001). In Carabetta v. Carabetta, 438 A.2d 109 (Conn. 1980), the parties did not secure a marriage license. The domestic relations statute provided that "[n]o persons shall be married without a license." However, the Connecticut Supreme Court held that the statutory requirement was "directory" rather than "mandatory" and that the marriage was therefore not "null and void." The court further suggested that it would hold a marriage void only if the legislature expressly required that result.

But see Estate of DePasse, 118 Cal. Rptr. 2d 143 (Cal. App. 2002), holding that the marriage license requirement is mandatory and its absence cannot be cured by petition to declare the existence of the marriage after the death of one of the parties; In re Khalil, 2003 WL 1873739 (D.V.I 4/4/03), holding that a marriage license is necessary to a valid marriage and that making the license mandatory furthered a state objective of protecting minors.

What value is there in "directory" regulations? What reasons are there for determining that a license requirement is "directory" rather than "mandatory"?

NOTE: "VOID" AND "VOIDABLE" MARRIAGES

In a simple world, marriages would be either void or valid. This is not, however, a simple world. Analyzing the effect of both the formal and substantive defects in marriage sometimes requires an understanding of one of the genuinely arcane areas of law: the distinction between a "void" and a "voidable" marriage. What makes the distinction difficult is that, while a divorce supposes a valid marriage that is dissolved after some time, an annulment has been understood to declare the *invalidity* of the marriage *ab initio*. In point of law, an annulled marriage is one that never existed. One might ask, therefore, how there can be a difference between a void marriage and a voidable marriage, if the result in either case is the nonexistence of the marriage at any time.

The differences between the two kinds of marriage are in substantial respects procedural. A "voidable" marriage has at least potential validity. It is valid unless its nullity has been declared. Moreover, the nullity of a voidable marriage ordinarily can be sought only by one of the parties to the marriage and only during the lifetime of the marriage. If, for example, the parties marry at age 17 when the local law permits marriages only by persons who are 18 years or older, their marriage could be annulled at the instance of at least the underaged spouse, and if the annulment is granted, the formal result is that they were never married. However, the marriage can become a valid marriage, and if the parties never seek its annulment, the marriage will become valid when they continue to live as husband and wife after reaching the age of consent. *See, e.g.*, Powell v. Powell, 86 A.2d 331 (N.J. 1952); Jones v. Jones, 37 S.E.2d 711 (Ga. 1946). *See also* Medlin v. Medlin, 981 P.2d 1087 (Ariz. App. 1999).

A "void" marriage in theory requires no declaration of invalidity. Moreover, the voidness of the marriage can be declared at any time and, generally, at the instance of any interested party. Nor, in principle, can a void marriage ever become a valid marriage.

The distinction between void and voidable marriages has its roots in English ecclesiastical law. Marital disabilities were of two types: civil (which included insanity and prior marriage) and canonical (which included marriages within forbidden degrees of kinship). Civil disabilities rendered a marriage void; canon law disabilities made it voidable. *See* Note, "Void" and "Voidable" Under Marriage Consanguinity Statutes, 17 Iowa L. Rev. 254 (1932). The continued viability of this distinction is doubtful, and it may well be questioned whether any such distinction is worth retaining, since many of the implications of voidness have been eliminated. For example, the children of a void marriage were illegitimate; those of a voidable marriage were legitimate unless the marriage was annulled. *See* Matter of Moncrief's Will, 139 N.E. 550 (N.Y. 1923); 1 Homer H. Clark, Jr., Domestic Relations in the United States 238 (1987). However, modern statutes now generally treat children of an invalid marriage as legitimate under most circumstances. For a review of the various statutory treatments, *see* 1 H. Clark at 239-242.

Similarly, alimony is in principle inconsistent with a void marriage; nonetheless, some states provide for alimony upon annulment—*e.g.*, Conn. Gen. Stat. Ann. §46b-60 (1986); Or. Rev. Stat. §§ 107.095, 107.105 (1983).

C. THE AGREEMENT TO MARRY

1. *The Content of the Agreement*

LUTWAK V. UNITED STATES

344 U.S. 604 (1952)

MINTON, J. The petitioners, Marcel Max Lutwak, Munio Knoll, and Regina Treitler, together with Leopold Knoll and Grace Klemtner, were indicted on six counts in the Northern District of Illinois, Eastern Division. The first count charged conspiracy to commit substantive offenses set forth in the remaining five counts and conspiracy "to defraud the United States of and concerning its governmental function and right of administering" the immigration laws and the Immigration and Naturalization Service, by obtaining the illegal entry into this country of three aliens as spouses of honorably discharged veterans. Grace Klemtner was dismissed from the indictment before the trial. . . . The jury acquitted Leopold Knoll and convicted the three petitioners on the conspiracy count. The Court of Appeals affirmed, and we granted certiorari.

We are concerned here only with the conviction of the petitioners of the alleged conspiracy. Petitioner Regina Treitler is the sister of Munio Knoll and Leopold Knoll, and the petitioner Lutwak is their nephew. Munio Knoll had been married in Poland in 1932 to one Maria Knoll. There is some evidence that Munio and Maria were divorced in 1942, but the existence and validity of this divorce are not determinable from the record. At the time of the inception of the conspiracy, in the summer of 1947, Munio, Maria and Leopold were refugees from Poland, living in Paris, France, while Regina Treitler and Lutwak lived in Chicago, Illinois. Petitioner Treitler desired to get her brothers into the United States.

Alien spouses of honorably discharged veterans of World War II were permitted to enter this country under the provisions of the so-called War Brides Act. . . .

The first count of the indictment charged that the petitioners conspired to have three honorably discharged veterans journey to Paris and go through marriage ceremonies with Munio, Leopold and Maria. The brothers and Maria would then accompany their new spouses to the United States and secure entry into this country by representing themselves as alien spouses of World War II veterans. It was further a part of the plan that the marriages were to be in form only, solely for the purpose of enabling Munio, Leopold and Maria to enter the United States. The parties to the marriages were not to live together as husband and wife, and thereafter would take whatever legal steps were necessary to sever the legal ties. It was finally alleged that the petitioners conspired to conceal these acts in order to prevent disclosure of the conspiracy to the immigration authorities.

The conspiracy to commit substantive offenses consisted in that part of the plan by which each of the aliens was to make a false statement to the immigration authorities by representing in his application for admission that he was married to his purported spouse, and to conceal from the immigration authorities that he had gone through a marriage ceremony solely for the purpose of gaining entry into this country with the understanding that he and his purported spouse would not live together as man and wife, but would sever the formal bonds of the ostensible marriage when the marriage had served its fraudulent purpose. . . .

From the evidence favorable to the Government, the jury could reasonably have believed that the following acts and transactions took place, and that the petitioners conspired to bring them about. Lutwak, a World War II veteran, was selected to marry Maria Knoll, his aunt by marriage. He went to Paris where he went through a marriage ceremony with Maria. They traveled to the United States, entering the port of New York on September 9, 1947. They represented to the immigration authorities that Maria was the wife of Lutwak, and upon that representation Maria was admitted. They never lived together as man and wife, and within a few months Munio and Maria commenced living together in this country as man and wife, holding themselves out as such. Lutwak, in the meantime, represented himself to friends as an unmarried man. Lutwak and Maria were divorced on March 31, 1950.

Lutwak and Mrs. Treitler also found two women—Bessie Benjamin Osborne and Grace Klemtner—who were honorably discharged veterans of World War II, and who were willing to marry Munio and Leopold so that the brothers could come to the United States. Bessie Osborne was introduced to Treitler by Lutwak, and went to Paris accompanied by Treitler. There she went through a pretended marriage ceremony with Munio Knoll, and on their arrival at New York City, Munio was admitted on November 13, 1947, on the representation that he was married to Bessie Osborne. The marriage was never consummated and was never intended to be. The parties separated after entering the United States, and they never lived together as husband and wife at any time. Bessie Osborne's suit for divorce from Munio was pending at the time of the trial.

Still later, Grace Klemtner, who was also a World War II veteran and an acquaintance of Regina Treitler, went to Paris and went through a pretended marriage ceremony with Leopold. They then traveled to the United States, where Leopold was admitted on December 5, 1947, upon the representation that he was the husband of Grace Klemtner. They immediately separated after their entry into this country, and they never lived together as husband and wife at any time until about the time Grace Klemtner appeared before the grand jury which returned the indictment. This was approximately April 1, 1950, more than two years after the marriage ceremony in Paris. Bessie Osborne and Grace Klemtner received a substantial fee for participating in these marriage ceremonies....

Petitioners present three principal contentions: (1) Their conspiracy was not unlawful because the marriages involved were valid marriages; (2) the trial court erred in permitting the ostensible wives of these marriages to testify against their so-called husbands;...

I

At the trial, it was undisputed that Maria, Munio and Leopold had gone through formal marriage ceremonies with Lutwak, Bess Osborne and Grace Klemtner, respectively. Petitioners contended that, regardless of the intentions of the parties at the time of the ceremonies, the fact that the ceremonies were performed was sufficient to establish the validity of the marriages, at least until the Government proved their invalidity under French law. They relied on the general American rule of conflict of laws that a marriage valid where celebrated is valid everywhere unless it is incestuous, polygamous or otherwise declared void by statute. Neither side presented any evidence of the French law, and the trial court ruled that in the absence of such evidence, the French law would be presumed to be the same as American law. The court later instructed the jury that "if the subjects agree to a marriage only for the sake of representing it as such to the outside world and with the understanding that they will put an end to it as soon as it has served its purpose to deceive, they have never really agreed to be married at all." The petitioners claim that the trial court erred in presuming that the French law relating to the validity of marriages is the same as

American law, and they further contend that even under American law these marriages are valid.

We do not believe that the validity of the marriages is material. No one is being prosecuted for an offense against the marital relation. We consider the marriage ceremonies only as a part of the conspiracy to defraud the United States and to commit offenses against the United States. In the circumstances of this case, the ceremonies were only a step in the fraudulent scheme and actions taken by the parties to the conspiracy. By directing in the War Brides Act that "alien spouses" of citizen war veterans should be admitted into this country, Congress intended to make it possible for veterans who had married aliens to have their families join them in this country without the long delay involved in qualifying under the proper immigration quota. Congress did not intend to provide aliens with an easy means of circumventing the quota system by fake marriages in which neither of the parties ever intended to enter into the marital relationship; that petitioners so believed is evidenced by their care in concealing from the immigration authorities that the ostensible husbands and wives were to separate immediately after their entry into this country and were never to live together as husband and wife. The common understanding of a marriage, which Congress must have had in mind when it made provision for "alien *spouses*" in the War Brides Act, is that the two parties have undertaken to establish a life together and assume certain duties and obligations. Such was not the case here, or so the jury might reasonably have found. Thus, when one of the aliens stated that he was married, and omitted to explain the true nature of his marital relationship, his statement did, and was intended to, carry with it implications of a state of facts which were not in fact true.

Because the validity of the marriages is not material, the cases involving so-called limited purpose marriages,[1] cited by petitioners to support their contention that the marriages in the instant case are valid, are inapplicable. All of those cases are suits for annulment in which the court was requested to grant relief to one of the parties to a marriage on the basis of his own admission that the marriage had been a sham. Where the annulment was denied, one or more of the following factors influenced the court: (1) a reluctance to permit the parties to use the annulment procedure as a quick and painless substitute for divorce, particularly because this might encourage people to marry hastily and inconsiderately; (2) a belief that the parties should not be permitted to use the courts as the means of carrying out their own secret schemes; and (3) a desire to prevent injury to innocent third parties, particularly children of the marriage. These factors have no application in the circumstances of the instant case. . . . In the instant case . . . there was no good faith—no intention to marry and consummate the marriages even for a day. With the legal consequences of such ceremonies under other circumstances, either in the United States or France, we are not concerned. . . .

JACKSON, J., whom BLACK, J., and FRANKFURTER, J., join, dissenting. Whenever a court has a case where behavior that obviously is sordid can be proved to be

---

1. *E.g.*, Schibi v. Schibi, 136 Conn. 196, 69 A.2d 831; Hanson v. Hanson, 287 Mass. 154, 191 N.E. 673. These and other cases cited by petitioners are collected and discussed in a note, 14 A.L.R.2d 624 (1950).

criminal only with great difficulty, the effort to bridge the gap is apt to produce bad law. We are concerned about the effect of this decision in three respects.

1. We are not convinced that any crime has been proved, even on the assumption that all evidence in the record was admissible. These marriages were formally contracted in France, and there is no contention that they were forbidden or illegal there for any reason. It is admitted that some judicial procedure is necessary if the parties wish to be relieved of their obligations. Whether by reason of the reservations with which the parties entered into the marriages they could be annulled may be a nice question of French law, in view of the fact that no one of them deceived the other. We should expect it to be an even nicer question whether a third party, such as the state in a criminal process, could simply ignore the ceremony and its consequences, as the Government does here.

We start with marriages that either are valid or at least have not been proved to be invalid in their inception. The Court brushes this question aside as immaterial, but we think it goes to the very existence of an offense. If the parties are validly married, even though the marriage is a sordid one, we should suppose that would end the case. On the other hand, if the marriage ceremonies were for some reason utterly void and held for naught, as if they never had happened, the Government could well claim that entry into the United States as married persons was fraud. But between these two extremes is the more likely case — marriages that are not void but perhaps voidable. In one of these cases, the parties (on the trial) expressed their desire to stay married, and they were acquitted; and no one contends that their marriage is void. Certainly if these marriages were merely voidable and had not been adjudged void at the time of the entry into this country, it was not a fraud to represent them as subsisting. We should think that the parties to them might have been prosecuted with as much reason if they had represented themselves to be single. Marriages of convenience are not uncommon and it cannot be that we would hold it a fraud for one who has contracted a marriage not forbidden by law to represent himself as wedded, even if there were grounds for annulment or divorce and proceedings to that end were contemplated.

The effect of any reservations of the parties in contracting the marriages would seem to be governed by the law of France. It does not seem justifiable to assume what we all know is not true — that French law and our law are the same. Such a view ignores some of the most elementary facts of legal history — the French reception of Roman law, the consequences of the Revolution, and the Napoleonic codifications. If the Government contends that these marriages were ineffectual from the beginning, it would seem to require proof of particular rules of the French law of domestic relations.

NOTES AND QUESTIONS

1. A number of New York state court decisions have held limited-purposes marriages valid. *E.g.*, Bishop v. Bishop, 308 N.Y.S.2d 998 (1970); Anonymous v. Anonymous, 49 N.Y.S.2d 314 (1944); Delfino v. Delfino, 35 N.Y.S.2d 693 (1942). Other courts have taken the same view. In Schibi v. Schibi, 69 A.2d 831 (Conn. 1949), the parties married solely for the purpose of legitimating an unborn child.

They did not intend to, nor did they, cohabit or otherwise assume the relationship of husband and wife. Subsequently, the husband sought an annulment on the ground that the marriage was void for lack of mutual consent of the parties. That relief was denied.

> The law is clear that mutual consent is essential to a valid marriage. It is unquestioned that mutual consent by these parties was requisite to validity under the law of New York, where the ceremony was performed, and that without it the marriage was void and the Superior Court had jurisdiction so to decree. In his complaint, the plaintiff alleges as the only basis for relief that at the time of the ceremony there was neither consent nor intent to incur the obligations of a marriage contract, and his prayers for relief are that the purported marriage be annulled and declared void. The sole question presented to the court for determination was whether the marriage was void because there was no mutual consent of the parties. That there was such mutual consent is implicit in the court's conclusion that the parties were legally married. Whether this conclusion is supported by the subordinate facts is the question decisive of the appeal.
>
> . . . The result reached is in accord with this general principle relative to the effect of prenuptial agreements: "Once a marriage has been properly solemnized and the obligations of married life undertaken, its validity cannot be affected by an antenuptial agreement not to live together, nor by an agreement previously entered into that the marriage should not be valid and binding, nor because one or even both of the parties did not intend it to be a permanent relation." That prenuptial agreements designed to negative the effect of a marriage are generally void as against public policy is well exemplified by these authorities. . . .

Id. at 832-834. *See also* De Vries v. De Vries, 195 Ill. App. 4 (1915); Bishop v. Bishop, 308 N.Y.S.2d 998 (1970); Bove v. Pinciotti, 46 Pa. D. & C. 159 (Pa. 1942). If it were conceded that validity would be determined by New York law, or that French law (absent contrary evidence) is the same as New York law, would that affect the outcome in *Lutwak?* Why does the majority opinion treat the validity of these marriages as "immaterial"?

2. Assume that one of the defendants, after serving his or her time in prison, married some third person. Would he or she be subject to prosecution for bigamy in New York? If one of the defendants were hospitalized, would the person whom he or she had married in France be responsible for that expense?

3. The validity of a marriage for limited purposes is important in almost any area where marriage confers a benefit or avoids a burden. Consider the following examples:

a. In United States v. Mathis, the defendant's former wife had cooperated with investigating authorities (the Alcohol, Tobacco, and Firearms Division of the Treasury Department). Mathis told her that, if she would remarry him, friends would give her $25,000; if she did not, she and her baby would be killed. She and the defendant remarried after her (inculpatory) grand jury testimony but before trial. At trial, she invoked the husband-wife testimonial privilege, which the court rejected. "It is well established that an exception to the husband-wife privilege exists if the trial judge determines that the marriage is a fraud. Lutwak v. United States, 344 U.S. 604 (1953). . . ." 559 F.2d 294, 298 (5th Cir. 1977). *See also* Archina v. People, 307 P.2d 1083 (Colo. 1957).

b. Mpirilis v. Hellenic Lines, Ltd., 323 F. Supp. 865 (S.D. Tex. 1970), involved a wrongful death action under the Jones Act to recover damages by reason of the fatal injuries suffered by the decedent while working on a ship in New York harbor. The plaintiff and the decedent were married on the day of the latter's arrival in the United States, allegedly so that he could gain entry into this country on a preferred basis. Assuming that the parties agreed not to assume any of the normal duties, obligations, or incidents of marriage, should the plaintiff be entitled to wrongful death recovery? Is the case in any way distinguishable from Lutwak v. United States?

4. The specific problem presented in *Lutwak*—fraud on immigration authorities—has been the subject of considerable litigation and congressional action. Its magnitude is a matter of dispute. According to studies done by the Immigration and Naturalization Service (INS) itself, some 30 percent of all marriage-based applications for permanent resident visas ("green cards") are founded on fraud, and 50,000 spurious marriage petitions are filed each year. This figure has been doubted by commentators, and it has been suggested that the rate of fraudulent applications is closer to 4 percent. *See* Note, The Constitutionality of the INS Sham Marriage Investigation Policy, 99 Harv. L. Rev. 1238, 1240-1241 (1986).

Wherever the truth about the frequency of fraudulent claims of marriage may lie, Congress responded by enacting the Marriage Fraud Amendments of 1986, 8 U.S.C. §§ 1154(h), 1255(e). Those amendments provide that an alien who marries a citizen receives only a conditional immigration status, with the bona fides and continuance of the marriage to be reexamined after two years. Procedures adopted by the INS may include a visit to the couple's residence to see whether they actually reside together and interviews with neighbors, employers, and others to determine the existence of a marital relationship. *See* Note, The Constitutionality of the INS Sham Marriage Investigation Policy, above, at 1241-1242.

The amendments have been upheld against constitutional challenge. Almario v. Attorney General, 872 F.2d 147 (6th Cir. 1989); Smith v. Immigration and Naturalization Service, 684 F. Supp. 1113 (D. Mass. 1988). *See also* Joe A. Tucker, Assimilation to the United States: A Study of the Adjustment of Status and the Immigration Marriage Fraud Statutes, 7 Yale L. & Pol'y Rev. 20 (1989).

PROBLEMS

1. Virgil and Gretta engaged in sexual intercourse at a time when they were unmarried. Several months later, Virgil saw Gretta at a party, where she told him that she was pregnant by him. They decided to marry in order to "give the baby a name." They also agreed, however, that they would not cohabit after the marriage, that there would be no sharing of incomes or support (except for the child), and that they would get a divorce after the child turned one year old.

They marry and go their separate ways. Virgil has, however, fallen in love with Beatrice in the meantime. Beatrice is Roman Catholic and has serious problems with marrying someone who is divorced. Virgil decides to seek an annulment of his marriage to Gretta rather than a divorce. Will the annulment be granted?

2. Roy and Dale have been friends for some time. At a party one evening, their friends decide to entertain themselves by making fun of Roy and Dale's friendship and whether it will ever "go anywhere." Because they had had a couple of drinks and because they were tired of being teased, Roy and Dale decide to go through a marriage ceremony; but, after a few days, when the joke has worn off, they plan to secure an annulment. They do not intend to cohabit or live together or in any other way act as husband and wife.

They go through a marriage ceremony before a justice of the peace. A week later, Roy brings an annulment action. Should the annulment be granted?

2. Capacity to Agree

EDMUNDS V. EDWARDS

287 N.W.2d 420 (1980)

BRODKEY, J. This case involves an action brought in the District Court for Douglas County on May 23, 1977, by Renne Edmunds, guardian of the estate of Harold Edwards (hereinafter referred to as Harold), against Inez Edwards (nee Ryan, hereinafter referred to as Inez), to annul the marriage of his ward Harold to Inez, which occurred on May 10, 1975. In his petition, the guardian alleged that the marriage was void for the reason that Harold did not have the mental capacity to enter into a marriage contract on that date, which allegation was specifically denied by Inez. In its order entered on November 27, 1978, following trial of the matter, the District Court found that Harold was mentally retarded, as that phrase is commonly used in medical science, but not to a degree which, under the law of the State of Nebraska, is of such a nature as to render him mentally incompetent to enter into the marriage relation, and that at the time of the marriage between Harold and Inez, Harold had sufficient capacity to understand the nature of the marriage contract and the duties and responsibilities incident to it, so as to be able to enter into a valid and binding marriage contract. The court therefore found that the marriage of Harold and Inez, which occurred on May 10, 1975, was, in fact and in law, a valid marriage and continues to exist as a valid marriage under the laws of the State of Nebraska, and is in full force and effect. The guardian has appealed to this court from that order. We affirm.

Harold was born on August 7, 1918, and was institutionalized at the Beatrice State Home as mentally retarded on September 25, 1939. He was a resident at the Beatrice State Home for a period of approximately 30 years. It was during this period that he first met Inez, who was also a patient of the home, and Bill Lancaster, who lived with Harold in Omaha after their release from the Beatrice State Home, and who has continued to reside with Harold and Inez since their marriage. Harold was placed in Omaha on November 14, 1969, and started a new life under the auspices of the Eastern Nebraska Community Office of Retardation (ENCOR), which was established in 1968 to provide alternatives for institutionalization of retarded persons at the Beatrice State Home and to assist in the normalization of the retarded in local communities. After coming to Omaha, Harold obtained employment as a food service worker in the Douglas County Hospital on

February 16, 1970, and lived in a staffed ENCOR apartment from that time until shortly before his marriage in 1975. . . . While under the auspices of ENCOR, Harold and Inez developed a romantic interest in each other and eventually decided to get married. The date of the marriage was postponed in order to afford the couple the opportunity to have premarital sex counseling and marriage counseling from the pastor of their church in Omaha. They were married by Reverend Verle Holsteen, pastor of the First Baptist Church in Omaha, Nebraska, and their friends, staff members of ENCOR, and out-of-state relatives attended the wedding in that church. The guardian did not bring this action to annul the marriage for a period of approximately 2 years after the date of the marriage ceremony. . . .

The guardian first called his medical expert, Dr. Robert Mitchell, a psychologist connected with Creighton University in Omaha. Dr. Mitchell expressed the opinion that he did not believe Harold was competent to enter into a valid marriage, but admitted on cross-examination that being mildly mentally retarded did not automatically preclude a person from marriage. He also testified that he had asked Harold during his examinations and consultations what marriage meant, to which Harold responded "For life," and also "You stay married forever." . . . Dr. Mitchell also testified: "It is much better, I think, to refer to Mr. Edwards as a person who is fifty-nine years of age who is not as bright as most people. But he has had fifty-nine years of experience, and he is an adult, and physiologically he is matured, as well."

The medical expert witness called by the defendant was Dr. Frank J. Menolascino, a psychiatrist specializing in the field of mental retardation, and author of numerous books and articles upon the subject. He was well acquainted with Harold, having first met him in 1959 when he was doing work at the Beatrice State Home, and had seen Harold many times since that time. He had examined Harold in December 1977, and again in July 1978, during the week Dr. Menolascino testified. He testified that Harold was not functioning below the mildly retarded range and that the tests reflected that a great deal of Harold's difficulty appeared to be primarily a lack of training. . . . Dr. Menolascino was asked: "Doctor, do you believe that you have an opinion as to whether Mr. Edwards was capable of understanding the nature of a marriage within the paradigm you have discussed in May of 1975?" and he answered: "Yes, he was able to." . . . On cross-examination Dr. Menolascino was asked: "In your opinion, do you think that Harold Edwards understands the fact that he is liable for Mrs. Edwards' bills if she goes to a store and runs up some bills?" to which he replied: "Yes." He was then asked: "Do you think he understands the fact that if he gets a divorce he might have to pay alimony?" His reply to that question was: "I am not sure. I am not sure. . . ."

In addition to the medical witnesses who testified, there was also evidence adduced from various lay witnesses. Renne Edmunds, the guardian, . . . testified: "It was my conclusion that he [Harold] could not only not manage a fund of thirty thousand, he couldn't manage the small purchases, as well." . . . Harry John Naasz, an adviser for ENCOR, who was Harold's supervisor, testified that he had assisted Harold in making preparations for the marriage including obtaining of blood tests and the marriage certificate. He had discussed the forthcoming wedding with Harold: "Can you tell us what you discussed concerning the marriage? A. We discussed what it would mean, what it would mean living together, sharing their lives. Q. And what did Harold express to you? A. He wanted to get married. Q. What did he say that led you to believe that he might understand marriage? A. He mentioned to me that he understood, too that it was a commitment to each other, that Inez would be living there." Mr. Naasz did admit in his testimony that at the beginning he did have some question in his mind about whether Harold understood marriage. He later referred the couple for marriage counseling. . . .

Also testifying at the trial was Elizabeth Cartwright, an employee of ENCOR, who monitors Harold and Inez's finances. She testified that when Harold gets paid at the Douglas County Hospital he signs his check, takes it to the bank, deposits all the money except $40, and gives Inez $20 and he keeps $20. She does not have to go to the bank with him. Elizabeth Cartwright also testified that Inez is quite a bit sharper than Harold and she helps him around. . . .

We now examine some established rules of law which we believe are applicable to this case. We first consider the nature of the marriage contract. Section 42-101, R.R.S.1943, provides: "In law, marriage is considered a civil contract, to which the consent of the parties capable of contracting is essential." Although by statute, marriage is referred to as a "civil contract," we have held: "That it is not a contract resembling in any but the slightest degree, except as to the element of consent, any other contract with which the courts have to deal, is apparent upon a moment's reflection. . . . What persons establish by entering into matrimony, is not a contractual relation, but a social *status*; and the only essential features of the transactions are that the participants are of legal capacity to assume that *status*, and freely consent so to do." . . .

Another statutory provision of which we must take cognizance in this appeal is section 42-103, R.R.S.1943, which provides: "Marriages are void . . . (2) when either party, at the time of marriage, is insane or mentally incompetent to enter into the marriage relation; . . ." This statute was reiterated, and other applicable rules with reference to competency to enter into a marriage relationship were reviewed in Homan v. Homan, 181 Neb. 259, 147 N.W.2d 630 (1967), wherein we stated: "The petition alleged that the ward was mentally incompetent at the time of the marriage. By statute a marriage is void "when either party is insane or an idiot at the time of marriage, and the term idiot shall include all persons who from whatever cause are mentally incompetent to enter into the marriage relation."

"A marriage contract will not be declared void for mental incapacity to enter into it unless there existed at the time of the marriage such a want of understanding as to render the party incapable of assenting thereto. Mere weakness or imbecility of mind is not sufficient to void a contract of marriage unless there be such a mental defect as to prevent the party from comprehending the nature of the contract and from giving his fee [sic] and intelligent consent to it.

"Absolute inability to contract, insanity, or idiocy will void a marriage, but mere weakness of mind will not unless it produces a derangement sufficient to avoid all contracts by destroying the power to consent. A marriage is valid if the party has sufficient capacity to understand the nature of the contract and the obligations and responsibilities it creates. . . ."

It is the general rule that the existence of a valid marriage is a question of fact. In this case the trier of fact was the court and the court had all the foregoing evidence, summarized above, before it. Concededly, much of the evidence with reference to the capacity of Harold to enter into the marriage contract was conflicting and disputed. . . . However, it is also the well-established rule that where the evidence on material questions of fact is in irreconcilable conflict, this court will, in determining the weight of the evidence, consider the fact that the trial court observed the witnesses and their manner of testifying, and therefore must have accepted one version of the facts rather than the opposite. This rule has been applied both in annulment actions and in divorce actions.

Applying this rule to the present case, we conclude, therefore, that the trial court was correct in dismissing the guardian's petition to annul the marriage of his ward, and that its action in this regard should be and hereby is affirmed.

NOTES AND QUESTIONS

1. Frank Menolascino & Michael L. Egger, Medical Dimensions of Mental Retardation xx-xxii (1978):

> The term *mental retardation* refers to the combined diagnostic criteria of impairments in intellectual ability and socially adaptive behavior. The term implies both a symptom of an underlying developmental disorder and an assessment of an individual's potential ability to learn. In brief, retarded persons learn slowly, and at chronological maturity their capacity to understand and adapt to social-vocational challenges will be, to varying degrees, less than average. . . .
>
> The President's Committee on Mental Retardation (1963) has estimated that 3% of our nation's citizens at some time during their lives are diagnosed as being mentally retarded to some degree. By this estimate, some 6-1/2 million children and adults are afflicted with this 'developmentally delaying' disorder. . . .
>
> Levels of retardation are usually discussed according to severity and the concomitant expected potentials for learning and general development. The levels of mental retardation are usually classified as mild, moderate, severe, and profound.
>
> The mildly retarded are almost always capable of learning to do productive work. Nearly all can learn academic subjects to varying degrees, and most are capable, as adults, of living independently and becoming self-supporting—*if* they have received appropriate care, training, and other services during childhood, adolescence, and early adulthood.
>
> Moderately retarded persons nearly always can learn to care for themselves, can profit to varying degrees from classroom instruction, and can learn to do simple routine tasks. . . . [M]ost are able to become at least partially self-supporting and may live in the community with some degree of supervision.
>
> Severely retarded persons generally require intensive services at all stages of life. They are capable of learning to care for themselves, and many can become marginally productive as adults, under supervision in a sheltered work setting. . . .
>
> The profoundly retarded nearly always require major medical and/or nursing supervision to remediate physical and medical disabilities and maintain life. . . .
>
> The President's Committee on Mental Retardation in 1973 . . . estimated the percentages of levels of mental retardation among the total population of America's retarded citizens . . . : 89% mildly retarded, 6.0% moderately retarded, 3.5% severely retarded, and 1.5% profoundly retarded. These percentages clearly indicate that the majority of the mentally retarded are more like the normal population than different from it.

2. The action to annul Harold's marriage was brought by the guardian of his estate. Persons under a disability may be placed under the care of a conservator, guardian, or both. Although the use of these terms, and the powers that go with them, differ greatly from jurisdiction to jurisdiction, conservators are usually appointed to protect the property of those who are unable to manage their property and affairs effectively—for example, UPC § 5-401 (Official 1991 Text). A conservator has a duty to receive a ward's income, to decide how much of the estate should be used for living expenses, and to prevent loss or waste of the ward's property or business.

Guardianship of the person is a more general notion and, indeed, can mean that the guardian has the same powers, rights, and duties as a parent possesses with respect to an unemancipated child. *See* UPC § 5-309.

3. Is there any inconsistency between appointment of a guardian of Harold's estate and a decision to permit him to marry? *See* Ertel v. Ertel, 40 N.E.2d 85 (Ill. App. 1942) ("In Illinois, less mental capacity is required to enable a person to enter into the marriage contract than is required for the execution of ordinary business transactions").

4. Mental deficiency and disease have always been a concern with respect to the existence of competence to agree to marry. State restrictions on marriage by the developmentally disabled and the mentally ill may also reflect, however, a eugenic concern that found strong support during the late nineteenth and early twentieth centuries. Belief in the hereditary sources of mental illness and faith in scientific solutions to social evils, combined with a growing concern about the health of the American family, seemed to suggest the value of standards for conjugal fitness that would reduce the incidence of "feeble-minded" children.

> Advocates of hereditary restrictions touted them as necessary weapons to defend the nation from degeneration. Feminist and pioneering social scientist Elizabeth Cady Stanton declared in 1879 that the "law of heredity should exclude many from entering the marriage relation." Ten years earlier she had insisted that only those "who can give the world children with splendid physique, strong intellect, and high moral sentiment, may conscientiously take on themselves the responsibility of marriage and maternity." Similarly, sociologist George Howard complained in 1904 that "under pleas of 'romantic love' we blandly yield to sexual attraction in choosing our mates, ignoring the welfare of the race." Appealing for a "higher standard of conjugal choice," he contended that experience "shows that in wedlock natural and sexual selection should play a smaller and artificial selection a larger role." Here, he declared, "the state has a function to perform."

Michael Grossberg, Governing the Hearth: Law and the Family in Nineteenth Century America 148 (1985).

5. In upholding a statute permitting sterilization of "mental defectives," Justice Holmes provided the following justification:

> The attack is not upon the procedure but upon the substantive law. . . . The judgment finds . . . that Carrie Buck "is the probable potential parent of socially inadequate offspring, likewise afflicted, that she may be sexually sterilized without detriment to her general health and that her welfare and that of society will be promoted by her sterilization," and thereupon makes the order. . . . [W]e cannot say as

a matter of law that the grounds [for sterilization] do not exist, and if they exist they justify the result. We have seen more than once that the public welfare may call upon the best citizens for their lives. It would be strange if it could not call upon those who already sap the strength of the State for these lesser sacrifices, often not felt to be such by those concerned, in order to prevent our being swamped with incompetence. It is better for all the world, if instead of waiting to execute degenerate offspring for crime, or to let them starve for their imbecility, society can prevent those who are manifestly unfit from continuing their kind. The principle that sustains compulsory vaccination is broad enough to cover cutting the Fallopian tubes. Three generations of imbeciles are enough.

Buck v. Bell, 274 U.S. 200, 207 (1927). Buck v. Bell has never been expressly overruled, although its current vitality has been sharply questioned in light of Skinner v. Oklahoma, 316 U.S. 535 (1942). The accuracy and acceptability of the premises of the eugenic movement have also been widely impeached. *See* Matter of Moe, 432 N.E.2d 712 (Mass. 1982); Elyse Ferster, Eliminating the Unfit—Is Sterilization the Answer?, 27 Ohio St. L.J. 591, 602-604 (1966); Michael Kindregan, Sixty Years of Compulsory Eugenic Sterilization: "Three Generations of Imbeciles" and the Constitution of the United States, 43 Chi.-Kent L. Rev. 123, 134-140 (1966). Most cases now permitting sterilization arise from a request by a parent or guardian for a court order permitting that procedure. *See, e.g.*, Matter of Moe, above.

6. The controversy over the meaning and inheritability of intelligence is heated and sometimes virulent. Several different aspects of this dispute should be kept in mind.

a. *Questions regarding the meaning of intelligence.* Most scientists agree that intelligence has something to do with the capacity to understand abstract concepts, to solve problems, and to express oneself verbally and quantitatively. However, these capacities are themselves imprecise and reflect a variety of mental qualities. Moreover, intelligence, unlike some other characteristics, is affected strongly by environmental factors (including cultural and educational opportunities, as well as diet) particularly during the early years of life. Nonetheless, intelligence tests measure something. They may not test intelligence, but they do predict in a general way occupational and professional success in our society.

b. *Questions regarding the measure of intelligence.* For many social purposes, it would be fair to say that intelligence *only* means relative performance on an intelligence quotient test. Questions about the design of these tests are now familiar to everyone. These tests were not standardized across socioeconomic status and race. Intelligence testing proponents, including minority group as well as majority group members, argue that the tests nonetheless are useful because they provide predictions for success in various educational and professional settings, and, to the extent they reflect cultural bias, that bias is also part of the educational and professional settings in question. However, because the design of these tests is directed to tasks associated with education and professional activity, the tests' utility in connection with *other* kinds of activities is even more speculative.

c. *Questions regarding the determinants of intelligence.* While alleles related to various conditions (such as Down's syndrome) that may involve intelligence levels have been identified, specific genes contributing to normal levels of intelligence have never been found. Accordingly, the case for the inheritability of intelligence is based on indirect, often probabilistic analyses of variation among groups of persons. Linda R. Maxson & Charles H. Daugherty, Genetics: A Human Perspective 209 (2d ed. 1989):

> Among the most compelling data is the increasing similarity in IQ of persons of increasing genetic relatedness. The average difference in IQ between genetically unrelated persons chosen at random is about 8 points. Therefore, knowledge of the IQ of one person provides little basis for predicting the IQ of any other person at random — a correlation of 0. However, as the genetic relatedness of pairs increases, the average IQ difference decreases and the correlation increases. Those persons most closely related are monozygotic twins, who are genetically identical. The correlation of IQ between monozygotic twins is almost .90; average IQs of monozygotic twins differ by an average of only about 3-4 points. . . .
>
> These data strongly indicate the genetic influence on intelligence, but influence of the environment is also clear. The correlation of IQ values among persons reared together is always higher than for persons reared apart, even for monozygotic twins. Increasing the environmental similarity always increases the similarity in IQ, just as does increasing genetic relatedness.

3. *Fraud and Duress*

WOLFE V. WOLFE

389 N.E.2d 1143 (Ill. 1979)

MORAN, J. After Judith Wolfe, plaintiff, filed a complaint for divorce in the circuit court of Cook County, James Wolfe, defendant, counterclaimed for an annulment of the marriage on the basis of fraud. . . .

In 1963, the parties discussed marriage but, when plaintiff informed defendant that she had previously been married and divorced, defendant explained that he, a Roman Catholic, was forbidden by his religion to marry her. In November of that year, however, plaintiff told defendant that she had learned from a friend in Arizona that her former husband had been killed in an auto accident and that she would receive a copy of the death certificate. Under these circumstances, defendant's church considered plaintiff a widow and defendant was free to marry her. Preparatory to marriage, plaintiff underwent conversion to Catholicism and, as a requirement thereof, executed a Sponsa in which she stated, under oath, that her former husband was dead.

Shortly before the couple married, in March of 1965, plaintiff had shown defendant a copy of the purported death certificate of her former husband. A child was born of the marriage in 1966.

In November 1973 the couple separated, and the following month, plaintiff sued for divorce. On May 10, 1974, defendant filed a counterclaim for annulment which alleged that plaintiff had fraudulently induced him to consent to marriage by misrepresenting that her former husband was dead.

At trial, defendant testified that, because of his religious convictions, he would not have married plaintiff had he not believed her to be a widow, and that he first learned that her former husband was still alive on February 1, 1974. The ex-husband was, in fact, called as a witness. The Sponsa and the copy of the purported death certificate were introduced into evidence. During examination by defendant's counsel, plaintiff admitted that, at the time she swore to and signed the Sponsa, she knew that her former husband was not dead. When questioned about the purported death certificate, plaintiff invoked the constitutional privilege against self-incrimination.

The evidence in this case clearly and convincingly showed that plaintiff had perpetrated a fraud upon defendant in order to obtain his consent to the marriage. Although such fraud would render the ordinary contract void, a marriage contract can be voided only if the nature of the fraud itself affects the essentials of the marriage. What constitutes the "essentials" of marriage cannot be expressly delineated, for what is essential to one marriage may not be equally significant to another. Whether a fraud goes to the essentials of a marriage must be determined on the basis of the facts in an individual case. . . .

In Bielby v. Bielby (1929), 333 Ill. 478, 165 N.E. 231, wherein it was determined that no fraud existed, the court . . . stated:

> The degree of fraud sufficient to vitiate an ordinary contract will not afford sufficient grounds for the annulment of a marriage. It is not sufficient that the complainant relied upon false representations and was deceived. False representations as to fortune, character, and social standing are not essential elements of the marriage, and it is contrary to public policy to annul a marriage for fraud or misrepresentations as to personal qualities.

With this background in mind, we turn to the issue before us: Did the fraud, under the circumstances of this case, go to the essentials of the marital relationship, rendering it impossible for defendant to perform the duties and obligations of his marriage? . . .

Sub judice, defendant has established that he is a loyal practitioner of his faith and has lived according to the rules and dictates of his church. In the absence of certain modifying circumstances, which apparently did not exist here, the defendant's religion prohibits marriage with a divorced person whose former spouse is still living. Under the facts of this case we believe that this marriage would not have occurred but for the fraud, executed for the purpose of inducing defendant's consent. Furthermore, since discovering the fraud, defendant is unable to continue marital cohabitation with plaintiff. It can be seen that this disability is the product of a canon of defendant's religion, placed upon him by his church. This is to be distinguished from a mere subjective, personal aversion. To deny defendant an annulment would cause the defrauded party to bear the consequences of the deception and allow the deceiver to proceed with impunity.

Under the circumstances of this case, we hold that the fraud goes to the essentials of the marital relationship, defendant's knowledge of which has rendered it impossible for him to continue to perform the duties and obligations of his marriage. As stated by the appellate court, "It is not in the public interest to protect such a marriage to the serious detriment of the defrauded party."

We recognize that the parties lived together as husband and wife for several years, and that a child of the marriage exists. Although we consider lengthy marital cohabitation to be a factor militating against the granting of an annulment, we do not consider it to be controlling here. Similarly, the existence of a child, although a factor, will not bar an annulment inasmuch as the status of the child, under Illinois law, is unchanged.

Based upon the foregoing, we conclude that defendant is entitled to an annulment. . . .

Judgment affirmed.

NOTES AND QUESTIONS

1. The law of annulment has been heavily influenced by the law of ecclesiastical courts applied in England until 1857. As late as 1897, even after assumption of civil jurisdiction over matrimonial affairs, the rule was that a marriage could be annulled only for "error personae," which meant that the wrong person was married. Errors of condition or quality ("error fortunae") were not sufficient to avoid the marriage. *See* Harry W. Vanneman, Annulment of Marriage for Fraud, 9 Minn. L. Rev. 497 (1925), reprinted in Association of American Law Schools, Selected Essays on Family Law 335, 336 (1950). An example of "error personae" (as well as an instance of the remedial effects of polygamy) can be found in the story of Jacob, Leah, and Rachel, Genesis 30:15-28.

2. Although American cases do not go as far as the traditional English view, most—as *Wolfe* indicates—have restricted annulment for fraud to misrepresentations going to. the "essentials" of marriage. An influential early American case, Reynolds v. Reynolds, 85 Mass. (3 Allen) 605 (1862), expressed the following rationale for this limitation:

> The great object of marriage in a civilized and Christian community is to secure the existence and permanence of the family relation, and to insure the legitimacy of offspring. It would tend to defeat this object, if error or disappointment in personal qualities or character was allowed to be the basis of proceedings on which to found a dissolution of the marriage tie. The law therefore wisely requires that persons who act on representations or belief in regard to such matters should bear the consequences which flow from contracts into which they have voluntarily entered, after they have been executed, and affords no relief for the results of a "blind credulity, however it may have been produced."

Id. at 607. The plaintiff in *Reynolds*, who had never engaged in sexual relations with the defendant prior to marriage, received an annulment based on his wife's undisclosed pregnancy by another. Where is the misrepresentation? And why does this misrepresentation go to the "essentials" of marriage? See 1 Homer H. Clark, Jr., The Law of Domestic Relations in the United States 195-198 (2d ed. 1987).

Under the traditional view of fraud, in what sense is agreement necessary to marriage? A cause of action for fraud in an ordinary contracts case involves a representation of fact, known to be false, that is intended to and does deceive the other party to his or her detriment. How does this approach to fraud compare to the way that fraud was defined for purposes of annulling a marriage?

3. The traditional English view of the fraud that will justify annulment, approximated by some American cases, stands at one end of the spectrum of

possible positions. New York, which sharply restricted divorce until relatively recently, is usually said to stand at the other end:

> [T]he fraud [required for annulment] need no longer "necessarily concern what is commonly called the essentials of the marriage *relation*—the rights and duties connected with cohabitation and consortium attached by law to the marital status. Any fraud is adequate which is 'material, to that degree that, had it not been practiced, the party deceived would not have consented to the marriage' and is 'of such nature as to deceive an ordinarily prudent person.'" Although it is not enough to show merely that one partner married for money and the other was disappointed [citing Woronzoff-Daschkoff v. Woronzoff-Daschkoff, 104 N.E.2d 877, 880 (N.Y. 1952)], and the decisions upon the subject of annulment have not always been uniform, there have been circumstances where misrepresentations of love and affection, with intention to make a home, were held sufficient, likewise in case of fraudulent representations concerning the legitimacy of children of the wife of a supposedly prior marriage, or concerning prior marital status. Concealment of prior marital status was held to be sufficient in Costello v. Costello; concealment of affliction with tuberculosis in Yelin v. Yelin; failure to reveal treatment of a mental disorder (schizophrenia, catatonic type) was held to be enough in Schaeffer v. Schaeffer; material misrepresentation of age in Tacchi v. Tacchi. . . .

Kober v. Kober, 211 N.E.2d 817, 819 (N.Y. 1965). In *Kober* itself, the New York Court of Appeals held that the husband's fraudulent concealment of his membership in the Nazi party during World War II and fanatical anti-Semitism were sufficient bases for annulment. *Kober* endorses a test similar to that used for ordinary contracts cases. If that is the test applied in New York, why can't false representations regarding wealth or social position suffice?

4. *Wolfe* purports to employ the traditional requirement that only fraud going to the essentials of marriage will justify annulment. How does the court define what is "essential"? Does its approach differ from the traditional notion of what is essential? Does it differ from the rule adopted by the New York courts?

5. Duress, like fraud, is usually said to vitiate the consent necessary for marriage. This claim arises only occasionally now. However, the older cases generally held that duress did not exist when a man agreed to marry after being threatened with prosecution for the crimes of seduction or bastardy. A review and criticism of these cases appear in Walter Wadlington, Shotgun Marriage by Operation of Law, 1 Ga. L. Rev. 183 (1966). Under this approach, to what extent is entrance into marriage a matter of "contract"?

6. If fraud is sufficient to invalidate a marriage, the question arises whether a marriage invalidated by fraud is void or voidable. Arnelle v. Fisher, 647 So. 2d 1047 (Fla. Dist. Ct. App. 1995), holds that a marriage to which one party's consent was procured through undue influence is voidable and not void. As a result, the marriage cannot be attacked or annulled after the death of one of the parties. *See* Hilary Lim, Messages from a Rarely Visited Island: Duress and Lack of Consent in Marriage, 4 Feminist Legal Stud. 195 (1996).

PROBLEMS

1. Plaintiff Elizabeth Princess married the defendant, Kermit, two years ago. Prior to the marriage, Kermit seemed the ideal spouse: handsome, sober,

hard-working, and sympathetic. Over the last two years, however, Elizabeth has found that her husband has a serious drinking problem, which he did not reveal; has no genuine interest in seeking a job; and is entirely unconcerned about his physical appearance or his manners. She has filed a complaint seeking an annulment on the ground that he failed to disclose his drinking problem and misrepresented his interest in seeking employment. Kermit has filed a motion to dismiss the bill for failure to state a claim. What arguments would be made by the parties in the hearing on that motion? *See* Johnston v. Johnston, 22 Cal. Rptr. 2d 253 (Cal. App. 1993) (where plaintiff alleged that defendant had "turned from a prince into a frog").

2. Mr. Patel, a native of India now resident in your city, has come to your office for advice. He married his wife, who is also a native of India, nine months ago. Patel is a member of a high caste in Indian society; his wife falsely represented that she is a member of the same caste. He has now learned that she is a member of the lowest ("Untouchable") class. Mr. Patel explains that this marriage violates the Hindu caste system, which is important both religiously and culturally, and embarrasses him and his family. He also tells you that, had he known of his wife's caste, he would not have married her. What advice would you give Patel?

3. Wallace and Susannah met as freshmen in college and, after dating for several months, engaged in nonmarital sexual intercourse, resulting in Susannah's pregnancy. Susannah wished to marry so that their child would be legitimate. Wallace did not wish to do so, at least initially. Susannah warned Wallace that she not only seek would to have him declared the father of the child but also would prosecute him criminally for fornication if he did not marry her. Fornication is a class B misdemeanor, punishable by imprisonment for not more than six months. Under this threat, Wallace married Susannah. Subsequently, he realized that a prosecution was unlikely because Susannah would herself be subject to the same charge. Wallace seeks an annulment on the ground of duress. Will an annulment be granted?

NOTE: NAMES

It is often assumed that, as part of the marriage contract, a married woman assumes her husband's name, and, indeed, this is common practice. While there is some dispute on this question, the common law seems to treat this practice as a matter of custom rather than as a legal requirement. *See* Stuart v. Board of Supervisors of Elections, 295 A.2d 223 (Md. App. 1972); State ex rel. Krupa v. Green, 177 N.E.2d 616 (Ohio App. 1961). It is, as well, common for a Latina to adopt a combined name on marriage, retaining her maiden name and adding her husband's name (with or without a hyphen). While legal process can be invoked to change a name, resort to that process is generally not required. One may change one's name by usage, or not. The only general limitation on change (by whatever strategy) is that the name change must not be designed to frustrate creditors or for some other illegitimate purpose. One might not, therefore, be able to change one's name to "State Tax Department."

A more complicated question has to do with naming children, originally and especially after divorce. Three kinds of rules are generally applied when a dispute arises: a presumption favoring maintenance of the child's current name, a "best interests" test, and (more recently) a presumption favoring the choice of the custodial parent. *See* Merle H. Weiner, "We Are Family": Valuing Associationalism in Disputes over Children's Surnames, 75 N.C. L. Rev. 1625, 1630-1631 (1997). Professor Weiner's article suggests that all three standards are flawed in theory or in application because they undervalue the importance of surnames as markers of associations, an approach that better reflects the interests of children and the meaning of divorce.

D. SUBSTANTIVE RESTRICTIONS ON MARRYING

1. *The Constitutional Framework*

ZABLOCKI V. REDHAIL

434 U.S. 374 (1978)

MARSHALL, J. At issue in this case is the constitutionality of a Wisconsin statute, Wis. Stat. §§ 245.10(1), (4), (5) (1973), which provides that members of a certain class of Wisconsin residents may not marry, within the State or elsewhere, without first obtaining a court order granting permission to marry. The class is defined by the statute to include any "Wisconsin resident having minor issue not in his custody and which he is under obligation to support by any court order or judgment." The statute specifies that court permission cannot be granted unless the marriage applicant submits proof of compliance with the support obligation and, in addition, demonstrates that the children covered by the support order "are not then and are not likely thereafter to become public charges." No marriage license may lawfully be issued in Wisconsin to a person covered by the statute, except upon court order; any marriage entered into without compliance with § 245.10 is declared void; and persons acquiring marriage licenses in violation of the section are subject to criminal penalties. . . .

Appellee Redhail is a Wisconsin resident who, under the terms of § 245.10, is unable to enter into a lawful marriage in Wisconsin or elsewhere so long as he maintains his Wisconsin residency. . . . In January 1972, when appellee was a minor and a high school student, a paternity action was instituted against him in Milwaukee County Court, alleging that he was the father of a baby girl born out of wedlock on July 5, 1971. After he appeared and admitted that he was the child's father, the court entered an order on May 12, 1972, adjudging appellee the father and ordering him to pay $109 per month as support for the child until she reached 18 years of age. From May 1972 until August 1974, appellee was unemployed and indigent, and consequently was unable to make any support payments.

On September 27, 1974, appellee filed an application for a marriage license with appellant Zablocki, the County Clerk of Milwaukee County, and a few days later the application was denied on the sole ground that appellee had not obtained a court order granting him permission to marry, as required by § 245.10. Although appellee did not petition a state court thereafter, it is stipulated that he would not have been able to satisfy either of the statutory prerequisites for an order granting permission to marry. First, he had not satisfied his support obligations to his illegitimate child, and as of December 1974 there was an arrearage in excess of $3,700. Second, the child had been a public charge since her birth, receiving benefits under the Aid to Families with Dependent Children program. It is stipulated that the child's benefit payments were such that she would have been a public charge even if appellee had been current in his support payments.

On December 24, 1974, appellee filed his complaint in the District Court, on behalf of himself and the class of all Wisconsin residents who had been refused a marriage license pursuant to §245.10(1) by one of the county clerks in Wisconsin.

II

In evaluating [the statute] under the Equal Protection Clause, "we must first determine what burden of justification the classification created thereby must meet, by looking to the nature of the classification and the individual interests affected." Since our past decisions make clear that the right to marry is of fundamental importance, and since the classification at issue here significantly interferes with the exercise of that right, we believe that "critical examination" of the state interests advanced in support of the classification is required.

The leading decision of this Court on the right to marry is Loving v. Virginia, 388 U.S. 1 (1967). In that case, an interracial couple who had been convicted of violating Virginia's miscegenation laws challenged the statutory scheme on both equal protection and due process grounds. The Court's opinion could have rested solely on the ground that the statutes discriminated on the basis of race in violation of the Equal Protection Clause. But the Court went on to hold that the laws arbitrarily deprived the couple of a fundamental liberty protected by the Due Process Clause, the freedom to marry. The Court's language on the latter point bears repeating:

> The freedom to marry has long been recognized as one of the vital personal rights essential to the orderly pursuit of happiness by free men.
> Marriage is one of the "basic civil rights of man," fundamental to our very existence and survival.

Id., at 12, quoting Skinner v. Oklahoma ex rel. Williamson, 316 U.S. 535 (1942).

Although *Loving* arose in the context of racial discrimination, prior and subsequent decisions of this Court confirm that the right to marry is of fundamental importance for all individuals. Long ago, in Maynard v. Hill, 125 U.S. 190 (1888), the Court characterized marriage as "the most important relation in life," and as "the foundation of the family and of society, without which there would be neither civilization nor progress." In Meyer v. Nebraska, 262 U.S. 390 (1923), the Court recognized that the right "to marry, establish a home and bring up children" is a central part of the liberty protected by the Due Process Clause, id., at 399, and in Skinner v. Oklahoma ex rel. Williamson, supra, 316 U.S. 535 (1942), marriage was described as "fundamental to the very existence and survival of the race," 316 U.S., at 541.

More recent decisions have established that the right to marry is part of the fundamental "right of privacy" implicit in the Fourteenth Amendment's Due Process Clause. In Griswold v. Connecticut, 381 U.S. 479 (1965), the Court observed:

> We deal with a right of privacy older than the Bill of Rights—older than our political parties, older than our school system. Marriage is a coming together for better or for worse, hopefully enduring, and intimate to the degree of being sacred. It is an association that promotes a way of life, not causes; a harmony in living, not political faiths; a bilateral loyalty, not commercial or social projects. Yet it is an association for as noble a purpose as any involved in our prior decisions.

Id., at 486.

Cases subsequent to Griswold and Loving have routinely categorized the decision to marry as among the personal decisions protected by the right of privacy. . . .

It is not surprising that the decision to marry has been placed on the same level of importance as decisions relating to procreation, childbirth, child rearing, and family relationships. As the facts of this case illustrate, it would make little sense to recognize a right of privacy with respect to other matters of family life and not with respect to the decision to enter the relationship that is the foundation of the family in our society. . . .

By reaffirming the fundamental character of the right to marry, we do not mean to suggest that every state regulation which relates in any way to the incidents of or prerequisites for marriage must be subjected to rigorous scrutiny. To the contrary, reasonable regulations that do not significantly interfere with decisions to enter into the marital relationship may legitimately be imposed. The statutory classification at issue here, however, clearly does interfere directly and substantially with the right to marry.

Under the challenged statute, no Wisconsin resident in the affected class may marry in Wisconsin or elsewhere without a court order, and marriages contracted in violation of the statute are both void and punishable as criminal offenses. Some of those in the affected class, like appellee, will never be able to obtain the necessary court order, because they either lack the financial means to meet their support obligations or cannot prove that their children will not become public charges. These persons are absolutely prevented from getting married. Many others, able in theory to satisfy the statute's requirements, will be sufficiently burdened by having to do so that they will in effect be coerced into forgoing their right to marry. And even those who can be persuaded to meet the statute's requirements suffer a serious intrusion into their freedom of choice in an area in which we have held such freedom to be fundamental.

III

When a statutory classification significantly interferes with the exercise of a fundamental right, it cannot be upheld unless it is supported by sufficiently important state interests and is closely tailored to effectuate only those interests. Appellant asserts that two interests are served by the challenged statute: the permission-to-marry proceeding furnishes an opportunity to counsel the applicant as to the necessity of fulfilling his prior support obligations, and the welfare of the out-of-custody children is protected. We may accept for present purposes that these are legitimate and substantial interests, but, since the means selected by the State for achieving these interests unnecessarily impinge on the right to marry, the statute cannot be sustained.

There is evidence that the challenged statute, as originally introduced in the Wisconsin Legislature, was intended merely to establish a mechanism whereby persons with support obligations to children from prior marriages could be counseled before they entered into new marital relationships and incurred further support obligations. Court permission to marry was to be required, but apparently permission was automatically to be granted after counseling was completed. The statute actually enacted, however, does not expressly require or provide for any counseling whatsoever, nor for any automatic granting of permission to marry by the court, and thus it can hardly be justified as a means for ensuring counseling of the persons within its coverage. Even assuming that counseling does take place—a fact as to which there is no evidence in the record—this interest obviously cannot support the withholding of court permission to marry once counseling is completed.

With regard to safeguarding the welfare of the out-of-custody children, appellant's brief does not make clear the connection between the State's interest and the statute's requirements. At argument, appellant's counsel suggested that, since permission to marry cannot be granted unless the applicant shows that he has satisfied his court-determined support obligations to the prior children and that those children will not become public charges, the statute provides incentive for the applicant to make support payments to his children. This "collection device" rationale cannot justify the statute's broad infringement on the right to marry.

First, with respect to individuals who are unable to meet the statutory requirements, the statute merely prevents the applicant from getting married, without delivering any money at all into the hands of the applicant's prior children. More importantly, regardless of the applicant's ability or willingness to meet the statutory requirements, the State already has numerous other means for exacting compliance with support obligations, means that are at least as effective as the instant statute's and yet do not impinge upon the right to marry. Under Wisconsin law, whether the children are from a prior marriage or were born out of wedlock, court-determined support obligations may be enforced directly via wage assignments, civil contempt proceedings, and criminal penalties. And, if the State believes that parents of children out of their custody should be responsible for ensuring that those children do not become public charges, this interest can be achieved by adjusting the criteria used for determining the amounts to be paid under their support orders.

There is also some suggestion that [the statute] protects the ability of marriage applicants to meet support obligations to prior children by preventing the applicants from incurring new support obligations. But the challenged provisions . . . are grossly underinclusive with respect to this purpose, since they do not limit in any way new financial commitments by the applicant other than those arising out of the contemplated marriage. The statutory classification is substantially overinclusive as well: Given the possibility that the new spouse will actually better the applicant's financial situation, by contributing income from a job or otherwise, the statute in many cases may prevent affected individuals from improving their ability to satisfy their prior support obligations. And, although it is true that the applicant will incur support obligations to any children born during the contemplated marriage, preventing the marriage may only result in the children being born out of wedlock, as in fact occurred in appellee's case. Since the support obligation is the same whether the child is born in or out of wedlock, the net result of preventing the marriage is simply more illegitimate children.

The statutory classification . . . thus cannot be justified by the interests advanced in support of it. The judgment of the District Court is, accordingly,

Affirmed.

STEWART, J., concurring in the judgment. I cannot join the opinion of the Court. To hold, as the Court does, that the Wisconsin statute violates the Equal Protection Clause seems to me to misconceive the meaning of that constitutional guarantee. The Equal Protection Clause deals not with substantive rights or freedoms but with invidiously discriminatory classifications. The paradigm of its violation is, of course, classification by race. . . .

The problem in this case is not one of discriminatory classifications, but of unwarranted encroachment upon a constitutionally protected freedom. I think that the Wisconsin statute is unconstitutional because it exceeds the bounds of permissible state regulation of marriage, and invades the sphere of liberty protected by the Due Process Clause of the Fourteenth Amendment.

Marriage is a privilege not a right

I

I do not agree with the Court that there is a "right to marry" in the constitutional sense. That right, or more accurately that privilege, is under our federal system peculiarly one to be defined and limited by state law. A State may not only "significantly interfere with decisions to enter into marital relationship," but may in many circumstances absolutely prohibit it. Surely, for example, a State may legitimately say that no one can marry his or her sibling, that no one can marry who is not at least 14 years old, that no one can marry without first passing an examination for venereal disease, or that no one can marry who has a living husband or wife. But, just as surely, in regulating the intimate human relationship of marriage, there is a limit beyond which a State may not constitutionally go.

The Constitution does not specifically mention freedom to marry, but it is settled that the "liberty" protected by the Due Process Clause of the Fourteenth Amendment embraces more than those freedoms expressly enumerated in the Bill of Rights. And the decisions of this Court have made clear that freedom of personal choice in matters of marriage and family life is one of the liberties so protected [citing Roe v. Wade; Loving v. Virginia; Griswold v. Connecticut; Pierce v. Society of Sisters; Meyer v. Nebraska].

It is evident that the Wisconsin law now before us directly abridges that freedom. The question is whether the state interests that support the abridgment can overcome the substantive protections of the Constitution.

The Wisconsin law makes permission to marry turn on the payment of money in support of one's children by a previous marriage or liaison. Those who cannot show both that they have kept up with their support obligations and that their children are not and will not become wards of the State are altogether prohibited from marrying.

If Wisconsin had said that no one could marry who had not paid all of the fines assessed against him for traffic violations, I suppose the constitutional invalidity of the law would be apparent. For while the state interest would certainly be legitimate, that interest would be both disproportionate and unrelated to the restriction of liberty imposed by the State. But the invalidity of the law before us is hardly so clear, because its restriction of liberty seems largely to be imposed only on those who have abused the same liberty in the past.

Looked at in one way, the law may be seen as simply a collection device additional to those used by Wisconsin and other States for enforcing parental support obligations. But since it operates by denying permission to marry, it also clearly reflects a legislative judgment that a person should not be permitted to incur new family financial obligations until he has fulfilled those he already has. Insofar as this judgment is paternalistic rather than punitive, it manifests a concern for the economic well-being of a prospective marital household. These interests are legitimate concerns of the State. But it does not follow that they justify the absolute deprivation of the benefits of a legal marriage. . . .

The Wisconsin law makes no allowance for the truly indigent. The State flatly denies a marriage license to anyone who cannot afford to fulfill his support obligations and keep his children from becoming wards of the State. We may assume that the State has legitimate interests in collecting delinquent support payments and in reducing its welfare load. We may also assume that, as applied to those who can afford to meet the statute's financial requirements but choose not to do so, the law advances the State's objectives in ways superior to other means available to the State. The fact remains that some people simply cannot afford to meet the statute's financial requirements. To deny these people permission to marry penalizes them for failing to do that which they cannot do. Insofar as it applies to indigents, the state law is an irrational means of achieving these objectives of the State.

As directed against either the indigent or the delinquent parent, the law is substantially more rational if viewed as a means of assuring the financial viability of future marriages. In this context, it reflects a plausible judgment that those who have not fulfilled their financial obligations and have not kept their children off the welfare rolls in the past are likely to encounter similar difficulties in the future. But the State's legitimate concern with the financial soundness of prospective marriages must stop short of telling people they may not marry because they are too poor or because they might persist in their financial irresponsibility. The invasion of constitutionally protected liberty and the chance of erroneous prediction are simply too great. A legislative judgment so alien to our traditions and so offensive to our shared notions of fairness offends the Due Process Clause of the Fourteenth Amendment. . . .

REHNQUIST, J., dissenting. . . . I would view this legislative judgment in the light of the traditional presumption of validity. I think that under the Equal Protection

Clause the statute need pass only the "rational basis test," and that under the Due Process Clause it need only be shown that it bears a rational relation to a constitutionally permissible objective. The statute so viewed is a permissible exercise of the State's power to regulate family life and to assure the support of minor children, despite its possible imprecision in the extreme cases envisioned in the concurring opinions.

NOTES AND QUESTIONS

1. The majority declares that marriage is a "fundamental liberty" and that state regulations substantially burdening access to marriage will be subject to strict scrutiny. There are two aspects to this approach. One involves the heightening of judicial scrutiny for laws that classify, not because the classification is suspect, but because of the importance or "fundamental" quality of the interest that is distributed or burdened unequally. Disagreement about whether scrutiny of classifications should be heightened for that reason lies behind the separate analyses of Justices Marshall and Stewart.

Assuming the majority's position, that heightened scrutiny of classifications can result from the nature of the interest as well as from the classification involved, the further question is whether a particular interest should be regarded as "fundamental." Previous cases had held the following to fall into the category of "fundamental liberty": the right to have offspring (e.g., Skinner v. Oklahoma, 316 U.S. 535 (1942)); the right to vote (e.g., Harper v. Virginia State Board of Elections, 383 U.S. 663 (1966)); the right to travel interstate (e.g., Shapiro v. Thompson, 394 U.S. 618 (1969)); and certain aspects of the right to privacy in making important decisions (e.g., Roe v. Wade, 410 U.S. 113 (1973)). On the other hand, the interest of children in public education has not been held a fundamental right (Plyler v. Doe, 457 U.S. 202 (1982)).

Justice Marshall concludes that marriage is a fundamental liberty that has long been recognized on the basis of a line of cases beginning with Maynard v. Hill. *Maynard* upheld the right of a state to enact a statute allowing dissolution divorce against a challenge that this remedy constituted an abridgement of the right to contract. Does it support the conclusion that marriage is a fundamental liberty?

Griswold v. Connecticut (discussed in Chapter 2) is also relied upon by Justice Marshall. To what extent does it entail the existence of a fundamental right to marry? To what extent do the other cases establish that proposition?

2. The majority opinion observes that it will not employ strict scrutiny for regulations that do not "significantly interfere with decisions to enter into the marital relationship . . . ," thus seeking to distinguish its unanimous decision in Califano v. Jobst, 434 U.S. 47 (1977), earlier in the same term. *Jobst* sustained a section of the Social Security Act that provided for termination of a dependent child's benefits upon marriage to an individual not entitled in his or her own right to benefits under the Act. Jobst himself was dependent because of a disability and married a woman who was also disabled but did not receive benefits under the Act. The Court applied the rational-basis standard, observing that this approach "is not rendered invalid simply because some persons who might otherwise have married

were deterred by the rule or because some who did marry were burdened thereby." 434 U.S. at 54. *Compare* the following analyses of the relationship between *Zablocki* and *Jobst*, which appear in various opinions in the former decision.

[Justice Marshall (for the Court):] As the opinion for the Court [in *Jobst*] expressly noted, the rule terminating benefits upon marriage was not "an attempt to interfere with the individual's freedom to make a decision as important as marriage." The Social Security provisions placed no direct obstacle in the path of persons desiring to get married, and—notwithstanding our Brother Rehnquist's imaginative recasting of the case . . .—there was no evidence that the laws significantly discouraged, let alone made "practically impossible," any marriages. Indeed, the provisions had not deterred the individual who challenged the statute from getting married, even though he and his wife were both disabled. [Justice Marshall also observed that because of the availability of other federal benefits, total payments to the Jobsts were only $20 per month less than they would have been had Mr. Jobst's child benefits not been terminated.] 434 U.S. at 374, n.12.

[Justice Stevens (concurring in the judgment):] When a state allocates benefits or burdens, it may have valid reasons for treating married and unmarried persons differently. Classification based on marital status has been an accepted characteristic of tax legislation, Selective Service rules, and Social Security regulations. As cases like *Jobst* demonstrate, such laws may "significantly interfere with decisions to enter into the marital relationship." That kind of interference, however, is not a sufficient reason for invalidating every law reflecting a legislative judgment that there are relevant differences between married persons as a class and unmarried persons as a class.

A classification based on marital status is fundamentally different from a classification which determines who may lawfully enter into a marriage relationship. The individual's interest in making the marriage decision independently is sufficiently important to merit special constitutional protection. It is not, however, an interest which is constitutionally immune from evenhanded regulation. Thus, laws prohibiting marriage to a child, a close relative, or a person afflicted with venereal disease, are unchallenged even though they "interfere directly and substantially with the right to marry." The Wisconsin statute has a different character.

Under this statute, a person's economic status may determine his eligibility to enter into a lawful marriage. . . . This type of statutory discrimination is, I believe, totally unprecedented, as well as inconsistent with our tradition of administering justice equally to the rich and to the poor. 434 U.S. at 403-404.

[Justice Rehnquist (dissenting):] Earlier this Term the traditional standard of review was applied in Califano v. Jobst, despite the claim that the statute there in question burdened the exercise of the right to marry. The extreme situation considered there involved a permanently disabled appellee whose benefits under the Social Security Act had been terminated because of his marriage to an equally disabled woman who was not, however, a beneficiary under the Act. This Court recognized that Congress, in granting the original [Social Security] benefit, could reasonably assume that a disabled adult child remained dependent upon his parents for support. The Court concluded that, upon a beneficiary's marriage, Congress could terminate his benefits, because "there can be no question about the validity of the assumption that a married person is less likely to be dependent on his parents for support than one who is unmarried." Although that assumption had been proved false as applied in that individual case, the statute was nonetheless rational. "The broad legislative classification must be judged by reference to characteristics typical of the affected classes rather than by focusing on selected, atypical examples."

The analysis applied in *Jobst* is equally applicable here. Here, too, the Wisconsin Legislature has "adopted this rule in the course of constructing a complex social welfare system that necessarily deals with the intimacies of family life." . . . [T]he extent of the burden imposed by this statute [does not] so differentiate it from that considered in *Jobst* as to warrant a different result. In the case of some applicants, this statute makes the proposed marriage legally impossible for financial reasons; in a similar number of extreme cases, the Social Security Act makes the proposed marriage practically impossible for the same reasons. I cannot conclude that such a difference justifies the application of a heightened standard of review to the statute in question here.

434 U.S. at 407-408.

PROBLEMS

1. Medicaid rules imputing to the recipient all income and assets of a spouse (assuming they are living together) may have the effect of keeping many older couples from marrying. J. L. Matthews, Social Security, Medicare and Pensions 7:6 (5th ed. 1991). Does *Zablocki* suggest the unconstitutionality of this deeming provision?

2. The state in which you live has enacted a statute requiring all persons marrying for the first time to undergo counseling through a state-licensed agency. The agency charges a fee of $50 for two counseling sessions. These sessions address management of finances and interpersonal relations. After attendance at two sessions, persons wishing to marry receive a certificate of compliance with the statutory counseling requirement, and a marriage license will be issued (all other requirements also being satisfied). Will such a statute be upheld against a constitutional challenge?

2. Particular Restrictions

a. Monogamy

POTTER V. MURRAY CITY

760 F.2d 1065 (10th Cir. 1985)

HOLLOWAY, C.J. In this suit [brought under 42 U.S.C. § 1983] the plaintiff-appellant Royston E. Potter (plaintiff) challenges Utah's proscription against polygamy or plural marriage. His principal claim is that the termination of his employment as a city police officer for the practice of plural marriage violated his rights to the free exercise of his religion and his right to privacy. . . .

In Reynolds v. United States, 98 U.S. (8 Otto) 145 (1878), the Supreme Court affirmed a criminal conviction of a Mormon for practicing polygamy and rejected the argument that Congress' prohibition of polygamy violated the defendant's right to the free exercise of religion. Plaintiff argues that *Reynolds* is no longer controlling because later cases have "in effect" overturned the decision. We disagree.

Plaintiff principally relies on Wisconsin v. Yoder. 406 U.S. 205 (1972). There the Supreme Court held that the religious belief of the Amish that their salvation requires life in a church community apart from the world necessitated that they be exempted from a state law requirement that children attend public school beyond the eighth grade. *Yoder* explained that for a state to compel school attendance beyond the eighth grade when there is a claim that it "interferes with the practice of a legitimate religious belief, it must appear either that the State does not deny the free exercise of religious belief by its requirement, or that there is a state interest of sufficient magnitude to override the interest claiming protection under the Free Exercise Clause." As Chief Justice Burger stated, "The essence of all that has been said and written on the subject [of the free exercise clause] is that only those interests of the highest order and those not otherwise served can overbalance legitimate claims to the free exercise of religion."

The parties have stipulated here for the purpose of the motions for summary judgment that plaintiff's practice of plural marriage is the result of a good faith religious belief. The plaintiff has made an undisputed showing that his two wives consented to the plural marriage, and that the wives and five children of the marriages receive love and adequate care and attention and do not want for any necessity of life. Plaintiff points out that the State defendants have not presented any empirical evidence that monogamy is superior to polygamy, nor has the Utah legislature ever considered whether its anti-polygamy laws are wise. Hence plaintiff argues that under *Yoder*, summary judgment should have been entered in his favor rather than for the defendants.

We cannot disregard *Reynolds*, however, because in *Yoder* and afterwards the Supreme Court has recognized the continued validity of *Reynolds*. In *Yoder*, *Reynolds* was one of four cases that the Court cited in support of the proposition that "[i]t is true that activities of individuals, even when religiously based, are often subject to regulation by the States in the exercise of their undoubted power to promote the health, safety, and general welfare, or the Federal Government in the exercise of its delegated powers." Since *Yoder*, the Court has said that "[s]tatutes making bigamy a crime surely cut into an individual's freedom to associate, but few today seriously claim such statutes violate the First Amendment or any other constitutional provision." . . . Moreover, *Reynolds* has been cited with approval since *Yoder*. . . .

Monogamy is inextricably woven into the fabric of our society. It is the bedrock upon which our culture is built. In light of these fundamental values, the State is justified, by a compelling interest, in upholding and enforcing its ban on plural marriage to protect the monogamous marriage relationship. . . .

Plaintiff argues that his constitutional right to privacy prohibits the State of Utah from sanctioning him for entering into a polygamous marriage. Again we disagree.

We find no authority for extending the constitutional right of privacy so far that it would protect polygamous marriages. We decline to do so. . . .

Plaintiff further argues that Utah's laws prohibiting polygamy have fallen into desuetude. He says that there have been fewer than 25 prosecutions in Utah since 1952 for such offenses, that there are at least 5,000 to 10,000 polygamist family members in the State, and that during Chief Gillen's thirty year tenure he had never arrested anyone nor seen anyone arrested or prosecuted for violating Utah's anti-bigamy statute. Thus he says that invoking laws which have long been in disuse to sanction him is a violation of the constitutional guarantees of due process and equal protection. We disagree.

Polygamy has been prohibited in our society since its inception. *See Reynolds*, 98 U.S. at 164-65. The prohibitions continue in full force today. We cannot agree that the discharge of plaintiff for engaging in bigamy violated any constitutional guarantee. The showing made did not establish the enforcement of a "basically obsolete or an empty law whose function has long since passed." The showing of minimal numbers of prosecutions does not establish an abandonment of the State's laws and an irrational revival of them here. "[M]ere failure to prosecute other offenders is no basis for a finding of denial of equal protection."

NOTES AND QUESTIONS

1. Reynolds v. United States, 98 U.S. 145 (1878), is the root case addressing the constitutionality of prohibitions against plural marriage. A Mormon defendant challenged the constitutionality of federal law making bigamy a crime in the territory of Utah. He introduced evidence that polygamy was the duty of male members of the Church of Jesus Christ of Latter-Day Saints, violation of which duty entailed "damnation in the life to come." The Court sustained the statute and defendant's conviction.

Polygamy has always been odious among the Northern and Western nations of Europe and, until the establishment of the Mormon Church, was almost exclusively a feature of the life of Asiatic and African people. At common law, the second marriage was always void. 2 Kent, Com. 79, and from the earliest history of England polygamy has been treated as an offense against society.

By the statute of 1 James I (ch. 11), the offense, if committed in England or Wales, was made punishable in the civil courts, and the penalty was death. As this statute was limited in its operation to England and Wales, it was at a very early period re-enacted, generally with some modifications, in all the Colonies. In connection with the case we are now considering, it is a significant fact that on the 8th of December, 1788, after the passage of the act establishing religious freedom, and after the convention of Virginia had recommended as an amendment to the Constitution of the United States the declaration in a bill of rights that "All men have an equal, natural, and unalienable right to the free exercise of religion, according to the dictates of conscience," the legislature of that State substantially enacted the Statute of James I, death penalty included, because, as recited in the preamble, "it hath been doubted whether bigamy or polygamy be punishable by the laws of this Commonwealth." 12 Hening's Stat. 691. From that day to this we think it may safely be said there has never been a time in any State of the Union when polygamy has not been offence against society, cognizable by the civil courts and punishable with more or less severity. In the face of all this evidence, it is impossible to believe that the constitutional guaranty of religious freedom was intended to prohibit legislation in respect to this most important feature of social life. Marriage, while from its very nature a sacred obligation, is nevertheless, in most civilized nations, a civil contract, and usually regulated by law. Upon it society may be said to be built, and out of its fruits spring social relations and social obligations and duties, with which government is necessarily required to deal. In fact, according as monogamous or polygamous marriages are allowed, do we find the principles on which the government of the people, to a greater or less extent, rests. Professor Lieber says, polygamy leads to the patriarchal principle, and which, when applied to large communities, fetters the people in stationary despotism, while that principle cannot long exist in connection with monogamy. . . . . An exceptional colony of polygamists under an exceptional leadership may sometimes exist for a time without appearing to disturb the social condition of the people who surround it; but there cannot be a doubt that, unless restricted by some form of constitution, it is within the legitimate scope of the power of every civil government to determine whether polygamy or monogamy shall be the law of social life under its dominion.

Id. at 164-166. The Utah Supreme Court has also rejected a claim that the ban on plural marriage violates the federal Constitution. State v. Green, 99 P.3d 820 (Utah 2004). For a discussion of the claim in *Reynolds* that polygamy is related to despotism and monogamy to democracy, *see* Maura I. Strassberg, Distinctions of Form or Substance: Monogamy, Polygamy, and Same-Sex Marriage, 75 N.C. L. Rev. 1501 (1997).

2. The relationship between religious tradition and legal doctrine was very clear in the nineteenth century, when political theory and judicial discourse more comfortably invoked moral language. The identification of civilization and Christianity was deep and widespread, and standard legal texts such as Thomas Cooley's *Constitutional Limitations* took the position that Christianity was part of state common law jurisprudence for various purposes, and most especially those related to marriage and the family. Thomas J. Cooley, A Treatise on the Constitutional Limitations Which Rest upon the Legislative Power of the States of the American Union 472 (1868). *See* Sarah Barringer Gordon, The Mormon Question: Polygamy and Constitutional Conflict in Nineteenth Century America 54-77 (2002).

The United States Supreme Court was not quite as explicit in *Reynolds*, but quite clear in Church of Jesus Christ of Latter-Day Saints v. United States, observing that "the organization of a community for the spread and practice of polygamy is, in a measure, a return to barbarism. It is contrary to the spirit of Christianity and of the civilization which Christianity has produced in the Western world." 136 U.S. 1, 48-49 (1890).

3. As *Reynolds* indicates, monogamy is not the universal form of marriage. A statute in Iraq provides that "[m]arriage to more than one woman shall not be permitted except with the permission of a judge and for such permission to be given the following two conditions must be fulfilled: (a) the husband must have the financial ability to support more than one wife and (b) there must be some lawful benefit." The judge is not to give permission if a lack of equity between the wives is feared. The Law of Personal Status, Law No. 188, art. 3 (3-6) (1959) (Iraq),

reprinted in Dawoud Sudqi El Alami & Doreen Hinchcliffe, Islamic Marriage and Divorce Laws of the Arab World 63, 66 (1996). A Kuwaiti statute allows plural marriage, although it prohibits a husband from requiring a second wife to live with his first wife without her consent, Law No. 51 of 1984 Concerning Personal Status, art. 85 (Kuwait) (reprinted in *id.* at 130), and a Lebanese statute limits plural marriage to three wives. The Law of the Rights of the Family of 16 July 1962, art. 31 (Leb.) (reprinted in *id.* at 152). For a thoughtful discussion of these and other aspects of marriage, *see* Carol Weisbrod, Universals and Particulars: A Comment on Women's Human Rights and Religious Marriage Contracts, 9 S. Cal. Rev. L. & Women's Stud. 77 (1999). Although not universal, monogamy is the most common form of marriage. *See* Claude Levi-Strauss, The Family, in The View from Afar 39, 44-45 (J. Neugroschel & P. Hoss trans., 1985).

4. One aspect of the Mormon experience was the adoption of polygamy by one group within a society that was otherwise monogamous. Variety in marital regimes within one nation is found now in countries that are home to populations with differing religions. Until the 1970s, Malaysian law included a number of laws relating to marriage and divorce. Muslims were (and still are) subject to Islamic law, which is regulated at the state level. Non-Muslims were governed by five statutes on marriage and three for divorce, as well as by customary laws of the Chinese and Hindus, among others. The complexity presented by that legal regime is discussed in Mehrun Siraj, Women and the Law: Significant Developments in Malaysia, 28 Law & Soc'y Rev. 561 (1994), and is illustrated by the problems in distribution of the estate of a Chinese Christian who solemnized his first marriage according to the Christian Marriage Ordinance and then contracted another marriage according to Chinese custom (which permits plural wives). *Id.* at 562. Malaysian law was revised in 1976 and prohibits polygamy except for Muslims marrying under Islamic law. *Id.* at 563-565.

During the same period, efforts were made to reform Islamic law, and a model Islamic Family Law Act was drafted. Each state passed its own version of the model. The version adopted in the state of Kelantan requires a married man to obtain the court's permission before taking another wife. If it is satisfied that the prospective wife and her *wali* (marriage guardian) consent to the marriage and that the man is able to support another family, it will approve the plural marriage. The financial inquiry seems to be largely pro forma. Although the law does not require notification of the husband's current wife or wives that he intends to marry again, the current practice is to do so. *Id.* at 566-567. To what extent would consent and financial capacity requirements remove objections to plural marriage in this country?

5. In practice, plural marriages continue to exist within our formally monogamous legal regime. Polygamous practices declined from the time of its rejection by the Mormon church in 1890 through the 1930s and 1940s. Since that time, however, there has been something of a resurgence in public advocacy of and participation in polygamous marriage. Although firm data are understandably lacking, some estimate that from 30,000 to 50,000 people are engaged in plural marriage in the western part of the United States. On contemporary polygamy in Utah, *see* Irwin Altman & Joseph Ginat, Polygamous Families in Contemporary Society (1996). *See also* Irwin Altman, Polygamous Family Life: The Case of Contemporary Mormon Fundamentalists, 1996 Utah L. Rev. 367. These studies

examine how wives and husbands achieve viable dyadic and communal relationships within plural families.

6. The first session of the United Nations Commission on the Status of Women in 1947 identified as a principal aim, in the field of marriage, "freedom of choice, dignity of the wife, monogamy, and equal right to dissolution of marriage." Legal Status of Married Women (Reports submitted by the Secretary-General). Why should monogamy be regarded as important to the recognition of equal rights for women? Is it relevant that women in Utah gained the franchise in 1870 and that the National Woman Suffrage Association (founded by Elizabeth Cady Stanton and Susan B. Anthony) resolved, days after the *Reynolds* decision, that the federal government "should forbear to exercise federal power to disenfranchise the women of Utah, who have had a more just and liberal spirit shown them by Mormon men than Gentile women in the States have yet perceived in their rulers"? *See* Carol Weisbrod & Pamela Sheingorn, Reynolds v. United States: Nineteenth Century Forms of Marriage and the Status of Women, 10 Conn. L. Rev. 828, 850-856 (1978).

For a discussion of women and polygamy in the multiracial, multireligious Malaysian setting, *see* Sirhaj, above, at 577-580.

The same issues are under discussion currently, supported in part by the description of access to marriage as a fundamental liberty in Zablocki v. Redhail and in part by acute interest in nontraditional marriage forms and particularly same-sex marriage. David L. Chambers summarizes recent sympathetic accounts of modern polygamous families in Polygamy and Same-Sex Marriage, 26 Hofstra L. Rev. 53, 70-74 (1997). He suggests that movements to legalize plural marriages should be supported unless they genuinely pose significant harms. While recognizing that much research on that question must be done, Professor Chambers also suggests that we should not treat as an adequate harm that women in plural marriages are, or regard themselves as, subordinate to their husbands if their lives are otherwise tolerable. Professor Chambers also recognizes that one cannot look only to the (he suggests successful) experiences of Mormon polygamy, since abandonment of the requirement of monogamy would permit plural marriage apart from any religious commitments. *Id.* at 82.

The Salt Lake Tribune, June 28, 1998, at A1 et seq., gives a more worrisome account of the economic and social conditions of Mormon fundamentalist polygamous families living in entirely or almost entirely polygamous towns in southern Utah and northern Arizona. The article, titled Polygamy on the Dole, reports that the average family sizes in Hilldale, Utah, and Colorado City, Arizona, are 8.55 and 7.97, respectively. Average household incomes are, however, half or less than half of the state averages: $21,822 in Hilldale (compared with a Utah average of $41,316) and $19,663 in Colorado City (compared with an Arizona average of $35,426). A third of the families in Hilldale and 61 percent of the families in Colorado City are reported to be living in poverty and, consequently, families in these communities draw far more than their shares of welfare benefits and educational subsidies.

The Salt Lake Tribune article reconfirms the long-standing observation that, although polygamy is relatively common and well known, state prosecutors are not inclined to prosecute those who engage in plural marriage.

7. What did Professor Lieber mean when he said that polygamy is related to despotism, and monogamy to democratic forms of government? Is this simply

nineteenth-century parochialism, or might something in the nature of polygamous family life be expected to affect attitudes toward social and political organization?

8. More generally, the Court in *Reynolds* assumes that there is a relationship between the organization and values of the family and those of the government at large. This relationship has been a staple of Western thought.

> In the seventeenth and eighteenth centuries, the household was an extension and reflection of the community at large. This notion is conventionally expressed by the preachers' description of the family as "a little commonwealth, a little church. . . . John Demos suggests that the family was joined "in a relation of profound reciprocity" with the society as a whole, such that "one might almost say that they are continuous with one another."

Lee E. Teitelbaum, Family History and Family Law, 1985 Wis. L. Rev. 1135, 1138-1139.

Modern courts and commentators are no less likely to view the family as a building block of society and to see family relations as both mirror and source of general social and political values. What does this association mean and what are its implications, assuming that it exists? Is the view of the family as a building block consistent with the modern emphasis on individual choice in defining the obligations and duration of marriage?

9. This relationship is also explored in Sarah Barringer Gordon, *supra* at 172-178, observing, *inter alia*, that for some time Utah was also a "divorce mill" state, with the loosest jurisdictional and substantive requirements in the country. It was sufficient for jurisdiction that the petitioner was "a resident or wishes to become one," and sufficient for granting a divorce that the court found that "the parties cannot live in peace and union together, and that their welfare requires a separation." *Id.* at 175.

10. It may seem odd that *Reynolds* was decided at approximately the same time that serial polygamy—divorce followed by remarriage—became common and the subject of heated controversy. *See generally* William O'Neill, Divorce in the Progressive Era (1967). What relationships might exist between these two issues? *See* Carol Weisbrod, Family, Church and State: An Essay on Constitutionalism and Religious Authority, 26 J. Fam. L. 741, 758-759 (1987-1988).

11. Would *Reynolds* be decided the same way after Zablocki v. Redhail? Does it matter that divorce followed by remarriage was rare in 1878 and is now almost statistically normal? *See generally* Andrew Cherlin, The Trends: Marriage, Divorce, and Remarriage, in Family in Transition 80 (Arlene Skolnick & Jerome Skolnick eds., 1986). Is the difference between polygamy and serial monogamy constitutionally significant?

12. Bigamy is, of course, a crime as well as an impediment to marriage. Generally, bigamy is committed when a person having a living spouse marries another. In many jurisdictions, bigamy is a strict liability offense—that is, even a reasonable mistake about the termination of the first marriage is no defense. *E.g.*, State v. Hendrickson, 245 P. 375 (Utah 1926) (evidence of the defendant's good faith belief that his first wife had obtained a divorce inadmissible). English law once took the same position but now allows a defense of reasonable mistake concerning the death of the first spouse (Regina v. Tolson, [1889] 23 Q.B.D. 168) or the existence

of a valid divorce decree (Regina v. Gould, [1966] 2 W.L.R. 643). Some recent American cases and statutes adopt the latter view as well; *e.g.*, People v. Vogel, 299 P.2d 850 (Cal. 1956); Ill. Rev. Stat. ch. 38, §11-12(b).

A specific exception to criminal liability for bigamy is provided by Enoch Arden statutes (or decisions to the same effect). The situation they address resembles that of the Tennyson poem providing the name: the disappearance for many years—usually five to seven under most statutes—of a spouse without explanation. Some statutes provide only a defense to the crime of bigamy. *E.g.*, Del. Code Ann., tit. 11, §§381, 384 (1953). Other statutes, however, also provide a procedure for judicial declaration of the death of the absent spouse and, accordingly, offer protection to a marriage contracted subsequent to the proceeding. *E.g.*, N.Y. Dom. Rel. Law §§220, 221; Pa. Stat. Ann., tit. 48, §§1-8 (1965).

Perhaps it should be said that the resemblance between poetry and life is imperfect. Enoch Arden, after a ten-year absence, saw the happiness of his wife Annie, her second husband, and their children, and resolved brokenheartedly that they would not know of his return until after his death.

b. Relationship

STATE V. SHARON H.

429 A.2d 1321 (Del. Super. 1981)

STIFTEL, J. [Sharon H. and Dennis H., who were half-sister and half-brother, were charged with entering a prohibited marriage. They were born to the same mother, but of different fathers. Sharon was adopted at the age of ten days by the W. family; Dennis was raised in various state programs. They met each other after reaching adulthood and were married.]

Title 13 of the Delaware Code, §101(a)(1) provides:

§101. Void and Voidable Marriages
(a) A marriage is prohibited and void between:
    (1) A person and his or her ancestor, descendant, brother, sister, uncle, aunt, niece, nephew or first cousin. . . .

Title 13 of the Delaware Code, §102 provides:

§102. Entering into a prohibited marriage; penalty
The guilty party or parties to a marriage prohibited by §101 of this title shall be fined $100, and in default of the payment of the fine shall be imprisoned not more than 30 days.

Section 101(a)(1) of Title 13 is what is commonly termed a consanguinity statute. These statutes exist in one form or another in the majority of the states of our nation. In general, a consanguinity statute prohibits marriages between blood relatives in the lineal, or ascending and descending lines. The historical basis for these statutes is rooted in English Canonical Law, which enforced what is considered to be a Biblical prohibition on incestuous relationships.

Another reason advanced for the enactment of incest and consanguinity statutes is a generally accepted theory that genetic inbreeding by close blood relatives tends to increase the chances that offspring of the marriage will inherit certain unfavorable physical characteristics. Even if this theory is accepted, it is unlikely that it was the original basis for consanguinity statutes, given the relative newness of the theory and the ancient history of these statutes; however, it is possible that this theory served as an additional basis for the revision and reenactment of the various statutes.

In any case, it is clear that consanguinity statutes were designed to prohibit marriages between blood relatives. The Delaware consanguinity statute is no exception. Although the language of the statute has been modified over the years, the clear intention of each statute has been the prohibition of marriages between blood relatives.

The present version of Delaware's consanguinity statute, 13 Del. C. § 101(a)(1), expressly prohibits marriages between brother and sister. Although the Delaware Courts have never addressed the issue, other courts which have applied similar statutes have concluded that the policy behind the prohibition of marriages or sexual relations between blood relatives requires the Court to include relatives of half-blood in the prohibition. Given the obvious intent of 13 Del. C. § 101(a)(1) to prohibit marriages between blood relatives, it is clear that a reasonable interpretation of 13 Del. C. § 101(a)(1) would prohibit the marriage between the appellees. . . .

Having concluded that 13 Del. C. § 101(a)(1) would normally prohibit marriage between the appellees, the question becomes whether the effect of 13 Del. C. § 919 is to destroy all ties between an adopted child and the child's natural relatives, including the ties of blood. . . . 13 Del. C. § 919(b) states:

> (b) Upon the issuance of the decree of adoption, the adopted child shall no longer be considered the child of his natural parent or parents, and shall no longer be entitled to any of the rights or privileges or subject to any of the duties or obligations of a child with respect to the natural parent or parents. . . .

Appellees contend that the proper interpretation of this statute is that 13 Del. C. § 919 ends all relationships between an adopted child and its natural relatives, including blood relationships, and so the blood relationship prohibited by 13 Del. C. § 101(a)(1). After looking at the plain language of the statute, however, I conclude that the General Assembly did not intend that 13 Del. C. § 919 have such an effect.

NOTES AND QUESTIONS

1. All states prohibit marriages (and sexual relations) between persons closely related by blood—that is, through a common ancestor. And all agree in prohibiting such relationships between parent and child, brother and sister, and grandparent and grandchild. Moreover, most states—like the court in *Sharon H.*—interpret these prohibitions as applying to persons related by the half as well as the whole blood. *E.g.*, Cal. Civ. Code Ann. § 4400 (West 1983); Ill. Ann. Stat.,

ch. 40, ¶ 212 (Smith Hurd 1984); Ipscott v. Maryland, 684 A.2d 439 (Md. 1996). In fact, attempted marital relationships involving persons so closely related rarely occur, and nonmarital relations between them are addressed by the criminal law.

The relationships that do result in domestic relations litigation typically are those between first cousins, uncles and nieces, and aunts and nephews, as well as certain nonconsanguineous relations—that is, between people related by marriage or "affinity" rather than by blood.

2. It is common to dismiss genetic bases for incest restrictions on the ground that taboos against incest are far older than the science of genetics. Certainly genetics as a science is relatively recent; its origins are usually associated with the research of the Austrian monk Gregor Mendel (1822-1884), who discovered the principles of inherited characteristics through painstaking experiments on inheritance in peas. Most of what we know about genetics has developed during the twentieth century, impelled by the Watson-Crick model of DNA, which (with the closely related molecule RNA) constitutes the genetic material of all living organisms.

Two things might be said about the relationship of genetic concerns and consanguinity. One is that observations about inheritance might informally have been made by earlier societies and transformed into taboos. The other is that it is quite clear that the mating of closely related persons does present a genuine basis for genetic concern. This concern is particularly strong with respect to the inheritance of harmful recessive alleles (gene forms). A large number of traits in humans have been identified as the result of the expression of recessive alleles. Among these are phenylketonuria (leading to mental retardation); amyotrophic lateral sclerosis (Lou Gehrig's disease); Bloom's syndrome (dwarfism with skin changes and susceptibility to cancer); and cystic fibrosis. These examples are taken from Linda R. Maxson & Charles H. Daugherty, Genetics: A Human Perspective 71-73 (2d ed. 1989).

When two humans reproduce, the offspring receives all of its genetic material from its parents. Moreover, it receives one allele for each type of gene from each parent. The selection of which alleles it will receive is random—that is, receipt of one allele for some trait has nothing to do with the receipt of any other allele.

Some alleles are dominant and others are recessive. When a person inherits two differing alleles, the trait associated with the allele that is expressed is dominant; that which is not expressed is recessive. The expression of most harmful recessive genes occurs at a low frequency among humans because it takes place only when both alleles (one received from each parent) are identical for this trait. Suppose, for example, a normal allele D and a recessive allele d (which is lethal when, but only when, paired with another allele d). A parent might have either a DD or Dd combination of alleles. If both parents are DD, neither carries the d allele and a child cannot inherit it. But if one parent is Dd, he or she is a carrier of the d allele. It has not been expressed in the parent because it is not paired with another d. And if the other parent is also a Dd, then it is possible that the child will inherit one d allele from the father and one from the mother, which is the only condition under which this recessive trait will be expressed. And it is more likely that both parents will be Dd if they are related than if they are not, and the more closely they are related the greater the likelihood of similar patterns.

3. Whatever weight we give to genetic concerns, it is plain that social concerns strongly influence restrictions on sexual relations and marriage between

close kin. For one thing, cultural restrictions are not always interpretable in terms that would make genetic sense. Historians and anthropologists have long wondered why a number of societies allow marriage between children born to the same father but different mothers but proscribe marriages in the reverse situation. This was the law among the Athenians, where one might marry a half-sister by the father but not by the mother, the Jews (*see* Genesis 20:12), and the Kwakiutl Indians of British Columbia. Claude Levi-Strauss, On Marriage Between Close Kin, in The View from Afar 88-89 (Joachim Neugroschel & Phoebe Hoss trans., 1985). Concern for heredity certainly does not explain an incest prohibition that is stricter on the maternal than on the paternal side.

Levi-Strauss concludes that the incest prohibition should be regarded not only negatively but positively—that is, as a division of the rights of marriage between families. It arises

> only so that families (however defined by each society) could intermingle. . . . As Edward Burnett Tyler understood a century ago . . . man knew very early that he had to choose between "either marrying-out or being killed-out": the best, but not the only, way for biological families not to be driven to reciprocal extermination is to link themselves by ties of blood. Biological families that wished to live in isolation, side by side with one another, would each form a closed group, self-perpetuating and inevitably prey to ignorance, fear, and hatred. In opposing the separatist tendency of consanguinity, the incest prohibition succeeded in weaving the web of affinity that sustains societies and without which none could survive.

Id. at 54-55. Does Levi-Strauss's location of the deep structure of incest prohibitions in a universal need for social links adopt a particular view of human nature?

4. The Delaware statute involved in State v. Sharon H., like many, also prohibits marriage between uncles and nieces, aunts and nephews, and first cousins. Would those prohibitions survive a constitutional challenge after Zablocki v. Redhail? What arguments would be made for and against the validity of these proscriptions?

PROBLEMS

1. Venus and Adonis are adopted sister and brother. They come from different birth families, but were adopted when they were very young and have lived together with their adoptive parents for the last ten years. Venus is now 20 and Adonis 21. They have fallen in love and wish to marry. Would they be barred from doing so under the statute applied in *Sharon H*? Should they be barred from marrying?

2. Murray was married for many years to Aphrodite, who died last year. Aphrodite brought a daughter, Delilah, to the marriage. Delilah lived and grew up in the home with Murray and Aphrodite. After her mother's death, Delilah moved back into the house to take care of Murray. Murray proposed marriage to Delilah, and she accepted. They sought a marriage license but were turned down by the county clerk, who knows them both. State law prohibits marriage between a father and his "daughter." What arguments might be made in connection with their challenge to the denial of their application to marry?

c. Different Sexes

GOODRIDGE V. DEPARTMENT OF PUBLIC HEALTH

798 N.E.2d 941 (2003)

MARSHALL, C.J. Marriage is a vital social institution. The exclusive commitment of two individuals to each other nurtures love and mutual support; it brings stability to our society. For those who choose to marry, and for their children, marriage provides an abundance of legal, financial, and social benefits. In return it imposes weighty legal, financial, and social obligations. The question before us is whether, consistent with the Massachusetts Constitution, the Commonwealth may deny the protections, benefits, and obligations conferred by civil marriage to two individuals of the same sex who wish to marry. We conclude that it may not. The Massachusetts Constitution affirms the dignity and equality of all individuals. It forbids the creation of second-class citizens. In reaching our conclusion we have given full deference to the arguments made by the Commonwealth. But it has failed to identify any constitutionally adequate reason for denying civil marriage to same-sex couples. . . .

Whether the Commonwealth may use its formidable regulatory authority to bar same-sex couples from civil marriage is a question not previously addressed by a Massachusetts appellate court. It is a question the United States Supreme Court left open as a matter of Federal law in Lawrence [v. Texas, 123 S. Ct. 2472 (2003)] at 2484, where it was not an issue. There, the Court affirmed that the core concept of common human dignity protected by the Fourteenth Amendment to the United States Constitution precludes government intrusion into the deeply personal realms of consensual adult expressions of intimacy and one's choice of an intimate partner. The Court also reaffirmed the central role that decisions whether to marry or have children bear in shaping one's identity. The Massachusetts Constitution is, if anything, more protective of individual liberty and equality than the Federal Constitution; it may demand broader protection for fundamental rights; and it is less tolerant of government intrusion into the protected spheres of private life.

Barred access to the protections, benefits, and obligations of civil marriage, a person who enters into an intimate, exclusive union with another of the same sex is arbitrarily deprived of membership in one of our community's most rewarding and cherished institutions. That exclusion is incompatible with the constitutional principles of respect for individual autonomy and equality under law.

The plaintiffs are fourteen individuals from five Massachusetts counties. As of April 11, 2001, the date they filed their complaint, the plaintiffs Gloria Bailey, sixty years old, and Linda Davies, fifty-five years old, had been in a committed relationship for thirty years; the plaintiffs Maureen Brodoff, forty-nine years old, and Ellen Wade, fifty-two years old, had been in a committed relationship for twenty years and lived with their twelve year old daughter; the plaintiffs Hillary Goodridge, forty-four years old, and Julie Goodridge, forty-three years old, had been in a committed relationship for thirteen years and lived with their five year old daughter . . . ; and the plaintiffs David Wilson, fifty-seven years old, and

Robert Compton, fifty-one years old, had been in a committed relationship for four years and had cared for David's mother in their home after a serious illness until she died.

The plaintiffs include business executives, lawyers, an investment banker, educators, therapists, and a computer engineer. Many are active in church, community, and school groups. They have employed such legal means as are available to them—for example, joint adoption, powers of attorney, and joint ownership of real property—to secure aspects of their relationships. Each plaintiff attests a desire to marry his or her partner in order to affirm publicly their commitment to each other and to secure the legal protections and benefits afforded to married couples and their children. . . .

In March and April, 2001, each of the plaintiff couples attempted to obtain a marriage license from a city or town clerk's office. . . . In each case, the clerk either refused to accept the notice of intention to marry or denied a marriage license to the couple on the ground that Massachusetts does not recognize same-sex marriage. Because obtaining a marriage license is a necessary prerequisite to civil marriage in Massachusetts, denying marriage licenses to the plaintiffs was tantamount to denying them access to civil marriage itself, with its appurtenant social and legal protections, benefits, and obligations.

On April 11, 2001, the plaintiffs filed suit in the Superior Court against the department and the commissioner seeking a judgment that "the exclusion of the [p]laintiff couples and other qualified same-sex couples from access to marriage licenses, and the legal and social status of civil marriage, as well as the protections, benefits and obligations of marriage, violates Massachusetts law." The plaintiffs alleged violation of the laws of the Commonwealth. . . .

The department, represented by the Attorney General, admitted to a policy and practice of denying marriage licenses to same-sex couples. It denied that its actions violated any law or that the plaintiffs were entitled to relief. The parties filed cross motions for summary judgment.

A Superior Court judge ruled for the department. . . .

After the complaint was dismissed and summary judgment entered for the defendants, the plaintiffs appealed. . . .

. . . G. L. c. 207, governing entrance to marriage, is a licensing law. The plaintiffs argue that because nothing in that licensing law specifically prohibits marriages between persons of the same sex, we may interpret the statute to permit "qualified same sex couples" to obtain marriage licenses, thereby avoiding the question whether the law is constitutional.

We interpret statutes to carry out the Legislature's intent, determined by the words of a statute interpreted according to "the ordinary and approved usage of the language." The everyday meaning of "marriage" is "[t]he legal union of a man and woman as husband and wife," Black's Law Dictionary 986 (7th ed. 1999), and the plaintiffs do not argue that the term "marriage" has ever had a different meaning under Massachusetts law. This definition of marriage, as both the department and the Superior Court judge point out, derives from the common law. Far from being ambiguous, the undefined word "marriage," as used in G. L. c. 207, confirms the General Court's intent to hew to the term's common-law and quotidian meaning concerning the genders of the marriage partners.

The intended scope of G. L. c. 207 is also evident in its consanguinity provisions. Sections 1 and 2 of G. L. c. 207 prohibit marriages between a man and certain female relatives and a woman and certain male relatives, but are silent as to the consanguinity of male-male or female-female marriage applicants. The only reasonable explanation is that the Legislature did not intend that same-sex couples be licensed to marry. We conclude, as did the judge, that G. L. c. 207 may not be construed to permit same-sex couples to marry.

III

A

The larger question is whether, as the department claims, government action that bars same-sex couples from civil marriage constitutes a legitimate exercise of the State's authority to regulate conduct, or whether, as the plaintiffs claim, this categorical marriage exclusion violates the Massachusetts Constitution. . . .

The plaintiffs' claim that the marriage restriction violates the Massachusetts Constitution can be analyzed in two ways. Does it offend the Constitution's guarantees of equality before the law? Or do the liberty and due process provisions of the Massachusetts Constitution secure the plaintiffs' right to marry their chosen partner? In matters implicating marriage, family life, and the upbringing of children, the two constitutional concepts frequently overlap, as they do here. Much of what we say concerning one standard applies to the other.

We begin by considering the nature of civil marriage itself. Simply put, the government creates civil marriage. In Massachusetts, civil marriage is, and since pre-Colonial days has been, precisely what its name implies: a wholly secular institution. No religious ceremony has ever been required to validate a Massachusetts marriage.

In a real sense, there are three partners to every civil marriage: two willing spouses and an approving State. While only the parties can mutually assent to marriage, the terms of the marriage—who may marry and what obligations, benefits, and liabilities attach to civil marriage—are set by the Commonwealth. Conversely, while only the parties can agree to end the marriage (absent the death of one of them or a marriage void *ab initio*), the Commonwealth defines the exit terms.

Civil marriage is created and regulated through exercise of the police power. "Police power" (now more commonly termed the State's regulatory authority) is an old-fashioned term for the Commonwealth's lawmaking authority, as bounded by the liberty and equality guarantees of the Massachusetts Constitution and its express delegation of power from the people to their government. In broad terms, it is the Legislature's power to enact rules to regulate conduct, to the extent that such laws are "necessary to secure the health, safety, good order, comfort, or general welfare of the community." . . .

Marriage also bestows enormous private and social advantages on those who choose to marry. Civil marriage is at once a deeply personal commitment to another human being and a highly public celebration of the ideals of mutuality, companionship, intimacy, fidelity, and family. . . . Because it fulfils yearnings for security, safe haven, and connection that express our common humanity, civil marriage is an esteemed institution, and the decision whether and whom to marry is among life's momentous acts of self-definition.

Tangible as well as intangible benefits flow from marriage. The marriage license grants valuable property rights to those who meet the entry requirements, and who agree to what might otherwise be a burdensome degree of government regulation of their activities. The Legislature has conferred on "each party [in a civil marriage] substantial rights concerning the assets of the other which unmarried cohabitants do not have."

The benefits accessible only by way of a marriage license are enormous, touching nearly every aspect of life and death. The department states that "hundreds of statutes" are related to marriage and to marital benefits. . . .

It is undoubtedly for these concrete reasons, as well as for its intimately personal significance, that civil marriage has long been termed a "civil right." See, e.g., Loving v. Virginia, 388 U.S. 1, 12 (1967) ("Marriage is one of the 'basic civil rights of man,' fundamental to our very existence and survival"). The United States Supreme Court has described the right to marry as "of fundamental importance for all individuals" and as "part of the fundamental 'right of privacy' implicit in the Fourteenth Amendment's Due Process Clause." Zablocki v. Redhail, 434 U.S. 374, 384 (1978). See Loving v. Virginia, supra ("The freedom to marry has long been recognized as one of the vital personal rights essential to the orderly pursuit of happiness by free men").

Without the right to marry—or more properly, the right to choose to marry—one is excluded from the full range of human experience and denied full protection of the laws for one's "avowed commitment to an intimate and lasting human relationship." Because civil marriage is central to the lives of individuals and the welfare of the community, our laws assiduously protect the individual's right to marry against undue government incursion. Laws may not "interfere directly and substantially with the right to marry." Zablocki v. Redhail, supra at 387.

Unquestionably, the regulatory power of the Commonwealth over civil marriage is broad, as is the Commonwealth's discretion to award public benefits. Individuals who have the choice to marry each other and nevertheless choose not to may properly be denied the legal benefits of marriage. But that same logic cannot hold for a qualified individual who would marry if she or he only could.

B

For decades, indeed centuries, in much of this country (including Massachusetts) no lawful marriage was possible between white and black Americans. That long history availed not when the . . . United States Supreme Court . . . held that a statutory bar to interracial marriage violated the Fourteenth Amendment, Loving v. Virginia, 388 U.S. 1 (1967). As . . . *Loving* make[s] clear, the right to marry means little if it does not include the right to marry the person of one's choice, subject to appropriate government restrictions in the interests of public health, safety, and welfare. In this case, as in . . . *Loving*, a statute deprives individuals of access to an institution of fundamental legal, personal, and social significance—the institution of marriage—because of a single trait: skin color in *Perez* and *Loving*, sexual orientation here. . . .

The Massachusetts Constitution protects matters of personal liberty against government incursion as zealously, and often more so, than does the Federal Constitution, even where both Constitutions employ essentially the same language. . . .

The individual liberty and equality safeguards of the Massachusetts Constitution protect both "freedom from" unwarranted government intrusion into protected spheres of life and "freedom to" partake in benefits created by the State for the common good. Whether and whom to marry, how to express sexual intimacy, and whether and how to establish a family — these are among the most basic of every individual's liberty and due process rights. And central to personal freedom and security is the assurance that the laws will apply equally to persons in similar situations. "Absolute equality before the law is a fundamental principle of our own Constitution." The liberty interest in choosing whether and whom to marry would be hollow if the Commonwealth could, without sufficient justification, foreclose an individual from freely choosing the person with whom to share an exclusive commitment in the unique institution of civil marriage. . . .

The plaintiffs challenge the marriage statute on both equal protection and due process grounds. With respect to each such claim, we must first determine the appropriate standard of review. Where a statute implicates a fundamental right or uses a suspect classification, we employ "strict judicial scrutiny." For all other statutes, we employ the "rational basis test." For due process claims, rational basis analysis requires that statutes "bear[] a real and substantial relation to the public health, safety, morals, or some other phase of the general welfare." For equal protection challenges, the rational basis test requires that "an impartial lawmaker could logically believe that the classification would serve a legitimate public purpose that transcends the harm to the members of the disadvantaged class."

The department argues that no fundamental right or "suspect" class is at issue here,[2] and rational basis is the appropriate standard of review. For the reasons we explain below, we conclude that the marriage ban does not meet the rational basis test for either due process or equal protection. Because the statute does not survive rational basis review, we do not consider the plaintiffs' arguments that this case merits strict judicial scrutiny.

The department posits three legislative rationales for prohibiting same-sex couples from marrying: (1) providing a "favorable setting for procreation"; (2) ensuring the optimal setting for child rearing, which the department defines as "a two-parent family with one parent of each sex"; and (3) preserving scarce State and private financial resources. We consider each in turn.

The judge in the Superior Court endorsed the first rationale, holding that "the state's interest in regulating marriage is based on the traditional concept that marriage's primary purpose is procreation." This is incorrect. Our laws of civil marriage do not privilege procreative heterosexual intercourse between married people above

---

2. Article 1 of the Massachusetts Constitution specifically prohibits sex-based discrimination. See *post* at 344-345, 798 N.E.2d at 970-971 (Greaney, J., concurring). We have not previously considered whether "sexual orientation" is a "suspect" classification. Our resolution of this case does not require that inquiry here.

every other form of adult intimacy and every other means of creating a family. General Laws c. 207 contains no requirement that the applicants for a marriage license attest to their ability or intention to conceive children by coitus. Fertility is not a condition of marriage, nor is it grounds for divorce. People who have never consummated their marriage, and never plan to, may be and stay married. While it is certainly true that many, perhaps most, married couples have children together (assisted or unassisted), it is the exclusive and permanent commitment of the marriage partners to one another, not the begetting of children, that is the sine qua non of civil marriage.

Moreover, the Commonwealth affirmatively facilitates bringing children into a family regardless of whether the intended parent is married or unmarried, whether the child is adopted or born into a family, whether assistive technology was used to conceive the child, and whether the parent or her partner is heterosexual, homosexual, or bisexual. If procreation were a necessary component of civil marriage, our statutes would draw a tighter circle around the permissible bounds of nonmarital child bearing and the creation of families by noncoital means. The attempt to isolate procreation as "the source of a fundamental right to marry" . . . overlooks the integrated way in which courts have examined the complex and overlapping realms of personal autonomy, marriage, family life, and child rearing. Our jurisprudence recognizes that, in these nuanced and fundamentally private areas of life, such a narrow focus is inappropriate.

The "marriage is procreation" argument singles out the one unbridgeable difference between same-sex and opposite-sex couples, and transforms that difference into the essence of legal marriage. Like "Amendment 2" to the Constitution of Colorado, which effectively denied homosexual persons equality under the law and full access to the political process, the marriage restriction impermissibly "identifies persons by a single trait and then denies them protection across the board." Romer v. Evans, 517 U.S. 620, 633 (1996). In so doing, the State's action confers an official stamp of approval on the destructive stereotype that same-sex relationships are inherently unstable and inferior to opposite-sex relationships and are not worthy of respect.

The department's first stated rationale, equating marriage with unassisted heterosexual procreation, shades imperceptibly into its second: that confining marriage to opposite-sex couples ensures that children are raised in the "optimal" setting. Protecting the welfare of children is a paramount State policy. Restricting marriage to opposite-sex couples, however, cannot plausibly further this policy. "The demographic changes of the past century make it difficult to speak of an average American family. The composition of families varies greatly from household to household." Troxel v. Granville, 530 U.S. 57, 63 (2000). Massachusetts has responded supportively to "the changing realities of the American family," and has moved vigorously to strengthen the modern family in its many variations. Moreover, we have repudiated the common-law power of the State to provide varying levels of protection to children based on the circumstances of birth. The "best interests of the child" standard does not turn on a parent's sexual orientation or marital status.

The department has offered no evidence that forbidding marriage to people of the same sex will increase the number of couples choosing to enter into opposite-sex marriages in order to have and raise children. There is thus no rational relationship between the marriage statute and the Commonwealth's proffered goal of protecting the "optimal" child rearing unit. Moreover, the department readily concedes that people in same-sex couples may be "excellent" parents. These couples (including four of the plaintiff couples) have children for the reasons others do—to love them, to care for them, to nurture them. But the task of child rearing for same-sex couples is made infinitely harder by their status as outliers to the marriage laws. While establishing the parentage of children as soon as possible is crucial to the safety and welfare of children, same-sex couples must undergo the sometimes lengthy and intrusive process of second-parent adoption to establish their joint parentage. While the enhanced income provided by marital benefits is an important source of security and stability for married couples and their children, those benefits are denied to families headed by same-sex couples. . . . Given the wide range of public benefits reserved only for married couples, we do not credit the department's contention that the absence of access to civil marriage amounts to little more than an inconvenience to same-sex couples and their children. Excluding same-sex couples from civil marriage will not make children of opposite-sex marriages more secure, but it does prevent children of same-sex couples from enjoying the immeasurable advantages that flow from the assurance of "a stable family structure in which children will be reared, educated, and socialized." . . .

No one disputes that the plaintiff couples are families, that many are parents, and that the children they are raising, like all children, need and should have the fullest opportunity to grow up in a secure, protected family unit. Similarly, no one disputes that, under the rubric of marriage, the State provides a cornucopia of substantial benefits to married parents and their children. The preferential treatment of civil marriage reflects the Legislature's conclusion that marriage "is the foremost setting for the education and socialization of children" precisely because it "encourages parents to remain committed to each other and to their children as they grow."

In this case, we are confronted with an entire, sizeable class of parents raising children who have absolutely no access to civil marriage and its protections because they are forbidden from procuring a marriage license. It cannot be rational under our laws, and indeed it is not permitted, to penalize children by depriving them of State benefits because the State disapproves of their parents' sexual orientation.

The third rationale advanced by the department is that limiting marriage to opposite-sex couples furthers the Legislature's interest in conserving scarce State and private financial resources. The marriage restriction is rational, it argues, because the General Court logically could assume that same-sex couples are more financially independent than married couples and thus less needy of public marital benefits, such as tax advantages, or private marital benefits, such as employer-financed health plans that include spouses in their coverage.

An absolute statutory ban on same-sex marriage bears no rational relationship to the goal of economy. First, the department's conclusory generalization—that same-sex couples are less financially dependent on each other than opposite-sex couples—ignores that many same-sex couples, such as many of the plaintiffs in this case, have children and other dependents (here, aged parents) in their care. The department does not contend, nor could it, that these dependents are less needy or deserving than the dependents of married couples. Second, Massachusetts marriage laws do not condition receipt of public and private financial benefits to married individuals on a demonstration of financial dependence on each other; the benefits are available to married couples regardless of whether they mingle their finances or actually depend on each other for support.

The department suggests additional rationales for prohibiting same-sex couples from marrying, which are developed by some amici. It argues that broadening civil marriage to include same-sex couples will trivialize or destroy the institution of marriage as it has historically been fashioned. Certainly our decision today marks a significant change in the definition of marriage as it has been inherited from the common law, and understood by many societies for centuries. But it does not disturb the fundamental value of marriage in our society.

Here, the plaintiffs seek only to be married, not to undermine the institution of civil marriage. They do not want marriage abolished. They do not attack the binary nature of marriage, the consanguinity provisions, or any of the other gate-keeping provisions of the marriage licensing law. Recognizing the right of an individual to marry a person of the same sex will not diminish the validity or dignity of opposite-sex marriage, any more than recognizing the right of an individual to marry a person of a different race devalues the marriage of a person who marries someone of her own race. If anything, extending civil marriage to same-sex couples reinforces the importance of marriage to individuals and communities. . . .

We also reject the argument suggested by the department, and elaborated by some amici, that expanding the institution of civil marriage in Massachusetts to include same-sex couples will lead to interstate conflict. We would not presume to dictate how another State should respond to today's decision. But neither should considerations of comity prevent us from according Massachusetts residents the full measure of protection available under the Massachusetts Constitution. The genius of our Federal system is that each State's Constitution has vitality specific to its own traditions, and that, subject to the minimum requirements of the Fourteenth Amendment, each State is free to address difficult issues of individual liberty in the manner its own Constitution demands.

Several amici suggest that prohibiting marriage by same-sex couples reflects community consensus that homosexual conduct is immoral. Yet Massachusetts has a strong affirmative policy of preventing discrimination on the basis of sexual orientation. See G. L. c. 151B (employment, housing, credit, services); G. L. c. 265, §39 (hate crimes); G. L. c. 272, §98 (public accommodation); G. L. c. 76, §5 (public education). . . .

The marriage ban works a deep and scarring hardship on a very real segment of the community for no rational reason. The absence of any reasonable relationship between, on the one hand, an absolute disqualification of same-sex couples who wish to enter into civil marriage and, on the other, protection of public health, safety, or general welfare, suggests that the marriage restriction is rooted in persistent prejudices against persons who are (or who are believed to be) homosexual. "The Constitution cannot control such prejudices but neither can it tolerate them. Private biases may be outside the reach of the law, but the law cannot, directly or indirectly, give them effect." Limiting the protections, benefits, and obligations of civil marriage to opposite-sex couples violates the basic premises of individual liberty and equality under law protected by the Massachusetts Constitution. . . .

SPINA, J. dissenting. . . .

1. *Equal protection*. . . . [T]he marriage statutes do not discriminate on the basis of sexual orientation. As the court correctly recognizes, constitutional protections are extended to individuals, not couples. The marriage statutes do not disqualify individuals on the basis of sexual orientation from entering into marriage. All individuals, with certain exceptions not relevant here, are free to marry. Whether an individual chooses not to marry because of sexual orientation or any other reason should be of no concern to the court. . . .

Unlike the *Loving* and *Sharp* cases, the Massachusetts Legislature has erected no barrier to marriage that intentionally discriminates against anyone. Within the institution of marriage, anyone is free to marry, with certain exceptions that are not challenged. In the absence of any discriminatory purpose, the State's marriage statutes do not violate principles of equal protection. This court should not have invoked even the most deferential standard of review within equal protection analysis because no individual was denied access to the institution of marriage.

Due process. The marriage statutes do not impermissibly burden a right protected by our constitutional guarantee of due process implicit in art. 10 of our Declaration of Rights. There is no restriction on the right of any plaintiff to enter into marriage. Each is free to marry a willing person of the opposite sex.

Substantive due process protects individual rights against unwarranted government intrusion. The court states, as we have said on many occasions, that the Massachusetts Declaration of Rights may protect a right in ways that exceed the protection afforded by the Federal Constitution. However, today the court does not fashion a remedy that affords greater protection of a right. Instead, using the rubric of due process, it has redefined marriage. . . .

SOSMAN, J., dissenting. In applying the rational basis test to any challenged statutory scheme, the issue is not whether the Legislature's rationale behind that scheme is persuasive to us, but only whether it satisfies a minimal threshold of rationality. Today, rather than apply that test, the court announces that, because it is persuaded that there are no differences between same-sex and opposite-sex couples, the Legislature has no rational basis for treating them differently with respect to the granting of marriage licenses. Reduced to its essence, the court's opinion concludes that, because same-sex couples are now raising children, and withholding the benefits of civil marriage from their union makes it harder for them to raise those children, the State must therefore provide the benefits of civil marriage to same-sex couples just as it does to opposite-sex couples. Of course, many people are raising children outside the confines of traditional marriage, and, by definition, those children are being deprived of the various benefits that would flow if they were being raised in a household with married parents. That does not mean that the Legislature must accord the full benefits of marital status on every household raising children. Rather, the Legislature need only have some rational basis for concluding that, at present, those alternate family structures have not yet been conclusively shown to be the equivalent of the marital family structure that has established itself as a successful one over a period of centuries. People are of course at liberty to raise their children in various family structures, as long as they are not literally harming their children by doing so. That does not mean that the State is required to provide identical forms of encouragement, endorsement, and support to all of the infinite variety of household structures that a free society permits.

Based on our own philosophy of child rearing, and on our observations of the children being raised by same-sex couples to whom we are personally close, we may be of the view that what matters to children is not the gender, or sexual orientation, or even the number of the adults who raise them, but rather whether those adults provide the children with a nurturing, stable, safe, consistent, and supportive environment in which to mature. Same-sex couples can provide their children with the requisite nurturing, stable, safe, consistent, and supportive environment in which to mature, just as opposite-sex couples do. It is therefore understandable that the court might view the traditional definition of marriage as an unnecessary anachronism, rooted in historical prejudices that modern society has in large measure rejected and biological limitations that modern science has overcome.

It is not, however, our assessment that matters. Conspicuously absent from the court's opinion today is any acknowledgment that the attempts at scientific study of the ramifications of raising children in same-sex couple households are themselves in their infancy and have so far produced inconclusive and conflicting results. Notwithstanding our belief that gender and sexual orientation of parents should not matter to the success of the child rearing venture, studies to date reveal that there are still some observable differences between children raised by opposite-sex couples and children raised by same-sex couples. Interpretation of the data gathered by those studies then becomes clouded by the personal and political beliefs of the investigators, both as to whether the differences identified are positive or negative, and as to the untested explanations of what might account for those differences. . . . Even in the absence of bias or political agenda behind the various studies of children raised by same-sex couples, the most neutral and strict application of scientific principles to this field would be constrained by the limited period of observation that has been available. Gay and lesbian couples living together openly, and official recognition of them as their children's sole parents, comprise a very recent phenomenon, and the recency of that phenomenon has not yet permitted any study of how those children fare as adults and at best minimal study of how they fare during their adolescent years. The Legislature can rationally view the state of the scientific evidence as unsettled on the critical question it now faces: Are families headed by same-sex parents equally successful in rearing children from infancy to adulthood as families headed by parents of opposite sexes? Our belief that children raised by same-sex couples should fare the same as children raised in traditional families is just that: a passionately held but utterly untested belief. The Legislature is not required to share that belief but may, as the creator of the institution of civil marriage, wish to see the proof before making a fundamental alteration to that institution.

Although ostensibly applying the rational basis test to the civil marriage statutes, it is abundantly apparent that the court is in fact applying some undefined stricter standard to assess the constitutionality of the marriage statutes' exclusion of same-sex couples. . . .

Shorn of these emotion-laden invocations, the opinion ultimately opines that the Legislature is acting irrationally when it grants benefits to a proven successful family structure while denying the same benefits to a recent, perhaps promising, but essentially untested alternate family structure. Placed in a more neutral context, the court would never find any irrationality in such an approach. For example, if the issue were government subsidies and tax benefits promoting use of an established technology for energy efficient heating, the court would find no equal protection or due process violation in the Legislature's decision not to grant the same benefits to an inventor or manufacturer of some new, alternative technology who did not yet have sufficient data to prove that that new technology was just as good as the established technology. That the early results from preliminary testing of the new technology might look very promising, or that the theoretical underpinnings of the new technology might appear flawless, would not make it irrational for the Legislature to grant subsidies and tax breaks to the established technology and deny them to the still unproved newcomer in the field. While programs that affect families and children register higher on our emotional scale than programs affecting energy efficiency, our standards for what is or is not "rational" should not be bent by those emotional tugs. Where, as here, there is no ground for applying strict scrutiny, the emotionally compelling nature of the subject matter should not affect the manner in which we apply the rational basis test.

OPINIONS OF THE JUSTICES TO THE SENATE

802 N.E.2d 565 (Mass. 2004)

[On December 11, 2003, the Massachusetts legislature adopted, pending decision by the Massachusetts Supreme Judicial Court, Senate Bill 2175, "An Act Relative to Civil Unions." Section 2 of that bill seeks to "provide eligible same-sex couples the opportunity to obtain the benefits, protections, rights and responsibilities afforded to opposite sex couples by the marriage laws of the commonwealth, without entering into a marriage." The bill includes a new Chapter 207A of the Massachusetts statutes establishing civil unions, open to same-sex couples eligible on grounds of age, non-relationship, and other standard categories, but not to opposite-sex couples. Section 3 of 207A provides that "[p]ersons eligible to form a civil union with each other under this chapter shall not be eligible to enter into a marriage with each other under chapter 207."

A second bill adopted at the same time, Senate Bill 2176, seeks an opinion by the Supreme Judicial Court on the question of whether the pending statute (S.B. 2175) complies with the equal protection and due process requirements of the state constitution.]

. . . We have now been asked to render an advisory opinion on Senate No. 2175, which creates a new legal status, "civil union," that is purportedly equal to "marriage," yet separate from it. The constitutional difficulty of the proposed civil union bill is evident in its stated purpose to "preserv[e] the traditional, historic nature and meaning of the institution of civil marriage." Senate No. 2175, §1. Preserving the institution of civil marriage is of course a legislative priority of the highest order, and one to which the Justices accord the General Court the great-est deference. We recognize the efforts of the Senate to draft a bill in conformity with the *Goodridge* opinion. Yet the bill, as we read it, does nothing to "preserve" the civil marriage law, only its constitutional infirmity. . . .

The same defects of rationality evident in the marriage ban considered in *Goodridge* are evident in, if not exaggerated by, Senate No. 2175. Segregating same-sex unions from opposite-sex unions cannot possibly be held rationally to advance or "preserve" what we stated in *Goodridge* were the Commonwealth's legitimate interests in procreation, child rearing, and the conservation of resources. Because the proposed law by its express terms forbids same-sex couples entry into civil marriage, it continues to relegate same-sex couples to a different status. The holding in *Goodridge*, by which we are bound, is that group classifica-tions based on unsupportable distinctions, such as that embodied in the proposed bill, are invalid under the Massachusetts Constitution. The history of our nation has demonstrated that separate is seldom, if ever, equal. . . .

The bill's absolute prohibition of the use of the word "marriage" by "spouses" who are the same sex is more than semantic. The dissimilitude between the terms "civil marriage" and "civil union" is not innocuous; it is a considered choice of language that reflects a demonstrable assigning of same-sex, largely homosexual, couples to second-class status. The denomination of this difference by the separate opinion of Justice Sosman (separate opinion) as merely a "squab-ble over the name to be used" so clearly misses the point that further discussion appears to be useless. If, as the separate opinion posits, the proponents of the bill believe that no message is conveyed by eschewing the word "marriage" and replacing it with "civil union" for same-sex "spouses," we doubt that the attempt to circumvent the court's decision in *Goodridge* would be so purposeful.

NOTES AND QUESTIONS

1. One measure of the social meaning of *Goodridge* is the number of amicus curiae briefs filed. The record lists 24 appearances by amici. Participants included the Massachusetts Bar Association; the Urban League of Eastern Massachusetts; the Massachusetts Family Institute; the National Association for Research and Therapy of Homosexuality; the Common Good Foundation; the states of Nebraska, Utah, and a number of others; the Catholic Action League of Massachusetts; the National Legal Foundation; the Marriage Law Project; the Religious Coalition for the Freedom to Marry; the Ethics & Religious Liberty Commission; the Coalition gaie et lesbienne du Quebec; the Free Market Foundation; the Boston Bar Association; the Massachusetts Psychiatric Society; and Agudath Israel of America.

2. Two other state supreme courts, in cases decided in the ten years preced-ing *Goodridge*, also held that limiting marriage to opposite-sex couples violated provisions of their state constitutions. In Baker v. Vermont, 744 A.2d 864 (Vt. 1999), the Vermont Supreme Court held that denial to same-sex couples of the privileges associated with marriage violated the state "common benefits" clause. As in *Goodridge*, the court held that same-sex couples were excluded from marriage

under Vermont statutes as a matter of statutory interpretation, but that the law, as interpreted,

> effectively excludes them from a broad array of legal benefits and protections incident to the marital relation, including access to spouse's medical, life and disability insurance, hospital visitation and other medical decisionmaking privileges, spousal support, instate succession, homestead protections, and many other statutory protections.

744 A.2d at 870. That deprivation denied the applicants equal access to public benefits and protections for the community as a whole and could not be justified by any claimed state interest in protecting a link between marriage and procreation.

The court held that plaintiffs are entitled to the same benefits and protections afforded by Vermont law to opposite-sex couples, but left the current law in place for "a reasonable period" to enable the legislature to consider and enact legislation consistent with that requirement. The Vermont legislature responded by enacting a civil union statute that provides same-sex couples who enter a civil union the same privileges available to married couples, 15 Vt. Stat. Ann. §§ 1201 et seq., but formally distinguishes a civil union from marriage. The terms of civil union in Vermont and other jurisdictions are examined in Chapter 4.

The Supreme Court of Hawaii held that prohibition of same-sex marriage constituted a form of sex-based discrimination violating the Hawaii Equal Rights Amendment. Baehr v. Lewin, 852 P.2d 44 (Haw. 1993). The majority in Baehr v. Lewin concluded that the prohibition of same-sex marriage was a sex-based classification in the same sense that statutes prohibiting interracial marriage were held to involve a race-based classification in Loving v. Virginia, 388 U.S. 1, 8 (1967). The result of this decision was a remand to the state trial court to hold hearings to determine whether the state could demonstrate that its denial of marriage to same-sex couples was supported by compelling state interests and was narrowly drawn to avoid unnecessary abridgements of constitutional rights.

In 1996, the Hawaii Circuit Court held the state's ban on same-sex marriage unconstitutional. Baehr v. Miike, 1996 WL 694236 (Haw. 1st Cir. 1996), aff'd, 950 P.2d 1234 (Haw. 1997). The trial court found that the defendant presented only

> meager evidence with regard to the importance of the institution of traditional marriage, the benefits which that relationship provide to the community and, most importantly, the adverse effects, if any, which same-sex marriage would have on the institution of traditional marriage and how those adverse effects would impact on the community and society.

In response, the Hawaii legislature initiated an amendment to the Hawaii Constitution providing that the legislature "shall have the power to reserve marriage to opposite sex couples," which was ratified in 1998. The Hawaii Supreme Court held that the marriage amendment removed any constitutional objection to the statute limiting access to marriage and rendered plaintiffs' complaint moot. Baehr v. Miike, 994 P.2d 566 (Haw. 1999). The legislature also enacted a "reciprocal beneficiaries" statute, Haw. Rev. Stat. Ann. § 572C-1 et seq. (Michie Supp. 1997). Substantive provisions of this statute appear in Chapter 4.

3. *Baker* and *Baehr*, like *Goodridge*, rested on state constitutional grounds. When the earlier cases were decided, it seemed that the United States Supreme Court was unlikely to find any federal constitutional basis for a right to marry by same-sex couples because of its decision in Bowers v. Hardwick, 478 U.S. 186 (1986). In *Bowers*, a majority of the Court upheld a Georgia statute criminalizing sodomy (defined as a sexual act involving the sex organs of one person and the mouth or anus of another). Although the statute did not address homosexual, as opposed to heterosexual, acts of these types, the majority approached the case as presenting the issue of whether "the Federal Constitution confers a fundamental right upon homosexuals to engage in sodomy and thus invalidates the laws of the many States that still make such conduct illegal. . . ." Having postured the case in this way, the Court concluded that there was no such right.

The decision in *Bowers* was repudiated, however, in Lawrence v. Texas, 539 U.S. 558 (2003), decided shortly before *Goodridge*. The issue in *Lawrence* was the same as that in *Bowers*: the validity of a state statute making it a crime for two persons of the same sex to engage in intimate sexual conduct, including contact between any part of the genitals of one person and the mouth or anus of another person. Justice Kennedy, writing for a majority of five, reviewed the historical and theoretical premises of the *Bowers* majority and rejected them. To the extent that the opinion was based on historical grounds, the majority in *Lawrence* found those grounds "not without doubt and, at the very least . . . overstated." To the extent that the opinion rested on a long tradition regarding homosexual conduct as immoral, that "history and tradition are a starting point but not the ending point of the substantive due process inquiry."

> The sweeping references by Chief Justice Burger to the history of Western civilization and to Judeo-Christian moral and ethical standards did not take account of other authorities pointing in an opposite direction. A committee advising the British Parliament recommended in 1957 repeal of laws punishing homosexual conduct. The Wolfenden Report: Report of the Committee on Homosexual Offenses and Prostitution (1963). Parliament enacted the substance of those recommendations 10 years later. Sexual Offences Act 1967, § 1.
>
> Of even more importance, almost five years before *Bowers* was decided the European Court of Human Rights considered a case with parallels to *Bowers* and to today's case. An adult male resident in Northern Ireland alleged he was a practicing homosexual who desired to engage in consensual homosexual conduct. The laws of Northern Ireland forbade him that right. . . . The court held that the laws proscribing the conduct were invalid under the European Convention on Human Rights. Dudgeon v. United Kingdom, 45 Eur. Ct. H.R. (1981) & ¶ 52. Authoritative in all countries that are members of the Council of Europe (21 nations then, 45 nations now), the decision is at odds with the premise in *Bowers* that the claim put forward was insubstantial in our Western civilization.
>
> In our own constitutional system the deficiencies in *Bowers* became even more apparent in the years following its announcement. The 25 States with laws prohibiting the relevant conduct referenced in the Bowers decision are reduced now to 13. . . .
>
> Two principal cases decided after *Bowers* cast its holding into even more doubt. In Planned Parenthood of Southeastern Pa. v. Casey, 505 U.S. 833 (1992), the Court reaffirmed the substantive force of the liberty protected by the Due Process Clause.

The *Casey* decision again confirmed that our laws and tradition afford constitutional protection to personal decisions relating to marriage, procreation, contraception, family relationships, child rearing, and education. In explaining the respect the Constitution demands for the autonomy of the person in making these decisions, we stated as follows:

> These matters, involving the most intimate and personal choices a person may make in a lifetime, choices central to personal dignity and autonomy, are central to the liberty protected by the Fourteenth Amendment. At the heart of liberty is the right to define one's own concept of existence, of meaning, of the universe, and of the mystery of human life. . . .

The second post-*Bowers* case of principal relevance is Romer v. Evans, 517 U.S. 620 (1996). There the Court struck down class-based legislation directed at homosexuals as a violation of the Equal Protection Clause. . . . We concluded that the provision was "born of animosity toward the class of persons affected" and further that it had no rational relation to a legitimate governmental purpose. . . .

Bowers was not correct when it was decided, and it is not correct today. It ought not to remain binding precedent. *Bowers v. Hardwick* should be and now is overruled.

The present case does not involve . . . public conduct or prostitution. It does not involve whether the government must give formal recognition to any relationship that homosexual couples seek to enter. The case does involve two adults who, with full and mutual consent from each other, engaged in sexual practices common to a homosexual lifestyle. The petitioners are entitled to respect for their private lives. . . . Their right to liberty under the Due Process Clause gives them the full right to engage in their conduct without intervention of the government.

123 S. Ct. at 2481-2484. For early commentary on *Lawrence*, *see* Laurence H. Tribe, Lawrence v. Texas: The "Fundamental Right" That Dare Not Speak Its Name, 117 Harv. L. Rev. 1893 (2004); Suzanne B. Goldberg, Equality Without Tiers, 77 S. Cal. L. Rev. 481 (2004).

4. Romer v. Evans, 517 U.S. 620 (1996), is cited by the majority in *Lawrence* as a second recent case inconsistent with the Court's earlier decision in Bowers v. Hardwick. The decision itself invalidated "Amendment 2" to the Colorado Constitution, adopted by statewide referendum, which precludes any legislative, executive, or judicial action extending protection against discrimination to homosexuals, homosexual conduct, or homosexual relationships. Justice Kennedy, for a six-member majority, held that the amendment's classification failed to meet the test of a rational relationship to a legitimate state purpose. The breadth of the amendment indicated that it was explained only by animus to a class, unrelated to any specific state purpose, and that classifications with the sole aim of generally disadvantaging a group are invalid. The majority does not address or cite Bowers v. Hardwick.

5. In Standhardt v. Superior Court ex rel. County of Maricopa, 77 P.3d 451 (Ariz. App. 2003), the plaintiffs relied on *Lawrence* for the proposition that denial of access to marriage denied same-sex couples due process of law. The court disagreed.

> First, as the State points out, elsewhere in its decision the Court explicitly stated that the case before it "[did] not involve whether the government must give formal recognition to any relationship that homosexual persons seek to enter." . . . It therefore follows that the Court did not intend by its comments to address same-sex marriages.

Petitioners mistakenly equate the "purposes" for which persons in a homosexual relationship may seek autonomy with the personal choices described in *Casey*, including the choice to marry. . . . In other words, "[p]ersons in a homosexual relationship may seek autonomy" to make "intimate and personal choices" that reflect "one's own concept of existence, of meaning, of the universe, and of the mystery of human life" free from government compulsion. . . . [W]e view the language in question as acknowledging a homosexual person's right to define his or her own existence, and achieve the type of individual fulfillment that is a hallmark of a free society, by entering a homosexual relationship. We do not view the language as stating that such a right includes the choice to enter a state-sanctioned, same-sex marriage. . . .

The court then held that the Arizona state constitutional provision ensuring a right to privacy did not extend to same-sex marriage and analyzed the constitutionality of the rule limiting marriage to opposite-sex couples under the rational-basis test. It concluded that the state's interest in "encouraging procreation and child-rearing within the stable environment traditionally associated with marriage" was rationally related to the rule. *See also* Morrison v. Sadler, 2003 WL 23119998 (Ind. App. 2003); Lewis v. Harris, 2003 WL 191114 (N.J. Super. 2003).

6. The ABA Section of Family Law Working Group on Same-Sex Marriage and Non-Marital Unions has issued a white paper that analyzes the law in all the 50 states as of early 2004. It is available at *http://www.abanet.org/family/whitepaper/home.html* (last visited Aug. 24, 2004).

7. Among the many discussions of same-sex marriage are Harry D. Krause, Marriage for the New Millennium: Heterosexual, Same Sex—or Not at All?, 34 Fam. L.Q. 271 (Summer 2000); Jennifer Wriggins, Marriage Law and Family Law: Anatomy, Interdependence, and Couples of the Same Gender, 41 B.C. L. Rev. 265 (2000); Mark Strasser, Marital Acts, Morality, and the Right to Privacy, 30 N.M. L. Rev. 43 (2000); Pamela S. Katz, The Case for Legal Recognition of Same-Sex Marriage, 8 J.L. & Pol'y 61 (1999); William N. Eskridge, Jr., Comparative Law and the Same-Sex Marriage Debate: A Step-by-Step Approach Toward State Recognition, 31 McGeorge L. Rev. 641 (2000); Michael Wald, Same-Sex Couple Marriage: A Family Policy Perspective, 9 Va. J. Soc. Pol'y & L. 291 (2001).

8. Constitutional issues aside, how should a legislature think about the desirability and importance of recognizing, or not recognizing, same-sex marriages? Should one look at the functions expected of marriage and inquire whether recognizing same-sex marriage would advance or detract from those functions? *See* David L. Chambers, What If? The Legal Consequences of Marriage and the Legal Needs of Lesbian and Gay Male Couples, 95 Mich. L. Rev. 447 (1996). Would recognition of same-sex marriage provide stability for relationships that will in any event occur, or would it prejudice fundamental relationships between women and men? *Compare* William Eskridge, Jr., The Case for Same-Sex Marriage: From Sexual Liberty to Civilized Commitment (1996), *and* Arthur S. Leonard, Going for the Brass Ring: The Case for Same-Sex Marriage, 82 Cornell L. Rev. 572 (1997), *with* Lynne Marie Kohm, A Reply to "Principles and Prejudice": Marriage and the Realization That Principles Win Over Political Will, 22 J. Contemp. L. 293 (1996).

For that matter, is it evident that recognition of same-sex marriage, as opposed perhaps to other forms of family recognition, is desirable from the perspective of lesbian and gay couples? *See, e.g.*, Paula L. Ettelbrick, Wedlock Alert:

A Comment on Lesbian and Gay Family Recognition, 5 J.L. & Pol'y 107 (1996); Barbara J. Cox, The Lesbian Wife: Same-Sex Marriage as an Expression of Radical and Plural Democracy, 33 Cal. W. L. Rev. 155 (1997).

NOTE: INTERNATIONAL DEVELOPMENTS IN SAME-SEX MARRIAGE

Canada In December 2004 the Supreme Court of Canada in In the Matter of Section 53 of the Supreme Court Act, R.S.C. 1985, c. S-26, 2004 SCC 79, held that national legislation that would permit same-sex marriage is permitted by the Canadian Charter of Rights and Freedoms. The decision was issued in response to a query from the national government, which has proposed legislation that says, "Marriage, for civil purposes, is the lawful union of two persons to the exclusion of all others." Because of the federal government's announced intention to introduce this legislation, the court declined to give its own opinion on whether excluding same-sex couples from marriage violates the Charter, though courts in six provinces and one territory have held that it does. The Supreme Court also held that the Charter protects religious officials from being compelled to perform same-sex marriages if such marriages are contrary to their religious beliefs. The opinion is available at *http://www.lexum.umontreal.ca/csc-scc/en/rec/html/2004scc079. wpd.html* (last visited Dec. 9, 2004).

The leading provincial opinion holding that denying same-sex couples the right to marry violates the Canadian Charter of Rights and Freedoms is Halpern et al. v. Canada (Attorney General), [2002] O.J. No. 2714. In that case, the Court of Appeal for Ontario relied on principles of human dignity, embodied in the Charter (and the Ontario Human Rights Code). Section 15(1) of the Charter provides that "[e]very individual is equal before the law and under the law has the right to the equal protection and equal benefit of the law without discrimination and, in particular, without discrimination based on race, national or ethnic origin, colour, religious, sex, age or mental or physical difficulty." The court found that the common law definition of marriage creates a formal distinction between opposite-sex couples and same-sex couples on the basis of their sexual orientation, that the Supreme Court of Canada had previously recognized sexual orientation as a ground analogous to those enumerated in § 15(1) in that it involves a "deeply personal characteristic that is either unchangeable or changeable only at an unacceptable personal cost, and that this differential treatment imposed a substantial burden on claimants in a way perpetuating or promoting the view that the individual is less capable or worthy of recognition or value as a human being or as a member of Canadian society. In making this last determination, the standard is whether a reasonable person in circumstances similar to the claimant would find that the challenged law differentiates in a manner that demeans his or her dignity."

The Attorney General of Canada argued that the amendment of 68 federal statutes to give same-sex couples the same benefits as opposite-sex couples (and corresponding amendments at the provincial level) provided same-sex couples equal treatment under the law. The Ontario court rejected that submission. For one thing, not all benefits and obligations had been extended to cohabiting couples. In addition, § 15(1) guarantees access to fundamental societal institutions as well as to economic benefits. Here, same-sex couples are excluded from such an institution, marriage, and that exclusion perpetuates the view that same-sex relationships are less worthy of recognition than oppose-sex relationships. In that respect, the exclusion "offends the dignity of persons in same-sex relationships."

Finally, the Ontario court considered whether the common law definition of marriage could be considered a reasonable limit on a Charter right in a free and democratic society. That conclusion would follow if the party supporting the challenged law proved that the objective of the law is pressing and substantial and the means chosen are reasonable and justifiable. The court considered several justifications. It concluded that the fact that marriage has always been defined as heterosexual is not in itself an objective capable of justification. It also concluded that the purposes of uniting the opposite sexes, encouraging the birth and raising of children, and companionship were ultimately expressions of the denial of dignity to same-sex couples.

Halpern declared invalid the common law definition of marriage to the extent that it refers to "one man and one woman" and reformulated the definition as "the voluntary union for life of two persons to the exclusion of all others." In announcing this remedy, the court rejected the Attorney General's request that the marriage statute simply be declared invalid, leaving it to the legislature to reconsider the entire question. The court similarly rejected a request for a suspension of the declaration of invalidity for some period of time, seeing no evidence that a declaration without a period of suspension posed any harm to the public, threatened the rule of law, or denied anyone the benefit of legal recognition of their marriage.

Europe   The Netherlands was the first country to recognize same-sex marriage. The Dutch Civil Code was amended in 2000, effective April 1, 2001, to recognize same-sex marriages. Title 5, Article 30(1) provides that "[a] marriage may be entered into by two persons of a different or of the same sex." Katharina Boele-Woelki, Registered Partnership and Same-Sex Marriage in the Netherlands, in Legal Recognition of Same-Sex Couples in Europe 231 (Katharina Boele-Woelki & Angelika Fuchs eds., 2003) (statute translated by Ian Sumner). Belgium followed suit in 2001. Belgium Bill, Belgische Kamer van Volksvertegernwoodigers. 52 Session de la 502 legislature, Doc. 59 216555/001, Jan. 20, 2003. Chapter II, Article 3 provides that "[t]wo persons of different sex or of the same sex can contract marriage. If a marriage is contracted between persons of the same sex, article 315 of the current Code is not applicable" (trans. editor).

The Dutch law recognizes virtually no differences between opposite-sex and same-sex marriages. Same-sex couples may adopt children on the same basis as other couples; indeed, there may be some advantage of same-sex couples seeking to adopt the child of a partner because, unlike opposite-sex marriage adoptions, the durational care period (three years) does not seem to apply. The major difference between opposite-sex and same-sex marriages has to do with the presumption of parentage for the female spouse of a married woman who gives birth during their marriage. In addition, as a constitutional matter, neither the king nor the queen may enter into a same-sex marriage. Boele-Woelki, *supra* at 41, 43-44.

During the first 20 months after the Act Opening Marriage to Same-Sex Couples became effective, 4,136 same-sex marriages (with slightly more male-male unions) were entered in the Netherlands. The number of opposite-sex marriages during the same time was 160,582. It is difficult to predict future incidence, but the initial rate may well have been at the high end because a number of couples taking advantage of the new law had likely already concluded registered partnerships (civil unions) under Dutch law, which were converted to marriages when that became possible. *Id.* at 45.

The Belgian law is somewhat more restrictive than the Dutch version. Like the Dutch law, the presumption of paternity (Art. 315 of the Belgian Civil Code) does not apply to a same-sex spouse. In addition, there is no provision for joint parental responsibility or for adoption by a same-sex partner or a same-sex couple. Belgian private international law also restricts more sharply the opportunity to marry for international couples. A marriage will be allowed only when the marriage is allowed by the national law of each partner—meaning, currently, a Belgian could marry only another Belgian (of the same sex) or a partner from the Netherlands. Equal Marriages for Same-Sex Couples, Equality and Marriage: Around the World (Feb. 2003), *available at http://www.samesexmarriage.ca/equality/world.html*; Allison O'Neill, Note: Recognition of Same-Sex Marriage in the European Community: The European Court of Justice's Ability to Dictate Social Policy, Cornell L. Rev. (forthcoming). Under Dutch private international law, the question of eligibility to marry will be determined by Dutch law if at least one of the parties is a Dutch national or habitual resident. Boele-Woelki, *supra* at 42-43.

In 2004 the Spanish prime minister announced that he would introduce legislation to permit gay marriage throughout the country, although the country's Roman Catholic bishops are organizing opposition to the plan. Tracy Wilkinson, Church Moves to Derail Spain's Same-Sex Marriage Bill, Los Angeles Times, July 21, 2004.

No other country has recognized same-sex marriage, and in some cases the barriers are juridical as well as social and political. German law recognizes same-sex partnerships for various purposes, but those partnerships are said to be considered not only different from but in some sense inferior to marriage. *See* Karsten Thorn, The German Law on Same-Sex Partnerships, in Legal Recognition of Same-Sex Couples in Europe 84 (Katharina Boele-Woelki & Angelika Fuchs eds., 2003), which emphasizes the significance of the provision of the German Constitution under which the state is obliged to promote marriage and the family—a provision that is understood to be limited to opposite-sex marriage. Because of that provision, it would be inappropriate to place a same-sex relationship on the same level as a "true" marriage. *Id.* at 85. For additional information on international developments in the legal treatment of unmarried partners, see Chapter 4.

South Africa The Supreme Court of Appeal of South Africa held in Fourie and Bonthuys v. Minister of Home Affairs (No. 232/2003, Nov. 30, 2004) that the common law institution of marriage should be extended to same-sex couples, relying on a provision of the South African constitution that prohibits discrimination on the basis of sexual orientation. (Bill of Rights § 9(3)). The court said that the definition of marriage should be changed from "the union of one man and one woman" to "the union of two persons to the exclusion of all others for life." However, same-sex couples will not be able to marry until legislation regarding formalities is amended. The case is available at *http://wwwserver.law.wits.ac.za/sca/judgment.php?case_id = 12942* (last visited Dec. 9, 2004). The court's decision could be appealed to the South African Constitutional Court.

NOTE: DEVELOPMENTS IN TRANSSEXUAL MARRIAGE

Marriage involving a transsexual partner presents the question of how one defines sex or gender. Courts in six states have decided cases involving the marriage of a postoperative transsexual person; all but one have held that such marriages are not permitted. In Littleton v. Prange, 9 S.W.3d 223 (Tex. App. 1999), *cert. denied*, 121 S. Ct. 174 (2000), the court refused to recognize a marriage between a transsexual woman (that is, a male-to-female transsexual) and a male. It held that the "sex" of Littleton (the transsexual partner) had been "immutably fixed by our Creator at birth," and that her self-conception as a female and sex reassignment surgery did not alter that initial identify. *See also* Kantaras v. Kantaras, 2004 WL 1635003 (Fla. Dist. Ct. App. 2d Dist.); In re A Marriage License for Nash, 2003 WL 23097095 (Ohio App. 11th Dist.); In re Estate of Gardiner, 42 P.3d 120 (Kan. 2002); Frances B. v. Mark B., 355 N.Y.S.2d 712 (N.Y. App. Div. 1974). M.J. v. J.T., 355 A.2d 204 (N.J. Super. 1976), *cert. denied*, 364 A.2d 1076 (N.J. 1976), is the only case that permitted transsexual marriage. The result of the Texas case, and the rationales of both the Texas and New Jersey decisions, are criticized in Martha M. Ertman, Marriage as a Trade: Bridging the Public/Private Distinction, 36 Harv. C.R.-C.L. L. Rev. 79, 88-89 (2001). Littleton v. Prange is also discussed in Julie A. Greenberg, When Is a Man a Man, and When Is a Woman a Woman?, 52 Fla. L. Rev. 745 (2000), reviewing both scientific and policy considerations.

The European Court of Human Rights has changed its view on the treatment of transsexuals. In Goodwin v. United Kingdom, (2002) 35 E.H.R.R. 18 ECHR, the court held that U.K. law denying a male-to-female transsexual the right to change a number of official government records that listed her as male, resulting in her treatment as male for purposes of inter alia Social Security, national insurance, pensions, and retirement age, violated European Convention Articles 8 (guaranteeing respect for one's private life) and 12 (securing the fundamental right of a man and woman to marry and to found a family). The latter changes previous doctrine that the inability of transsexuals to marry a person of the sex opposite to their re-assigned gender was not in breach of Article 12 of the Convention.

> Reviewing the situation in 2002, the Court observes that Article 12 secures the fundamental right of a man and woman to marry and to found a family. The second aspect is not however a condition of the first and the inability of any couple to conceive or parent a child cannot be regarded as per se removing their right to enjoy the first limb of this provision. . . .
>
> It is true that the first sentence refers in express terms to the right of a man and woman to marry. At the date of this case it can no longer be assumed that these terms must refer to a determination of gender by purely biological criteria. There have been major social changes in the institution of marriage since the adoption of

the Convention as well as dramatic changes brought about by developments in medicine and science in the field of transsexuality. The Court has found above, under Article 8 of the Convention, that a test of congruent biological factors can no longer be decisive in denying legal recognition to the change of gender of a post-operative transsexual. There are other important factors—the acceptance of the condition of gender identity disorder by the medical professions and health authorities within Contracting States, the provision of treatment including surgery to assimilate the individual as closely as possible to the gender in which they perceive that they properly belong and the assumption by the transsexual of the social role of the assigned gender. Furthermore, Article 9 of the recently adopted Charter of Fundamental Rights of the European Union departs, no doubt deliberately, from the wording of Article 12 of the Convention in removing the reference to men and women. . . .

While it is for the Contracting State to determine inter alia the conditions under which a person claiming legal recognition as a transsexual establishes that gender re-assignment has been properly effected or under which past marriages cease to be valid and the formalities applicable to future marriages (including, for example, the information to be furnished to intended spouses), there is no justification for barring the transsexual from enjoying the right to marry under any circumstances.

In February 2003, the Family Court of Australia, in a lengthy opinion reviewing European and Australian authorities, upheld a lower court decision holding valid a marriage by a female-to-male transsexual with hormone treatment and irreversible surgery and a woman against a challenge by the attorney general. Attorney-General (Cth) v Kevin, 172 FLR 300 (2003). *See also* Attorney General v. Otahuhu Family Court, [1995] 1 NZLR 603.

Most of the decisions allowing marriage by transsexuals seem to restrict their approval to postoperative transsexuals. The New Zealand court was plainly troubled by this requirement and decided that while it would not require that sexual function be possible, the couple "must present themselves as having what appear to be the genitals of a man and a woman. . . ." [1995] 1 NZLR at 612. The appellate court in *Kevin* emphasized the importance of irreversible surgery as an indicator of commitment to the new sexual identity, *see* 172 FLR at 635, thereby avoiding the risk of authorizing what turns out to be a same-sex marriage.

For an extensive analysis of case law and scientific discussion regarding transsexual marriage, *see* Terry S. Kogan, Transsexuals, Intersexuals, the Same-Sex Marriage, BYU L. Rev. (forthcoming 2004), raising the question, among others, whether the important criterion should be physical capacity or appearance or psychological condition.

d. Age

IN RE BARBARA HAVEN

---

86 Pa. D. & C. 141 (Orphans' Ct. 1953)

LAUB, Petitioner has invoked the provisions of the Act of March 24, 1927 . . . which provides that in special cases a judge of the orphans' court may authorize the issuance of a marriage license where one or both of the parties are under 16 years of age.[3] The child in this case is a female of the age of 14 years and eight months and desires to marry the son of her father's second wife, a young man 22 years of age. Her father has given his consent and now asks us to do likewise.

The testimony which we took at the hearing discloses that this attractive well-developed girl is physically suited for marriage. She has, however, achieved only the eighth grade in school and, although apparently intelligent, her marks are not of the best. She testified that she has been in love with her stepbrother for two years; has planned marriage almost from the inception of her acquaintance with him, and believes that her love for him is genuine and permanent. He is her first "steady" beau although she did attend school dances with other boys when she was 12 years old.

The young man in this case, Robert Bihler, is a typical, fine American youth. He is industrious and ambitious. There is no observable reason why he should not be married and it is evident that he is suited to become the head of a family.

The social aspects of marriage have become so impressed upon us that law-making bodies everywhere have seen fit to impose safeguards against ill-advised unions. Thus, waiting periods, medical examinations, age restrictions, marriages within certain degrees of consanguinity and affinity, and many other controls have been universally imposed by State legislatures in order to preserve and maintain the utmost purity and integrity of the marriage state. . . .

At common law a boy under 14 or a girl under 12 could not be married: Blackstone, book 1, chap. 15(2). But our legislature enacted the current law, apparently concluding that one in the sunlight of youth, standing on the threshold of life, should not walk precipitously into the marriage chamber, but first should look with calm deliberation whether the step is both desirable and safe. In this concept there has been ample support in aphorism and precept. Certainly it is based upon common experience and logic.

The statute in question . . . fulfills a two-fold function in protecting marriage as an estate and in placing a restraining hand upon the shoulder of impetuous youth. Our duty directs our attention to the interest of society in marriage, but it also commands us to consider the best interest of the minor as well.

The prime reason advanced in behalf of the present position is the young lady's protestation of affection for the boy. Love has many emotional counterfeits, each as likely as the other, but time and mature appreciation are the only devices which detect the real from the spurious. . . .

All of this was within the knowledge and contemplation of the legislature when it enacted the present law. When it conferred jurisdiction upon us to set aside the general rule in favor of special cases it could not have meant that our decision was to be exercised in commonplace situations such as obtains here.

In only a minority of cases do applicants seek marriage licenses without believing sincerely that they are in love and without a compelling desire to unite. . . .

---

3. Pa. Stat. tit. 48, §19 (1930) reads: "[N]o licenses to marry shall issue, if either applicant therefore be under the age of sixteen years: Provided, that a judge of the orphans' court shall have discretion to authorize a license to be issued by the clerk of the orphans' court in special cases. . . ."

Therefore, that which calls for action by us must truly be within the legislative concept of something "special," not something based upon the usual, ordinary or the mere urgent desire of the parties.

The proof offered here merely places these young people within the general category. Both are physically fit; both are fine, young citizens. But, in holding the marriage age to 16, the legislature must have realized that there is more to marriage than physical and mental development. It requires mature understanding and judgment; mature emotional stability. Above all, there must be a deep and abiding concept of marriage as more spiritual than physical, more an estate than a condition. In its wisdom the law-making body felt that an appreciation of these elements must be absent in a young girl of the age of the present applicant. It certainly felt that in fulfilling the function as protector of children, the law should not, in the absence of the most compelling circumstances, consent to the marriage of one so young. . . .

NOTES AND QUESTIONS

1. There is considerable evidence that teenage marriages are high-risk enterprises, in terms of both the likelihood of divorce and the quality of marital satisfaction. Generally speaking, youthful marriages correlate with lower income, higher unemployment, and lower satisfaction with financial condition. For a review of research on the significance of marital age, *see* Lynn Wardle, Rethinking Marital Age Restrictions, 22 J. Fam. L. 1 (1983-1984).

2. At the same time, as Professor Wardle also notes, a positive correlation between youth at the time of marriage and marital dissolution does not establish causation. Indeed, it is a canon of statistical inference that correlation does not imply causation. There are at least two reasons for rejecting the appealing inference that one variable causes another with which it is highly associated. One has to do with the question of direction of the inference. For example, a positive correlation can be found between class attendance and grades. One possible interpretation of this relationship is that people who go to class learn more and thus receive higher grades. Law teachers often favor this inference. Another plausible explanation, however, is that good grades lead students who attain them to enjoy classes more, and thus to attend them more frequently, than those who do not.

Moreover, there is always the possibility that some third variable produces covariance between two factors that are examined. Suppose we find a correlation between consumption of ice cream and drownings. It seems unlikely that eating ice cream throws large numbers of people into serious depression and results in their drowning themselves, or even causes them to swim more poorly. It also seems unlikely that depressed people on the point of suicide by drowning eat ice cream ritually. However, something else might explain the strong positive relationship: temperature. The warmer the weather, the more people go swimming (and thus the drowning rate is higher); similarly, the warmer the weather, the more ice cream people eat.

What variables, other than youth itself, might explain the apparent relationship between age and marital success?

3. Do age restrictions reflect state interests other than the risk of divorce, such as concern about sexual imposition? If so, what weight should be given to the father's consent to Barbara's marriage?

4. One must, after *Zablocki*, consider the constitutional posture of age restrictions. Is an age restriction the kind of burden on marriage that invokes strict scrutiny? If so, could any age restriction survive "strict scrutiny" as it was applied in *Zablocki*? Indeed, could any factor that is continuous rather than discrete—that is, which is distributed at all points of a continuum rather than categorically—be required to avoid overinclusiveness and underinclusiveness and survive?

5. Constitutional issues may also arise with parental consent to youthful marriages. In Kirkpatrick v. Dist. Ct., 43 P.2d 998 (2002), the Nevada Supreme Court considered the constitutionality of its state statute permitting a minor under the age of 16 to marry with the consent of one parent and the district court's authorization. Under that statute, the district court permitted petitioner's 15-year-old daughter to marry a 48-year-old man. Although the daughter's mother had provided consent, the father—who had joint legal custody and maintained an ongoing personal and custodial relationship with his daughter—had no knowledge that his daughter was planning to and ultimately did undergo a marriage in Nevada. Because he received neither notice nor an opportunity to be heard before his daughter was given judicial permission to marry, the statute was held to have been unconstitutionally applied in this instance.

E.　CONFLICT OF LAWS

IN RE MAY'S ESTATE

114 N.E.2d 4 (N.Y. 1953)

LEWIS, C.J. In this proceeding, involving the administration of the estate of Fannie May, deceased, we are to determine whether the marriage in 1913 between the respondent Sam May and the decedent, who was his niece by the half blood which marriage was celebrated in Rhode Island, where concededly such marriage is valid is to be given legal effect in New York where statute law declares incestuous and void a marriage between uncle and niece.

The question thus presented arises from proof of the following facts: The petitioner Alice May Greenberg, one of six children born of the Rhode Island marriage of Sam and Fannie May, petitioned in 1951 for letters of administration of the estate of her mother Fannie May, who had died in 1945. Thereupon, the respondent Sam May, who asserts the validity of his marriage to the decedent, filed an objection to the issuance to petitioner of such letters of administration upon the ground that he is the surviving husband of the decedent and accordingly, under section 118 of the Surrogate's Court Act, he has the paramount right to administer her estate. . . .

The petitioner, supported by her sisters Ruth Weisbrout and Evelyn May, contended throughout this proceeding that her father is not the surviving spouse of her mother because, although their marriage was valid in Rhode Island, the marriage never had validity in New York where they were then resident and where they retained their residence until the decedent's death.

The record shows . . . the respondent Sam May had resided in Portage, Wisconsin; that he came to New York in December, 1912, and within a month thereafter he and the decedent both of whom were adherents of the Jewish faith went to Providence, Rhode Island, where, on January 21, 1913, they entered into a ceremonial marriage performed by and at the home of a Jewish rabbi. The certificate issued upon that marriage gave the age of each party as twenty-six years and the residence of each as "New York, N.Y." Two weeks after their marriage in Rhode Island the respondent May and the decedent returned to Ulster County, New York, where they lived as man and wife for thirty-two years until the decedent's death in 1945. Meantime the six children were born who are parties to this proceeding. . . .

We regard the law as settled that, subject to two exceptions presently to be considered, and in the absence of a statute expressly regulating within the domiciliary State marriages solemnized abroad, the legality of a marriage between persons *sui juris* is to be determined by the law of the place where it is celebrated. Van Voorhis v. Brintnall, 86 N.Y. 18, 24. . . .

Incidental to the decision in Van Voorhis v. Brintnall, supra, which followed the general rule that ". . . recognizes as valid a marriage considered valid in the place where celebrated," this court gave careful consideration to, and held against the application of two exceptions to that rule viz., cases within the prohibition of positive law; and cases involving polygamy or incest in a degree regarded generally as within the prohibition of natural law.

We think the Appellate Division in the case as bar rightly held that the principle of law which ruled Van Voorhis v. Brintnall and kindred cases cited, supra, was decisive of the present case and that neither of the two exceptions to that general rule is here applicable.

The statute of New York upon which the appellants rely is subdivision 3 of section 5 of the Domestic Relations Law which, insofar as relevant to our problem, provides:

§ 5. Incestuous and void marriages

A marriage is incestuous and void whether the relatives are legitimate or illegitimate between either:

3. An uncle and niece or an aunt and nephew.

If a marriage prohibited by the foregoing provisions of this section be solemnized it shall be void, and the parties thereto shall each be fined not less than fifty nor more than one hundred dollars and may, in the discretion of the court in addition to said fine, be imprisoned for a term not exceeding six months. Any person who shall knowingly and wilfully solemnize such marriage, or procure or aid in the solemnization of the same, shall be deemed guilty of a misdemeanor and shall be fined or imprisoned in like manner.

Although the New York statute quoted above declares to be incestuous and void a marriage between an uncle and a niece and imposes penal measures upon the parties thereto, it is important to note that the statute does not by express terms regulate a marriage solemnized in another State whereas in our present case, the marriage was concededly legal. . . .

As section 5 of the New York Domestic Relations Law (quoted supra) does not expressly declare void a marriage of its domiciliaries solemnized in a foreign State where such marriage is valid, the statute's scope should not be extended by judicial construction. Van Voorhis v. Brintnall, supra. Indeed, had the Legislature been so disposed it could have declared by appropriate enactment that marriages contracted in another State which if entered into here would be void shall have no force in this State. Although examples of such legislation are not wanting, we find none in New York which serve to give subdivision 3 of section 5 of the Domestic Relations Law extraterritorial effectiveness. Accordingly, as to the first exception to the general rule that a marriage valid where performed is valid everywhere, we conclude that, absent any New York statute expressing clearly the Legislature's intent to regulate within this State marriages of its domiciliaries solemnized abroad, there is no "positive law" in this jurisdiction which serves to interdict the 1913 marriage in Rhode Island of the respondent Sam May and the decedent.

As to the application of the second exception to the marriage here involved between persons of the Jewish faith whose kinship was not in the direct ascending or descending line of consanguinity and who were not brother and sister, we conclude that such marriage, solemnized, as it was, in accord with the ritual of the Jewish faith in a State whose legislative body has declared such a marriage to be "good and valid in law," was not offensive to the public sense of morality to a degree regarded generally with abhorrence and thus was not within the inhibitions of natural law. . . .

DESMOND, J. (dissenting). . . . The general rule that "a marriage valid where solemnized is valid everywhere" (*see* Restatement, Conflict of Laws, § 121) does not apply. To that rule there is a proviso or exception, recognized, it would seem, by all the States, as follows: "unless contrary to the prohibitions of natural law or the express prohibitions of a statute." Section 132 of the Restatement of Conflict of Laws states the rule apparently followed throughout America: "A marriage which is against the law of the state of domicil of either party, though the requirements of the law of the state of celebration have been complied with, will be invalid everywhere in the following cases: . . . (b) incestuous marriage between persons so closely related that their marriage is contrary to a strong public policy of the domicil." . . .

. . . Section 5 of the Domestic Relations Law, the one we are concerned with here, lists the marriages which are "incestuous and void" in New York, as being those between parent and child, brother and sister, uncle and niece, and aunt and nephew. All such misalliances are incestuous, and all, equally, are void. The policy, language, meaning and validity of the statute are beyond dispute. It should be enforced by the courts.

NOTES AND QUESTIONS

1. Recognition by one state of marriages contracted in another state is generally a matter of policy governed by principles of choice of law rather than a

matter of compulsion under the full faith and credit clause, unless the marriage has been the subject of a judicial proceeding (as through an annulment action or declaratory judgment proceeding).

2. Section 283 of The Restatement (Second) of Conflict of Laws provides as follows:

(1) The validity of a marriage will be determined by the local law of the State which, with respect to the particular issue, has the most significant relationship to the spouses and the marriage. . . .

(2) A marriage which satisfies the requirements of the State where the marriage was contracted will everywhere be recognized as valid unless it violates the strong public policy of another State which has the most significant relationship to the spouses and the marriage at the time of the marriage.

According to the reporter for the Second Restatement,

[T]his formulation reflects the three underlying values of (a) State interest, (b) protection of the expectations of the parties and (c) the general policy favouring the validation of marriages. Subsection (2) calls, as a general rule, for the application of the law of the State of celebration provided that the marriage would be valid under that law. . . .

The formulation further makes clear that a marriage good under the law of the State of celebration should not be overthrown unless this is required by the "strong public policy" of the State of most significant relationship.

. . . In making this determination, the forum should first inquire whether the courts of the State of most significant relationship would have invalidated the marriage if the question had come before them. The fact that these courts would not have done so provides, of course, conclusive evidence that no strong policy of this State is involved. If, on the other hand, these courts would have invalidated the marriage . . . the forum would have good reason to do likewise. It would in all probability invalidate the marriage . . . if the parties were still domiciled in the State which was that of most significant relationship at the time of the marriage. The situation would be somewhat different, however, if by the time the action arose the parties had moved to a different State. . . . [A] State will naturally have less interest in having its invalidating rule applied in a case where the parties to the marriage have moved away than it would have if they had remained its local domiciliaries. . . .

Willis L. M. Reese, Marriage in American Conflict of Laws, 26 Int'l & Comp. L.Q. 952, 965-969 (1977).

While there is no comprehensive definition of the "state with the most significant relationship to the spouses and the marriage," it is generally agreed that a state where both parties were domiciled at the time of the marriage (wherever celebrated) would qualify, as would a state in which one of the spouses was domiciled and in which both spouses resided after the marriage.

3. In Catalano v. Catalano, 170 A.2d 726 (Conn. 1961), a resident of Connecticut married his niece, an Italian citizen, in Italy. Their marriage was valid under Italian law. The uncle (Fred) returned to this country immediately; his niece joined him after several years. Fred died shortly thereafter, and his niece sought a widow's allowance from Fred's estate. The Connecticut court, applying Connecticut law, held that her marriage to Fred was contrary to its public policy—a decision

based in part on statutory declarations that incestuous marriages are "void" and the existence of a substantial criminal penalty (up to ten years in prison) for incest.

In what respect do the analyses in *May's Estate* and *Catalano* differ? What are the indicia of a "strong public policy" against recognition of marriages that are valid in the state of celebration?

The outcome in *Catalano* is relatively uncommon. *See, e.g.,* Mason v. Mason, 775 N.E.2d 706 (Ind. App. 2002) (first-cousin marriage does not violate strong state policy); In re Loughmiller, 629 P.2d 156 (Kan. 1981) (same).

4. In Wilkins v. Zelichowski, 140 A.2d 65 (N.J. 1958), the parties were domiciled in New Jersey. They could not marry in that state because the wife was under the age of 18. Romantically, they ran away from home and married in Indiana, whose laws permit women under the age of 18 to marry. They returned to New Jersey, and shortly thereafter a child was born. Unfortunately, the husband was convicted of car theft and placed in a reformatory; the wife then sought an annulment of the marriage. Although the trial court found that an annulment would not illegitimate the child under New Jersey law and would in fact serve the child's best interests, it denied relief because the marriage was valid in the state of celebration. The Supreme Court of New Jersey reversed, concluding that New Jersey was the only state with an interest in the marital status and that recognition of the marriage would conflict with that state's strong public policy.

Is the decision in *Zelichowski* consistent with that in *May's Estate*? *See* Reese, above, at 960:

> There is surely no reason to suppose the policy embodied in the New York statute in *May's Estate* was any weaker than that embodied in the [New Jersey] statute in *Zelichowski*. And it seems clear that in both cases the statutory policy would have been served by application of the statute to invalidate the marriage. The cases, however, can be reconciled, it is felt, on the ground that they involved different choice-of-law values. It will be recalled that protection of the expectations of the parties is one value, and perhaps the principal value, supporting the rule that a marriage which meets the requirements of the State of celebration will usually be held valid elsewhere. Protection of that value is undoubtedly the basic explanation for the result in *May's Estate*. . . . By way of contrast, the wife sought annulment in *Zelichowski* and therefore it was clear that at least her expectations would not be disappointed by the invalidation of the marriage. . . .

What were the parties' expectations when they went to Indiana? Why isn't the husband's expectation disappointed by an annulment?

5. The cases we have dealt with to this point involve evasionary, or at least migratory, marriages. How does the situation differ when first cousins live and marry in one state, which permits them to do so, and later move to a second state whose laws would not permit them to marry?

> . . . [M]any states distinguish between the validity of a marriage and the ability to enjoy its "incidents." There was a time when courts treated marriage as a simple yes-or-no, up-or-down proposition: A marriage was either valid, in which case it was valid for all purposes, or it was not, in which case it was invalid for all purposes. Particularly in this century, however, judges have been willing to draw finer lines, applying the place of celebration rule to the question of validity while saving the

public policy exception for particular "incidents" of being married. The right to cohabit, for example, is a usual incident of being married, but not a necessary one. A man married to two wives in India might be able to move to Kansas without being prosecuted for bigamy, but Kansas might forbid the three of them from living together. At the same time, the surviving wives might both be permitted to inherit as spouses under the state's law of succession.

Larry Kramer, Same-Sex Marriage, Conflict of Laws, and the Unconstitutional Public Policy Exception, 106 Yale L.J. 1965, 1971 (1997). *See* In re Dalip Singh Bir's Estate, 188 P.2d 499 (Cal. App. 1948), in which a native of the Punjab Province of India legally married two wives. He later moved to California, where he died intestate. Both women sought to inherit as his wives. The California Court of Appeals held that recognition of both marriages for inheritance purposes did not violate strong public policy, but that the result would be different "if the decedent had attempted to cohabit with his two wives in California." *See also* People v. Ezeonu, 588 N.Y.S.2d 116 (Sup. Ct. 1992), in which a New York court convicted a Nigerian man of statutory rape of his 13-year-old "second wife." Relying on statutory language describing such marriages as "absolutely void," the court rejected the polygamous second marriage, which had been validly celebrated in Nigeria and recognized by Nigerian custom, refusing to give it local effect when the couple changed domicile to New York.

THE DEFENSE OF MARRIAGE ACT

In response to the Hawaii decision in Baehr v. Lewin discussed at page 207, above, Congress adopted the Defense of Marriage Act (DOMA), Pub. L. No. 104-199 (1996). The substantive provisions of the Act, as codified, are

28 U.S.C. § 1738(c) No State, territory, or possession of the United States or Indian tribe, shall be required to give effect to any public act, record, or judicial proceeding of any other State, territory, possession, or tribe respecting a relationship between persons of the same sex that is treated as a marriage under the laws of such other State, territory, possession, or tribe, or a right or claim arising from such relationship.

1 U.S.C. § 7 In determining the meaning of any Act of Congress, or of any ruling, regulation, or interpretation of the various administrative bureaus and agencies of the United States, the word "marriage" means only a legal union between one man and one woman as husband and wife, and the word "spouse" refers only to a person of the opposite sex who is a husband or wife.

LARRY KRAMER, *SAME-SEX MARRIAGE, CONFLICT OF LAWS, AND THE UNCONSTITUTIONAL PUBLIC POLICY EXCEPTION*

106 Yale L.J. 1965 (1997)

[Professor Kramer argues generally that the "public policy" doctrine allowing states to refuse recognition to marriages valid in the place of celebration because they disagree with the policy of the state of celebration is inconsistent with an equality requirement of the Full Faith and Credit Clause. "What is forbidden is a state's refusal to apply another state's law, otherwise applicable under forum choice-of-law rules, on the ground that it promotes a policy the forum finds repugnant. The measure of repugnance in this sense is fixed by the federal Constitution, and states have no business selectively ignoring or refusing to recognize the constitutional laws of sister states because they do not like them. A case that has contacts with another state such that the forum deems it outside the forum's sphere of interest (as defined by forum choice-of-law rules) does not slip back into that sphere because of the content of the other state's law. . . . States retain the power to regulate the marriages of domiciliaries according to their own dictates, including the power to adopt choice-of-law rules establishing the circumstances in which another state's law will apply. The only limitation proposed here is that, if a state adopts a choice-of-law practice that recognizes marriages celebrated elsewhere, the rule or approach it uses cannot be designed or selectively manipulated to disfavor particular laws because their content is deemed especially odious. Whether a state refines its traditional rules or adopts some form of modern analysis for marriage cases, the state's courts must apply that approach without basing their decisions on whether or how strongly they disapprove of a particular state's policy."]

There is a further complication. Part II argued that states cannot make an exception to their ordinary choice-of-law rules when those rules say to apply Hawaii law just because they dislike Hawaii's policy choices. Anticipating such an argument, opponents of gay and lesbian marriage went to Congress for permission. Congress responded with the Defense of Marriage Act, which purports to authorize states to do what I just argued the Full Faith and Credit Clause prohibits. . . .

Can the national legislature really do this? Congress purported to act under the second half of Article IV, section 1, which says, "And the Congress may by general Laws prescribe the Manner in which such Acts, Records and Proceedings shall be proved, and the Effect thereof." For those who like to play with texts, this so-called Effects Clause provides a splendid opportunity for exegetics: What are "general Laws"? Do "Acts, Records and Proceedings" include common law decisions or just statutes? Does the Clause apply only to how laws and judgments are proved, or can Congress prescribe substantive rules as well? Each of these questions has, in fact, produced its fair share of commentary over the years. There is, however, "a substantial consensus" today that, whatever mysteries remain, the Effects Clause does indeed authorize Congress to make binding choice-of-law rules for the states. Yet this consensus is confined to Congress's power to enact choice-of-law rules at all. No one has ever found it necessary to ask just how far Congress can go, because Congress has never legislated even a single choice-of-law rule for states. (Note how extraordinary DOMA is in this light: Congress was content to let the states slug it out on issues like slavery, miscegenation, divorce, and abortion—but this, it seems, goes too far.) We are dealing with a completely open question. . . .

If asked, most commentators today would probably [conclude that] the Full Faith and Credit Clause imposes certain judicially defined limits on states, analogous to limits imposed under the dormant Commerce Clause. These have the status of federal common law and can thus be displaced by Congress, which has nearly unlimited power under the Effects Clause to prescribe alternative rules. Hence, a state violates the Full Faith and Credit Clause by applying its law without a legitimate interest, and also, if I am right, by refusing to apply another state's law on public policy grounds. If Congress decides differently, however, it has power under the Effects Clause to authorize states to take these otherwise prohibited steps. On this view of Congress's power, then, DOMA is constitutional. . . .

There are a number of problems with this interpretation, which I was originally inclined to accept. To begin, the text of the Clause says that full faith and credit shall be given in each state to the laws and judgments of every other state. . . . It does not say that only some faith and credit need be given, but rather that the faith and credit given shall be full. This unqualified "full" and mandatory "shall" lose some (though obviously not all) of their meaning if Congress can simply legislate the requirement away or relieve states of whatever obligations the Full Faith and Credit Clause imposes. . . .

[T]he Full Faith and Credit Clause is more than a strategy to minimize friction. It represents the very idea of what it means to be in a Union. States are required to recognize and respect each other's laws because that is what members of a federation do. It may sometimes produce tension, but that inheres in the relationship, less a "cost" than an intrinsic characteristic. . . .

[C]ommitment to Union is itself a fundamental constitutional value. As such, Congress should not be permitted to redefine its terms at will or to legislate away the minimum requirements of mutual respect and recognition it entails any more than Congress can suppress speech or legislate inequality. . . .

[A]ssuming I am right and that states cannot make [a public policy exception], should it also be unconstitutional for Congress to do so? On the one hand, it is easier to imagine plausible reasons for Congress to authorize a content-based exception to ordinary choice-of-law rules. On the other hand, given the controversial nature of the issues, the likelihood that Congress will act for improper reasons is also much greater. To put the point bluntly, which of the following explanations seems more plausible: that the members of Congress who supported DOMA did so because they were concerned about interstate friction, or that they did so because they shared the same distaste of same-sex marriage as their state-level compatriots? In light of the tension between the public policy exception and the Full Faith and Credit Clause, this too should be prohibited to Congress.

NOTES AND QUESTIONS

1. 28 U.S.C. § 1738(c) declares that states are not required by the Full Faith and Credit Clause to recognize valid same-sex marriages entered in another state. The constitutionality of this provision has been controversial. The Supreme Court has never held that marriage is a public act requiring full faith and credit; however, the Court also has never held that it is not. Among the issues presented are whether the Full Faith and Credit Clause extends to public acts of this kind and, if it does, whether its command is categorical or subject to limitation in cases of strong contrary state policy.

A large literature on same-sex marriage and its recognition by other states has emerged. It includes Jennifer Brown, Competitive Federalism and the Legislative Incentives to Recognize Same-Sex Marriage, 68 S. Cal. L. Rev. 745 (1995); Evan Wolfson, Crossing the Threshold: Equal Marriage for Lesbians and Gay Men and the Intra-Community Critique, 21 N.Y.U. Rev. L. & Soc. Change 567 (1994); Alice Wooley, Excluded by Definition: Same-Sex Couples and the Right to Marry, 45 U. Toronto L.J. 471 (1995); William N. Eskridge, Jr., The Case for Same-Sex Marriage (1996); Lynn D. Wardle, A Critical Analysis of Constitutional Claims for Same-Sex Marriage, 1996 BYU L. Rev. 1; Developments in the Law — The Law of Marriage and Family: Constitutional Constraints on Interstate Same-Sex Marriage Recognition, 116 Harv. L. Rev. 2028 (2003).

2. Both before and after the enactment of DOMA, a number of states adopted express statutory provisions declaring a public policy against recognizing same-sex marriages. As of mid-2004, 38 states had DOMAs, four of them in their respective state constitutions. ABA Section of Family Law, Working Group on Same-Sex Marriage and Non-Marital Unions, White Paper: An Analysis of the Law Regarding Same-Sex Marriage, Civil Unions, and Domestic Partnerships 9 (2004). This strategy gained impetus after the decisions in *Goodridge* and Lawrence v. Texas. The Virginia legislature enacted a new provision, Va. Code § 20-12.1, in 2004, which included legislative findings that

> both the United States Supreme Court in Lawrence v. Texas, and the Massachusetts Supreme Court in Goodridge v. Department of Health, failed to consider the beneficial health effects of heterosexual marriage, as contrasted to the life-shortening and health compromising consequences of homosexual behavior, and this to the detriment of all citizens regardless of their sexual orientation or inclination.

Accordingly, the statute provides that "the Commonwealth of Virginia is under no constitutional or legal obligation to recognize a marriage, civil union, partnership contract or other arrangement purporting to bestow any of the privileges or obligations of marriage under the laws of another state or territory of the United States unless such marriage conforms to the laws of this Commonwealth."

The breadth of this provision is unusual in several respects, including its explicit rejection of civil unions and "other arrangements purporting to bestow any of the privileges or obligations of marriage." How far will this statute reach?

3. 1 U.S.C. § 7, above, states that the term *marriage* for purposes of federal statutes and regulations includes only a lawful marriage between one man and one woman, and the term *spouse* refers only to a lawfully married person of the opposite sex. Does the statute reach more broadly than it should? Will the requirement of a "lawful" marriage affect the coverage of federal legislation? Does it follow that all lawful marriages are marriages for purposes of federal legislation? If so, how would that affect the outcome in Lutwak v. United States, set out at page 158, above?

In general, federal law defers to state law defining domestic relations. Does establishment of a special federal rule for marriages of homosexual couples raise an issue under *Romer*?

PROBLEM

Suppose that the Massachusetts legislature amends the marriage act to include same-sex couples.

A. Ronald and Richard, two male residents of Utah who have enjoyed a long-term relationship, travel to Massachusetts, receive a marriage license, and have their marriage solemnized according to the requirements of Massachusetts law. They return to Utah after one week and continue to reside together. Two years later, Ronald sues Richard for divorce in Utah and asks for spousal maintenance. If Richard contests the divorce on the ground that there was no marriage, what will be the result?

B. Same facts as A, except that after two years of postmarital residence in Utah, Richard is killed in an automobile accident arising out of his employment. Ronald seeks to inherit as a surviving spouse and also to recover workers' compensation benefits.

C. Suppose that, in both situations A and B, the parties are two female residents of Massachusetts who married and continued to live in Massachusetts for two years. They then moved to Utah, where they lived together until the events described above.

Alternatives to Ceremonial Marriage

4

A. INTRODUCTION

Most of the time we think of marriage as a relationship clearly distinct from others, begun by a formal ceremony and ended by death or formal divorce. However, many people who have not gone through a valid ceremonial marriage live together and share their lives much as people who have been ceremonially married do. While this phenomenon is not new, the rate of cohabitation has increased dramatically over the last 30 years throughout the Western world. This chapter examines legal doctrines that in some circumstances and to varying extents result in the people in these households being treated as members of families.

RENATA FORSTE, *PRELUDE TO MARRIAGE OR ALTERNATIVE TO MARRIAGE?*

---

4 J. L. & Fam. Stud. 91-92 (2002)

Cohabitation's popularity in the U.S. as a living arrangement began to emerge during the 1960s and 1970s. Initially a deviant behavior, it was still uncommon during the early 1970s; for example in 1968 the case of a single cohabiting college student was considered significant. In contrast, today cohabitation has become a generally common life course experience, particularly among young people. Census estimates indicate that in 1977 there were 1.1 million cohabiting couples, about 1.5% of all households in the U.S. Twenty years later in 1997, the number of cohabiting households had grown to 4.9 million or 4.8% of all households. Demographic studies indicate that this increase in cohabitation has occurred across all education levels and race and ethnic groups. Cohabitation is now found in almost all segments of American society.

It is expected that cohabitation rates will likely increase in the future as younger cohorts, more accepting of cohabitation, replace older cohorts. In addition, there is some evidence that cohabitation rates are increasing even among the elderly. However, in general, the likelihood of individuals forming informal unions peaks prior to age 40, begins to decline during middle-age, and is least prevalent among the elderly. It is estimated that of individuals aged thirty-five to thirty-nine, half have cohabited.

Marriage rates have declined in the U.S. since the 1970s, yet couples have continued to form unions at about the same rate as in previous decades. Now, however, more of these first unions are cohabiting relationships rather than formal marriage. Over half of first unions formed in the early 1990s began with cohabitation. In addition, couples forming unions following divorce are particularly likely to cohabit first rather than marry.

* * *

Judith Seltzer in a recent review of literature on nonmarital families notes the heterogeneity of cohabiting couples, but concludes that cohabitors fall generally into three categories: (1) cohabiting couples that would marry, but lack the economic resources to do so, (2) cohabiting couples that want an alternative to marriage based more on equality, and (3) cohabitors for whom cohabitation is an extension of the courtship process prior to marriage. The first two categories of cohabitors do not marry — either out of necessity or choice; cohabitation for them serves as an alternative to marriage. In contrast, the third category of cohabiting couples define cohabitation more as a type of coresidential engagement, a temporary prelude to formal marriage.

MARY ANN GLENDON, *MARRIAGE AND THE STATE:* *THE WITHERING AWAY OF MARRIAGE*

62 Va. L. Rev. 663, 684-687, 692-693 (1976)

Cohabitation, or "living together," is only one aspect of diversity in American marriage behavior, using the word *marriage* broadly. Defining exactly what turns a sexual relation into "marriage" is difficult, but it is useful to follow the lead of the family sociologist Rene Konig, by thinking of the shadow institution of legal marriage as a set of heterosexual unions undertaken with some idea of duration and manifested to the relevant social environment. . . .

Motivations to enter informal rather than legal marriage include economic advantages as in the case of many elderly people,[1] inability to enter a legal marriage, unwillingness to be subject to the legal effects of marriage, desire for a "trial

---

1. In many cases the Social Security system inflicts financial penalties on elderly citizens who remarry. Although individuals who receive old-age assistance by virtue of their own participation are entitled to their full benefits regardless of marital status, 42 U.S.C. §402(a) (1970), widows and widowers who participate only through the earnings of their deceased spouses ordinarily have their benefits cut in half by remarriage. *Id.* §402(e)(4),

marriage," and lack of concern with the legal institution. This lack of concern is nothing new among groups accustomed to forming and dissolving informal unions without coming into contact with legal institutions. Among these groups legal marriage is but an aspect of the irrelevance of traditional American family law, law that is viewed as being property-oriented and organized around the ideals of a dominant social group. Lack of concern with marriage law has been growing, however, among many who definitely are not outside the mainstream of American life. Until recently these converts accepted unquestioningly the traditional structures of the enacted law, but they now find that on balance the enacted law offers no advantages over informal arrangements.

. . . In the past our legal response to cohabitation has been to pretend it is marriage and then attribute to it the traditional incidents of marriage. Thus, what in effect were cohabitation cases were disguised as cases involving presumptively legal marriage, estoppels, and implied agreements to pay for service. Because informal marriage exists in every society, every legal system has had to provide some ways to deal with the problems it generates. Professor Walter Weyrauch has convincingly demonstrated that this is the correct way to view not only the institution of common law marriage, but the myriad devices of the law of proof and presumptions that are the functional equivalent of common law marriage in those states that do not recognize it. In this view, naturally, the gradual decline in the number of jurisdictions that recognize the doctrine of common law marriage loses significance because other devices have simultaneously arisen to bring about functionally analogous legal effects, usually through the provision of economic benefits, such as alimony, inheritance rights, wrongful death, or workmen's compensation benefits to members of a de facto family.

The interesting question now becomes whether the increase in, and increased visibility and respectability of, informal marriage will bring about a casting-off of these legal fictions and the direct attribution of economic consequences to de facto dependency.

B. COMMON LAW MARRIAGE, PRESUMPTIONS OF MARRIAGE, AND PUTATIVE SPOUSES

As Glendon says, the traditional legal treatment of cohabitants was either to regard their relationship as wholly unlawful or to assimilate it into marriage through a variety of doctrines. This section considers three of the most important and widely

---

(f)(5). Also, the right of a surviving spouse, under some state laws, *e.g.*, N.Y. Estates, Powers & Trusts L. §5-1.1 (McKinney 1967), as amended (McKinney Pock. Pt. 1975-1976), to elect a statutory share of the decedent spouse's estate despite his will constitutes an obstacle to elderly couples who wish to preserve their separate estates for their individual families by previous marriage. The necessity of an antenuptial agreement to disclaim such rights is, at best, a nuisance and, at worst, an illusion, should the agreement for some reason be invalidated in court.

used of these doctrines: common law marriage, the putative spouse doctrine, and presumptions of marriage validity. Other devices include limitations on standing to attack the validity of marriage (see Chapter 3) and the validity of divorce (see Chapter 11).

1. Common Law Marriage

American common law marriage derives from English marriage law prior to the Marriage Act of 1753. Ecclesiastical courts did not require that couples marry in church; they also recognized people as married if they exchanged promises to marry in the present tense (*sponsalia per verba de praesenti*) or in the future followed by consummation (*sponsalia per verba de futuro*). However, the 1753 Marriage Act, known as Lord Hardwicke's Act, which provided that only marriages celebrated in church or in a public chapel in the presence of two witnesses would thereafter be valid, officially abolished nonceremonial marriage. Exceptions were made for the royal family, Quakers, and Jews. Nonceremonial marriages were recognized in the English colonies as well.

MICHAEL GROSSBERG, *GOVERNING THE HEARTH*

68-69, 79, 83-84, 86-90, 101 (1985)

[Some colonists deliberately avoided formal marriage as part of their rejection of traditional religious attitudes, while others formed informal unions out of necessity, due to the lack of regular clergy and lay officials empowered to celebrate marriage.] The presence of informal marriage in colonial America may be clear but its legal status was not. . . . In all likelihood, though, the clouded distinction between legality and validity in English law and the uncertainty engendered by the decentralized, informal colonial legal system led to ad hoc, localized solutions. Despite the clear preferences of provincial statutes, informal marriage probably received judicial acquiescence, if not endorsement, and thus the dual nuptial system lingered in the colonies after it had disappeared in the mother country. . . .

[After the American Revolution, judges and legislatures initially endorsed common law marriage.] Republican marriage law made matrimony much easier for a couple to enter, rechristened "irregular marriage" as "common law marriage," and significantly eased the rules governing proof of valid unions.[2] . . .

The continuing practice of irregular marriage, combined with unreliable public records and laissez faire government, made it difficult for couples to substantiate their marriages. However, judges placed the weight of the law behind those living as husband and wife. They did so by formally receiving into American common law the old rule that marriage could be presumed from the acknowledgements, cohabitation, and reputation of a couple. . . .

---

2. Chancellor Kent was a leader in this movement. *See* James Kent, Commentaries on American Law (1827), XXVI (6). —Ed.

At the heart of the judiciary's incorporation of the presumption of marriage lay a persistent inclination to find matrimony whenever a man and a woman lived together. . . . In a clear policy decision favoring practice over form, courts refused to dissolve marriages and break up families for lack of evidence of a wedding ceremony. . . .

The tolerance of informal marriage by jurists . . . evoked growing criticism in mid-century America. By the 1870s an organized reform campaign questioned the intent and methods of American family law. Reformers, legislators, social scientists, journalists, evangelical Protestants, and other interested parties assailed marriage law for its laxity and its failure to protect society from marital instability. . . .

Marriage reform in late nineteenth-century America is an example of what social critic Stan Cohen has labeled a "moral panic." . . . Cohen argues that such mass phenomena erupt when a "condition, episode, person or group of persons emerges to become defined as a threat to societal values and interests; its nature is presented in a stylized and stereotypical fashion by the mass media; the moral barricades are manned by editors, bishops and politicians and other right-think-ing people; socially accredited experts pronounce their diagnoses and solution; ways of coping are evolved, or (more often) resorted to; the condition then disap-pears, submerges or deteriorates." Sometimes panics pass and are forgotten. But other times, he suggests, the panic "has more serious and long term repercussions and it might produce changes in legal and social policy or even in the way in which societies conceive themselves." Such social scares offer a means of express-ing deep-seated fears and help focus those concerns on the most visible symbols of the crisis, what Cohen terms "folk devils." In nineteenth-century American domestic relations, panics over family life led to persistent efforts to compel deviant couples to adhere to orthodox republican matrimonial practices. Legal coercion became one of the most trusted weapons of reform. . . .

[One prominent expression of this change was a concerted attack on com-mon law marriage. Once championed as supporting virtue by giving the legal effect of marriage to relationships that functioned as marriage, common law mar-riage came to be seen as a prime cause of social disintegration and immorality.] . . . [B]y the early twentieth century [common law marriage] met almost universal public condemnation. The 1918 Minnesota Law Review reported that such unions were "becoming quite a rare occurrence, and the instances in which [they are] being presented to the courts are fewer still." But common-law marriage remained a legal option in most jurisdictions.

See also Ariela R. Dubler, Wifely Behavior: A Legal History of Acting Married, 100 Colum. L. Rev. 957 (2000).

IN RE MARRIAGE OF WINEGARD

257 N.W.2d 609 (Iowa 1977)

MASON, J. . . . John and Sally, 53 and 30 years of age respectively at time of trial, first met in 1962, shortly after Sally commenced working in the office of John's

Burlington business enterprise, Winegard Company. At the time, Sally was single and John was married and the father of two children. At some time in 1964 or 1965 John's first marriage was dissolved. In May of 1963 John and Sally commenced an erratic relationship which ultimately led to the present controversy.

Five months after John and Sally started seeing one another Sally married one Lonnie Anderkin and moved to Ohio. This union produced a child, Wendy Lynn, who was born in September of 1964. This marriage was apparently subjected to more than its share of marital and financial difficulties. At one point, Sally and Anderkin received a $500 loan from John. Subsequently, Sally returned to Burlington and asked John for financial assistance in order to obtain a dissolution of her marriage to Anderkin. Apparently, John gave her $50 on two different occasions which she used to commence two abortive dissolution actions in Iowa. During this period, which apparently was late 1965 and early 1966, John and Sally dated each other and traveled together.

In October of 1966 John accompanied Sally and her daughter to Las Vegas, Nevada, where Sally intended to commence divorce proceedings against Anderkin. Sally's legal and living expenses were paid by John. On December 7 Sally was granted a divorce from Anderkin, who appeared in the proceedings through counsel. During the six-week interval prior to the divorce decree, John divided his time between Las Vegas and Burlington. On the day the decree was issued, John and Sally returned to Burlington and at some point during the trip marriage was proposed by John and declined by Sally.

Upon their return to the Burlington area, John and Sally dated intermittently until February 1967, when Sally returned to Ohio and began living with her ex-husband Anderkin. A few months later, Anderkin went into military service and Sally moved in with his parents. The record is unclear with respect to Sally's activities in the following 15-18 months, but it is clear she married one Frank Gilvin in Dayton, Ohio, on October 31, 1968.

Sally's second marriage was apparently as troubled as her first and she once again returned to the Burlington area with John's financial assistance. Subsequently, John again accompanied her to Las Vegas, paying all expenses involved, and Sally was granted a default divorce from Gilvin on September 3, 1969.

Evidently, upon the divorce from Gilvin, Sally and John returned to Burlington where their relationship became matrimonially inclined. On April 4, 1970, John and Sally entered into an antenuptial agreement whereby, in essence, Sally waived ". . . all statutory or common law rights that she may have as the wife of John during John's lifetime and/or as the surviving spouse in the property or estate of John. . . ." In exchange for said waiver, John agreed to secure insurance on his life in the face amount of $100,000 and to name Sally as primary beneficiary thereof. The agreement stated its execution was prompted by the fact John and Sally ". . . are contemplating marriage and may be married in the near future. . . ."

Shortly after the execution of said agreement, John and Sally traveled to Hawaii with the intention of being married there. However, upon their arrival in Hawaii, John told Sally he wanted to delay their marriage plans, explaining he had waited until the day before their departure to tell his daughter of their matrimonial intentions and he felt she needed more time to adjust to the situation. John and Sally returned to Burlington unmarried.

In September of 1970, just a few months after her trip to Hawaii with John, Sally returned to Ohio and renewed her living arrangement with her ex-husband Anderkin. Again, Sally's revived relationship with her former husband only lasted for 3-4 months and she returned to the Burlington area in December of that year.

Following Sally's return, her relationship with John was rekindled and on February 14, 1971, he gave her an engagement ring. On March 29 John and Sally reaffirmed the previously executed antenuptial agreement and left for Las Vegas again with the intention to be married upon their arrival in that city. Once again, however, John and Sally returned to Burlington a few days later without having participated in a marriage ceremony. Apparently, abandonment of their plans was at John's request.

Sally testified at trial that on their return flight John asked if she still wanted to get married and she responded she did. At this point, John placed a wedding band on Sally's finger. Confused about his actions, Sally asked John if they were going to be married upon their return to Iowa. John allegedly responded that a marriage ceremony was unnecessary in Iowa and asserted they were "just as much married as anybody else there." Sally expressed concern over what to tell others with respect to their marital status and was directed by John to say they had been married in Las Vegas. In addition, John told Sally she could use his name.

In his version of the events which transpired during their Las Vegas journey, John admitted he intended to be married in that city, but maintained he changed his mind shortly after arriving there. John testified he informed Sally of his decision in their hotel room and there gave her the wedding band. He denied any symbolic significance in the gift of the ring, explaining he was only motivated by the fact he no longer had use for it. In response to Sally's expressed fear of potential embarrassment, John testified he told Sally she could move into his home temporarily and could use his name. He denied telling Sally they were "as much married as anybody else in Iowa," stated he recalled no in-flight conversation concerning their relationship and asserted he clearly told Sally he did not wish to marry her.

Immediately upon her return from Nevada, Sally and her daughter began living with John in his Burlington home. Various individuals were informed by Sally that she and John had in fact been married. John did nothing to deny or dispute his alleged marital relationship with Sally. The couple received wedding gifts from a number of people, including John's mother and brother and John's attorney. John and Sally received mail addressed to and traveled together as Mr. and Mrs. John Winegard. They attended family gatherings and sent out Christmas cards with "John and Sally Winegard" engraved thereon. Sally's picture appeared in the local newspaper and she was referred to therein as Mrs. John Winegard. In addition, Sally was given or had access to numerous credit cards, some of which listed the owner thereof as Mrs. John Winegard.

John and Sally's home life was apparently fairly stable until December 1971, eight months after their Las Vegas trip. At that time, Sally testified she felt John was involved with another woman and confronted him with her suspicions. John confirmed her belief and from that point on the parties' relationship deteriorated. February 6, 1973, Sally's petition for dissolution of marriage was filed. . . .

The trial court concluded John and Sally Winegard were husband and wife by virtue of a common law marriage. However, for purposes of determining the propriety of an order allowing temporary attorney fees in a dissolution proceeding, the marriage relation need not be established by a preponderance. If the proof be such as to make out a fair presumption of the fact of the existence of the marital relationship, then it is sufficient to warrant the court in granting an order for temporary attorney fees. . . .

. . . [W]e turn to some of the decisions of this court which recognize the principles applicable when a common law marital relationship is alleged.

Recently, in In re Marriage of Grother, 242 N.W.2d 1 (Iowa 1976), this court summarized those principles in these words:

". . . The burden was on . . . (petitioner) as proponent of the marriage to prove it by a preponderance of evidence. . . . A claim of common-law marriage is regarded with suspicion and is closely scrutinized. It was necessary for . . . (petitioner) to prove an intent and agreement *in praesenti* to be married by both parties together with continuous cohabitation and public declaration that they were husband and wife. . . ." (Emphasis in original.)

In In re Estate of Dallman, 228 N.W.2d 187, 190 (Iowa 1975), are the following pertinent comments:

"Although, as aforesaid, common-law marriages are recognized in this jurisdiction, one element essential to the proof of such relationship is a general and substantial 'holding-out' or open declaration thereof to the public by both parties thereto. In fact such 'holding-out' or open declaration to the public has been said to be the acid test.

"In other words, there can be no secret common-law marriage."

With respect to the requirement that the parties presently intend to be husband and wife, this court in Gammelgaard v. Gammelgaard, 247 Iowa 979, 980, 77 N.W.2d 479, 480, said:

". . . To establish the existence of such a marriage there must be shown a present intent to be husband and wife, followed by cohabitation. Proof of cohabitation is not in itself sufficient. . . . But such proof, as well as evidence of conduct and of general repute in the community where the parties reside, is admissible as tending to strengthen a showing of a present agreement to be husband and wife, and as bearing upon the question of intent."

The following additional comments upon the intent necessary to establish a common law marital relationship are contained in McFarland v. McFarland, 51 Iowa 565, 570, 2 N.W. 269, 273-274:

". . . It is true that cohabitation does not of itself constitute marriage. On the other hand, no express form in this State is necessary more than at common law. It is sufficient if the parties cohabiting intend present marriage, and it is immaterial how the intention is evidenced. The woman, indeed, may be entitled to marital rights if she intends present marriage, and the man does not, provided they cohabit and provided his conduct is such as to justify her in believing that he intends present marriage." . . .

The record discloses the following bearing on the existence of the marital relationship: (1) Sally's intent and belief with respect to her relationship with John; (2) opinions of various witnesses that the community generally regarded the parties as married; (3) continuous cohabitation by the parties since April of 1971; (4) John's failure to deny his alleged marriage; (5) John's acquiescence in Sally's use of his name and her representations to the community they were in fact married; (6) Sally's receipt of a wedding band from John; (7) hotel registrations and travel reservations wherein the parties were listed as Mr. and Mrs. John Winegard; (8) receipt of wedding gifts without objection by John; (9) payment by John of retail charge accounts incurred by Sally as Mrs. John Winegard; (10) mail received and sent by the parties as Mr. and Mrs. John Winegard; (11) John's consent to Sally's ownership of and designation as beneficiary under an insurance policy on his life wherein Sally was referred to as "insured's wife"; and (12) checks endorsed by John directing payment to the order of "Sally Winegard." . . .

John contends there is no direct evidence of an intent and agreement *in praesenti* by the parties to be husband and wife. Even assuming, as John maintains, Sally's testimony with respect to John's alleged statements on the return flight from Las Vegas is without credibility, it is well established circumstantial evidence may be relied upon to demonstrate a common law marriage. The record herein regarding the continuous cohabitation of the parties and the declaration or holding out to the public they were in fact husband and wife constitutes circumstantial evidence which tends to create a fair presumption that a common law marital relationship existed.

One final contention advanced by John in an attempt to refute the existence of a marital relationship between him and Sally centers upon the airborne conversation between them wherein John allegedly made reference to the recognition of common law marriages in Iowa. Specifically, John maintains that since that conversation, if it in fact took place, occurred in air space over a state other than Iowa, Sally has not demonstrated, as she must, that said unknown state recognizes common law marriages. John's contention is without merit. The actions of the parties, subsequent to the controverted airborne conversation, are sufficient to create the presumption required.

In light of the foregoing authorities we conclude from our de novo review the proof is sufficient to create a fair presumption of the existence of the marital relationship. Such quantum of evidence meets the standard required to justify the granting of an order for temporary attorney fees under the present factual circumstances.

NOTES AND QUESTIONS

1. At the conclusion of the trial on the merits, the court held that John and Sally were married and awarded Sally $75,000 in lieu of alimony. On appeal the Iowa Supreme Court affirmed the finding of a common law marriage and raised Sally's award to $140,000. In re Marriage of Winegard, 278 N.W.2d 505 (Iowa 1979). The court also held that John was estopped to attack and lacked standing to attack the validity of Sally's two Nevada divorces from her first two husbands. See Chapter 11, Section B (jurisdiction to grant divorces).

2. What are the elements of common law marriage, according to this court? In principle, the essence of common law marriage is that the parties intended to be married. At what point did Sally form this intent? At what point did John? Whose intent controls?

3. The doctrine of common law marriage does not provide a way to avoid the substantive requirements for marriage; it addresses only the issue of formalities. If John's first marriage or either of Sally's previous marriages had never been ended and all the other facts were the same, John and Sally could not have had a common law marriage. Yet with surprising frequency people do purport to marry while they are still legally married to someone else, either because they haven't bothered to get a divorce or because the divorce is not yet final. When the parties reside in a state that permits common law marriage, courts typically find that such a marriage commenced if and when the first marriage ended. *See, e.g.,* Hall v. Duster, 727 So. 2d 834 (Ala. Civ. App. 1999). For such situations the Uniform Marriage and Divorce Act (hereinafter UMDA) §207(b) proposes the following statutory remedy for states that do not generally allow common law marriage: "Parties to a marriage prohibited under this section who cohabit after removal of the impediment are lawfully married as of the date of the removal of the impediment." Under this statute, would John and Sally have been married?

4. In the late 1880s more than half the states allowed common law marriages to be formed within their boundaries, but today only nine states and the District of Columbia do so. The states are Alabama, Colorado, Iowa, Kansas, Montana, Rhode Island, South Carolina, Texas, and Utah. Since 1991, five states—Georgia, Idaho, Ohio, Oklahoma, and Pennsylvania—have abolished common law marriage by statute or judicial decision. A New Hampshire statute provides, "Persons cohabiting and acknowledging each other as husband and wife, and generally reputed to be such, for the period of 3 years, and until the decease of one of them, shall thereafter be deemed to have been legally married." N.H. Rev. Stat. §457:39 (1992). Under this statute, would the Winegards have been married?

5. Contrary to the trend in other states, in 1987 the Utah legislature enacted a statute that provides that a couple is married even if they have not participated in a valid ceremony if a court or administrative agency finds that they (a) are capable of giving consent; (b) are legally capable of entering a solemnized marriage under the provisions of this chapter; (c) have cohabited; (d) mutually assume marital rights, duties, and obligations; and (e) hold themselves out as and have acquired a uniform and general reputation as husband and wife. Utah Code Ann. Tit. 30 §1-4.5. Under this statute, would the Winegards have been treated as married?

The prosecutor of Juab County, Utah, invoked the statute in the prosecution of Tom Green for polygamy in 2001. Green obtained a marriage license and formally married and then almost immediately formally divorced each of his five wives. At any one time he was ceremonially married to at most one woman. However, he lived simultaneously with all five women in a family compound, and he and several of his "wives" appeared on multiple radio and TV shows, extolling the virtues of polygamy. Under Utah law, polygamy is defined as purporting to marry another person or cohabiting with another person while already married. The prosecutor argued that, notwithstanding the ceremonial marriages and divorces, Green and at least one of the women had a common law marriage under the statute set out above and that, therefore, Green had either purported to marry or cohabited with his other "wives" while having a living wife, in violation of the statute. Does the evidence support Green's conviction? For a discussion, *see* Ryan

D. Tenney, Note, Tom Green, Common-Law Marriage, and the Illegality of Putative Polygamy, 17 BYU J. Pub. L. 141 (2002). In State v. Green, 99 P.3d 820 (Utah 2004), the court rejected Green's claims that the bigamy statute was unconstitutionally vague as applied to him and that he was not given adequate notice that the common law marriage statute could be used against him in the way that it was.

The Utah statute was intended to reduce public assistance to families with children. In Utah stepparents, but not unmarried cohabitants, are obligated to support their stepchildren during their marriage to the children's custodial parent. Accordingly, a family may be eligible for assistance if the custodial parent is living with but not married to a partner, while the family would become ineligible if the cohabitants were married. Does this statute seem likely to accomplish its purpose? Might it be used to increase other public expenditures for family members? *See* Note, David F. Crabtree, Recognition of Common-Law Marriages, 1988 Utah L. Rev. 273.

6. Common law marriage is more important than one might conclude from looking only at the number of states in which such marriages can be contracted. Under choice-of-law rules, a state may recognize a common law marriage entered into in another jurisdiction even when the forum state itself does not allow common law marriages. As we saw in Chapter 3, the traditional choice-of-law rule is that a marriage valid where entered into is valid everywhere, but a state may refuse to recognize a marriage entered into in another state if to do so would violate a strong public policy of the forum state. If the parties were actually domiciled in a state that allows common law marriage, other states will generally recognize the parties' common law marriage. The problem arises when the parties were domiciled in a state that does not allow common law marriage but had some level of contact with a state that does.

According to Professor Clark, the states' approaches can be sorted into three groups. Some states do not have a strong policy against common law marriage; they therefore are willing to treat their domiciliaries as having entered into a common law marriage in another state even when the parties' contact with that state was just a short visit. At the other extreme, some states have such a strong policy against common law marriage that they will not recognize an alleged common law marriage between parties not domiciled in the common law marriage state at the time of the alleged marriage. In the third group of states, parties do not have to have been domiciled in the common law marriage state, but they must have established a residence there; visits alone are not sufficient. Homer H. Clark, Jr., The Law of Domestic Relations in the United States §2.4 at 57-59 (2d ed. 1988).

7. In principle, common law marriage differs from ceremonial marriage only in the way in which it is entered. Consequently, a formal divorce action is necessary to dissolve a common law marriage. However, the Utah statute quoted above provides that a proceeding to establish a common law marriage must be brought within a year after the relationship has ended. Does this statute create a form of common law divorce? *Compare* Texas Family Code §2.401(b), which provides that if an action to prove the existence of a common law marriage is not brought within two years of when the parties quit living together, it is rebuttably presumed that the parties did not agree to be married.

PROBLEMS

1. Sandra Renfro and Dave Winfield began dating in 1981, and she became pregnant by him. When Sandra told Dave, they agreed to be informally married, she says, but Dave didn't want a formal marriage because he believed that his public image would suffer if it were widely known that he had conceived a child outside marriage. They spent the nights of April 11-13 in a Dallas hotel, registering as "Mr. and Mrs. Dave Winfield." Dave says that he never intended to marry Sandra and doesn't remember staying in the hotel. The next week Sandra told her mother that she and Dave had married in Dallas. Her mother believed they were married, although Dave never told her so. Later in April Dave asked Sandra to look for a home for them in Houston. Sandra found a condominium, which Dave bought, telling his secretary that it was for his family. In September the baby was born, and Sandra gave the baby the last name of Renfro. Dave kept his personal belongings in the condominium and stayed there most of the time that fall when he was not traveling for business reasons. Dave's secretary says that over a two-year period Dave spent about one-third of his time at the condominium. When Dave was there, he did errands and worked around the house. The mailbox at the condominium originally had the name Winfield, but that name was taken off and replaced with Renfro.

In October Dave told a friend that he and Sandra had planned to get married after the baby was born but that the wedding had been postponed. In early December 1982 Sandra met with Dave's brother to purchase health insurance. She indicated on the application that she was not married. Dave paid for the insurance. Sandra filed her 1982 and 1983 income tax returns as a single person, at Dave's direction. He paid her taxes. Sandra never used the last name Winfield because Dave told her not to, and neither of them wore a wedding ring.

At Christmas 1982 Dave, Sandra, the baby, and her child from a former marriage visited Dave's family in Minnesota. Dave's mother called both children her grandchildren, and she hung a photograph of the children in her living room.

In the spring of 1983 Sandra at times traveled with Dave, but at other times that spring Dave traveled with Tonya Turner, whom he had been dating since 1981. Throughout this time Dave was seeing other women, as Sandra knew. When Sandra went to Dave's baseball games, at Dave's instruction she did not sit in the section for team members' families, and Dave and Sandra registered in hotels as Dave Winfield and Sandra Renfro. Tonya testified that Dave told her he was not married to Sandra. In the fall of 1983 a neighbor gave a party for Dave and Sandra and introduced them as Mr. and Mrs. Dave Winfield. Dave did not object or correct her.

Sandra filed for a divorce in 1988. Dave replied, alleging that they were not married. During the legal proceedings Dave ceremonially married Tonya Turner. Assuming that Texas allows common law marriage, were Sandra and Dave common law married?

2. In addition to the facts above, assume that Sandra and Dave vacationed for a month in 1983 in Pennsylvania, another state that allows common law marriage. While there, they went to a softball game, and the announcer told the

crowd that Dave Winfield and his wife were in the audience. Dave introduced Sandra to a sports writer as his wife, and the writer published a story identifying them as Mr. and Mrs. Dave Winfield. If Dave and Sandra did not enter into a common law marriage in Texas, did they do so in Pennsylvania? If so, would Texas recognize it?

3. Ernest and Irene, who were both widowed and retired, participated in a wedding ceremony performed by a minister, but they did not obtain a marriage license. Irene believed that if she remarried, she would lose her pension benefits as the surviving spouse of her first husband. After the wedding, Ernest and Irene lived together, referred to themselves as husband and wife, and were generally known among their friends as spouses. They filed their income taxes as single people and did not notify the Social Security Administration or the administrators of their private pensions that they were married. Ernest has died, and Irene claims rights as his surviving widow on the theory that they had a common law marriage. Ernest's brother, who is executor of his estate, has denied her claim. What arguments should the parties make?

2. *Presumptions of Marriage and Putative Spouses*

SPEARMAN V. SPEARMAN

policy = no beneficiary proceeds go to widow

482 F.2d 1203 (5th Cir. 1973)

RONEY, C.J. At the time of his death, on October 1, 1969, Edward Spearman was insured by Metropolitan Life Insurance Company under Group Policy No. 17000-G in the amount of $10,000. The policy provided that, if no beneficiary were designated, the proceeds were to be paid to the "widow" of the insured. The parties stipulated that the policy designated no beneficiary.

After Spearman's death, both defendants claimed to be his "widow" and claimed the proceeds of his life insurance policy. The first wife, Mary Spearman, is a resident of Alabama and was married to insured on October 2, 1946, in Russell County, Alabama. Two children, twin girls, were born of this marriage, and both carry the surname of Spearman. The second wife, Viva Spearman, a resident of California, married insured on June 7, 1962, in Monterey County, California. This marriage produced no offspring.

1st Mary
2nd Viva

Metropolitan filed this interpleader action and paid the proceeds of the policy into the registry of the District Court. . . .

The decision in this case turns on the definition of the term "widow" as used in the life insurance policy. The policy itself does not define "widow," nor does the Federal Employees' Group Life Insurance Act provide any guidance. This question is not however, one of first impression. In Tatum v. Tatum, 241 F.2d 401 (9th Cir. 1957), the Ninth Circuit, by looking to judicial interpretations of an analogous federal statute, the National Service Life Insurance Act, 38 U.S.C.A. §701 et seq., determined that the term "widow" meant "lawful widow." . . .

definition of "widow"

California law is in accord with the general rule which provides that a second marriage cannot be validly contracted if either spouse is then married.

Rule

In a contest between conflicting marriages under California law, once the first wife presents evidence that her marriage has not been dissolved, then the burden of persuasion shifts to the second wife to establish that her spouse's marriage to his first wife had been dissolved. Otherwise, the first wife is deemed to have established her status as the lawful wife. According to the California rule, as in most states, the process of establishing which wife enjoys the status of lawful wife involves these shifting presumptions and burdens of persuasion:

1. Initially, when a person has contracted two successive marriages, a presumption arises in favor of the validity of the second marriage. Absent any contrary evidence, the second wife is deemed to be the lawful wife.

2. The presumption of validity accorded the second marriage is, however, merely a rule of evidence. It is a rebuttable presumption, the effect of which is to cast upon the first wife the burden of establishing the continuing validity of her marriage by demonstrating that it had not been dissolved by death, divorce, or annulment at the time of the second marriage.

3. California formerly required the first wife to prove that her husband had not dissolved their marriage by showing that no record of either divorce or annulment existed in any jurisdiction in which the husband may have resided. This strict burden has now been somewhat relaxed. The current rule is that, to rebut the presumption of validity inuring to the second or subsequent marriage, the first spouse need examine the records of only those jurisdictions in which either she or her husband have been in fact domiciled.

4. If the first wife shows that an examination of the pertinent records of such jurisdictions and all of the available evidence demonstrate that her marriage remains undissolved, the burden of demonstrating the invalidity of the first marriage then shifts to the party asserting its invalidity, the second wife in this case. Unless the second wife then can establish that her husband's first marriage has been dissolved, the first wife qualifies as the "lawful widow." . . .

Even if the second wife cannot qualify as the insured's "widow," she may nevertheless be entitled to one-half of the proceeds of the life insurance policy as insured's "putative spouse."

A putative spouse is one whose marriage is legally invalid but who has engaged in (1) a marriage ceremony or a solemnization, on the (2) good faith belief in the validity of the marriage. According to Estate of Foy, 109 Cal. App. 2d 329, 240 P.2d 685 (1952),

> [t]he term "putative marriage" is applied to a matrimonial union which has been solemnized in due form and good faith on the part of one or of both of the parties but which by reason of some legal infirmity is either void or voidable. The essential basis of such marriage is the belief that it is valid.

109 Cal. App. 2d at 331-332, 240 P.2d at 686.

The theory under which the "putative spouse" is entitled to recover a share of the insurance proceeds is that, as the insured's "putative spouse," she is entitled to share in the property accumulated by the family unit during its existence. The general rule, therefore, is that the "putative spouse" is entitled to the same share in this property as would have been accorded a de jure spouse under the community property laws. . . .

Applying these rules to the facts before it, the District Court first looked to the law of Alabama and concluded that Mary, the first wife, was validly married in Alabama in 1946. The subsequent marriage to Viva in 1962 in California was valid under California law, unless there was a preexisting marriage. At this point, the presumption in favor of the most recent marriage to Viva required Mary to show that her marriage had not been dissolved or annulled at the time of the insured's marriage to Viva. This showing she successfully made by establishing that no petition for annulment or divorce had been filed, by either herself or the insured, in any of their known domiciles since 1946. . . . After Mary had rebutted the presumption of validity initially attaching to Viva's marriage, the burden of persuasion shifted to Viva. This burden failed for want of proof: Viva introduced no credible evidence that either Mary or the insured had ever been a party to any legal proceeding that had annulled or dissolved their marriage. The District Court then correctly ruled that Mary had established the continuing validity of her marriage to the insured and that Viva had failed to establish otherwise.

. . . The District Court found that Viva could not qualify as the insured's "putative spouse" because she could not meet the requirement of a good faith belief in the existence of a valid marriage. . . . The evidence before the District Court showed that Viva knew (1) that the insured had fathered two children by Mary Spearman, (2) that Mary and both children carried the Spearman name, (3) that Mary had secured a support decree against the insured, (4) that the insured returned to Alabama each year on his vacation, and (5) that while on these vacations the insured lived in the same house with Mary and his two children. On these facts, the District Court's finding of an absence of good faith was amply supported. As the District Court stated in its thorough opinion, "Viva admits that she was aware of the possibility, if not the likelihood, of [insured's] prior marriage to Mary, and, yet, she took no steps to perfect her marital status."

Viva contends that the District Court's view of the "bona fide belief" requirement rests upon an erroneous interpretation of the California decisions. She argues that these decisions require only that the "putative spouse" have neither actual knowledge of invalidity nor a belief that the marriage was invalid. Under Viva's view, then, so long as she did not actually know of her marriage's invalidity and maintained a belief in its validity, no matter how unreasonable that belief may have been, she qualified as the insured's "putative spouse." We decline to adopt such a test of good faith. Rather, we think that the District Court correctly held that a good faith belief in the validity of the marriage must be posited on a view of the facts known to the spouse in question. . . .

Affirmed.

NOTES AND QUESTIONS

1. *Spearman* invokes the presumption that the most recent of a series of marriages is valid. Another commonly invoked presumption that might apply on facts like these is that a marriage validly entered into continues. Both presumptions are applied in many contexts besides that of *Spearman*. Can you think of any? What factual and policy assumptions underlie these presumptions?

In *Spearman*, Viva would benefit from the presumption that the most recent marriage is valid, while Mary would invoke the presumption that a valid marriage continues. How should this case of "clashing presumptions" be resolved?

> . . . The Supreme Court of Pennsylvania has specifically instructed courts . . . to perform a balancing test by weighing the evidence in the record to determine which of two presumptions, one in favor of continuation of the first marriage and the other in favor of the validity of the second marriage, is more easily sustained by the evidence. . . . In adjusting that balance, we think no mechanical rule will suffice. Instead, we think the court should consider the conduct of both parties and their respective contributions to the stability of the family each chose to support or deny in light of the value our society attributes to traditional families and evolving conditions of family life in this nation.

Huff v. Director, 40 F.3d 35, 37 (3d Cir. 1994).

2. *Spearman* allows a first spouse to satisfy the burden of proving that the marriage never ended by a search of divorce records in the state where the parties to the first marriage were domiciled because only states in which one spouse or the other was domiciled may constitutionally assert jurisdiction to divorce them. See Chapter 11. However, not all courts agree that this is sufficient. *See, e.g.*, Yarbrough v. Celebrezze, 217 F. Supp. 943 (M.D.N.C. 1963) (first wife's search of divorce records of various states without finding any divorce obtained by husband did not rebut presumption); Spears v. Spears, 178 Ark. 720, 12 S.W.2d 875 (1928) (similar). What more could the party alleging the validity of the first marriage possibly do? The court in Johnson v. Johnson, 239 Ga. 714, 238 S.E.2d 437 (1977), applied a rule even more favorable to the first marriage. It requires the party relying on the first marriage to prove only that both parties to the first marriage were alive at the time of the second marriage. The party relying on the second marriage then has the burden of proving the dissolution of the first marriage.

3. Why did the court in *Spearman* conclude that Viva did not in good faith believe she was married? Even taking an objective view of good faith, as the court does, are there other "reasonable" explanations for Viva's belief that she was married, even knowing what she did about Edward's relationship with Mary? Both presumptions about the validity of marriage and the putative spouse rule, like common law marriage, are sufficiently indeterminate that courts can apply them flexibly to do justice in individual cases. Why might the court in *Spearman* have been unwilling to find that Viva had a spouse's property rights in the insurance proceeds?

With *Spearman*, compare Central States v. Gray, 2003 U.S. Dist. LEXIS 18282 (N.D. Ill.). John married Susie in 1965, and they formally separated in 1971. No divorce decree was ever issued. In 1973 Susie married Milton. John married Patricia in 1984, and they divorced in 1997. John and Gwendolyn were married in 2000; he died in 2001. Susie and Gwendolyn both claimed to be entitled to the surviving spouse benefit under John's pension plan. The court found that Gwendolyn was John's putative spouse, saying, "Good faith on the part of Gwendolyn is presumed; we have no reason to believe that she was aware that John's prior marriage to Susie was not dissolved." Applying a statute permitting the court to apportion property between a legal spouse and a putative spouse "as appropriate in the circumstances and in the interests of justice," the court awarded the entire spousal benefit to Gwendolyn. In addition to finding that Gwendolyn's belief was held in good faith, the court concluded that Susie was estopped to claim the benefit because she had "accepted the benefits" of a terminated marriage by marrying Milton.

4. The putative spouse doctrine derives from Spanish and French law and was first recognized in states, such as California, whose domestic relations law derived from civil law. Finding that one is a putative spouse does not necessarily give that person all the rights of a true spouse. Instead, as *Spearman* indicates, the putative spouse doctrine was originally used to provide marital property rights. For example, the Supreme Court of Nevada recently held that the putative spouse doctrine permits an award of property but not spousal support when the validity of the marriage is successfully challenged. Williams v. Williams, 97 P.3d 1124 (Nev. 2004). For the history, scope, and modern application of the doctrine, *see* Christopher L. Blakesley, The Putative Marriage Doctrine, 60 Tulane L. Rev. 1 (1985); Monica Hof Wallace, The Pitfalls of a Putative Marriage and the Call for a Putative Divorce, 64 La. L. Rev. 71 (2003).

5. Application of the presumptions about marriage validity produces a conclusion about which one of two or more marriages is valid. In contrast, the putative spouse doctrine admits of the possibility that two or more people would have spousal rights. Does it therefore amount to legalization of bigamy?

PROBLEMS

1. Irene and Bill were ceremonially married in Texas in 1956 when Irene was 17, a year younger than the minimum marriage age. They lived together until she was 22. Under Texas law their marriage was "ratified" and thus validated by their living together after she became 18. They separated in 1961 without having had children. Bill moved to Pennsylvania. In 1962 Irene filed for divorce from Bill, but the action was dismissed for lack of prosecution. There is no record of their being divorced in the counties in Texas and Pennsylvania in which each of them lived from 1961 until the present.

In 1965 Irene began living with Tom Bennett, with whom she had three children. She is named "Irene Bennett" on the children's birth certificates, even though she was never ceremonially married to Tom.

In 1967 Bill ceremonially married Ethel in Pennsylvania. On the application for the marriage license Bill said that he had never been married. He had told Ethel about his marriage to Irene but said that it had been annulled. Following the wedding ceremony, Bill and Ethel held themselves out and lived as a married couple for 15 years. They had two children. Bill, who was an employee of the federal government, recently died in an automobile accident. Both Irene and Ethel claim benefits as his surviving spouse. What arguments should each make?

2. Assume instead that Bill died in 1971 and that Ethel collected surviving spouse benefits until 1989. In that year Irene came forward and claimed that she was really the surviving spouse, entitled to the benefits. Does the time delay matter? Why or why not?

C. LEGAL ALTERNATIVES TO MARRIAGE

According to traditional principles, if a couple lived together without being ceremonially married and was not eligible for or did not satisfy the requirements for a common law marriage or of the putative spouse doctrine, their relationship was "meretricious," the legal equivalent of prostitution. Legally, they were at best roommates, at worst outlaws. However, with the dramatic rise in open nonmarital cohabitation, the law has changed. The first part of this section considers judicially created doctrines that give the parties some rights against each other. The second part examines a range of statutory approaches to giving unmarried cohabitants "familial" rights and duties between themselves, in relation to third parties, or both. (The legal position of unmarried parents and their children is covered in Chapter 12.) Finally, the last part of this section examines approaches taken in other Western countries.

Much of the debate about whether and to what extent the law should recognize cohabitation as giving rise to legal rights and duties is based on political and religious concerns about "undermining marriage." The following articles suggest additional reasons for uncertainty even among those who believe that legally regulated cohabitation should be available as an alternative to marriage.

ANN LAQUER ESTIN, *ORDINARY COHABITATION*

76 Notre Dame L. Rev. 1381, 1385-1391 (2001)

For some couples, cohabitation is understood to be a stage in the marriage process. Sixty percent of opposite-sex cohabitants in the United States go on to marry each other, and this often happens quickly. . . . As cohabitation rates have increased, marriage rates have declined, and the average age at first marriage has consistently increased. By 1995, more than half of all "first unions" began as cohabitation relationships.

Numerous studies have found that cohabiting relationships are less stable than married relationships and that marriages preceded by cohabitation are less stable than those in which the couple did not live together prior to their marriage. It is not clear, however, whether cohabitation causes the increase in the chances for divorce. Over time, the patterns have shifted; fewer cohabiting couples are going on to marry each other, and more are breaking up.

. . . Divorce interacts with cohabitation in interesting ways. Many divorced individuals choose to cohabit with a partner before entering into a second marriage or as an alternative to a second marriage. . . . As divorce rates increase, the standard for a successful long-term marriage increases as well, making a trial period seem more important. The fear of divorce may itself prevent some couples from marrying. Some demographers believe that the fact that cohabitation is available as an alternative to marriage has helped to stabilize divorce rates. Marriage may appear more stable than cohabitation because individuals in less promising relationships today choose not to marry.

Some couples choose cohabitation rather than marriage as an ethical matter, based on their personal values and their views of marriage as an institution. In her report of qualitative empirical research conducted in the United Kingdom, Carol Smart characterizes these as "reflexive relationships." By "reflexive relationships," she means

> those in which the couples spectate upon the reasons for entering a relationship, who seek (jointly) to define the nature of that relationship and its boundaries and qualities, who monitor the progress of the relationship and put in place contingency plans (like wills) to manage unforeseen or even foreseen changes.

Her study, as well as the anecdotal accounts of unmarried couples that appear regularly in the news media, suggests that these long-term cohabiting couples are more likely to value equality and independence. What percentage of cohabiting couples fit this description is impossible to determine, however, from the statistical demographic evidence.

Although some couples view cohabitation as a transition to marriage, and others make a deliberate decision to reject marriage, many couples fit into a third group. For these couples, moving in together and remaining in an unmarried relationship is largely a response to circumstances. Carol Smart's study describes cohabitation in "risk relationships," which she defines as "relationships . . . that are based on taking a chance (which can be a gradual process) or seizing an opportunity (which can be quite spontaneous) when faced with significant life events." Smart's study also revealed that men and women had different perspectives on these relationships. The women "expected the relationships to last only if the men were prepared to change in some fundamental way." Although the women were interested in marriage, they were uncertain whether marriage to this particular man was a good idea. The men in this study were also waiting to see if the relationship would work out, but their concerns centered more on remaining independent, and they were "alert to the need to be able to get away cleanly."

For couples in this third group, the choice of cohabitation may be strongly influenced by economic factors. . . .Various studies report that cohabitation is more common among couples with less education and fewer economic resources. Men's circumstances are particularly significant here; women are more likely to marry when there is a better supply of "marriageable" men, defined in terms of income, education, and employment.

The economic profiles of cohabiting couples tend to be different from married couples. As a group, cohabitants are more likely than married couples to have relatively comparable earnings and more likely to remain together where their earnings remain equal. This is in contrast to married couples, who are somewhat more likely to remain together where there is a specialization of labor. The evidence also suggests that cohabitants are more likely to make the transition to marriage where the male partner's earnings and education are higher.

Rates of marriage and cohabitation are notably different between racial and ethnic groups. Census data indicates that Hispanic women are more likely to marry at an early age, and African-American women are less likely to marry at all. When nonmarital unions are included in the household formation picture, however, racial differences are reduced, since African-American couples are more likely to cohabit than white couples. To what extent these differences are a function of economic circumstances is uncertain. Although it is clear that job opportunities and earning power have diminished significantly for African-American men, the empirical evidence suggests that neither women's increased earning power nor men's decreased earning power fully explains the lower rates of marriage for African-Americans.

* * *

Beyond these three groups, same-sex couples form another large category of cohabitants. Whatever their values and motivations, these couples do not now have the right to marry. As a consequence, their cohabitation cannot be understood as a transitional stage prior to marriage or as a deliberate rejection of marriage. Most likely, however, there are similar differences between the "reflexive" and "risk" relationships within this group, at least to the extent that some couples plan their cohabitation carefully and monitor the progress of their relationship, while others act more spontaneously.

Judith Seltzer points out that cohabiting couples are very diverse in part "because they are forming their relationships under a rapidly changing set of social rules about marriage, cohabitation, and childbearing outside of marriage." Steven Nock characterizes cohabitation as an "incomplete institution." The instability of the rules fosters experimentation, and makes it difficult to understand what cohabitation means. Without established social norms and expectations, cohabiting couples need to invent the rules for their relationship as it unfolds. Frequently, these rules are based on equality principles, and there is evidence to suggest that cohabitation relationships are more stable where couples have an equal balance of power. Equality is difficult, however, to achieve and to maintain over a long period of time.

Renata Forste, *Prelude to Marriage or Alternative to Marriage?*

4 J. L. & Fam. Stud. 91, 101 (2002)

Recognizing the role cohabitation plays in family formation in the U.S. is critical in determining family policy. If cohabitation is an alternative form of marriage, then issues such as financial obligations to partners, inheritance rights, and health and social security benefits require attention. If, however, cohabitation more closely resembles a form of being single as opposed to being married, then such issues are irrelevant.

Given the tentative nature of cohabiting relationships, changing family policy in support of this type of family form could potentially increase its stability. If the current nature of cohabiting unions promotes instability, then treating cohabiting relationships more like marriage in terms of community property laws, tax cuts, health and social security benefits could encourage greater long term investment behavior among partners. However, if the tentative nature of cohabiting relationships is due more to the selective nature of cohabitation, that is people less committed to their partners cohabit rather than marry, then policies providing marriage-like benefits to cohabiting couples may not be sufficient to encourage long term partner commitment. Policies supportive of joint investment and partner commitment among cohabiting couples, therefore, may or may not change the tenuous nature of these relationships.

Although much of the debate regarding cohabiting couples focuses on homosexual couples, the vast majority of cohabiting couples are heterosexual. For homosexual couples, cohabitation is an alternative to marriage given that legal marriage is not currently an option in most states. If domestic partner policies are developed with only homosexual couples in mind, there may be unintended consequences for the heterosexual majority of cohabiting couples for whom cohabitation acts as a prelude to formal marriage. Policy debates regarding domestic partners need to consider the heterogeneity of cohabiting partnerships and not just focus on a small minority of coresidential unions.

In sum, some couples choose cohabitation because they cannot afford to marry. For these couples, improving economic well-being may lead to an increase in formal marriage over cohabitation. Other couples choose cohabitation because they do not want to make a long-term commitment to a partner or because they consider cohabitation part of the engagement process leading to formal marriage. Such couples may or may not benefit from a contractual arrangement recognizing the formation or dissolution of their union. Given that most cohabiting couples either break up or marry within a relatively short period of time, such contracts may only create a legal quagmire for cohabitors. High earning cohabiting couples that shun marital responsibilities may be the most likely to benefit from contractual agreements recognizing their domestic partnership.

1. *Judicially Created Solutions*

MARVIN V. MARVIN[3]

18 Cal. 3d 660, 134 Cal. Rptr. 815, 557 P.2d 106 (1976)

TOBRINER, J. Plaintiff avers that in October of 1964 she and defendant "entered into an oral agreement" that while "the parties lived together they would combine their efforts and earnings and would share equally any and all property accumulated as a result of their efforts whether individual or combined." Furthermore, they agreed to "hold themselves out to the general public as husband and wife" and that "plaintiff would further render her services as a companion, homemaker, housekeeper and cook to . . . defendant."

Shortly thereafter plaintiff agreed to "give up her lucrative career as an entertainer (and) singer" in order to "devote her full time to defendant . . . as a companion, homemaker, housekeeper and cook"; in return defendant agreed to "provide for all of plaintiff's financial support and needs for the rest of her life."

Plaintiff alleges that she lived with defendant from October of 1964 through May of 1970 and fulfilled her obligations under the agreement. During this period

---

3. While actor Lee Marvin and Michelle Triola Marvin lived together, he won an Oscar for *Cat Ballou* in 1965 and starred in other films, including *The Dirty Dozen* in 1967 and *Paint Your Wagon* in 1969. — Ed.

the parties as a result of their efforts and earnings acquired in defendant's name substantial real and personal property, including motion picture rights worth over $1 million. In May of 1970, however, defendant compelled plaintiff to leave his household. He continued to support plaintiff until November of 1971, but thereafter refused to provide further support.

On the basis of these allegations plaintiff asserts two causes of action. The first, for declaratory relief, asks the court to determine her contract and property rights; the second seeks to impose a constructive trust upon one half of the property acquired during the course of the relationship.

Defendant demurred unsuccessfully, and then answered the complaint. Following extensive discovery and pretrial proceedings, the case came to trial. Defendant renewed his attack on the complaint by a motion to dismiss. Since the parties had stipulated that defendant's marriage to Betty Marvin did not terminate until the filing of a final decree of divorce in January 1967, the trial court treated defendant's motion as one for judgment on the pleadings augmented by the stipulation.

After hearing argument the court granted defendant's motion and entered judgment for defendant. Plaintiff . . . appealed from the judgment.

2. *Plaintiff's complaint states a cause of action for breach of an express contract*

* * *

Defendant first and principally relies on the contention that the alleged contract is so closely related to the supposed "immoral" character of the relationship between plaintiff and himself that the enforcement of the contract would violate public policy. . . .

Although the past decisions hover over the issue in the somewhat wispy form of the figures of a Chagall painting, we can abstract from those decisions a clear and simple rule. . . . The fact that a man and woman live together without marriage, and engage in a sexual relationship, does not in itself invalidate agreements between them relating to their earnings, property, or expenses. Neither is such an agreement invalid merely because the parties may have contemplated the creation or continuation of a nonmarital relationship when they entered into it. Agreements between nonmarital partners fail only to the extent that they rest upon a consideration of meretricious sexual services. Thus the rule asserted by defendant, that a contract fails if it is "involved in" or made "in contemplation" of a nonmarital relationship, cannot be reconciled with the decisions. . . .

3. *Plaintiff's complaint can be amended to state a cause of action founded upon theories of implied contract or equitable relief*

. . . We are aware that many young couples live together without the solemnization of marriage, in order to make sure that they can successfully later undertake marriage. This trial period preliminary to marriage, serves as some assurance that the marriage will not subsequently end in dissolution to the harm of both parties. We are aware, as we have stated, of the pervasiveness of nonmarital relationships in other situations.

The mores of the society have indeed changed so radically in regard to cohabitation that we cannot impose a standard based on alleged moral considerations that have apparently been so widely abandoned by so many. Lest we be misunderstood, however, we take this occasion to point out that the structure of society itself largely depends upon the institution of marriage, and nothing we have said in this opinion should be taken to derogate from that institution. The joining of the man and woman in marriage is at once the most socially productive and individually fulfilling relationship that one can enjoy in the course of a lifetime.

We conclude that the judicial barriers that may stand in the way of a policy based upon the fulfillment of the reasonable expectations of the parties to a nonmarital relationship should be removed. As we have explained, the courts now hold that express agreements will be enforced unless they rest on an unlawful meretricious consideration. We add that in the absence of an express agreement, the courts may look to a variety of other remedies in order to protect the parties' lawful expectations.[4]

The courts may inquire into the conduct of the parties to determine whether that conduct demonstrates an implied contract or implied agreement of partnership or joint venture, or some other tacit understanding between the parties. The courts may, when appropriate, employ principles of constructive trust or resulting trust. Finally, a nonmarital partner may recover in *quantum meruit* for the reasonable value of household services rendered less the reasonable value of support received if he can show that he rendered services with the expectation of monetary reward.

Since we have determined that plaintiff's complaint states a cause of action for breach of an express contract, and, as we have explained, can be amended to state a cause of action independent of allegations of express contract, we must conclude that the trial court erred in granting defendant a judgment on the pleadings.

The judgment is reversed and the cause remanded for further proceedings consistent with the views expressed herein.

(The concurring and dissenting opinion of Justice Clark is omitted.)

NOTES AND QUESTIONS

1. Could Michelle Marvin have argued that she had a common law marriage? Could she have argued that she was a putative spouse? Was her understanding of her situation significantly different from that of Sally Winegard or Viva Spearman?

If the Marvins had been married, could Michelle have enforced a contract such as that alleged in this case? Why or why not? Does enforcing express agreements between cohabitants give them greater freedom to determine their

4. We do not seek to resurrect the doctrine of common law marriage, which was abolished in California by statute in 1895. (*See* Norman v. Thomson (1898) 121 Cal. 620, 628, 54 P. 143; Estate of Abate (1958) 166 Cal. App. 2d 282, 292, 333 P.2d 200.) Thus we do not hold that plaintiff and defendant were "married," nor do we extend to plaintiff the rights which the Family Law Act grants valid or putative spouses; we hold only that she has the same rights to enforce contracts and to assert her equitable interest in property acquired through her effort as does any other unmarried person.

relationship than married people have? *See* J. Thomas Oldham & David S. Caudill, A Reconnaissance of Public Policy Restrictions upon Enforcement of Contracts Between Cohabitants, 18 Fam. L.Q. 93 (1984); Grace G. Blumberg, Cohabitation Without Marriage: A Different Perspective, 28 UCLA L. Rev. 1125 (1981). If so, does that mean that the *Marvin* holding "undermines marriage"?

2. Virtually all courts have followed *Marvin* in holding that the "meretricious" aspect of an unmarried cohabitant relationship may be severed from the economic aspects for purposes of determining whether the parties entered into an enforceable contract. *But see* Hewitt v. Hewitt, 394 N.E.2d 1204 (Ill. 1979) (reprinted in Chapter 1 at page 10); Rehak v. Mathis, 239 Ga. 541, 238 S.E.2d 81 (1977); Schwegmann v. Schwegmann, 441 So. 2d 316 (La. App. 1983). What aspects of relationships such as these are purely economic? In what sense are they severable from the romantic and sexual aspects of the relationship?

3. The great majority of courts today allow cohabitants to make some kind of claim against each other when the relationship ends, at least in principle. Carol Bruch, Cohabitation in the Common Law Countries a Decade After *Marvin*: Settled In or Moving Ahead? 22 U.C. Davis L. Rev. 717 (1989). Some courts have followed *Marvin* in extending express contract and equitable remedies to cohabitants. *See, e.g.,* Boland v. Catalano, 521 A.2d 142 (Conn. 1987); Suggs v. Norris, 364 S.E.2d 159 (N.C. App. 1988); Carol v. Lee, 712 P.2d 923 (Ariz. 1986); Watts v. Watts, 405 N.W.2d 303 (Wis. 1987). In two states, statutes require that cohabitants' contracts be in writing to be enforceable. Minn. Stat. §§513.075, 513.076; Tex. Fam. Code §1.108. The Minnesota Supreme Court has held that the writing requirement does not apply to cases in which the claimant seeks not an interest in property of the cohabitant but rather "to preserve and protect her own property." In re Estate of Eriksen, 337 N.W.2d 671 (Minn. 1983). In Posik v. Layton, 695 So. 2d 759 (Fla. App. 1997), the court said that an agreement for support between cohabitants is subject to the statute of frauds writing requirement. Other courts have held that express contracts are enforceable, but that equitable remedies are not available. *See, e.g.,* Tapley v. Tapley, 449 A.2d 1218 (N.H. 1982); Carnes v. Sheldon, 311 N.W.2d 747 (Mich. App. 1981); Morone v. Morone, 413 N.E.2d 1154 (N.Y. 1980).

For a detailed analysis of case law throughout the country, *see* Ann Laquer Estin, Ordinary Cohabitation, 76 Notre Dame L. Rev. 1381 (2001).

4. The variety in the states' approaches to the rights and duties of cohabitants presents complex choice-of-law problems. For example, if a couple enters into a cohabiting relationship in California and moves to another state that does not recognize equitable remedies before the relationship ends, which state's law applies? Professor William A. Reppy, Jr., who has written extensively on choice-of-law issues when a marriage ends by death or divorce, addresses the choice-of-law problems attendant to cohabitation in Choice of Law Problems Arising When Unmarried Cohabitants Change Domicile, 55 SMU L. Rev. 273 (2002).

5. Do the theories for recovery between the partners endorsed in *Marvin* apply to same-sex couples? Carol S. Bruch, Cohabitation in the Common Law Countries a Decade After *Marvin*: Settled In or Moving Ahead?, 22 U.C. Davis L. Rev. 717, 723 n.19 (1989) ("[S]ame sex couples have been accorded relief under *Marvin* principles in increasing numbers"). *But see* Comment, Applying

Marvin v. Marvin to Same-Sex Couples: A Proposal for a Sex-Preference Neutral Cohabitation Contract Statute, 25 U.C. Davis L. Rev. 1029 (1992) (arguing that the case law is inconsistent and creates uncertainty).

6. Do the *Marvin* remedies give any rights to third parties who deal with one or both of the partners? For example, would a creditor to whom Michelle owed money be able to use any of the theories to recover from Lee?

7. The final outcome of *Marvin* illustrates some of the difficulties in applying the range of remedies endorsed by the state supreme court. On remand the trial court found no express or implied contract to share property between Lee and Michelle. The court also found that Michelle was not entitled to an equitable trust or a quantum meruit award because she "suffered no damage resulting from her relationship with defendant, including its termination and thus [Lee] did not become monetarily liable to plaintiff at all," that she "actually benefited economically and socially from the cohabitation of the parties," that "a confidential and fiduciary relationship never existed between the parties with respect to property," that Lee "was never unjustly enriched as a result of the relationship of the parties or of the services performed by plaintiff for him or for them," and that Lee "never acquired any property or money from plaintiff by any wrongful act." Nevertheless, the trial court ordered Lee to pay Michelle $104,000 as rehabilitative support to enable her to get back on her feet. The court relied on footnotes in the supreme court opinion implying that remedies other than those that the court had specifically endorsed might be available on the right facts. 18 Cal. 3d 660, 684-685, nn.25, 26, 134 Cal. Rptr. 815, 557 P.2d 106. The Court of Appeals reversed, saying, "The difficulty in applying either of these footnotes in the manner in which the trial court has done in this case is that . . . there is nothing in the trial court's findings to suggest that such an award is warranted *to protect the expectations of both parties*" (emphasis added). Marvin v. Marvin, 176 Cal. Rptr. 555 (Cal. App. 1981). Compare the approach to these issues in the following case.

IN THE MATTER OF THE ESTATE OF ROCCAMONTE

808 A.2d 838 (N.J. 2002)   1941 - Mary + Nicolcan
                                            model

PRESSLER, P.J.A.D. (temporarily assigned).

* * *

Plaintiff Mary Sopko was born in 1925. In 1941 she married Nicholas Sopko, who was then in the army and, following his war assignment, she returned alone to Bloomfield, New Jersey, obtaining employment as a model in New York City's garment center. When her husband returned from army service, they lived together in New Jersey, she continued to work, and in 1952, she gave birth to their daughter, Sandra. In the 1950s she met Arthur Roccamonte, the owner of a trucking business servicing the garment industry. He was also then married and had two children. Roccamonte pursued plaintiff, and they embarked on an affair that endured for the rest of his life. Plaintiff's husband left her, and she and

Roccamonte lived together intermittently until the mid-1960s when she left New Jersey and went to California for the purpose of ending her relationship with Roccamonte, who had refused her requests that he divorce his wife and marry her. Roccamonte, however, wanted her to return, telephoned her repeatedly, and promised that if she came back to him, he would divorce his wife and, so plaintiff asserts, he would provide for her financially for the rest of her life. Relying on his promises, she returned to New Jersey, divorced her husband, and took up residency in Glen Ridge.

In 1970 Roccamonte leased an apartment in an upscale building in Glen Ridge where he and plaintiff lived together as husband and wife. Plaintiff's daughter lived with them. In 1973 the building was converted to cooperative ownership, Roccamonte purchased an interest which he titled in plaintiff's name, and they lived together in that apartment as husband and wife until his death. He never divorced his wife, explaining to plaintiff that a divorce would place his business in jeopardy. He continued throughout his life to support his wife and children generously. Although Roccamonte was extremely private respecting his business affairs, indeed secretive, there is no doubt that he was a man of considerable wealth and that the lifestyle he afforded plaintiff and the financial support he provided her was consistent with his affluence. He paid for substantial improvements to the apartment, gave her cash of $600 a week, and bought her clothes and jewelry. They took frequent vacations and regularly dined at expensive restaurants. Roccamonte also supported plaintiff's daughter, paying her college tuition and medical expenses. Plaintiff continued to work in the garment industry until 1990, for a time as a model and later as a salesperson, earning a take-home pay, she testified, averaging about $250 weekly. During their years together, plaintiff committed herself to her relationship with Roccamonte, conducting herself in private and in public as a loyal and devoted wife.

As time passed and she grew older, plaintiff became increasingly concerned about her own financial future in the event that she survived Roccamonte. She expressed these concerns to him, and he repeatedly assured her, she testified, that she had no cause for worry as he would see to it that she was provided for during her life. He repeated that promise in the presence of others, including a friend of plaintiff, who so testified, and her brother, with whom the couple frequently visited, who also so testified. Roccamonte, however, died intestate. On his death, plaintiff received the proceeds of an insurance policy on his life in the amount of $18,000 and of a certificate of deposit in her name in the amount of $10,000. She also had title to the apartment, the maintenance cost of which was then approximately $950 per month, and her jewelry. She had, moreover, received two weekly payments of $1,000 immediately after Roccamonte's death from his son, who was managing the trucking business. She testified to her belief that these payments represented the periodic support Roccamonte had intended her to receive from the business after his death, but the payments were characterized by Roccamonte's son as merely the proceeds of his father's last paycheck.

Not having been otherwise provided for and believing, therefore, that Roccamonte had failed to keep his promise to her of support for her life, plaintiff, in October 1995, some seven months after his death, commenced this palimony action against Roccamonte's estate seeking a lump-sum support award. . . .

. . . The trial judge rendered his oral decision dismissing the complaint, for reasons we hereafter discuss, on September 25, 2000. Plaintiff's appeal from the memorializing order ensued, and *Roccamonte II* was decided in November 2001. The Estate's appeal as of right was argued before this Court on September 10, 2002. By that time seven and a half years had passed since Roccamonte's death. Plaintiff is now 77 years old, and her attorney represented to us that she has exhausted her assets and is living in poverty, dependent entirely on social security payments of under $1,000 a month and food stamps. She makes a home with her disabled daughter, who is in receipt only of social security disability payments.

We address the proofs and the trial court's findings thereon respecting the first issue, whether an enforceable contract was made, in the context of what are now well-settled principles in this jurisdiction respecting the right of an unmarried person to enforce her cohabitant's promise to support her for life. In Kozlowski v. Kozlowski, 80 N.J. 378, 403 A.2d 902 (1979), we recognized that unmarried adult partners, even those who may be married to others, have the right to choose to cohabit together in a marital-like relationship, and that if one of those partners is induced to do so by a promise of support given her by the other, that promise will be enforced by the court.

We made clear in *Kozlowski* that the right to support in that situation does not derive from the relationship itself but rather is a right created by contract. Because, however, the subject of that contract is intensely personal rather than transactional in the customary business sense, special considerations must be taken into account by a court obliged to determine whether such a contract has been entered into and what its terms are. To begin with, as we held in *Kozlowski*, the palimony contract may be oral and usually is because "[p]arties entering this type of relationship usually do not record their understanding in specific legalese. . . ." The contract may also be express or implied. Consequently the existence of the contract and its terms are ordinarily determinable not merely by what was said but primarily by the parties' "acts and conduct in the light of . . . [their] subject matter and the surrounding circumstances." We thus concluded that a general promise of support for life, broadly expressed, made by one party to the other with some form of consideration given by the other will suffice to form a contract. And if such a promise of support for the promisee's lifetime is found to have been made, without any further specification or elaboration of its terms, and that promise is broken, the court will construe and enforce it by awarding the promisee "a one-time lump sum . . . in an amount predicated upon the present value of the reasonable future support defendant promised to provide, to be computed by reference to . . . [the promisee's] life expectancy. . . ."

* * *

. . . [T]he Estate argues that even if a promise were made, it would fail for want of consideration. The Estate takes the position that because sexual favor as the sole consideration would render the palimony contract unenforceable as meretricious, the consideration . . . must include domestic services, and plaintiff, it argues, was not required by Roccamonte to perform such services. That argument, however, misperceives the fundamental point of our palimony cases. The principle we recognized and accepted is that the formation of a marital-type relationship between unmarried persons may, legitimately and enforceably, rest upon a promise by one to support the other. A marital-type relationship is no more exclusively dependent upon one partner's providing maid service than it is upon sexual accommodation. It is, rather, the undertaking of a way of life in which two people commit to each other, forgoing other liaisons and opportunities, doing for each other whatever each is capable of doing, providing companionship, and fulfilling each other's needs, financial, emotional, physical, and social, as best as they are able. And each couple defines its way of life and each partner's expected contribution to it in its own way. Whatever other consideration may be involved, the entry into such a relationship and then conducting oneself in accordance with its unique character is consideration in full measure. There is no doubt that plaintiff provided that consideration here until her obligation was discharged by Roccamonte's death.

The Estate also argues that no valid palimony agreement could have been entered into because plaintiff was not entirely dependent economically on Roccamonte but was, rather, employed during most of the relationship. . . . [W]e see no reason why complete dependency is a *sine qua non* of a valid palimony agreement. The issue is, more pertinently, one of economic inequality, and the relevant question is whether the promisee is self-sufficient enough to provide for herself with a reasonable degree of economic comfort appropriate in the circumstances. If one of the partners is not economically self-sufficient, albeit a wage earner, the promise of support by the other is no less legally significant than if she were entirely economically dependent. The difference is only in the amount of promised support that must be fixed in order to reach a reasonable lump-sum payment.

In any event, we are dealing here with a woman whose income, when she was working, was barely at subsistence level, if that, in a relationship with a partner of financial substance. We note, illustratively, that his payment of the monthly maintenance fee on their apartment alone was roughly equivalent to her earnings. It is unlikely that plaintiff would not have taken steps to increase her own income had she been required to be self-supporting during the years of the relationship. Beyond that, at the time of their liaison, plaintiff had no young children at home requiring her care. Presumably she could have occupied her time with charitable work, with country-club membership and other entertainments, with polishing floors and furniture and otherwise "housekeeping," or, as she did, with a modestly paying job related to her partner's business, which enabled them, as she testified, to travel to work together in New York City and engage in a social life there. The fact that plaintiff chose to be employed cannot reasonably be deemed to result in her forfeiture of the support promise in view of her modest salary, the gross disproportion between her economic means and her partner's, and the gross disproportion between her earnings and the standard of living provided by Roccamonte. In any event, plaintiff was seventy years old when Roccamonte died, was no longer working, and at that time was relying exclusively on him for her support.

The question then is whether the promise of support for life was actually made. . . .

[handwritten: yes the promise & support was made]

. . . We are compelled to conclude that the evidence permits no conclusion other than that the promise of support for life was made, if not expressly as it appears to have been, then, ineluctably, by implication, and we so find as a fact by the exercise of our original jurisdiction. It is not disputed that Roccamonte's final break from his family and his marital-like relationship with plaintiff resulted from his successful efforts to induce plaintiff's return to him after she had moved to California to make a new life for herself because she had despaired of Roccamonte's willingness ever to divorce his wife and marry her. There is no reasonable inference that can be drawn from her abandonment of that plan at his insistence and the resulting reunion other than that she relied on his representations, express or implied, that her future would be neither prejudiced nor compromised. It is also beyond dispute that Roccamonte was concerned for plaintiff's economic well-being and provided for her lavishly during their twenty-five years together as well as during the first extended period of their relationship. In the circumstances and in view of the proofs, it appears highly unlikely that he intended to leave her to an impoverished old age or that she took the risk, when she reunited with him, of an impoverished old age. The promise, clearly implied, if not express, that he would see to it that she was adequately provided for during her lifetime, whether or not she survived him, seems to us to have been both the corollary for and the condition of their relationship for the last quarter century of Roccamonte's life.

The novel issue that we have not heretofore addressed is whether the promise of support for life is enforceable against the promisor's estate. As a conceptual matter, it is no different from enforcement of any other contract, other than a contract for personal services, made by a decedent during his lifetime. . . .

[handwritten right margin: Issue 3 promise enforceable against estate]

Had plaintiff died first, the duty of Roccamonte to support her for life would have been fulfilled and discharged. Just as clearly, the obligations she assumed were discharged upon his death because her continued performance was thereby rendered impossible. . . . But the obligation undertaken by Roccamonte to support plaintiff for life if she were the survivor is another matter altogether. It obviously cannot be said that termination of his obligation in the event of his death and her survival was within the parties' contemplation. Indeed, the intention of the parties appears to have been exactly to the contrary. Moreover, Roccamonte's promise of support was not a promise to perform personal services. It was a promise intended to provide financial compensation to plaintiff for keeping to her bargain until the discharge of her obligations. She did so, and is therefore entitled to the monetary benefit of that bargain. Roccamonte's duty to provide that benefit was, therefore, not discharged by his death and must, consequently, be discharged by his estate.

* * *

. . . We leave to the trial judge the determination of an appropriate level of support in the circumstances and the resolution of such questions as whether the Estate is entitled to a credit on the lump-sum payment for the amount of the certificate of deposit in plaintiff's name, the life insurance proceeds, and her receipt of social security benefits. . . .

NOTES AND QUESTIONS

1. Before this case was decided, the New Jersey courts had held that contracts between cohabitants are not per se unenforceable. Here, the estate argued that Mary gave no consideration and hence that there was no contract. What was the factual basis for this argument? Why did the court reject it? Why did the estate argue that Mary had a job and was not entirely dependent on Arthur? Would the case have been decided differently if she had been independently wealthy, but Arthur had supported her anyway?

2. A crucial factual question is whether Arthur had really implicitly promised to support Mary. What evidence suggests that he did? Does living together mean he made this promise? What about the fact that he didn't write a will and provide for her? Would the case have been decided differently if he had written a will and left her out?

3. We know that Michelle Marvin did not succeed in proving to the California courts that she and Lee had a contract. Would the *Roccamonte* court have found in Michelle's favor? Note that even though Mary ultimately prevailed, the litigation lasted more than seven years, and she received less than she would have had she been Arthur's widow. Professor Ann Estin has observed,

> Taken together, the legal norms of ordinary cohabitation developed in the quarter century since *Marvin* are not particularly generous. Only a small percentage of cohabitants will have even a possibility of legal recovery when their relationships end. To the extent that these rules have any effect on the choice between cohabitation and marriage, they are likely to encourage marriage for anyone seeking financial security and to encourage cohabitation rather than marriage for anyone seeking to avoid financial commitments.

Ann Laquer Estin, Ordinary Cohabitation, 76 Notre Dame L. Rev. 1381, 1402-1403 (2001).

4. Arthur Roccamonte's estate argued that if there were a contract, it was a personal services contract that required him to be alive and to provide support personally. The court rejected the argument, since Mary's expectations could be protected by awarding her a money judgment. To allow the estate to be closed and distributed to Arthur's heirs, the court directed that her claim be reduced to a lump sum, rather than ordering the estate to make periodic payments to her.

5. Could Mary have claimed successfully that she was entitled to equitable relief if the court had found her contract claim unproven? To prevail on a claim for equitable relief, based on having worked for one's cohabitant, a claimant must prove that the work was not done gratuitously. If the claimant kept the house, cared for the children, and did other kinds of domestic work, should a court presume that the work was gratuitous? What if one cohabitant works in the other's start-up business, with the understanding that neither will be able to take out money unless and until the business becomes successful? For a case denying recovery on such facts on the theory that the woman did not prove that she expected to be paid for her work, *see* Featherston v. Steinhoff, 575 N.W.2d 6 (Mich. App. 1997).

In Salzman v. Bachrach, 996 P.2d 1263 (Colo. 2000) (en banc), Roberta Salzman and Erwin Bachrach agreed to sell their homes and use the proceeds to build a home for them both. He designed the home; she contributed about twice as much as he to the building costs. She paid the mortgage and most of the living expenses, and he did not pay rent. About a year after they moved in, Bachrach quit-claimed his interest in the new house to Salzman to enable her to obtain a favorable mortgage, to give her tax advantages, and to ward off her former husband's threat to terminate spousal support on the ground that she was cohabiting and needed less support. Eventually their relationship went on the rocks, and Salzman asked Bachrach to move out. When he refused, she changed the locks on the door and posted a "No Trespassing" sign on the property, with the added phrase "This means you Erwin." He sued for a partition of the home, alleging that they were joint venturers. She responded that he had negligently designed the home, poorly managed its construction, misrepresented himself as an architect, and miscalculated the cost of the home. The Colorado Supreme Court affirmed the intermediate appellate court's *Constructive Trust* finding that Bachrach had established a claim for a constructive trust. The elements of a claim are (1) at the plaintiff's expense (2) the defendant received a benefit (3) under circumstances that would make it unjust for the defendant to retain the benefit without paying. With regard to the third element, the court found that "absent some countervailing consideration, the answer to this question is that it would be unjust to allow Salzman to keep Bachrach's entire contribution to the home." *See also* In re Real Estate of Shockley v. Foraker, 2004 WL 51260 (Del. Ch. 2004).

6. Are cohabitants in a confidential relationship with each other, so that fiduciary duties arise between them? If so, what are the legal consequences of such a finding? Williams v. Lynch, 666 N.Y.S.2d 749 (App. Div. 1997), held that the plaintiff's evidence was sufficient to support a finding that the parties' relationship was analogous to that of husband and wife and that as a result "plaintiff reasonably trusted defendant and relied on him to protect her interests." *Id.* at 751. On the other hand, Maglica v. Maglica, 78 Cal. Rptr. 2d 101 (Cal. App. 1998), held that, although the parties' relationship was like a common law marriage, fiduciary duties do not arise from that relationship alone because to impose them would amount to judicial reinstatement of common law marriage. Unless one party entrusts property to the other, no fiduciary relationship arises, the court said. *See also* Wilcox v. Trautz, 693 N.E.2d 141 (Mass. 1998) (agreement between cohabitants is not governed by the requirements applicable to premarital agreements, including that the terms be fair and reasonable; instead, ordinary rules of contract law apply).

-cohabitants = partnership

7. Where cohabitants have operated a business together outside the home, courts are generally willing to apply partnership principles to determine ownership of the business when the relationship ends. For example, in Bass v. Bass, 814 S.W.2d 38 (Tenn. 1991), a man and woman worked long hours for a number of years in businesses titled in his name. The woman was never paid for her work. When he died, she successfully claimed ownership of half of the business. Similarly, in In re Estate of Thornton, 499 P.2d 864 (Wash. 1972), a man and woman were treated as business partners where they ran a cattle operation together for many years. The administrator of the man's estate argued that the woman was not entitled to compensation because of the familial context. In an opinion reminiscent of the dissenting judge's opinion in Murdoch v. Murdoch, (see Chapter 2, page 40), the court held that she could claim compensation because her work was not merely domestic. *See also* Simpson v. Simpson, 172 A.2d 168 (Pa. 1961).

Can a cohabitant make a claim on this theory if she is paid for her work in the business? If she is not an equal manager? *See* Harman v. Rogers, 510 A.2d 161 (Vt. 1986), rejecting a cohabitant's partnership claim under these circumstances.

CONNELL V. FRANCISCO

898 P.2d 831 (Wash. 1995) (en banc)

GUY, JUSTICE. Petitioner Richard Francisco and Respondent Shannon Connell met in Toronto, Canada, in June 1983. Connell was a dancer in a stage show produced by Francisco. She resided in New York, New York. She owned clothing and a leasehold interest in a New York apartment. Francisco resided in Las Vegas, Nevada. He owned personal property, real property, and several companies, including Prince Productions, Inc. and Las Vegas Talent, Ltd., which produced stage shows for hotels. Francisco's net worth was approximately $1,300,000 in February 1984.

Connell, at Francisco's invitation, moved to Las Vegas in November 1983. They cohabited in Francisco's Las Vegas home from November 1983 to June 1986. While living in Las Vegas, Connell worked as a paid dancer in several stage shows. She also assisted Francisco as needed with his various business enterprises. Francisco managed his companies and produced several profitable stage shows.

In November 1985, Prince Productions, Inc. purchased a bed and breakfast, the Whidbey Inn, on Whidbey Island, Washington. Connell moved to Whidbey Island in June 1986 to manage the Inn. Shortly thereafter Francisco moved to Whidbey Island to join her. Connell and Francisco resided and cohabited on Whidbey Island until the relationship ended in March 1990.

While living on Whidbey Island, Connell and Francisco were viewed by many in the community as being married. Francisco acquiesced in Connell's use of his surname for business purposes. A last will and testament, dated December 11, 1987, left the corpus of Francisco's estate to Connell. Both Connell and Francisco had surgery to enhance their fertility. In the summer of 1986, Francisco gave Connell an engagement ring.

From June 1986 to September 1990 Connell continuously managed and worked at the Inn. She prepared breakfast, cleaned rooms, took reservations, laundered linens, paid bills, and maintained and repaired the Inn. Connell received no compensation for her services at the Inn from 1986 to 1988. From January 1989 to September 1990 she received $400 per week in salary.

Francisco produced another profitable stage show and acquired several pieces of real property during the period from June 1986 to September 1990. . . . Connell did not contribute financially toward the purchase of any of the properties, and title to the properties was held in Francisco's name individually or in the name of Prince Productions, Inc.

Connell and Francisco separated in March 1990. When the relationship ended Connell had $10,000 in savings, $10,000 in jewelry, her clothes, an automobile, and her leasehold interest in the New York apartment. She continued to receive her $400 per week salary from the Inn until September 1990. In contrast,

Francisco's net worth was over $2,700,000, a net increase since February 1984 of almost $1,400,000. In March 1990, he was receiving $5,000 per week in salary from Prince Productions, Inc.

Connell filed a lawsuit against Francisco in December 1990 seeking a just and equitable distribution of the property acquired during the relationship. The Island County Superior Court determined Connell and Francisco's relationship was sufficiently long term and stable to require a just and equitable distribution. The Superior Court limited the property subject to distribution to the property that would have been community in character had they been married. The trial court held property owned by each party prior to the relationship could not be distributed. In addition, the Superior Court required Connell to prove by a preponderance of the evidence that the property acquired during their relationship would have been community property had they been married.

. . . [The Court of Appeals reversed both holdings, and Francisco successfully petitioned the Supreme Court for review.]

A meretricious relationship is a stable, marital-like relationship where both parties cohabit with knowledge that a lawful marriage between them does not exist.

Relevant factors establishing a meretricious relationship include, but are not limited to: continuous cohabitation, duration of the relationship, purpose of the relationship, pooling of resources and services for joint projects, and the intent of the parties.

. . . The Superior Court found Connell and Francisco were parties to a meretricious relationship. This finding is not contested.

Historically, property acquired during a meretricious relationship was presumed to belong to the person in whose name title to the property was placed. "[I]n the absence of any evidence to the contrary, it should be presumed as a matter of law that the parties intended to dispose of the property exactly as they did dispose of it." Creasman v. Boyle, 31 Wash. 2d 345, 356, 196 P.2d 835 (1948). This presumption is commonly referred to as "the *Creasman* presumption."

. . . In 1984, this court overruled *Creasman*. Lindsey, 101 Wash. 2d at 304, 678 P.2d 328. In its place, the court adopted a general rule requiring a just and equitable distribution of property following a meretricious relationship. . . . Lindsey, 101 Wash. 2d at 304, 678 P.2d 328.

In *Lindsey*, the parties cohabited for less than 2 years prior to marriage. When they subsequently divorced, the wife argued the increase in value of property acquired during the meretricious portion of their relationship was also subject to an equitable distribution as if the property were community in character. We agreed, citing former RCW 26.09.080[5]

. . . Francisco contends the Court of Appeals misinterpreted *Lindsey* when it applied all the principles contained in RCW 26.09.080 to meretricious relationships.

---

5. Former RCW 26.09.080 provides:

In a proceeding for dissolution of the marriage, legal separation, declaration of invalidity, or in a proceeding for disposition of property following dissolution of the marriage by a court which lacked personal jurisdiction over the absent spouse or lacked jurisdiction to dispose of the property, the court shall, without regard to marital misconduct, make such disposition of

Holding [handwritten margin note]

We agree. A meretricious relationship is not the same as a marriage. . . . As such, the laws involving the distribution of marital property do not directly apply to the division of property following a meretricious relationship. Washington courts may look toward those laws for guidance.

Once a trial court determines the existence of a meretricious relationship, the trial court then: (1) evaluates the interest each party has in the property acquired during the relationship, and (2) makes a just and equitable distribution of the property. The critical focus is on property that would have been characterized as community property had the parties been married. This property is properly before a trial court and is subject to a just and equitable distribution.

While portions of RCW 26.09.080 may apply by analogy to meretricious relationships, not all provisions of the statute should be applied. The parties to such a relationship have chosen not to get married and therefore the property owned by each party prior to the relationship should not be before the court for distribution at the end of the relationship. However, the property acquired during the relationship should be before the trial court so that one party is not unjustly enriched at the end of such a relationship. We conclude a trial court may not distribute property acquired by each party prior to the relationship at the termination of a meretricious relationship. Until the Legislature, as a matter of public policy, concludes meretricious relationships are the legal equivalent to marriages, we limit the distribution of property following a meretricious relationship to property that would have been characterized as community property had the parties been married. This will allow the trial court to justly divide property the couple has earned during the relationship through their efforts without creating a common law marriage or making a decision for a couple which they have declined to make for themselves. Any other interpretation equates cohabitation with marriage; ignores the conscious decision by many couples not to marry; confers benefits when few, if any, economic risks or legal obligations are assumed; and disregards the explicit intent of the Legislature that RCW 26.09.080 apply to property distributions following a marriage.

Rule → [handwritten margin note]

limit to Community property [handwritten margin note]

Francisco argues the Court of Appeals erred in requiring the application of a community-property-like presumption to property acquired during a meretricious relationship. We disagree.

---

the property and the liabilities of the parties, either community or separate, as shall appear just and equitable after considering all relevant factors including, but not limited to:

(1) The nature and extent of the community property;

(2) The nature and extent of the separate property;

(3) The duration of the marriage; and

(4) The economic circumstances of each spouse at the time the division of property is to become effective, including the desirability of awarding the family home or the right to live therein for reasonable periods to a spouse having custody of any children.

In 1989 the Legislature amended RCW 26.09.080, replacing "spouse having custody of any children" with "with whom the children reside the majority of the time." Laws of 1989, ch. 375, §5, amending Laws of 1973, 1st Ex. Sess., ch. 157, §8.

In a marital context, property acquired during marriage is presumptively community property. When no marriage exists there is, by definition, no community property. However, only by treating the property acquired in a meretricious relationship similarly can this court's reversal of "the *Creasman* presumption" be given effect. Failure to apply a community-property-like presumption to the property acquired during a meretricious relationship places the burden of proof on the non-acquiring partner. This would overrule In re Marriage of Lindsey, 101 Wash. 2d 299, 678 P.2d 328 (1984) and reinstate the presumption expressed in Creasman v. Boyle, 31 Wash. 2d 345, 196 P.2d 835 (1948). The Court of Appeals properly rejected the resurrection of "the *Creasman* presumption." . . .

CONCLUSION

In summary, we hold that property which would have been characterized as separate property had the couple been married is not before the trial court for division at the end of the relationship. The property that would have been characterized as community property had the couple been married is before the trial court for a just and equitable distribution. There is a rebuttable presumption that property acquired during the relationship is owned by both of the parties and is therefore before the court for a fair division.

We reverse the Court of Appeals in part, affirm in part, and remand the case to the Superior Court for a just and equitable distribution of property.

[The dissenting opinion of Justice Utter is omitted.]

NOTES AND QUESTIONS

1. Does *Connell* create a new status relationship for unmarried cohabitants? If so, what is the basis for finding that the status exists? If not, what is the basis for dividing some of the property acquired during the parties' relationship according to community property principles?

2. As *Connell* indicates, even though Washington is a community property state, all property acquired by either spouse is subject to equitable division when the parties divorce. Why doesn't the court apply this rule to cohabitants? How would you argue for a contrary rule?

3. Do you think that the approach of *Marvin* or that of *Connell* is more consistent with the expectations of most cohabitants? If, as often happens, parties have inconsistent expectations, what principle should govern their property rights?

4. Does *Connell* authorize a court to award support to an economically weaker partner at the end of a meretricious relationship?

5. The Washington Supreme Court limited some of the expansive language in Connell in In re Marriage of Pennington, 14 P.3d 764 (Wash. 2000) (en banc), holding that lower courts had erred in finding meretricious relationships in two cases in which one of the parties had a spouse for at least part of the time they lived together. In each relationship, one of the parties was married to someone else at the outset, though by the time the parties broke up divorces had occurred, and in

both cases the parties' relationships were on again–off again to some extent. Based on these facts, the Supreme Court said that the parties' cohabitation was not "continuous" and that they did not have a mutual intent to live in a meretricious relationship. Saying that the meretricious relationship doctrine is still tied to its equitable underpinnings, the court said that its purpose was to prevent the unjust enrichment of one party at the other's expense and found no basis for granting a remedy in either case.

In Gormley v. Robertson, 83 P.3d 1042 (Wash. App. 2004), a division of the Washington Court of Appeals held that a person in a same-sex relationship could claim the benefit of the meretricious relationship doctrine. The court rejected the holding of another division of the court of appeals, Vasquez v. Hawthorne, 994 P.2d 240 (Wash. App. 2000), *rev'd and vacated on other grounds*, 33 P.3d 735 (Wash. 2001). The *Vasquez* court, interpreting *Connell*, held that a same-sex relationship cannot be a "quasi-marital relationship" because the parties cannot marry. *Gormley* rejected this argument, saying that one of the key elements of the doctrine is "knowledge by the partners that a *lawful* marriage between them does not exist." 83 P.3d at 1045 (italics in original).

6. Does the meretricious spouse doctrine give rights to third parties who deal with one or both of the parties?

7. Courts in a few other states have applied their divorce property laws to cohabitants upon a showing of an implied agreement between the parties to hold property as if they were married or on the basis of the court's equitable powers. *See, e.g.*, Eaton v. Johnston, 681 P.2d 606 (Kan. 1984); Pickens v. Pickens, 490 So. 2d 872 (Miss. 1986); Western States Construction, Inc. v. Michoff, 840 P.2d 1220 (Nev. 1992); Shuraleff v. Donnelly, 817 P.2d 764 (Or. App. 1991).

8. The provisions relating to domestic partners in the ALI Principles of the Law of Family Dissolution rejected the contract-based approach that underlies *Marvin* and instead adopt the approach of applying generally applicable family law principles to cohabitants as their relationship more closely resembles a marriage. The particular provisions of the principles are "inspired" by the law of Canada, Australia, and New Zealand and look to the case law of Washington and Oregon. Principles of the Law of Family Dissolution: Analysis and Recommendations, Chapter 1: Introductory Materials, Topic 1: Summary Overview of the Remaining Chapters. This chapter is printed in 8 Duke J. Gender L. & Pol'y 1-85 (2001). The materials on domestic partnerships appear at pp. 29-32. Section 6.03 of the ALI Principles provides specifically that two persons of the same or opposite sex are regarded as domestic partners if they share a primary residence and life together for a significant period of time. If the parties have a child together, the Principles propose that the parties should be regarded as domestic partners once they have maintained a common household for a particular period of time (to be established by the state; the example given in the commentary is two years). If they do not have a child, they are rebuttably presumed to be domestic partners after they have lived together for a (longer) period of time (e.g., three years). Parties who are domestic partners are subject to the property division and spousal support provisions applicable when married couples divorce, unless they have agreed to the contrary. ALI Principles §§6.01, 6.04, 6.05, 6.06.

Favorable commentary on the ALI domestic partner proposals includes Mary Coombs, Insiders and Outsiders: What the American Law Institute Has Done for

Gay and Lesbian Families, 8 Duke J. Gender L. & Pol'y 87 (2001); Martha M. Ertman, The ALI Principles' Approach to Domestic Partnership, 8 Duke J. Gender L. & Pol'y 107 (2001); Ira Mark Ellman, "Contract Thinking" Was Marvin's Fatal Flaw, 76 Notre Dame L. Rev. 1365 (2001); Grace Ganz Blumberg, The Regularization of Nonmarital Cohabitation; Rights and Responsibilities in the American Welfare State, 76 Notre Dame L. Rev. 1265, 1282-1283 (2001). Not all commentators are so positive, however.

LYNN D. WARDLE, DECONSTRUCTING FAMILY: A CRITIQUE OF THE AMERICAN LAW INSTITUTE'S "DOMESTIC PARTNERS" PROPOSAL

2001 BYU L. Rev. 1189,1200-1201, 1208, 1232-1233

The definition of "domestic partners" is extremely broad and overinclusive, exceeding the reasonable expectations of marriage or marriage-like economic interdependence. Its breadth will invite litigation and encourage the assertion of domestic partnership claims in cases when there is no just basis for them. Two unmarried people are deemed to be domestic partners and subject to the provisions of chapter 6 if "for a significant period of time [they] share a primary residence and a life together as a couple." The requirement that they cohabit for "a significant time" and that they have lived "as a couple" are so subjective as to invite judges to simply resort to personal preferences in deciding the issue.

The definition of domestic partners in chapter 6 is so broad that it could include persons who did not intend to intermingle their economic lives or incur any financial support or property sharing obligations. Arguably, it could even include persons who actually and demonstrably intend not to intermingle their economic lives or incur any financial support or property sharing obligations. Any two people unmarried to each other who live together as a couple in a primary residence for a significant time and who do not explicitly and properly agree not to be domestic partners may nevertheless be found to be domestic partners.

* * *

The biggest single flaw of chapter 6 is that it fails to create rights and remedies that are customized for domestic partnership; it extends exactly the same economic property interests and compensatory rights to domestic partners as are provided to couples who are in the much more significant, committed, economically interdependent relationship of marriage. Marital property interests are based on the time-verified fact that most parties who marry make a long-term (presumably life-long) commitment to share their lives and their total family and personal interests, and they make significant adjustments in their economic life based on those interdependency commitments. However, it is far from clear that most nonmarital couples have similar expectations and make similar sacrifices in reliance on their expectations. Indeed, the existing social science evidence points in exactly the opposite direction, indicating that parties living in nonmarital cohabitation have very different expectations and characteristics than parties who are married. In the face of the overwhelming evidence of such significant differences, chapter 6

irrationally extends full, equal marital property and compensatory payment rights
to domestic partners.

* * *

The potentially profound social effects of conferring legal equivalence upon
alternative relationships has not been wisely considered by the ALI Principles.
Chapter 6 relies on what the ALI Reporters perceive to be recent social changes
to justify a significant revision of the basic institution of marriage and family life.
It is far from clear, however, that the drafters have not mistaken a mere temporary
lifestyle fad for a significant social change, confusing a flashy but transitory generational blip in a few demographic cohorts for real lasting social change. Nothing
could be more common; every generation sees its time as a time of pivotal social
change and perceives its fads as constituting great political progress and social
reformation. But after a few brief decades, after a few natural calamities, a few
wars, a few years of economic troubles, the fads fade and the vaunted new
lifestyles wilt and largely disappear. In the meantime, however, large numbers of
the affected generation will suffer from the tragic (and unnecessary) deprivation
and impoverishment of their family life wrought by social engineers whose deval-
uation of marriage and marriage-based families facilitated and encouraged
couples and families to discard the only solid foundation for secure family relations in order to pursue shabby counterfeit "functional equivalents" like domestic
partnership.

See also Milton C. Regan, Jr., Calibrated Commitment: The Legal Treatment of
Marriage and Cohabitation, 76 Notre Dame L. Rev. 1435, 1447-1448 (2001); David
Westfall, Forcing Incidents of Marriage on Unmarried Cohabitants: The American
Law Institute's Principles of Family Dissolution, 76 Notre Dame L. Rev. 1467,
1473, 1478 (2001).

PROBLEMS

1. Harry and Margaret engaged in an intimate relationship for seven years
but never actually lived together. He was an executive, she an actress. At the end
of the relationship she sued, claiming that he expressly promised to support her
in return for her acting as his hostess and companion. He defended on the basis
that they had never lived together. Is cohabitation necessary under _Marvin?_
Under _Roccamonte?_ Under _Connell?_

What if Harry and Margaret had lived together for four days a week over a
long period but Harry maintained a separate dwelling?

2. Fifteen years ago Wendy, who was single, and Max, who was separated but
not divorced from his wife, began living together. At the time both worked for
Large Construction Co., he as a machine operator and she as a bookkeeper.

Within a few months they decided to start an equipment rental business, W & M Rentals. Max provided the start-up money from his savings and maintained the equipment, and Wendy kept the books and managed the rental end. The business license was issued in Wendy's name alone, in the hopes that this would keep Max's wife from having a claim to the business. Max continued to work for Large Construction Co. and worked at W & M nights and on weekends.

After three years W & M had become quite successful, and Max had grown tired of working for Large. He and Wendy agreed that he would quit to work only for W & M and that W & M would expand into the construction business. As the business grew larger and more successful, it demanded more sophisticated accounting than Wendy could provide. She was becoming increasingly busy with volunteer work and entertaining business clients, so eight years ago she quit working for W & M and since then has devoted herself to these other endeavors. Since that time all of the assets of the business have been titled in Max's name. He told Wendy that it was too inconvenient to have her name on anything when she wasn't in the office.

Five years ago Max's wife died. Wendy and Max discussed getting formally married but never went through with the plans, in part because a number of their business and social acquaintances assumed that they were married. Wendy has, however, always used her birth surname, and she and Max have never filed a joint income tax return. They have joint bank accounts and charge accounts and own their residence as joint tenants with right of survivorship. They have no children.

Wendy and Max's state recognizes common law marriage, the putative spouse doctrine, and all the *Marvin* remedies, and uses usual business partnership law.

If Wendy becomes ill and is provided emergency medical services, on what theory or theories can the hospital recover the costs of her care from Max? If Max and Wendy are domiciled in a common law property state, on what theory or theories may Wendy claim some or all of the assets of W & M?

2. Statutory Solutions: Domestic Partnerships, Civil Unions, Reciprocal Beneficiary Relationships, and More

In the aftermath of the litigation regarding same-sex marriage (see Chapter 3), legislatures in three states — Hawaii, Vermont, and New Jersey — have enacted laws that permit some unmarried partners to register their relationships and thereby to be entitled to some benefits that the law otherwise provides only to spouses. California has also enacted such legislation without the spur of litigation. Because the courts in Hawaii and Vermont held that denying same-sex couples the benefits of marriage violated provisions of the state constitutions, the laws all grant partners who register some of these benefits. However, no two of the four sets of laws are exactly the same. The differences express competing views about who should be eligible to enter these relationships as well as precisely which benefits of marriage should be extended to the parties who register. Selected provisions of each state's legislation are set out here.

HAWAII H.B. 118 (1997), CODIFIED AS HAW. REV. STAT. CH. 572C AND IN SCATTERED SECTIONS OF THE REST OF THE CODE. CHAPTER 572C

Section 572C-4 Requisites of a valid reciprocal beneficiary relationship. In order to enter into a valid reciprocal beneficiary relationship, it shall be necessary that:

(1) Each of the parties be at least eighteen years old;

(2) Neither of the parties be married nor a party to another reciprocal beneficiary relationship;

(3) The parties be legally prohibited from marrying one another under chapter 572;

(4) Consent of either party to the reciprocal beneficiary relationship has not been obtained by force, duress, or fraud; and

(5) Each of the parties sign a declaration of reciprocal beneficiary relationship as provided in section -5.

Section 572C-5 Registration as reciprocal beneficiaries; filing fees; records.

(a) Two persons, who meet the criteria set out in section -4, may enter into a reciprocal beneficiary relationship and register their relationship as reciprocal beneficiaries by filing a signed notarized declaration of reciprocal beneficiary relationship with the director. For the filing of the declaration, the director shall collect a fee of $8, which shall be remitted to the director of finance for deposit into the general fund.

(b) Upon the payment of the fee, the director shall register the declaration and provide a certificate of reciprocal beneficiary relationship to each party named on the declaration. The director shall maintain a record of each declaration of reciprocal beneficiary relationship filed with or issued by the director.

Section 572C-6 Rights and obligations. Upon the issuance of a certificate of reciprocal beneficiary relationship, the parties named in the certificate shall be entitled to those rights and obligations provided by the law to reciprocal beneficiaries. Unless otherwise expressly provided by law, reciprocal beneficiaries shall not have the same rights and obligations under the law that are conferred through marriage under chapter 572.

Section 572C-7 Termination of reciprocal beneficiary relationship; filing fees and records; termination upon marriage.

(a) Either party to a reciprocal beneficiary relationship may terminate the relationship by filing a signed notarized declaration of termination of reciprocal beneficiary relationship by either of the reciprocal beneficiaries with the director. For the filing of the declaration, the director shall collect a fee of $8, which shall be remitted to the director of finance for deposit into the general fund.

(b) Upon the payment of the fee, the director shall file the declaration and issue a certificate of termination of reciprocal beneficiary relationship to each party of the former relationship. The director shall maintain a record of each declaration and certificate of termination of reciprocal beneficiary relationship filed with or issued by the director.

(c) Any marriage license subsequently issued by the department to any individual registered as a reciprocal beneficiary shall automatically terminate the individual's existing reciprocal beneficiary relationship.

(d) If either party to a reciprocal beneficiary relationship enters into a legal marriage, the parties shall no longer have a reciprocal beneficiary relationship and shall no longer be entitled to the rights and benefits of reciprocal beneficiaries.

The main purpose of the Hawaii reciprocal beneficiaries law was to extend to registrants rights against third parties similar to those that spouses have. *See* Haw. Rev. Stat. §572C-2. For example, the law provides that reciprocal beneficiaries may be covered by health insurance, have hospital visitation and health care decision-making rights, have the same rights as a spouse in a decedent's estate, and may sue for wrongful death of their partners. *See* Haw. H.B. 118 (1997).

VERMONT LEGISLATURE, ACT NO. 91 (H. 847) (1999) CODIFIED AT VT. STAT. ANN. TIT. 15 §1201 ET SEQ. (2000)

---

§ 1202. Requisites of a Valid Civil Union. For a civil union to be established in Vermont, it shall be necessary that the parties to a civil union satisfy all of the following criteria:

(1) Not be a party to another civil union or a marriage.

(2) Be of the same sex and therefore excluded from the marriage laws of this state.

(3) Meet the criteria and obligations set forth in 18 V.S.A. chapter 106.

§ 1203. Person Shall Not Enter a Civil Union with a Relative

(a) A woman shall not enter a civil union with her mother, grandmother, daughter, granddaughter, sister, brother's daughter, sister's daughter, father's sister or mother's sister.

(b) A man shall not enter a civil union with his father, grandfather, son, grandson, brother, brother's son, sister's son, father's brother or mother's brother.

(c) A civil union between persons prohibited from entering a civil union in subsection (a) or (b) of this section is void.

§ 1204. Benefits, Protections and Responsibilities of Parties to a Civil Union

(a) Parties to a civil union shall have all the same benefits, protections and responsibilities under law, whether they derive from statute, administrative or court rule, policy, common law or any other source of civil law, as are granted to spouses in a marriage.

(b) A party to a civil union shall be included in any definition or use of the terms "spouse," "family," "immediate family," "dependent," "next of kin," and other terms that denote the spousal relationship, as those terms are used throughout the law.

(c) Parties to a civil union shall be responsible for the support of one another to the same degree and in the same manner as prescribed under law for married persons.

(d) The law of domestic relations, including annulment, separation and divorce, child custody and support, and property division and maintenance shall apply to parties to a civil union.

* * *

(f) The rights of parties to a civil union, with respect to a child of whom either becomes the natural parent during the term of the civil union, shall be the same as those of a married couple, with respect to a child of whom either spouse becomes the natural parent during the marriage.

§ 1205. *Modification of Civil Union Terms.* Parties to a civil union may modify the terms, conditions, or effects of their civil union in the same manner and to the same extent as married persons who execute an antenuptial agreement or other agreement recognized and enforceable under the law, setting forth particular understandings with respect to their union.

§ 1206. *Dissolution of Civil Unions.* The family court shall have jurisdiction over all proceedings relating to the dissolution of civil unions. The dissolution of civil unions shall follow the same procedures and be subject to the same substantive rights and obligations that are involved in the dissolution of marriage in accordance with chapter 11 of this title, including any residency requirements.

Sections 5160-5164 require and provide for civil union licenses, similar to marriage licenses, and designate who is authorized to "certify" civil unions, analogous to those authorized to celebrate marriages.

The Vermont legislation also includes creates the status of "reciprocal beneficiaries." The only people who can register as reciprocal beneficiaries are blood relatives who are unable to marry or join in civil union, such as siblings or an aunt and a niece. The legislation gives registrants a narrow range of privileges, such as hospital visitation rights and rights to make medical decisions if the other person is incapacitated." Vt. Stat. Ann. Ch. 25.

CAL. STATS. 2003, C. 421 (A.B. 205) — THE CALIFORNIA DOMESTIC PARTNER RIGHTS AND RESPONSIBILITIES ACT OF 2003, EFFECTIVE JAN. 1, 2005, CODIFIED AS SECTIONS OF THE CALIFORNIA FAMILY CODE

Family Code § 297. (a) Domestic partners are two adults who have chosen to share one another's lives in an intimate and committed relationship of mutual caring.

(b) A domestic partnership shall be established in California when both persons file a Declaration of Domestic Partnership with the Secretary of State pursuant to this division, and, at the time of filing, all of the following requirements are met:

(1) Both persons have a common residence.

(2) Neither person is married to someone else or is a member of another domestic partnership with someone else that has not been terminated, dissolved, or adjudged a nullity.

(3) The two persons are not related by blood in a way that would prevent them from being married to each other in this state.

(4) Both persons are at least 18 years of age.

(5) Either of the following:

(A) Both persons are members of the same sex.

(B) One or both of the persons meet the eligibility criteria under Title II of the Social Security Act as defined in 42 U.S.C. Section 402(a) for old-age insurance benefits or Title XVI of the Social Security Act as defined in 42 U.S.C. Section 1381 for aged individuals. Notwithstanding any other provision of this section, persons of opposite sexes may not constitute a domestic partnership unless one or both of the persons are over the age of 62.

(6) Both persons are capable of consenting to the domestic partnership.

(c) "Have a common residence" means that both domestic partners share the same residence. It is not necessary that the legal right to possess the common residence be in both of their names. Two people have a common residence even if one or both have additional residences. Domestic partners do not cease to have a common residence if one leaves the common residence but intends to return.

Family Code §297.5. (a) Registered domestic partners shall have the same rights, protections, and benefits, and shall be subject to the same responsibilities, obligations, and duties under law, whether they derive from statutes, administrative regulations, court rules, government policies, common law, or any other provisions or sources of law, as are granted to and imposed upon spouses.

(b) Former registered domestic partners shall have the same rights, protections, and benefits, and shall be subject to the same responsibilities, obligations, and duties under law, whether they derive from statutes, administrative regulations, court rules, government policies, common law, or any other provisions or sources of law, as are granted to and imposed upon former spouses.

(c) A surviving registered domestic partner, following the death of the other partner, shall have the same rights, protections, and benefits, and shall be subject to the same responsibilities, obligations, and duties under law, whether they derive from statutes, administrative regulations, court rules, government policies, common law, or any other provisions or sources of law, as are granted to and imposed upon a widow or a widower.

(d) The rights and obligations of registered domestic partners with respect to a child of either of them shall be the same as those of spouses. The rights and obligations of former or surviving registered domestic partners with respect to a child of either of them shall be the same as those of former or surviving spouses.

(e) To the extent that provisions of California law adopt, refer to, or rely upon, provisions of federal law in a way that otherwise would cause registered domestic partners to be treated differently than spouses, registered domestic partners shall be treated by California law as if federal law recognized a domestic partnership in the same manner as California law.

* * *

Family Code §298.5. (a) Two persons desiring to become domestic partners may complete and file a Declaration of Domestic Partnership with the Secretary of State.

(b) The Secretary of State shall register the Declaration of Domestic Partnership in a registry for those partnerships, and shall return a copy of the registered form and a Certificate of Registered Domestic Partnership to the domestic partners at the mailing address provided by the domestic partners.

(c) No person who has filed a Declaration of Domestic Partnership may file a new Declaration of Domestic Partnership or enter a civil marriage with someone other than their registered domestic partner unless the most recent domestic partnership has been terminated or a final judgment of dissolution or nullity of the most recent domestic partnership has been entered. This prohibition does not apply if the previous domestic partnership ended because one of the partners died.

Family Code §299. . . .

(d) The superior courts shall have jurisdiction over all proceedings relating to the dissolution of domestic partnerships, nullity of domestic partnerships, and legal separation of partners in a domestic partnership. The dissolution of a domestic partnership, nullity of a domestic partnership, and legal separation of partners in a domestic partnership shall follow the same procedures, and the partners shall possess the same rights, protections, and benefits, and be subject to the same responsibilities, obligations, and duties, as apply to the dissolution of marriage, nullity of marriage, and legal separation of spouses in a marriage, respectively, except as provided in subdivision (a) [which creates a summary dissolution procedure for domestic partnerships which is parallel to the procedures for marriages], and except that, in accordance with the consent acknowledged by domestic partners in the Declaration of Domestic Partnership form, proceedings for dissolution, nullity, or legal separation of a domestic partnership registered in this state may be filed in the superior courts of this state even if neither domestic partner is a resident of, or maintains a domicile in, the state at the time the proceedings are filed.

NEW JERSEY DOMESTIC PARTNERSHIP ACT, PUB. L. 2003, CH. 246 (2004), CODIFIED AT N.J.S.A. 26:8A-1 ET SEQ.

C.26:8A-2 Findings, declarations relative to domestic partners. The Legislature finds and declares that:

* * *

d. All persons in domestic partnerships should be entitled to certain rights and benefits that are accorded to married couples under the laws of New Jersey, including: statutory protection through the "Law Against Discrimination," P.L.1945, c.169 (C.10:5-1 et seq.) against various forms of discrimination based on domestic partnership status, such as employment, housing and credit discrimination; visitation rights for a hospitalized domestic partner and the right to make medical or legal decisions for an incapacitated partner; and an additional exemption from the personal income tax and the transfer inheritance tax on the same basis as a spouse. The need for all persons who are in domestic partnerships, regardless of their sex, to have access to these rights and benefits is paramount in view of their essential relationship to any reasonable conception of basic human dignity and autonomy, and the extent to which they will play an integral role in enabling these persons to enjoy their familial relationships as domestic partners and to cope with adversity when a medical emergency arises that affects a domestic partnership, as was painfully but graphically illustrated on a large scale in the aftermath of the tragic events that befell the people of our State and region on September 11, 2001. . . .

C.26:8A-4 Affidavit of Domestic Partnership; establishment, requirements. a. Two persons who desire to become domestic partners and meet the requirements of subsection b. of this section may execute and file an Affidavit of Domestic Partnership with the local registrar upon payment of a fee, in an amount to be determined by the commissioner, which shall be deposited in the General Fund. Each person shall receive a copy of the affidavit marked "filed."

b. A domestic partnership shall be established when all of the following requirements are met:

(1) Both persons have a common residence and are otherwise jointly responsible for each other's common welfare as evidenced by joint financial arrangements or joint ownership of real or personal property, which shall be demonstrated by at least one of the following:

(a) a joint deed, mortgage agreement or lease;

(b) a joint bank account;

(c) designation of one of the persons as a primary beneficiary in the other person's will;

(d) designation of one of the persons as a primary beneficiary in the other person's life insurance policy or retirement plan; or

(e) joint ownership of a motor vehicle;

(2) Both persons agree to be jointly responsible for each other's basic living expenses during the domestic partnership;

(3) Neither person is in a marriage recognized by New Jersey law or a member of another domestic partnership;

(4) Neither person is related to the other by blood or affinity up to and including the fourth degree of consanguinity;

(5) Both persons are of the same sex and therefore unable to enter into a marriage with each other that is recognized by New Jersey law, except that two persons who are each 62 years of age or older and not of the same sex may establish a domestic partnership if they meet the requirements set forth in this section;

(6) Both persons have chosen to share each other's lives in a committed relationship of mutual caring;

(7) Both persons are at least 18 years of age;

(8) Both persons file jointly an Affidavit of Domestic Partnership; and

(9) Neither person has been a partner in a domestic partnership that was terminated less than 180 days prior to the filing of the current Affidavit of Domestic Partnership, except that this prohibition shall not apply if one of the partners died; and, in all cases in which a person registered a prior domestic partnership, the domestic partnership shall have been terminated in accordance with the provisions of section 10 of P.L.2003, c.246 (C.26:8A-10).

c. A person who executes an Affidavit of Domestic Partnership in violation of the provisions of subsection b. of this section shall be liable to a civil penalty in an amount not to exceed $1,000. The penalty shall be sued for and collected pursuant to the "Penalty Enforcement Law of 1999," P.L.1999, c.274 (C.2A:58-10 et seq.).

C.26:8A-5 Notice of termination of domestic partnerships to third parties; requirements a. A former domestic partner who has given a copy of the Certificate of Domestic Partnership to any third party to qualify for any benefit or right and whose receipt of that benefit or enjoyment of that right has not otherwise terminated, shall, upon termination of the domestic partnership, give or send to the third party, at the last known address of the third party, written notification that the domestic partnership has been terminated. A third party that suffers a loss as a result of failure by a domestic partner to provide this notice shall be entitled to seek recovery from the partner who was obligated to send the notice for any actual loss resulting thereby.

b. Failure to provide notice to a third party, as required pursuant to this section, shall not delay or prevent the termination of the domestic partnership.

C.26:8A-6 Obligations of domestic partners. a. The obligations that two people have to each other as a result of creating a domestic partnership shall be limited to the provisions of this act, and those provisions shall not diminish any right granted under any other provision of law.

b. Upon the termination of a domestic partnership, the domestic partners, from that time forward, shall incur none of the obligations to each other as domestic partners that are created by this or any other act.

* * *

e. Domestic partners may modify the rights and obligations to each other that are granted by this act in any valid contract between themselves, except for the requirements for a domestic partnership as set forth in section 4 of P.L.2003, c.246 (C.26:8A-4).

* * *

g. A domestic partner shall not be liable for the debts of the other partner contracted before establishment of the domestic partnership, or contracted by the other partner in his own name during the domestic partnership. The partner who contracts for the debt in his own name shall be liable to be sued separately in his own name, and any property belonging to that partner shall be liable to satisfy that debt in the same manner as if the partner had not entered into a domestic partnership.

C.26:8A-10 Jurisdiction of Superior Court relative to termination of domestic partnerships. a. (1) The Superior Court shall have jurisdiction over all proceedings relating to the termination of a domestic partnership established pursuant to section 4 of P.L.2003, c.246 (C.26:8A-4), including the division and distribution of jointly held property. The fees for filing an action or proceeding for the termination of a domestic partnership shall be the same as those for filing an action or proceeding for divorce pursuant to N.J.S.22A:2-12.

(2) The termination of a domestic partnership may be adjudged for the following causes:

(a) voluntary sexual intercourse between a person who is in a domestic partnership and an individual other than the person's domestic partner as defined in section 3 of P.L.2003, c.246 (C.26:8A-3);

(b) willful and continued desertion for a period of 12 or more consecutive months, which may be established by satisfactory proof that the parties have ceased to cohabit as domestic partners;

(c) extreme cruelty, which is defined as including any physical or mental cruelty that endangers the safety or health of the plaintiff or makes it improper or unreasonable to expect the plaintiff to continue to cohabit with the defendant; except that no complaint for termination shall be filed until after three months from the date of the last act of cruelty complained of in the complaint, but this provision shall not be held to apply to any counterclaim;

(d) separation, provided that the domestic partners have lived separate and apart in different habitations for a period of at least 18 or more consecutive months and there is no reasonable prospect of reconciliation; and provided further that, after the 18-month period, there shall be a presumption that there is no reasonable prospect of reconciliation;

(e) voluntarily induced addiction or habituation to any narcotic drug, as defined in the "New Jersey Controlled Dangerous Substances Act," P.L.1970, c. 226 (C.24:21-2) or the "Comprehensive Drug Reform Act of 1987," N.J.S.2C:35-1 et al., or habitual drunkenness for a period of 12 or more consecutive months subsequent to establishment of the domestic partnership and next preceding the filing of the complaint;

(f) institutionalization for mental illness for a period of 24 or more consecutive months subsequent to establishment of the domestic partnership and next preceding the filing of the complaint; or

(g) imprisonment of the defendant for 18 or more consecutive months after establishment of the domestic partnership, provided that where the action is not commenced until after the defendant's release, the parties have not resumed cohabitation following the imprisonment.

(3) In all such proceedings, the court shall in no event be required to effect an equitable distribution of property, either real or personal, which was legally

and beneficially acquired by both domestic partners or either domestic partner during the domestic partnership.

(4) The court shall notify the State registrar of the termination of a domestic partnership pursuant to this subsection.

b. In the case of two persons who are each 62 years of age or older and not of the same sex and have established a domestic partnership pursuant to section 4 of P.L.2003, c.246 (C.26:8A-4), the domestic partnership shall be deemed terminated if the two persons enter into a marriage with each other that is recognized by New Jersey law.

* * *

NOTES AND QUESTIONS

1. Who is eligible to enter into a reciprocal beneficiary relationship in Hawaii? A civil union in Vermont? A domestic partnership in California? In New Jersey? What explains these limitations?

2. How does registering under each of the statutes affect the rights and duties of the partners between themselves? How are their rights and duties vis-à-vis third parties affected?

3. What are the differences in the procedures for entry into and exit from the relationships? What might explain these differences?

4. Does any of these statutes create a relationship equivalent to marriage? Why or why not? Are any of these relationships a desirable alternative to marriage?

Professor Polikoff has set out the argument for preferring a broadly inclusive domestic partner regime to marriage:

> Almost all domestic partnership models extend eligibility for registration to one of the following three categories of relationships: 1) same-sex couples only; 2) same-sex and opposite-sex couples; and 3) same-sex couples and individuals related to each other to a degree that would prevent them from marrying. Each of these categories is flawed. A small number of jurisdictions extend eligibility to a wider group of relationships and should be considered models for future registration schemes.
>
>   The three dominant categories express distinct underlying visions. Allowing only same-sex couples to register validates marriage as the proper norm. Thus, opposite-sex couples, who are permitted to marry, must marry to obtain relationship-based rights and responsibilities. This category does not support alternative family structures; rather it acknowledges the value of gay and lesbian couples and expresses the inequity of denying such couples access to some, or even most, of the incidents accorded spouses. Eligibility criteria customarily eliminate two individuals of the same sex who would be prohibited from marrying were they of opposite sex, thus evidencing marriage as the analogous relationship. Two sisters, or a grandmother and a granddaughter, no matter how emotionally and economically intertwined, cannot register. Conjugal relationships, whether opposite-sex or same-sex, are therefore supported above equally committed relationships between relatives.

The category that includes same-sex couples and relatives unable to marry similarly validates marriage as the proper norm because it excludes opposite-sex couples. This category does, however, recognize the importance of certain familial, non-conjugal, relationships and allows those in such relationships certain benefits.

Extending eligibility to both same-sex and opposite-sex couples validates the choice of heterosexuals to remain unmarried and thus has the potential to chip away at the privileged legal status of marriage. Such regimes, however, are geared toward conjugal relationships, even though engaging in sexual relations is not specified as an eligibility criterion. Intent to recognize only conjugal relationships is evidenced by exclusion from registration of all those who would be unable to marry under state incest laws.

In contrast to these three dominant models, the District of Columbia expresses a broad vision of what relationships matter. Its eligibility criteria extend to two individuals in "a familial relationship . . . characterized by mutual caring and the sharing of a mutual residence." Same-sex couples, opposite-sex couples, and those in non-conjugal relationships are thus all qualified to register.

* * *

When advocates for same-sex marriage invoke the very two-tiered structure that privileges marriage as a reason why lesbians and gay men must have access to the favored tier, they accept that two-tiered structure as a natural and unquestioned phenomenon. Worse still, advocates often extol marriage as a badge of maturity, commitment, and citizenship. Such arguments place gay and lesbian advocacy on the wrong side of an intense culture war. To be sure, opponents of same-sex marriage populate that side of the culture war as well. But what all on that side share is a conviction that the good of marriage is so profound and basic to a well functioning society that law and policy can single out marriage for "special rights" unavailable to other emotionally and economically interdependent units. On the other side of the culture war are those, like myself, who value equally all family forms and who therefore want just social policies that facilitate maximum economic well-being and emotional flourishing for all, not only for those who marry.

Nancy D. Polikoff, Ending Marriage as We Know It, 32 Hofstra L. Rev. 201, 218-230 (2003). *See also* Grace Ganz Blumberg, Legal Recognition of Same-Sex Conjugal Relationships: The 2003 California Domestic Partner Rights and Responsibilities Act in Comparative Civil Rights and Family Law Perspective, 51 UCLA L. Rev. 1555 (2004).

5. Does interstate recognition of civil unions pose the same issues as interstate recognition of same-sex marriage? Courts in at least four states have been asked to recognize Vermont civil unions as creating marriage or a marriage-like relationship, with mixed results. In Burns v. Burns, 560 S.E.2d 47 (Ga. App. 2002), the court held that a civil union was not a marriage within the meaning of language in a divorce decree that "[t]here shall be no visitation nor residence by the children with either party during any time where such party cohabits with or has overnight stays with any adult to which such party is not legally married. . . ." Because the court said that the mother's civil union with her partner was not a

marriage, it enforced the order and denied the mother visitation with her children. In contrast, in Langan v. St. Vincent's Hospital of New York, 765 N.Y.S.2d 411 (N.Y. Sup. Ct. 2003), the court held that John Langan was entitled to bring an action for wrongful death as the surviving spouse of his partner, Neal Spicehandler. It distinguished earlier cases holding that surviving domestic partners could not bring wrongful death suits by invoking the common law rules on interstate recognition of marriage, in effect treating the civil union as a marriage for these purposes.

Two courts outside Vermont have been asked to dissolve civil unions; both cases involved partners who could not terminate their relationships in Vermont because they could not satisfy the state's residency requirement. In Salucco v. Alldredge, 17 Mass. L. Rptr. 498, 2004 WL 864459 (Mass. Super.), the court exercised its general equity jurisdiction to dissolve the civil union, holding that Goodridge v. Dept. of Public Health, 440 Mass. 309 (2003) and Opinions of the Justices to the Senate, Feb. 3, 2004 (both reproduced in Chapter 3), require that same-sex couples who enter into a civil union must be given the same rights and responsibilities that opposite sex married couples have. However, the court in Rosengarten v. Downes, 802 A.2d 1066 (Conn. 2002), *cert. granted in part* 806 A.2d 1066 (Conn. 2002), held that a court with jurisdiction over "matters . . . concerning family relationship" did not have subject matter jurisdiction to dissolve a civil union. The court said, "Implicit in the plaintiff's argument that jurisdiction exists . . . is that we must recognize the validity of the Vermont civil union as a matter concerning family relations. If Connecticut does not recognize the validity of such a union, then there is no res to address and dissolve. . . . [Two statutes] expressly state that Connecticut does not endorse or authorize, respectively, civil unions or any other relationship between unmarried persons. On the basis of these enactments, we conclude that because the legislature expressly refused to endorse or authorize such unions it could not have intended civil unions to be treated as family matters within the jurisdiction of the Superior Court. . . ."

Both the California and New Jersey domestic partnership acts give effect to domestic partnerships, civil unions, or reciprocal beneficiary relationships validly entered into outside the state. N.J.S.A. 26:8A-C.26:8A-6; Cal. Fam. Code 299.2. However, statutes or constitutional provisions in Nebraska and Texas explicitly deny recognition to civil unions from other states. Neb. Const., Art. I, §29; Vernon's Tex. Code Ann., Family Code, §6.204. Litigation challenging the Nebraska provision as an unconstitutional bill of attainder is pending. Citizens for Equal Protection, Inc. v. Bruning, 290 F. Supp. 2d 1004 (D. Neb. 2003).

6. A number of local communities have enacted domestic partner registration ordinances, usually for the purpose of extending "spousal" benefits to the domestic partners of municipal employees, permitting partners to obtain public recognition of their relationships by registration, or both. See William C. Duncan, Domestic Partnership Laws in the United States: A Review and Critique, 2001 BYU L. Rev. 961; Craig A. Bowman & Blake M. Cornish, A More Perfect Union: A Legal and Social Analysis of Domestic Partnership Ordinances, 92 Colum. L. Rev. 1164 (1992).

Such local ordinances have been challenged on the ground that a municipality lacks authority to enact legislation altering family relationships. Among the decisions rejecting the argument are Tyma v. Montgomery County, 801 A.2d 148 (Md. 2002); Lowe v. Broward County, 766 So. 2d 1199 (Fla. Dist. Ct. App. 2000); Crawford v. City of Chicago, 710 N.E.2d 91 (Ill. App. 1999); Schaefer v. City & County of Denver, 973 P.2d 717 (Colo. Ct. App. 1998); Slattery v. City of New York, 686 N.Y.S.2d 683 (N.Y. Sup. Ct.), *aff'd as modified*, 266 A.D.2d 24, 697 N.Y.S.2d 603 (N.Y. App. Div. 1999); City of Atlanta v. Morgan, 492 S.E.2d 193 (Ga. 1997). A Pennsylvania court has accepted this argument, but an appeal has been granted. Devlin v. Philadelphia, 809 A.2d 980 (Comm. Ct. Pa. 2002), *appeal granted*, 833 A.2d 1115 (Pa. 2003).

7.Grace Ganz Blumberg, The Regularization of Nonmarital Cohabitation: Rights and Responsibilities in the American Welfare State, 76 Notre Dame L. Rev. 1265, 1282-1283 (2001):

> Independently of any legislation or court action, and for that reason generally less observed, American employers have increasingly been treating nonmarital cohabitants equally with married persons for purposes of employee benefits. The trend is particularly pronounced with large corporations. The significance of this development lies in the central role that employment benefits play in the American welfare system. By welfare system, I mean not merely "welfare" in the popular sense (public assistance), but rather the entire structure of rights and obligations that secure the welfare of individuals and families in the United States.
>
> After World War II, while other countries were establishing national health systems, American employers increasingly provided health insurance as an employment benefit for workers and their families. Although this approach has been supplemented by relatively limited public provisions for low-income families and the aged, employment has persisted as the dominant source of health coverage, and employment benefits have frequently been expanded to include the full panoply of benefits usually associated with a highly developed welfare state.

As of mid-2004, the Human Rights Campaign counted 7,360 employers that offered domestic partner health benefits, including 212 Fortune 500 companies, 6,811 private-sector companies, 10 state governments, 130 city and county governments, and 198 colleges and universities. *http://www.hrc.org* (last visited 7/19/04).

Private employment benefits plans which cover employees' same-sex partners but not the partners of employees in heterosexual relationships have been challenged as unconstitutional, or violative of Title VII, generally without success. Irizarry v. Board of Education of the City of Chicago, 251 F.3d 604 (7th Cir. 2001); Foray v. Bell Atlantic, 56 F. Supp. 2d 327 (S.D.N.Y. 1999), Cleaves v. City of Chicago, 68 F. Supp. 2d 963 (N.D. Ill. 1999).

PROBLEM

You are an analyst for the legislature of the hypothetical state of Emeraldia. You have been asked to discuss the advantages and disadvantages of the Hawaii, Vermont, California, and New Jersey legislation. Please write your memo.

3. Nonmarital Cohabitation in Other Western Countries

In Canada, much of Western Europe, Australia, and New Zealand, recent legislation gives cohabitants at least some rights traditionally reserved for married couples.

Canada Canadian law provides that all unmarried couples, opposite- and same-sex, who have lived together for at least one year are entitled to the same benefits and are, for purposes of federal law, under the same obligations as married couples. The Modernization of Benefits and Obligations Act, S.C. 2000, was enacted in response to the holdings of the Canadian Supreme Court in M. v. H., [1999] 2 S.C.R. 3 (S.C.C.), that a statute which imposed support obligations on heterosexual but not homosexual cohabitants violated the Canadian Charter of Rights and Freedoms, and in Miron v. Trudel, [1995] 2 S.C.R. 418 (S.C.C.) that a statute which provided benefits to spouses but not unmarried cohabitants violated the Charter. As a result of this legislation, Canadian federal law treats unmarried couples of the same and opposite-sex who have lived together for at least a year in the same way that it treats married couples.

However, provincial, rather than federal, law governs family property rights, and there the picture is mixed. In Saskatchewan, Manitoba, the Northwest Territories, and Nunavut the same law of property applies to married couples and to some cohabitants. In Alberta adults in "interdependent relationships," which may be same- or opposite-sex relationships, have the rights and obligations of spouses for purposes of property, support, and inheritance rights. In the other common law provinces, the property law that governs married couples does not apply to unmarried cohabitants. Instead, the common law separate-property system based on title, supplemented by contract and equitable principles, applies. However, some provinces have legislation providing different treatment for certain kinds of property, such as pensions or residences, and in several provinces unmarried couples may opt into the marital property regime by contract. In addition, legislation in all of the common law provinces extends support obligations to some unmarried couples. Nova Scotia and Manitoba also permit cohabitants to register as domestic partners, thereby obtaining the same rights and obligations as spouses with regard to family property, inheritances, and support. Berend Hovius, Property Division for Unmarried Cohabitees in the Common Law Provinces, 22 Can. Fam. L.Q. 175 (2004); Nicholas Bala, Controversy Over Couples inCanada: The Evolution of Marriage and Other Adult Interdependent Relationships, 29 Queen's L.J. 41 (2003), *available at http://qsilver.queensu.ca/law/papers/evolutionapril.htm*. In Quebec, which follows the civilian legal tradition, an implied partnership theory and unjust enrichment principles are used to distribute property between cohabitants. Quebec has no legislation that imposes support duties on cohabitants, though a 1999 statute recognizes de facto spouses for purposes of pensions, social assistance, and taxation, and same- and opposite-sex partners may enter a civil union and thereby obtain many of the rights and duties of spouses. *Id.*

The Canadian Supreme Court in 2003 rejected a claim that the Nova Scotia law treating the property rights of unmarried cohabitants differently from those of married couples violated the Charter. In *Nova Scotia v. Walsh*, (2002), 32 R.F.L. (5th) 81 (S.C.C.), the court emphasized the great variety among cohabiting opposite-sex couples and concluded that such couples should be able to make choices about rights and duties between themselves. It also concluded that the different treatment was not discriminatory because it was not demeaning and instead respected personal autonomy.

Australia and New Zealand Australian federal law regulates marriage and divorce, but these laws do not apply to unmarried cohabitants. Instead, all Australian states and territories have legislation providing for property distribution at the end of de facto relationships. These statutes do not require proof of a contract or facts that would give rise to a constructive or resulting trust or other traditional equitable remedy. However, the eight statutes vary substantially in terms of the nature of the parties' rights and of the relationships covered. In the Northern Territories, South Australia, and Tasmania only heterosexual cohabitants are covered, while statutes in Victoria, Western Australia, and Queensland apply to same- and opposite-sex couples. In the Australian Capital Territory and New South Wales the property distribution act applies to de facto relationships (same- and opposite-sex couples) and to relationships between two adult persons, whether or not related by family, who are not married or in a de facto relationship but who live together and one or both provide the other with domestic support and personal care. Lindy Willmott, Ben Mathews & Greg Shoebridge, Defacto Relationships Property Adjustment Law—A National Direction, 17 Austl. J. Fam. L. 37 (2003).

In New Zealand, as of February 2002, the same law of property and spousal support applies to married and unmarried couples, including same-sex couples. To fall within this regime, unmarried couples must have lived together three years or have a child living with them, or one of the partners must have made a substantial contribution to the relationship. Property (Relationships) Act 1976, as amended by Property (Relationships) Amendment Act 2001. *See* Bill Atkin, The Challenge of Unmarried Cohabitation—The New Zealand Response, 37 Fam. L.Q. 303 (2003).

United Kingdom In England and Wales unmarried cohabitants may have property rights based on contract and equitable principles; in some parts of the U.K. limited case law gives some rights vis-à-vis third parties. *See* David Burles, "Promises, Promises"—*Burns v Burns* 20 Years On, 33 Family Law 834 (Nov. 2003). Legislation that would allow same-sex partners to register and obtain many of the rights and duties of married couples is under consideration. In 2003 the British government announced its intention to introduce legislation that would create registered partnerships for same-sex couples only. Rights and duties of partners would be similar to those provided to opposite-sex married couples. Civil Partnership: A Framework for the Legal Recognition of Same-Sex Couples, *available at http://www.womenandequalityunit.gov.uk/lgbt/ partnership.htm*

Western Europe   On the European continent statutes increasingly assimilate cohabitation into marriage, with the Scandinavian countries leading the way. Since 1989 Denmark has allowed same-sex couples to enter into registered partnerships, as have Norway since 1993, Sweden since 1994, Iceland since 1996, and Finland since 2002. In all these countries the registered partner relationship is very similar to marriage, except that in most countries parent-child rights and duties do not arise because of the relationship, and registration is limited to same-sex couples to preserve the preferred position of marriage. The Netherlands and Belgium, which also allow same-sex marriage, have permitted registered partnerships since 1998 and 2000, respectively. In both countries both same- and opposite-sex couples may enter into a registered partnership. The Dutch registered partnership is similar to that in Scandinavia, while the Belgian legislation creates a relationship similar to the French PCS (below). Kees Waaldjik, Others May Follow: The Introduction of Marriage, Quasi-Marriage, and Semi-Marriage for Same-Sex Couples in European Countries, 38 N. Eng. L. Rev. 569 (2004). *See also* Kees Waaldjik, Chronological overview of the main legislative steps in the process of legal recognition of homosexuality in European countries, *available at http://athena.leidenuniv.nl/rechten/meijers/index.php3?c = 128* (last updated April 2003).

The French *Pakte Civil de Solidarite* (PCS), created in 1999 and which applies to same- or opposite-sex couples, is a form of registered partnership. Registrants "obtain most of the rights and obligations traditionally associated with marriage in the fields of social welfare, housing, tax law and property rights, but a few significant distinctions will remain in the areas of inheritance and children, as well as in the event of a possible breakdown of the relationship." Eva Steiner, The Spirit of the New French Registered Partnership Law—Promoting Autonomy and Pluralism or Weakening Marriage? 12 Child. & Fam. L.Q. 1 (2000).

Since 2001, Germany has permitted same-sex couples to register as domestic partners and to receive the same inheritance and tenancy rights as married couples. The law does not give same-sex couples the same welfare and tax rights that married couples have, and does not permit them to adopt. Waaldjik, above.

Eleven of Spain's 17 regions and autonomous cities have enacted legislation that gives some legal rights to unmarried cohabitants. They are Catalonia (1998), Aragon (1999), Navarra (2000), Valencia (2001), Balearic Islands (2001), Madrid (2002), Asturias (2002), Andalucia (2002), Basque Country (2003), Canary Islands (2003), and Extremadura (2003). Some of the acts require that the parties register as cohabitants to receive rights, while others provide that rights and duties attach automatically after the parties have cohabited for a certain amount of time or have had a child together. Joan Marsal Guillamet & Elena Lauroba Lacasa, Some Steps Towards Same-Sex Marriage in Spain, (working paper presented to the North American Regional Conference, International Society for Family Law, June 2003). *See also* Gabriel Garcia Cantero, The Catalan Family Code of 1998 and Other Autonomous Region Laws on *De Facto* Unions, in The International Survey of Family Law 397 (Andrew Bain ed., 2001).

Legislation in Croatia, Hungary, Lithuania, Portugal, and the Swiss cantons of Geneva and Zurich also give rights to unmarried cohabitants in some circumstances. Robert Wintemute, The Massachusetts Same-Sex Marriage Case: Could Decisions from Canada, Europe, and South Africa Help the SJC? 38 New Eng. L. Rev. 505 (2004). On Croatia, *see also* Dubravka Hrabar, The Protection of Weaker Family Members: The Ombudsman for Children, Same-Sex Unions, Family Violence and Family Law, in The International Survey of Family Law 111 (2004). On Lithuania, *see* Sarunas Keserauskas, "Moving in the Same Direction"? Presentation of Family Law Reforms in Lithuania, in *id.* at 314, 332-334. For additional information on European developments generally, *see* Caroline Forder, European Models of Domestic Partnership Laws: The Field of Choice, 17 Can. J. Fam. L. 371 (2000).

South America   The trend to assimilate cohabitation to marriage is quite pronounced in Latin America. Wolfram Muller-Freinenfels, Cohabitation and Marriage Law—A Comparative Study, 1 Int'l J.L. & Fam. 259, 262 (1987). For example, in several countries a court may approve the registration of a nonmarital relationship that retroactively gives all the effects of marriage. In some countries one partner alone can make such a request; in other countries the request must be made by the parties jointly. The minimum time period ranges from ten years in Panama to three years in Guatemala to two years in Bolivia. In Cuba no time limit is set; instead, a judicial finding that the relationship is monogamous and permanent is required. *Id.* at 264. In addition, in some countries a cohabitation relationship of sufficient duration gives rise to community property rights. *Id.* at 265. In contrast, in 2003 the Colombian Congress defeated proposed legislation that would have provided some property rights to same-sex couples, with the prevailing legislators arguing that the act would undermine the family. Patricia Alzate Monroy, Legal Update from Colombia: The Project for a Law Giving Equal Status to Same-Sex Couples is Finally Sunk, in The International Survey of Family Law 99 (2004).

FAMILY DISSOLUTION

II

FAMILY DISSOLUTION

Divorce Grounds and Procedures

5

A. INTRODUCTION

It is possible to trace the history of divorce to the tension between the Christian doctrine of the indissolubility of marriage and Roman (secular) law that came to tolerate and practice free divorce. The Anglo-American tradition, however, derives most directly from the Christian tradition. Anglo-American law, following canon law, distinguished among three procedures: annulment, separation, and divorce. A decree of annulment, theoretically based on a defect existing at the time of the original contract of marriage (such as fraud, lack of consent, or bigamy), declared that the marriage had never existed in law.

Judicial separation was long referred to as divorce "from bed and board," or *a mensa et thoro*. Judicial separation provides a very specific and limited form of relief. Its major consequence is to free one party from the obligation to cohabit. Spouses had a right of separation in only certain, narrowly defined circumstances: typically, cruelty or endangerment, neglect, desertion, and intemperance. Spouses who found themselves in immediate physical danger generally had adequate grounds for a legal separation. Separation statutes ordinarily authorized courts to divide property, order payment of alimony, and make custody awards if there were children.

Divorce *a mensa*, or judicial separation, was for some time regarded as a dangerous remedy by the courts. Because the spouses were not free to remarry, they were left formally with a choice between celibacy and loneliness on the one hand and adultery on the other. Moreover, a guilty husband's support duty continued in force despite the separation. Accordingly, this form of relief was thought appropriate only when circumstances made it necessary. As the court in Evans v. Evans, 1 Hag. Con. 35, 37, 161 Eng. Rep. 466, 467 (1790), put it in explaining why only serious cruelty would justify divorce *a mensa*,

That the duty of cohabitation is released by the cruelty of one of the parties is admitted, but the question occurs, What is cruelty? . . . This . . . must be understood, that it is the duty of Courts . . . to keep the rule extremely strict. The causes must be grave and weighty, and such as show an absolute impossibility that the duties of married life can be discharged. In a state of personal danger no duties can be discharged . . . but what falls short of this is with great caution to be admitted. Ending that essential aspect of marriage seemed justified only when one party has behaved so as to make cohabitation dangerous or otherwise unthinkable.

And, indeed, judicial separations were rare in this country in the nineteenth century. This is not, of course, the same thing as saying that separations were rare, only that formal relief was uncommon. As Hendrik Hartog has shown, there was little that courts could do to prevent a separation that was agreeable to both parties, whether because of other opportunities or lack of mutual sympathy. While one spouse could complain of unilateral separation for an extended time (abandonment), there was no one to complain in instances of consensual separation. Courts could not practically compel spouses to live together or force them to secure a divorce. In practice, as Hartog suggests, "By the 1840s, perhaps earlier, separating had become an exercise of unchallengeable private freedom." Hendrik Hartog, Man and Wife in America: A History 30 (2000).

While annulment and separation were remedies available from courts for some time, divorce in the sense we know it — termination of the marital relationship — was not available in England or much of the United States until relatively recently. Except for those few persons with enough wealth and influence to secure a private bill of divorce from Parliament, England was a "divorceless society" until enactment of the Marital Causes Act of 1857.

Most of the southern colonies followed English law of the time and did not recognize judicial divorce. However, a number of northern colonies (especially those more influenced by Protestant than by Church of England doctrine, such as Massachusetts) did permit judicial termination of marriages. *See* Nelson M. Blake, The Road to Reno 36-39 (1977). After the American Revolution, the northern states generally adopted laws providing for judicial divorce, and by 1800 every New England state and many mid-Atlantic states had done so. However, divorce remained rare or unknown in the southern states until after the Civil War. And because dissolution divorce was adopted by legislatures rather than courts in those states, its availability is considered wholly a matter for legislatures. There is no inherent equitable jurisdiction regarding divorce.

Throughout much of the nineteenth century and the first half of the twentieth, the divorce issue was much debated. The debate sometimes concerned whether judicial divorce should be allowed. It sometimes centered on the existence of "divorce mill" states: jurisdictions that granted divorces easily and without much regard for marital domicile. These states seem always to have existed in one place, originally in Connecticut and then in a number of western states (Indiana, then Utah and Idaho, and most famously Nevada). The grounds on which divorce should be allowed has occupied much of our attention in the last half-century.

In all of these debates, the themes that we encountered at the outset reappear. Religion continues to play a prominent part in discussions of divorce, although less overtly than it did in the nineteenth century, when courts and commentators more comfortably invoked religious argument. We have already seen the influence of religious argument in connection with plural marriage. Views on marriage must be related to laws on divorce, since the distinctive effect of dissolution divorce is that it dissolves a marriage. The Archbishop of Canterbury may be considered the primary opponent of no-fault divorce in England, and it is claimed that his opposition in the 1960s to a bill permitting divorce after seven years' separation accounted for withdrawal of that proposed legislation. *See* Olive M. Stone, The Matrimonial Causes Act and Reconciliation Bill 1963, 3 J. Fam. L. 87 (1963); J. Herbie DiFonzo, No-Fault Marital Dissolution: The Bitter Triumph of Naked Divorce, 31 San Diego L. Rev. 519, 532 (1994). In this country, religious opposition to judicial divorce, and then to no-fault divorce, is long-standing and well established. To take only one example, opposition by the Roman Catholic Church largely accounted for the limitation of divorce in New York to cases of adultery until 1967, although many efforts to liberalize the law had arisen during the preceding three decades. *See* Herbert Jacob, The Silent Revolution: The Transformation of Divorce Law in the United States 30-37 (1988).

The countervailing position had both religious and secular roots. The religious roots can be found in the Protestant view regarding divorce as an acceptable solution to marital failure. The secular roots can be found in the tradition of Roman law and, more recently, in a strong version of liberalism that values individual choice and the pursuit of satisfaction and doubts the capacity of government to better assess what is good and virtuous than can individuals.

While the divorce issue has commanded a great deal of public and heated discussion, it is part of a larger set of trends related to the incidence and stability of marriage in this country. It is certainly true that divorce has become far more common and had become, by the turn of the twenty-first century, statistically normal. This trend extends back over a century, although the rate seems to have reached a plateau at slightly less than 50 percent of all marriages. However, Larry L. Bumpass suggests that "[t]he plateau . . . must be interpreted in light of this history, and in recognition of the similar plateau that preceded the sharp upturn of the late 1960s. It is likely that the processes underlying this long-term decrease in the stability of marriages have not yet fully run their course." Larry L. Bumpass, The Declining Significance of Marriage: Changing Family Life in the United States 3 (1994).

More generally, demographers and others who study family and household relationships have noted the declining importance of marriage in this country and abroad. The proportion of all households headed by married couples fell from 77 percent in 1950 to 61 percent in 1980 and 55 percent in 1993. The 2000 census puts that figure at slightly under 52 percent. A number of phenomena other than divorce also have contributed to that decline.

We have already observed one substantial factor: a substantial increase in unmarried cohabitation (see pages 229-230 in Chapter 4). Other phenomena related to the marriage rate among households include a substantial increase in the age of first marriage (from the 1960s to now, up 4 years, to 24 years of age for women and 26 for men), a notable decrease in the age of first intercourse (with the proportion of youths between 15 and 20 years old doubling over the last two decades and 75 percent of teenagers reporting having intercourse before age 20), and finally, unlike most other countries, an increase in unintended pregnancies and childbearing, with most of the increase occurring among white women. Bumpass, above.

The question, of course, is what to make of all of this. So far as our current subject, divorce, is concerned, it would be fair to consider the change in divorce laws a natural experiment in domestic relations. It is not an experiment carried out in a laboratory with carefully developed and sharply focused hypotheses, conducted under controlled conditions, but a wide-ranging series of experiments affecting, over the last 25 years, millions of people. The divorce reform experiment rested, of course, on a series of premises. Underlying those premises was, as Carl Schneider points out in an article excerpted below, a significant shift in the nature of public discourse — one that deemphasized moral discourse in favor of instrumental claims, and especially the psychological goal of individual satisfaction. Carl E. Schneider, Moral Discourse and the Transformation of American Law, 83 Mich. L. Rev. 1803 (1985). For spouses, it was said, divorce was a liberating experience, allowing escape from marriages that had ended emotionally but whose continuation was required by prior divorce policy. From a family therapeutic point of view, the situation at divorce was not one of "no fault" but "equal fault," providing no basis for holding the marriage together and, indeed, an occasion for concluding that a clean break would be desirable. Law and therapy agreed that divorce reform meant greater happiness or satisfaction for members of the divorcing family. See Barbara Dafoe Whitehead, The Divorce Culture 53-65 (1997).

Contrary to the earlier belief that divorce is catastrophic for children, supporters of divorce reform further asserted that ending a troubled marriage would ease the situation of children in homes where the marital relationship had broken down by removing them from conflict between their parents. E.g., Susan Gettleman & Janet Markovitz, The Courage to Divorce 86-87 (1974) (suggesting that divorce "can liberate children"). Even more optimistically, it was suggested that "creative divorce" might make children more sensitive and tolerant. See Mal Krantzler, Creative Divorce: A New Opportunity for Growth 211 (1974). For a review of the early literature setting forth the benefits of divorce for children, see Barbara Dafoe Whitehead, supra at 84-91.

There is, however, something of a counterrevolutionary movement. Legislators in a number of states have proposed bills to reintroduce fault grounds, lengthier waiting periods, or both, either generally or where only one spouse seeks divorce. See Laura Bradford, Note, The Counter-Revolution: A Critique of Recent Proposals to Reform No-Fault Divorce Laws, 49 Stan. L. Rev. 607, 618 (1997). These proposals seem to rest on beliefs that no-fault divorce has led to escalating divorce rates, the disintegration of families, and harm to children who will be raised in single-parent households. To date, three states have taken a relatively small step in this direction: the creation of "covenant marriage." The first statute recognizing this form of marriage was Louisiana HB 756, enacted June 23, 1997. This legislation, codified in La. Stat. Ann. §9:272 et seq. (West 1999), allows parties to choose between "regular marriage," allowing no-fault divorce if the parties have lived separate and apart for 180 days, and covenant marriage, in which the parties formally agree that a "[c]ovenant marriage is for life." Parties to a covenant marriage are exempted from the generally applicable divorce provisions under La. Civ. Code §§102-103 (1999) and agree to seek a dissolution only "when there has been a complete and total breach of the marital covenant commitment. . . ." La. Stat. Ann. §272 (West 1999).

To a considerable extent, both the divorce revolution and the proposed counterrevolution rest on empirical claims about the effectiveness and effects of law. How does one evaluate such claims? As with any extant or proposed social innovation, one might ask whether this change produced the promised results and whether it produced any unexpected or undesired outcomes. One might further ask whether divorce reform or counterrevolution will address the more general question of marital stability, and whether that question needs addressing. Finally, and perhaps most important, one might ask what kinds of values should shape discourse about marriage and divorce.

CARL E. SCHNEIDER, *MORAL DISCOURSE AND THE TRANSFORMATION OF FAMILY LAW*

83 Mich. L. Rev. 1803, 1806-1810, 1819, 1827 (1985)

In this paper . . . I propose as a fruitful area of generalization the relationship between morals and family law, for few approaches offer so clear an insight into "the ends which the several rules of family law seek to accomplish" or "the reasons why those ends are desired." This is true for several reasons.

First, while morals and law need not coincide, any law must cope with the way the people it regulates regard their moral relations. This is particularly true of family law: moral issues are central to family life and family self-governance, and hence central to the context in which family law operates. . . . Moral issues arise specially often in the family, where their effect can be specially momentous and their resolution specially hard. For in marrying we take responsibilities for the welfare and happiness of someone who, trusting our assurances, has trusted that welfare and happiness to us; and in having children, we take responsibilities for the welfare and happiness — even the existence — of people who must trust that welfare and happiness to us. . . .

Second, while morals and law need not coincide, the moral views of citizens and of lawmakers shape, properly, their opinions about the law. Once again, this is specially true of family law. Because people have tenacious and passionate beliefs about family morals, because many people believe that law should vindicate right in matters so important, moral principles are deliberately and expressly incorporated in statute and case law. And for these same reasons, moral sentiments influence lawmakers unawares. . . .

Fourth, the relationship between morals and family law merits attention because American views about morals, especially family morals, have changed abundantly. We need to know how thoroughgoing those changes are and how they have influenced our thinking and our family law, in order that we may eventually ask how desirable those changes are and how far they should affect family law. . . .

We come now to the first formulation of my hypothesis. Four forces in American institutions and culture have shaped modern family law. They are the legal tradition of noninterference in family affairs, the ideology of liberal individualism, American society's changing moral beliefs, and the rise of "psychologic man." These forces have occasioned a crucial change: a diminution of the law's discourse in moral terms about the relations between family members, and the transfer of many moral decisions from the law to the people the law once regulated. I do not mean that this change is complete or will ever be completed. I do not suppose that it is occurring in every aspect of family law, or everywhere in the country with equal speed. I emphasize that there are other trends, and that there is a considered and considerable reaction to the trend impelled by a revived conservatism and a politicized fundamentalism. But I do suggest that the change is widespread jurisdictionally, institutionally, and doctrinally; that it is deep-seated; and that it is transforming family law. . . .

Divorce is among the clearest examples of the change I discern. For over a century, divorce law reflected and sought to enforce society's sense of the proper moral relations between husband and wife. Indeed, the law of divorce was virtually the only law that spoke directly or systematically to an ideal of marital relations. That ideal included duties of life-long mutual responsibility and fidelity from which a spouse could be relieved, roughly speaking, only upon the serious breach of a moral duty by the other spouse. In the last two decades, however, every state has statutorily permitted some kind of no-fault divorce. These reforms exemplify the trend I hypothesize because (1) they represent a deliberate decision that the morality of each divorce is too delicate and complex for public, impersonal, and adversarial discussion; (2) they represent a decision that the moral standard of life-long fidelity ought no longer be publicly enforced; and (3) they represent a decision to diminish the extent of mutual spousal responsibility that will be governmentally required.

It is, of course, true that no-fault divorce rests in part on a moral view about the relations of people to each other and about the proper scope of government influence over people's lives. Thus I am far from suggesting that the decision to adopt no-fault divorce was itself amoral or immoral. Rather, my point is that, before no-fault divorce, a court discussed a petition for divorce in moral terms; after no-fault divorce, such a petition did not have to be discussed in moral terms. Before no-fault divorce, the law stated a view of the moral prerequisites to divorce; after no-fault divorce, that law is best seen as stating no view on the subject. Before no-fault divorce, the law retained for itself much of the responsibility for the moral choice whether to divorce; after no-fault, most of that responsibility was transferred to the husband and wife. . . .

I have described a series of doctrinal developments that support the hypothesis that moral discourse in family law has diminished and that responsibility for moral decisions has been transferred from the law. This description not only supports that hypothesis; it also allows us to amplify it, for there has been an associated change in the nature of the moral discourse—namely, a change away from aspirational morality. The family law we inherited from the nineteenth century sought not just to regulate family life, but to set a standard of behavior not readily attainable. That law enunciated and sought to enforce an ideal of lifelong marital fidelity and responsibility. Attempts to diminish the responsibilities of one spouse to the other were denied legal force by prohibitions against altering the state-imposed terms of the marriage contract. Divorce was discouraged, was justified primarily by serious misconduct by a spouse, and was available only to the innocent. Marital responsibility in the form of alimony continued even where the marriage itself had ended. The old family law also enunciated what might be called an ascetic ideal. Sexual restraint in various forms was a prominent part of this ideal. Laws prohibiting fornication, cohabitation, and adultery confined sexual relations to marriage; laws declining to enforce contracts based on meretricious consideration and laws giving relief in tort for interference with the marital relationship sought to achieve the same effect indirectly. Sexual relations were confined to monogamous marriage by laws prohibiting polygamy and to exogamous marriage by laws prohibiting incest. . . .

Modern family law, as this survey suggests, not only rejects some of the old standards as meaningless, undesirable, or wrong; it also hesitates to set standards that cannot readily be enforced or that go beyond the minimal responsibility expressed in the cant phrase "Do your own thing, as long as you don't hurt anybody else." The standard embodied in that phrase, with its emphasis on its first clause, is emphatically not aspirational; that standard can instill neither the inspiration nor the empathy to encourage people to anticipate ways in which their conduct might be harmful, much less to shape their conduct so that it is actively helpful. . . .

. . . In some sense every legal decision is a "moral" decision. For instance, one might say that a resolution of a legal issue in terms of economic efficiency is also a resolution in moral terms, since there is available a moral basis for resolving legal issues on economic grounds. . . . Nevertheless, legal actors and those they govern distinguish between decisions made on moral grounds and decisions made on social, economic, psychological, or "legal" grounds. . . .

B.   THE TRADITIONAL DIVORCE SYSTEM

1.   Grounds for Divorce

This section examines the grounds for and defenses or bars to divorce under the traditional fault system. Until the last half-century, an action for divorce could be successful only when these conditions were met. The grounds and defenses themselves retain importance in many jurisdictions, where both fault and no-fault grounds may be asserted in a dissolution proceeding. The assumptions behind a fault-based system are no less important than the grounds, both in themselves and in assessing the desirability of a return, wholly or in part, to the traditional standards for divorce.

The fault system, reflecting public disfavor of divorce except in extreme situations, was embodied in statutes articulating the grounds for divorce with more or less specificity. The New Hampshire statute of 1901 is illustrative:

NEW HAMPSHIRE PUBLIC STATUTES CHAPTER 175, §5 (1901)

§5. Causes of divorce, what are.

A divorce from the bonds of matrimony shall be decreed in favor of the innocent party for either of the following causes:

I. Impotency of either party.

II. Adultery of either party.

III. Extreme cruelty of either party to the other.

IV. Conviction of either party of crime punishable in this state with imprisonment for more than a year, and actual imprisonment under such conviction.

V. When either party has so treated the other as seriously to injure health.

VI. When either party has so treated the other as seriously to endanger reason.

VII. When either party has been absent three years together, and has not been heard of.

VIII. When either party is an habitual drunkard, and has been such for three years together.

IX. When either party has joined any religious sect or society which professes to believe the relation of husband and wife unlawful, and has refused to cohabit with the other for six months together.

X. When either party, without sufficient cause, and without the consent of the other, has abandoned and refused, for three years together, to cohabit with the other.

XI. When the husband has willingly absented himself from the wife for three years together, without making suitable provision for her support and maintenance.

XII. When the wife of any citizen has willingly absented herself from her husband without his consent for three years together.

XIII. When the wife of any citizen has gone to reside beyond the limits of this state, and has remained absent and separate from her husband ten years together, without his consent and without returning to claim her marriage rights.

XIV. When the wife of any alien or citizen of another state, living separate, has resided in this state for three years together, her husband having left the United States with the intention of becoming a citizen of some foreign country, and not having during that period come into this state and claimed his marital rights, and not having made suitable provision for his wife's support and maintenance.

Modern divorce statutes often include provisions resembling those incorporated in the New Hampshire law, even when they also include "no-fault" grounds. As of 2004, 32 states retained traditional fault grounds for divorce, including the states with a covenant marriage option. Linda D. Elrod & Robert G. Spector, A Review of the Year in Family Law, chart 4, 37 Fam. L.Q. 527, 580 (2004).

KUCERA V. KUCERA

117 N.W.2d 810 (N.D. 1962)

STRUTZ, J. (on reassignment). The plaintiff brought this action for divorce, alleging extreme mental cruelty. The defendant in his answer denies the material allegations of the plaintiff's complaint and counterclaims on grounds of adultery and extreme cruelty.

The record discloses that the parties were married on September 17, 1955. At the time of the marriage, the plaintiff was pregnant by another man, a certain Mr. K_____, and the child who was born to her, less than seven months after the marriage, admittedly is not the child of the defendant. The plaintiff herself, testifying in this case, stated that she had had no sexual relations with the defendant prior to their marriage. She contends, however, that this child, having been born into the family of the defendant after their marriage and the defendant having married the plaintiff with full knowledge of her pregnant condition, should be held to have been adopted at its birth by the defendant and that the defendant is liable for its support as one standing *in loco parentis*.

The record further discloses that the parties themselves were extremely doubtful whether the marriage would be a successful one, even before it was consummated. The plaintiff testified that they had agreed, before marriage, that "if the marriage didn't work out we could get a divorce in a year, but it would give the child a name."

After the birth of this child, a second child was born and, for a period of more than two years before the commencement of this action, the parties ceased to have any marital relations. The defendant testified positively that:

We have had no sexual relations since Robin was born.

The plaintiff does not deny this. There is evidence in the record that the defendant did call the plaintiff names and that, on at least one occasion, he struck her. He also called the first child, who admittedly is not his child, some obscene names.

The differences of the parties finally were brought to a head when the defendant, returning home unexpectedly one evening from the college where he was working on a thesis, discovered Mr. K_____, the man who had fathered the plaintiff's first child, in the home with the plaintiff. The plaintiff thereupon admitted that Mr. K_____ had been calling on her for a period of more than six months, as often as once a week. This was in the month of March 1959. The parties continued to live under the same roof until the end of the school year in June, when this action was commenced by the plaintiff.

On this record the trial court granted to the plaintiff a decree of divorce, and ordered the defendant to make monthly payments for the support of the plaintiff and for the support of the two children born during the marriage. From this judgment the defendant has appealed, demanding a trial de novo. . . .

The plaintiff's cause of action is based on an allegation of extreme cruelty. "Extreme cruelty" is the infliction by one party to a marriage of grievous bodily injury or grievous mental suffering upon the other. Sec. 14-05-05, N.D.C.C.

A divorce may be granted in North Dakota on the grounds of grievous mental suffering, even though such suffering produces no bodily injury.

Does the record disclose conduct on the part of the defendant which would tend to so wound the feelings of the plaintiff that her health was impaired, and were the actions of the defendant such as to destroy the ends of the marriage? We have examined the entire record carefully. The plaintiff did testify to some instances in which the defendant's language and custom was such that she alleges it caused her extreme mental anguish. While the evidence supporting the plaintiff's cause of action is not very strong, the trial court did find that such evidence was sufficient to entitle her to a divorce.

The defendant, however, has counterclaimed for a divorce on grounds of extreme cruelty and on grounds of adultery. On reading the entire record, we believe that the plaintiff also was guilty of conduct which, standing alone, would entitle the defendant to a decree of divorce. For a period of more than six months, the plaintiff was allowing Mr. K_____, the man who was the father of her first child, to call on her at the home of the parties. True, the plaintiff contends that he called against her wishes, but the plaintiff does admit that these calls were continued, more or less regularly, for a period of more than six months. The plaintiff must have given some cooperation to Mr. K_____, at least to the extent of informing him as to what hours the defendant would be absent from the home.

The plaintiff has denied positively any acts of adultery during the six months of such visits. It is difficult to believe that the man who was the father of her child continued to call on her for more than six months without resuming such relationship as they had had prior to the marriage of the plaintiff and the defendant. While the court, ordinarily, will not require direct evidence on a charge of adultery, the trial court did believe the statements of the plaintiff when she testified that she had had no relations with Mr. K_____ during these visits. While the evidence is such that it is difficult to believe the plaintiff's testimony on this point, we cannot say that the evidence is so strong that the trial court clearly erred in this finding. . . .

Although the defendant failed to prove his charge of adultery to the satisfaction of the trial court, we do believe that he did prove a cause of action on the ground of extreme cruelty. Here, the defendant had married the plaintiff knowing that she had had previous relations with Mr. K_____ and that she was pregnant and with child by Mr. K_____ at the time of the marriage of the parties. Thereafter, he discovered that, for more than six months, the plaintiff was visited by the same Mr. K_____ in the home of the parties. Certainly that is sufficient evidence to substantiate a charge of extreme cruelty.

But that is not all. The defendant introduced evidence which would have justified a decree of divorce in his favor on grounds of desertion. He testified that "we have had no sexual relations since Robin was born," which was well over two years before the commencement of this action. The plaintiff did not deny this, nor did she try to justify her refusal to have reasonable sexual relations with the defendant, for physical or health reasons. She merely testified, "I couldn't stand to have sexual relations with him," and then admitted that her refusal was not due to physical or health reasons. . . .

Our statute defines "willful desertion" to include "persistent refusal to have reasonable matrimonial intercourse as husband and wife when health or physical condition does not make such refusal reasonably necessary. . . ." Sec. 14-05-06, Subsec. 1, N.D.C.C.

It is true that the defendant alleged only extreme cruelty and adultery as grounds for divorce in his counterclaim. But, under the Rules of Civil Procedure now in force in North Dakota, when issues not raised by the pleadings are tried by express or implied consent of the parties, they shall be tried in all respects as if they had been raised by the pleadings. . . .

Therefore, since the defendant did prove a cause of action for divorce on grounds of desertion as well as on grounds of extreme cruelty, we have a situation where both parties have established a cause of action for divorce.

Section 14-05-10 of the North Dakota Century Code provides:

"Divorces must be denied upon showing: . . .
"4. Recrimination; . . . ."

Section 14-05-15 reads:

"Recrimination is a showing by the defendant of any cause of divorce against the plaintiff in bar of the plaintiff's cause of divorce. . . ."

This court repeatedly has held that the above statutes are an absolute bar to divorce in a case where both the plaintiff and the defendant plead and prove facts constituting statutory grounds for divorce against each other.

This court, in these and other cases, pointed out that, where the Legislature has given the same legal effect to every recognized cause for divorce, it is not for the court to determine the gravity of the different causes which are proved.

Thus, where recrimination is proved, as it was in this case, a divorce must be denied to both of the parties. This is true even though we believe the legitimate ends of the marriage have been destroyed and a divorce perhaps would be the better solution for the difficulties facing the parties. The provisions of our statute on recrimination are mandatory, and a divorce "must be denied" upon a showing of recrimination. The court has no discretion in the matter and must follow the mandatory wording of the law.

The judgment of the trial court granting a divorce to the plaintiff must therefore be reversed, and a new judgment shall be entered denying a divorce to either party.

SIMPSON V. SIMPSON

716 S.W.2d 27 (Tenn. 1986)

FONES, J. Plaintiff's original complaint sought a divorce on the ground of irreconcilable differences but was later amended to assert cruel and inhuman treatment and abandonment and non-support. Defendant filed a pro se answer denying that he had been guilty of cruel and inhuman treatment or abandonment and non-support. The case was tried on 22 May 1984 and 10 September 1984. Defendant was represented by counsel at the trial. Plaintiff's proof consisted of her testimony and the testimony of two corroborating witnesses. Defendant did not testify and the only evidence he presented was the testimony of Dr. Adolph Seigmann in support of his defense of insanity. . . .

The parties were married 4 March 1973. She was twenty years of age and he was twenty-nine. . . .

Plaintiff testified that their trouble began about three months after they were married. She testified that he has repeatedly told her that she was dumb, unattractive, called her a "bitch" and threatened to "push her face in." He constantly criticized her cooking and her housekeeping and said he could not understand how she could hold a job because she was not a good worker. She testified that he frequently called her at work, as many as two and three times a day, to complain about something she had not done at home or had done wrong according to his view or to report that he could not find some object. On one occasion he called her at work and asked if she had taken his checkbook; and receiving a negative response, he demanded that she search her purse. He picked her up after work and immediately searched her purse himself. When they got home, her dresser drawers were "turned over." It was later discovered that he had left his checkbook in his parents' car. Plaintiff testified that these constant calls at work were very disturbing and upsetting to her.

Defendant complained that she did not make enough money to provide him with the things he wanted. In the spring before the separation, although they had no money for such things, he bought equipment for his parents' new boat and charged two to three hundred dollars to accounts that plaintiff was responsible for. On occasion when she would try to talk to him about their problems, he would threaten to "punch [her] face in."

In July 1982, plaintiff's parents paid her plane fare so that she could visit them in El Paso, Texas, during her vacation. When she returned, defendant met her at the plane and "was very quiet and withdrawn." Later that night, after she had gone to bed, he told her that it was unfair that she could go on vacation and he could not. He found some souvenirs that she had bought and threw them around the room and went to the kitchen and ran the garbage disposal for an unusual period of time. Plaintiff went in to investigate and found that he was throwing all of the food in the refrigerator down the garbage disposal. When she asked what was going on, defendant ordered her out of the room.

Plaintiff was afraid to stay in the house with him and called a friend, Carol Schraw, who agreed to pick her up and provide her a place to stay. Plaintiff then called the police. Defendant came into the bedroom and asked if she had called the police. She responded in the affirmative. Defendant immediately headed for the closet where he kept his handguns. Plaintiff ran out of the house and left with Ms. Schraw, who had arrived to pick her up. She resided with Ms. Schraw about ten days. After the plaintiff and defendant had a long talk, defendant promised to control his temper and try to work things out and plaintiff returned to their home.

A few months later, defendant returned to the pattern of abuse described herein. Plaintiff moved out of their home and filed a complaint for divorce on the ground of irreconcilable differences.

Soon thereafter defendant called and asked to take her to lunch to discuss their problems. Plaintiff reluctantly agreed, and defendant picked her up and drove to Bowling Green, Kentucky. After they were on Interstate 65 headed for Kentucky, plaintiff asked where they were going and defendant pulled a handgun from under the seat and showed it to plaintiff. Defendant told plaintiff there was a Bible, writing paper and stamps under the seat and that she should write to her father because he was going to kill her. Plaintiff became ill twice and defendant stopped to allow her to "be sick by the road side." On each occasion defendant warned plaintiff that if she attempted to get away or attract attention, "something drastic would happen." In Bowling Green, defendant allowed plaintiff to go to a restroom in a gas station. When plaintiff came out, he canvassed the restroom to see if she had left a message of distress.

Plaintiff testified that on the trip to Bowling Green defendant made a lot of promises to do better if she would return home and live with him and that she promised to do so only because she felt it was the only way to get back to Nashville. Plaintiff persuaded defendant to take her to the place where she was residing; but first defendant went by their house, gathered up all of his handguns and put them in the car. Defendant told her that he was going to distribute them to the members of his family and that, if he was picked up by the police, he would get out on bail, get access to one of those guns and kill her or a member of her family. Plaintiff testified that she was afraid to live with defendant.

Defendant's acts of cruelty were adequately corroborated by plaintiff's witnesses Patricia Wallenburg and Carol Schraw.

At the conclusion of the hearing on 22 May 1984 defendant moved for a dismissal of plaintiff's complaint on the ground of defendant's insanity and submitted the deposition of Dr. Adolph Seigmann, taken 17 April 1984 for use in evidence and filed 21 May in support of the alleged insanity. The trial judge took the motion under advisement and adjourned the hearing for a later setting. On 27 July the trial judge entered an order denying defendant's motion and setting 10 September 1984 as the date to hear the remainder of the proof.

Doctor Seigmann was the only witness that testified at the second hearing. . . .

Doctor Seigmann testified that defendant was suffering from a psychosis known as paranoid schizophrenia, that he had probably been so afflicted since age twenty to twenty-two and that "schizophrenia is never ending." But, he said, defendant would appear to be normal when not under the influence of a "severe episode." His testimony was ambiguous and contradictory on the question of whether defendant had lucid intervals. He appeared to express the opinion that defendant was able to control his behavior and act and appear normal at all times except when he was having a severe episode. . . .

. . . [T]he trial judge asked two questions to ascertain whether, if the cruel and inhuman treatment complained of by plaintiff consisted of fits of rage and temper tantrums, the defendant would be responsible for these actions. To each question Dr. Seigmann responded, "I don't think so." It appears that the trial judge based his decree on the answers to those two questions when he dismissed plaintiff's complaint, "for lack of statutory grounds . . . owing to insanity of defendant."

The Court of Appeals granted plaintiff a divorce on the grounds of cruel and inhuman treatment. In granting that relief, the intermediate court reasoned that mentally ill persons may be held liable in tort if malice or evil intent is not a necessary element. Since the abolition of interspousal immunity in Davis v. Davis, 657 S.W.2d 753 (Tenn. 1983), "it would be anomalous to hold that a spouse can obtain a recovery in a tort action against a mentally ill spouse but cannot obtain a divorce based upon the same facts." Defendant's abduction of his wife and threats to kill her were tortious acts incompatible with the marital relationship, the court reasoned, and "a spouse's mental illness cannot provide a defense to a complaint for divorce based upon tortious conduct that constitutes cruel and inhuman treatment." . . .

The courts of our sister states have had considerable difficulty in determining when insanity constitutes a bar to an action for divorce. The cases may be classified generally into two groups. Some courts appear to subscribe to the view that insanity is a good defense to an action for divorce without consideration as to the degree or character of insanity that is relied upon as a defense. The majority of the courts and the better reasoned cases consider the degree and the character of the insanity and what direct effect the degree and character of the insanity has upon the plaintiff's proof adduced to make out the cause of action upon the ground for divorce asserted. . . .

This Court has not decided a case wherein insanity has been asserted as a defense to a divorce action on the ground of cruel and inhuman treatment. We think the rule should be that a defendant in a divorce action asserting insanity as a defense to the commission of acts of cruelty must prove that at the time of such conduct, as a result of mental disease or defect, he or she lacked sufficient capacity either to appreciate the wrongfulness of his or her conduct or the volition to control his or her acts. This is the civil equivalent of the insanity rule we adopted in Graham v. State, 547 S.W.2d 531 (Tenn. 1977), applicable to criminal cases. . . . Thus, to successfully defend a divorce action based upon cruel and inhuman treatment, defendant has the burden of proving that he or she was not in remission at the time of the commission of all or a sufficient number of the acts of cruelty relied upon by plaintiff and that plaintiff's proof does not warrant dissolution of the marriage. . . .

The testimony of Dr. Seigmann fails to establish that defendant, as a result of mental illness, lacked capacity to appreciate the wrongfulness of his conduct or the volition to control his actions at the time he committed acts of cruel and inhuman treatment more than sufficient to warrant dissolution of this marriage.

Doctor Seigmann referred several times to the importance of defendant having a "support system." The answers upon which the trial judge relied in his finding were given by Dr. Seigmann under pressure after his having been told by the trial judge what opinion was required to avoid the loss of his patient's "support system." Whatever probative value his opinion might have had, if it had been unambiguous, was destroyed by the trial judge's informing the witness what opinion he would have to express for insanity to constitute a defense to the wife's suit.

The proof was uncontradicted that defendant had inflicted extreme cruelty upon his wife. Beginning three months after the marriage ceremony and continuing for approximately ten years, he had followed a continuing course of abuse and humiliating treatment that consisted of considerably more cruel acts than of fits of rage and temper tantrums. Defendant wholly failed to carry the burden of proving that the many acts of cruelty he committed over that ten year period were committed when, as a result of mental illness, he lacked the capacity to appreciate the wrongfulness of his conduct or the volition to control his actions. Thus plaintiff will be awarded a divorce on the ground of cruel and inhuman treatment.

NOTES AND QUESTIONS

1. The principal cases indicate the content of the most commonly invoked grounds for divorce under the fault system.

a. *Adultery*. Adultery ordinarily is defined as voluntary sexual intercourse by a married person with a person who is not his or her spouse. The element of voluntariness excludes rape from the definition of "adultery." In the traditional view, homosexual relations were not defined as adulterous, but cases seem now inclined to treat them in the same way as extramarital heterosexual relations. *See, e.g.,* Owens v. Owens, 274 S.E.2d 484 (Ga. 1981).

It is one of the oddities of adultery that it typically can be proved by direct evidence only when it did not in fact occur — that is, where one supposedly guilty spouse, typically the husband, agrees to provide the other with manufactured evidence that he has committed adultery so that she can establish a ground for divorce. This practice, which became a cottage industry in New York when adultery was the only available basis for absolute divorce, is discussed later in this section. Absent agreement of this kind, adultery is rarely committed in the presence of others and must be proved by circumstantial evidence. The circumstances that may give rise to an inference that adultery did occur include inclination and opportunity. Whether circumstantial proof actually offered in a divorce case is sufficient is largely a matter for the trial court to decide, as *Kucera*, above, page 295, indicates.

b. *Cruelty*. The definition of "cruelty" was originally developed in connection with divorce *a mensa et thoro*, before absolute divorce was judicially available. The older cases on cruelty required violence or at least intentionally and seriously injurious conduct that reasonably led to fear for life or health.

Although it might reasonably be asked whether the restrictive limitations on the definition of "cruelty" developed in the context of judicial separation or limited divorce should have applied once absolute divorce became available, *see* Lee E. Teitelbaum, Cruelty Divorce Under New York's Reform Act: On Repeating Ancient Error, 23 Buff. L. Rev. 1 (1973), the law in many jurisdictions imported those restrictions, at least initially. Over time, threats to mental as well as physical well-being came to be recognized, more or less generously. However, many courts, while extending the definition of "cruelty," also expressed concern that the definition not be so broad as to reach "mere" incompatibility. Some courts required proof of physical harm to support a divorce based on mental cruelty; some required expert evidence where the effect was emotional rather than physical. Perhaps the most common form of cruelty, at least in reality, may be called general marital unkindness. This includes a variety of forms of misconduct, including ridicule, harassment, false accusations of unfaithfulness, child abuse, relative abuse, and the like. *E.g.,* Stevenson v. Stevenson, 369 P.2d 923 (Utah 1962) (husband falsely accused wife of infidelity, emotional and mental illness, giving him a venereal disease, and — you may think ironically — paranoia). For a collection of cases granting divorce under these circumstances, *see* 2 Homer H. Clark, Jr., Domestic Relations 31-32 (2d ed. 1987).

Ultimately, the law concerning cruel treatment varied substantially at both the formal law and law-in-action levels. Not only did jurisdictions differ considerably in what their appellate decisions required to prove cruelty, but the decisions of trial courts, at least in uncontested cases, seemed to vary from what appellate courts said was needed. Nonetheless, as is evident in *Kucera,* evidentiary decisions by trial courts were often sustained if there was anything to support the trial judge's decision.

Illustrating the maintenance of traditional doctrine for fault-based divorce even where no-fault grounds are available, the New York Court of Appeals held that medical proof remains important, if not always essential, to establishing cruel and inhuman treatment in a long-term marriage. Cruel and inhuman treatment requires a course of conduct "which is harmful to the physical or mental health of the plaintiff, making cohabitation unsafe or improper, and when the marriage is of long duration a high degree of proof of serious or substantial misconduct. . . ." Doyle v. Doyle, 625 N.Y.S.2d 693, 693-694 (N.Y. 1995).

c. *Desertion.* This ground, sometimes called "abandonment" and often described in terms of "willful" desertion, requires departure from the home without the consent of the other and without justification. If there has been consent, it is said, there is no marital wrong and therefore no abandonment. What makes out consent is somewhat disputable, but generally failures to object and offers to reconcile may constitute evidence of consent. *See* 2 Homer H. Clark, Jr., The Law of Domestic Relations in the United States §14.3 (2d ed. 1987).

Justification for departure from the home is a more complicated business. The strictest view is that departure is justified only when the abandoned spouse has engaged in conduct that would itself provide grounds for divorce. If so, the ground serves little purpose. Other jurisdictions view justification more broadly to include conduct that in some way makes cohabitation impossible. *See* 2 H. Clark, above, at 17-18.

Many statutes, like the New Hampshire law, specify a minimum period, ordinarily between one and five years. And, as in New Hampshire, the period must usually be continuous.

In the ordinary desertion, the offending spouse leaves the marital home. However, some cases, including *Kucera,* recognize a "constructive" abandonment — meaning, as the term *constructive* always does, that no such thing occurred. These cases involve conduct by the offending spouse that amounts to marital misconduct on other grounds, which may or may not statutorily be specified. In Kreyling v. Kreyling, 23 A.2d 800 (N.J. 1942), the husband refused to engage in sexual intercourse without the use of a contraceptive. This refusal was held an unjustified course of conduct by the defendant and an instance of constructive desertion. Is it evident how such a decision permits a judicial expansion of the grounds for divorce?

d. *Impotence.* The New Hampshire statute makes impotence a ground for divorce. Does its inclusion seem logical, given the theory of divorce? However, logical or not, some statutes do include preexisting conditions as a basis for divorce.

2. The fault scheme recognized several defenses to divorce. Ordinarily, these are treated as affirmative defenses that must be specifically pleaded and proved.

a. *Insanity.* Insanity is generally recognized as a defense to divorce actions founded on adultery and desertion, as *Simpson*, above, page 297, indicates. Is there any reason for doubt to be expressed with respect to the applicability of that defense to divorce based on cruelty? *See generally* Walter Wadlington, A Case of Insanity and Divorce, 56 Va. L. Rev. 12 (1970).

b. *Connivance.* The theory of divorce is that the misconduct of one spouse has destroyed the marital relationship. Fault grounds may be considered instances of misconduct so grave that such a result may be supposed. In particular circumstances, however, it may appear that either the conduct was not in fact wrongful as to the petitioning spouse or cannot be said to have destroyed the marriage.

One set of circumstances where misconduct otherwise justifying divorce may not suffice arises when the "offending" conduct was in fact agreed to (connived at) by the spouse now seeking the divorce. As a practical matter, this defense is almost entirely limited to adultery, although a similar principle is evident in the requirement that desertion, to support a divorce, must be nonconsensual. For a recent and classic instance, *see* Hollis v. Hollis, 427 S.E.2d 233 (Va. App. 1993). The wife, who wished to divorce her husband, encouraged him to have an affair with someone he met at a Christmas party. In particular, she urged him and the corespondent to rent an apartment for a year and live there as man and wife and, when they did so, sent flowers and a congratulatory note. She then sought a divorce on the grounds of adultery.

Suppose, however, that the petitioning spouse suspects that the other is about to commit adultery and absents himself or herself to permit the gathering of evidence of the wrong. This seems not to be considered connivance. But it has been held connivance where the petitioning spouse simply does not care whether adultery occurs, although he or she does not consent to any such act. *See* 2 H. Clark, Domestic Relations, above, at 55. What is the basis for such a distinction?

c. *Condonation.* Condonation is a defense to most of the grounds of divorce, although its application to cruelty is somewhat unclear. Condonation occurs when the injured spouse, knowing of a marital wrong, continues or resumes marital cohabitation. Although the essence of the defense is said to be forgiveness, that state of mind may be inferred from resumption of marital relations itself.

However, the circumstances in which marital relations are resumed may be important. The New York Supreme Court, Appellate Division, held that an estranged couple's attempt at reconciliation, even where it involves an isolated resumption of cohabitation, or sexual relations, or both, does not, as a matter of law, preclude granting a divorce to a spouse who otherwise had a valid claim for abandonment. "Rather, the trial court should examine the totality of the circumstances surrounding the purported reconciliation, before determining its effect, if any, upon the pending marital proceeding. Among the many factors for the trial court to consider are whether the reconciliation and any cohabitation were entered into in good faith, whether it was at all successful, who initiated it and with what motivation." Haymes v. Haymes, 646 N.Y.S.2d 315, 319 (App. Div. 1996). The court relied in part on prior decisions holding that cohabitation, especially if not in good faith, does not condone a course of cruel conduct in the same way it would condone adultery. *See also* Aronson v. Aronson, 691 A.2d 758 (Md. Ct. Spec. App. 1997) (resumption of sexual relations is evidence of condonation); Nemeth v. Nemeth, 481 S.E.2d 181 (S.C. App. 1997) (no condonation resulting from two nights of cohabitation without sexual relations after wife confessed adultery).

In principle, condonation is conditional; it is forgiveness conditioned on the absence of future wrongdoing. An offense, once condoned, may be "revived" if the offending spouse does not treat the condoning spouse properly. Indeed, the initial wrong may be revived even if the offending spouse's subsequent misconduct is not sufficiently grave to constitute an independent basis for divorce. *Id.* at 63-64.

d. *Recrimination.* The defense of recrimination was raised in *Kucera.* Professor Clark describes recrimination as "a rare combination of silliness, futility and brutality." Homer H. Clark, Jr., Domestic Relations 704 (2d ed. 1979). What is his point?

Some jurisdictions do not recognize recrimination as a bar to divorce but instead look to "comparative rectitude" when both spouses have committed marital fault. *E.g.*, Hendricks v. Hendricks, 257 P.2d 366 (Utah 1953) (where reciprocal claims rest on various acts and omissions alleged to constitute cruelty to the other and neither party is guilty of adultery or felony, the trial court should determine which party was less at fault, grant a divorce, and adjust the spouses' rights).

3. The doctrine of collusion is often listed as a defense to divorce, but in some sense it is a special doctrine. Unlike the other defenses, collusion need not be pleaded or proved. Rather, for reasons obvious by its nature, this bar is ordinarily raised by the court *sua sponte.* The doctrine of collusion is also the clearest evidence of a public interest in the control of marital dissolution.

This bar arises from an agreement between the parties to frustrate the divorce procedure in some way. It may take the form of an agreement to create the appearance of marital wrongdoing when none has in fact occurred. The industry of supplying fictitious evidence of adultery is a familiar example. The defendant and plaintiff would arrange for one of them, usually the husband, to be in bed in a hotel room with an anonymous woman, partially clothed. A photographer would gain entry and "surprise" the couple in that position, and the photograph would provide evidence of adultery. In England, the practice was even simpler; the hotel bill was sent home by the husband, and witnesses testified that he stayed at the hotel and occupied a bedroom with a woman not his wife. Note, Collusive and Consensual Divorce and the New York Anomaly, 36 Colum. L. Rev. 1121 (1936), in AALS, Selected Essays on Family Law 976, 980-981 (1950). This "ordinary hotel evidence" featured in the divorce of Wallis Simpson from her husband Ernest, prior to her marriage to King Edward VIII. *See* H. Montgomery Hyde, Lord Justice 457 (1964). *See also* Lawrence M. Friedman, A Dead Language: Divorce Law and Practice Before No-Fault, 86 Va. L. Rev. 1497, 1512-1515 (2000), on this subject generally and on Dorothy Jarvis, who was the "unknown blonde" in 100 New York divorces, particularly.

Collusion may also arise, or be inferred, from agreements not to defend a case. On the other hand, consent expressed through an agreement to settle the rights of the parties or to grant suit money to the plaintiff is not in principle improper. The line between illegal and legal agreement has often been unclear, and this uncertainty presented problems in the drafting of separation agreements. Even ordinary provisions that one party will sue and the other not defend may be dangerous to include.

Of course, collusion is difficult to identify, since neither party has any interest in its detection. In order to assist courts in avoiding fraud of this sort, England and a few American states created an official whose business it was to root out this "most insidious and surreptitious menace to the courts." *See* Charles S. Connolly, Divorce Proctors, 34 B.U. L. Rev. 1 (1954).

Both the doctrine of collusion and the institution of the divorce proctor reflect the idea that the state is the third party in the marriage contract. The same may be said of the common requirement, mentioned in passing in *Simpson*, above, page 297, that the plaintiff's evidence be corroborated. If this is true, does the state have the power to force a divorce, or separation for policy reasons, against the wishes of the parties?

PROBLEMS

1. A divorce action is brought alleging cruel and inhuman treatment. Plaintiff husband testifies that his wife had for several years repeatedly nagged and scolded him for fancied wrongs on his part and had frequently accused him wrongly of adultery. This, plaintiff says, has resulted in a general decline in his health, loss of sleep, and increased nervousness on his part. Assuming these facts are proved, will a divorce be granted?

2. Plaintiff husband sues for divorce on the ground of his wife's cruelty. Among the counts of cruelty alleged was assault by the wife to force plaintiff into sexual intercourse. Defendant also was alleged to have battered her husband and tormented him by pulling his hair, ears, and nose and by kicking him in his injured leg. In fact, an assault of the sexual variety occurred the night before plaintiff's departure from the matrimonial home. On that occasion, plaintiff did have intercourse with defendant "in order to get some rest and end the attack"; he left home permanently the next morning. Assuming these facts, will the divorce be granted?

If a divorce would not be granted on these facts, would it be more likely available if defendant had kicked plaintiff in his leg once more on the morning that he left home?

3. Plaintiff wife sues for divorce on the ground of adultery. In order to gather evidence, plaintiff told defendant that she was going out of town on business. Instead, she hired a detective, and together they followed defendant to a meeting with *X*. Husband and *X* had dinner together and then went together to *X*'s apartment. Defendant and *X* were in the apartment with the lights out for four hours, until plaintiff and her detective knocked on the door.

Will a divorce be granted on these facts? Would it matter if plaintiff herself had committed adultery?

4. Plaintiff sues for divorce on the grounds of defendant's adultery. During pretrial negotiations, defendant admits having committed adultery and agrees to provide plaintiff with the name of the person with whom he committed the act. Defendant further agrees to pay the costs of the litigation and plaintiff's attorney's fees. Is there any obstacle to the speedy granting of a divorce on these facts?

2. *Divorce Procedure*

Judicial divorce procedure varied substantially during the nineteenth century. Although divorce proceedings were generally governed by rules of civil procedure, they often retained a special quality and were subject to special rules. Perhaps the most striking aspect of divorce procedure is the unwillingness of courts to follow the generally applicable principle that the parties themselves decide whether and how they will conduct a legal dispute. In most areas of private law, courts are not concerned with how a dispute is settled, but only that the dispute be resolved peaceably. Indeed, it is generally considered preferable that disputes be resolved extrajudicially if possible, and judges are free and indeed encouraged to urge parties to settle. Consequently, parties have considerable practical latitude to decide what the law does and does not allow. If a plaintiff files a suit alleging that the defendant, willfully and with malice, called the plaintiff a banana and the defendant decides to pay the plaintiff $35 in damages rather than file a motion to dismiss, nobody will complain. It is assumed that they are entitled to determine their interests in the matter.[1]

In many cases, the defendant may choose not even to participate by not filing an answer or otherwise responding to the complaint. Ordinarily, inaction will be taken as an admission of the facts alleged and will result in a default judgment upon motion of the plaintiff. *See* Federal Rules of Civil Procedure Rule 55.

Traditionally, these principles did not apply to divorce cases. It would be fair to say that procedure in divorce cases was not only generally adversarial but more adversarial than in other litigation. As a formal matter, only the spouses were (and are) parties to most divorce cases.[2] The state is not a party,[3] nor are children of

---

1. There are, of course, exceptions to the authority of parties to determine the outcome of a case by themselves. Some settlements, such as those in class action proceedings, must be approved by a court. *See, e.g.*, Federal Rules of Civil Procedure Rule 23(e): "A class action shall not be dismissed or compromised without the approval of the court. . . ." Such a requirement is explained by the existence of an unusual interest in the matter, held by persons not personally before the court (that is, class members).

2. There are occasional exceptions, as where a third party claims an interest in property that may be disposed of in the course of a divorce action or, in some states, where grandparents are authorized to intervene with respect to custody issues. For a survey of these exceptions, *see* Wm. David Taylor, Third-Party Practice in Divorce Cases, 26 Fam. L.Q. 5 (1992).

3. Although traditional practice in England and some states did require the notification of a public official (in England, the Queen's proctor, whose curious role is discussed at page 305, above).

the marriage regarded as parties. The Michigan Supreme Court, rejecting a suit
by four minor children to set aside a divorce granted to their mother against their
father on the ground that the divorce was collusive, observed as follows:

> The jurisdiction over divorce is purely statutory, and the legislative authority has not
> seen fit to allow any but the parties to intervene in such suits. The husband and wife
> are the only persons recognized as parties.
>
> It is true that the interests of children are in some important respects more
> nearly affected by such proceedings than by those which merely concern rights of
> property. . . . But no court in this country has any power to compel discordant
> husbands and wives to live together, and we do not perceive that any legal rights
> of these infants have been invaded, however much they may have been affected
> otherwise.
>
> It is for the Legislature to determine to what extent public policy requires the
> power of intervention to be vested in any but the parties to divorce suits. There are
> certainly some reasons why it might be wise to have children represented, but
> whether their ultimate prosperity would be furthered by permitting strangers to
> intervene in their behalf between parents, is a question which would probably be
> considered very carefully before any action is taken to permit it. In the mean time
> the courts have no right to sanction any such intervention. . . .

Baugh v. Baugh, 37 Mich. 59, 61-62 (1877).

Third parties other than children may seek to intervene in divorce matters
and are also usually denied party status. *See, e.g.,* Luthen v. Luthen, 596 N.W.2d
278 (Minn. App. 1999) (mother of the husband's out-of-wedlock child not entitled to intervene in divorce to seek property division order that would protect her
child support); Nielson v. Thompson, 982 P.2d 709 (Wyo. 1999) (judgment
denied creditors right to intervene in divorce action involving debtor spouse to
protect their claimed interest in his receiving assets against which they might
execute).

Even though, or perhaps because, only the husband and wife are formal
parties, divorce courts were traditionally unwilling to rely on the parties' determinations of their own interests. Unlike most civil matters, the law is not agnostic about the settlement of marital issues, and, unlike other civil matters, the
remedy sought has traditionally been disfavored. As we have just seen, the circumstances under which a marriage ended were specifically defined by statute
and, at least in principle, afforded relief only in extreme cases. Those statutes
required not only that one spouse have committed particular forms of marital
misconduct but also that the plaintiff not have connived at or condoned the
offense and be himself or herself innocent of marital wrongdoing. Because this
public interest often conflicted with private desires, there was substantial reason
for concern that the parties would both want an outcome prohibited by law.
Thus, many cases hold that a divorce cannot be given by stipulation or default.
Similarly, judgment on the pleadings and summary judgment were often said to
be inappropriate in divorce cases.

> It is the policy of this jurisdiction that no divorce should be granted except on the
> basis of a hearing in open court at which evidence is adduced. The purpose of that
> policy is to prevent collusion in divorce cases. It has been figuratively said, time and

time again, that the public is a third party in every divorce case and has an interest in the preservation of the marriage bond, and that, therefore, no divorce should be granted until after the court hears evidence.

This policy is in part embodied in the District of Columbia Code, Title 16, Section 419, which prohibits the granting of a decree for divorce on default, without proof; and further which provides that any admission contained in a defendant's answer may not be taken as proof of the facts admitted thereby.

Rea v. Rea, 124 F. Supp. 922, 922 (D.D.C. 1954) (disapproving summary judgment in divorce cases). *See also* Brunges v. Brunges, 587 N.W.2d 554 (Neb. 1998), following the view that divorce cases cannot be resolved by stipulation. Both parties filed pleadings stating that the marriage was irretrievably broken. The trial court relied on these pleadings and granted the petition without taking evidence, although the divorce statute requires a hearing at which testimony or deposition evidence is presented. The Nebraska Supreme Court noted that, ordinarily, a court may rely on admissions in pleadings but that, under the dissolution statute, a hearing must be conducted in divorce cases.

Various other rules also expressed the state's reluctance to end a marriage and suspicion of suits to do so. In ordinary civil litigation, affirmative defenses are waived if not specially pleaded in the answer. In divorce matters, however, courts were often authorized to consider affirmative defenses such as condonation and recrimination even if the defendant did not raise that bar. In addition, as late as 1968, more than half of the states took the position that the uncontradicted testimony of one or both spouses was not sufficient to establish grounds for divorce, but must be corroborated in some degree by other evidence or testimony. Homer H. Clark, Jr., Domestic Relations 399-400 (1968).

Concern for preserving marriages was also reflected in various strategies to delay proceedings in the hope of reconciliation. One traditional device treated the initial divorce decree as an interlocutory order or, as it was sometimes called, a decree *nisi* ("unless"). As the name implies, this decree was not final; the parties remained married to each other and, unlike a judicial separation, were not even expected to live apart. Interlocutory decrees were a post-trial strategy for ensuring that grounds for divorce genuinely existed and for encouraging reconciliation. At the end of the interlocutory period, a final decree would be entered unless some legal bar to that relief appeared or the parties themselves terminated divorce proceedings. On interlocutory decrees in general, *see* Note, Interlocutory Decrees of Divorce, 56 Colum. L. Rev. 228 (1956).

A number of states adopted "cooling off" periods prior to trial, a period of delay (anywhere from 20 days to six months) between the time of filing and hearing. These provisions are summarized as of 1968 in Homer H. Clark, Jr., Domestic Relations, above, 387-389. Some jurisdictions added conciliation procedures providing counseling for parties seeking to end their marriage. *See, e.g.,* Louis H. Burke, Conciliation—A New Approach to the Divorce Problem, 30 Cal. St. B.J. 199 (1955). Mandatory conciliation, which was tried in Europe as well as in this country, was generally regarded a failure. *See, e.g.,* Brigitte Bodenheimer, The Utah Marriage Counseling Experiment: An Account of Changes in Divorce Law and Procedure, 7 Utah L. Rev. 443 (1961).

C.   THE ADOPTION OF NO-FAULT DIVORCE

LAWRENCE FRIEDMAN, *RIGHTS OF PASSAGE: DIVORCE LAW IN HISTORICAL PERSPECTIVE*

63 Or. L. Rev. 649, 662, 666-667 (1984)

. . . In almost every state, perjury or something close to it was a way of life in divorce court. . . . In theory, a collusive divorce was illegal. Certainly, perjury was a crime, and so was the manufacture of evidence. Judges had to be aware of what was going on in front of their noses. Yet the system flourished, and the divorce rate grew steadily. There were 7,380 divorces in 1860, or 1.2 per 1000 marriages. There were 167,105 divorces in 1920, or 7.7 per 1000 marriages. The overwhelming majority were collusive and consensual, in fact if not in theory. The legal system winked and blinked and ignored. . . .

. . . The real divorce revolution, arguably, was not the passage of the no-fault statutes. These statutes were a delayed ratification of a system largely in place; a system that was expensive, dirty, and distasteful, perhaps, but a system that more or less worked. If one asks who created that system, the answer is ordinary people and their lawyers. Their demand for easy divorce, their pressure on the system, led to concrete patterns of legal behavior that flourished for a century. Lower court judges, all over the country, accepted the system, but it was not their idea. The structure of divorce law, as it existed between 1870 and 1970, evolved quietly in obscure places, without disturbing the surface of law or altering official norms.

In its middle period, divorce law was a compromise between the instrumental demand for divorce and the opposing moral postulate. The situation was, by common agreement, a mess: costly, ineffective, destructive. Yet it lasted for generations. This sort of clash between instrumental and normative goals, and this sort of stalemate, is by no means rare in the law. Prostitution has been mentioned as another example. Prostitution has been persistently illegal, and persistently tolerated after a fashion. In some cities, at one time, there were even ordinances defining the boundaries of the red light districts which had no legal right to exist. Perhaps wherever there is complexity of doctrine, and a sharp division between theory and practice, a split between instrumental and normative goals is a likely cause. Law is not inherently irrational, or technical, or "legalistic," or confused. A muddled, dualistic system, like the divorce law of 1900 or 1940, cries out for some essentially social explanation.

In the middle of the twentieth century, it was clear to everybody that the system of divorce was a fake: "a solemn if silly comic melodrama," "beneath the dignity of the American court"; a system that "cheapens not only the tribunal but the members of the legal profession who are . . . involved." The question was: What to do about it? One suggestion was to increase the role of the court and to reduce the element of sham. It was felt that a judge should have authority to deal with the entire human drama that lay behind a bill of divorce, and that skilled professionals should be attached to the court to help him. The goal was to set up a true "divorce court," a court of family justice.

This was indeed the philosophy of the Report of the Governor's Commission on the Family, issued in California in 1966. The report called for the destruction of the old system, and paved the way for the California no-fault law of 1970. The Commission demanded an end to "dissimulation, hypocrisy, and . . . perjury." A new law was needed to "allow the therapeutic processes of the Family Court to function with full effectiveness." The "standard" the Commission suggested would "permit — indeed . . . require — the Court to inquire into the whole picture of the marriage."

California did change its law in 1970, and in the next decade, so did almost every state. Yet the "therapeutic" path was most decidedly not the one taken. Instead, the whole house of cards collapsed. For divorces at least — child custody of course is a different animal — the judge did not gain more power and discretion. Instead, in practice he lost what little power he had. No-fault reduced divorce to even greater routine. The social-work or family-court ideal faded away. . . .

Anyone who thinks about conditions of modern life can quickly come up with explanations for the triumph of no-fault; too many, in fact. There is, to begin with, the so-called sexual revolution, which downplays traditional morality, takes away some of the aura that surrounded chastity, and champions a rich, full sex life. There is the cumulative effect of the divorce rate itself; the status is so common that much of its stigma is gone. There is the new role of women, and the new conception of marriage, early signs of which William O'Neill had discovered in the Progressive era. There is the new individualism, with its emphasis on personal choice.

All of these are changes in general culture.

The no-fault divorce revolution was not solely an American phenomenon, as Mary Ann Glendon observes in Abortion and Divorce in Western Law 66-67 (1987):

> Between 1969 and 1985 divorce law in nearly every Western country was profoundly altered. Among the most dramatic changes was the introduction of civil divorce in the predominantly Catholic countries of Italy and Spain, and its extension to Catholic marriages in Portugal. Other countries replaced or amended old strict divorce laws. . . . The chief common characteristics of all these changes were the recognition or expansion of nonfault grounds for divorce, and the acceptance or simplification of divorce by mutual consent. When California in 1969 became the first Western jurisdiction completely to eliminate fault grounds for divorce, the move was thought by some to pre-figure the direction of reforms in other places. But it soon became clear that the purist approach was not to find wide acceptance. That same year England, too, passed a new divorce law which purported to make divorce available only when marriage had irretrievably broken down. But since the English statute permitted marriage breakdown to be proved by evidence of traditional marital offenses as well as by mutual consent or long separation, it did not really

repudiate the old fault system. As it turned out, compromise statutes of the English type (resembling those already in place in Australia, Canada, and New Zealand) became the prevailing new approach to the grounds of divorce.

The following materials suggest the experience under the American no-fault divorce regime and the issues it presents.

1. Grounds for Divorce

UNIFORM MARRIAGE AND DIVORCE ACT

§302 [Dissolution of Marriage; Legal Separation]

(a) The [_____] court shall enter a decree of dissolution of marriage if:

(1) the court finds that one of the parties, at the time the action was commenced, was domiciled in this State, or was stationed in this State while a member of the armed services, and that the domicil or military presence has been maintained for 90 days next preceding the making of the findings;

(2) the court finds that the marriage is irretrievably broken, if the finding is supported by evidence that (i) the parties have lived separate and apart for a period of more than 180 days next preceding the commencement of the proceeding, or . . .

(ii) there is serious marital discord adversely affecting the attitude of one or both of the parties toward the marriage;

(3) the court finds that the conciliation provisions of Section 305 either do not apply or have been met;

(4) to the extent it has jurisdiction to do so, the court has considered, approved, or provided for child custody, the support of any child entitled to support, the maintenance of either spouse, and the disposition of property; or has provided for a separate, later hearing to complete these matters.

(b) If a party requests a decree of legal separation rather than a decree of dissolution of marriage, the court shall grant the decree in that form unless the other party objects.

§305 [Irretrievable Breakdown]

(a) If both of the parties by petition or otherwise have stated under oath or affirmation that the marriage is irretrievably broken, or one of the parties has so stated and the other has not denied it, the court, after hearing, shall make a finding whether the marriage is irretrievably broken.

(b) If one of the parties has denied under oath or affirmation that the marriage is irretrievably broken, the court shall consider all relevant factors, including the circumstances that gave rise to filing the petition and the prospect of reconciliation, and shall:

(1) make a finding whether the marriage is irretrievably broken; or

(2) continue the matter for further hearing not fewer than 30 nor more than 60 days later, or as soon thereafter as the matter may be reached on the

court's calendar, and may suggest to the parties that they seek counseling. The court, at the request of either party shall, or on its own motion may, order a conciliation conference. At the adjourned hearing the court shall make a finding whether the marriage is irretrievably broken.

(c) A finding of irretrievable breakdown is a determination that there is no reasonable prospect of reconciliation.

The UMDA was the result of a compromise worked out in the early 1970s, when the Family Law Section of the American Bar Association objected to the original draft put out by the commissioners. *See* Harvey Zuckman, The ABA Family Law Section v. NCCUSL: Alienation, Separation and Forced Reconciliation over the Uniform Marriage and Divorce Act, 24 Catholic U. L. Rev. 61 (1974); Henry H. Foster & Doris Jonas Freed, Divorce Reform: Brakes on Breakdown, 13 J. Fam. L. 443 (1973-1974).

A New Hampshire statute, Rev. Stat. Ann. §458:7-a (1990), provides a different model. It continues to incorporate fault grounds, which have been recognized since 1901, but now also permits divorce on the ground of irreconcilable differences:

A divorce from the bonds of matrimony shall be decreed, irrespective of the fault of either party, on the ground of irreconcilable differences which have caused the irremediable breakdown of the marriage. In any pleading or hearing of a libel for divorce under this section, allegations or evidence of specific acts of misconduct shall be improper and inadmissible, except where child custody is in issue and such evidence is relevant to establish that parental custody would be detrimental to the child or at a hearing where it is determined by the court to be necessary to establish the existence of irreconcilable differences. If, upon hearing of an action for divorce under this section, both parties are found to have committed an act or acts which justify a finding of irreconcilable differences, a divorce shall be decreed and the acts of one party shall not negate the acts of the other nor bar the divorce decree.

Revised Stat. Ann. §458:7-b provides that no divorce shall be granted when "there is a likelihood for rehabilitation of the marriage" or when "there is a reasonable possibility of reconciliation."

The following case raises questions about the meaning of "irreconcilable" differences in no-fault provisions.

DESROCHERS V. DESROCHERS

---

347 A.2d 150 (N.H. 1975)

KENISON, C.J. The parties married in September 1970. Their only child, a daughter, was born in January 1973. The parties separated in May of that year and the wife brought this libel for divorce the following September. A month later the parties agreed to and the court approved arrangements for custody, visitation and support. The defendant did not support his wife and child from the time of separation until the temporary decree. He made the payments called for by the decree from its entry until June 1975. In July 1974, the Hillsborough County Superior Court, Loughlin, J., held a hearing and made certain findings of fact. The critical portion of these findings is: "[T]he action was originally brought because the defendant did not work steadily and stated that he, when he learned that the plaintiff was pregnant, wanted a boy instead of a girl; if the plaintiff bore a girl he would like to put the child up for adoption. After the birth of the child [a daughter] the defendant became very attached to the child, has visited the child weekly except on two occasions, and has been faithfully making support payments under the temporary order of $25.00 a week. The defendant claims that he loves his wife, does not want a divorce. The wife claims that she no longer loves her husband, but since the filing of the divorce he has been an industrious worker and is very attached to the child." The superior court transferred without ruling the question "whether, on all the findings of fact, cause exists for granting a divorce under the provisions of RSA 458:7-a." This appeal was argued in September 1975. At the argument, counsel informed the court that the defendant had stopped making support payments and had gone to Nevada in June 1975. At that time he had written to his attorney expressing his desire to remain married. . . .

RSA 458:7-a (Supp. 1973) is the product of a national discussion regarding the proper grounds for divorce. It follows in important respects the California Family Law Act of 1969. . . . A consensus has emerged that a period of separation due to marital difficulties is strong evidence of the irremediable breakdown of a marriage. . . . When asked to interpret a statute similar to RSA 458:7-a, the Florida court of Appeal stated: "The Legislature has not seen fit to promulgate guidelines as to what constitutes an 'irretrievably broken' marriage. It is suggested that this lack of definitive direction was deliberate and is desirable in an area as volatile as a proceeding for termination of the marital status. Consideration should be given to each case individually and predetermined policy should not be circumscribed by the appellate courts of this State.

"Thus, we are hesitant to set forth specific circumstances which trial courts could utilize as permissible indices of an irretrievable breakdown of the marital status. Were we to attempt to do so, we feel that the basic purpose of the new dissolution of marriage law would be frustrated. Such proceedings would either again become primarily adversary in nature or persons would again fit themselves into tailor-made categories or circumstances to fit judicially defined breakdown situations. It is our opinion that these two problems are the very ones which the Legislature intended to eliminate." Riley v. Riley, 271 So. 2d 181, 183 (Fla. App. 1972).

The existence of irreconcilable differences which have caused the irremediable breakdown of the marriage is determined by reference to the subjective state of mind of the parties. While the desire of one spouse to continue the marriage is evidence of "a reasonable possibility of reconciliation," it is not a bar to divorce. If one spouse resolutely refuses to continue and it is clear from the passage of time or other circumstances that there is no reasonable possibility of a change of heart, there is an irremediable breakdown of the marriage. The defendant may attempt to impeach the plaintiff's evidence of his or her state of mind regarding the relationship. If the trial court doubts plaintiff's evidence that the marriage has irremediably broken down, the court may continue the action to determine if reconciliation is possible. However, if the parties do not reconcile, dissolution should be granted. . . .

The question whether a breakdown of a marriage is irremediable is a question to be determined by the trial court. RSA 458:7-a contemplates the introduction of factual testimony sufficient to permit a finding of irreconcilable differences which have caused the irremediable breakdown of the marriage. Nevertheless there are limits to the inquiry. "In the first place, there is the natural tendency to withhold information of a personal nature from anyone but a trusted and discreet adviser; secondly, any probing into personal matters against the wishes of the party examined would be objectionable . . .; and thirdly, the parties have come to court for a purpose. Their answers, which may be perfectly honest ones, will inevitably be slanted in the direction of their ultimate goal, which is divorce." Within these limits the trial court must be adequately informed before acting in matters of such importance. But the statute does not contemplate a complete biopsy of the marriage relationship from the beginning to the end in every case. This is a difficult task, but judges face similar problems in other cases.

The separation of the parties for two and one-half years and the plaintiff's persistence in seeking a divorce during that period is evidence from which the trial court could find that this marriage has irremediably broken down.

Remanded.

NOTES AND QUESTIONS

1. The doctrine that proof of grounds of divorce requires granting that relief was applied in Earls v. Earls, 42 S.W.3d 879 (Tenn. App. 2000). The wife suffered a catastrophic accident, leaving her quadriplegic. After approximately one year, the husband filed for divorce, alleging irreconcilable differences and inappropriate marital conduct. The wife agreed that the parties had irreconcilable differences but resisted the divorce because she desired to continue being covered by the husband's employer-provided group medical insurance. The trial court declined to grant the husband a divorce or to declare the parties divorced.

The evidence revealed that, during the wife's slow and difficult rehabilitation period, each party became discouraged and depressed. Mr. Earls was frustrated because he believed that Mrs. Earls was not pursuing her rehabilitation as vigorously as she could, and Mrs. Earls became depressed and angry about the cruel blow fate had dealt her. Each party became the target of the other's frustration and anger, and eventually the pressure and strain drove the parties apart. They began to argue frequently and to call each other names.

On this record, the appellate court reversed the trial court, holding that the evidence established both irreconcilable differences and inappropriate marital conduct (on both sides). It held that when any ground for divorce is proved, including inappropriate marital conduct, the General Assembly has empowered the courts to "grant a divorce to the party who was less at fault or, if either or both parties are entitled to a divorce, declare the parties to be divorced, rather than awarding a divorce to either party alone." Accordingly, a Tennessee court should grant a divorce from the bonds of matrimony whenever there is evidence of continued misconduct by one or both spouses that makes continued cohabitation unacceptable. Mrs. Earls' concern regarding her future medical care should have been addressed in the division of the marital estate and in spousal support and should not have influenced the decision on whether to grant a divorce.

Compare Koon v. Koon, 969 S.W.2d 828 (Mo. App. 1998). The wife alleged that she and her husband had "separated on March 19, 1996," and that the marriage was irretrievably broken "because [Husband] has behaved during the marriage in such a way that [Wife] cannot reasonably be expected to live with him." Under the Missouri statute, a finding that the marriage is irretrievably broken, when contested, must be supported by evidence of various kinds of misconduct by the defendant, such that the wife could not be expected to continue to live with the husband. At trial, the wife testified that her husband tried to control everything she did and that they often argued over how and where money should be spent. She also testified that when the husband was working temporarily in Virginia, she was much happier than when he was at home. In her opinion, there was no hope for reconciliation. The husband testified that he did not believe the marriage was irretrievably broken and that he did not want the court to dissolve the marriage.

In rendering judgment, the trial court found that the parties' marriage was irretrievably broken, but also specifically stated it did "*not* find that [Husband] has behaved in such a way that [Wife] could not reasonably be expected to live with him." On these findings, the appellate court reversed the trial court, holding that no divorce could be granted on these facts.

2. In what sense is the marriage broken where one spouse wishes to continue that marriage?

3. Why do the opposing spouses in *Desrochers* and *Earls* wish to prevent divorce? Should it matter?

4. *Compare* Missouri Annotated Statutes §452.320, which authorizes a divorce on the ground that a marriage is irretrievably broken only when both parties agree. If one of the parties denies that the marriage is irretrievably broken, a divorce can be granted only on a finding that the respondent has engaged in marital fault or that the parties have lived separate and apart for 12 months by mutual consent, or 24 months without such agreement, prior to the date of the petition. In In re Marriage of Mitchell, 545 S.W.2d 313 (Mo. App. 1976), the court refused to grant a divorce to a husband, although the husband testified that he no longer loved his wife and had had intercourse with another woman and although efforts at counseling and reconciliation had failed. Is this an approach preferable to that taken in *Desrochers*?

5. *See also* Hadjimilitis v. Tsavliris, [2003] 1 F.L.R. 81. A wife applied for divorce on the grounds of her husband's unreasonable behavior. They had married in 1990 and had three children. The family was very wealthy, living in a luxurious home with servants and owning other properties, including a yacht. The wife filed for divorce in March 2001, alleging that the husband was very controlling, routinely subjecting her to public humiliation and undermining her, and had no interest in wife's viewpoint or mental well-being. The husband defended the divorce, arguing that the marriage could be saved through counseling and

criticizing his wife's behavior, accusing her of having affairs and not being a fit wife or mother. The court held that the wife should be granted the divorce, concluding that it was clear that the marriage had irretrievably broken down and that wife could not reasonably be expected to live with husband. In giving evidence, the wife came across as a "subdued and somewhat compliant individual." The husband appeared to believe strongly in the sanctity of marriage and that problems should be worked through. However, he was not prepared to take any responsibility himself for the relationship problems. There was ample evidence from the wife's witnesses as to the husband's bullying behavior toward her. He admitted to often raising his voice to the wife but contended that it was wholly justified by the need to "chide and correct her." The court granted a divorce to the wife but not the husband.

6. When states first adopted judicial divorce, often in the mid-nineteenth century, those statutes were challenged on a number of grounds, including the claim that they interfered with contracts (in this case, of marriage). The United States Supreme Court ultimately upheld dissolution divorce, observing that "[marriage] is an institution, in the maintenance of which in its purity the public is deeply interested, for it is the foundation of the family and of society, without which there would be neither civilization nor progress." Maynard v. Hill, 125 U.S. 190, 211 (1888). No-fault divorce statutes were also challenged on various constitutional grounds, and upheld. In Waite v. Waite, 64 S.W.3d 217 (Tex. App. 2001), the court rejected claims that the statute was invalid under the Free Exercise and Establishment clauses of the First Amendment as well as state constitutional grounds, relying in part on Maynard v. Hill to support the authority of state government to regulate entrance into and exit from marriage.

2. No-Default Divorce Procedure

BODDIE V. CONNECTICUT

401 U.S. 371 (1971)

HARLAN, J. Appellants, welfare recipients residing in the State of Connecticut, brought this action in the Federal District Court for the District of Connecticut on behalf of themselves and others similarly situated, challenging, as applied to them, certain state procedures for the commencement of litigation, including requirements for payment of court fees and costs for service of process, that restrict their access to the courts in their effort to bring an action for divorce.

It appears . . . that the average cost to a litigant for bringing an action for divorce is $60.00. Section 52-259 of the Connecticut General Statutes provides: "There shall be paid to the clerks of the supreme court or the superior court, for entering each civil cause, forty-five dollars. . . ." An additional $15.00 is usually required for the service of process by the sheriff, although as much as $40 or $50 may be necessary where notice must be accomplished by publication. . . .

Assuming, as we must on this motion to dismiss the complaint, the truth of the *undisputed* allegations made by the appellants, it appears that they were unsuccessful in their attempt to bring their divorce actions in Connecticut courts, simply by reason of their indigency. . . .

. . . A three-judge court . . . concluded that "a state may [limit] access to its civil courts and particularly in this instance, to its divorce courts, by the requirement of a filing fee or other fees which effectively bar persons on relief from commencing actions therein."

. . . We now reverse. Our conclusion is that, given the basic position of the marriage relationship in this society's hierarchy of values and the concomitant state monopolization of the means for legally dissolving this relationship, due process does prohibit a state from denying, solely because of inability to pay, access to its courts to individuals who seek judicial dissolution of their marriages. . . .

As this Court on more than one occasion has recognized, marriage involves interests of basic importance in our society. It is not surprising, then, that States have seen fit to oversee many aspects of that institution. Without a prior judicial imprimatur, individuals may freely enter into and rescind commercial contracts, for example, but we are unaware of any jurisdiction where private citizens may covenant for or dissolve marriages without state approval. Even where all substantive requirements are concededly met, we know of no instance where two consenting adults may divorce and mutually liberate themselves from the constraints of legal obligations that go with marriage, and more fundamentally the prohibition against remarriage, without invoking the State's judicial machinery. . . .

. . . [W]e conclude that the State's refusal to admit these applicants to its courts, the sole means in Connecticut of obtaining a divorce, must be regarded as denying them an opportunity to be heard upon their claimed right to a dissolution of their marriages, and, in the absence of a sufficient countervailing justification for the State's action, a denial of due process.

The arguments for this kind of fee and cost requirement are that the State's interest in the prevention of frivolous litigation is substantial, its use of court fees and process costs to allocate scarce resources is rational, and its balance between the defendant's right to notice and the plaintiff's right to access is reasonable.

In our opinion, none of these considerations is sufficient to override the interest of the plaintiff-appellants in having access to the only avenue open for dissolving their allegedly untenable marriages. Not only is there no necessary connection between a litigant's assets and the seriousness of his motives in bringing suit, but it is here beyond present dispute that appellants bring these actions in good faith. Moreover, other alternatives exist to fees and cost requirements as a means for conserving the time of courts and protecting parties from frivolous litigation, such as penalties for false pleadings and affidavits. . . .

In concluding that the Due Process Clause of the Fourteenth Amendment requires that these appellants be afforded an opportunity to go into court to obtain a divorce, we wish to reemphasize that we go no further than necessary to dispose of the case before us, a case where the *bona fides* of both appellants' indigency and desire for divorce are here beyond dispute. We do not decide that access for all individuals to the courts is a right that is, in all circumstances, guaranteed by the Due Process Clause of the Fourteenth Amendment so that its exercise may not be placed beyond the reach of any individual, for, as we have already noted, in the case before us this right is the exclusive precondition to the adjustment of a fundamental human relationship. The requirement that these appellants resort to the judicial process is entirely a state-created matter. Thus we hold only that a State may not . . . preempt the right to dissolve this relationship without affording all citizens access to the means it has prescribed for doing so.

Reversed.

BLACK, J., dissenting. This is a strange case and a strange holding. Absent some specific federal constitutional or statutory provision, marriage in this country is completely under state control, and so is divorce. . . . It is not by accident that marriage and divorce have always been considered to be under state control. The institution of marriage is of peculiar importance to the people of the States. . . . The States, therefore, have particular interests in the kinds of laws regulating their citizens when they enter into, maintain and dissolve marriages. The power of the States over marriage and divorce is complete except as limited by specific Constitutional provisions.

The Court here holds, however, that the State of Connecticut has so little control over marriages and divorces of its own citizens that it is without power to charge them practically nominal initial court costs when they are without ready money to put up those costs. . . .

NOTES AND QUESTIONS

1. Does it follow from *Boddie* that states cannot impose any fees on indigents seeking divorce? Does the indigent plaintiff have a right to have costs of publication, which can be quite expensive, paid by the state or county? If so, will the kind of notice given be affected? *See* Dungan v. Dungan, 570 S.W.2d 183 (Tenn. 1979) (ordering, in lieu of publication, service by registered mail to the defendant's last address and posting in three public places); Johnson v. Johnson, 329 A.2d 451 (D.C. App. 1974) (authorizing publication in only one newspaper, which was the least expensive).

2. The fees actually involved in *Boddie* were, as Justice Black observes, "nominal." Because indigency was conceded, the Court had no occasion to consider what counts as indigency sufficient to excuse divorce plaintiffs from responsibility for those costs.

Is receipt of welfare itself sufficient? *See* Hightower v. Hightower, 235 N.W.2d 313 (Iowa 1975), requiring that plaintiff show that she is unable to pay the fees without affecting her ability to purchase basic necessities. There, a young woman with seven children living on AFDC and a small monthly wage was held able to pay fees amounting to $27. *See also* Tomashefski v. Tomashefski, 369 A.2d 839 (Pa. Super. 1976).

3. Does it follow from *Boddie* that the plaintiff in a divorce case should be entitled to counsel, either in all cases or in those involving complicated issues of property or custody? Most courts reject a general right to counsel in divorce cases:

. . . [T]he *Boddie* case does not support, or by rationale imply, an obligation of the State to assign, let alone compensate, counsel as a matter of constitutional right. The *Boddie* case held narrowly that because the State's regulation of marriage and divorce, in the generic sense, is an assumption of governmental power, the State could not deny access to its courts in matrimonial actions by exacting a court fee from indigent matrimonial suitors. . . . Of course, counsel is always desirable, and in complicated matrimonial litigation would be essential. But however desirable or necessary, representation by counsel is not a legal condition to access to courts.

In re Smiley, 330 N.E.2d 53, 56 (N.Y. 1975) (Breitel, J.). *See* Annotation, 85 A.L.R. 3d 983 (1978).

On the other hand, the Alaska Supreme Court upheld a right to appointed counsel in certain custody cases in Flores v. Flores, 598 P.2d 893, 896 (Alaska 1979):

We have noted on previous occasions that "[c]hild custody determinations are among the most difficult in the law." Although the legal issues in a given case may not be complex, the crucial determination of what will be best for the child can be an exceedingly difficult one as it requires a delicate process of balancing many complex and competing considerations that are unique to every case. A parent who is without the aid of counsel in marshalling and presenting the arguments in his favor will be at a decided and frequently decisive disadvantage which becomes even more apparent when one considers the emotional nature of child custody disputes. . . . This disadvantage is constitutionally impermissible where the other parent has an attorney supplied by a public agency.

4. Some statutes expressly permit courts to appoint counsel for parties in divorce matters as an exercise of discretion. *See* McKinney's New York Family Court Act §§261, 262 (1983). The same result may be reached as a matter of inherent judicial authority.

Traditional fault-based divorce procedure not only assumed but required the parties to adopt an adversarial posture. Most modern statutes include fault grounds (together with no-fault bases). When divorce is sought on fault grounds, the posture of divorce procedures remains substantially adversarial. Most divorces now rest, however, on no-fault grounds, and the question arises whether recognizing divorces on those grounds implies the elimination or reduction of public interest in the outcomes of divorce proceedings.

MANION V. MANION

143 N.J. Super. 499, 363 A.2d 921 (1976)

SUSSER, J.C.C. This case raises the novel question of whether, in an action for divorce based on . . . (18 months separation), a motion to enter final judgment by default pursuant to R. 4:43-2 is properly brought where the same is supported solely by affidavits. . . .

On June 25, 1976, the wife, plaintiff herein, filed a motion pursuant to R. 4:46 seeking summary judgment for the following: (a) dissolving the marriage; (b) incorporating a property settlement and support agreement entered into by the parties on April 12, 1976; and (c) permitting the plaintiff to resume her maiden name.

. . . In the present case there has been a default and no answer or appearance by an adversary. Therefore, the court agreed to consider plaintiff's motion as one for the entry of final judgment by default based on affidavits alone. . . .

The newly adopted Divorce Act of 1971 was not an abdication of the State's interests in the bonds of matrimony and of the role the family structure plays in our modern society. There is no indication in either the legislative history or in the post reform decisional law that the state is now any less concerned with the institution of marriage and the family structure. Our Supreme Court has said:

> The law regards divorce actions as imposing special responsibilities upon the court and attorney as officers of the court. This is because in every suit for divorce the State is in fact if not in name a third party having a substantial interest. The public is represented by the conscience of the court [citations omitted], and "The law regards these actions which tend to disrupt the marriage status with regret — certainly it does not encourage them." [citations omitted] In re Backes, 16 N.J. 430, 433-34, 109 A.2d 273, 274 (1954).

Because of this particularly significant state interest it is of paramount importance that each divorce proceeding be treated individually and specially with a view toward the parties interest as well as the public interest. . . .

Although the new Divorce Act manifests a public policy to terminate dead marriages, this is not to be construed as terminating the State's interest.

. . . [T]here are those civil cases where judgment may be entered without the necessity of oral testimony once a default has been entered. However, manifestly, this is not such a situation. The court, as the public's conscience and protector of state interests, is compelled to be satisfied that the statutory mandates have been fulfilled and its judgment is in the best interest of all concerned. To accomplish this it is beneficial, if not essential, that the court have the opportunity to hear the direct examination of the nondefaulting party and to have the party present and in a position to respond to any questions the court might desire to pose. The interests of the State and the public would not be best served by turning our matrimonial courts into divorce mills where boiler plate forms are inserted at one end and divorce judgments are catapulted out of the other. The scale is easily tipped in favor of requiring oral testimony to prove the essential elements in a cause of action for divorce rather than by affidavit. Therefore, plaintiff's motion is denied.

NOTES AND QUESTIONS

1. Section 302 of The Uniform Marriage and Divorce Act requires a court to make several findings as a condition of entering a decree of dissolution, including a finding that the marriage is irretrievably broken. Does this requirement mandate the result in *Manion*?

Many state statutes also expressly require hearings in all divorce cases. *See* 2 Homer H. Clark, Jr., Domestic Relations 98 (1987). Davis v. Davis, 16 P.3d 478 (Okla. App. 2000), applied a statute providing that, in divorce cases, the "court may admit proof of the admissions of the parties to be received in evidence, carefully excluding such as shall appear to have been obtained by connivance, fraud, coercion or other improper means. . . . *But no divorce shall be granted without proof*" (emphasis added). In this case, neither party testified, no evidence was produced prior to the granting of the divorce, and the court held that the divorce decree was invalid.

The requirement of a hearing does not, however, imply a lengthy hearing. Studies of no-fault divorce hearings report average times of less than 30 minutes. *See* Stephen L. Sass, The Iowa No Fault Dissolution of Marriage Law in Action, 18 S.D. L. Rev. 629, 650 (1973); Alan H. Frank, John J. Berman & Stanley F. Mazur-Hart, No Fault Divorce and the Divorce Rate: The Nebraska Experience — An Interrupted Time Series Analysis and Commentary, 58 Neb. L. Rev. 1, 61-65 (1978).

2. What is the status of the bar of collusion under a no-fault regime? In McKim v. McKim, 6 Cal. 3d 673, 493 P.2d 868, 872 (1972), the California Supreme Court held that collusion did bar the granting of a no-fault divorce.

. . . [U]nder [the wife's theory] it would be proper for the parties to agree that one of them would present false evidence that their differences were irreconcilable and their marriage had broken down irremediably. The obtaining of a decree of dissolution by such an agreement would be a fraud on the court.

On the other hand, the Iowa Supreme Court concluded that "collusion is no longer relevant [in divorce proceedings]. In truth, if it were demonstrated the parties were in collusion to bring about a termination of the marriage relationship, it would further evidence the fact of marital breakdown." In re Marriage of Collins, 200 N.W.2d 886, 890 (Iowa 1972).

On what assumptions might the California and Iowa courts have come to their differing conclusions? Are their perceptions of the meaning of "marital breakdown" the same? Of the existence or nature of a continuing public interest in the regulation of divorce?

Should concern about collusion depend on whether the state has adopted a "pure" no-fault system or retains fault grounds together with no-fault grounds?

3. Is there any role for the divorce proctor, discussed at page 305, above? In Bhaiji v. Chauhan, [2003] 2 FLR 485, the Queen's proctor intervened in a series of five uncontested divorce actions. All of the suits involved young people of Indian ethnicity; in each one, one of the parties was a U.K. citizen and long-standing resident and the other an Indian citizen recently come to reside in the U.K. Each marriage had been brought to court for dissolution on the ground that respondent behaved in such a way that petitioner could not reasonably be expected to live with him or her. Each petition was presented by the petitioner acting in person; no solicitor was involved until the Queen's proctor intervened. There were "curious similarities" in the language of some of the petitions, leading the court to conclude that all petitions (with one possible exception) were drafted by the same person.

Four of the five suits were dismissed, and the remaining suit was allowed to be withdrawn. The court commented:

> The Queen's Proctor's intervention in undefended suits for divorce, whether (as in these suits) prior to decree nisi or following decree nisi but prior to decree absolute, is now exceedingly rare. The consequence has been a hearing of equal rarity, namely a hearing of a suit, undefended by the respondent, in open court upon oral evidence. In almost all undefended suits the evidence is in the form of an affidavit by which the petitioner verifies the allegations in his or her petition. If, on the face of such evidence, the petitioner is entitled to a decree, the district judge will without a hearing so certify and, on a later date, will formally pronounce a decree nisi in open court. The judge's duty pursuant to s.1(3) of the Matrimonial Causes Act 1973 to enquire, so far as he reasonably can, into the facts alleged by the petitioner is thus emasculated almost to invisibility. This appraisal only on paper of undefended suits is described in rr 2.24 and 2.36 of the Family Proceedings Rules 1991 as the "special procedure." The label was coined almost 30 years ago when an exception to the need for an oral hearing of every suit, even if undefended, was introduced in very limited circumstances. . . . The procedure is no longer special: on the contrary it is almost universal. The continued use of the label, though trivial, well illumines the time-warp in which the law and practice governing the dissolution of marriage have become caught.

[2003] 2 FLR 485, para. 5.

4. Several states have adopted summary dissolution procedures *E.g.*, Cal. Fam. Code §§2400 et seq. (West 1994); Colo. Rev. Stat. §14-10-120.3 (1987); Or. Rev. Stat. §§107.485, 107.490, 107.500 (1993). These procedures, which are often restricted to marriages with no minor children, typically dispense with any requirement of a hearing as long as the parties have agreed to the distribution of any marital property and abandoned spousal maintenance claims. The California version follows:

California Family Code — Summary Dissolution
§2400. [Conditions]

(a) A marriage may be dissolved by the summary dissolution procedure provided in this chapter if all of the following conditions exist at the time the proceeding is commenced:

(1) Either party has met the jurisdictional requirements of Chapter 3 . . . with regard to dissolution of marriage.

(2) Irreconcilable differences have caused the irremediable breakdown of the marriage and the marriage should be dissolved.

(3) There are no children of the relationship of the parties born before or during the marriage or adopted by the parties during the marriage, and the wife, to her knowledge, is not pregnant.

(4) The marriage is not more than five years in duration at the time the petition is filed.

(5) Neither party has any interest in real property wherever situated [with the exception of a short-term residential lease].

(6) There are no unpaid obligations in excess of four thousand dollars ($4,000) incurred by either or both of the parties after the date of their marriage, excluding the amount of any unpaid obligation with respect to an automobile.

(7) The total fair market value of community property assets, excluding all encumbrances and automobiles . . . is less than twenty-five thousand dollars ($25,000) and neither party has separate property assets, excluding all encumbrances and automobiles, in excess of twenty-five thousand dollars ($25,000).

(8) The parties have executed an agreement setting forth the division of assets and the assumption of liabilities of the community, and have duly executed any documents, title certificates, bills of sale, or other evidence of transfer necessary to effectuate the agreement.

(9) The parties waive any rights to spousal support.

(10) The parties, upon entry of the judgment of dissolution of marriage . . . irrevocably waive their respective rights to appeal and their rights to move for a new trial.

(11) The parties have read and understand the summary dissolution brochure provided for in Section 2406.

(12) The parties desire that the court dissolve the marriage. . . .

Sec. 2403. When six months have expired from the date of the filing of the joint petition for summary dissolution, the court may, upon application of either party, enter the judgment dissolving the marriage. The judgment restores to the parties the status of single persons. . . . The clerk shall send a notice of entry of judgment to each of the parties at the party's last known address.

§2406. [Brochure supplied by court.] [This section requires courts to supply a brochure, in "nontechnical" English and Spanish language versions, describing summary dissolution proceedings. The brochure summarizes the procedure. It advises that the parties should consult a lawyer, explains the availability of legal aid lawyers, that spousal support will not be available, and that a permanent adjudication of rights will occur.]

D. EVALUATING DIVORCE REFORM

The "natural experiment" embodied in the adoption of no-fault divorce laws incorporated a number of premises, stated or not. Those included the failure of the traditional divorce system, which was characterized by massive fraud, unfairness (especially to those without wealth who could not travel to "divorce mill" states), and insult to the professionalism of judges and lawyers. They included as well perceptions of harm to the parties, who might be condemned to a marriage that was a union in name only and to consequent misery. They included the assumption that the value of marriage was to be judged instrumentally — that is, according to its tendency to promote the happiness and satisfaction of the parties. And, as the Introduction notes, the underlying assumptions of advocates of no-fault divorce were that, instrumentally, divorce would facilitate the happiness of parties to an unsuccessful relationship and would ease the suffering of children living with strife between their parents.

A "counterrevolution," as critics of no-fault divorce sometimes describe their approach, must challenge these premises, establish their own guiding assumptions, and provide approach(es) to the definition and management of marital difficulty that are better than those of the legal system they question. The following materials illustrate some of the grounds for challenge and some of the proposals for further reform of divorce law.

PAULA MERGENHAGEN DEWITT, *BREAKING UP IS HARD TO DO*

American Demographics, Oct. 1992, at 53

In 1991, almost 1.2 million American marriages dissolved, according to the National Center for Health Statistics (NCHS). Divorcing couples now account for about 2 percent of married couples each year. In 1970, 700,000 divorces accounted for just 1.5 percent of the married population. While the number of divorces increased 71 percent, the number of married couples increased only 19 percent. The result: "domestic relations cases" accounted for one-third of all civil cases filed in general jurisdiction courts in 1990. . . .

Divorce is highly concentrated in the first years of marriage. Over one-third of those divorced in 1988 were married four years or less, according to NCHS. Many of these marriages were doomed from the start. Almost 40 percent of divorced respondents to a Gallup poll reported that problems were present when they married or early in marriage.

Just slightly over half of married persons are under the age of 45, but this group accounted for 84 percent of those divorced in 1988. Younger baby boomers in their late 20s and early 30s are especially prone to divorce. In fact, 42 percent of those divorced in 1988 were aged 25 to 34.

Women now file for divorce in six out of ten cases, according to NCHS. And more than half of divorced women told the Gallup Organization that it was their idea to separate, compared with only 44 percent of divorced men. This is a reversal from 1970, when most divorces were the man's idea. The likely reason for the reversal is financial. Women with jobs and resources of their own are less likely to stay in an unhappy marriage.

NORVAL GLENN, *IS THE CURRENT CONCERN ABOUT AMERICAN MARRIAGE WARRANTED?*

9 Va. J. Soc. Pol'y & L. 5, 5-6, 9-10, 12-13, 15-18, 21-24, 28, 30, 33, 44-46 (2001)

Family issues, especially those relating to marriage, are prominent in public discussions in the United States. Some Americans, especially many religious conservatives, have long been concerned about the state of marriage. That concern has recently spread across the political spectrum to centrists and even to many liberals and secular humanists. There is now an active pro-marriage movement. . . . Those groups include participants in the "divorce reform" movement, who work for a retreat from the more extreme forms of no-fault divorce; the Coalition for

Marriage, Family, and Couples Education; the Communitarian Network; the Institute for American Values and its affiliated Council on Families; and traditional pro-family and pro-marriage organizations such as the Family Research Council and Focus on the Family. . . . Similarly, numerous politicians and public policy makers give at least verbal support to pro-marriage efforts. . . .

My task in this essay is to assess the extent to which the current concern about the institution of marriage is warranted. First, I address the effects of marriage on individuals and on society. . . .

In the decades since [publication of Jessie Bernard's 1972 book, The Future of Marriage, arguing that American marriage typically is highly beneficial to husbands but is distinctly harmful to wives], an enormous amount of cross-sectional evidence has accumulated showing that in a variety of ways married persons fare better than unmarried ones. Married persons are advantaged over unmarried ones in satisfaction with almost all aspects of life, in almost all dimensions of physical health, in most aspects of mental health, in longevity, in financial success, and in avoiding trouble with the law, to name just a few of the ways. Most of the differences by marital status are similar for men and women, though the ones pertaining to physical health are rather consistently greater for men than for women. . . .

On the other hand, there is little evidence that even poor or mediocre marriages positively affect well-being. The quality of marriage seems to make a huge difference; on some dimensions of well-being, such as reported happiness, persons in poor or even mediocre marriages fair [sic] less well than unmarried persons. . . . Clearly, the positive association of marriage with well-being depends on the fact that a large proportion of marriages are of high quality. . . .

Considerable recent research has compared the estimated effects of marriage and nonmarital cohabitation on well-being. Heterosexual cohabitors in the United States are diverse and cohabit for a variety of reasons, with only a small minority having stable long-term relationships. Because many of the emotional and psychological benefits of marriage derive from the security of the relationship, it is hardly surprising that cohabiting couples without plans to marry generally do not seem to derive the benefits that married couples do from their relationships.

The quality of marriage affects not just the spouses in them, but also their children. The importance of marriage's effect on children has long been recognized by family scholars and researchers. . . .

During the past two decades, nearly all researchers have come to agree that parental marital situations have important effects on children, and that the effects of marital failure are generally negative. There still is considerable disagreement about how severe, widespread, and enduring the negative effects of divorce are, but the focus of the debate has shifted to which negative effects result from pre-separation marital conflict and which result from the separation and its aftermath. Those who believe the separation and its aftermath have important negative effects do not always agree on the mechanisms by which the apparent effects come about, some emphasizing economic influences and others such factors as the lack of paternal influence. There are related issues, of course, concerning the effects of paternal absence and economic deprivation in the case of children born to unmarried mothers. . . .

The societal consequences of good marriages are more than just the sum of the benefits to individual spouses and to their children. For instance, marriage apparently increases the productivity and earnings of men. A recent study indicates that levels of criminal activity are reduced by the development of quality marital bonds, and other research has shown that when men marry they tend to cease or cut back on behavior destructive to themselves and to others. Marriage seems to induce men to become good members not only of their families, but also of their communities and of society at large. . . .

Some trends in American marriage are so well known that I need not dwell on them here. For instance, few need to be reminded that divorce in this country increased steeply during the late 1960s and the 1970s, with the crude divorce rate (and most refined divorce rates) more than doubling during that decade and a half. . . .

Although these changes are well known, their details deserve close scrutiny, and some less well-known marriage-related trends also warrant attention. For instance, it is not well known that the divorce rate in the United States has declined recently. The number of divorces per 1,000 married women age 15 and older peaked around 1980 and has declined slowly since then. For those concerned about marital instability, however, this news may not be as good as it first appears. Some of the decline in the 1980s resulted from a decrease in the proportion of married women who were in the early, and more divorce-prone, stages of their marriages; consequently, the decline in divorces may not reflect an increase in marital stability. . . . A more important change would be an increase in the stability of longer-term marriages with children, and it is not clear that this increase has occurred. . . .

* * * *

Perhaps the most serious widespread misconception about a marriage-related trend is the belief that modern-day couples who stay married have better marriages than did the couples in stable marriages prior to the increase in divorce in the 1960s and 1970s. Some commentators have argued that the divorce boom tended to raise the quality of existing marriages because greater divorce proneness resulted from an increased reluctance of persons in poor marriages to remain in them, rather than from a greater tendency for marriages to deteriorate. . . .

More recent data tell a different story. Data from the General Social Surveys show a modest but statistically significant decline in reported marital happiness from 1972 through the mid-1990s. If it were true that divorce increased only because people became less willing to stay in poor marriages, reported marital happiness should have increased substantially. The fact that it did not indicates an increased tendency for marriages to go bad. More direct evidence on the increase in marital failure is provided by the substantial decline in the percentage of ever-married non-widowed persons who were in first marriages they reported to be "very happy." . . . [These declines were found across virtually all age levels and for both black and white respondents.]

* * *

Although not all news about American marriage is bad, the current concern about its condition seems clearly warranted. The social scientific evidence for the importance of marriage to adults, children, adolescents, and the society as a whole is about as conclusive as social science evidence can be, as is the evidence that several trends of the last half of the 20th century lessened the individual and social benefits of marriage. Whether such terms as "crisis" are appropriate in characterizing the state of marriage is more debatable. Exaggerating the ills of the institution might lead to despair rather than constructive action, and pro-marriage activists will gain more support for their efforts if they avoid the image of hysterical alarmists. However, "crisis" and similar terms have often been applied to conditions that almost certainly have been less consequential than the problems that now afflict marriage in this country. . . .

Ira Mark Ellman, *The Misguided Movement to Revive Fault Divorce, and Why Reformers Should Look Instead to the American Law Institute*

11 Int'l J.L., Pol'y & Fam. 216, 219-226 (1997)

Some opponents of pure no-fault divorce believe that no-fault provisions are a cause of rising divorce rates, and that revision of the divorce laws will therefore help reverse that trend. With that goal in mind, some propose a waiting period for a year or more before divorce will be granted, at least for couples with minor children. Even longer waiting periods, up to five years, have been urged before allowing a unilateral no-fault divorce, and some would bar them altogether. Would such proposals work to reduce marital break-up? At one level the claim that the divorce laws affect the rate of divorce seems necessarily true. If divorce were entirely barred, as it was in Ireland until very recently, then there would be no divorces at all. And so it also seems plausible to think that if divorce were allowed, but more difficult to obtain, then the divorce rate would decline. The obvious problem, however, is that while legal barriers can affect the rate of formal divorce, it is far less clear they can affect the rate of actual marital demise. . . .

There are many reasons to think that the law is a minor player in affecting divorce rates. The American divorce rate has been climbing steadily since 1860. . . . There was a very large jump in the divorce rate following World War II, followed by a decline to prior levels and an uncharacteristic period of stability during the 1950s. The climb then resumed, and by the mid 1960s had become very steep. The divorce rate was 2.1 per 1000 people in 1950, grew to 2.9 by 1968, and peaked at 5.3 in 1979. That is, the divorce rate began climbing more than a decade before the no-fault movement began, and peaked at about the time no-fault was adopted nationwide. Since then it declined, first to 5.0, where it held steady through 1986, and more recently to 4.5 per 1000 — 15 percent less than in 1981. Indeed, recent analyses of 1988 data suggest that 43 percent of marriages end in divorce, not more than 50 percent, an estimate that is frequently heard. . . .

Of course, it is true that divorce rates are higher today than in the 1960s. The long-term historical pattern of rising divorce rates "is a wide-spread phenomenon in western societies" despite their varying divorce laws. Indeed, divorce laws vary within the United States as well. . . . But while there are marked regional variations in the United States, they are entirely unrelated to regional patterns in divorce laws: the two regions most resistant to pure no-fault divorce laws, the South and the Northeast, have the highest and lowest divorce rates, respectively. Cultural patterns, by contrast, have clear effects on divorce rates. Some religious groups have far lower divorce rates than others, and interfaith marriages, which have increased, have higher divorce rates than intrafaith marriages. . . .

Some no-fault critics are less concerned with deterring divorce than deterring bad marital behaviour. They are therefore less interested in abolishing no-fault grounds for divorce, or imposing lengthy waiting periods, than in making marital fault a factor in allocating marital property or awarding alimony. They believe such fault-based financial rules will improve marital conduct. . . .

. . . If one has in mind the suppression of truly bad behaviour, like interspousal violence, then divorce law seems neither the simplest nor the most effective available tool. The behaviour one seeks to suppress is already a violation of the criminal law and actionable in tort, and in some states the tort claim can even be joined with the dissolution action. Undoubtedly more could be done to improve these remedies. But the claim that the violent actor undeterred by these sanctions will nevertheless cease that violence to avoid its consideration at divorce — a divorce he may not yet even contemplate — seems rather implausible. . . .

CAROL WEISBROD, *ON THE EXPRESSIVE FUNCTIONS OF FAMILY LAW*

22 U.C. Davis L. Rev. 991, 1004-1007 (1989)

Family law is a particularly important point at which to examine problems of the expressive function of law. It already contains many examples of messages. Proposals are heard to the effect that it should contain more, despite the acknowledgement that the effectiveness of law is limited. For example, Max Rheinstein concluded that law was not a prime determinant of behavior in relation to marital stability. Mary Ann Glendon notes that the relation between law and behavior is uncertain, and that other factors are critical. . . .

Even if we assume some effectiveness, the problem remains "what message?" One possibility is a message of facilitation of private choice, which may finally lead to the proposition that marriage is not a useful legal idea. Another message would try to invoke the now-gone consensus of the Christian nation.

The fact that the consensus is gone is a point on which we agree. However, that agreement creates a problem, since we want our law of the family to be not merely not evil, but affirmatively good. As Lee Teitelbaum suggests,

> It does not seem enough . . . to content ourselves with saying only that some rule cannot be shown to produce evil. While that may suffice for a commercial contract or the occasional tort, there is some feeling that family relationships should be founded on rules and practices we can call good.

But what we can call "good," and how to justify the description, is precisely the issue that remains unclear. "Like just about every other long-standing institution," Clifford Geertz tells us, " — religion, art, science, the state, the family — law is in the process of learning to survive without the certitudes that launched it." The process is association in law with the realists and so we return to Grant Gilmore. He wrote in 1951:

> At twenty years distance we may with the prescience of hindsight pass judgment. Llewellyn and his coconspirators were right in everything they said about the law. They skillfully led us into the swamp. Their mistake was in being sure that they knew the way out of the swamp: they did not, at least we are still there.

Decades later, it is as true in family law as in much else. But there is something in family law that makes the matter peculiarly difficult. The problem is centrally that we care so much, and that law, finally, can do so little. As to this, it may be that the public is more sensitive to reality than some lawyers. Here is Trollope, particularly acute on the failure of the law to provide anything approaching an adequate remedy in certain situations. In Kept in the Dark, involving the concealment of a wife's previous engagement, the wife, rejected by her husband, considers the law's relevance to her situation. The idea of the "limits of law" could not be more clearly set out.

> She could not force him to be her companion. The law would give her only those things which she did not care to claim. He already offered more than the law would exact, and she despised his generosity. As long as he supported her the law could not bring him back and force him to give her to eat of his own loaf, and to drink of his own cup. . . . He had said that he had gone, and would not return, and the law could not bring him back again.

The strength of inquiries into the expressive functions of law is that they focus not only on the formal content of the decision, but also on its effect and tone. They direct attention away from the decision maker, powerful and authoritative, and towards the audiences which the decision both addresses and reflects. While emphasis on rule and decision making gets us to clarification and thus simplification, emphasis on rhetoric gets us to complexity and contradiction. Given the circumstances, while we must somehow still decide things, we might do well to announce our decisions in a less certain voice.

NOTES AND QUESTIONS

1. Has readier access to divorce meant freedom for unhappy spouses to enter new and happier relationships? In addition to the Glenn excerpt above, data regarding the divorce rate for previously married spouses may be relevant. It appears that their divorce rate is higher than that for first marriages, but the difference seems to occur only during the early years of the marriage. See Andrew Cherlin, Marriage, Divorce, Remarriage 29 (1992).

2. Has the availability or frequency of divorce affected the happiness of husbands and wives equally?

3. What do you make of the competing claims regarding the relationship between change in divorce laws and the increased rate of divorce? What are the

problems in determining whether a change in law caused a change in behavior? This issue can be divided into several categories. One is whether a law designed to control or change behavior does so. *See, e.g.,* David L. Chambers, Making Fathers Pay: The Enforcement of Child Support (1979) (jailing fathers who do not pay child support); Richard O. Lempert, Desert and Deterrence: An Assessment of the Moral Bases of the Case for Capital Punishment, 79 Mich. L. Rev. 1177 (1981) (review of debate on deterrent effect of capital punishment). *See also* Richard A. Posner, Against Constitutional Theory, 73 N.Y.U. L. Rev. 1, 11-12 (1998). A second is whether a legal change that was not designed to change, but simply to permit or facilitate, certain behavior has nonetheless also changed that behavior. On the history and social context of divorce reform, *see* Herbert Jacob, The Silent Revolution (1998).

4. Does the availability of divorce affect attitudes toward marriage, either generally or for children whose parents have divorced? What plausible assumptions might one make in either direction? For one study supporting the view that Americans expect their own marriages to endure, *see* Lynn Baker & Robert Emery, When Every Relationship Is Above Average: Perceptions and Expectations of Divorce at the Time of Marriage, 17 Law & Hum. Behav. 439 (1993). On the intergenerational effect of divorce, *see* Paul R. Amato, Explaining the Intergenerational Transmission of Divorce, 58 J. Marriage & Fam. 628 (1996); L. L. Bumpass, T. C. Martin & J. A. Sweet, The Impact of Family Background and Early Marital Factors on Marital Disruption, 12 J. Fam. Issues 22 (1991).

PATRICIA H. SHIONO & LINDA SANDMAN QUINN, *EPIDEMIOLOGY OF DIVORCE*

4 The Future of Children: Children and Divorce 15, 21-26 (Spring 1994)

The changes in the marriage, divorce, and remarriage rates over the past 70 years have had a profound effect on the living arrangements of children. A growing number of children are being raised by single parents or by stepparents. In 1990, there were 64.1 million children under 18 in the United States; the vast majority (45.2 million, or 70.5%) lived in two-parent households (Figure 4). Most children (37 million, or 57.7%) lived with their biological parents, 11.3% (7.2 million) lived in married step families, and 1.5% (1 million) lived with adoptive parents. Approximately one quarter of the children lived in single-parent households; 9.5% (6 million) lived with a divorced, single parent, 7.7% (4.9 million) lived with a never-married parent, 7.6% (4.9 million) lived with a separated or widowed parent, and 4.7% (3 million) lived in a house with no parent present.

Trends in the composition of families for children living with one parent also have changed dramatically over time. In 1940, approximately 40% of children in one-parent families lived with widowed mothers, and very few children lived with never-married mothers. Between 1940 and 1960, as separation and divorce became more common, so did the number of children in one-parent families with a separated or divorced mother.

After 1960, the proportion of children in one-parent families with a never-married mother increased greatly, from 3.4% in 1960 to 28.2% in 1988. At the same time, there were large declines in death rates among married men so, by 1988, only 5% of children in one-parent families lived with widowed mothers. . . .

Figure 4
THE AMERICAN FAMILY TODAY: LIVING ARRANGEMENTS OF
CHILDREN UNDER AGE 18 IN 1990

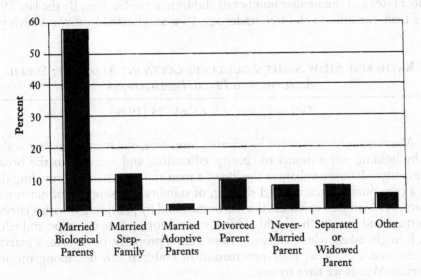

Sources: Norton, A. J., and Miller, L. F. U.S. Bureau of the Census. *Marriage, divorce and remarriage in the 1990's.* Current Population Reports. Series P-23, No. 180. Washington, DC: U.S. Government Printing Office, 1992, Table N; and Saluter, A. F. U.S. Bureau of the Census. *Marital status and living arrangements: March 1990.* Current Population Reports, Series P-20, No. 450. Washington, DC: U.S. Government Printing Office, May 1991, Tables 4 and 5.

There have been large changes in the living arrangements of American children in one-parent families by ethnic group. In the past 50 years, the proportion of white children living with a divorced or separated mother has been increasing. Among white families, the rapidly decreasing proportion of children living with widowed mothers has gradually been replaced by increases in the proportions of children living with single mothers. In contrast, the biggest change in living arrangements for African-American children has been the exponential growth in the proportion living with never-married mothers. Prior to the 1960s, only 4% of African-American children lived with never-married mothers. This proportion increased to 16% in 1970 and in 1988 had become the most common form of living arrangement for African-American children (52%). (There are no comparable data about Hispanic families.)

The trends over time in the number of children affected by divorce generally followed the changes in the divorce rates. However, decrease in family size, the increasing number of births to single women, and the shorter duration of marriage all modify the relationship between divorce rates and the number of children affected by divorce. Each year prior to the 1960s, fewer than 400,000 children were affected by divorce. As the number of divorces rose in the late 1960s, so did the number of children affected by divorce. The number of children affected by divorce during the 1960s and 1970s rose dramatically and was generally higher than the number of divorces because the average families that divorced in that era had more than one child. In later years, the number of children affected by divorce was lower than the number of divorces because of the slight decline in the divorce rates and the smaller number of children in the families. By the late 1970s, more than one million children under age 18 were affected by divorce each year.

KATHERINE SHAW SPAHT, LOUISIANA'S COVENANT MARRIAGE: SOCIAL ANALYSIS AND LEGAL IMPLICATIONS

59 La. L. Rev. 63, 63-69, 75 (1998)

Marriage cultivates virtue by offering love, care, and nurture to its members, and by holding out a model of charity, education, and sacrifice to the broader community. Marriage enhances the life of a man and a woman by providing them with a community of caring and sharing, of stability and support, of nurture and welfare. . . . Marriage enhances the life of the child by providing it with a chrysalis of nurture and love, with a highly individualized form of socialization and education. It might take a whole village to raise a child properly, but it takes a marriage to make one. . . . [For] [t]he procreation of children can be among the most important Words we have to utter.

To preserve and to nurture those most important Words, our children, motivated the covenant marriage legislation, legislation that permits a husband and a wife to obligate themselves legally to a stronger, more enduring union. The covenant marriage and its legal consequences more closely resemble the promises made by each spouse in the wedding ceremony. The children of the marriage are third party beneficiaries of the promises made by their parents and benefit in both tangible and intangible ways—economically, physically, psychologically, and emotionally. Judith Wallerstein's unique twenty-five year longitudinal study of children of divorce establishes what the average citizen intuited before the post-modern era:

> Unlike the adult experience, the child's suffering does not reach its peak at the breakup and then level off. On the contrary. Divorce is a cumulative experience for the child. Its impact increases over time. At each developmental stage the impact is experienced anew and in different ways. . . .

Divorce abrogates children's rights to be reasonably free from adult cares and woes, to enjoy the association of both parents on a daily basis, to remain innocent of social services and therapy, and to spend family time in ways that are not dictated by the courts. . . . [D]ivorce involves a radical redistribution of hardship, from adults to children, and therefore cannot be viewed as a morally neutral act.

As poignant as these findings and conclusions are, social scientists are increasingly convinced that the weakening and virtual collapse of marriage explain the exploding phenomenon of cohabitation. Maggie Gallagher in her book *The Abolition of Marriage: How We Destroy Lasting Love* persuasively argues that there is an indisputable connection between the weak institution we now call marriage, which is defined in no small part by divorce law, and the irregular living arrangement known as cohabitation.

There seems to be a tipping point at which marriage becomes so fragile and divorce so common that an increasing number of women decide it may be safer to dispense with marriage altogether: Illegitimacy surges in the wake of a surge in divorce.

David Popenoe and Barbara Dafoe Whitehead, two names well known among social scientists and in the popular culture, have completed a massive study of countries throughout the West and conclude that in countries where marriage as an institution is weakest, cohabitation is the most widespread. In other words, if marriage is a weak institution, what's the point of it, a conclusion that has so alarmed Popenoe and Whitehead that they have founded "The Marriage Project" at Rutgers University. . . .

Another, less obvious objective of the legislation, which is reflected in who may perform the mandatory pre-marital counseling, is to revitalize and reinvigorate the "community" known as the church. Reinvigoration results from inviting religion back "into the public square" for the purpose of performing a function for which religion is uniquely qualified—preserving marriages. . . . A minister, priest, or rabbi may perform the required pre-marital counseling. Likewise, as in the case of performance of the ceremony, the legislation provides a secular alternative to who may provide the counseling, a marriage counselor. Furthermore, the work of preserving marriages through counseling when difficulties arise necessitates the same time-consuming personal investment which a minister, priest, or rabbi can perform well, not only by virtue of the commitment of his time, but also by virtue of his moral authority. The religious cleric communicates . . . the religious view of marriage and the "community's" expectation that the couple will devote serious effort to preserving their marriage.

Because the legislation "invites" religion back to the public square, the legislation is careful not to "dictate" the content of the counseling beyond its basic contours.

STEVEN L. NOCK, LAURA SANCHEZ, JULIA C. WILSON & JAMES D. WRIGHT, COVENANT MARRIAGE TURNS FIVE YEARS OLD

10 Mich. J. Gender & L. 169, 170-173, 186-187 (2003)

Covenant marriage legislation proposes that the individual and social problems caused by marital dissolution can be lessened by helping people take their marriage vows more seriously and by making divorce more difficult to obtain. Currently, less than two percent of all newly contracted marriages in Louisiana are covenant marriages. This study used the only existing data of newlywed covenant and standard couples married since passage of Louisiana's covenant marriage law in 1997 to analyze the social and demographic factors of covenant couples, the dynamics behind making the decision to have a covenant marriage rather than a standard marriage, and gendered differences in satisfaction with covenant marriage. . . .

Louisiana's covenant marriage statute sets stricter criteria for forming or dissolving a legal marriage. Couples wishing to enter a covenant marriage in

Louisiana . . . must participate in premarital counseling with a state-recognized secular or religious counselor. . . .

Covenant marriage establishes limited grounds for divorce. Divorce may be granted for the traditional marital faults including infidelity, physical or sexual abuse of a spouse or child, a felony life or death-penalty conviction, or abandonment of at least one year. A no-fault provision for divorce permits termination after a two-year waiting period of living separate and apart (no-fault divorce in a standard marriage requires six months). . . .

Based on interviews with key players in Louisiana's passage of the 1997 legislation and newspaper accounts, two principal aims of Louisiana's covenant marriage statute emerge. First, covenant marriage is accompanied by an array of symbolic and political goals, demonstrating an urge to "do something" to challenge what has been called the "Divorce Culture" and to return marriage to a privileged status in society. Louisiana legislators wanted to have an impact on how marriage, divorce, family, and related concepts are thought about and publicly discussed, a goal shared by legislators in other states now trying various methods to reconsider several notions of fault in marital dissolution.

Second, and perhaps more substantively, the law intends that couples ask questions of themselves and their intended spouses about the nature and depth of their commitment to the relationship. Only in states with covenant marriage must marrying couples decide which system of laws will govern their marriages. . . .

Those who elect covenant marriage differ from other newlyweds in five ways. First, the dynamics of how couples discovered and selected their marriage option indicates that covenant spouses have a far different trajectory toward marriage than standard spouses.

The covenant marriage option is meaningful to these couples not only as a personal vow to each other, but also as a public statement of their beliefs about what marriage as an institution entails. Our findings show that covenant married couples mostly learned about the option from a religious authority, that the vast majority are pleased with their choice, that practically none wished for a standard marriage or felt that the difference between the two options does not matter. Not surprisingly, covenant couples are far more likely to believe that covenant marriage is better for society.

Second, people who choose covenant marriage are much less likely to have cohabited, or to have children with someone other than their current marriage partner. Not only does this indicate that they bring far fewer demands from previous relationships to their marriages, it suggests that they really are standing outside of some of the more common relationship and family trends noted over the past few decades.

Third, people who choose covenant marriage have different beliefs than those who select standard marriage. They are better educated and also hold more traditional attitudes. They believe they have a responsibility to marry and have children. They are more religious in both faith and practice than standard married couples, and more likely to agree with one another about their religious beliefs and practices. . . .

Finally, covenant spouses enjoy greater support and approval from friends and relatives before getting married, and also six months after their wedding.

Covenant marriage clearly appeals to a distinct group who differ from the "average" person approaching marriage. . . . The behaviors, beliefs, and strategies for dealing with conflict found among covenant couples are likely, in our opinion, to produce more stable marriages regardless of the legal regime. Such a possibility indicates that the existence of covenant marriage, per se, may be primarily symbolic in the long run. . . .

Covenant marriages are rare and probably attract more attention. The deliberations leading to the choice of a covenant marriage may have salutatory consequences. If so, then the law may be found to exert some influence on the small number of people who opt for covenant marriages. Even if it does, the aggregate effect on divorce or abuse rates (for the state) will be quite small unless the option becomes significantly more popular.

ELIZABETH S. SCOTT, *DIVORCE, CHILDREN'S WELFARE, AND THE CULTURE WARS*

9 Va. J. Soc. Pol'y & L. 95, 95-106, 107-108, 111 (2001)

Are children harmed when their parents divorce? If so, should parents' freedom to end marriage be restricted? These questions have generated uncertainty and controversy in the decades since legal restraints on divorce have been lifted. During the 1970s and 80s, the traditional conviction that parents should stay together "for the sake of the children" was supplanted by a view that children are usually better off if their unhappy parents divorce. By this account, divorcing parents should simply try to accomplish the change in status with as little disruption to their children's lives as possible.

This stance has been challenged sharply by conservative family-values advocates who see divorce and marital instability as the key to societal decline. In their view, children whose parents divorce are damaged in their moral, social, and emotional development, and society ultimately pays a high price through increased teen pregnancy, school drop-outs, poverty, and delinquency. These advocates argue that marriage can only be saved if the government restricts divorce by reinstituting fault grounds and discouraging unhappy spouses from selfishly defecting from their responsibilities. In contrast, liberals and some feminists oppose any restrictions on the freedom of unhappy spouses to divorce, in part because they suspect (correctly for the most part) that the ultimate agenda for many conservatives is a return to the era of traditional marriage and gender roles. Liberals tend to discount concerns about the harm to children of divorce and assume that parents only end marriages that are intolerable.

The upshot, as the recent controversy surrounding the introduction of covenant marriage legislation confirms, is that divorce, particularly when children are involved, has become the focus of a raging battle in the "Culture Wars." Opinion on this issue is deeply polarized, and moderate voices are seldom heard. Nonetheless, polls suggest that public opinion is more uncertain and nuanced than are the views of advocates—for example, many people oppose general government restrictions on divorce, and yet make an exception for couples with young children.

A growing body of social science research on the impact of divorce on children indicates that the issue is more complex than either conservatives or liberals
would have us believe. Among the most important studies of the past decade is a
longitudinal study of families conducted by Paul Amato and Alan Booth. Contrary
to the conservative line that divorce is always bad for children, Amato and Booth
found that children who are exposed to serious conflict in their parents' marriage
are better off when conflict is reduced by divorce. On the other hand, we should
not reassure ourselves that children generally are better off if their unhappy parents divorce. A surprisingly high percentage of marriages that end in divorce
involve low or moderate levels of conflict—what Amato calls "good enough"
marriages. Those divorces appear to have quite a negative impact on the long
term well-being of the children involved. In short, those children whose parents'
marriages are not highly conflictual would be better off if their parents stayed
together. . . .

A large body of social science research demonstrates clearly that children
whose parents divorce generally fare poorly compared to children who grow up
in intact families. Children of divorce suffer economic hardship because their
family income declines. Their academic adjustment tends to be inferior, and they
have more adjustment and behavior problems than children whose parents stay
together. Many children of divorce are resilient, of course, and recover from the
dislocation of divorce. It is clear, however, that divorce represents a significant risk
factor that threatens the well-being of children.

Or does it? An important question about the differences found between children of divorce and children in intact families is whether the problems of the former should be attributed mostly to the divorce or to their exposure to conflict
between their parents before the divorce. . . . In the past generation, researchers
have shed light on this question and have made significant progress in sorting out
the harmful impact of interparental conflict on children from the impact of
divorce itself. In the 1990s, Paul Amato and Alan Booth evaluated the well-being
of the adult children of couples who had participated in their longitudinal study,
including a group whose parents had divorced since the study began in 1980. . . .
The researchers found that the impact of divorce on the well-being of children as
young adults was strongly correlated with the level of conflict between the parents during marriage. Those children whose parents' marriages were characterized by high levels of conflict were better off when their parents divorced than
when they remained together. No surprise here. What is somewhat surprising is
that the researchers found that children whose parents ended marriages that
involved low or moderate levels of conflict (perhaps a majority of divorces) did the
worst of all the groups on all measures of well-being—worse than children whose
parents remained in low-conflict marriages and worse than children from high-
conflict marriages that ended in divorce. Other researchers have confirmed this
finding. It points to the conclusion that a large percentage of divorces have a
harmful impact on the children, and the effect is greatest where the parents' decision to end the marriage seems least justified.

Parents who end low-conflict marriages are an interesting and puzzling
group because they seem to choose divorce even though their marriages are not
that bad—even by their own reports. In the Amato and Booth study, these

spouses reported general happiness, little hostility and indeed expressed affection and respect for their spouses shortly before divorce. They engaged in activities together and generally gave little sign that divorce was likely. So, why did they divorce? The reasons Amato lists are not primarily related to the quality of the marriage. Rather, these individuals left their marriages because (compared to those who remained married) they were less subject to constraints that create barriers to divorce. These constraints include financial costs of divorce, religious beliefs, and close community ties. When asked to explain their decisions, those who left low-conflict marriages reported mid-life crises, dissatisfaction with their spouse's personality, or, in some cases, no reason that they could articulate.

The readiness of parents to leave "good enough" marriages may reflect changing attitudes toward marriage and marital commitment that grew out of cultural changes in the 1960s and 70s. In a 1985 article, Carl Schneider described this trend, arguing that religion and morality have declined as influences on behavior, having been supplanted by individual motivation to achieve personal happiness and self-realization. . . . If this account is accurate, then the attitude that an unsatisfying marriage should be set aside even if it is not miserable, makes some sense. Divorce, on this view, allows each spouse to pursue fulfillment elsewhere.

The social science research challenges two comforting assumptions that have contributed to widespread tolerance of divorces involving children. First, it seems less certain, in light of the Amato and Booth findings, that most parents reluctantly make this difficult decision only when their marriage is truly unbearable, and that in doing so they carefully weigh their children's interests. Those parents who end "good enough" marriages may be optimistic about their children's adjustment to divorce, perhaps believing that their children's well-being is contingent on their own happiness. However, the second assumption—that children are generally better off if their unhappy parents divorce—no longer seems viable in light of the mounting research evidence. . . .

Ideally, as Amato suggests, policy reform would discourage parents in low-to-moderate conflict marriages from divorcing, while encouraging divorce among those couples whose marriages are conflictual. Realistically, however, it seems unlikely that changes in legal policy could facilitate divorce among couples who remain together in highly conflictual marriages without destabilizing marriage more broadly. Under no-fault divorce law, no legal barriers discourage divorce, and so we must conclude that unhappy couples who stay together do so for powerful religious, moral, or other reasons that are not readily subject to influence. The policy goal must be a more limited one of discouraging divorce among low-conflict couples with children while avoiding additional barriers that unduly deter divorce in high-conflict marriages.

Although it is clear that social norms supporting marital commitment have weakened substantially, the extent to which no-fault divorce law has played a role in this change is uncertain. The interaction between law and social norms is complex, and the direction of influence is not clear. Nonetheless, it is possible that no-fault divorce reforms may have contributed to the inclination of parents in "good enough" marriages to divorce by inadvertently destroying restrictions on divorce that served as useful precommitment mechanisms. Whatever its deficiencies, traditional divorce law created barriers that reinforced the initial commitment that most couples have when they get married. By imposing substantial costs on the decision to divorce (the requirement of proving fault), divorce law discouraged unhappy spouses from leaving marriage because of transitory dissatisfaction or routine stresses—boredom, mid-life crises, and the like. Thus, it seems likely that divorces of the kind that seem to be most harmful to children were less common under the fault regime. . . . In general, unhappy spouses likely pursued this option only when continuing in marriage was intolerable and most couples in "good enough" marriages stayed together.

The no-fault reforms removed these legal barriers and made divorce easier. . . . The upshot is that spouses who are not deterred by other barriers (religion, social disapproval, financial constraints), or who have attractive alternatives (other relationships perhaps), are more likely to leave marriage than might have been true a generation ago. . . .

The next question is whether there are legal reforms that could ameliorate the costs created by no-fault divorce law. Social conservatives offer a simple solution—turn back the clock to the traditional regime of fault-based divorce law. In my view, this is not likely to be a satisfactory solution. There were many good reasons to abandon the requirement of proving fault as the basis for divorce. . . .

Instead, a useful government role could be to assist couples to achieve their goal of lasting marriage by providing an option not currently available in most states—a voluntary legally enforceable commitment term. My proposal is that couples entering marriage be allowed to choose either marriage regulated by conventional no-fault rules or marriage that could only be legally terminated after an extended waiting period (of two years, for example.) Perhaps the second option would only apply to divorces involving children, although some couples might want the security of this legal commitment, whether or not they have children. The recently enacted covenant marriage statutes adopt a similar approach to the one that I am proposing. However, these statutes include fault grounds for divorce as well as a waiting period. This undermines their appeal by hearkening back to an era to which most people have no desire to return and it encourages collusion and strategic behavior by spouses eager for a quick exit.

. . . [A] period of mandatory delay . . . would create a barrier to divorce, making the decision to leave marriage more costly. It might also promote more thoughtful decision-making about divorce. . . . Finally—and this is more intangible—the waiting period defines the relationship as one that is not easily set aside, and this may subtly influence the attitudes and behavior in marriage of couples who have undertaken this commitment. In general, parties who anticipate that their relationship will continue into the future have an incentive to cooperate that disappears when exit is always an option. . . .

Whether couples would be inclined to undertake this commitment (and thus whether the reform will have a significant impact on divorce) depends on the social meaning that this commitment option assumes. This is very hard to predict. . . .

Many people today are uneasy about any legally enforceable commitment in marriage and suspect that proposals to allow or encourage such commitment are part of a reactionary social agenda. . . . Thus, it is not surprising that many feminists oppose covenant marriage, despite the fact that it may provide greater security in marriage for some women. . . .

In my view, the liberal response [also] reflects . . . political concerns that are usually unarticulated. . . . A claim that children are better off if their parents stay together implies that the traditional nuclear family of two married parents and their children is the optimal family form and that single-parent families are inferior. . . . The fear is that divorced and single mothers and their children may be stigmatized by policies that discourage divorce.

NAOMI R. CAHN, *THE MORAL COMPLEXITIES OF FAMILY LAW*

50 Stan. L. Rev. 225, 227-236 (1997)

Two recent books, *The Divorce Culture* by Barbara Dafoe Whitehead and *In Defense of Single-Parent Families* by Nancy Dowd, provide a framework for addressing the "morality" of single-parent families and the crisis of moral discourse within a family law itself. *The Divorce Culture* suggests that a cultural focus on personal happiness has caused a dramatic increase in the divorce rate. Ms. Whitehead argues that parental selfishness is responsible for the decline of the American family and that children have a morally based claim to require their parents to stay together. In contrast, *In Defense of Single-Parent Families* argues that these families are harmed more by the stigma surrounding single parenthood than by single parenthood itself. . . .

Both authors agree that divorce is largely responsible for the increase in single-parent families. . . .

According to Whitehead, [traditional attitudes regarding divorce as a serious disruption] have changed as a result of the divorce revolution of the past two decades. Divorce itself—and, in turn, the family—has been redefined. As both a personal and a social matter, Whitehead contends, divorce is no longer perceived as an event with far-reaching consequences for family and society; instead, it is regarded as highly personal, individualized experience. Whitehead traces the development of what she calls "expressive divorce" to an increasing societal emphasis on personal psychological happiness within marriage. . . .

Whitehead . . . explores the dramatic contrast between adults' short stories of liberation, which are evident even in the socially conservative etiquette books, and the extensive research literature documenting the devastating impact of divorce on children. The numerous studies cited by Whitehead highlight that children are the real "victims" of divorce, often suffering a range of negative consequences, including decreased economic status and increased emotional difficulties. . . .

. . . [I]n the wake of divorce and other trends in family development, Whitehead identifies a new ideology of the family, which celebrates what she terms the "Love Family." The Love Family is based on choice and voluntary affiliation with another adult rather than on the permanent commitment traditionally associated with marriage. . . . As evidence of this, Whitehead cites the decreasing proportion of parents who believe it is important to stay married for the sake of their children's well-being. Consequently, she contends, the new Love Family lacks stability, since it is not based on a long-term commitment to children. Once again, children are most harmed by this new ideology because they are no longer raised within a secure relationship. Although Whitehead does acknowledge that divorce may be appropriate in high-conflict families, she cites with approval the conclusion of two researchers that, outside of such situations, parents should try to resolve their differences rather than undergo a divorce.

Whitehead does not endorse the movement to abolish no-fault divorce laws, but instead urges a cultural shift toward "sacrifice" for children and away from the individual self-fulfillment that she sees at the core of the divorce culture. . . .

Dowd agrees with Whitehead that children should be the focus of the debate over divorce. By contrast, however, she seeks to turn the discussion away from "family form" in order to focus on the economic and cultural problems that single-parent families face. . . . Dowd explores the legal treatment of single-parent families, highlighting how the law fails to support single parenthood. She shows how the single-parent family form is labeled as deviant and how this "deviance" label becomes self-fulfilling as a result of policies that do not support single-parent families. Finally, Dowd advocates that our culture provide greater economic and social support to single-parent families.

Of the myths that Dowd explores, the first—and perhaps the most important—is the myth that single parenthood causes poverty through the intergenerational transfer of a culture of poverty. Dowd acknowledges that single-parent families are disproportionately poor. However, she argues that the poverty of single-parent families is not inherent in family form, but instead results from policies and practices that do not support single parents . . . [including] insufficient welfare, sex discrimination in the workplace, or the gendered division of labor that occurs within the family unit. . . .

Dowd also examines how the law supports these and other myths by, for example, failing to provide adequate financial support to children who live in single-parent families. In discussing single-parent families caused by divorce, Dowd is particularly critical of the traditional structure of family roles, asserting that "every parent is a single parent, generally following a gendered parenting role." On divorce, then, these roles lead to a dramatic economic downturn in the lives of women and children. Women earn less in the workplace and are typically the primary caretakers, unable to work longer hours. Moreover, Dowd asserts, the law sustains this gendered caretaking by failing to establish adequate financial support in the form of alimony, property division, or child support awards.

NOTES AND QUESTIONS

1. Louisiana was the first state to adopt covenant marriage. The principal drafter of the Louisiana statute, Professor Katherine Shaw Spaht, was prompted by a divine calling to promote divorce reform and enlisted an evangelical Protestant state legislator in her cause who, in turn, consulted a group of pastors in his district to draft a bill expressing the biblical ideal for marriage. W. Bradford Wilcox, Sacred Vows, Public Purposes: Religion, The Marriage Movement and Marriage Policy 8-9 (2002).

In addition to Louisiana, Arizona and Arkansas also offer an option of "covenant marriage" either as an initial marital state or through conversion of an earlier marriage to the covenant form. Ariz. Rev. Stat. Ann. §§25-901 to 906 (West 2000 and Supp. 2001); Ark. Code Ann. §§9-11-801 to 9-11-811 (Michie 2002). The Arizona statute provides for divorce on fault grounds but also on no-fault grounds (separation for at least one year after a separation decree or two years without such a decree or where both spouses agree to the dissolution). Ariz. Rev. Stat. Ann. §25-903. The Arkansas statute allows dissolution only for fault grounds and where the parties have been separated without reconciliation for two years after entrance of a decree of separation, and also provides that if there is a minor child of the marriage, the waiting period will be two and one-half years from the date of the separation judgment. Ark. Code Ann. §9-11-808. These statutes are analyzed in Chauncey E. Brummer, The Shackles of Covenant Marriage: Who Holds the Keys to Wedlock, 25 U. Ark. Little Rock L. Rev. 261 (2003).

2. While covenant marriage statutes include a provision for converting an "ordinary" marriage to a covenant marriage, those in Louisiana and Arkansas offer no method for conversion of a covenant to a non-covenant marriage. Brummer, *supra* at 289. Do marrying parties have the kind of information they need to be held to their agreement without the possibility of rescission? *See* Gary Becker, A Treatise on the Family 327-329 (1991).

> If participants in marriage markets have complete information about all prospects, divorce would be a fully anticipated response to a demand for variety in mates or to life-cycle changes in traits. Most divorces would then occur after many years of marriage, because traits change gradually. The facts, however, suggest the opposite: about 40 percent of all divorces (and annulments) occur prior to the fifth year of marriage, and separation usually precedes divorce by a year or more.
>
> If, however, participants had highly imperfect information, most divorces would occur early in marriage by virtue of the fact that information about traits increases rapidly after marriage. Several years of marriage is usually a far more effective source of information on love and many other traits than all the proxies available prior to marriage. I suggest that marriages fail early primarily because of imperfect information in marriage markets and the accumulation of better information during marriage. This suggestion is supported by the fact that unexpected changes in earnings and health do raise the probability of divorce.
>
> Women who divorced early in their marriage report that "difficult" spouses and value conflicts were major sources of their discontent, presumably because these traits are much better assessed after a few years of marriage. Personality conflict, sexual incompatibility, and similar traits should be less important sources of later than of earlier divorces; little additional information about these traits is acquired after a few years of marriage. On the other hand, some information, including information about other women and about earnings potential, is acquired more slowly and should be more important in later divorces.

3. Covenant marriage can be understood as an effort to express, both privately and publicly, the conditions of trust, goodwill, and optimism of the parties at the beginning of their marriage. Manuel Utset observes that "[t]here is wide agreement among commentators, as well as transacting parties, that [these conditions] are valuable assets at the beginning of all cooperative ventures. However, while these three factors provide important benefits at the beginning of ventures,

they also bias the predictions parties make regarding future conflicts that require prophylactic action." Manuel Utset, A Theory of Self-Control Problems and Incomplete Contracting: The Case of Shareholder Contracts, 2003 Utah L. Rev. 1329, 1376-1377.

These feelings of trust, goodwill, and optimism can be characterized as hot psychological states that parties are in at the time of incorporation. . . . When shareholders try to predict how much their preferences may change during the venture, they will tend to project their current preferences, as shaped by feelings of trust, goodwill, and optimism, onto their predictions of those future preferences. This can lead shareholders to incorrectly predict: (1) how long these feelings will last, and (2) what their preferences will actually be once trust, goodwill, and optimism begin to fade.

Shareholders undoubtedly know that these feelings can be challenged during the venture as the parties come into conflict over such things as business policy, and that, in certain instances, these feelings may disappear completely. However, due to the projection bias, shareholders will tend to underappreciate how much their preferences will actually change once they are back in a cold state—i.e., a state in which trust, goodwill, and optimism have been significantly weakened or in which they have ceased to motivate preferences altogether.

. . . [P]redictions about future hot-state preferences made by shareholders while in a cold state can lead them to underappreciate the need to adopt shareholder contracts to regulate their future hot-state actions. The further preference-distortions caused by trust, goodwill, and optimism should increase the magnitude of shareholder mispredictions regarding the need to adopt shareholder contracts.

A caveat is in order. The argument in this Section is not that the existence of trust, goodwill, optimism, and familial love at the beginning of a venture is necessarily more harmful than it is helpful. Instead, the point made in this Section is that the cost-benefit analysis of parties regarding whether to rely on these feelings at the beginning of the venture is complicated by the need to account for the projection bias and the potential for overappreciating the self-regulation viability of trust, goodwill, and love. . . .

2003 Utah L. Rev. at 1378-1380. Does Professor Utset's analysis suggest the undesirability of holding parties to covenant marriage, or does it suggest the value of holding parties to agreements based on trust, or does it suggest that the answer might depend on the attitudes of the parties when they come to think about terminating their marriage?

4. The Arkansas covenant marriage statute also prohibits the parties from suing each other in tort, unless they are judicially separated. Ark. Code Ann. §9-11-809. Why should covenant marriage entail a return to the common law doctrine of spousal immunity, which had been abandoned in Arkansas as to both intentional and negligent torts? See Brummer, supra at 286.

5. If parties enter into a covenant marriage, or some other variation (such as a marriage with an extended waiting period when there are children of the marriage or requiring fault grounds if there are children), and one of the spouses seeks a divorce in a jurisdiction that offers pure no-fault divorce grounds, will the restrictions of the state where the marriage was entered be given effect?

As we will see in Chapter 11, dealing with jurisdiction, divorce can take place in any state in which either of the married parties is domiciled. See Williams v. North Carolina, 317 U.S. 287 (1942); Williams v. North Carolina, 325 U.S. 226

(1945). Moreover, the forum state, assuming jurisdiction, may and ordinarily does apply its own rules for divorce, even if they differ substantially from the rules in effect in the place where the parties were married. Consequently, the enforceability in other states of limits on divorce associated with covenant marriage, for example, is doubtful. *See* Brian H. Bix, Choice of Law and Marriage: A Proposal, 36 Fam. L.Q. 255, 259-260 (2002); Katherine Shaw Spaht & Symeon C. Symeonides, Covenant Marriage and the Law of Conflicts of Law, 32 Creighton L. Rev. 1085 (1999).

Professor Bix suggests that the inability of marrying parties to know what rules will apply to dissolution undermines the capacity of couples to choose the rules that fit their preferences and circumstances, to convey to the other the type of marital relationship they are expecting, and to choose rules that would encourage investment in the marriage by both parties. Accordingly, he proposes that parties should be able to choose the law to be applied to the marriage, including its termination. This choice could be provided either by legislative creation of a variety of options or by premarital contracts. In addition, Professor Bix proposes the adoption of either federal legislation or uniform state laws regarding the law to be applied in the event of issues related to the marriage. *Id.* at 264-271. *See also* F. H. Buckley & Larry E. Ribstein, Calling a Truce in the Marriage Wars, 2001 U. Ill. L. Rev. 561 (2001), which urges a similar proposal.

6. Professor Spaht, along with many others, expresses concern about the exclusion of religion from the "public square." In this, they follow the view of Richard John Neuhaus, whose much-cited *The Naked Public Square* suggests that "the operative values" of the American people, values "overwhelmingly grounded in religious belief," have been "systematically excluded from policy consideration." Richard John Neuhaus, The Naked Public Square 37 (1984). The issue is not whether religious organizations can and do participate in public issues. Churches have played major roles at the local level in connection with proposals regarding marriage and divorce, and have routinely filed amicus briefs in cases involving same-sex marriage, homosexual relations, and other issues affecting families and marriage. Rather, it is a particular kind of religious discourse that Pastor Neuhaus and Professor Spaht think has disappeared. How was that discourse conducted previously? Is Professor Spaht's argument consistent with the older form of religious and moral discourse?

7. Followers of what is generally regarded as traditional liberal theory regard individual choice as the primary political value. The authority of the state is limited and does not expect any particular set of beliefs from its citizens regarding what is good or virtuous. In some views, liberalism and its emphasis on government neutrality respond to the loss of faith in a human telos and objective moral truths. June Carbone, From Parents to Partners 37-38 (2000).

Professor Carbone contrasts with this the communitarian approach to liberalism, exemplified by the political theorist William Galston, which rejects the notion that liberalism does not hold views about civic virtue. Rather, he argues that the distinctive feature of liberalism is its unwillingness to move from convictions about the nature of the good to public coercion of individuals to accept those convictions.

With regard to the family, Galston argues that "from the standpoint of the economic well-being and sound psychological development," the evidence indicates that the intact two-parent family is generally preferable to the available alternatives. William A. Galston, Liberal Purposes: Goods, Virtues and Diversity in the Liberal State 284 (1991). To advance that goal, Galston recommends "braking" mechanisms that would require divorcing parents to take some time for reflection before proceeding and all absent parents to pay for their children's support. William A. Galston, A Liberal Democratic Case for the Two-Parent Family, 1 The Responsive Community 14, 23-25 (1990-1991). Galston's views are summarized, analyzed, and compared with those of other family theorists (particularly economist Gary Becker, political theorist Susan Muller Okin, and lawyer Martha Fineman) in June Carbone, From Parents to Partners (2000) (*passim*).

Professor Carbone also projects the following discussion between Professor Galston and Professor Martha Fineman. Both agree that the primary purpose of the family is to provide for children. Professor Galston argues that a stable marriage of two parents best serves these goals.

> [Professor Fineman] . . . argues that the association between children's well-being and the two-parent family is at least in part circular. Children need food, clothing, shelter, love, and affection. The nuclear family meets those needs by dividing responsibility between homemaking mothers and breadwinning fathers, but it is not the only way to insure children's well-being. Many societies recognize nurturing roles for a host of adults . . . or provide for families' material needs in ways that are not so dependent on a single breadwinner. . . . Efforts to promote the two-parent family, whether in the form of joint custody or welfare cuts, often work to children's detriment. . . .
>
> At this point, the dispute between Galston and Fineman becomes an empirical one. Galston cites [evidence] linking the drug crisis, the education crisis, and the problems of teen pregnancy and juvenile crime to broken families; Fineman challenges the studies' validity and their ability to establish a causal relationship. Galston claims that government action can strengthen the two-parent family to the benefit of children; Fineman argues that such intervention is more likely to worsen their lot. . . .

June Carbone, From Parents to Partners 42-43 (2000).

8. Proponents of traditional restrictions on divorce and those who support divorce reform differed on the implications of divorce for children. There now seems to be general agreement that children of divorce experience substantial difficulties for at least some time, although the duration is unclear. In addition to the foregoing materials, *see* Judith Wallerstein & Sandra Blakeslee, Second Chances: Men, Women, and Children a Decade After Divorce (1989); E. Mavis Hetherington, Margaret Stanley-Hagen & Edward R. Anderson, Marital Transitions: A Child's Perspective, 44 Am. Psychol. 303 (1989).

These and other studies have much to do with the proposed counterrevolution in divorce policy and with more specific proposals, such as limiting divorce where the spouses have minor children. For an argument regarding the morality of such a limitation, *see* Elizabeth S. Scott, Rehabilitating Liberalism in Modern Divorce Law, 1994 Utah L. Rev. 687, 731-734 (arguing that Mill's "harm principle" should be transformed into an affirmative obligation on parents and spouses to "rescue" their children from injuries that might follow divorce).

9. It is also clear that single-parent families are far more likely to be poor than are two-parent families. This affects the prospects for both mother and children.

And we also know that government policy in the United States provides less financial support for families than government policy in Western Europe:

> This public support [provided in other countries] can have a significant impact on the well-being of single-parent families. After all government transfer payments, the average income of single-parent families in the United States is about 54% of that of a two-parent family. In France the comparable percentage is 76%, and in Norway it is 86%. Similarly, most other Western countries have substantial public child care for children older than two, and many have paid maternity leave. . . .
>
> After all government transfer payments, in 1991 the poverty rate in the United States for single-parent families was 59.5%. In Sweden and Denmark, the poverty rate for such families is less than 10%. Of course, such support for families is not cheap. One study estimates that the United States spends 4% of its GDP on social protection programs for the non-aged, compared to 13% for Sweden.

J. Thomas Oldham, ALI Principles of Family Dissolution: Some Comments, 1997 Ill. L. Rev. 801, 820-821. How would this problem best be addressed, or should it be addressed?

10. On what basis can we judge the effectiveness and desirability of single-parent families, which inevitably emerge for some time after any divorce? How do we measure their effectiveness? With what do we compare their effectiveness if we can measure it—with two-parent families in general, or with two-parent families where the parents remain married despite long-standing marital discord?

E.   LAWYERS AND THE DIVORCE PROCESS

The divorce process includes not only substantive and procedural law but the activities of lawyers and other professionals who participate in marital dissolutions. The first two subsections of this section deal with aspects of the lawyer-client relationship that present special issues in matrimonial cases and arise largely in the formally, if not practically, adversarial setting of traditional divorce litigation. The last part of the section considers proposals to change the method by which matrimonial disputes are resolved and the role of lawyers in alternative approaches to dispute resolution.

1.   Creating the Lawyer-Client Relationship

KLEMM V. KLEMM

142 Cal. Rptr. 509 (Cal. App. 1977)

BROWN, J. The ultimate issue herein is to what extent one attorney may represent both husband and wife in a noncontested dissolution proceeding where the written consent of each to such representation has been filed with the court. . . .

At the dissolution hearing Attorney Catherine Bailey appeared for the wife. It developed that Bailey is a friend of the husband and wife and because they could not afford an attorney she was acting without compensation. The attorney had consulted with both the husband and wife and had worked out an oral agreement whereby the custody of the minor children would be joint, that is, each would have the children for a period of two weeks out of each month, and the wife waived child support.

The trial judge granted an interlocutory decree and awarded joint custody in accord with the agreement. However, because the wife was receiving aid for dependent children payments from the county, he referred the matter of child support to the Family Support Division of the Fresno County District Attorney's office for investigation and report.

The subsequent report from the family support division recommended that the husband be ordered to pay $25 per month per child (total $50) child support and that this amount be paid to the county as reimbursement for past and present A.F.D.C. payments made and being made to the wife. Bailey, on behalf of the wife, filed a written objection to the recommendation that the husband be required to pay child support.

At the hearing on the report and issue of child support on April 25, 1977, Bailey announced she was appearing on behalf of the husband. She said the parties were "in agreement on this matter, so there is in reality no conflict between them." No written consents to joint representation were filed. On questioning by the court the wife evinced uncertainty as to her position in the litigation. The wife said, "She [Bailey] asked me to come here just as a witness, so I don't feel like I'm taking any action against Dale." The judge pointed out that she (the wife) was still a party. When first asked if she wanted Bailey to continue as her attorney she answered "No." Later she said she would consent to Bailey's being relieved as her counsel. She then said she didn't believe she could act as her own attorney but that she consented to Bailey's representing the husband. After this confusing and conflicting testimony and a request for permission to talk to Bailey about it, the judge ordered, over Bailey's objection, that he would not permit Bailey to appear for either the husband or the wife because of a present conflict of interest and ordered the matter continued for one week.

At the continued hearing on May 2, 1977, Bailey appeared by counsel, who filed written consents to joint representation signed by the husband and wife and requested that Bailey be allowed to appear for the husband and wife (who were present in court). The consents, which were identical in form, stated:

I have been advised by my attorney that a potential conflict of interest exists by reason of her advising and representing my ex-spouse as well as myself. I feel this conflict is purely technical and I request Catherine Bailey to represent me.

The court denied the motion,[4] and the husband and wife have petitioned this court for a writ of mandate to direct the trial court to permit such representation.

_____

4. The court grounded its ruling upon the following reasoning: "[Under] our canons of ethics and rules of conduct it would be improper for Miss Bailey to appear in this

Rule 5-102 of the State Bar Rules of Professional Conduct states:

(A) A member of the State Bar shall not accept professional employment without first disclosing his relation, if any, with the adverse party, and his interest, if any, in the subject matter of the employment. A member of the State Bar who accepts employment under this rule shall first obtain the client's written consent to such employment.

(B) A member of the State Bar shall not represent conflicting interests, except with the written consent of all parties concerned.

The California cases are generally consistent with rule 5-102 permitting dual representation where there is a full disclosure and informed consent by all the parties, at least insofar as a representation pertains to agreements and negotiations prior to a trial or hearing. Where, however, a fully informed consent is not obtained, the duty of loyalty to different clients renders it impossible for an attorney, consistent with ethics and the fidelity owed to clients, to advise one client as to a disputed claim against the other.

Though an informed consent be obtained, no case we have been able to find sanctions dual representation of conflicting interests if that representation is in conjunction with a trial or hearing where there is an actual, present, existing conflict and the discharge of duty to one client conflicts with the duty to another. As a matter of law a purported consent to dual representation of litigants with adverse interests at a contested hearing would be neither intelligent nor informed. Such representation would be per se inconsistent with the adversary position of an attorney in litigation, and common sense dictates that it would be unthinkable to permit an attorney to assume a position at a trial or hearing where he could not advocate the interests of one client without adversely injuring those of the other.

However, if the conflict is merely potential, there being no existing dispute or contest between the parties represented as to any point in litigation, then with full disclosure to and informed consent of both clients there may be dual representation at a hearing or trial.

In our view the case at bench clearly falls within the latter category. The conflict of interest was strictly potential and not present. The parties had settled

---

proceeding on behalf of the respondent where there is not in the court's opinion a theoretical conflict, but an actual conflict of interest in this respect: This proceeding is to determine what amount, if any, the respondent will pay on account of child support to the petitioner Gail Klemm. At this point in time the court is advised and at the April 25th hearing that Mrs. Klemm was receiving public assistance, the end result being that whatever amount ordered paid and in fact paid would be paid to the Family Support Division and would not actually be realized by the petitioner in that if such amounts would become a part of the overall monthly grant.

"However, there is obviously a potential if not actual point in time when the petitioner may not be receiving public assistance in which case whatever order, if any, is made to her benefit on account of child support in this proceeding would be the amount subject to modification that she would receive on account of child support at least for some period of time."

their differences by agreement. There was no point of difference to be litigated. The position of each inter se was totally consistent throughout the proceedings. The wife did not want child support from the husband, and the husband did not want to pay support for the children. The actual conflict that existed on the issue of support was between the county on the one hand, which argued that support should be ordered, and the husband and wife on the other, who consistently maintained the husband should not be ordered to pay support.

While on the face of the matter it may appear foolhardy for the wife to waive child support,[5] other values could very well have been more important to her than such support — such as maintaining a good relationship between the husband and the children and between the husband and herself despite the marital problems — thus avoiding the backbiting, acrimony and ill will which the Family Relations Act of 1970 was, insofar as possible, designed to eliminate. It could well have been if the wife was forced to choose between A.F.D.C. payments to be reimbursed to the county by the husband and no A.F.D.C. payments she would have made the latter choice.

Of course, if the wife at some future date should change her mind and seek child support and if the husband should desire to avoid the payment of such support, Bailey would be disqualified from representing either in a contested hearing on the issue. There would then exist an actual conflict between them, and an attorney's duty to maintain the confidence of each would preclude such representation.

The conclusion we arrive at is particularly congruent with dissolution proceedings under the Family Law Act of 1970, the purpose of which was to discard the concept of fault in dissolution of marriage actions, to minimize the adversary nature of such proceedings and to eliminate conflicts created only to secure a divorce. It is contrary to the philosophy of that act to create controversy between the parties where none exists in reality.

We hold on the facts of this case, wherein the conflict was only potential, that if the written consents were knowing and informed and given after full disclosure by the attorney, the attorney can appear for both of the parties on issues concerning which they fully agree. . . .

A word as to procedure. Initially, the trial court is entitled to accept properly executed written consents to joint representation at their face value. The judge is entitled to presume the attorney is familiar with the law and code of professional ethics and has complied with the proper standards. However, if the judge has any question regarding whether the proper standards have been observed, it is his duty to either require counsel to inquire further or inquire himself regarding the circumstances of the execution of the written consents and the state of mind of the clients for the purpose of making the necessary factual determination in this regard.[6]

---

5. It is to be noted that the parties' agreement that the children should not receive support would not prevent the court from awarding child support either at the hearing or at some time subsequent thereto. Therefore, the children's rights are not in issue nor are they jeopardized.

6. A trial court has the inherent and statutory power to intervene on its own initiative to inquire into any appearance of impropriety, control the proceedings to remedy the defect, and even disqualify an attorney if that appears necessary.

Finally, as a caveat, we hasten to sound a note of warning. Attorneys who undertake to represent parties with divergent interests owe the highest duty to each to make a full disclosure of all facts and circumstances which are necessary to enable the parties to make a fully informed decision regarding the subject matter of the litigation, including the areas of potential conflict and the possibility and desirability of seeking independent legal advice. Failing such disclosure, the attorney is civilly liable to the client who suffers loss caused by lack of disclosure. In addition, the lawyer lays himself open to charges, whether well founded or not, of unethical and unprofessional conduct. Moreover, the validity of any agreement negotiated without independent representation of each of the parties is vulnerable to easy attack as having been procured by misrepresentation, fraud and overreaching. It thus behooves counsel to cogitate carefully and proceed cautiously before placing himself/herself in such a position.

NOTES AND QUESTIONS

1. As the opinion in *Klemm* indicates, clients with a common purpose (such as establishing a partnership or concluding a real estate transaction) often retain a single lawyer to carry out that purpose. This is generally permitted, especially in transactional matters but also in some litigative settings:

> So long as the American legal system broadly permits parties to make individual or collective decisions to bypass entitlements that they otherwise might claim, it cannot be objectionable that jointly represented parties have forgone some claims or defenses against each other in favor of what they regard as a more valuable position jointly asserted. In appreciation of the values of party autonomy, the law has generally permitted joint representation, even among parties with differing interests, so long as their interests are not too antagonistic and so long as they properly consent.

Charles Wolfram, Modern Legal Ethics 349-350 (1986). *Compare* Rule 1.7(a) of the American Bar Association (ABA) Model Rules of Professional Conduct, which provides that a lawyer shall not represent a client if the representation of that client will be directly adverse to another client, unless (1) the lawyer reasonably believes that the representation will not adversely affect the relationship with the other client and (2) each client consents. It also recognizes that it is usually impossible in litigation to take a position on behalf of one client that is not harmful to the interests of the other.

2. As we have seen, however, every divorce action — unlike almost any other legal matter — has at least a formal litigative component. Should matrimonial cases be considered transactional in nature (like contracts or wills) or litigative in character?

A number of decisions, and some current ethics opinions, take the position of the trial judge in *Klemm*, which prohibits one lawyer from representing both parties in matrimonial cases. *E.g.*, Bartlett v. Bartlett, 444 N.Y.S.2d 157, 158 (App. Div. 1981); Ohio Bar Formal Op. 30, 1 Fam. L. Rep. 3109 (1975); N.Y. City Bar Op. 258 (1980). The American Academy of Matrimonial Lawyers Standards of Conduct 2.20 (1991) likewise states, "An attorney should not represent both husband and wife even if they do not wish to obtain independent representation." The Academy expresses concern that "it is impossible for the attorney to provide impartial advice to both parties, and even a seemingly amicable separation or divorce may result in bitter litigation over financial matters or custody." Comment to 2.20.

3. Where divorcing spouses cannot afford independent representation and a lawyer or legal services office will not represent both, it often happens that the lawyer represents one spouse and the other goes unrepresented. In addition to obvious concerns for fairness, this situation presents problems in reaching a negotiated resolution.

The ABA Model Rules of Professional Conduct state generally that "[i]n dealing on behalf of a client with a person who is not represented by counsel, a lawyer should not state or imply that the lawyer is disinterested." Rule 4.3. When would the unrepresented client be so misled in a divorce setting?

The Comment to Rule 4.3 goes on to say that the lawyer should "not give advice to an unrepresented person other than the advice to obtain counsel." A broad interpretation of the phrase "giving advice" would create obvious problems for a lawyer representing a client even in an uncontested divorce where the other spouse was unrepresented. *See* Nathan Crystal, Ethics Problems in Marital Practice, 30 S.C. L. Rev. 321, 354 (1979). And, indeed, a broad interpretation has sometimes been articulated, even to the point of saying that a lawyer for plaintiff could not submit to the defendant a document waiving service of summons and the right to contest jurisdiction. ABA Informal Op. 1140 (1970). *See also* ABA Formal Op. 58 (1931) (lawyer cannot meet with unrepresented opposing party to secure latter's consent to divorce). However, a later opinion permits some kinds of communication with, but not advice to, the opponent. ABA Informal Op. 1269 (1973). *See generally* Crystal, above, at 354-356.

The Academy of Matrimonial Lawyers has adopted an approach that allows discussions with unrepresented parties but urges that counsel, at the earliest opportunity, inform the opposing party as follows:

1. I am your spouse's lawyer.
2. I do not and will not represent you.
3. I will at all times look out for your spouse's interests, not yours.
4. Any statements I make to you about this case should be taken as negotiations or argument on behalf of your spouse and not as advice to you as to your best interest.
5. I urge you to obtain your own lawyer.

4. Conflicts of interest are troublesome because they create concerns about the loyalty of the lawyer to his or her client. These concerns in turn arise from two sources. One has to do with whether a lawyer will fully advise or zealously represent a party if that same lawyer owes an identical duty to an opposing party. The other source of concern is the lawyer's duty to preserve a client's confidences.

Simultaneous representation of two clients in a common matter as in *Klemm* presents both of these sets of concerns. However, a conflict reflecting the second concern may also arise when a lawyer clearly represents only one party and the other is independently represented if the lawyer representing one party has *previously* represented the other. The critical question is whether there is reason to believe that that lawyer acquired confidential information during the first representation that would be relevant to the present matter. If it appears that the lawyer may have done so and the former client has not consented to the lawyer's current representation, the lawyer may be disqualified on motion of the former client. *See* Rule 1.9 of the ABA Model Rules of Professional Conduct; Cleland v. Cleland, 404 A.2d 905 (Conn. Super. 1979).

Both Rule 1.9 and *Cleland* use the "substantial relationship" test, which focuses on whether the scope of the prior representation is such that information relating to the current case would have been pertinent to the earlier representation. Courts differ on the specificity with which they examine similarities between the former and current matters, but most require a particularized inquiry into scope of representation, as opposed to information actually transmitted:

> Essentially, then, disqualification questions require three levels of inquiry. Initially, the trial judge must make a factual reconstruction of the scope of the prior legal representation. Second, it must be determined whether it is reasonable to infer that the confidential information allegedly given would have been given to a lawyer representing a client in those matters. Finally, it must be determined whether that information is relevant to the issues raised in the pending case against the former client.

Westinghouse Electric Corp. v. Gulf Oil Corp., 588 F.2d 221, 225 (7th Cir. 1978).

In *Cleland,* the plaintiff wife sought to disqualify the husband's lawyer and his law firm. The law firm had represented her in the recent past in connection with estate planning and preparation of her will. Should the motion to disqualify be granted? What would a client engaged in estate planning tell her lawyer, and how would that information be relevant in a divorce suit?

5. In general, any conflict of interest affecting a member of a firm and any confidential information received by a firm member are imputed to all members of the firm. In Borden v. Borden, 277 A.2d 89 (D.C. App. 1971), the court applied the rule of imputed knowledge to a legal aid office. As we saw in connection with Boddie v. Connecticut, 401 U.S. 371 (1971), indigents are not generally entitled to counsel in divorce actions. Accordingly, such an interpretation of ethics rules may mean that where both spouses are indigent and only one legal aid agency serves the community, one party *must* go without representation. However, the Alaska Supreme Court took a somewhat less absolute position in Flores v. Flores, 598 P.2d 893 (Alaska 1979). *Flores* concluded that a legal services office is not an ordinary law firm and could represent both spouses if it maintained separate offices and records and if it protected access to files. Since those conditions did not exist in the circumstances actually presented, representation of both spouses was disapproved.

The ABA Model Rules of Professional Conduct suggest that lawyers employed in the same unit of a legal services organization constitute a firm, but the same is not necessarily true of lawyers employed in separate units. What constitutes a separate unit apparently depends on "the particular rule that is involved, and on the specific facts of the situation." Comment 2 to Rule 1.10. If the lawyers are in the same unit, whatever that means, the categorical rule of disqualification set out in Rule 1.10(a) seemingly applies.

6. In addition to conflicts between current clients and between a current and a former client, a conflict between the interest of a client and the lawyer himself or herself may also exist. Although most of the cases in this connection arise from transactions involving a client's property, a growing body of law and commentary concerns sexual relations between clients and attorneys. This issue is discussed at pages 365-366.

PROBLEMS

1. Alma and Gustav Mahler have been married for ten years and now have agreed to divorce. Gustav is employed as a mechanic by an aircraft company, making about $30,000 a year; Alma has not worked outside the home for several years. They have been discussing matters for some time and have agreed that Alma will have custody of their two children (ages two and five). Gustav will have visitation for one day each weekend and will pay child support according to the state child support guidelines. Alma will seek employment. Their real and personal property consists of a house, in which they have $28,000 equity, two cars worth approximately $8,000 each, and about $10,000 in personal property (mostly household furnishings). Alma will keep the house, the furnishings, and one car.

Alma and Gustav have both come to your office for assistance in securing the divorce. They want you to represent both of them, and they do not want a second attorney, who would, in their view, add unnecessarily to the expense of the divorce and perhaps create problems. Would you and should you represent Alma and Gustav?

2. Assume Alma comes to you two years after receiving a divorce. She and her former husband, Gustav, had reached an agreement between themselves, identical with the agreement described in Problem 1. Arnold Becker, an experienced divorce lawyer, represented both. Last week, however, Alma was talking with a friend of hers, also divorced, who mentioned that she has received an interest in her ex-husband's pension plan. Alma was not aware that she might have some interest in Gustav's pension plan and wants to know if she can still receive something for it. How would you advise her?

3. Jean and Taylor Smith are divorcing. Taylor Smith is represented by Haddock & Carp, a law firm that has previously represented him in connection with his business interests. The firm also represented both Jean and Taylor when they challenged a lien on their home initiated by an electrician who charged what they considered, and the court agreed, to be an exorbitant amount for replacing the wiring in their home. Jean Smith now seeks to disqualify Haddock & Carp from representing Taylor. Should she succeed?

4. Suppose that, in Problem 3, Taylor's lawyer had previously represented him in a bankruptcy proceeding. Would that affect your analysis?

NOTE: FEE ARRANGEMENTS

Most courts take the view that contingent fees are not allowed in domestic relations cases. The court in Meyers v. Handlon, 479 N.E.2d 106 (Ind. App. 1985), summarizes the usual justifications for this prohibition:

. . . [W]e discern at least five reasons for the traditional disapproval of contingent fee contracts. They are: 1) the public policy favoring marriage; 2) disapproval of giving attorneys a financial incentive to promote divorce; 3) the statutory availability of attorney fee awards making contingent fees unnecessary; 4) the potential for overreaching or undue influence in a highly emotional situation; and 5) a need for the court to make an informed distribution of property which includes the obligation of attorney fees. . . .

The reason cited in virtually every case dealing with this issue is the State's interest in preserving the marital relationship and discouraging divorce. It is thought that a contingent fee contract in contemplation of divorce gives an attorney some incentive to actually promote the divorce or hinder possible reconciliation. Such a financial interest in derogation of marriage offends public policy. . . .

. . . The evolution away from restrictive divorce laws occurred, in our opinion, not because of a diminished societal interest in preserving the marriage relationship but in recognition that society's interest was rarely served by prolonging the agonies of a dying marriage. This does not, however, lessen the impropriety of an attorney having a financial stake in promoting a hostile, adversarial atmosphere between the parties. . . .

The fourth reason . . . is potential for overreaching and undue influence. . . . Divorce and the resulting division of the marital property creates an emotional atmosphere in which distraught parties are especially vulnerable to agreeing to a contract which turns out to be oppressive. . . .

The final reason . . . is the concern that the trial court's duty to provide an equitable property settlement and establish support for minor children or a disabled spouse may be thwarted by the existence of a contingent fee arrangement — especially where the court has not been informed of its existence. . . .

Id. at 109-111. *See also* Sobieski v. Maresco, 143 So. 2d 62 (Fla. Dist. Ct. App. 1962); Baskerville v. Baskerville, 75 N.W.2d 762 (Minn. 1956); Shanks v. Kilgore, 589 S.W.2d 318 (Mo. App. 1979); Glasscock v. Glasscock, 403 S.E.2d 313 (S.C. 1991). Rule 1.5(d)(1) of the ABA Model Rules of Professional Conduct also prohibits "any fee in a domestic relations matter, the payment of which is contingent upon the securing of a divorce or upon the amount of alimony or support, or property settlement in lieu thereof. . . ." Comment [6] of Section 1.5 provides that the prohibition does not apply to "legal representation in connection with the recovery of post-judgment balances due under support, alimony, or financial orders because such contracts do not implicate the same policy concerns." The Comments provide no explanation for the prohibition generally. Why don't the policy concerns present in the initial divorce proceeding also present in post-judgment actions?

The court in Meyers v. Handlon notes in passing that, unlike most cases, the fees of one party to a divorce can be shifted to the other party, and this arguably makes contingent fees unnecessary. Implicitly, this argument suggests that contingent fees are allowed only as a necessary evil. It is true that, with some exceptions, American (unlike English) practice usually leaves each party to pay his or her own legal fees regardless of the outcome of the case. It is not true, however, that contingent fees are permitted only when necessary — that is, only when the client cannot pay an hourly or set fee rate. Rule 1.5(c) of the ABA Model Rules of Professional Conduct states generally that "[a] fee may be contingent on the outcome of the matter for which service is rendered . . . ," without any requirement that clients be unable to pay an hourly or project rate. If a client in a contract or tort matter may choose to pay a contingent fee, or if a lawyer in such cases may ask for such a fee, these fees serve purposes other than making legal services available when they otherwise would not be. How convincing, then, is the "lack of necessity" argument?

There has been some attrition from the general view that contingent fees are never proper in divorce cases. Over the last two or three decades, a number of decisions have permitted some form of contingent fee, particularly when dissolution has already occurred or the basis for the divorce is noncontroversial.

In Oliver v. Doga, 384 So. 2d 330 (La. 1980), the Louisiana Supreme Court permitted a contingent fee for the representation of a wife in connection with division of community property. The parties had already separated but had not yet divorced; however, the representation was limited to the property division issue. *See also* Burns v. Stewart, 188 N.W.2d 760 (Minn. 1971) (contingent fee enforced where husband had deserted wife, making prospects of reconciliation negligible, and fee charged wife was reasonable); In re Cooper, 344 S.E.2d 27 (N.C. App. 1986) (contingent fee enforceable if not for procurement of divorce but only for resolution of financial issues). *Compare* Ballesteros v. Jones, 985 S.W.2d 485 (Tex. App. 1998), upholding a contingent fee arrangement in a divorce case. The arrangement was for counsel to receive one-third of the settlement recovery; the resulting claim was for $90,000. The court noted that contingent fee arrangements are rarely justified in divorce actions, but held that the issues here — including need for proof of a common law marriage — were sufficiently complex and the outcome sufficiently uncertain that a contingent fee was permissible and that there was in this case no glaring or flagrant disparity between the fee paid and the value of the services rendered.

As noted above, courts often shift responsibility for fees in divorce cases from one party to another. Such awards are usually entered and/or upheld when the party lacks sufficient funds to pay the agreed (reasonable) fee in whole or in part, or where the spouse seeking relief will have substantially fewer resources than the other. *See* Cordone v. Cordone, 752 A.2d 1082 (Conn. App. 1999). All or partial fees may also be awarded when the court finds that one spouse has engaged in dilatory or other improper tactics. *E.g.*, Hendricks v. Hendricks. 784 N.E.2d 1024 (Ind. App. 2003); Do v. Superior Court (Nguyen), 135 Cal. Rptr. 2d 855 (Cal. App. 2003). An allowance of attorneys' fees will be overturned only when there is an abuse of discretion, that is, when it appears that the trial court could not reasonably have concluded as it does. *Compare* In re Marriage of Robinson and Thiel, 35 P.3d 89 (Ariz. App. 2001) (abuse of discretion to spouse with far fewer resources) *with* In re Marriage of Duncan, 108 Cal. Rptr. 2d 833 (Cal. App. 2001) (no abuse of discretion where both parties had sufficient financial resources to pay for their litigation, even though husband had substantial earned income and wife had none). A fee award may also be denied where there is no evidence to support the amount awarded. *See* Viera v. Viera, 698 So. 2d 1308 (Fla. App. 1997); Humberger v. Humberger, 1998 WL 610604 (Idaho App. 1998); Taylor v. Taylor, 508 S.E.2d 50 (S.C. App. 1998).

"Performance" or "value-added" fees — fees that reflect the outcome reached rather than the amount or kind of work done — have become common in many legal settings. A New York court has considered the extent to which such fees are "contingent" and therefore improper where contingent fees are prohibited in domestic relations cases. The wife had agreed to pay her attorney a "bonus" of $2 million in light of the favorable results achieved in the divorce action — an agreement by the husband to pay her $15 million in property and alimony after his initial offer of $750,000. The wife sought to avoid a $1 million payment and rescind the performance agreement because it was executed 24 hours before the husband signed the separation agreement, which provided for an uncontested divorce. The trial court entered summary judgment in favor of the client, finding the agreement amounted to a contingent fee on the property and alimony arrangement and was violative of the disciplinary rule barring such arrangements. The Appellate Division reversed the summary judgment and remanded, noting that the separation agreement was complete at the time the fee agreement was made and that the issue was whether any contingency remained after that point. Weinstein v. Barnett, 640 N.Y.S.2d 77 (App. Div. 1996).

An element of performance-based compensation has often been recognized in judicial awards of lawyers' fees in divorce cases. See Sexton v. Sexton, 469 S.E.2d 608 (S.C. 1996), holding that beneficial results achieved by parties on appeal and remand are relevant to the adequacy of an attorneys' fees award. A Florida court, while recognizing bonus fees, held that retainer agreements would be construed in the client's favor against the drafting law firm and that where the obligation to pay a "bonus" was not clear, the attorney could not collect. May v. Sessums, 700 So. 2d 22 (Fla. Dist. Ct. App. 1997).

In a pair of heart-warming decisions, the Pennsylvania Supreme Court authorized a trial court to imprison a husband for failure to pay court-ordered attorneys' fees, Sinaiko v. Sinaiko, 664 A.2d 1005 (Pa. Super. Ct. 1995), and the Texas Court of Appeals held that the husband's obligation to pay attorneys' fees in lieu of temporary support was not a "debt" for purposes of the Texas constitutional prohibition on imprisonment for debt. Ex parte Kimsey, 915 S.W.2d 523 (Tex. Ct. App. 1995).

PROBLEMS

1. Martha Allen visits your office to discuss her divorce action, which has been in negotiation for some time. She has been married for 18 years, and a considerable amount of property is involved. Her husband's attorney is a well-known, aggressive divorce lawyer. Martha Allen has lost confidence in her current attorney because "he just doesn't seem interested in my problems and isn't willing to take on my husband's lawyer." She tells you that she has heard good things about you but wants to be quite sure that you are really committed to her success. Accordingly, she would prefer a fee arrangement in which you receive one-third of whatever she receives in property distribution. Assume that you believe that the distribution would be sufficient to provide a reasonable fee. May you enter into the proposed fee arrangement? Would you?

2. In the same situation as that in Problem 1, there is little property to be distributed because most of John Allen's wealth is in his professional practice,

which is not considered marital property in this jurisdiction. However, it seems likely that Martha Allen will receive spousal maintenance, either through permanent alimony or through reimbursement alimony (which will have to be paid over a number of years). She is willing to pay you one-third of what she receives in maintenance but does not want to pay an hourly rate. How would you respond to her proposal?

2. Counseling and Client Relations

The allocation of authority between lawyers and their clients is both important and complex. Rule 1.2(a) of the ABA Model Rules of Professional Conduct provides as follows:

> A lawyer shall abide by a client's decision concerning the objectives of representation, subject to paragraphs (c), (d), and (e), and shall consult with the client as to the means by which they are to be pursued. A lawyer shall abide by the client's decision whether to accept an offer of settlement of a matter.

In principle, it seems that the client should have the authority to decide whether to pursue a potentially available legal remedy, whether to propose a settlement, and whether to accept an offered settlement. The Comment to Rule 1.2 explains, however:

> A clear distinction between objectives and means sometimes cannot be drawn, and in many cases the client-lawyer relationship partakes of a joint undertaking. In questions of means, the lawyer should assume responsibility for technical and legal tactical issues, but should defer to the client regarding such questions as the expense to be incurred and concern for third persons who might be adversely affected.

The practical difficulty in distinguishing between the responsibilities of clients and lawyers is reflected in theoretical disagreement regarding those roles. One view maintains that the primary duty of lawyers is to assist their clients' expressions of their own dignity and autonomy, rather than themselves decide what is good and wise. *E.g.*, Monroe H. Freedman, Understanding Legal Ethics 43-64 (1990); Charles J. Fried, The Lawyer as Friend: The Moral Foundations of the Lawyer-Client Relationship, 85 Yale L.J. 1060, 1071 (1976). The other urges lawyers to take responsibility for acts on behalf of clients and be guided by their own senses of both client interests and just conduct. *E.g.*, David Luban, Lawyers and Justice: An Ethical Study (1988); William W. Simon, Ethical Discretion in Lawyering, 101 Harv. L. Rev. 1083, 1113-1119 (1988).

What is not disputed is that lawyers act as advisors to their clients, however their respective responsibilities are defined and allocated. However, even here the question of the lawyer's proper sphere reintroduces itself. A distinction may be drawn between technical advice relating to legal rights and advice that is more general. The latter class of advice or counseling can also be considered more or less broadly. Nontechnical counseling can be limited, perhaps to the relative costs and benefits of pursuing an arguably available legal position. It can also be far broader, addressing the client's emotional condition, long-term hopes, desires, and prospects. The more broadly counseling is understood, the greater the potential for assimilating the roles of lawyer and client.

A broader counseling role has been increasingly recognized over the last several decades. Model Rule 2.1 provides that "[i]n representing a client, a lawyer shall exercise independent professional judgment and render candid advice. In rendering advice, a lawyer may refer not only to law but to other considerations such as moral, economic, social and political factors, that may be relevant to the client's situation."

Domestic relations lawyers especially have been expected to go beyond technical legal advice in counseling clients. Because divorce itself has traditionally been, and still is, regarded as undesirable, lawyers have been urged to counsel their clients to explore reconciliation rather than pursue dissolution. This expectation still remains. Standard 2.2 of the American Academy of Matrimonial Lawyers Standards of Conduct provides:

> An attorney should advise the client of the emotional and economic impact of divorce and the possibility or advisability of reconciliation.

Comment

The duty of vigorous advocacy in no way prohibits the matrimonial lawyer from counseling the client to be cautious in embarking on divorce. The divorce process exacts a heavy and economic and emotional toll. An attorney should ask if reconciliation might be possible, or at least whether the client is receptive to counseling. If the client exhibits uncertainty or ambivalence, the lawyer should assist in obtaining a counselor. In no event should an attorney urge a client to file suit, unless necessary to protect the client's interests.

It is generally assumed that a lawyer's role in family matters is to act not only as an advocate, but to some extent as a counselor and advisor. And the [ABA Rules of Professional Conduct] specifically permit the lawyer to address moral, economic, social and political factors, which may be relevant to the client's situation. . . .

If the client has begun counseling in hopes of reconciliation, the matrimonial lawyer should attempt to mitigate litigation-related activities that might prejudice marital harmony. It is important, however, that the attorney be mindful that clients may make damaging admissions during joint marriage counseling. One spouse may use a "breathing spell" afforded by counseling to deplete the marital estate. The lawyer should advise the client of these risks and take precautions to protect the client in the interim.

The special situation of the lawyer-client relationship in matrimonial matters provides a paradigm case for "client-centered counseling," an approach that has been broadly advocated in the clinical legal literature. *See* David A. Binder & Susan C. Price, Legal Interviewing and Counseling: A Client-Centered Approach (1977); Ira C. Ellman, Lawyers and Clients, 34 UCLA L. Rev. 717 (1987). At base, a client-centered approach emphasizes the desirability of enabling clients to make their own decisions.

JAMES R. ELKINS, *A COUNSELING MODEL FOR LAWYERING
IN DIVORCE CASES*

53 Notre Dame L. Rev. 229 (1977)

Separation and divorce are significant and traumatic events in an individual's life. The dissolution of a marriage and an ongoing family unit is seldom a happy occasion. Frequently, separation and divorce involve intense anger, bitterness, and disillusionment; ambivalence, anxiety, depression, and guilt may also be experienced. . . .

Influenced by his use of directive interviewing in the context of other legal settings, the attorney traditionally seeks to obtain the "relevant" facts in order to determine grounds for divorce . . . and factors which will influence the amount of child and spousal support, child custody, and visitation rights. Typically, lawyers want those facts which are relevant to legal problems and are not concerned with facts relevant to the client's feelings. Given this orientation to ascertaining the facts, the lawyer forcefully guides the client's responses by direct questions designed to elicit the facts needed for producing a legal result. . . .

The most serious drawback of the traditional approach is that it does not allow for the expression of client feelings, which is essential to a satisfactory attorney-client relationship. Thus, the initial problem can be viewed as structuring a relationship in which the client can express feelings easily and constructively. Such a relationship will be dependent upon the attorney's understanding that "feelings can be facts, too." The underlying premise that feelings are facts is based upon an understanding that behavior which appears to be irrational or self-destructive may be a tacit way of communicating feelings. . . .

The first issue of concern to the domestic relations counselor is finding an appropriate model by which to fashion a more constructive and growth-oriented relationship. In developing a framework for dealing with domestic relations clients, the attorney can profitably turn to the counselor for guidance. An attorney following the counseling model views himself as a member of a "helping profession"; he is concerned with more than the mere application of technical legal skills. Thomas Shaffer notes that "counselors" are perceptive to verbal and non-verbal signals, empathic and congruent, adept at listening, and open to the client. An attorney following a model based on counseling theories expresses a preference "for client-centered indices of concern . . . he seeks a capacity for acceptance . . . for understandings . . . and for congruence (awareness of the feelings within himself). . . .

A. ACTIVE LISTENING

. . . Active listening entails listening to determine what the client is really saying. . . . Finding out what the client is "really saying" will require the attorney to "[r]ead between the lines; listen for metaphors; measure the emotional charge in . . . (the client's) remarks; look for the irrational." "I want a divorce" may really mean "sympathize with me; tell me I've been mistreated, but talk me out of it." . . .

B. POTENTIAL OBSTACLES TO THE CLIENT-CENTERED APPROACH

1.   Client dependency

In response to client expectations and psychological needs, the attorney in a domestic relations case is often cast in a strong, supportive role. Feelings of dependence on the client's part may arise from a variety of factors: the client's expectation that the lawyer will "step in and straighten things out"; the client's attempt to avoid responsibility for making a decision; the client's "magical expectation . . . that the lawyer is able to accomplish any manipulation or transaction which the client desires"; the client's inflated view of the legal profession; the client's low self-esteem; and, finally, the attorney's psychological need to occupy a dominant role in the interaction. . . .

How should the attorney approach the client who has a rescue attitude? Carl Rogers points out that the natural tendency in such a situation is to try to convince the client that feelings of powerlessness and low self-esteem are exaggerated, and that there is no logical reason for him to feel that way. This attempt, however, may not always be successful:

. . . The counselor is giving more genuine help if he assists the client to face these feelings openly, recognize them for what they are, and admit that he has them. . . .

2.   Understanding the client's world

. . . It is essential that the lawyer determine what the client wants and expects. To what degree is the client seeking "information, support, love, friendship, skills, problem solution, decision-making, a way out of unpleasantness, movement toward a goal, change in inner feelings"? What kind of role is the attorney asked to play in providing what the client wants? And are the client's expectations and role demands compatible with the attorney's image of his professional role? . . .

. . . [C]lient behavior may be viewed as "irrational" if the attorney fails to look beyond the surface to search for underlying motivations. . . . It is helpful to adhere to a theory that all behavior is adaptive and has an underlying motivation linked to the client's view of the world. The client's world and the attorney's world are not mutually inclusive; on the contrary, they are in some respects mutually exclusive. Thus, behavior which is defined as irrational by the attorney may stem from that part of the client's world which does not intersect with the attorney's. . . .

Austin Sarat & William B. Felstiner, *Law and Strategy in the Divorce Lawyer's Office*

20 Law & Soc'y Rev. 93 (1986)

[This research is based on observations of one side of 40 divorce cases in Massachusetts and California, including observation and tape recording of lawyer-client sessions, attending court and mediation hearings and trials, and interviewing lawyers and clients about these events. Approximately 115 lawyer-client conferences were tape-recorded.

The conference on which the following discussion is based was between a lawyer with a good educational background who had practiced for 14 years and his client. The client was a middle-class wife in her late thirties, with no children. The house was the major asset. The client and her husband had initially sought to resolve their dispute through mediation. The husband, however, hired a lawyer and secured an ex parte restraining order barring the wife from entering the property at any time. That order ended all hope of mediation, and the client hired the lawyer involved in this conference. At the time of this conference, a judge had upheld the restraining order but left open the question of whether it might be set aside on grounds of bad faith by the husband.]

Clients look to lawyers to explain how the legal system works and to interpret the actions and decisions of legal officials. Despite their lack of knowledge about and contact with the law, clients are likely to have some general notions that the law works as a formally rational legal order, one that is rule governed, impersonal, impartial, predictable, and relatively error free. How do lawyers respond to this picture? . . .

[The lawyer in this case describes to his client a legal system that depends on insider knowledge possessed by lawyers, that is highly unpredictable in outcome, and that cannot even be explained adequately to outsiders.] . . .

In total, the lawyer's description of the legal process involves an open acknowledgement of human frailties, contradictions between appearance and reality, carelessness, incoherence, accident, and built-in limitations. The picture presented is both cynical and probably considered by lawyers to be realistic. Whereas others claim that legal actors, particularly appellate judges, present the law in highly formalistic terms and work to curtail inconsistencies and contradictions in legal doctrine, many of the lawyers that we observed engaged in no such mystification. . . .

Given such a legal process, how should divorce disputes be managed? This concern is central in most of the cases that we observed, and it is an issue that may recur as lawyer and client discuss each of the major controversies in a divorce case. . . .

While many clients think of the legal process as an arena for a full adversarial contest, most divorce disputes are not resolved in this manner. Although not all lawyers are equally dedicated to reaching negotiated agreements, most of those we observed advised their clients to try to settle the full range of issues in the case. This is not to say that these divorces were free of conflict, for the negotiations themselves were often quite contentious. . . .

The conference we are examining revolves around two major issues: (1) whether to ignore or contest the restraining order; and (2) what position to take concerning disposition of the family residence. Much of the conference is devoted to discussing the restraining order—its origins, morality, and legality; the prospects for dissolving it; the lawyer's stake in contesting it; and the client's emotional reaction to it. Substantively the order is not as important as the house itself, which received much less attention and generated much less controversy. Both issues, however, force the lawyer and client to decide whether they will retain control of the case by engaging in negotiations or cede control to the court for hearing and decision. The lawyer definitely favors negotiations.

> *Lawyer:* Okay. What I would like your permission to do then is to meet with Foster [opposing counsel], see if I can come up with or negotiate a settlement with him. . . . My feeling is, Jane, that if we reach that point, both lawyers are prepared to make a recommendation on settlement to their respective clients, if either of the clients, either you or Norb, find something terribly disagreeable with the proposal that we have, the lawyers have come to between themselves, then the case just either can't be settled or it's not ripe for settlement. But we would have given it the best shot. . . .

The client in this case is reluctant to begin settlement negotiations until some attention is paid to the restraining order. While she acknowledges that she wants a reasonable property settlement, she reminds her lawyer that that is not her exclusive concern:

> *Client:* Yes, there's no question in my mind that [a property settlement] is my first goal. However, that doesn't mean that it's my only goal. . . .

The lawyer responds by acknowledging that he considers the restraining order to be legally wrong and that he believes it could be litigated. Thus, he confirms his client's position and inclination on legal grounds. Yet he dissents from her position and opposes her inclination to fight on other grounds. . . .

. . . [T]he lawyer is worried that an effort to fight the restraining order would interfere with the resolution of the case, that is, of the outstanding property issue. Although the lawyer considers the restraining order to be a legal mistake, its effect would end upon final disposition of the house. In the meantime, the client can either live with the order or pay for additional hearings. He believes that it would be unwise for her to fight further, not only because the contest would be costly but also because it would postpone or derail entirely negotiations about the house and other tangible assets. . . .

. . . Time and again in our study we observed lawyers attempting to focus their client's attention on the issues the lawyers thought to be major while the clients often concentrated on matters that the lawyers considered secondary. . . . His sense of justice and of the long-term best interests of his client lead him to transform this dispute from a battle over the legality and morality of the restraining order to a negotiation over the more narrow and tangible issue of the ultimate disposition of the house and other assets, which he believes can and should be settled. . . .

In attempting this transformation, the lawyer allies himself with [his client's] therapist:

> *Lawyer:* I agree with Irene that that [fighting the restraining order] is not the best way. . . . It's probably the worst way. This [negotiating] hopefully is the best way.

This reliance on the therapist is noteworthy because it is often assumed that a therapeutic orientation is antithetical to the adversarial inclination of law and the legal profession. . . . [T]he settlement preference of no-fault divorce corresponds to the movement in family therapy toward the "constructive divorce." It could well be that various professionals dealing with divorce have simultaneously registered and reinforced the emergence of new cultural mores concerning marriage and its dissolution. However we interpret this observation, it is clear that this lawyer, and most of those we observed, construct an image of the appropriate mode of disposition of a case that is at odds with the conventional view in which lawyers are alleged to induce competition and hostility, transform noncontentious clients into combatants, and promulgate a "fight theory of justice." . . .

* * *

. . . In divorce . . . cases, the lawyer must help redefine the client's orientation toward the legal process. . . . [T]his means that lawyers must help their clients view the emotional process of dissolving an intimate relationship in instrumental terms. . . . [L]awyers and clients struggle, although rarely explicitly, with the issue of what part of the client's personality is relevant to the legal process. . . .

The negotiation of the legal self in this case begins by focusing on the relative importance of emotions engaged by the legal process and the symbolic aspects of the divorce as opposed to its financial and material dimensions. Throughout this conference the lawyer warns his client not to confuse the realms of emotion and finance and instructs her that she can expect the legal process to work well only if emotional material is excluded from her deliberations.

This emotional material is rather complex and difficult for both lawyer and client to sort out. The client is, in the first instance, eager to let her lawyer know that she feels both anger and mistrust toward many participants in the legal process. . . .

The client continues to express her anger throughout the conference, especially when the conversation turns directly to her husband's lawyer.

> Client: The other option I see could have been that Norb would have gotten different legal advice from the beginning. So the thing, I suppose, that I'm concerned about, I'm concerned about Foster. I distrust him as thoroughly as I do Norb, and I think you have been very measured in your statements about him. I think he's a son-of-a-bitch, and there's nothing I've seen that he's done that changed my mind about that. . . .

The client's mistrust is not reserved exclusively for the opposition. She is, to an extent, wary of her own lawyer as well. . . . The predicament in which the client finds herself—needing to trust a stranger when trust has just been betrayed by an intimate—is one that faces and perplexes divorce clients generally. . . .

By playing down the question of trust the lawyer is telling the client that the emotional self must be separated from the legal self. Gestures and symbolic acknowledgement of wrongs suffered belong to some realm other than law. He is, in addition, defending himself against a kind of emotional transference. Much of the emotion talk in this conference involves the lawyer himself, directly or indirectly. In the discussion of trust the client makes the lawyer into a kind of husband substitute. . . . The client described him as her "knight in shining armor," an image of protection and romance; she acknowledges having sexual fantasies about him. . . . These demands on her lawyer typify the kind of environment in which divorce lawyers work. . . .

NOTES AND QUESTIONS

1. A study of Dutch matrimonial lawyers bears a number of resemblances to Sarat and Felstiner's research.

> Working within the margins set by legal rules and institutional practices, the accepted norms governing legal practice, and more general social norms of "reasonableness," "fairness" and what is "good for the children," and taking account of the reasonable wishes of the client, lawyers try to achieve a mutually acceptable divorce settlement with which the parties and their children will be able to live. Their objective, in other words, is a "reasonable divorce" in which the problems are dealt with outside of court, as much as possible directly by the parties, but when necessary with the help and advice of their lawyers.
>
> The most striking characteristic of divorce practice is the central place most lawyers give to conflict minimalization and a nonadversarial approach. Most of them try consciously to reduce the level of aggression in divorce cases — to exert, as one put it, a "neutralizing, regulating influence" on their clients and the process itself. . . .
>
> Lawyers' control over the legal procedure makes available various techniques for cooling off conflict. Simple delay is often used to this end.
>
> Lawyers frequently exert considerable pressure on their own clients to be reasonable. When possible they cooperate with the lawyer for the other party in seeking to get their clients to agree to a reasonable settlement. . . . [T]he key to their role is a common strategy from which they seldom diverge: the maintenance of a stance of relative neutrality. They keep their professional distance from the client, letting the client understand that while they are there to offer certain kinds of professional help, they will not allow themselves to be coopted into the client's quarrels. . . .
>
> The idea that lawyers polarize and escalate conflict finds little support in our observations or interviews. Very little polarization occurs at all. When it does, it seems to be largely a result of interaction processes between the parties themselves. Some clients expect their lawyers to be far more aggressive than they are willing to be and criticize them for failing to be "hard" enough.

John Griffiths, What Do Dutch Lawyers Actually Do in Divorce Cases?, 20 Law & Soc'y Rev. 135, 163-167 (1986).

A study of lawyers in the Australian legal system is likewise inconsistent with the notion that lawyers and courts are entrenched in an adversarial mindset that exacerbates rather than resolves interpersonal and social conflict. Family lawyers in both the public and private sectors believed it was best to settle cases, and three-quarters of those lawyers said they would go to court only if efforts at settlement had proved fruitless. These expectations were supported by case outcomes; less than 8 percent of a sample of 812 cases resulted in a hearing and judicial decision, and three-quarters of the cases were resolved before a pre-hearing conference. It may be that lawyer negotiations are more successful at producing full settlements than is mediation. Rosemary Hunter, Adversarial Mythologies: Policy Assumptions and Research Evidence in Family Law, 30 J.L. Soc'y. 156, 159-162 (2003). *See also* John Eekelaar et al., Family Lawyers: The Divorce Work of Solicitors 13, 16-17 (2000).

2. Do the lawyers described by Sarat & Felstiner in this country and Griffiths in the Netherlands follow a client-centered approach? May they understand the client's world but not adopt it as their own? What reasons are there for distinguishing those two worlds?

3. Who should win the struggle over the client's legal identity? Is the lawyer engaging in an illegitimate form of manipulation? Or is the client seeking from the legal system something that it is not prepared to provide?

4. Should the legal system provide an opportunity for divorcing parties to express the anger, anxiety, bitterness, and other emotions that Elkins describes? Does it do so, in effect, through the role of lawyers in divorce matters?

5. As the introductory discussion indicates, in principle the client is entitled to make the substantive decisions about the conduct of his or her case. The client may decide whether to seek, or accept, sole or joint custody; what to seek by way of property distribution; whether to ask for or forgo alimony. If, after advising the client, the lawyer is profoundly dissatisfied with the client's position, he or she may withdraw *if* that can be accomplished without material adverse effect on the client's interests or if, among other things, the client insists on an illegal course of action or one that the lawyer considers repugnant or imprudent. Model Rule 1.14(b). How ready should a lawyer be to withdraw?

6. Lawyers who engage in divorce practice have been grouped in several ways. Divorce law generally was a part of general or small office practice, although a small group of lawyers, usually in urban centers in the United States, could be said to specialize in this field. *See* Hubert J. O'Gorman, Lawyers and Matrimonial Cases: A Study of Informal Pressures in Private Professional Practice 65-80 (1963); Jerome E. Carlin, Lawyers on Their Own 95 (1962). With the growth in divorce rates and other factors, more lawyers devote considerable portions of their practice to divorce or, more broadly, to family law. *See* Craig A. McEwen, Richard T. Maiman & Lynn Mather, Divorce Lawyer Role Conceptions and the Specialization of Divorce Law Practice, Annual Meeting of the Law and Society Association (June 1991).

It remains true, however, that lawyers who engage in substantial divorce practice tend to have lower-income clients and to work in relatively small law firms. In addition, women attorneys tend to be more heavily involved in divorce practice than men. Half of the women lawyers studied by McEwen, Maiman, and Mather concentrated on divorce practice, compared with only 28 percent of the men; or, looking in the other direction, half of the divorce specialists in the study were women. *Id.* at 12-13.

7. The high rates of participation by women in family law practice has been predicted and observed frequently. Some of the explanations are ideological, relating to assumptions about the values women bring to the legal profession. *See* Lee

E. Teitelbaum, Antoinette Sedillo Lopez & Jeffrey Jenkins, Gender, Legal Education, and Legal Careers, 41 J. Legal Educ. 443, 448 (1992). Some may be structural, to the extent that women find or seek employment in small firms that may allow them greater opportunities to balance professional and familial or personal activities. *See* Terence C. Halliday, Six Score Years and Ten: Demographic Transitions in the American Legal Profession, 1850-1980, 20 Law & Soc'y Rev. 53, 75 (1986). And yet others may arise from a form of market demand, to the extent that wives seeking divorce may prefer women lawyers. *See* McEwen, Maiman & Merry, above, at 24-25.

8. If there is a tendency for women lawyers to prefer representing wives, and for wives to prefer being represented by women lawyers, would that affect the kinds of approaches taken by attorneys in the studies described above? How? For good or ill?

9. Both Elkin and Sarat & Felstiner discuss the phenomenon of transference. In some instances, that may lead to opportunities for sexual relations between clients and attorneys. A growing body of law and commentary addresses that issue.

A relatively limited restriction was adopted in American Bar Association Standing Committee on Ethics and Professional Responsibility. Formal Opinion 92-364 (July 9, 1992) observes that sexual involvement with a client may constitute a breach of fiduciary duty when the relationship results from the client's dependence, may interfere with the lawyer's professional judgment, and may otherwise impair the representation provided by the lawyer. The opinion advises lawyers to refrain from sexual relationships with clients and observes that discipline may result if the lawyer's representation is actually impaired. Rule 3-120(B) of the California Rules of Professional Conduct seemingly reaches a similar conclusion. The California rule provides that a lawyer shall not

> (1) Require or demand sexual relations with a client incident to or as a condition of any professional representation; or (2) Employ coercion, intimidation, or undue influence in entering into sexual relations; or (3) Continue representation of a client with whom the member has had sexual relations if such sexual relations cause the member to perform legal services incompetently. . . .

In June 2002, the American Bar Association House of Delegates approved language in Model Rule 1.8(j) recommended by the Ethics 2000 Commission. That rule prohibits a lawyer from having sex with a client unless a consensual sexual relationship existed prior to the beginning of professional representation.

Broader, sometimes per se, bans on sexual relations with clients have been advocated and sometimes adopted. The New York Code of Professional Responsibility, DR. 1-102(A)(7), 22 NYCRR §1200.3(A)(7) (West 1995), provides that "[a] lawyer shall not: . . . Begin a sexual relationship with a client during the course of the lawyer's representation of the client." Standard 2.16 of the American Academy of Matrimonial Lawyers Standards of Conduct states that "[a]n attorney should never have a sexual relationship with a client or opposing counsel during the time of the representation." *See also* Committee on Professional Ethics & Conduct v. Hill, 436 N.W.2d 57, 59 (Iowa 1989) ("Sexual contact between an attorney and client in a professional context constitutes professional impropriety");

In re DiSandro, 680 A.2d 73 (R.I. 1996) (although no ethics rule specifically requires it, an attorney must refrain from sexual relations with the client or withdraw from the case). *But compare* Shirk v. Shirk, 561 N.W.2d 519 (Minn. 1997) (holding that a sexual relationship between a client and her attorney that is contrary to professional rules does not itself result in incompetent representation providing grounds to vacate a decree).

For a survey of the issues presented, *see* Caroline A. Forell, Lawyers, Clients, and Sex: Breaking the Silence on the Ethical and Liability Issues, 22 Golden Gate U. L. Rev. 611 (1992). For a critique of disciplinary rules of the kinds adopted by New York state and the ABA, *see* Linda Fitts Mischler, Personal Morals Masquerading as Professional Ethics: Regulations Banning Sex Between Domestic Relations Attorneys and Their Clients, 23 Harv. Women's L.J. 1 (2000).

PROBLEMS

1. During a hotly contested custody litigation, you realize that you, the other attorney, and the parents are not going to reach any interim or permanent settlement. You are also convinced that the children are undergoing terrible emotional strain because of the conduct of their parents. You feel the best recourse is to ask the court to appoint a guardian ad litem for the children.

a. Must you discuss this step with your client?

b. If your client directs you not to seek such an appointment, may you do so anyway? Are there any other actions you might take?

2. You represent the wife in a petition for an increase in child support. You have negotiated a deal for an amount above the state child support guidelines and feel you will not do any better in court. You so inform the wife, but she still wants more and refuses to settle. Can you accept the offer on your client's behalf? If not, should you seek to withdraw, and can you properly do so?

3. Alternative Dispute Resolution

Jessica Pearson & Nancy Thoennes, Mediating and Litigating Custody Disputes: A Longitudinal Evaluation

17 Fam. L.Q. 497, 497-498 (1984)

One result of the upsurge in divorce is that the court is overwhelmed by the demands being made upon it. Over half of the cases filed in all trial courts are concerned with matrimonial actions. Approximately 10 percent of divorce cases go to full scale legal battles over custody. Many court systems are so overloaded that delays of nine to ten months are common for no-fault divorces and contested cases often have to wait for a year or two to be scheduled.

Court congestion is not the only problem with the adversarial system. Many feel it is simply inappropriate when applied to the resolution of marital disputes. According to one writer, the adversarial model increases trauma and escalates conflict. Another writer argues that the adversarial system encourages "dog and cat fights" that run counter to the best interests of the child. Lawyers are accused of being poorly trained to deal with the psychological aspects of divorce and of encouraging their clients to take extreme positions that are unnecessarily divisive. Judicial proceedings are criticized for failing to address unresolved feelings about the marriage and separation that often precipitate custody conflicts in the first place. Others feel that adversarial interventions foster low commitment to the eventual agreement and fail to enhance the cooperative, communication and problem-solving skills of the parties. Still others fault the coercive nature of adjudication as well as the "twin dragons" of cost and delay.

THOMAS E. CARBONNEAU, *ALTERNATIVE DISPUTE RESOLUTION: MELTING THE LANCES AND DISMOUNTING THE STEEDS*

160-162 (1989)

The legal system does not openly respond to the emotions experienced by divorcing spouses. . . .

In an attempt to deal with marital conflict in manageable practical terms, the legal process of divorce focuses primarily upon objective conduct and the disposition of financial matters. . . . The courts are not meant nor equipped to provide relief in the form of therapy or counselling. From the perspective of intra- and inter-personal conflict, they merely proffer remedies for resolving "surrogate," albeit concrete, conflicts, thereby avoiding the more fundamental personal grievances of the implicated individuals.

The divorcing couple's perception of the legal setting for divorce is, in many respects, inconsonant with the objective attributes of judicial adjudication. The spouses misunderstand the legal system's assessment of, and approach to, their problems and infuse their underlying personal conflicts into the legally cognizable claims. The courts, then, are confronted with an emotional tug-of-war that they allow to masquerade as a set of practical concerns. . . .

Moreover, the "battleground" atmosphere of the courtroom devalues rationality and invites the spouses to adopt a distorted view of their situation and to engage in single-minded advocacy. The spouses' conflicts are usually exacerbated rather than attenuated by the gamesmanship of adversarial posturing. Legal proceedings, in fact, become an invitation to extend the conflictual relationship and to engage in an exercise of personal vindication. Litigation is a socially acceptable means by which to portray matrimonial conflicts, to dramatize a sense of having been victimized, and to unravel the plight of a personal dilemma that could not be redressed in the reality of the marriage. . . . The usual result is further acrimony. . . .

Without compromising its essential ordering and stabilizing mission, the legal process for divorce might be supplemented by alternative mechanisms. The human complexity of divorce disputes calls for a choice of remedies. Rather than obliging spouses to deal with the breakdown of their relationship through the prism of adversarial contentiousness, alternative processes would permit them to face their emotional and practical dilemma squarely, allowing them to assume responsibility for, and a measure of control over, the conclusion of their matrimonial relationship. As a general rule, the parties should gain a sense of achievement, acceptance, and a more lucid understanding of their former relationship from such an experience. It might enhance their capacity to engage in parenting after divorce and provide them with insight as to future relationships. In addition, nonadversarial proceedings would lessen state intrusion into the couple's private life.

A considerable amount of interest in "alternative dispute resolution" has arisen from a variety of sources: academic commentary, the legal and other "helping" professions, and the popular media. In its 1991 Standards of Conduct, the American Academy of Matrimonial Lawyers added its support through Standard 1.4, providing that "[a]n attorney should be knowledgeable about alternate ways to resolve matrimonial disputes," and which also observes:

> Matrimonial law is not simply a matter of winning or losing. At its best, matrimonial law should result in disputes being resolved fairly for all parties, including children. Parties are more likely to abide by their own promises than by an outcome imposed by a court.

The phrase "alternative dispute resolution" itself refers to a variety of methods of handling disputes that are considered alternatives to adversarial litigation. Two such methods of resolution, negotiation and arbitration, are hardly new approaches to the management of disputes or, in the case of negotiation, even to the management of matrimonial disputes. They have, however, been the subject of heightened interest as perceptions of the costs, dangers, and ineffectiveness of litigation have become more acute.

a. Negotiation

As we have seen, whatever the various literatures may say, lawyers are inclined to settle domestic relations matters through negotiation. The same conclusion is reached in the following study of divorce cases in the Dane County (Madison, Wisconsin) Family Court Division. The study, which examined divorces granted to spouses with one or more minor children, involved both a review of court files and interviews with a subset of participants.

MARYGOLD S. MELLI, HOWARD S. ERLANGER & ELIZABETH CHAMBLISS, *THE PROCESS OF NEGOTIATION: AN EXPLORATORY INVESTIGATION IN THE CONTEXT OF NO-FAULT DIVORCE*

40 Rutgers L. Rev. 1133, 1142 (1988)

Over the last two decades, many studies, including ours, have found that the predominant mode of dispute resolution is not litigation, but negotiation. Of the

349 files examined in the first phase of our study, only 32 involved a dispute between the parties that had to be settled by a judge. Several commentators have noted that, given findings such as these, to speak of negotiation as "alternative dispute resolution" is nonsensical. Marc Galanter has argued: "On the contemporary American legal scene the negotiation of disputes is not an alternative to litigation. . . . [I]t is not some marginal peripheral aspect of legal disputing in America; it is the central core." . . .

Negotiation was certainly not a "marginal peripheral aspect" of the divorce cases we studied in Dane County. The great bulk of the cases ended not as a result of litigation but due to negotiated settlements. Negotiation is not just the typical outcome; it is also the *expected* mode of dispute resolution in the minds of the parties and their lawyers. Contrary to the conventional view that the parties expect a judge to decide their case but *may* settle before trial, these parties saw settlement as the solution, and the judicial process as the alternative. . . .

The literature on negotiation stresses that the influence of the courts is pervasive, even when the parties and their lawyers negotiate on their own. . . . Mnookin & Kornhauser have described the process as one of "bargaining in the shadow of the law." The primary influence of the courts is said to result from the administration and enforcement of legal rules that guide and limit the parties' negotiations. If negotiation fails, the courts will decide.

In our interviews, there was evidence consistent with this conventional view of the importance of the courts. Parties who settled were clearly influenced by their lawyers' predictions of how the court would decide. One husband, who was reluctant to settle because he thought the settlement was unfair, gave in based upon his attorney's advice:

> I told [my lawyer] a number of times how I felt, but he pulls out a stack of law statutes and law books and says, "the judge is going to look at or take that into consideration." That came up a number of times . . . she had a right to ask for it or a right to collect it.

A wife stated: "I really didn't know whether [the settlement] was fair or not. I had no idea, so that was one place I consulted my attorney. She said realistically in her experience she felt that was probably about all I could expect to get . . . so I felt that was adequate." . . .

However, most striking about our interviews was evidence that demonstrated the minimal role of the judge as reviewer of the substance of the parties' agreement. In divorce cases the influence of the court is believed to be more significant than in other types of civil disputes, because even fully stipulated cases must be reviewed by a judge. However, we found the role of the judge as reviewer to be extremely limited. In only one of the 349 court files was the stipulation of the parties not approved by the court. In this case, the custodial parent was receiving Aid to Families with Dependent Children (AFDC). At the final hearing at which the divorce was granted . . . the state child support agency objected that the amount to which the parties had stipulated was not sufficient to support the children and the custodial parent agreed only because the state was providing support through AFDC. As a result, the court increased the amount of support when it entered the child support order. . . .

Much of the literature on negotiation has assumed that settlements represent solutions to which both parties agree. Therefore, a negotiated settlement is seen as much more acceptable to the parties than one imposed by the court. . . .

. . . [O]ur interviews suggest that much negotiation in divorce proceedings does not involve people who want the flexibility to arrange their affairs to the best advantage of each. Divorcing couples are usually in a major life crisis and one or both are bitter; the resulting "settlement" does not represent genuine agreement but a "best I can get" solution. In other words, true agreement between the parties is much less common than the frequency of settlements might indicate. We have data on satisfaction with the settlement for 41 of the 44 parties interviewed. Twenty of these were satisfied; six said they were satisfied but nonetheless felt that the settlement was unfair to them, while 15 were very dissatisfied. The following are typical comments from the latter 21 parties, who constituted half the group for which we have data; clearly their settlements do not represent consensual agreements.

I said to [my lawyer] "you cannot make me sign those papers . . . you're talking about 14 years of my life . . . I'm still carrying on the responsibility for two kids . . . if I stay [in the house] till the kids are out of school I'll owe [my husband] $26,000. . . ."

Well, I was worn down. . . . I cried through the whole thing, I could hardly say yes, I could hardly sign. [But I did and] I walked out of there and cried for probably two weeks straight. . . .

This characteristic of divorce negotiation—that it often results in settlements which are not agreeable to one or both of the parties—may help explain a current problem in the divorce courts: the high volume of post-divorce litigation.

NOTES AND QUESTIONS

1. The observation that few disputes of any kind are resolved in the courtroom has been demonstrated in a variety of contexts. The rate of disposition by plea is well known and is usually placed at between 90 percent and 95 percent of all cases. *E.g.*, Milton Heumann, Plea Bargaining: The Experiences of Prosecutors, Judges, and Defense Attorneys 28 (1978) (not-guilty plea rate in Connecticut has averaged about 10 percent since 1880). H. Laurence Ross concludes in his study of dispute resolution in civil matters that "the principal institution of the law in action is not trial; it is settlement out of court." H. Laurence Ross, Settled Out of Court 7 (2d ed. 1980).

2. Negotiated resolution of divorce matters has also been common for some time. In addition to the materials in the preceding section, a study in 1929 indicated that, even though fault divorce was then universal, only about 10 percent of the divorce cases studied resulted in contested hearings. Leon C. Marshall & Geoffrey May, The Divorce Court 199-200 (1932-1933). The authors concluded that the reason for this rate was agreement by the parties before the final hearing. *Id.* at 219. *See also* Robert J. Levy, Comment on the Pearson-Thoennes Study and on Mediation, 17 Fam. L.Q. 525, 530 (1984).

3. While negotiated settlements are common across fields, it does not follow that all negotiations are alike. In divorce, perhaps unlike in many other areas, much of the negotiating is done by the parties themselves. Moreover, the participation of clients in negotiating with each other and with their lawyers may be profoundly affected by the emotional context of the divorce. *See* Melli, Erlanger & Chambliss, above, at 1152-1153. Griffiths suggests that "lawyer and client are busy with two different divorces: the lawyer with a legal divorce, the client with a social and emotional one." John Griffiths, What Do Dutch Lawyers Actually Do in Divorce Cases?, 20 Law & Soc'y Rev. 135 (1986). Lawyers and clients may also be busy with several different negotiations: the lawyers between themselves and with their own clients and the clients between themselves and with their own lawyers.

4. A recent large empirical study of divorce, custody, and visitation in two California counties is consistent with the foregoing research but provides additional material for consideration. Eleanor Maccoby and Robert Mnookin, in Dividing the Child: Social and Legal Dilemmas of Custody (1992), examined the level of conflict between divorcing parties using two sources: interviews with parents (conducted about three years after separation) and court records. Their data "suggest that the common perception that conflict is the norm for divorcing parents is largely unfounded." *Id.* at 159. Parents assessed the level of conflict in their own divorce at very low levels. On a ten-point scale, the median rating for conflict over custody was 2.0. Median ratings for conflict over visitation and child support were both at 2.50, and the median rating for conflict over spousal support was at 1.0. An examination of court records indicates that 50 percent of all divorces were entirely uncontested, and an additional 29 percent were settled without any contest in the pleadings. Of the remaining 20 percent, 11 percent were settled through mediation, 5 percent were settled after a court-ordered custody evaluation, 2 percent were settled during trial, and only 1.5 percent were ultimately resolved by judicial determination. *Id.* at 134-138. Maccoby and Mnookin also found that "contrary to popular perception, most divorce decrees do not reflect a trade-off between custody and money issues. We believe that child support schedules and community property rules substantially constrain such trade-offs." *Id.* at 160.

The authors suggest that their data confirm the effectiveness of procedural devices to reduce conflict, such as mandatory mediation and preferences for joint custody. How do the data do so? Are there other explanations for the low levels of reported conflict?

5. The common law of fraud, of course, applies to lawyers and imposes a minimum standard of conduct for negotiations. *See* Russell Korobkin, Michael Moffitt & Nancy Welsh, The Law of Bargaining, 87 Marq. L. Rev. 839 (2004). Similarly, Rule 4.1 of the Model Rules of Professional Conduct provides that "[i]n the course of representing a client a lawyer shall not knowingly: (a) make a false statement of material fact or law to a third person." Model Rule 8.4 has language that suggests an even broader set of restrictions. For a discussion, *see* Peter R. Jarvis & Bradley F. Tellam, A Negotiation Ethics Primer for Lawyers, 31 Gonz. L. Rev. 549 (1995).

James J. White finds a central dilemma in requirements of truthfulness in connection with negotiation:

> On the one hand the negotiator must be fair and truthful; on the other he must mislead his opponent. Like the poker player, a negotiator hopes that his opponent will overestimate the value of his hand. Like the poker player, in a variety of ways he must facilitate his opponent's inaccurate assessment. The critical difference between those who are successful negotiators and those who are not lies in the capacity both to mislead and not to be misled.

James J. White, Machiavelli and the Bar: Ethical Limitations on Lying in Negotiations, 1980 Am. B. Found. Res. J. 926-927. Walter W. Steele, Jr., Deceptive Negotiating and High-Toned Morality, 39 Vand. L. Rev. 1387 (1986), provides an alternative view:

> In a broad sense, justifications exist for this less than honest standard for negotiating. A lawyer's devotion to a client's interest is so compelling that some lawyers feel justified, if not compelled, to employ some deception when negotiating. This view point assumes that clients have a right to a lawyer who engages in deception. Unfortunately, the Model Code of Professional Responsibility and its modern cousin, the Model Rules of Professional Conduct, do not adequately address whether or not clients have a right to a deceptive lawyer.
>
> Another justification for less than honest and straight-forward negotiating is the belief that a convention exists among lawyers to mislead during negotiations. This viewpoint, when carried to its logical conclusion, means that lawyers expect to negotiate with one another much like the proverbial used car salesperson. What a curious postulate for a learned and "high-toned" profession to adopt. . . .
>
> A final justification for less than honest and straight-forward negotiating is that deceit is inherent to negotiation. Are misrepresentations essential to negotiations? Certainly non-lawyer negotiators engage in deception from time to time. Should we expect something else from lawyers? Consider the negotiating standards of two holy men, one a willing buyer and the other a willing seller. If their personal commitments to holiness prevented them from making the slightest misrepresentation or from engaging in any abuse of their bargaining positions, how would the ultimate outcome of the negotiations differ from the outcome achieved by two lawyer negotiators? If deceit is truly inherent to negotiation, the outcome achieved by the holy men could not be defined as the product of a negotiation. But if the result achieved by their methods is somehow better or fairer than the result achieved by lawyers, then perhaps the legal definition of negotiation should be changed.
>
> None of these rationalizations of deceptive negotiation is fully satisfactory. As a consequence, each prevaricating negotiator relies upon one or some combination of them. Each negotiator feels more or less justified to deceive or abuse power when negotiating, depending upon how well the chosen rationalizations satisfy the moral imperative of that particular negotiator. The result might be thought of as a disco dance floor full of negotiators, some more adroit than others, some more at ease with the music that others, and each very definitely free to "do his own thing." Obviously, what is missing is a specific and reasonably thorough set of standards for negotiating.

Mnookin, Peppet, and Tulumello ask:

> Aren't I supposed to be a zealous advocate?
>
> An attorney is supposed to champion the client's cause, and as a consequence, many lawyers claim that a duty of "zealous advocacy" requires them to do everything that isn't clearly forbidden. But this often places lawyers in an uncomfortable position. Because defending a client's interests is paramount, attorneys may fear that adopting any negotiating strategy other than extreme hard bargaining violates a basic duty to the client.

Robert Mnookin, Scott Peppet & Andrew Tulumello, Beyond Winning: Negotiating to Create Value in Deals and Disputes 292-293 (2000). Under the Model Rules, this is nonsense. Rule 1.3. requires "reasonable diligence" on behalf of a client. Comment 1 to Model Rule 1.3 states that "a lawyer should act with commitment and dedication to the interests of the client and with zeal in advocacy upon the client's behalf. However, a lawyer is not bound to press for every advantage that might be realized for a client. A lawyer has professional discretion in determining the means by which the matter should be pursued." This comments suggests that attorneys retain significant flexibility in defining the bounds of zealous representation. The client's interest, broadly conceived, may be better served by a more constrained and reasoned approach to negotiation than by initiating a contest of wills or a war of attrition. So long as the client understands the risks and benefits of a problem-solving stance, there is no inherent contradiction between problem solving and advocacy. Indeed, sometimes blindly going to war—even if the client insists on it—may disserve the client's broader interests. As Elihu Root once said, "About half of the practice of a decent lawyer consists in telling would-be clients that they are damned fools and should stop."

6. A number of lawyers in many jurisdictions seek to engage in "collaborative lawyering." In collaborative lawyering, the lawyers and clients agree to negotiate from the outset of the case using a problem-solving approach. Their agreements typically involve including protocols adopting early commitment to negotiation, interest-based joint problem solving, collaboration with professionals in other disciplines, and intentional development of a new legal culture through activities of local practice groups. They also contain a provision disqualifying both lawyers from representing their clients if either party chooses to proceed in litigation. Pauline H. Tessler, Collaborative Law: USA (2001) provides the fullest description of this approach.

Although many aspects of negotiations are commonly recommended for domestic relations lawyers, the withdrawal and disqualification provisions raise questions. One might ask whether the threat of having to secure new counsel invites abuse by inappropriately or excessively pressuring some parties to settle when it would be in their interest to litigate. See John Lande, Possibilities for Collaborative Law: Ethics and Practice of Lawyer Disqualification and Process Control in a New Model of Lawyering." 64 Ohio St. L.J. 1315, 1316 (2003). Model Rule of Professional Conduct 1.2(C) allows a lawyer to limit the scope of representation "if the limitation is reasonable under the circumstances and the client gives informed consent." Would the possibility of undue pressure to settle raise questions about the "reasonableness" of such a limitation? Would it be important to know how frequently collaborative lawyering negotiations fail to produce a result? Would parties be able to judge the acceptability of collaborative relations between their attorneys and the acceptability of results reached through this process beforehand? On the difficulties contracting parties have in accurately predicting their preferences over time, *see* Manuel Utset, A Theory of Self-Control Problems and Incomplete Contracting: The Case of Shareholder Contracts, 2003 Utah L. Rev. 1329.

PROBLEMS

1. You represent the wife in a divorce action she has brought because of her husband's adultery. She wants you to get everything from her husband that can be had and indicates that she will not allow her husband visitation of their two teenage children if she does not get what she thinks is due her. How will you approach negotiations in this case?

2. In the course of a divorce negotiation, counsel for the husband indicates that her client wishes joint physical and legal custody. It is clear that the wife wishes sole physical and legal custody and that she has been the primary caretaker of the children throughout the marriage. In fact, the husband is not much interested in joint physical custody, but very much wants joint legal custody. Has the husband's lawyer behaved unethically? What could and should the husband's lawyer have done?

3. Your client, Anthony Ciulla, has told you that he feels very guilty about the end of his marriage, and is willing to give his wife all the marital property except one automobile and is willing to pay her substantial alimony, even though she has been employed throughout the marriage. You have advised him that, under the circumstances, a court is unlikely to require more than an equal distribution of marital property and would almost surely not award spousal maintenance. Nonetheless, Anthony does not want any contest with his wife and instructs you to accept any offer that leaves him an automobile and provides alimony of not more than $1,000 per month.

Opposing counsel opens negotiations by saying, "My client wants to be reasonable. She thinks that 80 percent of the marital property will suffice. But she really does not want to fight about this, and there is some flexibility. Will your client give her the 75 percent?" How do you answer?

b. Arbitration

Considerable interest has been expressed in arbitration as a substitute for traditional divorce procedure, on the basis that arbitration is less adversarial and more economical in terms of time and money. This interest has been most strongly expressed in connection with the resolution of child custody issues.

ALLAN R. KORITZINSKY, ROBERT M. WELCH & STEPHEN W.
SCHLISSEL, *THE BENEFITS OF ARBITRATION*

14 Fam. Advoc. 45 (No. 4 1992)

Family law arbitration is the process by which adversaries, usually the husband and wife or ex-husband and ex-wife, agree to submit one or more issues in controversy to a neutral third party, who will resolve the issues in a way that will be final and binding. The arbitrator's decision, if reached properly, will be affirmed by the court as a party of its judgment.

This agreement to arbitrate may occur during a divorce action or after the marriage has been dissolved. It might be contained in a written agreement signed by the parties as part of a divorce settlement or a pre- or postmarital agreement. . . .

The parties have an opportunity to agree on an arbitrator. The arbitrator may conduct the hearing in a confidential, private setting at a time and place convenient to all parties. The "arbitration decision," or award, is submitted to the court for confirmation. . . .

Some of the benefits of arbitration in family law are:

1. *Selection of Decision Maker.* The parties and their attorneys can choose as the arbitrator a family law specialist who has expertise in representing either spouse, as well as knowledge in the area of family law. In many court systems, judges are assigned to family law cases without regard to their background, training, interest, or experience.

2. *Convenient Forum for Hearing.* The arbitration hearing can be scheduled at the convenience of the participants, with none of the interruptions or delays that are so frequent in the courts. . . .

3. *Procedural Flexibility.* The parties and their attorneys can agree to submit expert or other witness testimony at a time and place convenient for all witnesses, by telephone, sworn affidavits, reports, or any other agreed-upon method.

4. *Speedy and Less Costly.* Arbitration is likely to cost significantly less than a trial, especially when considering a lawyer's trial preparation time for cases that are adjourned or postponed. . . .

5. *Final and Binding.* The parties can stipulate that the decision or award of the arbitrator is final and binding, with limited rights of review and appeal. . . . Because a written record is not necessary (except possibly for child custody matters), the parties save substantial time and money.

ARBITRATION'S DETRIMENTS

1. *Lack of Discovery.* The parties generally are not protected by discovery rules and have to resort to the courts to compel discovery when items are not produced involuntarily. . . .

2. *Nonapplicability of Evidentiary and Other Rules.* The [Uniform Arbitration Act] contemplates little discovery other than witness subpoenas; the production of books, records, documents, and other evidence; and depositions of witnesses who cannot be subpoenaed or who will be unavailable to attend the hearing (sec. 7, UAA). To resolve these issues, the parties may provide in the arbitration agreement that some or all of the rules of evidence and other procedural rules apply. They also may enlarge the scope of discovery that will be allowed prior to or during the arbitration process. However, this may be counterproductive to the arbitration process itself. . . .

3. *Nonbinding Nature of Certain Issues.* Court decisions indicate that custody and possibly child support may not be subject to final and binding arbitration, with resulting limited court review and appeal rights. . . .

4. *Lack of Enforcement.* An arbitrator does not have the power to enforce the arbitration award or enter a decree of divorce. This is not a detriment, though, as the UAA specifically provides that the decision or award *shall* be confirmed by the court in a judgment or decree unless vacated or changed by that court.

The distinctive feature of arbitration is its binding character. Arbitrators, unlike mediators (discussed below), are employed to resolve disputes rather than to facilitate resolution by the parties. Arbitration is, of course, a routine feature in labor law and collective bargaining and, to a substantial and perhaps increasing extent, in commercial disputes. On the evolution and status of arbitration, *see* Thomas E. Carbonneau, Alternative Dispute Resolution 105 et seq. (1989).

FLAHERTY V. FLAHERTY

477 A.2d 1257 (N.J. 1984)

GARIBALDI, J. The question posed in this appeal is whether an arbitration provision in a separation agreement, entered into by the parties prior to their divorce and incorporated in their divorce judgment, is enforceable. The Chancery Division and the Appellate Division enforced the arbitration provision. We granted certification, and now modify and affirm, as modified, the Appellate Division's judgment. . . .

Roger makes two basic claims. The first is that arbitration of domestic disputes between former spouses regarding alimony and child support should not, as a matter of public policy, be permitted to be settled outside the courts, and therefore the arbitration clause in the Agreement should not be enforced. The second is that the arbitration award in this case was erroneous and should be overturned.

Although it is clear that marital separation agreements are enforceable in this state insofar as "they are just and equitable," this Court has never before addressed the question of the enforceability of an arbitration clause in a separation agreement.

In this state, as in most American jurisdictions, arbitration is a favored remedy. It permits parties to agree to resolve disputes outside of the court system. A court generally will enforce an arbitration agreement unless it violates public policy.

In recent years arbitration has been used more frequently as a viable means of resolving domestic disputes that arise under separation agreements. In other jurisdictions around the country courts have consistently enforced arbitration clauses to settle matrimonial disputes. *See* Sterk, "Enforceability of Agreements to Arbitrate: An Examination of the Public Policy Defense," 2 Cardozo L. Rev. 481, 493 (1981).

Our arbitration statute recognizes the validity of arbitration as a means of resolving contractual disputes between parties. . . . New Jersey has long recognized the validity and enforceability of separation agreements between divorcing spouses. Enforcement of arbitration clauses pertaining to alimony as within such agreements is a logical extension of the view . . . that parties should be granted as much autonomy as possible in the ordering of their personal lives. Since parties may settle spousal support rights and obligations by contract, there is no policy reason to prohibit their submitting disputes arising out of such contracts to binding arbitration. It is fair and reasonable that parties who have agreed to be bound by arbitration in a formal, written separation agreement should be so bound. Rather than frowning on arbitration of alimony disputes, public policy supports it. We recognize that in many cases arbitration of matrimonial disputes may offer an effective alternative method of dispute resolution. As commentators have noted, the advantages of arbitration of domestic disputes include reduced court congestion, the opportunity for resolution of sensitive matters in a private and informal forum, reduction of the trauma and anxiety of marital litigation, minimization of the intense polarization of parties that often occurs, and the ability to choose the arbitrator. In this sensitive and intensely private area of domestic disputes, arbitration expressly contracted for by the spouses is highly desirable. We accordingly hold today that under the laws of New Jersey, parties may bind themselves in separation agreements to arbitrate disputes over alimony. As is the case with other arbitration awards, an award determining spousal support would be subject to the review provided in N.J.S.A. 2A:24-8.

Our inclination to embrace arbitration in all phases of matrimonial disputes is tempered, however, by our knowledge that in such cases competing public policy considerations abound. Accordingly, the principal issue involved here is whether public policy prohibits arbitration from resolving child support and custody disputes.

Although it is generally accepted that spouses may enter enforceable agreements to arbitrate alimony disputes, some commentators have suggested that arbitration is unsatisfactory to resolve disputes concerning child support or custody because of the court's traditional role as *parens patriae*. Traditionally, courts under the doctrine of parens patriae have been entrusted to protect the best interests of children. Children's maintenance, custody-visitation, and overall best interests have always been subject to the close scrutiny and supervision of the courts despite any agreements to the contrary. Some commentators see arbitration as a dangerous encroachment on this jurisdiction. Since parents cannot by agreement deprive the courts of their duty to promote the best interests of their children, it is argued that they cannot do so by arbitration.

Detractors notwithstanding, there has been a growing tendency to recognize arbitration in child support clauses. We do not agree with those who fear that by allowing parents to agree to arbitrate child support, we are interfering with the judicial protection of the best interests of the child. We see no valid reason why the arbitration process should not be available in the area of child support; the advantages of arbitration in domestic disputes outweigh any disadvantages.

Nevertheless, we recognize that the courts have a nondelegable, special supervisory function in the area of child support that may be exercised upon review of an arbitrator's award. We therefore hold that whenever the validity of an arbitration award affecting child support is questioned on the grounds that it does not provide adequate protection for the child, the trial court should conduct a special review of the award. This review should consist of a two step analysis. First, as with all arbitration awards, the courts should review child support awards as provided by N.J.S.A. 2A:24-8. Second, the courts should conduct a *de novo* review unless it is clear on the face of the award that the award could not adversely affect the substantial best interests of the child.

An arbitrator's award that grants all the requested child support would generally satisfy this second test because it is always in the child's best interest to have as much support as possible. . . . Thus, only an arbitrator's award that either reduced child support or refused a request for increased support could be subject to court review beyond the review provided by statute, because only such an award could adversely affect the interests of the child. However, even awards reducing support would be subject to court review only if they adversely affected the *substantial* best interests of the child. . . .

NOTES AND QUESTIONS

1. Judicial enforcement of arbitration clauses and acceptance of arbitration decisions have varied widely. Arbitrability and acceptance of arbitration awards are not identical. *Flaherty*, because it answers the arbitrability question affirmatively, must also consider whether to accept the decree. What standards does *Flaherty* apply to the acceptance issue? On the question of enforcement of arbitration clauses in custody cases, *see also* Kelm v. Kelm, 2000 WL 664720 (Ohio App.), refusing enforcement of an agreement to arbitrate.

2. Suppose that the parties include a provision in their separation agreement stating that the noncustodial spouse need not pay child support if visitation provisions are violated. The agreement also includes an arbitration provision. State court decisions hold that noncompliance with visitation orders does not affect the child support obligation. What should the result be if an arbitrator finds repeated interference with the noncustodial parent's visitation rights? Would judicial review be effective?

3. The *Flaherty* court indicates that it will review the arbitration award *de novo* if the award could adversely affect the child's best interests. If such review is common, what efficiencies come with use of arbitration?

4. The use of arbitration seems to be recognized readily in "mundane" issues, such as property division and alimony. Does it follow that an arbitrator will be bound by the terms of an agreement in which a wife waives any claim to alimony? For a negative answer, *see* 2 Homer H. Clark, Jr., Domestic Relations 161-162 (2d ed. 1989).

PROBLEM

You are a law clerk to Judge Wilson, who sits on the Family Court of your county. Pending before her is the case of Mr. and Ms. Feld, an orthodox Jewish couple with six children. The Felds decided to divorce and voluntarily submitted their custody dispute for arbitration to a Beth Din (a religious court). The Beth Din divided custody between the parents, with the three oldest placed with the father and the three youngest with the mother. The father has filed a divorce petition in Judge Wilson's court. The petition seeks incorporation of the religious court's decree in the civil order, relying on a state statute providing generally for judicial enforcement of decisions reached by an arbitrator to whom a dispute has been submitted by the parties. Judge Wilson asks for your analysis of the father's request.

c. Mediation

JESSICA PEARSON & NANCY THOENNES, *MEDIATING AND LITIGATING CUSTODY DISPUTES: A LONGITUDINAL EVALUATION*

17 Fam. L.Q. 497, 498-499 (1984)

Mediation is a process in which a third party, the mediator, encourages the disputants to find a mutually agreeable settlement by helping them to identify the issues, reduce misunderstandings, vent emotions, clarify priorities, find points of agreement, explore new areas of compromise and possible solutions. Rooted in African moots, socialists' comrades' courts, psychotherapy and labor mediation rather than Anglo-American jurisprudence, mediation stresses informality, open and direct communication, reinforcement of positive bonds and avoidance of blame. As a "cooperative" dispute resolution process, its central purpose is to "reorient the parties toward each other not by imposing rules on them, but by helping them to achieve a new and shared perception of their relationship, a perception that will direct their attention toward one another."

... The benefits attributed to the process are far-reaching. When compared to the adversarial system, mediation is believed to be more expeditious, inexpensive, private, procedurally simple and amenable to truth-finding and the complete airing of grievances. Supposedly, it is able to deal with the causes of problems, reduce the alienation of the litigants, and lead to the development of satisfying agreements that are perceived as fair and acceptable over time. Further, unlike adjudication, mediation presumably aids disputing parties in resuming workable relationships with one another.

Family mediation supporters contend that the process will enhance the adjustment of children . . . following separation and divorce by promoting parental cooperation, reinforcing parent-child bonds and encouraging visitation.

NOTES AND QUESTIONS

1. Mediation has commanded wide support as the preferred method of alternative dispute resolution for divorce — especially child custody issues. A small sampling of the favorable literature includes Joan Blades, Family Meditation: Cooperative Divorce Settlement (1985); O. J. Coogler, Structured Meditation in Divorce Settlement (1978); John M. Haynes, Divorce Meditation: A Practical Guide for Therapists and Counselors (1981); Jay Folberg, Mediation of Child Custody Disputes, 19 Colum. J.L. & Soc. Probs. 413 (1985).

California has been a leader in revising the procedure as well as the substance of divorce law. Its mandatory mediation law requires that all custody and visitation disputes be mediated prior to consideration by the county superior court. Cal. Civ. Code §4607(a) (West Supp. 1990). Several states have followed suit in either requiring or encouraging mediation as a precursor or adjunct to judicial proceedings. For a summary of the California statute and a brief review of experience under it, see Trina Grillo, The Mediation Alternative: Process Dangers for Women, 100 Yale L.J. 1545, 1551-1555 (1991).

While a number of states require parenting agreements for custody to include provisions for alternative dispute resolution, some courts take the position that a parenting agreement is, in effect, a custody provision and therefore subject to modification by the court. See In re Marriage of Duffy, 718 N.E.2d 286 (Ill. App. 1999). But if the parties include a provision for mediation prior to litigation of custody issues, a court can enforce such an agreement by dismissing a postdivorce motion filed before mediation. Gould v. Gould, 523 S.E.2d 106 (Ga. App. 1999). It does not necessarily follow that the court is bound to accept the result of the mediation. See Wayno v. Wayno, 756 So. 2d 1024 (Fla. App. 2000).

2. Mediation may be carried out by lawyers, by professionals in other fields, or in teams. How mediation is conducted may well depend on the discipline from which the mediator comes. See Russell M. Coombs, Noncourt-Connected Mediation and Counseling in Child-Custody Disputes, 17 Fam. L.Q. 469 (1984).

An early concern of both proponents and doubters of mediation in family law matters was the absence of standards of professional conduct for lawyers acting in this role rather than as advocates. Two kinds of fears arose. One was that general rules of professional conduct would apply; the other was that they would not. On the one hand, attorneys acting as mediators might find themselves charged with a failure to comply with ethics requirements drawn from the advocacy role, most obviously with respect to conflicts of interest but in other respects as well. See, e.g., Coombs, above, at 492. On the other hand, if generally applicable ethical rules directed to advocacy did not apply, lawyer-mediators would be left without guidance or constraint in their dealings with clients.

The American Bar Association did come to grips in some degree with the role played by attorneys who seek to assist two clients in resolving problems. Rule 2.2 of The Model Rules of Professional Conduct recognized a professional role for lawyers as "intermediaries," and permitted assumption of this role under the following conditions: (1) consent of each client after consultation concerning the implications of common representation, including the advantages and risks involved and its effect on the attorney-client privilege; (2) a reasonable belief by the lawyer that the matter can be resolved in a way consistent with the client's best interests with little risk of prejudice to the interests of any client; and (3) the lawyer's reasonable belief that he or she can undertake the common representation impartially. A lawyer must withdraw as an intermediary on the request or any client or if any of the above conditions are no longer satisfied and, upon withdrawal, may not continue to represent any of the clients in this matter.

It should be noted that "intermediation" is not the same thing as "mediation." What the ABA calls "intermediation" involves legal representation of multiple clients who have, or at least initially believe they have, a common goal. A lawyer acts as intermediary if he or she represents a buyer and seller or, where permitted, both spouses seeking a divorce.

The 2004 version of the ABA Model Rules of Professional Conduct deletes Rule 2.2, presumably on the theory that joint representation is adequately covered by Rule 1.7, which deals generally with conflict of interest between current clients. Model Rule 1.7(b) provides that, even if representation would usually be prohibited because of a conflict of interest, a lawyer may represent more than one client if (1) he or she reasonably believes that it will be possible to provide competent and diligent representation to each affected client; (2) the representation is not prohibited by law; (3) the representation does not involve the assertion of a claim by one client against another represented in the same litigation or proceeding before a tribunal; and (4) each client gives informed consent, confirmed in writing. Comment [18] to Rule 1.7 defines informed consent in a manner generally consistent with former Rule 2.2. If the assumption is that Rule 2.2 is unnecessary in view of Rule 1.7, do you agree?

The Model Rules now also recognize the lawyer's role in alternative dispute resolution as a "third-party neutral," whether as mediator, arbitrator, conciliator, or evaluator. Model Rule 2.4 states that a lawyer serves that role when he or she assists two or more persons *who are not clients of the lawyer* to reach a resolution of some dispute or issue between them. Rule 2.4(b) requires a lawyer in this capacity to inform unrepresented parties that the lawyer is not representing them and, if it appears necessary, explain the difference between a lawyer's role as a third-party neutral and the role of a lawyer who represents a client.

The ABA Section on Mediation has adopted its own standards for lawyers engaged in mediation, which, with some modification, were approved by the ABA House of Delegates in 1984. Standards of Practice for Lawyer Mediators in Family Disputes, 18 Fam. L.Q. 363 (1984). Those standards approach the mediation process in the following terms:

Each of the mediation participants should have independent legal counsel before reaching the agreement. . . . If the participants, or either of them, choose to proceed without independent counsel, the mediator shall warn them of any risk involved in not being represented, including where appropriate, the possibility that the agreement they submit may be rejected as unreasonable in light of both parties' legal right or may not be binding on them.

3. Despite the wide interest and support for mediation, some doubts have nonetheless been raised about the capacity of mediation to achieve the results claimed for that process. Those questions arise in several connections.

a. *Questions about efficiency.* Adjudication is described as and, as we have seen, certainly can be a costly enterprise from the perspectives of both parties and courts. And, as we have also seen, mediation is assumed to be less costly on both counts. The small body of research does not, however, clearly demonstrate substantial savings in time and money. The Pearson and Thoennes study finds the following:

> Successful mediation clients move through the court system faster than their adversarial counterparts [an average of 9.7 months], but unsuccessful mediation respondents travel slowest [an average of 13.4 months]. . . . In the purely adversarial samples [those cases in which mediation was never tried,] . . . the average number of months between filing and final orders are [about 11.5 months]. . . . Since mediation often requires the postponement of an investigation and the continuation of a hearing on custody and visitation issues, it is not surprising that cases move faster for those who either mediate or litigate than for those who try both.
>
> Mediation appears to translate into modest savings in attorneys' fees. The average legal fee paid by the successful mediation group was $1630. For the unsuccessful mediation group, it was $2000. And for the rejecting and control groups it was $1800 and $2360, respectively. It is unclear why individuals in the rejecting group pay lower legal fees than their counterparts in the control and unsuccessful mediation groups. Nevertheless, individuals who attempt to mediate do not experience excessive legal fees.

Pearson & Thoennes, above, at 507-508. Do these data also suggest that those who chose to litigate did not pay excessive legal fees? Is it possible to say whether one method of dispute resolution is systematically and significantly less expensive to the public than another?

With respect to the public cost of litigation, differences between mediation and litigation again do not seem significant. In another report by the same authors, the total cost of the sample of mediated cases amounted to about $40,000, based on an assumption of 4.0 hours of bench time per hearing. The public cost for nonmediated cases was about $45,500. Pearson & Thoennes, Mediation and Divorce: The Benefits Outweigh the Costs, 4 Fam. Adv. 26, 29 (1982). Even this comparison may, however, be incomplete.

> [T]he calculation of expense assumes a greater use of custody investigations in nonmediated cases than mediated cases, which in turn supposes some systematic reason for believing that mediation mitigates the need for such investigations. In addition, the cost of mediation services was based on the costs of the Custody Mediation Project, *excluding* program overhead.

Other confounding factors may also be involved. The self-selection of couples for mediation in the Denver Project strongly suggests that the mediating group was more disposed toward settlement than either the control group or the group that rejected the offer of mediation, and this by itself may have reduced time and therefore cost.

Lee E. Teitelbaum & Laura DuPaix, Alternative Dispute Resolution and Divorce: Natural Experimentation in Family Law, 40 Rutgers L. Rev. 1093, 1115 (1988). *See also* Carol J. King, Burdening Access to Justice: The Cost of Divorce Mediation on the Cheap, 73 St. John's L. Rev. 375 (1999), suggesting that requiring parties to undergo divorce mediation at their expense presents serious financial and quality problems.

b. *Questions about satisfaction.* To a considerable extent, interest in mediation has been promoted by a broad sense that divorcing parties experience high levels of dissatisfaction with the process, the results, and the conduct of attorneys. The dedication to a standard work on mediation pointedly illustrates this perception: "I am indebted to my former wife and the two attorneys who represented us in our divorce for making me aware of the critical need for a more rational, more civilized way of arranging a parting of the ways." O. J. Coogler, Structured Meditation in Divorce Settlement (1978). Dissatisfaction with the legal process, bad enough by itself, also is said to increase the risk of future conflict among all participants.

The Pearson and Thoennes study reported favorably on the expressed satisfaction of those who used mediation. "The vast majority (92 percent) of all successful mediation clients are satisfied with the process and would mediate again in the future or recommend it to a friend. Although unsuccessful mediation clients are less enthusiastic, most (61 percent) would recommend it to a friend." Successful mediation clients also reported high levels of satisfaction with their final agreements; 75 percent of that group said that they were satisfied, while no more than 60 percent of the remaining groups did so. And only 15 percent of the successful mediating group, but 30 to 40 percent of the others, reported substantial noncompliance with the terms of their agreement. 17 Fam. L.Q. at 505.

These results seem to confirm the assumptions of mediation proponents. Some caution in accepting this conclusion is, however, appropriate. For one thing, the group that engaged in mediation was not random but self-selected; accordingly, couples who chose to mediate may well have differed from those who did not. The sample reporting the greatest satisfaction included more younger couples with shorter marriages and younger children, and this group may have fewer difficult issues to resolve at divorce. *See* Teitelbaum & DuPaix, above, at 1120. Moreover, the mediation project provided mediation services without charge, while the alternative (litigation) approach is at least believed to be expensive. That economy may in itself provide a sense of satisfaction. Finally, the fact of participation in an "experiment" can itself affect attitudes. *Id.* at 1119. *See also* Kenneth Kressel, The Process of Divorce (1985), for methodological questions about mediation research; Robert J. Levy, Comment on the Pearson-Thoennes Study and on Mediation, 17 Fam. L.Q. 525, 530 (1984), for questions about the research discussed above.

c. *Questions about fairness.* It is generally believed that mediation will produce a sense of fairness in the process because of its consensual and voluntary nature. Although results from some research support this conclusion, others do so far less strongly. *Compare* Pearson & Thoennes, above, at 505, *with* K. Kressel, above, at 187.

Special concerns about the fairness of informal settlements for women in divorce have arisen:

> Feminist critics of mediation [in divorce] have often suggested that divorce and custody mediation tend to disempower women. Although a complete analysis is not available, there is reason to think that women are significantly more likely to regard mediation as threatening and balanced against them than are men. While women did report that mediation helped them in understanding themselves and their spouses, they were also far more likely than men to report a sense of being pressured into agreement, a lack of comfort in expressing their feelings, and a sense that mediators essentially dictated the terms of the agreement.

Teitelbaum & DuPaix, above, at 1120-1121. For an extensive and thorough analysis of mediation and divorce from both academic and practice perspectives that also expresses concern about the implications of mandatory mediation for divorcing women, *see* Grillo, above; Penelope E. Bryan, Killing Us Softly: Divorce Mediation and the Politics of Power, 40 Buff. L. Rev. 441 (1992).

One primary concern is the perceived imbalance of power between women for whom custody is the most important "good" to come from divorce and husbands who may exchange their claims to joint or sole custody for financial concessions. However, Maccoby and Mnookin's research did not find evidence of such bargaining. On the contrary, they found, as we have seen, that divorce decrees do not often embody an exchange between custody and money issues. Moreover, they report little in the way of strategic behavior by spouses. Eleanor Maccoby & Robert Mnookin, Dividing the Child: Social and Legal Dilemmas of Custody 160 (1992).

A more pervasive critique of the effect of mediation and the interjection of the helping professions in child custody matters has been offered by Professor Fineman.

MARTHA A. FINEMAN, *DOMINANT DISCOURSE, PROFESSIONAL LANGUAGE, AND LEGAL CHANGE IN CHILD CUSTODY DECISIONMAKING*

101 Harv. L. Rev. 727, 756, 765 (1988)

Social workers view divorce as occasioning the birth of an ongoing, albeit different, relationship, with mediators and social workers as its midwives and monitors.... The continued involvement is not only with each other but with the legal system as well. This ideal is obviously very different from the traditional legal system, which seeks an end or termination of a significant interaction at divorce: a division, distribution, or allocation of the things acquired during marriage—an emancipatory model—and with its "ending," the permission for a "new life" for the participants and the withdrawal of active legal interference in their relationship.

The helping professions' ideal process "avoids" or "reduces" conflict and is typified by mediation. Helping professionals believe that mediation, employing a therapeutic process, is within their exclusive domain because lawyers, unlike social workers, ignore the underlying causes of divorce and give little regard to the "real reason" for the split-up. . . .

The rhetorical symbolism employed by social workers and mediators is politically powerful. It empowers the helpers and may allow them to eclipse the interests of those who are designated as the very ones to be helped. For example, although the helping professions' vision portrays mediation as allowing custody decisions to be made with sharing and caring rather than conflict and contention, mediation may in fact merely hide rather than eliminate conflict, allowing the stronger of the two parents to dominate and control the weaker.

The adoption of the mediators' image has important substantive implications with significant political and social ramifications. One of the most harmful assumptions underlying social workers' discourse is that a parent who seeks sole custody of a child has some illegitimate motivation. Mediators may acknowledge exceptions to this generalization . . . , but the general assumption is that the parent who is willing to live up to the idea of shared custody and control is the one with the child's real interests at heart.

. . . A mother who resists sharing her child with her ex-husband is characterized as having "issue overlay"; she protests too much. Such women may be characterized as clinging and overly dependent on the role identification as wife and mother. . . .

Lost in the rhetoric of the social worker are real concerns. There is little or no appreciation of the many real problems that joint custody and the ideal of sharing and caring can cause. The prospect of a continued relationship with an ex-spouse may be horrifying to contemplate, but the sharing ideal assumes that a relationship between the noncustodial parent and the child cannot proceed without it. Also unsettling is the extent to which allegations of mistreatment, abuse, or neglect on the part of husbands toward either their wives or children are trivialized, masked, or lost amid the psychological rhetoric that reduces mothers' desires to have custody and control of their children to pathology.

We should be deeply skeptical of these views of women and mothers. . . .

PROBLEMS

1. Evan and Mary Braun are ending their marriage. They approach you to write up what they have agreed to. In reviewing their proposed agreement, it seems that Evan has agreed to give virtually all of the property to his wife and to pay her alimony (although she has worked throughout the marriage). Evan seems to feel guilty about the breakdown of their relationship and as a result wishes the divorce to go as easily as possible. How do you proceed in dealing with the Brauns?

2. Michael and Sue Heikkonen are ending their 20-year marriage. Both express resistance to hiring individual lawyers for all of the usual reasons. During

the interview, Michael does most of the talking; Sue speaks only when spoken to and always agrees with her husband. Michael is a salesman for a computer company; Sue has not been employed since their youngest child (now age 8) was born. She was previously a secretary in the company for which Michael then worked. Michael thinks that each should keep his or her own separate property, which accounts for most of the parties' wealth in this case. He has inherited a substantial amount of money; his wife has inherited none. Sue wants custody of their two children; Michael wants joint legal custody (although his travel schedule makes physical custody impossible). Michael is willing to pay child support according to state guidelines and is opposed to alimony that will discourage Ms. Heikkonen from finding employment. Sue does not want to find employment outside the home until the children are out of high school. Accordingly, she thinks alimony is necessary. How will you approach this mediation?

Suppose that, in the course of discussions, Sue tells you that she will give up on her alimony claim and seek work if Michael abandons any claim to joint custody.

3. You are a lay leader in your local church as well as a prominent attorney. Your church strongly discourages divorce. Two members of that church come to you for counseling and assistance in connection with their marriage, which has been weak for some time. They know you as a religious leader and as a leader of the bar, where you have specialized in trusts and estates for many years. Is there any reason why you should not serve as a mediator or intermediary?

Property Division and Spousal Support

6

about what constitutes a "family," and why and how family membership changes a person's rights and duties.

A. OVERVIEW

This chapter and Chapters 7 and 8 concern orders that courts use to allocate the economic rights and obligations of parents and former spouses. This chapter covers property division and spousal support (also called alimony or maintenance) at the time of divorce. Chapter 7 concerns initial child support orders. Chapter 8 deals with modification, termination, and enforcement of support orders and the federal income tax and bankruptcy treatment of obligations.

As we will see, there is debate about whether the justifications and criteria for making these awards differ. As a practical matter, courts and lawyers always consider the relationship among these orders to arrive at a complete picture of the postdivorce economic circumstances of former spouses and their children. On the other hand, practicality also dictates distinguishing and labeling these orders because very important "collateral" consequences of an order — its modifiability and terminability, its tax and bankruptcy consequences — turn on this distinction. Property division orders are not modifiable, but support orders are. Property division and child support have no income tax consequences, while spousal support is deductible to the payor and income to the payee. Support is not dischargeable in bankruptcy, while property division obligations sometimes are.

These issues are the stuff of which a large portion of domestic relations practice is made. This reason alone justifies extended treatment of them. But determination of the economic consequences of divorce is not merely the point at which theoretical and principled understandings about the nature of the family and family law are practically implemented. When courts and legislatures decide what constitutes property and how it should be divided, when and why spousal support is required, and how to divide financial obligations to children between parents who no longer live in the same household, they reexamine fundamental questions about what constitutes a "family," and why and how family membership changes a person's rights and duties.

1. Historical Justifications of and Criteria for Economic Awards

A commonly told story of changes in the law of property division and support over the last century assumes that before the no-fault revolution the law sharply distinguished property from support orders. Property was supposed to have been awarded to the spouse who owned it during marriage, and support orders carried the entire burden of providing for dependent women and children. Moreover, the fault theory of divorce shaped the availability of support, for a wife[1] found at fault was not entitled to alimony and was likely to lose custody of the children and so not be entitled to support for them either. As fault-based divorce covertly turned into consensual divorce, according to this story, the presence or absence of formal grounds became bargaining tools used to shape the economic consequences.

Neither the law nor the reality was ever this simple. In some jurisdictions at some times the criteria for property division were not sharply distinct from those for spousal and child support, and scholarly articles written in the early twentieth century debated whether "alimony" was in the nature of support or property division. F. Granville Munson, Some Aspects of the Nature of Permanent Alimony, 16 Colum. L. Rev. 217 (1916). See also Chester G. Vernier & John B. Hurlbut, The Historical Background of Alimony Law and Its Present Structure, 6 Law & Contemp. Probs. 197 (1939). Nor were property awards based solely on simple assessments of who owned what during marriage:

> In the nineteenth century, a property settlement apparently was awarded to the wife under the same theory that ongoing support or alimony would be awarded today (i.e., for future needs), rather than as a division of the accumulated assets of the marriage. The legal profession termed this property settlement "alimony," but because the word often was used rather indiscriminately, authority existed for the proposition that "alimony" was meant to include maintenance not only for the wife but also for those children committed to her custody.

Donna Schuele, Origins and Development of the Law of Parental Child Support, 27 J. Fam. L. 807, 827 (1988-1989), citing Schichtl v. Schichtl, 55 N.W. 309, 309-310 (Iowa 1893); Boggs v. Boggs, 49 Iowa 190, 191 (1878); Campbell v. Campbell, 37 Wis. 206 (1875).

It is commonly believed that equitable distribution arose in common law property states only in the latter half of the twentieth century, and that community property states do not permit equitable distribution. In fact, a few common law property states have provided for equitable distribution since the nineteenth century. See, e.g., Gen. Stat. Kan. §4756 (1889); Okla. Stat. Ann.,

---

1. Traditionally men were not entitled to alimony. Orr v. Orr, 440 U.S. 268 (1979), excerpted in Chapter 2, held that this limitation violates equal protection.

tit. 12, §1278 (West 1976) (enacted in 1893). These statutes are discussed in Comment, The Development of Sharing Principles in Common Law Property States, 28 UCLA L. Rev. 1269, 1294-1299 (1981). By the early twentieth century, statutes in all the community property states except Louisiana empowered divorce courts to divide community property "equitably." Harriet S. Daggett, Division of Property upon Dissolution of Marriage, 6 Law & Contemp. Probs. 225, 231 (1930), citing McKay, Community Property 39 et seq. (1910). However, today more community property states require title-based distribution. See below.

Thus, the criteria for and purposes of the various types of economic orders in fault-based divorce law overlapped, at least in some jurisdictions, just as they often do today. However, the demise of the fault-based system did generate a conceptual crisis for spousal support and property division orders by eliminating or limiting the effect of a finding of fault on the division of economic resources.

2. Economic Orders in the No-Fault Era

The divorce revolution implied far more than a change in the grounds for marital dissolution. Divorce policy now sought to relieve spouses of a relationship that was "socially dead" so that they might seek new and more satisfying relationships. Given this policy, several propositions initially seemed obvious. One was that judicial decrees should end, as far as possible, all personal and economic ties between the spouses. Second, the abandonment of fault grounds, coupled with the emerging emphasis on gender equality, implied that both spouses should become equal and independent social and economic actors after divorce and that neither spouse should be especially burdened by the divorce decree.

These developments had a number of theoretical and practical implications for economic orders at divorce.[2] Most generally, these orders sought to end the relationship between formerly married parties. Support as a "pension" for the wronged spouse was obviously inconsistent with the new disinterest in fault and with a goal of terminating the previous relationship. Fortunately, an approach to marital property emerged that provided a vehicle for distributing wealth without long-term support. Drawing on social perceptions about the importance of women's work in the (unpaid) domestic economy and the legal theory of community property, legislatures and courts came to regard assets acquired during marriage as the result of the contributions of both spouses. While those contributions differed in kind and in origin, they nonetheless were considered important and, in some approaches, of equal value.

Understood in this new way, the theory that property should be distributed according to spousal contribution, rather than according to title or beneficial

---

2. However, Professor Herma Hill Kay has written that the advocates of no-fault divorce did not intend or even contemplate that this change would undermine the traditional bases for economic awards. Herma Hill Kay, Equality and Difference: A Perspective on No-Fault Divorce and Its Aftermath, 56 U. Cin. L. Rev. 1, 62-63 (1987).

ownership in specific items of wealth, did not seem controversial in principle. However, a number of questions presented themselves.

The first part of this chapter introduces some problems of principle and practice in connection with property distributions. Most obvious are questions about the definition and valuation of the parties' contributions to the acquisition of property.

The no-fault era property division statutes generally permit transfers of wealth from one spouse to the other who is dependent and needy as a qualification of the "contribution" theory, and spousal support is available for the same reason. A related approach provides support, but only on a limited basis, to allow a spouse who lacks education and training an opportunity to acquire skills. However, the first wave of writing accompanying no-fault divorce provided little theoretical justification for imposing an obligation on one spouse to provide for the other's needs after the marriage had ended. One answer that has developed is to regard support orders at least partially as compensation to the family for contributions that could not adequately be reflected in a property award.

These problems of theory and practice are heightened under current economic circumstances. Until relatively recently, the principal forms of wealth were tangible or intangible property (such as stocks or houses) that could be separated from the activity that generated them (employment). However, the most important forms of modern wealth for many families are directly associated with employment: pension plans and insurance, for example. How should the current forms of wealth be treated within the traditional distinction between property and alimony? And how does one reconcile the current nature of wealth with the desires to end marriage at the point of divorce and at the same time to recognize contributions to the marriage? The third part of this section takes up these questions in some detail.

3. Criticism of No-Fault Economics

Less than ten years after the beginning of the "no-fault revolution," critics began to argue that the revolution had caused unprecedented economic disaster for the women and children of divorce. The best known of these critics, Dr. Lenore Weitzman, along with several colleagues, studied divorce awards and the postdivorce economic status of men, women, and children in California in the early 1970s.[3] Virtually no one disagrees with Weitzman's fundamental claim that,

---

3. Weitzman's book, The Divorce Revolution (1985), collects and analyzes these data. Much of the work was published earlier in a series of articles, including Lenore J. Weitzman & Ruth B. Dixon, Child Custody Awards: Legal Standards and Empirical Patterns for Child Custody, Support and Visitation After Divorce, 12 U.C. Davis L. Rev. 471 (1979); Ruth B. Dixon & Lenore J. Weitzman, Evaluating the Impact of No-Fault Divorce in California, 29 Fam. Rel. 297 (1980); Lenore J. Weitzman & Ruth B. Dixon, The Alimony Myth: Does No-Fault Divorce Make a Difference? 14 Fam. L.Q. 141 (1980); Lenore J. Weitzman, The Economics of Divorce: Social and Economic Consequences of Property, Alimony and Child Support Awards, 28 UCLA L. Rev. 1181 (1981).

on average, women and children suffer badly in their economic position after divorce.[4]

However, Weitzman's analysis of the reasons for the problem is disputed. Weitzman largely blames the change from fault to no-fault divorce grounds for the poor position of women and children. This change in the law, she said, had two adverse effects. The change in grounds, which essentially was a change from consensual to unilateral divorce (see Chapter 5), deprived women of bargaining power — that is, they could no longer extract favorable economic settlements by refusing to go along with a divorce, and the change gave judges more discretion over economic awards, which they exercised to the disadvantage of women. Weitzman, The Divorce Revolution at 26-28, 63-66. *See also* Lenore J. Weitzman, Bringing the Law Back In, 1986 Am. B. Found. Res. J. 791, 793-794; Ira M. Ellman, The Theory of Alimony, 77 Cal. L. Rev. 1, 6-8 (1989); Robert H. Mnookin & Lewis Kornhauser, Bargaining in the Shadow of the Law: The Case of Divorce, 88 Yale L.J. 950, 950-954 (1979); Martha L. Fineman, Implementing Equality: Ideology, Contradiction and Social Change: A Study of Rhetoric and Results in the Regulation of the Consequences of Divorce, 1983 Wis. L. Rev. 789, 802.

More recent studies and reanalyses of existing data undermine these claims. Professor Marsha Garrison studied changes in the divorce law of New York and concluded that changes in the law governing spousal support and property division had much more effect than did the changes in grounds. Marsha Garrison, The Economics of Divorce: Changing Rules, Changing Results in Divorce

---

4. Perhaps the most widely quoted of Weitzman's statistics is that one year after legal divorce men's standard of living rose 42 percent, while women experienced a 73 percent loss. Weitzman, The Divorce Revolution at 339. However, others have cast doubt on the accuracy of these numbers. *See, e.g.,* Saul D. Hoffman & Greg J. Duncan, What Are the Economic Consequences of Divorce? 25 Demography 641 (1988); Greg J. Duncan & Saul D. Hoffman, Economic Consequences of Marital Instability, in Horizontal Equity, Uncertainty and Economic Well-Being 427 (M. David & T. Smeeding eds., 1985); Greg J. Duncan & Saul D. Hoffman, A Reconsideration of the Economic Consequences of Marital Dissolution, 22 Demography 485 (1985); Saul D. Hoffman, Marital Instability and the Economic Status of Women, 14 Demography 67 (1977).

Other studies that support Weitzman's claim of a basic disparity between men and women following divorce, if not her figures, include: Heather R. Wishik, Economics of Divorce: An Exploratory Study, 20 Fam. L.Q. 79 (1986); Alaska Women's Commission, Family Equity at Issue: A Study of the Economic Consequences of Divorce on Women and Children (Research Summary Oct. 1987); James B. McLindon, Separate but Unequal: The Economic Disaster of Divorce for Women and Children, 21 Fam. L.Q. 351 (1987); Rosalyn B. Bell, Alimony and the Financially Dependent Spouse in Montgomery County, Maryland, 22 Fam. L.Q. 225 (1988); Barbara R. Rowe & Alice M. Morrow, The Economic Consequences of Divorce in Oregon After Ten or More Years of Marriage, 24 Willamette L. Rev. 463 (1988); Barbara R. Rowe & Jean M. Lown, The Economics of Divorce and Remarriage for Rural Utah Families, 16 J. Contemp. L. 301 (1990).

For a more complex analysis, concluding that since the 1950s women's poverty rate has increased relative to that of men even though the absolute rate of poor women has not increased and suggesting explanations for the gender disparity, *see* Sara S. McLanahan, Annemette Sorensen & Dorothy Watson, Sex Differences in Poverty, 1950-1980, 15 Signs 102 (1989).

Reform at the Crossroads 1 (S. Sugarman & H. Kay eds., 1990). During the time period that Garrison studied, a spouse in New York could block a divorce because no-fault divorce was available only by mutual consent. The study did not show that no-fault (unilateral) divorce undermines women's bargaining position.[5] The bargaining hypothesis has also been criticized on the basis that it assumes that most of the people who want out of marriage are husbands and that most wives want, or are at least willing, to stay married. Marygold S. Melli, Constructing a Social Problem: The Post-Divorce Plight of Women and Children, 1986 Am. B. Found. Res. J. 759, 770-771; Stephen D. Sugarman, Dividing Financial Interests on Divorce in Divorce Reform at the Crossroads, above, at 130, 135 n.17.

   More fundamentally, as several authors have pointed out, changes in the law, especially the law of divorce grounds, do not have a wide-ranging impact on the postdivorce economic position of most divorcing people. As Professor Marygold Melli has written, "The bottom line is that Weitzman's data do not show any substantial changes in the economic situation of women and children under no-fault divorce; it was bad before no fault, and it continues to be bad now." Marygold S. Melli, above, at 770. *See also* Stephen D. Sugarman, above. In fact, most divorcing people do not have much property to divide. In most states the median net value of marital assets is $25,000 or less. Marsha Garrison, The Economic Consequences of Divorce, 32 Fam. & Conciliation Cts. Rev. 10, 11 (1994). The Census Bureau reported that in 1989 two-thirds of divorced women received no property settlement.[6] Moreover, relatively few divorced women have ever been awarded spousal support, even though all states permit courts to order it. According to Census data collected between 1887 and 1922, only 9 percent to 15 percent of divorced women were awarded alimony.[7] In 1991 the Census Bureau reported that only 15.5 percent of divorced or separated women were

---

   5. However, Garrison cites work by Elizabeth Peters that "provides some support for the bargaining hypothesis." *Id.* at 80, citing Elizabeth Peters, Marriage and Divorce: Informational Constraints and Private Contracting, 76 Am. Econ. Rev. 437 (1986).

   6. Bureau of the Census, Child Support and Alimony 1989 (Current Population Reports, Series P-60, No. 173) at 2 (1991). The earliest to make this point was William J. Goode, After Divorce 217 (1956). Other studies reporting similar results include Marsha Garrison, Good Intentions Gone Awry: The Impact of New York's Equitable Distribution Law upon Divorce Outcomes, 57 Brooklyn L. Rev. 621, 660, table 9 (1991) (summarizing several studies); The Divorce Revolution at 57; Lenore J. Weitzman, The Economics of Divorce: Social and Economic Consequences of Property, Alimony and Child Support Awards, 28 UCLA L. Rev. 1181, 1202 (1981); James B. McLindon, Separate but Unequal: The Economic Disaster of Divorce for Women and Children, 21 Fam. L.Q. 351, 381-384 (1987).

   7. Lenore J. Weitzman & Ruth B. Dixon, The Alimony Myth: Does No-Fault Divorce Make a Difference?, 14 Fam. L.Q. 141, 180 (1980), citing P. Jacobson, American Marriage and Divorce 126 (1959). A large empirical study conducted in Ohio in 1933 found that divorcing wives asked for some kind of financial award in 2,500 of a total of 6,586 divorce, annulment, and alimony actions, and that in 23 percent of these 2,500 cases they were awarded periodic payments and awards in gross in 10.5 percent of the 2,500. John S. Bradway, Foreword, 6 Law & Contemp. Probs. 183 (1939), and Edward W. Cooey, The Exercise of Judicial Discretion in the Award of Alimony, 6 Law & Contemp. Probs.

awarded spousal support.[8] About 18 percent of women divorced before 1970 received awards, while 12 percent to 13 percent of those divorced in 1970 or later did so.[9]

Whether the change in divorce grounds caused or aggravated the postdivorce economic position of women and children is of more than theoretical interest. Consistent with her conclusion that no-fault divorce did have such an adverse impact, Weitzman recommended that states not adopt pure no-fault divorce. Weitzman, The Divorce Revolution, ch. 11. In contrast, those who do not believe that the change in grounds significantly affected the economic consequences of divorce reject this solution.

MARYGOLD S. MELLI, CONSTRUCTING A SOCIAL PROBLEM: THE POST-DIVORCE PLIGHT OF WOMEN AND CHILDREN, 1986 Am. B. Found. Res. J. 759, 770-772:
[T]o the extent that Weitzman lays the blame [for the impoverishment of many divorced women] on the concept of no-fault divorce and gender-neutral rules, she is not only wrong but also may have done us a disservice in our search for a viable solution. There are at least three ways in which this may be the case. First, by emphasizing the bargaining power of innocent spouses under fault divorce, Weitzman ignores the fate of mothers who decide to end a marriage and who therefore would suffer the economic hardship of a guilty spouse. . . . Traditional marriage and the role it requires of women can be devastating on the self-confidence and self-esteem of women. For women who are affected in this way, divorce may be seen as the best solution. . . .

213, 213-214 (1939), both discussing Leon C. Marshall & Geoffrey May, The Divorce Court—Ohio (1933).

8. Bureau of the Census, Child Support and Alimony: 1989 (Current Population Reports, Series P-60, No. 173) Table L (1991).

9. Bureau of the Census, Child Support and Alimony: 1983 (Supplemental Report, Current Population Reports, Special Studies, Series P-23, No. 148 (Oct. 1986). *See also* Lenore J. Weitzman, above, at 1181, 1221-1222 (1981); Heather R. Wishik, Economics of Divorce: An Exploratory Study, 20 Fam. L.Q. 79 (1986); Alaska Women's Commission, Family Equity at Issue: A Study of the Economic Consequences of Divorce on Women and Children (Research Summary Oct. 1987); Rosalyn B. Bell, Alimony and the Financially Dependent Spouse in Montgomery County, Maryland, 22 Fam. L.Q. 225 (1988); Robert E. McGraw et al., A Case Study in Divorce Law Reform and Its Aftermath, 20 J. Fam. L. 443, 473 (1982); Barbara R. Rowe & Alice M. Morrow, The Economic Consequences of Divorce in Oregon After Ten or More Years of Marriage, 24 Willamette L. Rev. 463, 477 (1988); Barbara R. Rowe & Jean M. Lown, The Economics of Divorce and Remarriage for Rural Utah Families, 16 J. Contemp. L. 301, 311 (1990). James B. McLindon, Separate but Unequal: The Economic Disaster of Divorce for Women and Children, 21 Fam. L.Q. 351 (1987) (in 1970-1971, New Haven, Conn., before adoption of no-fault divorce, 50 percent of divorced women received more than a nominal award; after adoption, 30 percent did). Between 1979 and 1985 the average alimony payment declined, in constant dollars, by 21 percent, and the average child support award also declined in constant dollars between the late 1970s and mid-1980s. Marsha Garrison, The Economic Consequences of Divorce, 32 Fam. & Conciliation Cts. Rev. 10, 14-15 (1994) (citing multiple sources, including Census data).

Second, Weitzman's preoccupation with the contemporary no-fault-divorce structure and gender-neutral rules . . . leads her to inaccurately credit fault divorce with economic protections for women and children that it in fact never provided. It also results in failure to give sufficient recognition to the efforts now developing in the law to provide more adequate post-divorce economic protection for wives and children. . . .

Finally, by assuming that the disastrous economic consequences of divorce were caused by a change in the law, The Divorce Revolution makes the problem appear to be a simple one: a few more changes in the law and the problems will be rectified. It is undoubtedly true . . . that changes in some laws may incrementally affect the economic status of divorced women and children. . . . But the consequences of divorce for those women who devote their major energies to homemaking and the children for whom they care is a problem that has long preceded the current controversies. It defies easy solution and has survived any number of divorce reforms.

MARSHA GARRISON, *THE ECONOMIC CONSEQUENCES OF DIVORCE,* 32 Fam. & Conciliation Cts. Rev. 10, 18-19 (1994): The median income of married couples is more than double that of households headed by women and, when there are children, more than triple that of single mothers. The result is that the poverty rate for single-mother families with children is more than five times that of married couples with children. For Black single mothers, the picture is even more bleak; 69% of these families have incomes below the poverty line.

The economic advantage of marriage is sufficiently great that even male-headed households have a significantly smaller median income than that of married couples. . . .

The economic disadvantage of divorce as compared to marriage is thus clear and inevitable. But this disadvantage does not result from divorce law and cannot be cured by it; no divorce law can provide a standard of living for families that experience divorce that is commensurate with that enjoyed by the marital household. With increasing numbers of two-earner families, the economic disadvantage of divorce as compared to marriage will not abate and will likely grow. We can be confident that divorce will almost always occasion a decline in standard of living as compared to marriage. All that divorce law can accomplish is fair apportionment of that disadvantage.

It is thus important to distinguish poverty caused by divorce law, which is preventable, from poverty that flows from divorce (or predates it) and is thus unpreventable. . . . Evidence on this question is still scanty but accumulating.

First, it is now apparent that many women who are poor after divorce were also poor before divorce. Recent Census data suggests that divorce is approximately twice as likely among couples with incomes below the poverty line as compared to others. Among families with children, census researchers have reported that 21% of those that experienced the loss of the father from the household during a 2-year survey period were already poor, a poverty rate generally double that of married-couple households with children. Among mothers living in married-couple families who formed mother-child families within the year, 26% of White mothers and 39% of Black mothers were already poor.

Moreover, those mother-child families that were poor before parental separation are most likely to remain poor. One expert has thus estimated that more than 60% of poor Black mothers were poor before forming mother-child families. A large proportion of poor single-mother families thus represent continuing poverty rather than poverty occasioned by family dissolution.

Second, an increasingly large segment of poor mother-child families reflects nonmarriage rather than divorce. . . .

The already poor and the never-married are not the only women represented in the poverty statistics, of course. According to census research from the mid-1980s, almost twice as many mother-child households were poor following divorce as had been during marriage: 35.5% versus 19%. Not all of that increase was preventable, however; for families at the margin of poverty, the increased expenses of two households would likely drive both into poverty under any divorce regime.

See also Mary Ann Glendon, The New Family and the New Property 83-85 (1981). Views about the modern role of family and private, rather than public, obligation also substantially affect judgments about how much we should try to use property division and support orders to restructure families' postdivorce lives. Consider the following perspectives.

SUSAN W. PRAGER, *SHARING PRINCIPLES AND THE FUTURE OF MARITAL PROPERTY LAWS*, 25 UCLA L. Rev. 1, 5-6, 12 (1981): Although the views of those favoring separate property and those advocating sharing principles ultimately diverge, both stem from a concern for equality. This preoccupation with equal rights concerns may dangerously skew our vision of marital property policy questions and create a deceptive mode of analysis. The recent literature is dominated by the notion that equality is the critical, perhaps exclusive, factor in *shaping* the property rights of married people. It suggests that to the extent that there is economic inequality a sharing oriented system is required. When inequality is not present, a system based on individual rights is appropriate.

While it is certainly true that in recent years sharing principles have been advanced because of the economic inequalities created by the traditional marriage, it is questionable whether once those inequalities disappear the need for sharing principles will vanish as well. As long as marriage and other similar close personal relationships continue to reflect sharing behavior, there is a place for sharing principles in marital property law. Marital sharing principles are not dependent upon a social structure in which one or the other spouse relinquishes the earner role. Rather the need for the sharing philosophy stems from the dynamics of marriage and similar relationships.

. . . In marriage most of us seek an alliance with another individual who will believe in us, be loyal to us, help us function in a demanding, often hostile world, and who will help make life satisfying. In exchange we will try to do the same. In many senses these needs and the expectations they create shape the frame of mind with which decisions are made during marriage. The expectation of stability and continuity and the desire for a shared life suggest that married people are unlikely to make decisions on an individually oriented basis; rather the needs of each person tend to be taken into account. Thus married people will often make decisions differently than they would if there were no marriage or marriage-like relationship functioning. . . .

. . . The choice of a separate property system may reflect the judgment that, regardless of how the spouses actually make choices, from a societal viewpoint their decisions *ought* to be made on an individual basis. Thus, the marital property law becomes a tool of social engineering, designed to encourage independence. A separate property system encourages each person to function as an earner by refusing to compensate a spouse who remains in the home for some significant period.

The absence of sharing principles can thus be used to discourage the establishment of dependency relationships. But if many couples in fact make decisions with the special exigencies of the marital relationship in mind, a system of property law which assumes decisions ought to be made on an individual basis may produce two quite different ill effects. First, one spouse may ultimately be treated unfairly if the couple does not alter its behavior to conform to the individualistic orientation of the separate property model. Second, if behavior is indeed responsive to a legal structure which dictates putting oneself first, other social values will suffer. By dictating that a married person behave as if unmarried with respect to certain choices or suffer the consequences of subsequent property disadvantage for not doing so, the individually oriented model works to reward self-interested choices which can be detrimental to the continuation of the marriage. At the same time it punishes conduct of accommodation and compromise so important to furthering and preserving the relationship. From a social engineering standpoint, an individualistic property system will begin to produce behavior that is at cross-purposes with other values, such as stability and cooperation in marital relationships.

J. Thomas Oldham, Putting Asunder in the 1990s, 80 Cal. L. Rev. 1091, 1125-1126 (1992): Divorce reform is still struggling to respond to the increasing practice of serial marriage in American society. Most divorcing spouses eventually remarry. Indeed, one argument advanced in support of no-fault divorce was that people should be able to establish a happy domestic life; if a first marriage appeared to be a mistake, the spouses should be free to dissolve the first union and initiate another.

Obviously, such a policy is not unrelated to the post-divorce economic problems of women and children. Many divorcing families already are in a difficult economic situation. Once the divorced father remarries, particularly if he establishes a new family, his connections with the first family will probably diminish. . . .

What posture should divorce law take toward the divorced father? Should he be encouraged to remarry, should substantial barriers to remarriage be created, or should the law be neutral? If the father remarries, this may affect his inclination and ability to provide resources to his former spouse and his children. Many, myself included, would find it unfair to burden unduly the noncustodial parent's ability to remarry. Thus, the challenge for the no-fault divorce system is whether it can adequately provide for the custodial parent and the children without placing unreasonable burdens upon the ex-husband's remarriage options. Satisfying both of these goals may require the talents of the magicians Penn and Teller. Many divorcing families already are pressed financially before they divorce. Maintaining two households frequently is quite difficult, even before a divorcing spouse contemplates establishing a new relationship.

It must be recognized that divorce normally will be a financial hardship for both spouses as well as for the children. Marital roles will change and probably become more onerous for most custodial parents, at least until they remarry; this is unfortunate, but given current American family policy it seems inevitable. About 60% of married women living with their spouse work outside the home. In contrast, about 75% of divorced women are in the work force. It is unrealistic to suggest that a divorcing housewife should not be "forced . . . to play multiple roles against her will after the marriage ends." One must strike a fair balance between a desire to use private law to compensate women for roles assumed during marriage and the concern about unduly burdening men's remarriage prospects.

CARL E. SCHNEIDER, *RETHINKING ALIMONY: MARITAL DECISIONS AND MORAL DISCOURSE,* 1991 B.Y.U. L. Rev. 197, 243-245: . . . Family law generally, and the law of alimony and marital property particularly, try to regulate two of the most intimate, complex, and consequential things in people's lives — their closest personal relations and their money. People want, and perhaps expect, such a law to make its decisions individually and meticulously, giving its full attention to the whole situation in which the specific parties were acting and to the differences between the specific parties and the rest of the world. Because morality matters deeply to most people, they will consider their moral relations a central part of that full situation and those differences. . . .

Another obstacle to eliminating moral discourse from family law is that there are important reasons for wanting to retain it. The family is a central social institution which affects people in many of the most basic aspects of their lives. The obligations family members assume to each other, then, will have important social consequences, consequences in which the law has a legitimate interest. . . . Thus some people on the right argue in favor of traditional alimony rules partly on the ground that they strengthen the family by enforcing the obligations and the sense of obligation family members are taken to owe each other. And thus some people on the left argue in favor either of restricting alimony (for example, by making alimony available only for rehabilitative purposes) or of expanding alimony . . . as a means of promoting women's moral claims to autonomy and self-sufficiency. . . .

The social interest in alimony which has traditionally had special weight has to do with another of the law's functions — the protective function. It is a basic function of law to protect citizens against harms done them by their fellows. Because spouses do and should be able to depend on each other, and because spouses are for that and other reasons peculiarly vulnerable to each other, spouses can easily and severely injure each other in many ways. Alimony has traditionally been understood to be one way in which the law protects former spouses from the financial component of such injuries. Since those financial injuries can be devastating, this social purpose ought not be easily discarded. And it is a purpose which can be best served where the law undertakes the moral inquiry into whether such an injury has been done.

B. PROPERTY DIVISION AT DIVORCE

In all states, the steps in dividing property at divorce are the same: The first is to determine which property is subject to the court's dispositional authority under state law. Then the property is valued, and the court allocates the divisible party between the spouses according to the governing legal principles. The final order implements the decisions and may provide who gets exactly what assets. The most important issues in principle are those that determine which property is divisible and in what shares. States can be divided into three groups based on how they resolve these issues. A key variable that distinguishes these three systems is the amount of discretion available to the judge.

Title-Based Distribution   Under this type of system, courts have little or no express discretion over property division, for the governing principle is that property is awarded to the spouses as they owned it during the marriage. Thus, distribution at divorce depends on the principles of property ownership discussed in Chapter 2. In a common law property jurisdiction using a pure title system, the spouse in whose name property was titled would receive it at divorce, subject to any claims of the other spouse based on the equitable ownership principles discussed in Chapter 2. A court in a community property jurisdiction using a pure title system would award separate property to the owner and divide the community property equally.

Today no common law property state relies on title-based distribution. It is used in a limited form in California, Louisiana, and New Mexico, the three community property states that mandate equal division of community property with very few exceptions and require that separate property be awarded to the spouse who owned it during marriage. Cal. Fam. Code §2550 (West 1994); La. Civ. Code Ann. art. 1290, 1308, 2336, 2341; La. Code Civ. Pro. Ann. art. 82; N.M. Stat. Ann. §40-4-7 (1998); Michelson v. Michelson, 86 N.M. 107, 520 P.2d 263 (1974). For a general discussion *see* William A. Reppy, Jr., Major Events in the Evolution of American Community Property Law and Their Import to Equitable Distribution States, 23 Fam. L.Q. 163, 164, n.3, n.5 (1989). Where community property must be divided equally, division in kind is generally not required. *See, e.g.,* In re Marriage of Fink, 160 Cal. Rptr. 516, 603 P.2d 881 (1980).

Pure Equitable Distribution   This type of system is at the opposite end of the discretion spectrum, for the judge has discretion to divide all the property of both spouses as is "just and proper" or through some equivalent formula. Despite the similarity in terminology, "equitable distribution" is very different from the "equitable ownership" principles we examined in Chapter 2. Determining who is the equitable owner of property during marriage is critical to implementing a title-based system of divorce property division, since the equitable owner will prevail over a titleholder who is not the equitable owner. In a state that mandates equitable distribution of all property, which spouse owned property legally or equitably during marriage may be relevant but is not determinative of who will get it at divorce. In 2004, Connecticut, Iowa, Kansas, Massachusetts, Montana, New Hampshire, North Dakota, Oregon, South Dakota, Utah, and Vermont allowed courts to divide all the parties' property equitably. Linda D. Elrod & Robert G. Spector, A Review of the Year in Family Law, 36 Fam. L.Q. 577 (2004). In some of these states, however, property is still characterized as marital or separate and ordinarily only marital property is divided.

Equitable Distribution of Marital or Community Property This system gives judges more discretion over property division at divorce than does a title system, but less than an equitable distribution system, and it has become the system most commonly used in this country. In most of the community property states — Arizona, Idaho, Nevada, Texas, Washington, and Wisconsin — equitable rather than equal division of community property is mandated, and these states also permit equitable distribution of separate property under limited circumstances. In addition, most common law property states have gone to a form of a "deferred marital property," which was first fully developed in the Nordic countries. In 2004, the common law states using this system were Alabama, Arkansas, Colorado, Delaware, D.C., Florida, Georgia, Hawaii, Illinois, Indiana, Kentucky, Maine, Maryland, Michigan, Minnesota, Mississippi, Missouri, Nebraska, Nevada, New Jersey, New York, North Carolina, Ohio, Oklahoma, Pennsylvania, Rhode Island, South Carolina, Tennessee, Virginia, West Virginia, Wisconsin, and Wyoming. Elrod & Spector, above. Under this system, as long as the marriage lasts, each spouse owns and manages assets that he or she brings into or acquires during the marriage. But when the marriage ends, the assets are shared as if they had been acquired in a community property state.

The current and original versions of section 307 of the Uniform Marriage and Divorce Act set out alternative approaches to what property is subject to division and on what basis.

UNIFORM MARRIAGE AND DIVORCE ACT §307

Alternative A (for common law property states)
(a) In a proceeding for dissolution of a marriage . . . the court, without regard to marital misconduct, shall . . . finally equitably apportion between the parties the property and assets belonging to either or both however and whenever acquired, and whether the title thereto is in the name of the husband or wife or both. In making apportionment the court shall consider the duration of the marriage, any prior marriage of either party, any antenuptial agreement of the parties, the age, health, station, occupation, amounts and sources of income, vocational skills, employability, estate, liabilities, and needs of each of the parties, custodial provisions, whether the apportionment is in lieu of or in addition to maintenance, and the opportunity of each for future acquisition of capital assets and income. The court shall also consider the contribution or dissipation of each party in the

acquisition, preservation, depreciation, or appreciation in value of the respective estates, and the contribution of a spouse as a homemaker or to the family unit.

Alternative B (for community property states)

In a proceeding for dissolution of the marriage . . . the court shall assign each spouse's separate property to that spouse. It also shall divide community property, without regard to marital misconduct, in just proportions after considering all relevant factors including:

(1) contribution of each spouse to acquisition of the marital property, including contribution of a spouse as homemaker;

(2) value of the property set apart to each spouse;

(3) duration of the marriage; and

(4) economic circumstances of each spouse when the division of property is to become effective, including the desirability of awarding the family home or the right to live therein for a reasonable period to the spouse having custody of any children.

NOTES AND QUESTIONS

1. As originally drafted, §307 of the Uniform Marriage and Divorce Act (UMDA) did not provide different rules for common law and community property states. Instead, like Alternative B, it provided that each spouse was to receive his or her separate property and that the marital property was to be divided "without regard to marital misconduct, in such proportions as the court deems just after considering" all the factors listed in Alternative B except the duration of the marriage. The original version defined "marital property" as "all property acquired by either spouse subsequent to the marriage" except (1) property acquired by gift, bequest, devise, or descent; (2) property acquired in exchange for property acquired prior to the marriage or in exchange for property acquired by gift, bequest, devise, or descent; (3) property acquired by a spouse after a decree of legal separation; (4) property excluded by valid agreement of the parties; and (5) the increase in value of property acquired prior to the marriage.

This version was initially rejected by the Family Law Section of the American Bar Association, and the version you see above was adopted. However, most common law property states now divide property into marital and nonmarital shares and allow only the former to be distributed at divorce. Emily Osborn, Comment, The Treatment of Unearned Separate Property at Divorce in Common Law Property Jurisdictions, 1990 Wis. L. Rev. 903, 918-939. The American Law Institute Principles of the Law of Family Dissolution, published in 2002 and dealing extensively with the economic consequences of divorce, also recommend this system, with the notable exception that in long-term marriages separate property gradually is converted into marital (and hence divisible) property. ALI, Principles of the Law of Family Dissolution §§4.03, 4.12 (2002).

2. Is a deferred marital property system illogical, in that it treats spouses as economic individuals while they are married but as an economic unit when they divorce? If a spouse in a state with a deferred marital property system, seeing

divorce coming, begins to give away property, perhaps to children or parents, does the other spouse have any remedy? Should the other spouse be able to avoid these transfers while the parties are still married? Should the divorce court be able to avoid them? In common law property states a similar problem has arisen in applying the elective share statutes when one spouse dies. Courts in some of these states created or applied principles of fraudulent and illusory transfers to protect the rights of spouses under the elective share statutes. Some courts have followed this lead for divorce. *See, e.g.,* In re Adams, 538 N.E.2d 1286 (Ill. App. 1989); Rock v. Rock, 587 A.2d 1133 (Md. App. 1991); Booth v. Booth, 371 S.E.2d 569 (Va. App. 1988). Taking fault into account when dividing property can sometimes provide a partial solution. The role of fault is discussed later in this section.

3. Courts in common law property states have generally held that a statute providing for equitable distribution of property at divorce does not violate due process, even though it permits a court to award one spouse property that was owned by the other spouse during marriage. For example, in Rothman v. Rothman, 320 A.2d 496, 499, 501 (N.J. 1974), the New Jersey Supreme Court said,

> A state may, in the exercise of the police power, enact a statute to promote the public health, safety, morals or general welfare. Such a state, because of retroactive application or otherwise, may diminish in value or totally destroy an individual's right, whether in property as such or arising out of contract, provided that the public interest to be promoted sufficiently outweighs in importance the private right which is impaired. . . . It has long been well settled and now stands unchallenged that marriage is a social relationship subject in all respects to the state's police power.

However, the Arizona Supreme Court in Hatch v. Hatch, 547 P.2d 1044 (Ariz. en banc 1976), suggested that an unequal division of community property would violate due process except in unusual circumstances. The Texas courts have suggested that awarding one spouse's separate property to the other would violate due process. Eggemeyer v. Eggemeyer, 554 S.W.2d 137 (Tex. 1977), *appeal after remand*, 623 S.W.2d 462 (Tex. App. 1981); Cameron v. Cameron, 641 S.W.2d 210 (Tex. 1982).

The Uniform Marital Property Act (UMPA) provides that property acquired by either spouse before adoption of the act remains the separate property of that spouse. The drafters perceived that changing separate to marital property *during* an ongoing marriage might be unconstitutional. However, on the basis of the principle exemplified in *Rothman*, the drafters saw no problem in providing that separate property that would have been marital property had it been acquired after the act was adopted is treated as marital property when the marriage terminates by death or divorce. UMPA §§17 and 18, with commentary. (The UMPA does not include rules for property division at divorce or death, leaving these matters to other provisions of state law.) In essence, these rules defer the effect of the adoption of the UMPA on property acquired before adoption until the dissolution of the marriage. *Compare* the quasi–community property statutes, discussed later in this section.

PROBLEM

Hamilton and Wilma marry when both are 21. Neither brings significant assets into the marriage, and neither inherits or is given property during the marriage. Throughout the marriage Wilma was a homemaker, and Hamilton was a well-paid employee who skillfully invested his excess income in stocks and bonds, always taking title in his name alone. When they divorce, their assets consist of the family home, purchased during the marriage from Hamilton's earnings and titled in joint tenancy, and the securities that Hamilton purchased.

In a common law state using a pure title system, what property would be divisible? In a community property system using a pure title system? In a common law property state that has adopted Alternative A of §307, what property would be subject to division? In a community property state that had adopted Alternative B? In a common law property state that had adopted the original version of §307?

1. The Meaning of "Equitable Distribution"

Equitable distribution statutes vary considerably in form but little in substance. Some, like UMDA §307, contain lists of factors that judges must consider, while others do not. Appellate courts often interpret the latter kind of statute as requiring consideration of factors similar to those contained in the statutory lists. As many as 38 factors have been identified. Note, Property Division and Alimony Awards: A Survey of Statutory Limitations on Judicial Discretion, 50 Fordham L. Rev. 415, 439 n.170 (1981). All statutes give judges substantial discretion. Lists of factors do not provide much structure, for they do not tell judges what weight or priority to give to the factors.

What these statutes do, then, is to grant judges discretion without providing either governing principles or ultimate goals. However, as a practical matter, judges will probably adopt, consciously or unconsciously, some framework within which to make decisions, either from a sense that such a framework is necessary to ensure a measure of consistency or to achieve efficiency. And good lawyers will construct a theory of their cases so that they can do more than simply present scattered pieces of evidence.

Legislatures and courts are developing principles for property division, as the next cases illustrate. As you study them and the materials that follow, consider what goals are being pursued and to what extent these goals are realistic or even desirable.

IN THE MATTER OF THE MARRIAGE OF PIERSON

653 P.2d 1258 (Or. 1982)

TANZER, J. . . . This dissolution ends a 24-year marriage. The parties are in their early forties. Wife earns $30,000 per year as a public administrator; husband earns $20,000 as a teacher. Their children are grown. Neither party seeks support. The parties have divided their personal property. They have agreed to bear their own attorney fees. The sole task of the court is to equitably divide four items of real property.

The parties bought their family home and accompanying acreage in the 1960's. Two years before this proceeding, wife moved out and husband remained. It now has a value of $90,000.

When wife moved out, she withdrew the family savings of $13,000, added $3,000 or $4,000 of her own and purchased a house on Kathy Street. This was done with the cooperation of husband. The Kathy Street residence has an equity valued at $24,310.

Wife then purchased a condominium. She moved out of the Kathy Street house and into the condominium. The equity in the condominium is valued at $2,500.

Wife's father died intestate in April, 1975. The parties separated in August, 1978. The father's estate was distributed in April, 1979, one year before the filing of this proceeding in April, 1980. Wife's inheritance is a plot of farm land. Husband evaluates wife's equity in her share of the inheritance at $181,200; wife evaluates it as $131,200. Neither previous court made a specific finding as to its value.

The parties agreed that the Kathy Street house should be sold and the proceeds divided evenly between them. Husband agreed that wife should receive the condominium. The parties disagreed as to the disposition of the property inherited by the wife. The wife contended that she was entitled to an award of one-half of the non-inherited property and that her inheritance should be awarded to her outside of the property division equation. Husband asserted that the inheritance should be considered as part of the marital assets, one-half of which should be awarded to him.

The trial court awarded the family home to husband, ordered the Kathy Street residence sold and the proceeds divided evenly, and awarded the condominium and the inheritance to the wife. The valuations are reflected in this table:

	Husband	Wife
Family home	$ 90,000	
Kathy Street residence	12,155	$ 12,155
Condominium		2,500
Wife's inherited share of her father's farm		131,200-181,200
	$102,155	$145,855-195,855

The wife appealed, contending that the trial court should have awarded equal shares in the "marital assets," exclusive of her inheritance. The Court of Appeals affirmed without opinion.

Only the property division is in issue. The court is called upon to divide the property in a manner which is "just and proper in all the circumstances," ORS 107.105(1)(e). . . . In summary, we review the exercise of equitable discretion in the property division in an attempt to identify the principles which should guide the court's discretion.

[ORS 107.105(1)(e) provides: "Whenever the court grants a decree of annulment or dissolution of marriage or of separation, it has power further to decree as follows (e) For the division or other disposition between the parties of the real or personal property, or both, of either or both of the parties as may be just and proper in all the circumstances. The court shall consider the contribution of a spouse as a homemaker as a contribution to the acquisition of marital assets. There is a rebuttable presumption that both spouses have contributed equally to the acquisition of property during the marriage, whether such property is jointly or separately held. . . ." The court construed this statute as permitting equitable distribution of all property owned by either party, whenever and however acquired. It held that "marital assets" subject to the rebuttable presumption of equal contribution include all property acquired by either spouse during the marriage, even those acquired by gift or inheritance. Thus, the farm that wife inherited from her father was marital property subject to the presumption, but the presumption was rebutted because she inherited it after the parties separated. Husband did not contest the trial court's finding that he had been compensated for his work on the farm during the marriage.]

. . . That does not mean, however, that we accept the wife's contention that she should receive her inherited property entirely plus exactly one-half of the remaining property.

Property division is not a function solely of arithmetic. Absent overriding considerations, marital assets should be divided as equally as practical. Where, as here, one spouse is equitably entitled to receive a marital asset because he or she acquired it free from any contribution of the other spouse, the asset can initially be removed from the equation. Thus, unless additional considerations dictate otherwise, wife should retain her inheritance.

The equation of property division and the entitlement of a party to individually acquired property may be disturbed in order to accomplish broader purposes of a dissolution. There are social objectives as well as financial ones to be achieved and that may result in an uneven financial division. As we said in *Haguewood*, 292 Or. at 206-207:

"Dissolution of a marriage is analogous in many ways to dissolution of a partnership or other joint financial venture. . . . The analogy is not complete, however. Unlike a business dissolution, a marital dissolution often requires the achievement of certain social as well as financial objectives which may be unique to the parties. . . . For example, the parties to a long-term marriage should be awarded the resources for self-sufficient, post-dissolution life apart insofar as possible within the limitations of the capabilities and property of the parties. . . ."

. . . The need in this case is to enable both spouses to emerge from the marriage and recommence life on a sufficient economic footing. Fortunately, there is sufficient property and income to serve that need. Where the income and property of one spouse is greater, the achievement of economic self-sufficiency of both parties is not necessarily best served by an equal division of the marital assets. In dividing the non-inherited marital assets, we therefore take into account that the wife has greater income and, because of the inheritance, greater financial resources.

We are also influenced by two practical considerations: a forced sale can cost much of the value of property, and imposition of a judgment lien on property tends to drain income and to continue, rather than sever, the financial relationship of the parties. Where economic self-sufficiency, a fair division, and other purposes of a decree can be achieved without ordering a sale or imposing a lien, it is preferable to avoid those divisional devices. That means that a division with a slight imbalance may be preferable to one which is exactly even. These considerations all suggest that the non-inherited property be divided as cleanly as possible. Because the husband has less income and less property, he should receive the greater share of the non-inherited property, but the imbalance should be reduced to avoid unreasonable disproportionality.

We therefore modify the decree to award the entire Kathy Street house to wife. This lessens the imbalance, avoids the necessity of sale and gives wife more flexibility. We acknowledge that the parties agreed to the sale of the Kathy Street house and division of the proceeds, but the husband did so in conjunction with his unsuccessful claim upon the inheritance and the wife did so in conjunction with her unsuccessful demand for one-half of the non-inherited property. The resulting imbalance ($90,000 to $26,810) is so disproportionate that a judgment lien against the house, consistent with husband's ability to pay or refinance, although an undesirable device, seems the only equitable way to transfer some value to wife. We therefore also modify the decree to provide for a $20,000 judgment lien against the family home in favor of the wife, payable in equal monthly payments at the statutory rate of interest over 10 years from the effective date of this decision. The modified schedule of distribution of the non-inherited assets would then be as follows:

	Husband	Wife
Family home and judgment lien	$70,000	$20,000
Kathy Street house		24,310
Condominium		2,500
Subtotal	$70,000	$46,810
Plus inheritance	–	131,200-181,200
TOTAL	$70,000	$178,010-228,010

Affirmed as modified. No costs to either party.

[The dissenting opinion of Peterson, J., is omitted.]

NOTES AND QUESTIONS

1. Perhaps the most fundamental issue of equitable distribution is whether property awards should be based on each spouse's contributions to the acquisition of assets during the marriage, or should seek to allow the former spouses to live their postdivorce lives as independent actors by dividing property according to need. To say that these are two primary theories for property division does not necessarily mean that legislatures or courts adopt one to the exclusion of the other, or that they seek to accomplish only these goals. Which theory, if either, is dominant in UMDA §307? In the statute construed in *Pierson*? In the opinion of the court?

As we have seen, modern property division law also seeks to minimize post-divorce contacts between the spouses. To what extent is this goal reflected in *Pierson*?

2. Much of the reform in property division law in the last 20 years has focused on how to deal with couples in which one partner, usually the woman, stayed out of the labor market to work as a homemaker. By 2000, of 55 million wives, 22 million were not in the labor force for a variety of reasons. U.S. Bureau of the Census, Census 2000 Summary File 3 (SF3), p.44. Family Type by Employment Status (Internet Release).

In a common law property jurisdiction using the traditional title-based system of property division, a spouse (almost always the wife) who did not work outside the home throughout all or most of the marriage would ordinarily receive little or no property at divorce because her work as a homemaker was not recognized as a financial contribution to the acquisition of property titled in her husband's name. *See* Chapter 2, Section B.1. Though she might well be in great financial need after a divorce, the only way of providing for her was alimony, where that was available. As *Pierson* and UMDA §307 indicate, an important reason that common law property states moved to equitable division of property at divorce was a changed understanding of fairness to homemakers.

Under statutes such as that in *Pierson*, that require that homemaking be considered a contribution to the acquisition of property, how should homemaking be valued? In wrongful death suits homemaking is broken down into component jobs, and the market value of these jobs is determined. Under this approach how should the components of homemaking be characterized? Many of the jobs to which a homemaker's work might be compared are very low paying. For example, should the care of young children be compared to babysitting or to teaching? Should running the household be compared to housecleaning or to managing a small business? Should the characterization vary from family to family so that a homemaker who takes care of her home herself is compared only to a cleaning person while one who has hired help is compared to a manager? Should this method of analysis be used for purposes of property distribution at divorce?

In some southern states the courts developed equitable distribution by expanding resulting and constructive trust remedies to count general economic contributions to the family and then homemaking as a contribution to the acquisition of property. In some of these states such awards are called "lump-sum alimony," but in substance they are divisions of property. *See, e.g.,* Burgess v. Burgess, 286 S.E.2d 142 (S.C. 1982), Canakaris v. Canakaris, 382 So. 2d 1197 (Fla. 1980); Jenkins v. Jenkins, 278 So. 2d 446 (Miss. 1973); LaRue v. LaRue, 304 S.E.2d 312 (W. Va. 1983). In 1994 the Mississippi Supreme Court officially adopted equitable distribution of all assets, abandoning the resulting trust and lump-sum alimony alternatives. Ferguson v. Ferguson, 639 So. 2d 921 (Miss. 1994).

In Marvin v. Marvin, 557 P.2d 106 (Cal. 1976), set out in Chapter 4, the California trial court on remand found that Lee Marvin's support of Michelle Marvin adequately compensated her for her services. Has the homemaker wife similarly been adequately compensated, so that she should have no claim to property that her husband earned during the marriage? Is the spouse different from the cohabitant? If we take the view that marital support can compensate for homemaking, should living a lavish lifestyle be treated as more complete compensation than living simply?

3. The statute in *Pierson* creates a presumption that the parties contributed equally to the acquisition of marital property. Statutes or case law in many other states creates a presumption that marital property will be divided equally. What is the difference between a presumption in favor of a finding of equal contribution and one in favor of equal division?

Sometimes presumptions express assumptions about general factual truths, and sometimes they express policy choices. Upon what is a presumption in favor of a finding of equal contribution based? A presumption in favor of equal division? Community property and presumptions in favor of equal division can be understood as eliminating the difficulties of quantifying contributions by valuing the contributions of homemakers as equal to those of income producers.

Empirical research shows that, on average, women receive half or more of the net assets under equitable distribution regimes. However, studies of settled cases have found great variability in how people divide assets. For example, in her New York study, Professor Marsha Garrison found that only one-fifth of the couples divided their net worth relatively equally, and the variation was largely inexplicable. Marsha Garrison, Good Intentions Gone Awry: The Impact of New York's Equitable Distribution Law on Divorce Outcomes, 57 Brook. L. Rev. 621, 673-674, tables 18 and 20 (1991).

In a related study, Garrison found that judges strongly tended toward equal division of marital assets. When they deviated from equal division, they tended to give greater weight to the parties' relative contributions to the acquisition of the property than to their need. Marsha Garrison, How Do Judges Decide Divorce Cases? An Empirical Analysis of Discretionary Decision Making, 74 N.C. L. Rev. 401, 452-458 (1996).

Is there a point beyond which the policy of equal sharing no longer applies? The cases are divided; for a discussion *see* David N. Hofstein, Ellen Goldberg Weiner & Christopher Marrone, Equitable Distribution in Large Marital Estate Cases, 17 J. Am. Acad. Matrimonial L. 307 (2001).

4. The *Pierson* opinion, like many others, analogizes marriage to a business partnership. However, it also observed that the analogy of marriage to a business partnership is not perfect. What does it mean here to call marriage a partnership? In what sense is marriage not to be treated as if it were actually a partnership when the spouses divorce?

When a business partnership is dissolved and the business is ended, all the assets of the partnership are divided equally after returning the "capital investment" of each partner. Only rarely is an unequal division of the remaining assets justified. The rules in the few community property states that require return of separate property to the owner and equal division of community property produce results similar to the business partnership rules. However, when one partner carries on a business, as frequently happens, the withdrawing partner usually may choose between forcing the remaining partner(s) to buy out his/her interest and leaving his/her capital in the business with a right to share future profits. If property division were based on these principles, what would the typical order look like? *See* Cynthia Starnes, Divorce and the Displaced Homemaker: A Discourse on Playing with Dolls, Partnership Buyouts and Dissociation Under No-Fault, 60 U. Chi. L. Rev. 67 (1993). For a critique of the partnership analogy *see* Ira Mark Ellman, The Theory of Alimony, 77 Cal. L. Rev. 1 (1989).

Sometimes spouses are partners in the conventional business sense, and courts may apply partnership law rather than family law principles to determine ownership of the business assets when the marriage and business partnership both break up. For example, in Leathers and Leathers, 779 P.2d 619 (Or. App. 1989), the court found that the spouses had been partners in an oil business throughout their 22-year marriage and applied partnership law to award a share of the business to the wife. If the court had applied domestic relations principles, it might have been unable to give the wife much or any of the property because of a restrictive premarital agreement the parties had signed. However, because it chose to use business law principles, the court did not fully explore issues of the enforceability and scope of the premarital agreement. For discussion of these issues see Chapter 10.

5. Until 2000, the English courts in effect took the view that ordinarily marital property was to be awarded to the husband except to the extent of the wife's needs. In White v. White [2000] 3 WLR 571, [2000] FLR 981, the House of Lords reinterpreted the English statute regarding property division at divorce to include considerations of contribution, including homemaker contributions, as well as need. The *White* court rejected the earlier view as inconsistent with the principle that there should be no discrimination between husbands and wives, asking why the husband should receive all the property in excess of the financial needs of both parties. While the court explicitly declined to say that there is a presumption of an equal division or even that an equal division is a starting point, it said that a court must justify a division that is not equal. *White* is available on the House of Lords Web site at *http://www.parliament.the-stationery-office.co.uk/ pa/ld199900/ldjudgmt/jd001026/white-1.htm*. For a preliminary analysis and commentary *see* Peter Duckworth & David Hodson, White v. White — Bringing Section 25 Back to the People, 42 Fam. L. 24 (Jan. 2001).

6. In *Pierson* the court awarded the husband, whose income was less than wife's, more than half of the marital assets to enable him to begin his postmarital life "with a reasonable degree of self sufficiency." How did the court decide what amount to award husband to achieve this goal?

If need is the controlling factor in property division, a number of questions arise. Should the goal be to ensure that both parties will be in similar economic circumstances after the divorce? Must courts project the economic conditions of the spouses into the future? If so, how far into the future? Can courts make accurate predictions? And even if we can determine what unequal division of property will provide both parties economic self-sufficiency, why is it fair to require the person who receives less than half to finance his or her former spouse's life after the divorce? These issues also arise in determining whether a person is entitled to spousal support, the topic of the next section of this chapter. The ALI Family Dissolution Principles recommend a presumption in favor of dividing marital property equally that could be rebutted by a showing that the former spouse is entitled to compensation for reasons that would justify an award of spousal support or that the former spouse improperly disposed of marital property. ALI, Principles of the Law of Family Dissolution §4.09 (2002).

Professor Fineman has argued that courts applying a rebuttable presumption for an equal division will tend to divide property equally and that therefore they will not consider need in dividing property. Martha L. Fineman, Implementing Equality: Ideology, Contradiction and Social Change: A Study of Rhetoric and Results in the Regulation of the Consequences of Divorce, 1983 Wis. L. Rev. 789. A study of appellate decisions in six states found that Fineman's prediction tends to be true, and the author therefore concluded that courts rarely base property division on need. Suzanne Reynolds, The Relationship of Property Division and Alimony: The Division of Property to Address Need, 56 Fordham L. Rev. 827 (1988). However, Professor Krauskopf interprets Reynolds's data differently:

> [T]he trial judges in the six-state study probably did include need in their decision making, but valued the contributions unequally. . . . If the judge then divided the assets equally, he would have given [the spouse who made the lesser contribution] an "extra" . . . for need. The court would have used property to meet needs. [However, she concluded that] we cannot know whether the court ignored need altogether or gave [one spouse] something for need.

Joan M. Krauskopf, Theories of Property Division/Spousal Support: Searching for Solutions to the Mystery, 23 Fam. L.Q. 253, 274-275 (1989).

7. A minority of state statutes list marital fault as a factor that may be considered in property division, and some, like UMDA §307, explicitly exclude "marital misconduct" as a factor. The others either call simply for equitable distribution or for equitable distribution with lists of factors that do not include language clearly connoting fault. Most courts today exclude marital fault as a factor in property division, and even where fault can be considered, courts often relegate it to a minor role. Brett R. Turner, The Role of Marital Misconduct in Dividing Property upon Divorce, 15 Divorce Litigation 117 (2003).

In more than forty states "economic misconduct" is a factor in property division. Linda D. Elrod & Robert G. Spector, A Review of the Year in Family Law, 36 Fam. L.Q. 577 (2004). Under statutes that do not address fault but include lists of factors, courts sometimes justify the consideration of economic fault on the basis that it pertains to the parties' contributions to the acquisition or dissipation of assets. What does "economic misconduct" mean? The Illinois Court of Appeals found economic misconduct "where one spouse uses marital property for his or her own benefit for a purpose unrelated to the marriage at a time where the marriage is undergoing an irreconcilable breakdown." Klingberg v. Klingberg, 386 N.E.2d 517, 521 (Ill. App. 1979). Courts in other states have generally adopted this definition of economic misconduct. Kittredge v. Kittredge, 803 N.E.2d 306 (Mass. 2004); Jeffcoat v. Jeffcoat, 649 A.2d 1137 (Md. App. 1994) (collecting and discussing cases).

In *Kittredge*, the trial court found that the husband lost $400,000 by gambling over the course of the marriage, but the judge counted only $40,000 against the husband as economic waste. The wife appealed, and the Massachusetts Supreme Judicial Court affirmed.

> . . . [W]e do not accept the wife's argument that illegality automatically equates with dissipation of marital assets. The concept of dissipation, or, as it is sometimes called,

"waste," has taken on various attributes, potentially covering both lawful and unlawful conduct. It is those attributes, not a simple determination of unlawfulness, that govern the determination whether particular expenditures by a spouse constitute dissipation of marital assets. . . .

. . . "Conduct" that has harmed the marriage or the marital estate may be viewed negatively, and considered as a factor that would diminish that spouse's equitable share of marital property. However, it is conduct having an adverse impact on the marriage or the marital estate, not simply conduct that is in some other sense considered "good" or "bad," that is to be weighed. An equitable division of marital property is intended to effect fairness between the parties in light of all of the circumstances, not to punish "bad" behavior or enforce the criminal laws. Thus, the fact that a spouse's "conduct" during the marriage included unlawful conduct, and that the marital estate is less valuable as a result of that unlawful conduct, is but one circumstance, not necessarily determinative in itself, for a judge to consider in equitably distributing property . . .

Courts have also identified dissipation as a factor that affects a spouse's "contribution" to the marital assets, in the sense that it offsets or diminishes the value of whatever positive contributions that spouse has made. Thus, determination whether a spouse's expenditures constitute dissipation considers them in the light of that spouse's over-all contribution, including whether the expenditures have rendered the spouse unable to support the other spouse from the much-diminished estate at the time of divorce. . . .

Applying principles of equitable distribution, various courts have found dissipation in a spouse's gambling. However, that finding of dissipation has not been predicated on some inherent feature of gambling (either lawful or unlawful) but rather on the circumstances of the gambling activity in question—its timing, the gambler's intent to deprive the other spouse, and the resulting inability to meet financial obligations to the other spouse—that make it equitable for the gambling spouse to bear the brunt of the losses that he or she has incurred. . . .

The specific facts of the husband's gambling in this case do not support characterizing his entire $400,000 loss as a dissipation of assets for purposes of an equitable division of property. . . . The husband's gambling occurred throughout the parties' marriage—it was not something that started in response to the breakdown of the marriage or in anticipation of divorce. There is no suggestion that the husband intended to deprive the wife of her share of the marital estate, or that he gambled away the money rather than see it go to her. At no time was the husband derelict in his support of the wife and children—to the contrary, the wife and children were more than comfortably provided for at all times, leading "an upper class lifestyle," with college and graduate education for the children. And, notwithstanding the magnitude of the husband's gambling losses, the marital estate to be divided now supplies the wife with ample means to maintain that same "upper class lifestyle" following divorce. Thus, the husband's gambling losses did not and will not undermine the family's financial security or cause sacrifices in their high standard of living. Finally, while the wife did not herself participate in her husband's gambling, she was aware of it for many years and, whatever concerns she may have harbored about it, there is no evidence that she did anything to protest it. On these facts, the husband's gambling was not a form of "conduct" that harmed the marriage, nor did it prevent him from making a very substantial financial "contribution" to the marital estate. As such, the judge did not err in refusing to treat the entirety of the gambling losses as dissipation.

803 N.E.2d at 314-317.

8. Tort suits between spouses or recently divorced former spouses have become increasingly common. Most are for the intentional torts of assault or battery, but successful suits have also been brought for intentional infliction of emotional distress, tortious infliction of a venereal disease, negligence, fraud, and on miscellaneous other theories. *See* Robert G. Spector, Marital Torts: Actions for Tortious Conduct Occurring During the Marriage, 5 Am. J. Fam. L. 71 (1991); Kristin J. Krohse, Note: No Longer Following the Rule of Thumb — What to Do with Domestic Torts and Divorce Claims, 1997 U. Ill. L. Rev. 923; Leonard Karp & Cheryl L. Karp, Marital Torts: Beyond the Normal Ebb and Flow — Infliction of Emotional Distress in Domestic Violence Cases, 28 Fam. L.Q. 389 (1994).

PROBLEMS

1. Theresa and Nandor lived throughout their married life in a state whose statutory and case law create a rebuttable presumption of equal division of the property and mandate that the court consider "the contributions of each spouse to the acquisition of the property, including the contribution of a spouse as homemaker." Both Theresa and Nandor worked, and they contributed roughly equal amounts of money to running the household, but Theresa has done most of the homemaker work. Is Theresa therefore entitled to more than half the property?

Nandor spent his excess earnings on "toys," and Theresa invested hers in stocks. Has Theresa contributed more to the acquisition of the stocks than has Nandor? Has Nandor committed economic waste?

2. During a time when Betty and Walt were experiencing marital difficulties, Walt gave his son from a prior marriage a very large gift when the son graduated from high school. Betty and Walt divorced six months later. Did Walt's gift amount to "economic misconduct"?

3. Mary and Victor were married four years ago. Before the marriage Victor was a successful psychiatrist earning $50,000 a year; after they were married he quit. Mary is heir to the Johnson & Johnson fortune; she receives more than $1 million annually from a family trust. During the marriage they lived on Mary's income, and they purchased real property worth almost $4 million. At trial Mary presented convincing evidence that Victor was negotiating for her murder. The courts have previously held that the statutes embody a partnership concept of marriage for purposes of property division and that fault is not a factor to be considered in dividing the property. Can Victor's actions be considered in dividing the property?

4. During marriage counseling Wilma admits that she never loved or felt sexually attracted toward her husband, Harry. Soon after, they divorce on grounds of irreconcilable differences. Harry then sues Wilma for fraud, alleging that if she had not professed great love and passion for him while they were courting, he would never have married her or transferred property into her name that he owned before marriage. Wanda moves to dismiss the tort suit on public policy grounds. Should the motion be granted?

5. Cherry and Dave were married in 1996 and separated in April 2001 when Cherry sought a domestic violence restraining order which precluded Dave from

owning or possessing a firearm. Dave, who was a deputy sheriff, lost his job because of the firearm restriction. The court awarded Dave a car and his pension benefits, and Cherry received household goods, a car, and her pension benefits. If the court had divided the pension benefits earned during the relationship equally, Dave would have been ordered to pay Cherry an additional $15,250. To justify the award, the judge made findings that included: "By virtue of the obtaining of the permanent domestic violence protection order, the petitioner's ability to obtain gainful employment or meaningful retirement benefits in the future is severely limited due to his education and training." The judge also commented to Cherry's counsel, "I just don't see that if she's going to put him out of a job, what does she expect him to pay and what does she expect him to do?" Cherry has appealed. Assuming that the law in this state does not allow a judge to take noneconomic fault into account in dividing property, what arguments should the parties make on appeal?

2. *Characterization of Property as Separate or Marital*

In states in which only community or marital property is divisible, characterizing assets as "community/marital" or "separate/nonmarital" is crucial. Even in states that permit division of all property, the principles that underlie characterization may affect how a judge exercises discretion because these principles express commonly held beliefs about fairness and the spouses' expectations. Statutes and case law generally provide that separate property includes (1) property owned by either spouse before marriage, (2) property acquired by a spouse after the marriage by gift or inheritance, and (3) property acquired after the marriage in exchange for separate property. However, many assets cannot readily be characterized on the basis of these rules alone. For example, they do not tell us whether income produced by or the increase in value of separate property is separate or marital, whether separate property that has been mixed ("commingled") with marital property is separate or marital, or whether an asset's character has been changed or "transmuted" by a voluntary act of the owner, such as a change in title, issues with which the next case deals.

O'BRIEN V. O'BRIEN

508 S.E.2d 300 (N.C. App. 1998)

HORTON, Judge. Plaintiff-husband and defendant-wife were married on 24 May 1975, separated on 7 August 1995, and divorced on 24 September 1996. No children were born of the marriage. Following their separation, plaintiff instituted this equitable distribution action on 28 December 1995.

The evidence before the trial court tends to show that in 1986, after receiving an inheritance from her father of approximately $163,000.00, defendant opened an investment account with Wheat First Securities. She deposited about $158,000.00 of her inheritance, as well as a $10,000.00 gift from her Aunt Mabel

Dozier Stone (Aunt Mabel), into this investment account. On the advice of her broker, defendant had the investment account listed in the joint names of the parties, with a right of survivorship. From November 1986 until July 1989, the parties deposited a total of $4,550.00 of marital funds into this investment account, and withdrew $38,658.00 from the investment account for marital purposes. This investment account remained with Wheat First Securities until July 1989, at which time it was transferred to Interstate Johnson Lane when the parties' investment broker changed firms. At the time of the transfer, the investment account was valued at $138,161.00 or nearly $30,000.00 less than the initial deposit.

The investment account remained at Interstate Johnson Lane until January 1991, when it again followed the investment broker to his new position at Shearson Lehman. At the time of the transfer to Shearson Lehman, the investment account had depreciated as a result of market forces, and was valued at $119,714.00. Also, during this time Aunt Mabel was in poor health and was attempting to deplete her estate by distributing portions to her intended beneficiaries in order to avoid estate tax consequences. Therefore, Aunt Mabel made gifts to plaintiff and defendant in December 1992 and January 1993 for $10,000.00 each, for a total of $40,000.00. Along with each gift Aunt Mabel included a note describing the purpose of her gifts. The 28 December 1992 note to plaintiff read, in pertinent part, as follows:

> Dear Dick:
>   I have enclosed a check for $10,000 which is part of the inheritance I am leaving Mabel. Since the law allows only $10,000 per family member, I am sending this gift for her in your name to remove assets from my estate that would otherwise be taxed at a very high rate if left in the estate. Please deposit upon receipt.
>   . . .
>   Mabel D. Stone

Aunt Mabel's 15 January 1993 note contained similar language, stating that she had "enclosed a check for $10,000 which is part of the inheritance that I am leaving to Mabel." Of this $40,000.00 in gifts from Aunt Mabel, $24,990.00 was deposited into the investment account at Shearson Lehman, and $9,970.00 was used to purchase a 1993 Volvo 850 automobile for defendant.

In addition to the $24,990.00 in gift money invested in the investment account, the investment account increased in value by approximately $44,000.00 due to dividends, share reinvestment gains and market value gains. Further, approximately $6,500.00 in management fees were charged against the investment account, and $1,035.00 was withdrawn from the investment account. In May 1994, the Shearson Lehman investment account was valued at $181,452.00. The investment account remained at Shearson Lehman until May 1994, when it was transferred to Scott & Stringfellow. While the investment account was at Scott & Stringfellow, defendant received an inheritance from Aunt Mabel's estate totaling $62,841.00, of which she deposited $56,851.00 into the investment account. The investment account remained there until the parties' separation in August 1995. After hearing all of the evidence, the trial court found that the $40,000.00 in gifts from Aunt Mabel were intended to be gifts to defendant in the total amount of $40,000.00, and not gifts to plaintiff. Further, the trial court determined that other than $4,550.00 of marital funds deposited in the investment account when it was with Wheat First Security, all of which was withdrawn and spent for marital purposes, no other marital property or earnings of the parties was ever deposited to or invested in the investment account. Consequently, the trial court determined the investment account to be the separate property of defendant and not subject to distribution. In sum, the trial court found $308,465.12 of the total estate to be the separate property of defendant and $277,578.57 to be marital property. After determining that an equal division of the marital property would be equitable, the trial court awarded plaintiff $158,677.28 of the marital estate, and awarded defendant $118,901.29 of the marital estate. In addition, the trial court ordered plaintiff to pay defendant a distributive award of $19,888.00 in order to equalize the distribution. On appeal, plaintiff contends the trial court erred by (1) classifying the investment account and the gifts from Aunt Mabel as defendant's separate property rather than the marital property of the couple; . . . and (4) failing to award plaintiff an unequal distribution of the marital property and debt.

I.

. . . In an equitable distribution case filed before 1 October 1997, the trial court must undergo a three-step analysis: (1) identify what is marital property and what is separate property; (2) calculate the net value of the marital property; and (3) distribute the marital property in an equitable manner. In this case, we are concerned with the first step, the classification of the investment account as either marital property or separate property.

The main contention raised by plaintiff's appeal is that the trial court improperly classified the investment account as defendant's separate property. According to plaintiff, although the money used to begin the investment account was part of defendant's inheritance, the investment account should nevertheless be classified as marital property for the following reasons: (1) marital funds were commingled with the inherited funds, thus "transmuting" the investment account from separate property to marital property; (2) defendant has failed to "trace out" the $4,550.00 in marital funds which were deposited into the investment account; and (3) plaintiff actively participated with defendant in managing the investment account by making certain decisions which ultimately led to the increased value of the investment account. For purposes of clarity, we will address each of these points separately.

Before addressing plaintiff's contentions, we note that in order to determine the nature of certain property, it is helpful to consult the definitions of martial property and separate property provided in N.C. Gen. Stat. §50-20(b), which defines the terms as follows:

(1) "Marital property" means all real and personal property acquired by either spouse or both spouses during the course of the marriage and before the date of the separation of the parties, and presently owned, except property determined to be separate property . . . in accordance with subdivision (2) . . . of this subsection. . . . It is presumed that all property acquired after the date of marriage

and before the date of separation is marital property except property which is separate property under subdivision (2) of this subsection. This presumption may be rebutted by the greater weight of the evidence.

(2) "Separate property" means all real and personal property acquired by a spouse before marriage or acquired by a spouse by bequest, devise, descent, or gift during the course of the marriage. . . . Property acquired in exchange for separate property shall remain separate property regardless of whether the title is in the name of the husband or wife or both and shall not be considered to be marital property unless a contrary intention is expressly stated in the conveyance. The increase in value of separate property and the income derived from separate property shall be considered separate property.

N.C. Gen.Stat. §50-20(b) (Cum.Supp. 1997). Furthermore, in cases such as this there are dual burdens of proof. First, the party seeking to classify the investment as marital property must show by the preponderance of the evidence that the property is presently owned, and was acquired by either of the spouses during the course of the marriage and before the date of separation. Thereafter, the party seeking to classify the investment account as separate property must show by the preponderance of the evidence that the property falls within the statutory definition of separate property. If both parties meet their burdens, "'then under the statutory scheme of N.C.G.S. §50-20(b)(1) and (b)(2), the property is excepted from the definition of marital property and is, therefore, separate property.'"

A. "TRANSMUTATION" OF SEPARATE PROPERTY INTO MARITAL PROPERTY

According to plaintiff, although the initial deposit into the investment account was without question the separate property of defendant, the subsequent actions by the parties of commingling marital funds with separate funds "transmuted" the nature of the investment account from separate property to marital property. The doctrine of transmutation is well developed in Illinois, where it was first adopted by judicial decision and later by legislative enactment. Under this theory, "the affirmative act of augmenting nonmarital property by commingling it with marital property" creates a rebuttable presumption that all the property has been transmuted into marital property. In re Marriage of Smith, 86 Ill. 2d 518, 56 Ill.Dec. 693, 427 N.E.2d 1239, 1245-46 (Ill. 1981).

However, as plaintiff concedes, this Court has expressly rejected the theory of transmutation. We find, therefore, that the mere commingling of marital funds with separate funds alone does not automatically transmute the separate property into marital property.

B. "TRACING OUT" OF SEPARATE FUNDS

Next, plaintiff contends that regardless of whether the investment account was transmuted into marital property, defendant failed to meet her burden of "tracing out" her separate property. Here, it is clear that the investment account was begun during the marriage and prior to the date of separation. However, it is equally clear that the initial deposit into the investment account was from defendant's separate property, consisting of her inheritance from her father's estate. Therefore, defendant has met her burden of establishing the separate nature of the property.

Despite the fact that defendant has met her burden of proving the separate nature of the investment account, plaintiff contends defendant must also "trace out" her separate property from the $4,550.00 of marital funds which were deposited into the investment account. However, the $4,550.00 of marital funds deposited into the investment account was the only deposit of marital funds into the investment account. Further, soon after this deposit, $38,658.00 was withdrawn from the account.

After considering this evidence, the trial court concluded that the $4,550.00 deposit of marital funds was entirely consumed by the subsequent withdrawal, such that no marital funds remained in the investment account. Since there is competent evidence in the record to support this finding, we are bound by it. Therefore, after these marital funds were removed, the only funds remaining in the investment account were separate funds. This being the case, we find that defendant has met her burden of "tracing out" her separate property.

C. ACTIVE VS. PASSIVE APPRECIATION OF THE INVESTMENT ACCOUNT

Finally, plaintiff contends that he actively participated in the management of the investment account, such that the account should be treated as marital property. It is well recognized that there is a distinction between active and passive appreciation of separate property. Active appreciation refers to financial or managerial contributions of one of the spouses to the separate property during the marriage; whereas, passive appreciation refers to enhancement of the value of separate property due solely to inflation, changing economic conditions or other such circumstances beyond the control of either spouse. Furthermore, the party seeking to establish that any appreciation of separate property is passive bears the burden of proving such by the preponderance of the evidence.

The issue of the characterization of the appreciation of investment accounts, mutual funds, and other stocks or securities, as active or passive has not been previously addressed in North Carolina. . . . Therefore, we will look to other jurisdictions for guidance.

In Deffenbaugh, 877 S.W.2d 186, the Missouri Court of Appeals was presented with the question of whether the appreciated value of 425 shares of a mutual fund was marital or separate property. The evidence tended to show that the shares were originally purchased with the wife's separate property. According to the husband, he regularly looked at the quarterly statements, corresponded with and spoke to the investment broker, and regularly gave advice to his wife. However, the court held that these activities "were within the purview of ordinary and usual spousal duties; and as such, did not transform the increased value of the original shares of the mutual fund into [separate] property." Id. Further, the Missouri Court of Appeals has repeatedly held that several factors must be shown in order for a spouse to be awarded a proportionate share of the increase in value of the other spouse's separate property, including: (1) a contribution of substantial services; (2) a direct correlation between those services and the increase in value; (3) the amount of the increase in value; (4) the performance of the services during the marriage; and (5) the value of the services, lack of compensation, or inadequate compensation.

[handwritten: Use the multifactorial approach of MO court of appeals]

We believe that the multi-factorial approach of the Missouri Court of Appeals is consistent with the public policy considerations incorporated in our Equitable Distribution Act, and we adopt that approach. We hold, therefore, that if either or both of the spouses perform substantial services during the marriage which result in an increase in the value of an investment account, that increase is to be characterized as an active increase and classified as a marital asset. In making the determination of whether the services of a spouse are substantial, the trial court should consider, among other relevant facts and circumstances of the particular case, the following factors: (1) the nature of the investment; (2) the extent to which the investment decisions are made only by the party or parties, made by the party or parties in consultation with their investment broker, or solely made by the investment broker; (3) the frequency of contact between the investment broker and the parties; (4) whether the parties routinely made investment decisions in accordance with the recommendation of the investment broker, and the frequency with which the spouses made investment decisions contrary to the advice of the investment broker; (5) whether the spouses conducted their own research and regularly monitored the investments in their accounts, or whether they primarily relied on information supplied by the investment broker; and (6) whether the decisions or other activities, if any, made solely by the parties directly contributed to the increased value of the investment account.

[handwritten margin: Holding]

Here, the trial court did not find that the actions of the spouses in jointly meeting with the wife's broker and routinely choosing between investment alternatives based on the recommendation of the investment broker rose to the level of substantial activity. The trial court determined that the defendant-wife had established by the preponderance of the evidence that any appreciation of the investment account was purely passive. After careful review, we find that the trial court's findings support its conclusions of law. Therefore, we overrule this assignment of error.

[handwritten margin: Found that this was passive]

II.

. . . Next, plaintiff contends the trial court erred by finding the two $10,000.00 checks written by Aunt Mabel to plaintiff were the separate property of defendant. In its 2 April 1997 order, the trial court made the following findings with regard to Aunt Mabel's intent:

[handwritten margin: 2 checks]

14. In December [1992] and January [1993], defendant's Aunt Mabel Dozier Stone was in ill health. [Aunt Mabel] was attempting to distribute a portion of her estate to intended beneficiaries prior to her death in order to avoid estate tax consequences. In December [1992], [Aunt Mabel] wrote two $10,000 checks — one payable to defendant individually and one payable to plaintiff individually. In January [1993], [Aunt Mabel] wrote two more $10,000 checks — one to plaintiff individually and one to defendant individually. She also wrote a letter to plaintiff describing her intent and design that the checks payable to plaintiff were in fact gifts for the defendant. [Aunt Mabel's] intention in making the $40,000 in payments was to make a gift to defendant in the total amount of $40,000 and not to make any gift to plaintiff of any of said sum. . . . Plaintiff was not an object of [Aunt Mabel's] bounty or gift-giving.

He was not the intended recipient of the funds being given. With regard to these checks, plaintiff was merely a conduit for [Aunt Mabel's] gift to defendant.

According to plaintiff, there was no competent evidence in the record to support this finding. Additionally, plaintiff contends that "as a matter of law the aunt's intent is irrelevant given that the aunt had to have been making a gift to [plaintiff] in order to comply with federal gift tax law."

. . . [T]he trial court's findings in this case are adequately supported by the record evidence, and these findings justify its conclusions. It is clear that plaintiff was not the object of Aunt Mabel's bounty, but was a mere conduit for the gift to defendant. As such, we overrule this assignment of error. Further, we find plaintiff's federal estate tax argument to be without merit.

* * *

[The court affirmed the trial court order dividing the marital property equally because the husband did not present sufficient evidence to overcome the state's strong policy in favor of equal division.]

NOTES AND QUESTIONS

1. *Presumptions.* The statute construed in *O'Brien*, like those in many other states, creates a presumption that all property acquired during the marriage is marital. What is the effect of this presumption? What policy underlies it?

2. How did the court determine the character of the gifts from Aunt Mabel? For purposes of the federal estate and gift tax, half of these transfers were gifts to the husband. Why didn't this characterization control who owned the gifts for purposes of the O'Briens' divorce?

3. *O'Brien* deals with two of the most difficult issues that arise when distribution of property depends on first categorizing it as marital or separate: how to determine when an asset's character has changed from separate to marital (or vice versa) and how to treat the appreciation in value of separate property.

Courts in community property states, where characterization has been required for a long time, have more experience with issues of characterization than do those in common law property states. However, the resolutions that these courts have reached should not necessarily be imported into common law property states because community property rules are sometimes shaped by considerations of rights and duties of the spouses during marriage. For example, in some community property states, characterization rules sought to protect the separate property of wives when they were still legally disabled from managing property. The means to achieve this goal was to maximize the amount of property classified as separate. Such an approach might, however, be inconsistent with a goal of maximizing the amount of property that is divisible at divorce. Bea Ann Smith, The Partnership Theory of Marriage: A Borrowed Solution Fails, 68 Tex. L. Rev. 689, 698-706 (1990), and sources cited therein. Professor Reppy has also pointed out that courts in community property states faced with a characterization problem must consider the effect of the decision on the property rights of the spouses during marriage and at the death of one spouse, as well at divorce. William A. Reppy, Jr., Major Events in the Evolution of American Community Property Law and Their Import to Equitable Distribution States, 23 Fam. L.Q. 163, 164-165 (1989).

Recent surveys conclude that not only do courts in different states decide characterization issues differently, but even cases within the same state are sometimes inconsistent. The authors of these analyses conclude that the inconsistencies in case law cannot be explained by the form of the statute and that many courts do not even insist on the literal application of statutory language. Mary Moers Wenig, Increase in Value of Separate Property During Marriage: Examination and Proposals, 23 Fam. L.Q. 301, 318 (1989); Joseph W. McKnight, Defining Property Subject to Division at Divorce, 23 Fam. L.Q. 193, 206 (1989).

In addition to the sources cited, *see also* Brett R Turner & Lawrence J Golden, Equitable Distribution of Property (2nd ed. 1994); J. Thomas Oldham, Divorce, Separation and the Distribution of Property (1987 with annual updating).

4. *Transmutation.* In most states that have addressed the issue, the owner of property may change or transmute its character by a voluntary act manifesting this intent. Marital or community property can be transmuted into the separate property of one or both spouses, and separate property of one spouse can be transmuted into marital or community property or separate property of the other spouse. In some community property states transmutation of community property into separate property requires a written agreement.

The most common transmutation issue is whether a change in how an asset is titled changes its character. Say that the owner of a premarital house (originally separate property) changes the title to joint tenancy with right of survivorship. The first question is whether the change in title changes the character of the house at all. This issue is closely related to an issue discussed in Chapter 2, under what circumstances a change in title establishes that one spouse made a gift of property to the other. The original owner may claim that title was changed only to avoid probate and to give the other spouse ownership of the property at death but not to give that spouse any rights during the marriage or at divorce. The courts are divided on the effect of such evidence. Some courts have held that a change in title automatically transmutes property. Most courts say that transmutation is presumed. Finally, some courts say that a change in title does not create a presumption in favor of transmutation but that intent to transmute may be proven by this and other evidence. See Brett R. Turner, The Effect of Interspousal Transfers upon Classification of Separate Property: A 2003 Update, 15 Divorce Litigation 61 (2003); Laura W. Morgan & Edward S. Snyder, When Title Matters: Transmutation and the Joint Title Gift Presumption, 18 J. Am. Acad. Matrimonial L. 335 (2003).

How does *O'Brien* treat the wife's having changed title to her inheritance? What is the position of the Illinois court, which *O'Brien* rejects? What policy does each approach express?

If the court finds that the character of the property has changed, a second question may arise: Into what kind of property was the asset transmuted? In some states, placing title to an asset that was originally separate property in the joint names of both spouses transmutes the asset into jointly owned separate property of each, while in other states the asset becomes marital property.

Transmutation problems can also arise when one spouse buys a gift for the other with separate or marital funds. Usually gifts are separate property. The issue is whether applying this rule to interspousal gifts is inconsistent with the fundamental policy underlying community property and deferred marital property regimes. In California spousal gifts usually remain marital property, except that gifts of clothes and jewelry are separate unless they are "substantial." Other community property states do not necessarily agree. If separate property is used to make a gift, some courts say that the property is transmuted into marital property, and others say that it becomes the separate property of the other spouse. Common law property states are also divided on the effect of interspousal gifts. In some, case law or statutes say that such a gift is marital property, while in others the gift becomes the separate property of the recipient.

5. *Appreciation of separate property.* Community property and common law property states approach classification of the appreciation in value of separate property in fundamentally different ways. The differences derive partly from the purposes that classification serves in the two kinds of states. In common law property states the only purpose of classification is to divide the spouses' property when they divorce. In community property states, however, classification is important during the marriage and affects rights of third parties. Thus, in community property states rules tend to make it easy for third parties, such as creditors, to determine what the character of property is.

Most community property states follow the "inception of title" rule. Under this rule, the character of an asset is determined when it is acquired. Thus, property acquired as separate property remains separate property even though community property is invested in it, and vice versa. (Property has a mixed character if it is initially acquired partly with community funds and partly with separate funds.) The treatment of increases in value depends on the cause of the increase. If the increase is attributable to market forces, inflation, or the like, the increase in value takes the same character as the original capital investment in the asset. Thus, separate property that increases in value during the marriage because of market forces continues to be entirely separate property, and the community has no claim to it. However, if the increase in value of separate property is attributable to the investment of community funds or the labor of one of the spouses, the community is entitled to reimbursement for the value of the contribution. The converse is true if separate funds or labor is invested in community property.

California case law provides the method most widely used in community property states for dealing with an increase in value of separate property that is partly attributable to passive forces (which creates more separate property) and partly attributable to community funds or efforts (for which the community is entitled to reimbursement). Two cases, Pereira v. Pereira, 103 P. 488 (Cal. 1909), and Van Camp v. Van Camp, 199 P. 885 (Cal. App. 1921), applied two different methods. Under *Pereira* a reasonable return on the separate investment is calculated and treated as separate property; the remainder of the increase in value is community property. Under *Van Camp* a fair salary for the labor of the spouse is calculated. If the spouse was paid less than this amount, the community receives enough of the increase to make up the difference, and the rest of the increase in value is separate property. While no hard and fast rules determine when each rule should be used, California case law provides that *Pereira* should be used when the appreciation in value is primarily attributable to community efforts, and *Van Camp* should be used when the primary cause is market factors and the like. In re Lopez, 113 Cal. Rptr. 58 (Cal. App. 1974). Commentators tend to prefer the rule that will, on the facts of the particular case, give the greater return to the primary source of the increase in value. For an analysis and application of this approach *see* J. Thomas Oldham, Separate Property Businesses That Increase in Value During Marriage, 1990 Wis. L. Rev. 585. *See also* Cynthia Samuels, Restoration of the Separate Estate from Community Property After the Equal Management Reform: Some Thoughts on Louisiana's Reimbursement Rules, 56 Law & Contemp. Probs. 273, 276 (Spring 1993).

Common law property states have not always followed the community property approach, which provides a structured, if complicated, way of treating increase in value. In many of these states increases in value caused by market or other passive forces are allocated proportionately according to the contributions of separate and marital funds. Under this "source of funds" rule, increases in the value of separate property attributable to marital funds or efforts are marital property, and increases attributable to market changes and the like are separate in some states and marital in others.[10]

In a common law property state that treats passive increases in the value of separate property as separate property, the *Pereira-Van Camp* problem can arise. In addition to the *Pereira* and *Van Camp* solutions, some of these states grant trial courts substantial discretion to resolve the problem on a case-by-case basis.

The ALI Family Dissolution Principles provide that the increase in value of separate property is marital if attributable to a spouse's labor and separate if due to other causes. In mixed cases the Principles recommend an approach similar to that used in *Pereira*. ALI, Principles of the Law of Family Dissolution §§4.04, 4.05 (2002).

6. In all states income produced by marital property — rents, dividends, interest, and the like — is also marital property. The states are divided, though, in their treatment of income from separate property. Four community property states — Idaho, Louisiana, Texas, and Wisconsin — follow the Spanish rule, which treats income from separate property as community property. The other five community property states follow the American rule that such income is separate property. Thomas R. Andrews, Income from Separate Property: Towards a Theoretical Foundation, 56 Law & Contemp. Probs. 171 (Spring 1993).

Equitable distribution statutes that address this issue usually say that income from nonmarital property is nonmarital. The Comment to UMDA §307 says that income from nonmarital property is marital property. A 1990 survey found that five of sixteen states with statutes that allow division only of marital property follow this rule, and eight say that the income is nonmarital property. (The other states had not yet addressed the issue.) Emily Osborn, Comment, The Treatment

---

10. While §307 of the UMDA says that increases in value of separate property are separate, one of the reporters for the UMDA has written that the drafters had in mind assets such as bonds, which increase in value without owner effort and for which tracing and identification are easy. Robert J. Levy, An Introduction to Divorce-Property Issues, 23 Fam. L.Q. 147, 154 (1989).

of Unearned Separate Property at Divorce in Common Law Property Jurisdictions, 1990 Wis. L. Rev. 903, 918-930.

The ALI Family Dissolution Principles treat income from separate property as they treat appreciation in value: Income is marital if attributable to a spouse's labor and separate if due to other causes. ALI Principles, above. For detailed discussion of these issues see the Reporter's Note to §4.04.

7. Separate property may be mixed with marital property intentionally, as when a separately owned asset is brought into the marriage and is paid off or maintained with marital funds, or unintentionally, as when a bank account owned before marriage earns interest in a state that treats the income from separate property as marital. In a few states, property cannot be partly separate and partly marital; in these states commingling separate property with marital property automatically converts the separate property into marital property. In most states, though, it is legally possible to *trace* separate funds in and out of bank accounts and other property. Tracing can be quite difficult, however, as, for example, when separate and marital funds are mixed in a bank account and then many withdrawals are made over the years. Ordinarily, the spouse who claims to own separate property carries the burden of tracing the funds. If the spouse cannot carry this burden, commingled property will be entirely marital.

8. Property acquired during premarital cohabitation is generally not treated as marital property when the parties divorce. However, some courts have held that property acquired "in anticipation of marriage" is marital property. Mangone v. Mangone, 495 A.2d 469 (N.J. Super. 1985); In re Marriage of Crouch, 410 N.E.2d 580 (Ill. App. 1980); Grishman v. Grishman, 407 A.2d 9 (Me. 1979); In re Marriage of Altman, 530 P.2d 1012 (Colo. App. 1974); Stallings v. Stallings, 393 N.E.2d 1065 (Ill. App. 1979); In re Marriage of Schriner, 410 N.E.2d 572 (Ill. App. 1980). *Contra*: Rolle v. Rolle, 530 A.2d 847 (N.J. Super. 1987).

Treating property acquired in anticipation of marriage as marital property blurs the distinction between the property remedies available to cohabitants and spouses at the break-up of their relationships. Why is this distinction made in the first place? Given the distinction, should property acquired in anticipation of marriage be treated as marital property? What facts would show that property was acquired in anticipation of marriage?

9. A number of legislatures and courts have considered when a marriage ends for purposes of defining "marital property." The possibilities include

(1) The date of separation (*see, e.g.*, Cal. Fam. Code §771 (West 1994) (property acquired while parties live separate and apart is separate property); N.C. Gen. Stat. §50-20 (1991); Pa. Consol. Stat. §3501(a)(4) (1991); Deitz v. Deitz, 436 S.E.2d 463 (Va. App. 1993); In re Estate of Osicka, 461 P.2d 585 (Wash. App. 1969) (property acquired by either spouse after a permanent separation and separation agreement is separate property)

(2) The date the petition for dissolution was filed (*see, e.g.*, Painter v. Painter, 320 A.2d 484 (N.J. 1974); *but see* Smith v. Smith, 371 A.2d 1 (N.J. 1977) (termination date for identification of marital property could be date of a separation agreement accompanied by a separation in fact)

(3) The date the decree is entered (*see, e.g.*, Askins v. Askins, 704 S.W.2d 632 (Ark. 1986); Centazzo v. Centazzo, 509 A.2d 995 (R.I. 1986))

(4) The date of the prehearing settlement conference (*see* Minn. Stat. §518.58 (2003))

What are the advantages and disadvantages of each of these rules?

10. A related but different question is when property is valued for purposes of division. Most jurisdictions appear to value assets as of the date of judgment of divorce, though courts in some states have said that the date of valuation is to be decided case by case. Harriet N. Cohen & Patricia Hennessey, Valuation of Property in Marital Dissolutions, 23 Fam. L.Q. 339, 344-346 (1989); Annot., Proper Date for Valuation of Property Being Distributed Pursuant to Divorce, 34 A.L.R.4th 63 (1984).

11. *See* Charlotte K. Goldberg, Value and Volatility: The New Economy and Valuing Businesses at Divorce, 35 Fam. L.Q. 451 (2001), for a detailed discussion of some of the issues raised in these notes.

PROBLEMS

1. Howard is a waiter. A substantial portion of his income comes from tips. Are these gifts from a third party and hence separate property or wages and hence marital property?

2. On Edwin and Julie's wedding day Julie's father gives them $10,000. Is this Julie's separate property or marital property? What if Edwin gives Julie a necklace worth $5,000, purchased from his premarital funds? If Julie gives Edwin a valuable painting on their fifth anniversary, purchased from marital funds, does the painting remain marital property or does it become Edwin's separate property?

3. In 1983 Wanda purchased a house, taking title in her own name. She made the down payment and mortgage payments with her own funds. When she married Henry in 1985, the equity in the house was worth $20,000. Two days after the wedding Wanda changed the title of the house to herself and Henry as joint tenants with right of survivorship, and the two began contributing equally to the mortgage payments from their earnings. The equity in the house is now worth $60,000, or $40,000 more than its value when they married. Of this $40,000, $20,000 was attributable to the payoff of principal that they made through their mortgage payments, and $20,000 was attributable to inflation and other market factors. Wanda and Henry are now divorcing. They live in a common law property state where only marital property is divisible at divorce. The statute defines "marital property" as all property acquired by either spouse subsequent to the marriage except (1) property acquired by gift, bequest, devise, or descent and (2) property acquired in exchange for property acquired prior to the marriage or in exchange for property acquired by gift, bequest, devise, or descent. The statute also provides that all property acquired by either spouse subsequent to the marriage is presumed to be marital property regardless of how it is titled and that this presumption may be overcome by showing that the property was acquired in one of the two ways listed above.

Assuming that no cases have interpreted this statute and that Wanda wants as much of the value of the house as possible to be characterized as her separate, nonmarital property, what arguments should she make? How should Henry argue that some or all of the house is marital property?

4. While Herb and Winnie were married and living together, Herb won the lottery. He receives his winnings in annual installments over 20 years. If Herb and Winnie divorce three years after he has won, are the remaining 17 years of payments marital property or Herb's separate property? What if Herb and Winnie had been living separately for two years when Herb won the lottery?

5. W was part owner of a closely held corporation before she married H. After the business H and W worked full-time for the business. Each of them drew a salary from the business, and the business paid W dividends. Are assets purchased with the dividends W's separate property or marital property? How about assets the spouses purchased with their wages?

6. Before his marriage to Kathleen, John inherited a small lakeside resort from his first wife, which was and always has been titled in his name alone. He ran the resort throughout his 20-year marriage to Kathleen, and the parties lived in a house that was part of the resort. Kathleen, who worked as a nurse during the marriage, also helped run the resort. John finished paying the mortgage on the resort with money that it earned during the marriage. The parties had no children, but the wife's ten children from a former marriage lived with the parties and helped run the resort. Over the 20 years, the resort more than doubled in value from $151,000 to $398,000, in part because of market conditions and in part because of improvements that John made over the years. The parties made no attempt to keep their finances separate during the marriage, and each put inherited money, as well as their earnings, into a joint account from which all the bills for the family and for the resort were paid. John's inheritance amounted to $25,000, and Kathleen's to $90,000. The parties dispute the character of the increase in value of the resort property. In this jurisdiction, the passive increase in value of separate property remains separate. What arguments should each party make?

3. *Choice-of-Law Issues*

When spouses acquire property in one state but are divorced in another, choice-of-law problems may arise. For example, H and W, who is a homemaker, marry and live for most of their lives in a common law property state. They own $200,000 in personal property, all of which was saved from H's earnings and all of which remains titled in H's name alone. H and W retire to a community property state and shortly thereafter divorce. Under traditional choice-of-law principles, the court in the community property state will apply its own law to determine what property is subject to division, but it will apply the law of the state where the property was acquired to determine whether it is community or separate property. Thus, the $200,000 will be characterized as H's separate property. (Remember that even in common law states that characterize property as marital or nonmarital at divorce, the common law title system described in Chapter 2 governs ownership during the marriage.) If the state in which they are living at divorce permits division only of community property, W will be entitled to none of the assets even though, had the couple been divorced in their original home state, the court could have awarded her some of these assets.

Legislatures in some community property states have solved this problem by enacting "quasi-community property" statutes, which provide that if property would have been community property had it been acquired in the state, it is treated as community property for purposes of property division at divorce. Cal. Fam. Code §125 (West 1994); Ariz. Rev. Stat. Ann. §25-318 (1976); Tex. Fam. Code §3.63(b). In the absence of such legislation, courts in some community property states have solved the problem by applying the substantive property division law of the state in which the property was acquired. Berle v. Berle, 546 P.2d 407 (Idaho 1976); Braddock v. Braddock, 542 P.2d 1060 (Nev. 1975); Hughes v. Hughes, 573 P.2d 1194 (N.M. 1978). This approach creates difficult problems of tracing, apportionment, and determining the effect of a post-acquisition change in the law of the state in which the property was acquired.

Similar issues may arise if spouses acquire property in a community property state and are divorced in a common law property/equitable distribution state. In addition, choice-of-law issues may arise in determining whether property should be characterized as marital or community property or as separate or nonmarital property. Consider, for example, a husband and wife who first live in a common law (or community property) state that treats income from separate property as marital property and later move to a state that treats such income as nonmarital property. Courts in most common law property states have held that the state's own laws governing characterization as well as division should apply, which eliminates problems of relating inconsistent laws of different jurisdictions. William A. Reppy, Jr., Major Events in the Evolution of American Community Property Law and Their Import to Equitable Distribution States, 23 Fam. L.Q., 163, 191 (1989).

Other articles dealing with these choice-of-law issues include J. Thomas Oldham, Conflict of Laws and Marital Property Rights, 39 Baylor L. Rev. 1255 (1987); Eugene F. Scoles, Choice of Law in Family Property Transactions, Hague Academy, 209 Recueil des Cours 13 (1988-II); Russell J. Weintraub, Obstacles to Sensible Choice of Law for Determining Marital Rights on Divorce or in Probate: *Hanau* and the Situs Rule, 25 Hous. L. Rev. 1113 (1988).

For a discussion of jurisdiction to award property located in another state and enforcement of such orders, see Chapter 11.

4. Dividing Debts

Even though many property division statutes do not address division of debts, most courts have assumed that they have authority to allocate responsibility for paying debts. In many families this is, practically speaking, the most important issue.

GELDMEIER V. GELDMEIER

669 S.W.2d 33 (Mo. App. 1984)

REINHARD, J. . . . Husband and wife married in 1963. Their two children, Mark and Kelly, were born in 1964 and 1968, respectively. Husband, a bottler at Anheuser-Busch for the past fifteen years, was the principal breadwinner. His gross income during 1981 was $36,465.00, which included substantial overtime.

Husband had worked overtime in each of the past ten years, and testified that he regularly refused overtime work offered to him.

Wife was primarily a homemaker, although she had worked as a secretary at one point during the marriage. Wife completed her master's degree in clinical psychology shortly before the parties' dissolution. Although she was seeking employment in both her chosen profession and other fields, her job search had not proven fruitful at the time of trial.

In its order, the court divided the marital property and awarded wife custody of the two children and support of $80.00 per week, per child. Maintenance was set at $100.00 per month.

On appeal, husband contends that the court "divided the marital property and debts in such a disproportionate manner that the effect of the division of the property was to award property to wife while awarding more debts than property to the husband."

The disposition of marital property is governed by §452.330 RSMo. 1982:

> The court shall set aside to each spouse his property and shall divide the marital property in such proportions as the court deems just after considering all relevant factors. . . .

The court possesses broad discretion in the division of marital property. Its division must be just and equitable, but an equitable division need not be equal. Moreover, in reviewing this matter, we are bound to sustain the trial court's order unless there is no substantial evidence to support it or it is against the weight of the evidence.

Clearly, the court in its distribution of marital property was aware of the statutory framework within which it was required to act. The marital home, valued at approximately $40,000.00, was the major asset and was encumbered by two separate notes, secured by deeds of trust, for $16,400.00 and $15,000.00. ($16,400.00 was the amount still owed on the parties' original home mortgage; the latter $15,000 was borrowed to pay marital debts.) The court awarded the marital home to wife, who had custody of the minor children. In turn, the court ordered:

> petitioner [wife] [to] execute a note and deed of trust in favor of Respondent [husband] in the amount of Seven Thousand Five Hundred ($7500.00) Dollars, with no interest, payable on the earliest happening of one of the following events: (1) The emancipation of the minor child, Kelly Ann Geldmeier. (2) The marriage of petitioner. (3) The sale of the house by petitioner.

In its decree the court recognized that this note represented husband's interest in the marital home.

As to the other marital property, the court awarded wife the 1973 Cutlass automobile, valued at $800.00; household furniture worth $500.00 and personal property in her possession. Husband received, in addition to his interest in the marital home, a 1974 Chevelle automobile, valued at $450.00; a $500.00 boat; his interest in the Anheuser-Busch pension plan, worth approximately $2,000.00 and including insurance plans connected with the plan; his $1,100.00 interest in a life insurance policy, with directions that the children be named as beneficiaries until their emancipation; $2,500.00 from the recent sale of stock, and the remaining value of his Anheuser-Busch stock fund, worth approximately $3,000.00.

debts

As to the parties' outstanding debts, the court ordered wife to pay the debt to her parents; husband to pay the debt to his parents. Wife was ordered to pay the first note for $16,400.00, secured by a deed of trust, and husband the second note of $15,000.00. By implication, husband is responsible for signature and student loans totalling approximately $6,500.00, for which payments are withheld from his weekly salary. Husband was also ordered to discharge all other debts, which amounted to $600.00, and hold wife harmless.

According to husband, the net result of the property division was that he received no assets, since the debts he was ordered to pay exceeded the property he received. We recognize that, were we to total the balance sheets of each party, husband winds up with a negative balance. However, a balance sheet approach is not necessarily the just approach to distribute marital assets. Here, the court was confronted with a difficult financial situation. By its order, it sought to divide the property in such a manner that the children, placed in wife's custody, would not be wrenched from the security of the family home during their minority. The court's order that husband assume responsibility for the lion's share of outstanding marital debts is supported by the evidence, since only husband at that time possessed the ability to assume those obligations. Moreover, its order concerning the debts does not alter the fact that, consistent with §452.330, RSMo. Supp. 1982, the court set aside to husband portions of the marital property. Therefore, we can find no abuse of discretion in the court's property division.

KAROHL, P.J. I not only concur in the result I concur in the opinion. However, in order that the opinion not be misunderstood to approve a distribution of marital property of an amount greater than the total value of the marital property before the court at the time of the hearing, I believe the following comments are necessary.

In summary, the total marital assets before the court had a value of $19,450, consisting of: Equity in house — $8,600; automobiles — $1,250; furniture — $500.00; boat — $500.00; pension plan — $2,000; life insurance — $1,100; stock and proceeds of recent stock sale — $5,500, for a total of $19,450. The court awarded the wife a total of $17,400 in marital property summarized as follows:

Marital home	$40,000.00
Less First Deed of Trust	16,400.00
Less Third Deed of Trust in favor of husband	7,500.00
	$16,100.00
1973 Cutlass	800.00
Household furniture	500.00
	$17,400.00

The court awarded the husband marital personal property having a value of $9,550. However he was ordered to pay the $15,000 balance on the second deed of trust on the marital home and received in return a note and third deed of trust for $7,500, for a net deduction of $7,500. Therefore, on balance the husband received $2,050 of marital property. Although both parties were ordered to pay certain general debts they were not debts constituting liens on any of the marital property divided by the court.

In the event the balance due on the second deed of trust had been greater than $17,050, the decree would have so divided the marital property as to give the husband a negative balance. I do not believe that result is authorized by §452.330, RSMo. Supp. 1982.

NOTES AND QUESTIONS

1. Among the methods discussed in the case law for dividing debts are these:

a. Equitable division of all — treat as distinct issues the division of assets and the division of debts, dividing each "equitably." Relevant factors include ability to pay, which spouse was the principal financial manager or incurred the debt, and so forth.

b. Divide debts proportionately to division of assets — treat division of assets and debts as distinct issues but allocate responsibility for debts in the same proportion that assets are awarded.

c. Total netting out — from the total value of the divisible assets subtract the total amount of divisible debts. Divide the remainder (if any).

d. Netting out of specific assets — when an asset is specifically encumbered, value the asset at the difference between its market value and the debt (sometimes expressed by saying that until the debt is paid, the asset is not yet fully acquired; at the time of divorce the asset is acquired only to the extent that it is free of debt). Some courts extend this method to include debts traceable to the acquisition of a specific asset. Other assets and debts are divided equitably. Some courts say that if an asset is worth less than the amount of the debt incurred in acquiring it, the value of that item is simply reduced to zero; the balance of the debt is not used to reduce the net value of any other item.

Which method is more consistent with a contribution theory of property division? With a need-based theory? Should the choice of theory for purposes of property division govern division of debts? *See* In re Marriage of Fonstein, 552 P.2d 1169, 1175 (Cal. 1976); In re Marriage of Eastis, 120 Cal. Rptr. 861 (Cal. 1975). *See also* Cal. Fam. Code §2622 (West 1994) (equal division is not required when marital assets exceed marital debts).

2. In most states that permit division only of marital property, only marital debts are divisible at divorce. Separate debts are the responsibility of the spouse who incurred them. However, courts that allocate marital debts on an "equitable" basis may take separate debts into account in determining ability to pay. The court in *Geldmeier* seems to have assumed that all of the debts were marital.

Rules for characterizing debts as community or separate were first developed in community property states to determine what assets creditors could reach. Generally, each spouse's separate property is liable for his or her debts, and community property is liable for community debts. The states vary in their treatment of the liability of separate property for community debts and the liability of community property for separate debts.

Ordinarily a debt is marital if it was incurred for the joint benefit of the parties or in acquiring a marital asset. Some courts have applied this test to characterize debts incurred during periods of separation as marital if they were incurred to pay family living expenses. *Compare* Alford v. Alford, 120 S.W.3d 810 (Tenn.

2003), rejecting the "joint benefit" test as confusing and difficult; marital debt defined consistently with the definition of marital property, that is, "all debts incurred by either or both spouses during the course of the marriage up to the date of the final divorce hearing." *See also* In re Marriage of Scoffield, 852 P.2d 664 (Mont. 1993); In re Marriage of Welch, 795 S.W.2d 640 (Mo. App. 1990).

3. The *Geldmeier* court allocated to each spouse debts owing to his or her parents without discussing their amount. Why?

4. An order or agreement between spouses regarding the allocation of debts does not bind creditors. Why not? *See, e.g.,* Srock v. Srock, 466 P.2d 34, 35-36 (Ariz. App. 1970). For consideration of the consequences to one spouse if the other files bankruptcy, see Chapter 8.

PROBLEM

John and Lois have no substantial debts and have the following marital assets: equity in home — $8,000, 1974 Chevelle — $450, 1973 Cutlass — $800, furniture — $500, boat — $500, pension plan — $2,000, stock and cash—$5,500. John's attorney proposes that Lois, the custodian of three young children, be awarded the equity in the home, the Chevelle, and the furniture, for a total of $8,950; and that husband receive the Cutlass, the boat, the pension plan, and the stock and cash, for a total of $8,800. John works full-time and earns $40,000 per year. Lois has a part-time job and earns approximately $600 per month. As attorney for Lois, would you accept this proposal, which gives each spouse property of substantially equal dollar value?

5.   *The Marital Home*

The major asset in *Geldmeier* was the family home. It could have been sold to satisfy the debts, but then the children would have been displaced. Even if the parties have no substantial debts, a similar problem arises if their only significant asset is the marital home and an equitable or equal division precludes awarding full ownership of the house to the custodial parent. The *Geldmeier* court sanctioned the common practice of ordering a division of the house but not requiring its immediate sale. Courts and legislatures in some states, however, have significantly limited the authority of trial courts to delay the sale of the family home for a long period of time because of the limitations such an order places on the ability of the spouse not occupying the home to make use of his or her share.

The *Geldmeier* trial court specifically said that the husband, who did not occupy the house, was not entitled to interest on the amount representing his share of the house. Was this fair? If instead of fixing a dollar amount for the spouse who does not occupy the home, a court orders the proceeds of the future sale of the home to be divided according to some formula, the nonoccupying spouse is not ordinarily guaranteed any return.

Instead of awarding ownership of the home to one spouse, with the obligation to pay the other some amount on sale, some courts order continued joint ownership of the house with sale ordered at some future date, and permit the custodial parent to remain in the house until the sale. In such cases, the court should allocate responsibility for the mortgage payments until the house is sold. If the non-occupying spouse is ordered to pay the mortgage, half the payments might be characterized as spousal or child support.

Empirical studies find that the spouse with physical custody of the children is still likely to be awarded possession of the house, though this tendency decreased over the 1970s and 1980s.[11]

Of course, if the spouse who receives the home does not have enough income to pay the mortgage, taxes, and upkeep, the home will have to be sold anyway.

See also Martha F. Davis, The Marital Home: Equal or Equitable Division, 50 U. Chi. L. Rev. 1089 (1983); Peter M. Moldave, The Division of the Family Residence Acquired with a Mixture of Separate and Community Funds, 70 Cal. L. Rev. 1263 (1982).

C. SPOUSAL SUPPORT AT DIVORCE

Spousal support, or alimony, as it was traditionally known, was originally developed by the ecclesiastical courts as an incident of legal separation. The rules regarding it were transferred wholesale to alimony following absolute divorce without much consideration of whether they were appropriate in this different context. The traditional law of alimony and its origins are described in the following excerpt.

CHESTER G. VERNIER & JOHN B. HURLBUT, *THE HISTORICAL BACKGROUND OF ALIMONY LAW AND ITS PRESENT SRUCTURE*

6 Law & Contemp. Probs. 197, 198-200 (1939)

Permanent alimony . . . is an incident of the Ecclesiastical divorce *a mensa et thoro*. . . . Then, as now, pecuniary provision for the injured wife was necessary as

---

11. *See* Marsha Garrison, Good Intentions Gone Awry: The Impact of New York's Equitable Distribution Law upon Divorce Outcomes, 57 Brook. L. Rev. 621, 681, Table 24 (1991); Barbara R. Rowe & Alice M. Morrow, The Economic Consequences of Divorce in Oregon After Ten or More Years of Marriage, 24 Willamette L. Rev. 463, 472-473 (1988); James B. McLindon, Separate but Unequal: The Economic Disaster of Divorce for Women and Children, 21 Fam. L.Q. 351 (1987); Alaska Women's Commission, Family Equity at Issue: A Study of the Economic Consequences of Divorce on Women and Children (Research Summary Oct. 1987); Heather R. Wishik, Economics of Divorce: An Exploratory Study, 20 Fam. L.Q. 79 (1986) (Vermont, 1982-1983). *But see* Barbara R. Rowe & Jean M. Lown, The Economics of Divorce and Remarriage for Rural Utah Families, 16 J. Contemp. L. 301 (1990) (women awarded the house outright in 52.7 percent of the cases, joint ownership ordered 32.1 percent of the time, and men received sole ownership the rest of the time; no statistically significant relationship between having custody and getting the house).

a matter of social economy. Inequality of economic opportunity as a fact was not obscured by modern notions of "equal rights." Her technical legal status permitted such relief without resort to novel doctrines. In legal contemplation, the marital tie upon which the husband's legal duty to maintain her rested was not severed by the divorce decree. There were, however, other considerations present. The discriminatory common law scheme of marital property rights was in full bloom. Only very serious and aggravated types of marital transgressions entitled the wife to divorce. It is no wonder that her application for permanent alimony was treated with sympathy, and with liberality when the circumstances permitted liberality.

The primary object of the order for permanent alimony was to provide continuing maintenance for the wife. In form at least there was no pretense of effecting a division of property. The order was invariably for periodic payments, usually commencing at the date of the divorce sentence. The amount of the award rested in broad discretion of the Ecclesiastical judge. The ultimate considerations, of course, were the needs of the wife and the ability of the husband to pay. The marital delinquency of the husband standing established, the amount was usually greater than that given as temporary alimony. While provision for the custody and maintenance of children was without the province of the Ecclesiastical judge, the husband's obligation to support the children was not ignored in fixing the amount which he could appropriately be called upon to pay for the wife's support. Actually, however, the order for permanent alimony involved more than a mere judicial measurement of the husband's legal duty as husband to support the wife. If he acquired wealth from the wife by virtue of the marriage, he could not be compelled to disgorge, but that fact was of influence in fixing the amount of the award. Finally, in the minds of some of the judges at least, the notion of punishment depending upon the degree of the husband's moral delinquency played some part in the process. By balancing the above considerations the wife might be allotted as much as one-half of the combined income of the spouses, and often as much as one-third.[12]

While apparently there is no reported precedent in the Ecclesiastical courts on the matter, it has been assumed that permanent alimony to the guilty wife against whom the husband secured a separation was judicially unthinkable. This unenlightened view, totally blind to the fact that a guilty wife may starve as quickly as an innocent one, found technical justification in the theory that the husband's duty to support continued only so long as she cohabited with him or lived apart because of his misconduct. . . . Alimony to the innocent husband seems never to have been suggested to the Ecclesiastical judges, but such an award would presumably have been also unthinkable because the wife was under no duty to maintain him.[13]

---

12. Some courts arrived at the figure of a third of the husband's income as alimony by analogizing to dower. Edward W. Cooey, The Exercise of Judicial Discretion in the Award of Alimony, 6 Law & Contemp. Probs. 213, 221 (1939) (discussing cases). —Ed.

13. Orr v. Orr, 440 U.S. 268 (1979), *supra* at Chapter 2, Section B.4.e, held that a formal rule that makes spousal support available only to one sex is unconstitutional. As a practical matter, though, most spousal support awards are for the benefit of women.

Even though relatively few divorced women have ever been awarded spousal support, the issue has been and continues to be emotionally and symbolically important, as the following passage, written in 1939, suggests.

Catherine G. Peele, *Social and Psychological Effects of the Availability and the Granting of Alimony on the Spouses*

6 Law & Contemp. Probs. 283, 287-290 (1939)

It is not surprising that generally there is much emotion associated with the giving or receiving of alimony. Alimony perpetuates, in most instances, a relationship passionately undesired and in a way that continues and even increases former antagonisms. Although we can safely assume that the average individual will react emotionally to an alimony decree, it is difficult to know in advance what slant this will take, so many elements are involved. It easily becomes a sort of legal poultice that draws to a head the underlying domestic poison that the divorce is expected to drain away.

. . . [I]n general it may be said that men react in one of two ways to the idea of paying money to a woman from whom they are separated or divorced. If the man believes that his wife was in the wrong and was almost solely to blame for the ensuing separation or divorce, he will often resent having to pay alimony, especially if the woman has means of her own, has no small children, or is thought by him to be capable of earning her own living. . . .

If, on the other hand, the man has a guilty conscience and secretly thinks that he was at fault and that his behavior was the cause of the marital break, the paying of alimony may constitute penance, and may justify him in his own eyes for what he did. Such a man will have a great inner need to pay alimony and may wish to pay more than he can well afford to pay, or may urge a reluctant ex-wife to accept it. It is as if he were saying to the world at large that after all he was willing to do the handsome thing by his former wife, and therefore he can not be greatly blamed for what he did. He thinks, as many people do, that the giving of money should be adequate recompense to anybody for anything that might have been done to them.

Or his guilt may not be involved in the manner in which the marriage tie was broken, but in the knowledge of what has happened to his family since then. One sees instances of men who put aside all thoughts of what is happening to the members of the families of which they were formerly the heads, and as a substitute mail a check. They pride themselves on providing liberal financial support and so hide the fact that they are refusing to assume any other responsibility. Thus, paying alimony, doing all the court requires, may enable a man to feel that he has bought his freedom, when otherwise he would have had to feel that what was happening to his former wife or his children was some concern of his.

. . . On the other hand, to others the making of alimony payments has an opposite meaning, and constitutes for them a reason for maintaining to some extent their former relationship with their families. A man who thinks of money as power and has no sense of guilt in connection with the marital break, may want to pay alimony as a means of retaining his authority in his former home. He may feel that as long as he is contributing regularly to his former wife's support he has the right to demand that he be given a voice in the management of the household of which he formerly was a part. . . .

Thus, the payment of alimony can be a symbol of power to both the man and the woman concerned, and this is probably the usual reason why some women state, as many do, that they will accept support for their children from the children's father, but that they will not under any circumstances take any money for themselves. . . .

On the other hand, a woman may think of alimony as meaning power, not her former husband's power over her, but her power over him. She may cherish this power merely for its nuisance value, hoping that having to pay it constitutes a constant source of annoyance to him. Or she may know that as long as he has to pay alimony he can not afford to marry again, or to live in accordance with the style in which he would like to live. Her desire to punish him may be a much more important factor in her insistence on receiving alimony than is her need for financial support. . . .

Perhaps the wives who are out for vengeance make themselves the most conspicuous, but as a matter of fact a woman may be humiliated by the knowledge that she is receiving support only because of a legal decree as frequently as the man may balk at the threat of compulsion contained in the decree. Anybody who comes into contact with cases of separation and divorce knows that there are many more women who do without what they need rather than take legal means to force their former husbands to support them, than there are women who use the courts to harass their ex-spouses.

1. Changing Attitudes Toward Spousal Support in the No-Fault Era

Consistent with the modern preference for ending spousal obligations at divorce, the law in most states during the 1960s and 1970s disfavored awards of spousal support. When awarded, the spousal support was supposed to facilitate the economic independence of the spouses from each other. During the 1970s and early 1980s a number of legislatures enacted statutes limiting the duration of spousal support awards. *See, e.g.*, Ind. Code Ann. §§31-15-7-1, 31-15-7-2 (Lexis) (limit of two years unless spouse or child in custody of spouse is physically or mentally incapacitated); Kan. Stat. Ann. §60-1610(b)(2) (Supp. 1990) (limit of 121 months, subject to reinstatement). *See also* Ore. Rev. Stat. §§107.407, 107.412 (if after ten years of spousal support payments the recipient has not made a reasonable effort to become financially self-supporting, the payor may petition to terminate support).

Studies of spousal support awards during the 1970s and 1980s found that from one-third to 98 percent were for a limited time; in most of the studies half or more of the awards were of limited duration.[14]

---

14. *See, e.g.*, U.S. Dept. of Commerce, Bureau of the Census, Child Support and Alimony: 1983 (Supplemental Report, Current Population Reports, Special Studies, Series P-23, No. 148 (Oct. 1986); Lenore J. Weitzman & Ruth B. Dixon, The Alimony Myth:

During the 1980s, however, sentiment began to shift again as the divorce rate rose and the poor economic position of divorced women and their children became more widely known. Realizing that most divorcing people do not have enough property to provide support for dependent spouses and children, courts, commentators, and legislators again considered the desirability of dividing post-divorce income between spouses. Some legislatures and courts have rejected a preference for limited-term awards or have even created a preference for indefinite awards in some circumstances. *See, e.g.*, Minn. Stat. Ann. §518.552(3) (West 1994) (limited-term orders not preferred, if "there is some uncertainty as to the necessity of a permanent award, the court shall order a permanent award leaving its order open for further modification"); Walter v. Walter, 464 So. 2d 538 (Fla. 1985) (rejecting preference for short-term rather than permanent alimony).

Based on her analysis of cases decided in the mid-1980s, Professor Krauskopf concluded that appellate courts usually uphold awards of indefinite support to women who were homemakers for more than 20, and perhaps more than 15, years. Joan M. Krauskopf, Rehabilitative Alimony: Uses and Abuses of Limited Duration Alimony, 21 Fam. L.Q. 573, 579-580 (1988).[15] However, Professor Garrison found that in New York the number of long-married wives who were awarded spousal support declined from the 1970s to the 1980s, and more of the awards that were made contemplated temporary, rather than permanent, support. Garrison, above, at 700-701.

Long-term spousal support to provide for dependent spouses continues to be controversial. The following readings suggest the nature of the debate.

Does No-Fault Divorce Make a Difference? 14 Fam. L.Q. 141, 161-162 (1980); Robert E. McGraw et al., A Case Study in Divorce Law Reform and Its Aftermath, 20 J. Fam. L. 443, 475 (1982); Harriet N. Cohen & Adria S. Hillman, New York Courts Have Not Recognized Women as Equal Marriage Partners, 5 Equitable Distrib. Rep. 93 (1985); Alaska Women's Commission, Family Equity at Issue: A Study of the Economic Consequences of Divorce on Women and Children 17 (Oct. 1987); Heather R. Wishik, Economics of Divorce: An Exploratory Study, 20 Fam. L.Q. 79 (1986); James B. McLindon, Separate but Unequal: The Economic Disaster of Divorce for Women and Children, 21 Fam. L.Q. 351 (1987); Marsha Garrison, Good Intentions Gone Awry: The Impact of New York's Equitable Distribution Law on Divorce Outcomes, 57 Brook. L. Rev. 621, 698, table 37 (1991).

15. Most marriages that end in divorce are of short to medium duration, however, and many of the people are relatively young. Half of all divorcing couples have been married approximately seven years, and half the wives are 33.2 years old or younger. Census Bureau, Statistical Abstract of the United States, 1998 Table 160 (118th ed. 1998). Of all divorcing couples, 63 percent have been married less than ten years, and only 12 percent have been married 20 years or longer. National Center for Health Statistics, Dept. of Health & Hum. Serv., 43 Monthly Vital Statistics, Report 9 (Supp. Mar. 22, 1995).

HERMA HILL KAY, *EQUALITY AND DIFFERENCE: A PERSPECTIVE ON NO-FAULT DIVORCE AND ITS AFTERMATH*

56 U. Cinn. L. Rev. 1, 79-85 (1987)

I asked earlier whether, in order to implement equality between the sexes, legal significance should be accorded at the dissolution of the family unit to the consequences of choices made concerning sex roles during the existence of the family relationship. It seems clear that, at least in the short run, the answer to that question must be an affirmative one. It is necessary to take steps to alleviate the situation of those women who are trapped in circumstances neither they nor their husbands anticipated, and that they cannot now avoid. . . .

In the long run, however, I do not believe that we should encourage future couples entering marriage to make choices that will be economically disabling for women, thereby perpetuating their traditional financial dependence upon men and contributing to their inequality with men at divorce. I do not mean to suggest that these choices are unjustified. For most couples, they are based on the presence of children in the family. The infant's claim to love and nurturance is a compelling one both on moral and developmental grounds. Throughout history, the choice of the mother as the primary nurturing parent has been the most common response to the infant's claim. . . . But other choices are possible. . . . Serious discussion of the possibility of shared parenting for children, and for infants in particular, as a way of achieving equality between women and men is very recent. . . .

I do not propose that the state attempt to implement this view of family life by enacting laws requiring mothers to work or mandating that fathers spend time at home with their children. But since, as I noted earlier, Anglo-American family law has traditionally reflected the social division of function by sex within marriage, it will be necessary to withdraw existing legal supports for that arrangement as a cultural norm. No sweeping new legal reforms of marriage and divorce will be required, however, to achieve this end. It will be enough, I think, to continue the present trend begun in the nineteenth century toward the emancipation of married women, and implemented more recently by gender-neutral family laws, as well as the current emphasis on sharing principles in marital property law.

PAULA ENGLAND & GEORGE FARKAS, *HOUSEHOLDS, EMPLOYMENT AND GENDER*

44-45, 55-56 (1986)

By "human capital" economists refer to the stock of attributes in a person that can be put to use in serving some end. When that end is productivity on the job, attributes such as intelligence, strength, education, and skills are relevant. Similarly, we can think of those qualities helpful in person-to-person interaction as a form of human capital as well. These include the ability to provide empathy, companionship, sexual and intellectual pleasure, social status, or earnings. Individuals "invest" in human capital whenever they forgo something desirable in the present to develop a personal attribute which will pay off in the future, whether in a job or household relationship.

. . . [M]any of the highest-return investments within the household sector are to relationship-specific rather than general human capital. To call an investment relationship-specific means that it has value only within the current relationship, and would be of no benefit in a different one. . . . Of course, investments may be anywhere along a continuum from those useless in a new relationship to those whose benefits are completely transferable to a new relationship. . . .

Marital investments that transfer poorly to a new relationship include learning what shared leisure activities both partners enjoy, learning what division of labor is most efficient with this partner, decorating the house in a style both partners like, learning to fight and make up with this partner, learning this partner's sexual preferences, and developing relationships with in-laws. In addition, the tremendous investments of time, caring and money that parents make in children bear fruit not only in the children's futures, but also in the satisfaction parents derive from the relationship. Investment in children with one partner contributes relatively little to improving one's relationship with a new partner. . . .

. . . [M]en typically make fewer relationship-specific investments than women, accumulating instead resources which are as useful outside as within their current relationship. Thus, while both men and women work at the relationship-specific issues of learning to get along with the other person, women are usually the expressive-emotional specialists, focusing heavily on personal relationships and empathic understanding. Of course, some of these efforts are potentially useful in future relationships as well — examples include skills at listening, pleasing, and compromising. Yet much of the investment in these emotional skills is by its very nature specific to the particular relationship. In addition, women typically take the major responsibility for child rearing, heavily investing their own time for the future benefit of the children, but also for the benefit of the particular marriage. Thus women's effort is skewed toward investments which are most valuable within the particular relationship.

The relationship-specific nature of learning to get along with a particular husband can be seen by questioning what value such learning has for the woman if she becomes divorced. Furthermore, what good are kin links with the current husband's family (links she has invested time and emotion in) once she is divorced or when she is remarried? And, especially, are the children, in whom she has invested so much, an asset in finding a new partner? More likely they are a hindrance. Of course, the earnings of employed women are something they can transfer out of the relationship. . . . Yet, even women with earnings seldom earn as much as their partners. . . . Thus, whether employed outside the home or not, wives tend to accumulate fewer resources that are of value outside the current relationship.

While women are taking major responsibility for the instrumental and expressive work of the household, men are advancing their careers. Even blue-collar men not getting promotions are accumulating years of seniority that usually increase their earnings. A husband's increased earning power will, of course, benefit the man's wife as long as the relationship persists, but it continues to benefit the husband should he leave the relationship. That is, earning power is "liquid," readily transferable to a new life.

IRA MARK ELLMAN, *THE THEORY OF ALIMONY*

77 Cal. L. Rev. 1, 48-52 (1989)

. . . [M]arital specialization makes sense for most couples, with one spouse concentrating more heavily on the market while the other focuses more heavily on domestic matters. If the spouses view their marriage as a sharing enterprise, they will usually conclude that they are both better off if the lower earning spouse spends more on their joint domestic needs, and allows the higher earning spouse to maximize his or her income. A problem arises only if their mutual commitment to share breaks down, in which case the spouse who has specialized in domestic aspects of the marriage — who has invested in the marriage rather than the market — suffers a disproportionate loss. . . .

[Alimony is intended to compensate for] the "residual" loss in earning capacity that arises from the kind of economically rational marital sharing behavior we have just seen. This is a residual loss in the sense that it survives the marriage. . . . Nonetheless, spouses are not necessarily liable for every loss their former mate incurs. . . . The function of alimony is . . . to reallocate the postdivorce financial consequences of marriage in order to prevent distorting incentives. Because its purpose is to reallocate, it is necessarily a remedy by one spouse against the other. . . . [B]y eliminating any financial incentives or penalties that might otherwise flow from different marital lifestyles, this theory maximizes the parties' freedom to shape their marriage in accordance with their nonfinancial preferences. . . .

A system of alimony that compensates the wife who has disproportionate postmarriage losses arising from her marital investment protects marital decision-making from the potentially destructive pressures of a market that does not value marital investment as much as it values career enhancement.

J. THOMAS OLDHAM, *PUTTING ASUNDER IN THE 1990s*

80 Cal. L. Rev. 1091, 1110-1111 (1992)

Men and women have different earning capacities for many reasons. Although some of these reasons, such as discrimination, education levels, and career choice, are not directly related to roles assumed during marriage, a general argument could be made that all of these factors indirectly stem from society's assumption that women will bear primary child care responsibilities. Discrimination based on this assumption can place women at a considerable economic disadvantage. Employers might be concerned about pregnancy or other leave time, parents might provide less encouragement or education for daughters, and women themselves might choose less "desirable" careers that can more easily accommodate child care responsibilities. . . .

Even if one accepts the view that almost all of the wage gap stems from actual or potential child care responsibilities, it does not follow that the full cost of these employment disabilities should be borne by the divorcing husband.

I believe it is fair only to ask the divorcing husband to share the costs of decisions in which he participated and that some mechanism should be found that isolates the effects of decisions made during marriage. It is not fair to ask the husband to compensate the wife for all career damage she incurred on the expectation that one day she would assume child care responsibilities. Even if the husband should be responsible for such damage, a goal of post-divorce equal living standards is not justified by compensation for career damage. Individual spouses have different levels of intelligence and education and have different career interests at the time of marriage; these all would cause income inequalities for reasons largely unrelated to sex. Thus, even a very broad concept of career damage due to child care responsibilities does not justify a goal of post-divorce equal living standards.

JOAN WILLIAMS, *IS COVERTURE DEAD? BEYOND A NEW THEORY OF ALIMONY*

82 Geo. L.J. 2227, 2255-2258 (1994)

Ellman's exclusive focus on reimbursing the wife for losses in her earning capacity presents two separate problems. First, his model for measuring a wife's losses omits the losses typically experienced by lower-status wives. A service-sector or pink-collar worker does not suffer the same direct decrease in earnings as the attorney who leaves the partnership track, but she may well lose opportunities and other employment benefits. Sociological studies show that working-class women who start out in "women's work" often respond to attractive job opportunities; thus, a wife who started out as a clerical worker might have ended up a machinist. Moreover, even working-class wives who reenter the workforce after divorce doing the same job they did before may have sacrificed subtler benefits. For example, informal seniority and flexibility often are granted to valued, long-term workers; these informal benefits can prove extremely important for a mother with a sick child.

Ellman's exclusive focus on *detriment* to the wife also presents a deeper problem: it ignores the *benefits* conferred upon husbands by the dominant family ecology. A wife who shoulders childrearing and other domestic responsibilities allows her husband *both* to perform as an ideal worker *and* to have his children raised according to norms of parental care that Ellman himself explicitly embraces. Husbands receive this benefit regardless of whether or not the wife has received the kind of detriment Ellman is willing to recognize.

Ellman, like other commentators, also overlooks the important fact that divorcing fathers *retain the primary benefit they garner from the domestic ecology even after the marriage has ended.* In the 90 percent of divorces in which mothers are awarded sole physical and legal custody—and even in states such as California where joint custody is favored—mothers typically remain the child's primary caretaker. Thus, even after divorce, noncustodial fathers continue to receive the benefits of the dominant family ecology: they can continue to perform as ideal workers while their children are raised according to norms of parental care. . . .

My analysis of the dominant family ecology suggests an approach to post-divorce entitlements very different from Ellman's. Ellman perpetuates the "he who earns it" rule; I consider it a holdover from coverture. Although the husband clearly owns "his" wage vis-a-vis his *employer*, this does not necessarily determine the issue of whether he owns it vis-a-vis his *family*. My analysis of the dominant family ecology suggests that the wages of the family should be jointly owned. . . . I will argue that the way to accomplish this is by equalizing the incomes of the two post-divorce households.

2. Applying the Changing Views

The Uniform Marriage and Divorce Act (UMDA) was drafted early in the no-fault era, and it tends to reflect the clean-break perspective that disfavors spousal support. However, it also contains the seeds of change.

Uniform Marriage and Divorce Act §308

(a) In a proceeding for dissolution of marriage . . . the court may grant a maintenance order for either spouse only if it finds that the spouse seeking maintenance:

(1) lacks sufficient property to provide for his reasonable needs; and

(2) is unable to support himself through appropriate employment or is the custodian of a child whose condition or circumstances make it appropriate that the custodian not be required to seek employment outside the home.

(b) The maintenance order shall be in amounts and for periods of time the court deems just, without regard to marital misconduct, and after considering all relevant factors including:

(1) the financial resources of the party seeking maintenance, including marital property apportioned to him, his ability to meet his needs independently, and the extent to which a provision for support of a child living with the party includes a sum for that party as custodian;

(2) the time necessary to acquire sufficient education or training to enable the party seeking maintenance to find appropriate employment;

(3) the standard of living established during the marriage;

(4) the duration of the marriage;

(5) the age and the physical and emotional condition of the spouse seeking maintenance; and

(6) the ability of the spouse from whom maintenance is sought to meet his needs while meeting those of the spouse seeking maintenance.

NOTES AND QUESTIONS

1. Parts (a) and (b) of §308 both refer to the amount of marital property awarded to the claimant spouse, his or her ability to be self-supporting, and minor children in his or her custody. What is the difference between these sections? *See* Commentary to §308; In re Marriage of Johnsrud, 181 Mont. 544, 548-549, 572 P.2d 902, 904-905 (1977); Farmer v. Farmer, 506 S.W.2d 109 (Ky. 1974).

The UMDA's preference for using property division, rather than spousal support, as the primary vehicle for financial settlement between spouses furthers the goal of providing the parties with a "clean break." Property division awards are final, eliminating subsequent modification problems. Further, property division awards are more advantageous to the recipient than support awards because they do not present continuing enforcement problems (if the award calls for only one lump-sum payment or transfer), and to the payors because they provide financial certainty and ability to plan.

2. Even though courts sometimes say that they award spousal support to keep the recipient off the welfare rolls, most courts have held that a person who can earn just enough to subsist is not self-supporting for these purposes, at least if the marital standard of living was substantially higher. *See, e.g.,* In re Marriage of Kuppinger (Cal. App. 1975); Casper v. Casper, 510 S.W.2d 253, 255 (Ky. 1974); Lepis v. Lepis, 416 A.2d 45 (N.J. 1980).

PROBLEM

Donald and Joan divorced after an 11-year marriage. The total value of the marital assets is $112,605.67. The trial court has ordered Donald to pay Joan $50,000 as her share, $25,000 immediately and the rest at $500 a month plus interest until paid off. In determining whether Joan is eligible to receive support under UMDA §308, the income that the lump-sum payment of $25,000 will produce will be treated as available income. Should she also be expected to invade the principal to support herself? Should the $500 a month that she will receive be treated as income available for her expenses?

TURNER V. TURNER

385 A.2d 1280 (N.J. Super 1978)

IMBRIANI, J.C.C. . . . . Our statute does not mandate alimony. It provides that a "court *may* award alimony to either party." N.J.S.A. 2A:34-23 (emphasis supplied). In the past alimony has been liberally granted and without time limitation, but terminable upon death of either or remarriage of the recipient. . . .

. . . "[W]hile women were formerly excluded from the employment market, then accepted on a limited basis, they are now widely accepted by industry." What began as an elitist movement for "women's liberation" only a decade ago, now appears to have taken root as a profound and deep social change. Indeed, today there are many women who have considerable skills and are able to command salaries far in excess of what many men earn. It is imperative that courts recognize that society has changed. . . .

. . . In the past we dealt with men of means who had the ability to maintain two households. Now we deal with the store clerk, the assembly line operator, the building custodian and a host of other blue collar workers. Unlike litigants of the past, these men cannot maintain one household, much less two, in the same style to which they and their former wives were accustomed. In this milieu should a divorced woman be required, as a matter of law, to put her skills to use, and if she has none, to develop appropriate skills, if possible, to acquire a job?

In the past our attention was riveted upon the needs of the rejected wife. This was because most men in the matrimonial courts had the ability to maintain two households. But today our primary attention is addressed to what the man can afford to pay. The solution often becomes complicated because it is not uncommon for many men to remarry and raise new families.

The law should provide both parties with the opportunity to make a new life on this earth. Neither should be shackled by the unnecessary burdens of an unhappy marriage. This is not to suggest that women of no skills, or those who suffer a debilitating infirmity, or who are of advanced age (whatever that may be) should be denied alimony for as long as needed. But such women are the exception, not the rule.

If we are to encourage a woman to seek employment, what better way is there than to direct that alimony will be rehabilitative in nature and will cease on some predetermined date? A permanent award of alimony *in futuro* with the hope that a woman will seek employment has not and will not work.

Some ask why impose a time limit? Is it not sufficient to permit a man to petition the court for modification of alimony when there is a change of circumstances? Such an inquiry misconceives the problem. What is needed is a system which will *encourage* a woman to develop skills and seek employment — not one that will address a situation when and if it should arise. The court must design a blueprint for the future which will have "teeth" to compel a recipient of alimony to obtain employment.

Our cases are replete with language that a divorced woman is entitled to be maintained in the style of life to which she became accustomed during coverture. Yet we all know that in the vast majority of cases we hear today that is not possible. Where the parties were required to spend during coverture practically all of their income, with little or no savings, to maintain a certain living style, it takes no great insight to appreciate that following the divorce neither will have access to the same amount of funds and both will have to scale down their style of living.

This is not unique to divorced couples. Even where we have a happy marriage, when the man dies his widow must fend for herself on the reduced income of a pension; for some there is no pension. To live even close to her previous style of life, the widow must seek employment.

We know that when a woman has maintained the household for many years, while caring for the family, she has been deprived of the opportunity to acquire marketable skills, and has lost whatever such skills she once possessed. During this time her husband has developed and improved his employment skills. Under these circumstances, it would be inequitable to thrust a woman into the employment market without first ascertaining whether she has the potentiality to obtain suitable employment and, if so, to afford her sufficient time to acquire employment skills. If the court finds that such a potentiality exists, it can determine the time a woman would need to acquire such skills and award her rehabilitative alimony during that time. It may even direct that marital assets subject to equitable distribution shall be first used to pay educational costs she may need to develop or upgrade her skills.

Such a program affords multiple advantages to the woman. She will receive financial assurances within an appropriate period to plan her future with a minimum of financial concern, but nonetheless with the foreknowledge that alimony will cease on a predetermined date. She can look forward to pursuing a career of her own which will yield valuable emotional and psychological dividends. She can enjoy the self-fulfillment and rewards of entry into the employment market a goal of the modern day women's movement.

Rehabilitative alimony, since awarded for a brief period of time, may well be for a sum greater than would have been awarded as permanent alimony. Further, the allowance of rehabilitative alimony does not preclude an allowance of permanent alimony where the woman's ability to earn is less than her needs that will be necessary to maintain her same style of living. Where appropriate, both can be awarded. For instance, if a woman requires $500 a week to maintain her style of living, and the court determines that with a two-year training period she could earn $100 a week, there should be nothing to preclude an award of $400 a week permanent alimony and $100 a week rehabilitative alimony that would cease in two years.

The advantage to the man is evident. He can now make meaningful plans for his own personal and financial future. In the past a woman could remarry without being inhibited by the burdens of an earlier marriage. But this path was not available to many men who found alimony a significant obstacle. . . .

This court is satisfied that rehabilitative alimony is a valuable technique and one that is available today in New Jersey. There is no statute or case directly prohibiting its use.

The facts of this case are unusual. The parties have been married for 22 years. There are three children, one of whom is emancipated; the wife has custody of the others, who are 13 and 17 years of age. The 17-year-old will graduate high school in June 1979 and probably go on to college. The 13-year-old has not displayed college potentiality at this moment.

The wife is 45 years of age and has attended Ohio State University. In the past seven years she has taken part-time employment, including as a reading teacher at a private school. Several years ago she matriculated at Kean College and will graduate in August 1978 (some six months hence) with a degree as a Reading Specialist. She presently works at Kean College and receives a salary of $50 a week plus free tuition. Upon graduation she anticipates earning $12,000 a year. In addition, when the house is sold in the summer of 1979 (because it will be too large for only the wife and one child) the wife will have received equitable distribution from all sources of at least $80,000 in cash. The husband will provide support for the children, including their college expenses. Her obligations will essentially be limited to maintaining herself.

The husband is 49 years of age and a civil engineer who earned $31,000 in 1977. In addition, he receives a military pension of about $5,000 a year, of which more is said infra.

What makes this case unique is that the husband was involved in an airplane accident while in the U.S. Navy two years before marriage. He lost his left leg. His right leg sustained serious damage and its condition has progressively deteriorated. He is seriously concerned that he may also lose his right leg, which he believes will prevent his continued employment. It is because of this concern that this family has lived a relatively frugal life and has always implemented a savings program. As a result of the injuries received in the airplane accident, he receives a government pension, [which his wife concedes was vested prior to the marriage and is not subject to equitable distribution.]

Considering (1) the substantial sums that each will receive by way of equitable distribution, (2) the earning ability that both will enjoy by the time the house is sold, and (3) the necessity that the husband save a greater sum than usual because of his physical condition, fairness and equity dictate that rehabilitative alimony of $50 a week be awarded to the wife, which shall cease on September 1, 1979. By that time the wife will have completed one full year of employment in her new position as a reading specialist. She will have only the 15-year-old child at home, whom the husband will support. The interest income she will earn from her share of the marital assets, together with her salary and child support payment, will adequately satisfy her needs and enable her to maintain the style of living to which she is accustomed.[16]

IN RE THE MARRIAGE OF LAROCQUE

406 N.W.2d 736 (Wis. 1987)

[The trial court awarded Rosalie LaRocque limited-term spousal support of $1,500 per month for 5 months and then $1,000 per month for 13 months. The court of appeals affirmed the circuit court's decision on the amount but not on the duration of maintenance, concluding that the circuit court abused its discretion in terminating maintenance at the end of the 18 months. This appeal followed.]

ABRAHAMSON, J. Daniel and Rosalie LaRocque were married in 1959; they filed for divorce in 1982. When the divorce was granted in 1984, Mrs. LaRocque was 46 years old, Mr. LaRocque was 48, and only one of the LaRocques' five children was still a minor (age 17).

Mrs. LaRocque received a bachelor's degree in psychology in June of 1959. During the first two years of the marriage, she held several full-time positions including secretary, clerk and teacher. Thereafter, she worked outside the home sporadically, as a part-time substitute teacher and as a member of the school board. At the time of the divorce she was not certified to teach in a public school. During the marriage, her principal occupation was as a full-time homemaker and caretaker of the parties' five children. She also assisted Mr. LaRocque in his various election campaigns. Her total income from employment outside the home during the marriage amounted to $5660.

Mr. LaRocque received a law degree in 1962. During the marriage he was employed as a lawyer in private practice, an assistant district attorney, a district attorney for Marathon County, and a circuit court judge. In 1984 he was appointed judge of the Wisconsin Court of Appeals. When the divorce action was commenced, his annual income was $49,966; when the divorce was granted, his

---

16. After *Turner* was decided, Arnold v. Arnold, 401 A.2d 261 (N.J. App. Div. 1979), specifically disapproved of rehabilitative alimony, but the *Turner* approach was implicitly approved in Lepis v. Lepis, 416 A.2d 45 (N.J. 1980).

annual income was $60,000. His earnings during the marriage totaled $548,987. The family annual income had increased from $1763 in 1959 to $50,235 in 1980 and $60,000 at the time of the divorce. . . .

The circuit court divided the property, awarding Mrs. LaRocque the household furniture and appliances ($4043), the family car ($2000), the parties' income tax refund ($3000), and the family home subject to the two mortgages (net value $34,431), for a total value of $43,474. Mrs. LaRocque had foreseeable future expenditures for house repairs, broker's fees and taxes on the sale of the house, 1984 property taxes, and legal fees. Mr. LaRocque was awarded the retirement fund with the vested portion valued at $54,340.

During the separation period Mr. LaRocque paid the family bills of over $1600 per month and paid Mrs. LaRocque $372 every two weeks. Mrs. LaRocque submitted several budgets for expenses in maintaining herself and the children living at home; the budgets ranged from $1654 to $2317 per month. She testified that her standard of living had declined over the two-year separation and that she could not meet her minimum existing expenses on less than $1654 per month, exclusive of property and income taxes and the second mortgage payment. Mr. LaRocque submitted no budget; he listed $225 per month as an apartment rental expense.

In awarding maintenance, the circuit court found that Mrs. LaRocque could work as an elementary school teacher upon certification and that the entry level salary for elementary school teachers in the Wausau district was $12,000 a year and the average salary $25,000 a year. The circuit court further found that Mrs. LaRocque's present earning capacity was between $12,000 and $15,000 per year and her future earning capacity was at least $25,000 per year. The circuit court concluded that the entry level salary upon her certification as a teacher would provide Mrs. LaRocque with a standard of living reasonably comparable to the one enjoyed during marriage inasmuch as the parties' median annual income during the marriage was approximately $18,000 and the average annual income was $20,000 and as many as five children shared that income during the marriage. Thus, according to the circuit court, as an entry level teacher Mrs. LaRocque could earn more than one half of the average annual income during marriage.

The circuit court's memorandum decision explained that the 18 months' maintenance it awarded would enable Mrs. LaRocque to take whatever schooling she deemed appropriate to enhance her earning ability. It went on to say that after the last child reached majority Mrs. LaRocque could sell the house and, with the proceeds from the sale, pursue whatever course she thought would produce an adequate income.

The circuit court also acknowledged that Mr. LaRocque had indicated he would continue to provide for the children who would be going to college and that Mr. LaRocque did not have liquid funds available from the retirement fund.

Thus the circuit court arrived at a maintenance award of $1500 per month for 5 months and then $1000 per month for 13 months. Mrs. LaRocque appealed, arguing that both the amount and duration of the maintenance award were inadequate. . . .

A circuit court determining a maintenance award and an appellate court reviewing a maintenance award must begin with sec. 767.26, Stats. 1985-86, which provides that the court may grant an order requiring maintenance payments to either party for a limited or indefinite length of time after considering:

(1) The length of the marriage.

(2) The age and physical and emotional health of the parties.

(3) The division of property made under 767.255.

(4) The educational level of each party at the time of marriage and at the time the action is commenced.

(5) The earning capacity of the party seeking maintenance, including educational background, training, employment skills, work experience, length of absence from the job market, custodial responsibilities for children and the time and expense necessary to acquire sufficient education or training to enable the party to find appropriate employment.

(6) The feasibility that the party seeking maintenance can become self-supporting at a standard of living reasonably comparable to that enjoyed during the marriage, and, if so, the length of time necessary to achieve this goal.

(7) The tax consequences to each party.

(8) Any mutual agreement made by the parties before or during the marriage, according to the terms of which one party has made financial or service contributions to the other with the expectation of reciprocation or other compensation in the future, where such repayment has not been made, or any mutual agreement made by the parties before or during the marriage concerning any arrangement for the financial support of the parties.

(9) The contribution by one party to the education, training or increased earning power of the other.

(10) Such other factors as the court may in each individual case determine to be relevant.

These factors are the touchstone of analysis in determining or reviewing a maintenance award. They reflect and are designed to further two distinct but related objectives in the award of maintenance: to support the recipient spouse in accordance with the needs and earning capacities of the parties (the support objective) and to ensure a fair and equitable financial arrangement between the parties in each individual case (the fairness objective). . . .

We conclude that the circuit court abused its discretion in this case by misapplying (or failing to apply) several of the statutory factors and by not giving full play to the objectives of maintenance. By construing the support objective too narrowly and disregarding the fairness objective, the circuit court mistook subsistence to be the objective of maintenance and awarded an inadequate amount.

The circuit court offered three principal reasons for concluding that Mrs. LaRocque needed only $1500 per month for 5 months, to be reduced to $1000 per month for 13 months after the minor child graduated from high school: (1) Mrs. LaRocque would eventually have the proceeds of the sale of the house available to her; (2) the award comports with the standard of living of the parties; (3) Mr. LaRocque might pay college expenses for their adult children. Examining each of the circuit court's reasons, we do not find these reasons persuasive.

While the circuit court should consider the property division in awarding maintenance, sec. 767.26 (3), we disagree with the circuit court's implication that

Mrs. LaRocque use the proceeds from the sale of the house, her share of the property division, to support herself. . . .

It is difficult to understand why, and the circuit court does not explain why, Mrs. LaRocque should liquidate her capital to obtain funds to pay living and retraining expenses, while Mr. LaRocque retains full use of his $60,000 a year salary and keeps his retirement fund (the property he received in the property division) untouched and secure for his retirement years. The property division should provide Mrs. LaRocque as well as Mr. LaRocque with a nest egg for retirement or a reserve for emergencies.

. . . Sec. 767.26(6) requires the circuit court to consider the feasibility of the party seeking maintenance becoming self-supporting at a standard of living reasonably comparable to that enjoyed during the marriage and the length of time necessary to achieve this goal if the goal is feasible. The legislature thus has expressly declared that the standard of living for maintenance is a standard of living comparable to the one enjoyed during the marriage. . . .

The increased expenses of separate households may prevent the parties from continuing at their pre-divorce standard of living, but both parties may have to bear the sacrifices that the cost of an additional household imposes. A court must not reduce the recipient spouse to subsistence level while the payor spouse preserves the pre-divorce standard of living. In this case, while Mrs. LaRocque's budgets were unchallenged, the circuit court implicitly rejected them and awarded limited term maintenance in an amount less than the lowest monthly budget Mrs. LaRocque submitted.

[The court rejected the trial court's conclusion that the marital standard of living was $20,000 per year, a figure reached by averaging the total income earned during the marriage. It said instead that the proper measure was the lifestyle that the parties enjoyed in the years immediately before the divorce, when the husband's income was $60,000 and expected to increase and expenses might decrease.]

The circuit court's final reason for limiting Mrs. LaRocque's maintenance was that Mr. LaRocque had stated he would help pay the college expenses of the adult children. Apparently the circuit court considered this factor relevant under sec. 767.26(10). We find it difficult to understand why in awarding maintenance the circuit court credited Mr. LaRocque's payment of college expenses for adult children — particularly when such payment is unstipulated and as yet unrealized — but did not consider the expenses Mrs. LaRocque incurred by having adult children live with her. . . .

In regard to fairness, the other objective of a maintenance award, the circuit court appears not to have given any weight at all to this objective of maintenance or to such statutory factors as the length of the marriage, the educational level of each party at the time of the marriage and the time of the divorce, and the contribution by one party to the education, training or increased earning power of the other.

Where a spouse has subordinated his or her education or career to devote time and energy to the welfare, career or education of the other spouse or to managing the affairs of the marital partnership, maintenance may be used to compensate this spouse for these nonmonetary contributions to the marriage. In adopting the 1977 Divorce Reform Act the legislature stated that it intended that "a spouse who has been handicapped socially or economically by his or her contribution to a marriage shall be compensated for such contributions at the termination of the marriage, insofar as this is possible, and may receive additional education where necessary to permit the spouse to become self-supporting at a standard of living reasonably comparable to that enjoyed during the marriage." 1977 Wis. Laws, c. 105, sec. 1.

The LaRocques were married for 25 years. Both parties contributed to the marriage. The record is replete with evidence of Mrs. LaRocque's contributions to Mr. LaRocque's education and increased earning power. Because the wife's contribution in this marriage was as homemaker and the husband's as wage-earner, the husband leaves the marriage with the "asset" of a stream of income which the wife's contributions helped him to develop. The wife, however, does not leave the marriage with a stream of income; a career as homemaker — although of economic value to the family and society — all too frequently does not translate into money-making ability in the marketplace. Because the parties had accumulated some but not a great deal of property during their marriage, the court in this case cannot rely on the property distributed to the wife to "compensate" her for her contribution to the marriage and her loss of a stream of income.

The maintenance award produced a substantial disparity between the post-divorce incomes of the parties. Mrs. LaRocque was granted maintenance for 18 months and probably can earn $1000 per month as long as she can work. Within 18 months of the divorce Mr. LaRocque will have the use of his entire income of $60,000 per year or $5000 per month and his full retirement funds without any further obligation to support Mrs. LaRocque. The circuit court did not consider whether this result satisfied the fairness objective of maintenance. . . .

This court has said that when a couple has been married many years and achieves increased earnings, it is reasonable to consider an equal division of total income as a starting point in determining maintenance.

If the circuit court had considered the fairness objective of maintenance and had applied the *Bahr-Steinke* standard of starting at an equal division of income of the parties in this case, the starting figure of the maintenance award would be $2500 per month, a figure consistent with Mrs. LaRocque's highest budget figure. . . .

. . . We reverse the decision of the court of appeals regarding the amount of maintenance, and we remand this matter to the circuit court.

The circuit court has to consider the statutory factors enumerated in sec. 767.26 to determine whether to award limited or indefinite maintenance. The circuit court's determinations of the amount of maintenance and the duration of maintenance are intertwined. We agree with the court of appeals that the circuit court's judgment terminating maintenance after 18 months is not supported by the record and is an abuse of discretion. . . .

In determining whether to grant limited-term maintenance, the circuit court must take several considerations into account, for example, the ability of the recipient spouse to become self-supporting by the end of the maintenance period at a standard of living reasonably similar to that enjoyed before divorce; the ability of the payor spouse to continue the obligation of support for an indefinite time; and the need for the court to continue jurisdiction regarding maintenance.

Because limited-term maintenance is relatively inflexible and final, the circuit court must take particular care to be realistic about the recipient spouse's future earning capacity. The circuit court must not prematurely relieve a payor spouse of a support obligation lest a needy former spouse become the obligation of the taxpayers.

In this case, in awarding limited-term maintenance the circuit court considered, as it was required to consider under sec. 767.26(5), Mrs. LaRocque's earning capacity and her ability to become self-supporting. The circuit court apparently concluded that the limited-term maintenance award was adequate to enable Mrs. LaRocque to become self-supporting at a standard of living similar to that enjoyed before the divorce.

Mrs. LaRocque acknowledged that she could get a $12,000-per-year job but she believed such a job would not provide advancement or career possibilities. Because $12,000 was inadequate to meet her budget, she asked for maintenance sufficient to retool herself for a job with career potential, job satisfaction and greater earnings so that she could become self-supporting at the pre-divorce standard of living. Although Mrs. LaRocque had expressed interest in a career as a psychologist, the circuit court considered only a career as a teacher.

The circuit court apparently determined the length of time it would take Mrs. LaRocque to acquire certification to teach, the expenses of earning the certification, the likelihood of her obtaining employment in Wausau, and the time it would take her to earn $25,000 per year starting at the low end of the pay scale, but it did so on the basis of conjecture, not facts. Without facts of record, the court assumed that a woman in her mid-forties who had been a full-time homemaker for more than twenty years could readily enter the job market and within 18 months of the divorce support herself at a pre-divorce standard of living.

Like the court of appeals, we conclude that nothing in the record indicates whether Mrs. LaRocque would be certified and employable as a teacher within 18 months, whether teaching jobs were available in Wausau, whether there was a good likelihood she would be hired and, if so, how long it would take her as an entry level teacher to reach the salary of $25,000. Without such facts the circuit court could not appropriately award limited-term maintenance. Accordingly, we conclude, as did the court of appeals, that the circuit court abused its discretion in awarding limited maintenance for 18 months. We therefore affirm that part of the court of appeals decision remanding the issue of the duration of maintenance.

CAROL ROGERSON, *SPOUSAL SUPPORT AFTER MOGE*

14 Can. Fam. L.Q. 386-387 (1997)

[In 1992 the Canadian Supreme Court rejected the clean-break approach to spousal support in long-term marriages and adopted instead a theory similar to that articulated in *LaRocque*. Moge v. Moge [1992] 43 R.F.L. (3) 345 (S.C.C.) Surveying cases decided since *Moge*, Professor Rogerson concluded that the trend toward short-term, low-level spousal support awards has been reversed and that more spouses are getting more support for longer periods of time.] Despite the gloss of a compensatory analysis, the expanded role for spousal support post-*Moge* appears to be driven, in large part, by a concern with responding to post-divorce need and preventing post-divorce poverty, rather than by principles of providing fair compensation to women for their unpaid labour in the home and providing for the equitable sharing between the spouses of the economic consequences of the marriage. Although there are exceptions, many lawyers and judges continue to feel more comfortable with a traditional understanding of spousal support as a private scheme of income security rather than with a compensatory model, and continue to rely upon the conventional concept of need (and its corollary, self-sufficiency) to structure and give content to the compensatory principle. As a result it is those spouses who demonstrate the greatest economic need and who will experience the greatest economic hardship after marriage breakdown — whether by reason of age, illness, lack of skills, or a poor economy — who are viewed as the most sympathetic candidates for spousal support, while those who have youth, good health, and employability in their favour are seen as self-sufficient economic actors, despite their past and ongoing responsibilities for the care of children.

While there may be more spousal support post-*Moge* and somewhat less post-divorce poverty, I fear that in the course of things the radical message of *Moge* with respect to the value of women's work in the home and their entitlement to compensation from their husbands has been diluted. While *Moge* has undoubtedly wrought some very positive developments in terms of how we treat those members of our society — mainly women — who assume primary responsibility for the care of children, much remains to be done. The current political climate is, unfortunately, not one that will render that an easy task.

From a broad political perspective, it is no surprise that the compensatory message of *Moge* is being subtly reshaped into a message of the obligation of family members to provide for each other's economic needs. In a period of diminishing public resources and a recessionary economy, the family has re-emerged as a central economic institution and a locus of economic security for vulnerable citizens. Our political language of rights and entitlements is being replaced with the language of obligations and responsibilities with particular emphasis on the obligations of family members to care for each other. The fact that many citizens in need have no family resources to draw upon is lost from sight, as is the fact that it is women who will assume responsibility for many of the caring functions being delegated to the family, but whose claims of entitlement to compensation for their work are being delegitimated.

In Bracklow v. Bracklow, (1999) 1 S.C.R. 420, 44 R.F.L. (4th) 1, the Canadian Supreme Court upheld a spousal support order where the wife had become too ill to work, even though the marriage was of relatively short duration and the couple had been more or less economic equals during the marriage. Carol Rogerson, Spousal Support Post-*Bracklow*: The Pendulum Swings Again? 19 Can. Fam. L.Q. 185 (2001), discusses and criticizes *Bracklow*, which, she argues, broadens the basis for awarding spousal support beyond that provided for in *Moge*. *Moge* is easy to apply in long-term traditional marriages that tend to produce permanent awards. Its application is less clear in cases in which wives worked but were secondary earners with primary responsibility for the children; especially marriages of medium duration. The main issue in such a case, Rogerson argues, is whether the support obligation will terminate eventually (generous rehabilitative alimony) or whether it should be permanent. While *Bracklow* does not answer this question, it does deal with another difficult class of cases, those in which one spouse has a clear need for support but no basis for claiming that the need arose because of the roles adopted during marriage. In *Bracklow* the parties had lived together for four years and then were married for three more. When they separated the wife was 43, and her children from a former relationship were grown. The Canadian Supreme Court said that the traditional basis for spousal support — mutual interdependence with support orders based on need and ability to pay — survives. *See also* Carol Rogerson, The Canadian Law of Spousal Support, 38 Fam. L.Q. 69 (2004).

NOTES AND QUESTIONS

1. How do courts measure need? Typically, the parties submit detailed budgets to prove their needs. Must a court take those budgets at face value? In Simmons v. Simmons, 409 N.E.2d 321 (Ill. App. 1980), the wife claimed needs for food and transportation higher than actual costs during marriage. She explained that she ate out four or five nights a week because she did not like to eat alone at home and that she took a cab to work. On what basis would a judge validly determine whether these were "needs"?

2. You are the trial judge in *LaRocque*. When the case comes back before you on remand, Mr. LaRocque presents credible evidence that Mrs. LaRocque could renew her teaching credentials and get an entry-level teaching job in Wausau within 18 months and that she might expect to reach a salary of $25,000 in another three years. Mrs. LaRocque has decided that she would like to become a psychologist, and she estimates that it will take her seven years to finish her education and begin a practice.

For how long should you order Mr. LaRocque to pay support? Why? What if the controlling precedent is *Turner*? *See also* Morgan v. Morgan, 366 N.Y.S.2d 977 (1975), *rev'd*, 383 N.Y.S.2d 343 (1976); In re Marriage of Francis, 442 N.W.2d 59 (Iowa 1989). What if a long-term homemaker has no plans and no wish to start a new career? Under *Turner*, what support would be ordered, if any? Under *LaRocque*?

3. The courts in both these cases concluded that at the time of the divorce the wife needed spousal support while she retrained herself to become capable of self-support at a reasonable level. In both cases it was uncertain how long this period might be. Why did the *Turner* court opt for limited-term (apparently renewable) support, while the *LaRocque* court held that a similar order was impermissible? As a practical matter, what is the difference between a limited-term, renewable spousal support award and a modifiable indefinite award of spousal support? *See* Joan M. Krauskopf, Rehabilitative Alimony: Uses and Abuses of Limited Duration Alimony, 21 Fam. L.Q. 573, 579-580 (1988).

In some states limited-term support awards may be modified if a spouse is not able to become self-supporting at the end of the support period. *See, e.g.,* Polette and Polette, 781 P.2d 1253 (Or. App. 1989); Bentz v. Bentz, 435 N.W.2d 293 (Wis. 1988); Dixon v. Dixon, 319 N.W.2d 846 (Wis. 1982); In other states limited-term alimony is not modifiable. *See, e.g.,* Self v. Self, 861 S.W.2d 360 (Tenn. 1993).

4. What justification does the *Turner* court give for requiring the husband to support the wife through her period of retraining? What is the *LaRocque* court's justification for imposing a support obligation on the husband? How should a spouse's contributions and sacrifices be valued and translated into a dollar figure? Does the reason that she became a homemaker matter? What if her husband had asked her not to work outside the home? What if he encouraged her to develop a career but she decided not to? What if they simply never discussed the matter?

What is the relationship, if any, between these measures and the marital standard of living? Is dividing the parties' total income equally the same thing as maintaining the marital standard of living, as *LaRocque* suggests? Are there other justifications for dividing the total income?

The opinion of the Minnesota Court of Appeals in Chamberlain v. Chamberlain, 615 N.W. 2d 405 (Minn. App. 2000), explicitly addresses the policy tension evident in *Turner* and *LaRocque*. The parties were divorcing after a 20-year marriage. The court, apparently quoting the husband, said the wife is "in good health, 50 years old, at the top of her teaching career, did not play the role of a traditional homemaker for most of the marriage, needs no further education or rehabilitation, and does not suffer health problems that affect her ability to work. In addition, she received a substantial property award as a result of the dissolution." *Id.* at 412. The husband, therefore, argued, that the trial erred when it awarded her permanent spousal support of $2,400 per month. The appellate court rejected his argument that she was entitled to no support because the parties had enjoyed a very lavish lifestyle throughout the marriage, supported by debt and the husband's $200,000/year income, and the spousal support statute required the court to consider the marital standard of living in determining spousal support issues. The court observed that as of 1984 the Minnesota spousal support statute disfavored permanent maintenance; a court had to find "exceptional circumstances" to justify an award. In 1985 the statute was amended in three places to require the court to consider the marital standard of living and to direct courts to order permanent support in questionable cases so as to preserve the option of modifying the award if circumstances change. However, the appellate court in this case found that the amount of support awarded was excessive, considering the parties' income and the housing needs of the wife.

5. The ALI Family Dissolution Principles propose that "compensatory spousal payments" be ordered to compensate a spouse for financial losses occasioned by the marriage, rather than to relieve need:

A spouse frequently seems in need at the conclusion of a marriage because its dissolution imposes a particularly severe loss on him or her. The intuition that the former spouse has an obligation to meet that need arises from the perception that the need results from the unfair allocation of the financial losses arising from the marital failure. This perception explains why we have alimony, and why all alimony claims cannot be adjudicated by reference to a single standard of need.

ALI, Principles of the Law of Family Dissolution §5.02 Comment, at 789 (2002). Section 5.03(2) provides for awards to compensate for:

(a) In a marriage of significant duration, the loss in living standard experienced at dissolution by the spouse who has less wealth or earning capacity (§5.04).

(b) An earning capacity loss incurred during marriage but continuing after dissolution and arising from one spouse's disproportionate share, during marriage, of the care of the marital children or of the children of either spouse (§5.05).

(c) An earning capacity loss incurred during marriage and continuing after dissolution, and arising from the care provided by one spouse to a sick, elderly, or disabled third party, in fulfillment of a moral obligation of the other spouse or of both spouses jointly (§5.12).

Section 5.03(3) adds that awards may be made to compensate for :

(a) The loss either spouse incurs when the marriage is dissolved before that spouse realizes a fair return from his or her investment in the other spouse's earning capacity (§5.15).

(b) An unfairly disproportionate disparity between the spouses in their respective abilities to recover their pre-marital living standard after the dissolution of a short marriage.

Under these provisions, would Mrs. Turner or Mrs. LaRocque be entitled to compensatory payments?

Commentary on the ALI spousal support provisions includes June Carbone, The Futility of Coherence; The ALI's Principles of the Law of Family Dissolution, 4 J.L. & Fam. Stud. 43 (2002); Cynthia Lee Starnes, Victims, Breeders, Joy and Math: First Thoughts on Compensatory Spousal Payments Under the Principles, 8 Duke J. Gender L. & Pol'y 137 (2001); Tonya L. Brito, Spousal Support Takes on the Mommy Track: Why the ALI Proposal is Good for Working Mothers, 8 Duke J. Gender L. & Pol'y 151 (2001).

6. The debate over spousal support policy occurs in other countries as well. *See, e.g.,* Belinda Fehlberg, Spousal Maintenance in Australia, 18 Int'l J. Law, Pol'y & Fam. 1 (2004), observing that, notwithstanding the debate, support awards are relatively rare in Australia.

7. The widespread adoption of child support guidelines (*see* Chapter 7) has stimulated interest in spousal support guides. Guidelines, it is argued, reduce the potential for arbitrary exercises of discretion as well as the costs of divorce, leaving more money for the post-divorce family. However, their development has been hindered by lack of agreement on the purposes of spousal support and the large number of factors considered relevant. The ALI Family Dissolution Principles recommend that jurisdictions adopt a formula that will yield presumptive levels and durations of spousal support. ALI, Principles of the Law of Family Dissolution §§5.05-5.07 (2002).

For discussion of guidelines used in Maricopa County, Arizona, California, Florida, some Kansas counties, Maine, some Michigan counties, Nevada, New Mexico, Ohio, Oregon, Pennsylvania, Texas, and some counties in Virginia, *see* Twila B. Larkin, Guidelines for Alimony: The New Mexico Experiment, 38 Fam. L.Q. 29 (2004); Virginia R. Dugan & Jon A. Feder, Alimony Guidelines: Do They Work? 25 Fam. Advoc. 20 (2003). The Maricopa County guidelines are based on the ALI recommendation. Ira Mark Ellman, The Maturing Law of Divorce Finances: Toward Rules and Guidelines, 33 Fam. L.Q. 801, 812 (1999). *See also* Victoria M. Ho & Jennifer J. Cohen, Are Alimony Guidelines in Our Future? 15 Divorce Litig. 189, 191 (Nov. 2003).

In the era of fault-based divorce a wife's misconduct could either bar her from receiving alimony or limit the amount, and in some places the husband's fault could be a factor in increasing the amount. As of winter 2004, the following states did not permit consideration of marital fault in spousal support awards: Alaska, Arizona, Arkansas, California, Colorado, Delaware, Hawaii, Illinois, Indiana, Iowa, Kansas, Maine, Minnesota, Montana, Nebraska, Nevada, New Mexico, Ohio, Oklahoma, Oregon, Vermont, Washington, and Wisconsin. Linda D. Elrod & Robert G. Spector, A Review of the Year in Family Law, Chart 1, 36 Fam. L.Q. 577 (2004). In a few jurisdictions a person against whom a fault-based divorce is awarded cannot be awarded support, and in some others fault is a factor courts may consider.

June Carbone, *The Futility of Coherence: The ALI's Principles of the Law of Family Dissolution,* Compensatory Spousal Payments

4 J.L. & Fam. Stud. 43, 72-76 (2002)

The most fundamental choice the ALI makes is to deem fault irrelevant to divorce proceedings. . . . The ALI acknowledges that it is possible "to avoid the punitive nature of a fault award by casting it as compensation for the financial costs of splitting one household in two." It then rejects the possibility, however, because of the lack of consensus on what would constitute grounds for divorce, and concludes: "In sum, courts that purport to allocate the unavoidable costs of dissolution by assessing the cause of the marital failure are in fact rewarding failure and punishing sin. They are not compensating one spouse for a harm 'caused' by the other."

I would have preferred that the ALI separate the notion of "sin" from breach of contract. Fault in family law has historically conflated the two, castigating adulterers, for example, both because they have acted shamefully and because they have imposed financial ruin on their families. It is possible to separate the condemnation associated with extracurricular sex, however, from breach of contract. The latter is removed from the moral realm; there is no condemnation comparable to the adulterer's for a party that reneges on a commercial agreement. The obligation is simply to compensate the other party for the consequences of a decision to leave a less than optimal relationship; to compensate one spouse "for a harm 'caused'" by the other's decision to leave. For all that I believe that the two notions are different, however, I would not ultimately come to a different conclusion about the wisdom of the result. Even if breach of contract is defined in terms of the unexcused decision to end a marriage, the ALI is right that it will be difficult to define what constitutes excuse (or, in contract terms, anticipatory breach) and, perhaps more critically, the process of determining breach will impose significant costs of its own. If the financial results turn on the determination, each party will acquire an incentive to charge the other with wrongdoing, the initial charges will inspire anger if not countercharges, and the process of resolution, even if predictable from the outset, will engender more bitterness among parties who under the best of circumstances have difficulty putting anger and bitterness aside. The cost of coherence is simply too high.

If the ALI rejection of fault considerations can be justified, however, then the issue arises whether its decision to protect the interests most associated with breach of contract principles can also be defended. I believe that it can. Consider . . . Carl Schneider's Applebys of Milan, Michigan:

He is fifty-eight; she is fifty-six; they have been married for thirty-five years. He has been a salesman all his life, she is a housewife. Their only child, Meg, is now thirty-two and living in New Mexico. Mrs. Appleby has always spent most of her time at home, in large part because her husband has always insisted on it and because he becomes angry when she does not. Mrs. Appleby consequently has few friends of her own, and what social life the couple has revolves around Mr. Appleby's friends. Mr. Appleby has been spending less and less time at home, and Mrs. Appleby has become more and more distressed. One evening, he tells her that he has fallen in love with his nineteen-year-old secretary and wants a divorce so that he can marry her. . . . Mr. Appleby has never earned much, and they have never saved much. If they are divorced, all his modest income will be consumed supporting his new wife and her twin sons. Mrs. Appleby has a high-school education and hasn't been on the job market for thirty-five years. Now change the facts slightly. Eliminate the child. Give Mr. Appleby some restraint. He's tired of Mrs. Appleby and finds that some of the young women in the office are flirting with him. He takes one to dinner, but stops short of romantic involvement. Instead, the experience heightens his dissatisfaction with his home life, and he requests a divorce. He begins dating after the separation, becomes intimately involved only after the divorce decree becomes final, and marries his nineteen-year-old secretary a year later. Without adultery, his behavior stands on different moral grounds. Yet, in breach of contract terms, the principle is the same: his conduct ends a marriage Mrs. Appleby would prefer to continue.

* * *

The Applebys present the classic — and the best continuing — case for an expectation award. Mrs. Appleby's greatest loss is her misguided expectation that the marriage would continue with the status and associations it conferred and the support provided by Mr. Appleby's income. . . . It is Mr. Appleby's breach of the obligation to remain married that disappoints Mrs. Appleby's expectations, and that triggers the duty to provide compensation. Yet, if he is expected to sustain the standard of living she enjoyed while married, he could not also enjoy the same standard of living with his nineteen-year-old second wife and her twin sons. What justifies protection of her expectation interest without protection of his, and without a determination that he, not she, caused the end of the marriage?

The short answer is that the Appleby case . . . represents not only the best case for application of the Principles, but a typical case of those likely to receive a large expectation-based award. While women initiate the majority of divorces, they typically do so after relatively few years of marriage. By age 45, the rate at which men and women initiate divorce evens out. Older women are less likely to initiate divorce than younger women, their opportunities for remarriage decline with age, and the greater their dependence on their husband's income, the less likely they are to seek divorce without what has historically been legally cognizable grounds. The ALI crafts its principles to provide the largest expectation awards for the women most likely to suffer from breach of the promise to remain married.

* * *

Finally, in [this case] public policy issues stand alongside the matters of private justice. Even if she were at fault, Mrs. Appleby would be left destitute by the absence of an award, and public policy considerations in every divorce era have suggested that some support be provided. . . . . The interests of justice are more complicated than vindication of contract rights might suggest. Providing awards in these cases protects a greater array of interests than denying payment altogether, and at a lower overall price for the divorce system than trying to tailor award to the fault-based equities of each case.

NOTES AND QUESTIONS

1. Professors Brinig and Crafton have argued that a regime that does not take marital fault into account for purposes of awarding spousal support encourages people to engage in bad marital behavior, including domestic violence. Margaret F. Brinig & Steven M. Crafton, Marriage and Opportunism, 23 J. Legal Stud. 869 (1994). Professors Ellman and Lohr criticize the methodology of this study and the assumptions upon which the article is based on a variety of grounds, arguing that Brinig and Crafton did not prove their thesis and that use of fault may even produce results contrary to those hypothesized. Ira Mark Ellman & Sharon Lohr, Marriage as Contract, Opportunistic Violence, and Other Bad Arguments for Fault Divorce, 1997 U. Ill. L. Rev. 719 (1997).

2. Even if general fault is not a factor, economic misconduct may be. However, drawing the line between these two types of fault is as difficult here as it is when the distinction must be made for purposes of property division. See Harvey L. Golden & J. Michael Taylor, Fault Enforces Accountability, 10 Fam. Advoc. 11, 12-13 (1987); Donald C. Schiller, Alimony — Should Marital

Misbehavior Be a Factor? *in* Alimony: New Strategies for Pursuit and Defense 10, 11-14 (American Bar Assn. Family Law Section 1988); Barbara B. Woodhouse, Sex, Lies, and Dissipation: The Discourse of Fault in a No-Fault Era, with Comments by Katharine T. Bartlett, 82 Geo. L.J. 2525 (1994).

PROBLEMS

1. Winnie and Harold are divorcing following an 18-year marriage. Both are 45. Before the marriage and for the first two years after the wedding Winnie taught school. She quit when their first child was born and never went back. The marital property was divided equally. The trial court awarded Winnie sufficient spousal support for two years to enable her to renew her teaching certificate without having to work; at that point the award was to be reduced by 50 percent and was to continue for an indefinite duration. The judge justified this award as encouraging Winnie to become self-supporting while recognizing that she was unlikely ever to be able to earn enough to enable her to live at the marital standard of living. Winnie has appealed, arguing that this award amounts to a prospective modification of indefinite spousal support without requiring proof of changed circumstances. Can the award be defended?

Two months before the initial two-year period of the award is over, Winnie moves to modify it on the ground that she has not completed the training necessary to renew her teaching certificate and so is not able to be self-supporting at the level expected at the time of divorce. She has been working part-time and looking unsuccessfully for full-time work. A vocational expert called by Harold testifies that she has been "minimally involved" in preparing for a career.

Harold first moves to dismiss Winnie's petition on the basis of *res judicata*. What arguments should the parties make?

If Harold loses the *res judicata* argument, what additional arguments should he make, and how should Winnie respond?

2. Hank and Wendy were married for 15 years. Both worked throughout the marriage. During the marriage Hank invented a process to produce wooden parts for curved windows and started his own business based on the invention. By the time of the divorce the business had sales of more than $1 million a year. Wendy was awarded 40 percent of the total marital assets (mostly stock in Hank's company), worth $283,465, as her share of the property. Hank and Wendy did not change their standard of living much when Hank's invention began to pay off, and Wendy earns enough to live at nearly the marital standard of living.

Has Wendy sacrificed education or career opportunities so as to entitle her to spousal support? Does her employment prove that she did not sacrifice? Has a homemaker necessarily made such a sacrifice? Under *LaRocque*'s fairness principle, should Wendy share in Hank's high income through spousal support? If she receives an award on this basis, has she been compensated twice for her contributions, since she received a share of the stock in his company?

3. Throughout Wilma and Fred's 20-year marriage, Wilma worked to support herself and Fred and their two children when the children were young. She was also the children's primary caretaker. Fred drank heavily much of the time and

worked only sporadically at unskilled jobs. Wilma has filed for divorce. Fred claims spousal support. On what theories might he be entitled to support? How should Wilma's lawyer argue against an award?

3.   Spousal Support for the Caregiving Parent?

PROBLEM

Wanda has filed for divorce from her husband, Herman, alleging incompatibility. They have two children, ages three and six years old. Wanda was employed as a teacher until her older child was born; since then she has remained at home. Wanda has requested spousal support sufficient to enable her to continue caring for her children. Herman opposes any award of permanent alimony and offers evidence that Wanda can obtain employment as a teacher earning $24,000 per year. Herman offers to pay day-care costs for the children, the total cost of which will be $10,000 per year for both children. What arguments should each party make at the hearing on Wanda's request for spousal support? In addition to the materials you have already read, consider the following.

EMPIRICAL DATA ON WORKING PARENTS

In 2003, both parents were employed in 60.7 percent of two-parent families. In 30.5 percent of two-parent families, only the father was employed, and in 5.5 percent only the mother was. Another way of looking at this phenomenon is by the labor force participation of mothers. In 2003, about 70 percent of mothers with children under age 18 were employed. Employment is more common among single mothers and among mothers of older children. Almost 78 percent of unmarried mothers were employed, compared to about 69 percent of married mothers. Of mothers with children younger than one year, 53.7 percent were employed. About 56 percent of unmarried mothers with infants younger than one were employed, compared to about 53 percent of married mothers. Bureau of Labor Statistics, Employment Characteristics of Families Summary (April 20, 2004).

THE GENERAL STATE OF THE LAW

UMDA §308(a)(2) provides that a caretaker of children may be eligible for spousal support even though she or he is otherwise capable of self-support,[17] and many cases have held that custodial parents of young children should receive spousal support to enable them to remain at home with the children. When spousal support is awarded because the recipient has custody of the children, it usually terminates at the latest when the youngest child attains the age of majority.

---

17. Professor Levy initially recommended that child support awards, rather than spousal support, include money for the custodian's maintenance. Robert J. Levy, Uniform Marriage and Divorce Legislation: A Preliminary Analysis 145 (1969).

As a practical matter, spousal and child support are often insufficient to provide for the needs of the children and the custodial parent, so the parent must work anyway. A review of state case law published in 1993 concluded that appellate case law in only one state, Missouri, consistently supports awarding long-term spousal support to enable a parent to stay at home with children, though sporadic cases from other states are noted. In other states the premium on self-sufficiency and the assumption that a relatively young person can be and should be self-sufficient prevail. Ann Laquer Estin, Maintenance, Alimony, and the Rehabilitation of Family Care, 71 N.C. L. Rev. 721, 729-738 (1993).

THE POLITICS AND SOCIAL VALUE OF CAREGIVING

ANN LAQUER ESTIN, *MAINTENANCE, ALIMONY, AND THE REHABILITATION OF FAMILY CARE,* 71 N.C. L. Rev. 729-738 (1993): In an earlier era, although family care was not compensated, and usually not legally recognized, it was clearly understood to be central to the family's functioning and it was structurally supported through a variety of legal and social devices — devices which have eroded over the past generation. Caregiving is even less recognized today. Despite the language of modern divorce statutes, caregiving is perceived not as an independent contribution to the family, but only as one half of a traditional gender-structured marriage pattern. . . .

Recent years have seen a dramatic polarization of views about family policy issues, and as these issues have become increasingly politicized, the significance of caregiving is further obscured. Women's traditional caregiving roles are either glorified and described as imminently in danger, or treated as the fundamental obstacle to full gender equality. In this debate, private choices around the organization of work and family life take on an added burden of moral and political significance. Those who glorify caregiving have seemed blind to its hazards, and those who demean it have seemed blind to its value. . . .

Despite our often polarized and politicized view of the family, there should be little dispute that caregiving is an essential attribute of family life, worthy of recognition in the law of divorce. . . . Support payments to caregivers would have two benefits: facilitating the care of children in the difficult period after divorce, and allocating to both parents the costs of putting children first *during* marriage. The literature in this area of family law suggests only one disadvantage to caregiver support remedies: the risk that they will foster traditional family roles, economic dependence, and the corresponding gender roles that many men and women find oppressive.

Although the argument against mandating traditional family roles may be strong, the argument against tolerating those roles is not. . . . There is no social consensus about the wisdom or value of moving toward gender-neutral marriage, in which family care and market labor are equally allocated.

TWILA PERRY, *ALIMONY: RACE, PRIVILEGE, AND DEPENDENCY IN THE SEARCH FOR THEORY,* 82 Geo. L.J. 2481, 2483-2484, 2513 (1994): Statistics indicate that Black women are awarded alimony at a significantly lower rate than white women. . . . It also appears that women in higher income marriages are more likely to receive alimony than women in lower income marriages. In light of this data, it is important that we examine the implications of women scholars devoting substantial attention to an issue that is of practical importance to relatively few women, and especially so few women of color. . . .

. . . [T]he marriage paradigm that has, to a great extent, shaped the discourse on developing a theory of alimony . . . has little relevance to the realities faced by most poor women of color and . . . , accordingly, most of the approaches to alimony based on it have little practical relevance to the lives of these women. I define the issue, however, as more than one of mere irrelevance or exclusion — I argue that the search to develop a theory of alimony may have serious negative implications for poor women of color, especially Black women. Specifically, the paradigmatic model of marriage and divorce has the potential to reinforce the subordination and marginalization of Black women in two ways: first by reinforcing privilege or an image of privilege for middle and upper-middle class white women in both marriage and divorce, and second, by reinforcing a hierarchy among women in which their value is determined by the presence or absence of legal ties to men, particularly affluent men. . . .

Although no-fault divorce has been appropriately criticized for its failure to protect women economically, it has generated one positive result. To some degree, no-fault divorce has served as an equalizer among women. In calling off the bargain that formerly ensured some women compensation for giving up their careers to care for their home, the law, since no-fault, has been sending a similar message to all women: it is not wise to depend on a man for your lifelong economic survival. The privilege of choice, that many middle or upper-middle class women once may have taken for granted is, more than ever, in jeopardy.

Indeed, it can be said that in some ways the lives of white mothers, either as a result of divorce or because they were never married, are becoming more similar to those of Black mothers. . . . The way that no-fault divorce has pulled the rug out from under women at some of the more comfortable levels of society can be seen as an opportunity for women from different social and economic backgrounds to consider their commonalities. . . . There may be increased connection and cooperation among women of diverse backgrounds if they all see themselves as having to play the multiple roles of parent and worker, without assuming economic dependence on a man.

D. DIVORCE AND NEW PROPERTY

1. Introduction

Traditionally interests that may broadly be characterized as "new property," such as pensions and other employment benefits, goodwill in small businesses, professional licenses, and educational degrees were not considered divisible property but as potential sources of income from which spousal support could be paid.

Since the 1970s, lawyers have aggressively and often successfully argued that these forms of wealth should be treated as property subject to division.[18]

As we have seen, former spouses who can be self-supporting often are not entitled to spousal support and so cannot share in employment-related interests through alimony. However, capacity for self-support does not bar property division. In addition, to the extent that an equal division of community or marital property is required or favored, courts that want to award one spouse the family home have often been able to find that the other spouse's interests in pension plans or business goodwill are intangible assets that offset such awards.[19] These circumstances have spurred efforts to expand the pot of interests called "property" for purposes of distribution at divorce.

On the other hand, if wealth associated with employment is treated as divisible property, distributions of pension benefits or professional goodwill will not be modifiable. Sometimes spouses want to characterize these interests as property precisely so that the court orders will not be changeable. However, some courts have been reluctant to deal with the interests in such a final fashion and have for that reason refused to call them "property."

If these interests are to be treated as property, courts ordinarily must assign a present value to them in the course of determining the total property division. However, because these interests typically take the form of a stream of payments of money payable over time, valuing them is difficult. If there were established markets in these interests, valuation could be determined by looking at market price. Often, though, there is no such market, and courts must use other techniques for assigning value. The following explains basic techniques that can be used.

NOTE: VALUING STREAMS OF PAYMENTS

Let's say that you have a goose that lays a golden egg every two weeks. What is it worth? The goose is surely worth more than what its meat and feathers would bring after its death. The meat and feathers constitute the goose's *salvage value*. Assets that produce income are almost always going to be worth more than their

---

18. In addition to the reasons discussed in the text, a well-known California decision on lawyer malpractice liability has probably motivated lawyers to press these claims as well. In Smith v. Lewis, 530 P.2d 589 (Cal. in bank 1975), the court held that an attorney had committed malpractice when he assumed that the husband's retirement benefits were separate property without researching the issue, at a time when the law was not entirely clear. The court awarded damages of $100,000.

19. Professor Herma Hill Kay has suggested that the California cases treating professional goodwill as divisible community property may be merely an effort to raise the total value of the community property to the point that the wife can receive the house as her half and the husband the goodwill as his half. Mary Ann Glendon, The New Family and the New Property 81, n.114 (1981). Lenore Weitzman found that the wives of men with substantial pensions were more likely than other wives to be awarded the family home in a home-pension trade-off. Lenore J. Weitzman, The Economics of Divorce: Social and Economic Consequences of Property, Alimony and Child Support Awards, 28 UCLA L. Rev. 1181, 1198-1199 (1981).

salvage value, although their total value includes their salvage value. Most of the assets we will discuss in this chapter are intangibles anyway.

We might try to value the goose by asking how much we paid for it, but what if we paid 59 cents because no one realized that it would lay golden eggs when it grew up? The goose's *book value* would be 59 cents, but this value is historical. It tells us nothing about the changes that have occurred in the goose or in the market for geese and thus has no necessary relationship to the goose's present market value. Besides, some of the assets we will discuss have no book value.

Since we expect that the goose will continue laying a golden egg every two weeks for some indefinite period of time, we are really trying to measure how much that stream of eggs is worth now. If we knew for sure how long the goose would continue to lay eggs and what the price of gold would be, we could easily calculate the total worth of the eggs that the goose will lay. But this sum would not be the value today of those eggs because of the *time value of money*. For example, let's say that the constant profit on one golden egg is $10 (the price we can get for the egg minus the costs of food and other expenses of producing it). A buyer would not pay $10 today for an egg to be delivered in one year because the buyer could invest the same $10 in an interest-bearing account and at the end of the year have $10 plus the interest it earned. Thus, the price today of one egg to be delivered in a year should be an amount that, when invested, will produce $10 in a year. Assuming an interest rate of 8 percent, the amount that must be invested today to earn $10 in one year is $10 divided by 1 plus the interest rate (here, 1.08), or $9.26. (The general formula is Present Value = Future Value divided by 1 + the interest rate. Fortunately, present-value tables are widely available.) This method of determining value is called the *discounted cash flow method*.

The critical choice in determining the present value is deciding what interest rate we assume. The higher the interest rate, the lower the present value will be. The interest rate depends on the current value of money and how uncertain our estimate is of the value of a thing. Valuing the goose is uncertain because we do not and cannot know for certain such critical facts as how long the goose will live, how long it will lay eggs, whether it will continue to lay regularly, and what the price of gold will be. Generally speaking, the more uncertain, or riskier, an investment is, the higher the interest rate will be, since people demand higher rates of return for risky investments. The discussion of assets in this chapter will include how interest rates, or rates of return, are chosen for purposes of valuing them. To the extent that the calculations take into account future uncertainties, they are based on actuarial assumptions for the hypothetical person, which almost always turn out to be inaccurate when applied to the real people involved.

2. *Pensions and Other Employment-Related Benefits*

Employment-related benefits, provided either by the employer or through public programs such as Social Security, are for many people the most important elements of economic security. Until the 1970s, though, these benefits hardly figured in economic settlements accompanying divorce. Employees' pension rights and other benefits were often very ephemeral; many plans provided that an employee had no absolute right to a pension unless he or she worked for the employer for many years and was employed by that employer at the time of retirement. Courts tended to hold that, under these conditions, pension rights could not be considered property.

Pension rights became more substantial and more common after 1975, the year in which the Employee Retirement Income Security Act (ERISA), 29 U.S.C. §§1001 et seq., became effective.[20] Pension plans that are "qualified" under ERISA and related provisions of the Internal Revenue Code provide employers and employees with substantial federal income tax advantages. (The employer's contributions to the plan are deductible as a business expense, and the contributions to the plan and the income they produce are not income to an employee until retirement benefits are paid.) Most important for our purposes, employees covered by qualified plans are guaranteed that even after relatively short periods of employment, their interests in the plan will vest — that is, they will eventually be entitled to receive benefits through the plan. ERISA has made pension rights more substantial and thus more important at divorce, though they are not universal.

Retirement plans differ according to who pays for the plan and how benefits are determined. Both the employer and the employee contribute toward the cost of a *contributory* plan. Only the employer contributes to a *noncontributory* plan. If a plan is contributory, the employee's contributions are immediately vested, so the employee is entitled to them even if he or she quits participating in the plan before retirement. The employee's interest in the amount attributable to the employer's contributions may not vest until the employee has worked for a defined period of time, although ERISA limits how long the employer can delay vesting of pension rights.

Even if an employee's pension rights are vested, this does not mean the employee has an immediate right to payment. Employers can and typically do specify the earliest time at which an employee is eligible to draw retirement benefits — that is, when the benefits *mature*. Before this time the benefits are *unmatured*.

In *defined contribution* plans, each employee has a separate account, and the amount of the employee's benefits will depend on how much is in the account through contributions, interest earned, and any other increase in value when the employee begins to draw benefits. In *defined benefit* plans, an employee's benefits are determined on the basis of a formula, usually based on years of service and salary, which does not depend on the amount of contributions. Individual accounts are not maintained for each employee. Either type of plan can be contributory or noncontributory.

The next case discusses these differences further in the context of deciding whether to treat pension rights as divisible property at divorce.

---

20. Between 1975 and 1987 the number of private pension plans more than doubled, from 340,000 to 870,000, and annual contributions to pension plans rose to $95 billion from $37.1 billion. Peter J. Strauss, Robert Wolf & Dana Shilling, Aging and the Law 110 (1990).

Laing v. Laing

741 P.2d 649 (Alaska 1987)

Compton, J. . . . The trial court awarded Kenneth his pension with a present value of $27,000 and awarded Marla offsetting marital assets. Kenneth challenges the award on the grounds that there was insufficient evidence to support the $27,000 figure and that Marla's share should not have been awarded in a lump sum. We first address the issue whether the trial court properly characterized Kenneth's nonvested pension as marital property. . . .

Alaska thus follows the majority rule that "vested" pension and retirement benefits are subject to division by a divorce court. Annotation, Pension or Retirement Benefits as Subject to Award or Division by Court in Settlement of Property Rights Between Spouses, 94 A.L.R.3d 176, 182 [hereafter Annot., Pension Rights]. Whether the majority rule can also be applied with regard to Kenneth's nonvested[21] pension rights is a question of first impression in Alaska. Jurisdictions are split on this issue. Those in which nonvested pensions are held not to be divisible marital property rely primarily on the notion that such interests are too speculative and cannot be said to constitute a property right.

The trend, however, is to consider pensions as marital property regardless of whether they have vested.

Supporting this trend is the reasoning that the contingent nature of a nonvested pension presents simply a valuation problem, not bearing on the non-employee spouse's entitlement to a just share of the marital assets. Pension benefits are generally viewed as deferred compensation for services rendered and the employee spouse's right thereto is a contractual right. . . . One commentator provides another persuasive reason for characterizing even nonvested pensions as divisible marital assets:

The non-employee spouse's contribution to the pension asset is exactly the same whether the pension be labeled a mere *expectancy*, or a *contingent future interest*.

L. Golden, Equitable Distribution of Property 172 (1983) (emphasis in original). We are persuaded that the contingencies that may prevent the employee spouse from ever collecting his or her nonvested pension should not bar the non-employee spouse from recovering a share if the pension is in fact paid out. Indeed, a contrary rule would frustrate the statutory command that Alaska courts effect a "just division of the marital assets." This obviously requires that the trial court consider the financial circumstances of each party. It would be wholly inconsistent with this policy to ignore the existence of so substantial an asset as a party's pension

---

21. The term *nonvested* is used here to mean that if Kenneth's employment were to terminate immediately he would be entitled to no future retirement or pension benefits. The term is not used, as some courts have done, to indicate merely that the pension rights have not matured. When a pension or retirement benefits plan is vested but not matured, an employee is absolutely entitled to benefits, though he is not entitled to actual payments until some future date. (citations omitted)

rights. In this regard, we adopt the rule representing the current trend and recognize nonvested pension rights as a marital asset.

B. VALUATION AND DIVISION

The trial court assigned a present value of $27,000 to Kenneth's pension, awarded it to him and awarded Marla offsetting assets. Kenneth asserts that there was insufficient evidence to support the present value figure adopted by the trial court. For the reasons stated below we reject generally the present value method of dividing nonvested pensions and remand the case.

Courts have used two primary methods of valuing and dividing pension benefits, whether vested or nonvested, upon divorce: the present value approach and the reserved jurisdiction approach.[22]

In the present value approach, a court faced with a nonvested pension factors the contingencies to collection into a "reduced to present value" calculation. A similar reduction to present value can easily be obtained for a vested pension. The court determines a fraction of the present value representing the marital contribution to the accrued pension benefits. The numerator of this fraction is the number of years the pension has accrued during the marriage; the denominator is the total number of years during which the employee spouse's pension has accrued. Once this calculation is complete, the court may award the pension interest to the employee spouse and give the non-employee spouse an offsetting amount of other assets.

Citing the goal that a property settlement should provide a final resolution of a divorcing couple's financial affairs, a number of courts have stated that the present value approach is preferred where a present value can be attached to the pension and where there exist other marital assets sufficient to satisfy the non-employee spouse's claim without undue hardship on the employee spouse.

We nonetheless find this method unacceptable. Since the non-employee spouse receives his or her share in a lump sum at the time of the divorce, the method unfairly places all risk of possible forfeiture on the employee spouse. While the probability of forfeiture is supposedly factored in to reduce the present value amount determined at the time of the divorce, it is clear that the non-employee spouse has taken only a reduction in the amount of the award whereas the employee spouse loses the entire amount awarded to the non-employee spouse in the event of forfeiture. We find this approach to be inherently unfair.

---

22. A third possible method of division is to award the nonemployee spouse a percentage of the employee spouse's contribution to the plan plus interest. (citations omitted) We reject this method because it ignores employer contributions which, to the extent they were made during marriage, ought to be considered a marital asset.

Resort to this method is usually justified on the ground that uncertainties in valuation of a particular retirement plan prevents any other method of valuation. (citation omitted) But the reserved jurisdiction method, of which we approve, would appear to cover any such circumstance and would more fairly compensate the nonemployee spouse for his or her contribution to this marital asset.

In the other scheme used by the courts for valuation and division of a pension, the reserved jurisdiction approach, the trial court retains jurisdiction and orders the employee spouse to pay to the former spouse a fraction of each pension payment actually received. This scheme more evenly allocates the risk of forfeiture between the parties, although it also runs counter to our expressed preference for finalizing a couple's financial affairs as soon as possible.

However, reserving jurisdiction does not necessarily mean that a protracted pay-out to the former spouse will follow vesting. Once vesting occurs, that portion of the pension which is marital property can be calculated as of the time of the divorce. The non-employee spouse's share of this figure may, in appropriate cases, be payable in a lump sum or in installments which do not particularly have to be keyed to the time that the pension benefits are actually received.

We are persuaded that reserving jurisdiction more closely parallels the societal goals of retirement benefits generally — that is, to provide financial security to participants. A present lump sum award to the non-employee spouse calculated on a pension which has not vested does not necessarily promote this purpose. The fact is that nonvested pensions are sometimes forfeited, often for reasons which properly should be within the power of the employee to decide, and sometimes for reasons which are entirely beyond the control of the employee. There is no reliable way to factor the contingency of forfeiture into a present value calculation. Thus, we are willing to accept a degree of continued financial entanglement insofar as that may be necessary to effect a just division of nonvested pension rights.

We adopt the following approach for dividing nonvested pension rights after divorce. First, because the nonvested pension may, by definition, be forfeited in its entirety, it should not be considered when the trial court makes the initial property division at the time of the divorce. If and when the employee spouse's pension rights vest and if the parties are unable to reach an agreement on their own, the non-employee spouse may at any time thereafter seek an order dividing the pension. This is to be done in the same manner as if the pension had been vested at the time of the divorce. Realistically, there is such a variety of pension plan designs that it is impossible to develop any one detailed formula that will produce an equitable result in every instance. Once the pension has vested, the trial court can determine whether the present value or the retained jurisdiction approach is appropriate in a given case and adapt that approach to the specific circumstances presented.

As one possible resolution, we direct the trial court on remand to investigate the applicability of the Retirement Equity Act of 1984 (REACT), Pub. L. No. 98-397, 98 Stat. 1426 (1984). REACT applies to retirement benefit plans covered by the Employee Retirement Income Security Act of 1974 (ERISA), Pub. L. No. 93-406, 88 Stat. 829 (1974). The record does not indicate whether Kenneth's UNO-CAL pension was such a plan. Under REACT, a "qualified domestic relations order" (QDRO) can be filed with the administrator of the employee spouse's pension plan. 29 U.S.C. 1056(d)(3). If and when the employee spouse's pension vests and matures, the plan administrator makes appropriate payments directly to the non-employee former spouse in accordance with the QDRO. 29 U.S.C. 1056(d)(3)(A). See generally Troyan, Pension Evaluation for Marriage Dissolution

Actions: A Pension Evaluator's Perspective, in J. McCahey, Valuation and Distribution of Marital Property 16 §§45.26-45.39, at 45-105 to 45-136.

REACT thus solves the problem of continuing financial entanglement between former spouses. Moreover, because payments are made directly by the plan, the non-employee spouse is sure to receive the payments to which he or she is entitled.[23] In certain circumstances, REACT allows the non-employee spouse to convert his or her share of the benefits to pay status independently of the employee spouse. 29 U.S.C. §1056(d)(3)(E).

We reverse and remand for a reevaluation of Kenneth's nonvested pension. If Kenneth's UNOCAL plan is not covered by ERISA, we direct the trial court to retain jurisdiction so that an appropriate division may be made if and when Kenneth's pension becomes vested.

[Dissenting opinion of Justice Burke, concluding that trial court's use of the present value method of distribution was proper in this case, omitted.]

NOTES AND QUESTIONS

1. The court's analysis assumes that the principal problem with treating pensions as property is that they may be "mere expectancies" rather than "contingent future interests." What problem is the court addressing? Is a vested pension right more or less contingent than a nonvested one? Is a matured right more or less contingent than an unmatured one? Why should the contingent nature of pension rights mean that they are not property for purposes of divorce?

Virtually all courts and many statutes now treat vested pension rights as property subject to division, and most treat nonvested rights in the same way.

2. Another important feature of traditional property is its transferability. Pension benefits typically are not transferable because ERISA requires that an employee's interests not be assignable or alienable. Why doesn't this feature lead courts to conclude that pensions are not property divisible at divorce?

3. *Laing* discusses the two basic ways that courts divide pensions. Under the "present value" or "offset" approach, the court determines the present value of the employee spouse's right to receive payments from the pension in the future, awards those rights to the employee, and awards the nonemployee spouse other marital property in lieu of his or her share of the pension.

Under the "if, as, and when" approach, each spouse receives a fractional share of each pension payment as it comes due. Before the Retirement Equity Act of 1984 was enacted, courts usually implemented this method by ordering the employee to pay the non-employee his or her share of each payment as it came in. In some jurisdictions the pension plan administrator was supposed to pay the nonemployee directly, on the theory that the court order dividing the pension constituted an assignment to the nonemployee of part of the employee's rights. The safest way to

---

23. It is important to note that REACT affects only the method by which a non-employee spouse may collect ERISA pension benefits. The fact and amount of his or her entitlement to the former spouse's pension is determined by state law. 29 U.S.C. §1056(d)(3)(B).

ensure that the plan would make these payments was to join the plan as a party to the divorce action, but it was not always clear whether this was possible.

What are the advantages and disadvantages of each of these approaches? *Laing* criticizes the use of the offset method for nonvested pensions but suggests that it might be appropriate for a vested pension. Why? The *Laing* court focuses only on negative changes in an employee's retirement prospects, but positive changes can also occur. For a discussion of the methods of division, *see* Elizabeth Barket Brandt, Valuation, Allocation, and Distribution of Retirement Plans at Divorce; Where Are We? 35 Fam. L.Q. 469 (2001). *See also* Marvin Snyder, Challenges in Valuing Pension Plans, 35 Fam. L.Q. 235 (2001).

In note 22 the *Laing* court discussed and rejected a third method of dividing the pension. What is wrong with this approach?

4. When nonvested pensions were not treated as property, the income from a pension could be considered in determining spousal support. Trial judges sometimes award spousal support "in lieu of" dividing a pension. Are there advantages to handling pensions this way? Appellate courts usually hold that this solution is reversible error. Why?

5. In jurisdictions that permit only marital property to be divided at divorce, a pension earned in part before marriage and in part during marriage must be divided into marital and nonmarital shares. Most courts use the "time rule," which *Laing* describes. The value of the pension rights is multiplied by a fraction whose numerator is the number of years the pension accrued during the marriage and whose denominator is the total number of years the pension accrued. Thus, if at the time of divorce the employee spouse has accrued rights for 20 years and if the spouses have been married for 15 of those years, 15/20, or three-quarters, of the pension rights are marital property.

Some courts use an accrual method to determine the marital share. Under this method the present value of accrued benefits on the date of the marriage is subtracted from the present value of the total accrued benefits on the date of the divorce, and the difference is the value of the benefits earned during marriage. If the pension benefit amounts are linked to the employee's salary, some courts determine the marital share by dividing the total salary the employee received during the marriage by the total salary received throughout the entire period of employment and multiplying this fraction by the total pension benefits. Thus, if an employee earned $150,000 during the marriage and $300,000 throughout his or her employment with the company, $150,000/$300,000, or half, of the pension benefits would be marital property.

In re Marriage of Hunt, 909 P.2d 525 (Colo. 1995), involved husbands' appeals from orders that used the time rule to divide their pension interests. The husbands argued that this method improperly allowed their former wives to share in increases in value of the pensions attributable to increases in the husbands' postdivorce pay raises. After reviewing both the time rule and the accrual rule, the court upheld use of the time rule, particularly where the pension division is deferred. The court said:

The "time rule" formula recognizes that post-divorce pension benefit enhancements defy easy categorization. Typically, there is commingling of effort undertaken during the marriage and after the marriage which together enhance the value of the future benefit. The employee spouse's ability to enhance the future benefit after the marriage frequently builds on foundation work and efforts undertaken during the marriage. Hence, the theory underlying the "time rule" formula is called the "marital foundation" theory. We agree with the cases . . . that accept the "marital foundation" theory. Thus, we find that although sometimes related to effort, post-dissolution enhancement must be treated identically to passive increases such as cost-of-living increases or increases ascribable to pension plan changes in order to equitably apportion the risks of delay inherent in the deferred distribution and reserve jurisdiction methods for distribution of benefits.

909 P.2d at 534. Further, the court said that the time rule "removes courts from the complicated, time-consuming, inefficient, and hopelessly flawed task of evaluating the enhancement and denominating the enhancement as either marital, separate, passive or some combination thereof." *Id.* at 535. *Contra* Koelsch v. Koelsch, 713 P.2d 1234 (Ariz. 1986).

In McClary v. Thompson, 65 S.W.3d 829 (Tex. App. 2002), a husband argued that under Texas community property law, the inception of title analysis should be used to determine the character of a pension which the husband began to contribute to before marriage and which he contributed to earn throughout the marriage. The court rejected his argument, distinguishing pensions from other assets which are analyzed under the inception of title principle, such as real estate, on the basis that the pension is employee compensation earned during the marriage. The court held that benefits that accrue during the marriage are community property, and benefits earned before the marriage are premarital separate property. For a discussion of the inception of title rule, see page 420.

For a detailed description of the issues that arise in dividing a defined benefit pension so that each former spouse owns his or her own share, *see* Brett R. Turner, A Possible New Alternative for Deferred Distribution of Retirement Benefits: The Separate Interest Approach, 13 (11) Divorce Litig. 1 (2001). *See also* Elizabeth Barket Brandt, Valuation, Allocation, and Distribution of Retirement Plans at Divorce; Where Are We? 35 Fam. L.Q. 469 (2001).

6. For pension plans governed by ERISA, employees have the option of receiving their benefits in the form of a joint and survivor annuity, which provides for periodic payments to the retired employee and after the employee's death to the surviving spouse. If an employee divorces before retirement, REA allows the nonemployee former spouse to retain joint and survivor annuity benefits, if that the QDRO expressly so provides. A QDRO can also assign *only* survivor benefits to the nonemployee spouse, which means that the nonemployee will receive benefits only at the death of the employee. If the former spouse is the full survivor beneficiary, the employee cannot designate any future spouse as a beneficiary.

The benefits that a former spouse may receive under a joint and survivor annuity should be distinguished from that spouse's share of the employee's benefits. If the plan is a defined contribution plan, the QDRO should in effect establish two separate accounts, one for each spouse, so that the rights of neither will be affected by the other's death (assuming that the rights are vested). However, if the plan is a defined benefit plan and if the employee dies before the nonemployee has begun to draw benefits, ordinarily the nonemployee will lose whatever rights he or she may have had. If the nonemployee is already receiving benefits when the employee dies, he or she will continue to receive them because the nonemployee will have selected a form of benefit related to his or her own life expectancy rather than to the life expectancy of the employee.

Whether an employee's survivors will be entitled to any kind of death benefit if the employee dies before retiring depends on the terms of the plan. To the extent that the funds in the pension were contributed by the employee, there will be a death benefit, and often plans provide a death benefit as to the employee's vested rights based on the employer's contributions. The employee designates who gets the death benefit.

7. Employees may have a number of other kinds of benefits, which may or may not be intended to provide for retirement. Many of these are treated as defined contribution plans for purposes of property distribution at divorce. They include individual retirement accounts, Keogh plans, profit-sharing plans, stock bonus plans, employee stock ownership plans, and thrift and savings plans. The well-known divorce dispute between Gary Wendt, the president and CEO of GE Capital Services, and his wife of 32 years, Lorna, ultimately turned on questions of the valuation and method of dividing of stock options. Wendt v. Wendt, 757 A.2d 1225 (Conn. App. 2000).

One issue that commonly arises is whether unexercised stock options are property at all. The Pennsylvania Supreme Court concluded that employee stock options, which were earned during the marriage, but have not vested and cannot be exercised until after the parties' separation, should be treated like pension benefits. They are thus divisible marital property, which should be valued to take into account any uncertainty about their future realization. Fisher v. Fisher, 769 A.2d 1165 (Pa. 2001). *Contra* In re Huston, 967 P.2d 181 (Colo. App. 1998) (concluding that unvested stock options are a mere expectancy and therefore not property. *See also* Fountain v. Fountain, 559 S.E.2d 25 (N.C. App. 2002); In re Frederick, 578 N.E.2d 612 (1991); DeJesus v. DeJesus, 687 N.E.2d 1319 (N.Y. 1997); In re Marriage of Huston, 967 P.2d 181 (Colo. App. 1998); Kapfer v. Kapfer, 419 S.E.2d 464 (1992). A number of courts have also treated accrued vacation and sick leave that can be cashed in when an employee retires as divisible property. *See, e.g,* Schober v. Schober, 692 P.2d 267 (Alaska 1984); Lesko v. Lesko, 457 N.W.2d 695 (Mich. App. 1990); Ryan v. Ryan, 619 A.2d 692 (N.J. Super 1992). *Contra* Thomasian v. Thomasian, 556 A.2d 675 (Md. App. 1989).

Recent articles on stock options include David S. Rosettenstein, Exploring the Use of the Time Rule in the Distribution of Stock Options on Divorce, 35 Fam. L.Q. 263 (2001), and The ALI Proposals and the Distribution of Stock Options and Restricted Stock on Divorce: The Risks of Theory Meet the Theory of Risk, 8 Wm. & Mary J. Women & L. 243 (2002); Tracy A. Thomas, The New Marital Property of Employee Stock Options, 35 Fam. L.Q. 497 (2001); Diana Richmond, The Challenges of Stock Options, 35 Fam. L.Q. 251 (2001); Robert J. Durst II, Stock Options: A Significant but Unsettled Issue in the Distribution of Marital Assets, 17 J. Am. Acad. Matrimonial L. 275 (2001).

8. One of the most valuable employment-related benefits is the right to participate in group health or life insurance, because group insurance may not

require proof of insurability and group rates are often substantially lower than the cost of similar coverage under an individual policy. Often an employee's dependents, including a spouse, can participate in the group plan, but those plans typically provide that coverage terminates when a person no longer qualifies as a dependent — for example, when a spouse becomes a divorced former spouse. Federal and state statutes now protect divorced spouses against loss of health insurance coverage. The Consolidated Omnibus Budget Reconciliation Act of 1985 (COBRA) amended the Internal Revenue Code and related sections of ERISA and the Public Health Service Act to require that health insurance plans permit divorced spouses to continue participating in their former spouses' plans for up to 36 months following a divorce. 26 U.S.C. §4980B (1990). Spouses must pay premiums to continue participating. In addition, some states have statutes, some of them pre-dating COBRA, that give divorced people the right to continue participating in group health insurance programs through their former spouses' employment for a limited time.

PROBLEMS

1. Wanda was awarded her pension, and Herman received other property as an offset for his share. Wanda's pension has matured, and she is receiving monthly payments from it. Should these monthly payments be considered income to Wanda from which she could be ordered to pay Herman spousal support, or would that allow Herman to double-dip? If the pension was divided by awarding Herman a fractional share of each payment, should these payments be treated as his income in determining spousal support issues?

2. When Winnie and Harold were divorced, Harold was working as a high-level manager at Big Company. Six years later Harold was offered an attractive early retirement package that significantly increased the amount of his retirement benefits. If Winnie had received an increased share of marital property in lieu of an interest in Harold's pension, would she have a claim to some portion of these benefits that were not anticipated when they divorced? If she had been awarded her share in the pension retirement benefits in the form of an "if, as, and when" order, would she be entitled to share in the enhanced package of benefits?

3. During her marriage to Gerald, Mary was awarded stock options. At the time that the options were to expire, the community did not have the funds to exercise the options, and so Mary used her separate funds to exercise the options and purchase the stocks. At the time, the options were worth $50,000, and the purchase price was $40,000. Mary and Gerald are divorcing. The stocks are worth $ 135,000. What portion of the stocks is community or marital property? What portion, if any, is Mary's separate property?

NOTE: SOCIAL SECURITY, MILITARY, AND OTHER PENSIONS

Approximately 95 percent of all American workers are covered by Social Security. Workers may also be covered by other federal retirement programs, such as the Railroad Retirement Act or a military pension provision. Numerous cases, including several from the Supreme Court, have considered whether these retirement benefits should be treated like the private pension in *Laing*. Typically, state courts have treated federal pensions like other pensions and have applied their marital property law to them. However, the Supreme Court has held that statutory provisions that prevent covered employees from assigning or alienating their pension rights were intended to prevent courts from treating these rights as marital property, and, under the supremacy clause of the Constitution, this federal purpose controls.

The first of these cases was Hisquierdo v. Hisquierdo, 439 U.S. 572 (1979), which dealt with a husband's pension benefits under the federal Railroad Retirement Act. The Supreme Court concluded that the anti-assignment and anti-alienation provisions are intended to ensure that the benefits actually reach the beneficiary and that treating the benefits as divisible community property conflicts with this purpose. The Railroad Retirement Act applies to relatively few people, but other federal pension statutes also contain anti-assignment and anti-alienation clauses like those in the railroad act.

Military Retirement Benefits   In McCarty v. McCarty, 453 U.S. 210 (1981), the Court held that states could not treat military retirement benefits as marital property, based on the statutes' anti-assignment and anti-alienation clauses and Congress's underlying purposes for creating military retirement benefits. As in *Hisquierdo*, the Court held that a state divorce court could not award the spouse who was not in the military either a share of the retirement benefit itself or an offsetting share of other, divisible property. In 1982, in response to *McCarty*, Congress enacted the Uniformed Services Former Spouses' Protection Act (USFSPA), 10 U.S.C. §§1072, 1076, 1086, 1401, 1408, 1447, 1448, 1450, which provides that each state's divorce courts may treat disposable military retired pay or retainer pay according to the state law governing division of marital property.

USFSPA allows former spouses of military personnel to obtain court-ordered payments of property settlements directly from the appropriate military finance center if during the marriage the spouse who was a member of the armed forces performed at least ten years of service credited toward earning the retirement benefits. The former spouse's claim cannot exceed 50 percent of the service member's disposable retired or retainer pay. (When two or more former spouses have claims, direct payments cannot exceed in the aggregate 65 percent.) If the ten-year test is not met, the divorce court can still treat the pension as divisible marital property, but the division can be enforced only by the offset method or by ordering the military spouse to pay a share of pension payments to the former spouse. Similarly, the court can also award the spouse who was not in the military more than 50 percent of the benefits, but amounts above 50 percent cannot be collected directly from the military finance center. Former spouses of military personnel may also receive direct payment of court-ordered spousal or child support regardless of the length of the marriage. Military personnel may designate their former spouses as beneficiaries of death benefits as well.

Military personnel who are disabled may receive disability benefits if they waive a corresponding amount of retirement pay, and it is often to their benefit to do so because disability payments are exempt from federal, state, and local income taxes, while retirement pay is not. In Mansell v. Mansell, 490 U.S. 581 (1989), the Supreme Court considered whether a wife whose former husband made such a waiver after the divorce court had awarded her a share of his military retirement benefits was entitled to a share of his disability benefits. Under California state law, if a former spouse receives disability pay in lieu of retirement benefits, that portion of the disability pay is divisible community property. The California courts applied this rule, interpreting USFSPA as eliminating federal preemption of state law regarding military retirement pay. The Supreme Court, however, held that USFSPA did not completely eliminate federal preemption and concluded that military disability pay is not divisible marital property because the USFSPA definition of "disposable retired or retainer pay" excludes retirement pay waived to receive disability payments. The effect was that the former wife lost almost 30 percent of the monthly retirement income she would otherwise have received as community property. Justices O'Connor and Blackmun dissented, saying USFSPA should be interpreted as eliminating federal preemption so as to allow states to treat military pensions in the same way that they treat other pensions. Since Mansell, many cases concerning military retirees' postdivorce waiver of retirement pay to receive disability benefits have been decided. Most state courts have found a way to protect the retirees' former spouses. Commonly, separation agreements or court orders contain indemnity provisions, which are not considered to violate the USFSPA because the retiree is free to use any assets to satisfy the obligation. Surratt v. Surratt, S.W.3d (Ark. App. 2004), citing and discussing cases. But see Halstead v. Halstead, 596 S.E.2d 353 (N.C. App. 2004) (error for court to award spouse an unequal distribution of the military retirement benefits, where the inequality was calculated to replace the amount that spouse lost because of the disability pay election).

Civil Service Pensions   The Civil Service Act allows treatment of civil service benefits as marital property divisible at divorce, 5 U.S.C. §8345(j)(1).

Social Security   Most courts have held that Social Security benefits are not property subject to division and that their value may not be considered in the division of property. Some courts reach this conclusion based on the anti-assignment and anti-alienation provisions of the Social Security Act, 42 U.S.C. §407. Further, the Social Security Act exempts from the anti-alienation protections actions to enforce a beneficiary's legal obligations to support a spouse, former spouse, or children. 42 U.S.C. §659. This exemption specifically does not apply to "any payment or transfer of property or its value by an individual to the spouse or former spouse of the individual in compliance with any community property settlement, equitable distribution of property, or other division of property between spouses or former spouses." 42 U.S.C. §659(i)(3)(B)(ii). (Though Social Security benefits may not be treated as divisible marital property, payments that a former spouse receives may be treated as income from which spousal support can be paid.)

Finally, the divorced spouses are entitled to receive Social Security benefits on the account of the divorced spouse if they were married for at least ten years. 42 U.S.C. §402(b)(1). The benefit payable to a divorced spouse of a covered worker does not reduce the benefit payable to the worker. 42 U.S.C. §403(a)(3). If a divorced spouse worked and contributed enough to Social Security to be entitled to benefits independently, he or she must choose between these independent benefits and those based on the employment of the former spouse. The maximum that a person may receive on the account of a former spouse who is still living is 50 percent of the latter's benefit. Thus, a person whose independent benefits are greater than the benefits on the account of the former spouse loses the latter altogether. A divorced spouse may apply for dependency benefits when he or she reaches age 62 if the former spouse is also at least 62, even though the latter is not yet collecting Social Security.

In addition, a spouse who collects Social Security on the account of a former spouse must remain single to receive benefits. A person who has been married and divorced more than once may draw benefits on the account of whichever former spouse will provide the greatest benefits. And more than one former spouse may be able to claim benefits on the account of the same earner. For example, assume that Q, a wage earner, and R, a homemaker, were married for 13 years and divorced. Q then married S, who was also a homemaker, and they were divorced after 11 years. R remarried T, another wage earner, and they divorced after 15 years. R, who is not independently entitled to Social Security, may draw benefits on the account of either Q or T, and both R and S may draw benefits on the account of Q.

NOTE: ASSIGNING PRESENT VALUES TO AND DIVIDING PENSIONS

Defined-contribution and defined-benefit plans are valued in fundamentally different ways. Valuing an employee's interest in a defined-contribution plan is in principle simple. Since each employee has a separate account, the employee's interest is worth the current fair market value of the assets in the account. *See, e.g.,* Kanta v. Kanta, 479 N.W.2d 505 (S.D. 1991), and cases cited therein. If the assets are cash or its equivalent, the value will be the total amount of contributions plus any income they have earned. Valuation is more difficult if the assets are themselves more difficult to value, such as real estate.

Since defined-benefit plans do not maintain separate accounts for each employee, valuation of interests in these is more difficult. The problem is similar to valuing the goose that laid the golden eggs. Some courts have looked to convenient alternate figures to assign a value to a defined-benefit plan, such as what death benefit the employee's survivors would receive if the employee died now. But these values have no necessary relationship to the actual present value of the employee's right to receive payments from the pension in the future. Instead, actuarial principles are used to discount the value of those future payments to a present value. For examples of this process, *see* Kalinoski v. Kalinoski, 9 Fam. L. Rptr. 3033, 3037-3039 (Pa. Ct. Common Pleas 1982); Bishop v. Bishop, 440 S.E.2d 591 (N.C. App. 1994).

Often pension plans permit employees to choose from several alternative methods of payout, which may or may not be actuarially equivalent. While a lawyer may well be able to determine the value of benefits in a defined-contribution plan alone, most lawyers lack the expertise to value defined-benefit plan benefits.

Instead, they hire experts. The lawyer's responsibility here is to understand what kinds of analyses various experts perform so that an appropriate one can be chosen. In addition, a lawyer must understand generally the method that the expert uses to value a pension and, specifically, what assumptions about interest rates, mortality, and so on the expert made. These experts do not necessarily know family property law and so may not know that benefits earned after the divorce are not divisible or, in states that permit division only of property acquired during the marriage, that benefits attributable to premarital employment are not divisible. The lawyer must explain these rules to the expert and ensure that the calculations are consistent with them.

NOTES AND QUESTIONS

1. Much has been written about the choice of interest rate to be used in determining the present value of a pension. This choice is important because varying the interest rate by just 1 percent can produce a difference in the present value of as much as 24 percent, depending on the age of the person and other factors. Acceptable interest rates for these purposes include those that long-term bonds pay and those published monthly by the Pension Benefit Guaranty Corporation, an agency of the U.S. government that insures private defined-benefit pension plans. The corporation's interest rates are generally considered realistic and responsive to changing economic conditions.

2. Present-value calculations also require assumptions about the employee's life expectancy. Should standard mortality tables be used to estimate this, or are the tables used by the Pension Benefit Guaranty Corporation better? If an employee has a known medical problem, should the life expectancy be reduced to reflect this? What if the employee is unusually healthy?

3. When an employee who is still working will retire is often uncertain, and many pension plans allow for a range of possible retirement dates. Should the earliest possible retirement date be used in the present-value calculation? The average date? What if the benefits of an employee who takes early retirement are reduced? What if an employee who retires early receives a bonus?

4. For what risks should the value of the benefits be further discounted? The risk that the employee will die before retiring? The risk that the pension rights will become worthless because the employer goes bankrupt? Others?

NOTE: QUALIFIED DOMETIC RELATIONS ORDERS

As we have seen, the "if, as, and when" method of dividing a pension may require that an employee spouse pay the nonemployee a share of each payment received, creating the potential for enforcement problems and general friction. Another problem can arise if the employee has the right to choose when to retire. The nonemployee former spouse will probably want to begin receiving his or her share of the benefits at the employee's earliest possible retirement date, but the employee may not want to retire then. In In re Marriage of Gillmore, 629 P.2d 1 (1981), the trial court refused to order a husband who was eligible to be but not yet retired to pay his wife her share of his retirement benefits. The Supreme Court of California reversed, holding that the trial court's action impermissibly impaired the wife's interest by depriving her of the immediate enjoyment of it. The court said that the husband did not have to retire; it gave him the choice of paying her a lump sum equal to the present value of her interest or monthly payments of the amount she would have received if he had retired. The court in *Laing* solved the problem similarly, you will notice.

The Retirement Equity Act of 1984 (REA) solves these problems for pensions subject to ERISA. It provides that a divorce court may enter a qualified domestic relations order (QDRO), which directs the pension plan administrator to pay a portion of an employee's benefits to someone other than the employee. 29 U.S.C. §1056(d). The order can require that payments to the nonemployee begin before the employee actually retires, beginning on or after the earliest date on which the employee could retire. While most attention has been paid to using QDROs to effect division of pension rights through property distribution, they can also be used to effect payment of spousal or child support. The nonemployees to whom these payments are made are called "alternate payees."

REA imposes seven requirements that an order must meet to be a QDRO. If the order satisfies these requirements, the plan administrator must comply with it; if it does not, ERISA forbids the administrator to comply. To be a QDRO, an order must designate with specificity:

1. The name and the last known mailing address of the participant and the name and mailing address of each alternate payee;
2. The amount or percentage of the participant's benefits to be paid to each alternate payee or the manner in which the amount or percentage is to be determined;
3. The number of payments of the period to which the order applies; and
4. Each plan to which the order applies.

In addition, the order may *not* require a plan to:

5. Provide any type or form of benefit, or any option, not otherwise provided by the plan;
6. Provide increased benefits (determined on the basis of actuarial value[24]);
7. Pay benefits to an alternate payee that must be paid to another alternate payee under a previous QDRO.

REA makes clear that division of a pension through a QDRO does not violate the anti-assignment and anti-alienation requirements of ERISA. However, payment of benefits to one other than the covered employee without a QDRO does violate these requirements.

---

24. This requirement may require alternate valuations. For further discussion, *see* William M. Troyan, Pension Evaluation in Light of the Retirement Equity Act of 1984, 11 Fam. L. Rptr. 3005, 3006-3009 (1985).

A defined-contribution plan is divided by providing that the nonemployee receive an amount or percentage of the account balance. Because a defined-benefit plan has no account balance, the QDRO uses a flat figure or a formula to designate how much will be paid to the nonemployee.

REA only applies to plans governed by ERISA; therefore, QDROs are available only for these plans. Most retirement plans sponsored by private companies are governed by ERISA, and QDROs can also be used to divide IRC §403(b) tax-deferred annuities, which are often available to employees of universities and not-for-profit hospitals. The largest group of plans not covered are those provided for federal, state, and local government employees. Some states have legislation allowing QDROs to be used for state and local government pensions. In addition, some cases hold that anti-assignment and anti-alienation provisions in public employee retirement benefit plans do not prevent courts from dividing pension rights at divorce because the provisions were intended to protect family members as well as employees. *See, e.g.,* In re Marriage of Branstetter, 508 N.W.2d 638 (Iowa 1993); Moran v. Moran, 612 A.2d 26 (R.I. 1992).

For more information *see* David Clayton Carrad, QDRO Malpractice 2.0: The Next Generation, 14 Divorce Litig. 5 (May 2002).

3. Personal Injury Awards, Disability Pay, and Similar Interests

Implicit in classifying pension rights earned during the marriage as marital property is the assumption that they are compensation for labor performed during the marriage, rather than income after the marriage, even though they also clearly function as postretirement income. Other forms of wage-replacement payments, such as disability pay, workers' compensation, and personal injury recoveries, potentially present similar classification problems. The Kentucky Supreme Court, in Holman v. Holman, 84 S.W.3d 903, 906-907 (Ky. 2002), citing Gragg v. Gragg, 12 S.W.3d 412, 417 (Tenn. 2000), discussed the approaches:

> Those courts which hold that disability benefits constitute marital property have advanced several rationales for this conclusion. Under one approach, which has been referred to as the "mechanistic approach," courts consider whether disability benefits have been specifically excepted from the definition of marital property by statute. Disability benefits will be considered marital property unless there is a statutory provision specifically excluding disability benefits from the marital estate.
>
> Another rationale given in support of the mechanistic approach is that disability benefits should be considered marital property because the policy premiums were paid with marital funds or the marital estate acquired the benefits as a form of compensation for spousal labor during the marriage, much like a pension.
>
> However, the majority of courts considering the proper classification of disability benefits have adopted the analytical approach which focuses on the nature and purpose of the specific disability benefits at issue. Under this approach, benefits which actually compensate for disability are not classified as marital property because such benefits are personal to the spouse who receives them and compensate for loss of good health and replace lost earning capacity. However, where the facts warrant, courts utilizing the analytical approach will separate the benefits into a

retirement component and a true disability component, with the retirement component being classified as marital property and the disability component being classified as separate property. This approach has been applied both to disability benefits paid in connection with insurance coverage maintained by the disabled spouse's employer and to disability benefits paid in connection with a private policy of disability insurance acquired with marital funds during the marriage.

In addition to the approaches noted by the Tennessee Supreme Court is an approach recommended by the American Law Institute which, similar to the "analytical approach" or "purpose analysis," classifies such benefits according to the nature of the property they replace rather than by the source of the funds used to acquire the benefit: "Disability pay and workers' compensation benefits are marital property to the extent they replace income or benefits the recipient would have earned during the marriage but for the qualifying disability or injury."[25] Such benefits are therefore classified "as marital property to the extent they replace earnings during the marriage, and as separate property to the extent they replace earnings before or after the marriage, without regard to how or when the benefit was acquired."[26]

* * *

Pension and retirement benefits compensate individuals who live past retirement age. Such benefits constitute deferred compensation for services rendered and function as a substitute for life savings. . . . On the other hand, disability benefits do not substitute for savings but instead "protect against the inability of an individual to earn the salary or wages to which he or she was accustomed in the immediate past." Generally, therefore, disability benefits replace income which is lost before retirement. Logic dictates that disability benefits and income should be treated in the same manner since disability benefits are income replacement. Since the future income of each spouse is not classified as marital property, disability benefits which replace future income should not be classified as marital property.

We recognize that marital funds were used to acquire Appellant's disability coverage, but that does not change the character of the property the disability benefits replace. Disability coverage itself has been analogized to a form of term insurance "from which the marital partnership derived a full measure of protection during the marriage." Like the proceeds of property insurance that take their character from the nature of the property they replace and not from the source of the funds used to pay the insurance premium, Appellant's disability benefits should be classified according to the nature of the wages they replace rather than the source of the funds used to acquire his disability coverage.

NOTES AND QUESTIONS

1. Should classification of these rights depend on when they were earned, as classification of pensions does? If not, why not?

2. In Marsh v. Marsh, 437 S.E.2d 34, 36 (S.C. 1993), the court rejected the "analytic approach" to classification, which requires determination of the purpose

---

25. Principles of the Law of Family Dissolution: Analysis and Recommendations §4.08(2)(b) (American Law Institute, Proposed Final Draft, Part I, 1997).

26. *Id.* at §4.08(2)(b), comment (b).

of a personal injury award, in favor of the "literal or mechanistic approach." It concluded, therefore, that the award was marital property because it was received during the marriage. The court emphasized that classification was merely the first step in dividing the property.

> Classifying the property as marital merely gives the family court the authority to divide the award as the equities presented in the particular case may require. For example, the award or settlement may be the only asset of the marriage. The injured spouse who has collected against his or her tortfeasor or another liable party may be in better health and financial status than the other spouse who may have no responsible party from whom to collect. . . . Stretching the plain language of our statute which defines marital property to exclude personal injury awards and settlements, as other courts have done, would merely render the family court unable to award the portion of the proceeds which is deemed post-divorce economic loss or personal to the non-injured spouse. Therefore, applying the so-called analytic approach under our equitable division law would result in a more mechanical and rigid distribution than an application of the so-called mechanistic approach.
>
> Our well-developed statutory and common law of equitable distribution is premised on providing the family court the flexibility to view each case based on the individual circumstances peculiar to the parties involved and to fashion a division of the parties' assets in a manner that is uniquely fair to the parties concerned. We find the analytic approach would frustrate this policy. Accordingly, we hold proceeds of a personal injury settlement acquired during the marriage are marital property subject to the family court's jurisdiction.

What are the advantages of this approach? Is it consistent with the legislative scheme inherent in providing that only marital property is subject to equitable division?

3. For a thorough review and analysis of these issues, *see* Grace G. Blumberg, Marital Property Treatment of Pensions, Disability Pay, Workers' Compensation, and Other Wage Substitutes: An Insurance, or Replacement Analysis, 33 UCLA L. Rev. 1250 (1986).

PROBLEMS

1. Shirley, a plaintiff's personal injury attorney, and Howard are divorcing. They disagree about whether contingent fees that Shirley hopes to recover for some of the cases she worked on during the marriage are divisible marital property. Case 1 has been settled, but no payments have been made at the time of the divorce. In case 2, Shirley's client won a favorable jury verdict, but the case is on appeal. Case 3 is in the discovery stages. What arguments should Shirley and Howard make regarding the fees in each of these cases?

2. Hank inherited a Christmas tree farm from his parents during his marriage to Wilma. He worked on the farm, which remained his separate property. Wilma had a job in town. At the time of Hank and Wilma's divorce they disagree about whether immature trees, which will be ready to harvest in ten years, are divisible marital property. What arguments should each side make?

3. Virginia's mother created a trust during Virginia's marriage to Alex. Virginia is entitled to one-sixth of the income for her life. At her death her interest

goes to her children. When Virginia and Alex divorce, what portion of the trust, if any, is marital property subject to division?

4. Professional Practices and Other Closely Held Businesses

When one or both spouses own an interest in a small business, either as a sole proprietor, a partner, or a shareholder in a close corporation, dividing this interest may be the most important issue at divorce. Is the business interest divisible property at all? If so, how should this interest be valued (since there will probably not be a readily ascertainable market value) and divided?

When a spouse owns a personal service business, such as a professional practice, the problems are compounded. The practice likely owns some tangible assets — equipment, books, and accounts receivable — but, compared to a hardware store, these assets represent relatively little of the total value of the business. Expertise and services provided by the professional are relatively more important. Thus, there are real problems of defining what constitutes the property in the practice.

MAY V. MAY

589 S.E.2d 536 (W. Va. 2003)

DAVIS, Justice. . . .

The parties were married on June 23, 1979. . . .

On May 22, 2000, Mrs. May filed for divorce. On September 24, 2001, the Circuit Court of Hancock County granted the parties a divorce on the grounds of irreconcilable differences. The decree granting the divorce left unresolved the issue of the distribution of marital property. That issue was subsequently litigated in front of the family court judge.

During the proceeding before the family court judge, the parties presented expert testimony on the valuation of Dr. May's solo dental practice. Dr. May's expert valued the dental practice at $55,000.00, which included a 20% discount for lack of marketability. Mrs. May's expert placed a fair market value on the dental practice at $120,000.00. The fair market value included a value for goodwill.

By order entered on February 26, 2002, the family court judge adopted the dental practice valuation proffered by Mrs. May's expert. Mrs. May's equitable distribution payment for her interest in the dental practice was payable to her in the amount of $889.00 per month from June 1, 2004, to May 31, 2012. . . . From these rulings, Dr. May filed an appeal directly to this Court.

* * *

A. GENERAL DEFINITION OF GOODWILL

Goodwill may be defined generally as:

[T]he advantage or benefit, which is acquired by an establishment, beyond the mere value of the capital stock, funds, or property employed therein, in consequence of general public patronage and encouragement, which it receives from constant or habitual customers, on account of its local position, or common celebrity, or reputation for skill or affluence, or punctuality, or from other accidental circumstances or necessities, or even from ancient partialities or prejudices.

Essentially, goodwill is "the favor which the management of a business has won from the public, and probability that old customers will continue their patronage." Further, marketable "[g]oodwill associated with a business is an asset distributable upon dissolution of a marriage." However, "[w]here no market exists for goodwill, it should be considered to have no value."

B. GOODWILL IN DIVORCE LITIGATION: ENTERPRISE AND PROFESSIONAL

Essentially, there are two types of goodwill recognized by courts in divorce litigation: enterprise goodwill (also called commercial or professional goodwill) and personal goodwill (also called professional goodwill). A good working definition of enterprise goodwill is:

> Enterprise goodwill attaches to a business entity and is associated separately from the reputation of the owners. Product names, business locations, and skilled labor forces are common examples of enterprise goodwill. The asset has a determinable value because the enterprise goodwill of an ongoing business will transfer upon sale of the business to a willing buyer.

Courtney E. Beebe, "The Object of My Appraisal: Idaho's Approach to Valuing Goodwill as Community Property in *Chandler v. Chandler*," 39 Idaho L. Rev. 77, 83-84 (2002). Personal goodwill has been described as follows:

> [P]ersonal goodwill is associated with individuals. It is that part of increased earning capacity that results from the reputation, knowledge and skills of individual people. Accordingly, the goodwill of a service business, such as a professional practice, consists largely of personal goodwill.

Diane Green Smith, "'Til Success Do Us Part: How Illinois Promotes Inequities in Property Distribution Pursuant to Divorce by Excluding Professional Goodwill," 26 J. Marshall L. Rev. 147, 164-65 (1992). As discussed later in this opinion, the goodwill calculated by Mrs. May's expert was personal goodwill.

C. JURISDICTIONAL CONSIDERATION OF GOODWILL AS MARITAL PROPERTY

There is a split of authority on whether enterprise goodwill and/or personal goodwill in a professional practice may be characterized as marital property and thus equitably distributed. Three different approaches have developed.[27] We will

---

27. Our research revealed that the following jurisdictions have not squarely decided the issue of whether personal goodwill or enterprise goodwill of a professional practice

review each approach before determining the rule of law we now adopt in West Virginia.

1. No Distinction A large number of courts (13) *make no distinction* between personal and enterprise goodwill. These jurisdictions have taken the position that both personal and enterprise goodwill in a professional practice constitute marital property.[28] A case which best illustrates this position is Poore v. Poore, 75 N.C. App. 414, 331 S.E.2d 266 (1985).

Poore

In *Poore*, the wife sued for divorce from her husband. The husband was a dentist and the sole owner and operator of an incorporated dental practice. At the trial level, the husband produced expert evidence as to the value of his dental practice. The husband's expert opined that the practice had a net value of $7,549.00 and had no goodwill. The wife's expert contended that the dental practice had a value of $232,000.00, which included a value for personal goodwill. The trial court rejected the evidence by both experts and found that the dental practice had a value of $73,561.00. The trial court also found that the dental practice had no goodwill. Both parties appealed. An issue on appeal that is relevant to this case involved the wife's contention that the dental practice had goodwill.

did the dental practice have good will?

In addressing the issue of valuing a professional practice in general, the court in *Poore* made the following observations:

> The valuation of each individual practice will depend on its particular facts and circumstances. In valuing a professional practice, a court should consider the following components of the practice: (a) its fixed assets including cash, furniture, equipment, and other supplies; (b) its other assets including accounts receivable and the value of work in progress; (c) its goodwill, if any; and (d) its liabilities. Among the valuation approaches courts may find helpful are: (1) an earnings or market approach, which

---

constitutes marital property: Alabama, Georgia, Idaho, Iowa, Maine, and Vermont. In Ohio, the state Supreme Court has not addressed the issue. Consequently, there appears to be an unresolved split of authority among the Ohio appellate court districts. . . . Additionally, in Endres v. Endres, 532 N.W.2d 65 (S.D. 1995), the South Dakota Supreme Court found that enterprise goodwill in a professional practice is marital property, but expressly declined to decide whether personal goodwill in a professional practice is marital property.

28. *See* Wisner v. Wisner, 129 Ariz. 333, 631 P.2d 115 (App. 1981) (medical practice); In re Foster, 42 Cal. App. 3d 577, 117 Cal. Rptr. 49 (1974) (medical practice); In re Marriage of Huff, 834 P.2d 244 (Colo. 1992) (law practice); Heller v. Heller, 672 S.W.2d 945 (Ky. App. 1984) (accounting practice); Kowalesky v. Kowalesky, 148 Mich. App. 151, 384 N.W.2d 112 (1986) (dental practice); In re Marriage of Stufft, 286 Mont. 239, 950 P.2d 1373 (1997) (law practice); Ford v. Ford, 105 Nev. 672, 782 P.2d 1304 (1989) (medical practice); Dugan v. Dugan, 92 N.J. 423, 457 A.2d 1 (1983) (law practice); Moll v. Moll, 187 Misc. 2d 770, 722 N.Y.S.2d 732 (2001) (stockbroker); Poore v. Poore, 75 N.C. App. 414, 331 S.E.2d 266 (1985) (dental practice); Mitchell v. Mitchell, 104 N.M. 205, 719 P.2d 432 (App. 1986) (accounting practice); Sommers v. Sommers, 660 N.W.2d 586 (N.D. 2003) (medical practice); In re Marriage of Hall, 103 Wash. 2d 236, 692 P.2d 175 (1984) (medical practice).

bases the value of the practice on its market value, or the price which an outside buyer would pay for it taking into account its future earning capacity; and (2) a comparable sales approach which bases the value of the practice on sales of similar businesses or practices. Courts might also consider evidence of offers to buy or sell the particular practice or an interest therein.

Turning to the issue of valuing goodwill in a professional practice, the *Poore* Court stated:

> The component of a professional practice which is the most controversial and diffi-cult to value, and yet often the most valuable, is its goodwill. Goodwill is commonly defined as the expectation of continued public patronage. It is an intangible asset which defies precise definition and valuation. It is clear, however, that goodwill exists, that it has value, and that it has limited marketability. . . .
> There is no set rule for determining the value of the goodwill of a professional practice; rather, each case must be determined in light of its own particular facts. The determination of the existence and value of goodwill is a question of fact and not of law, and should be made with the aid of expert testimony. . . . Among the factors which may affect the value of goodwill and which therefore are relevant in valuing it are the age, health, and professional reputation of the practitioner, the nature of the practice, the length of time the practice has been in existence, its past profits, its com-parative professional success, and the value of its other assets.
> Various appraisal methods can be and have been used to value goodwill. Any legitimate method of valuation that measures the present value of goodwill by tak-ing into account past results, and not the postmarital efforts of the professional spouse, is a proper method of valuing goodwill. One method that has been widely accepted in other jurisdictions is to determine the market value of the goodwill, *i.e.*, the price that a willing buyer would pay to a willing seller for it. Another method that has been received favorabl[y] is a capitalization of excess earnings approach. . . . Under this approach, the value of goodwill is based in part on the amount by which the earnings of the professional spouse exceed that which would have been earned by a person with similar education, experience, and skill as an employee in the same general locale. It has also been suggested that the value of goodwill be based on one year's average gross income of the practice, or a percentage thereof, and that evidence of sales of comparable practices is relevant to the determination of its value.

The court in *Poore* reversed the trial court's ruling on the issue of the value of the dental practice and remanded the matter for reconsideration of the goodwill issue consistent with its opinion.

The underlying rationale for the position taken by *Poore* and the courts that follow its position was succinctly stated in Golden v. Golden, 270 Cal. App. 2d 401, 75 Cal. Rptr. 735 (1969):

> [I]n a divorce case, the good will of the husband's professional practice as a sole prac-titioner should be taken into consideration in determining the award to the wife. . . .
> [I]n a matrimonial matter, the practice of the sole practitioner husband will continue, with the same intangible value as it had during the marriage. Under the principles of community property law, the wife, by virtue of her position of wife, made to that

value the same contribution as does a wife to any of the husband's earnings and accumulations during marriage. She is as much entitled to be recompensed for that contribution as if it were represented by the increased value of stock in a family business.

2. Minority View   On the other hand, a minority of courts (5) have taken the position that neither personal nor enterprise goodwill in a professional practice constitutes marital property.[29] The case which best illustrates the position taken by these courts is Singley v. Singley, 846 So. 2d 1004 (Miss. 2002).

Singley

In *Singley*, the husband, who maintained a solo dental practice, filed for divorce. During the proceedings, an expert, appointed by the court, valued the husband's dental practice at $145,000.00. The valuation included goodwill. The trial court refused to admit evidence of the husband's expert on the issue of the value of his dental practice. The trial court thereafter equitably divided the value of the dental practice. The husband appealed to the state's mid-level appellate court arguing, among other things, that goodwill should not have been included in the valuation of his dental practice. The appellate court disagreed and affirmed the trial court's ruling. The husband thereafter appealed to the state Supreme Court.

* * *

The opinion in *Singley* further held:

We disagree with the Court of Appeals that goodwill may be included in the valuation of a business when the issue of that valuation concerns distribution in a divorce action. We join the jurisdictions that adhere to the principle that goodwill should not be used in determining the fair market value of a business, subject to equitable division in divorce cases.

The *Singley* court gave the following justification for its determination that goodwill in a professional practice is not marital property:

The term goodwill as used in determining valuation of a business for equitable distribution in a domestic matter is a rather nebulous term clearly illustrating the difficulty confronting experts in arriving at a fair, proper valuation. Goodwill within a business depends on the continued presence of the particular professional individual as a personal asset and any value that may attach to that business as a result of that person's presence. Thus, it is a value that exceeds the value of the physical building housing the business and the fixtures within the business. It becomes increasingly difficult for experts to place a value on goodwill because it is such a nebulous term

[handwritten margin notes: Singley; does not like goodwill b/c hard to determine]

29. *See* Powell v. Powell, 231 Kan. 456, 648 P.2d 218 (1982) (medical practice); Chance v. Chance, 694 So. 2d 613 (La. App. 1997) (medical practice); Singley v. Singley, 846 So. 2d 1004 (Miss. 2002) (dental practice); Donahue v. Donahue, 299 S.C. 353, 384 S.E.2d 741 (1989) (dental practice); Smith v. Smith, 709 S.W.2d 588 (Tenn. Ct. App. 1985) (law firm).

subject to change on a moment's notice due to many various factors which may suddenly occur, i.e., a lawsuit filed against the individual or the death and/or serious illness of the individual concerned preventing that person from continuing to participate in the business. It is also difficult to attribute the goodwill of the individual personally to the business. The difficulty is resolved however when we recognize that goodwill is simply not property; thus it cannot be deemed a divisible marital asset in a divorce action.

3. Majority View "[T]he majority of states [24] differentiate between 'enterprise goodwill,' . . . and 'personal goodwill[.]'" Courts in these states take the position that personal goodwill is not marital property, but that enterprise goodwill is marital property.[30] One of the leading cases discussing and adopting the distinction between personal goodwill and enterprise goodwill is the decision in Yoon v. Yoon, 711 N.E.2d 1265 (Ind. 1999).

In *Yoon*, the wife was granted a divorce from her husband. In granting the divorce the trial court assigned a value of $2,519,366.00 to the husband's medical practice. This figure included a value for goodwill. The husband appealed to a mid-level appellate court. There, the valuation was upheld. The husband then appealed to the state Supreme Court. In addressing the issue of goodwill, the Indiana Supreme Court stated:

> Goodwill has been described as the value of a business or practice that exceeds the combined value of the net assets used in the business. Goodwill in a professional practice may be attributable to the business enterprise itself by virtue of its existing arrangements with suppliers, customers or others, and its anticipated future customer base due to factors attributable to the business. It may also be attributable to the individual owner's personal skill, training or reputation. This distinction is

---

30. *See* Richmond v. Richmond, 779 P.2d 1211 (Alaska 1989) (law practice); Tortorich v. Tortorich, 50 Ark. App. 114, 902 S.W.2d 247 (1995) (dental practice); Eslami v. Eslami, 218 Conn. 801, 591 A.2d 411 (1991) (medical practice); E.E.C. v. E.J.C., 457 A.2d 688 (Del. 1983) (law practice); McDiarmid v. McDiarmid, 649 A.2d 810 (D.C. App. 1994) (law practice); Thompson v. Thompson, 576 So. 2d 267 (Fla. 1991) (law practice); Antolik v. Harvey, 7 Haw. App. 313, 761 P.2d 305 (1988) (chiropractic business); In re Marriage of Head, 273 Ill. App. 3d 404, 210 Ill. Dec. 270, 652 N.E.2d 1246 (1995) (medical practice); Yoon v. Yoon, 711 N.E.2d 1265 (Ind. 1999) (medical practice); Prahinski v. Prahinski, 75 Md. App. 113, 540 A.2d 833 (1988) (law practice); Goldman v. Goldman, 28 Mass. App. Ct. 603, 554 N.E.2d 860 (1990) (medical practice); Roth v. Roth, 406 N.W.2d 77 (Minn. App. 1987) (chiropractic business); Hanson v. Hanson, 738 S.W.2d 429 (Mo. 1987) (medical practice); Taylor v. Taylor, 222 Neb. 721, 386 N.W.2d 851 (1986) (medical practice); In re Watterworth, 821 A.2d 1107 (N.H. 2003) (medical practice); Travis v. Travis, 795 P.2d 96 (Okla. 1990) (law practice); Matter of Marriage of Maxwell, 128 Or. App. 565, 876 P.2d 811 (1994) (self-employed advertising copywriter); Butler v. Butler, 541 Pa. 364, 663 A.2d 148 (1995) (accounting firm); Moretti v. Moretti, 766 A.2d 925 (R.I. 2001) (professional landscaper); Guzman v. Guzman, 827 S.W.2d 445 (Tex. App. 1992) (accounting firm); Sorensen v. Sorensen, 839 P.2d 774 (Utah 1992) (law practice); Howell v. Howell, 31 Va. App. 332, 523 S.E.2d 514 (2000) (law practice); Peerenboom v. Peerenboom, 147 Wis. 2d 547, 433 N.W.2d 282 (App. 1988) (dental practice); Root v. Root, 65 P.3d 41 (Wyo. 2003) (medical practice).

sometimes reflected in the use of the term "enterprise goodwill," as opposed to "personal goodwill."

Enterprise goodwill is an asset of the business and accordingly is property that is divisible in a dissolution to the extent that it inheres in the business, independent of any single individual's personal efforts and will outlast any person's involvement in the business. It is not necessarily marketable in the sense that there is a ready and easily priced market for it, but it is in general transferrable to others and has a value to others. . . .

In contrast, the goodwill that depends on the continued presence of a particular individual is a personal asset, and any value that attaches to a business as a result of this "personal goodwill" represents nothing more than the future earning capacity of the individual and is not divisible. Professional goodwill as a divisible marital asset has received a variety of treatments in different jurisdictions, some distinguishing divisible enterprise goodwill from nondivisible personal goodwill and some not.

Accordingly, we join the states that exclude goodwill based on the personal attributes of the individual from the marital estate.

[B]efore including the goodwill of a self-employed business or professional practice in a marital estate, a court must determine that the goodwill is attributable to the business as opposed to the owner as an individual. If attributable to the individual, it is not a divisible asset and is properly considered only as future earning capacity that may affect the relative property division.

* * *

4. West Virginia   In our examination of the three views on the issue of goodwill in a professional practice, we believe the majority view represents the soundest legal approach. Therefore, we hold that "enterprise goodwill" is an asset of the business and may be attributed to a business by virtue of its existing arrangements with suppliers, customers or others, and its anticipated future customer base due to factors attributable to the business. Additionally, we hold that "personal goodwill" is a personal asset that depends on the continued presence of a particular individual and may be attributed to the individual owner's personal skill, training or reputation.

Furthermore, we hold that in determining whether goodwill should be valued for purposes of equitable distribution, courts must look to the precise nature of that goodwill. Personal goodwill, which is intrinsically tied to the attributes and/or skills of an individual, is not subject to equitable distribution. It is not a divisible asset. It is more properly considered as the individual's earning capacity that may affect property division and alimony. On the other hand, enterprise goodwill, which is wholly attributable to the business itself, is subject to equitable distribution.

* * *

D. VALUATION OF GOODWILL

Finally, once a professional practice has been determined to possess distributable goodwill, a value must be placed thereon. "[T]here are a variety of acceptable methods of valuing the goodwill of a professional practice, and no single method is to be preferred as a matter of law." . . . The Court in In re Marriage of Hall, 103 Wash. 2d 236, 692 P.2d 175, 179 (1984), pointed out that "[i]n valuing goodwill five major formulas have been articulated." *Hall* discussed the valuation methods as follows:

> Under the straight capitalization accounting method the average net profits of the practitioner are determined and this figure is capitalized at a definite rate, as, for example, 20 percent. This result is considered to be the total value of the business including both tangible and intangible assets. To determine the value of goodwill the book value of the business' assets are subtracted from the total value figure.
>
> The second accounting formula is the capitalization of excess earnings method. Under the pure capitalization of excess earnings the average net income is determined. From this figure an annual salary of average employee practitioner with like experience is subtracted. The remaining amount is multiplied by a fixed capitalization rate to determine the goodwill.
>
> The IRS variation of capitalized excess earnings method takes the average net income of the business for the last 5 years and subtracts a reasonable rate of return based on the business' average net tangible assets. From this amount a comparable net salary is subtracted. Finally, this remaining amount is capitalized at a definite rate. The resulting amount is goodwill.
>
> The fourth method, the market value approach, sets a value on professional goodwill by establishing what fair price would be obtained in the current open market if the practice were to be sold. This method necessitates that a professional practice has been recently sold, is in the process of being sold or is the subject of a recent offer to purchase. Otherwise, the value may be manipulated by the professional spouse.
>
> The fifth valuation method, the buy/sell agreement method, values goodwill by reliance on a recent actual sale or an unexercised existing option or contractual formula set forth in a partnership agreement or corporate agreement. Since the professional spouse may have been influenced by many factors other than fair market value in negotiating the terms of the agreement, courts relying on this method should inquire into the presence of such factors, as well as the arm's length nature of the transaction.

Hall, 692 P.2d at 178-80.

* * *

E. RESOLUTION OF INSTANT APPEAL

In the instant proceeding, Mrs. May's expert placed a fair market value on the dental practice at $120,000.00, which included a value of $80,568.00 for goodwill. It appears Mrs. May's expert used the IRS variation of capitalized excess earnings method to calculate a value for goodwill in Dr. May's dental practice. The family court judge adopted the valuation by Mrs. May's expert. For the reasons set forth herein, we find that the family court judge erred in adopting the goodwill portion of the report compiled by Mrs. May's expert.

During one of the hearings in this matter, Mrs. May's expert gave the following testimony regarding the nature of the goodwill assigned to the dental practice.

Q.   Well, did you include [enterprise] goodwill —
A.   In that value of Dr. May's practice what I included was the personal goodwill of Dr. May.

* * *

Q.   What is enterprise goodwill?

* * *

A.   [Enterprise] goodwill is that goodwill which is tied and associated with the goodwill of the total practice itself. [Enterprise] goodwill normally must be involved with more than one practitioner in the office — in the practice.
Q.   How does that apply to Dr. May? Isn't he a solo practitioner?
A.   He has only personal goodwill, he has no [enterprise] goodwill.
Q.   But you included personal goodwill in your evaluation?
A.   I did, that is correct.
Q.   And is not personal goodwill the attributes and/or skills of a person?
A.   Personal goodwill?
Q.   Yes.
A.   It is definitely tied into the professional himself, the doctor.
Q.   It's the intangibles that go along with Hillman May in this case itself; is that right?
A.   I am sorry, what?
Q.   It was not very clear. I can understand why you didn't understand it. Personal goodwill would be completely and totally tied to Dr. May, to Hillman May himself?
A.   Correct.
Q.   If he walked out the door and finished practicing tomorrow, that value of goodwill would be gone?
A.   It would stay with him.
Q.   I'm sorry, it would be gone for the practice? I want to make that very clear.
A.   Yes.
Q.   And you think that personal goodwill is something appropriate, again, to valuation?
A.   It's usually the highest single asset.

The above testimony makes clear that the $80,568.00 goodwill assigned to Dr. May's dental practice, by Mrs. May's expert, was personal goodwill. Insofar as we have declined to follow the jurisdictions that permit personal goodwill to be a marital asset, it was error for the family court judge to accept the personal goodwill valuation portion of the report issued by Mrs. May's expert.

* * *

ALBRIGHT, Justice, concurring. . . .

The majority builds on the still vital equitable distribution principle set forth in Tankersley v. Tankersley, 182 W. Va. 627, 390 S.E.2d 826 (1990): that the starting point for valuing a business is fair market value, with the net value of a business calculated by deducting the debts related to the business from the total market value. By recognizing goodwill as a component of the valuation process and a distinction between enterprise and personal goodwill to determining the distributable value of sole proprietorships, professional practices and, by extension, other non-corporate forms of business or practices such as partnerships, the majority has provided needed uniform direction for the lower courts. In time, this concept may eventually be extended to include closely held corporations where one of the litigants is a major stockholder whose involvement in a business may represent a significant portion of overall goodwill. By defining and adopting a distinction between the intangible assets of "enterprise" and "personal" goodwill and providing that only enterprise goodwill is subject to equitable distribution, the majority has established a consistent foundation on which determinations regarding both equitable distribution and alimony can be made. As I indicated before, the benefits of this approach may well be extended to apply not only to sole proprietorships, professional practices and other non-corporate forms of business but also to closely held corporations. Clearly, the categorization of goodwill decreases the likelihood that future earning capacity — personal goodwill — will be improperly considered as part of the valuation process while increasing the probability that it will be correctly factored into the determination of alimony.

* * *

Two issues which I believe require further comment include the discount for lack of marketability and spousal contribution. While the majority did not find a discount for marketability appropriate in this case, the reason for doing so was not related to any one valuation method. Rather, this conclusion was reached because the recommendation was made on the factually unsupported assumption of Dr. May's expert that the practice would be hard to sell. Consequently, in my view such discounts are a viable tool in the valuation process when they are appropriate to the valuation method being employed and the circumstances, supported by documented evidence, so warrant.

As a point of clarification with regard to spousal contribution, the majority implies what Hoak v. Hoak, 179 W. Va. 509, 370 S.E.2d 473 (1988), explicitly decided: the contribution a spouse makes to the home during the time a person is earning a professional degree or by assisting in the establishment of a professional practice plays no part in determining the portion of a professional practice's value which is subject to equitable distribution. Rather, these contributions may be considered in appropriate circumstances for award of reimbursement alimony.

While I expect that this opinion will generate additional valuation concerns for this Court to address, the majority has made significant strides in this area of equitable distribution of marital property with which I unhesitatingly concur.

NOTES AND QUESTIONS

1. Surely the tangible assets of a business, including a professional practice, may be divisible property, as may intangible assets, such as accounts receivable. In what ways is goodwill so different from these other types of assets that it should not be treated as divisible property? What arguments support treating it as property?

In some other legal contexts, goodwill is treated as property, but in others it is not. For example, under the Internal Revenue Code, goodwill is not subject to depreciation, loss of goodwill is not compensated for in eminent domain proceedings, and its loss does not produce an income tax deduction. However, since 1993 the Internal Revenue Code has provided that goodwill may be amortized over a 15-year period. IRC §197.

When professionals are associated in practice, their partnership agreement or corporate charter often includes provisions and formulas that permit the partner(s) continuing in the practice to buy out the interest of a partner who dies, resigns, etc. When the formula produces an amount greater than the withdrawing partner's fractional share of the tangible assets and accounts receivable, have the partners in effect acknowledged that the practice has goodwill? When a practice is sold or a partner withdraws, the selling or withdrawing practitioner often signs a covenant not to compete to prevent that partner from continuing to trade on his or her reputation in competition with that of his or her successors. Is this a device that requires the partner to leave his or her share of the goodwill in the business?

What is the relevance of the legal treatment of goodwill in other contexts to the question presented by *May*?

2. What is the difference between "enterprise" and "professional" or "personal" goodwill? Why did the *May* court conclude that Mrs. May's expert was referring to personal rather than enterprise goodwill? What arguments support the *May* court's holding that only enterprise goodwill is divisible at divorce? How would you argue that all goodwill should be divisible?

The ALI Family Dissolution Principles recommend that goodwill be treated as property, whether it is marketable or not. They also say that to the extent goodwill is not marketable, spousal earning capacity, labor, or skills should not be included in the value. ALI, Principles of the Law of Family Dissolution §4.07(3) (2002).

3. Some courts say that divisible goodwill can exist only in a partnership and not in a sole practice. *See, e.g.*, Nail v. Nail, 486 S.W.2d 761 (Tex. 1972); Sorensen v. Sorensen, 839 P.2d 774 (Utah 1992). What would be the basis for the distinction? This rule means that a person married to a professional who practices with others may share in goodwill at divorce, while one married to a sole practitioner will not.

4. Some courts explicitly require that goodwill be salable for it to be treated as divisible property. For example, in some states ethical rules forbid lawyers to sell their law practices. In those states a doctor, dentist, or accountant may have professional goodwill while a lawyer would not. Other professions may have ethical limitations that affect the salability of practices. This approach creates the

anomaly that some professionals may have goodwill while others may not. What arguments support this position?

Where lawyers are ethically prohibited from selling their practices, the ban is based on a lawyer's obligation to preserve client confidences. Charles Wolfram, Modern Legal Ethics 879-880 (1986); EC 4-6 (a lawyer should not attempt to sell a law practice as a going business because to do so would involve the disclosure of confidences and secrets). In practice, however, this prohibition is sometimes circumvented by inflating the value of other assets or by having the buyer associate with the seller for a few months. Rule 1.17 of the ABA Model Rules of Professional Conduct allows the sale of law practices, including goodwill, but it requires that the seller give actual written notice to each client before the sale. Lawyers are also ethically prohibited from entering into partnership agreements that include covenants not to compete. Charles Wolfram, above, at 885; DR 2-108(A); ABA Model Rules of Professional Conduct, Rule 5.6.

5. If goodwill is divisible property, is it to be characterized as separate or marital, where that distinction matters? Is it separate if "brought into the marriage"? If so, are the profits it produces also separate? How do we distinguish profits attributable to the labor of the working spouse (which is marital property)? How should we account for the decrease in value over time of "old" goodwill while "new" goodwill is built up? *See* Mary Moers Wenig, Increase in Value of Separate Property During Marriage: Examination and Proposals, 23 Fam. L.Q. 301, 324-326 (1989).

6. As *May* discusses, valuation of goodwill (and small businesses generally) is notoriously difficult. If the same or a similar business has recently sold, valuation is not a problem because market value is widely accepted as the gold standard for this issue. Where there is not a ready market for the kind of business being valued, accounting methods are ordinarily used. These methods all look to the flow of income that the business produces and, using a "capitalization rate," calculate what amount of money would have to be invested at that rate of interest to produce the stream of income. The problems with these methods are obvious. Technical issues include how to calculate the income stream that is to be capitalized and what interest rate to choose. More generally, it can be argued that these methods produce figures that have no necessary relationship to what the business person would realize on sale or withdrawal from the business, to the extent that is important.

7. A popular way of dividing pensions is to use a QDRO to divide the pension into separate portions for each spouse. This solution is particularly useful when the spouses do not have enough other property to balance the pension or when valuing the pension is difficult. Since similar problems arise in valuing and dividing small businesses, can a similar solution be employed? That is, can the business be divided in kind by awarding each of the spouses a fraction of it? What problems would be created? Bowen v. Bowen, 96 N.J. 36, 473 A.2d 73 (1984).

8. In an empirical study of judicially decided divorce cases in New York, Professor Marsha Garrison found that when husbands owned a business or a professional license, they were much more likely to receive substantially more than half of the marital wealth. In this study, husbands, not wives, were invariably the ones who held this kind of asset. Marsha Garrison, How Do Judges Decide

Divorce Cases? An Empirical Analysis of Discretionary Decision Making, 74 N.C. L. Rev. 401, 457 (1996).

In 1990 Professor Grace Ganz Blumberg participated in colloquia in five California cities about treatment of goodwill. The participants were lawyers, judges, and accountants. She observed,

> [A] substantial minority of participants expressed remarkable resistance to the generous [California] appellate law on [goodwill]. Relatively few attorneys or accountants, although rather more trial court judges, totally rejected capitalization measures. Instead, many embraced arguably incorrect valuation practices that tend to downvalue goodwill, even practices specifically disapproved by state appellate law.
>
> The sex divide was dramatic. Everyone of the few women panelists promoted generous definitions of goodwill and criticized unwarranted and unlawful limiting valuation practices. A fair number of men, particularly accountants, agreed with them. On the other side, only male participants opposed capitalization and sought to limit valuation improperly. Such men were prone to detect "feminist bias" in women participants, including this writer, who did not agree with them. Yet there was only one woman panelist who represented a feminist organization; all the rest could best be described as "successful professional women."
>
> I was struck by this charge of "feminist bias" because the personal bias of any professional would be to oppose goodwill recognition. All colloquia participants, men and women, were "economically male."

Grace G. Blumberg, Identifying and Valuing Goodwill at Divorce, 56 Law & Contemp. Probs. 217, 220-221 (Spring 1993).

9. For more information see Patrice Leigh Ferguson and John E. Camp, Valuation Basics and Beyond: Tackling Areas of Controversy, 35 Fam. L.Q. 305 (2001); Randall B. Wilhite, The Effect of Goodwill in Determining the Value of a Business in a Divorce, 35 Fam. L.Q. 351 (2001); Ann Bartow, Intellectual Property and Domestic Relations: Issues to Consider When There Is an Artist, Author, Inventor, or Celebrity in the Family, 35 Fam. L.Q. 383 (2001); Alicia Brokars Kelly, Sharing a Piece of the Future Post-Divorce: Toward a More Equitable Distribution of Professional Goodwill, 51 Rutgers L. Rev. 569 (1999).

PROBLEMS

1. Robert started a State Farm Insurance Agency during his marriage to Linda. His agreement with State Farm provides that he may not sell any brand of insurance except State Farm and that all information about policyholders are trade secrets belonging to State Farm, as are the agency's computer system and business records. If Robert and State Farm ever terminate their relationship, Robert may keep the office and sell other companies' insurance, but he cannot solicit State Farm policyholders for one year. The agency has been the most profitable insurance agency in the state for the last ten years, and Robert works ten to eleven hours a day, seven days a week. The agency pays Robert considerably more than the industry average for insurance agents. Does Robert's agency have goodwill? Why or why not?

2. Vincent and Marilyn are divorcing, and they dispute the value of the Green 'n' Tidy Landscape business, which Vincent founded during the marriage and has operated for 15 years. The business has six employees in addition to Vincent, all of whom do manual labor. He is the only person who deals with clients. Marilyn's expert included a value for goodwill in his calculation of the value of the business, based on the amount by which its earnings exceed a fair salary for Vincent and a fair rate of return on the tangible assets of the business. Vincent's expert's valuation did not include an amount for goodwill, based on the state supreme court's holding in an earlier case that a professional practice of a sole practitioner does not have a goodwill value for purposes of divorce. Should the court find that the business has divisible goodwill? Why or why not?

3. Would a well-known entertainer have professional goodwill that could be divisible marital property? *See* Piscopo v. Piscopo, 557 A.2d 1040 (N.J. Super. 1989) (entertainer Joe Piscopo), discussed in Jay E. Fishman, Celebrity as a Business and Its Role in Matrimonial Cases, 17 Am. J. Fam. L. 203 (2004).

5. Degrees, Licenses, Jobs, and Earning Capacity

PROBLEM

Judith and Phillip were married 17 years ago, when Judith was a second-year medical student and Phillip was beginning his internship. He later did a residency in cardiology, and she did a residency in pediatrics. Both Judith and Phillip took out loans to pay for their medical school expenses, which they have paid off. While Judith was in medical school, Phillip supported both of them from his very modest salary as a resident.

After completing her residency, Judith was hired as an assistant professor at State University Medical School, and Phillip opened a private cardiology practice with a partner. Judith became a professor rather than entering private practice so that she would have a flexible schedule to care for their three children.

Phillip, who is now 41, earned an average of $150,000 (net) per year during the last three years. Judith, age 40, is an untenured professor with no expectation of tenure in the foreseeable future, although she is widely published and is one of the ten top pediatric geneticists in the nation. She earned $70,000 last year.

Judith and Phillip are now divorcing. They have agreed that Judith will have custody of the three children and that Phillip will pay child support. They disagree, however, about spousal support and property division. Based on the materials that you have already read on property division and spousal support and the materials in this chapter that precede and follow this problem, consider these questions:

1. Is Judith eligible for spousal support?
2. Does Judith or Phillip have "professional goodwill" subject to equitable distribution?
3. Is either Judith or Phillip entitled to compensation for helping the other develop his or her career? If so, why? What is the measure of

compensation? Some form of reimbursement is the most common remedy. Is this adequate? If one spouse is awarded periodic payments for helping the other, are the payments terminable on the recipient's remarriage? Are they modifiable? Is a spouse entitled to compensation only when the divorce occurs shortly after one spouse has finished putting the other through school?

As you answer these questions, consider the following materials.

CASE LAW AND STATUTES

MAHONEY V. MAHONEY

91 N.J. 488, 453 A.2d 527 (1982)

The Court must decide whether the plaintiff's [MBA] degree is "property" for purposes of N.J.S.A. 2A:34-23, which requires equitable distribution of "the property, both real and personal, which was legally and beneficially acquired . . . during the marriage." . . .

[T]his Court has frequently held that an "expansive interpretation [is] to be given to the word 'property.'" . . . This Court, however, has never subjected to equitable distribution of an asset whose future monetary value is as uncertain and unquantifiable as a professional degree or license. . . . A professional license or degree is a personal achievement of the holder. It cannot be sold and its value cannot readily be determined. A professional license or degree represents the opportunity to obtain an amount of money only upon the occurrence of highly uncertain future events. By contrast, [a] vested but unmatured pension entitle[s] the owner to a definite amount of money at a certain future date.

The value of a professional degree for purposes of property distribution is nothing more than the possibility of enhanced earnings that the particular academic credential will provide. In Stern v. Stern, 66 N.J. 340, 345, 331 A.2d 257 (1975), we held that a lawyer's earning capacity, even where its development has been aided and enhanced by the other spouse . . . should not be recognized as a separate, particular item of property within the meaning of N.J.S.A. 2A:34-23. Potential earning capacity . . . should not be deemed property as such within the meaning of the statute.

Equitable distribution of a professional degree would similarly require distribution of "earning capacity" — income that the degree holder might never acquire. The amount of future earnings would be entirely speculative. Moreover, any assets resulting from income for professional services would be property acquired after the marriage; the statute restricts equitable distribution to property acquired during the marriage.

Valuing a professional degree in the hands of any particular individual at the start of his or her career would involve a gamut of calculations that reduces to little more than guesswork. As the Appellate Division noted, courts would be required to determine far more than what the degree holder could earn in the new career. The admittedly speculative dollar amount of earnings in the "enhanced" career [must] be reduced by the . . . income the spouse should be assumed to have been able to earn if otherwise employed. In our view . . . [this] is ordinarily nothing but speculation, particularly when it is fair to assume that a person with the ability and motivation to complete professional training or higher education would probably utilize those attributes in concomitantly productive alternative endeavors.

Even if such estimates could be made, however, there would remain a world of unforeseen events that could affect the earning potential — not to mention the actual earnings — of any particular degree holder. A person qualified by education for a given profession may choose not to practice it, may fail at it, or may practice in a specialty, location or manner which generates less than the average income enjoyed by fellow professionals. The potential worth of the education may never be realized for these or many other reasons. An award based upon the prediction of the degree holder's success at the chosen field may bear no relationship to the reality he or she faces after the divorce.

Moreover, the likelihood that an equitable distribution will prove to be unfair is increased in those cases where the court miscalculates the value of the license or degree. The potential for inequity to the failed professional or one who changes careers is at once apparent; his or her spouse will have been awarded a share of something which never existed in any real sense. The finality of property distribution precludes any remedy for such unfairness. "Unlike an award of alimony, which can be adjusted after divorce to reflect unanticipated changes in the parties' circumstances, a property division may not [be adjusted]." . . .

Even if it were marital property, valuing educational assets in terms of their cost would be an erroneous application of equitable distribution law. As the Appellate Division explained, the cost of a professional degree "has little to do with any real value of the degree and fails to consider at all the nonfinancial efforts made by the degree holder in completing his course of study." Once a degree candidate has earned his or her degree, the amount that a spouse — or anyone else — paid towards its attainment has no bearing whatever on its value. The cost of a spouse's financial contributions has no logical connection to the value of that degree. . . .

This Court does not support reimbursement between former spouses in alimony proceedings as a general principle. Marriage is not a business arrangement in which the parties keep track of debits and credits, their accounts to be settled upon divorce. Rather, as we have said, "marriage is a shared enterprise, a joint undertaking . . . in many ways it is akin to a partnership." But every joint undertaking has its bounds of fairness. Where a partner to marriage takes the benefits of his spouse's support in obtaining a professional degree or license with the understanding that future benefits will accrue and inure to both of them, and the marriage is then terminated without the supported spouse giving anything in return, an unfairness has occurred that calls for a remedy. . . .

To provide a fair and effective means of compensating a supporting spouse who has suffered a loss or reduction of support, or has incurred a lower standard of living, or has been deprived of a better standard of living in the future, the Court now introduces the concept of reimbursement alimony into divorce proceedings. The concept properly accords with the Court's belief that regardless of the appropriateness of permanent alimony or the presence or absence of marital property to be equitably distributed, there will be circumstances where a supporting spouse should be reimbursed for the financial contributions he or she made to the spouse's successful professional training. Such reimbursement alimony should cover all financial contributions towards the former spouse's education, including household expenses, educational costs, school travel expenses and any other contributions used by the supported spouse in obtaining his or her degree or license.

O'BRIEN V. O'BRIEN

489 N.E.2d 712 (N.Y. 1985)

In this divorce action, the parties' only asset of any consequence is the husband's newly acquired license to practice medicine. The principal issue presented is whether that license, acquired during their marriage, is marital property subject to equitable distribution under Domestic Relations Law §236(B)(5). . . . We now hold that plaintiff's medical license constitutes "marital property" within the meaning of Domestic Relations Law §236(B)(1)(c) and that it is therefore subject to equitable distribution pursuant to subdivision 5 of that part. . . .

[The court then discussed New York equitable distribution law, which allows division of all marital property, defined as "all property acquired by either or both spouses during the marriage and before the execution of a separation agreement or the commencement of a matrimonial action, regardless of the form in which title is held." The court concluded that "the New York Legislature deliberately went beyond traditional property concepts when it formulated the Equitable Distribution Law. Instead, our statute recognizes that spouses have an equitable claim to things of value arising out of the marital relationship and classifies them as subject to distribution by focusing on the marital status of the parties at the time of acquisition. Those things acquired during marriage and subject to distribution have been classified as 'marital property' although, as one commentator has observed, they hardly fall within the traditional property concepts because there is no common-law property interest remotely resembling marital property."]

The determination that a professional license is marital property is . . . consistent with the conceptual base upon which the statute rests. As this case demonstrates, few undertakings during a marriage better qualify as the type of joint effort that the statute's economic partnership theory is intended to address than contributions toward one spouse's acquisition of a professional license. Working spouses are often required to contribute substantial income as wage earners, sacrifice their own educational or career goals and opportunities for child rearing, perform the bulk of household duties and responsibilities and forgo the acquisition of marital assets that could have been accumulated if the professional spouse had been employed rather than occupied with the study and training necessary to acquire a professional license. . . .

Plaintiff's principal argument, adopted by the majority below, is that a professional license is not marital property because it does not fit within the traditional view of property as something which has an exchange value on the open market and is capable of sale, assignment or transfer. The position does not withstand analysis for at least two reasons. First, as we have observed, it ignores the fact that whether a professional license constitutes marital property is to be judged by the language of the statute which created this new species of property previously unknown at common law or under prior statutes. Thus, whether the license fits within traditional property concepts is of no consequence. Second, it is an overstatement to assert that a professional license could not be considered property even outside the context of section 236(B). A professional license is a valuable property right, reflected in the money, effort and lost opportunity for employment expended in its acquisition, and also in the enhanced earning capacity it affords its holder, which may not be revoked without due process of law. That a professional license has no market value is irrelevant. Obviously, a license may not be alienated as may other property and for that reason the working spouse's interest in it is limited. The Legislature has recognized that limitation, however, and has provided for an award in lieu of its actual distribution.

Plaintiff also contends that alternative remedies should be employed, such as an award of rehabilitative maintenance or reimbursement for direct financial contributions. . . . [N]ormally a working spouse should not be restricted to that relief because to do so frustrates the purposes underlying the Equitable Distribution Law. Limiting a working spouse to a maintenance award, either general or rehabilitative, not only is contrary to the economic partnership concept underlying the statute but also retains the uncertain and inequitable economic ties of dependence that the Legislature sought to extinguish by equitable distribution. Maintenance is subject to termination upon the recipient's remarriage and a working spouse may never receive adequate consideration for his or her contribution and may even be penalized for the decision to remarry if that is the only method of compensating the contribution. As one court said so well, "[t]he function of equitable distribution is to recognize that when a marriage ends, each of the spouses, based on the totality of the contributions made to it, has a stake in and right to a share of the marital assets accumulated while it endured, not because that share is needed, but because those assets represent the capital product of what was essentially a partnership entity." The Legislature stated its intention to eliminate such inequities by providing that a supporting spouse's "direct or indirect contribution" be recognized, considered and rewarded. Turning to the question of valuation, it has been suggested that even if a professional license is considered marital property, the working spouse is entitled only to reimbursement of his or her direct financial contributions. By parity of reasoning, a spouse's down payment on real estate or contribution to the purchase of securities would be limited to the money contributed, without any remuneration for any incremental value in the asset because of price appreciation. Such a result is completely at odds with the statute's requirement that the court give full consideration to both direct and indirect contributions "made to the acquisition of such marital property by the party not having title, including joint efforts or expenditures and contributions and services as a spouse, parent, wage earner and homemaker." If the license is marital property, then the working spouse is entitled to an equitable portion of it, not a return of funds advanced. Its value is the enhanced earning capacity it affords the holder and although fixing the present value of that enhanced earning capacity may present problems, the problems are not insurmountable. Certainly they are no more difficult than computing tort damages for wrongful death or diminished earning capacity resulting from injury and they differ only in degree from the problems presented when valuing a professional practice for purposes of a distributive award, something the courts have not hesitated to do. The trial court retains the flexibility and discretion to structure the distributive award equitably, taking into consideration factors such as the working spouse's need for immediate payment, the licensed spouse's current ability to pay and the income tax consequences of prolonging the period of payment and, once it has received evidence of the present value of the license and the working spouse's contributions toward its acquisition and considered the remaining factors mandated by the statute, it may then make an appropriate distribution of the marital property including a distributive award for the professional license if such an award is warranted. When other marital assets are of sufficient value to provide for the supporting spouse's equitable portion of the marital property, including his or her contributions to the acquisition of the professional license, however, the court retains the discretion to distribute these other marital assets or to make a distributive award in lieu of an actual distribution of the value of the professional spouse's license.

NOTES AND QUESTIONS

1. No state courts follow *O'Brien* in treating a degree as property except two panels of the Michigan Court of Appeals. *See* Postema v. Postema, 471 N.W.2d 912 (Mich. App. 1991); Wiand v. Wiand, 443 N.W.2d 464 (Mich. App. 1989). The ALI Family Dissolution Principles recommend against treating licenses, degrees, and the like as divisible property. ALI, Principles of the Law of Family Dissolution §4.07(1), (2) (2002).

2. Even though few states treat degrees as property, most are willing to give relief to the spouse who is divorced at or near the end of the other spouse's professional schooling. However, as the following excerpt indicates, the states are far from uniform in the relief they provide.

ANN LAQUER ESTIN, *MAINTENANCE, ALIMONY, AND THE REHABILITATION OF FAMILY CARE*, 71 N.C. L. Rev. 721, 759-762 (1993): In dozens of cases addressing the "diploma dilemma," courts in different jurisdictions have invented new remedies, labeled with titles such as "property division alimony," "reimbursement alimony," "equitable restitution," or "equitable redemption alimony." In some states, reimbursement approaches directed to the diploma problem have been incorporated in maintenance and property division statutes. . . .

Although the restitution and reimbursement cases reflect more willingness to grant compensation to one marital partner, they also reflect deep tension between the economically rooted notion of restitution and the courts' ideal of marriage. Courts determined to compensate the supporting spouse in diploma dilemma cases have come up with theories that allow reimbursement, but they have also wrestled with restitution and family law principles in an effort to identify what types of losses or contributions should be reimbursed. As a result, the cases vary significantly in their definition of the types of marital support for which compensation may be ordered. At a minimum, reimbursement remedies cover the actual costs of a partner's education and professional training: tuition, books, and fees. Some remedies extend further to include payments for the educated partner's living expenses. Most courts specify that compensation is not appropriate for homemaking rather than financial support.

In some jurisdictions, courts compute restitution awards or reimbursement alimony far more broadly, including the lost earnings of the spouse who was educated during the marriage. In others, courts have computed their awards based on the lost opportunities of the spouse who worked instead of attending school. This leads in some cases to an award intended to cover the costs of an "equal educational opportunity" for the supporting spouse. In the most extreme cases, courts have authorized reimbursement remedies based on the present value of the educated spouse's increased future earnings. This method renders the "reimbursement" award indistinguishable from a property division award valuing then "dividing" the degree or license itself.

California Family Code §2641

(a) "Community contributions to education or training" as used in this section means payments made with community or quasi-community property for education or training or for the repayment of a loan incurred for education or training, whether the payments were made while the parties were resident in this state or resident outside this state.

(b) Subject to the limitations provided in this section, upon dissolution of marriage or legal separation of the parties:

(1) The community shall be reimbursed for community contributions to education or training of a party that substantially enhances the earning capacity of the party. The amount reimbursed shall be with interest at the legal rate, accruing from the end of the calendar year in which the contributions were made.

(2) A loan incurred during marriage for the education or training of a party shall not be included among the liabilities of the community for the purpose of division pursuant to this division but shall be assigned for payment by the party.

(c) The reimbursement and assignment required by this section shall be reduced or modified to the extent circumstances render such a disposition unjust, including, but not limited to, any of the following:

(1) The community has substantially benefitted from the education, training, or loan incurred for the education or training of the party. There is a rebuttable presumption, affecting the burden of proof, that the community has not substantially benefitted from community contributions to the education or training made less than 10 years before the commencement of the proceeding, and that the community has substantially benefitted from community contributions to the education or training made more than 10 years before the commencement of the proceeding.

(2) The education or training received by the party is offset by the education or training received by the other party for which community contributions have been made.

(3) The education or training enables the party receiving the education or training to engage in gainful employment that substantially reduces the need of the party for support that would otherwise be required.

(d) Reimbursement for community contributions and assignment of loans pursuant to this section is the exclusive remedy of the community or a party for the education or training and any resulting enhancement of the earning capacity of a party. However, nothing in this subdivision limits consideration of the effect of the education, training, or enhancement, or the amount reimbursed pursuant to this section, on the circumstances of the parties for the purpose of an order for support pursuant to Section 4320.

(e) This section is subject to an express written agreement of the parties to the contrary.

See also Indiana Code §31-15-7-6 (Lexis):

When the court finds there is little or no marital property, it may award either spouse a money judgment not limited to the property existing at the time of final separation. However, this award may be made only for the financial contribution of one (1) spouse toward tuition, books, and laboratory fees for the higher education of the other spouse.

PUBLIC OPINION

In a survey of the attitudes of married professional students and their spouses about treating a professional degree earned during marriage as marital property, the researchers asked their subjects to evaluate vignettes, which were structured to test the importance of (1) financial support provided by the nonstudent for living expenses and educational costs, (2) nonmonetary sacrifices of the nonstudent, (3) the duration of the marriage after the student earned the degree and the extent of assets the couple had accumulated during the marriage, and (4) differences in the future earning capacities of the spouses at the time of divorce. The study found that all four factors had statistically significant effects on the subjects' judgments. Financial support was by far the strongest factor, followed by comparative earning capacity, sacrifice, and duration of the marriage/assets accumulated.

Demographics accounted for little of the variation in the responses. Women were likely to award slightly more than men, and people who strongly supported feminism were likely to award more than those who strongly opposed feminism. Nonstudents who thought they contributed more than their spouses to living expenses were likely to give lower awards than nonstudents who thought their spouses contributed the majority of their living expenses. (The researchers' explanation was that these nonstudents did not feel much empathy for nonstudent spouses perceived as dependent.) Dental students and their spouses were likely to give slightly higher than average awards, while the awards of business students and their spouses were slightly lower than average. Rebecca R. Eisner & Ruth

Zimmerman, Individual Entitlement to the Financial Benefits of a Professional Degree: An Empirical Study of the Attitudes and Expectations of Married Professional Students and Their Spouses, 22 U. Mich. J.L. Reform 333 (1989).

EMPIRICAL INFORMATION

MEDIAN ANNUAL INCOME BY EDUCATIONAL ATTAINMENT—2000

	Men	Women
Less than 9th	$20,466	$15,399
9th-12th	24,437	17,209
High school graduate (includes GED)	32,493	23,719
Some college, no degree	38,652	27,190
Associate's degree	41,067	30,178
Bachelor's degree	53,505	38,208
Master's degree	65,052	47,049
Professional degree	91,324	56,345
Doctorate degree	75,631	55,620

Source: U.S. Census Bureau, Population Profile of the United States: 2000 (Internet Release) 12-3.

Parent-Child Support Duties   7

However controversial continuation of spousal support duties after divorce may be, everyone agrees that the parent-child relationship and the need for child support continue after and are in principle unaffected by changes in the relationship between the child's parents. Nonetheless, orders directed to parents inevitably and significantly affect the shape of the household in which children live, and this circumstance raises its own theoretical and practical problems. The following excerpt explains the development of the parents' legal duty to support their children and introduces some of the complexities in implementing that duty.

Leslie Harris, Dennis Waldrop & Lori R. Waldrop, *Making and Breaking Connections Between Parents' Duty to Support and Right to Control Their Children*

69 Or. L. Rev. 689, 692-708 (1990)

At least from the early seventeenth century, the English Poor Laws imposed a legal duty on parents to support their poor children to minimize the financial burden on the community. Well into the nineteenth century, however, the English courts refused to hold parents legally responsible for the support of their children outside this context.[1]

In contrast, during the nineteenth century American courts and legislatures established that under the private law, parents have a legal duty to support their children. The judicial path was not smooth, however. . . . Over the century, though, the judicial trend was to make parents' duty to support their children legally enforceable.

---

1. *See*, e.g., Shelton v. Springett, 138 Eng. Rep. 549, 550 (1851); Mortimore v. Wright, 151 Eng. Rep. 502, 504 (1840); *see also* 1 W. Blackstone, Commentaries on the Laws of England 446-454 (Christian ed. 1807).

State legislatures also enacted statutes providing that parents had a duty to support their children.[2] The final draft of the New York Field Draft Civil Code declared the existence of such a duty.[3] . . .

The hesitation to make child support a legally enforceable duty did not reflect a belief that parents had no obligation. Blackstone, for example, discussed at length parents' moral duty to maintain and educate their children. Courts feared, however, that if this duty were legally enforceable, parents would lose control over their children to third parties or to the children themselves. . . .

When the courts did impose a legal support duty on parents, they protected parental control by structuring rules regarding the scope of the duty and the means of enforcing it which maximized parental discretion and made legal enforcement difficult. In addition, the expressed justification for requiring parents to support their children seems to have changed. In the eighteenth century Blackstone based parents' moral duty to support their children on their having begotten the children and, by implication, voluntarily undertaken to care for them. In contrast, some nineteenth century courts began to justify requiring parents to support their children as a corollary to their right to custody. Nineteenth century code drafters also grounded the support duty in the parent's right to custody. Custody includes not only physical custody—living with and caring for a child day to day—but also legal custody—the authority to determine how children will live and behave. Thus, such codes effectively linked parents' support duty to their right to exercise control over their children. . . .

The nineteenth century jurists' linkage of support duties and control rights seems consistent with their general inclination to define human relations in contractarian terms. One nineteenth century family law author even conceived parental authority over children as part of a contract between parents and children:

> The parent shows himself ready, by the care and affection manifested to his child, to watch over him, and to supply all his wants, until he shall be able to provide them for himself. The child, on the other hand, receives these acts of kindness; a tacit compact between them is thus formed; the child engages, by acts equivalent to a positive undertaking to submit to the care and judgment of his parent so long as the parent, and the manifest order of nature, shall coincide in requiring assistance and advice on the one side, and acceptance of them, and obedience and gratitude on the other.[4]

While discussions of parent-child relationships today may not use such blunt language, they still are often perceived as being based on exchange. Consider, for example, the claim that one reason absent fathers do not pay child support is that

---

2. In 1936, Vernier wrote that all states except Kansas had civil statutes imposing this obligation. 4 C. Vernier, American Family Laws § 234, at 57 (1936).

3. "It is the duty of the father, the mother, and the children, of any poor person who is unable to maintain himself by work, to maintain such persons to the extent of their ability." N.Y. Code Commrs. Draft of a Civil Code for the State of New York § 97 (Final Draft 1865).

4. D. Hoffman, Legal Outlines (1836), quoted in Michael Grossberg, Governing the Hearth, 235 (1985).

their loss of contact with and control over their children attenuates their sense of responsibility to the children. This claim is partly empirical, but it also assumes that people's values and behavior are based on exchange. . . .

Current rationales for parental authority tend to justify it instrumentally as serving the best interests of children and society. Examples include claims that parents are in the best position to know and care about their children's needs, that giving parents authority encourages them to assume and discharge the responsibilities of parenthood, and that diffusing authority over how children will be raised promotes cultural and social diversity. . . .

Making parents' duty to support their children legally enforceable inherently limits the parents' control to some extent. However, in the intact family children cannot sue their parents to enforce this duty, for such suits would interfere too much with parental autonomy.[5] The available common law and statutory enforcement mechanisms—the necessaries doctrine and family expense statutes—protect parental control by making enforcement difficult. In addition, the scope of the support duty is defined by parental choices about their lifestyle and their children's lifestyle.

In the nineteenth century the courts extended the necessaries doctrine, which was originally used to enforce a husband's duty to support his wife, to include parental support.[6] . . .

In approximately twenty states, legislatures have enacted family expense statutes,[7] which, like the necessaries doctrine, permit creditors to sue parents for goods and services supplied to their children without requiring a prior promise by the parents to pay. Parental liability under these statutes is usually broader than under the necessaries doctrine. For example, the creditor may not have to prove that an item was a "necessary." Nevertheless, the statutes preserve some control for parents, since liability exists only for family expenses. Further, the statutes permit only suits by creditors; they do not authorize one family member to sue another for support.

As a practical matter, neither the necessaries doctrine nor a family expense statute is a very effective means of enforcing support obligations. Third parties are likely to be reluctant to rely on these statutes in supplying goods or services to a child, because if a parent refuses to pay, the supplier must bring suit. Thus, both as a matter of substantive law and in practice, the necessaries doctrine and the family expense statute present relatively little threat to parental control. . . .

The most common situation in which courts require parents to support their children, even though they do not have physical or legal custody of them, is when

---

5. J. Madden, The Law of Persons and Domestic Relations 392 (1931); Mandelker, Family Responsibility Under the American Poor Laws: 1, 54 Mich. L. Rev. 497, 499 n.4; Comment, Parent and Child—Child's Right to Sue Parent for Support, 15 N.C.L. Rev. 67 (1936); Comment, Extent of a Parent's Duty of Support, 32 Yale L.J. 825 (1923). Similarly, cohabiting spouses cannot sue each other for support. See, e.g., McGuire v. McGuire, 157 Neb. 226, 59 N.W.2d 336 (1953).

6. The necessaries doctrine is covered in Chapter 2.

7. 1 Homer Clark, The Law of Domestic Relations in the United States, §7.1, at 433-434 (2d ed. 1987).

the parents are separated or divorced.[8] An essential feature of such orders is that they impose a support duty on a person who no longer has legal authority to control the child.

During the nineteenth century as divorce became more common, the question of whether noncustodial fathers should be required to support their children arose increasingly. . . . Some noncustodial fathers argued that the legal duty to support arose from the right to custody, and that, therefore, they no longer had any such duty. Some fathers also argued that since they no longer had a right to their children's services, they should not be required to support them. Ultimately, courts usually rejected these blanket principles and ordered men who were at fault for the marital breakdown to pay child, as well as spousal, support. To the extent the noncustodial fathers' duty to support their children remained an open question, nineteenth century legislatures often resolved it by enacting separate maintenance and divorce statutes that empowered courts to award child support.

These judicial and statutory developments established that when parents divorce and children live with only one parent, the link between custody and support can be broken as well. Nevertheless, historical judicial reluctance to require divorced fathers to pay adequate sums for their children's support and to enforce support orders may be attributable in part to the lingering belief that support duties should coincide with custodial rights.

The first three parts of this chapter concern how the theoretical and principled issues discussed above play out in the determination of the amount of child support owed by a nonresidential parent. The last two parts consider the boundaries of intrafamilial support duties — when must parents support adult children, and when must adult children support their aging parents?

A. THE PREVAILING CHILD SUPPORT MODEL

The extent to which judges' discretion should be limited by a formula or guideline was a recurring issue in the law of spousal support and property division. Not

---

8. Courts also commonly order unmarried fathers not living with their children to pay child support. At least since Elizabethan times the support duty of unmarried fathers has been enforced when a child is receiving public assistance. However, outside this context unmarried fathers had no common law duty to support their children. Simmons v. Bull, 21 Ala. 501 (1852); Nixon v. Perry, 77 Ga. 530, 3 S.E. 253 (1887); Furillio v. Crowther, 16 Eccl. 302 (1826); Cameron v. Baker, 171 Eng. Rep. 1190 (1824); Hard's Case, 91 Eng. Rep. 22 (1795). Nineteenth century statutes also did not impose a support duty on unmarried fathers outside the poor laws. For a discussion of the treatment of nonmarital children in nineteenth century America, *see* Michael Grossberg, Governing the Hearth ch. 6 (1985).

surprisingly, this issue has also arisen for child support. Federal legislation enacted during the 1980s mandates that all states use child support guidelines. 42 U.S.C. § 667. A Senate report explained the reasons for requiring guidelines:

> Although the child support enforcement program has greatly strengthened the ability of children to have support orders established and collected, there remains a continuing problem that the amounts of support ordered are in many cases unrealistic. This frequently results in awards which are much lower than what is needed to provide reasonable funds for the needs of the child in the light of the absent parent's ability to pay. In some instances, however, there are also awards which are unrealistically high.
>
> Some States have established guidelines to be used by the courts in setting the amount of child support orders. Where these guidelines exist, overall award levels tend to be somewhat higher than where the amount of the order is entirely discretionary with each judge. Moreover, the existence of guidelines tends to assure that there is reasonable consideration given both to the needs of the child and the ability of the absent parent to pay. This provides some protection for both parties.

S. Rep. No. 387, 98th Cong., 2d Sess. 40, reprinted in 1984 U.S. Code Cong. & Admin. News 2397, 2436. Federal regulations provide that child support guidelines must "take into consideration all earnings and income of the absent parent, be based on specific descriptive and numeric criteria and result in a computation of the support obligation." 45 C.F.R. § 302.56. This amount must be rebuttably presumed to be the correct amount of child support, and a deviation must be supported by specific findings based on criteria specified by state law. "Such criteria must take into consideration the best interests of the child. Findings that rebut the guidelines shall state the amount of support that would have been required under the guidelines and include a justification of why the order varies from the guidelines." Id.

Early child support guidelines required parents to share the "costs" of raising a child. While this approach has substantial intuitive appeal, no state today bases its guidelines on this approach. The following excerpt explains the difficulties with the cost approach and describes the approaches most widely used in the U.S.

ROBERT G. WILLIAMS, *GUIDELINES FOR SETTING LEVELS OF CHILD SUPPORT ORDERS*

21 Fam. L.Q. 281, 287-289, 290-293, 295 (1987)

Why has an equitable level of child support been so difficult to determine by the courts? The root of the problem is that most expenses related to child rearing are commingled with expenditures benefiting all household members. In a recent economic study, Espenshade estimates that over one-half of family expenditures on children fall into just three categories: food, housing and transportation.[9] It is

---

9. The reference is to T. J. Espenshade, Investing in Children: New Estimates of Parental Expenditures (1984), which was considered the most authoritative study then

apparent that, on an individual case basis, it is difficult to separate out a child's share of these major household expenses. . . .

. . . Since most expenditures made on behalf of children are intertwined with general household expenditures, it is not only virtually impossible to disentangle them reliably, but many costs of children become hidden in the larger pool of spending for the total household. Consequently, the full children's share of expenditures in those categories is generally not recognized, with the result that even parents may underestimate the true costs of bringing up their own children. . . .

. . . What are the costs of children above the minimum level needed for basic subsistence? Economists agree that, above the minimum level, there is no absolute "cost" of rearing a child. Studies of household expenditure patterns make it clear that parents with higher income spend more on their children because they can afford to do so. A more accurate way of posing this question, then, is: What are the normal levels of spending on children within households above the poverty level? Estimating these normal levels of spending is the only method that economists have of estimating costs of children in such households.

The best available evidence on this subject comes from the aforementioned Espenshade study. The study is based on data from 8,547 households drawn from the 1972-1973 Consumer Expenditure Survey, a national survey of household expenditure patterns conducted by the Bureau of Labor Statistics. . . .

As can be seen from Espenshade's estimates for three socioeconomic levels, amounts spent on children in intact households go up as family income increases. Based on Espenshade's figures, we have derived estimates for the proportion of net income expended for two children by income level of the parents. These estimates . . . show that spending on children can be validly described as proportions of household income, although the proportions decline as household income increases. Thus, spending on one child varies from 26.0 percent of net income at low-income levels to 19.2 percent at the upper end of the income range. Similarly, spending on two children decreases from 40.4 percent at low-income levels to 29.7 percent in high income households.

A third question relevant to determining levels of child support is: How is spending on children affected by the number of children in the family? From Espenshade's findings, we can develop estimates of the proportion of current family consumption devoted to one, two, and three children. . . . [E]stimates of expenditures on children as a proportion of current family consumption are 26.2 percent for one child, 40.7 percent for two children, 51.0 percent for three children, and 57.5 percent for four children. . . .

---

available. After this article was written, the Department of Health and Human Services commissioned Dr. David Betson to do an updated analysis of family expenditures on children. His study, which also uses a marginal expenditures approach, estimates that a two-parent family spends 25 percent of its income on one child, 35 percent on two children, and 40 percent on three children. David Betson, Alternative Estimates of the Cost of Children from the 1980-86 Consumer Expenditure Survey, Final Report to the U.S. Dept. of Health & Hum. Serv., Office of the Asst. Sec'y for Planning & Evaluation 57 (1990). Some states' child support guidelines still use the Espenshade estimates, while others use the Betson figures. — Ed.

There is a common misperception that the declining increments primarily reflect economies of scale in rearing children. Instead, these figures seem to indicate a decreasing level of expenditures for each child as family size increases. Espenshade estimates, for example, that virtually equal amounts are spent on each child in a two-child family, but that the spending level for each represents only about three-fourths the amount that would have been spent on one child alone.

* * *

A. FLAT PERCENTAGE GUIDELINE

This simplest type of guideline sets child support as a percentage of obligor income, with the percentage varying according to the number of children. Some percentage guidelines are based on gross income (before tax) while others are based on net income (after mandatory deductions). . . .

The Wisconsin percentage of income standard may be the most well-known example of a flat percentage guideline. Child support orders are determined only on the basis of the obligor's gross income and the number of children to be supported. The percentages of obligor gross income allocated to child support are 17 percent for one child, 25 percent for two children, 29 percent for three children, 31 percent for four children and 34 percent for five or more children. The percentage of income standard is designed to be comparable to a tax in simplicity of structure and ease of application. It is intended for use in conjunction with mandatory income withholding for all child support orders from the date a child support order is established. . . .

Under the percentage of income standard, the child support obligation is not adjusted for the income of the custodial parent. The standard assumes that each parent will expend the designated proportion of income on the child, with the custodial parent's proportion spent directly. There is no adjustment for other factors such as child care expenses, extraordinary medical expenses, or age of child. . . .

B. INCOME SHARES MODEL

. . . The income shares model is based upon the precept that the child should receive the same proportion of parental income that would have been received if the parents lived together. Thus, the income shares model calculates child support as the share of each parent's income estimated to have been allocated to the child if the parents and child were living in an intact household. . . .

Computing child support under the income shares model involves three basic steps:

1. Income of the parents is determined and added together.
2. A basic child support obligation is computed based on the combined income of the parents. This obligation represents the amount estimated

to have been spent on the children jointly by the parents if the household were intact. The estimated amount, in turn, is derived from economic data on household expenditures on children. A total child support obligation is computed by adding actual expenditures for work-related child care expenses and extraordinary medical expenses.

3. The total obligation is then pro-rated between each parent based on their proportionate shares of income. The obligor's computed obligation is payable as child support. The obligee's computed obligation is retained and is presumed to be spent directly on the child. This procedure simulates spending patterns in an intact household in which the proportion of income allocated to children depends on total family income.

The income shares model has been specified in both net income and gross income versions. It incorporates a self-support reserve for the obligor, under which the formula is not applied in determining child support until an obligor's income exceeds the poverty level (although a minimum order is set on a case-by-case basis).

C. DELAWARE MELSON FORMULA

The Delaware Child Support Formula was developed by Judge Elwood F. Melson and was adopted by the Delaware Family Court for statewide use beginning in January 1979. As stated in a recent report of the Delaware Family Court, the basic principles of the Melson child support formula are as follows:

1. Parents are entitled to keep sufficient income for their most basic needs to facilitate continued employment.

2. Until the basic needs of children are met, parents should not be permitted to retain any more income than required to provide the bare necessities for their own self-support.

3. Where income is sufficient to cover the basic needs of the parents and all dependents, children are entitled to share in any additional income so that they can benefit from the absent parent's higher standard of living.

NOTES AND QUESTIONS

1. The following example of the operation of the Wisconsin percentage guideline and a generic Income Shares formula, based on parents' gross income, is adapted from Robert G. Williams, Development of Guidelines for Child Support Orders: Advisory Panel Recommendations and Final Report II-106 through II-108 (Office of Child Support Enforcement 1987).

Father lives alone, and the two children live with Mother. Father's gross monthly income is $1,600. Mother has a gross monthly income of $1,200 and spends $150 per month on work-related child care.

INCOME SHARES FORMULA

1. Calculate the parents' total monthly income and each parent's proportionate share of the total:

$$\text{Total} = \$1,600 + 1,200 = \$2,800$$

$$\text{Father's share} = 1,600/2,800 = 57.14\%$$

$$\text{Mother's share} = 1,200/2,800 = 42.86\%$$

2. Calculate the total child support obligation by adding the basic obligations (read applicable tables) to child care costs and extraordinary medical expenses. Here, assume that the applicable table says that the basic support obligation for two children for parents earning a total of $2,800 per month is $646.

$$\text{Total} = \$646 + \$150 + \$796$$

3. Calculate noncustodial parent's share by multiplying total child support obligation by his or her proportion from step 1.

$$57.14\% \text{ of } \$796 = \$454.83$$

WISCONSIN FORMULA

1. Percent of Obligor's gross income for 2 children = 25%
2. 25% of $1,600 = $400.

2. In 25 states guidelines are established by statute, in 18 by court rule, and in the remainder by administrative rule. National Conference of State Legislatures, Which Branch of Government Establishes Each State's Child Support Guidelines, available at *http://www.ncsl.org/programs/cyf/branch.htm* (last visited Oct. 5, 2004). Thirty-three states have guidelines based on the Income Shares model; 13 states and the District of Columbia use a percentage of income approach; Alabama and Hawaii use hybrids, and the Delaware and Montana approaches are unique. Linda D. Elrod & Robert G. Spector, A Review of the Year in Family Law, Chart 3, 36 Fam. L.Q. 579 (2004).

3. All three of the models that Williams discusses are based on the principle that parents should share their income with their children, and the size of that share is determined by how much an average intact family (both parents and all children living together) would spend on the children. What arguments support this as the most appropriate measure of the duty of parents when the family is not intact?

4. Which type of formula is most sensitive to variations in the situations of individual families? What price is paid for individualization, and what costs are associated with less individualized approaches?

5. The trend toward child support guidelines is international. *See, e.g.,* J. Thomas Oldham, Lessons from the New English and Australian Child Support Systems, 29 Vand. J. Transnat'l L. 691 (1996); Anna Worwood, Countdown to "D-Day" for Fathers, March [2003] Fam. L. 19 (discussing the English Child Support, Pension and Social Security Act 2000, which became effective in 2003 and which establishes a presumptive amount of child support based on the nonresident parent's net income, the number of children for whom support will be ordered, the number of nights the children stay with the nonresident parent, and the number of other children for whom the parent is financially responsible).

NANCY THOENNES ET AL., *THE IMPACT OF CHILD SUPPORT GUIDELINES ON AWARD ADEQUACY, AWARD VARIABILITY AND CASE PROCESSING EFFICIENCY*

25 Fam. L.Q. 325, 342-345 (1991)

. . . [After adoption of child support guidelines] the average monthly award increased 5 percent in Colorado, 28 percent in Hawaii, and 16 percent in Illinois. When we examine gains made in each state among various income categories following adoption of the guideline, we find that average order levels increased significantly at the middle-income level in Colorado, at the low-income level in Illinois, and at all income levels in Hawaii.

In Illinois, increases in award levels were primarily caused by significant improvement in employment and earning levels among mothers and fathers in the postguideline time period. In Colorado and Hawaii, where there were no significant differences in economic factors between the pre- and postguideline samples, the gains were largely dependent on the level of awards in each state's preguideline sample. Specifically, Colorado experienced modest gains in award levels at the lower- and upper-income levels because its preguideline awards were high relative to those of the other states. By contrast, Hawaii experienced the most dramatic gains because it had the lowest starting points among all income levels and, therefore, had the most room for improvement. . . .

Further analysis of our case data revealed that much of the increase was due to a reduction in zero-dollar awards among families with unemployed noncustodians and female obligors: following adoption of the guidelines, the proportion of cases with unemployed noncustodians without support orders dropped 15 percentage points and the proportion of cases with female obligors without support orders dropped 30 percentage points. By contrast, the incidence of zero-dollar awards among families with employed noncustodians and male obligors remained the same. . . . These findings suggest that as a result of guidelines, orders are being imposed in a more gender-neutral manner with a greater proportion of mothers being ordered to pay. In addition, guidelines are creating the expectation that obligors should contribute to the support of their children regardless of their employment status and earning capacity. . . .

Based on our research, not one guideline appears to produce consistently higher or lower awards. The Income Shares Model produced the highest awards with low-income families, the Melson Formula produced the highest awards in middle-income families, and the Percentage of Income Approach produced the highest awards in upper-income families. . . . Moreover, following adoption of the guidelines, average awards for various income categories are very comparable across the states. . . .

A review conducted for the federal Office of Child Support Enforcement, based on multiple sources of information including case record analysis in 11 states and reports from state child support agencies, found that formulas and guidelines produce a more uniform treatment of similar cases than discretionary decisions by judges. ABA Center on Children and the Law, for CSR, Inc., I. Evaluating Child Support Guidelines: Findings and Conclusions (1996). The same study found that courts deviated from the presumptive formula mount in 17 percent of the cases.

B. CHALLENGES TO THE PREVAILING MODEL

States must review their child support guidelines at least once every four years to ensure that they produce "appropriate" orders. In conducting these reviews, the states must consider "economic data on the cost of raising children," and they must analyze case data to determine the extent to which orders deviate from the guidelines. 45 C.F.R. § 302.56. As states have gone through this process, and as more information about the operation of guidelines has become available, critics have challenged both the theoretical assumptions and empirical foundations of existing guidelines. The two most widely discussed alternatives are those proposed by the American Law Institute's Principles of the Law of Family Dissolution and by proponents of the cost-shares approach.

Leslie Harris, *The Proposed ALI Child Support Principles*

35 Willamette L. Rev. 717, 727-733 (1999)

In a memorandum introducing the *Principles*, the reporter explained that existing child support guidelines, "unlike the earlier need-based discretionary rubric, . . . are neither intended nor designed to register and reflect the need of the child in the residential household. They do not, in any meaningful manner, consider the resources independently available to the residential household."[10]

---

10. Grace G. Blumberg, Reporter's memorandum to the members of the Institute, Mar. 7, 1998, ALI, Principles of the Law of Family Dissolution xxix (Tent. Dr. 3, Pt. II, 1998).

Therefore, the combined amount that the parents spent or would spend on the child if all lived in the same household has little directly to do with how much should be spent on the child living with only one parent.

Perhaps the most essential fact the marginal expenditures model fails to take into account is that the costs of the two households together are greater than one household alone because of loss of economies of scale. How this economic burden should be distributed, particularly with regard to its impact on the child, is a critical question that the marginal expenditures model simply does not address.

As it turns out, if the child's parents have equal amounts of income before child support is paid, the marginal expenditures model spreads the loss of economies of scale equally between the households. However, when the parents' incomes are unequal, child support guidelines based on the marginal expenditures model perpetuate, and can exacerbate, the difference in the two households' standards of living. . . .

As in first generation child support formulas, the *Principles* provide that parents will share income with their child or children. Unlike many first generation formulas, the ALI version explicitly acknowledges that each parent's interests sometimes diverge from those of the child, as well as from each other's. It seeks a balance among these interests that can be defended on principle.[11] The *Principles* evaluate the need for and adequacy of child support awards by comparing the economic standard of living in the households of the parents, rather than looking only at the relative income of the parents. Where the household of the residential parent has a lower standard of living, the *Principles* call for increased child support to narrow the gap; where the residential parent's household has a higher standard of living, child support is lower. . . .

1. THE INTERESTS OF THE CHILD

A common aspiration expressed in judicial opinions and popular discussions concerning child support is that the child should not suffer economically because the parents are not living together. However, the *Principles* do not attempt to achieve this goal because doing so would infringe too greatly on the rights of the nonresidential parent. For the same reason, the *Principles* do not adopt the modest-sounding goal that the child should not suffer disproportionately as compared to other family members. The *Principles* argue that to achieve even this goal, it would be necessary to use an equal living standards formula for child support. The *Principles* reject this formula because of its intrusion on the nonresidential parent's interests. . . .

To avoid this, the *Principles* compromise the child's interests and provide instead that the goals of the child support formula should be to: (1) allow the child to "enjoy a minimum decent standard of living when the resources of both

---

11. See Principles § 3.03.

parents together are sufficient to achieve such result without impoverishing either parent"; (2) allow the child to "enjoy a standard of living not grossly inferior to that of the child's higher income parent"; and (3) prevent the child from suffering "loss of important life opportunities that the parents are economically able to provide without undue hardship to themselves or their other dependents."[12]

2. THE INTERESTS OF THE RESIDENTIAL PARENT

The most fundamental interest of the residential parent recognized by the *Principles* is not to bear disproportionately the direct and indirect costs of child rearing.[13] . . .

3. THE INTERESTS OF THE NONRESIDENTIAL PARENT

The *Principles* argue that the marginal expenditure principle, which, as discussed above, is the basis for most child support formulas today, fundamentally expresses a principle of justice for the nonresidential parent: to contribute no more to the support of the children than if the parent were living with the children in a two-parent household.[14] The *Principles* accept this measure as a starting point but do not allow it to prevail in all situations.

> At bottom, the marginal expenditure principle reflects a strong cultural belief in the primacy of the earner's claim to his earnings. . . . It is true that any transfer of income to the child's residential household may also be enjoyed by other members of the household, including the residential parent. This is an inevitable and unavoidable effect of any child support transfer, and is not itself an adequate reason for limiting or disapproving child support. Nevertheless, the payor parent has an interest in limiting the measure of his child support obligation to his relationship to the child, rather than to the residential household.[15]

* * *

[T]his notion of justice arguably overstates the nonresidential parent's claim. The continuity of marginal expenditure measure may be understood to be predicated on the notion that, insofar as he is the dominant earner, the nonresidential parent should be held harmless by divorce, that is, he should be no worse off economically after divorce than he was during marriage. Yet being no worse off suggests, in the alternative, that he should not be heard to complain so long as he does not suffer a decline in his standard of living. To the extent that he will not suffer a decline in his

---

12. This analysis is sent out at Principles § 3.03 and comments thereto. — Ed.
13. Principles § 3.03, comment d at 6.
14. *Id.* at § 3.03, comment e at 7-8.
15. *Id.* at 18.

standard of living (using household equivalence measures), there is no persuasive reason he should not pay more than what he would have spent on the children were he living with him. This does not imply equalization of household standards of living. In view of the lost economies of scale, the standard of living in the child's residential household will necessarily drop well below the preseparation standard if the standard of living of the higher income nonresidential parent is held constant.[16]

Although the *Principles* do not use "maintenance of the support obligor's marital standard of living" as the basis for any part of the child support obligation, they use this standard as a touchstone for determining whether the obligor is being treated fairly in particular circumstances. Indeed, to evaluate the fairness of proposed orders, the *Principles* consistently compare the standard of living of each household after payment of child support to the standard of living that the parties would enjoy if they all lived in the same household.

[The *Principles* begin by establishing a "base amount" of child support, which is the amount that would be required under a well-constructed marginal expenditure formula. When the residential parent's income is lower than the nonresidential parent's, as is true in most cases, a supplement is added to the base amount, so as to make the standards of living in the two households closer, though not equal. As the income of the residential parent approaches that of the nonresidential parent, the amount of the supplement decreases. When the two parents' households have equal incomes, the supplement is completely eliminated, leaving the base alone as the amount of child support owed. When the income of the residential parent's household is greater than the nonresidential parent's, the ALI Principles call for the child support obligation to be decreased below the base amount. ALI, Principles of Family Dissolution § 3.05.]

Economist R. Mark Rogers, a leading proponent of the cost-shares approach to child support, argues that most existing formulas overstate the costs of raising children because they use intact family data to estimate child costs rather than acknowledging that, in response to increased costs of two households, families will simply spend less on children; fail to account for tax benefits associated with children; and fail to account for time that children spend with nonresidential parents. He also argues that the Espenshade and Betson estimates of the marginal costs of raising children are economically suspect. *See* R. Mark Rogers & Donald J. Bieniewicz, Child Cost Economics and Litigation Issues: An Introduction to Applying Cost Shares Child Support Guidelines (2002), *available at http://www.guidelineeconomics.com/analysis/RMR_published.html* (last visited Oct. 5, 2004).

---

16. *Id.* § 3.03, Reporters Note to comment e at 18.

JO MICHELL BELD & LEN BIERNAT, *FEDERAL INTENT FOR STATE*
CHILD SUPPORT GUIDELINES: INCOME SHARES, COST SHARES,
AND THE REALITIES OF SHARED PARENTING

37 Fam. L.Q. 165, 173-174, 177-180 (2003)

. . . The cost shares alternative was developed in the mid-1990s by affiliates of the Children's Rights Council (CRC), a non-profit organization with both national and state chapters "that works to assure children meaningful and continuing contact with both their parents and extended family regardless of the parents' marital status." Its proponents argue that cost shares guidelines are fundamentally different from income shares guidelines, principally in the estimation of child costs and the allocation of these estimated costs between the parents. These differences, in their view, make the model superior to income shares.

While it is true that there are important differences between the prevailing income shares model for child support guidelines and the cost shares model, there are some fundamental similarities as well. Both approaches attempt to establish a clear relationship between child support guidelines and expenditures on children by parents, although the underlying estimates for those expenditures are indeed quite different in the two models. Both approaches base support on the incomes of both parents, with the cost shares model reflecting a Melson-style method of determining each parent's income available for child support. But the cost shares model makes assumptions about expenditure patterns and cost offsets in separated families that income shares models do not routinely make. . . .

* * *

The cost shares model borrows several principles from existing income shares guidelines but reflects a very different set of economic assumptions about expenditures on children in separated families. Cost shares guidelines use a Melson formula approach to the determination of income; rely on estimates of expenditures on children in single-parent families after offsets for "tax benefits attributable to the children;" and apply a joint physical custody cross-credit approach to the calculation of the final support obligation. A cost shares order for support is calculated as follows:

(1) Determine each parent's share of their combined income available for child support. As in all three Melson formula states, a cost shares guideline subtracts a self-support reserve from a parent's net income to arrive at his or her income available for child support. The calculation of net income under cost shares includes "an imputed child support order for other biological or adopted children residing with the parent," which is not present in any of the Melson formula states. In addition, the self-support reserve under cost shares is slightly higher than the highest reserve under existing Melson guidelines. . . .

(2) Determine the parents' combined "basic" expenditures on the children. Cost shares guidelines estimate expenditures on the children quite differently than do income shares guidelines. First, cost shares uses estimated single-parent spending as the standard for spending by separated parents. Where the income

shares approach adds together the incomes of the parents and estimates what two-parent families with that level of income spend for children's share of housing, food, transportation, and other pooled expenses, the cost shares approach averages the parents' incomes and estimates what a single-parent family with that level of income spends for these needs. Effectively, this means that the children will be allocated a share of only half the combined income of the parents. Second, "fixed expenses" incurred by either parent (i.e., expenses that do not move with the children between households) are then subtracted from this estimate of single-parent spending on the children. The exact categories of expense in the "fixed expense" component vary with different versions of the cost shares model, but may include expenditures by each parent for housing for the children, medical insurance premiums, and court-ordered life insurance premiums. The remaining amount is considered the "basic child cost" subject to apportionment between the parents.

(3) Determine each parent's "total incurred child cost." The cost shares model also makes very strong assumptions about the way in which children's expenses are distributed between parents who live in separate households. The model assumes that each parent's spending on the children is determined solely by the amount of time the children spend in each household. There is no assumption that custodial parents incur a larger share of the costs by virtue of their status as custodial parents. Consequently, each parent's "total incurred child cost" is calculated as follows:

a. Apportion the basic child cost between the parents according to each parent's percentage of parenting time. The resulting amount is presumed to be the parent's "incurred basic child costs."

b. Add to each parent's incurred basic child costs any other actual expenditures for the children by each parent. Such expenditures include the "fixed expenses" previously subtracted from the estimates of total basic costs (e.g., life insurance premiums, medical insurance premiums, housing), as well as expenses not included in the table of "basic child costs" (e.g., child care, education). The resulting amount for each parent is presumed to be that parent's total expenditures for the children.

c. Calculate the "tax benefit attributable to the children" for each parent and subtract this benefit from the parent's total expenditures for the children to arrive at the parent's "total incurred child costs." Like the definition of "fixed expenses," the definition of "tax benefit attributable to the children" may vary with different versions of the model, but the authors generally describe it as the difference between the after-tax income of the parent after receiving his or her actual child-related tax benefits, and the after-tax income of the parent assuming single taxpayer/no dependents status.

(4) Determine the final order for support through a cross-credit calculation. This step resembles the formula used in some states to establish support for extended parenting time, but without the multiplier that is typically applied to child costs to reflect the increased cost of caring for children in separate households. Each parent's obligation to the other parent is calculated by multiplying the parent's share of their combined monthly income available for child support by the other parent's total incurred child costs. The parent who owes the higher amount to the other parent is the obligor, and pays the difference between the two obligations to the other parent.

NOTES AND QUESTIONS

1. Child support formulas are, to varying degrees, opaque and therefore likely to be applied mechanically, as well as likely to be viewed with suspicion by those who use them. Most obviously, all of the formulas use some kind of standardized measure to determine how much money parents at various levels of income "should" spend on their children. Parents and their attorneys regularly question where these amounts come from, and even experts who understand the economic analysis upon which the measures are founded debate the validity of various methodologies. In addition to the challenge from the proponents of the cost-shares formula, *see, e.g.*, Mark Lino, Expenditures on Children by Families: U.S. Department of Agriculture Estimates and Alternative Estimators, 11 J. Legal Econ. 31 (Fall 2001); Laura W. Morgan & Mark C. Lino, A Comparison of Child Support Awards Calculated Under States' Child Support Guidelines with Expenditures on Children Calculated by the U.S. Department of Agriculture, 33 Fam. L.Q. 191 (1999).

Professor Ellman argues that no methodology is value-neutral and that drafters of child support guidelines must, therefore, directly confront the value choices that inhere in the task. Ira Mark Ellman, Fudging Failure: The Economic Analysis Used to Construct Child Support Guidelines (forthcoming 2004 University of Chicago Legal Forum, available at *http://papers.ssrn.com/sol3/cf_dev/AbsByAuth.cfm?per_id=227652*). What are these choices? How would drafters go about balancing the interests of children and their parents? Would it be desirable to return to the preguideline days when judges decided child support based on individualized assessments of children's needs and parents' ability to pay?

2. Those who support the cost-shares approach often argue that existing guidelines establish support levels that are too high and unfairly burden obligor parents. *See* R. Mark Rogers, Wisconsin-Style and Income Shares Child Support Guidelines: Excessive Burdens and Flawed Economic Foundation, 33 Fam. L.Q. 135 (1999). *See also* Ronald K. Henry, Child Support at a Crossroads: When the Real World Intrudes upon Academics and Advocates, 33 Fam. L.Q. 235 (1999); However, the cost-shares approach has not been adopted by any state and has attracted criticism. *See, e.g.*, Jo Michelle Beld & Len Biernat, Federal Intent for State Child Support Guidelines: Income Shares, Cost Shares, and the Realities of Shared Parenting, 37 Fam. L.Q. 165 (2003); Laura W. Morgan, The "Cost Shares" Model of Child Support Guidelines (2004), *available at http://www.supportguidelines.com/articles/article.html* (last visited Oct. 5, 2004). What objections do you see?

3. Existing guidelines and the more generous ALI Principles have also been criticized for producing orders that are too low to provide adequately for children. The preferred alternative of these critics is often the equal living standards (ELS) model, proposed in Judith Cassetty, G. K. Sprinkle, Ralph White & Bill Douglass, The ELS (Equal Living Standards) Model for Child Support Awards, in Essentials of Child Support Guidelines Development: Economic Issues and Policy Considerations 329 (1986). This model, which would have the judge order sufficient child support to equalize the living standards in the households of the child's two parents, clearly links the nonresidential parent's obligation both to the income of the residential parent and to the living standard in the residential

parent's household. *See* Marsha Garrison, The Economic Consequences of Divorce: Would Adoption of the ALI Principles Improve Current Outcomes? 8 Duke J. Gender L. & Pol'y 119 (2001); Marsha Garrison, An Evaluation of Two Models of Parental Obligation, 86 Cal. L. Rev. 41 (1998). However, the ELS model has been adopted in no state. What problems do you see that might explain its lack of political acceptance?

Noncustodial parents often justify their resistance to paying child support by their claim that the money "isn't really going to the kids." Such a claim raises at least two issues. The first is deciding which expenditures really "go to the kids" and which benefit the custodial parent. The second issue is the form of child support orders. The typical order requires the obligor to pay a fixed sum to the other parent rather than pay specific expenses. Further, if the obligor supplies goods or services directly to the child, the obligor does not usually get an offset for them against the child support ordered. Should courts require the obligor to pay expenses directly rather than bundling everything into a lump sum? Should courts require recipients of child support to account for the money? Or are these kinds of limitations inconsistent with the custodial parents' prerogatives?

4. In several states obligors have brought constitutional challenges to child support guidelines on a variety of due process and equal protection grounds, though without success. *See* Georgia Dept. Human Res. v. Sweat, 580 S.E.2d 206 (Ga. 2003); Gallaher v. Elam, 104 S.W.3d 455 (Tenn. 2003); Stillman v. State, 87 P.3d 200 (Colo. App. 2003); Parents Opposed to Punitive Support v. Gardner, 998 F.2d 764 (9th Cir. 1993).

5. Additional commentaries on the ALI child support proposals include Karen Syma Czapanskiy, ALI Child Support Principles: A Lesson in Public Policy and Truth-Telling, 8 Duke J. Gender L. & Pol'y 259 (2001); Leslie Joan Harris, The ALI Child Support Principles: Incremental Changes to Improve the Lot of Children and Residential Parents, 8 Duke J. Gender L. & Pol'y 245 (2001).

6. Several commentators have proposed that households should generally be treated as economic units for purposes of support duties, thus eliminating inter-household support payments altogether in many circumstances. For example, Judge R. Michael Redman suggests that the noncustodial parent should remain financially responsible for the children until the custodial parent remarries. At that point the custodial stepparent would replace the noncustodial parent unless and until the custodial parent remarries somebody else. R. Michael Redman, The Support of Children in Blended Families: A Call for Change, 25 Fam. L.Q. 83, 89 (1991). *See also* Leslie Joan Harris, Reconsidering the Criteria for Legal Fatherhood, 1996 Utah L. Rev. 461. Professor David Chambers has observed,

> . . . Without great prodding, most parents who have never lived with their children — most typically, fathers who are the subject of paternity suits — never pay support at all. Even divorced fathers who have lived with their children typically pay regularly for only a short time, then pay less, and then often pay nothing. . . . Neither love nor a sense of moral responsibility induces most absent parents to pay as much as they could.
>
> Current patterns of visitation are similar. Most fathers of children from outside of marriage do not see their children at all. Every study of divorced, noncustodial fathers confirms a pattern somewhat comparable to their patterns of payment

of support: visits begin with frequency and then typically taper off within a few years. . . .

Many people attribute noncustodial parents' low rates of payment and visitation to indifference to their children's welfare. It is nonetheless possible to ascribe more sympathetic causes for declining feelings of responsibility over time. Although a minority of divorced, noncustodial fathers sustain a vital relationship with their children years after separation, many fathers who see their children no more frequently than once a week or every other week find the visitation relationship unnatural and unsatisfying. Over time, they feel less and less a part of their children's lives. . . .

If the noncustodial parent remarries, he develops a new center for his life and derives satisfactions from new children with whom he shares life day-to-day. . . .

David Chambers, The Coming Curtailment of Compulsory Child Support, 80 Mich. L. Rev. 1614, 1623-1624 (1982).

What arguments support such a change? What problems can you see, and how would you modify this proposal to deal with them?

C.   PARTICULAR ISSUES IN APPLYING CHILD SUPPORT FORMULAS

PETERSON V. PETERSON

434 N.W.2d 732 (S.D. 1989)

BRADSHAW, C.J. . . . Janey and Gregory were married on August 12, 1967. Megan, who is now 14 years old, and Ryan, now 11 years old, were born to this marriage. The marriage lasted for seventeen years until, because of Gregory's misfeasance, Janey instituted an action for divorce.

On May 2, 1985, Janey was granted a divorce. The judgment and decree of divorce gave custody of Megan and Ryan to Janey, decreeing that Gregory pay $250 per month, per child, for the support of the children. The trial court concluded further that Janey should receive one-half of the property amassed during the marriage through the joint efforts of the parties, and 30 per cent of the property which had been donated to Gregory by his father. Janey also received, as part of the property award, $115,063 in cash. She thus obtained a total property award, after deducting liabilities, of $329,858. . . .

[Janey moved to adjust upward the amount of child support Gregory was required to pay. The trial judge granted the motion and raised Gregory's monthly child support obligation from $500 to $665. Janey appealed, arguing that "the trial court misinterpreted SDCL 25-7-7 when it failed to include certain items in Gregory's gross income in determining support."]

* * *

Janey argues that the lower court abused its discretion by, first, not considering money earned (but never actually received) by Gregory which was put back into the family business, and, second, by awarding a sum that is mathematically at a lower percentage of net income than that given other income brackets under the statute.

SDCL 25-7-7 defines monthly gross income to include, in pertinent part, amounts received from the following sources: (1) Compensation paid to an employee for personal services, whether called salary, wages, commissions, bonus or other designations; (2) Gain or profit from a business or profession, farming included, usually called self-employment income; . . . (4) Interest, dividends, rentals, royalties or other gain derived from investment of capital assets. . . . Furthermore, SDCL 25-7-7 states that "[g]ross income from . . . rentals, royalties, . . . or other sources, are the net profits or gain shown on any or all schedules filed as part of the obligor's federal income tax returns for any business with which he is associated. . . ." The statute goes on to provide that the court may allow or disallow deductions from an obligor's monthly gross income which, although listed on the obligor's federal income tax return, do not require the disbursement of cash.

In the present case, Gregory's 1986 federal income tax return lists, among other items, net rental income from a truck stop in Worthington, Minnesota, and interest income from a contract for deed. According to the evidence, Gregory never received these monies; instead, they were utilized to keep the truck stop in a reasonable state of repair. Consequently, Gregory avers, these funds added nothing to his income.

In the proceedings below, Janey implored the trial court to determine Gregory's net monthly income to be $4,514.66, which included earnings from the Worthington property and Ronning Enterprises. Gregory, by contrast, urged the trial court to delete from his monthly gross income the funds from the Worthington property and Ronning Enterprises, thereby reducing his net monthly income to $3,213.16. The lower court determined that Gregory had a monthly gross income, excluding the two sums of money he never receives, of approximately $5,029.00, or a net monthly income of $3,212.00. Thus, the trial judge, though cognizant of Gregory's unreceived income, refused to include it when he computed Gregory's monthly gross income.

Reading SDCL 25-7-7 as a whole, . . . we are unable to hold that the trial judge erred in interpreting the statute. Pursuant to its terms, SDCL 25-7-7 includes in an obligor's monthly gross income only those amounts received by the obligor. Here, Gregory did not receive the rental or interest income, he was without power to guide the disposition of this income, and the expenditure of the income did not inure to his benefit. With these facts as a foundation, we hold that the trial judge acted within the bounds of his discretion when he refused to include within Gregory's monthly gross income rental and interest income listed on Gregory's federal income tax return.

Additionally, Janey demonstrates that the trial judge misused his discretion when he arrived at an amount of child support to be paid by Gregory, who has a net monthly income exceeding $1,500. We disagree.

When confronted with an obligor with a net monthly income greater than $1,500, the trial judge must use a discretion which is tempered by the requirement that it have a sound basis in the available evidence. This discretion is to include an appraisal of the realistic needs of the children and the obligor's ability to satisfy these requisites. The trial court must consider the financial condition of both parents, including the mother's new spouse.

SDCL 25-7-7 specifically requires that, if net monthly income exceeds the $1,500 level, the amount of child support shall be at an appropriate level, and in no instance may the amount of support be less than that required at the $1,500 level. The statute requires support payments of between $462 and $495 for the support of two children at the $1,500 level. The lower court ordered support of $665 per month,[17] which exceeds the amount required at the $1,500 level. This is all that SDCL 25-7-7 requires. The statute does not require a mathematical analysis of percentages but rather requires that support be at an appropriate level, and not be less than that required at the $1,500 level. The trial court must do more than a mere mathematical extrapolation from the table in SDCL 25-7-7.

The trial judge had access to the affidavits of Gregory and Janey, as do we. Janey's affidavit contains an enumeration of the children's monthly expenses. Likewise, Gregory, in his affidavit, outlines his current financial situation, including his present monthly gross and net incomes. The conclusion of the trial court that the support of the children should be raised to $665 per month is adequately supported by the record. . . .

This evidentiary showing, allied with the trial judge's general finding that Gregory and Janey each have enough income and resources to adequately provide for Megan and Ryan, convinces us that the trial judge possessed sufficient evidence from which he could discern, as a matter of law, that Gregory's child support obligation should be elevated to the level established by the trial court. Hence, we find no abuse of discretion, and the trial judge's determination shall stand.

SABERS, J. (dissenting in part and concurring in result in part). I dissent because the child support award is wholly inadequate under the evidence in this record.

Under SDCL 25-7-7, when the obligor's net monthly income exceeds $1,500 the circuit court must exercise its discretion in setting the child support obligation. This discretion is not unfettered, but must have a sound basis in the evidence. Havens v. Henning, 418 N.W.2d 311 (S.D.1988). In *Havens*, the custodial parent petitioned the court to increase the father's child support obligation for two remaining minor children. The circuit court found that the father's net monthly income was $2,100 and increased the child support obligation to $334 per child per month or a total support award of $668. The award was challenged and upheld because of the increased net income of the father since the divorce, the increased cost of living, and the increased cost of raising children as they get older.

In this case, the trial court found that the defendant's gross monthly income was approximately $5,029 per month and that he had additional monthly income of $1,301.50 from the Worthington, Minnesota truck stop and a Ronning Enterprises project which the court refused to consider. The court awarded $665 per month as the total child support. This award was unreasonable because the

---

17. Gregory also pays for the following items for the benefit of the children: insurance premiums of $148.00 per month, camp expenses, skiing expenses, and airline expenses.

defendant's net monthly income in this case is at least twice the amount of the net monthly income of the father in *Havens* and yet the child support award is $3.00 per month less.

The court also erred in failing to address the current financial needs of the minor children and disregarding the income of $1,301.50 from the Worthington and Ronning Enterprises projects. The majority opinion approves the trial court's omission on the claimed basis that "Gregory did not receive the rental or interest income, he was without power to guide the disposition of this income, and the expenditure of the income did not inure to his benefit." None of these statements have any real basis in fact and there is no proof in the record to support these positions. Gregory did receive the rental or interest income and he had power to guide the disposition of this income, and the expenditure of the income inured to his benefit.

SDCL 25-7-7 does not exclude these items, it includes them. As indicated in the majority opinion SDCL 25-7-7 defines monthly gross income to include, in pertinent part, "amounts received from the following sources: (2) Gain or profit from a business or profession, . . . (4) Interest, dividends, rentals, royalties or other gain derived from investment of capital assets." As further stated in the majority opinion, the statute goes on to provide that the court may allow or disallow deductions from a obligor's property as monthly gross income, which, although listed on the obligor's federal income tax return, do not require the disbursement of cash. Even if these funds were utilized to keep the truck stop in a reasonable state of repair, he received the income, he guided the disposition of this income, and the expenditure inured to his benefit. Clearly this income does not qualify as a deduction under the statute and an obligor should not be able to avoid his lawful obligations simply by utilizing the funds to make repairs.

Exhibit 3, the 1986 United States individual income tax return of the father, is even more startling. Line 17 of Schedule D shows net long-term gain of $335,070. Only forty percent of this figure ($134,028) is subject to tax and appears on line 13 as "taxable" capital gain. This, and other income totaled $207,068 which, after an IRA deduction of $2,000 and $12,000 for alimony resulted in a "taxable" income or adjusted gross income of $193,068. In other words, the taxable income may have been under $200,000, but the real income for 1986 was almost $400,000.

For this court to limit the child support award to $332.50 per month per child is incredible. Strange as it may seem, this amount is near the poverty line for one person. It is even more incredible when one considers the father's real income for 1986 was $394,110. I would reverse and remand to the trial court to properly reconsider child support in accordance with South Dakota law and the guidelines set forth in SDCL 25-7-7. . . .

[The opinion of Justice Henderson, concurring in part, is omitted.]

NOTES AND QUESTIONS

1. The court in *Peterson* says that the child support statute "includes in an obligor's monthly gross income only those amounts received by the obligor,"

which the court takes to mean amounts that the obligor receives in cash. Does the statute impose this limitation? How does the dissent interpret "receives"?

The majority concluded that income that the father had to report for purposes of the federal income tax was not income for purposes of the child support guidelines. Generally, courts have held that just because an item is deductible for purposes of the federal income tax it is not necessarily deductible for purposes of calculating child support. *See, e.g.,* Turner v. Turner, 586 A.2d 1182 (Del. 1991); In re Sullivan, 794 P.2d 687 (Mont. 1990). Should income and expenses be treated the same for purposes of both income taxes and child support? Why or why not?

2. Child support guideline definitions of income are usually very inclusive, and courts have construed them broadly. Retirement income, Social Security payments, lottery winnings, personal injury settlements, spousal support, and inheritances have been treated as income. *See, e.g.,* In the Interest of A.M.D., 78 P.3d 741 (Colo. 2003); Wood v. Wood, 403 S.E.2d 761 (W. Va. 1991); In re Micaletti, 796 P.2d 54 (Colo. App. 1990); Genna Rosten, Consideration of Obligor Spouse's or Parent's Personal Injury Recovery or Settlement in Fixing Alimony or Child Support Award, 59 A.L.R. 5th 489 (2004).

An emerging issue is how stock options should be treated for purposes of calculating child support. While of undoubted economic value, stock options present difficult issues for a number of reasons, including difficulties in assigning value to them and questions about the extent to which courts should pressure parents to exercise options by attributing income to parents who own the options. Discussions include Susan Isard, Note, Stock Options and Child Support: The Price of Accuracy, 14 Hastings Women's L.J. 215 (2003); Kristy Watson, Acting in the Best Interests of the Child: A Solution to the Problem of Characterizing Stock Options as Income, 69 Fordham L. Rev. 1523 (2001).

On the deduction side, legitimate business expenses are generally deductible for owners of small businesses. Rimkus v. Rimkus, 557 N.E.2d 638 (Ill. App. 1990); In re Smith, 791 P.2d 1373 (Mont. 1990). Employees cannot usually deduct their expenses, though.

3. The other major issue in *Peterson* is how to set child support when the income of one or both parents is higher than the top amount on the child support scale. The *Peterson* court, like most other courts, refuses simply to extrapolate the percentages in the scale to the parents' actual income. Why? How did the court decide what amount of support the father owed? Justice Sabers criticized the amount of the child support order on the basis that it was only a little above the poverty level for one person. Is this argument persuasive? How would you argue that the amount set by the trial court was too low, considering the father's income?

Some courts have held that the guidelines simply do not apply in this situation and that the case should be decided under preguideline law. Wylie v. Wylie, 568 So. 2d 812 (Ala. Civ. App. 1990); Battersby v. Battersby, 590 A.2d 427 (Conn. 1991); Brandt v. Brandt, 565 So. 2d 397 (Fla. Dist. Ct. App. 1990). Other courts begin with the guideline amount that would apply if the parents' income were equal to the guideline maximum and then exercise discretion to add amounts to reflect the additional income. *See, e.g.,* Voishan v. Palma, 609 A.2d 319 (Md. 1992); In re Lalone, 469 N.W.2d 695 (Iowa 1991); Hoffman v. Hoffman, 805 S.W.2d 848 (Tex. App. 1991); In re LeBlanc, 800 P.2d 1384 (Colo. App. 1990).

The Kentucky Court of Appeals, emphasizing that "no child needs three ponies," rejected the share of the wealth approach used in some states in the case of high income parents. Downing v. Downing, 45 S.W.3d 449 (Ky. App. 2001). Pearson v. Pearson, 751 N.E.2d 921 (Mass. App. 2001), also cites the "three pony rule" to explain its refusal to award child support in high income cases on a pure income share basis. Pearson cites as source of the phrase Morgan, Child Support and the Anomalous Cases of the High-Income and Low-Income Parent: The Need to Reconsider What Constitutes "Support" in the American and Canadian Child Support Guideline Models, 13 Can. J. Fam. L. 161 (1996). For further discussion of these issues *see* Kathleen A. Hogan, Child Support in High Income Cases, 17 J. Am Acad. Matrimonial L. 349 (2001).

4. In several high-income cases, including a number involving professional athletes, the court acknowledged that the parent is likely to receive a very high income for only a short time. In some states, courts may enter orders in such cases that contemplate or even require that some current child support be saved to provide for the child in the future after the parent's income goes down. *See, e.g,* Nash v. Mulle, 846 S.W.2d 803 (Tenn. 1993); In re Paternity of Tukker M.L., 544 N.W.2d 417 (Wis. 1996), both allowing a court to order the establishment of an educational trust fund. This approach is not permitted in other states, which say that child support can be ordered only to provide for the child's current needs. *See, e.g.,* Lang v. Koon, 806 N.E.2d 956 (Mass. App. 2004), reversing a child support order that included an amount that would have allowed the children's custodial parent to save money for the children's college. The court said that support orders must address current circumstances, and that only in very limited cases are orders for future education justified, where the children have special needs or profligate parents. Since neither was shown here, the judge said, "it remains the responsibility of the individual parents, without judicial intervention, to plan in advance for anticipated college expenses." For further information *see* Judith G. McMullen, The Professional Athlete: Issues in Child Support, 12 Marquette Sports L. Rev. 411 (2001).

5. Despite earlier commentary, which suggests that parents commonly settle for child support below the presumptive guideline amount, the majority of courts have held that this is not permissible unless a downward deviation is otherwise justified under the state's criteria for rebutting the presumption established by the formula. *See, e.g.,* Cox v. Cox, 776 P.2d 1045 (Alaska 1989); Ching v. Ching, 751 P.2d 93 (Haw. App. 1988); Peerenboom v. Peerenboom, 433 N.W.2d 282 (Wis. Ct. App. 1988). The Department of Health & Human Services has also taken the position that states should require parties who stipulate child support to justify child support obligations that deviate from the presumptive amount calculated under the guidelines. 56 Fed. Reg. 22,347 (May 15, 1991).

On the other hand, in general, parents may enter into enforceable contracts for more child support than a court could order or for a longer term, and if the parents agree, courts ordinarily may incorporate such agreements into their orders.

NOTE: CHILDREN'S MEDICAL EXPENSES

Federal and state laws require that child support decrees specifically address how children's medical expenses will be paid. For employed parents this can usually be done most economically by ordering a parent whose employer provides insurance to include the children in his or her plan. States must have laws preventing employers from denying enrollment to employees' children not living with the employee parent, born outside marriage, or not claimed as a dependent by the employee parent for federal income tax purposes. 42 U.S.C. § 1396g-1. This section also provides that the insurance plan must allow the child to be enrolled outside limited enrollment seasons, and if the noncustodial parent does not enroll the child, the plan must allow the custodial parent to enroll the child. The insurance plan must provide the child the same documents about the plan that it gives participants, and it must permit the custodial parent to submit claims without the approval of the noncustodial parent. It cannot eliminate coverage for the child unless it receives written evidence that a court order requiring coverage is no longer in effect or that the child is covered by other, comparable health insurance. *Id.*

ERISA requires covered group health plans to honor a qualified medical child support order (QMCSO). 29 U.S.C. § 1169. This order creates or recognizes the right of a child to benefits from a parent's group health care plan. QMCSOs, which bear an obvious resemblance to the QDROs (discussed in Chapter 6) must include the following information:

- The name and last known mailing address of the plan participant and each "alternate recipient" covered by the order (an "alternate recipient" is a child entitled by the court order to enroll in the plan);
- A reasonable description of the type of coverage to be provided by the plan, or the method by which coverage is to be determined;
- The period to which the order applies; and
- Each plan to which the order applies.

The QMCSO cannot require the plan to provide a type or form of benefit that it does not otherwise provide. Insurance plans must have procedures for determining the validity of QMCSOs and communicating the decisions to affected parties promptly. Since the QMCSO only applies to the plan named in the order, if the parent employee changes jobs, a new QMCSO must be obtained.

States' child support guidelines vary substantially in their treatment of the costs of children's health insurance and payment for uninsured medical expenses. For recent examples, *see* Jo Michelle Beld & Len Biernat, Federal Intent for State Child Support Guidelines: Income Shares, Cost Shares, and the Realities of Shared Parenting, 37 Fam. L.Q. 165, 177-178 and sources cited in footnotes (2003).

PROBLEMS

1. Father's employer pays for an apartment and a company car for Father. Should the fair market value of these fringe benefits income for purposes of calculating child support? What about contributions that the employer makes to Father's retirement account?

In a jurisdiction that bases child support on net income, should Father be able to deduct mandatory amounts withheld from his pay to fund his pension? How about extra amounts that he contributes voluntarily to the pension? What if

Father is self-employed and regularly contributes to a retirement plan over which he has sole control?

2. Father, a certified public accountant, is a minority shareholder in a closely held accounting firm; the other shareholders are his father and two brothers. Mother, a medical doctor, is a sole practitioner whose practice is incorporated. Last year each business retained some of its earnings rather than paying them out as dividends. Should the retained earnings be included as income if the jurisdiction follows the test adopted in *Peterson*? What if the jurisdiction adopted the approach for which the dissent advocates?

Now assume that both Father's and Mother's corporations make contributions to retirement plans for them. Should this money be treated as income under the *Peterson* majority's test? Under the dissent's approach?

3. Emilio and Carey have two children, born in 1994 and 1996. In 1997 Emilio stipulated to a court order requiring him to pay Carey child support of $3,500 per month, to maintain medical insurance for the children, and to pay their reasonable uninsured medical and dental expenses. Emilio has also voluntarily paid for child care, a housekeeper, vacations, food, transportation, private schools, and a four-bedroom house in Malibu.

In 2003 Carey moved to modify the child support order to comport with recently modified child support guidelines. The parties cannot agree about the amount of Emilio's annual income. He says that it exceeds $1 million per year and agrees to pay any reasonable amount of child support. Carey claims that his income is closer to $12 million per year. Carey has served a discovery request on Emilio for two years' worth of documents, including bank records relating to accounts in his name alone or jointly with any other person or for any business enterprise in which he has an interest; income records, including copies of 1099 forms, W-2 forms, payroll check stubs or receipts, gifts, loans, commissions, rents, interest, dividends, and annuities; books of account; records of loans made by him and monies owed to him; records of employment and fringe benefits he has received; records of stock brokerage accounts; records of his debts and liabilities; and documentation of his monthly expenses. She has also demanded additional documents pertaining to his income and lifestyle and trust documents, wills, codicils, and estate planning documents executed since he married his current wife.

Emilio objects to these discovery requests on the grounds that they are unduly burdensome and an unreasonable invasion of his privacy. What arguments should Emilio and Carey make at the hearing on the discovery motions?

MARYGOLD S. MELLI, *GUIDELINE REVIEW: CHILD SUPPORT*
AND TIME SHARING BY PARENTS

33 Fam. L.Q. 219, 220-221 (1999)

. . . In the late 1980s when the states began to formulate mandatory guidelines to be used in setting the amount of child support, they focused on the most common arrangement, sole physical custody and on the need to ensure that the costs of raising the child in that household would be shared equitably by the nonresidential parent. Therefore, the focus was on the child raising costs in the residential household and little attention was paid to the fact that the nonresidential parent might incur costs when spending time with the child. However, in the last decade there has been increasing recognition that there are a number of situations in which child-related expenditures by the nonresidential parent arise. One reason for this increased concern may be the growing involvement of fathers—who are overwhelmingly the nonresidential parents in spending time with their children. A number of studies have shown that over the last decade or so there has been an increase in the amount of time that divorced fathers spend with their children.

While the percentage of income model did not include an adjustment for visitation, the income shares and Melson models have always provided for adjustments when each parent has the children for a substantial amount of time, generally defined as at least 25 to 35 percent of the time. Robert G. Williams, Guidelines for Setting Levels of Child Support Orders, 21 Fam. L.Q. 281 (1987). This approach has been criticized, based on the claim that nonresidential parents who spend less time than this with their children still incur substantial expenses. William V. Fabricius & Sanford L. Braver, Non-Child Support Expenditures on Children by Nonresidential Divorced Fathers: Results of a Study, 41 Fam. Ct. Rev. 321 (2003). This claim is also one of the foundations of the argument in favor of the cost-shares formula approach, above. Supporters of the current model respond that the study by Frabricius and Braver is methodologically flawed and argue that is it not a good idea to calibrate child support to visitation time because visitation tends to decline over time and because such calibration is likely to promote continuing hostilities between parents over how much visitation should and does occur. Irwin Garfinkel, Sara McLanahan, & Judith Wallerstein, Visitation and Child Support Guidelines, 42 Fam. Ct. Rev. 342 (2004). In turn, Fabricius and Braver dispute the substantive accuracy of these claims. William V. Fabricius & Sanford L. Braver, Expenditures on Children and Visitation Time: A Reply to Garfinkel, McLanahan, and Wallerstein, 42 Fam. Ct. Rev. 350 (2004).

Despite this empirical uncertainty, the trend is for child support guidelines to incorporate adjustments for shared parenting time, including for cases in which the children are with the residential parent more than 70 percent of the time. In 2004, 28 states' child support rules provided for adjustments for shared parenting time. Linda D. Elrod & Robert G. Spector, A Review of the Year in Family Law, Chart 3, 36 Fam. L.Q. 579 (2004). See also Stephanie Giggetts, Application of Child Support Guidelines to Cases of Joint-, Split-, or Similar Shared-Custody Arrangements, 57 A.L.R.5th 389 (2004). In the common case where the residential parent's income is lower than the nonresidential parent's, the result is a reduced child support award unless the total amount to be shared is increased to recognize the increased costs of the child being in two households, as the drafters of the income shares model recommended. See Williams, above.

While the argument favoring a closer link between parenting time and child support was originally made in support of lowering the support payments of nonresident parents, the next case explores how this principle should be employed when the residential parent's income is substantially higher than that of the nonresidential parent.

COLONNA V. COLONNA

855 A.2d 648 (Pa. 2004)

Justice NEWMAN. . . .

Appellant, Mary M. Colonna (Mother), and Appellee Robert J. Colonna (Father), were married in 1983 and separated in 1996. . . . At the time of separation, Father sought primary legal and physical custody of the parties' four children, who at the time ranged in age from nine to three years old. Pending the outcome of Father's custody petition, the parties agreed to a temporary order of shared legal and physical custody, pursuant to which the children lived three and one-half days per week with each parent. . . .

On November 19, 1997, the trial court ordered Father to pay Mother $6,132.00 per month ($73,584.00 per year) in child support and to provide health insurance for Mother and the children. The trial court also ordered Father to pay the interest portion of the mortgage on the marital home; homeowners, personal property and automobile insurance; private school tuition; and other expenses. . . .

By Order dated May 4, 1998, the trial court awarded primary legal and physical custody to father during the school year, and primary legal and physical custody to Mother during the summer. Mother has partial custody of one or more of the children on Tuesday and Thursday during the school year, and Father has partial custody of one or more of the children on Tuesday and Thursday during the summer. The parties alternate holidays and weekends throughout the year, and each parent has two weeks with the children for summer vacation.

On July 24, 1998, Father sought to terminate child support on the basis that he was now the children's primary custodian. . . . A hearing was held before a master in October of 1998, at which time Father introduced his 1997 tax return indicating monthly net income of $16,130.00 ($193,560.00 per year), which was a significant decrease from the monthly net income of $85,942.00 ($1,031,304.00 per year) shown on his 1996 tax return. He presented evidence of living expenses and reasonable needs in the amount of $14,834.23 per month ($178,010.76 per year). The master assessed Mother a net earning capacity of $4,607.00 per month ($55,284.00 per year). Mother presented the same reasonable needs as she did during the 1997 support hearing, namely $28,208.00 per month ($338,496.00 per year) for herself and the children, with $21,106.00 per month ($253,272.00 per year) attributable to the children. She maintained that her expenses were the same as they had been when the parties shared custody equally.[18] The master concluded

---

18. We note that a parent incurs certain fixed costs related to providing the children with a home in which to exercise his or her period of partial custody. Costs such as mortgage or rent payments, insurance, utilities, etc. remain the same whether the children are in a parent's custody or not.

that Mother's earning capacity was unchanged, but that Father's monthly net income was now $16,130.00 ($193,560.00 per year).

The master determined that Mother had custody 27% of the year, and Father had custody 73% of the year. She was troubled by the disparities in the parties' income and the fact that Mother has certain fixed expenses incident to her alternating weekend and summer custody. . . . [The master recommended that Father be ordered to pay Mother $294 per month in child support, based on the findings that at the level of their combined incomes, the parents' combined child support obligation should be $5,868 per month. The master allocated this between the parents proportionately to their incomes and to the amount of time the children spent with each of them.]

Mother and Father both filed exceptions to the master's recommendation. By Order dated April 27, 1999, the trial court sustained Mother's exceptions in part, and ordered Father to pay $810.00 per month ($9,720.00 per year) for support of the children. "This order award was calculated using the presumptive minimum under the new guidelines multiplied by the percentage of Mother's custody time." In an Opinion in support of the Order, the trial court stated:

> In this proceeding, the hearing officer recommended a child support amount which was offset by [Mother's] obligation to husband for child support. I agreed with the hearing officer's decision that it was not appropriate in this case to terminate support based solely on the custodial situation. However, [Father] had not filed for child support against [Mother] and I found that it was inappropriate to offset any child support due [Mother] by any amount that she would owe [Father]. Therefore, I awarded [Mother] support based on the guidelines reduced to the percentage of her partial custody time.

Father appealed to the Superior Court, which reversed in a published Opinion. The Superior Court concluded that for purposes of calculating child support, the custodial parent is the obligee and the non-custodial parent is the obligor. Because the children spend 73% of the time with Father and 27% with Mother, the Superior Court determined that Father, as the obligee, does not owe child support to Mother, who is the obligor. . . .

We adamantly disagree with this conclusion. Like the master and the trial court, we are troubled by the disparity in the parties' incomes and are concerned that the refusal to consider this as a factor when fashioning a support order may be contrary to the best interests of the children. We must always be mindful of the fact that the support laws work in conjunction with our custody laws. The General Assembly has declared:

> [I]t is the public policy of this Commonwealth, when in the best interest of the child, to assure a reasonable and continuing contact of the child with both parents after a separation or dissolution of the marriage and a sharing of the rights and responsibilities of child rearing by both parents. . . .

23 Pa.C.S. § 5301. Where the parent who does not have primary custody has a less significant income than the custodial parent, it is likely that he or she will not be able to provide an environment that resembles the one in which the children

are accustomed to living with the custodial parent. While a downward adjustment in lifestyle is a frequent consequence of divorce that affects both adults and children, we would be remiss in failing to ignore the reality of what happens when children are required to live vastly different lives depending upon which parent has custody on any given day. To expect that quality of the contact between the non-custodial parent and the children will not be negatively impacted by that parent's comparative penury vis-à-vis the custodial parent is not realistic. Issuing a support order that allows such a situation to exist clearly is not in the best interests of the children.

Therefore, where the incomes of the parents differ significantly, we believe that it is an abuse of discretion for the trial court to fail to consider whether deviating from the support guidelines is appropriate, even in cases where the result would be to order child support for a parent who is not the primary custodial parent. . . .

In a case such as the instant matter, the trial court should inquire whether the non-custodial parent has sufficient assets to provide the children with appropriate housing and amenities during his or her period of partial custody. We specifically note that the term "appropriate" does not mean equal to the environment the children enjoy while in the custodial parent's care, nor does it mean "merely adequate." The determination of appropriateness is left to the discretion of the trial court, upon consideration of all relevant circumstances.

* * *

. . . Because we conclude that a parent with primary custody may be ordered to pay child support to a parent with partial custody, we reverse the Order of the Superior Court and remand the case to the trial court for a determination of support for the parent with partial custody.

Chief Justice CAPPY, dissenting. Because I believe that a custodial parent should not be obligated to pay child support to a noncustodial parent, I must respectfully dissent.

The majority has declared that where "the incomes of the parents differ significantly, we believe that it is an abuse of discretion for the trial court to fail to consider whether deviating from the support guidelines is appropriate. . . ." The majority further decrees that "the trial court should inquire whether the non-custodial parent has sufficient assets to provide the children with appropriate housing and amenities during his or her period of partial custody." The majority provides an exceedingly vague definition of "appropriate housing and amenities," stating that "the term 'appropriate' does not mean equal to the environment the children enjoy while in the custodial parent's care, nor does it mean 'merely adequate.'" Finally, the majority specifically states that this ruling is not limited to those high income cases where the combined net income of the parents exceeds $15,000.00 per month, but rather encompasses all situations where there is a "significant disparity in income."

I find this analysis to be troubling for several reasons. First, I can perceive no objective standards within the rule it sets forth. How does a trial court determine what is "appropriate housing and amenities"? Furthermore, what constitutes a "significant disparity" in income? I am concerned that we are providing the trial courts and the practicing bar precious little guidance as to how the majority's rule should be applied.

Second, I find the majority's approach disquieting because I believe it transforms a child support action into a quasi-equitable distribution action. In my view, the majority's new rule is not so much addressing whether the needs of the children are being met (which is a proper subject of a child support action), but rather is focused on augmenting the wealth of the noncustodial parent. While such a focus may be proper in an equitable distribution matter, it has no place in a child support action. A child support action should not be used to jerry-rig a new balance between the respective financial positions of the spouses.

Finally, and most importantly, I am not in accord with the majority's foundational premise concerning the relationships between parents and children. The majority appears to be of the belief that if there is a disparity in income, the parent-child relationship will perforce be corrupted by the wealthier parent's desire to "buy the affection of the children. . . ." The majority goes so far as to state that it is unrealistic to believe that a noncustodial parent's relationship with her child will not suffer where the custodial parent is more wealthy than the noncustodial parent. The majority believes we should capitulate to what it perceives to be a social reality, and redistribute the wealth so that the affections of the child will not be alienated due to a parent's inability to provide the child with material advantages comparable to those provided by the wealthier parent.

I am disturbed by this approach. First, I can find no basis in the law for the proposition that a noncustodial spouse must be enabled, via payments from the custodial parent, to provide material advantages and entertain her children in the same lavish fashion as may the custodial parent. This simply has not been the law of this Commonwealth.

Furthermore, I am disturbed by the philosophy underpinning this rule. Unlike the apparent view of the majority, I do not believe that the health of any given parent-child relationship is measured by a parent's ability to provide a surfeit of expensive possessions or experiences for her child. Rather, the parent-child relationship thrives, or withers, based on the availability of intangibles such as love, attention, and affection. While it may be true that we live in a highly materialistic culture, does this fact stand in contradiction to the timeless realities of parenting? Or, to put it colloquially, *can* money buy love? I think not. And, more importantly, I balk at this court's implication that not only are a child's affections for sale, but also that our judiciary should be in the business of fostering the market for such a "commodity."

For the foregoing reasons, I respectfully dissent.

NOTES AND QUESTIONS

1. In *Colonna* if the custodial relationship had been reversed, so that the mother had the children 73 per cent of the time, the father would surely have been ordered to pay child support. In such a case, should the amount that he spends while the children are with him reduce the amount of support that he

pays? If the children live with each parent half the time and the parents' incomes are widely disparate, as in *Colonna*, should child support be ordered from the wealthier to the poorer parent? Does it logically follow that if the residential parent's income is very high, he or she should pay child support to the nonresidential parent for periods of "visitation"? Why or why not?

If the parties had two children, and one lived fulltime with the mother and the other fulltime with the father, would the same principles apply that govern in cases of shared custody?

2. In *Colonna*, the father's income was almost four times that of the mother's. What if his income had only been twice hers; should the court have ordered him to pay support to her then? By how much must their incomes differ before a court enters an order as in *Colonna*?

NOTE: CHILD SUPPORT OBLIGATIONS OF LOW-INCOME PARENTS

When a parent has little or no income, the first issue that must be considered is whether additional income should be imputed to the parent on the theory that he or she could reasonably be expected to earn more. The question of when income should be imputed to a parent is similar to the question of when a support obligation should be reduced because the obligor's income has decreased, to the extent that both depend on a judgment about whether the obligor parent should be expected to earn more than he or she does. Modification of support based on reduced income is covered in Chapter 8.

Parents with very low incomes who cannot earn more are generally not totally exempt from child support. Many guidelines provide for a minimum child support obligation, such as $25 or $50 per month, since all parents are obligated to support their children. In Marriage of Gilbert, 945 P.2d 238 (Wash. App. 1997), however, the court held that a rule that provided for a minimum monthly order of $25 violated the federal requirement that amounts determined by a child support formula must be treated as creating a rebuttable presumption. The court ordered that henceforth the rule should be treated as creating such a presumption.

Most guidelines and courts that have considered the issue have held that public assistance payments, from either Supplemental Security Income (based on disability or old age) or Temporary Assistance to Needy Families, is not "income" from which a parent may be ordered to pay child support. *See, e.g.,* Marrocco v. Giardino, 767 A.2d 720 (Conn. 2001); Dept. of Public Aid ex rel. Lozada v. Rivera, 755 N.E.2d 548 (Ill. App. 2001); Angela. F. Epps, To Pay or Not To Pay, That Is the Question: Should SSI Recipients Be Exempt From Child Support Obligations? 34 Rutgers L.J. 63 (2003). In comparison, most guidelines and courts include Social Security Disability payments received by parent or a child in the calculation of child support, though the states vary in their approaches. *See* Tori R. A. Kricken, Child Support and Social Security Dependent Benefits: A Comprehensive Analysis and Proposal for Wyoming, 2 Wyo. L. Rev. 39 (2002).

A number of courts have held that child support orders should be issued against incarcerated parents, even though the parent has no ability to pay while in prison; the payments become a debt which the parent is expected to pay upon release. *See, e.g.,* Holt v. Geter, 809 So. 2d 68 (Fla. Dist. Ct. App. 2002). *See also* Bergen Cty. Bd. of Servs. v. Steinhauer, 683 A.2d 856 (Ch. Div. 1996) (majority of courts modify or suspend an incarcerated parent's support obligations; public policy favors granting modification or suspension if obligor is incarcerated and without assets so as to avoid unenforceable order); Karen Rothschild Cavanaugh & Daniel Pollack, Child Support Obligations of Incarcerated Parents, 7 Cornell J.L. & Pub. Pol'y 531, 532 (1998); Frank J. Wozniak, Loss of Income Due to Incarceration as Affecting Child Support Obligation, 27 A.L.R.5th 540 (2004).

D. SUPPORT FOR OLDER CHILDREN

LESLIE HARRIS, DENNIS WALDROP & LORI R. WALDROP, *MAKING AND BREAKING CONNECTIONS BETWEEN PARENTS' DUTY TO SUPPORT AND RIGHT TO CONTROL THEIR CHILDREN*

69 Or. L. Rev. 689, 717-720 (1990)

Today we ordinarily think of parents' support duty as terminating when a child attains the age of majority. However, in the nineteenth and into the twentieth century the determination of when parents were no longer required to support their children depended on the child's actual capacity for self-support and submission to parental control.

Older adolescents, especially boys, were considered capable of at least partial self-support and often worked for wages. So long as a minor child lived with or was supported by the parents and had not been emancipated, the father was entitled to the child's earnings. By the same token, a parent was obligated to support a minor child so long as the child remained under the parent's control. A parent might discharge, at least partially, the duty to support a minor child capable of earning wages by giving the child the right to retain the wages. Some authorities went so far as to say that a parent was not required to support a child to the extent that the child could earn money. Further, a parent was not required to support a minor child capable of self-support who left the parent and struck out on his or her own. Some courts expressed this idea by saying that parents were not obligated to support minor children who were emancipated. "Emancipation" is a term with multiple meanings, depending on the context in which it is used. In a formal sense, emancipation means the termination of some or all of the mutual rights and duties of the parent-child relationship, and it could occur by mutual agreement or when one party acted wrongfully, as when a father abandoned or forced a child out. In the latter situation the father was not entitled to the child's earnings. . . .

These rules were formulated in a time when children, especially boys, often attained functional adulthood in late adolescence, even though they were still legally minors. Parents were probably less worried about children remaining dependent for unreasonably long periods than they were that the children would strike out on their own when the parents felt they were still needed at home to work. In this context, the rules can be understood primarily as giving legal effect to circumstances as they actually existed. To some extent the rules also suggested that minors should remain subject to parental authority unless the parents acquiesced in their independence.

In the early 1970s most states lowered the age of majority to 18, the age at which most children are just finishing high school. However, social conditions have changed so that many young people continue in school well into their twenties, remaining economically, and to some extent personally, dependent on their parents. Many parents voluntarily support older children, but the question is whether parents are or should be legally obligated to continue to support them. . . .

CHILDERS V. CHILDERS

575 P.2d 201 (Wash. en banc 1978)

HICKS, A.J. . . . The parties were married in April 1953. They have three sons, born 1954, 1956 and 1959. Husband is a medical doctor practicing alone in King County. At trial, he was 53 years of age and wife was 45 years of age. . . .

Husband appealed to the Court of Appeals from that portion of the decree which requires him to pay . . . tuition, books and miscellaneous educational fees of each son. . . .

RCW 26.08.110, the statute in effect prior to enactment of the 1973 Dissolution of Marriage Act, provided that support could be ordered only for minor children of a marriage. . . .

The 1973 dissolution act, RCW 26.09, eliminated all reference to minority, and granted the court authority to order support for dependent children to whom a duty of support is owed. . . .

. . . We have no doubt that a change in the law was intended by the change in wording from the old support statute (referring to "minor," a fixed and arbitrary status) to the new support statute (referring to "dependent" and "emancipated," both of which are statuses to be determined under the facts of each case). The legislature may well have decided as a result of the lower majority age,[19] that support obligations should no longer hinge on minority, but that trial courts should have discretion to determine when a duty of support is owed, or ceases to be, and when a child is dependent, or ceases to be.

. . . We construe the dissolution act as basing any support obligation on dependency, not minority, and ending the obligation at emancipation, not majority. . . . Since the trial court is empowered under RCW 26.09 to order support to continue past a child's majority, we turn now to determine if there is an abuse of discretion in so ordering under the facts of this case.

The Childers' boys are children of the marriage. The other criteria set out in RCW 26.09.100 are that they be dependent and that their father owe them a duty of support. Both are matters of fact.

19. The Washington legislature lowered the age of majority to 18 in 1971. — Ed.

Although the legislature has defined dependent child variously throughout the code as 18 and under, under 21, or simply in financial need, the chapter before us contains no definition. . . . A dependent is, in our view and as used in this context, one who looks to another for support and maintenance, one who is in fact dependent, one who relies on another for the reasonable necessities of life. Dependency is a question of fact to be determined from all surrounding circumstances, or as the legislature put it: "all relevant factors." RCW 26.09.100. Age is but one factor. Other factors would include the child's needs, prospects, desires, aptitudes, abilities, and disabilities, and the parents' level of education, standard of living, and current and future resources. Also to be considered is the amount and type of support (i.e., the advantages, educational and otherwise) that the child would have been afforded if his parents had stayed together.

We find no abuse of discretion in the trial court's determination that the Childers' boys were dependents. They lived at home and were not self-sustaining at the time the decree was entered. As to their status as dependents continuing through 4 years of continuous pursuit of a baccalaureate degree, we think it reasonable to assume that a medical doctor, himself with years of higher education which brings him a higher than average income, would willingly treat his sons as dependents if they chose and showed an aptitude for college, but for the fact of the divorce. Where, as here, the children would have most likely remained dependent on their father past 18 while they obtained a college education, it is within the discretion of the trial court to define them as dependents for that purpose.

This brings us to the language "duty of support." That there *is* a parental duty of support owing to children has been clear since 1881:

> The expenses of the family and the education of the children are chargeable upon the property of both husband and wife, or either of them, and in relation thereto they may be sued jointly or separately.

Code of 1881, § 24079. . . .

We stated long ago that this duty of support can extend to education, the type and extent to be determined under the facts of each case. Reference is often had to Washington's example in this area, with the reasoning from the case of Esteb v. Esteb, 138 Wash. 174, 244 P. 264, 246 P. 27, 47 A.L.R. 110 (1926) most frequently cited. In *Esteb* we held that the court has the legal right to require a divorced father to provide funds for a college education for his minor daughter whose custody was in the mother. We quote extensively the reasoning, at pages 178, 182, 244 P. at 265, 267:

> As to the amount of education that should be considered necessary, courts have never laid down a hard and fast rule. . . .
> Applying the rule as stated by the courts and the textwriters, it will be seen that the question of what sort of an education is necessary, being a relative one, the court should determine this in a proper case from all the facts and circumstances.
> Nor should the court be restricted to the station of the minor in society, but should, in determining this fact, take into consideration the progress of society, and the attendant requirements upon the citizens of today. . . . An opportunity [in the 1800s] for a common school education was small, for a high school education less,

and for a college education was almost impossible to the average family, and was generally considered as being only within the reach of the most affluent citizens. While there is no reported case, it is hardly to be doubted that the courts at that time would have even held that a high school education was not necessary, inasmuch as very few were able to avail themselves of it. But conditions have changed greatly in almost a century that has elapsed since that time. Where the college graduate of that day was the exception, today such a person may almost be said to be the rule. . . . That it is the public policy of the state that a college education should be had, if possible, by all its citizens, is made manifest by the fact that the state of Washington maintains so many institutions of higher learning at public expense. It cannot be doubted that the minor who is unable to secure a college education is generally handicapped in pursuing most of the trades or professions of life, for most of those with whom he is required to compete will be possessed of that greater skill and ability which comes from such an education.

. . . Thus, it has long been the law in Washington that a divorced parent may have a duty of support for college education if it works the parent no significant hardship and if the child shows aptitude. . . .

[The Court of Appeals construed the statute as not allowing courts to order divorced parents to support children beyond the age of 18 because, it concluded, to hold otherwise would violate the privileges and immunities section of the Washington state constitution and the equal protection clause of the Fourteenth Amendment.] We turn to the issue of the claimed constitutional infirmity which the Court of Appeals raised and decided sua sponte. The fact that married parents *may* legally bid their children "a fiscal farewell" at age 18 when some divorced parents *may* be legally required to provide financial support when they are able but do not choose to do so, led the Court of Appeals to its conclusion. The fact that most married parents choose willingly to make financial sacrifices for their children's education, including college and regardless of age, seems to have been disregarded. . . .

It is not the policy of this State to require divorced parents to provide adult children with a college education in all circumstances. If an absolute duty of support for such a purpose were imposed on divorced parents, there would perhaps be an unreasonable classification. Instead, what exists is the long standing special powers the courts have had (in equity, regardless of legislation) over the children of broken homes to assure that their disadvantages are minimized.

. . . That the divorced parent, especially noncustodial, will sometimes not willingly provide what he otherwise would have but for the divorce, we recognized long ago in Esteb v. Esteb, 138 Wash. 174, 184, 244 P. 264, 267, 246 P. 27 (1926):

Appellant's counsel strenuously argued that it is the father's right to determine what education he will give his children, and that, if he decides not to give them a college education, and to save his money for other purposes, the courts should not interfere.

This rule is a salutary one, and should always be applied to a proper case. Whenever a father has the custody of a child, the law presumes that he will provide for the child's education in that vocation for which it is best fitted, and which will enable it to meet the conditions of modern life. But can the courts indulge that presumption, where the custody of the child has been taken from the father? . . .

Parents, when deprived of the custody of their children, very often refuse to do for such children what natural instinct would ordinarily prompt them to do. . . . In most cases the father, who is the one who holds the purse strings, and whose earning capacity is greater than that of the mother, is the one who is able to give the minor a proper education. To adopt the rule contended for by appellant would be to put the court, in providing for the custody of the child, in the dilemma of knowing that if the child is given to the mother the father would, in very many cases, refuse to give it an education greater than that required under the penalty of the law, and that the mother could not do so.

. . . In the 1973 act, the legislature simply allows the courts to secure for the children what they would have received from their parents except for the divorce, limited to that which is necessary for the children's and society's well-being and that which will not work an undue hardship on parents. Nothing more is expected of divorced parents than married parents, and nothing less.

In all probability more married parents will be making sacrifices financially for their children 18 and up than will the divorced parents who, in the sound discretion of the trial court, will have a legally imposed duty to do so. Even if the legislation does create a classification, it rests upon a reasonable basis. It is based on considerations already mentioned, and the facts known to the legislature and this court as well as to the layman, of the disruptions to homelife, bitterness and emotional upset which attend most marital breaks. The irremediable disadvantages to children whose parents have divorced are great enough. To minimize them, when possible, is certainly a legitimate governmental interest.

Note too that the governmental interest at stake here extends beyond the children to our nation as a whole. A well-educated citizenry is one of the major goals of a democratic society.

Under an equal protection challenge, a statutory classification such as is claimed to exist in this case, is measured against the rational relationship test and upheld if rationally related to some legitimate government interest. We do not utilize a strict scrutiny test because the classification is not suspect, nor is there any fundamental right not to provide support for one's children past age 18. We have no trouble asserting that a rational relationship exists between the legislative scheme before us and the compelling State interest in seeing that children are properly provided for within the boundaries of the needs of the children and what parents can afford. . . .

. . . We reverse the Court of Appeals in regard to support of the Childers's sons terminating at age 18.

JUDITH S. WALLERSTEIN & SANDRA BLAKESLEE, *SECOND CHANCES: MEN, WOMEN & CHILDREN A DECADE AFTER DIVORCE*

157-160 (1989)

In most divorced families, it is not clear who will pay for higher education. The mother's income plus child support does not generally provide savings for college tuition. Since fathers are usually financially more secure than mothers, it is fathers who can most afford to pay the bulk of college tuition. Many fathers provide child support payments, with more or less regularity, when their children are young, but the support does not rise when the children become teenagers and expenses go up steeply. And it usually stops abruptly at age eighteen — just when the child is ready to enter college. Children of divorce feel less protected economically; unlike children from intact families, whose parents usually continue to support them through college and sometimes even beyond, the children of divorce face an abrupt, premature end to an important aspect of their childhood. . . .

From an early age, these children are aware of money: It is scarce. Growing up, they know full well when their court-ordered child support payments will stop. If they have college plans, they face losing financial support when they most need it, and many adolescents seem to lower their ambitions in the face of this loss. At the ten-year mark, only one in ten children in high school said they knew there would be enough money for them to go to college. But even those raised by well-to-do parents feel more vulnerable than peers from equally well-to-do families. When fathers in our study do help children with college, they are twice as likely to help boys as girls. . . .

For reasons I don't understand, many fathers who pay all their child support over the years and maintain close contact with their children draw the line at college. While they can afford it, value education, and have cordial relations with their children, they do not offer even partial support through college. One-quarter of these men hold advanced degrees in medicine, law, or business administration, and the majority have college educations. But when I ask about college for their children, they don't want to discuss it. They don't plead poverty. Rather, they tend to say, "I paid my child support through the years. I met all my obligations. I've given my wife thousands of dollars, and now it's up to her." They do not say, "I am worried about my boy's future and how he's going to make it through college." On the contrary, these fathers seem strangely at peace about not helping their biological children with higher education and content to avoid the sacrifices that parents in intact families expect of themselves. A middle-class father living with his children does not question his moral obligation to set aside college savings. A middle-class father who only visits his children may see his obligations differently. Since he sees the child only occasionally, there is a distancing — both physical and psychological — between himself and his child. He sees paying for college as a voluntary act, one that is not very compelling in most cases. . . .

WILLIAM V. FABRICIUS, SANFORD L. BRAVER & KENDRA DENEAU,
*DIVORCED PARENTS' FINANCIAL SUPPORT OF THEIR CHILDREN'S
COLLEGE EXPENSES*

41 Family Court Review 224, 234-236, 238 (2003)

When we took into account divorced mothers' and fathers' financial situations and their ability to pay for college expenses, we found that, by students' reports, mothers and fathers voluntarily contributed remarkably similar proportions of their financial resources to their children's college education. This occurred in a state that has no statute or case law holding parents to a duty to college support. . . .

One dramatic factor [that may have affected parents' contributions] was legal custody arrangements. Equal numbers of students were from joint legal as from sole mother custody. In joint custody families, fathers contributed more than mothers did, and fathers with joint legal custody contributed more than fathers without did. In sole maternal custody families, mothers contributed more than fathers did, and mothers with sole custody contributed more than mothers with joint custody did. A similar result was found for dual or father residential custody. Among mother residential custody families, controlling for legal custody, fathers' contributions steadily increased with the amount of access they had to their children, to the point that they contributed more than mothers, whereas mothers' contributions remained constant. These findings suggest that when either parent feels parentally disenfranchised or that they have "lost" their child, they are likely to contribute less to college expenses. . . .

A potential problem in regarding both of these custody factors as causal for fathers is that "committed" fathers, the kind who requested and/or obtained these custody arrangements, may have been the very ones who would have paid more anyway, regardless of custody arrangements. There are several arguments against this "self-selection" possibility, however. First, the self-selection possibility implies that fathers for the most part had the residential custody arrangements they desired. But we know from previous work on other recent cohorts of this group of students that students reported that fathers wanted more time with their children. This was especially true of fathers who saw their children minimally or not at all, some, and a moderate amount. The percentages of these fathers who their now-adult children judged to have wanted more time with them are 63%, 78%, and 78%, respectively. Second, it is difficult to imagine that fathers who were predisposed to contribute certain amounts sorted themselves into corresponding categories of access arrangements; yet fathers' contributions increased steadily across the categories of increasing time with their children.

NOTES AND QUESTIONS

1. Children's economic prospects are much improved if they receive advanced training. *See* the data on the economic value of education in Chapter 6 at page 500. However, at some point parents expect that the children will "quit going to school and go to work," or at least pay for their own additional training. Should courts ever order parents in "intact families," that is, those in which both parents live with their children, to pay for advanced education? Should the answer be different if the family is not "intact," that is, if the parents do not live together?

In contrast to *Childers* and the decisions of other state supreme courts, in Curtis v. Kline, 666 A.2d 265 (Pa. 1995), the Pennsylvania Supreme Court held that a statute allowing courts to order divorced parents to pay support for adult children attending school violates the equal protection clause:

It will not do to argue that this classification is rationally related to the legitimate governmental purpose of obviating difficulties encountered by those in non-intact families who want parental financial assistance for post-secondary education, because such a statement of the governmental purpose assumes the validity of the classification. Recognizing that within the category of young adults in need of financial help to attend college there are some having a parent or parents unwilling to provide such help, the question remains whether the authority of the state may be selectively applied to empower only those from non-intact families to compel such help. We hold that it may not. In the absence of an entitlement on the part of any individual to post-secondary education, or a generally applicable requirement that parents assist their adult children in obtaining such an education, we perceive no rational basis for the state government to provide only certain adult citizens with legal means to overcome the difficulties they encounter in pursuing that end.

2. Most child support guidelines do not address specifically parental responsibility for supporting children in college. *See* Linda D. Elrod & Robert G. Spector, A Review of the Year in Family Law: Children's Issues Remain the Focus, 37 Fam. L.Q. 527, Chart 3 (2004). In the absence of a statute explicitly authorizing support for an adult child attending school, courts are divided about whether they may make such awards. Some courts base orders on statutes that declare a parental duty to support children in need. *See, e.g.,* Paxton v. Paxton, 89 P. 1083 (Cal. 1907); Elchinger v. Elchinger, 135 So. 2d 347 (La. Ct. App. 1961); Haxton v. Haxton, 705 P.2d 721, 730-731 (Or. 1985). In states without such statutes, courts base their holdings on common law principles. *See, e.g.,* Patetta v. Patetta, 817 A.2d 327 (N.J. Super. A.D. 2003).

At a minimum most states have adjusted the date of termination of child support to require support for children older than 18 who are still dependent in the sense of living at home going to high school. Verna v. Verna, 432 A.2d 630 (Pa. Super. 1981); Ariz. Rev. Stat. §25-320(c) (2004); Tenn. Code Ann. §34-1-102(b) (2004); Tex. Fam. Code §151.001(b) (2004). Some states require child support to continue until a child is 19 or finishes high school or its equivalent, whichever occurs first. Cal. Fam. Code §§3900, 3901; S.D. Codified Laws Ann. §25-5-18.1.

3. In some states, the principles that determine when divorced parents must pay for their children's postsecondary education also apply to children born outside marriage. *See, e.g,* Ex parte Jones (Jones v. Williams), 592 So. 2d 608 (Ala. 1991). However, in other states a court may order divorced parents to pay child support for children attending post-secondary education such orders are not permitted if the parents were never married; their support obligations end when their children turn 18. *See, e.g.,* Iowa Code §252A.3 (1983). Would this distinction violate equal protection?

4. In states that authorize courts to award postmajority support, the court must still find that the child will benefit from the award and that the parents can afford to pay. How should a court go about determining when a child is benefiting from post-high school education? When parents can afford to pay?

5. The highest Italian appeals court ruled in 2002 that a parent must support his 29-year-old son with a law degree:

The court ruled that Marco was not responsible for keeping himself "where labor conditions do not satisfy his specific qualifications, his attitudes and his real interests, so long as there is a reasonable possibility of satisfying his aspirations within a limited time, and support is compatible with the economic possibilities of the family."

When couples marry here, they pledge to support their children until they have fulfilled their aspirations. This commitment is reinforced by the Constitution, which does not set a time limit on the parental obligation. But in practice, the recent trend has been for children to extend their dependence on their parents.

Alan Riding, Italian Court Rules That Son Knows Best About Leaving Home, New York Times, April 6, 2002. The article reports that 35.4 percent of Italian men between ages 30 and 34 but only 18.3 percent of women still lived with their parents.

6. Courts are divided about whether parents may be ordered to support adult disabled children who are incapable of self-support. The modern trend is to impose a support duty. *See* Riggs v. Riggs, 578 S.E.2d 3 (S.C. 2003) (collecting cases). *See also* Ariz. Rev. Stat. Ann. §25-320(B) (2004); Del. Code Ann. tit. 13, §501 (1981); Mo. Rev. Stat. §452.340.4; S.C. Code Ann. §20-7-90 (Law. Co-op. 1985). *But see* Smith v. Smith, 447 N.W.2d 715 (Mich. 1989).

Lewis v. Dept. of Soc. Serv., 61 S.W.3d 248 (Mo. App. 2001), concerned the interaction of parental support duties and adult children's eligibility for public benefits based on disability. Jennifer, who at the time of this litigation was older than 18, received Supplemental Security Income benefits because of her disability of $337 to $482 per month. The state child support enforcement agency brought an action to increase the father's child support obligation from the $25 per week ordered in the 1978 divorce decree. The trial court did not consider the SSI payments in calculating the father's support duty. The Missouri court of appeals affirmed on appeal, saying that the SSI benefits were "intended to 'offset the additional financial burden incumbent with children who are physically or mentally disabled' and to defray a portion of the extraordinary expenses related to Jennifer's condition."

7. With some frequency, parents who have been ordered to pay support for older children attending school seek reduction or elimination of their obligation because the children are not behaving as the parents think they should. These cases raise starkly the issue of the extent to which support and control should be linked. Some courts hold that, at least if the parent's commands are "reasonable," the child who disobeys has "emancipated" him or herself, meaning that the parent is no longer obliged to pay support. *See, e.g.,* Roe v. Doe, 272 N.E.2d 567 (N.Y. 1971). Other courts ask whether the children's behavior is reasonable; if so, parents must continue to pay the support. *See, e.g.,* Newburgh v. Arrigo, 443 A.2d 1031, 1038 (N.J. 1982); Milne v. Milne, 556 A.2d 854 (Pa. Super. 1989); Bedford v. Bedford, 563 A.2d 102 (Pa. Super. 1989). Others hold that parents obligated to support their adult children may not condition their payments on their children's behavior. *See, e.g.,* Miller and Miller, 660 P.2d 205 (Or. App. 1983); Smith and Smith, 606 P.2d 694 (Or. App. 1980). What are the relative advantages and disadvantages of each of these approaches?

PROBLEMS

1. Molly and Frank's divorce decree requires Frank to pay $450 per month as child support for their two children, Ollie and Terry. The decree is silent about

what happens when Ollie, the older child, becomes 18, which is the age of majority in this jurisdiction. You are Frank's attorney. He has asked you whether he may cut his child support check in half in the month after Ollie becomes 18 without going to court. Molly claims that he cannot reduce his child support until he successfully moves to modify the decree because of Ollie's having attained the age of majority. What advice would you give Frank and why? What course of action would you advise and why?

2. If child support continues for an adult child attending school, should it be paid to the child or to the former custodial parent? Should child support continue during the summer and at other times when school is not in session?

3. Susan's parents' divorce decree requires her father to pay for her tuition, room and board and books while she is in school until age 22 so long as she maintains passing grades. Susan, who is now 19 and who has passing grades, recently moved out of the dorm into an apartment against her father's wishes. Her father, who does not deny that he has the financial ability to pay for Susan's schooling, has moved to terminate his support obligation because of her refusal to live where he believes that she should and because of her general lifestyle, which he regards as irresponsible and immoral.

4. If an adolescent child in the legal custody of one parent moves to the other parent's house following a series of fights with the custodial parent, has the child forfeited a right to child support? Does it matter whether the parent with legal custody "threw the child out"? What if, after leaving, the child refuses to visit or speak to the parent with legal custody? Would the situation be different if the child went to live with a friend's parents?

E. SUPPORT FOR PARENTS

Families now provide a great deal of support for their adult members. In 1988 approximately 3,250,000 persons provided financial support to more than 5,400,000 adults not living in the household with them. Almost all of those receiving such support were relatives, and parents made up the largest group of non-household adults receiving support. These numbers increased, even between 1986 and 1988. While the number of children receiving support during that period decreased absolutely (from about 7.9 million to about 7 million) and as a portion of all persons receiving support (from 65.0 percent to 56.2 percent), the number of adults receiving support rose by more than 25 percent, and the number of parents increased by some 40 percent (to 1,665,000). The average annual payment by children to their parents was $1,330. Bureau of the Census, United States Dept. of Commerce, Who's Helping Out? Support Networks Among American Families: 1988 2, 6-7 (1992).

The trend toward increased support of parents has been evident at least since 1960 and will likely increase sharply until the baby boom generation reaches 65 (in 2030). At that time, the ratio of retirement-aged persons to the working-age population will have increased from its current level of 20 per 100 persons to

37 per 100. *Id.* at 1. Does it follow that because adult children do often provide support for their parents, they generally should be required to do so? At the hearing on his motion, what arguments should the attorneys for each party make?

AMERICAN HEALTHCARE CENTER V. RANDALL

513 N.W.2d 566 (S.D. 1994)

AMUNDSON, J. . . . Appellant Robert Randall (Robert) is the only child of Harry and Juanita Randall. Although he grew up in Aberdeen, Robert has not resided in South Dakota since in 1954. Robert is now a resident of the District of Columbia.

Following an accident which required Juanita's hospitalization, Robert came back to Aberdeen and checked into various nursing homes to place his mother. In the fall of 1990, Juanita was admitted to the Arcadia Unit of Americana Healthcare Center (Americana) in Aberdeen, South Dakota. The Arcadia Unit is specifically designed to deal with individuals who possess mental problems such as Alzheimer's disease. . . .

At that time, in view of Juanita's limited income, Robert discussed the possibility of financial assistance from Medicaid with various Americana personnel. Later that month, Robert completed an application for long-term care medical assistance for Juanita. In November, the South Dakota Department of Social Services (DSS) denied this application because Juanita had not exhausted all of her assets. At the time, Juanita's only assets were [the house and mutual funds that had been conveyed to a trust].

Juanita's bill was two months delinquent at the time Americana learned of the rejected Medicaid application. Americana then contacted Robert about his mother's unpaid bills. Because of Juanita's financial position, Robert, as her legal guardian, filed . . . a Chapter 7 bankruptcy petition . . . and discharged the Americana bill for Juanita individually and Robert, as her guardian, on October 30, 1991. Meanwhile, Americana filed this suit to collect the unpaid bills. . . .

In June of 1991, Robert was requested to remove his mother from Americana because of the unpaid bills. Despite this request, Juanita remained at Americana until her death on December 8, 1991. At the time of Juanita's death, the unpaid balance for her care was $36,772.30. . . .

Prior to trial, the court granted Robert's motion for summary judgment as to Robert Randall as guardian of the person and estate of Juanita because of the discharge in bankruptcy, but denied summary judgment to Robert Randall individually. . . . At the summary judgment hearing, Americana raised its claim under SDCL 25-7-27 for the first time.[20]

---

20. SDCL 25-7-27 states:

Every adult child, having the financial ability so to do shall provide necessary food, clothing, shelter or medical attendance for a parent who is unable to provide for himself; provided that no claim shall be made against such adult child until notice has been given such adult child that his parent is unable to provide for himself, and such adult child shall have refused to provide for his parent.

On September 3, 1992, Robert renewed his motion for summary judgment on the additional ground that SDCL 25-7-27 was unconstitutional and requested a continuance. . . . The trial court stated that it was premature to rule on the constitutionality of the statute at that time and denied the continuance.

A court trial was held September 22, 1992. At the conclusion of Americana's case, Robert moved for directed verdict on the grounds that Americana had failed to establish either an oral or written contract to act as guarantor for his mother's nursing home bills. . . . The trial court granted Robert's motion for directed verdict on Americana's claims for liability based on an oral or written contract of guarantee. . . . The trial court found in favor of Americana on its SDCL 25-7-27 claim. This appeal followed. . . .

At common law, an adult child was not required to support a parent. Such an obligation could only be created by statute. Such statutes trace their beginnings from the Elizabethan Poor Law of 1601 in England. Swoap v. Superior Court, 10 Cal. 3d 490, 111 Cal. Rptr. 136, 516 P.2d 840, 848 (1973). South Dakota adopted the current version of SDCL 25-7-27 in 1963.

The North Dakota Supreme Court considered a claim premised on a similar statutory provision in Bismarck Hospital & Deaconesses Home v. Harris, 68 N.D. 374, 280 N.W. 423 (1938). That court stated:

> If the person against whom liability is sought to be established refuses to pay for services rendered, an action may be brought against him by such third party. In such action, the plaintiff must establish the kinship of the parties, the financial ability of the person sought to be charged, the indigence of the person to whom relief was furnished, the reasonable value of the services, and that such relief was an immediate necessity. Id. 280 N.W. at 426.

Robert claims SDCL 25-7-27 violates equal protection because it discriminates against adult children of indigent parents. The trial court held that it did not. Any legislative act is accorded a presumption in favor of constitutionality and that presumption is not overcome until the act is clearly and unmistakably shown beyond a reasonable doubt to violate fundamental constitutional principles. Since Robert challenges the constitutionality of the statute, he bears the burden of proving the act unconstitutional.

. . . No quasi-suspect classification or fundamental right has been implicated in this case, thus, a rational basis analysis will be applied to this support statute. . . .

Under the rational basis test, South Dakota uses a two-pronged analysis when determining whether a statute violates the constitutional right to equal protection under the laws. Lyons v. Lederle Laboratories, 440 N.W.2d 769, 771 (S.D. 1989). First, does the statute set up arbitrary classifications among various persons subject to it and, second, whether there is a rational relationship between the classification and some legitimate legislative purpose. Id.

When applying the first prong of the *Lyons* test, it is clear that SDCL 25-7-27 does not make an arbitrary classification. Rather, "it is the moral as well as the legal duty in this state, of every child, whether minor or adult, to assist in the support of their indigent aged parents." An adult child is liable under SDCL 25-7-27 upon the same principle that a parent is liable for necessary support furnished to their child.

Much like the plaintiffs in Swoap v. Superior Court of Sacramento County, Robert argues that the only support obligations which are rational are those arising out of a relationship voluntarily entered into. 10 Cal. 3d 490, 111 Cal. Rptr. 136, 516 P.2d 840, 851 (1973). For instance, the obligation to support a child or spouse is at least initially voluntary, therefore, it is rationally based. Robert argues that, since children do not voluntarily enter into the relationship with their parents, it is arbitrary to force this obligation upon them. Id. The fact that a child has no choice in the creation of a relationship with its parents does not per se make this an arbitrary classification. The fact that an indigent parent has supported and cared for a child during that child's minority provides an adequate basis for imposing a duty on the child to support that parent. Id. . . .

It is certainly reasonable to place a duty to support an indigent parent on that parent's adult child because they are direct lineal descendants who have received the support, care, comfort and guidance of that parent during their minority. If a parent does not qualify for public assistance, who is best suited to meet that parent's needs? It can reasonably be concluded that no other person has received a greater benefit from a parent than that parent's child and it logically follows that the adult child should bear the burden of reciprocating on that benefit in the event a parent needs support in their later years. Swoap, 516 P.2d at 851. Consequently, this statute does not establish an arbitrary classification.

The second prong of the test requires a rational relationship between this classification and some legitimate state interest. Clearly, this state has a legitimate interest in providing for the welfare and care of elderly citizens. SDCL 25-7-27 prevents a parent from being thrown out on the street when in need of specialized care. Placing this obligation for support on an adult child is as legitimate as those interests recognized by this court in the past when applying the rational basis test. . . .

The primary purpose of this statute is to place financial responsibility for indigent parents on their adult children when a parent requires such assistance. Although the legislature repealed similar laws in the past, SDCL 25-7-27 has survived. Therefore, SDCL 25-7-27 serves a legitimate legislative interest, especially under the facts of this case, where indigency was voluntarily created by the trust and there would have been sufficient assets to pay for the parent's care had the trust not been created. Robert has not been denied his right to equal protection under the law. . . .

In conclusion, we affirm the trial court's decision in all respects.

SWOAP V. SUPERIOR COURT

516 P.2d 840 (Cal. 1973)

[Children held liable to reimburse the state for public assistance provided to their indigent parents' support argued that the statute imposing the duty on the children was unconstitutional on several grounds. Employing reasoning much like that in *Randall*, the California Supreme Court rejected the challenge.]

TOBRINER, J., dissenting. The majority propose, by the instant opinion, to establish a new constitutional standard for determining when the state may compel some of its citizens to pay for benefits which the state, in its wisdom, decides to provide to other citizens. Under the test proposed by the majority, a state can charge one class of citizens with the costs of providing public programs to another class whenever there is simply some "rational relationship" between the group of benefitted individuals and those who must pay the bill. Applying this "minimal rationality" test in the instant case, the majority hold that since the class of children have generally benefitted from parents, the state can require those children whose parents happen to be poor to reimburse the state for the cost of public old age assistance, regardless of whether a particular child is otherwise legally obligated to provide such support to his parent. . . .

Under the majority's newly propounded "rationality" test, a government intent on reducing the general tax burden could single out insulated minority classes to bear a disproportionate share of the tax burden of a whole range of public services. Thus, for example, the "mere rationality" standard would permit the state not only to charge adult children with the costs of old age benefits but would authorize public savings by charging such children for the costs of subsidized housing projects, medical care, recreational centers, reduced public transportation fares and the various other social programs the state decides to make available to its senior citizens. Although the children of the recipients of such benefits may have had no preexisting obligation to pay for such services, the majority's constitutional test would presumably sanction such charges on the ground that children as a whole have benefitted from parents. Moreover, since the circumstances of the individual case are assertedly irrelevant, the state presumably could require even a child who had been abandoned by his parents to pay the costs of these varied public programs. . . .

It might be possible to understand the reasons for the majority's uprooting of a consistent line of precedent and creation of a novel constitutional ruling if the legislation challenged in the instant case offered the promise of unquestionably beneficial social consequences; under such circumstances one might expect to find the court questioning past decisions that impeded the salutary result. The statutes in question here, however, offer no such beneficent social consequences.

On the contrary, almost all observers agree that the social effects of the challenged relative responsibility provisions are harsh and self-defeating. "[A] large body of social work opinion [has long maintained] that liability of relatives creates and increases family dissension and controversy, weakens and destroys family ties at the very time and in the very circumstances when they are most needed, imposes an undue burden upon the poor . . . and is therefore socially undesirable, financially unproductive, and administratively infeasible." (ten Broek, 17 Stan. L. Rev. at pp. 645-646.) As Justice Friedman, writing for the Court of Appeal in the instant case, observed: "[The challenged provisions] strike most aggressively and harshly at adult children occupying the lower end of the income scale. The enforced shift of subsistence funds from one generation to the other distributes economic desolation between the generations. It galls family relationships. It injects guilt and shame into elderly citizens who have made their contributions to society and have become dependent through life's vicissitudes."

Jenny Baxter, a 75-year-old Californian receiving Old Age Security benefits, eloquently summarized the true effect of the relative responsibility laws: "No one is born into this world with a debt to their parents for their birth and contributions until their maturity. That is the parents' contribution to life and society. When the child reaches maturity, he starts a new separate unit and in turn makes his contribution to life and society as did his parents, carrying on the generation cycle on through eternity. The children should not be saddled with unjust demands that keep them at or near poverty level with no hope to escape it, just because a parent still breathes. And aged parents should not have to live their remaining lives facing the heartbreaking experience of being such a burden to their children. Many would prefer death but are afraid of retribution for taking their own lives. Their grief — a living death."

NOTES AND QUESTIONS

1. Does it follow that, because parents support their children when young, children should support their parents when needy? Is there a general duty of reciprocity, as the court in *Randall* assumes? Are the parents providing some good or service without benefiting themselves? Is there an expectation of reciprocity by parents and children? Do parents generally expect that their children will use their resources to support them?

The view expressed by Jenny Baxter, quoted in Justice Tobriner's dissent, seems to be widely shared. While elderly parents often think that they are entitled to have their health care needs provided by government or by private insurance, only about 10 percent believe that adult children should provide the needed financial support. Alvin Schorr, U.S. Dept. of Health & Human Serv., Pub. No. 3-11953, ". . . Thy Father & Thy Mother . . .": A Second Look at Filial Responsibility and Family Policy 12 (1980). Thirty states have filial responsibility statutes on the books, though they are rarely enforced. Seymour Moskowitz, Adult Children and Indigent Parents: Intergenerational Responsibilities in International Perspective, 86 Marq. L. Rev. 401 (2002). *See also* Peter Laslett, Is There a Generational Contract? Justice Between Age Groups and Generations 24, 28-29 (Peter Laslett & James S. Fishkin eds., 1992).

2. Are family responsibility laws explained by the notion of the family as an economic unit? Is the family such a unit at the time that support by children is sought? *See* Lee E. Teitelbaum, Intergenerational Responsibility and Family Obligation: On Sharing, 1992 Utah L. Rev. 765, 776-777.

3. Five years before she entered the nursing home, the mother in *Randall* transferred most of her assets into an irrevocable trust, which named her as the income beneficiary but prevented the trustee from using the corpus of the trust for her benefit. Her son Robert, the appellant in *Randall*, was both trustee and residual beneficiary of the trust. As his mother's guardian, Robert used the income from the trust and his mother's Social Security benefits to pay legal fees incurred by forming the guardianship, the bankruptcy proceedings, and an unsuccessful pursuit of Medicaid benefits instead of paying for her care in the nursing home. While Robert's actions were not illegal or a breach of fiduciary duty, the court expressed its disapproval of his choices and was distinctly untroubled that he would have to pay his mother's bill from the trust assets that he received. 513 N.W.2d at 574.

Presbyterian Medical Center v. Budd, 832 A.2d 1066 (Pa. Sup. 2003), involved similar facts. A daughter had used her power of attorney to transfer her mother's assets to herself, rather than spending them on her mother's care, resulting in the mother neither having the money to pay for her own care nor being eligible for Medicaid (because of the transfer of assets to the daughter). The nursing home sued the daughter for these costs, and the court rejected the claims that the daughter was liable based on contract or fraud, finding that the facts did not support these claims. However, the court held that the daughter was liable under the state relative responsibility statute.

In each case, if the child had not received assets from the parent during the parent's lifetime, would the child still have been liable under the relative responsibility laws? Why or why not?

4. In both *Randall* and *Budd* the children attempted to obtain Medicaid benefits to pay for their mothers' custodial care. Medicaid is a public assistance program only for people whose assets and income fall below poverty levels. If Juanita Randall had not transferred her property into the irrevocable trust, she definitely would not have been eligible for Medicaid, and the transfer itself may have disqualified her, or her income may have been too high for her to qualify. In 1993, federal rules that determine whether a person can transfer assets into a trust and still be eligible for Medicaid were substantially tightened. Omnibus Budget Reconciliation Act of 1993 § 13611, codified at 42 U.S.C. § 1396p. Under these rules, if a person gratuitously transfers assets to another outright within three years of applying for Medicaid, the applicant is disqualified from eligibility for a period of time, as in *Budd*. If the applicant transfers property into a trust, the "look back" period is five years.

5. In determining an unmarried person's eligibility for Medicaid, generally all the applicant's income, including gifts of cash or its equivalent, is considered available to pay for care. This rule limits the ability of a person's children or others to make voluntary contributions to the care of a person. However, trusts created by a Medicaid applicant or by a third party for the benefit of the applicant which provide that none of the money can be used for food, clothing or shelter but can only be used for other needs, such as transportation, entertainment, and so on. are not considered resources and so do not disqualify the beneficiary from receiving Medicaid. The trusts are called special needs or supplemental needs trusts.

6. For additional perspectives, *see* Margaret F. Brinig, The Family Franchise: Elderly Parents and Adult Siblings, 1996 Utah L. Rev. 393; Usha Narayanan, The Government's Role in Fostering the Relationship Between Adult Children and Their Elderly Parents: From Filial Responsibility Laws . . . To What? A Cross Cultural Perspective, 4 Elderlaw J. 369 (1996).

Modification, Termination, Enforcement, and Tax and Bankruptcy Treatment of Orders

8

A. INTRODUCTION

We have already seen that the family can be imagined as a hub surrounded by other social and legal institutions. This image may again come to mind in this chapter, which examines the policies and rules relating to modification and enforcement of orders and to taxation and bankruptcy treatment of property transfers and obligations imposed incident to family break-up.

As we saw in earlier chapters, it is often difficult to distinguish clearly between awards dividing property and those providing for spousal support. The same is true of spousal and child support obligations. However, the classification of an order as property division, spousal support, or child support is centrally important in the issues considered in this chapter.

B. MODIFICATION AND TERMINATION OF SUPPORT

Traditionally and still today in most jurisdictions, support duties terminate at the death of the obligor or the recipient. However, in a number of states, a court may order the obligor's estate to continue to pay spousal support, or the parties may agree in writing to such an extension. Note, Alimony, Till Death Do Us Part, 27 J. Fam. L. 859 (1989); *see also* ALI Principles of the Law of Family Dissolution § 5.07 (2000). In approximately 20 states, statutes or case law permit child support liability to be imposed on a parent's estate under some circumstances. *See, e.g.,* §750 Ill. Comp. Stat. Ann. 5/510(d); Nev. Rev. Stat. §125B.130; Koidl v. Schreiber, 520 A.2d 759 (N.J. App. 1986); Caldwell v. Caldwell, 92 N.W.2d 356

(Wis. 1958); L.W.K. v. E.R.C., 735 N.E.2d 359 (Mass. 2000). The ALI Principles recommend that state law should not provide for automatic termination of child support upon the death of the obligor; instead, the court should have discretion to modify or terminate the order or commute the obligation to a lump sum. ALI Principles, *supra*, § 3.25. This proposal is derived from the Model Marriage and Divorce Act, which has been adopted in Arizona, Colorado, Illinois, Kentucky, Minnesota, Missouri, Montana and Washington. *Id.*, at 569, Reporter's Note to comment b.

The traditional rule is that, unlike property awards, spousal and child support are modifiable upon a showing of a "substantial (or material) change of circumstances." This phrase gives judges considerable discretion to alter previously established support obligations. This section considers generally how courts and legislatures have given meaning to this phrase and the extent to which judicial discretion is narrowed by statute or case law.

As you consider these materials, think about how the problems raised in the cases relate to what you have already learned about the justifications and criteria for imposing support duties in the first place. Are the policies reflected in initial awards carried forward to solve modification problems? Are postdecree changes in circumstances treated the same when spousal support and child support are at stake? Consider, for example, how increases in an obligor's income are treated. Courts typically say that since divorce terminates the marital relationship, an increase in the payor's income alone—that is, without a showing of the recipient's increased need—is not grounds for modifying spousal support because a person is not entitled to share in a former spouse's postdivorce efforts or good fortune. However, divorce does not terminate the parent-child relationship, and therefore a parent's increase in income may be grounds for increasing child support.

1. *"Foreseeable" Changes in Circumstances*

In many cases a major issue is the tension between the value of rules that promote stability in orders and those that allow courts to respond to changes in individual circumstances. The Uniform Marriage and Divorce Act (UMDA) strongly emphasizes stability; § 316 provides that to be a ground for modifying a spousal or child support order, a change of circumstances must be "so substantial and continuing as to be unconscionable." Sometimes courts deal with the tension between stability and flexibility by saying that change that was "foreseeable" is not a ground for modification. This test cannot be taken literally, however. Many changes that are widely regarded as sufficient for modifying a support order, such as the increased cost of supporting children as they mature, are also entirely foreseeable.

Indeed, some of these "foreseeable" changes are so predictable that courts and commentators have sought ways to adjust support orders for them automatically. Before widespread use of child support guidelines, cost-of-living adjustments (COLAs) in support orders to adjust for inflation were often proposed. While many courts approved inclusion of COLA provisions, others rejected them because they fail to account for actual changes in income and other factors relevant to need and ability to pay. J. Thomas Oldham, *Abating the Feminization of Poverty: Changing the Rules Governing Post-Decree Modification of Child Support Obligations,* 1995 BYU L. Rev. 841, 850-853. On the other hand, while it is predictable that parents will spend more to support older children than young ones, courts rarely approve orders automatically increasing child support as children grow older. Instead, they ordinarily require motions to modify previous orders to permit individualized determination of needs and ability to pay. *Id.* at 853-856.

The advent of child support guidelines produced a clear difference between modification of child support and alimony with regard to some "foreseeable" changes. Federal legislation requires states to implement a regular review process that will ensure that child support orders are updated at least every three years.[1] That requirement effectively abrogates the traditional approach under which a child support order, like an alimony order, could be modified only on the initiative of the party who proved a substantial change of circumstances.

2. *"Voluntary" Versus "Involuntary" Decreases in the Payor's Income*

A decrease in an obligor's ability to pay is a commonly asserted ground for modifying support. Involuntary decreases, such as when the obligor is laid off from work, are generally treated as a sufficient reason to decrease support. However, courts are not so tolerant of "voluntary" reductions in income, as the next case illustrates.

DEEGAN V. DEEGAN

603 A.2d 542 (N.J. App. 1992)

LONG, J.A.D. Plaintiff, Edna Deegan and defendant Ross Deegan were divorced in 1985. The Judgment of Divorce, which incorporated an oral property settlement agreement, provided, among others, that defendant would pay alimony to plaintiff in the amount of $250.00 per week. The agreement also provided that plaintiff would receive one-third of defendant's annual vacation pay and one-third of the value of his pension from the proceeds of the sale of the marital home.

. . . On April 27, 1990, defendant retired, four months short of his 62nd birthday. On August 22, 1990, he moved for an order terminating alimony. In support of the motion, the 62-year-old defendant filed a certification stating that he had previously shared his pension with his former wife thus eliminating that asset as a source for alimony. He set forth the reasons for his decision to retire:

---

1. The legislation actually imposes this requirement only when Title IV-D support enforcement services (which are described in the next section of this chapter) are being provided in the case. 42 U.S.C. § 1305.

In reaching the decision to retire I considered many factors. First of all, the steam-fitter's union, for whom I had worked for 42 years, offered a single sum pension option which was quite attractive. Secondly, work at the time was very slow and there was a real possibility that I would be laid off. Thirdly, working as a steamfitter involves a great deal of physical labor, including bending, lifting, climbing, and working in the elements. On August 14, 1989, I turned 60 years of age and this sort of labor has become increasingly more difficult for me over the years.

. . . [Plaintiff] characterized his decision to retire as totally voluntary and asked the court not to allow him to stop the support she needed to survive.

Without a plenary hearing, the judge denied defendant's motion, and granted plaintiff's cross-motion reasoning as follows:

The plaintiff, — the defendant seeks to terminate his alimony obligation pursuant to a judgment of divorce dated November the 12th of 1985 which is $250.00 a week because he has decided to retire at age sixty. He suggests to the court that he took a lump-sum pension benefit and has now invested that which generates income of approximately $13,100.00 per year and that is the extent of his income vis a vis his 1989 income of $54,000.00.

Individuals who have obligations and in particular alimony and child support obligations cannot voluntarily retire and then say to the court, we have a substantial change of circumstances, I don't have the income to comply with the previous judg-ment of divorce. When he retired, he knew he had this obligation to this woman and he continues to have this obligation to this woman, and he will continue to pay the alimony of $250.00 per week.

He'll just have to secure some other additional work to supplement his pen-sion of $13,100.00 which I'm sure will not be difficult for him. He's been in the labor market for forty-two years. He is a healthy individual. There's no allegations that he is in bad health. So he does have the ability. He'll just have to go out and find a job to generate the income. So his application to terminate alimony will be denied.

Defendant appeals, claiming that the trial judge erred in determining that he had failed to meet the burden of establishing that he had undergone changed cir-cumstances. . . .

Spousal support agreements are always subject to modification pursuant to N.J.S.A. 2A:34-23 upon a showing of changed circumstances. . . . A party seeking modification "must demonstrate that changed circumstances have substantially impaired the ability to support himself or herself." An analysis of "changed cir-cumstances" is not limited to what the parties might have contemplated at the time of the divorce. To the contrary, the analysis focuses on "whether the change in circumstances is continuing and whether the agreement or decree has made explicit provision for the change."

Whether circumstances have really changed so as to warrant modification requires a court to study the parties' financial condition at the time of the divorce, as well as at the time of the application. Where the change is involuntary, all that is required is an analysis of the alterations in the parties' financial circumstances. However, where the change is a voluntary one, other considerations come into play. . . .

[Cases from other states addressing elective retirement] can be broadly characterized as falling into several different categories. The first is what might be denominated a bright line category. In those cases, the voluntariness of the change in circumstances, in itself, is viewed as barring an application for modification. In other words, if a party, not otherwise under compulsion, voluntarily chooses a change in life style which reduces his or her financial circumstances, he or she may not base an application for modification of an alimony award on that voluntary change. This rule has the virtue of simplicity, but little else. Indeed, it has been revisited in Florida, and rejected as "too severe." Pimm v. Pimm, 568 So. 2d 1299, 1300 (Fla. Dist. Ct. App. 1990).

In the second category of voluntary retirement cases are evaluated solely based upon the motives of the party seeking to make the change. If the change is made in good faith, the application for modification is approved. By comparison, a bad faith change, i.e., one based upon the desire to reduce alimony obligations, will be disapproved as a basis for modification.

A variation on the good faith theme is found in the "sole purpose" category of cases. In these cases, it is said that if the "sole" motivation for the change is to avoid support obligations, good faith is absent. The problem with the sole purpose standard was recognized in Sifers v. Sifers, 544 S.W.2d 269 (Mo. App. 1976), where the court opined that it is likely that a party moving for modification will always be able to advance at least one legitimate reason for retirement. In Smith v. Smith, 419 A.2d 1035 (Me. 1980), the Supreme Court of Maine adopted a "primary purpose" rule which included a *Dilger* [v. Dilger, 576 A.2d 951 (Ch. Div. 1990)] like analysis:

> The better rule appears to be that retirement of the payor spouse for the primary purpose of avoiding alimony does not of itself bring about the substantial change in the payor's circumstances needed to justify a reduction in alimony. Such a rule does not place an undue burden on the payor spouse who retires in complete good faith. On the other hand, as compared with the sole-purpose rule, the primary-purpose rule allows a more searching inquiry into the financial circumstances of the retiring party and makes it more difficult for a parsimonious payor spouse to disguise his motives for retiring.

The final category includes cases in which any negative impact on the payee spouse is considered sufficient to bar modification based upon voluntary retirement.

As can be seen, many of these categories overlap. For example, the sole and primary purpose cases are really good faith cases expressed another way. Likewise, the bright line cases are another articulation of negative impact. Regardless of the ultimate outcome, all of these courts have focused to one extent or another on two issues: the motive of the payor spouse and the effect on the payee.

We have grappled with this question and have concluded that the considerations enunciated In re Marriage of Smith, 396 N.E.2d 859, 863 (Ill. App. Ct. 1979) are a good starting point:

> Relative factors are the age, health of the party, his motives in retiring, the timing of the retirement, his ability to pay maintenance even after retirement and the ability of the other spouse to provide for himself or herself.

We also agree with Judge Bassler in *Dilger*, supra, 576 A.2d 951, that the "reasonableness" of the early retirement should be a factor, as should the expectations of the parties and the opportunity of the dependent spouse to prepare to live on the reduced support. In short, whether a spouse may voluntarily retire will depend on the individual circumstances of a particular case.

We have also concluded that, in the final analysis, even in a case in which the retiring spouse has been shown to have acted in good faith and has advanced entirely rational reasons for his or her actions, the trial judge will be required to decide one pivotal issue: whether the advantage to the retiring spouse substantially outweighs the disadvantage to the payee spouse. Only if that answer is affirmative, should the retirement be viewed as a legitimate change in circumstances warranting modification of a pre-existing support obligation.

Thus, where a payor spouse has substantial reasons for retiring (i.e., health concerns) and the effect on the payee spouse is minimal (due, for example, to other available income, qualifying for social security, or new employment) the balance will be struck in favor of the payor. Where, on the other hand, the payor spouse simply wants a new life and the payee spouse will become destitute without support, the payee's interests will prevail. Where the interests are in equipoise the payor spouse's application will fail because he or she is unable to show that the advantage substantially outweighs the disadvantage to the payee. Each of these scenarios is straightforward. In most cases, the factors will be less obvious and the balancing process more complicated. Where the sole problem is timing, the trial judge may condition approval on a preparatory hiatus during which the movant may retire or not as he or she chooses but during which the financial obligations will continue.

This ruling should not be viewed as a limitation on freedom of choice or freedom of action. By it, the payor spouse whose good faith early retirement or other life style change would not deleteriously affect the former spouse is free to follow his or her star. Where a significant disadvantage to the payee spouse is foreseen, the payor spouse is still not precluded from such a change. Any party is free to retire, take a vow of poverty, write poetry or hawk roses in an airport, if he or she sees fit. The only limitation is discontinuance of the financial aid the former spouse requires. The reason for this is that the duty of self-fulfillment must give way to the pre-existing duty which runs between spouses who have been in a marriage which has failed.

It goes without saying that issues of possible voluntary early retirement and the like should be resolved in the first instance at the time of the divorce in a negotiated agreement. No thoughtful matrimonial lawyer should leave an issue of this importance to chance and subject his or her client to lengthy future proceeding such as we have here.

Turning back to this case, we reverse and remand the matter to the trial judge for a full review of the financial circumstances of both parties in light of the standards we have set forth. He may accept further certifications or require a plenary hearing if there are disputed material facts in issue.

Reversed and remanded.

NOTES AND QUESTIONS

1. In intact marriages, an income-earning spouse may reduce his or her income. The other spouse may strongly object because of the adverse impact on

their lifestyle and future options. Courts will not ordinarily entertain a suit to require a current spouse not to reduce his or her income. How are such disputes resolved? Does the fact that the parties no longer live in the same household justify the different approach to justiciability of the dispute?

How would a judge determine "whether the advantage to the retiring spouse substantially outweighs the disadvantage to the payee spouse" as required by *Deegan*?

2. The approaches described in *Deegan* also appear in cases interpreting child support guidelines, which impute income to a parent under certain circumstances. Some jurisdictions provide for imputed income only if it is proved that the parent diminished his or her income for the "bad faith" purpose of minimizing child support. For a review of cases, *see* Lewis Becker, Spousal and Child Support and the "Voluntary Reduction of Income" Doctrine, 29 Conn. L. Rev. 647 (1997). *See also* Elizabeth Trainor, Basis for Imputing Income for Purpose of Determining Child Support Where Obligor Spouse Is Voluntarily Unemployed or Underemployed, 76 A.L.R.5th 191 (2004); Karen A. Cusenbary, Decrease in Income of Obligor Spouse Following Voluntary Termination of Employment as Basis for Modification of Child Support Award, 39 A.L.R.5th 1 (2004).

3. Under the Melson formula for calculating child support, described in Chapter 7, a petition to modify downward cannot be granted sooner than two and a half years after the original order in the absence of a substantial change in circumstances brought about by no fault of the petitioner, changes in day care expenses, or changes in other child support obligations of the obligor. Thus, if the obligor's loss of income is voluntary, he or she must still pay at the original level for the first two and a half years. After that, the same level of income will be attributed to a parent who has voluntarily lost employment until he or she can demonstrate that he or she "has been actively seeking employment commensurate with his/her current skills, education, and training" for a sufficient period of time. Sentner v. Sentner, 799 A.2d 1154 (Del. 2002) (discussing Report of the Family Court Judiciary, The Family Court of the State of Delaware: Delaware Child Support Formula Evaluation and Update (Oct. 1, 1998)).

4. When circumstances warrant imputing income, the next problem is how much income to impute, since support awards are not supposed to be based on "speculative" estimates of earning ability, but rather actual earning ability. Where the obligor has the qualifications for jobs that are readily available, determining earning ability is not so difficult, but as the match between the obligor's skills and the requirements of available jobs decreases, the line between speculating and legitimate imputation of income is harder to discern. For example, in Hutchinson v. Hutchinson, 9 P.3d 815 (Or. App. 2003) (en banc), at the time of the modification hearing, Husband, who earlier had earned $240,000 per year, had been unemployed for a year. His efforts to find work at a comparable salary had been unsuccessful because of downturns in the economy, his age, and the specialized nature of his experience. He sought a reduction in spousal support from $6,000 per month to $250 per month. An expert witness for his former wife testified that Husband was qualified for jobs with actual openings that paid $50,000 to $60,000 per year and that he could probably find work paying $120,000 within a year. The trial court modified the spousal support obligation, based on the assumption that Husband could earn $120,000 per year. The appellate court reversed, characterizing the finding as "speculative" but concluding that he could earn $60,000

per year. Why was the higher figure "speculative"? Because jobs paying that much are scarcer? Because the expert testified that Husband would probably have to look longer to find such a job? If Husband turned down a high-paying job that would have required him to move several states away because he wanted to stay close to his children, who lived for most of the time with Wife, should the amount of income that he would have earned had he accepted the job be attributed to him? *See* Wrenn v. Lewis, 818 A.2d 1005 (Me. 2003).

5. When loss of income is involuntary because the obligor becomes disabled, the obligor's children may be eligible for Social Security or other benefits. Most courts give the obligor a dollar-for-dollar credit for the benefits a child receives. Cases to this effect that summarize case law from other states include Pontbriand v. Pontbriand, 622 A.2d 482 (R.I. 1993); Brewer v. Brewer, 244 Neb. 731, 509 N.W.2d 10 (1993). The theory of these cases is that the benefits substitute for a parent's lost earning power and replace support the child would have obtained from the parent. A minority of courts merely consider the child's receipt of benefits as a change in circumstances that may but does not necessarily justify modification of the child support duty. The New York Court of Appeals in Graby v. Graby, 664 N.E.2d 488 (N.Y. 1996), took this approach, analogizing the child's Social Security benefits to other government benefits such as welfare, which parents do not purchase. The court noted, "In many cases, granting the noncustodial parent a credit for Social Security disability benefits earmarked for dependent children might effectively abolish the child support obligation of that parent, who has regular and consistent income, and at the same time disproportionately reduce the resources available to the children." 664 N.E.2d at 491.

PROBLEMS

1. When Martha and Fred were divorced, Fred was awarded custody of their child, and Martha was ordered to pay child support. At the time Martha was an untenured teacher in the local school system. Because of budget cuts she has been laid off work. She could get a job as a secretary, earning half as much as she made as a teacher. However, she expects that the school system will be rehiring in a year or so and has decided to go back to school to get her master's degree because that will move her higher on the rehire list and increase her pay if she is rehired as a teacher. She has moved to eliminate her child support obligation temporarily, until she is rehired. Under the tests discussed in *Deegan*, how would her motion be analyzed? If the court finds that her motion should be denied, should the court impute income to her at the rate that a secretary would make, or that a teacher would make?

2. Joe Hill was ordered to pay support for his two children, who are in their mother's custody, when he was divorced two years ago. Joe works in a manufacturing plant, and his union has called a strike because wage negotiations with the employer have been stalled for six months. The union does not have a strike fund, so that if Joe goes on strike he will have no income. If he does participate in the strike and then moves to reduce his child support obligation because of his loss in income, should the court grant the motion under the tests discussed in *Deegan*?

3. New Families—Spousal Support, Remarriage, and Cohabitation

Traditionally, as we have seen, alimony was considered a continuation of the support duty imposed by marriage. Therefore, it terminated when the recipient remarried because her new spouse's support duty replaced the former spouse's support obligation. Traditional legal principles had little to say about the effect of cohabitation on alimony because open cohabitation without marriage was not socially acceptable. The following materials consider the impact on spousal support duties of two important changes—the changing justifications and criteria for requiring someone to support a former spouse following divorce, and the high incidence of unmarried cohabitation.

PETERSON V. PETERSON

434 N.W.2d 732 (S.D. 1989)

BRADSHAW, C.J. [The facts of this case are set out more fully in Chapter 7 at page 519.] Janey Peterson (Janey) appeals from a judgment terminating her right to receive alimony from Gregory A. Peterson (Gregory). . . .

$1000 - 7yr

Finally, the court decree provided the following language: (Gregory) is ordered to pay to (Janey) as alimony the sum of $1,000 per month for a seven-year period starting with the first month after the entry of judgment herein, . . . after said seven-year period, (Gregory) shall pay to (Janey) $500 per month, . . . for an additional 10 years unless during this last 10-year period (Janey) dies or *remarries*, at which time this portion of the alimony shall cease. (emphasis supplied)

Gregory petitioned the trial court to amend its divorce judgment and extinguish his duty to provide alimony when he learned that Janey had remarried on August 1, 1987. Janey resisted. . . .

The trial judge granted [the motion]. . . . [P]ursuant to our ruling in Marquardt v. Marquardt by Rempfer, 396 N.W.2d 753 (S.D. 1986), his obligation to pay alimony was cancelled.

Trial Court granted the motion

Janey [appeals,] contending . . . that the trial court misconstrued *Marquardt*. . . .

Janey seeks an affirmative resolution of this issue by advancing three alternative assertions: (1) That the language of the trial court's alimony award indicates by implication that Gregory's duty to pay alimony would not cease if Janey remarried during the initial seven years following the parties' divorce; (2) That the alimony award was an integral part of the property settlement segment of the divorce decree; and (3) That extraordinary circumstances exist, i.e., Janey's new husband is unable to support her, which require the perpetuation of her alimony payments. These contentions will be addressed seriatim.

Janey

In *Marquardt*, supra, we opined that "[p]roof that the spouse receiving spousal support payments has remarried establishes a prima facie case requiring the court to terminate the support payments unless [the recipient of the support payments can show] extraordinary circumstances which justify continuation of the payments." By adopting this stance, we rejected the automatic termination rule espoused in Voyles v. Voyles, 644 P.2d 847 (Alaska 1982), and other cases. These automatic termination jurisdictions have allowed alimony to continue, despite remarriage, if the parties' agreement or the decree of the court expressly provided that the flow of alimony was to remain unimpeded by the recipient spouse's remarriage. Janey urges us to adopt this exception in this case.

We must repeat, in order to fully comprehend the gist of Janey's argument, the succeeding pertinent language of the alimony award: (Gregory) is ordered to pay to (Janey) as alimony the sum of $1,000 per month for a seven-year period starting with the first month after the entry of judgment herein. . . . After said seven-year period, (Gregory) shall pay to (Janey) $500 per month . . . for an additional 10 years unless during this last 10-year period (Janey) dies or remarries, at which time this portion of the alimony shall cease.

Since this language fails to provide that alimony payments will end if Janey remarries during the first seven years, Janey maintains that "it clearly implies that remarriage does not operate to terminate alimony during the first seven years." This assertion is without merit.

Janey's reliance on the *Voyles* exception is misplaced because the *Voyles* exception, by its terms, applies only where there is an express statement that alimony is to survive notwithstanding the remarriage of the recipient spouse. Silence in a divorce decree or a voluntary agreement, as to the occurrence of remarriage, falls short of a specific declaration that alimony will endure in the event the recipient spouse remarries. Thus, the parties to a divorce must, to avail themselves of the *Voyles* deviation, point to either a statement in an agreement or divorce decree which provides that the payor spouse will pay alimony, irrespective of the recipient spouse's remarriage, or evidence that the parties intended that the alimonial obligation would survive past the date of the payee spouse's remarriage. Here, since Janey has shown neither the amount of evidence required nor an agreement that alimony would continue after her remarriage, her argument must collapse.

Next, Janey argues that the alimony award was an intrinsic part of the property settlement segment of the divorce decree. . . . We refuse to countenance this contention on the basis of the facts before us.

In Lien v. Lien, 420 N.W.2d 26 (S.D. 1988) (Lien II), we held that payments, though denominated as "support," were, in fact, part of a property division between the parties. As such, they were not terminable under *Marquardt*. We reached that conclusion due to the husband's insistence, at trial, that the payments be labeled "support" so that he could avoid the adverse tax consequences attendant to a total cash award of property.

It is apparent from a reading of *Lien II*, supra, that when deciding whether an award of alimony is, in reality, a portion of a property settlement, a court must scrutinize the language of the divorce decree, the circumstances encompassing it, and the end sought to be achieved by the parties. After conducting this examination in the present case, we are left with the conviction that the alimony award was not a disguised property settlement.

Here, the divorce decree provided that Janey receive the parties' right, title, and interest in and to Karen's, Inc. (a retail store), the family residence, the personal property situated within the home, a 1978 station wagon, and $115,063 to be paid in cash within six months of the date of the decree. This amounted to a total property award of $329,858. The cash award was, in the trial judge's words, necessary to "effectuate the property division."

Based on this language, it is obvious that this money, not the periodically paid alimony, was an integral part of the property settlement necessary to accomplish an equitable division of property. The wording of the divorce decree, coupled with the circumstances of the divorce, indicates that the monthly payments made by Gregory to Janey were for her support and were not meant to accomplish an equitable property division. Thus, this contention of Janey's must also fail. . . .

Janey's final position under this alimony issue is that extraordinary circumstances exist which require the continuation of her alimony payments. Janey argues that since she has not profited economically from her second marriage, she needs the alimony to live in the style to which she had become accustomed prior to her divorce from Gregory. In one of her affidavits, Janey says that "I did marry Timothy W. Johnson on August 1, 1987; however, his income, together with my child support, is not sufficient to provide for me and my two minor children." The following passage, extracted from the opinion in Nugent v. Nugent, 152 N.W.2d 323, 329 (N.D. 1967), capsulizes our view of Janey's assertion:

> [W]e do not believe that such factors [that the husband's fault caused the divorce, that the wife contributed to the household while the husband obtained a medical degree, and that the wife's new husband was unable to provide for her in the same fashion as her previous mate] constitute extraordinary circumstances as would justify the continuation of the alimony payments in this case, [wife] having voluntarily elected to marry another, who now must assume the responsibility for her support.

Additionally, we have said "it is 'illogical and unreasonable' that a spouse should receive support from a present spouse and a former spouse at the same time." *Marquardt*, supra at 754.

Since Janey has shown no extraordinary circumstances to rebut the prima facie requirement that alimony should terminate, we hold that the trial court was correct and did not abuse its discretion in terminating Janey's alimony.

[The concurring opinions of Justice Morgan and Justice Henderson are omitted.]

NOTES AND QUESTIONS

1. Janey first argued that the language of the decree on its face provided that the payments would not terminate during the first seven years after the divorce. What argument supports this construction of the language? Why do you think the court rejected the argument?

The *Peterson* court is not alone in requiring that language very specifically provide that spousal support will survive the recipient's remarriage to be enforceable. *See, e.g.*, Moore v. Jacobsen, 817 A.2d 212 (Md. 2003); Hardesty v. Hardesty, 581 S.E.2d 213 (Ala. App. 2003); Holm v. Holm, 678 N.W.2d 499 (Neb. 2004).

2. Janey's second argument is that the clause requiring Gregory to pay her $1,000 a month for seven years was part of the property division and so not

modifiable. Ambiguity about the character of an award is commonly found in divorce decrees (and separation agreements). Sometimes this ambiguity is the result of sloppy drafting, and sometimes it is created deliberately so that the obligation will be treated as property division for some purposes and as spousal support for other purposes. As you will see in the rest of this chapter, statutes and courts have created different tests to classify an award as property division or spousal support for purposes of modification and termination, for enforcement, for income taxes, and for bankruptcy. However, as *Peterson* illustrates, ambiguity about these issues often invites subsequent litigation. The alternative is for courts and lawyers to address collateral consequences explicitly.

In the face of ambiguous language, the *Peterson* court, like most courts, uses a totality-of-the-circumstances test to determine whether the obligation is spousal support or property division. Which factors suggest that the $1,000 a month duty was spousal support? Which suggest that it was property division?

3. Under *Peterson*, spousal support terminates on remarriage absent a showing of "exceptional circumstances." What circumstances did Janey allege, and why did the court find that they were not exceptional? How would the *Peterson* court define "exceptional circumstances"? What rationale today supports a rule that spousal support always terminates on the recipient's remarriage? What justifies the *Peterson* court's approach, which has been adopted in many jurisdictions?

The ALI Family Dissolution Principles provide that periodic payments to a former spouse should automatically terminate at the obligee's remarriage unless "the original decree provides otherwise" or "the court makes written findings establishing that termination of the award would work a substantial injustice because of facts not present in most cases. . . ." ALI, Principles of the Law of Family Dissolution § 5.07 (2002).

4. The Oregon Supreme Court in Bates and Bates, 733 P.2d 1363 (Or. 1989) (en banc), adopted a different formulation for determining when spousal support should terminate on remarriage: when remarriage "supplants the purposes behind the initial award." 733 P.2d at 1366. If this standard had been applied in *Peterson*, would spousal support have been terminated? How does a court faced with a motion to modify ascertain what the purposes behind the initial award were?

In New Jersey, the state supreme court has held that the touchstone for determining the adequacy of a spousal support award is whether it assists "the supported spouse in achieving a lifestyle that is reasonably comparable to the one enjoyed while living with the supporting spouse during the marriage." Lepis v. Lepis, 416 A.2d 45 (N.J. 1980). In Crews v. Crews, 751 A.2d 524 (N.J. 2000), the court held that a motion to modify based on changed circumstances should be decided with reference to this standard. To facilitate that determination, it directed trial courts when setting initial awards to make findings establishing the standard of living during the marriage and evaluating whether the award will enable the parties to enjoy a lifestyle reasonably comparable to the marital standard. In Weishaus v. Weishaus, 849 A.2d 171 (N.J. 2004), the divorcing parties reached a financial settlement but could not agree whether the provisions would enable the former wife to maintain the marital standard of living, and they asked the court to enter a final order consistent with their agreement that did not include the findings that *Crews* calls for. The trial judge refused, and the wife appealed, arguing that the findings should not be required if they stood in the way of settlement. How should the case have been decided and why?

PROBLEMS

1. Wanda and Herbert were divorced after a 30-year marriage. Wanda had quit work two years after the marriage to raise their four children, and she had never worked in the market after that. Herbert was the owner of a successful small business. When Herbert and Wanda divorced, the court awarded Wanda more than half of the marital property other than the business and ordered Herbert to pay her $1,500 per month indefinitely as spousal support. Judge Anderson said that the award was partially in recognition of Wanda's claim to an interest in the business. The judge explained that she thought spousal support, which is modifiable, was fairer than property division because it required the parties to share the risk that the business might fall on hard times. The judge said that the award was also justified by Wanda's lost earning capacity and the length of the marriage. Two years later Wanda married Simon, who was disabled in a workplace accident and receives a small disability pension. Herbert has moved to terminate spousal support. Under the *Peterson* rule, how should a court rule on the motion and why? Under *Bates*?

2. If Wanda's spousal support were terminated and Simon died six months after the wedding, leaving no estate for Wanda to inherit, should she be able to have her support from Herbert reinstated? Why or why not?

IN RE MARRIAGE OF DWYER

825 P.2d 1018 (Colo. Ct. App. 1991)

ROTHENBERG, J. Rodney C. Dwyer, husband, appeals from an order of the trial court extending the duration of maintenance payable to Anne E. Dwyer, wife. We affirm. . . .

Husband's first contention is that since the wife is cohabitating with an adult male, maintenance should be terminated as a matter of law under § 14-10-122(2), C.R.S. (1987 Repl. Vol. 6B). We disagree.

Section 14-10-122(2) provides:

> Unless otherwise agreed in writing or expressly provided in the decree, the obligation to pay future maintenance is terminated upon the death of either party or the *remarriage* of the party receiving maintenance. (emphasis added)

Initially, we note that husband does not suggest that wife's new relationship constitutes a valid common law marriage which would concededly be a "remarriage" within the meaning of § 14-10-122(2). Rather, he argues that § 14-10-122(2) should apply to cohabitation as well as remarriage.

Although no Colorado case is directly on point, a majority of the jurisdictions that have addressed this issue have held that a former spouse's unmarried cohabitation is not, in and of itself, sufficient ground for suspending, reducing, or terminating maintenance. *See* Alibrando v. Alibrando, 375 A.2d 9 (D.C. 1977); Sieber v. Sieber, 258 N.W.2d 754 (Minn. 1977); Garlinger v. Garlinger, 137 N.J. Super. 56, 347 A.2d 799 (1975). *See generally* Thomas J. Oldham, The Effect of Unmarried Cohabitation by a Former Spouse upon His or Her Right to Continue to Receive Alimony, 17 J. Fam. L. 249 (1978).

The rationale for adopting this approach is that unmarried cohabitants do not assume the reciprocal obligations of marriage, including the common law duty of support.

An additional rationale was used by the Kentucky supreme court which also rejected the same argument made by husband here. The Kentucky court reasoned that such an interpretation of its statute, which is identical to ours, would violate the plain meaning of the statutory term "remarriage."

We agree with both rationales and, therefore, hold as a matter of law that the existence of cohabitation in and of itself is not tantamount to "remarriage" for purposes of § 14-10-122(2).

Finally, we note that there is no evidence that the wife's cohabitation here did in fact diminish or eliminate her need for continuing maintenance. To the contrary, wife introduced into evidence a written agreement which she and her cohabitant had executed approximately two years before the hearing. The agreement explicitly stated that the parties thereto would not be legally responsible for each other's support and their separate assets and liabilities would remain separate.

Further, wife testified that she pays $200 per month rent, that she and her cohabitant contribute jointly to other household expenses, and that living in this arrangement has resulted in only a modest reduction of her monthly housing and food expenses. Thus, apart from an incidental reduction of her living expenses, her cohabitant does not contribute to her support.

In sum, the record here supports the trial court's finding that the wife needed continuing maintenance. . . .

NOTES AND QUESTIONS

1. Perhaps the most common argument for distinguishing cohabitation from remarriage for purposes of terminating spousal support is that cohabitants do not have a duty to support each other, while married persons do. However, in a state that automatically terminates spousal support upon remarriage, doesn't the *Dwyer* rule discourage remarriage?

2. In a state where remarriage may be a change in circumstances warranting reduction or elimination of spousal support, how should cohabitation be treated? Why do you suppose that Mrs. Dwyer and her cohabitant entered into a written agreement not to support each other? Assume the agreement is binding between the parties. How should it affect Mr. Dwyer's support duty?

3. Should spousal support be reduced or eliminated when the recipient becomes platonic roommates with someone else? Should this situation be distinguished from *Dwyer*?

4. In Combs v. Combs, 787 S.W.2d 260 (Ky. 1990), the Kentucky Supreme Court considered under what circumstances a recipient's cohabitation with

another person would constitute a sufficient change in circumstances to warrant modifying spousal support. It directed courts to consider:

1. Duration — It should never be the intention of the Court to allow for maintenance reduction based upon casual "overnights" or dating. A showing of substantially changed circumstances . . . based upon cohabitation, necessarily involves proof of some permanency or long-term relationship.
2. Economic Benefit — The relationship must be such to place the cohabitating spouse in a position which avails that spouse of a substantial economic benefit. The scope and extent of the economic benefit should be closely scrutinized. If the "cohabitation" does not change the cohabitating spouse's economic position, then reductions should not be permitted.
3. Intent of the Parties — Does it appear that the cohabitating spouse is avoiding re-marriage to keep maintenance? Does it appear from the circumstances that the cohabitating parties intend to establish a "lasting relationship"?
4. Nature of the Living Arrangements — Does it appear that the cohabitation is merely a space sharing situation or is there one common household?
5. Nature of the Financial Arrangements — Is there a "pooling of assets"? Is there actually a joint or team effort in the living arrangement? Who pays the bills and how are they paid?
6. Likelihood of a Continued Relationship — Does it appear that the relationship will continue in the future? Do the parties intend the relationship to continue indefinitely?

What assumptions about the rationale for terminating support underlie these factors? Is the approach here the same as that adopted by *Peterson* for determining when remarriage terminates spousal support? Should the test be the same in the two situations? If this test were applied to *Dwyer*, would spousal support terminate? If it were applied to *Peterson*? For a similar list of statutory factors *see* W. Va. Code §48-5-707 (2001).

5. Several jurisdictions have adopted statutes terminating spousal support if the recipient forms a relationship with a new partner. *E.g.*, Ala. Code §30-2-55 (1992) ("living openly or cohabiting with a member of the opposite sex"); Ill. Rev. Stat. ch. 750 ¶ 5/510(c) (1992) ("cohabits with another person on a resident, continuing conjugal basis"); Pa. Cons. Stat. §3706 (1992) ("cohabitation with a person of the opposite sex who is not a member of the family of the petitioner within the degrees of consanguinity"); P.R. Laws Ann. tit. 31, §385 (1992) (wife "lives in public concubinage or observes licentious behavior").

Several other states provide that cohabitation may be grounds for modifying or terminating spousal support. *E.g.*, Cal. Fam. Code §4323 (Deering 1993) ("cohabiting with a person of the opposite sex" creates a rebuttable presumption of decreased need for support); Ga. Code Ann. §19-6-19 (2002) (voluntary cohabitation, defined as "dwelling together continuously and openly in a meretricious relationship with another person, regardless of the sex of the other person"); N.Y. Dom. Rel. Law §248 (Consol. 1993) ("wife is habitually living with another man and holding herself out as his wife"); Okla. Stat. tit. 43 § 134(C) (2004) ("voluntary cohabitation," defined as "dwelling together continuously and habitually of a man and a woman who are in a private conjugal relationship not solemnized as a marriage according to law, or not necessarily meeting all the standards of a common-law marriage"). For collected cases, *see* Diane M. Allen, Divorced or Separated Spouse's Living with Member of Opposite Sex as Affecting Other Spouse's Obligation of Alimony or Support Under Separation Agreement, 47 A.L.R.4th 38 (2004).

6. If state law provides that spousal support does not automatically terminate upon cohabitation or remarriage, but rather is a possible change in circumstances, is it contrary to public policy to enforce an agreement providing for automatic termination? Consider the view of Justice O'Hern, dissenting from a decision upholding the enforceability of such an agreement in Konzelman v. Konzelman, 729 A.2d 7, 17-21 (N.J. 1999):

> When viewed through the Gaussian filter employed by the Court, the anti-cohabitation clause appears as a pleasant piece of bargaining between equals. Although the Court properly declines to presume that all women are passive players in this arena, it fails to afford proper weight to the uneven economic playing field upon which the contest takes place. . . .
>
> The majority downplays the woman's loss of freedom or autonomy by asserting that the case is not about sex, but that it is about money, the freedom of contract, and whether the anti-cohabitation provision entered into was "voluntary, knowing and consensual," and based upon "mutuality, voluntariness and fairness." It offends our intelligence for defendant to suggest that the anti-cohabitation clause in this case is not about sex. If the clause were not about sex, why then is cohabitation with another person of the same sex permitted without a reduction in support? For reasons rooted in our past, "social conventions [still seek to] . . . deny women the same chance of sexual happiness as men. . . ." Alan Ryan, Cultural Perversions, N.Y. Times Book Review at 16 (Mar. 14, 1999) (reviewing Martha C. Nussbaum, Sex and Social Justice (1999)). There is a double standard at play here that views women as having a lesser need than men for companionship of the opposite sex, "yet . . . universally punishe[s] [women] if they display evidence to the contrary. . . ." Natalie Angier, Men, Women, Sex and Darwin, N.Y. Times Magazine, Feb. 21, 1999, at 51.
>
> The danger against which courts have guarded in the past concerns "the numerous ways in which a spouse can use [economic power associated with spousal support] to exert unjust and inappropriate control over the recipient's personal life." Sara Z. Moghadam, The Maryland Survey: 1995-96: C. Dismissing the Purpose and Public Policy Surrounding Spousal Support, 56 Md. L. Rev. 927, 927 (1997). . . .
>
> Mrs. Konzelman is punished for her choice of companionship while Mr. Konzelman is relieved of the burden to demonstrate that his former partner's financial status is any better because of her new relationship. That approach ignores the economic needs and dependency test that underpins an alimony obligation. The trial court found that Mrs. Konzelman's financial status had improved only to the extent of $170 per week because of her relationship.
>
> Mrs. Konzelman was married for twenty-seven years. The record does not disclose whether she left work to raise her children, thereby decreasing her potential for earnings. That is often the case. . . .
>
> Dependency acquired during the marriage based on the marital roles assumed by the parties is at the heart of an alimony obligation. It is manifestly unfair to relieve

Mr. Konzelman of all alimony obligations based upon Mrs. Konzelman's choice of companionship with another man, when economic need is the true measure of alimony. The law is casting this partner of twenty-seven years into poverty for what, a sin? If her relationship ends, she will not even have, from the partners' once-shared earning capacity, a dollar a week to live on while Mr. Konzelman will be permitted to reap the benefits of an increased earning capacity built up during the marriage. . . .

In Melletz, supra, Judge Dreier punctured the hypocrisy attendant to anti-cohabitation clauses by asking the rhetorical question: could a divorced wife obtain a similar promise from her husband in return for less alimony? 271 N.J.Super. at 365-66, 638 A.2d 898. . . .

III

Finally, the enforcement of anti-cohabitation clauses imposes a needless burden on the judiciary and the matrimonial bar. This trial consumed thirteen days over three months and included twenty-six witnesses. The evidence included the reports and testimony of several private investigators, one of whom watched Mrs. Konzelman's home seven days a week for 127 days. It would not have taken thirteen days or a spy in her yard to determine that Mrs. Konzelman's companion contributed $170 a week to the household. As a result of the Court's ruling, each Konzelman hearing here-inafter will result in an exhaustive (and exhausting) inquiry into whether the situation involved something more than "a mere, romantic, casual or social relationship. . . ." (Does this mean that there is a platonic defense to anti-cohabitation clauses?) Such tasteless inquiries into the private lives of divorced women, when unnecessary, are beneath the dignity of the judiciary.

In addition, by approving anti-cohabitation clauses, the Court will force attorneys and parties to bargain over the fair value of the clause. The Court's holding invites husbands to seek such clauses, perhaps as a bargaining chip. There are only two purposes for the clause, either to eliminate the need to examine changed economic circumstances or to retain control over the divorced spouse. Either way, there will be a price. Wives will not wish lightly to contemplate the kind of surveillance this woman endured. It is regrettably the way of the world that only the wealthy will want to or will be able to buy the clause. I would not add to the already emotionally charged denouement of a marriage this unseemly bit of bargaining. . . .

I would reverse the judgment of the Appellate Division and reinstate that of the trial court reducing Mrs. Konzelman's alimony by $170 per week.

PROBLEM

Helen and Martin were divorced in 1993 after a 31-year marriage. Helen had a GED and had not worked outside the home. Martin was a very successful optometrist. Helen was awarded permanent spousal support because the court found that her employment opportunities were limited to minimum-wage jobs. Martin has filed a motion to terminate spousal support because Helen has been living with Vic for almost three years in the home that she received in the divorce from Martin. The evidence shows that neither Helen nor Vic maintains another residence, that they share household expenses more or less evenly, that they have an exclusive sexual relationship, and that they are open about their relationship and socialize with friends and family as a couple. Vic and Helen do not intend to marry, neither has provided for the other by will, and each has arranged for his or her oldest child to manage things if he or she becomes incompetent. They do not have joint bank accounts, their car titles are not held jointly, and Helen has not put Vic's name on the title to the house. Helen has no income aside from the spousal support she receives from Martin, although she could earn $700 a month if she worked full-time at a minimum wage job.

Under the approach in *Dwyer*, how should the court rule on Martin's motion and why? Under the statutes cited in notes 4 and 5 above?

4.   New Families — Child Support

One way of understanding cases and statutes that terminate spousal support when the recipient remarries or cohabits is that the appropriate family unit for allocating economic responsibility is the one that functions as a day-to-day household. On the other hand, rules that do not make termination of spousal support automatic express the view that the economic consequences of a previous marriage are so important that they should continue to have an impact despite the reconfiguring of the family. This section considers the similar, but even more complicated, problems in determining how decisions by parents to remarry or assume financial responsibility for children from a new marriage should affect their child support obligations.

Most divorced adults, including parents with custody, remarry, and never-married parents often marry as well. About half of all marriages every year are remarriages for one or both spouses, and about 65 percent of those adults have children from a previous relationship. B.A. Chadwick & T.B. Heaton, Statistical Handbook on the American Family (2d ed, 1999). In 1996, 17 percent of all children lived in blended families, that is, families consisting of parents and their new spouses, with or without new children. U.S. Census Bureau, From Birth to Seventeen: The Living Arrangements of Children, 2000 in Population Profile of the United States: 2000, 6-2 (Internet release, last visited Oct. 14, 2004).

When a parent has children from several relationships, it would be possible to apply child support guidelines by adding the number of children and then prorating for the children whose support is actually at issue in this particular case. However, no jurisdiction does this. Instead, the presumptive child support obligation is calculated based on the number of children being provided for in the particular case. *See* Paula Woodland Faerber, Empirical Study: A Guide to the Guidelines: A Longitudinal Study of Child Support Guidelines in the United States, 1 J.L. & Fam. Stud. 151, 156 (1999). The following case addresses two issues that recur in determining child support for parents with multiple families.

AINSWORTH V. AINSWORTH

574 A.2d 772 (Vt. 1990)

DOOLEY, J. The parties were divorced on April 30, 1986. They stipulated then that defendant was to pay child support in the amount of $35 per week for each of their two children for a total of $70 per week. Mr. Ainsworth remarried on August 15, 1987, and established a new home with his wife and her son at that time. On September 21, 1987, plaintiff filed a motion for modification pursuant to 15 V.S.A. §660, seeking increased support in an amount to be determined under the guidelines mandated by the statute that was effective on April 1, 1987. . . .

. . . [T]he parties agreed that if defendant had a preexisting support obligation to his stepson, the correct guideline figure based on the parties' gross incomes would be $121 per week for both children, and if he did not, the figure would be $141 per week. The trial court ruled that the stepfather did not have a preexisting support obligation to his stepson and that the correct figure under the guideline was accordingly $141.

As to the second question, the court held that the guideline figure of $141 per week was greater than was appropriate under the circumstances and would not leave sufficient financial resources for the needs of the defendant. Accordingly, the court held that a departure from the guideline amount was warranted and increased defendant's support obligation to $90 a week, $20 more than under the original order. . . .

The first question we face is whether the trial court can find an order based on the guidelines "inequitable" because of the expenses of supporting another child when the support obligation for that other child did not preexist the one for the child or children included in the guideline calculation. We believe that the trial court has this power.

We start with the wording chosen by the Legislature to describe when the court should deviate from the guidelines. The term "equitable" normally means "[j]ust; conformable to the principles of justice and right." Black's Law Dictionary 482 (5th ed. 1979). Thus, the use of the term "inequitable" must give the trial court authority to look at whether a guideline-based amount is just under the circumstances. . . .

While the wording chosen by the Legislature makes clear that it intended to give trial courts discretion to ensure support awards are just, this is an area where we must be careful to define the nature and scope of that discretion so that it is not used to create inequity or to undermine the standardization that the Legislature intended. If we allow the trial courts to consider any variation in the needs of the children or the living situation or expenses of the parents, we would return to the preguideline law where a wide range of support amounts was permissible in almost every case. In short, the "escape valve" of §659 would eat up the rule and destroy the predictability of amounts and the maintenance of the standard of living of the children that are the desired results of a guideline system.

Our examination of the statutory scheme demonstrates, however, that this case involves the type of situation where the Legislature intended that the court exercise discretion consistent with the policies of the act. That intent is demonstrated by the exclusion from gross income of certain support payments. While the drafting is not a model of clarity, we conclude that the exclusion covers amounts being paid pursuant to preexisting support orders.

It is important to analyze what is covered by the exclusion and what is not.

First, as we construe the legislative intent, it requires that there be an actual support order. Second, it requires that the order, not merely the obligation, be preexisting at the time the calculation is made. Third, it requires that payments be made on the order.

The limits of the second requirement are particularly important. It shows that the Legislature was primarily concerned about the timing of the orders. If a noncustodial parent is subject to two child support orders, the amount paid under the first order is always deductible under §653(5)(E)(i) from that parent's income in determining the amount of the second order, even though the child covered by the second order might have been born before the child covered by the first order.

There are practical reasons why the Legislature created a rule allowing a parent to deduct the expenses of other support obligations only in limited circumstances. They are explained in People in Interest of C.D., 767 P.2d at 811-12, in describing the identical Colorado rule:

> Inherent in the statutory scheme is a legislative recognition that child support obligations which have been previously imposed by a court have been determined to be both necessary and reasonable in amount in proper judicial proceedings. Non-ordered support obligations, on the other hand, have not been judicially scrutinized either as to their necessity or their reasonableness, and the General Assembly accordingly has not provided for automatic income adjustments based upon those obligations, whether or not they are actually paid.
>
> In addition, jurisdictional and practical impediments render the support schedule an ill-suited device to determine the necessity for, and the reasonableness of, support obligations for persons who are not parties to the proceedings before the court. . . . [T]he mere fact that a parent may have some legal duty to support other children does not indicate the extent of the support needs of the other children, . . . whether those needs are or can be met by other persons . . . [or] an obligor's actual contribution to those needs. The use of the statutory schedule under these circumstances requires the court to make assumptions concerning these matters which may not be wholly warranted.
>
> These reasons involve practical considerations—a formula guideline system using mathematical calculations may consider only specific, liquidated amounts that are paid periodically. It would be unfair, however, to consider amounts paid under existing support obligations only when they are the subject of court orders. By allowing consideration of payments made to discharge support obligations in instances where they have been scrutinized by a court and can be fit within mathematical formulas and allowing courts to deviate from support amounts calculated under the guidelines when such amounts are "inequitable," the Legislature must have intended that the courts use their discretion to consider the expenses connected with second families. The use of discretion in this area prevents the guideline system from being wholly arbitrary.

For the above reasons, we answer the first question in this case in the affirmative. The trial court may, under §659, find that calculating a support order based on the guidelines would be inequitable because of a parent's expenses in supporting other dependents.

II.

The second question is whether the court's discretion under §659 extends to situations where the expenses are for the support of a second wife and a stepchild.

The trial court found that Vermont law does not create a general obligation for stepparents to support stepchildren, but went forward to consider the expenses connected with supporting the stepchild in exercising its discretion under §659.

The trial court found no obligation of support in this case because the statutory support obligation of stepparents is limited to situations where the financial resources of the natural parents are inadequate to provide the child with a reasonable subsistence. Although the stepparent support statute contains the language cited, it also states that the duty it imposes is "coextensive" with the duty to support a natural child. Therefore, we disagree with the trial court and find that the statute creates a general obligation of support. . . .

III.

Having decided that the trial court could find the application of the guidelines to be inequitable in this case, we must address whether the court properly exercised its discretion in setting a support amount. We emphasize here that the fact that the court finds the application of guidelines to be "inequitable" in a particular case does not mean that it must automatically order a substantially lower support amount. . . . It is particularly important to emphasize that consideration of a case under §659 does not necessarily mean a lower support amount in second-family cases. We have held that a change in financial circumstances "resulting from a deliberate and voluntary act, absent a sufficient reason for the sacrificing of income," will not support a modification of a child support order. We recently applied this principle in a case in which the noncustodial parent remarried and had three children of the second marriage. See Isham v. Isham, 568 A.2d 421, 423 (1989). We held that it was within the discretion of the trial court to deny a modification of defendant's support obligation to a child of his first marriage since the court could find that he had voluntarily reduced his income available for child support.

The voluntary nature of second-family obligations is not the only consideration in establishing the child support order under §659. The statute lists eight factors the court must consider. We agree with the trial court in this case that the financial resources of the new spouse of the parent is also a relevant consideration. A parent should not be able to rely on second-family expenses without consideration of second-family income and resources. . . .

. . . We adopt the view, as with custody decisions, that the trial court's findings and conclusions must show it considered the factors specified in §659(a) as well as other relevant factors and must show the reasons for the deviation from the guidelines and the amount of support ordered.

The findings and conclusions here are incomplete and much too sketchy to meet the above requirements. The court had evidence from both parties on their income and expenses. The evidence from the defendant showed a high level of consumer debt connected with the purchase of a house and furnishings for his new family. Although the court found that defendant's new spouse had "financial resources as represented by her education and former work experience," it apparently considered her to have no potential income when it set the support amount. In any event, the court never specified how, based on the evidence and its findings, it arrived at the figure of $90 per week as the new child support amount. Nor can we conclude that the court considered all the factors specified in §659(a)(1)-(8) and considered the extent to which the defendant's expenses were voluntarily incurred in the face of his obligation to the children of his first marriage.

Because the findings and conclusions do not specify the reasons for the amount of support awarded and show consideration of the statutory factors, we must reverse and remand for a new hearing. Reversed and remanded.

MORSE, J., dissenting. Because I believe the Court misconstrues the child support guidelines law, I respectfully dissent.

Under 15 V.S.A. §659(a), the trial court may exercise discretion in establishing child support only if it "finds that a child support order based on the support guidelines would be inequitable." This determination of inequitability is a prerequisite to the court's exercise of discretion in setting an amount more or less than the guideline figure. . . .

In adopting the new child support statute, the legislature stated its purpose as follows:

> The legislature . . . finds and declares as public policy that parents have the responsibility to provide child support and that child support orders should reflect the true costs of raising children and approximate insofar as possible the standard of living the child would have enjoyed had the marriage not been dissolved.

15 V.S.A. §650. That policy is reiterated in §654 of the legislation:

> The rule shall be based on the concept that children should receive the same proportion of parental income after separation or divorce of their parents as they would receive if their parents were living together in one household.

The priority is clear. Children come first. Their living standard should not drop "insofar as possible."

. . . Defendant concedes on appeal that his "expenses were all related to a purchase of a home and furnishings for that home." Notably, defendant has not alleged the existence of any involuntary expenses such as unexpected medical costs, nor has he alleged an involuntary reduction in disposable income, such as would arise from being laid off. In fact, his gross income from his primary job had increased about forty-five percent since the divorce decree, from $18,000 to $26,000 per year. (In addition, he earned $2,000 a year from a part-time job.) His claim that a guideline-based order would be inequitable is based solely on voluntary undertakings, expenses common for one in his circumstances. These expenses include payments on his $37,700 home mortgage as well as considerable short-term consumer debt on his four credit cards.

Defendant's brief purports to compare the parties' financial situations, alleging that plaintiff currently has a monthly disposable income of $8 while defendant suffers a shortfall of $642. This alleged discrepancy is not determinative of the issue. The courts should not further burden a custodial parent for living frugally in order to provide for her children in need and reward the noncustodial parent who, despite a higher gross income, has gone into debt. The legislature has determined that his children come first, before the obligations of his new home and furnishings; he must share, in the same proportion as his gross income compares to plaintiff's, in the cost of their upbringing.

. . . If defendant's new house and furnishings came before his children, he would not be honoring his "responsibility to provide child support [where] child support orders should reflect the true costs of raising children," and the children's needs would not be met by "the parents in proportion to their respective gross incomes." . . .

Whether or not defendant has a duty to support his stepson pursuant to 15 V.S.A. §296, such a duty should not dilute his duty to pay child support to his natural children under 15 V.S.A. §656(a). . . .

I am not of the view that defendant has no obligation to support his stepson. I would hold only that any such obligation must not be subtracted from his gross income in calculating the guideline child support figure. In this sense defendant's obligation to his stepchild is no different than his obligation to pay taxes. He may have a legal duty to pay both, but neither enters into the calculation of his child support obligation under the statutory guidelines.

It may be useful to compare the situation of a parent who is subject to a child support order stemming from a former marriage. In such a case, the earlier child support obligations, if actually paid, may reduce the parent's obligations to the children of the second marriage under the new statutory framework. Children of the second marriage receive diminished support relative to children of the first marriage. The legislature had to choose where to place the inevitable hardship—all things being equal—resulting from the assumption of second-family responsibilities. It chose to keep child support, as dictated by the guidelines in the usual case, intact for children who were already the beneficiaries of a child support order. This is as it should be. The decision to assume added familial responsibilities should include an evaluation of the added cost, without factoring in a reduction in support to children of the divorce to help finance the second family. In short, the Court's decision today reduces the cost equation at the expense of children of divorce.

I would not fashion a per se rule. Expenses for children in a second family in some instances might well warrant a departure from the guidelines. It is not necessary to broaden discretion under §659(a)'s inequitability standard, however, to, in the words of the Court, "prevent the guideline system from being wholly arbitrary." This case involves expenses related to defendant's stepchild and second wife which were neither onerous nor extraordinary. The trial court found that the stepson's mother—a college graduate, a violinist, and experienced as a secretary with administrative skills, who wished to be with her family rather than work the six months prior to the hearing—has "financial resources as represented by her education and her former work experience." We cannot ignore this finding unless it is clearly erroneous, and no one argues that it is clearly erroneous. Moreover, as defendant concedes in his brief, "Mr. Ainsworth's expenses were all related to a purchase of a home and furnishings for that home." It is on these facts that I would conclude that the trial court's determination of inequitability under §659(a) was not permitted. . . .

NOTES AND QUESTIONS

1. In applying child support guidelines, the great majority of states provide that spousal support and child support actually paid pursuant to court order are deductible from the payor's income. However, formulas used to calculate the

presumptive amount of child support rarely take into account the needs of a subsequent spouse or subsequent biological, adoptive, or stepchildren. Marianne Takas, The Treatment of Multiple Family Cases Under State Child Support Guidelines 20 (OCSE 1991).

How does the *Ainsworth* court justify treating a person's duty to support different classes of dependents differently?

A number of states, like Vermont, give courts discretion to deviate from the calculated amount because of new support duties. How does the *Ainsworth* court define when exercise of discretion in such circumstances is warranted? Cases endorsing the general approach include Clark v. Tabor, 830 S.W.2d 873 (Ark. App. 1992); In re C.D., 767 P.2d 809 (Colo. App. 1988); Short v. Short, 577 So. 2d 723 (Fla. Dist. Ct. App. 1991); People ex rel. Browning v. Melton, 536 N.E.2d 133 (Ill. App. 1989); State ex rel. Dix v. Plank, 780 P.2d 171 (Kan. App. 1989); In re Marriage of Ladely, 469 N.W.2d 663 (Iowa 1991). *But see* Gilley v. McCarthy, 469 N.W.2d 666 (Iowa 1991); In re Hall, 798 P.2d 117 (Mont. 1990); Hoover v. Hoover, 793 P.2d 1329 (Nev. 1990); Steuben County Dept. Soc. Serv. ex rel. Padgett v. James, 569 N.Y.S.2d 32 (App. Div. 1991); Ainsworth v. Ainsworth, 835 P.2d 928 (Or. App. 1992); Falrey v. Liskey, 401 S.E.2d 897 (Va. App. 1991).

The ALI Family Dissolution Principles provide for a deduction from the obligor's income of child support actually paid under a prior order or agreement. If the prior child lives with the obligor, the obligor gets a deduction for the amount of support that the parent would pay if the child lived with the child's other parent. ALI, Principles of the Law of Family Dissolution § 3.14(3) (2002). The *Principles* give the fact finder discretion to grant a deduction when the obligor has subsequently borne children. *Id.* § 3.16(1)(c).

2. The dissenter in *Ainsworth* tends to favor what has been called the "First Family First" approach. At the other extreme is the "Second Family First" approach. In a suit to modify support for children in the first marriage, the court imputes an amount of support for the children in the second family from child support guidelines and deducts this amount from the parent's income before calculating child support for the children in the first family. What policies underlie this approach?

3. Mary Ann Glendon in The New Family and the New Property 71-72 (1981) notes that much of the problem with child support is that persons of limited means divorce, remarry, and produce new families, incurring more obligations than they can fulfill. She discusses "other, more experienced, polygamous societies," that is, Muslim countries, but suggests that they have not been more successful in dealing with the economic consequences of multiple families:

> In countries where Muslims are still legally permitted to have more than one wife at a time, they are admonished by religious law not to take more wives than they can afford. At least this is a common interpretation of 4 Koran, Verse 4: "[M]arry of the women who seem good to you, two, or three or four; and if ye fear that you cannot do justice, then one only. . . ." Yet this counsel, like much traditional Western marriage law, seems merely the expression of a moral ideal, with little or no legal sanction.

4. Constitutional challenges to child support schemes that give financial preference to prior children have generally been rejected. In Gallaher v. Elam,

104 S.W.3d 455 (Tenn. 2003), a father argued that the Tennessee child support guidelines, which give obligors a deduction for child support paid pursuant to a court order but not for support paid without an order, including for children living with the obligor, violate equal protection. The state supreme court rejected the argument that strict or heightened scrutiny should be applied to the rule, holding that it did not infringe upon the father's right to be a parent or his right to have a relationship with the children and that the classification made by the statute among children did not justify enhanced scrutiny. The court then found the distinction drawn by the rule to be rational, saying:

[T]he Guidelines [are] designed to ensure that the voluntary acts of obligors (e.g., choosing to have additional children) do not reduce their existing court-ordered child support obligations. It is rational to require obligors to be under a court order to support their children before those children can be considered in calculating the amount of support for another child because such a requirement ensures that the obligor is legally liable for the amount of child support claimed as a deduction. Furthermore, the obligor's children who are not receiving support pursuant to a court order and who live with the obligor inherently benefit from the obligor's household expenditures. Children who do not live with the obligor do not enjoy this benefit. Thus, both policy and fact justify the classification at issue. Moreover, the trial court is not flatly prohibited from considering non-court-ordered support. Chapter 1240-2-4-.04(4) of the Guidelines provides that courts may deviate from the Guidelines in cases of "extreme economic hardship." We conclude that the state has a rational, legitimate interest in requiring obligors to be under a court order to support their children before these children may be considered in calculating the amount of support for another child. . . .

See also Pohlmann v. Pohlmann, 703 So. 2d 1121 (Fla. Dist. Ct. App. 1997); Feltman v. Feltman, 434 N.W.2d 590 (S.D. 1989).

5. Canadian provinces use a percentage of income model, based on the payor's gross income and the number of children to set the amount of child support. A payor's duty to support a pre-existing or second family is a potential reason for the judge to deviate from this amount. D.A. Rollie Thompson, The Second Family Conundrum in Child Support, 18 Canadian J. Fam. L. 227 (2001).

6. The new child supported by Mr. Ainsworth was his stepchild, and under Vermont law stepparents are obligated to support stepchildren with whom they live to the same extent as their legal parents are. Most states adhere to the common law rule that stepparents have no duty to support their stepchildren based on their status alone. A number of states' statutes impose a support duty on stepparents under some circumstances. In addition to Vermont, see, e.g., Mo. Rev. Stat. § 568.040; Mont. Code Ann. § 40-6-217 (1991); N.D. Cent. Code § 14-09-09; N.H. Rev. Stat. Ann. § 546-A-1; Okla. Stat. Ann. tit. 10 § 15; Or. Rev. Stat. § 109.053; S.D. Cod. Laws Ann. § 25-7-8. A few states make live-in partners of the custodial parent at least secondarily liable for the support of the custodial parent's child. E.g., Hawaii Rev. Stat. § 577-4; S.E.M. v. D.M.M., 664 S.W.2d 665 (Mo. App. 1984).

In a state that does not impose a legal duty of support on stepparents, should the fact that a stepparent does support a stepchild be a ground for deviating from the amount calculated under the guidelines formula?

Empirical studies show that custodial stepparents almost always support their stepchildren. David Chambers, Stepparents, Biologic Parents, and the Law's Perceptions of "Family" After Divorce in Divorce Reform at the Crossroads 102, at 105 (Stephen D. Sugarman & Herma Hill Kay eds., 1990). Recognizing this economic reality, workers' compensation and unemployment compensation statutes generally provide that stepchildren who are dependent on a stepparent are covered by state workers' compensation laws. *See, e.g.*, Ariz. Rev. Stat. Ann. § 23-1064; Conn. Gen. Stat. § 31-234; Ga. Code Ann. § 34-9-13(a)(1) (1982); Ind. Code Ann. § 22-3-3-19(b) (West 1981); La. Rev. Stat. § 23:1021(3); N.C. Gen Stat. § 97-2(12) (1985). *See also* Roush v. Director for the Division of Employment Security, 387 N.E.2d 126 (Mass. 1979) (stepchildren covered by unemployment compensation laws).

Chapter 12 considers the circumstances under which courts impose support duties on stepparents after a marriage between parent and stepparent ends.

7. Often a parent's new spouse earns income. How did the *Ainsworth* court deal with the father's new wife's income?

Most child support guidelines provide that the income of a parent's new spouse is not income for purposes of calculating the basic obligation. *See, e.g.*, Jorgensen v. Jorgensen, 640 P.2d 202 (Ariz. 1982); In re Marriage of Kessler, 441 N.E.2d 1221 (Ill. App. 1982).

In some community property states, courts have held that half of the earnings of the new spouse, which are community property, belong to the obligated parent and are to that extent considered in calculating the child support obligation. DeTevis v. Aragon, 727 P.2d 558 (N.M. App. 1986). Matherne v. Matherne, 571 So. 2d 888 (La. App. 1990), held that a trial court has discretion to apply the guidelines to the combined income of the payor and new spouse, but in Crockett v. Crockett, 575 So. 2d 942 (La. App. 1991), the court held that where the father was involuntarily unemployed and the new wife's income was not sufficient to meet the expenses of a family, her income should not be included under the guidelines.

Courts in other community property states as well as common law property states have interpreted statutes providing that spouses are not liable for each other's premarital debts to mean that a noncustodial stepparent's income cannot be considered in calculating his or her spouse's child support obligation. Hines v. Hines, 707 P.2d 969 (Ariz. App. 1985); Duffey v. Duffey, 631 P.2d 697 (Mont. 1981). *See also* Van Dyke v. Thompson, 630 P.2d 420 (Wash. 1981) (en banc), and Abitz v. Abitz, 455 N.W.2d 609 (Wis. 1990).

Even though a stepparent's income cannot be considered in calculating the basic support obligation, many cases decided before and after the advent of guidelines have held that courts may consider the extent to which the new spouse's income increases the parent's ability to pay and so may justify an increase in an award. *E.g.*, Spivey v. Schneider, 217 S.E.2d 251 (Ga. 1975); Tedford v. Dempsey, 437 So. 2d 410 (Miss. 1983); Rann v. Rann, 283 N.Y.S.2d 426 (Fam. Ct. 1967); Ainsworth and Ainsworth, 835 P.2d 928 (Or. App. 1992); Commonwealth ex rel. Travitsky v. Travitsky, 326 A.2d 883 (Pa. Super. 1974); Shank v. Shank, 444 A.2d 1274 (Pa. Super. 1982); Renaud v. Renaud, 373 A.2d 1198 (R.I. 1977). A California statute provides that the income of a parent's new spouse or nonmarital partner "shall not be considered when determining or modifying child support, except in an extraordinary case where excluding that income would lead to extreme and severe hardship to any child subject to the child support award, in which case the court shall also consider whether including that income would lead to extreme and severe hardship to any child" supported by the parent or the parent's new spouse or nonmarital partner. Cal. Fam. Code § 4057.5 (2004).

A number of courts have also held that a custodial parent's remarriage can reduce the needs of the children, leading to reduced support from the noncustodial parent. *See, e.g.,* Gardner v. Perry, 405 A.2d 721 (Maine 1979); Beverly v. Beverly, 317 N.W.2d 213 (Mich. App. 1981); Snyder v. Snyder, 499 N.E.2d 320 (Ohio App. 1985); Abitz v. Abitz, 455 N.W.2d 609 (Wis. 1990); Thies v. MacDonald, 187 N.W.2d 186 (Wis. 1971).

What is the practical difference between including a stepparent's income in calculating the basic child support obligation and finding that the custodial parent's ability to pay has increased because of his or her new spouse's income? North Dakota courts have explicitly recognized the tension between rules that say a stepparent is not obligated to support stepchildren and those that say parents should support their children even if they are not employed and has attempted to structure a compromise. For a description, *see* Spilovoy v. Spilovoy, 511 N.W.2d 230 (N.D. 1994).

PROBLEMS

1. Madelyn and Tom were divorced in 1992. Madelyn was granted primary physical custody of their two children, and Tom was ordered to pay child support. Madelyn married George in 1993. In 1994 Madelyn filed a motion to increase child support. Tom submitted interrogatories seeking extensive information about gifts that Madelyn received from George, including entertainment, travel, restaurant meals, and all amounts that George paid directly or indirectly to third parties on her behalf. Madelyn refused to answer the interrogatories on the grounds that the information sought is irrelevant, and Tom has filed a motion to compel. The child support guidelines in this state are of the Income Shares type, and they define income as "income from any source including but not limited to salaries, wage, commissions, bonuses, dividends, severance pay, pensions, interest, trust income, annuities, capital gains, social security benefits, workers' compensation benefits, gifts, prizes, and alimony or spousal support received." In this jurisdiction stepparents are not legally obligated to support their stepchildren. Information is discoverable if it is relevant to the subject matter of the litigation. How should the court rule on Tom's motion? Why?

2. When Mary and Fred were divorced, she received sole custody of their child, Carl. Mary married Sam a year ago, and they now have a new baby. Mary has decided to quit work and stay home to care for Carl, the baby, and Amy, Sam's child from a former relationship. Carl goes to kindergarten three hours a day, and Amy is in school six hours a day. Before she quit work, Mary earned $35,000 a year. Fred has asked the court to impute this much income to Mary when it recalculates child support for Carl. What arguments can be made in support of this request? How should Mary respond?

5. A Comparison: Child Support Duties When the Family Receives Public Assistance

For centuries Anglo-American societies have imposed duties on family members to support dependent relatives who would otherwise receive or are receiving public assistance. We have already seen two circumstances in which such obligations are imposed today. Chapter 2 considered Medicaid eligibility rules, which sometimes provide that the income of an applicant's spouse is deemed to be available for support of the applicant. The section in Chapter 7 about adult children's duty to support their parents dealt with statutes whose original purpose was reducing or eliminating the public obligation to support needy elders.

Until 1996, public assistance for poor families with children was called Aid to Families with Dependent Children (AFDC), and basic eligibility rules were determined at the national level, just as rules about eligibility for Medicaid still are. The national AFDC standards included a variety of relative responsibility rules. The relative responsibility rules imposed support obligations on families of applicants for public assistance that are not legally enforced for other families. For example, Pub. L. No. 97-35 §2306(a) (1981), provided that a custodial stepparent's income had to be included in determining a child's eligibility, regardless of whether state law imposed a general obligation on stepparents to support stepchildren. Pub. L. No. 98-369, §2640(a) (1984), provided that the income of grandparents had to be included in determining a child's eligibility if the child's parent was younger than 18 and living in the grandparents' home. These rules typically operated by requiring that income of a responsible relative be deemed available to an applicant for assistance, which could have the effect of making the person ineligible or reducing his or her grant, regardless of whether the relative actually provided financial assistance to the applicant.

In Bowen v. Gilliard, 483 U.S. 587 (1987), the Supreme Court upheld another rule that imposed family support duties on welfare families that are different from those of other families. The court rejected constitutional challenges to a federal rule that required a parent who lived with children who were half-siblings to include all the children in the family unit that applied for AFDC. Before the rule was adopted, such a parent might choose to exclude a child from the family group when that was financially advantageous. For example, if the parent received child support on behalf of one of three children, the family might be better off financially if the parent applied for assistance as a family consisting of him or herself and only two children. The challenged rule eliminated this option, and suit was brought alleging a violation of the Equal Protection Clause. Finding no basis for invoking heightened scrutiny, the Court wrote:

> The rationality of the amendment denying a family the right to exclude a supported child from the filing unit is also supported by the Government's separate interest in distributing benefits among competing needy families in a fair way. Given its perceived need to make cuts in the AFDC budget, Congress obviously sought to identify a group that would suffer less than others as a result of a reduction in benefits. When considering the plight of two five-person families, one of which receives no income at all while the other receives regular support payments for some of the minor children, it is surely reasonable for Congress to conclude that the former is in greater need than the latter. . . .

483 U.S. at 599. The Court also rejected the argument that the rule violated the Takings Clause:

> The basic requirement that the AFDC filing unit must include all family members living in the home, and therefore that support payments made on behalf of a member of the family must be considered in determining that family's level of benefits, does not even arguably take anyone's property. . . . Nor does the simple inclusion of the support income in the benefit calculation have any legal effect on the child's right to have it used for his or her benefit. To the extent that a child has the right to have the support payments used in his "best interest," he or she fully retains that right. Of course, the effect of counting the support payments as part of the filing unit's income often reduces the family's resources, and hence increases the chances that sharing of the support money will be appropriate. . . . But given the unquestioned premise that the Government has a right to reduce AFDC benefits generally, that result does not constitute a taking of private property without just compensation.
>
> The only possible legal basis for appellees' takings claim, therefore, is the requirement that an applicant for AFDC benefits must assign the support payments to the State, which then will remit the amount collected to the custodial parent to be used for the benefit of the entire family. This legal transformation in the status of the funds, the argument goes, modifies the child's interest in the use of the money so dramatically that it constitutes a taking of the child's property. As a practical matter, this argument places form over substance, and labels over reality. Although it is true that money which was earmarked for a specific child's or children's "best interest" becomes a part of a larger fund available for all of the children, the difference between these concepts is, as we have discussed, more theoretical than practical. . . .

483 U.S. at 605-606.

The 1997 Personal Responsibility and Work Opportunity Reconciliation Act (PRWORA), Pub. L. No. 104-193, eliminated AFDC and replaced it with Temporary Assistance to Needy Families (TANF). Among the many changes that PRWORA made was the elimination of many federal eligibility rules, including the relative responsibility rules. States now establish their own eligibility rules, and many continue to use the relative responsibility rules.

Critics have argued that this "dual system of family law" is unprincipled. *See, e.g.,* Jill Elaine Hasday, Parenthood Divided: A Legal History of the Bifurcated Law of Parental Relations, 90 Geo. L.J. 299 (2002); Amy E. Hirsch, Income Deeming in the AFDC Program: Using Dual Track Family Law to Make Poor Women Poorer, 16 N.Y. Rev. Law & Soc. Change 713 (1987-1988); Jacobus ten Broek, California's Dual System of Family Law: Its Origin, Development and Present Status, Parts 1, 2 and 3, 16 Stan. L. Rev. 257, 900 (1964); 17 Stan. L. Rev. 614 (1965). *But see* Thomas P. Lewis & Robert J. Levy, Family Law and Welfare Policies: The Case for "Dual Systems," 54 Cal. L. Rev. 748, 775-776, 779 (1966).

PROBLEMS

1. Joell Sanders and her seven children receive welfare. Vertis Lott is the father of one of her children. The state welfare department, as assignee of that child's support right, sued Lott for child support. The hearing officer, applying the state child support guidelines, found that, based on Lott's income, the presumed amount he owes is $82 per week. Lott showed that an order of $42 per

week would reimburse the state in full for its payments on behalf of his child and cover food stamps and incidental expenses. Lott has asked the court to reduce his child support obligation to $42 per week, claiming that the facts constitute "extraordinary circumstances" justifying a deviation from the presumed amount. Should his motion be granted? Why or why not?

2. Under state law, parents do not have a legal duty to support their children 18 years and older, except that they must support children between the ages of 18 and 21 who are living with their parents and receiving welfare. Ellen and John Jones share their home with their 19-year-old daughter, Doris, and Doris's child, Bobby. Ellen and John seek a declaratory judgment that the statute requiring them to support Doris violates equal protection and substantive due process. The state relies on Bowen v. Gilliard to support the rule. Can *Bowen* be distinguished? Why or why not?

C. ENFORCEMENT

TIMOTHY S. GRALL, *CUSTODIAL MOTHERS AND FATHERS AND THEIR CHILD SUPPORT: 2001*

Current Population Reports P60-225 (U.S. Census Bureau Oct. 2003)

In the spring of 2002, an estimated 13.4 million parents had custody of 21.5 million children under 21 years of age whose other parent lived somewhere else. About 5 of every 6 custodial parents were mothers (84.4 percent) and 1 in 6 were fathers (15.6 percent), proportions statistically unchanged since 1994. Overall, 27.6 percent of all children under 21 living in families had a parent not living in the home.

* * *

About 31.2 percent of custodial mothers have never been married. The remaining ever-married mothers included 43.7 percent who were divorced or separated and 25.1 percent who were currently married or widowed. The majority of custodial fathers were divorced or separated (56.2 percent), while 24.5 percent were currently married or widowed and 20.3 percent had never been married. The age of custodial mothers increased somewhat between 1994 and 2002. In 1994, one-quarter (25.4 percent) were 40 years of age or older. By 2002, the proportion had increased to approximately one-third (34.3 percent).

Among custodial mothers, over half (56.0 percent) were non-Hispanic White, about one-fourth (26.7 percent), were Black, and 15.0 percent were Hispanic. Custodial fathers were more likely than mothers to be non-Hispanic White (70.5 percent), less likely to be Black (15.3 percent), and statistically as likely to be Hispanic (11.1 percent). Over half (57.7 percent) of custodial parents had only one child, but custodial mothers were more likely than fathers to have two or more children living with them in 2002 (43.7 percent and 34.2 percent, respectively).

The proportion of custodial parents and their children living below the poverty level declined from 33.3 percent in 1993 to 23.4 percent in 2001. Despite the steady decline in poverty for custodial-parent families, the rate remained about four times higher than the rate for married-couple families with related children in 2001 (6.1 percent).

Poverty levels varied among many custodial-parent groups. Although the poverty rate of custodial mothers fell from 36.8 percent in 1993 to 25.0 percent in 2001, it was still significantly higher than the rate of custodial fathers, 14.7 percent. Poverty rates were at least 55 percent for custodial parents who did not work or those who were participants in public assistance programs in 2001. Young (under 30 years of age), Black, or never-married custodial parents also tended to have higher rates of poverty (about 36 percent) than other members of their respective demographic groups. Custodial parents working full-time, year-round had considerably lower poverty rates, at just 7.8 percent.

Of the 13.4 million custodial parents in April 2002, 7.9 million (59.1 percent) had some type of support agreement or award for their children. . . . [A]n overwhelming majority of agreements were reported by the custodial parent as legal (established by a court or other government entity), while nonlegal, informal agreements or understandings represented only a very small proportion. The remaining included 5.5 million custodial parents who had no child support agreements, and 300,000 where legal arrangements were pending.

When the 5.9 million custodial parents without any agreements or those with informal agreements were asked why a legal agreement was not established, the reason most often cited was that they did not feel the need to go to court or get legal agreements (32.7 percent). Among the other reasons given were that the other parent provided what they could for support (26.3 percent), and they felt the other parent could not afford to pay (23.3 percent). . . .

Custodial mothers were more likely than fathers to have child support awards. About 63.0 percent of custodial mothers and 38.6 percent of fathers had child support agreed or awarded to them. There was considerable variation in award rates based on the demographic characteristics of custodial mothers. Child support award rates were about 50 percent for custodial mothers who had income below the poverty level, who were Black or Hispanic, who had less than a high school diploma, who had never married or were separated, or who were under 30 years of age. Custodial mothers who were non-Hispanic White or divorced had significantly higher award rates (over two-thirds). . . .

About three-quarters of custodial parents received at least some child support payments. Approximately 6.9 million of the 7.9 million custodial parents with child support agreements or awards in 2002 were due payments from those awards. Among these parents who were due support in 2001, 73.9 percent received at least some payments directly from the noncustodial parent, a proportion unchanged since 1993. The average annual amount of child support received for these parents receiving at least some support was $4,300, and did not differ between mothers and fathers.

The proportion of custodial parents receiving every payment they were due increased from 36.9 percent to 46.2 percent between 1993 and 1997, and the 2001 proportion remained unchanged at 44.8 percent. Among these parents, the average amount received was $5,800, and did not differ significantly between mothers and fathers.

While the proportion of custodial parents receiving full payments increased since 1993, the proportion receiving some of the payments due fell from 38.9 percent in 1993 to 28.6 percent in 1999 and was unchanged in 2001. Average child support received by these parents amounted to $2,100 per custodial-parent family.

Of the 1.5 million custodial parents below poverty and due child support in 2001, 65.6 percent received at least some payments, which included those receiving the full amount (30.8 percent) and less than the full amount of support due (34.7 percent). . . . The average amount of child support received by custodial-parent families below poverty who received any payments was $3,000, accounting for 40.2 percent of their total family income.

* * *

The 6.9 million custodial parents who were due child support under the terms of agreements or current awards were due an average of $5,000 in 2001; an aggregate of $34.9 billion in payments due. Of this amount, about $21.9 billion (62.6 percent) was received, averaging $3,200 per custodial-parent family. The average amount of support received in 2001 was about 12.1 percent higher, in real terms, than in 1993. The average amount of child support due increased by 16.8 percent during this same time. In 2001, custodial mothers received $19.8 billion of the $31.9 billion in support that was due (62.1 percent) and custodial fathers received $2.1 billion — 68.3 percent of the approximate $3.0 billion that was due.

Overall, custodial parents reported receiving $22.8 billion directly from the noncustodial parent for support of their children in 2001, which included $900 million received by parents without current awards or agreements.

* * *

Child support was more likely to be received by parents with custody and visitation agreements. A large majority (85.3 percent) of the 6.9 million custodial parents due child support payments in 2001 had arrangements for joint child custody or visitation privileges with the noncustodial parents, and approximately three-fourths (77.1 percent) of these parents received some support payments. Of the custodial parents due child support but who did not have joint custody or visitation arrangements, about half (55.8 percent) received any payments.

For the 6.5 million custodial parents without agreements, or with agreements but not due child support, 68.6 percent had arrangements with the noncustodial parents for visitation privileges or some type of shared custody.

Custodial parents with agreements or awards were more likely to receive noncash support. Many noncustodial parents provided assistance in the form of noncash support, such as gifts or expenses. About 61.0 percent of all custodial parents received at least one type of noncash support for their children. If the custodial parent had a child support agreement or award, two-thirds (65.8 percent) received some type of noncash support, compared with 54.1 percent without awards.

The most common type of noncash support was gifts for birthdays, holidays, or other occasions, (58.2 percent), followed by clothes (39.3 percent), food or groceries

(28.5 percent), medical expenses (other than health insurance) (18.7 percent), and full or partial payments for child care or summer camp (10.1 percent). . . .

Total requests for assistance related to child support declined between 1994 and 2002. About 36.5 percent of custodial parents contacted a child support enforcement office (IV-D office), state department of social services, or other welfare or TANF office for child support assistance in 2001. This number dropped 15.5 percent, from 5.8 million to 4.9 million, between 1994 and 2002. Also, the total number of contacts for assistance decreased 19.2 percent during this time, from 13.0 million to 10.5 million. Contacts were made for many reasons, but the most likely were to collect child support that was due (27.9 percent), to establish a legal agreement or court award (23.1 percent), to obtain welfare or public assistance (14.2 percent), and to locate the noncustodial parent (13.1 percent). . . .

1. Private Enforcement Mechanisms — Liens, Trusts, and Insurance

Under some circumstances judges (and lawyers drafting separation and other agreements) can do much to eliminate or minimize enforcement problems. For example, if a transfer of property is to take effect at the time the decree or agreement is signed, all the necessary documents should be available at the time of execution so that the transfer can be completed immediately. For executory terms, the decree or agreement should establish definite time limits and procedures for carrying out obligations.

The decree or agreement can also employ devices that preclude or discourage noncompliance and make enforcement easier, such as liens and trusts to secure payment of future money obligations. In some states statutes explicitly authorize courts to order that trusts for dependents be established incident to divorce.

To protect a dependent person against the premature death of a supporting former spouse or parent, some states allow courts to order the obligor to maintain life insurance for the benefit of the obligee in a sufficient amount to provide the ordered support. *E.g.*, Moore v. Moore, 543 So. 2d 252 (Fla. 1989), applying Fla. Stat. §61.08(3); Or. Rev. Stat. §§107.810-107.830. *See also* Or. Rev. Stat. §107.105(f) ("If a spouse has been awarded spousal support in lieu of a share of property, the court shall . . . order the obligor to provide for and maintain life insurance in an amount commensurate with the obligation and designating the obligee as beneficiary for the duration of the obligation. . . ."). *See also* Jacobitti v. Jacobitti, 641 A.2d 535 (N.J. 1994), affirming an order requiring an elderly obligor to establish an alimony trust for his wife rather than purchasing life insurance for his benefit, since he was unlikely to be insurable. In other states, though, such an order is considered postmortem alimony and can only be entered with the agreement of the parties.

The rest of this section considers mechanisms for enforcing duties to transfer property or to pay support when the original decree or agreement did not include enforcement mechanisms or the mechanisms were ineffective.

2. Jailing "Deadbeat" Parents

Both federal and state law provide that in some circumstances failure to pay child support is a crime, and obligors who fail to pay court-ordered support for their dependents may be held in contempt of court and jailed in all states.

Both remedies require proof that the obligor knew of the support duty and willfully refused to pay while having the ability to do so. The following case, an appeal from a finding of criminal contempt, addresses constitutional challenges that may be raised any time an obligor faces incarceration for failure to pay support.

MOSS v. SUPERIOR COURT

950 P.2d 59 (Cal. 1998)

BAXTER, Justice. . . .

The "Declaration for Contempt" in this matter, executed by Tamara S. Ortiz on June 22, 1995, alleged that a judgment of dissolution filed March 17, 1992, ordered Brent N. Moss to pay $241.50 each, or a total of $483 a month support for the two children of the marriage, one-half due on the first and one-half due on the fifteenth day of each month, commencing on January 15, 1992. The order was modified on November 1, 1994, after which $385 was to be paid monthly, with semimonthly payments of $192.50. The declaration alleged that Brent had knowledge of the order and was able to comply with each order when it was disobeyed. No payments were made from July 1, 1994, through June 15, 1995. A total of $5,210 was due and unpaid.

Brent was unemployed when the support order was made. The amount to be paid was based on his ability to earn $1,671 gross income per month.

. . . The superior court issued an order to show cause on June 17, 1995, directing Brent to appear and show cause why he should not be found guilty of contempt for willful disobedience of the support order.

At the November 7, 1995, hearing on the order to show cause, Tamara testified that she and Brent, her then husband, were present when the support order was made and that he had not paid any support at all since July 1, 1994.

. . . On cross-examination Tamara testified that Brent did not have a car and at times had no food in his house. She was not aware of him having a job in the past four years, and did not know if he had any money or any ability to pay.

Betty Lou Moss, Brent's mother, testified that she provided Brent with a home. She paid the utilities expenses most times, but on other times he did so. He worked at odd jobs, and she did not know how much he earned from them. Brent often ate at her home. She did not know if he purchased food on his own. When the children were with him, they slept at his house, but he brought them to Betty Moss's home to eat. Betty Moss did not know if Brent ever fed them at his house. She did not remember how long it had been since Brent had a job. He did not discuss jobs with her. He did odd jobs like lawn mowing once in a while, but she did not know how much he earned. When she asked him about getting a job he said he was trying. He did not tell her what he was trying, however.

No other evidence was presented.

Counsel for Brent did not dispute the existence of a valid order for support, his client's knowledge of that order, and possible "willfulness," but argued that there had been no evidence of ability to comply with the support order....

The court agreed that the burden of proving inability to comply lay with Brent and observed that there had been no evidence whatsoever that Brent was not able to work. The court found that Brent did have the ability to pay something in child support, as the evidence permitted an inference that he was receiving money from some source other than his mother. In partial explanation of that conclusion, the court stated that Brent was well dressed and had to be doing something to buy his own clothes and feed himself when he did not eat at his mother's home. The court also stated that Brent was "a person who could get a job flipping hamburgers at McDonald's.... I don't know why he couldn't get a job at minimum wage. He's, in my mind, chosen not to." Brent's attorney then conceded that Brent had the ability to work. When asked later if there was a finding of ability to work, however, the court said only that Brent had "the ability to get money. Now, whether you want to say it's the ability to work, which there is no evidence that he can't, or the ability to get money from his mother, which he apparently freely does as he needs to . . . I am left with the inference that he has money from another source." . . .

The court found Brent guilty of 24 counts of contempt. . . .

Brent's petition for a writ of mandate sought to set aside the contempt judgment on the ground that, although he raised the issue of inability to pay, Tamara presented no evidence that he had any resources with which to pay child support and therefore had the ability to comply with the order. . . . Relying on [*Ex parte*] *Todd*, 50 P. 1071 (1897), [*In re*] *Jennings*, 184 Cal. Rptr. 53 (1982), and *In re Brown*, 136 Cal.App.2d 40, 288 P.2d 27 (1955), he also claimed that, while the amount of support fixed by a child support order may be based on ability to earn, a finding of contempt may not be based on ability to earn. The Court of Appeal set aside the contempt judgment, holding that the evidence was not sufficient to prove that Brent had the ability to pay, . . . and we granted the petition for review of real party in interest for the purpose of doing so.

For the reasons stated below, we conclude that, insofar as *Todd* may apply to child support obligations, it should be disapproved. . . .

* * *

. . . In *Todd* the contemner discontinued making court-ordered alimony payments to his ex-wife. After a hearing on an order to show cause re contempt, the court found that the contemner had no money or other means of payment and had not committed a fraud on his creditors by disposing of property. The court also found that the contemner had been allowed a month within which to seek employment so that he could earn money to make the weekly alimony payments, but had made no effort to obtain employment. He was committed to jail until he paid the $200 then due.

This court held: "This order was clearly in excess of the power of the court, which cannot compel a man to seek employment in order to earn money to pay alimony, and punish him for his failure to do so."

Todd was followed by *Brown, supra,* 136 Cal.App.2d 40, 288 P.2d 27, a case in which the habeas corpus petitioner had been sentenced to a five-day jail term for failure to comply with a judgment ordering him to pay alimony. The affidavit in support of the contempt citation was construed by the Court of Appeal to allege that the contemner had insufficient money to comply due to his being unemployed. The court concluded that there had been a sufficient showing of ability to work, but this was inadequate. "If ability to work in remunerative employment was, in a pertinent legal sense, ability to comply with the mandate of the judgment, and if it had been alleged that petitioner wilfully refused to work for the express purpose of avoiding compliance with his obligations, the affidavit would have been sufficient. But mere ability to work is not the same as ability to pay." . . .

The habeas corpus petitioner in *Jennings, supra,* 133 Cal.App.3d 373, 184 Cal.Rptr. 53, had been sentenced to 60 days in jail following a finding that he was in contempt of court for failure to pay spousal support and attorney fees. He claimed that, since there was proof that he did not have the ability to pay, the order was in excess of the court's jurisdiction because it imprisoned him for a debt that he could not pay. At the time of proceedings the petitioner, an architect, was unemployed and had no assets, but the contempt court found that he had the ability to earn $80,000 per year. He had received unrestricted personal loans and unemployment insurance during the period in which alimony payments were due. The contempt court found that he had "willfully and unjustifiably quit working to avoid his financial obligation of spousal support" and had allowed his business interests to depreciate to the point at which they were practically useless. Because the contemner had voluntarily ceased work, the court had made the support order on the basis of his ability to earn, rather than on his current earnings.

The court found with respect to each count that the petitioner had the ability to pay the support obligation in full and had willfully and intentionally failed to do so, and even though he had the ability to employ himself, he had deliberately refused to employ himself so as to be unable to make the payments.

Relying on its understanding of *Todd* and *Brown,* the *Jennings* court held that the contempt order was in excess of the court's jurisdiction because it was based on capacity to earn rather than actual ability to pay. The court recognized that it is permissible to base an order for support on earning capacity rather than actual income when there is evidence of an attempt to avoid family financial responsibilities by refusing to seek employment. It concluded nonetheless that a contempt sanction could not be imposed for failure to comply with the support order. . . .

INVOLUNTARY SERVITUDE

We shall assume, as did the *Jennings* court, that the *Todd* holding was based on the constitutional proscriptions of involuntary servitude or imprisonment for debt. . . .

A. THIRTEENTH AMENDMENT

Section 1 of the Thirteenth Amendment of the federal Constitution provides: "Neither slavery nor involuntary servitude, except as a punishment for crime whereof the party shall have been duly convicted, shall exist within the United States, or any place subject to their jurisdiction."

The Thirteenth Amendment, unlike the Fourteenth Amendment, prohibits conduct by private persons as well as governmental entities. It has been construed and applied primarily to circumstances in which one individual sought to compel work by another. In its decisions applying the Thirteenth Amendment, the United States Supreme Court has recognized that many fundamental societal obligations involving compelled labor do not violate the proscription of involuntary servitude. It has never held that employment undertaken to comply with a judicially imposed requirement that a party seek and accept employment when necessary to meet a parent's fundamental obligation to support a child is involuntary servitude.

In those decisions in which a Thirteenth Amendment violation has been found on the basis of involuntary servitude, the court has equated the employment condition to peonage, under which a person is bound to the service of a particular employer or master until an obligation to that person is satisfied. A court order that a parent support a child, compliance with which may require that the parent seek and accept employment, does not bind the parent to any particular employer or form of employment or otherwise affect the freedom of the parent. The parent is free to elect the type of employment and the employer, subject only to an expectation that to the extent necessary to meet the familial support obligation, the employment will be commensurate with the education, training, and abilities of the parent.

* * *

The United States Supreme Court has consistently recognized that the Thirteenth Amendment does not prevent enforced labor as punishment for crime, and does not prevent state or federal governmental entities from compelling the performance of civic duties such as jury service, military service, and road work. A parent's obligation to support a minor child is a social obligation that is no less important than compulsory military service, road building, jury service and other constitutionally permissible enforced labor. Even if the necessity of accepting employment in order to meet this obligation were somehow analogous to those forms of compelled labor, we have no doubt that this form of labor would be recognized as an exception to the ban on involuntary servitude found in the Thirteenth Amendment. It is clear to us, however, that employment undertaken to meet a child support obligation is not analogous to government-controlled labor and does not otherwise create a condition of peonage or slavery. Unlike those recognized exceptions to the Thirteenth Amendment in which labor is compulsory, undertaking employment because an income is necessary to enable a parent to comply with a valid court order to support a child does not impose on the parent any government control over the type of employment, the employer for whom the parent's labor will be performed, or any other aspect of the parent's individual freedom that might be associated with peonage or slavery.

* * *

Article I, section 6, provides: "Slavery is prohibited. Involuntary servitude is prohibited except to punish crime." When considering involuntary servitude issues we have assumed that the protection extended by article I, section 6, is coextensive with that accorded by the Thirteenth Amendment. . . .

* * *

We conclude, therefore, that article I, section 6 of the California Constitution, affords Brent no greater rights than does the Thirteenth Amendment to the federal Constitution. . . .

IMPRISONMENT FOR DEBT

. . . Article I, section 10, states in pertinent part: "A person may not be imprisoned in a civil action for debt or tort, or in peacetime for a militia fine."

It has long been settled that this provision does not apply to imprisonment for crime. "Imprisonment for debt, as such imprisonment is defined in our constitutional guaranties, is necessarily imprisonment in a civil action for debt. As such imprisonment existed in the English common law, it was a provisional remedy strictly analogous to the present-day remedy of attachment of goods. It is against such attachments that the constitutional guaranties against imprisonment for debt are directed. They have no application whatever to imprisonment for crime, and legislative bodies are free to provide for punishment by imprisonment of offenders who commit acts denominated by the said legislative bodies as offenses against the public, provided, of course, that other constitutional limitations are not violated."

More recently, in *In re Trombley* (1948) 31 Cal.2d 801, 193 P.2d 734 this court considered the application of the prohibition of imprisonment for debt. . . . We stated that . . . we would examine any statute which makes nonpayment of an obligation a crime in light of the constitutional provision to ensure that the constitutional prohibition of imprisonment for debt is not circumvented by mere form. . . .

* * *

Article I, section 10, no longer includes an express fraud exception to its prohibition of imprisonment for debt. That change has no substantive effect on the scope of the prohibition, however, and the fraud exception is still recognized. The obligation to pay child support, one which arises out of both statute and court order, is indistinguishable for purposes of the fraud exception [from other obligations that have been held not within the prohibition of Article I, section 10.]

Family support obligations are not ordinary debts subject to the constitutional prohibition of imprisonment for debt. It is held that the obligation to make such payments is not a "debt" within the meaning of the constitutional guaranty against imprisonment for debt.

Even were the obligation considered a debt, however, the *Trombley* rationale would be applicable. Children are dependent on their parents for the necessities of life and it is essential to the public welfare that parents provide support with which to care for their needs. To paraphrase the *Trombley* court, a parent who knows that support is due, has the ability to earn money to pay that support, and still willfully refuses to seek and accept available employment to enable the parent to meet the support obligation acts against fundamental societal norms and fair dealing, and necessarily intentionally does an act which prejudices the rights of his children. This conduct would fall within the fraud exception to the constitutional prohibition of imprisonment for debt.

We conclude therefore, that neither the constitutional prohibition of involuntary servitude nor the bar to imprisonment for debt precludes imposition of a contempt or criminal sanction on a parent who, having the ability to do so, willfully fails to pay court-ordered child support, or when necessary to make payment possible willfully fails or refuses to seek and accept available employment for which the parent is suited by virtue of education, experience, and physical ability.

* * *

BURDEN OF PROOF

. . . The trial court based its contempt judgment on evidence that the support order had been made, Brent had notice of the order, an inference that Brent must have had some income to meet those needs not met by his mother, and its observation that Brent had the ability to earn money to pay something toward his support obligation. Brent had argued that he needed only to raise the question of ability to comply in order to shift to Tamara the burden of presenting evidence sufficient to prove beyond a reasonable doubt that he had the present financial ability to comply with the order.

Brent's argument reflects a basic misunderstanding of the allocation of burden in support proceedings. Ability to comply with a support order is not an element of the contempt which must be proven beyond a reasonable doubt by the petitioner. Inability to comply is an affirmative defense which must be proven by a preponderance of the evidence by the alleged contemner.

We observe initially that assigning the burden to prove an affirmative defense by a preponderance of the evidence to a defendant in a criminal proceeding, and thus to an alleged contemner in a criminal contempt proceeding, is constitutionally permissible. The Supreme Court so held in *Martin v. Ohio* (1987) 480 U.S. 228, 107 S.Ct. 1098, 94 L.Ed.2d 267, when it considered the validity under the due process clause of the Fourteenth Amendment of an Ohio statute pursuant to which self-defense was an affirmative defense in a prosecution for murder. . . .

The rule applied by the high court was consistent with the court's earlier decision in *Patterson v. New York* (1977) 432 U.S. 197, 97 S.Ct. 2319, 53 L.Ed.2d 281. There the court considered a New York law that placed the burden on a murder defendant to prove an affirmative defense of extreme emotional disturbance by a preponderance of the evidence in order to reduce the offense to manslaughter. The court emphasized, as it did again in *Martin v. Ohio, supra*, 480 U.S. at page 232, 107 S.Ct. at page 1101, that defining the elements of an offense and the procedures, including the burdens of producing evidence and of persuasion, are matters committed to the state. A state's decision in that regard does not offend the due process clause "unless 'it offends some principle of justice so rooted in the traditions and conscience of our people as to be ranked as fundamental.'" Thus the state may not label as an affirmative defense a traditional element of an offense and thereby make a defendant presumptively guilty of that offense unless the defendant disproves the existence of the element. Due process does not require that the state prove the nonexistence of a constitutionally permissible affirmative defense, however.

The California Legislature has made inability to pay — which encompasses both present financial inability and inability to obtain remunerative employment in order to pay — an affirmative defense. Proof of ability to pay is not an element of a contempt based on a failure to comply with a child support order. . . . The United States Supreme Court has confirmed that whether ability to comply is to be an element of the contempt or an affirmative defense, and whether Code of Civil Procedure section 1209.5 shifts the burden of persuasion or simply imposes a burden of producing some evidence showing inability to comply are questions of state law. (*Hicks v. Feiock* (1988) 485 U.S. 624, 629, 108 S.Ct. 1423, 1428, 99 L.Ed.2d 721.)

As the Court of Appeal explained on remand of the *Feiock* matter from the Supreme Court, ability to pay has traditionally been considered an affirmative defense in contempt proceedings. . . .

The Legislature's decision that ability to comply should not be an element of a child support contempt offense and to permit the contemner to escape punishment if inability is established reflects a policy like those underlying the rule of convenience made applicable to many defenses that are dependent on information or evidence accessible to or in the control of the defendant. As the court recognized in *Feiock:* "The contemner is the person in the best position to know whether inability to pay is even a consideration in the proceeding and also has the best access to evidence on the issue, particularly in cases of self-employment. Considerations of policy and convenience have led courts to sanction placement of the burden of establishing a defense on defendants under similar circumstances."

Although the *Feiock* court correctly recognized that ability to pay is not an element of the contempt offense, it went on to state that the alleged contemner need only raise the issue of ability to pay and that the petitioner must then prove the contempt beyond a reasonable doubt, including ability to pay. Because ability to pay is not an element of the child support contempt offense, we do not agree and disapprove *In re Feiock, supra,* 215 Cal.App.3d 141, 263 Cal. Rptr. 437, in that respect. As the court had earlier acknowledged, the elements of this contempt are only a valid court order, the alleged contemner's knowledge of the order, and noncompliance. If the petitioner proves those elements beyond a reasonable doubt the violation is established. He or she need go no farther. To prevail on the affirmative defense of inability to comply with the support, order, the contemner must prove such inability by a preponderance of the evidence.

* * *

[Over a dissent, the court held that its conclusion that the respondent has the burden of proof on the issue of ability to pay should be applied prospectively only.]

NOTES AND QUESTIONS

1. In what sense could it be said that Brent Moss was "able" to pay $385 per month, as required by the support order? The court insists that jailing him for nonpayment does not constitute involuntary servitude because the order "does not bind the parent to any particular employer or form of employment or otherwise affect the freedom of the parent. The parent is free to elect the type of employment and the employer, subject only to an expectation that to the extent necessary to meet the familial support obligation, the employment will be commensurate with the education, training, and abilities of the parent." Is this convincing? Is Moss free to decline work that he does not enjoy? Could a parent who left a high-paying job for one that provided lower pay and more job satisfaction successfully claim that he or she was "unable" to pay child support at a level based on the original job? For further discussion *see* Walter W. Klein, Moss v. Superior Court: Enforcing Child Support Orders with New Rules for Contempt Actions, 29 Sw. U. L. Rev. 529 (2000).

2. In a jurisdiction that treats ability to pay as an element of nonsupport, what kind of evidence would be sufficient to establish that an obligor was able to pay? In State v. Nuzman, 95 P.3d 252 (Or. App. 2004), the mother testified that when the order was entered, the father was capable of working as a bartender. Over the next 17 years, however, she received small support payments from him on only two occasions, and she had no contact with him or even knowledge of his whereabouts. A clerk who worked for the attorney handling the case testified that the file did not contain any information indicating that the father had a criminal record or that he was receiving disability payments. The clerk also testified that in the usual course of business the office checks criminal records and disability rolls for the names of delinquent obligors every three months. From this, the attorney argued, it should be inferred that the father was not incarcerated or disabled during the time he had not paid support. Would this be enough evidence to prove beyond a reasonable doubt that the father had the ability to pay? Would it make any difference if the file contained 17 years' worth of printouts showing that the father was not incarcerated or receiving disability payments?

3. If an obligor becomes unemployed involuntarily and is unable to find work, his or her support obligation will be modified downward, as we have already seen. However, many people do not seek downward modifications of support orders as soon as they have grounds. Instead, they stop paying and wait. Until the mid-1980s, in some states a court could have retroactively decreased a child support obligation in recognition of these changes. However, federal law now requires states to provide that overdue child support is a judgment by operation of law. 42 U.S.C. § 666(a)(9). The purpose of the requirement and the effect of the change are to prevent courts from retroactively modifying child support obligations. Retroactive downward modification of spousal support obligations is still possible in some states, however.

If a parent who becomes involuntarily unemployed does not seek an immediate modification but also quits paying court-ordered child support, can he or she successfully claim inability to pay in a contempt action?

4. When an obligor falls behind on support obligations because of loss of employment, courts today typically issue "seek work" orders, which, as their name suggests, require the obligor to look for work and to report on those efforts to the court. *See, e.g.*, In re Marriage of Dennis, 344 N.W.2d 128 (Wis. 1984).

5. Sometimes an obligor who fails to pay support attempts to justify this action on the basis that he or she is not receiving access to the child as required by a court order because of the actions of the residential parent, the child or both. Ordinarily, access and child support are independent in the sense that a residential parent's failure to allow the other parent access does not excuse the nonresidential parent from paying child support. Homer H. Clark, Jr., The Law of Domestic Relations in the United States § 16.6 at 682 (2d ed. 1988). *But see* Or. Rev. Stat. Ann. § 107.431(1)(d) (1983) (court may modify a child support order when "the parent or other person having custody of the child or a person acting in that parent or other person's behalf has interfered with or denied without good cause the exercise of the parent's visitation rights").

Some courts distinguish visitation interference, which is not a defense to nonpayment of support, from active concealment of a child, which is. The leading case is Damico v. Damico, 872 P.2d 126 (Cal. 1994). The bases for the distinction are that a parent whose child is actively concealed cannot invoke other remedies to gain access and that if the payor does not know where the child is, he or she cannot make payments and the purpose of the order, to provide for the child, is defeated. *See* Marcia L. Retchin, Concealment of the Child as a Defense to Child Support, 6 Divorce Litig. 169 (1994). In Comer v. Comer, 927 P.2d 265 (Cal. 1996), the California Supreme Court limited *Damico*, holding that even if a child has been "actively concealed," the parent deprived of visitation may be required to pay child support arrearages that accrued during the concealment if the concealment ends while the child is still a minor because the child can still benefit from payment of the arrearages. *Comer* was extended in In re Marriage of Walters, 70 Cal. Rptr. 2d 354 (Cal. App. Dist. 2 1997). The court held that a father must comply with an order to pay child support to a trustee where the mother concealed herself and their daughter until the daughter reached majority, since the money would be used to reimburse the state for public assistance paid for the child while she was in hiding. For further discussion of enforcement of custody and visitation rights, see Chapter 9.

6. In most jurisdictions, the formal rule is that an obligor cannot satisfy an order to pay a specific sum in support by purchasing goods or services instead, and obligors are not entitled to offset the costs of such purchases against the amount they owe. Leslie J. Harris, Dennis Waldrop & Lori R. Waldrop, Making and Breaking Connections Between Parents' Duty to Support and Right to Control Their Children, 69 Or. L. Rev. 689, 712 (1990). Again, however, some courts use their equitable powers to make exceptions, especially when the custodial parent has consented to substituting purchases for payments. *See also* Or. Rev. Stat. § 107.135(7)(a) ("The court may allow a credit against child support arrearages for periods of time, excluding reasonable parenting time unless otherwise provided by

order or judgment, during which the obligor, with the knowledge and consent of the obligee or pursuant to court order, has physical custody of the child.").

7. Since Elizabethan times, willful failure to support a dependent has been a crime, and many states have criminal nonsupport statutes on the books. *See, e.g.,* Model Penal Code §230.5. These statutes have fallen into disuse in many places, though they are being used more frequently in some places as a result of current interest in child support enforcement. In addition, failure to pay child support may be a crime under the federal Child Support Recovery Act. The criminal provision, also known as the Deadbeat Parents Punishment Act, 18 U.S.C. §228, authorizes imprisonment for six months for willful failure to pay support for a child who lives in another state for more than a year and for up to two years imprisonment for traveling in interstate commerce with intent to evade a support obligation or for willfully failing to pay support for a child in another state for more than two years. Claims that the act violates the Tenth Amendment or the Commerce Clause have been unsuccessful. *See* U.S. v. Klinzing, 315 F.3d 803 (7th Cir. 2003) (collecting and discussing cases). In U.S. v. Bigford, 365 F.3d 859 (10th Cir. 2004), the court held that a parent who is charged with violating the Act may challenge the validity of the underlying child support order on the ground that the court lacked personal jurisdiction over him or her, distinguishing cases which have held that a parent may not attack the substantive validity of the order in the criminal proceeding. On jurisdiction to enter a child support, see Chapter 11 below.

Under the federal statute, ability to pay is an element of the crime, which is rebuttably presumed from proof that a support obligation was in effect at the time of the failure to pay. 18 U.S.C. §228(b). If this presumption is construed as shifting the burden of persuasion on the issue of ability to pay to the defendant, it is unconstitutional. U.S. v. Grigsby, 85 F. Supp. 2d 100 (D.R.I. 2000). However, the presumption may be constitutional if it is construed so that the prosecution bears the burden of persuasion on this issue. For more information on presumptions in criminal cases, *see* Leslie J. Harris, Constitutional Limits on Criminal Presumptions as an Expression of Changing Concepts of Fundamental Fairness, 77 J. Crim. L. & Criminology 308 (1986).

8. David Oakley was convicted in Wisconsin of intentionally refusing to pay child support for his nine children as a repeat offender. The trial judge sentenced Oakley to three years in prison the first count, imposed and stayed the execution of an eight-year sentence on two more counts and imposed a five-year term of probation to follow his incarceration; the judge also imposed as a condition of probation that Oakley not have any more children unless he could demonstrate that he was supporting his existing children and had the ability to support another child. Oakley sought postconviction relief, arguing that the condition unconstitutionally limited his right to procreate, citing Skinner v. Oklahoma, 316 U.S. 535 (1942), and Zablocki v. Redhail, 434 U.S. 374 (1978) (page 176 of this text). The divided Wisconsin Supreme Court affirmed in State v. Oakley, 629 N.W.2d 200 (Wis. 2001). The majority, emphasizing that Oakley was convicted of felony intentional refusal to support, scrutinized the probation condition for reasonableness. It found that the condition was not overly broad because it did not eliminate his right to procreate and that it was reasonably related to the goal of rehabilitation. The dissenting justices argued that the means chosen to achieve

the state goals here were, as in *Zablocki*, not sufficiently closely tailored to the state goals.

9. Courts are divided about whether contempt proceedings can be used to enforce property division orders. Some courts say that the constitutional prohibition of debtors' prison precludes this use of contempt. *E.g.*, Stone v. Stidham, 393 P.2d 923 (Ariz. 1964); Bradley v. Superior Court, 310 P.2d 634 (Cal. 1957); McAlear v. McAlear, 469 A.2d 1256 (Md. 1984). Other courts have found no constitutional impediment to the use of the contempt power to enforce monetary obligations in property division. *E.g.*, Harvey v. Harvey, 384 P.2d 265 (Colo. 1963); Haley v. Haley, 648 S.W.2d 890 (Mo. App. 1982); Harris v. Harris, 390 N.E.2d 789 (Ohio 1979); Hanks v. Hanks, 334 N.W.2d 856 (S.D. 1983).

Courts also differ when decisions concerning the availability of contempt to enforce property orders are based on nonconstitutional grounds. Cases holding that contempt does not lie in such circumstances include Ball v. Ball, 440 So. 2d 677 (Fla. Dist. Ct. App. 1983). Cases that permit courts to use contempt include In re Marriage of Ramos, 466 N.E.2d 1016 (Ill. App. 1984); Elliot v. Elliot, 431 A.2d 55 (Me. 1981); Schaheen v. Schaheen, 169 N.W.2d 117 (Mich. App. 1969); Hudson v. Hudson, 521 So. 2d 40 (Ala. App. 1987); DeGrace v. DeGrace, 520 A.2d 987 (Vt. 1986).

NOTE: CIVIL OR CRIMINAL CONTEMPT?

Brent Moss faced a criminal contempt action for his failure to pay child support, and he was, therefore, entitled to the constitutional protections generally afforded defendants in criminal proceedings, including the right to have the facts constituting the contempt proven by the prosecution beyond a reasonable doubt. Hicks v. Feiock 485 U.S. 624, 629 (1988). If instead his former wife had brought a civil contempt action against him, the hearing would not have had to provide these criminal safeguards. Defendants in criminal contempt actions are also entitled to claim the privilege against self-incrimination, jury trial, and other constitutional safeguards. *See* United Mine Workers of America v. Bagwell, 512 U.S. 821, 826-827 (1994).

In its first case dealing with the distinction between civil and criminal contempt, the U.S. Supreme Court observed that "It may not be always easy to classify a particular act as belonging to either of these two classes." Bessette v. W. B. Conkey Co., 194 U.S. 324, 329 (1904). The problem arises because neither the nature of the proceeding nor the kind of behavior leading to the sanction provides a basis for categorizing. An individual may be held in civil contempt for acts arising out of a criminal case. For example, a witness's refusal to testify may be treated as a civil contempt, even in a murder prosecution. An individual may also be held in criminal contempt for acts arising in a civil matter, as where a plaintiff or her lawyer curses the judge. Nor is the contemnor's behavior a clear indicator of the kind of contempt. Nonpayment of child support may be civil or criminal.

In Hicks v. Feiock, above, an appeal from a California decision holding a child support obligor in contempt for nonpayment, the Supreme Court discussed the test for distinguishing civil from criminal contempt:

The question of how a court determines whether to classify the relief imposed in a given proceeding as civil or criminal in nature, for the purposes of applying the Due Process Clause and other provisions of the Constitution, is one of long standing, and its principles have been settled at least in their broad outlines for many decades. . . . [T]he labels affixed either to the proceeding or to the relief imposed under state law are not controlling and will not be allowed to defeat the applicable protections of federal constitutional law. This is particularly so in the codified laws of contempt, where the "civil" and "criminal" labels of the law have become increasingly blurred.

Instead, the critical features are the substance of the proceeding and the character of the relief that the proceeding will afford. . . . The character of the relief imposed is thus ascertainable by applying a few straightforward rules. If the relief provided is a sentence of imprisonment, it is remedial if "the defendant stands committed unless and until he performs the affirmative act required by the court's order," and is punitive if "the sentence is limited to imprisonment for a definite period." If the relief provided is a fine, it is remedial when it is paid to the complainant, and punitive when it is paid to the court, though a fine that would be payable to the court is also remedial when the defendant can avoid paying the fine simply by performing the affirmative act required by the court's order. . . .

In repeatedly stating and following the rules set out above, the Court has eschewed any alternative formulation that would make the classification of the relief imposed in a State's proceedings turn simply on what their underlying purposes are perceived to be. Although the purposes that lie behind particular kinds of relief are germane to understanding their character, this Court has never undertaken to psychoanalyze the subjective intent of a State's laws and its courts, not only because that effort would be unseemly and improper, but also because it would be misguided. In contempt cases, both civil and criminal relief have aspects that can be seen as either remedial or punitive or both: when a court imposes fines and punishments on a contemnor, it is not only vindicating its legal authority to enter the initial court order, but it also is seeking to give effect to the law's purpose of modifying the contemnor's behavior to conform to the terms required in the order. . . . For these reasons, this Court has judged that conclusions about the purposes for which relief is imposed are properly drawn from an examination of the character of the relief itself.

485 U.S. at 631-635. In United Mine Workers of America v. Bagwell, above, the Supreme Court considered what kind of procedural safeguards must be provided in a much more complex case, involving claims that a union had repeatedly violated an injunction regarding activities during a strike and which resulted in the union being fined millions of dollars. The court declined to adopt a simple test for determining whether the contempt was civil or criminal and instead used multiple factors, including the complexity of the order allegedly violated and the severity of the penalty, to conclude that due process required criminal procedural safeguards. For further discussion see Margit Livingston, Disobedience and Contempt, 75 Wash. L. Rev. 345 (2000).

For purposes of determining whether an indigent person has the right to counsel in a contempt proceeding, many courts have abandoned the civil-criminal distinction. For example, in Mead v. Batchlor, 460 N.W.2d 493 (Mich. 1990), the court held that a person must be afforded the right to counsel, including the right to free counsel if indigent, before he or she can be incarcerated for nonpayment of support, regardless of whether the contempt proceeding is civil or criminal. The court based its holding on prior Supreme Court cases holding that due process requires provision of counsel before a person is deprived of physical liberty.

PROBLEMS

1. Oliver faithfully complied with an order requiring him to pay $300 per month to his former wife, Paula, for the support of their child, Carlo, until he lost his job as a skilled worker in a plywood mill when the mill closed. While he received unemployment compensation, Oliver looked for work and continued to pay child support. He could not find another mill job, however, and since his unemployment compensation ran out, Oliver has only worked sporadically at odd jobs. He stopped paying child support. Because Oliver was at home much of the time, Carlo, now four, began to spend most of his time at Oliver's house.

A month ago Paula, whose hours at work had just been cut, demanded that Oliver pay her the amounts he owes her for the last five months. She says that she cannot afford to maintain the house for herself and Carlo without this money, and she believes that Oliver could get steady work if he only tried harder. When Oliver refused, Paula angrily told him he could not see Carlo anymore unless he paid up. Oliver has not seen Carlo since, even though the divorce degree provides that he is entitled to visit for eight hours every Saturday.

Two weeks ago Oliver was served with a motion to show cause why he should not be held in (civil) contempt for failing to comply with the child support order. What defenses should his attorney assert on his behalf? How should Paula's attorney respond?

2. Barbara Chadwick filed for divorce in 1992. During pretrial proceedings, her husband Beatty informed the court that he had transferred $2.5 million of marital funds to satisfy an alleged debt to a company in Gibraltar. Barbara's attorney then learned and revealed to the court further information that suggested that the debt might be a sham. The trial judge determined that the transfer was an attempt to defraud Barbara and ordered Beatty to return the $2.5 million to an account over which the court had jurisdiction. Beatty refused to comply, and Barbara moved to have him held in civil contempt. The court found that Beatty had the present ability to comply with the order, held him in civil contempt, and ordered him jailed until he complied with the order. Beatty refused to comply and has been in jail ever since. He has applied eight times to state trial courts and six times to the federal court for release. His latest petition argues that the facts amply demonstrate that there is no possibility that he will ever comply with the order and that, therefore, the action has ceased to be one for civil contempt and has become a punitive, criminal contempt. He then argues that because he was jailed without being accorded the usual constitutional criminal procedure protections, he must be released or retried. What arguments should the attorneys for Barbara and Beatty make on the issue of whether the contempt action is civil or criminal?

3. The State-Federal Child Support Enforcement Program

Support orders enforced by levying on an obligor's property or by using contempt powers suffer from limitations in addition to the legal ones that we have been examining. As a practical matter, obligees ordinarily need attorneys to draft the appropriate documents and shepherd cases through court. And both kinds of devices are available only to enforce past-due support; neither operates prospectively.

Responding to mounting evidence of problems in child support enforcement, in 1975 Congress enacted Title IV-D of the Social Security Act, Pub. L. 93-647, which created the federal Office of Child Support Enforcement. The legislation requires each state to establish a child support enforcement agency, also called a IV-D agency. Additional requirements have been imposed since then. Major provisions are codified at 42 U.S.C. §§ 651-662, 666. A state that does not comply with these requirements loses substantial federal funding for its welfare program. In addition, the federal government pays a percentage of the costs of the states' enforcement programs and provides other financial incentives, which are based in part on the amount of support money collected.

The state IV-D agency must provide certain services, including establishment of support duties, establishment of paternity, and location of absent parents. States cannot charge custodial parents receiving welfare benefits for these services, although they may charge parents who are not receiving welfare a modest application fee. In the mid-1990s it was estimated that at least 60 percent of all child support enforcement actions are brought by IV-D agencies. Paul K. Legler, The Coming Revolution in Child Support Policy; Implications of the 1996 Welfare Act, 30 Fam. L.Q. 519, 522 (1996). In most states the agency attorney who provides these services does not represent the residential parent; instead, like criminal prosecutors, they are said to represent the state. For a discussion of the complex practical and ethical issues that this role presents for attorneys *see* Barbara Glesner Fines, From Representing "Clients" to Serving "Recipients": Transforming the Role of the IV-D Child Support Enforcement Attorney, 67 Fordham L. Rev. 2155 (1999).

Expedited Processes   To expedite the collection of child support, states must have an administrative or quasi-judicial process for obtaining and enforcing support orders in IV-D cases. Some states also handle non-IV-D cases through their administrative processes. Most states that use an administrative process give their courts concurrent original jurisdiction in support cases and provide for appellate judicial review of administrative orders. Federal regulations require that states provide obligors with due process safeguards. Administrative orders must have the same force and effect as court orders, each party must receive a copy of the order, and the state must have written procedures for ensuring that the presiding officers are qualified. 45 C.F.R. § 303.101(c) (1987). Neither the presiding officer nor the parent's advocate must be an attorney. 45 C.F.R. § 303.101(c)(4) (1987).

Enforcement by Wage Withholding   Perhaps the most important enforcement devices are those that allow wage withholding. States must require wage withholding in all child support cases unless a court or administrative agency hearing officer finds good cause, put in writing, not to implement withholding immediately, or the parties agree not to implement withholding immediately. A delinquency equal to one month's amount of support that occurs after one of these exceptions takes effect results in mandatory income withholding, regardless of the good cause finding or parties' agreement. 42 U.S.C. §§ 666(a)(1), 666(b).

Where income withholding is triggered by an alleged arrearage, the obligor is entitled to prior notice and a hearing. The exact procedures for giving notice and allowing contests vary from state to state. The Federal Consumer Credit Protection Act, 15 U.S.C. §§ 1671-1677, limits how much of a person's wages may be withheld. The basic limit is 50 percent of disposable earnings for a non-custodial parent who is not supporting a second family. This amount is much higher than the amount of an obligor's wages that can be withheld to enforce other debts.

Other Enforcement Devices   States must provide a number of other ways to enforce child support, including:

- Judicial authority to impose liens against real and personal property for amounts of overdue support;
- Judicial authority to require obligors to post a bond or give some other guarantee to secure payment of overdue support;
- Allowing failure to pay child support to be reported to consumer credit bureaus;
- Withholding state tax refunds payable to a parent of a child receiving child support services, if the parent is delinquent in making payments; and
- Suspending the driver's licenses and professional, occupational, and recreational licenses of delinquent obligors.

In addition, the IRS must withhold federal tax refunds due to delinquent child support obligors, and parents who owe child support may be denied federal loans.

Efforts to Locate Parents   Federal legislation requires the establishment of a national directory of new hires, which contains employment information about everyone hired in the United States, and of similar state directories. The legislation also requires creation of national and state registries of child support orders. These databases will be linked so that orders can be matched with obligors quickly. States must also have automated, centralized systems for recording the payment and dispersal of child support.

The Program's Effectiveness   The Office of Child Support Enforcement offered the following assessment of the effectiveness of its program.

DHHS, OFFICE OF CHILD SUPPORT ENFORCEMENT, *CHILD SUPPORT ENFORCEMENT FY 2003 PRELIMINARY DATA REPORT*

June 2004

* * *

Child support collections continued to increase and reached an all-time high of $21.2 billion in fiscal year 2003. That's a 5% increase over last year, even as the caseload declined. And it's a 33% increase over 1999.

But the real story behind these numbers is that 90% of the collections were distributed to families. Only 10% went to reimburse state and Federal governments for TANF payments or foster care costs. Payments to families increased 6% over last year and 41% from 1999. This is true across the country. The percent of payments going to families was 86% or more in 47 states. In 7 states, the percentage going to families exceeded 95%.

That's pretty startling, considering that this program started out as a means of recovering the costs of public assistance payments, a sort of reimbursement to the taxpayers for "welfare" expenditures on children.

Of course, much of the change is attributable to the change in our caseload: now, only 17% of our cases are families currently receiving TANF or foster care, and only 9% of our collections are for these cases. Former assistance cases make up 46% of our caseload and 40% of our collections; in other words, the biggest category of families we are helping is former public assistance recipients: we're ensuring that these are two-income households, financially secure, where parents won't have to return to the welfare rolls.

But this change also represents a real turn-around in our conception of what our program is for. We now view child support as primarily a means of getting reliable income to families, not as a means of recovering the taxes spent on public assistance. We take it as a given that the money parents earn should support their children directly, especially when those parents have worked their way off of dependence on public assistance.

* * *

ARREARS INCREASE TO $96 BILLION

The other number that drew my attention immediately when I reviewed this report is the increasing unpaid child support debt, which is approaching $100 billion, according to states' reports of the accumulated arrears over all the years since the program began.

In 1999, 53% of the child support cases had arrearages owed. In 2003, the proportion was up to 68%. We obtained collections in 60% of these cases, so we know that child support professionals are working hard on them and that obligors are trying to work on their debts. But we collected an average of $600 per arrearage case, while the average amount of arrears per arrearage case is $9,000. So, even though we're collecting significant amounts of arrears, we don't seem to be making a dent in the problem, and the overall debt continues to grow.

Clearly, we need to design and implement more effective strategies to collect arrears from those who have the ability to pay and refuse to do so. And, we need to do more to help low-income parents who want to meet their obligations and are struggling to do so.

We know that about half of the debt is owed to the government, and not to the families. And we know what we collected about 58% of current support due in 2003. We need to be more aggressive about leveraging older debt owed to the government as an incentive to obtain more reliable payments of current support to families. If we do, I suggest that state and Federal governments will do better as families become more self-sufficient and less dependent on Medicaid and other public benefits than they have been doing in collecting old child support debt owed to those governments for long-ago welfare payments.

And, I think we need to be much more creative about avoiding the accumulation of arrears in the first place, using data to set affordable orders, modifying orders simply and promptly when family circumstances change, initiating contact when a payment is missed the first time, providing exceptional customer service in the very early months after an order is entered to establish consistent voluntary compliance — instead of waiting until huge debt thresholds are reached before we take drastic enforcement action.

* * *

Sherri Z. Heller, Ed.D.
Commissioner
U.S. Office of Child Support Enforcement

CHILD SUPPORT ENFORCEMENT PROGRAM BACKGROUND, RESULTS,
AND SUMMARY TABLES

* * *

PROGRAM RESULTS FOR FY 2003

* * *

Caseload   OCSE defines a child support case as a parent (mother, father, or putative father) who is now or eventually may be obligated under law for the support of a child or children receiving services under the title IV-D program.

A *current assistance case* is one in which the children are: (1) recipients of Temporary Assistance for Needy Families (TANF) under title IV-A of the Social Security Act or (2) entitled to Foster Care maintenance payments under title IV-E of the Social Security Act. In addition, the children's support rights have been assigned by a caretaker to the state and a referral to the state IV-D agency has been made. A *former assistance case* is a case in which the children were formerly receiving title IV-A (AFDC or TANF) or title IV-E Foster Care services. A *never assistance case* is a case in which the children are receiving services under the title IV-D program, but are not currently eligible for and have not previously received assistance under titles IV-A or IV-E of the Social Security Act. This includes cases in which the family is receiving IV-D services as a result of a written application for IV-D services (including cases in which children are receiving state, not title IV-E, foster care services) or a case in which they are Medicaid recipients *not* receiving additional assistance.

In the Child Support Enforcement program there were 15.9 million cases reported during fiscal year 2003. This represents a 0.9 percent decrease in caseload since fiscal year 2002. In FY 2003, there were 2.8 million current assistance cases, 7.4 million former assistance cases, and 5.8 million never assistance cases reported.

* * *

Orders Established . . .   There were 1.2 million orders for child support established in fiscal year 2003. *Never assistance* orders made up 44 percent of the support orders established for fiscal year 2003, *current assistance* orders accounted for 20 percent, and *former assistance* accounted for 36 percent

Collections   Collection data are shown under the following reporting categories: *current IV-A* and *IV-E assistance* ($1.8 billion), *former assistance* ($8.5 billion), and *never assistance* ($10.9 billion). . . . Total child support collections were $21.2 billion for fiscal year 2003. This was a 5.2 percent increase in collections from the previous fiscal year.

Child support payments are collected through various methods, such as income withholding, unemployment compensation interception, and state or Federal income tax refund offsets. Income withholding accounts for 66 percent of total collections received (almost $16.7 billion) in FY 2003. Money collected and sent to families totaled almost $19.0 billion in FY 2003, an increase of 6 percent since FY 2002.

Collections per Full-Time Equivalent Staff   There were over 61,000 FTE staff working in the child support program in the states and jurisdictions in fiscal year 2003. Child support collected nationally per full-time equivalent staff (FTE) was over $346,000.

Expenditures and Incentives   In fiscal year 2003, total administrative expenditures were $5.2 billion, a 0.6 percent increase from fiscal year 2002. The Federal share of expenditures was $3.4 billion and the state share was $1.8 billion. The Federal government reimburses states for 66 percent of the majority of allowable expenditures and 90 percent for laboratory paternity costs.

For FY 2003, the majority of states (26) showed increases in total expenditures from the previous fiscal year. However, most of those states (17) showed an increase of less than 10 percent.

* * *

Collections Due and Distributed   The total amount of current support due for fiscal year 2003 was over $27.1 billion. About $15.7 billion, or 58 percent, of that amount was collected and distributed. The total amount of arrearages reported for all previous fiscal years was $95.8 billion, and over $6.5 billion was collected and distributed. There were 10.8 million cases with arrears due in fiscal year 2003 and 6.4 million of these cases had collections. Hence, 60 percent of obligors owing arrears made some payment toward their arrears in fiscal year 2003. In addition, there were $1.2 billion in interstate collections forwarded to other states in that year.

Other Statistics   In fiscal year 2003, program increases were noted for *total cases in which a collection was made*. At 8.0 million cases, this is a 2.1 percent increase over the number of paying cases for fiscal year 2002.

There were 11.5 million *cases with an order established* in fiscal year 2003. This is a 2 percent increase over the number of cases with orders reported in the previous fiscal year.

The *total number of children* in CSE cases totaled almost 17.6 million in fiscal year 2003. This represents a slight decrease from the 17.9 million reported for fiscal year 2002.

Cost-effectiveness represents the amount of child support collected for every $1.00 expended on the program. The *CSPIA cost-effectiveness ratio* was $4.33 for fiscal year 2003.

* * *

4.   *The Continuing Challenge of Childhood Poverty*

As Custodial Mothers and Fathers and Their Child Support: 2001, above at page 578, discusses, despite vigorous efforts to enforce child support, children's poverty rates, and particularly the poverty rates of children living with single mothers, remain very high. Child support enforcement alone cannot solve the problem of childhood poverty, for a variety of reasons. As the letter from Commissioner Heller, above at page 596, suggests, many obligors who do not pay are themselves too poor to pay at a level sufficient to bring their children out of poverty. Public assistance payments are too low to provide families with incomes above the poverty level. Some current proposals to address the problem view providing for children as primarily the responsibility of the parents, and therefore focus on trying to improve parents' financial capability. The work requirements of TANF can be understood in this light, as can federal and state initiatives to promote marriage and to help poor fathers gain employment. For detailed, current information about federal initiatives, *see* the DHHS Fatherhood Initiative Web site, *http://www.fatherhood.hhs.gov/index.shtml* (last visited Oct. 12, 2004). Other commentators argue for a more substantial public role in insuring the economic well-being of all children, including the development of some form of child support assurance program.

U.S. COMMISSION ON INTERSTATE CHILD SUPPORT, *SUPPORTING OUR CHILDREN: A BLUEPRINT FOR REFORM*

257-259 (1992)

Child Support Assurance is a plan to guarantee every child a certain level of financial security. It has three prongs: awards established pursuant to a support guideline, increased enforcement through such means as immediate income with-holding, and insured minimum benefits. The first two prongs are already man-dated through federal legislation. The third program has been the subject of much debate in the past few years. This debate has been coupled with proposals to federalize all or part of the child support program. . . .

. . . The Commission notes, with interest, proposals for programs in which the federal government insures that children receive a certain financial benefit. . . . If an obligor fails to pay his or her ordered support amount, the federal govern-ment would forward to the custodial parent the difference between the assurance amount and the awarded support. Some members of the Commission feel that the current economic plight of children dictates that Congress take action to estab-lish a national system to ensure that children receive a minimum level of financial security. Other members, concerned that child support assurance will only be another form of welfare, entirely oppose such programs.

Child support assurance differs from welfare in several important ways. First, the assured support payment is not income tested. Any custodial parent is eligible to receive an assured payment. Second, it does not discourage work. . . . A child support assurance plan does *not* base the amount of assured payment on a parent's earning. Therefore, during the fragile transition period when a [parent receiving welfare] is attempting to be self-supporting, the parent receives the child support assurance payment in addition to his or her earnings. Third, child support assurance will lead to enhanced support for our nation's children since a parent will be unable to receive the assured payment unless the parent cooperates with the government officials attempting to enforce support. Fourth, it does not stigmatize the recipient as does welfare. Recipient of child support assurance has no connotation of "being on the public's dole" since any-one qualifies, regardless of income. Finally, child support assurance properly focuses society's attention on the obligated parent. Rather than the public's pointing a finger at the custodial parent as so often occurs with welfare, the public's concern will be directed toward the parent who has abrogated his or her support responsibility.

On child support assurance programs *see also* Congressional Budget Office, An Analysis of Alternative Child Support Assurance Programs (April 1996), *avail-able at http://www.cbo.gov/showdoc.cfm?index=4661&sequence=0* (last visited Oct. 12, 2004); The Century Foundation, Idea Brief: Child Support Assurance (April 2004), *available at http://www.tcf.org/4L/4LMain.asp?SubjectID=1&ArticleID=465* (last visited Oct. 12, 2004).

For further discussion of the extent to which responsibility to provide for dependent members of society, including children and their caretakers, should be understood as a private, family matter or an issue for the public as a whole, *see* Martha Albertson Fineman, The Neutered Mother, The Sexual Family and Other Twentieth Century Tragedies (1995); Martha Albertson Fineman, The Autonomy Myth (2004); Lee Anne Fennell, Relative Burdens; Family Ties and the Safety Net, 45 Wm. & Mary L. Rev. 1453 (2004); Ariela R. Dubler, In the

Shadow of Marriage: Single Women and the Legal Construction of the Family and the State, 112 Yale L.J. 1641 (2003); Jacobus ten Broek, California's Dual System of Family Law: Its Origin, Development, and Present Status, Parts 1, 2 and 3, 16 Stan. L. Rev. 257, 900 (1964); 17 Stan. L. Rev. 614, (1965).

D. TAXES

The relationship of federal tax policy to family groups, however defined, has posed fundamental questions for both tax policy and family law. One is whether the appropriate unit for imposing taxes is the individual or the family. The other is whether state variations in family law should affect federal tax liability.

The extent to which the tax code treats taxpayers differently, depending on their marital and parental status, has varied, although the current trend is toward differential treatment. As we shall see, the current trend is toward federalizing tax law so that otherwise similarly situated people are taxed in the same way, regardless of the domestic relations law of the state in which they live. Nevertheless, for purposes of the most fundamental tax issues—whether people are "married" and whether they are legally "parent and child"—state law generally controls. However, under the Defense of Marriage Act, Pub. L. No. 104-199 (1996), same-sex couples who are married or in civil unions are not treated as married for purposes of federal tax law and may not be so treated for purposes of state tax law if they move to other states that do not recognize their marriage or civil union. DOMA and interstate recognition of same-sex marriages and civil unions are discussed in Chapters 3 and 4, above.

1. Taxation of the Ongoing Family

Originally the income tax code implicitly assumed that the individual was the tax-paying unit. Married and unmarried people were taxed at the same rates, and the income from children's property was taxed at the children's rates rather than at their parents' rates. Because tax rates are progressive—that is, the rates increase as income goes up—a system that treats the individual as the taxing unit is likely to extract a different amount of tax from a family with two income earners than a family earning the same amount with one income earner.

To illustrate, imagine two families, the Joneses and the Smiths. Mr. Jones is employed in the marketplace, earning $60,000 per year, and Mrs. Jones is a homemaker. Both Mr. and Mrs. Smith work in the marketplace, each earning $30,000 per year. Further, assume that the income tax rate is 20 percent on the first $20,000 of income, 33 percent on income between $20,000 and $50,000, and 50 percent on income over $50,000. The tax owed by the Joneses (ignoring exemptions, deductions, and the like) is 20 percent of $20,000 ($4,000), 33 percent of $30,000 ($10,000), and 50 percent of $10,000 ($5,000) for a total of $19,000. The

Smiths owe 20 percent of $20,000 ($4,000) each, plus 33 percent of $10,000 ($3,333) each, for a total of $14,666.[2]

The first major challenge to this regime arose in response to two Supreme Court decisions that interpreted the Internal Revenue Code (IRC) as making state law rules about marital property ownership determinative of married people's income tax liability. Both cases involved couples in which the husband worked in the paid labor force and the wife was a homemaker.

In Lucas v. Earl, 281 U.S. 111 (1930), the spouses, who lived in a common law property state, entered into a contract providing that they would share equally all their income during their marriage. They therefore claimed that each of them owed taxes on half the husband's wages. If they had prevailed, their total tax bill would have been lower than if he had been taxed on all the income. However, the Supreme Court ruled against them, holding that income is taxed to the person who earned it by labor or investment of capital, regardless of whether it is validly assigned to someone else.[3] Since only the husband really earned the money, he was taxable on all of it. A few months later the Court decided Poe v. Seaborn, 282 U.S. 101 (1930), which involved a similar married couple who lived in a community property state and who also claimed that each of them owned half the husband's income and was taxable on it. The Court ruled in their favor because their state's marital property law treated them as equal owners of the income.

As word of the tax advantages of living in community property states got out, six common law property jurisdictions enacted community property legislation between 1939 and 1949. Carolyn C. Jones, Split Income and Separate Spheres: Tax Law and Gender Roles in the 1940s, 6 Law & Hist. Rev. 259, 266-274 (1988); Judith Younger, Marital Regimes: A Story of Compromise and Demoralization, Together with Criticism and Suggestions for Reform, 67 Cornell L. Rev. 45, 69-70 (1981).[4] Professor Jones has argued that more states did not adopt community property, despite the tax savings for citizens, because of philosophical hostility to the idea that a wife might have a property interest in a husband's earnings and because of the difficulty of combining community property principles with common law property rules. Jones at 269-270.

Congress eliminated the advantage enjoyed by residents of community property states in the Revenue Act of 1948, Pub. L. No. 471, ch. 168, § 301, which provided for joint returns and thus for income splitting between married couples, regardless of the underlying marital property regimes. The effect of the joint return is to treat married couples as an economic unit, at least for this purpose. As

---

2. This example is based on a top marginal income tax rate of 50%. The actual top marginal rate has been declining. The 2003 tax act provides that the top rate is 35%. This provision sunsets in 2010, when the top marginal rate will revert to 39.6 %.

3. This principle has been generalized as the "assignment-of-income" doctrine, which has a substantial impact throughout the income tax code.

4. The states were Michigan, Nebraska, Oklahoma, Oregon, Pennsylvania, and the territory of Hawaii. Colorado, Illinois, Kansas, Massachusetts, New Jersey, New York, South Dakota, and Wyoming considered but did not enact such legislation. Jones, 6 Law & Hist. Rev. at 268-269.

soon as the legislation was enacted, Congress had to deal with questions of tax rates—should married people be taxed at the same rate as single taxpayers? If they are taxed at a different rate, should it be higher or lower? Congress has not settled on answers to these questions, as variations in relative tax rates over the last 50 years demonstrate. *See generally* Boris I. Bittker, Federal Income Taxation and the Family, 27 Stan. L. Rev. 1389 (1975); Pamela B. Gann, Abandoning Marital Status as a Factor in Allocating Income Tax Burdens, 59 Tex. L. Rev. 1 (1980); Lawrence Zelenak, Marriage and the Income Tax, 67 S. Cal. L. Rev. 339 (1994).

The same legislation that created the joint income tax return also introduced the marital deduction and splitting of estates and gifts for purposes of the federal estate and gift tax. Younger, above. These changes introduced treatment of married people as an economic unit into these wealth transfer taxes. Today this process has been completed; under IRC §§ 2056 and 2523, spouses can now transfer unlimited amounts of property to each other without federal gift or estate tax consequences.

The Tax Reform Act of 1986 also changed the taxation of income from property belonging to children in ways that result in the family (parent and child) rather than the individual (child) being treated as the taxable unit. Rules regarding taxation of trusts were changed to make it much more difficult for parents to shift income to children for short periods of time,[5] and the method of taxing the unearned income of children younger than 14 was changed so that it is taxed at the higher of the parents' rate and the child's rate. IRC § 1(g).

Amendments to the Internal Revenue Code enacted in 2001 and 2003 eliminate the so-called marriage penalty. Beginning in 2005, the standard deduction for married couples will be 174 percent of that for singles, and it will increase until it reaches 200 percent of the standard deduction for singles in 2009. Joint filers will also be entitled to a wider tax bracket; eventually the upper limit of the 15 percent bracket for joint filers will be twice the upper limit for individuals. IRC §§ 63(c)(2) and (7).

Ordinarily, spouses are jointly and severally liable for the full amount of tax that either owes. However, under IRC § 6015 in circumstances an "innocent spouse," that is, a spouse who did not know or have reason to know that the amount of tax stated on a joint return was understated, may be exempt from liability for errors attributable to his or her spouse. For details *see* Robert S. Steinberg, Three At Bats Against Joint and Several Tax Liability: (1) Innocent Spouse (2) The Election to Limit Liability and (3) Equitable Relief, 17 J. Am. Acad. Matrimonial L. 403 (2001).

---

5. Before these changes, parents could establish "Clifford" trusts and similar trusts, which were relatively short-term trusts for the benefit of, for example, a child, the income from which was taxed at the beneficiary's rate rather than the grantor's. *See* Nitsche, 26 J. Fam. L. *supra* at 720-725, for a discussion of the prior rules and the 1986 changes. The rules for trusts other than grantor trusts have also been changed to make them less available as a way of shifting income from parents to children for tax purposes. *Id.* at 718-720.

2.   *Taxation of the Family After Divorce*

For some families, the income tax consequences of financial transfers incident to divorce are of substantial importance. Knowledgeable lawyers can do much good for families earning enough income to make tax planning important. Proper structuring of financial arrangements can reduce the amount of taxes that all the members collectively pay, leaving more money to support the former spouses and their children.

Two basic principles of tax law are at the heart of tax planning: (1) As previously mentioned, the income tax is progressive, so that people with higher incomes pay tax at a higher rate; (2) Property division and child support payments have no income tax consequences, but spousal support is a deduction for the payor and income for the recipient. Taken together, these principles generally make it more desirable from the perspective of income taxes for payments to be treated as alimony *if* the payor's income is significantly higher than the recipient's. In return for taking on the tax burden that spousal support imposes, the recipient can be given a greater absolute number of support dollars. During the 1980s the number of tax brackets was reduced and the highest tax rates were lowered, reducing the impact of the alimony deduction. However, in the right circumstances the benefit is still there.

During the same time period the value of personal exemptions rose. Thus, allocation between divorced parents of the exemptions for children is also an important tax issue.

Implicit in this structure is a major issue that we have already examined in other contexts: Is there a meaningful difference among the three major types of orders incident to divorce—property division, spousal support, and child support? If so, how do we distinguish among the types of orders? When the tax code provisions were first adopted, fewer states had equitable distribution laws, and spousal support, if ordered, was typically indefinite. As we have seen, though, under the modern law of equitable distribution of property and new forms of spousal support, such as rehabilitative and reimbursement alimony, it is debatable whether these types of orders are sharply distinct. Nevertheless, the tax code makes distinctions, although changes made by the Tax Reform Act of 1984 were intended to allow parties (or courts in litigated cases) to determine the tax consequences of postdivorce transfers—within limits. Other perennial issues in the tax treatment of postdivorce financial transfers are the same as those that arise in taxation of ongoing families—whether variations in state law should have an impact on federal income tax liability and what the basic taxing unit should be.

a.   Property Division—IRC § 1041

Before 1984, if the property of one spouse was transferred to the other, the property had increased in value from the time of its acquisition, and the spouses lived in a common law property state, the original owner was required to pay income taxes on the increase in value. United States v. Davis, 370 U.S. 65 (1962). The *Davis* rule often worked a real hardship, because the transferor spouse had to dip into other assets to pay the taxes. Because of this and because of ignorance, the rule was widely disobeyed. Moreover, the rule did not apply in community property states when community property was divided equally at divorce because this distribution was not considered a transfer of property owned by one spouse to the other. *See, e.g.,* Carrieres v. Commission, 64 T.C. 959 (1975), *acq.* 1976-2 C.B. 1, *aff'd per curiam,* 552 F.2d 1350 (9th Cir. 1977); Wren v. Commissioner, 24 T.C.M. (CCH) 290 (1965); Davenport v. Commissioner, 12 T.C.M. (CCH) 856 (1953); Walz v. Commissioner, 32 B.T.A. 718 (1935).

Once again spouses in community property states enjoyed an income tax advantage compared to those in common law property states because of differences in marital property ownership laws. And once again courts and legislatures in some common law property states attempted to change their rules to secure tax advantages for their citizens. Rather than adopting community property wholesale, however, these states provided that immediately before divorce (but not throughout the marriage) the spouses were deemed to own property jointly, so that divorce property division would not be treated as a transfer of property from one spouse to the other. Lower courts upheld this tactic in some cases. *E.g.,* Collins v. Commissioner, 412 F.2d 211 (10th Cir. 1969) (Okla.); Imel v. United States, 375 F. Supp. 1102 (D. Colo. 1974), *aff'd,* 523 F.2d 853 (10th Cir. 1975) (Colo.). Legislatures in other states enacted legislation that purported to produce this result. *E.g.,* Or. Rev. Stat. § 107.105(1)(f).

The Supreme Court never decided whether this strategy worked because Congress amended IRC § 1041, which governs the effect of property division at divorce, in 1984. Section 1041 now provides that, just as spouses may transfer unlimited amounts of property to each other during marriage and at death without estate or gift tax consequences, their property may also be divided at divorce without income tax consequences. If property was owned by one spouse during the marriage and transferred to the other at divorce, the transferee takes the basis of the original owner. This means that when the property is sold, the transferee spouse will owe income taxes on the capital gain in value of the property that accrued while the property was owned by the original owner as well as after the divorce.

More specifically, IRC § 1041 eliminates income tax consequences for property transfers "incident to divorce." A transfer falls in this category if it occurs within one year of the termination of the marriage, or within six years of termination of the marriage if made pursuant to a divorce decree or separation agreement. Other transfers are presumed not to be incident to divorce, but the taxpayer can rebut the presumption.

Section 1041 also provides for no income tax consequences if one spouse transfers property to a third party for the benefit of a former spouse if (1) the transfer is required by the decree or separation agreement, (2) the transfer is made pursuant to a written request from the former spouse, or (3) the transferor receives written consent or ratification from the former spouse.

Property transfers between former spouses incident to divorce are also free from gift tax under IRC § 2516.

Transfers of Pensions and Related Assets   As you recall from earlier chapters, if an employee's pension rights are covered by the Employee Retirement

Income Security Act (ERISA), some or all of those rights can be transferred to a former spouse by a Qualified Domestic Relations Order (QDRO). An alternate payee under a QDRO is treated as the recipient of benefits under the plan for tax purposes. This means that the alternate payee pays any income taxes owing on benefits as they are paid. The payments have no tax consequences for the employee; they are not income, and they are not deductible. IRC § 402. The code also permits transfers of Individual Retirement Accounts (IRAs) between former spouses under a divorce decree or written separation agreement without tax consequences. IRC § 408(d)(6). When such a transfer is made, the IRA becomes the IRA of the transferee.

Sale of Principal Residence   If married taxpayers sell their principal residence, up to $500,000 of capital gains is not recognized as income under provisions enacted by Congress in 1997. Single taxpayers may exclude from recognition up to $250,000 in capital gains. IRC § 121. To qualify for this exclusion, the taxpayer must have owned and lived in the residence for two of the five years before the date of sale. The exclusion can be claimed every two years, but only once during each two-year period. For divorced spouses, the former spouse who occupies the residence is entitled to the exclusion, and so is the former spouse who does not occupy the residence, as long as the former spouse who occupies the residence is entitled to use the residence under a divorce or settlement agreement. Thus, if at the time of divorce both parties remain owners but one is granted the right to occupy the house until the youngest child is 18, and the house is then sold, both parties are entitled to the capital gains exclusion.

b.   Spousal Support—IRC §§ 71 and 215

Under the prior version of IRC §§ 71 and 215, whether payments were deductible and includible as alimony depended on whether their purpose was support of the recipient spouse. The identification of the purpose of postdivorce payments was indeterminate and depended on underlying state law, which varied. Because of the flexibility of the rules, people with knowledgeable divorce lawyers could obtain alimony tax treatment for most or even all periodic cash payments between them.

In 1984 the test for treating payments as alimony for tax purposes changed, with the expressed goals of making the test objective and federalizing it so that the consequences of payments would be uniform across the states. If payments satisfy five requirements, they will be treated as alimony under IRC §§ 71 and 215 unless the separation agreement or divorce decree provides to the contrary:

(1)   Payments must be in cash or cash equivalent to or for the benefit of a former spouse.
(2)   Payments must be required by a
    (a)   written separation agreement, or
    (b)   divorce or separate maintenance decree, or
    (c)   other support decree such as an order of temporary support

(3) If the payments are made after a final decree of divorce or legal separa-
     tion, the payor and payee cannot live in the same household. The par-
     ties have a one-month grace period to establish separate households.
(4) Payments must end at the payee's death, and the payor cannot be
     required to make substitute payments to the payee's estate or third par-
     ties after the payee's death.
(5) The payments may not be treated as child support.

These requirements do not depend on the form of payment, and therefore lump-
sum as well as periodic payments may be treated as alimony.

However, if the size of payments treated as alimony declines precipitously in
the first three years, the payor will owe income taxes under the recapture rules.
These rules express the judgment that there is a real and significant difference
between spousal support and property division and that spouses should not be
able to disguise property division as spousal support. The recapture rules discourage front-end loading of payments. If recapture is required, the party who paid
alimony must declare the recaptured amount as income and pay taxes on it. The
recipient is entitled to a corresponding deduction.[6]

Even if payments are originally set up so that no amounts will be recaptured,
the calculations are based on actual payments, not obligations. Thus, if a payor
falls into arrears in the first or second year and then catches up in the third year,
a recapture may be created that would reverse the intended tax consequences of
the payments. The risk of recapture also makes modification of payments tricky
within the first three years.

In some circumstances amounts will not be recaptured, even though the calculation discussed here apparently calls for recapture:

---

6. A recapture calculation must be done only once, in the third year after payments
begin. The recapture formula requires comparison of the total amount paid during the
second year to the total paid in the third year and then comparison of the amount paid in
the first year to the amounts paid in the second and third years in the following way:

  I.   Subtract [the amount paid in Year 3 plus $15,000] from the amount paid in
       Year 2 to get R1.
  II. Average [the amount paid in Year 2 plus the amount paid in Year 3 minus R1].
       Add $15,000 to this amount, and subtract all from the amount paid in Year 1.
       This is R2.
  III. Total R1 and R2 to get the amount to be recaptured, if any.

For example, say that *A* pays *B* alimony of $30,000 in Year 1, $30,000 in Year 2, and
$5,000 in Year 3. The amount of recapture is calculated this way:

  I. $30,000 - (5,000 + 15,000) = 10,000 = $ R1.
  II. $30,000 - [(30,000 + 5,000 - 10,000)/2 + 15,000] = 30,000 - [12,500 + 15,000] = 2,500 = $ R2.
  III. $\$10,000 + \$2,500 = $ Amount to be recaptured in Year 3.

If either R1 or R2 is negative, it is treated as 0 for purposes of the rest of the calculations, so one negative number does not fully or partially cancel a positive number.

(1) If the payments cease within the three years because of the death of either party or the remarriage of the payee.

(2) If payments are made under temporary support orders.

(3) If the payments are to be made for at least three years and the amount is a fixed portion of the income from a business or property or from employment rather than a fixed dollar amount.

See generally Stephen P. Comeau, An Overview of the Federal Income Tax Provisions Related to Alimony Payments, 38 Fam. L.Q. 111 (2004).

c. Child Support

Child support payments are tax-free to the payee and not deductible to the payor. Where obligations are clearly designated as child support, applying this principle is easy. However, it is common for separation agreements to provide that one parent will pay a certain amount to the other as "family support," without designating explicitly how much is for child support.

In Commissioner v. Lester, 366 U.S. 299 (1961), the Supreme Court interpreted the prior version of IRC § 71 so that an amount was treated as child support only if it was explicitly fixed as such. Thus, even though an obligation to make payments was obviously for the purpose of child support, it was treated as spousal support for purposes of income taxes as long as it was not explicitly designated as child support.

The Tax Reform Act of 1984 reversed this rule. Now, amounts are treated as child support if they are clearly associated with a contingency relating to a child. IRC § 71(c)(2). This makes it much more difficult to obtain alimony treatment for undifferentiated spousal and child support. For example, say that *A* pays *B*, the custodian of the two children, $1,000 per month as family support, to be reduced by $200 per month when the first child turns 18 and $200 per month when the second child turns 18. Since no amount was fixed as child support, under the *Lester* rule all of this amount could be treated as alimony even though $400 was obviously child support. However, under the new rules, only $600 per month would be treated as alimony.

Internal Revenue Service Temp. Reg. § 1.71-1T, Q-18 provides that a contingency is presumed to be related to a child if:

(1) payments are to be reduced not more than six months before or after the date the child is to attain the age of 18, 21, or the local age of majority, or

(2) payments are to be reduced on two or more occasions which occur not more than one year before or after a different child of the payor spouse attains a certain age between the ages of 18 and 24, inclusive.

The presumption that payments are clearly related to a child contingency can be rebutted by showing that the timing of a change was calculated independently of considerations relating to children.

d. Dependency Exemptions, Child Tax Credits, Child Care Credits, Earned Income Credits, and Children's Medical Expenses

The parent who has custody may claim the dependency exemption for the child, as well as the child tax credit of $1,000 per child. IRC §§ 152, 24. If the parents have joint custody, the parent with whom the child lives for a longer period of time is entitled to the exemption and the credit. Both the dependency exemption and the tax credit are phased out for higher-income taxpayers, although the credit is phased out at a lower income level than the exemption. The majority of courts have held that a domestic relations court may order that the custodial parent assign the dependency exemption to the other parent. Leseberg v. Taylor, 78 P.3d 201 (Wyo. 2003). The child credit is partially refundable for low-income families. If a family does not owe any income tax, it will be entitled to a refund equal to the lesser of the family's child credit or 10 per cent of their earnings that exceed $10,000. The 10 per cent limit rises to 15 per cent in 2005, and the $10,000 cap will be adjusted annually for inflation. For a detailed analysis and criticism of the rules governing allocation of the dependency exemption for children *see* C. Garrison Lepow, The Flimflam Father: Deconstructing Parent-Child Stereotypes in Federal Tax Subsidies, 5 N.Y.U. J. Legis. & Pub. Pol'y 129 (2001-02).

Only the parent entitled to the dependency exemption is entitled education-related benefits, the Hope Scholarship and the lifetime learning credit. IRC § 25A.

The custodial parent alone is entitled to claim two other kinds of credits, both of which are phased out for higher-income taxpayers: the child care credit and the earned income credit. Neither of these credits can be assigned to the other parent, and if the parents have joint custody, the parent with physical custody for a longer time gets the credits. The child care credit reduces taxes for parents with earned income who must pay for child care to enable themselves to work. IRC § 21. Low-income custodial parents are also entitled to the earned income credit if they have earned income.

Allocation of one tax benefit associated with children — the deduction for medical expenses — depends only upon who pays. Regardless of who has custody, whichever parent pays a child's medical expenses may deduct them. IRC § 213(d)(5).

For more information on and a critique of current law regarding tax incident to divorce, *see* Deborah A. Geier, Simplifying and Rationalizing the Federal Income Tax Law Applicable to Transfers in Divorce, 55 Tax Law. 363 (2002).

PROBLEMS

1. When Harold and Wanda separated, Harold agreed to give Wanda $800 per month to support her and the children. They were separated, and Harold made the payments for eight months. At that point the court entered a final divorce decree, which required Harold to pay $535 per month as "child support" and $300 per month as "spousal support." The spousal support payments terminate when the youngest child becomes 21.

How much, if any, of the payments that Harold made while he and Wanda were separated may he deduct as alimony? Which of the two streams of payments required by the divorce decree may Harold deduct as alimony? If you were Harold's attorney and wanted to ensure that the $300 per month would be treated as alimony, what additional or different terms in the decree would you ask for?

2. When Millie and David were divorced, they agreed to hold their house as tenants in common, and that Millie and the children would have the right to occupy the house for ten years. At that point the house is to be sold and the proceeds divided equally. They have also agreed that David will make the mortgage payments on the house. How much of each payment is alimony for purposes of income taxes? If the divorce decree provided that Millie owned the house and that David was to pay the mortgage, how much of each payment would be treated as alimony for tax purposes?

E. BANKRUPTCY

An empirical study conducted in 2001 found that families in the worst financial trouble and who are most likely to declare bankruptcy are families with children. "Our study showed that married couples with children are more than twice as likely to file for bankruptcy as their childless counterparts. A divorced woman raising a youngster is nearly three times more likely to file for bankruptcy than her single friend who has no children." Elizabeth Warren, The Growing Threat to Middle Class Families, 69 Brook. L. Rev. 401, 402 (2004); *see also* Elizabeth Warren, The New Economics of the American Family, 12 Am. Bankr. Inst. L. Rev. 1 (2004). "Personal bankruptcy often follows a serious economic reversal. About two-third of all bankruptcies occur after one or both adults in a household have had a serious interruption in income, such as a layoff, cutback in hours, downsizing, outsourcing, or some other euphemism that means income has been cut sharply. Nearly half of all families file for bankruptcy in the aftermath of a serious medical problem. Divorce has hit more than one in five families in bankruptcy. In the 2001 sample, nearly nine out of ten filers listed at least one of these three reasons in explaining their bankruptcy petitions." Elizabeth Warren, Bankrupt Children, 86 Minn. L. Rev. 1003, 1022 (2002). The financial strains that lead to bankruptcy may undermine the marriage too, or the costs of divorce may force either or both former spouses into bankruptcy shortly after the divorce is final. Sheryl L. Scheible, Bankruptcy and the Modification of Support: Fresh Start, Head Start, or False Start? 69 N.C. L. Rev. 577, 578 (1991) (citing case study indicating that one-third of persons in bankruptcy had been divorced within the previous or following year).

The fundamental purpose of bankruptcy law is to give debtors a fresh start by freeing them from prebankruptcy debts while equitably dividing their assets among creditors. When a person declares bankruptcy, a trustee in bankruptcy is appointed to take control of the bankrupt's assets and devise a plan for using them to pay off the bankrupt's creditors to the extent possible.[7] Some assets, such as a homestead interest in real property, may be exempt from bankruptcy and will not be taken to satisfy the debtor's creditors. 11 U.S.C. § 522. In addition, if exempt assets are encumbered by judicial liens, under certain circumstances the liens will be avoided (that is, eliminated) as well.

Filing a bankruptcy proceeding activates a stay of all creditors' efforts to collect against the debtor. 11 U.S.C. § 362(a). A creditor may move to lift the stay, and the motion will be granted if lifting the stay will not be detrimental to the debtor's estate and if the creditor's rights are otherwise adequately protected. When the bankrupt person's assets are distributed in the bankruptcy, secured creditors generally are preferred to unsecured ones, though by statute certain unsecured creditors have priority over other unsecured creditors. Once the bankruptcy proceeding is concluded, the debtor starts anew with the exempt property that he or she retained, and any debts that were not paid from the bankruptcy estate are discharged. *See generally* Shayna M. Steinfeld & Bruce R. Steinfeld, A Brief Overview of Bankruptcy and Alimony/Support Issues, 38 Fam. L.Q. 127 (2004).

In recent years various courts and commentators have observed the increasing use of bankruptcy proceedings by former spouses to defeat the financial terms of their divorce decrees. Some cases, such as the next one, address the problem directly.

IN RE HUCKFELDT

39 F.3d 829 (8th Cir. 1994)

LOKEN, C.J. During their twelve years of marriage, Roger and Georgianne Huckfeldt accumulated over $250,000 in debts while Huckfeldt completed college, medical school, and six years of a residency in surgery, and Georgianne completed college and law school. These debts include $166,000 in student loans to Huckfeldt and $47,000 jointly borrowed from Georgianne's parents. The Huckfeldts divorced on March 26, 1992. The divorce decree ordered Huckfeldt to pay his student loans, one-half of the debt to Georgianne's parents, and other enumerated debts totaling some $241,000. The decree ordered Huckfeldt to hold Georgianne harmless for these debts but otherwise denied Georgianne's request for maintenance.

---

7. Individuals may undergo either of two kinds of bankruptcy proceedings. In a Chapter 7 proceeding, the debtor's assets are liquidated under the supervision of a trustee to pay off creditors to the extent possible. The discussion in the text largely assumes a Chapter 7 proceeding. People with a regular income and unsecured debt of less than $100,000 and secured debt of less than $350,000 may instead go through Chapter 13 proceedings, which allow the debtor to remain in control of his or her assets and to set up a reorganization plan to delay the payment of debts. In other words, a Chapter 13 proceeding allows the debtor to rehabilitate himself or herself and repay at least some debts. Similarly, businesses may reorganize and extend debt payment through Chapter 11 proceedings. Chapter 12 creates special proceedings for family farmers that are similar to but simpler than Chapter 11 proceedings.

On June 4, 1992, six months before Huckfeldt would complete his residency in surgery, he filed a voluntary Chapter 7 petition, listing assets of $1,250 and liabilities of $546,857. After filing the petition, Huckfeldt accepted a fellowship at Oregon Health Sciences University, a one or two year position paying $45,000 per year, substantially less than the income he could likely earn as a surgeon during the pendency of his Chapter 7 proceeding. Following Huckfeldt's petition, creditors of the debts assigned to him in the divorce decree began pursuing Georgianne for repayment. She filed for bankruptcy protection in March 1993.

In September 1992, Georgianne and her parents ("the Creditors") filed a motion to dismiss Huckfeldt's Chapter 7 petition on the ground that it was filed in bad faith. The Creditors alleged that Huckfeldt had threatened to file for bankruptcy during the divorce proceedings and had commenced this proceeding in defiance of the divorce decree for the purpose of shifting responsibility for assigned debts to Georgianne.[8] The Creditors further alleged that Huckfeldt "has deliberately taken steps to reduce his annual income" to avoid payment of his debts through a Chapter 7 liquidation. The Creditors argued that this bad faith warranted dismissal under sections 105, 109, 301, and 707 of the Bankruptcy Code.

After a hearing, the bankruptcy court granted the Creditors' motion to dismiss. After finding that Roger could be earning $110,000 to $120,000 per year, after all expenses except income tax, the court stated:

It is the purpose of the bankruptcy system to provide a fresh start for the honest but unfortunate debtor. It is not the purpose of the bankruptcy system to eliminate the obligations of a party who is capable of paying same. The Court believes debtor filed this bankruptcy petition in bad faith and with the deliberate intention of unloading debt, particularly that to his spouse, which he could shortly begin to repay. Further this Court believes it was the intent of the debtor to leave his ex-spouse with all the debts and obligations incurred over the twelve years and force her into a bankruptcy situation also. . . . Accordingly the Court concludes that this case was filed in bad faith and concludes that good faith is a requirement for the filing of a bankruptcy petition no matter what the chapter.

The district court affirmed, expressly holding that § 707(a) of the Code authorizes dismissal for bad faith. . . .

Section 707(a) provides that the bankruptcy court may dismiss a Chapter 7 proceeding only after notice and a hearing and only for cause. . . . In authorizing dismissal "for cause," the statute does not define "cause," beyond setting forth three specific examples. Use of the introductory word "including" means that these three types of "cause" are nonexclusive. . . .

Although Huckfeldt's briefs carefully avoid the issue, the initial question is whether the district court erred in holding that bad faith may be "cause" for

---

8. Absent "undue hardship," which Huckfeldt has not alleged, his student loans are nondischargeable. See 11 U.S.C. § 523(a)(8). Thus, this case primarily concerns whether he can avoid the joint debts that the divorce court ordered him to pay.

dismissal under § 707(a). That is an open issue in this circuit, and few other circuits have considered it. . . .

. . . Congress has defined the ultimate issue in § 707(a) cases as whether the Chapter 7 petition should be dismissed "for cause." As this case illustrates, some conduct constituting cause to dismiss a Chapter 7 petition may readily be characterized as bad faith. But framing the issue in terms of bad faith may tend to misdirect the inquiry away from the fundamental principles and purposes of Chapter 7. Thus, we think the § 707(a) analysis is better conducted under the statutory standard, "for cause." If the bankruptcy court elects instead to act under the inherent judicial power to punish a bad faith litigant, that action should not be taken under § 707(a). . . .

Huckfeldt filed a Chapter 7 petition to frustrate the divorce court decree and to push his ex-wife into bankruptcy. He then manipulated his immediate earnings to ensure that the Chapter 7 proceeding would achieve these non-economic motives. . . . Indeed, such conduct has long been considered unworthy of bankruptcy protection:

> [T]he petition in this case was not filed for the purpose of a just liquidation by composition with creditors but to defeat the wife from a right of possession in and to the real estate which was to be awarded to her under the divorce proceedings. This violates the purpose and intent of the statute . . . and, as said by the Supreme Court of the United States, under that situation, the proceedings will be halted at the outset.

In re Brown, 21 F. Supp. 935, 939 (S.D. Iowa 1938). Huckfeldt is not an "honest but unfortunate debtor" entitled to the equitable relief of a Chapter 7 liquidation. His petition was properly dismissed for cause.

The judgment of the district court is affirmed.

NOTES AND QUESTIONS

1. How would a court tell when a bankruptcy petition was filed for the purpose of defeating a former spouse's rights under a divorce decree rather than for other, good faith reasons? In *Huckfeldt*, if the former husband had had debts that creditors could not collect from his former wife, would that have shown that his petition was filed for a legitimate purpose?

2. Another way in which a person might defeat the claims of a former spouse by filing bankruptcy is illustrated in Farrey v. Sanderfoot, 500 U.S. 291 (1991). A Wisconsin divorce decree awarded the husband, Gerald Sanderfoot, the couple's home, and ordered him to pay his former wife, Jeanne Farrey, $29,208.44 to equalize the property division order. To secure this award, the decree provided that Farrey "shall have a lien against the real estate property of [Sanderfoot] for the total amount of money due her pursuant to this Order of the Court, i.e. $29,208.44, and the lien shall remain attached to the real estate property . . . until the total amount of money is paid in full." 500 U.S. at 293.

The Bankruptcy Code provides that if a security interest attaches to exempt property, such as the obligor's home, the property will not be sold. Instead, the debtor will retain the exempt property. Generally, liens on exempt property survive bankruptcy as well. However, 11 U.S.C. § 522(f) provides that *judicial* liens are eliminated ("avoided") by a bankruptcy proceeding under some circumstances. Less than a year after the divorce, Sanderfoot filed for Chapter 7 bankruptcy and claimed the home as exempt property. He also moved under § 522 to avoid Farrey's lien on the grounds that it was a judicial lien that impaired his exemption. Farrey argued in the trial court that the lien-avoidance statute could not be applied to deprive her of her interest in the marital home. She ultimately prevailed in the Supreme Court, but not on these grounds.

Instead, the Court interpreted § 522 as avoiding only those judicial liens that attach to property interests that the debtor owns before the lien attaches. 500 U.S. at 296. Sanderfoot had conceded for purposes of argument that the divorce decree gave him a wholly new interest in the home rather than adding his former wife's share to his preexisting share. 500 U.S. at 294. The Court therefore held that § 522 did not apply and that Farrey's lien survived Sanderfoot's bankruptcy.

The holding in Farrey v. Sanderfoot is quite technical, and Farrey's success depended on Sanderfoot's concession. As we have seen, though, a property division order might well be characterized as recognizing and confirming each spouse's predivorce ownership of the property, at least to some extent. Indeed, since Wisconsin is a community property state, a Wisconsin court might take that position. In fact, after *Farrey* was decided, this very question came before the Wisconsin Court of Appeals. The facts of Klemme v. Schoneman, 165 Wis. 2d 250, 477 N.W.2d 77 (Wis. App. 1991), are similar to those in *Farrey*. The husband received the marital home subject to a duty to pay the wife $5,800, which was secured by a lien on the property. He then filed for bankruptcy and claimed that the lien was avoidable. When the wife later attempted to foreclose the lien, the husband argued that he had possessed a community property interest in the house before the lien attached and that to the extent the lien attached to this interest it was avoided by the bankruptcy proceeding. The *Klemme* court declined to decide whether the husband's interest preexisted the divorce or was created by it. Instead, the court concluded that the lien was not a judicial lien but rather a mortgage and therefore was not subject to being avoided. Other courts facing this problem have reached the conclusion that the divorce decree creates a new interest to which the lien attaches, rather than fastening a lien onto a preexisting interest. *See, e.g.,* In re Catli, 999 F.2d 1405 (9th Cir. 1993).

The bankruptcy amendments of 1994 also made it more difficult for a debtor to avoid a lien on exempt property that secures rights created by divorce. If the underlying debt is for support, the new rules provide that the lien is not avoided. 11 U.S.C. § 522(f)(1). This exception does not apply to liens that secure property division debts, as in *Farrey*. Therefore, the rules discussed above continue to be important. For more information, *see* Sheryl Scheible Wolf, Divorce, Bankruptcy, and Metaphysics: Avoidance of Marital Liens Under § 522(f) of the Bankruptcy Code, 31 Fam. L.Q. 513 (1997).

3. If a former spouse successfully discharges obligations under a divorce decree by declaring bankruptcy, may the domestic relations court modify its decree to provide relief to the other spouse? In such cases, the obligee is often successful in modifying support obligations in the family law court, though it is improper for the domestic relations court to reinstate the discharged obligation

in effect. Alyson F. Finkelstein, A Tug of War: State Divorce Courts Versus Federal Bankruptcy Courts Regarding Debts Resulting from Divorce, 18 Bankr. Dev. J. 169 (2001). Some courts have even held that the property division provisions of the divorce decree may be revised under such circumstances. *See, e.g.,* Birt v. Birt, 86 P.3d 544 (Az. App. 2004), holding that a lower court erred when it refused to set aside a divorce judgment on the wife's motion after the husband obtained a discharge in bankruptcy of his obligations under the decree. The effect of the bankruptcy order was to leave the wife liable for all of the couple's substantial debts, rather than for only half as provided in the divorce decree, while allowing the husband to keep his share of property awarded in the decree. The appellate court ruled that the trial court correctly refused to reopen the divorce case on the ground that the bankruptcy action was newly discovered evidence or that the debt division provisions of the divorce decree were prospective in their application. However, it said, the trial court should have granted wife's motion to vacate the judgment for "any other reason justifying relief from the operation of the judgment," Ariz. R. Civ. Pro. 60(c)(60). The court said, "Husband's filing of bankruptcy, which he concedes was to avoid the terms of the dissolution decree, creates such a substantial injustice that it overrides the commitment to finality of judgments. . . ." 86 P.3d at 550. The opinion cites cases from North Dakota, New Mexico, Kansas, Minnesota, and Alabama that modify divorce decree provisions regarding property division or spousal support following one former spouse's successful declaration of bankruptcy.

The Bankruptcy Code provides that an order for spousal or child support is not dischargeable in bankruptcy. This means that after the proceedings are concluded, the obligor must continue paying support. 11 U.S.C. § 523(a)(5). In contrast, property division orders are dischargeable only under some circumstances. Application of this rule turns on characterizing an order as one for spousal support, child support, or property division. The following case deals with this issue.

SYLVESTER V. SYLVESTER

865 F.2d 1164 (10th Cir. 1989)

PER CURIAM. In January 1969, after seventeen years of marriage, appellant Wendell Sylvester and appellee Jane Sylvester obtained a divorce in Texas. The divorce decree incorporated a settlement agreement which provides in relevant part that, in recognition of the medical education and training of appellant acquired in large part through the earnings of his former wife and contributions by her parents, appellant agrees to meet a number of obligations: to pay his former wife $750.00 per month until their minor child reaches the age of 18; to pay his former wife $1,000 per month thereafter until his former wife remarries or either appellant or his former wife dies; to pay the taxes, insurance premiums, and note payments on the real property awarded to his former wife when the payments become due; to pay the premiums on the life insurance policies awarded to his former wife; to pay the college expenses of the minor child; and to pay for all indebtedness incurred by the parties before the divorce.

In July 1984, appellant filed a voluntary petition for relief under Chapter 11 of the Bankruptcy Code. . . . The bankruptcy court found that appellant's obligations in the settlement agreement were in the nature of alimony, maintenance, or support and thus were nondischargeable under 11 U.S.C. § 523(a)(5). . . .

The determination of whether an obligation arising out of a divorce settlement is in the nature of alimony, maintenance, or support is a matter of federal bankruptcy law. In determining dischargeability under § 523(a), the initial inquiry is the intent of the parties at the time they entered into their agreement.

Here, several facts demonstrate that the obligations imposed on appellant in the settlement agreement were intended to be in the nature of alimony, maintenance, or support: the settlement agreement segregates the property settlement provisions from appellant's obligations; the agreement states that the obligations imposed upon appellant are in consideration of appellee "relinquishing any rights that she might have against [appellant] for support"; the parties had a minor child at the time of the divorce and appellant had substantially more income than appellee; the agreement provides that appellant is to make payments directly to appellee over a substantial period of time; and the obligation to make monthly payments to appellee terminates on remarriage or death. Additionally, as the district court found, "[t]he provisions in the agreement in dispute had the actual effect of providing support to the appellee—enabling her to maintain a home . . . and have a monthly income." In light of those facts, we agree with the bankruptcy court and the district court that appellant's obligations are covered by § 523(a)(5) and therefore are not dischargeable in bankruptcy. . . .

Appellant's next argument is that even if the obligations at issue are in the nature of alimony, maintenance, or support, the bankruptcy court erred in not conducting an evidentiary hearing to determine his ex-wife's present need for support, citing In re Calhoun, 715 F.2d 1103, 1109 (6th Cir. 1983). In *Calhoun* the Sixth Circuit held that after determining that the parties to a divorce intended to create an obligation for support, the next inquiry is whether the obligation "has the effect of providing the support necessary to ensure that the daily needs of the former spouse and any children of the marriage are satisfied." Id. at 1109. In conducting this analysis, the bankruptcy court should "look to the practical effect of the discharge" of the obligation "upon the dependent spouse's ability to sustain daily needs. . . . If the [obligation] is not found necessary to provide such support, the inquiry ends and the debtor's obligation . . . must be discharged." Id. *See also*, e.g., In re Warner, 5 B.R. 434, 442-43 (Bankr. D. Utah 1980).

Although *Calhoun* supports appellant's argument, it is a minority approach which we decline to follow. A requirement that the former spouse's present need for support or changed circumstances be analyzed in determining dischargeability finds no support in either the language or the legislative history of § 523(a)(5). *See* In re Harrell, 754 F.2d 902, 906-07 (11th Cir. 1985). Furthermore, as the court in *Calhoun* recognized, such an inquiry would put federal courts in the position of modifying state matrimonial decrees. Calhoun, 715 F.2d at 1109 n.10. We decline to make such an intrusion into the area of domestic relations absent a clearer congressional mandate to do so. Therefore, we join the other circuits that have rejected the approach of the Sixth Circuit in *Calhoun*. E.g., Forsdick v. Turgeon, 812 F.2d 801, 804 (2d Cir. 1987); Draper v. Draper, 790 F.2d 52, 54 n.3 (8th Cir. 1986); In re Harrell, 754 F.2d 902, 907 (11th Cir. 1985).

Accordingly, the district court's affirmance of the bankruptcy court is affirmed.

NOTES AND QUESTIONS

1. The *Sylvester* court, like most bankruptcy courts, treats the parties' or the court's intent at the time of divorce as determining the character of an order. What factors in this case support the finding that the obligation was in the nature of support? What would have to change to result in a finding that the order was a division of property? For a discussion of the intent test and its application, *see* Shayna M. Steinfeld & Bruce R. Steinfeld, A Brief Overview of Bankruptcy and Alimony/Support Issues, 38 Fam. L.Q. 127 (2004).

2. *Sylvester* argues that a bankruptcy court should not reexamine a state court order to determine whether a support recipient actually needs the amount of support given because this would amount to a de facto modification of the state order. However, the bankruptcy of the obligor might itself be a sufficient change in circumstances to support modification of a support order. Therefore, would it not be more efficient to allow the bankruptcy court to make this determination?

On the other hand, by deciding that the character of an order is a federal rather than a state law question, Congress seems to have decided that whether an order is support or property for purposes of bankruptcy should not necessarily be decided in the same way that it would for purposes of modification. Should the analyses be the same? Why or why not? Is it more important that the same bankruptcy rules apply to everyone, regardless of the state they live in, or that the terms of their divorce decree be characterized in the same way for all purposes?

In Fitzgerald v. Fitzgerald, 9 F.3d 517 (6th Cir. 1993), the court that decided *Calhoun* limited the "present needs" test significantly, saying that it is applied only to determine whether something that was not labeled "support" in the divorce decree should be so treated, and not to reduce payments that everyone agreed were intended for support.

3. If the court finds that a debt arises from property division rather than support, the next issue likely to arise is whether it is dischargeable under § 523(a)(15). This section of the Bankruptcy Code says that property division orders are also nondischargeable unless:

(A) the debtor does not have the ability to pay such debt from income or property of the debtor not reasonably necessary to be expended for the maintenance or support of the debtor or a dependent of the debtor and, if the debtor is engaged in a business, for the payment of expenditures necessary for the continuation, preservation, and operation of such business; or

(B) discharging such debt would result in a benefit to the debtor that outweighs the detrimental consequences to [the creditor spouse, former spouse or child].

Most courts apply this test at the time of the hearing, though some courts use the time of the petition. Bernice B. Donald & Jennie D. Latta, The Dischargeability of Property Settlement and Hold Harmless Agreements in Bankruptcy: An Overview of §523(a)(15), 31 Fam. L.Q. 409, 415-416 (1997). The courts are split on who bears the burden of proof to establish these exceptions. Some put the burden of going forward with enough evidence to raise an issue on the debtor but put the burden of persuasion on the creditor; some put the burdens of production and persuasion on part (A) on the debtor and the burden of persuasion on part (B) on the creditor; some put the burden of persuasion on both issues on the debtor; and some put both on the creditor. *Id.* at 420-421. For further discussion *see* Peter C. Alexander, Building "A Doll's House": A Feminist Analysis of Marital Debt Dischargeability in Bankruptcy, 48 Vill. L. Rev. 381 (2003).

4. Several other provisions of the Bankruptcy Code provide special protection for former spouses and children who are creditors of the bankrupt person:

a. If a spouse files for bankruptcy while divorce proceedings are pending, the divorce court can grant the divorce and decide other matters that do not affect the debtor's estate, but it cannot issue orders that affect the estate unless the automatic stay mentioned above at pages 700-701 is lifted. Exceptions to the automatic stay include actions to establish, modify, or enforce child or spousal support and to establish paternity. 11 U.S.C. §362(b)(2).

b. The list of unsecured debts that are given a priority under the statute includes claims for support. 11 U.S.C. §507(a)(7).

c. A debtor's transfer of money or property to a spouse, former spouse, or child to satisfy a support debt is not a "preference" and so cannot be avoided by the trustee in bankruptcy. 11 U.S.C. §547(c)(7).

d. Child support creditors do not have to pay a filing fee when they intervene in a bankruptcy proceeding, although spousal support and property division creditors are not exempt from the fee.

5. If the person who files for bankruptcy is entitled to payments from a former spouse, the most important question is whether the right to those payments is an asset of the bankruptcy estate, subject to being used to pay off the person's debts. The Bankruptcy Code provides that spousal or child support that the bankrupt person receives is exempt from bankruptcy to the extent reasonably necessary for support of the bankrupt or his or her dependents if state law provides that such amounts are exempt from creditors. 11 U.S.C. §522(d)(10)(D). Property division debts are assets of the bankruptcy estate and are not exempt.

Child Custody

9

A. INTRODUCTION

During the colonial period in this country, and in England during the same time, custody disputes rarely came before the courts. Common law doctrine assigned to fathers sole custody of their legitimate children. A father not only had the sole right to custody while he lived; he could determine custody after death by appointing a testamentary guardian. The following excerpt describes the transition from a clear rule of paternal custody to judicial superintendence in the United States.

MICHAEL GROSSBERG, *GOVERNING THE HEARTH: LAW AND THE FAMILY IN NINETEENTH CENTURY AMERICA*

235-239 (1985)

Prerepublican Anglo-American law granted fathers an almost unlimited right to the custody of their minor legitimate children. Moored in the medieval equation of legal rights with property ownership, it assumed that the interests of children were best protected by making the father the natural guardian and by using a property-based standard of parental fitness. Custody law held children to be dependent, subordinate beings, assets of estates in which fathers had a vested right. Their services, earnings, and the like became the property of their paternal masters in exchange for life and maintenance. Literary critic Jay Fliegelman summarized the stark reality of the traditional law of parent and child: "[T]he debt is owed nature not nurture." These assumptions lingered on in the new republic. The influential University of Maryland law professor David Hoffman explained the dual nature of paternal authority in his 1836 Legal Outlines. First was "the injunction imposed on parents by nature, of rearing, and carefully watching over the moral, religious, and physical education of their progeny, and the impracticality of

621

advantageously discharging that duty, unless children yield implicit obedience to the dictates of parental concern, seeing that they are not of sufficient age and discretion to limit the measure of their submission or obedience." Second was "the presumed consent of the offspring." . . .

Professor Hoffman also emphasized that these parental rights conferred authority primarily on the father:

> If parental power arose not in truth from these principles, but from some fancied property given to the parent in his offspring, by the act of propagation, it would seem to follow . . . that this authority would appertain in the largest degree to the mother, since she not only has the pains and deprivations incident to gestation and parturition, but is the principal sharer in the cares which succeed the birth. Yet it is the father who holds and exercises the principal authority. . . .

In 1809 a South Carolina equity court heard Jennette Prather's demand for a separation from her husband and the custody of her children. She charged her mate with living openly in adultery. The judges easily complied with her first request, but hesitated in granting the second. Chancellor Henry De Saussure was mindful, he said, of the father being the children's "natural guardian, invested by God and the law of the country with reasonable power over them. Unless his parental power has been monstrously and cruelly abused, this court would be very cautious in interfering with the execution of it." The court finally denied the errant husband his full parental rights. It gave the custody of an infant daughter, though not of the older children, to Jennette. In doing so, the judges acknowledged that they were treading on uncertain legal ground.

The ambivalence of the South Carolina court reveals the conflicting pressures on the post-Revolutionary bench generated by custody disputes between mothers and fathers. Traditional male authority over the family remained a fundamental tenet of family law. But a growing concern with child nurture and the acceptance of women as more legally distinct individuals, ones with a special capacity for moral and religious leadership and for child rearing, undermined the primacy of paternal custody rights. . . .

The judicial disposition to emphasize child welfare in determining custody began to refashion the preferences of the common law. The "best interests of the child" became a judicial yardstick used to measure all claims for children. Its dramatic impact is most apparent in the resolution of disputes between the natural parents for their children.

B. STANDARDS FOR CUSTODY DETERMINATION

1. An Introduction to the "Best Interests" Standard

Professor Grossberg describes the transition in the American law of custody as a movement from paternal patriarchy to judicial patriarchy, by which he means (at least in part) the replacement of virtually unbounded paternal authority by virtually unbounded judicial authority (exercised, of course, by male judges). The doctrinal vehicle conveying that judicial power was the "best interests" doctrine. We have noted on a number of occasions the use in family law of "standards" rather than rules, and, plainly, the "best interests" doctrine must also fall in the "standards" category.

Although moving from a nearly absolute and therefore clear rule of paternal custody to a best-interest standard enhanced judicial authority over child custody decisions, the breadth of the latter standard creates problems of management for judges and parties alike. The difference between rules and standards is between an approach to legal decision making that employs apparently mechanical formulae (rules) and one that proceeds by the individualized application of generally stated social policies (standards).

The tension between rules and standards runs throughout the law of custody, but the fault lines change with each generation. When the best-interest standard first took hold, the courts were convinced that custody needed to be awarded to one, and only one, parent. Under the best-interest rubric, the determination of which parent gradually changed from a preference for fathers to a presumption, at least for children of "tender years," in favor of mothers. Under both approaches the participation of the other parent then depended on the cooperation of the custodial parent. Certainty in decision-making authority was considered essential.

More recently, with greater acceptance of shared parenting and more egalitarian gender roles, legislatures and courts have authorized joint custody awards that acknowledge both parents' contribution to child rearing. In some jurisdictions, the preference for joint custody has become a rule creating a legal presumption in favor of joint custody; in all jurisdictions, the law favors the continuing involvement of both parents and makes it difficult to deny a parent access to a child altogether.

The presumption of both parents' continuing involvement, in turn, places greater emphasis on disqualifying conduct — and determinations of unfitness. The U.S. Constitution recognizes "fit" parents as having a fundamental liberty interest in the care, custody, and management of their children, limiting the courts' discretion to award custody or visitation to others. *See, e.g.,* Troxel v. Granville, 530 U.S. 57 (2000). Chapters 12 and 13 explore the increasingly contentious law regarding how legal parenthood is determined. The materials in this chapter assume that legal parenthood has been decided and concern custody and visitation disputes between a child's legal parents or between a legal parent and a third party. The first part of this section introduces the meanings and application of the "best interests" standard, and the second examines joint custody. As we will see, both of these standards permit and sometimes even require courts to judge parents' conduct to determine their "fitness" to parent. The remainder of this section concerns the legal issues that arise from this inquiry.

PAINTER V. BANNISTER

140 N.W.2d 152 (Iowa), *cert. denied*, 385 U.S. 949 (1966)

STUART, J. . . . The custody dispute before us in this habeas corpus action is between the father, Harold Painter, and the maternal grandparents, Dwight and

Margaret Bannister. Mark's mother and younger sister were killed in an automobile accident on December 6, 1962 near Pullman, Washington. The father, after other arrangements for Mark's care had proved unsatisfactory, asked the Bannisters to take care of Mark. They went to California and brought Mark to their farm home near Ames in July, 1963. Mr. Painter remarried in November, 1964 and about that time indicated he wanted to take Mark back. The Bannisters refused to let him leave and this action was filed in June, 1965. Since July 1965 he has continued to remain in the Bannister home under an order of this court staying execution of the judgment of the trial court awarding custody to the father until the matter could be determined on appeal. For reasons hereinafter stated, we conclude Mark's better interests will be served if he remains with the Bannisters.

Mark's parents came from highly contrasting backgrounds. His mother was born, raised and educated in rural Iowa. Her parents are college graduates. Her father is agricultural information editor for the Iowa State University Extension Service. The Bannister home is in the Gilbert Community and is well kept, roomy and comfortable. The Bannisters are highly respected members of the community. Mr. Bannister has served on the school board and regularly teaches a Sunday school class at the Gilbert Congregational Church. Mark's mother graduated from Grinnell College. She then went to work for a newspaper in Anchorage, Alaska, where she met Harold Painter.

Mark's father was born in California. When he was 2 1/2 years old, his parents were divorced and he was placed in a foster home. Although he has kept in contact with his natural parents, he considers his foster parents, the McNelly's, as his family. He flunked out of a high school and a trade school because of a lack of interest in academic subjects, rather than any lack of ability. He joined the navy at 17. He did not like it. After receiving an honorable discharge, he took examinations and obtained his high school diploma. He lived with the McNelly's and went to college for 2 1/2 years under the G.I. bill. He quit college to take a job on a small newspaper in Ephrata, Washington in November 1955. In May 1956, he went to work for the newspaper in Anchorage which employed Jeanne Bannister. . . .

We are not confronted with a situation where one of the contesting parties is not a fit or proper person. There is no criticism of either the Bannisters or their home. There is no suggestion in the record that Mr. Painter is morally unfit. It is obvious the Bannisters did not approve of their daughter's marriage to Harold Painter and do not want their grandchild raised under his guidance. The philosophies of life are entirely different. As stated by the psychiatrist who examined Mr. Painter at the request of the Bannisters' attorneys: "It is evident that there exists a large difference in ways of life and value systems between the Bannisters and Mr. Painter, but in this case, there is no evidence that psychiatric instability is involved. Rather, these divergent life patterns seem to represent alternative normal adaptations." . . .

The Bannister home provides Mark with a stable, dependable, conventional, middle-class, middle-west background and an opportunity for a college education and profession, if he desires it. It provides a solid foundation and secure atmosphere. In the Painter home, Mark would have more freedom of conduct and thought with an opportunity to develop his individual talents. It would be more exciting and challenging in many respects, but romantic, impractical and unstable. . . .

Our conclusion as to the type of home Mr. Painter would offer is based upon his Bohemian approach to finances and life in general. We feel there is much evidence which supports this conclusion. His main ambition is to be a free lance writer and photographer. He has had some articles and picture stories published, but the income from these efforts has been negligible. At the time of the accident, Jeanne was willingly working to support the family so Harold could devote more time to his writing and photography. In the 10 years since he left college, he has changed jobs seven times. . . .

There is general agreement that Mr. Painter needs help with his finances. Both Jeanne and Marilyn, his present wife, handled most of them. Purchases and sales of books, boats, photographic equipment and houses indicate poor financial judgment and an easy come easy go attitude. He dissipated his wife's estate of about $4300, most of which was a gift from her parents and which she had hoped would be used for the children's education.

The psychiatrist classifies him as "a romantic and somewhat of a dreamer." An apt example is the plan he related for himself and Mark in February 1963: "My thought now is to settle Mark and myself in Sausalito, near San Francisco; this is a retreat for wealthy artists, writers, and such aspiring artists and writers as can fork up the rent money. My plan is to do expensive portraits ($150 and up), sell prints ($15 and up) to the tourists who flock in from all over the world. . . ."

The house in which Mr. Painter and his present wife live, compared with the well kept Bannister home, exemplifies the contrasting ways of life. In his words, "it is a very old and beat up and lovely home. . . ." They live in the rear part. The interior is inexpensively but tastefully decorated. The large yard on a hill in the business district of Walnut Creek, California, is of uncut weeds and wild oats. The house "is not painted on the outside because I do not want it painted. I am very fond of the wood on the outside of the house."

The present Mrs. Painter has her master's degree in cinema design and apparently likes and has had considerable contact with children. She is anxious to have Mark in her home. Everything indicates she would provide a leveling influence on Mr. Painter and could ably care for Mark.

Mr. Painter is either an agnostic or atheist and has no concern for formal religious training. He has read a lot of Zen Buddhism and "has been very much influenced by it." Mrs. Painter is Roman Catholic. They plan to send Mark to a Congregational Church near the Catholic Church, on an irregular schedule. . . .

Were the question simply which household would be the most suitable in which to raise a child, we would have unhesitatingly chosen the Bannister home. We believe security and stability in the home are more important than intellectual stimulation in the proper development of a child. There are, however, several factors which have made us pause.

First, there is the presumption of parental preference, which though weakened in the past several years, exists by statute. We have a great deal of sympathy for a father, who in the difficult period of adjustment following his wife's death, turns to the maternal grandparents for their help and then finds them unwilling to return the child. There is no merit in the Bannister claim that Mr. Painter permanently relinquished custody. It was intended to be a temporary arrangement. A father should be encouraged to look for help with the children from those who love them without the risk of thereby losing the custody of the children permanently. This fact must receive consideration in cases of this kind. However, as always, the primary consideration is the best interest of the child, and if the return of custody to the father is likely to have a seriously disrupting and disturbing effect upon the child's development, this fact must prevail.

Second, Jeanne's will named her husband guardian of her children and if he failed to qualify or ceased to act, named her mother. The parent's wishes are entitled to consideration.

Third, the Bannister's are 60 years old. By the time Mark graduates from high school they will be over 70 years old. Care of young children is a strain on grandparents and Mrs. Bannister's letters indicate as much.

We have considered all of these factors and have concluded that Mark's best interest demands that his custody remain with the Bannisters. Mark was five when he came to their home. The evidence clearly shows he was not well adjusted at that time. He did not distinguish fact from fiction and was inclined to tell "tall tales" emphasizing the big "I." He was very aggressive toward smaller children, cruel to animals, not liked by his classmates and did not seem to know what was acceptable conduct. As stated by one witness: "Mark knew where his freedom was and he didn't know where his boundaries were." In two years he made a great deal of improvement. He now appears to be well disciplined, happy, relatively secure and popular with his classmates, although still subject to more than normal anxiety.

We place a great deal of reliance on the testimony of Dr. Glenn R. Hawks, a child psychologist. The trial court, in effect, disregarded Dr. Hawks' opinions stating: "The court has given full consideration to the good doctor's testimony, but cannot accept it at full face value because of exaggerated statements and the witness's attitude on the stand." We, of course, do not have the advantage of viewing the witness's conduct on the stand, but we have carefully reviewed his testimony and find nothing in the written record to justify such a summary dismissal of the opinions of this eminent child psychologist.

Dr. Hawks is head of the Department of Child Development at Iowa State University. However, there is nothing in the record which suggests that his relationship with the Bannisters is such that his professional opinion would be influenced thereby. Child development is his specialty and he has written many articles and a textbook on the subject. He is recognized nationally, having served on the staff of the 1960 White House Conference on Children and Youth and as consultant on a Ford Foundation program concerning youth in India. He is now education consultant on the project "Head Start." He has taught and lectured at many universities and belongs to many professional associations. He works with the Iowa Children's Home Society in placement problems. Further detailing of his qualifications is unnecessary.

Between June 15th and the time of trial, he spent approximately 25 hours acquiring information about Mark and the Bannisters, including appropriate testing of and "depth interviews" with Mark. Dr. Hawks' testimony covers 70 pages of the record and it is difficult to pinpoint any bit of testimony which precisely summarizes his opinion. He places great emphasis on the "father figure" and discounts the importance of the "biological father." "The father figure is a figure that the child sees as an authority figure, as a helper, he is a nurturant figure, and one who typifies maleness and stands as maleness as far as the child is concerned."

His investigation revealed: ". . . the strength of the father figure before Mark came to the Bannisters is very unclear. Mark is confused about the father figure prior to his contact with Mr. Bannister." Now, "Mark used Mr. Bannister as his father figure. This is very evident. It shows up in the depth interview, and it shows up in the description of Mark's life given by Mark. He has a very warm feeling for Mr. Bannister."

Dr. Hawks concluded that it was not for Mark's best interest to be removed from the Bannister home. He is criticized for reaching this conclusion without investigating the Painter home or finding out more about Mr. Painter's character. He answered: "I was most concerned about the welfare of the child, not the welfare of Mr. Painter, not about the welfare of the Bannisters. In as much as Mark has already made an adjustment and sees the Bannisters as his parental figures in his psychological makeup, to me this is the most critical factor. . . ."

It was Dr. Hawks' opinion "the chances are very high (Mark) will go wrong if he is returned to his father." This is based on adoption studies which "establish that the majority of adoptions in children who are changed, from ages six to eight, will go bad, if they have had a prior history of instability, some history of prior movement. When I refer to instability I am referring to where there has been no attempt to establish a strong relationship." . . .

Mark has established a father-son relationship with Mr. Bannister, which he apparently had never had with his natural father. He is happy, well adjusted and progressing nicely in his development. We do not believe it is for Mark's best interest to take him out of this stable atmosphere in the face of warnings of dire consequences from an eminent child psychologist and send him to an uncertain future in his father's home. Regardless of our appreciation of the father's love for his child and his desire to have him with him, we do not believe we have the moral right to gamble with this child's future. He should be encouraged in every way possible to know his father. We are sure there are many ways in which Mr. Painter can enrich Mark's life.

For the reasons stated, we reverse the trial court and remand the case for judgment in accordance herewith.

ANNA FREUD, *PAINTER V. BANNISTER: POSTSCRIPT BY A PSYCHOANALYST*

7 The Writings of Anna Freud 247, 247-255 (1966-1970)

I can imagine plaintiff and defendants, father and grandparents of Mark, in spite of their tug of war, being sufficiently united in their concern for the child to seek expert advice concerning him instead of bringing the matter to the court. If the clinic to which they turned were the Hampstead one (or the Yale Child Study Center), the advice given would be based on psychoanalytic reasoning. The main difference between the legal and the clinical situation then would be that in the first instance the warring partners would have a solution imposed on them, while in the second instance they would be left free either to adopt or to reject the solution with which they are presented.

MARK'S PROBLEM

I do not think that we would find Mark's problem easier to handle than either the trial judge or Mr. Justice Stuart. . . . Mark was lucky enough to live in normal family circumstances until he was five. There is no reason to suspect that during these decisive years his father did not play the usual important role for him. This "normal" life came to an end only with the disastrous accident which, for reason of their deaths, deprived him of mother and sister and, for other reasons, soon thereafter deprived him of the presence of his father.

Disturbing as the accident was, it does not alter the fact that Mark grew up with parents of his own. We take it for granted that the sudden loss of mother and sibling coupled with the separation from his father, was deeply upsetting for him. There is no evidence to show how his relations with mother, father, and sister had developed, or how his personality had been shaped before the traumatic moment intervened. That he showed signs of maladjustment after the events, i.e., when he arrived at the grandparents, is not surprising, nor is this necessarily connected with mismanagement on the part of the father or other influences derived from the father's personality. Children frequently react with overt behavior problems to shocks, upsets, and disruptions in their lives, i.e., to events following which adults withdraw into a lengthy mourning process.

MARK'S PAST

In the absence of any other surviving member of the immediate family, the clinic would have to enlist the father's help for clarifying questions concerning Mark's past. We would want to know whether developmental progress was satisfactory or unsatisfactory until age five; whether Mark was in good affectionate contact with his mother, or his father, or with both; whether they considered him a clinging or an independent child; whether before losing his mother, he had reached the stage of obvious preference for her, accompanied by rivalry with and jealousy of his father; whether at this time he had impressed people as a manly or as an unmanly little boy; whether the parents considered him to be a "good" child, age adequately in control of his impulses, or whether they found him self-indulgent and difficult to manage. Data of this kind would give a clue whether or not the disruption of the family had caused him to undergo a change of personality.

Other relevant information concerning Mark would have to be elicited in the clinic's usual manner from the boy himself. The investigator would have to piece together in particular the residues of his infantile love life. What methods did Mark adopt to cope with his losses? Has he forgotten, denied, or repressed all memories of events before the accident? How far is the image of his dead mother still alive in his mind? Does it or does it not play an important role in his conscious fantasies or, perhaps inaccessible to consciousness, in his unconscious? To what extent has he transferred the feelings for his mother to his grandmother? If he has done so in an intense way, how would he react to a further separation, this time from her? Are there signs to be noted that he would be able to shift his affections, this time to a stepmother who is, so far, unknown to him? . . .

As regards Mark, we have no evidence so far to show what happened in his case. There is the contention that the boy's allegiance to his father has been transferred in its entirety to the grandfather. If this were proved to be true, inquiry would still be needed whether this shift was a wholly positive one or whether it was prompted, at least in part, by the boy's anger with the absent father, an anger which may well be smoldering under the surface and may burst out some time to the detriment of his development.

THE WARRING ADULTS

Since in the clinical situation both parties in the dispute have consulted us of their own free will, we can also count on their cooperation in investigating their own respective attitudes toward the child. . . .

With Mark's father and grandparents it is difficult to foresee the result of our investigations. In the father, there are signs of obvious, object-directed feelings for the child, alternating with periods of detachment, which may or may not be attributable to the man's immediate reaction to his tragic losses. On the other hand, there are also indications that, as a father, he is not disinclined to use his son selfishly, i.e., for his own aggrandizement as an author, a figure on TV, etc.

As for the grandparents, we are prepared to find that for them Mark represents the daughter whom they have lost and mourn. There is also the suspicion that in claiming Mark, they reclaim symbolically their daughter from the son-in-law, who from the start was unwelcome to them for many reasons. There also is little doubt that the grandparents love Mark himself, are attentive to his needs, and sacrifice for him some of the peace and quiet of their homelife to which every elderly couple is entitled.

The weight and truth of any of these pronouncements remain tentative until they are confirmed or disputed by probing interviews with the three adults in question.

LEGAL V. PSYCHOANALYTIC ASPECTS

Unlike the two courts, we are in the lucky position not to have to pronounce judgment. We merely formulate advice. When doing so, we disregard or minimize the importance of some of the facts which swayed the courts.

In disagreement with the trial judge, and in agreement with his expert, Dr. Hawks, we discount the importance of the "biological father" as such. The "blood ties" between parent and child as well as the alleged paternal and maternal "instincts" are biological concepts which, only too often, prove vague and unreliable when transferred to the field of psychology. Psychologically speaking, the child's "father" is the adult man to whom the child attaches a particular, psychologically distinctive set of feelings. When this type of emotional tie is disrupted, the child's feelings suffer. When such separations occur during phases of development in which the child is particularly vulnerable, the whole foundation of his personality may be shaken. The presence of or the reunion with a biological father to whom no such ties exist will not recompense the child for the loss which he has suffered. Conversely, the biological father's or mother's unselfish love for their child is by no means to be taken for granted. It happens often enough that biological parents fail in their duty to the child, while other adults who are less closely related to him, i.e., who have no "instinctive" basis for their feelings, successfully take over the parental role.

We place less emphasis than Mr. Justice Stuart on benefits such as a "stable, dependable background" with educational and professional opportunities. Important as such external advantages are, we have seen too often that they can be wasted unless they are accompanied by the internal emotional constellations which enable the children to profit from them. Children are known to thrive in socially and financially unstable situations if they are firmly attached to their parents, and to come to grief under the best social conditions when such emotional security is missing. . . .

FORMULATION OF ADVICE

It is not possible at this point to foretell whether, after investigation, our advice will be in line with the judgment of the trial court or with Mr. Justice Stuart. What can be promised is that it will be based not on external facts but on internal data. We shall advise that Mark had better stay with his grandparents provided that the following facts can be ascertained:

> that the transfer of his attachment from the parents to the grandparents is fairly complete and promises to be permanent during his childhood; i.e., that they have become the central figures toward whom his feelings are directed and around whom his emotional life revolves . . . that, given this new attachment, a further change is not advisable . . . ; that the grandparents, on their part, cherish Mark for his own sake, not only as a replacement for the daughter who was killed, nor as a pawn in the battle with their son-in-law.

Conversely, we shall advise that Mark had better be returned to his father if the following facts emerge:

> that Mr. Painter still retains his place as "father" in Mark's mind and that in spite of separation and new experiences the child's feelings and fantasies continue to revolve around him; that anger about the "desertion" (and perhaps blame for the mother's death) have not succeeded in turning this relationship into a predominantly hostile one; that the father cherishes Mark for his own sake; that it can be shown that Mr. Painter's using the child for publicity purposes was not due to lack of paternal consideration on his part but happened owing to the bitterness and resentment caused by the fight for possession of his son.

Provided that Mr. Painter, Mr. and Mrs. Bannister, and Mark would allow the clinic two or three weeks' time for investigation, I am confident that we should be able to guide them toward a potentially helpful solution of their difficult problem.

NOTES AND QUESTIONS

1. One way to conceptualize legal rules is in the form of a conditional imperative: If [fact *A*] + [fact *B*] exist, then *X* result follows. For example, If [goods are delivered to buyer] + [goods are retained by buyer] + [for an unreasonable time], then the goods have been accepted by the buyer. How does this concept of rules apply to the best-interest standard as it is employed in Painter v. Bannister?

2. The court in *Painter* notes the existence of a presumption favoring custody by a child's parents against all others. Who bore the burden of overcoming that presumption? What kind of factual showing did the court require to overcome the presumption? Did the court's use of the best-interest standard effectively eliminate the parental presumption? The *Bannister* court noted that the presumption of parental preference had been "weakened in the past several years." In 2000, however, in Troxel v. Granville, 530 U.S. 57 (2000), (see Chapter 12) the U.S. Supreme Court found the court-ordered grandparent visitation in accordance with a best-interest standard in that case to be an unconstitutional infringement of the mother's fundamental right to make decisions concerning the custody, care, and control of her child. Subsequent decisions have added real teeth to the presumption in favor of parents' custody and visitation preferences, and a number of courts require either a showing of parental unfitness or detriment to the child to overcome the presumption that parents will act in their children's best interests. If Painter v. Bannister were decided today, do you think the case would come out differently? Do you think constitutional protection is necessary to protect parents from the type of subjective judgments made in *Painter*? If you represented the Bannisters in an action today, is there additional evidence you would try to present? Would you characterize the existing evidence differently?

3. The *Painter* court treated the custody determination as a de novo proceeding although Mark had lived with his grandparents, with his father's consent, for almost two years when the action was filed. Had the grandparents secured a custody award when Mark initially moved in with them, in most states the father would have had to establish a substantial change in circumstances to justify a custody transfer, and that change would ordinarily need to involve Mark's or the grandparents' circumstances, rather than a change in the father's position. *See* C.R.B. v. C.C., 959 P.2d 375 (Alaska 1998) (the parental preference doctrine does not operate where a nonparent already has court-ordered custody of a child; as a result, a parent seeking to regain custody from a nonparent makes the same threshold showing of a substantial change in circumstances as is required where the suit is brought against a parent); In the Interest of Ferguson, 927 S.W.2d 766 (Tex. App. 1996) (presumption favoring parent does not apply where parent seeks modification of decree granting custody to nonparent). The characterization of the existing custody arrangement and the differing burdens of proof come up as

potential issues in most of the cases in this chapter. Consider whether you think the characterization changes the outcome of these cases.

4. Professor Freud observes that biological concepts often prove "vague and unreliable when transferred to the field of psychology." Vagueness is a matter of legal as well as psychological concern. Ordinarily, a statute will be declared void if persons "of common intelligence must necessarily guess as to its meaning and differ as to its application." Connally v. General Constr. Co., 269 U.S. 385, 391 (1926). How can the requirement of statutory definiteness be satisfied by the best-interest test? Is the answer to this a question of the meaning of the language in general or the meaning that has been given the language during the course of judicial application? See In the Matter of J. O. L., 409 A.2d 1073 (D.C. App. 1979).

5. Judgments regarding a child's best interests inevitably involve social scientific propositions. It is not surprising, therefore, that expert witnesses commonly play an important role in contested custody matters, as Dr. Hawks did in Painter v. Bannister. Their role is the subject of much controversy. Must the trier of fact give any weight to expert testimony? If one party produces expert evidence and the other does not, does it follow that the former will succeed? If not, why not? Could the grandparents have overcome a presumption in favor of the parent in a case like this without expert testimony?

6. Mark later chose to return to his father. Is this fact instructive in any way?

7. In considering these questions, the extent of our knowledge about child development and the decisions that will improve the child's circumstances is an issue of obvious importance. Consider the following summary of research concerning the adaptation of children to divorce.

JOAN G. WEXLER, *RETHINKING THE MODIFICATION OF CHILD CUSTODY DECREES*

94 Yale L.J. 757, 784-788 (1985)

In 1969, two prominent authorities, writing about the legislative reform of custodial adjudication, noted with concern that few empirical studies dealt with the effects of divorce and that those that did concentrated primarily on the consequences of divorce on parents rather than children. Although a number of pertinent variables still need to be studied, since 1970 there has been significant research done concerning the effects of divorce on children, and, in particular, concerning the process of divorce and the variables that contribute to a healthy adjustment to that process.

Recent social science research reveals that divorce is not a single stressful event confined to a certain moment, the date of the legal formality, but is instead a process that extends over time, beginning prior to the formal divorce with a state of family dissolution and ending some time after the divorce in some form of family reconstitution. In that process, the people involved learn to adapt and cope with their changed situations. To reach a new equilibrium, family members experiment along the way with a variety of coping mechanisms, some successful and some unsuccessful.

Several noteworthy research projects have focused on the post-divorce adjustment of children and their parents. Hetherington, Cox and Cox conducted a two-year longitudinal study of 48 white, middle-class, divorced families with preschool children and a carefully matched sample of intact families. The study examined responses to the crisis of divorce, including new patterns of family organization, and analyzed how the characteristics of family members and the differences in family structure contributed to the family members' responses to the divorce. Data were collected at intervals of two months, one year, and two years following the legal divorce.

The similar demographic characteristics of the families involved limits the significance of this study. It does, however, provide a thus far unique, in-depth analysis of divorcing families and an intact family control group over time. The study showed that families experience severe stress and disorganization during the first year following a formal divorce. Indeed, during that first year, family conflict escalates rather than declines. On almost every measure of parental behavior, divorced parents during the first twelve months after divorce were coping far less well than non-divorced parents. Divorced parents made fewer maturity demands on their children, were less consistent in their discipline, were less apt to reason with their children, communicated less well, and were less affectionate. The authors described a cycle of negative parent-child interaction, with the most notable effect on the mother-son relationship. Only after that first year of heightened tension did an increased sense of well-being begin to emerge. At the two-year follow-up, the most debilitating effects of the divorce on both parents and children had abated.

The other major longitudinal study of divorce and children, conducted by Wallerstein and Kelly, concerned the effectiveness of a divorce counseling service in Marin County, California; its subjects were families who had sought such assistance. Consequently, the families involved in this study not only had similar backgrounds but were also self-selected and therefore perhaps were not representative of all divorcing families. The study also lacked an intact family control group. Despite these methodological shortcomings, this research is evidently the only longitudinal study to assess the effects of divorce on children of different ages, is rich in qualitative data, and has been well received by social scientists.

The sample consisted of sixty divorced couples with 131 children who were between three and eighteen years old at the time of the marital separation. All family members were interviewed by a therapist during the six-week divorce counseling session. Although a divorce need not have occurred prior to this session, the parents had to have separated and legal proceedings had to have begun. Family members were interviewed again twelve to eighteen months later, and once again five years later. This five-year perspective enabled the researchers to distinguish several stages in the divorce process and to report on the experiences of the children and the adults during each of these periods.

Like the subjects in the study by Hetherington, Cox and Cox, the children in the Wallerstein and Kelly study took some time to adjust to their new situation. For example, at the first follow-up, nearly half of the pre-school group, over one-third of the 7- and 8-year-olds, and half of the 9- and 10-year-olds, either still displayed the dysfunctional behaviors observed in the initial interviews or were in even more deteriorated psychological conditions.

Eighteen months after separation, the "average" mother and father were still in transition, struggling with the process of adapting to a new environment and status. Particularly for the woman, life had not yet stabilized; close to half of the women were depressed to some considerable degree. A number of both men and women continued to rage at their former partners, seemingly unaffected by the passage of time. Substantiating the findings of Hetherington and her associates, Wallerstein and Kelly concluded that the stresses during the beginnings of a post-divorce relationship with the child were extraordinary, contributing particularly to a strain on the custodial parent's capacity to parent. On the other hand, at the second follow-up, almost five years after separation, most families had achieved overall stability.

Other researchers have corroborated and commented upon the importance of the time factor in parental adjustment to divorce. An intimate relationship between two individuals is not easily severed. The intensity of the emotional attachment, which may include aspects of concern and friendship as well as anger, revenge, pain, guilt, and distrust, has been found to diminish with time as an individual learns to separate his or her identity from that of the former spouse. Moreover, the adjustment of the children is linked to that of the custodial parent. One study found that the children's post-divorce social adjustment greatly depended upon the custodial parent's ability to achieve and maintain his or her own emotional and social adjustment.

It would seem, then, that custody controversies often represent the playing out, for a significant period of time after the formal divorce, of chronic, unresolved, and acrimonious marital problems. Many custody controversies during the transitional period prior to recovery from the divorce would seem to be no more than a reflection of the lack of adjustment to the psychological trauma of divorce.

Studies of the adjustment of children after divorce, some of which are cited by Dean Wexler, include Paul R. Amato and Alan Booth, A Generation at Risk: Growing Up in an Era of Family Upheaval (1997); Sara McLanahan and Gary Sandefur, Growing Up with a Single Parent: What Hurts, What Helps (1994); Christy S. Buchanan et al., Caught Between Parents: Adolescents' Experience in Divorced Homes, 62 Child Dev. 108 (1991); Judith S. Wallerstein & Sandra Blakeslee, Second Chances: Men, Women, and Children a Decade After Divorce (1989); Judith S. Wallerstein & Joan B. Kelly, Surviving the Breakup: How Children and Parents Cope with Divorce (1980); E. Mavis Hetherington et al., The Aftermath of Divorce, in Mother/Child, Father/Child Relationships 149 (Joseph H. Stevens, Jr. & Marilyn Mathews eds., 1978); E. Mavis Hetherington et al., The Development of Children in Mother-Headed Families, in The American Family: Dying or Developing 117 (Howard Hoffman & David Reiss eds., 1978).

2. The Primary Caretaker

Entirely predictably, courts faced with the dilemma between regimes of rules and standards have sought a middle ground through the use of what might be called intermediate rules. The following materials present one of the most important bases for decision making in custody cases. Does it solve the problems created by intermediate standards such as "the child's best interests"?

BURCHARD V. GARAY

42 Cal. 3d 531; 724 P.2d 486 (1986)

BROUSSARD, J. This case concerns the custody of William Garay, Jr., age two and one-half at the date of trial. Ana Burchard, his mother, appeals from an order of the superior court awarding custody to the father, William Garay.

As a result of a brief liaison between Ana and William, Ana became pregnant. Early in her term she told William that she was pregnant with his child, but he refused to believe that he was the father. William, Jr., was born on September 18, 1979.

After the birth, Ana undertook the difficult task of caring for her child, with the help of her father and others, while working at two jobs and continuing her training to become a registered nurse. William continued to deny paternity, and did not visit the child or provide any support.

In the spring of 1980 Ana brought a paternity and support action. After court-ordered blood tests established that William was the father, he stipulated to paternity and to support in the amount of $200 a month. Judgment entered accordingly on November 24, 1980. In December of that year William visited his son for the first time. In the next month he moved in with Ana and the child in an attempt to live together as a family; the attempt failed and six weeks later he moved out.

William asked for visitation rights; Ana refused and filed a petition for exclusive custody. William responded, seeking exclusive custody himself. The parties then stipulated that pending the hearing Ana would retain custody, with William having a right to two full days of visitation each week.

At the onset of the hearing Ana requested a ruling that William must prove changed circumstances to justify a change in custody. William opposed the motion, arguing that the court need only determine which award would promote the best interests of the child. The court deferred ruling on the motion. The evidence at the hearing disclosed that William, Jr., was well adjusted, very healthy, well mannered, good natured, and that each parent could be expected to provide him with adequate care.

. . . Applying the "best interests" test, [the court] awarded custody to William. Its decision appears to be based upon three considerations. The first is that William is financially better off — he has greater job stability, owns his own home, and is "better equipped economically . . . to give constant care to the minor child and cope with his continuing needs." The second is that William has remarried, and he "and the stepmother can provide constant care for the minor child and keep him on a regular schedule without resorting to other caretakers"; Ana, on the other hand, must rely upon babysitters and day care centers while she works and studies. Finally, the court referred to William providing the mother with visitation, an indirect reference to Ana's unwillingness to permit William visitation. . . .

. . . [A]lthough we conclude that the trial court correctly ruled that the case was governed by the best-interest standard, we find that it erred in applying that standard. The court's reliance upon the relative economic position of the parties is impermissible; the purpose of child support awards is to ensure that the spouse otherwise best fit for custody receives adequate funds for the support of the child. Its reliance upon the asserted superiority of William's child care arrangement suggests an insensitivity to the role of working parents. And all of the factors cited by the trial court together weigh less to our mind than a matter it did not discuss — the importance of continuity and stability in custody arrangements. We therefore reverse the order of the trial court. . . .

The trial court's decision referred to William's better economic position, and to matters such as homeownership and ability to provide a more "wholesome environment," which reflect economic advantage. But comparative income or economic advantage is not a permissible basis for a custody award. "[There] is no basis for assuming a correlation between wealth and good parenting or wealth and happiness." (Klaff, The Tender Years Doctrine: A Defense (1982) 70 Cal. L. Rev. 335, 350. . . .) If in fact the custodial parent's income is insufficient to provide proper care for the child, the remedy is to award child support, not to take away custody.

The court also referred to the fact that Ana worked and had to place the child in day care, while William's new wife could care for the child in their home. But in an era when over 50 percent of mothers and almost 80 percent of divorced mothers work, the courts must not presume that a working mother is a less satisfactory parent or less fully committed to the care of her child. A custody determination must be based upon a true assessment of the emotional bonds between parent and child, upon an inquiry into "the heart of the parent-child relationship . . . the ethical, emotional, and intellectual guidance the parent gives to the child throughout his formative years, and often beyond." (In re Marriage of Carney, supra, 24 Cal. 3d 725, 739.) It must reflect also a factual determination of how best to provide continuity of attention, nurturing, and care. It cannot be based on an assumption, unsupported by scientific evidence, that a working mother cannot provide such care — an assumption particularly unfair when, as here, the mother has in fact been the primary caregiver.

Any actual deficiency in care, whether due to the parent's work or any other cause, would of course be a proper consideration in deciding custody. But the evidence of such deficiencies in the present case is very weak — the testimony of William, disputed by Ana, that on one occasion Ana left the child alone briefly while she cashed a support check, and that sometimes the child was delivered for visitation in clothes that were shabby or too small. But these matters are trivial. The essence of the court's decision is simply that care by a mother who, because of work and study, must entrust the child to daycare centers and babysitters, is per se inferior to care by a father who also works, but can leave the child with a stepmother at home. For the reasons we have explained, this reasoning is not a suitable basis for a custody order.

The trial court recited other grounds for its order. One was that William was "better equipped psychologically" to care for the child. Ana has had emotional problems in the past, and reacted bitterly to the separation, but William's conduct has not been a model of emotional maturity. After they separated, Ana objected to William seeing the child and did not communicate about matters involving the child. But after William obtained custody pursuant to the trial court's order, he proved equally obdurate to Ana's visitation rights, leading the court to amend its order to spell out those rights.

All of these grounds, however, are insignificant compared to the fact that Ana has been the primary caretaker for the child from birth to the date of the trial court hearing, that no serious deficiency in her care has been proven, and that William, Jr., under her care, has become a happy, healthy, well-adjusted child. We have frequently stressed, in this opinion and others, the importance of stability and continuity in the life of a child, and the harm that may result from disruption of established patterns of care and emotional bonds. The showing made in this case is, we believe, wholly insufficient to justify taking the custody of a child from the mother who has raised him from birth, successfully coping with the many difficulties encountered by single working mothers. We conclude that the trial court abused its discretion in granting custody to William, Sr., and that its order must be reversed.

We acknowledge the anomalous position of an appellate court, especially a supreme court, in child custody appeals. Over four years have passed since the trial court awarded custody to William. Our decision reversing that order returns the case to the trial court which, in deciding the child's future custody, must hold a new hearing and determine what arrangement is in the best interests of the child as of the date of that hearing. Thus, the effect of our decision is not to determine finally the custody of William, Jr., but is to relieve Ana of the adverse findings of the trial court and of the burden of proving changed circumstances since the trial court order, and to make clear that in deciding the issue of custody the court cannot base its decision upon the relative economic position of the parties or upon any assumption that the care afforded a child by single, working parents is inferior.

The order is reversed.

BIRD, C.J., concurring. I write separately to underscore that the trial court's ruling was an abuse of discretion not only in its failure to give due weight to the importance of continuity and stability in custody arrangements but in its assumption that there is a negative relation between a woman's lack of wealth or her need or desire to work and the quality of her parenting. As this case so aptly demonstrates, outmoded notions such as these result in harsh judgments which unfairly penalize working mothers. . . .

Read in light of the record, the court's findings amount to "outmoded notions of a woman's rule being near hearth and home." In an era where over 50 percent of mothers and almost 80 percent of divorced mothers work, this stereotypical thinking cannot be sanctioned. When it is no longer the norm for children to have a mother at home all day, courts cannot indulge the notion that a working parent is ipso facto a less satisfactory parent. Such reasoning distracts attention from the real issues in a custody dispute and leads to arbitrary results. . . .

Stability, continuity, and a loving relationship are the most important criteria for determining the best interests of the child. Implicit in this premise is the recognition that existing emotional bonds between parent and child are the first consideration in any best-interests determination. . . .

. . . [T]here is no accepted body of expert opinion that maternal employment per se has a detrimental effect on a child. On the contrary, one recent study on maternal employment and child development has concluded that "[maternal] employment status had no negative relation to children's development over a 5-year period. . . . Thus, the trial court's presumption lacks any expert support. . . .

Yet, under the trial court's rationale, it is the mother — and not the father — who would be penalized for working out of the home. She and she alone would be placed in this Catch-22 situation. If she did not work, she could not possibly hope to compete with the father in providing material advantages for the child. She would risk losing custody to a father who could provide a larger home, a better neighborhood, or other material goods and benefits.

If she did work, she would face the prejudicial view that a working mother is by definition inadequate, dissatisfied with her role, or more concerned with her own needs than with those of her child. This view rests on outmoded notions of a woman's role in our society. Again, this presumption is seldom, if ever, applied even-handedly to fathers. The result — no one would take an unbiased look at the amount and quality of parental attention which the child was receiving from each parent.[1]

The double standard appears again when, as here, the father is permitted to rely on the care which someone else will give to the child. It is not uncommon for courts to award custody to a father when care will actually be provided by a relative, second wife, or even a babysitter. However, the implicit assumption that such care is the equivalent of that which a nonworking mother would provide "comes dangerously close to implying that mothers are fungible — that one woman will do just as well as another in rearing any particular children." This is scarcely consistent with any enlightened ideas of childrearing. . . .

NOTES AND QUESTIONS

1. The California Supreme Court in *Burchard* agreed with the trial court that the award to William was an initial custody determination to be determined in

---

1. *See also* In re Marriage of Estelle (Mo. App. 1979) 592 S.W.2d 277, in which the court affirmed a custody award to a working father, not remarried, as against an equally fit working mother. The reviewing court made no negative comments about the child's placement in day care, but rather emphasized that the father often prepared the child's breakfast and dinner and picked her up from the day care center himself. *Id.*, at p.278. It is difficult to imagine a mother's performance of these chores even attracting notice, much less commendable comment. . . .

See also Masek v. Masek (1975) 89 S.D. 62 [228 N.W.2d 334], in which a mother who taught music part-time lost custody to a father who worked full-time. The trial court noted that the mother slept until 9 a.m. on Saturdays, failed to prepare breakfast for her husband, who left for work at 7 a.m., and on occasion had run out of jam and cookies. It concluded from these facts that she was unfit for custody because her "primary interests are in her musical career and outside of the house and family."

accordance with a best-interest standard. Ana had argued that the court should treat the parties' earlier stipulation giving her custody as a court order, and William's subsequent request for custody as a motion to modify subject to a changed-circumstances standard.

2. What role does gender play in determining children's interests? Historically, courts recognized a maternal preference and presumed that children of "tender years" would be better off with their mothers. Many courts have declared such presumptions unconstitutional. *See, e.g.*, Pusey v. Pusey, 728 P.2 117 (Utah 1986). The "maternal preference and tender years" presumption, however, has not completely disappeared. South Carolina continues to allow the doctrine to be employed as a tie breaker, Woodall v. Woodall, 471 S.E.2d 154 (S.C. 1996), and a Florida court has held that abandonment of the doctrine does not make emotional ties between parent and child due to the child's age or sex irrelevant. Cherradi v. LaVoie, 662 So. 2d 751 (Fla. Dist. Ct. App. 1995).

3. Burchard v. Garay looks to the primary caretaker as the preferred custodian. Is that more than a socially acceptable strategy for reaching the same result produced by the maternal preference? Is the appropriate solution to replace notions of "mothers" and "fathers" with that of "parents"? For an analysis of the implications of gender neutralization, *see* Martha A. Fineman, The Neutered Mother, 46 Miami L. Rev. 653 (1992). *See also* Martha A. Fineman, The Neutered Mother, the Sexual Family, and Other Twentieth Century Tragedies Part 2 (1995); Carol Sanger, Separating from Children, 96 Colo. L. Rev. 375 (1996). For a discussion of the continuing role of "essentialist" assumptions about the capacities of women and men, *see* Mary Becker, Maternal Feelings: Myth, Taboo, and Child Custody, 1 Rev. L. & Women's Stud. 133 (1992).

4. How do societal expectations influence custody awards in an era of gender-neutral standards? Eleanor Maccoby and Robert Mnookin undertook a study of custodial arrangements in California including some 1100 families who filed for divorce in two counties between September 1984 and April 1985. Dividing the Child (1992). Maccoby and Mnookin were particularly interested in the success of a statutory scheme that went "beyond a formal insistence on gender neutrality" by enacting statutes designed to encourage continuing relations between children and both parents. *Id.* at 8. An emphasis on joint physical custody was one of those strategies, taking as its goal the gender neutralization of post-divorce custodial arrangements.

Maccoby and Mnookin found that, when interviewed shortly after separation, mothers almost universally wanted sole physical custody. They also found that a "surprisingly high" proportion of fathers wanted either sole or joint physical custody. However, while mothers almost uniformly followed their initial preferences with a formal petition for sole custody, fathers more often abandoned their stated preferences and requested a lesser custodial interest at the time of the divorce decree.

In the result, mothers had sole custody in 70 percent of the divorces studied. Approximately 10 percent of the divorces resulted in sole paternal custody, and 20 percent in joint physical custody. The authors found it difficult to explain the inconsistency between the legal context described above and the frequency of maternal custody and an even greater frequency of arrangements requiring only fathers to pay child support.

Maccoby and Mnookin conclude that "despite some revolutionary changes in the law to eliminate gender stereotypes and to encourage greater gender equity, the characteristic roles of mothers and fathers remain fundamentally different." *Id.* at 271. They also conclude that, while they expected that divorce bargaining would be substantially affected by the California legal regime, "much divorce decisionmaking takes place outside the law's shadow."

After reading Burchard v. Garay, could you interpret these data to be consistent with California policy regarding divorce and with the theory that decision making in divorce cases is significantly affected by the legal context in which bargaining takes place? *See* Lee E. Teitelbaum, Divorce, Custody, Gender, and the Limits of Law: On Dividing the Child, 92 Mich. L. Rev. 1808, 1834-1838 (1994).

If women are indeed far more likely to be primary caretakers than are men, would that circumstance create equal protection problems?

5. Burchard v. Garay indicates that placement of a child with his or her primary caretaker will serve the "best interests of the child," psychologically understood. Is this the only rationale for such placements, or might they be justified as a way of recognizing the investment of one parent in the rearing of the child? *See* David L. Chambers, Rethinking the Substantive Rules for Custody Disputes in Divorce, 83 Mich. L. Rev. 477 (1984).

AMERICAN LAW INSTITUTE, *PRINCIPLES OF THE LAW OF FAMILY DISSOLUTION § 2.08* (2002)

§ 2.08 Allocation of Custodial Responsibility

(1) Unless otherwise resolved by agreement of the parents . . . , the court should allocate custodial responsibility so that the proportion of custodial time the child spends with each parent approximates the proportion of time each parent spent performing caretaking functions for the child prior to the parents' separation . . . except to the extent required under § 2.11 [where there is credible evidence of abandonment, domestic abuse, or other serious misconduct by a parent] or necessary to achieve one or more of the following objectives:

(a) to permit the child to have a relationship with each parent which, in the case of a legal parent or a parent by estoppel who has performed a reasonable share of parenting functions, should be not less than a presumptive amount of custodial time set by a uniform rule of statewide application;

(b) to accommodate the firm and reasonable preferences of a child who has reached a specific age, set by a uniform rule of statewide application;

(c) to keep siblings together when the court finds that doing so is necessary to their welfare;

(d) to protect the child's welfare when the presumptive allocation under this section would harm the child because of a gross disparity in the quality of the emotional attachment between each parent and the child or in each parent's demonstrated ability or availability to meet the child's needs;

(e) to take into account any prior agreement . . . ;

(f) to avoid an allocation of custodial responsibility that would be extremely impractical or that would interfere substantially with the child's need for stability . . . ;

(g) [to deal with a parent's proposed relocation] . . . ;

(h) to avoid substantial and almost certain harm to the child.

NOTES AND QUESTIONS

1. In identifying the "primary caretaker," courts look to various factors. One list of relevant considerations appears in Garska v. McCoy, 278 S.E.2d 357, 363 (W. Va. 1981):

> While it is difficult to enumerate all of the factors which will contribute to a conclusion that one or the other parent was the primary caretaker parent, nonetheless, there are certain obvious criteria to which a court must initially look . . . : (1) preparing and planning of meals; (2) bathing, grooming and dressing; (3) purchasing, cleaning, and care of clothes; (4) medical care, including nursing and trips to physicians; (5) arranging for social interaction among peers after school, i.e., transporting to friends' houses or, for example, to girl or boy scout meetings; (6) arranging alternative care, i.e., babysitting, daycare, etc.; (7) putting child to bed at night, attending to child in the middle of the night, waking child in the morning; (8) disciplining, i.e., teaching general manners and toilet training; (9) educating, i.e., religious, cultural, social, etc.; and (10) teaching elementary skills, i.e., reading, writing, and arithmetic.

West Virginia became the first state to adopt a version of the American Law Institute (ALI) draft provision on custodial responsibility. W. Va. Code § 48-11-201 (1999). To what extent do the ALI Principles change the approach in Garska v. McCoy? How does § 2.08 seek to reconcile those interests, and is it likely to be more or less successful than the approach in *Garska*?

2. How does one measure the past caretaking functions that form the basis for post-divorce custodial responsibility under the ALI Principles? Section 2.03(6) of the Principles defines caretaking functions as tasks involving "interaction with the child or direct[ing] the interaction and care provided by others." Those functions resemble the functions described in Garska v. McCoy, and include feeding, bedtime and wake-up routines, care of the child when sick or hurt, bathing, grooming, personal hygiene, educational activities, disciplinary and training activities, arrangements for and communication with schools and teachers, moral guidance, and arrangement of alternative care. Caretaking functions are distinguished from "parental functions," which include provision of economic support, decision-making regarding the child's welfare, maintenance of the family home, financial planning, and "other functions . . . that are important to the child's welfare, and development."

The allocation described in the Principles takes only caretaking, and not parental, functions into account. Only time spent on caretaking activities is relevant; the degree of initiative or investment is not ordinarily to be considered.

Where the parents' time commitments to caretaking have changed over time, the Comment indicates that the longer (rather than the more recent) arrangement should be given priority on the ground that a different result would inadequately recognize the caretaking functions likely to have been most significant to the child and would provide an incentive for strategic behavior in anticipation of divorce. A substantial change that had endured for some time, however, should be given precedence.

PROBLEMS

1. Bryan and Shannan were married and had two young children. After the birth of their youngest child, Shannan became depressed and began taking medication and drinking heavily. Shannan entered a rehabilitation program and remained there for five and a half months. After four years of marriage, while Shannon was still in the rehabilitation program, Bryan filed for dissolution of the marriage. The trial court awarded Bryan sole physical custody. Five months later, Shannan asked for and received alternating weekend and holiday visitation.

A year after the initial custody award, Shannan moved to modify the custody award to grant her physical custody. Because Bryan worked long hours, the children were spending many hours with day care providers and Bryan's parents. Shannan had remarried and had another child. She was a full-time homemaker who could care for the children in her home during the day, and she argued that being with her would be in the child's best interests.

The trial court found that Shannan's recovery efforts had been successful and that she had been sober for more than a year. The judge ruled that it would be in the children's best interests to live with Shannan, since she could provide personal care for them. Bryan was granted visitation.

Bryan appeals, citing Burchard v. Garay. What arguments should the parties make?

2. This custody dispute involves the mother, Jennifer, and the child's unmarried father, Steve. Jennifer gave birth to her daughter in 1993, when she was 15 years of age and a sophomore in high school. Steve was three months older, and also in school. He acknowledged paternity immediately and now seeks sole custody.

Jennifer initially considered terminating her pregnancy, but ultimately decided to have the child and to raise her in her mother's house. Both parties are still in school. Jennifer has been the custodial parent during the child's life. The evidence indicates that, due to Jennifer's immaturity, the maternal grandmother and Jennifer's sister have raised the child virtually from its infancy. They have supplied almost all of the child's necessities, since neither parent has the earning capacity to provide support.

Jennifer is intelligent and has received a scholarship from the University of Michigan. She plans to live in resident housing during the period required for a bachelor's and, perhaps, a master's degree. She contemplates living at the university and placing the child in appropriate day care or schooling and in off-school times would return to her mother's home.

Steve resides with his parents and, in the early days, exercised visitation with his mother participating in caring for the child. He has a good relationship with his daughter. He is currently a student at the local community college and maintains part-time employment. Steve's mother is not employed outside the home and would welcome the opportunity to spend her entire time in raising the child when the father is at school or work. She is in good health and is 39 years old. What custodial order should be entered?

3. Marie and James are divorcing after a 20-year marriage. They have three minor children, ages 14, 13, and eight. For the last 17 years, James worked as a public school teacher and Marie stayed at home with the children. Three years before their separation, the youngest child began attending kindergarten and Marie began a nine-month course in computing at a local community college. This training led to her employment as a computer programmer in a bank. Her education and employment have occupied much of Marie's time, and James has assumed responsibility for after-school caretaking of their children. Marie and James agree that the children should have one primary home, and each wants primary custody. How should custody be allocated under the primary caretaker presumption and under the ALI Principles?

3. Joint Custody

We have already considered a number of areas of substantial change in family law doctrine and procedure. The grounds for divorce, the theory of alimony, the principles of property distribution at divorce, and the process for dissolving families have all changed dramatically over the last several decades. The shift from recognition of a sole parent with decision-making power to encouragement of the continuing involvement of both parents in the child's life may also be counted as a significant development.

Currently, the justifications for most custodial rules reflect empirical claims. The maternal preference initially proceeded not from a natural right but from a judicial belief that mothers were, for social or other reasons, better suited than fathers to care for children. Today, joint custody similarly follows from a deep conviction that children benefit from continuing contact with both parents. It is reasonable to wonder about the bases for these claims about how the world works.

Until relatively recently, courts generally agreed that all children of a family should be placed with a single custodial parent. Joint custody arrangements were disfavored or simply rejected on a number of grounds, including the notion that a single parent with primary responsibility provided consistency in discipline and moral education. Joint legal custody also seemed to threaten a continuation of the spousal conflict leading to divorce — a conflict that would now directly involve the children. Rejection of joint custodial arrangements was so general that Professor Clark's 1968 hornbook on domestic relations does not even mention joint custody. Homer H. Clark, Jr., The Law of Domestic Relations ch. 17 (1968).

Over the last 30 years, however, attitudes and legal rules concerning joint custody have changed. Current interest in joint custody is driven by the perception that custody disputes are acrimonious and harmful to children and that placement of custody with one parent tends to continue that acrimony, to alienate the noncustodial parent from (typically) his children, and to create continuously contentious relations between the divorced parents. As we will see, some states now articulate a preference for joint custody, and most permit it in appropriate cases. The most contentious remaining issue is not whether joint custody should be allowed, but when, and to what extent the courts use it to avoid having to choose between two otherwise fit parents.

TAYLOR V. TAYLOR

508 A.2d 964 (Md. 1986)

MCAULIFFE, J. The parties to this appeal are Judith Ann Taylor (Appellant) and Neil Randall Taylor, III (Appellee). The Taylors were married on November 26, 1977, and are the parents of Christina Lee Taylor, born April 9, 1979, and Neil Randall Taylor, IV, born August 5, 1980.

During the summer of 1982, the Taylors began experiencing marital difficulties and on September 10, 1982, they separated. Appellant left the marital home in Elkton, and took up residence with her parents in nearby Newark, Delaware. The children continued to reside in the marital home. On September 29, Appellee filed a Bill of Complaint in the Circuit Court for Cecil County seeking an absolute divorce and temporary and permanent custody of the children. Appellant filed an answer on November 3 in which she requested custody of the children pendente lite and permanently.[2]

On November 24 a "visitation schedule," signed only by counsel, was filed, detailing an apparent agreement between the parties, and specifying the days and times that each party would have the children.[3]

On December 7, Judge Donaldson Cole entered a pendente lite order granting the parties "joint custody" of the children "in consideration of the agreement of the parties." The order further provided that the children were to reside with Appellee in the family home, and incorporated by reference the visitation schedule previously filed.

On April 7, 1983, Appellant changed attorneys. Five days later she filed an amended and supplemental answer in which she requested that the order of December 7, 1982, be stricken, and that she be awarded care and custody of the children. . . . [F]ollowing a five day trial Judge H. Kenneth Mackey granted Appellee's request for an absolute divorce, and ordered continuation of the arrangement spelled out in the "visitation agreement," which he characterized as

---

2. Appellant's answer recited that at the time of separation the parties agreed the children would reside with Appellee in the marital home and Appellant would be free to be with the children on a daily basis, both in and out of the home. Appellant contended, however, that subsequent to that time it became apparent that Appellee was unable to cope with the responsibility of caring for the children, and additionally he would not allow Appellant to have the children with her in her mother's home.

3. The schedule provided that the children would be with Appellant each weekday morning, all day and overnight on each Tuesday, and on alternate weekends.

"a sort of joint custody." . . . We granted certiorari to consider the following two questions:

1) Whether a trial judge in Maryland has the authority to grant joint custody; and

2) Whether, if the trial judge did have the authority to grant such an award, he abused his discretion under the facts of this case.

I. DEFINITION OF JOINT CUSTODY

. . . The inability of courts and commentators to agree on what is meant by the term "joint custody" makes difficult the task of distilling principles and guidelines from a rapidly growing body of literature and case law. What one writer sees as an amorphous concept another sees as a structured legal arrangement. While it is clear that both parents in a joint custody arrangement function as "custodians" in the sense that they are actually involved in the overall welfare of their child, a distinction must be made between sharing parental responsibility in major decision-making matters and sharing responsibility for providing a home for the child.

Embraced within the meaning of "custody" are the concepts of "legal" and "physical" custody. Legal custody carries with it the right and obligation to make long range decisions involving education, religious training, discipline, medical care, and other matters of major significance concerning the child's life and welfare. Joint legal custody means that both parents have an equal voice in making those decisions, and neither parent's rights are superior to the other.[4]

Physical custody, on the other hand, means the right and obligation to provide a home for the child and to make the day-to-day decisions required during the time the child is actually with the parent having such custody. Joint physical custody is in reality "shared" or "divided" custody. Shared physical custody may, but need not, be on a 50/50 basis, and in fact most commonly will involve custody by one parent during the school year and by the other during summer vacation months, or division between weekdays and weekends or between days and nights.

With respect to physical custody, there is no difference between the rights and obligations of a parent having temporary custody of a child pursuant to an

---

4. The parent not granted legal custody will, under ordinary circumstances, retain authority to make necessary day-to-day decisions concerning the child's welfare during the time the child is in that parent's physical custody. Thus, a parent exercising physical custody over a child, whether pursuant to an order of visitation or to an order of shared physical custody, necessarily possesses the authority to control and discipline the child during the period of physical custody. Similarly, that parent has the authority to consent to emergency surgery or emergency major medical care when there is insufficient time to contact the parent having legal custody. We need not here consider the issues that may arise when the parent having legal custody cannot agree with the parent exercising physical custody concerning emergency medical care. This residuum of authority should be exercised so as not to conflict with the long-range decisions and policies made by the parent having legal custody.

order of shared physical custody, and one having temporary custody pursuant to an award of visitation. Thus, a determination to grant legal custody to one parent and to allocate physical custody between the parents may be accomplished either by granting sole custody to one parent and specified rights of visitation to the other, or by granting legal custody to one parent and specified periods of physical custody to each parent. In either instance the effect will be the same. . . .

II. AUTHORITY TO AWARD JOINT CUSTODY

Appellant argues that "[t]here is no express statutory authority for an award of joint custody in Maryland" and that in the absence of such authority a court of equity lacks jurisdiction to grant joint custody. . . . [W]e hold the authority to grant joint custody is an integral part of the broad and inherent authority of a court exercising its equitable powers to determine child custody. . . .

III. JOINT CUSTODY CONSIDERATIONS

This Court last considered the issue of joint custody in McCann v. McCann, 167 Md. 167, 172, 173 A.7 (1934), in which our predecessors denounced joint control of a child as an arrangement "to be avoided, whenever possible, as an evil fruitful in the destruction of discipline, in the creation of distrust, and in the production of mental distress in the child." Significant societal changes that have occurred over the ensuing half century mandate our re-examination of those views.

Proponents of joint custody point out that it offers an opportunity for a child to enjoy a meaningful relationship with both parents, and may diminish the traumatic effects upon the child that can result from a dissolution of the marriage. While sole custody may reduce the noncustodial parent to the second class status of a visitor, joint custody allows both parties to function as, and be perceived as, parents. The sharing of the burdens as well as the joys of childrearing may be particularly helpful in the many instances where both parents are employed. Where joint custody has been appropriate, benefits have accrued not only to the child, but to parents as well.

The principal criticism leveled at joint custody is that it creates confusion and instability for children at the very time they need a sense of certainty and finality in their lives. Additionally, it is said to present too great an opportunity for manipulation of the parents by the child. Critics also contend that the option of joint custody creates too great a temptation to the trial judge to avoid choosing one parent and disappointing the other by simply awarding custody to both. Certainly, joint custody is not appropriate in every case. Indeed, it has been suggested that it is appropriate only in a small minority of cases. But when appropriate, joint custody can result in substantial advantages to children and parents alike, and the feasibility of such an arrangement is certainly worthy of careful consideration. . . .

. . . The availability of joint custody, in any of its multiple forms, is but another option available to the trial judge. Thus, the factors that trial judges ordinarily consider in child custody cases remain relevant. The following discussion of factors particularly relevant to a consideration of joint custody is in no way intended to minimize the importance of considering all factors and all options before arriving at a decision.

Capacity of the Parents to Communicate and to Reach Shared Decisions Affecting the Child's Welfare. This is clearly the most important factor in the determination of whether an award of joint legal custody is appropriate, and is relevant as well to a consideration of shared physical custody. Rarely, if ever, should joint legal custody be awarded in the absence of a record of mature conduct on the part of the parents evidencing an ability to effectively communicate with each other concerning the best interest of the child, and then only when it is possible to make a finding of a strong potential for such conduct in the future.

With few exceptions, courts and commentators agree that joint custody is a viable option only for parents who are able and willing to cooperate with one another in making decisions for their child.

When the evidence discloses severely embittered parents and a relationship marked by dispute, acrimony, and a failure of rational communication, there is nothing to be gained and much to be lost by conditioning the making of decisions affecting the child's welfare upon the mutual agreement of the parties. Even in the absence of bitterness or inability to communicate, if the evidence discloses the parents do not share parenting values, and each insists on adhering to irreconcilable theories of child-rearing, joint legal custody is not appropriate. The parents need not agree on every aspect of parenting but their views should not be so widely divergent or so inflexibly maintained as to forecast the probability of continuing disagreement on important matters. . . .

Ordinarily the best evidence of compatibility with this criterion will be the past conduct or "track record" of the parties. We recognize, however, that the tensions of separation and litigation will sometimes produce bitterness and lack of ability to cooperate or agree. The trial judge will have to evaluate whether this is a temporary condition, very likely to abate upon resolution of the issues, or whether it is more permanent in nature. Only where the evidence is strong in support of a finding of the existence of a significant potential for compliance with this criterion should joint legal custody be granted. Blind hope that a joint custody agreement will succeed, or that forcing the responsibility of joint decision-making upon the warring parents will bring peace, is not acceptable. In the unusual case where the trial judge concludes that joint legal custody is appropriate notwithstanding the absence of a "track record" of willingness and ability on the part of the parents to cooperate in making decisions dealing with the child's welfare, the trial judge must articulate fully the reasons that support that conclusion.

Willingness of Parents to Share Custody. Generally, the parents should be willing to undertake joint custody or it should not be ordered. We are asked by Appellant, and by the Women's Legal Defense Fund as amicus curiae, to hold that a trial judge may never order joint legal custody over the objection of one parent. They argue, with some force, that unwillingness on the part of one parent to share custody inevitably presages intransigence or inability to cooperate in making decisions affecting the welfare of the child. While we agree that the absence of an express willingness on the part of the parents to accept a joint custody arrangement is a strong indicator that joint legal custody is contraindicated, we are unwilling to fashion a hard and fast rule that would have the effect of granting to either parent veto power over the possibility of a joint custody award. . . . On the other hand, joint custody may be inappropriate when opposed by the child, or when there are indications that the psychological or emotional needs of the child would suffer under a joint custody arrangement.

Preference of Child. The reasonable preference of a child of suitable age and discretion should be considered. In addition to being sensitive to the possible presence of the "lollipop" or "rescue" syndromes, the trial judge must also recognize that children often experience a strong desire to see separated parents reunited, and this motivation may produce an unrealistic preference for joint custody.

Potential Disruption of Child's Social and School Life. Joint physical custody may seriously disrupt the social and school life of a child when each parent has the child for half the year, and the homes are not in close proximity to one another. . . . However, distance is not a bar, and when the distance between homes is great, a joint custody arrangement may offer the only practical way to preserve to the child a meaningful relationship with each parent. Depending upon the age and emotional maturity of the child, similarity of the respective home environments may be desired, or exposure to dissimilar environments, cultures and opportunities for learning may be indicated.

Demands of Parental Employment. In some situations, joint physical custody will be appropriate only if the work hours of the parents are different, or there is flexibility in the demands of the employment of each.

Age and Number of Children. The factor of age obviously interrelates with other factors already discussed. The number of children involved may pose practical difficulties to a joint custody arrangement, but on the other hand may be helpful to both parents in bringing about a sharing of the pressures of single family parenting of a number of children. In rare cases, split custody may be preferred over single or joint custody.

Sincerity of Parents' Request. A number of interested observers have opposed the concept of joint custody absent mutual agreement on the ground that one spouse may interpose a demand for joint custody solely to gain bargaining leverage over the other in extracting favorable alimony, child support or property concessions.

Drawing upon the reasoning of King Solomon, writers have suggested that a parent truly interested in the welfare of a child will give up almost anything to protect the child, and thus the threat of enforced joint custody can be used to extract unwarranted concessions. While the remedy they suggest — denial of joint custody in the absence of parental agreement — is unnecessarily restrictive, we acknowledge the legitimacy of these concerns and highlight the necessity to carefully examine the motives and sincerity of each parent.

Financial Status of the Parents. Joint physical custody imposes financial burdens upon the parents because of the necessity of maintaining two homes for the child, with separate furnishings and often separate toys, equipment, and clothing.

Impact on State or Federal Assistance. Aid to families with dependent children and eligibility for medical assistance may be affected by the award of joint custody. The necessary showing of "absence" of a parent may be challenged when there is an award of joint custody that includes shared physical custody. Under current standards eligibility may be established in the presence of joint physical custody, provided joint legal custody does not also exist.

Benefit to Parents. Although the primary focus is properly upon the best interest of the child, it is also appropriate to consider the salutary effect that joint custody may have in the parents, not only because their feelings and interests are worthy of consideration, but also because their improved self-image as parents is likely to redound to the ultimate benefit of the child. . . .

IV. THIS CASE

In our review of the record to determine whether the trial judge abused his discretion, we are initially confronted with the problem of understanding the exact nature of the custody arrangement he intended. It is clear he intended to perpetuate the arrangement found to exist at the time of trial, which he charac-terized as "a sort of joint custody." This was basically the arrangement stipulated by the "visitation schedule" filed by counsel for the parties, which formed the basis of the pendente lite custody order. The trial judge described the arrange-ment as follows:

> Both parents teach school. The father's work day is from about 8:30 A.M. to 4:15 P.M. and the mother's 12:00 P.M. to 4:15 P.M. . . . In November 1982 the parties agreed upon a sort of joint custody of the children. Their base is in the father's home but the mother probably sees them more of their waking hours. The mother is in the home with the children Monday to Friday from 7:30 A.M. to 12:30 P.M.
>
> The mother has the children in her home from 4:15 P.M. to 8:00 P.M. Tuesday and on alternate [weekends] from 10:00 P.M. Saturday until 8:00 P.M. Sunday. The paternal grandmother babysits Monday to Friday from 12:30 P.M. to 4:15 P.M., i.e., from the time the mother leaves the children until the father gets home. The father pays his mother $29.00 weekly. The mother contributes no money for child support.

It is difficult to determine from an examination of the "visitation schedule" filed by the parties whether they were using "visitation" to mean custody, or whether the agreement assumed custody by Appellee with specific visitation rights reserved to Appellant. The temporary custody order provided for "joint custody," but also established a "visitation" schedule for Appellant. The final order, while perpetuating the existing arrangement with respect to physical care of the chil-dren, is silent on the question of legal custody.

We think it likely the trial judge intended to grant joint physical custody, but we would have to speculate concerning his intent as to legal custody. Any uncertainty should be resolved by the trial court, and we shall remand for that purpose. . . .

NOTES AND QUESTIONS

1. The Maryland courts rejected the possibility of joint custody in 1934. In 1986 in *Taylor*, the Maryland Supreme Court concluded that, in view of "significant

societal changes over the ensuing half century," this arrangement should be considered an option available to the trial judge.

Does the court have in mind changes in ideology? Joint custody may be supported by feminist interests insofar as it provides some relief from traditional gender-based assumptions about custody and by men to the extent is allows them seemingly greater access to their children, whom they are typically required to support after divorce. Joint custody is also consistent with the ideology of mediators and family therapists who strongly value cooperative post-divorce relations between parents. *See* Lee E. Teitelbaum & Laura DuPaix, Alternative Dispute Resolution and Divorce: Natural Experimentation in Family Law, 40 Rutgers L. Rev. 1093, 1108-1109 (1988). Or is joint custody supported by changes in beliefs about the importance of consistency and continuity of care? Or do the changes lie in changed expectations and/or realities concerning the employment of women, the readiness of men to assume caretaking responsibilities, or both? To what extent are these various assumptions founded in experience or research?

2. A number of states have not only accepted joint custody as a possible post-divorce arrangement but declared it to be the preferable arrangement. And a District of Columbia court has extended the legislative policy favoring joint custody by divorcing parents to a custody action between unmarried parents. Ysla v. Lopez, 684 A.2d 775 (D.C. App. 1996). On what assumptions would one establish such a preference or presumption? For empirical information relevant to those assumptions, see the data discussed in note 5, below. But even given a preference for joint custody in divorce cases, can one safely assume that the expression of policy found in legislative criteria for divorce applies generally to unmarried parents?

3. Some states that created presumptions favoring joint custodial awards later retreated from that position. In 1979, California adopted a statute not only permitting, but also incorporating a presumption in favor of, joint custody "where the parents have agreed to an award of joint custody." Cal. Civ. Code § 4600.5(a) (West 1979). A California task force recommended, however, that the existing joint custody provision be "clarified" to eliminate any presumption favoring joint custody, and the California Civil Code was amended in 1989 to state that there was neither a preference nor a presumption for or against any custodial arrangement. Cal. Civ. Code § 4600(d) (West Supp. 1989). A similar pattern of adoption of, and then retrenchment from, presumptions favoring joint custody can be found in Utah, whose legislature in 1988 adopted a rebuttable presumption in favor of joint legal custody and in 1990 abandoned that presumption. *See* Thronson v. Thronson, 810 P.2d 428, 429-432 (Utah App. 1991).

4. The court in *Taylor* emphasizes the importance of the willingness of parents to undertake joint custody. Not all courts do so, however. An Indiana intermediate court of appeals held that the objection of one parent does not bar a joint custody award. Periquet-Febres v. Febres, 659 N.E.2d 602 (Ind. App. 1995). Illinois has modified its statute to allow joint custody awards even when either parent or both parents object, but joint custody can be terminated either by the wish of the parties or by court order. In re Marriage of Lasky, 678 N.E.2d 1035 (Ill. 1997).

5. The initial research on joint custody involved small, not necessarily representative samples and self-selected couples, who tended to be joint custody

enthusiasts. Eleanor E. Maccoby and Robert R. Mnookin's book, *Dividing the Child* (1992), provided the first large-scale empirical study of joint custody in practice. It took place in two counties in California that strongly emphasized joint physical custody. Dividing the Child, at 10. Maccoby and Mnookin state that some 15 percent of their sample families initially settled on dual residence prior to entrance of a custody order (meaning that children spent at least one-third of their overnights with each parent) and 20 percent of the families received joint physical custody orders at divorce.

With regard to those initial living arrangements, Maccoby and Mnookin found acceptance of dual living arrangements in a broad range of families. Earlier research, in contrast, had suggested that it was limited to wealthier, better-educated families. In addition, Maccoby and Mnookin demonstrated that dual residence arrangements were established even when parents did not share a healthy (that is to say, nonhostile) view of their divorces and their partners. Ratings by mothers of the "hostility" of their divorces were only somewhat lower on average in cases of dual residence than when the child was living in one home, and the hostility ratings for fathers were identical. And, while fewer parents who rated their hostility at very high levels settled on dual residence, there were nonetheless many instances of high levels of hostility in the dual residence families. Dividing the Child, at 86-92.

It also does not appear that dual residence was reserved for parents with a shared ideological commitment to continuing joint parenthood. While Maccoby and Mnookin found that both parents were typically strongly committed to strong parental relations with their children, it was most often the case in dual residence families that fathers insisted on sharing time more equally than mothers would have wished. Dividing the Child, at 93.

These pre-divorce living arrangements often resulted in joint custody decrees when the divorce was complete. Indeed, joint physical custody orders were more common than dual residence prior to divorce. However, it also appeared that joint physical custody often was used as a compromise solution to sharp dispute. This compromise aspect was evident from the actual living patterns. In more than half of the cases with a joint custody decree, the child did not in fact have dual residence (that is, spend at least one-third of the time with each parent) and, where this was so, the children usually lived with their mothers. Dual residence arrangements are not in themselves stable. While only 19 percent of children in the mother's residence at the outset of the study were living with their fathers or in dual residence by its end, more than one-half of the children who lived initially in dual residences (or with their fathers) had moved into some different residential arrangement by two years after the divorce. Dividing the Child, at 167-170.

Dual residence and, in principle, joint physical custody imply shared physical care of the child. Joint *legal* custody has no such implications. This form of shared responsibility plainly has become the social and legal norm in California. A majority of both mothers (60 percent) and fathers (75 percent) preferred joint legal custody when interviewed after separation but prior to divorce. Moreover, these initial preferences were expressed in custody petitions. Overall, three-quarters of all awards incorporated joint legal custody. Dividing the Child, at 106-107.

In an article based on the research project that produced *Dividing the Child*, the authors report that joint *legal* custody, considered apart from residential arrangements, does not seem to have any effect on children. The appropriate focus of attention, they suggest, should be on joint physical custody and actual residential arrangements for children. Catherine R. Albiston, Eleanor E. Maccoby & Robert R. Mnookin, Does Joint Legal Custody Matter?, 2 Stan. L. & Pol'y Rev. 167 (1990).

Maccoby and Mnookin's research is the largest and most carefully designed study of custodial arrangements. Nonetheless, it too has limitations. It was conducted in California, whose legal climate may be said heavily to favor joint custodial arrangements. The families that actually chose to participate in the study were more likely to have requested and implemented joint physical custody than were nonparticipating families, skewing the results in that direction. And, of course, the rate of attrition from the original population of divorcing parents presents an inevitable problem for all research of this kind. *See* Lee E. Teitelbaum, Divorce, Custody, Gender, and the Limits of Law: On Dividing the Child, 92 Mich. L. Rev. 1808, 1814-1815 (1994).

6. Split physical custody occurs when each parent has physical care of at least one child. Many states recognize a presumption that siblings should not be separated on the ground that such an arrangement "deprives children of the benefit of constant association with one another." In re Marriage of Pundt, 547 N.W.2d 243, 245 (Iowa App. 1996); In re Marriage of Smiley, 518 N.W.2d 376, 380 (Iowa 1994). As is true of most custody rules, however, disapproval of split custody is not ironclad, and "circumstances may arise which demonstrate that separation may better promote the long-range best interests of children. Good and compelling reasons must exist for a departure." In re Marriage of Pundt, 547 N.W.2d 243, 245 (Iowa App. 1996).

The court in *Pundt* approved a split custody award:

We find several factors in this case which would support split physical care of the children. Both of the parents are capable of caring for the children. The custody evaluator recommended split physical care based on a finding Derrick was established in State Center. By staying in State Center, Derrick has stability in his home, school, and friends. Moreover, the parties were in split physical care arrangement from the time they separated in February 1994 until the dissolution decree was entered in April 1995. This situation does not appear to have been detrimental to the children.

Furthermore, we consider Derrick's stated preference to live with Ricky. When a child is of sufficient age, intelligence, and discretion to exercise an enlightened judgment, his or her wishes, though not controlling may be considered by the court, with other relevant factors, in determining child custody rights. A minor child's preference to live with one parent is relevant and cannot be ignored.

Derrick was twelve years old at the time this matter was tried. He will be fourteen in August of 1996. Derrick was able to express several reasons for his preference to reside with Ricky. These include his desire to preserve established friendships and extended family relationships. Derrick is also interested in athletics and believes his chances of participation in sports are better if he remains in State Center. Although Derrick's stated reasons for his preference may appear superficial, they are nevertheless profoundly important to him. The significance of Derrick's sentiments was cited as an important factor in the custody evaluator's recommendation to award Derrick's physical care to Ricky. . . .

We also find Derrick's preferences can be accommodated without the negative consequences traditionally associated with split physical care. As joint legal custodians Ricky and Jeanice will have equal participation in decisions affecting the children's legal status, medical care, education, extracurricular activities, and religious instruction. Additionally, the decree's provisions for liberal visitation and the parties' physical proximity should allow the children constant association with one another. Split physical care under these circumstances will facilitate rather than impede the custodial objectives referred to earlier.

547 N.W.2d at 245-246. Other cases approving split custody include Loll v. Loll, 561 N.W.2d 625 (N.D. 1997) (13-year-old twins could be separated based on children's individual needs); Bowman v. Bowman, 1997 WL 148059 (Ohio App. 1997) (decision based in part on on-camera interviews with children).

A much discussed case raising similar issues in a different setting is Adoption of Hugo, 700 N.E.2d 516 (Mass. 1998). The juvenile court placed a two-year-old special needs child whose parents had been found unfit with his paternal aunt rather than with his foster mother, who had custody of and planned to adopt Hugo's biological sister. The trial court found that the paternal aunt, who had raised her own developmentally disabled son, was prepared to devote greater time to Hugo and to work with him in areas of special need, and that trauma associated with Hugo's removal from his foster mother and sister would be overcome in the long run by the benefits of the aunt's care. The Massachusetts Supreme Judicial Court held that the juvenile court did not abuse its discretion.

Hugo's lawyers have asked the Supreme Court to declare that brothers and sisters have a constitutional right to be together, and claim that their position reflects a shift to "child centered" custodial decisions rather than an emphasis on the points of view of the contending adults. New York Times, *nytimes.com/library/national/122998*, at 1. Certiorari was denied, 119 S. Ct. 1286 (1999). What is the child's point of view about this matter, and how would one know? What is the issue about which the child's perspective is sought? Is it whether he or she wishes to remain with a sibling, or where he or she would best thrive? On the other hand, how confident can a court be of its judgment on the latter question, and what factors would make it more or less confident?

7. The desirability of joint custody is framed largely in terms of the best interests of children after divorce. Such a focus indulges two assumptions, often never made explicit. One is that we can indeed determine which of various custodial arrangements will, generally and in specific cases, advance the interests of those children. The second is that the best interests of the child is the only important consideration in custodial orders. Consider, however, the following analysis.

MARTHA A. FINEMAN, *DOMINANT DISCOURSE, PROFESSIONAL LANGUAGE, AND LEGAL CHANGE IN CHILD CUSTODY DECISIONMAKING*

101 Harv. L. Rev. 727, 734-735, 768-769 (1988)

The helping professions' discourse has presented shared parenting as the only truly acceptable custody policy. This is because they view joint custody as the only "fair" result. Ironically, although they might question the capacity of legal processes and institutions to resolve custody disputes in accordance with this ideal, they view law itself as possessing vast power to transform people's behavior. The helping professions therefore have little hesitation in resorting to law for the implementation of their social policies.

. . . The shared parenting discourse of the helping professions found rhetorical compatibility with other family law reform efforts that also incorporated notions of equality, partnership, and gender neutrality. The joint custody rhetoric of the helping professions, like other discourses, assumed and advocated equalitarianism — arguing that there are no differences between women and men, and that none should be promoted through gender-specific laws. Within the context of custody theory, this perspective denied and obscured recognition of anything "special" between mothers and children, innately or in fact. On this level, arguments for joint custody were consistent with feminist discourses that called for increasing male participation in child care to free women from anachronistic roles.

In focusing on ideal sex roles and equalitarian marriage, the helping professions' literature emphasized that traditional custody policy discriminated against men by unjustifiably favoring sole maternal custody. Not unlike the emerging fathers' rights discourse, their rhetoric asserted that there was no basis for maternal preference, which was grounded in the sexist assumption that men could not nurture but that women could. In real life, according to the helping profession, parents shared parenting and "parents are forever." . . .

. . . Custodial mothers' experience as primary caregivers during marriage and after divorce should have figured significantly in the establishment of new rules to govern the process and content of custody decisionmaking. Yet because of the domination of the social workers' rhetoric, which stressed shared parenting, custodial mothers' concerns were excluded. Thus reform is occurring with the exception, rather than the norm, providing the prototype for change.

In most marriages, one parent, normally the mother, assumes day-to-day primary care. Shared parenting in these situations seldom means equally divided responsibility and control; typically one parent sacrifices more than the other in order to care for the child. The sense of sharing in this context is not based on the actual assumption of divided responsibilities by the parents. Rather, the shared parenting can be viewed as based on the relationship between the parents who, because of the intimacy of their situation, share the potential for jointly exercising important decisionmaking responsibility for their children. Yet an unrealistic and idealized vision of shared parenting *independent* of the relationship (or lack thereof) between parents is now imposed on couples after divorce. This vision assumes that they will work out their relationship to make shared parenting successful. It is one thing for divorcing parents voluntarily to choose the shared parenting ideal, but quite another to impose it on parents who do not or cannot live up to its demands. There may be substantial costs to treating the deviant as the norm and fashioning rights outside the context of responsibility. In the divorce context, this amounts to furthering the interests of noncaretaking fathers over the objections and, in many instances, against the interests of caretaking mothers.

What are the "substantial costs to which Fineman refers? Some authors have suggested that "joint custody may provide a useful bargaining device for husbands, who may use it as a threat in connection with settlement of property, alimony, or child support levels." Lee Teitelbaum & Laura DuPaix, Alternative Dispute Resolution and Divorce: Natural Experimentation in Family Law, 40 Rutgers L. Rev. 1111 (1988). Maccoby and Mnookin, however, found little evidence of strategic behavior in their sample of California families. Regression analysis did not show that mothers who experienced more legal conflict had to give up support to win the custody they sought. Eleanor Maccoby & Robert Mnookin, Dividing the Child 155-156 (1992). They conclude that the absence of strategic behavior may reflect the infrequency of such behavior in reality and/or the California child support schedules and community property regime which, together, may have made it easier for mothers to resist strategic claims. *Id.* at 157.

A Wisconsin study found, however, that cases resulting in joint physical custody could be divided into two groups. The first group, which represented a little more than half of the joint physical custody total, produced approximately equal divisions of time between the two parents. The remaining cases resembled joint custody with visitation, with the mother assuming primary custody of the child in over 80 percent of these cases. Marygold S. Melli, Patricia R. Brown & Maria Cancian, Child Custody in a Changing World: A Study of Postdivorce Arrangements in Wisconsin, 1997 Ill. L. Rev. 773. The study concluded that "[c]ases where the outcome is equal shared custody had generally low levels of dispute, while those with an unequal shared custody award were the most contentious. This suggests that parents with equal shared time are very different from those who negotiate or are given an unequal shared custody award." *Id.* at 788. Maccoby and Mnookin, in what they termed the "most disturbing" result of their study, similarly separated cases that settled relatively early in the divorce process from the presumably higher-conflict cases that settled later. They found that 40 percent of the high-conflict cases resulted in joint physical custody, typically with primary mother residence, compared with 25 percent of the cases resolved earlier. Dividing the Child, at 58. This suggests that courts may be using the joint physical custody label to paper over the most difficult disputes. And while the "threat" of joint custody may not affect child support in cases that settle, the courts often assume in joint physical custody cases that parents contribute directly to the child in proportion with the amount of time specified in the award.

Some courts have sought to avoid the difficulties involved in choosing between parents or sole or joint custody by adopting "parenting plans" that specify each parent's responsibility without labeling the result. The ALI has made this approach central to its custody proposals.

Principles of the Law of Family Dissolution § 2.05 (2002)
§ 2.05 Parenting Plan: Proposed, Temporary, and Final
(1) An individual seeking a judicial allocation of custodial responsibility or decisionmaking responsibility . . . should be required to file with the court a proposed parenting plan. . . .
(2) Each parenting plan filed under Paragraph (1) should be required to be supported by an affidavit containing . . . [the names and addresses of involved

individuals, a description of the past allocation of caretaking and other parenting functions, the child's and caretakers' schedules, a description of the known areas of agreement and disagreement, and other relevant information].

(5) . . . [T]he court should order a parenting plan that is consistent with the custody provisions of §§ 2.08-2.12 [favoring continuation of the division of responsibility that existed during the marriage] and contains the following provisions:

(a) a provision for the child's living arrangements and for each parent's custodial responsibility, which should include either

(i) a custodial schedule that designates in which parent's home each minor child will reside on given days of the year; or

(ii) a formula or method for determining such a schedule in sufficient detail that, if necessary, the schedule can be enforced in a subsequent proceeding.

(b) an allocation of decisionmaking responsibility as to significant matters reasonably likely to arise with respect to the child; and

(c) a provision . . . for resolution of disputes that arise under the plan, and a provision establishing remedies for violations of the plan.

NOTES AND QUESTIONS

1. The ALI approach moves away from the use of labels (e.g., "sole custody," "joint custody") to allocate decision-making power in favor of more detailed plans that define the respective responsibilities of each parent. A parenting plan might specify, for example, that the mother, who coaches the child's soccer team, shall have custody on the days of every soccer game and practice, and sole decision-making power over team-related issues while the father shall attend parent-teacher conferences and have primary decision-making responsibility for homework disputes. Are more detailed plans likely to generate conflict as circumstances change (e.g., the child joins a more competitive team that practices more frequently and travels during the period the other parent is supposed to have custody) or prevent conflict by eliminating some of the ambiguity and discretion in more traditional awards?

2. Consider how you would draft a parenting plan in the following case. Father would ideally like joint legal decision-making power and physical custody of two children, ages 7 and 9, three weekends a month and one day during the week. Mother prefers an award of sole custody to her, and visitation for the father every other weekend and on rotating days during the week that change with her work schedule. If you represented the father, what kind of plan would you propose, and how might you try to persuade the mother to accept it? How would the result be different from an award of sole legal or physical custody to the mother, with visitation for the father? How would it differ from a joint custody award?

3. Parenting plans may produce results that resemble joint custody, sole custody, or some combination of the two, but they may also defer resolution of contentious issues. Consider how a court would approach the following dispute if a parenting plan had been in place.

LOMBARDO V. LOMBARDO

507 N.W.2d 788 (Mich. App. 1993)

HOLBROOK, Jr., J. . . . The parties were divorced on May 14, 1985, and awarded "joint custody, care, control and education" of their children Michael, Erin, and Robert. The original divorce judgment awarded physical custody of the children to plaintiff, but the judgment was amended later to transfer physical custody to defendant. Plaintiff was awarded visitation rights.

On the Traverse City school district's third-grade placement test, the parties' son Robert ranked fourth of nine hundred students. Robert completed a fourth-grade curriculum as a third grader at the Old Mission School. Robert was selected to attend the school district's talented and gifted program, which selects children from home schools and places them with other gifted children for education.

The parties disagree over whether to enroll Robert in the program for gifted children. Plaintiff thinks that Robert's attendance in the program is essential for him to reach his scholastic potential. After watching Robert's brother Michael go through the program, defendant believes that Robert would experience difficulty adjusting to the program and might narrow his focus on academics only. Unable to agree with regard to the issue, plaintiff filed a motion to order Robert into the program. Following a hearing regarding the matter, the trial court entered its order denying plaintiff's motion. The trial court found that an established educational environment was in place and that Robert was doing well in that environment. The trial court noted the problem of transporting Robert to the school and the segregated nature of the program. In the absence of any law regarding the subject, the trial court determined that the parent who is the primary physical custodian should make the decision. The trial court concluded that if a different standard of review was applicable, then there had not been a showing that keeping Robert at his current school was not in his best interest. . . .

. . . [P]laintiff argues that the trial court erred in determining that the parent who is the primary physical custodian of a child should decide where the child goes to school when the parents are joint custodians of the child and cannot agree concerning that issue. Plaintiff further argues that to the extent that the trial court considered the best interests of the child, it erred in its determination of the best interests of Robert under these circumstances. . . .

Defendant has primary physical custody of the children, and plaintiff has physical custody of the children for not less than 128 days each year. When a child resides with a parent, that parent decides all routine matters concerning the child. MCL 722.26a(4); MSA 25.312(6a)(4). Because the parties in this case were awarded joint custody of their children, they share the decision-making authority with respect to the "important decisions affecting the welfare of the child." MCL 722.26a(7)(b); MSA 25.312(6a)(7)(b). This Court has held that a trial court properly denies joint custody in a proceeding to modify the custody portion of a divorce judgment where the parties cannot agree on basic childrearing issues, in light of the state's interest in protecting the child's best interests. Unfortunately, the Legislature has not provided guidance concerning how to resolve disputes involving "important decisions affecting the welfare of the child" that arise between joint custodial parents. Citing Griffin v. Griffin, 699 P2d 407 (Colo. 1985), defendant argues that the parent who has primary physical custody of a child has the power to decide the type of educational program the child will experience. In *Griffin*, the divorce decree awarded custody of the parties' child to the petitioner mother. The petitioner and the respondent agreed in the divorce decree that they were to select jointly the child's schools. When the parties were unable to agree about the choice of schools for their child, the respondent father moved to enforce the education provision of the decree. Noting that the agreement did not provide a means of resolving deadlocks over school selection, the Colorado Supreme Court ruled that the agreement was unenforceable because the court has no power to force the parties to reach agreement. The *Griffin* court determined that "any attempt to enforce the agreement by requiring the parents to negotiate and reach a future agreement would be not only futile, but adverse to the interests of the child as well." The court in *Griffin* further determined that the power to control the child's education remained with the mother as the custodial parent in accordance with a Colorado statute that authorizes the custodial parent to make child-rearing decisions in the absence of an enforceable agreement concerning the child's education.

Griffin is similar to the present case where the parties have agreed through the use of joint custody to share the decision-making authority with respect to decisions concerning the welfare of the children. However, *Griffin* is distinguishable by the existence of the Colorado statute that authorizes the custodial parent to make child-rearing decisions in the absence of an enforceable agreement concerning the child's education.

We are mindful of the fact that a court is usually ill-equipped to fully comprehend and act with regard to the varied everyday needs of a child in these circumstances, because it is somewhat of a stranger to both the child and the parents in a marital dissolution proceeding. Von Tersch v. Von Tersch, 235 Neb. 263, 271; 455 N.W.2d 130 (1990). We also recognize that requiring the parent to meet and resolve the issue "exposes the child to further discord and surrounds the child with an atmosphere of hostility and insecurity." *Griffin*, supra at 410. However, joint custody in this state by definition means that the parents share the decision-making authority with respect to the important decisions affecting the welfare of the child, and where the parents as joint custodians cannot agree on important matters such as education, it is the court's duty to determine the issue in the best interests of the child.

We believe the trial court in this case clearly erred in determining that the parent who is the primary physical custodian has the authority to resolve any disputes concerning the important decisions affecting the welfare of the children. MCL 722.27(1)(c); MSA 25.312(7)(1)(c), provides that a court shall change a previous custody order only if there is clear and convincing evidence that it is in the best interests of the children. . . .

The controlling consideration in child custody disputes between parents is the best interests of the children. Parties to a divorce judgment cannot by agreement usurp the court's authority to determine suitable provisions for the child's best interest. West v. West, 241 Mich. 679, 683-684; 217 N.W. 924 (1928). Similarly, the court should not relinquish its authority to determine the best interests of the child to the primary physical custodian. Accordingly, we conclude that a trial court must determine the best interests of the child in resolving disputes concerning "important decisions affecting the welfare of the child" that arise between joint custodial parents.

We agree with plaintiff that the trial court did not make specific findings concerning the best interests of Robert. A trial court must consider, evaluate, and determine each of the factors listed at MCL 722.23; MSA 25.312(3), in determining the best interests of the child. The trial court in this case merely determined that plaintiff had failed to show that keeping Robert at his current school was not in his best interest. Consequently, we remand this case to the trial court to determine the best interests of Robert according to the relevant factors contained in MCL 722.23; MSA 25.312(3). . . .

NOTES AND QUESTIONS

1. *Compare* Brzozowski v. Brzozowski, 625 A.2d 597 (N.J. Super. Ct., Ch. Div. 1993). The father and mother had joint legal custody but the mother was the physical custodian. Their separation agreement defined "joint" custody as "mutual cooperation and decisionmaking regarding the child's health, education, and welfare." The agreement also provided for equal sharing of unreimbursed medical expenses and barred both parents from incurring non-emergency major medical expenses without the other's knowledge and consent.

After a bicycle accident, a doctor recommended elective surgery to correct an obstruction to their daughter's nose. The father secured two "second opinions" concluding that surgery at that time was neither necessary nor risky. The chancery court held that it was unwilling to interfere with the decision making of the residential parent and denied the father's application to prevent the operation in question.

> The contrary holding will produce applications, emergent and otherwise, to the court whenever the parties cannot reach agreement. *Cf.* Novak v. Novak, 446 N.W. 2d 422, 15 FLR 1622 (Minn. Ct. App. 1989), in which it was held that, where joint legal custodians disagree on the choice of schooling for the child, the trial court must resolve the dispute consistent with the child's best interests. Putting aside the real questions regarding judicial administration posed by this situation, any court should be reluctant to substitute whatever limited expertise it may have for the empirical knowledge and day-to-day experience of the parent with whom the child lives, except where there is a clear showing that an act or omission will contravene the best interests of the child. Here, no such showing has been made.

See also Debenham v. Debenham, 896 P.2d 1098 (Kan. App. 1995). Parents with joint custody disagreed over whether to send their child to private school. Although it affirmed the trial court order that the child should attend the private school chosen by the parent with primary physical custody, the Kansas Court of Appeals rejected a per se rule favoring decisions by the primary custodian. The appellate court also went out of its way to regret that the "legislature has declared joint custody and equal decisional rights as the public policy of this state." 896 P.2d at 1101.

2. How is the trial court to decide whether it is in Robert's best interest to be in the gifted or regular school program?

3. What meaning does joint legal custody have under the approach taken in *Brzozowski*?

PROBLEMS

1. Alicia Arguello wishes to appeal from the custody and visitation order of the Family Court. The court awarded custody to Alicia but gave Andy Arguello visitation for approximately 165 days per year, including most of the children's summer vacation, every other weekend during the school year, one night each week during the school year, eight nights at Christmas, three nights at Thanksgiving, two nights for Father's Day, and on his and the children's birthdays. What arguments would you make on her behalf?

2. As clerk to Justice Austin of the state supreme court, you have been asked to prepare an analysis of Andersen v. Andersen, pending before the court. The trial judge awarded joint legal and physical custody of the parties' two daughters. Neither party requested joint custody, but the court below found that arrangement met the statutory standard that custody orders should be in the best interests of the children.

The record indicates that the children, who are eight and ten years of age, desire to remain with their mother but expressed love for their father and wanted to spend substantial time with him. The trial judge found both parents to be fit, and that they wished equally to have close contact with their children. She also found Ms. Andersen to be sensible but somewhat bitter about the divorce and more partisan than Mr. Andersen; Mr. Andersen she found to be a rather "relaxed" person. Ms. Andersen resisted joint custody because she did not think she could cooperate with her former husband; Mr. Andersen did not object to joint custody, although he also did not seek it.

Please advise Justice Austin.

4. Judging Parenthood: What Makes Parents Unfit?

How do we "judge" parents? If custody decisions reflect shared norms that fathers should ordinarily have custody (the presumption in the nineteenth century), that mothers should ordinarily have custody (the presumption in the middle of the twentieth century), or that custody should ordinarily be shared (the presumption in some states today), individualized judgments may not be necessary. But if a custody decision involves choosing between fit parents, value judgments are inevitable. And if the parents' relationship with each other is so contentious they cannot agree on a custody arrangement, the parents might also be quite willing to believe the worst about the other parent and to allege parental misconduct in court. Historically, the courts often considered the factors that determined fault-based divorce, particularly adultery and abandonment, as factors in the subsequent custody award. With no-fault divorce, the custody award is often the only time in a dissolution proceeding that the court passes judgment on adult behavior. How should courts approach these determinations? Should the standards focus on commitment to the child or the qualities of the parent? This section explores the role of the courts in evaluating parental behavior that may influence custody determinations. The materials specifically consider the contentious issues of sexual behavior, race, religion, spousal abuse, and "unfriendly co-parenting" as they relate to the best interests of children.

MARTHA FINEMAN, *THE ILLUSION OF EQUALITY: THE RHETORIC AND REALITY OF DIVORCE REFORM*

79-80 (1991)

As equality and the concurrent concept of gender neutrality have been incorporated into custody decision making, such old, tested, gendered rules that permitted predictable, inexpensive decisions to be made without protracted litigation have been set aside. As a result, one problem confronting the new, formally degendered, family-law system is the need to create new, gender-neutral factors or processes to handle decision-making in individual cases. The result has been increased state regulation of the post-divorce family.

a. Sexual Activity

TAYLOR V. TAYLOR

110 S.W.3d 731 (Ark. 2003)

BROWN, J. . . .
On November 9, 1999, Rexayne Taylor and Wes Taylor were divorced. . . . [T]hey agreed to share joint custody of the children, with Rexayne Taylor being the primary custodial parent. . . .

In May 2000, a friend of Rexayne Taylor's, Kellie Tabora, who was an admitted lesbian, moved into her home and began paying her $500 a month for living expenses. On May 2, 2001, a little over a year later, Wes Taylor filed a petition to modify the divorce decree. In his petition, he alleged that there had been a change in circumstances warranting a custodial change for the two boys because his former wife's living conditions were not in the best interest of the children. Rexayne Taylor responded and denied the allegations.

On April 10 and 11, 2002, the circuit court held a hearing on Wes Taylor's petition. Rexayne Taylor and Kellie Tabora acknowledged that Kellie moved into Rexayne's home in May 2000. Rexayne testified that Kellie slept on the couch most of the time. She added, however, that, on occasion, they would sleep together in Rexayne's bed. Rexayne stated that she was not a lesbian, that she thought homosexuality was wrong, and that she and Kellie did not have a sexual relationship. She further testified that after Wes Taylor filed his petition in May 2001, Kellie slept in a separate bed in a separate room.

Kellie Tabora stated that although she was a lesbian, her last relationship had ended at least three years ago. She testified that she had slept in Rexayne's bed about half the time prior to the filing of Wes Taylor's petition, but that they had had no sexual contact while sleeping in the same bed. Kellie also testified that on three or four occasions, Rexayne's children slept with both women in the same bed. When asked what she would do if the children were teased about her presence in the home, Kellie said she would leave. She further testified that she did not condone a homosexual lifestyle or advocate it.

Wes Taylor presented additional witnesses who testified that he was a good father and that his boys seemed well adjusted. Each of his witnesses also testified that Rexayne Taylor was a good mother to the boys. Wes Taylor presented testimony from two witnesses that the boys had experienced a change in behavior because of Kellie Tabora's presence: his mother, Barbara Taylor, and his girlfriend, Lynelle Crotty. Mrs. Taylor testified that the difference in the boys' behavior when they are in Kellie's presence and not in her presence is that "they don't come to us when she's present." She further stated that since the divorce, the couple's oldest child, R.T., had experienced a change in personality and was now more withdrawn and cried more often. Lynelle Crotty agreed that R.T. was more withdrawn, while the youngest child, A.T., she believed, became confused when talking about his mother's friend. In addition, Wes Taylor presented several witnesses who testified that they would not allow their children to stay in Rexayne's home, knowing that an admitted lesbian lived there.

* * *

Upon learning of Rexayne Taylor's situation with Kellie Tabora, Wes Taylor expressed his concern about how this would affect the children. He told the circuit court that he believed that R.T. knew what "gay" meant and what a "lesbian" is, and that he did not want to wait until it was "too late" to do something about the situation. He said that in his opinion, he could provide a "more . . . normal home life and social life than Rexayne" could. In response, Rexayne Taylor presented testimony from both boys' elementary school teachers that they were well adjusted and enjoyable children. Neither teacher testified to any behavioral change in the boys. In addition, A.T.'s teacher testified that assuming the other children in the school did find out that A.T.'s mother was living with a lesbian, she did not think there would be any repercussions from his peers, although it was possible that they might tease him. Francis Henley, Rexayne's father, testified that he had not observed any changes in the children other than the fact that they were maturing and growing older. He added that he did not believe that Kellie Tabora's presence in their lives was making any difference.

Monica Smith, the mother of R.T.'s best friend, also testified as part of Rexayne Taylor's case. She stated that her boys often spent the night at Rexayne's home and that she was unaware of any unhealthy influences to which they may have been exposed. She also testified that neither R.T. nor A.T. had displayed any change in their behavior or demeanor. Rexayne Taylor took the stand and stated . . . she was always supportive of her children. She added that if the court was concerned about

Kellie and her continued presence in the home she would ask Kellie to move from her home in order to retain custody.

On April 17, 2002, the circuit court filed its letter opinion. . . .

. . . The court found that both Rexayne and Kellie Tabora had testified that Kellie had lived in Rexayne's home since May 2000, and from May 2000 until May 2001, she and Rexayne had slept in the same bed on numerous occasions. The court observed that both women had denied a sexual relationship and that the sleeping arrangements changed once Wes Taylor filed his petition. The court then made the following observations:

> The plaintiff here claims the circumstances of the expressed sexual preference of Kelli Tabora and the fact that she and defendant slept together for approximately one year requires the conclusion that sex occurs. But if the testimony of defendant and Kelli Tabora is accepted as the truth what is present here is that no actual inappropriate behavior but rather the appearance of inappropriate behavior exists. Is that harmful enough to require removal of these children from that environment? It would seem likely that if it is generally known by friends and acquaintances that defendant resides with and also sleeps with an admitted lesbian, that most will conclude sex is involved. This assumption on the part of the public would subject the children to ridicule and embarrassment and could very well be harmful to them. Therefore, it is the conclusion of this Court that residence of Kelli Tabora with defendant and the children even without sex is inappropriate behavior and is a circumstance that justifies changing of custody from defendant to plaintiff. It is at least poor parental judgment on the part of defendant to allow a well known lesbian to both reside with defendant and the children and sleep in the same bed with defendant.

The court declined to award Wes Taylor child support and restricted Rexayne Taylor's visitation rights with the boys to overnight visits when Kellie Tabora was not spending the night with her. . . .

* * *

As to her lifestyle and Kellie Tabora's residence, Rexayne Taylor argues that the circuit court made no finding of actual inappropriate behavior. Instead, the circuit court premised its ruling on the appearance of inappropriate behavior. She submits that the circuit court's conclusions do not rise above mere speculation and conjecture and that the great weight of evidence was that the children had not been the subject of ridicule due to her living arrangement. Her final point is that the circuit court's ruling punishes her and the children, not because she is having an illicit relationship, but because it may appear that way to others, and not because of any demonstrated harm that has come to the children, but because harm may possibly occur in the future.

Wes Taylor responds . . . that the danger in the situation, as noted by the witnesses, was that the public might find out about Rexayne Taylor's living situation and the boys would then be subjected to ridicule. . . . He further emphasizes that Arkansas courts have never condoned a parent's promiscuous conduct or lifestyle in the presence of a child. He concludes that the public is going to believe that Rexayne Taylor and Kellie Tabora were having a sexual relationship, whether they were or not, and that it is that perception which the circuit court found to be dangerous to the children's welfare and which would surely subject them to ridicule. . . .

* * *

We turn then to the circuit court's finding concerning Rexayne Taylor's living arrangement with an acknowledged lesbian. It is clear to this court that the circuit court was concerned about the boys' best interest. Yet, the court grounded its decision on the "appearance of inappropriate behavior" while, at the same time, crediting the two women's testimony that they did not have a sexual relationship. Based upon appearances, the circuit court concluded that the public's assumptions "would subject the children to ridicule and embarrassment and could very well be harmful to them." No finding was made that the children had in fact been harmed or affected by their mother's action of sleeping in the same bed with Kellie Tabora prior to the filing of the modification petition on May 2, 2001. To the contrary, the weight of the testimony, including that of each child's schoolteacher, was that the children were happy, well adjusted, outgoing, and well-parented children.

It is true that this court has held that a parent's unmarried cohabitation with a romantic partner, or a parent's promiscuous conduct or lifestyle, in the presence of a child cannot be abided. The instant case, however, is altogether different. Here, it appears from the circuit court's statements that the court was trying to protect the children from future harm based on future public misperception. A review of our caselaw reveals that this court has yet to address a situation in which a parent's current actions might bring about a future harm for a child based on the public's erroneous perception. We turn to other jurisdictions for guidance on this point.

* * *

[The court discussed cases from West Virginia, Oklahoma, Nebraska, and Illinois, all of which held that a mother's association with a lesbian or that she was a lesbian is not in itself a sufficient basis for modifying custody. Instead, the courts all held that the parent's conduct must be shown to have an adverse impact on the children, and they said that the potential for future harm was insufficient. In contrast, a Missouri court has held that custody may modified on the basis of a finding that a parent's open displays of affection with a same-sex partner may be emotionally harmful to children.]

. . . We note that in the case before us, there is no proof of a sexual relationship between Rexayne Taylor and Kellie Tabora. In fact, both women denied that any sexual contact had occurred in the past or was presently occurring. Moreover, the circuit court did not base its decision on the fact that the women were engaged in a sexual relationship. Wes Taylor correctly points out that this court has held that a trial court did not err in determining it was not in the children's best interest for their primary custodian who was involved in a homosexual relationship to "continue cohabitating with another adult with whom she admitted being romantically involved." But we contrast those circumstances with the instant case, where the circuit court credited Rexayne Taylor's and Kellie Tabora's testimony that they were not romantically or sexually involved.

Furthermore, Wes Taylor has failed to demonstrate any actual harm or adverse effect to the boys attributable to Kellie Tabora's presence in the household. Because no harm has been shown to the children, because there was no showing that the two women are engaged in a lesbian relationship, and because Kellie Tabora is no longer sleeping in Rexayne Taylor's bed, we disagree that a change of custody premised on appearances and on the potential for teasing in the future is sufficient to constitute a material change in circumstances. Clearly, it was in the best interest of the boys to stay in an environment in which, by all accounts, they were thriving.

We further disagree that a decision can be based on perceptions and appearances rather than concrete proof of likely harm. In this regard, we are persuaded by the reasoning of the Maryland Court of Appeals in a case involving visitation with a parent involved in a homosexual relationship:

> . . . If there is sound evidence demonstrating that a child is likely to be harmed down the road, but there is no present concrete finding of harm, a court may still consider a child's future best interests and restrict visitation. The need for a factual finding of harm to the child requires that the court focus on evidence-based factors and not on stereotypical presumptions of future harm.
>
> Therefore, before a trial court restricts the non-custodial parent's visitation, it must make specific factual findings based on sound evidence in the record. If the trial court does not make these factual findings, instead basing its ruling on personal bias or stereotypical beliefs, then such findings may be clearly erroneous and the order may be reversed. In addition, if a trial court relies on abstract presumptions, rather than sound principles of law, an abuse of discretion may be found.

Boswell v. Boswell, 352 Md. 204, 237, 721 A.2d 662, 678 (1998).

While we are well aware of the expression that "perception is reality," when dealing with the extreme seriousness of changing the custody of children from one parent to the other, we are convinced that evidence-based factors must govern. Here, there is not only the absence of proof that a homosexual relationship was occurring, but the great weight of evidence supported Rexayne Taylor's position that the boys were well adjusted and happy in their environment and had not been adversely affected by her living arrangement. We, therefore, hold that the circuit court abused its discretion in changing the custody of R.T. and A.T. from Rexayne Taylor to Wes Taylor. Accordingly, we reverse the order of the circuit court and remand.

NOTES AND QUESTIONS

1. The Arkansas Supreme Court in this case observed, "It is true that this court has held that a parent's unmarried cohabitation with a romantic partner, or a parent's promiscuous conduct or lifestyle, in the presence of a child cannot be abided." The court cited Taylor v. Taylor, 345 Ark. at 300 (2001), which upheld an order conditioning the mother's custody on her not permitting her partner to live in the residence or stay overnight in the home when the children were present. A number of decisions in other jurisdictions say that a parent's extramarital activity is in and of itself proof of unfitness and a reason to deny the parent custody. E.g., Jarrett v. Jarrett, 400 N.E.2d 421 (Ill. 1979), cert. denied, 449 U.S. 927; Dockins v. Dockins, 475 So. 2d 571 (Ala. Civ. App. 1985) (mother denied custody;

entertained paramour in home when children were present); Adam v. Adam, 436 N.W.2d 266 (S.D. 1989) (mother's extramarital affair harmful to five-year-old child); V. A. E. v. D. A. E., 873 S.W.2d 262 (Mo. App. 1994) (mother's affair resulting in child was "a factor in the custody equation").

Some courts that take a per se approach apply it only in extreme cases, however. For example, in Stacy v. Stacy, 332 S.E.2d 260 (W. Va. 1985), the West Virginia Supreme Court emphasized the role of its primary caretaker presumption:

> In Garska v. McCoy we held that "[w]ith reference to the custody of very young children, the law presumes that it is in the best interests of such children to be placed in the custody of their primary caretaker, if he or she is fit. . . .
>
> In the case before us it appears that the court failed to apply the principles of Garska v. McCoy, supra, in making the custody award. There was no finding of which parent was the primary caretaker and, indeed, most of the evidence at the final hearing did not go to the issue of which parent took primary responsibility for the children's care but to the allegedly adulterous behavior of the appellant.
>
> The record clearly indicates that the court did not deny custody to the appellant because she failed to qualify as the primary caretaker but because she was guilty of adultery. Although adultery in some circumstances may be grounds for a finding of unfitness as a parent, it is not always so. In Syllabus Point 4 of J. B. v. A. B., 161 W. Va. 332, 242 S.E.2d 248 (1978), we set forth the standard for determining when sexual misconduct should be considered in making a custody award:
>
>> Acts of sexual misconduct by a mother, albeit wrongs against an innocent spouse, may not be considered as evidence going to the fitness of the mother for child custody unless her conduct is so aggravated, given contemporary moral standards, that reasonable men would find that her immorality, per se, warranted a finding of unfitness because of the deleterious effect upon the child of being raised by a mother with such a defective character. . . .
>
>> Because the record indicates that the court did not make a finding as to which parent was the primary caretaker and because it appears that the court denied custody to the appellant solely because she was guilty of adultery, without finding that the adultery had any deleterious effect upon the children, the case is reversed. . . .

332 S.E.2d at 261-262.

2. Courts can accord various degrees of significance to parents' extramarital activity, short of treating it as a per se ground for denying custody. They can disregard it entirely; they can say that it is important when there is evidence that children have been adversely affected by that fact; they can say that nonmarital cohabitation is important when there is evidence that children will probably be affected adversely in the near future; they can presume that such cohabitation will harm the child and require the *parent* to prove that the child's best interests nonetheless require that he or she retain custody. Which of these are the most desirable approaches? *See* Julie Shapiro, Custody and Conduct: How the Law Fails Lesbian and Gay Parents and Their Children, 71 Ind. L.J. 623 (1996).

Is the central issue in cases involving parents' sexual conduct one of morality, of harm, or both? What is the connection between those issues?

3. *Taylor* involved the father's motion to modify an existing custody order, and the court held that the father had not met his burden of showing a "material change in circumstances." The *Taylor* court observed, "While we are well aware of the expression that "perception is reality," when dealing with the extreme seriousness

of changing the custody of children from one parent to the other, we are convinced that evidence-based factors must govern." In an initial determination of custody, might the court give greater weight to "perceptions" in the determination of the children's best interest?

4. The *Taylor* court treated the issue as one of nonmarital cohabitation rather than homosexuality. The opinion in M. A. B. v. R. B., 510 N.Y.S.2d 960 (Sup. Ct. Spec. Term 1986), reviews a number of decisions holding that homosexuality is not itself a sufficient reason for denying custody or visitation. In DeLong v. DeLong, 1998 WL 15536 (Mo. App. Jan. 20, 1998), the court rejected a rule that a homosexual parent is per se unfit in favor of the nexus test. The court required a showing of some connection between the parent's sexual conduct, whether homosexual or heterosexual, and harm to the child before that conduct could be considered relevant to the custody determination. Moreover, it expressly declared that "[g]eneralizations regarding the possible impact a parent's sexual conduct outside the presence of a child may have on a child are impermissible."

There are, however, decisions that suggest otherwise, particularly where the conduct is obvious to the child. For example, in Roe v. Roe, 324 S.E.2d 691, 691-694 (Va. 1985), the father had custody of the child because of the mother's illness. She sought a change of custody to her because the father was living in a homosexual relationship:

> After hearing the evidence, the [trial] court entered a custody order granting "joint, legal custody" of the child to the father and mother. The order provided that the child was to live with the father during the school year and with the mother during the summer vacation, and provided for extensive visitation by each parent when the child was living with the other. The order conditioned the father's custody upon his "not sharing the same bed or bedroom with any male lover or friend while the child is present in the home." We granted an appeal to the mother.
>
> The trial court found that there was little animosity between the parents. Aside from the central issue pervading this case, each parent had been a fit, devoted, and competent custodian. The court interviewed the little girl and found that she was a "very lovely, outgoing, bright and intelligent child . . . a very happy child [who] seemed to be well adjusted and outgoing." The court found that there was no evidence that the father's conduct had an adverse effect on the child, but that she did express a wish to live with her mother.
>
> The father openly admitted that he was living in an active homosexual relationship, sharing a bed and bedroom with a male friend in the same house with the child. The father's lover testified as a witness in order, the father says, that the trial court could ascertain that he was a person of good character whose influence in the home would not be harmful to the child.
>
> The father and his male friend both testified that they did not "flaunt" their homosexuality. The court, however, observed: "this relationship of sharing the same bed or bedroom with the child being in the home would be one of the greatest degrees of flaunting that one could imagine. It flies in the face of Brown v. Brown [218 Va. 196, 237 S.E.2d 89 (1977)], and it flies in the face of society's mores anyway." Apparently for this reason, the court conditioned the partial award of custody to the father on the requirement that he and his lover not share the same bed or bedroom. . . .
>
> . . . The moral climate in which children are to be raised is an important consideration for the court in determining custody, and adultery is a reflection of a

mother's moral values. An illicit relationship to which minor children are exposed cannot be condoned. Such a relationship must necessarily be given the most careful consideration in a custody proceeding. . . .

Although we decline to hold that every lesbian mother or homosexual father is per se an unfit parent . . . the father's continuous exposure of the child to his immoral and illicit relationship renders him an unfit and improper custodian as a matter of law. . . . [W]e have no hesitancy in saying that the conditions under which this child must live daily are not only unlawful but also impose an intolerable burden upon her by reason of the social condemnation attached to them, which will inevitably afflict her relationships with her peers and with the community at large. The father's unfitness is manifested by his willingness to impose this burden upon her in exchange for his own gratification.

The trial court was, as stated above, seriously concerned as to the impact of the father's conduct upon the child, but took the position that its worst features could be allayed by ordering him out of his lover's bedroom. We are not so persuaded. . . . We conclude that the best interests of the child will only be served by protecting her from the burdens imposed by such behavior, insofar as practicable. In the circumstances of this case, this necessitates not only a change of custody to the mother, but also a cessation of any visitations in the father's home, or in the presence of his homosexual lover, while his present living arrangements continue. . . .

In Bottoms v. Bottoms, 457 S.E.2d 102 (1995), the Virginia Supreme Court distinguished *Doe* in a custody dispute between a mother living with her lesbian companion and the child's maternal grandmother. The court held that while a homosexual parent is not per se unfit to have custody, the conduct "inherent in lesbianism" is punishable as a felony and is thus relevant in determining custody. It also found that, unlike *Doe*, there was proof that this and other conduct by the mother had harmed the child.

See also Ex parte D. W. W (R. W. v. D. W. W.), 717 So. 2d 793 (Ala. 1998), holding that even without evidence of adverse effect, the trial judge would have been justified in restricting the mother's visitation in order to limit her children's exposure to her "lesbian lifestyle." The court noted that exposing children to a "lifestyle . . . that is illegal under the laws of this state[,] and immoral in the eyes of most of its citizens, could greatly traumatize them." 717 So. 2d at 796.

5. Many theories concerning the etiology of homosexuality have found some support, but none has found acceptance. Some suggest that homosexuality is genetically and/or hormonally caused; others view homosexuality as a form of sexual assignment formed during the early years of life that will not be affected by later experiences or conditioning; and yet others consider homosexuality a learned behavior resulting largely from environmental influences. Does the theory one chooses (either explicitly or implicitly) bear on the relevance of sexual orientation to custody decisions? For an accessible review of current theories, *see* Simon Le Vay, The Sexual Brain 105-130 (1993).

A small-group study by Susan Golombak & Fiona Tasker, Do Parents Influence the Sexual Orientation of Their Children? Findings from a Longitudinal Study of Lesbian Families, 32 Developmental Psychol. 3 (1996), does not find a greater incidence of homosexuality in children raised by lesbian parents than in those raised by heterosexual parents, although the study does report a somewhat greater willingness to experiment on the part of the former. *See also* Judith Stacey & Timothy J. Biblarz, (How) Does the Sexual Orientation of Parents Matter? 66 Am. Soc. Rev. 159 (2001) (reviewing 21 studies and reaching similar conclusions) and Lynn D. Wardle, The Potential Impact of Homosexual Parenting on Children, 1997 U. Ill. L. Rev. 833, 839 (arguing that methodologically flawed and inadequate social science studies ignored increased development of homosexual orientation in children, emotional, and cognitive disadvantages caused by the absence of opposite sex parents and economic security).

6. The trial court in *Taylor* credited the women's testimony that, although they shared the same bed, they were not engaged in a sexual relationship. If you were an attorney in the case representing the father, how would you have approached the issue of credibility? What kind of evidence would you have sought to introduce? If two lesbians were living together and sharing a bed, should the court assume a sexual relationship? If a heterosexual man and woman were living together and sharing a bed, what assumption should the court make about their behavior? Should the issue turn primarily on their testimony? If the harm comes from exposure to homosexuality or the failure to condemn it, can the children in *Taylor* be said to suffer from a harm?

b. Race

PALMORE V. SIDOTI

466 U.S. 429 (1984)

BURGER, C.J. We granted certiorari to review a judgment of a state court divesting a natural mother of the custody of her infant child because of her remarriage to a person of a different race.

When petitioner Linda Sidoti Palmore and respondent Anthony J. Sidoti, both Caucasians, were divorced in May 1980 in Florida, the mother was awarded custody of their 3-year-old daughter.

In September 1981 the father sought custody of the child by filing a petition to modify the prior judgment because of changed conditions. The change was that the child's mother was then cohabiting with a Negro, Clarence Palmore, Jr., whom she married two months later. Additionally, the father made several allegations of instances in which the mother had not properly cared for the child.

After hearing testimony from both parties and considering a court counselor's investigative report, the court noted that the father had made allegations about the child's care, but the court made no findings with respect to these allegations. On the contrary, the court made a finding that "there is no issue as to either party's devotion to the child, adequacy of housing facilities, or respectability of the new spouse of either parent."

The court then addressed the recommendations of the court counselor, who had made an earlier report "in [another] case coming out of this circuit also involving the social consequences of an interracial marriage. Niles v. Niles, 299 So. 2d 162." From this vague reference to that earlier case, the court turned to the present case and noted the counselor's recommendation for a change in custody because "[t]he wife [petitioner] has chosen for herself and for her child, a lifestyle unacceptable to the father and to society. . . . The child . . . is, or at school age will be, subject to environmental pressures not of choice."

The court then concluded that the best interests of the child would be served by awarding custody to the father. The court's rationale is contained in the following: "The father's evident resentment of the mother's choice of a black partner is not sufficient to wrest custody from the mother. It is of some significance, however, that the mother did see fit to bring a man into her home and carry on a sexual relationship with him without being married to him. Such action tended to place gratification of her own desires ahead of her concern for the child's future welfare. This Court feels that despite the strides that have been made in bettering relations between the races in this country, it is inevitable that Melanie will, if allowed to remain in her present situation and attains school age and thus becomes more vulnerable to peer pressures, suffer from the social stigmatization that is sure to come."

The judgment of a state court determining or reviewing a child custody decision is not ordinarily a likely candidate for review by this Court. However, the court's opinion, after stating that the "father's evident resentment of the mother's choice of a black partner is not sufficient" to deprive her of custody, then turns to what it regarded as the damaging impact on the child from remaining in a racially mixed household. This raises important federal concerns arising from the Constitution's commitment to eradicating discrimination based on race.

The Florida court did not focus directly on the parental qualifications of the natural mother or her present husband, or indeed on the father's qualifications to have custody of the child. The court found that "there is no issue as to either party's devotion to the child, adequacy of housing facilities, or respectability of the new spouse of either parent." This, taken with the absence of any negative finding as to the quality of the care provided by the mother, constitutes a rejection of any claim of petitioner's unfitness to continue the custody of her child.

The court correctly stated that the child's welfare was the controlling factor. But that court was entirely candid and made no effort to place its holding on any ground other than race. Taking the court's findings and rationale at face value, it is clear that the outcome would have been different had petitioner married a Caucasian male of similar respectability.

A core purpose of the Fourteenth Amendment was to do away with all governmentally imposed discrimination based on race. Classifying persons according to their race is more likely to reflect racial prejudice than legitimate public concerns; the race, not the person, dictates the category. Such classifications are subject to the most exacting scrutiny; to pass constitutional muster, they must be justified by a compelling governmental interest and must be "necessary . . . to the accomplishment" of their legitimate purpose, McLaughlin v. Florida, 379 U.S. 184, 196 (1964). *See* Loving v. Virginia, 388 U.S. 1, 11 (1967).

The State, of course, has a duty of the highest order to protect the interests of minor children, particularly those of tender years. In common with most states, Florida law mandates that custody determinations be made in the best interests of the children involved. The goal of granting custody based on the best interests of the child is indisputably a substantial governmental interest for purposes of the Equal Protection Clause.

It would ignore reality to suggest that racial and ethnic prejudices do not exist or that all manifestations of those prejudices have been eliminated. There is a risk that a child living with a stepparent of a different race may be subject to a variety of pressures and stresses not present if the child were living with parents of the same racial or ethnic origin.

The question, however, is whether the reality of private biases and the possible injury they might inflict are permissible considerations for removal of an infant child from the custody of its natural mother. We have little difficulty concluding that they are not. The Constitution cannot control such prejudices but neither can it tolerate them. Private biases may be outside the reach of the law, but the law cannot, directly or indirectly, give them effect. . . .

Whatever problems racially mixed households may pose for children in 1984 can no more support a denial of constitutional rights than could the stresses that residential integration was thought to entail in 1917. The effects of racial prejudice, however real, cannot justify a racial classification removing an infant child from the custody of its natural mother found to be an appropriate person to have such custody.

The judgment of the District Court of Appeal is reversed.

NOTES AND QUESTIONS

1. What interests are at stake in this case? Do the child's interests include identification with a racial group?

2. Both *Palmore* and *Taylor* discuss the potential impact of peer and community reaction on children. How is *Palmore* relevant to cases about sexual orientation? How might it be distinguished?

3. Palmore v. Sidoti was considered and distinguished in Jones v. Jones, 542 N.W.2d 119 (S.D. 1996). The father was an enrolled member of the Sisseton-Wahpeton Dakota Nation who was adopted at age seven; the mother was a Caucasian. The father was employed on a family farm and earned about $22,000 per year, and the mother was a homemaker and nursing student. The father was a recovering alcoholic, and the mother suffered from depression and low self-esteem. They had three children, all of whom have Native American features. In its findings, the trial court noted the father's arguments that the children would be discriminated against if they moved from their home and the family farm and that he wished to continue to make the children aware of their culture and heritage. The trial court indicated that this was an example of the father's concern for "the totality of the upbringing of his children," but also stated that its decision had to be "made on a racially neutral basis." On appeal, this decision was affirmed against the mother's claim that race was impermissibly taken into account:

> While the trial court was not blind to the racial backgrounds of the children, we are satisfied that it did not impermissibly award custody on the basis of race. As noted, [the father] showed a sensitivity to the need for his children to be exposed to their ethnic heritage. All of us form our own personal identities, based in part, on our religious, racial and cultural backgrounds. To say, as [the mother] argues, that a court

should never consider whether a parent is willing and able to expose to and educate children on their heritage, is to say that society is not interested in whether children ever learn who they are. *Palmore* does not require this. . . .

In Davis v. Davis, 658 N.Y.S.2d 548 (App. Div. 1997), the appellate court upheld an order granting a wife's application for custody of her biracial child. It held that while race was one factor for consideration in custodial placement, the fact that the husband was an African-American now living in a biracial household whereas the wife's household was all white did not compel an award to the husband where there was no evidence that the child would be denied his biracial identity and where the wife was more flexible in dealing with the child's daily requirements and provided greater continuity of care.

PROBLEMS

1. Isabel and Ian Wright are divorcing and disagree about the proper custodian for their two children, a boy age four and a girl age seven. The couple have long disagreed about many issues, including those related to racial matters. Ian Wright has made disparaging remarks about minorities generally, and African Americans particularly, that offend Isabel. To make matters more acute, Isabel has admitted that she has fallen in love with Richard Addison, who is African American, and intends to divorce her husband in order to marry Richard. Ian offers the testimony of a qualified psychologist that their children have adopted their father's view of African Americans and would hate living with their mother and her new husband. What weight, if any, should the trial court place on this evidence?

2. Judith Fox received custody of her son, Reynard, age 6, after a bitterly contested divorce. She has married a Mexican American, and they are the only ethnically mixed couple in the neighborhood in which they reside. Allen Fox has sought custody and has offered the evidence of school teachers and school children that Reynard has been teased unmercifully by the Anglo children in the school and that he is not invited to birthday parties by their parents. Is this evidence relevant to the assignment of custody? Would the testimony of a psychologist that the child faces a significant risk of emotional distress as a result of the behavior of other children and parents in the community be relevant? Is it in a child's best interest to grow up without conflict or unusual discomfort?

c. Religion

The meanings of terms such as *fitness* or *best interests* change with time and place. At one time the parents' religion may be a central concern. At other times the emphasis may be on sexual behavior, physical characteristics and qualifications, or general commitments to mainstream values. Challenges to the center may come from the social and political left or right. In some cases, religious beliefs are founded on, or at least are related to, beliefs about sexual behavior, race, and the like, or religious beliefs themselves may be expressly at issue.

SHELLEY V. WESTBROOKE

37 Eng. Rep. 850 (Ch. 1817)

... A petition was presented in the name of the infant Plaintiffs, stating the marriage of their father and mother in the year 1811, and that they were the only issue of it; that about three years ago the father deserted his wife, and had since unlawfully cohabited with another woman; that thereupon the mother returned to the house of her father with the eldest of the infants and the other was soon after born; that they had since that time been maintained by their mother and her father, and that their mother had lately died. It was then stated that the father avowed himself an atheist, and that since his marriage he had written and published a work, in which he blasphemously derided the truth of the Christian revelation, and denied the existence of a God as creator of the universe; and that since the death of his wife, he had demanded that the children should be delivered up to him, and that he intended, if he could, to get possession of their persons, and educate them as he thought proper. Their maternal grandfather had lately transferred £2000 4 per cents. into the names of trustees, upon trust for them. ...

The Lord Chancellor gave his judgment in writing. ...

This is a case in which, as the matter appears to me, in which [the father's] conduct, which I cannot but consider as highly immoral, has been established in proof, and established as the effect of those principles: conduct nevertheless, which he represents to himself and others, not as conduct to be considered as immoral, but to be recommended and observed in practice, and as worthy of approbation.

I consider this, therefore, as a case in which the father has demonstrated that he must, and does deem it to be matter of duty which his principles impose upon him, to recommend to those whose opinions and habits he may take upon himself to form, that conduct in some of the most important relations of life, as moral and virtuous, which the law calls upon me to consider as immoral and vicious. ...

I cannot, therefore, think that I should be justified in delivering over these children for their education exclusively, to what is called the care to which Mr. S. wishes it to be intrusted. ...

The order restrained the father and his agents from taking possession of the persons of the infants, or intermeddling with them till further order; and it was referred to the Master, to enquire what would be a proper plan for the maintenance and education of the infants; and also to enquire with whom, and under whose care the infants should remain during their minority, or until further order.

IN RE MARRIAGE OF HADEEN

619 P.2d 374 (Wash. App. 1980)

CALLOW, C.J. Judith N. Hadeen, petitioner below ... appeals from the trial court's award of custody of four of the Hadeens' five daughters to Mr. Hadeen. The trial court awarded Mr. Hadeen custody of Lisa, age 15, Lynn, age 13, Lila, age 11, and LaVon, age 8. Mrs. Hadeen was awarded custody of the Hadeens' oldest daughter, Lori, age 17. This appeal presents the issues of whether religious acts may constitute a determinative factor in an award of custody, and, if so, what test must be used to protect the interests of children and the religious freedom of parents.

In the fall of 1977, a person who had previously been the Hadeens' minister returned from Canada and activated a Bellingham branch of the First Community Churches of America. The First Community Church is a fundamentalist Christian sect which demands much of its members' time, their total loyalty, and a subservience to the teachings of the church. The church teaches a strict code of discipline as a means of gaining parental control of children. Mrs. Hadeen admitted that on one occasion she had her other children hold her daughter Lisa while she spanked her with a Ping-Pong paddle for 2 hours. Mrs. Hadeen testified that usually only a few spankings were necessary. It is unclear whether Mr. Hadeen sanctioned Mrs. Hadeen's disciplinary practices. Witnesses testified that the church teaches enforced isolation and fasting as another means of discipline. The church also teaches that there are essentially two classes of people: "natural people" and "spirit filled people" who have repented, been baptized and received the Holy Spirit. There was testimony that children were taught to use foul language when speaking to other children who were "natural people," and that there was nothing wrong with lying to "natural people." Mrs. Hadeen denied that church members were taught not to associate with "natural" people. . . .

Mr. Hadeen testified that the church exercised control over its members to whatever extent possible. He said that he never treated his children violently, but had slapped and kicked Mrs. Hadeen in the children's presence following their separation. He did so, he testified, because on one occasion she would not talk to him and on another she cursed him and began "speaking in tongues."

Mrs. Hadeen's sister-in-law testified that the parties' religion had not had bad effects on the children and that their conduct was exemplary. Others testified similarly. Mr. Hadeen's sister-in-law testified that the church taught parents to spank their children until they stopped screaming. She further testified that ex-members were shunned. Another church member testified that ex-members were ostracized, and that some parents beat their children while others did not. According to this witness, the church came before family for Mrs. Hadeen.

The trial court interviewed three of the Hadeens' daughters in chambers. Lori testified that her grades are excellent and that she is active in basketball. She testified that the church did not force her or others to do anything. She said she did not visit her father because of the way he had treated her mother and tried to buy the children's affection. Lisa testified that her mother would not talk to her because she would not go to church. She left her mother because she beat her to force her to go to church. Lynn testified that she was in the seventh grade, played sports, had high grades, and did not like her father because he tried to bribe her. . . .

When the taking of testimony was complete, the trial court appointed a psychiatrist as an independent expert to evaluate (a) the children's interrelationship; (b) the parents' and children's interrelationship; (c) whether the children had personality problems; and (d) the problems, effects and desirability of split custody. . . .

Based on the records before it, the trial court entered the following findings of fact respecting custody:

a) That the four youngest children of the parties maintain strong emotional bonds with both parents.

b) That the Petitioner provides proper physical care for the children.

c) That the children are reasonably well adjusted with the exception of Lisa, who is having difficulties adjusting to the dissolution.

d) That both of the parties were members at one time in the First Community Churchs [sic] of America. The Respondent has subsequently removed himself from the church.

e) That the Petitioner, Judith Hadeen, is in complete submission to the First Community Church of America, to the exclusion of other reasonable relationships.

f) That the Petitioner's first fidelity is to the church, as is evidences [sic] by the Petitioner's rejection of the parties' minor child Lisa, and as evidenced by the Petitioner's move to Seattle with only a short time remaining in school and the subsequent move made in Seattle, all of which are not in the best interest of the parties' minor children.

g) That [the psychiatrist] recommends the children's custody be with the Petitioner, provided the problems caused by the Petitioner's religious involvement with the First Community Churches of America are satisfactorily resolved.

h) To award custody to the Petitioner, Judith Hadeen, would effectively cut Glen Hadeen off from his involvement with the children, and that the children need to have continued contact with both parents. That Lori Hadeen, the oldest of the parties' minor children, is deeply involved with the First Community Church of America, and she had close associations with her mother and the church. Because of her age Lori should be placed in the custody of her mother.

i) The best interest of the parties' other minor children is served by placing those children in the custody of the Respondent, Glen Hadeen, subject to reasonable rights of visitation for the Petitioner. Mrs. Hadeen assigns error to the last five of the findings. . . .

The best interests and welfare of the children are paramount in custody matters. The trial court must consider all relevant factors, including the parents' and children's wishes; the interrelationship of the children with their parents and others who may affect their best interests; the child's adjustment to his or her home, school, and community; and the mental and physical health of all concerned. . . . Whether the trial court considered and premised its decision upon considerations violative of the First Amendment's provision respecting religion requires our consideration of the principles used in determining the scope and application of the First Amendment's provision respecting religion.

The First Amendment provides in pertinent part, "Congress shall make no law respecting an establishment of religion, or prohibiting the free exercise thereof. . . ." This clause applies through the Fourteenth Amendment to the states, including the states' judiciary. The dual nature of the First Amendment's provision respecting religion encompasses the establishment clause, which guarantees government neutrality in matters touching upon religion, and the free exercise clause, which recognizes the individual's liberty in religious matters. The overall purpose respecting freedom of religion is to insure that no religion is advanced or favored, commanded or inhibited. . . .

Wisconsin v. Yoder considered whether compulsory school attendance laws past the eighth grade violated the right of Amish parents to exercise their religious beliefs. Noting that parents have the right to direct the religious upbringing of their children, Wisconsin v. Yoder, supra at 233-34, added: To be sure, the power of the parent, even when linked to a free exercise claim, may be subject to limitation . . . if it appears that parental decisions will jeopardize the health or safety of the child, or have a potential for significant social burdens. . . . The Court held that Amish parents could not be penalized for a violation of the compulsory attendance laws, but noted that the case before it was not a case in which "any harm to the physical or mental health of the child . . . has been demonstrated or may be properly inferred." Cases involving religion as an aspect of a custody dispute generally comport with the language of Wisconsin v. Yoder, regarding a showing that the parental decisions will jeopardize the child's health or safety. The showing that must be made and the test involved in the determination of when the jeopardy must arise are, however, subject to significant dispute.

We glean from . . . [prior] cases that religious decisions and acts may be considered in a custody decision only to the extent that those decisions or acts will jeopardize the temporal mental health or physical safety of the child. The question remains whether jeopardy to a child must be one of actual present impairment of the child's physical and/or mental well-being or a reasonable and substantial likelihood of impairment. We conclude that the . . . requirement of actual impairment is improvident and could lead a trial court to ignore a child's present welfare. We hold that the requirement of a reasonable and substantial likelihood of immediate or future impairment best accommodates the general welfare of the child and the free exercise of religion by the parents.

The trial court's finding that Mrs. Hadeen is in complete submission to the church to the exclusion of other "reasonable" relationships is a subjective conclusion which should have played no part in the trial court's decision unless Mrs. Hadeen's submission posed a substantial threat of endangering the children's mental or physical welfare. There was no evidence that Mrs. Hadeen neglected her children or did not provide them with her companionship because of her membership in the church. In fact, the trial court expressly found that the children were adjusted reasonably well.

Also unsupported by substantial evidence is the finding that the psychiatrist's recommendation of custody being with the mother was conditioned upon the mother's resolution of her involvement with the church. The psychiatrist stated that it was in the children's best interests to maintain contact with the father if that could be done without having the mother and father fight. He recommended that if the children were uncomfortable with visitation, then it would be in their best interests not to be forced to visit either parent. . . .

Reversed and remanded.

NOTES AND QUESTIONS

1. The "rejection" discussed by the *Hadeen* court is related to shunning or excommunication. More generally, it is an instance of the practice of exclusion,

which is a conventional sanction used by religious and social groups. How should this exclusion be dealt with in the custody context? Will entrance of a court decree ordering visitation with the parent to be shunned avoid the effects of rejection?

2. In Kendall v. Kendall 687 N.E.2d 1228 (Mass. 1997), *cert. denied*, 524 U.S. 953 (1998), the Massachusetts Supreme Judicial Court considered a case in which a trial court restricted a father, who had *joint* legal custody, from exposing his children to fundamentalist Christian doctrine. At the time of their marriage, the mother was Jewish and the father Catholic. Before marriage, the parties agreed that any children (they ultimately had three) would be raised in the Jewish faith. Several years after their marriage, the husband joined the Boston Church of Christ, a fundamentalist Christian church, and shares his church's belief that those of other faiths are "damned to go to hell." He has stated that he would like his children to accept Jesus Christ as their savior and that he would "never stop trying to save his children." The mother adopted Orthodox Judaism subsequently, and the oldest child began studying and adhering to Orthodox principles.

The trial court awarded the parents joint legal custody, with the mother having sole physical custody. The court also found it substantially damaging to the children to leave each parent free to expose the children without limitation to his or her religion and ordered both parents not to indoctrinate the children in a way that alienated them from the other parent. The father was further ordered not to take the children to his church or Sunday school or engage the children in prayer or Bible study that would promote rejection of their mother or their own Jewish self-identity. The order allowed, for example, the father to have pictures of Jesus Christ on the wall but did not allow taking the children to religious services where they would receive the message that those who do not accept Jesus Christ as their savior would burn in hell.

The court analyzed the issue as follows:

"[P]arents together have freedom of religious expression and practice which enters into their liberty to manage their familial relationships." Those individual liberties may be restricted where there is compelling interest. A parent's right to practice religion may be restricted only where limited exposure to that parent's beliefs is necessary to further the child's best interests. To do so, there must be an affirmative showing of harm caused by exposure to the conflicting religious teachings.

The determinative issue is whether the harm found to exist in this case to be so substantial so as to warrant a limitation on the defendant's religious freedom. . . . [P]roof of substantial harm "by implication" could be derived from testimony as to the child's general demeanor, attitude, school work, appetite, health or outlook. [This] court also opined that the "wholly uncorroborated testimony" of a parent was insufficient to demonstrate harm. By implication, the court suggested that a plaintiff should consult "church, school, medical or psychiatric authorities" to support a charge that a child has been harmed by exposure to the parent's religious beliefs. Moreover, the court specifically recommended the appointment of [a guardian ad litem]. . . .

Other states [addressing these issues] have struggled to define what constitutes substantial harm. Very few have actually ruled that substantial harm had been demonstrated.

We adhere to the line of cases requiring clear evidence of substantial harm. Application of the strict requirements in those cases comports with the protections of religious freedoms historically preserved under the Massachusetts Constitution.

The harm found to exist in this case presents more than . . . generalized fears. . . . Among the factors the judge cited to support her conclusion that substantial harm to the children had been demonstrated are the following findings: [that Jeffrey threatened to cut off the fringe of his son's religious clothing; that church services to which the children were taken included teaching that non-members would be damned to hell; that the oldest son may experience choosing a religion as choosing between his parents, which would likely cause him significant emotional distress; and that all three children are now emotionally distressed].

Whether the harm found to exist amounts to the "substantial harm" required to justify interference with the defendant's liberty interest is a close question, especially because there is considerable value in "frequent and continuing contact" between the child and both parents, and "contact with the parents' separate religious preferences." . . .

. . . [W]e conclude that the judge's findings support her order. . . .

Where, as here, the judge has found demonstrable evidence of substantial harm to the children, we reject the defendant's argument that the divorce judgment burdens his right to practice religion under the free exercise clauses of the Massachusetts and United States Constitution. Both . . . permit limitations on individual liberties where there exists a compelling interest. Promoting the best interests of the children is an interest sufficiently compelling to impose a burden on the defendant's right to practice religion and his parental right to determine the religious upbringing of his children. . . .

See also Johns v. Johns 918 S.W.2d 728 (Ark. App. 1996) (upholding trial court order to noncustodial parent requiring him to ensure church attendance over his free exercise objection); In re Jensen-Branch, 899 P.2d 803 (Wash. App. 1995) (reversing an order barring noncustodial father from teaching his children the precepts of his church, the Worldwide Church of God, where there was no evidence of harm to children).

3. A much discussed and sometimes litigated aspect of the relationship of religious belief to custody is presented in Osier v. Osier, 410 A.2d 1027 (Me. 1980). The trial court had granted custody to the father, largely on the basis of the mother's testimony that she would withhold her consent to a blood transfusion for her son even if it became medically necessary to safeguard the child's health. The court concluded "that the [mother's] religious beliefs are such that they would endanger the physical well-being or life of their child." The Maine Supreme Court reversed.

[I]n approaching a case of this sort the divorce court should make a preliminary determination of the child's best interest, without giving any consideration to either parent's religious practices, in order to ascertain which of them is the preferred custodial parent. Where that preliminary determination discloses that the religious practices of only the nonpreferred parent are at issue, any need for the court to delve into a constitutionally sensitive area is avoided.

If, on the other hand, that preliminary determination discloses a preference for the parent whose religious practices have been placed in issue, the divorce court, in fashioning an appropriate custody order, may take into account the consequences upon the child of that parent's religious practices. Because of the sensitivity of the constitutional rights involved, however, any such inquiry must proceed along a two-stage analysis designed to protect those rights against unwarranted infringement. To summarize that analysis briefly: first, in order to assure itself that there exists a factual situation necessitating such infringement, the court must make a threshold factual determination that the child's temporal well-being is immediately and substantially endangered by the religious practice in question and, if that threshold determination is made, second, the court must engage in a deliberate and articulated balancing of the conflicting interests involved, to the end that its custody order makes the least possible infringement upon the parent's liberty interests consistent with the child's well-being. . . .

If and only if the court is satisfied that an immediate and substantial threat to the child's well-being is posed by the religious practice in question, need it proceed to the second stage of the inquiry, requiring it to engage in an explicit balancing of the conflicting interests. In fashioning the appropriate order, the court should adopt a means of protecting the best interests of the child that makes the least possible intrusion upon the constitutionally protected interests of the parent. This balancing process requires the judge to conduct an evidentiary hearing on the alternative remedies available. . . . Although this court is not now willing to say that an order completely denying custody may never be appropriate where the temporal welfare of the child is genuinely threatened by a religious practice of the parent seeking custody, the divorce court should explore every reasonable alternative before resorting to such a drastic solution.

4. In the context of medical decision making based on a parent's religious objection, do we know how the group would receive a child healed by a procedure contrary to the group's beliefs but ordered by a court? Should the answer matter?

5. How do the approaches to parental religious beliefs and practices in *Hadeen* and *Osier* differ?

6. In *Hadeen*, the trial judge interviewed three of the daughters in chambers. This procedure is commonly authorized, sometimes by statute and sometimes by practice. Ohio Rev. Code Ann. §3109.04(A) and 3109.04(C) (1989) illustrate the former. It provides that the court "may allow any child who is twelve years of age or older to choose . . . the parent with whom the child is to live, unless the court finds that the parent so selected is unfit to take charge or unless the court finds . . . that it would not be in the best interest of the child to have the choice. . . ." The statute also provides that in determining the best interests of a child, "the court shall consider . . . [t]he wishes of the child regarding their [sic] custody if he is eleven years of age or older." What weight should be given to the child's preferences, and why?

STEPHEN WIZNER & MIRIAM BERKMAN, *BEING A LAWYER FOR A CHILD TOO YOUNG TO BE A CLIENT: A CLINICAL STUDY*

---

68 Neb. L. Rev. 330 (1989)

The widespread adoption of [appointing lawyers for children] has generated considerable professional and scholarly debate over the role of the child's legal representative in divorce litigation, especially in cases involving young children.

This debate encompasses diverse views, which include: (1) a child's lawyer in a custody case should play the classic advocate's role of employing all legal means to advance the child's expressed preference, regardless of the child's age or the lawyer's view of what would be in the child's best interests; (2) an attorney should refuse to represent a child who is too young to express a meaningful preference; (3) the attorney for the child has a duty to advocate her independent, professional judgment of the child's best interests, even if it is inconsistent with the child's expressed preference; (4) the child's attorney should act as a mediator, not an advocate, assisting the parents to negotiate a settlement of their dispute that may, or may not, give substantial weight to the child's preferences or the attorney's view of the best interests of the child; (5) the child's legal representative should act as a neutral, objective investigator, fact gatherer, and reporter, assisting the court in making a fully informed assessment of the needs of the child and how those needs can best be met; (6) counsel for the child should not act as a lawyer, but should serve only as a professional companion for the child, protecting her from the process, explaining the process to her, answering her questions, and influencing or "orchestrating" the conduct of the process so that the child is damaged as little as possible by the legal proceedings; (7) the appointment of independent legal counsel for a child disempowers the parents and undermines their ability to act in their child's best interests; and (8) a child's attorney should act to make the custody determination process more formal and public, to diminish the influence of mental health experts, and to advocate the abolition of the "best interest" standard in favor of a "primary caretaker" standard.

Some have argued that the child advocate in a divorce case must assume a variety of roles including confidante, counselor, investigator, negotiator, mediator, "orchestrator," and advocate. Depending on the age, maturity, intelligence, and emotional state of the child, as well as the circumstances of the case, some argue that the advocate should assume several or all of these roles simultaneously or at different times in a given case. Even those who hold this view may disagree on how to balance the various roles, how to evaluate and weigh the child's preferences, and what to do when a child is too young to state a meaningful preference. Others have argued that *none* of these roles are appropriate professional roles for lawyers, and that young children ought not have their own legal representatives in custody disputes.

PROBLEMS

1. Frank and Irene Jones are divorcing. They have two children. Irene is a devout member of a religious sect led by her father. Among this sect's principal tenets, shared by Irene, are beliefs that government is a manifestation of Satan and that all persons who are not members of the sect are God's enemies. Sect members also believe that they may ignore all acts of government, including tax laws and hunting and fishing regulations. There is no evidence that the children have been harmed, and they maintain a close bond with their mother.

What arguments will be made by either Frank or Irene? To what extent, if any, should the court consider the religious views of the sect and Irene?

2. The Reagans are also divorcing. The trial court has awarded custody of the children to their mother, Sheila Reagan, noting that although both parties enjoyed close relationships with their children, both were generally fit parents, and both had made appropriate arrangements for the children, the mother had a deep religious commitment while the father had no religious involvement. Arthur Reagan appealed. What arguments might be made for his position, and what will Sheila Reagan argue in response?

3. It is a bad year for marital stability. Juan and Anita Chavez are seeking a divorce. Both are Roman Catholics, and their three children have attended church regularly. The evidence indicates that Juan Chavez is highly observant, has participated in church-related activities, and believes that the children should attend parochial school. Anita is less observant and attends church only on major religious holidays, has no interest in church-related activities, and prefers that the children go to public school. Both wish primary custody of their children. May and should the trial judge take the relative religious commitments of the parents into account?

4. How, if at all, would your answer to each of these problems change if two of the children were eight and ten, the ten-year-old strongly preferred that the nonreligious parent receive custody, and the eight-year-old believed that he would go to hell if he did not follow the observances of the more religious parent?

d. Spouse Abuse

OPINION OF THE JUSTICES TO THE SENATE

691 N.E.2d 911 (Mass. 1998)

[The Massachusetts Supreme Judicial Court responded to questions from the Senate concerning the constitutionality of a bill establishing a presumption against awarding custody of a child to a parent where it appeared by a preponderance of the evidence that a parent had engaged in a pattern or serious incident of abuse. On such a showing, the burden of proof shifts to the challenged parent to prove that the child's best interests require placement with such parent.]

The Supreme Judicial Court and the Supreme Court of the United States have recognized that parents have a fundamental interest in their relationships with their children that is constitutionally protected. . . . However, parents' interests in their relationships with their children are not absolute, because "[t]he overriding principle in determining [the rights of a parent to custody] must be the best interests of the child."

There is a growing national awareness that children who witness or experience domestic violence suffer deep and profound harms. See, e.g., Cahn, Civil Images of Battered Women: The Impact of Domestic Violence on Child Custody Decisions, 44 Vand. L. Rev. 1041, 1055-1058 (1991). To better protect children, many States have adopted legislation making it more difficult for an abusive parent to obtain custody of a child in a divorce proceeding. Eleven States have adopted statutes creating presumptions similar to the one contained in Senate No. 2021.[5] . . .

In custody disputes between parents there is no constitutional or statutory entitlement to any particular form of custody. A parent seeking custody must simply present evidence of facts which demonstrate why such an award of custody serves the child's best interests. . . . Evidence of domestic violence is only one factor of many considered by a judge in making custody determinations. . . .

In determining whether the presumption and shifting of burden survive constitutional due process, the question is not whether the State may restrict parents' liberty interests in relating with their children, but rather, what standard of proof is constitutionally required for the State to do so. Senate No. 2021 would establish the presumption after proof by a "preponderance of the evidence." Both the Supreme Judicial Court and the Supreme Court of the United States have utilized the analysis contained in Mathews v. Eldridge, 424 U.S. 319 (1976), to balance these interests. This requires consideration of three distinct factors: (1) "the private interest that will be affected by the official action"; (2) "the risk of an erroneous deprivation of such interest through the procedures used, and the probable value, if any, of additional or substitute procedural safeguards"; and (3) "the Government's interest, including the function involved and the fiscal or administrative burdens that the additional or substitute procedural requirement would entail." We will examine each of the interests to determine whether the presumption created by Senate No. 2021 meets the requirements of due process.

1. *Private interests.* First we must identify the private interests. Creating a presumption that custody in a parent is not in the best interests of a child implicates the interest of the parent in his or her relationship with the child, as well as the child's interest in the relationship with his or her family. . . . [T]he presumption also implicates the child's right to be free from abusive or neglectful behavior.

Although parents have a fundamental, constitutionally protected interest in their relationships with their children, attainment of some of the children's best interest may involve some limitation on the liberties of one or the other of the parents. For example, in Kendall v. Kendall, 426 Mass. 238, 248 (1997), the court concluded that a parent's right to practice religion must be restricted when necessary to promote a child's best interests. In addition, if there is abuse or neglect, the State may require a partial or complete severance of the parent-child relationship to

---

5. "Four of the [eleven] states established presumptions, the other seven created rebuttable presumptions. The state statutes utilize different burdens of proof for establishing domestic violence as well as for rebutting the presumption." (Footnotes omitted.) Comment, Protecting New York's Children: An Argument for the Creation of a Rebuttable Presumption Against Awarding a Spouse Abuser Custody of a Child, 60 Alb. L. Rev. 1345, 1367 (1997). Some states make no mention of a standard for the presumption to attach, some require only credible evidence, and others require a preponderance of the evidence standard. To rebut the presumption, some States require the abusive parent to participate in special programs that address the underlying issues (e.g., anger management or programs for sexual offenders), and some require clear and convincing evidence that custody with the abusive parent is in the child's best interests. *Id.* . . .

protect a minor child from serious physical or emotional harm. Nevertheless, parents' interests in relating with their children are extremely important, and before the State may permanently deprive any parent of that interest, it should generally be required to meet a standard of proof higher than a preponderance of the evidence.

. . . [A] child's interest to be with his or her parents fluctuates with the child's interest to be free from abuse and neglect. . . . To allow a child to experience or witness domestic violence "is a violation of the most basic civil right, the most basic condition of civilized society: the right to live in physical security, free from the fear that brute force will determine the conditions of one's daily life." Therefore, the child's interest in being free from such abuse outweighs any interest a child has in family integrity. Because a child's interest in being free from the effects of domestic violence is extremely significant, proof by a preponderance of the evidence appears to be a sufficient standard to allow the rebuttable presumption to attach in custody disputes between parents.

2. *Risk of error.* . . .

A preponderance of evidence standard creates a greater risk of an erroneous deprivation of custody than a higher standard of proof. However, the presumption . . . "may be rebutted by a preponderance of the evidence that [a custody award to the challenged parent] is in the best interests of the child. . . ." [This allows the challenged parent an opportunity immediately to overcome the presumption.]

Another issue of concern is that one parent may make false allegations of abuse to gain an advantage in custody proceedings. The risk of success of such conduct is greater with a preponderance of the evidence standard than with a stricter standard of proof. However, parents acting in such a manner are clearly not acting in the child's best interests. Therefore, parents who make false allegations of abuse run the great risk that they will lose custody of their children. . . .

3. *The State's interest.* The final factor we must consider is the State's interest in the rebuttable presumption, and the burdens that a more demanding standard of proof would create for the child. The State, as parens patriae, has a "compelling interest in protecting the physical and psychological well-being of minors." It is thought by some that it is not in the best interests of a child to be in the custody of a perpetrator of domestic violence.[6] Thus, the State has a significant interest in protecting a child from residing with a parent who has a history

---

6. There is substantial evidence that children who witness or experience domestic violence suffer "a distinctly grievous kind of harm." *Custody of Vaughn*, 422 Mass. 590, 595, 664 N.E.2d 434 (1996). See Note, Domestic Violence and Custody Litigation: The Need for Statutory Reform, 13 Hofstra L. Rev. 407 (1985). Numerous articles addressing the effects of family violence on children support conclusions that (1) batterers are more likely to abuse their children than the average parent, see Comment, Protecting New York's Children: An Argument for the Creation of a Rebuttable Presumption Against Awarding a Spouse Abuser Custody of a Child, 60 Alb. L. Rev. 1345, 1352 (1997), and studies cited; (2) children exposed to domestic violence suffer both behavioral and developmental harm, see Comment, *supra* at 1351; and (3) that children exposed to domestic violence are more likely to be violent with their spouses or children. . . .

of committing acts of domestic violence, unless it is shown to be in the child's best interests.

A standard of proof stricter than the preponderance of the evidence would be inconsistent with the promotion of the State's interest. The burden of a stricter standard would fall entirely on the parent alleging abuse. A victim of domestic violence may not have the resources necessary to meet a higher standard of proof. . . . Because the purpose of Senate 2021 is to prevent children from witnessing or experiencing domestic violence, a standard of proof greater than a preponderance of the evidence would prevent many victims of abuse from proving the existence of domestic violence at custody proceedings, and a greater number of children would end up in the custody of a perpetrator of domestic violence.

. . . [T]he "preponderance of the evidence" standard . . . satisfies the requirements of due process under the State and Federal Constitutions.

NOTES AND QUESTIONS

1. An empirical study has questioned whether Massachusetts courts applying this standard take seriously the risks posed by abusive men in awarding custody and visitation. Jay G. Silverman, Cynthia M. Mesh, Carrie V. Cuthbert, Kim Slote & Lundy Bancroft, Child Custody Determinations in Cases Involving Intimate Partner Violence: A Human Rights Analysis, 94 Am. J. Pub. Health 951-957 (2004). This study indicates that judges are reluctant to limit visitation even in the face of persistent allegations of domestic violence.

2. North Dakota also has a statutory presumption against granting custody to a parent who has committed acts of domestic violence. The presumption is created by a showing of "credible evidence," and can be overcome only by "clear and convincing evidence" that the best interests of the child require that parent's participation as a custodial parent. . . ." N.D. Cent. Code § 14-09-06.2(1)(j). Would these standards for creation and rebuttal of the presumption satisfy the Mathews v. Eldridge test? See also Troxel v. Granville in Chapter 12. In Owan v. Owan, 541 N.W.2d 719 (N.D. 1996), there was evidence that both parents had engaged in some degree of violence toward each other. The North Dakota Supreme Court summarized a line of cases interpreting the statute generally and where both parents were involved:

> When there is credible evidence of domestic violence on the part of both parents, findings that ambiguously allude to the issue are insufficient to support a custody award. Rather, the trial court must make detailed findings on the domestic violence issue.
>
> We have detailed the procedure to be followed when there is evidence of domestic violence by both parents: . . . the trial court [must] measure the amount and extent of domestic violence inflicted by both parents. If the amount and extent of domestic violence inflicted by one parent is significantly greater than that inflicted by the other, the statutory presumption . . . will apply only to the parent who has inflicted the greater domestic violence, and will not apply to the parent who has inflicted the lesser. However, if the trial court finds that the amount and extent of the violence inflicted by one parent is roughly proportional to the violence inflicted

by the other parent, and both parents are otherwise found to be fit parents, the presumption against awarding custody to either perpetrating parent ceases to exist. In such a case, the trial court . . . may consider the remaining customary best-interests factors in making its custody decision.

541 N.W.2d at 722-723. A dissenting judge in *Owan* suggested that if the majority meant that a finding of domestic violence preempted consideration of all other factors relevant to the child's best interest, the effect would be a conclusive presumption that all parents who engage in domestic violence are unfit. Such a presumption, he argued, would be unconstitutional under Stanley v. Illinois, 405 U.S. 645 (1972). *Stanley* involved a presumption that unwed fathers as a class are unfit and therefore not entitled to notice in neglect proceedings involving their children. The Supreme Court struck down that presumption under the Due Process Clause. Although the Court acknowledged that many unwed fathers may not have a substantial relationship with their children, some unwed fathers do have such a relationship (including the father in that case), and a presumption precluding the opportunity to prove willingness and ability to care by a father was inconsistent with the state's interest in the child and with the father's constitutional interest in his child.

Do you agree with this analysis?

3. As we saw in Chapter 5, alternative dispute resolution, especially mediation, is widely promoted and used in domestic relations cases. Several jurisdictions have adopted mandatory mediation, and many authorize court-based mediation for these matters. *See* Andree G. Gagnon, Ending Mandatory Divorce Mediation for Battered Women, 15 Harv. Women's L.J. 272, 279-282 (1992).

The desirability of mediation in divorce cases involving spousal abuse is, however, sharply disputed. What reasons would lead to special concern about mediation in this setting? *See, e.g.,* John H. Haynes & Gretchen L. Haynes, Mediating Divorce 3-19 (1989); Lenore Walker, The Battered Woman 31, 35-37 (1979); Andree G. Gagnon, above, at 274; Douglas D. Knowlton & Tara L. Mulhauer, Mediation in the Presence of Domestic Violence: Is It the Light at the End of the Tunnel or Is a Train on the Track?, 70 N.D. L. Rev. 255, 264 (1994).

Most jurisdictions with mandatory or court-authorized mediation for divorce cases provide an exemption from mediation for abused parties. *See* Alison E. Gerencser, Family Mediation: Screening for Domestic Abuse, 23 Fla. St. U. L. Rev. 43 (1995). Those exemptions often require a court to determine whether mediation is desirable, or will be harmful, and often vest the court with considerable discretion in deciding whether to exempt a case involving alleged abuse from mediation. *E.g.,* N.C. Gen. Stat. §50-13.1(c) (1997) (waiver for "good cause"); Fla. Stat. Ann. §44.102 (1995) (court shall not refer for mediation in cases where it finds a history of domestic abuse that would "compromise" the mediation process); Or. Rev. Stat. §107.179 (1997) (court "may" waive mediation if it finds it "likely" that mediation will produce "severe emotional distress"). What difficulties arise with these kinds of provisions? What approach should be taken to the use of mediation where domestic violence is alleged?

4. In a little less than a decade, the courts have shifted from viewing domestic violence as a private matter between the parents to seeing it as a critical consideration in child custody decisions. The California legislature expressly declared

"that the perpetration of child abuse or domestic violence in a household where a child resides is detrimental to the child." Cal. Fam. Code §3020(a). The ALI Principles also systematically incorporate consideration of domestic violence into their approach to custody decision making. *See* Merle H. Weiner, Domestic Violence and Child Custody: Importing the American Law Institute's Principles of the Law of Family Dissolution into Oregon Law, 35 Willamette L. Rev. 643 (1999). *But see* Knight v. Knight 680 A.2d 1035 (Me. 1996) (resumption of visitation by father, who was a convicted murderer, could not be conditioned on certification by therapist that children were ready for visitation and could not be based exclusively on the children's willingness to visit).

PROBLEMS

1. Martha and George have a long history of bickering. On two occasions, George insulted Martha's intelligence and physical appearance to the point where Martha threw a plate and a pot at George, hitting him but doing no damage. It is uncontested that, while both Martha and George very much want custody of their two children, Alice and Ron, Martha has been the primary caretaker. Both children witnessed these incidents. Who should be awarded custody under a statute like that in Massachusetts? Like the statute in North Dakota?

2. Susan and Walter married ten years ago, shortly after graduating from college. They have a seven-year-old and a nine-year-old. Susan has been the primary caretaker, but Walter has been actively involved with the children. One day, shortly after he returned home from work, Susan told Walter she was leaving him for his best friend, Arthur. Susan moved out the next day, taking the children with her. Walter, who had no idea that Susan was dissatisfied with their relationship, was devastated. He tried to talk Susan into returning, to no avail. Several weeks later, Susan came by unexpectedly to pick up some of her belongings. She and Walter quarreled. Susan, who had been drinking, slapped Walter and Walter struck back, knocking her across the room and breaking her nose. Susan quickly obtained a restraining order keeping Walter away from her and the children. Walter did not contest the order and was not present at the hearing at which it was issued. He has not seen the children in the intervening six months. How should custody be allocated under the principles set out in the principal case and cases discussed in the notes?

3. During a domestic dispute, Ben struck Carmen in the face, blackening her eye. Carmen sought a divorce and sole custody of their two children, Robin, age five, and Alex, age four. A court-appointed custody evaluator reports that the children are closely attached to both parents, that Ben has not physically abused either the children or Carmen other than on this one occasion, and that Ben strongly desires joint legal custody and generous visitation, or if that is not possible, sole custody with generous visitation to Carmen. He also reports that Carmen remains very angry with Ben, does not want any more contact with him than is absolutely necessary, and wishes a limited and fixed visitation schedule that removes the chance of unplanned interaction with Ben as far as possible. How should these factors be considered and weighed in making a custody decision?

e. Unfriendly Co-parenting

RENAUD V. RENAUD

721 A.2d 463 (Vt. 1998)

JOHNSON, J. Daniel Renaud (father) appeals from a divorce judgment of the Franklin Family Court. He contends the court: (1) abused its discretion in awarding Gail Renaud (mother) sole legal and physical parental rights and responsibilities notwithstanding the court's finding that mother had interfered with the relationship between the child and father; and (2) erroneously divided the marital estate. We affirm.

The parties were married in October 1989. They had one child, a son, born in January 1994. In May 1996, the parties separated following father's disclosure that he was having an affair with a co-worker and wanted a divorce. At the time of trial in April and May of 1997, mother was living with the three-year-old child in the marital home, and father was living with the co-worker and her children.

Both parties worked full time in supervisory positions for the federal government. Before the separation, both shared in attending to the minor's childcare needs. Mother arranged her work schedule to have Fridays off to spend with the child. Father took the child to daycare in the morning, visited him there during the day, and brought him home at night. Mother generally took time off from work when the child was sick, purchased his clothes, and did his laundry. The court found that both parents provided the child with love, discipline, structure, and guidance, and that either would be fit to serve as the custodial parent.

Following the separation, father voluntarily moved out, and mother and child continued to reside in the family home. Almost immediately, mother began to impede father's contact with the child, forcing father to file a number of motions to establish an emergency visitation schedule. Following a hearing in July 1996, the court established a temporary visitation schedule. Thereafter, mother filed a succession of relief-from-abuse petitions, alleging that father had physically and sexually abused the minor. The allegations ranged from evidence of diaper rash, to sunburn, cuts and bruises, and inappropriate touching. These petitions further disrupted father's contact with the child, resulting in periods of noncontact and supervised visitation.

None of the abuse allegations was substantiated, and all of the petitions were ultimately dismissed. Indeed, the court found that father had never abused the minor, that the factual support for the "excessive number of motions and petitions" was "weak at best," and that mother had, in fact, "imagined abuse where there was no abuse." The court further found that mother's actions were the result of a heightened distrust of father because of his marital unfaithfulness, and that her "baseless suspicions had adversely affected [the minor] in that he is no longer as loving towards [father] as he once was." A team of psychiatric experts appointed by the court observed that the child interacted well with each parent, but noted that mother's repeated accusations had damaged the child's relationship with father, and warned that if such accusations continued they could seriously compromise the father-child relationship.

688   9.   Child Custody

The court awarded sole parental rights and responsibilities to mother, albeit "with some hesitation." The court found that the child had an extremely close emotional relationship with mother and that "upsetting that relationship [was] likely to be detrimental to [the child]." The court further observed that mother had sought counseling to overcome her emotional problems resulting from the divorce, and concluded that she would be able "in a reasonable period of time . . . [to] help repair the damage she caused to the relationship between [father] and [the child]," and could "actively encourage frequent and open contact" between them. To further ensure that this occurred, the court specifically ordered mother to encourage the child to develop a warm and loving relationship with father, forbade either parent from making disparaging remarks about the other in the minor's presence, and ordered extensive visitation with father totalling about fifty percent of the minor's time. This appeal followed.

I.

In light of the court's express findings that mother had undermined the child's relationship with father by filing excessive and baseless abuse allegations, father contends that the court's decision to award mother sole parental rights and responsibilities was a patent abuse of discretion. Like the trial court here, we are reluctant to condone any conduct by a parent that tends to diminish the child's relationship with the other parent. . . .

The paramount consideration in any custody decision, however, is the best interests of the child. . . . Children are not responsible for the misconduct of their parents toward each other, and will not be uprooted from their home merely to punish a wayward parent. . . . Nevertheless, a child's best interests are plainly furthered by nurturing the child's relationship with both parents, and a sustained course of conduct by one parent designed to interfere in the child's relationship with the other casts serious doubt upon the fitness of the offending party to be the custodial parent. . . .

This is not to say that evidence of alienation of affection automatically precludes the offending parent from obtaining custody. . . . The best interests of the child remains the paramount consideration. Courts should be wary, however, of overreliance on such otherwise significant considerations as the child's emotional attachment to, or expressed preference for, the offending parent, or on such factors as stability and continuity. For as one court has observed, "The desires of young children, capable of distortive manipulation by a bitter, or perhaps even well-meaning, parent, do not always reflect the long-term best interest of the children." Nehra v. Uhlar, 43 N.Y.2d 242, 372 N.E.2d 4, 7, 401 N.Y.S.2d 168 (N.Y. 1977). And although stability is undoubtedly important, the short-term disruption occasioned by a change of custody may be more than compensated by the long-term benefits of a healthy relationship with both parents.

Thus, where the evidence discloses a continual and unmitigated course of conduct by a parent designed to poison a child's relationship with the other parent, a change of custody from the offending parent may well be in the child's long-term best interests. . . .

A more subtle, but no less invidious, form of interference in parent-child relations may take the form of persistent allegations of physical or sexual abuse. In *Young*, for example, the court reversed an award of custody to the mother where the trial court had inexplicably ignored uncontradicted evidence that the mother had filed numerous false accusations of sexual abuse by the father. As the court observed, "these repeated uncorroborated and unfounded allegations of sexual abuse brought by the mother against the father cast serious doubt upon her fitness to be the custodial parent." . . . The situation is more difficult where the allegations of abuse, although ultimately found to be baseless, may initially be in doubt. Society has a strong interest in encouraging parents to take action if they suspect that their child is being abused. Accordingly, courts should infer an ulterior motive in the filing of such charges only where a parent knew, or reasonably should have known, that they were groundless. Here, the court found that the factual support for mother's relief-from-abuse petitions was "weak at best," and that mother "imagined abuse where there was no abuse" because of her emotional distress and distrust of husband. The record amply supports these findings, but the findings do not indicate whether mother knew or reasonably should have known that the petitions were groundless.

The record mitigates in favor of mother in this regard. The evidence showed that she did not act precipitously in filing the petitions, but consulted with the child's pediatrician and therapist, as well as her own therapist, about her suspicions. The child's pediatrician recalled at the first relief-from-abuse hearing that mother had expressed grave concern that father was neglecting the child's physical well-being, and did not appear to be acting out of malice or spite. Moreover, while he informed her that the child's physical condition did not necessarily suggest abuse or neglect, he also told her that if the child's sunburns continued he would "be quite alarmed," and would feel that the "caregiver [father] is not able to protect [the child] from an obvious source of harm." Although the court ultimately dismissed the petition, finding no evidence of abuse, it did express concern about the sunburn and bruises, and urged father to "re-double [his] efforts to be vigilant."

Facts concluding Mother's allegations were not groundless

Mother also expressed her concerns to the child's therapist. She was particularly anxious about statements by the child suggesting that father had manipulated the child's penis. The therapist recalled at the second relief-from-abuse hearing that mother "chiefly wanted guidance." Although he ultimately concluded that it was unlikely the child had been abused, he was sufficiently concerned to contact Social and Rehabilitation Services. Later, when mother informed him that she had filed a relief-from-abuse petition, the therapist reassured her that he would have done the same under the circumstances. Although the court again found the allegations of abuse to be groundless, it stressed that it was "not at all suggesting that the mother's reaction wasn't appropriate. She was obviously concerned. She was obviously worried. But we don't find anything devious about what she did here . . . basically as a concerned mother under the circumstances."

Mother's therapist also contacted SRS on mother's behalf after hearing her concerns. Like the pediatrician and the child's therapist, he believed that mother was primarily seeking expert guidance and reassurance that the child was being well cared for.

Thus, the record evidence does not support a finding that mother's purpose was to alienate the child from his father, or that her concerns were wholly unreasonable. It is particularly significant in this regard that mother repeatedly sought expert guidance before acting and received ambiguous messages, suggesting on the one hand that the physical evidence of abuse was weak, but on the other hand that her concerns were not entirely unfounded and certainly warranted investigation.

The trial court also focused on the relatively transient nature of mother's emotional distress, finding it "likely that, in a reasonable period of time, [mother] will be less distrustful of [father] and will help repair the damage she caused to the relationship between [father and child]." Although there was conflicting evidence on this point, substantial credible expert evidence supported the conclusion that mother's actions were a transient reaction to a highly volatile emotional situation, and that she had progressed to the point where she could within a reasonable period of time cooperate with father and foster a healthy relationship with the child. We note that the child's tender years may facilitate the healing process envisioned by the court, whereas an older child might not be so amenable to change.

Indeed, the evidence and the findings here contrast sharply with those in another case decided today. There, the family court awarded the father parental rights and responsibilities for two teenage boys, notwithstanding its express finding that the father had willfully poisoned the mother's relationship with the boys and had demonstrated no inclination to act otherwise. The court had also found that the mother had been the children's primary care provider before the separation, and was the custodian of choice in all other significant respects. We thus concluded that an award to the father in these circumstances would seriously impede the mother's opportunity to reestablish a healthy relationship with her sons in the future, and that reversal of the judgment was compelled. Here, in contrast, the court expressly found that mother's actions were transitory, unlikely to be repeated, and subject to cure.

Finally, we note that the court awarded father extremely liberal visitation, resulting in a nearly equal sharing of time with the child. This fact, coupled with the court's finding that a change of custody would be highly detrimental to the minor, and that mother would be able to foster a healthy relationship with father within a reasonable period of time, leads us to conclude that the court did not abuse its discretion in awarding parental rights and responsibilities to mother. We hasten to remind the parties, however, that the court's ruling is subject to future modification, and underscore the court's specific admonishment to mother to encourage a warm and loving relationship between father and child. . . .

Affirmed.

NOTES AND QUESTIONS

1. Compare *Renaud* with the decision of the New York Appellate Division in the custody fight between Mia Farrow and Woody Allen.

Woody and Mia began a relationship in 1980 without marrying. At the beginning of the relationship Mia had seven adopted children from an earlier marriage. She and Woody adopted a daughter, Dylan; Woody became close to Mia's youngest son, Moses, and adopted him; and Woody and Mia had a biological child, Satchel. Shortly after Woody's adoption of Dylan and Moses became final, Mia discovered that Woody was having an affair with her college-age daughter, Soon Yi Previn. During their ensuing dispute, Mia accused Woody of abusing Dylan. Woody sought custody of three children, arguing that Mia had fabricated the charges in an effort to alienate the children from him.

The trial court found that the evidence in support of the abuse charges was inconclusive. Nonetheless, the court observed:

It is true that Ms. Farrow's failure to conceal her feelings from the rest of the family and the acting out of her feelings of betrayal and anger toward Mr. Allen enhanced the effect of the situation on the rest of her family. We note though that the reasons for her behavior, however prolonged and extreme, are clearly visible in the record. On the other hand the record contains no acceptable explanation for Allen's commencement of the sexual relationship with Ms. Previn at the time he was adopting Moses and Satchel, or for the continuation of that relationship at the time he was supposedly experiencing the joys of fatherhood.

The court concluded that the children had been deeply disturbed by Woody's inappropriate relationship with their sister, and that contact "between Ms. Previn and her siblings in the context of the relationship with Mr. Allen would be virtually unavoidable even if Mr. Allen chose to insulate his children from the relationship." The court also held that even if the allegations of abuse were untrue, "[a]t the very least, the process of investigation itself has left the relationship between Mr. Allen and Dylan severely damaged." Accordingly, the appellate court upheld Mia's continued custody award, honored Moses's desire that Woody not have visitation, and granted Woody very limited supervised visitation with Dylan and Satchel. One judge dissented in part, observing that Woody had had a warm and loving father-son relationship with Satchel, but that the relationship was in jeopardy "in large measure because Mr. Allen is being estranged and alienated from his son by the current custody and visitation arrangement." The dissenting judge also observed that Mia had encouraged the estrangement, telling Satchel that he was seeing a doctor that "was going to help him not to see Mr. Allen anymore." Allen v. Farrow, 197 A.D.2d 327 (N.Y. App. Div. 1994).

Is the New York court's approach to Allen v. Farrow consistent with the approach of the Vermont court in *Renaud*? In each case, how did the court treat the father's act of infidelity? Did each mother's allegation of child abuse represent reasonable suspicion about someone who had given her reason for distrust or an unsupported allegation that poisoned the family relationships? Did both mothers try to undermine the father's relationships with the children, and how did the respective courts view their actions? How did the courts construe the children's interests? How much weight did the courts give to the children's interest in remaining in contact with both parents? Did the courts pass moral judgment on any part of the parents' behavior?

2. In the early 1990s, psychologist Richard Gardner argued that "parental alienation syndrome" should be recognized as a divorce phenomenon in which one parent, typically the mother, attempts to maintain the psychological bond with the child by undermining the child's relationship with the other parent. He recommended a transfer of custody to the non-alienating parent in egregious cases. The Parental Alienation Syndrome: A Guide for Mental Health and Legal Professionals (1992, 2d ed. 1998). Critics have noted that parental alienation syndrome is not a recognized diagnosis in the Diagnostic and Statistical Manual IV (DSM-IV) and that Gardner's work did not appear in peer-reviewed journals. Courts, however, can take parental willingness to cooperate into account without a formal diagnosis of a psychiatric "syndrome." See, e.g., C.J.L. v. M.W.B., 879 So. 2d 1169 (Ala. 2003), discussing the distinction between expert testimony establishing parental alienation syndrome and a custody evaluation documenting the mother's efforts to undermine the children's relationship with their father through, among other things, false accusations of child abuse. Other scholars have documented the negative impact that parental conflict has on children's well-being without using the term *parental alienation*. See, e.g., Janet R. Johnston & Linda E.G. Campbell, Impasses of Divorce (1988).

3. Many states, like Vermont, have a custody preference for the parent who will facilitate the child's continuing contact with both parents. See, e.g., California's "friendly parent" provision, Cal. Fam. Code § 3040(a)(1) ("the court shall consider, among other factors, which parent is more likely to allow the child frequent and continuing contact with the non-custodial parent"); Va. Code Ann. § 20-124.3(6) (Michie 1994) (directing the courts to consider, in determining the child's best interests, "[t]he propensity of each parent to actively support the child's contact and relationship with the other parent, the relative willingness and demonstrated ability of each parent to maintain a close and continuing relationship with the child, and the ability to cooperate in matters affecting the child"). The usual indicia of friendliness to maintaining "constructive" post-divorce relationships between the other parent and the child include willingness to permit visitation during the time between separation and divorce, and the absence of restrictions on the other parent's opportunity to visit. See, e.g., Owensby v. Lepper, 666 N.E.2d 1251 (Ind. App. 1996) (denial of visitation for seven months; custody awarded to father, although mother had actual custody of child prior to divorce); Marriage of Wang, 896 P.2d 450 (Mont. 1995) (requiring that father not work during visitation). Other indicia include negative comments regarding the other parent. E.g., Marriage of Finer, 920 P.2d 325 (Colo. App. 1996) (father awarded custody). A survey of cases indicating a preference for the "friendly parent" appears in Edward B. Borris, Parents' Ability and Willingness to Cooperate: "The Friendly Parent Doctrine" as a Most Important Factor in Recent Child Custody Cases, 10 Divorce Litig. 65 (Apr. 1998). For a critique of the doctrine, particularly in the context of allegations of abuse, see Mary Ann Mason, The Custody Wars 143-173 (1999).

4. False charges of spousal or child abuse are perhaps the most dramatic instances of bad relations between parents. The Massachusetts court in Opinion of the Justices to the Senate (on page 681, above) refers to that concern and notes that false allegations of this kind create a great risk that parents will lose

custody of their children. *See also* In re Marriage of Kunkel, 546 N.W.2d 634 (Iowa App. 1996) (custody to father, although mother, who made false allegations of physical abuse, had been primary caretaker); Campbell v. Campbell, 604 A.2d 33 (Me. 1992). In the latter case, the Maine Supreme Judicial Court announced the following standard for determining the relevance of false abuse claims:

> We hold that the parent's action is relevant to the divorce court's consideration only if the court finds by clear and convincing evidence both 1) that the parent willfully misused the protection process in order to gain a tactical advantage in the divorce proceeding, and 2) that in the particular circumstances of the divorcing couple and their children, that willful misuse tends to show that the acting parent will after the divorce have a lessened ability and willingness to work with the other parent in their joint responsibilities for the children.

604 A.2d at 34. *See* Borris, above, at 71-73.

How much risk does this standard create for a spouse who has been the object of domestic abuse? Would Mia Farrow bear a substantial risk under such a standard in accusing Woody Allen of abusing their three-year-old daughter Dylan on the basis of inconclusive evidence?

5. Emphasis on the willingness of one parent to maintain friendly relations with the other is consistent with the convictions of proponents of alternative dispute resolution for continuing and constructive post-divorce relations among parents and children and with the movement toward joint custody, discussed above *See* Lee E. Teitelbaum & Laura DuPaix, Alternative Dispute Resolution and Divorce: Natural Experimentation in Family Law, 40 Rutgers L. Rev. 1093, 1108-1109 (1988). To what extent does placing weight on friendly post-divorce relations undermine the contributions made by the caretaking parent during marriage? On what basis can one say that it is better for the child to be placed with a parent who did not perform the caretaking role during marriage rather than with his or her caretaker, even though he or she may be the angrier parent at divorce? Should the reason for the divorce matter? What would have happened in Allen v. Farrow if the court gave greater weight to friendly co-parenting?

As with the relatively recent interest in mediation of divorce issues and joint custody, an emphasis on friendly post-divorce relations reflects the prominence of family therapeutic principles. For a discussion of the relationship between the claims of helping professionals and judicial decision making and the risks created by this relationship, *see* Martha Albertson Fineman, Dominant Discourse, Professional Language, and Legal Change in Child Custody Decisionmaking, 101 Harv. L. Rev. 727 (1988), excerpted at page 653, above. An interdisciplinary group of lawyers, psychologists, social workers, and judges offers the following caveat about friendly parent doctrines:

> The sometimes unspoken foundation for [this doctrine] posits that, ideally, a child should be raised, even after the parents' divorce, by two cooperative parents. . . . Yet it is a truism — one that most judges would acknowledge, that the parent better able

to foster the child's relationship with the noncustodial parent is not necessarily the parent better able to pilot the child across the huge sea of concerns that determine the child's health, happiness, and passage to successful adulthood. . . . The problem — one that has been insoluble when efforts have been made to deconstruct other custody criteria — is giving content to the friendly parentism while minimizing the risk that its vague and indeterminate qualities will be misused to cover decisions based unduly on decisionmakers' personal values.

National Interdisciplinary Colloquium on Child Custody, Legal and Mental Health Perspectives on Child Custody Law: A Deskbook for Judges 73-74 (Robert J. Levy ed., 1998).

Should the emphasis on friendly co-parenting extend to the parent's lawyers? For a discussion of the relationship between therapeutic jurisprudence and collaborative styles of lawyering in family law, *see* Symposium: Therapeutic Jurisprudence and Preventive Law's Transformative Potential for Particular Areas of Legal Practice, 5 Psychol. Pub. Pol. & L. 951 (1999).

6. The therapy ordered in Allen v. Farrow did not succeed in repairing the father-daughter relationship. Dylan objected to seeing her father because of his relationship with her sister, and in a subsequent proceeding the court denied Woody's request for therapeutic visitation. The order was upheld on appeal. Allen v. Farrow, 215 A.D.2d 137, 626 N.Y.S.2d 125 (1995).

June Carbone, *From Partners to Parents: The Second Revolution in Family Law*

193-194 (2000)

Custody battles have become ground zero in the gender wars because they are among the few remaining family law disputes where courts judge adult behavior. Mia Farrow and Gail Renaud both felt wronged by their partners' infidelity. The fault system would have given voice to at least Gail's sense of betrayal (and Mia's, had she and Woody ever married), the tender years presumption would have given both mothers custody, and visitation was likely to happen informally, if it occurred at all. In the new system, the custody determination carries the full symbolic and practical weight of the adults' conflict. Maintaining parental ties is the new sine qua non of responsible parenthood — and a possible lever in the effort to exact revenge on the other spouse. The emphasis on parental cooperation then increases the importance of potentially disqualifying conduct: domestic violence, child abuse, and parental alienation carry greater significance as they become the limited exceptions to the principle of shared parenting. And, in this context, the courts still pass judgment. While neither the *Allen* nor the *Renaud* courts considered the father's infidelity to their partners, they ruled that Woody's behavior with Soon Yi . . . had harmed his children, and that Gail Renaud's baseless allegations against her faithless ex-husband were bad parenting. Custody decisions — and the connections between parents and children — hold the new moral center of family law.

C.   VISITATION AND ITS ENFORCEMENT

MORGAN v. FORETICH

546 A.2d 407 (D.C. Cir. 1988)

STEADMAN, J. The formal parties to this appeal are the divorced parents of a daughter, *H*, the ultimate real party in interest. She was born in 1982. On November 8, 1984, appellant Morgan was awarded custody of *H* and appellee Foretich was given liberal visitation. Almost continuously since that date, the parties have been in litigation on these issues. . . . Now before us is an appeal from an order of August 19, 1987, granting Foretich a two-week summer visitation with *H* and a subsequent order of civil contempt and imprisonment of Morgan for refusal to comply with the August 19 order.

Some of the background facts, through August of 1986, were recited in our previous opinions. In January 1985, within two months of the custody and visitation order of November 8, 1984, Morgan began to make accusations that Foretich was sexually abusing *H* during visitation. . . .

Matters first came to a head in February 1986, when Morgan refused to allow *H* to visit Foretich in accordance with the court-ordered visitation schedule. Hearings were held in June and July of 1986 on several motions, including Foretich's motions to hold Morgan in contempt and for change of custody and Morgan's motions for temporary suspension of visitation and to compel discovery. On July 17, 1986, Judge Dixon orally announced his finding that Morgan had failed to prove by a preponderance of the evidence that Foretich had abused *H*, and that Morgan had disobeyed the visitation orders without lawful justification or excuse. A series of further hearings and orders then ensued, resulting in a finding of contempt and order of incarceration in August 1986. . . . On appeal, we upheld the closure of the contempt hearings and affirmed the judgment of contempt.

Meanwhile, Judge Dixon had ordered that visitation be resumed. When Morgan again failed to comply, Judge Dixon found her in contempt and ordered her incarcerated on February 17, 1987. Morgan was released from jail on February 19, 1987, and on February 24, 1987, visitations resumed for the first time in over a year. From February 24 through April 1, 1987, the visits were supervised and lasted one hour. On April 1, Judge Dixon ordered that the visits be extended to four hours.

On April 6, 1987, Judge Dixon began a series of hearings on a motion by Foretich for a change of custody and termination of Morgan's parental rights and on Morgan's cross motion to suspend visitation, or, in the alternative, to require supervised visitation. . . .

During the course of the hearings on the motions, Judge Dixon entered several orders continuing to gradually expand the visitation schedule. On April 21, 1987, he ordered the first overnight unsupervised weekend visitations. Pursuant to further orders, *H* spent nine or ten weekends with Foretich. Several emergency stays of the weekend visitation orders sought by Morgan and H's guardian were denied by this court. H's guardian played some part in most of these weekend visits and submitted reports of her observations to Judge Dixon.

Then on August 19, 1987, with the hearings still not completed, Judge Dixon entered an order providing for an extended visitation from August 22 through September 6, 1987. In his six-page order, he noted, inter alia, that since H was scheduled to return to school on September 8, "[w]hatever the court's ultimate ruling may be on the pending motions, to further delay the defendant-father's entitlement to summer visitation with his child until that ultimate ruling results in a denial of said summer visitation by default."

Morgan appealed this visitation order that same day. Her emergency motion for stay pending appeal filed the following day was denied by this court on August 21. Morgan failed to comply with the visitation order. She secreted the child and refused to reveal her whereabouts. (To this day, H remains hidden.) On August 24, Judge Dixon issued an order to show cause why Morgan should not be held in contempt. . . .

After a hearing held on August 26, Judge Dixon held Morgan in contempt and ordered her incarcerated, effective August 28. He also ordered that the security posted one year earlier pursuant to this court's order be forfeited at the rate of $5,000 per day. On August 27, Morgan appealed the contempt judgment and sought a stay pending appeal. The stay was denied and Morgan was incarcerated on August 28, where she remains.

A principal issue before us is whether the record supports the trial court's action in ordering a two-week summer visitation. Our standard of review is well established. Trial court decisions as to visitation rights are reversible only for clear abuse of discretion. . . . [A] trial court judgment may not be set aside except for errors of law, unless it appears the judgment is "plainly wrong or without evidence to support it." Thus, to the extent that such decisions rest on factual foundations, such findings are binding unless clearly erroneous. Such is particularly the case where, as here, the findings rest in significant part on considerations of credibility. . . .

The critical factual determination challenged by Morgan was that sexual abuse of H by her father had not been proven, or, as the court put it, the evidence was "in equipoise." That finding, asserts Morgan, was "plainly wrong." . . .

A review of the record shows that there was probative evidence on both sides of the issue of abuse. The ultimate question, however, is not how we weigh the evidence but rather whether a finder of fact, fully and personally knowledgeable of not only the evidence presented in the April to August hearings but also the entire history of these proceedings from November 1985 forward, would be clearly erroneous in concluding that the alleged sexual abuse had not been proven and would commit a clear abuse of discretion in allowing a two-week visitation. We cannot so conclude. . . .

In this litigation, neither party can conclusively speak for H. She has her own champion, a court-appointed guardian. Although the guardian states that she is in clear disagreement with the trial court's order for the extended summer visitation, we think correct her assessment that she "cannot argue that the order was without evidence to support it or an abuse of Judge Dixon's discretion." . . .

The trial court here, as in many family division matters, has the deeply taxing and unenviable responsibility of struggling to deal justly with changing lives. Inherent in the process are new developments and events. One such development occurred at oral argument before us. In her brief to us, Morgan urged, as a "wiser and fairer" alternative, the appointment of a multidisciplinary team of neutral experts to evaluate H's case and to recommend an appropriate visitation schedule. The guardian from an early point in her service has consistently championed this step. In our order of May 29, 1987, we expressed our confidence that the trial court would consider the use of a court-appointed expert. Now, before us in oral argument, Foretich announced that he no longer opposed the creation of such a team. . . .

We take no firm position on this alternative or other surfacing issues not yet the subject of an appeal. But time moves on as the impasse continues. . . .

Probably neither our courts nor any courts anywhere in the world can deal in a perfect way with matters so intimately linked to a family unit formed and dissolved. We can but try. The little girl H grows older day by day. It is she, first and foremost, to whom the courts must seek to render justice as the process moves on. . . . [T]he orders appealed from are affirmed.

NOTES AND QUESTIONS

1. Denial of visitation is an extreme remedy, rarely approved. In Larroquette v. Larroquette, 293 So. 2d 628 (La. App. 1974), the father had visiting privileges with his eight-year-old daughter, which he exercised regularly. After about one year (during which the mother remarried), the mother testified that the daughter began to be upset when she returned from weekend visitation, which she attributed to the child's sleeping in the same bed with her father and his "concubine." Mr. Laroquette admitted that he was living in "open concubinage," but said that he would have the concubine out of the house during subsequent visits. The trial judge awarded visitation privileges every Saturday, with overnight privileges every other week, on condition that the visitation be exercised in his household only in the absence of persons other than relatives. The mother appealed. The appellate court held that visitation in the father's home should not be allowed, even on a conditional basis, but that the father should not be denied visitation altogether.

See also J. L. P. (H.) v. D. J. P., 643 S.W.2d 865 (Mo. App. 1982), where the husband appealed from a trial court order denying overnight visitation to a father who was homosexual and was living with a partner. The trial court order was affirmed, although the court observed that the record would have supported "an even broader prohibition upon the father's exercise of visitation in the presence of known homosexuals."

As these cases indicate, courts employ broad discretion in fashioning visitation arrangements. For other examples, see Schlick v. Schlick, 678 So. 2d 1176 (Ala. Civ. App. 1996) (order requiring custodial mother to install additional telephone line for child where she screened incoming calls and would not answer phone approved in defining father's visitation rights); In re Marriage of Elmer,

936 P.2d 617 (Colo. App. 1997) (order requiring supervision of exchanges for father's visits to minimize parental disputes that the child would witness). However, courts will find abuses of discretion from time to time. *See* Knight v. Knight 680 A.2d 1035 (Me. 1996) (resumption of visitation by father, who was a convicted murderer, could not be conditioned on certification by therapist that children were ready for visitation); Khan v. Khan, 654 N.Y.S.2d 34 (App. Div. 1997) (unsupervised visitation overturned because of father's history of violence against mother).

2. What weight should trial judges give to the child's expressed preference regarding visitation? Should that preference be given more weight than with respect to the determination of custody, or less weight? *See* Steven L. Novinson, Post-Divorce Visitation: Untying the Triangular Knot, 1983 U. Ill. L.F. 119, reviewing the arguments in both directions.

Although interference with visitation often is attributed to hostile custodial parents, children themselves may be unwilling to cooperate in visitation arrangements. A study of 59 children between the ages of 5 and 12 in Toronto, Ontario, who were involved in custody or visitation disputes reports that some 60 percent of the children held generally negative attitudes toward visitation, but only 10 percent completely refused to see a parent. Older children more often held negative attitudes toward visitation, and a history of parental violence was often present. Negative feelings were related to the quality of their own interactions with the parents (such as punitive or restrictive parenting) and to negative personality traits they associated with parents (lying, selfishness). Since the sample for this study comes from high-conflict families, it is especially plausible that attitudes were influenced by stories from the custodial parent or by interparental behavior. Helen Radovanovic et al., Child and Family Characteristics of Children's Post-Separation Visitation Refusal, 25 J. Psychiatry & L. 33 (1997).

3. Is visitation important only for the child's sake? What about for the non-custodial parent?

4. Anthony Lewis, in commenting on Morgan v. Foretich, reported a telephone conversation with Professor Joseph Goldstein of the Yale Law School and the Child Study Center at Yale. According to Dr. Goldstein, "It really doesn't make any difference if in a Rashomon sense each parent sees the world differently. One has to be responsible for the child's growth and development. It isn't that one is better than two. It's that the two cannot cooperate.

"The court gives a visitation order and then backs away. It is not responsible for the day before the visit or the day after. The custodial parent is. And his or her hands should not be tied with respect to critical judgments." In this case, Professor Goldstein said, the continued imprisonment of Dr. Morgan must be "in the service of some abstract notion of protecting the court's dignity, or enforcing the father's rights. But it deprives the child of her mother for an extended period when the continuity of that relationship is critical."

Mr. Lewis then talked with Dr. Foretich, "who asked several times what he should do. . . ." Mr. Lewis answered the question in the following way: "On reflection, my answer is that Dr. Foretich should think about the judgment of Solomon. In that story the law proposed to satisfy the two claimant mothers by dividing the child in half. But the real mother gave up her claim in order to save the child. The interest of the child mattered more than legal victory. Dr. Foretich would deserve respect if he made that principle his own now and dropped all his litigation. It would be painful, but it would serve his daughter's interest." Anthony Lewis, Abroad at Home, Limits of Law, N.Y. Times, Dec. 22, 1988, A23, col. 1.

Is the story of Solomon an apt metaphor? What happened to the mother who gave up her claim, and would the same result occur here?

5. The court in *Morgan* used the contempt sanction in an effort to secure compliance with its visitation order. Dr. Morgan remained in jail for just over two years and was released only when President Bush signed a bill limiting the period of incarceration for contempt to one year. Such bills were initiated in both the House of Representatives and the Senate, expressly to deal with Elizabeth Morgan's situation.

Eric Foretich continued to search for Hilary (i.e., *H.*). He finally located her in New Zealand, living with her maternal grandparents, and sought custodial rights there until he apparently lacked the financial resources to continue. On the latter years of this case, *see* Jonathan Groner, Hilary's Trial 251-276 (1991).

In September 1996, Congress passed the Elizabeth Morgan Act, which allowed Dr. Morgan to return with Hilary to the United States without being subject to the outstanding visitation order, and without the possibility of a new order absent Hilary's consent. In December 2003, the act was declared to be an unconstitutional bill of attainder that applied to only one person. By then, however, Hilary had reached the age of majority. *See* Foretich v. United States, 351 F.3d 1198 (2003).

Was Congress right to intervene in this case at any time? Is there some sanction other than incarceration that might have been effective in dealing with Morgan's refusal to comply with the court order? Would sanctions based on money (that is, withholding support) have affected this case? What should the system do if the child herself refuses to participate in court-ordered visitation? If this is seen to justify termination of child support, is the most relevant factor here the financial capacity of the custodial parent?

6. One commentator has suggested that custodial parents be granted a necessity defense in contempt proceedings such as Morgan v. Foretich when they believe in good faith that violating the court order is necessary to protect a child from further harm. Her proposal reflects convictions that proving sexual abuse is difficult and that the contempt sanction is, at least in this setting, ineffective or counterproductive. Susan B. Apel, Custodial Parents, Child Sexual Abuse, and the Legal System: Beyond Contempt, 38 Amer. U. L. Rev. 491 (1989). Would you support adoption of such a defense?

7. The principal case discusses contempt as a vehicle for enforcement of visitation rights. Other sanctions may also be available. An Illinois statute establishing criminal penalties for unlawful interference with visitation was upheld against a void for vagueness challenge in People v. Warren, 671 N.E.2d 700 (Ill. 1996), and a Louisiana court held that an ex parte order granting custody to the mother could form the basis for a prosecution of the father for parental kidnapping. State v. Arceneaux, 695 So. 2d 1148 (La. App. 1997).

BURGESS V. BURGESS

13 Cal. 4th 25, 913 P.2d 473 (1996)

MOSK, Justice. This matter requires us to determine whether a parent seeking to relocate after dissolution of marriage is required to establish that the move is "necessary" before he or she can be awarded physical custody of minor children. In this case, a parent with temporary physical custody of two minor children sought a judicial determination of permanent custody and expressed the intention to relocate with the children from Tehachapi to Lancaster, California, a distance of approximately 40 miles. The trial court ordered that it was in the "best interest" of the minor children to remain in the physical custody of that parent even if she moved to Lancaster; it ordered "liberal visitation" with the noncustodial parent. The Court of Appeal reversed, on the ground that the custodial parent failed to carry her burden of establishing that relocating with the minor children was "necessary."

We conclude that, in an initial judicial custody determination based on the "best interest" of minor children, a parent seeking to relocate does not bear a burden of establishing that the move is "necessary" as a condition of custody. Similarly, after a judicial custody order is in place, a custodial parent seeking to relocate bears no burden of establishing that it is "necessary" to do so. Instead, he or she "has the right to change the residence of the child, subject to the power of the court to restrain a removal that would prejudice the rights or welfare of the child."

Paul D. Burgess (hereafter the father) and Wendy A. Burgess (hereafter the mother), were married and had two children, Paul and Jessica. Both parents were employed by the State Department of Corrections at the state prison in Tehachapi and owned a home in a suburb. They separated in May 1992, when the children were four and three years old. The mother moved with the children to an apartment in Tehachapi; the father remained in their former home, pending sale of the property. The mother petitioned for dissolution shortly thereafter.

In July 1992, the trial court entered a "Stipulation and Order" dissolving the marriage and providing for temporary custody and visitation in accordance with a mediation agreement between the parties. The parents agreed that they "shall share joint legal custody of the children. The mother shall have sole physical custody of the children."

The mediation agreement expressly identified as "[a]t [i]ssue" the visitation schedule for the father "if the mother leaves Kern County." The parents agreed to a detailed schedule for weekly visitation by the father, as well as an alternative schedule for biweekly weekend visitation, depending on his work schedule.

At a hearing concerning custody in February 1993, the mother testified that she had accepted a job transfer to Lancaster and planned to relocate after her son's graduation from preschool in June. She explained that the move was "career advancing" and would permit greater access for the children to medical care, extracurricular activities, and private schools and day-care facilities. The travel time between Lancaster and her home in Tehachapi was approximately 40 minutes. The father testified that he would not be able to maintain his current visitation schedule if the children moved to Lancaster; he wanted to be their primary caretaker if the mother relocated.

The trial court issued a ruling providing that the father and the mother would share joint legal custody, with the mother to have sole physical custody. It retained the present visitation schedule, but provided that after June 1993, "the father will have visitation with the children, assuming the wife moves to Lancaster, on alternate weekends . . . with at least one three hour midweek visitation. . . ."

The father moved for reconsideration and for a change in custody. . . .

In July 1993, the trial court denied the motion for reconsideration. . . . Shortly thereafter, it held a hearing on the motion for change in custody. . . . He again testified that if his children relocated with the mother he would not be able to maintain his current visitation schedule; he sought a custody arrangement under which each parent would have the children for "[a]bout a month and a half." He also testified that he regularly traveled to Lancaster on alternate weekends, to shop and visit friends; he characterized the trip to Lancaster from his home as "an easy commute."

The mother testified that she had been working in Lancaster for four months and planned to move there. She identified several advantages to the children to living in Lancaster, including proximity to medical care and increased opportunities to participate in extracurricular activities. She also testified that the father objected to her move, at least in part, in order to retain control of her and the children. To her understanding, he did not want to change his work shift "because it keeps me in Tehachapi." She expressed her willingness to accommodate weekend visitation with the father as well as extended visitation in the summers.

In August 1993, the trial court issued an order on custody and visitation to the following effect. "The court finds that it is in the best interest of the minor children that the minors be permitted to move to Lancaster with the petitioner and that respondent be afforded liberal visitation. Due to the complexity of the work schedules of both of the parties, who are employed by the California Department of Corrections, the court requests that a four-way meeting be held by the parties within ten days from the date of this order to work out a mutually agreed upon visitation schedule. In the event that such a schedule cannot be worked out, then the parties are to attend mediation. The court suggests that during the summertimes and if school is on a year round basis, that respondent father be provided with 'large block of time' visitations."

The father appealed from both the order denying reconsideration and the order denying change in custody; the appeals were consolidated.

The Court of Appeal reversed. It formulated the following test for relocation cases. The trial court initially must determine whether the move "will impact significantly the existing pattern of care and adversely affect the nature and quality of the noncustodial parent's contact with the child. The burden is on the noncustodial nonmoving parent to show this adverse impact." If the impact is shown, the trial court must determine whether the move is "reasonably necessary," with "the burden of showing such necessity fall[ing] on the moving parent." If it concludes that the move is "necessary" — either because not moving would impose an unreasonable hardship on custodial parent's career or other interests or because moving will result in a discernible benefit that it would be unreasonable to expect the parent to forgo — the trial court "must resolve whether the benefit to the child in going with the moving parent outweighs the loss or diminution of contact with the nonmoving parent."

On the facts before it, the Court of Appeal concluded that "no showing of necessity was made." "[T]he reality here is that in moving, [the mother] primarily gained convenience." It reversed the orders and remanded for further proceedings consistent with the opinion. We granted review. We now reverse.

II.

. . . In an initial custody determination, the trial court has "the widest discretion to choose a parenting plan that is in the best interest of the child. . . ."

In addition, in a matter involving immediate or eventual relocation by one or both parents, the trial court must take into account the presumptive right of a custodial parent to change the residence of the minor children, so long as the removal would not be prejudicial to their rights or welfare. (Fam. Code, §7501 ["A parent entitled to custody of a child has a right to change the residence of the child, subject to the power of the court to restrain a removal that would prejudice the rights or welfare of the child."].) Accordingly, in considering all the circumstances affecting the "best interest" of minor children, it may consider any effects of such relocation on their rights or welfare. . . .

No abuse of discretion appears. After extensive testimony from both parents, the trial court not unreasonably concluded that it was in the "best interest" of the minor children that the father and the mother retain joint legal custody and that the mother retain sole physical custody, even if she moved to Lancaster.

The trial court's order was supported by substantial evidence concerning the "best interest" of the minor children. First, and most important, although they had almost daily contact with both parents during the initial period after the separation, the minor children had been in the sole physical custody of the mother for over a year at the time the trial court issued its order concerning permanent custody. Although they saw their father regularly, their mother was, by parental stipulation and as a factual matter, their primary caretaker. As we have repeatedly emphasized, the paramount need for continuity and stability in custody arrangements — and the harm that may result from disruption of established patterns of care and emotional bonds with the primary caretaker — weigh heavily in favor of maintaining ongoing custody arrangements (Burchard v. Garay, supra, 42 Cal.3d at p. 541, 229 Cal.Rptr. 800, 724 P.2d 486).

From the outset, the mother had expressed her intention to relocate to Lancaster. The reason for the move was employment related; the mother evinced no intention to frustrate the father's contact with the minor children. Moreover, despite the fact that the move was, as the Court of Appeal observed, primarily for the mother's "convenience," her proximity to her place of employment and to the children during the workday would clearly benefit the children as well. A reduced commute would permit increased and more leisurely daily contact between the children and their primary caretaker. It would also facilitate the children's participation, with their mother, in extracurricular activities. In the event of illness or emergency, the children could more promptly be picked up and treated, if appropriate, at their regular medical facility, which was also located in Lancaster.

Although it would be more convenient for the father to maintain a daily visitation routine with the children if they remained in Tehachapi, he would still, even under his present work schedule, be able to visit them regularly and often. The trial court's order of "liberal visitation" included overnight visits on alternative weekends and additional weekday visits each month. The father conceded that he regularly traveled to Lancaster and that he considered it an "easy commute." . . .

III.

The Court of Appeal concluded that the trial court abused its discretion in ordering that the mother should retain physical custody, on the ground that her relocation to Lancaster was not "necessary. . . ."

In an initial custody determination, a parent seeking to relocate with the minor children bears no burden of establishing that the move is "necessary." The trial court must — and here did — consider, among other factors, the effects of relocation on the "best interest" of the minor children, including the health, safety, and welfare of the children and the nature and amount of contact with both parents. We discern no statutory basis, however, for imposing a specific additional burden of persuasion on either parent to justify a choice of residence as a condition of custody.

The Court of Appeal relied on Family Code section 3020: "The Legislature finds and declares that it is the public policy of this state to assure minor children frequent and continuing contact with both parents after the parents have separated or dissolved their marriage, and to encourage parents to share the rights and responsibilities of child rearing in order to effect this policy, except where the contact would not be in the best interest of the child, as provided in [Family Code] [s]ection 3011."

In substance, the Court of Appeal concluded that Family Code section 3020 establishes an implicit requirement, limiting the trial court's discretion under Family Code section 3011, that, after separation or dissolution of marriage, the trial court may not award sole physical custody of the minor children to a parent unless he or she remains in the same locality or establishes that relocation is "necessary." . . .

The Family Code specifically refrains from establishing a preference or presumption in favor of any arrangement for custody and visitation. Thus, Family Code section 3040, subdivision (b), provides: "This section establishes neither a preference nor a presumption for or against joint legal custody, joint physical custody, or sole custody, but allows the court and the family the widest discretion to choose a parenting plan that is in the best interest of the child." Similarly, although Family Code section 3020 refers to "frequent and continuous contact," it does not purport to define the phrase "frequent and continuous" or to specify a preference for any particular form of "contact." Nor does it include any specific means of effecting the policy, apart from "encourag[ing] parents to share the rights and responsibilities of child rearing."

Moreover, construing Family Code section 3020 by implication to impose an additional burden of proof on a parent seeking to relocate would abrogate the presumptive right of a custodial parent to change the residence of the minor child. It has long been established that . . . the "general rule [is that] a parent having child custody is entitled to change residence unless the move is detrimental to the child."

As this case demonstrates, ours is an increasingly mobile society. Amici curiae point out that approximately one American in five changes residences each year. Economic necessity and remarriage account for the bulk of relocations. Because of the ordinary needs for both parents after a marital dissolution to secure or retain employment, pursue educational or career opportunities, or reside in the same location as a new spouse or other family or friends, it is unrealistic to assume that divorced parents will permanently remain in the same location after dissolution or to exert pressure on them to do so. It would also undermine the interest in minimizing costly litigation over custody and require the trial courts to "micromanage" family decisionmaking by second-guessing reasons for everyday decisions about career and family.

More fundamentally, the "necessity" of relocating frequently has little, if any, substantive bearing on the suitability of a parent to retain the role of a custodial parent. A parent who has been the primary caretaker for minor children is ordinarily no less capable of maintaining the responsibilities and obligations of parenting simply by virtue of a reasonable decision to change his or her geographical location.[7]

Accordingly, we decline to interpret Family Code section 3020, in the absence of express statutory language, to impose a burden of proof on a parent seeking to relocate with the minor children to establish "necessity." . . . .

Although this matter involved an initial order of custody and visitation, the same conclusion applies when a parent who has sole physical custody under an existing judicial custody order seeks to relocate: the custodial parent seeking to relocate, like the noncustodial parent doing the same, bears no burden of demonstrating that the move is "necessary."

Ordinarily, after a judicial custody determination, the noncustodial parent seeking to alter the order for legal and physical custody can do so only on a showing that there has been a substantial change of circumstances so affecting the minor child that modification is essential to the child's welfare. . . .

We conclude that the same allocation of the burden of persuasion applies in the case of a custodial parent's relocation as in any other proceeding to alter existing custody arrangements: "[I]n view of the child's interest in stable custodial and emotional ties, custody lawfully acquired and maintained for a significant period will have the effect of compelling the noncustodial parent to assume the burden of persuading the trier of fact that a change [in custody] is in the child's best interests." Similarly, the same standard of proof applies in a motion for change in custody based on the custodial parent's decision to relocate with the minor children as in any

---

7. An obvious exception is a custodial parent's decision to relocate simply to frustrate the noncustodial parent's contact with the minor children. "Conduct by a custodial parent designed to frustrate visitation and communication may be grounds for changing custody." (Burchard v. Garay, supra, 42 Cal. 3d at p. 540, fn. 11, 229 Cal. Rptr. 800, 724 P.2d 486; In re Marriage of Ciganovich, supra, 61 Cal. App. 3d at p. 294, 132 Cal. Rptr. 261 ["a custodial parent's attempt to frustrate the court's order has a bearing upon the fitness of that parent"].)

other matter involving changed circumstances: "[O]nce it has been established [under a judicial custody decision] that a particular custodial arrangement is in the best interests of the child, the court need not reexamine that question. Instead, it should preserve the established mode of custody unless some significant change in circumstances indicates that a different arrangement would be in the child's best interest."

The showing required is substantial. We have previously held that a child should not be removed from prior custody of one parent and given to the other "unless the material facts and circumstances occurring subsequently are of a kind to render it essential or expedient for the welfare of the child that there be a change." In a "move-away" case, a change of custody is not justified simply because the custodial parent has chosen, for any sound good faith reason, to reside in a different location, but only if, as a result of relocation with that parent, the child will suffer determent rendering it "essential or expedient for the welfare of the child that there be a change."

This construction is consistent with the presumptive "right" of a parent entitled to custody to change the residence of his or her minor children, unless such removal would result in "prejudice" to their "rights or welfare." (Fam. Code, § 7501.) The dispositive issue is, accordingly, not whether relocating is itself "essential or expedient" either for the welfare of the custodial parent or the child, but whether a change in custody is "essential or expedient for the welfare of the child."

At the same time, we recognize that bright line rules in this area are inappropriate: each case must be evaluated on its own unique facts. Although the interests of a minor child in the continuity and permanency of custodial placement with the primary caretaker will most often prevail, the trial court, in assessing "prejudice" to the child's welfare as a result of relocating even a distance of 40 or 50 miles, may take into consideration the nature of the child's existing contact with both parents — including de facto as well as de jure custody arrangements — and the child's age, community ties, and health and educational needs. Where appropriate, it must also take into account the preferences of the child. (Fam. Code, § 3042, subd. (a) ["If a child is of sufficient age and capacity to reason so as to form an intelligent preference as to custody, the court shall consider and give due weight to the wishes of the child in making an order granting or modifying custody."].)

Thus, for example, in In re Marriage of Rosson, supra, 178 Cal. App. 3d 1094, 224 Cal. Rptr. 250, the Court of Appeal affirmed the decision of the trial court that the mother's decision to move from Napa to San Francisco — a two-hour commuting distance — did require a change in physical custody. Under that standard we are announcing, it could properly consider the preferences of the children, aged 10 and 13, for remaining in Napa and take into account the facts that both parents had de facto physical custody of the children and that the father had assumed substantial parenting responsibilities relating to the children's academic, athletic, social, and religious activities. Similarly, In re Marriage of Selzer, supra, 29 Cal. App. 4th 637, 34 Cal. Rptr. 2d 824, the same Court of Appeal affirmed the trial court's determination that the custodial parent's decision to move from Ukiah to Santa Rosa — a one-hour commuting distance — did not require a change in physical custody. Again, under our standard, it could reasonably consider the presumption in favor of stability and continuity in the child's primary custodial relationship — in that case with her mother — and the child's lack of preference for changing the custody arrangement. It could also reasonably affirm the trial court's visitation order, which provided for increased visitation with the father and also required the mother to drive the child to Ukiah for visitation.

For the reasons discussed, we reverse the judgment of the Court of Appeal.

NOTES AND QUESTIONS

1. Limitations on movement, especially interstate movement, by a custodial parent to protect custodial rights present obvious federal and state constitutional issues. The Wyoming Supreme Court held that the rights of a parent and the duty of state courts to adjudicate custody did not themselves justify restricting the right to travel under the U.S. and Wyoming constitutions. As a result, the court held, a desire to relocate could not itself be a "material change of circumstance" enabling the court to reconsider a custodial placement:

> The right to travel enjoyed by a citizen carries with it the right of a custodial parent to have the children move with that parent. This right is not to be denied, impaired, or disparaged unless clear evidence before the court demonstrates another substantial and material change of circumstance and establishes the detrimental effect of the move upon the children.

Watt v. Watt, 971 P.2d 608, 615-616 (1999). An Idaho Court of Appeals also addressed the right to travel generally and applied strict scrutiny to a restriction on relocation. The court held, however, that in the circumstances of that case, the restriction did not directly burden the right of the parent herself to travel, served a compelling interest in preserving the children's rights, and was the least restrictive order possible under the circumstances. Ziegler v. Ziegler, 691 P.2d 773 (Idaho App. 1985). *See also* Bates v. Tesar, 81 S.W.3d 411 (Tex. App. 2002) (finding that trial court's domicile restriction did not violate due process).

In Saenz v. Roe, 119 S. Ct. 1518, 526 U.S. 489 (1999), the Supreme Court identified three aspects of the constitutionally based "right to travel":

> The "right to travel" discussed in our cases embraces at least three different components. It protects the right of a citizen of one state to enter and to leave another state, the right to be treated as a welcome visitor rather than an unfriendly alien when temporarily present in the second state, and for those travelers who elect to become permanent residents, the right to be treated like other citizens of that state.

119 S. Ct. at 1525. The first of these aspects is reflected in Edwards v. California, 314 U.S. 160 (1941) (invalidating limitations on free interstate passage by indigent persons). A second is the right of a nonresident traveler to visit another state without limitations unless substantial justification exists. The third aspect of the right to travel is the right of newly arrived citizens to the same privileges and immunities enjoyed by other citizens of the state. This third aspect was recognized in Shapiro v. Thompson, 394 U.S. 618 (1969), dealing with restrictions on access to welfare benefits for relatively recent arrivals in the state, and again in *Saenz* itself,

which limited maximum welfare benefits to newly arrived residents in California. As in Shapiro v. Thompson, strict scrutiny of laws affecting the rights of newly arrived citizens seems to be required.

Which of these aspects of the right to travel, if any, are implicated in custodial cases involving relocation? Do these cases also implicate a parent's liberty interest in the care, custody, and control of his or her children? *See* Frase v. Barhart, 840 A.2d 114 (Md. 2003) (overturning custody condition that required mother whose fitness had been questioned to apply for and live in a certain type of housing).

2. In the original *Burgess* decision, the move was only 40 miles and within the state. Subsequent cases suggest that where the move involves longer distances that will necessarily alter the children's relationship with the noncustodial parent, the courts may engage in more searching review. In re Marriage of Condon, 67 Cal. App. 4th 533, 73 Cal. Rptr. 2d 33 (1998), involved a mother's desire to take her two sons back to her native Australia. The court noted that allowing relocation to a foreign country, given the problems of distance, cost, cultural differences, and the difficulties of enforcing visitation rights, would often effectively raise problems distinct from problems raised by interstate and even intrastate moves, including introduction to cultural conditions far different from those experienced in this country and the greater distance and associated additional, perhaps prohibitive, costs of visitation ordinarily implicated by international relocation. A third concern is the difficulty of enforcing local custody and visitation orders in a foreign country. The appellate court considered this case to test the outer limits of the *Burgess* principle allowing relocation absent a showing that the move was inconsistent with the child's best interest, and suggested that in foreign relocation cases, the court should ordinarily consider such a move a termination of visitation rights and require a showing by the relocating parent that termination would be in the child's best interests. It also suggested the importance of flexibility and imagination in devising ways to deal with the various problems of international relocation.

The California Supreme Court revisited the move-away issue more generally in In re Marriage of LaMusga, 88 P.3d 81 (Cal. 2004), a case that involved a cross-country move and the conclusion that relocation would undermine the children's tenuous relationship with their father. In *LaMusga*, the court rejected the conclusion that a custodial parent with "a good faith reason to move . . . cannot be prevented directly or indirectly, from exercising his or her right to change the child residence" absent a "substantial showing" by the noncustodial parent that a change of custody is "essential" to prevent detriment to the child. Instead, the court indicated that a "noncustodial parent opposing such a change of residence bears the initial burden of showing that the move will cause some detriment to the children." Once this showing of detriment has been made, the trial court must then "weigh the likely effects on the child's welfare from moving with the custodial parent, against the likely effects from a change in custody" in accordance with a best-interest analysis. While many courts have concluded that the move itself cannot be the factor constituting detriment, the *LaMusga* court permitted consideration of the impact of the move on the relationship with the noncustodial parent as the principle factor establishing detriment in the case. The *LaMusga* court, in otherwise restraining too great a deference to the custodial parent's decision to move, cited *Condon* with approval.

3. The states vary considerably in the standards they apply to parental moves. Historically, courts disfavored removal of a child from the jurisdiction after divorce. Edwin J. Terry et al., Relocation: Moving Forward or Moving Backward?, 31 Tex. Tech. L. Rev. 983, 986 (2000). Some courts still employ a presumption against a move on the grounds that it will almost inevitably undermine the relationship with the noncustodial parent. See, e.g., White v. White, 650 A.2d 110, 113 (Pa. Super. Ct. 1994) (requiring moving parent to demonstrate that relocation will improve quality of life for parent and child).

As societal mobility has increased, however, many courts, like the California Supreme Court in Burgess, have relaxed their opposition to moves. Some states now recognize a presumption that the custodial parent should be able to move absent a showing of bad faith or detriment to the child. See, e.g., In re Francis, 919 P.2d 776 (Colo. 1996), holding that articulation by the custodial parent of a sensible reason for moving creates a presumption that the child should remain with the relocating parent and relocation should be denied only on a showing of endangerment. A similar position was taken by the Minnesota Supreme Court in Silbaugh v. Silbaugh, 543 N.W.2d 639 (Minn. 1996), holding that an evidentiary hearing on relocation is not required unless the objecting parent has made a prima facie case of endangerment or that the move was intended to deprive that parent of visitation. A Florida decision, Russenberger v. Russenberger, 669 So. 2d 1044 (Fla. 1996), also relies on a presumption that the custodial parent could relocate but found the presumption rebutted in that case by evidence casting doubt on the mother's motives for relocating.

Other states balance competing factors. The New York Court of Appeals modified its approach to relocation in Tropea v. Tropea, 642 N.Y.S.2d 575 (N.Y. 1996). In Tropea, the court rejected a lower court formula involving three steps: The court would (1) determine whether the proposed relocation would deprive the noncustodial parent of regular and meaningful access to the child, (2) where such disruption is established, presume that the move is not in the child's best interest, and (3) require the parent seeking relocation to demonstrate exceptional circumstances justifying the move. If these conditions were met, the court would consider other aspects of the child's best interests. The Court of Appeals found this test both difficult to apply and mechanistic. Difficulty of application arose from, for example, confusion regarding the notion of "meaningful access." The test was mechanical in, for example, avoiding inquiry into the need and motives for relocation and the effect of relocation on the child when the disruption did not amount to denial of meaningful access.

Rather, the Court of Appeals held, each relocation request must be considered on its own merits, with primary emphasis on the outcome likely to serve the child's best interests. While the impact of a move on the relationship between the child and noncustodial parent remains a central concern, the reasons for wanting to move, the noncustodial parent's interest in securing custody, the feasibility and desirability of a change in custody, the child's attachment to the parents, and all other relevant factors should be considered in each case.

Subsequent to the decision in Tropea, a New York Family Court held that the Tropea approach could not be applied to a mother's request to relocate to a distant state where she and her ex-husband equally shared custody of their ten-year-old daughter. Sara P. v. Richard T., 670 N.Y.S. 2d 964 (Fam. Ct. 1998). In this case, the mother remarried. She and her new husband decided to move to South Carolina, where she would not have to work because of his increased salary and would be closer to her family. Both parents sought primary residential custody. The court, granting the father's request for primary physical residence, acknowledged that a best-interest standard would be applied under *Tropea*, but said that a variety of factors other than those mentioned in *Tropea* — most of which have nothing to do with relocation itself, and seem to amount to an entirely new custody determination — should be considered in deciding the child's best interests.

All authority does not, however, presume the custodial spouse's authority to determine residence. Similarly, Pollock v. Pollock, 889 P.2d 633 (Ariz. App. 1995), holds that the relocating parent has the burden of proof, but need not prove substantial advantage to the child. The *Pollock* standard has been codified at Ariz. Rev. Stat. Ann. §25-408. New Jersey has adopted a 12-factor analysis, requiring consideration of "(1) the reasons given for the move; (2) the reasons given for the opposition; (3) the past history of dealings between the parties insofar as it bears on the reasons advanced by both parties for supporting and opposing the move; (4) whether the child will receive educational, health and leisure opportunities at least equal to what is available here; (5) any special needs or talents of the child that require accommodation and whether such accommodation or its equivalent is available in the new location; (6) whether a visitation and communication schedule can be developed that will allow the noncustodial parent to maintain a full and continuous relationship with the child; (7) the likelihood that the custodial parent will continue to foster the child's relationship with the noncustodial parent if the move is allowed; (8) the effect of the move on extended family relationships here and in the new location; (9) if the child is of age, his or her preference; (10) whether the child is entering his or her senior year in high school, at which point he or she should generally not be moved until graduation without his or her consent; (11) whether the noncustodial parent has the ability to relocate; (12) any other factor bearing on the child's interest." Baures v. Lewis, 770 A.2d 214, 229-230 (N.J. 1999).

A comprehensive review of law and policy concerning relocation appears in Carol S. Bruch & Janet M. Bowermaster, The Relocation of Children and Custodial Parents: Public Policy, Past and Present, 30 Fam. L.Q. 245 (1996).

4. It may seem unfair to limit the choices available to a custodial parent, particularly a custodial mother, in order to preserve the father's visitation rights when there is considerable reason to believe that those rights are rarely exercised and that their exercise decreases over time. A number of studies have reported high rates of "father dropout" where children live with their mothers. One study, reporting the results of a national sample study conducted in 1981, observed:

> The process of estrangement [of nonresident fathers] from the child appears to be an abrupt one, typically beginning soon after the marriage breaks up. . . . Fathers are more likely to see their children at least once a week if their marriage broke up during the past two years, though the rate of frequent contact appears to drop off sharply even sooner than that, after about 12 months.

Frank F. Furstenberg et al., The Life Cycle of Children of Divorce, 48 Am. Soc. Rev. 656, 664 (1983).

However, the Maccoby and Mnookin California study described earlier found very different results. The authors employed a relatively strict notion of what counts as visitation: daytime or overnight visits during typical two-week periods during the school year. Dividing the Child, *supra* at 171. Using that definition, they found that children had daytime or overnight visits with their fathers in three-quarters of the mother-residence families. Overnight visitation was the most common arrangement, followed by daytime visits and, least frequently, failure of substantial visitation. In the smaller group of father-residence families, about 40 percent of the mothers had overnight visitation with their children. Dividing the Child, at 171, Figure 8.4. At this early point in the divorce process, then, less than 20 percent of the children had no significant relationship with their fathers.

Although these levels of visitation are higher than most would suppose, they might be discounted somewhat because they were measured shortly after the parents separated. By the end of the study, one would expect a substantial drop in visitation by fathers. That was not the case. Where children lived in dual residence, substantial visitation was the case by definition. But even where the child lived primarily with one parent, substantial visitation with the nonresidential parent continued to be common. Moreover, visits most commonly involved overnight stays. The percentages of fathers whose children visited overnight remained relatively constant during the three and one-half years from the beginning to the end of the study, and the same is true of mothers whose children lived primarily with their fathers. There was some decline in daytime visitations by fathers and consequently an increase in families where children did not visit with their fathers. Dividing the Child, at 170-172. Nonetheless, all of the fathers with sole or dual residence, and more than 60 percent of the fathers whose children lived with their mother, maintained very substantial relations with their children.

And, of course, some of the other fathers maintained some relationship, although less than "substantial" as we have used that term. Only 13 percent of the children living with their mother had not seen their father within the past year, and only 7 percent of those living with their father had not seen their mother during that period.

Judith Wallerstein and other researchers, however, have concluded that the frequency or duration of visits from the noncustodial parent does not necessarily correlate with improvement in the child's well-being; the more important factors are the psychological adjustment of the custodial parent, the stability and welfare of the new household, and the quality of the contact between the noncustodial parent, the custodial parent, and the child. Judith S. Wallerstein & Tony J. Tanke, To Move or Not to Move: Psychological and Legal Considerations in the Relocation of Children Following Divorce, 30 Fam. L.Q. 305, 311-312 (1996).

5. One of the effects of mobility by the custodial spouse is prejudice to the noncustodial spouse's opportunity for visitation. Suppose that matters are reversed; the noncustodial parent voluntarily fails to visit the children after divorce (either because he or she has moved or through disinterest). Can the custodial spouse enforce such visits by modifying the decree to require them? Is visitation regarded as an obligation or a privilege? *See* Carol Bruch, Making Visitation Work: Dual Parenting Orders, 1 Fam. Advoc. 22, 26 (Summer 1978) (suggesting that courts order noncustodial parents to visit their children).

But see Hathcock v. Hathcock, 685 So. 2d 736 (Ala. App. 1996), holding that the father's obligation to visit was a moral but not a legal duty and could not be enforced by a monetary penalty. Why should the custodial parent's obligation to facilitate visitation be considered a legal duty enforceable by contempt, but visitation by the noncustodial parent considered only a moral obligation?

6. The American Law Institute Principles of the Law of Family Dissolution note that the basic principle of awarding custody in a way reflecting the time spent by each parent in caretaking functions may be affected by a parent's relocation. Section 2.08(1)(g) provides that when this is so, the court should apply the principles of §2.17(4), dealing with modification of an existing order. Those principles would justify an award of custody, with permission to relocate, to a parent who has been exercising a significant majority of the caretaking responsibility as long as the relocation is in good faith, for a legitimate purpose, and to a location that is reasonable in light of that purpose. Legitimate purposes for relocation include closeness to significant family or other support networks, significant health reasons, protecting the child's safety, pursuing a significant employment opportunity, and being with a spouse or partner.

If neither parent has exercised a significant majority of caretaking responsibilities, custody should be allocated according to the child's best interests in general.

PROBLEMS

1. Alma is the custodial parent for three children, ages four, six, and nine. She is a sales executive and expects to be transferred from her present home in Atlanta to San Francisco. Her former husband, Ralph, is employed at a job that does not allow him to make lengthy trips. He is very much opposed to any arrangement that will interfere with his continuing visitation (which he has carried out faithfully). Alma plans to accept the transfer and seeks your advice regarding her custodial situation. How would you advise her?

2. Suppose that Alma is not currently employed but has decided to enroll in law school. She has been accepted at an ABA-accredited law school in her home state of Georgia and at Stanford. Alma would greatly prefer to study at Stanford. Ralph, who has met his visitation obligations, seeks an order prohibiting Alma from moving with the children to any location more than 180 miles from Atlanta. Should that order be granted?

3. In Problem 2, Ralph also offers the testimony of a psychologist that the children's best interests would be served by continuing regular contact with him. Should this affect the outcome?

BERSANI V. BERSANI

565 A.2d 1368 (Conn. 1989)

FREEDMAN, J. On October 3, 1988, the plaintiff wife instituted an action against the defendant husband for dissolution of marriage. On November 11,

1988, the court awarded custody pendente lite of the parties' two minor children to the plaintiff and specific visitation rights pendente lite to the defendant.

On March 7, 1989, under an agreement of the parties, approved by the court, the plaintiff was required to give the defendant thirty days written notice of her intent to leave the country. After a hearing on May 9, 1989, the court denied a motion filed by the plaintiff in which she sought a court order permitting her to return to Spain with the children pending the final hearing in the dissolution action.

In early June, the defendant learned that the plaintiff had moved out of the house that she was occupying with the children. The defendant sought information concerning the whereabouts of the plaintiff and the children from the plaintiff's attorney. While the plaintiff's attorney acknowledges that she possesses the requested information, she has declined to disclose it on the ground that to do so would violate her obligation to maintain confidential information imparted to her by a client.

By motion dated June 7, 1989, the defendant seeks an order to compel the plaintiff's attorney to reveal the information claiming that the attorney-client privilege must yield to assure that a judicial determination is made and enforced respecting the best interests of the children.

On June 8, 1989, the court found the plaintiff in wilful contempt, ordered her to return to Connecticut and awarded temporary custody of the two children to the defendant.

On July 14, 1989, after a hearing that the plaintiff did not attend but at which she was represented by counsel, the marriage was dissolved and the court ordered, inter alia, that custody of the minor children was to be with the defendant.

The defendant acknowledges in his memorandum in support of his motion to compel that Rule 1.6 of the Rules of Professional Conduct precludes, except as specifically authorized, disclosures by an attorney of confidential information imparted to the attorney by a client in the course of the attorney's representation. He argues, however, that sustaining the privilege in the present circumstances would "tend to immunize a flagrant violation of this court's orders and to inflict an unjustifiable harm to the interests of the defendant and of the children."

The plaintiff argues in her memorandum of law in opposition to the defendant's motion to compel that, while the court has an obligation to apply the best interests of the child standard in custody disputes, "the issue presently before this court does not involve custody, it involves disclosure of privileged information." The plaintiff further argues that the "best interests of the child" does not provide an exception to the confidentiality rule. . . .

"The common-law rule of privileged communications has been stated as follows: 'Where legal advice of any kind is sought from a professional legal adviser in his capacity as such, the communications relating to that purpose, made in confidence by the client, are at his instance permanently protected from disclosure by himself or by the legal adviser, except the protection be waived.' 8 Wigmore, Evidence at 2292, p.554 (McNaughton Rev. 1961). . . ." Connecticut has not altered the rule by statute, as have some states. "The privilege is designed to remove client apprehension as to compelled disclosure by the attorney, and thereby encourage freedom of full disclosure by the client of all the facts relating to the subject matter of inquiry or litigation." C. Tait & J. LaPlante, Connecticut Evidence sec. 12.5 (1976).

Subsection (c)(2) of Rule 1.6 of the Rules of Professional Conduct provides that a lawyer may reveal information relating to the representation of a client to the extent that the lawyer believes that it is necessary to "[r]ectify the consequence of a client's criminal or fraudulent act in the commission of which the lawyer's services had been used." Rule 3.3(a)(2) of the Rules of Professional Conduct states that "[a] lawyer shall not knowingly . . . fail to disclose a material fact to a tribunal when disclosure is necessary to avoid assisting a criminal or fraudulent act by the client. . . ."

It is the opinion of this court that the plaintiff's wilful contempt in leaving the country in violation of the court's order constitutes a fraud on the court, a fraudulent act under Rule 1.6(c)(2). While it is clear to this court that the plaintiff's attorney did not assist or advise the plaintiff to violate the court's order, the attorney's present refusal to disclose her client's whereabouts does serve to assist the plaintiff in her ongoing violation of the court's order.

The New Jersey Supreme Court in Fellerman v. Bradley, 99 N.J. 493, 503, 493 A.2d 1239 (1985), stated that in the context of the "crime or fraud" exception to the attorney-client privilege, "our courts have generally given the term 'fraud' an expansive reading." In *Fellerman*, the failure of the defendant's attorney to disclose the whereabouts of his client prevented the court from enforcing a provision of the final judgment in a dissolution action, to which the defendant had previously agreed, requiring the defendant to pay an expert's fee. The court stated that "the client, through his attorney, attempted to perpetrate a fraud on the court — to 'mock' justice — by consenting to and subsequently flouting a judgment that obligated him to bear the costs of an accountant."

The situation in the present case presents more compelling facts than those in *Fellerman* to justify the expansion of the meaning of fraud in Rule 1.6(c)(2) beyond traditional tort or criminal law definitions to include those which constitute "a fraud on the court." The court in *Fellerman* concluded that the defendant's attempt to escape payment of a court ordered expense constituted a fraud on the court. The plaintiff's deliberate violation of the court's order in the instant case has extended ramifications because it impedes the court's ability to implement its subsequent orders regarding custody, orders made in the best interests of the two minor children. . . .

This court, mindful of the importance of the attorney-client privilege and the function it serves in our adversary system, must nevertheless weigh the benefits of that privilege against the state's vital interest as parens patriae in determining the best interests of the minor children. While the plaintiff would have this court hold that the issue before it does not involve custody, the issue of custody here is inextricably intertwined with the issue of attorney-client privilege. The facts reveal: (1) that the plaintiff has left the country with the children in direct violation of a court order; (2) that the plaintiff's attorney knows the precise whereabouts of her client and declines to disclose that information; (3) that the failure to disclose that information assists the plaintiff in her ongoing contempt of the court's order; and (4) that the court's ability to effectuate subsequent orders issued in the best interests of the children has been thwarted.

It is this court's opinion, that, under the circumstances, the attorney-client privilege does not apply to information imparted to an attorney by a client in the course of perpetrating a fraud on the court. Moreover, any claim of privilege must yield in these circumstances to the best interests of the children. Accordingly, the defendant's motion to compel counsel to reveal the whereabouts of the plaintiff and the children is granted.

NOTES AND QUESTIONS

1. Two related issues are presented in this case. One has to do with the scope of the lawyer-client privilege, which is defined by local rules of evidence. Many states have adopted Proposed Rule 503 of the Federal Rules of Evidence, which provides in subsection d(1) that there is "no privilege under this rule. . . . If the services of the lawyer were sought or obtained to enable or aid anyone to commit or plan to commit what the client knew or reasonably should have known to be a crime or fraud."

The most obvious instance occurs when a client engages a lawyer to provide legal assistance in connection with contemplated illegal activity. *E.g.*, United States v. Hodge & Zweig, 548 F.2d 1347 (9th Cir. 1977). *Hodge & Zweig* involved narcotics transactions. What is the criminal or fraudulent activity in *Bersani*?

Assuming criminality, *Bersani* would most closely resemble *Hodge & Zweig* if the client said to his lawyer, "I plan to abduct my child from my wife's lawful custody and want you to represent me in any ensuing civil or criminal matters." Is that what happened here?

2. The second issue concerns the reach of rules of professional conduct. Model Rule 1.6 provides that

[a] lawyer shall not reveal information relating to representation of a client unless the client consents after consultation. . . . A lawyer may reveal such information to the extent the lawyer reasonably believes necessary . . . to prevent the client from committing a criminal act that the lawyer believes is likely to result in imminent death or substantial bodily harm. . . .

The language of this Rule does not make explicit the relationship between the evidentiary privilege and ethical requirements. If information received by the lawyer *is* subject to the attorney-client evidentiary privilege, its disclosure over the objection of the client cannot be ordered. If, however, the information is not subject to the lawyer-client privilege, it may still be confidential as an ethical matter. Indeed, all information received by an attorney that relates to representation is subject to the general expectation of confidentiality set out in Rule 1.6. However, if confidential information is not privileged, it is subject to *involuntary* disclosure when ordered by a court. *See* Comment to Rule 1.6.

With this background, how would you characterize plaintiff wife's communication to her lawyer about her whereabouts? To whom, and under what circumstances, can that communication be disclosed?

3. Other cases requiring attorneys to disclose information in similar circumstances include Matter of Jacqueline F., 391 N.E.2d 967 (N.Y. 1979); Jafarian-Kerman v. Jafarian-Kerman, 424 S.W.2d 333 (Mo. App. 1967).

4. A duty to disclose may also arise when an attorney learns after the event that his or her client has committed a fraud on the court, usually through perjury or

other false statements. Model Rule 3.3(a) provides that "[a] lawyer shall not knowingly: . . . (2) Fail to disclose a material fact to a tribunal when disclosure is necessary to avoid assisting a criminal or fraudulent act by the client." Subsection (4) provides that "[i]f a lawyer has offered material evidence and comes to know of its falsity, the lawyer shall take reasonable remedial measures." The Comment to this rule indicates that the lawyer's duty to take remedial steps includes remonstrating with the client, seeking to withdraw, or ultimately disclosing the fraudulent conduct.

PROBLEMS

1. Suppose that the custodial mother has taken the children away because she believes the father is sexually abusing the children. The children are too young to testify, and, while there is some circumstantial evidence to support the mother's belief, you have advised her that a court is unlikely to find the evidence sufficient to eliminate the father's visitation rights. Should disclosure of the children's location be required in these circumstances?

2. During a deposition, your client states that he has no property or wealth other than that set out in interrogatories completed prior to the deposition. You have just learned that, six months prior to separating from his wife, your client opened a bank account in the neighboring state in which he has deposited $60,000 in cash proceeds from his business. What obligations, if any, do you have in this situation?

3. Your client, Alena Martinez, is in the middle of a hotly contested custody dispute. While it is agreed that Alena will have custody, Juan Martinez wants joint legal custody and extensive visitation. Alena Martinez opposes both, in part because she resents Juan's repeated adulteries, which provoked the divorce. Efforts to negotiate a specific visitation schedule have failed. Opposing counsel has proposed that the parties agree simply that Juan have "reasonable visitation." You know that Alena will not make it easy for Juan to see their children. Can you agree to this provision?

D. MODIFICATION OF CUSTODY AND VISITATION ORDERS

STATE EX REL. JOHNSON V. BAIL

938 P.2d 209 (Or. 1997)

GRABER, Justice. We are called on to decide what role, if any, a parent's illegal act of custodial interference plays in a court's decision with respect to that parent's motion to modify child custody. . . .

This child custody case involves the unmarried parents of a girl who was born on July 6, 1987. Father's paternity was established pursuant to statute. Mother had physical custody of the child from birth. Pursuant to ORS 109.175,[8] mother also had legal custody. Father visited the child two or three times a week during the first few weeks after her birth. At the time, mother and the child lived with mother's parents in Dallas, Oregon.

A dispute arose between the parties, and father made threats against mother and members of her family. Mother then moved to Salem with the child, without telling father their whereabouts. When father located mother a few months later, she moved to Willamina. When father again located her in late 1988, mother moved to California, without informing him, and took an assumed name. At that time, mother had legal custody of the child.

Meanwhile, father began court proceedings to establish visitation rights with the child. The trial court granted an order of visitation on November 5, 1987, but father was not able to see the child, because he did not know where she was. He then sought custody of the child. On December 23, 1988, the trial court issued an order changing the child's legal custody to father. Mother had not appeared in opposition to either motion. No judgment was entered.

About four years later, in late 1992, father and police located mother in California. Mother and child returned to Oregon. In February 1993, mother pleaded guilty to custodial interference in the second degree. Mother was sentenced to 20 hours of community service; she completed that sentence.

The child continued to live with mother after her return to Oregon. The child was reintroduced to father gradually, but suffered serious emotional problems as a result of that effort.

In 1993, mother filed a motion to modify the 1988 default order, seeking to return legal custody of the child to her. Following a trial in early 1994, at which two experts testified that it was in the child's best interests to remain with mother, the trial court granted custody to mother. . . .

Father appealed to the Court of Appeals, which affirmed the trial court's judgment. We allowed father's petition for review. Father's proposed rule of law is that a change in circumstances resulting directly or indirectly from a parent's illegal act of custodial interference should be disqualified, as a matter of equity, from triggering an analysis of a potential change in custody. That proposed rule of law is based on the Court of Appeals' holding in Welby and Welby, 89 Or. App. 412, 749 P.2d 602 (1988). For the reasons that follow, we affirm the decision of the Court of Appeals in the present case.

ORS 109.103 allows unmarried parents to initiate a civil proceeding to determine custody of their child in cases in which paternity has been established. The statute provides in part:

"The parents shall have the same rights and responsibilities regarding the custody and support of their child that married or divorced parents would have,

---

8. ORS 109.175 provides in part: "If paternity of a child born out of wedlock is established pursuant to . . . an order or judgment entered pursuant to . . . ORS 416.400 to 416.470, . . . the parent with physical custody at the time of filing of the . . . notice . . . has sole legal custody until a court specifically orders otherwise."

and the provisions of ORS 107.095 to 107.425 that relate to the custody or support of children shall be applicable to the proceeding."

In turn, ORS 107.135 gives the court the power to modify custody judgments. In addition, ORS 109.175 provides in part: "The first time the court determines who should have legal custody, neither parent shall have the burden of proving a change of circumstances." That wording implies, and we hold, that the burden of showing a change in circumstances does apply to a parent seeking a change of custody in subsequent proceedings.

The child custody statutes do not specify what the concept of a "change of circumstances" means. However, this court has established a two-step inquiry to be used in determining whether a court should modify a custody arrangement:

> A petitioner seeking a change of custody must show (1) that after the original judgment or the last order affecting custody, circumstances relevant to the capacity of either the moving party or the legal custodian to take care of the child properly have changed, and (2) that considering the asserted change of circumstances in the context of all relevant evidence, it would be in the child's best interests to change custody from the legal custodian to the moving party.

Ortiz and Ortiz, 310 Or. 644, 649, 801 P.2d 767 (1990). . . . In the absence of evidence of a change in circumstances since the last arrangement of custody, the court does not reach the second step in the analysis.

The requirement that there be a change in circumstances before a court will consider modifying custody is a rule of long standing. . . .

The rationale for the change-in-circumstances rule is that, unless the parent who seeks a change in custody establishes that the facts that formed the basis for the prior custody determination have changed materially by the time of the modification hearing, the prior adjudication is preclusive with respect to the issue of the best interests of the child under the extant facts. . . . The purposes served by the change-in-circumstances rule are "to avoid repeated litigation over custody and to provide a stable environment for children." The inquiry into whether there has been a change in circumstances since the time of the previous custody arrangement is a factual one that relates to the capability of one or both parents to care for the child.

As noted earlier in this opinion, the Court of Appeals has carved out an exception to the change-in-circumstances rule. In *Welby*, the court held that a parent "cannot rely on evidence" of a "strengthened relationship" with a child to establish a change in circumstances, if that strengthened relationship resulted from abduction and secreting of the child. In such a circumstance, the court held, the parent who engaged in the illegal conduct cannot meet the first step of the two-part inquiry into whether a court should modify a custody arrangement and, therefore, the court cannot reach the issue of the child's best interests.

Welby held, and father argues here, that certain kinds of criminal conduct prohibit proof of a change in circumstances. However, we are dealing here with a legislative scheme. The legislature could make that policy choice if it wishes, but at present no statute precludes inquiry into an otherwise sufficient change in circumstances simply because that change can be traced, in whole or in part, to a parent's unlawful act.

Neither do we find anything in the rationale behind or purposes of the change-in-circumstances rule, as heretofore announced by this court, to support father's proposed rule of law. Punishment of a parent's past misconduct and deterrence of potential misconduct by others in the future are functions of the criminal law, which prohibits custodial interference. By contrast, the overriding theme of the child custody statutes is the best interests of the child.

A child whose circumstances have changed is entitled, when a parent institutes a proper proceeding, to consideration of the child's best interests. If the change in circumstances results from the parent's illegal act, were the court to refuse to consider whether (1) the change in circumstances justifies a modification of custody and (2) a modification is in the best interests of the child, then the court would be punishing the child for the parent's misconduct. We are unwilling to do that. To the extent that this opinion is inconsistent with *Welby*, *Welby* no longer controls.

We now turn to an application of the change-in-circumstances rule. In the present case, a 1988 default order granted custody to father, when the child was 1-1/2 years old. When the court granted custody to mother in 1994, the child was nearly seven years old. The trial court found that circumstances had changed because of "the child's unfamiliarity with [father] and the risk now posed to the emotional stability of the child if [her] custody were awarded to [father]." On de novo review, the Court of Appeals also found a change in circumstances. Specifically, the Court of Appeals found that the child had experienced serious emotional problems for a period of several months after being reintroduced to father and that her emotional problems "will only be exacerbated if father were to be awarded sole custody of the child."

As noted, we accept the factual findings of the Court of Appeals. Indeed, father's counsel concedes before this court that, factually, there was a change in circumstances. He argues only that a change in circumstances resulting directly or indirectly from a parent's illegal act of custodial interference should be disqualified, as a matter of equity, from triggering an analysis of a potential change in custody. We have rejected that position above. We conclude that the first step of the modification analysis is satisfied.

The second step in our two-step inquiry focuses on whether the requested modification of custody is in the child's best interests. . . .

That "best interests of the child" inquiry is required by statute. . . . Additionally, ORS 107.137(3) provides:

"In determining custody of a minor child pursuant to ORS 107.105 or 107.135, the court shall consider the conduct, marital status, income, social environment or life style of either party only if it is shown that any of these factors are causing or may cause emotional or physical damage to the child."

Under that provision, a parent's "conduct" shall be considered only if it is causing or in the future may cause a specified harm to the child. A parent's illegal act is a kind of "conduct." If that conduct is causing or may cause the child emotional or physical damage, then the court must consider that illegal act in making its determination regarding custody. Conversely, unless a parent's illegal act is causing or may cause damage to the child, that conduct is not a consideration.

Here, the Court of Appeals, like the trial court, weighed the statutory factors and found that it was in the child's best interests to grant custody to mother, notwithstanding her illegal conduct. Father argues that the emotional problems that the child has experienced as a result of her reintroduction to him are due to mother's illegal conduct. Mother's conduct did cause harm to the child by depriving her of a relationship with her father and thereby making the child's reintroduction to father traumatic. Nonetheless, the evidence in the record is such as to entitle the trial court and the Court of Appeals to conclude, as they did, that it is in the child's best interests for custody to be with mother.

In summary: (1) If circumstances relating to the capability of one or both parents to care for their child have changed since the previous custody arrangement, then the requirement that there be a change in circumstances before a court will consider modifying custody is satisfied, whatever the reason for the change. (2) When determining custody in a modification proceeding, after finding a change in circumstances, the court is to consider a parent's "conduct" only if that conduct is "causing or may cause emotional or physical damage to the child." In this case, because there was a change in circumstances between the time of the 1988 custody order and the 1994 modification hearing, and because the evidence showed that it was in the child's best interests to continue living with mother notwithstanding her conduct, the trial court did not err in awarding custody to mother.

NOTES AND QUESTIONS

1. The requirement that a party seeking a change in custody show a "material" change in circumstances is almost universal. Burchard v. Garay, above, page 635, observed that this requirement entails identification of

> a prior custody decision based upon circumstances then existing which rendered that decision in the best interest of the child. The court can then inquire whether alleged new circumstances represent a significant change from preexisting circumstances, requiring a reevaluation of the child's custody.

The rationale for this approach is described as follows:

> In deciding between competing parental claims to custody, the court must make an award "according to the best interests of the child." This test, established by statute, governs all custody proceedings. The changed-circumstance rule is not a different test, devised to supplant the statutory test. . . . It provides, in essence, that once it has been established that a particular custodial arrangement is in the best interests of the child, the court need not reexamine that question. Instead, it should preserve the established mode of custody unless some significant change in circumstance indicates that a different arrangement would be in the child's best interests. The rule thus fosters the dual goals of judicial economy and protecting stable custodial arrangements.

724 P.2d 486, 488 (1986).

2. The difference in standards for a de novo determination of custody and a change in circumstances raises the issue of what constitutes a custody order. The California Supreme Court in Montenegro v. Diaz, 27 P.3d 289 (Cal. 2001), held

that "a stipulated custody order is a final judicial custody determination for purposes of the changed circumstance rule only if there is a clear, affirmative indication the parties intended such a result." In other words, the parties' agreement in, for example, Painter v. Bannister that the grandparents would care for Mark would not be "a final judicial custody determination" unless the parties both entered a stipulated order with the court *and* provided "clear, affirmative indication" that they intended the order to be a final judicial determination. If the grandparents had secured a custody award when Mark initially moved in with them, the father would have had to overcome a greater hurdle to justify a change in custody, notwithstanding the constitutional deference to parents. *See* Callahan v. Davis, 869 So. 2d 434 (Miss. 2004) (parent who voluntarily relinquishes custody of a minor child, through a court of competent jurisdiction, has forfeited the right to rely on the existing natural parent presumption and must show that a change in custody is in the child's best interests to modify custody to nonparents); C.R.B. v. C.C., 959 P.2d 375 (Alaska 1998); In the Interest of Ferguson, 927 S.W.2d 766 (Tex. App. 1996) (presumption favoring parent does not apply where parent seeks modification of decree granting custody to nonparent). *But see* Harris v. Smith, 752 N.E.2d 1283 (Ind. 2001) (even when a parent initiates an action to re-obtain custody of a child who has been in the custody of a third party, the burden of rebutting the presumption in favor of parental custody remains upon the third party).

3. The Uniform Marriage and Divorce Act (UMDA) adopts a strict approach to modification. No modification will be granted within two years of the initial order unless there is evidence of danger to the child's physical, mental, moral, or emotional health, and modification afterward is permitted only where new or previously unknown facts show (1) consent to modification by the custodian; (2) integration into petitioner's family with consent of the custodian; or (3) serious danger to the child's physical, mental, moral, or emotional health *and* harm caused by change in environment is outweighed by its advantages. *See* In re Custody of Dallenger, 568 P.2d 169 (Mont. 1977).

The ALI Principles of Family Dissolution also relax the requirements somewhat, providing that "a court may modify a court-ordered parenting plan if it finds, on the basis of facts that were not known or have arisen since the entry of the prior order and were not anticipated therein, that a substantial change has occurred in the circumstances of the child or of one or both parents and that a modification is necessary to the child's welfare." § 2.15(1). The Principles also permit modifications in the child's best interest if the parents agree, the modification reflects a de facto change already in place for at least six months, the change is necessary to accommodate an older child's preferences, and other circumstances. § 2.16.

Is so limited a basis for modification consistent with concern for the child's best interests? *Compare* King v. King, 477 P.2d 356, 360 (Alaska 1970) (change of circumstances simply "one of the factors to be weighed" in modification proceedings); Posey v. Bunney, 561 P.2d 400 (Idaho 1977) (best interests of child a controlling consideration in all custody proceedings).

How would the UMDA standard apply in cases of joint custody? Would modification from joint to sole custody be allowed when the parents disagree about important decisions relating to the child, or would some further showing be necessary? Should more than the collapse of amicable decision making be required? *See* In re Marriage of Wall, 868 P.2d 387 (Colo. 1994), interpreting the joint-custody statute to require only a showing that modification is in the child's best interests, rather than the material change of circumstance necessary for ordinary custody modifications.

4. Among the most common reasons that a change in custody is sought is remarriage of one of the parents. It is often said that remarriage of the noncustodial parent does not by itself constitute a "material change of circumstances." *See* Simons v. Simons, 374 A.2d 1040 (Conn. 1977). What about remarriage of the custodial parent? The ALI Principles expressly provide that neither a parent's remarriage nor cohabitation constitutes changed circumstances by itself. §215(3)(b).

What is the effect of holding that remarriage does not itself constitute a material change of circumstance?

5. How does the changed-circumstance rule apply to cases where the custodial parent, after some time, wishes to move? Who has the burden of establishing the material change? The standards for relocation discussed above often dovetail with the requirements for change of circumstances. The *Burgess* court, for example, held that

> [o]rdinarily, after a judicial custody determination, the noncustodial parent seeking to alter the order for legal and physical custody can do so only on a showing that there has been a substantial change of circumstances so affecting the minor child that modification is essential to the child's welfare. . . .
>
> We conclude that the same allocation of the burden of persuasion applies in the case of a custodial parent's relocation as in any other proceeding to alter existing custody arrangements. . . .

Does *LaMusga* change the standard for relocation to one that differs from the standard for modification? See note 2 above following *Burgess*. *Compare* ALI §2.17, which provides that "[t]he relocation of a parent constitutes a substantial change in circumstances . . . only when the relocation significantly impairs either parent's ability to exercise responsibilities the parent has been exercising or attempting to exercise under the parenting plan."

In states that impose greater barriers to relocation, the custodial, rather than the noncustodial, parent may bear the burden of justifying the move, and the standard may specifically tailored to the issue of relocation. *See, e.g., Tropea*, the New York decision noted above, which requires demonstration of "exceptional circumstances" to justify a move that would have the impact of the depriving the noncustodial parent of "regular and meaningful access."

The law of most states is that absent a court order restricting their movement, the custodial parent and the child are free to move to another jurisdiction. *See* Taylor (Mitten) v. Taylor, 849 S.W.2d 319, 322-323 (Tenn. 1993). *See also* In re Marriage of Lower, 269 N.W.2d 822, 825 (Iowa 1978) ("If a decree grants custody of a child to a parent who resides within the jurisdiction of the court, but the decree is silent concerning the place where the child is to live, the custodian may, in the absence of a statute to the contrary, remove the child from the state."); Jordan v. Jordan, 439 A.2d 26, 31 (Md. App. 1982). An exception may be recognized where removal of a child by the custodial parent to a foreign country is involved, but, even in that circumstance, most courts permit removal. *See, e.g.,*

Bozzi v. Bozzi, 413 A.2d 834 (Conn. 1979), and other cases collected at 30 A.L.R.4th 548 (1984).

These outcomes are sometimes explained simply as a matter of the terms of the decree. Where the decree is silent regarding relocation, the party seeking to impose such a restriction is in the position of seeking to modify the terms of the custodial order and must therefore show both changed circumstances and that the modification will serve the child's best interests. *Compare*, however, Scheiner v. Scheiner, 336 So. 2d 406 (Fla. App. 1976), *cert. denied*, 342 So. 2d 1103 (Fla. 1977) (although decree is silent, party seeking to move may be said to violate the decree). What arguments can be made in support of each result?

6. Are there interests other than those of the child that might also be taken into account? *See* D'Onofrio v. D'Onofrio, 365 A.2d 27, 29-30 (N.J. Super.), *aff'd*, 365 A.2d 716 (1976), addressing the best interest of the "new family unit," including the custodial parent and his or her new spouse. *See also* Henry v. Henry, 326 N.W.2d 497, 499 (Mich. App. 1982) (adopting *D'Onofrio*: the proper test "focuses on what is in the best interest of the new family unit, i.e., custodial parent and child, and not what is in the best interest of the child; the latter having been decided in the earlier custody hearings").

For a recent review of cases dealing with relocation, *see* Janet M. Bowermaster, Sympathizing with Solomon: Choosing Between Parents in a Mobile Society, 31 J. Fam. L. 791 (1992-1993).

7. An exception to the changed-circumstance requirement is sometimes recognized where the parties have not fully litigated the custody issue. *See* ALI Principles § 2.16(2)(d):

> The court may modify a parenting plan without a showing of changed circumstances if the modification is in the child's best interests and . . . is necessary to change a parenting plan that was based on an agreement that the court would not have ordered . . . had the court been aware of the circumstances at the time the plan was ordered, if modification is sought under this section within six months of the issuance of the parenting plan.

See also, e.g., Simons v. Simons, 374 A.2d 1040 (Conn. 1977). This exception may also take the form of a "prior unknown facts" rule, allowing modification without a showing of change in circumstance when the party seeking modification provides information that was not known and could not have been discovered by reasonable diligence prior to the initial decree. *E.g.*, Kallas v. Kallas, 614 P.2d 641 (Utah 1980).

PROBLEMS

1. Philip and Nancy Friedman were divorced four years ago. Both parents were raised as Orthodox Jews, strictly observing the Sabbath and the dietary laws. The children attended a yeshiva. The Friedmans were awarded joint legal custody. Nancy Friedman has physical custody, with visitation rights for Philip.

About two years after the divorce, Philip sought to modify the custody order to place sole custody in himself. Nancy Friedman cross-moved for sole custody. The father's motion was based on Nancy Friedman's lapse in religious observance.

Philip Friedman presented evidence indicating that his former wife had ceased attending Sabbath services and rarely took the children there, watched television on the Sabbath, and was thinking about moving the children to a public school. The children, aged 11 and 8, had different desires about custody: The older girl wanted to live with her father; the younger wished to continue living with her mother but not to be separated from her sister.

What arguments might be made regarding the motion and cross-motion?

2. Alex and Sharon Norris were divorced two years ago, and both wished to maintain joint custody of their three-year-old child. The trial court allowed joint custody and approved the residential arrangements agreed to by the parents, which placed the child primarily with the mother and provided for liberal visitation by the father.

The parties now seek to modify the existing custodial order. Sharon Norris wishes to move to New Hampshire, where her parents live; Alex Norris wishes to remain in the state. Alex seeks joint primary physical custody so that he and his daughter can continue to be with his extended family. The trial court concluded that Alex had the burden of showing "a substantial change of circumstances and that remaining in New Mexico would be in the child's best interests." The judge then found that the mother's motives for moving were legitimate and that the costs and benefits of moving or remaining in New Mexico were approximately equal. Accordingly, the trial court held that the child should remain in the physical custody of the mother.

Alex Norris has appealed the trial court order. What arguments should he make?

3. Mark and Grace Montoya divorced four years ago. Both are employed — she as an elementary school teacher, he as a high school football coach. They have one child, Richard, age four. Richard has been in his mother's custody and has had difficulty adjusting to the divorce. Richard is in pre-school, and then in day care. His teachers and the day care supervisor describe Richard as having "emotional or behavioral problems"; he is aggressive and does not share well. Mark Montoya recently married a woman with two children from her previous marriage. She does not work outside the home and would welcome Richard. Mark has moved for a change of custody, which Grace Montoya opposes. What arguments should be made in support of each position? What evidence should be sought to support the arguments?

Family Contracts

10

A. INTRODUCTION: STATUS AND CONTRACT REVISITED

The expression *family contracts* may refer to a wide variety of agreements. In addition to the agreement to marry, contracts affecting family relationships may include agreements between the spouses regarding religious upbringing of children, ownership of wealth during the marriage, and settlements in contemplation of divorce, or an agreement between the spouses and some third person to bear a child. A contract can also be an important vehicle for analyzing the rights and duties of unmarried cohabitants. (See Chapter 4.) In these and many other instances, a central problem is the fit between legal contract principles — designed to deal with arm's-length, usually commercial, transactions — and family relationships. Stewart Macaulay et al., Contracts: Law in Action (1992), a contracts book, includes a section on family contracts.

Despite the ubiquity of contract ideas and vocabulary in family law, that fit seems uncomfortable on its face. The typical remedy in contracts is expectation damages, paid in money. Specific performance is rarely available, although it can be ordered more easily in the context of the sale of goods or land than otherwise. Moreover, typical contract remedies principles prefer to reduce the consequences of enforcement. It is desirable, as Professor Farnsworth has suggested, to provide a remedy that will encourage promisees to deal with promisors in the future. Contract doctrines relating, for example, to mitigation or foreseeability provide the language in which these limits on remedies are expressed.

Money damages, however, do not seem adequate in many family law contexts. A surrogacy contract seeks to provide a child to parents who cannot bear a child, and nothing else would seem to do. The same may be said about promises between spouses to give a *get* (a Jewish religious divorce) or to raise a child in a particular religion. The preference of contract law for economic solutions rather than specific performance, and for reducing the consequences of enforcement, may bar realization of these expectations.

The tension between contracts and family relationships is long-standing and has been variously expressed. Toennies's distinction between *gesellschaft* (principles of exchange) and *gemeinschaft* (principles of community) and Hegel's comment that rights in the family do not exist until the family dissolves both reflect that tension.[1]

This sense of tension between rights defined in terms of economic exchange and the more complex, communitarian relationships we associate with family life continues in a more modern idiom. As Milton Regan has written,

> Appreciation of the social significance of marriage as a constitutive relationship, however, leads to some skepticism about claims that contract should be privileged over status as the source of obligations at divorce. First, the interdependence and vulnerability that characterize intimate relationships systematically create unique opportunities for overreaching. The cultivation of a relational sense of identity by definition indicates a disposition inclined to regard the parties' interests as largely coterminous. Such an attitude may undermine the willingness to engage in self-interested bargaining that normally makes us confident that a contract accurately reflects each party's preferences. The party who has a more individuated sense of self is likely to be the one to propose a contract in the first place, to distinguish more sharply the resources belonging to each party, and to seek to limit the other partner's access to assets. Yet this is not the sense of self that the law should necessarily privilege in family matters.

Milton Regan, Family Law and the Pursuit of Intimacy 149 (1993). For an overview of many of the complex themes involved in the question of contracts and the family, *see* Carl E. Schneider, Moral Discourse and the Transformation of American Family Law, 83 Mich. L. Rev. 1803, 1831-1832 (1985). *See also* Elizabeth S. Scott, Rational Decisionmaking About Marriage and Divorce, 76 Va. L. Rev. 9 (1990); June Carbone & Margaret F. Brinig, Rethinking Marriage: Feminist Ideology, Economic Change and Divorce Reform, 65 Tul. L. Rev. 953 (1991); Jeffrey E. Stake, Mandatory Planning for Divorce, 45 Vand. L. Rev. 397 (1992); Brian Bix, Bargaining in the Shadow of Love: The Enforcement of Premarital Agreements and How We Think About Marriage, 40 Wm. & Mary L. Rev. 145 (1998); Katharine B. Silbaugh, Marriage Contracts and the Family Economy, 93 Nw. U. L. Rev. 65 (1998); Barbara Stark, Marriage Proposals: From One-Size-Fits-All to Postmodern Marriage Law, 89 Calif. L. Rev. 1479 (2001); Howard Fink & June Carbone, Between Private Ordering and Public Fiat: A New Paradigm for Family Law Decision-making, 5 J.L. & Fam. Stud. 1 (2003). Earlier

---

1. "The right which the individual enjoys on the strength of the family unit and which is in the first place simply the individual's life within this unity, takes on the form of right (as the abstract moment of determinate individuality) only when the family begins to dissolve." Georg W. F. Hegel, Philosophy of Right §159, at 110-111 (Knox trans., 1952). *Cf.* Ferdinand Toennies on Sociology: Pure, Applied, and Empirical 160-169 (Werner Cahnman & Rudolf Herbele eds., 1971).

relevant writing includes Lenore J. Weitzman, Legal Regulation of Marriage: Tradition and Change, 62 Cal. L. Rev. 1169 (1974); Marjorie M. Schultz, Contractual Ordering of Marriage: A New Model for State Policy, 70 Cal. L. Rev. 207 (1982); Robert H. Mnookin & Lewis Kornhauser, Bargaining in the Shadow of the Law: The Case of Divorce, 88 Yale L.J. 950 (1979).

Why, then, do we continue to use contract language in connection with families? Part of the answer is that there are economic aspects to family relationships, perhaps now more than before. Moreover, contracts are important for other than economic transactions. We talk routinely about church covenants and the social contract. In this broader view, it is natural that relationships as important as those involved in marriage and the family should invoke the idea of contract. We may also note that the *idea* of contract (or promise, or agreement, or covenant) is not the same as a legal contract enforceable in court. The Uniform Commercial Code, for example, distinguishes between the agreement made in fact by the parties and the contract enforceable in court. The word *contract*, then, may be understood as referring to an image or metaphor, or even to a piece of paper useful in framing the expectations of the parties as an educational or counseling device but not intended to be legally enforceable.

It may also be that the difference between status and contract is overstated. The role of the courts and the state is evident in both. And, as Corbin noted many years ago, an overly strong emphasis on an agreement between strangers misses much of contract law.

> The legal relations consequent upon offer and acceptance are not wholly dependent, even upon the reasonable meaning of the words and acts of the parties. The law determines these relations in the light of subsequent circumstances, these often being totally unforeseen by the parties. In such cases it is sometimes said that the law will create that relation which the parties would have intended had they foreseen. The fact is, however, that the decision will depend upon the notions of the court as to policy, welfare, justice, right and wrong, such notions often being inarticulate and subconscious.

Arthur L. Corbin, Offer and Acceptance, and Some of the Resulting Legal Relations, 26 Yale L.J. 169, 206 (1917).

However, ignoring the contractual aspects of relationships presents similar dangers.

> [Contract] ideas are particularly important in a time of significant social uncertainty, much of it arising out of the impact of the current changes in the situation of women. The skeptical position on the use of contracts tends to the conclusion that an official state attitude towards such contracts must begin with a presumptive negative, based on the view that the law and theory of contract is most likely to be irrelevant. Analysis of these issues from within the field of contracts suggests that the state stance can often be more open to individual variation without sacrifice of collective judgment.

Carol Weisbrod, The Way We Live Now: A Discussion of Contracts and Domestic Arrangements, 1994 Utah L. Rev. 777, 782-783.

B. PREMARITAL AGREEMENTS

At least since the sixteenth century, spouses have used premarital agreements to alter the legal regimes for marital property ownership and management. The English Statute of Frauds of 1677 dealt with such contracts, requiring them to be in writing to be enforceable. Today, in the United States, they are still with us, but their acceptability waxes and wanes. As marital regimes ossify, contract offers a more flexible way to order individual relationships. As marriage laws seek to protect the vulnerable, premarital contracts may become more associated with the rich and powerful. The headlines belong to the famous; the premarital agreements of a baseball player or a Kennedy receive disproportionate attention, but their most common use may well be to keep the assets of a first marriage separate from the arrangements of a second one.

To be enforceable, premarital agreements must satisfy the usual contract requirements: They must be entered into voluntarily, supported by consideration, and satisfy the statute of frauds. Traditionally, and still today in most states, premarital agreements must also satisfy additional procedural requirements and are subject to greater judicial supervision of their substantive terms than are commercial contracts. The cases and statutes regulating premarital agreements can be divided into two broad categories: The Uniform Premarital Agreement Act (UPAA) and a number of state court decisions such as Simeone v. Simeone proceed from the belief that the parties should be relatively free to reach whatever agreements they like, and be able to rely on the enforceability of such contracts at separation or divorce. The ALI Principles and the decisions in other states place greater weight on the fairness of the result at the time of enforcement, even if that makes the result less predictable. The following materials first consider the common law decisions and then compare the UPAA and the ALI Principles. As you study these materials, consider whether the resolution of individual issues, such as the importance of representation by counsel, reflects different approaches to the enforceability of these agreements, and whether the traditional justifications for treating these agreements differently from commercial contracts still ring true.

SANDERS V. SANDERS

288 S.W.2d 473 (Tenn. App. 1955)

This is a suit between husband and wife while still living together, involving the validity of an antenuptial contract.

Referring to the parties as they appeared below the complainant, Dr. B. F. Sanders, a dentist, filed the original bill herein against his wife, Hazel B. Sanders, alleging that they were last married October 28, 1951, previous to which they had been twice married and divorced.

The bill alleges as a condition of their remarriage in October 1951, the defendant required the complainant to execute the following contract:

This instrument, made and entered into on this the 26th day of October, 1951, by and between Dr. B. F. Sanders, hereinafter called the first party, and Hazel Burnette, hereinafter called the second party.

Witnesseth

Whereas, The parties to this instrument are contemplating marriage and establishing a home together, and

Whereas, Each has property of their own and upon their marriage desire to pool their resources for the benefit of each other, and

Whereas, In order to avoid any future conflict as to their rights and interests in said property this instrument is made.

Now Therefore, For and in consideration of the mutual benefits to be derived therefrom the parties agree and bind themselves as follows:

1. The parties hereby agree to enter into the marriage relation and live together as husband and wife.

2. On or before the date of marriage all property belonging to the parties, including bonds, bank account and realty, shall be re-issued, re-deposited and deeds drawn so that each party shall be the joint owner, with right of survivorship, of all of the property at present owned and held by the parties separately and individually.

3. Each party obligates himself to purchase and hold all property, present and future, jointly with the other party and agrees to execute any instrument necessary to convey, sell, or encumber any property, real or personal, when it is to the best interest of both parties that same be conveyed, sold, or encumbered.

4. At the death of either party the property belonging to both shall be and become the absolute property of the other, free from claims of any and all other persons. To make effective and certain this section of the agreement a joint will of the parties is made and is placed in their safety deposit box in the First National Bank in the City of Harriman, Tennessee.

5. Should either party file a divorce against the other, then the party so filing shall by such filing forfeit to the other all right, title, and interest in all the property, real, personal or mixed, jointly held and owned by them.

The parties agree that the original of this instrument shall be deposited in escrow with J. E. Pearman to be held by him. The agreement cannot be revoked except by written consent of both parties and the holder in escrow shall not deliver the original to any one except a court of competent jurisdiction or to the parties to this instrument upon their mutual demand for the surrender thereof. The instrument is made in triplicate with each party hereto retaining a copy thereof, but the copy shall not be used in evidence or to serve any legal purpose whatsoever if the original is available.

In Witness Whereof the parties hereto have set their signatures on the day and date first above written.

The bill alleges as a further condition of the remarriage defendant required complainant to execute a joint will with her, by which each gave to the other all joint property except that if defendant died first, the estate in the hands of complainant was charged with the payment to defendant's parents, if living, $1,000 per year for ten years. Upon the death of the survivor the estate to be equally divided between heirs of complainant and parents of defendant. The bill gives notice that complainant revokes and declares void the will.

The bill also alleges that the antenuptial contract is void "being against public policy." As reasons for his desire to cancel the contract and revoke the will, he charges that defendant "in recent months has conceived the idea that she can treat the complainant as she pleases and that he must endure it." As examples of alleged mistreatment complainant charges that defendant refused to sign joint income tax return and refers to his grandson as "a little Bastard."

The bill further alleges: "Your complainant avers that he loves his wife, that he expects to live with her if she will permit him to do so, and will treat him right, and he expects to leave her a substantial amount of property and money on his death, but he would like to have the privilege of giving her something rather than being under a contract to give her all."

The bill prays that the contract and will be canceled and revoked, or in the alternative that the contract be declared void as a violation of public policy.

Defendant filed an answer and cross-bill averring that she and complainant were first married on December 24, 1938 and first divorced in February 1949. They remarried in April 1949; that complainant filed a divorce action against her in July 1949, which was dismissed in December 1949; that complainant filed a second divorce action against her March 23, 1951, to which she filed answer and cross-bill, and she was granted a second divorce on June 4, 1951 and remarried in October 1951.

The answer admits the execution of the foregoing contract, and avers that it was proposed by complainant to induce her consent to a remarriage; that he had it prepared by his attorneys and it was "made in consideration of and prior to their third marriage." . . .

The answer denies all wrongdoing alleged against defendant in the original bill. . . .

First: Is paragraph 5 of the antenuptial contract against public policy and void. This paragraph reads as follows:

> 5. Should either party file a divorce against the other, then the party so filing shall by such filing forfeit to the other all right, title, and interest in all the property, real, personal or mixed, jointly held and owned by them.

Under the circumstances it would seem that the effect of paragraph 5 of the contract should be determined by whether or not a subsequent divorce suit is instituted by either party in good faith and upon reasonable grounds. This would be a question of the construction of that provision rather than its validity.

The reasoning for the Chancellor holding that the contract in suit violated public policy is stated in his opinion, as follows:

> Here, we have in clause five of the contract a clause which would cause the party filing a divorce action to forfeit all of his right, title and interest in the joint property of parties. While it is desirable that the parties not seek a divorce, certainly neither husband nor wife should be forced to live with the other regardless of the conduct of the other party. For fear of a great financial loss, great hardship could

be imposed upon the party to such contract. He or she might be forced to endure abuse, insult, embarrassment or the grossest sort of cruel and inhuman treatment. To permit such an agreement to stand would impose a penalty for seeking a legal remedy for an impossible situation. I think it is definitely contrary to public policy.

If the forfeiture clause in the contract could have the effect stated, we would agree that same contravened public policy; but, with greatest respect for the learned Chancellor, we are constrained to hold otherwise for these reasons:

As held by the Chancellor, it is premature to declare fully the rights of the parties under the contract at this time; yet it is necessary to construe and determine the effect of the contract in order to determine whether it violates the public policy rule. To do this, it is proper to consider the purposes of the contract, and the situation of the parties when it was made.

The parties at the time the contract was executed were contemplating remarriage. Their previous married life had been [unusually] turbulent. Each had filed two divorce actions against the other. Each was possessed of valuable property which they were agreeing to pool into an estate by entireties. In that situation it was reasonable that each should want to avoid future divorce action and stipulate against it, and the forfeiture provision apparently seemed to them at the time as a good means to that end. There is no intimation in the record that the contract was not executed in good faith by the parties in the belief that it was valid in all its provisions. Should a contract made under those conditions be declared void because of its forfeiture provision?. . . .

Here the consideration for the contract was the consummation of the contemplated marriage and the pooling of the property of the parties. The forfeiture provision was no part of the consideration, and only imposes a penalty in the event either party should seek a divorce. We think that the provision is more nearly analogous to the forfeiture provision sometimes put in wills which . . . are uniformly held not to violate public policy.

Nor does the provision contract away the right of either party to sue for divorce. It only imposes an option to sue for divorce and recover such property as the Court may award if successful. If the divorce suit is prosecuted in good faith and upon reasonable grounds, although not successful, the property rights stipulated in the contract will not be forfeited. If, however, the divorce suit is not prosecuted in good faith and upon reasonable grounds, the party filing such suit will forfeit his or her right to the property.

For these reasons we are constrained to hold the learned Chancellor erred in decreeing that the contract violated public policy and is void. Therefore, the defendant's first assignment of error will be sustained and complainant's first assignment is overruled. . . .

As indicated, the decree of the Chancellor will be reversed, and a decree will be entered in this Court in accordance with this opinion. Thereafter the cause will be remanded to the Chancery Court of Roane County for such orders as may be necessary for the enforcement of the decree.

NOTES AND QUESTIONS

1. It has long been established that premarital agreements may deal with property rights of the spouses when the marriage terminates by death. Statutes often explicitly recognize that spouses may contract around the statutory provisions to protect surviving spouses. *E.g.*, UPC §2-213 (1990) (adopting the criteria for enforceability of the Uniform Premarital Agreements Act, below). However, according to traditional principles, terms that contemplated divorce were ordinarily viewed as contrary to public policy and thus unenforceable. The holding of *Sanders* was, therefore, unusual for its time. What were the rationales for the traditional rule? Why did the court in *Sanders* find this case to be exceptional? What was the significance of the unusual marital history of Mr. and Mrs. Sanders? Of the fact that Mr. Sanders's attorney drafted the agreement?

2. The landmark case of Posner v. Posner, 233 So. 2d 381 (Fla. 1970), *rev'd on other grounds*, 257 So. 2d 530 (1972), held that contracts concerning property division and spousal support at divorce are not inherently contrary to public policy. Most courts faced with the issue since then have taken the same view, concluding that no-fault divorce laws express a legislative policy of neutrality toward divorce and that, in an era of frequent divorce, public policy favors settling disputes amicably. *But see* McAlpine v. McAlpine, 653 So. 2d 520 (La. 1995), which holds that parties may not waive permanent spousal support by premarital agreement. The court invoked a provision of the Louisiana Civil Code that says that people may not make agreements contrary to laws enacted for the protection of the public interest and held that the public interest in providing for spousal support following divorce precluded enforcement of an absolute waiver.

Posner and many other cases require either that a premarital agreement make full and adequate provision for the spouses or that the spouses make full disclosure to each other. The next case considers whether to abandon even these limits.

SIMEONE V. SIMEONE

581 A.2d 162 (Pa. 1990)

FLAHERTY, J. At issue in this appeal is the validity of a prenuptial agreement executed between the appellant, Catherine E. Walsh Simeone, and the appellee, Frederick A. Simeone. At the time of their marriage, in 1975, appellant was a twenty-three year old nurse and appellee was a thirty-nine year old neurosurgeon. Appellee had an income of approximately $90,000 per year, and appellant was unemployed. Appellee also had assets worth approximately $300,000. On the eve of the parties' wedding, appellee's attorney presented appellant with a prenuptial agreement to be signed. Appellant, without the benefit of counsel, signed the agreement. Appellee's attorney had not advised appellant regarding any legal rights that the agreement surrendered. The parties are in disagreement as to whether appellant knew in advance of that date that such an agreement would be presented for signature. Appellant denies having had such knowledge and claims to have signed under adverse circumstances, which, she contends, provide a basis for declaring it void.

The agreement limited appellant to support payments of $200 per week in the event of separation or divorce, subject to a maximum total payment of $25,000. The parties separated in 1982, and, in 1984, divorce proceedings were commenced. Between 1982 and 1984 appellee made payments which satisfied the $25,000 limit. In 1985, appellant filed a claim for alimony pendente lite. A master's report upheld the validity of the prenuptial agreement and denied this claim. Exceptions to the master's report were dismissed by the Court of Common Pleas of Philadelphia County. The Superior Court affirmed.

We granted allowance of appeal because uncertainty was expressed by the Superior Court regarding the meaning of our plurality decision in Estate of Geyer, 533 A.2d 423 (Pa. 1987) (Opinion Announcing Judgment of the Court). The Superior Court viewed Geyer as permitting a prenuptial agreement to be upheld if it either made a reasonable provision for the spouse or was entered after a full and fair disclosure of the general financial positions of the parties and the statutory rights being relinquished. Appellant contends that this interpretation of Geyer is in error insofar as it requires disclosure of statutory rights only in cases where there has not been made a reasonable provision for the spouse. Inasmuch as the courts below held that the provision made for appellant was a reasonable one, appellant's efforts to overturn the agreement have focused upon an assertion that there was an inadequate disclosure of statutory rights. Appellant continues to assert, however, that the payments provided in the agreement were less than reasonable.

The statutory rights in question are those relating to alimony pendente lite. Other statutory rights, such as those pertaining to alimony and equitable distribution of marital property, did not exist in 1975. Those rights arose under the Divorce Code of 1980, and the Code expressly provides that marital agreements executed prior to its effective date are not affected thereby. 23 P.S. §103. Certainly, at the time the present agreement was executed, no disclosure was required with respect to rights which were not then in existence. The present agreement did expressly state, however, that alimony pendente lite was being relinquished. It also recited that appellant "has been informed and understands" that, were it not for the agreement, appellant's obligation to pay alimony pendente lite "might, as a matter of law, exceed the amount provided." Hence, appellant's claim is not that the agreement failed to disclose the particular right affected, but rather that she was not adequately informed with respect to the nature of alimony pendente lite.

The plurality opinion in Geyer expressly applied and followed this Court's decision in Hillegass Estate, 244 A.2d 672 (Pa. 1968), which held that a prenuptial agreement will be upheld if it either made a reasonable provision for the spouse or was entered after a full and fair disclosure of financial status. . . .

. . . Because the Superior Court viewed the present agreement as having made an adequate provision for appellant, it held that the agreement was valid regardless of whether there had been a full disclosure of statutory rights being surrendered. . . .

While the decision of the Superior Court reflects, perhaps, a reasonable interpretation of Geyer, we do not view this case as a vehicle to affirm that interpretation. Rather, there is need for a reexamination of the foundations upon which Geyer and earlier decisions rested, and a need for clarification of the standards by which the validity of prenuptial agreements will be judged.

There is no longer validity in the implicit presumption that supplied the basis for *Geyer* and similar earlier decisions. Such decisions rested upon a belief that spouses are of unequal status and that women are not knowledgeable enough to understand the nature of contracts that they enter. Society has advanced, however, to the point where women are no longer regarded as the "weaker" party in marriage, or in society generally. Indeed, the stereotype that women serve as homemakers while men work as breadwinners is no longer viable. Quite often today both spouses are income earners. Nor is there viability in the presumption that women are uninformed, uneducated, and readily subjected to unfair advantage in marital agreements. Indeed, women nowadays quite often have substantial education, financial awareness, income, and assets.

Accordingly, the law has advanced to recognize the equal status of men and women in our society. *See, e.g.,* Pa. Const. art. 1, §28 (constitutional prohibition of sex discrimination in laws of the Commonwealth). Paternalistic presumptions and protections that arose to shelter women from the inferiorities and incapacities which they were perceived as having in earlier times have, appropriately, been discarded. . . . It would be inconsistent, therefore, to perpetuate the standards governing prenuptial agreements that were described in *Geyer* and similar decisions, as these reflected a paternalistic approach that is now insupportable.

Further, *Geyer* and its predecessors embodied substantial departures from traditional rules of contract law, to the extent that they allowed consideration of the knowledge of the contracting parties and reasonableness of their bargain as factors governing whether to uphold an agreement. Traditional principles of contract law provide perfectly adequate remedies where contracts are procured through fraud, misrepresentation, or duress. Consideration of other factors, such as the knowledge of the parties and the reasonableness of their bargain, is inappropriate. . . . Prenuptial agreements are contracts, and, as such, should be evaluated under the same criteria as are applicable to other types of contracts. . . . Absent fraud, misrepresentation, or duress, spouses should be bound by the terms of their agreements.

Contracting parties are normally bound by their agreements, without regard to whether the terms thereof were read and fully understood and irrespective of whether the agreements embodied reasonable or good bargains. Based upon these principles, the terms of the present prenuptial agreement must be regarded as binding, without regard to whether the terms were fully understood by appellant. *Ignorantia non excusat.*

Accordingly, we find no merit in a contention raised by appellant that the agreement should be declared void on the ground that she did not consult with independent legal counsel. To impose a per se requirement that parties entering a prenuptial agreement must obtain independent legal counsel would be contrary to traditional principles of contract law, and would constitute a paternalistic and unwarranted interference with the parties' freedom to enter contracts.

Further, the reasonableness of a prenuptial bargain is not a proper subject for judicial review. *Geyer* and earlier decisions required that, at least where there had been an inadequate disclosure made by the parties, the bargain must have been reasonable at its inception. *See Geyer,* 516 Pa. at 503, 533 A.2d at 428. Some have even suggested that prenuptial agreements should be examined with regard to whether their terms remain reasonable at the time of dissolution of the parties' marriage.

By invoking inquiries into reasonableness, however, the functioning and reliability of prenuptial agreements is severely undermined. Parties would not have entered such agreements, and, indeed, might not have entered their marriages, if they did not expect their agreements to be strictly enforced. If parties viewed an agreement as reasonable at the time of its inception, as evidenced by their having signed the agreement, they should be foreclosed from later trying to evade its terms by asserting that it was not in fact reasonable. . . .

Further, everyone who enters a long-term agreement knows that circumstances can change during its term, so that what initially appeared desirable might prove to be an unfavorable bargain. Such are the risks that contracting parties routinely assume. Certainly, the possibilities of illness, birth of children, reliance upon a spouse, career change, financial gain or loss, and numerous other events that can occur in the course of a marriage cannot be regarded as unforeseeable. If parties choose not to address such matters in their prenuptial agreements, they must be regarded as having contracted to bear the risk of events that alter the value of their bargains. . . .

The present agreement recited that full disclosure had been made, and included a list of appellee's assets totalling approximately $300,000. Appellant contends that this list understated by roughly $183,000 the value of a classic car collection which appellee had included at a value of $200,000. The master, reviewing the parties' conflicting testimony regarding the value of the car collection, found that appellant failed to prove by clear and convincing evidence that the value of the collection had been understated. The courts below affirmed that finding. . . . Appellant's contention is plainly without merit.

Appellant's final contention is that the agreement was executed under conditions of duress in that it was presented to her at 5 P.M. on the eve of her wedding, a time when she could not seek counsel without the trauma, expense, and embarrassment of postponing the wedding. The master found this claim not credible. The courts below affirmed that finding, upon an ample evidentiary basis.

Although appellant testified that she did not discover until the eve of her wedding that there was going to be a prenuptial agreement, testimony from a number of other witnesses was to the contrary. . . . And the legal counsel who prepared the agreement for appellee testified that, prior to the eve of the wedding, changes were made in the agreement to increase the sums payable to appellant in the event of separation or divorce. He also stated that he was present when the agreement was signed and that appellant expressed absolutely no reluctance about signing. It should be noted, too, that during the months when the agreement was being discussed appellant had more than sufficient time to consult with independent legal counsel if she had so desired. Under these circumstances, there was plainly no error in finding that appellant failed to prove duress.

Hence, the courts below properly held that the present agreement is valid and enforceable. Appellant is barred, therefore, from receiving alimony pendente lite.

Order affirmed.

PAPADAKOS, J., concurring. . . . I cannot join the opinion authored by Mr. Justice Flaherty, because, it must be clear to all readers, it contains a number of unnecessary and unwarranted declarations regarding the "equality" of women. Mr. Justice Flaherty believes that, with the hard-fought victory of the Equal Rights Amendment in Pennsylvania, all vestiges of inequality between the sexes have been erased and women are now treated equally under the law. I fear my colleague does not live in the real world. If I did not know him better I would think that his statements smack of male chauvinism, an attitude that "you women asked for it, now live with it." If you want to know about equality of women, just ask them about comparable wages for comparable work. Just ask them about sexual harassment in the workplace. Just ask them about the sexual discrimination in the Executive Suites of big business. And the list of discrimination based on sex goes on and on.

I view prenuptial agreements as being in the nature of contracts of adhesion with one party generally having greater authority than the other who deals in a subservient role. I believe the law protects the subservient party, regardless of that party's sex, to insure equal protection and treatment under the law.

McDERMOTT, J., dissenting. Let me begin by setting forth a common ground between my position in this matter and that of the majority. There can be no question that, in the law and in society, men and women must be accorded equal status. I am in full agreement with the majority's observation that "women nowadays quite often have substantial education, financial awareness, income, and assets." However, the plurality decision I authored in Estate of Geyer, 516 Pa. 492, 533 A.2d 423 (1987), as well as the Dissenting Opinion I offer today, have little to do with the equality of the sexes, but everything to do with the solemnity of the matrimonial union. . . .

The subject of the validity of pre-nuptial agreements is not a new issue for this Court. A pre-nuptial agreement is the reservation of ownership over land, money and any other property, acquired in the past, present or future, from the most unique of human bargains. A pre-nuptial agreement may also prove an intention to get the best out of a marriage without incurring any obligation to do more than be there so long as it suits a purpose. Certainly, a prenuptial agreement may serve many purposes consistent with love and affection in life. It may answer obligations incurred prior to present intentions, obligations to children, parents, relatives, friends and those not yet born. It may answer obligations owed for prior help and affection. It may serve to keep matters right and fair, for innumerable reasons arising antecedent to the marriage. Indeed, it may prove a fidelity in persons to prior obligations that makes their intended promises the more secure. Moreover, society has an interest in protecting the right of its citizens to contract, and in seeing the reduction, in the event of a dissolution of the marriage, of the necessity of lengthy, complicated, and costly litigation. Thus, while I acknowledge the long-standing rule of law that pre-nuptial agreements are presumptively valid and binding upon the parties, I am unwilling to go as far as the majority to protect the right to contract at the expense of the institution of marriage. Were a contract of marriage, the most intimate relationship between two people, not the surrender of freedom, an offering of self in love, sacrifice, hope for better or for worse, the begetting of children and the offer of effort, labor, precious time and care for the safety and prosperity of their union, then the majority would find me among them.

In my view, one seeking to avoid the operation of an executed pre-nuptial agreement must first establish, by clear and convincing evidence, that a full and fair disclosure of the worth of the intended spouse was not made at the time of the execution of the agreement. This Court has recognized that full and fair disclosure is needed because, at the time of the execution of a pre-nuptial agreement, the parties do not stand in the usual arm's length posture attendant to most other types of contractual undertakings, but "stand in a relation of mutual confidence and trust that calls for the highest degree of good faith. . . ." In addition to a full and fair disclosure of the general financial pictures of the parties, I would find a pre-nuptial agreement voidable where it is established that the parties were not aware, at the time of contracting, of existing statutory rights which they were relinquishing upon the signing of the agreement. It is here, with a finding of full and fair disclosure, that the majority would end its analysis of the validity of a pre-nuptial agreement. I would not. An analysis of the fairness and equity of a pre-nuptial agreement has long been an important part of the law of this state. . . .

At the time of dissolution of the marriage, a spouse should be able to avoid the operation of a pre-nuptial agreement upon clear and convincing proof that, despite the existence of full and fair disclosure at the time of the execution of the agreement, the agreement is nevertheless so inequitable and unfair that it should not be enforced in a court of this state. . . . The majority holds to the view, without waiver, that parties, having contracted with full and fair disclosure, should be made to suffer the consequences of their bargains. In so holding, the majority has given no weight to the other side of the scales: the state's paramount interest in the preservation of marriage and the family relationship, and the protection of parties to a marriage who may be rendered wards of the state, unable to provide for their own reasonable needs. . . .

It is also apparent that, although a pre-nuptial agreement is quite valid when drafted, the passage of time accompanied by the intervening events of a marriage, may render the terms of the agreement completely unfair and inequitable. While parties to a pre-nuptial agreement may indeed foresee, generally, the events which may come to pass during their marriage, one spouse should not be made to suffer for failing to foresee all of the surrounding circumstances which may attend the dissolution of the marriage. Although it should not be the role of the courts to void pre-nuptial agreements merely because one spouse may receive a better result in an action under the Divorce Code to recover alimony or equitable distribution, it should be the role of the courts to guard against the enforcement of pre-nuptial agreements where such enforcement will bring about only inequity and hardship. It borders on cruelty to accept that after years of living together, yielding their separate opportunities in life to each other, that two individuals emerge the same as the day they began their marriage.

At the time of the dissolution of marriage, what are the circumstances which would serve to invalidate a pre-nuptial agreement? This is a question that should only be answered on a case-by-case basis. However, it is not unrealistic to imagine that in a given situation, one spouse, although trained in the workforce at the time of marriage, may, over many years, have become economically dependent upon the other spouse. In reliance upon the permanence of marriage and in order to provide a stable home for a family, a spouse may choose, even at the suggestion of the other spouse, not to work during the marriage. As a result, at the point of dissolution of the marriage, the spouse's employability has diminished to such an extent that to enforce the support provisions of the pre-nuptial agreement will cause the spouse to become a public charge, or will provide a standard of living far below that which was enjoyed before and during marriage. In such a situation, a court may properly decide to render void all or some of the provisions of the pre-nuptial agreement.

I can likewise conceive of a situation where, after a long marriage, the value of property may have increased through the direct efforts of the spouse who agreed not to claim it upon divorce or death. In such a situation, the court should be able to decide whether it is against the public policy of the state, and thus inequitable and unfair, for a spouse to be precluded from receiving that increase in the value of property which he or she had, at least in part, directly induced. I marvel at the majority's apparent willingness to enforce a pre-nuptial agreement in the interest of freedom to contract at any cost, even where unforeseen and untoward illness has rendered one spouse unable, despite his own best efforts, to provide reasonable support for himself. I would further recognize that a spouse should be given the opportunity to prove, through clear and convincing evidence, that the amount of time and energy necessary for that spouse to shelter and care for the children of the marriage has rendered the terms of a pre-nuptial agreement inequitable, and unjust and thus, avoidable.

NOTES AND QUESTIONS

1. *Simeone* remains one of the watershed cases embracing the right of married couples to reach their own agreements. Part of the reasoning of the case stems from its declaration that "the law has advanced to recognize the equal status of men and women in our society." What does the court mean by "equal status," and how do the concurrence and dissent differ in their consideration of gender equality?

What is the relationship between "equal status" and equal bargaining power? There are no published empirical studies of premarital agreements, but anecdotal evidence from family law attorneys and appellate cases indicates that these agreements may operate more frequently to the economic disadvantage of women than of men. *See* Gail F. Brod, Premarital Agreements and Gender Justice, 6 Yale J.L. & Feminism 229, 234-252 (1994); Barbara A. Atwood, Ten Years Later: Lingering Concerns About the Uniform Premarital Agreement Act, 19 J. Legis. 127 (1993). The reasons for the apparent disadvantage to women, the authors suggest, include the facts that premarital agreements are most common in second marriages, which frequently involve men quite a bit older and wealthier than the women they are marrying, and that agreements are commonly used to preclude or limit sharing of the parties' earnings and premarital wealth when the marriage ends by death or divorce.

2. The wife in *Simeone* claimed that the husband first presented her with the premarital agreement on the eve of the wedding and therefore she entered into it under duress. In what sense would this be duress? Why does the court reject her argument? *See also* DeLorean v. DeLorean, 511 A.2d 1257 (N.J. Super. 1986), rejecting a similar argument. In In re Bonds, 5 P.3d 815 (Cal. 2000), Barry Bonds

and his fiancée had rushed to the lawyer's office to complete an antenuptial agreement in time to make a flight to Las Vegas, where the wedding was scheduled for the following day. Despite the fact that Sun Bonds saw the agreement for the first time that afternoon, the California Supreme Court upheld the trial court's finding that "the temporal proximity of the wedding to the signing of the agreement was not coercive, because under the particular circumstances of the case, including the small number of guests and the informality of the wedding arrangements, little embarrassment would have followed from postponement of the wedding." *Id.* at 825-836.

3. The Pennsylvania cases prior to *Simeone* required full disclosure or fair and adequate provision before a premarital agreement would be enforced. What is the relationship between disclosure, a matter of the bargaining process, and fair and adequate provision, which pertains to the substance of the agreement? The Supreme Court of Nebraska explained the reasoning this way:

> At least three principles support our interpretation of the [disclosure] rule. First, . . . an agreement to marry gives rise to a confidential relationship. As a result, the parties to an antenuptial agreement do not deal at arm's length and must exercise candor and good faith in all matters bearing upon the contract.
>
> Secondly, parties to an antenuptial agreement are very often ill-matched in terms of bargaining power. As one court put it, "candor compels us to raise to a conscious level the fact that, as in this case, prenuptial agreements will almost always be entered into between people with property or an income potential to protect on one side and people who are impecunious on the other." Gant v. Gant, 329 S.E.2d 106, 114 (W. Va. 1985). Thus, a rule requiring full disclosure or independent knowledge serves to level the bargaining field for the party in the weaker position.
>
> Finally, unlike other private commercial contracts, the State has an interest and is a party to every marriage. . . . In the absence of antenuptial agreements, state laws govern the division of marital property and the awarding of alimony in the event of divorce. Often, antenuptial agreements alter the rights parties otherwise would have under those state laws. Consequently, it is altogether appropriate that parties entering into antenuptial agreements do so with knowledge of the holdings to which they are waiving any claim under state law. . . .

Randolph v. Randolph, 937 S.W.2d 815 (1996).

None of these requirements applies to ordinary contracts. Why should they apply to agreements between people about to be married? Should parties who are *engaged* to be married have fiduciary obligations to each other? Many states agree with *Randolph*, but California distinguishes between spouses, who do have such fiduciary obligations, and those contemplating marriage, who do not. In re Bonds, 5 P.3d 815 (Cal. 2000).

4. If spouses are required to make full disclosure to each other, what must be disclosed? Must each spouse know the details of the other's holdings, or is having a general idea sufficient? The *Randolph* court required that "the spouse seeking to enforce an antenuptial agreement must prove, by a preponderance of the evidence, either that a full and fair disclosure of the nature, extent, and value of his or her holdings was provided to the spouse seeking to avoid the agreement, or that disclosure was unnecessary because the spouse seeking to avoid the agreement had independent knowledge of the full nature, extent, and value of the proponent

spouse's holdings." 937 S.W.2d at 821. California, in contrast, places the burden of proof on the party challenging the premarital agreement. If you were advising a party on how to ensure sufficient disclosure to validate an agreement in a state following *Randolph*, what would you suggest?

5. Must each party's legal rights absent an agreement be disclosed, as the wife in *Simeone* argued? If so, does this mean as a practical matter that each person must have independent legal advice? Many courts suggest that independent legal advice is the best means of ensuring that an agreement is enforceable, but no statutes impose a requirement of counsel in all cases. California, in response to the *Bonds* case described above, enacted one of the strictest statutes in the country. It provides, inter alia, that

c) . . . it shall be deemed that a premarital agreement was not executed voluntarily unless the court finds in writing or on the record all of the following:

(1) The party against whom enforcement is sought was represented by independent legal counsel at the time of signing the agreement or, after being advised to seek independent legal counsel, expressly waived, in a separate writing, representation by independent legal counsel.

(2) The party against whom enforcement is sought had not less than seven calendar days between the time that party was first presented with the agreement and advised to seek independent legal counsel and the time the agreement was signed.

(3) The party against whom enforcement is sought, if unrepresented by legal counsel, was fully informed of the terms and basic effect of the agreement as well as the rights and obligations he or she was giving up by signing the agreement, and was proficient in the language in which the explanation of the party's rights was conducted and in which the agreement was written. The explanation of the rights and obligations relinquished shall be memorialized in writing and delivered to the party prior to signing the agreement. The unrepresented party shall, on or before the signing of the premarital agreement, execute a document declaring that he or she received the information required by this paragraph and indicating who provided that information.

Cal. Fam. Code §1615 (2004).

6. As a lawyer drafting a premarital agreement for one party, would you advise the other party to seek independent counsel? Would you explain why? In In re Marriage of Foran, 834 P.2d 1081 (Wash. App. 1992), the court refused to enforce a premarital agreement, prepared by the husband's lawyer, that in effect allowed the husband to increase his already substantial wealth at the expense of the marital community. Though the lawyer advised the wife to consult her own lawyer, he did not explain why. This advice, according to the court, was insufficient to hold her to the contract.

If you were advising a person about whether to sign a premarital agreement, how would you decide what advice to give? A lawyer drafting a premarital agreement faces potential malpractice charges if the agreement is not upheld. For that reason, many lawyers will refuse to draft such agreements.

It may, however, be in the interests of a client facing the losing end of such an agreement not to correct flaws that may strengthen arguments about its invalidity. If a client has little ability to change the terms of a one-sided agreement, and your participation increases the likelihood that the agreement will be upheld, should you represent the client? What is your obligation in a case in which you believe that the agreement is one-sided or unfair and the client intends to sign the agreement over your objections?

7. How should a court determine whether terms of an agreement are "fair and adequate"? Should the fairness of the terms be evaluated at the time of the agreement or at the time enforcement is sought? By their very nature premarital agreements are often intended to operate at some point far in the future, but they often fail to take account of the likelihood that the parties' circumstances will change dramatically. How would you draft a premarital agreement to deal with this problem?

GAIL F. BROD, *PREMARITAL AGREEMENTS AND GENDER JUSTICE*

6 Yale J.L. & Feminism 229, 283-284, 286 (1994)

The recent trend in the law has been to exalt the "freedom of contract" principle to the point where even an unconscionable premarital agreement may be enforced. But a freedom of contract regime enables the economically powerful to dictate the terms of the contract and sharpens the existing inequality in the distribution of wealth and resources. Until there is true economic and social parity between men and women, lawmakers must temper the relentless freedom of contract approach by considering countervailing policies and concerns.

Lawmakers considering premarital agreements should be guided by a fundamental public policy: the attainment of economic justice for the economically vulnerable spouse (and, incidentally, any children in his/her care) at the termination of marriage. . . . Courts should uphold a premarital agreement only if its substance effectuates the law's goal of guaranteeing the economically vulnerable spouse economic justice at the termination of marriage, or failing that, if the negotiating process that led to the unjust agreement was truly fair.

. . . Economic justice is attained if, at the end of marriage, a spouse's economic position is not significantly worse than it was before the marriage — taking into account the spouse's economic gains and losses (including opportunity gains and costs) that accrued during the marriage. . . .

It may be argued persuasively that an economically unjust premarital agreement should be unenforceable even if it was procured fairly. But this position elevates "economic justice" above all other public policies and ignores significant principles that militate in favor of enforcing even unjust agreements: first, society's concern with protecting the freedom of men and women to contract and to pass their family wealth to persons of their choosing; second, society's desire to promote the institution of marriage; and third, society's need to allow parties to settle voluntarily and amicably their property rights in advance of marriage, in lieu of engaging in litigation at the end of marriage. More importantly, to refuse to enforce an economically unjust premarital agreement that resulted from a fair bargaining process suggests that adults cannot be trusted to protect their own interests. Therefore, an economically unjust agreement should be enforceable, but only if the law guarantees that the agreement was fairly procured.

Conversely, an economically just agreement that was unfairly procured should not be enforceable.

CAROL WEISBROD, *PRACTICAL POLYPHONY: THEORIES OF THE STATE AND FEMINIST JURISPRUDENCE*

24 Ga. L. Rev. 985, 990-992 (1990)

One tension between feminist jurisprudence and liberal theory is rooted in the fact that the dominance perspective, at least, in its most extreme form, invites a generalized attack on female capacity. Liberal theory recognizes participation only by competent actors. Children, the insane and other incompetents cannot participate because they cannot, or cannot be permitted to, choose. Only if the consequences of subordination or suppression are viewed as essentially moderate — as a remediable injustice rather than a total annihilation of the autonomous self — can one go in the direction of immediate public participation by women within liberalism, and if the consequences of subordination are merely moderate, the evil cannot be so great as is sometimes suggested. If we start with the idea that the evil is that great, however, and if female consciousness is almost entirely controlled, then serious issues exist as to women and choice. Why should sexual activity initiated by women, for example, be any more voluntary than that initiated by men and consented to by women? Why should the "I do" of the marriage ceremony count? Why, as Carole Pateman formulates it, should a woman's "yes" be any more privileged, or any less open to invalidation, than her "no"? If everything becomes a false consciousness problem — but somehow exclusively for women and not for men — we would seem to be in deep trouble.

Some writing presented in the specific context of consent to sexual intercourse is, in effect, about taking women's consent (or lack of consent) seriously. *No means no.* Other writing, however, suggests, in effect, that women in this society are unable to consent freely, having been so molded by the culture that it is impossible for them to refuse certain options. Under this view, the problem is nothing so limited as, for example, how women who value "X" are to function in a "Y" professional world; the answer to that might well be to change the professional world, and indeed some feminist writing is addressed exactly to that issue. Instead, the problem is women's inability to value or to make choice at all. The current version of this view suggests that women are molded to be what they are; earlier political theorists believed that women fit this model naturally. Whatever its basis, however, the point here is that the dominance views — in effect an explanation of women's condition rather than a rejection of the traditional descriptions — are drawn so sharply that they seem to echo earlier debates over, for example, whether women had souls (a subject which Keith Thomas tells us was "half frivolously, half seriously" debated by theologians for many centuries) or could be held to full criminal accountability. The question sometimes seems to be once again the one Dorothy Sayers saw: Are women human?

BRIAN BIX, *BARGAINING IN THE SHADOW OF LOVE: THE ENFORCEMENT OF PREMARITAL AGREEMENTS AND HOW WE THINK ABOUT MARRIAGE*

40 Wm. & Mary L. Rev. 145, 182, 188 (1998)

When the court in *Simeone* and certain commentators advocated applying the standards from contract law to premarital agreements, they intended the agreements to be subject to minimal scrutiny. That perspective seems to depend, however, on a view of contract law that is decades behind the developments in contractual doctrine and commentary. A modern approach to contract law might reach results that, by enforcing some premarital agreements but not others, better reflect the intuitions of most people regarding the fair result in different cases. . . .

The court in *Simeone*, when it relegated premarital agreements to a contractual approach, seemed to have in mind some classical conception of contract encompassing caveat emptor, naïve "plain meaning" enforcement, and little attention to the relationship between the parties or the larger context within which the agreement was signed. If one could apply "contract principles" to premarital agreements, why not apply, by analogy, the quite different principles underlying Article 2 of the U.C.C.?

The U.C.C. obligates parties to exercise good faith in performing and enforcing the obligation of an agreement, construes contractual terms in light of the parties' course of performance and course of dealing and in light of trade usage, and implies various warranties unless they are expressly excluded. For contracts of indefinite duration, a party may terminate only after reasonable notice, and courts sometimes have held actions apparently authorized by the express wording of a contract to be bad faith actions in breach of the agreement. These changes from classical contract thinking are by no means limited to U.C.C. cases.

If courts apply *these* types of contract principles to premarital agreements, there will be far less reason for complaint. Perhaps courts could interpret the terms of premarital agreements that appear to be one-sided in more reasonable ways by using the tools of modern contract law, or by disallowing the strict enforcement of the express terms of some agreements as contrary to "good faith." . . .

A growing body of literature has discussed whether contracts governing long-term commercial relations should be considered, either by the law or at least by legal commentators, in a way significantly different from other contracts. Advocates of . . . different treatment argue that "beyond a certain point, contracts governing long-term relations come to appear less like individual bargains, in which all the terms can be discerned from the intentions of the parties at the time of formation, and more like *constitutions* governing polities — requiring similar modes of ongoing interpretation." Courts should understand the agreement between the parties — in particular, any *written* agreement between the parties — *in light of* the ongoing relationship, they argue, and the presumptive purpose of court (or arbitrator) intervention should be to maintain that relationship, even if slight deviation from or supplementation to the precise terms of the contract is required.

Those who oppose different treatment assert that with long-term agreements, as in most places, it is better to enforce terms strictly as written, as this will reflect better the choices and preferences of the parties. Such a method of interpretation, they argue, is more efficient and avoids the "freedom of contract" problem of foisting contractual obligations on parties who never consented to them. More subtle arguments for this position maintain that agreements that appear to be "incomplete" are so because of an asymmetry of information between the parties, or because of a fear that more "complete" provisions would encourage strategic behavior by one of the parties. . . .

[However,] one must distinguish legal standards that may in fact help to maintain the relationship from those that will have no such effect because they will be applied only in endgame situations. Premarital agreements — at least the vast majority of those subject to court action and academic commentary — purport to control the endgame situation: they affect the disposition of property upon separation, divorce and death. Though the enforceability of such provisions may have indirect effects on maintaining the relationship at earlier points, the terms of such agreements become relevant only when the marriage relationship is already over.

Though it appears, therefore, that the flexible approaches suggested by some courts and commentators for long-term agreements may have a place in understanding the modern approach to contract law, they are not applicable to divorce-centered premarital agreements, which do not govern the day-to-day maintenance of the marriage relationship. The approaches to long-term agreements aimed at maintaining relationships would, however, be highly relevant if and when states start enforcing agreements focused on the actions and obligations of parties *during* marriage.

Although both the traditional theories justifying contract law and the ideas underlying the influential economic analysis of law assume that people act rationally to protect their own interests, recent work in psychology has begun to question that assumption. There are particular situations and circumstances in which parties are particularly unlikely to act in a rational way, and the law — especially contract law — should respond to that reality.

Premarital agreements are good examples of contracts that illustrate problems with rational judgment, as they involve long-term planning and the consideration of possible negative outcomes at a time when the parties are most likely to be optimistic that such negative outcomes will occur. Parties need protection in this situation because they are unlikely to be able to think clearly for themselves regarding the consequences of divorce at any time, and certainly not immediately before marriage. . . . [E]ven those who are well educated in such matters, e.g., law students in a family law course, carry an unduly optimistic view about the chances that their marriage will last. More general studies in psychology have confirmed that people tend to evaluate causal theories in a self-serving manner; though people may know that fifty percent of marriages end in divorce, they convince themselves — with little grounding for their conclusions — that they have characteristics that will put them in the portion that will endure. People who assume that they will not divorce will not work hard to maintain a fair deal contingent on divorce occurring, just as parties do not bargain for reasonable terms on the failure of installment payments, as they do not expect to ever fail in their payments. Additionally, parties may have some sense of the consequences of failure one year from now, but it may be harder to foresee and plan for the consequences of failure fifteen years from now — after one or both partners have made sacrifices in their careers and perhaps after children have been born.

The National Conference of Commissioners on Uniform State Laws (NCCUSL) drafts proposed uniform acts in an effort to promote more consistent state legislation. These acts become law if enacted by the individual state legislatures. NCCUSL accordingly attempts to draft acts of broad applicability and acceptability. The Uniform Premarital Agreement Act (UPAA), set forth below, has been adopted by roughly half the states between the mid-1980s and the late 1990s.

The American Law Institute (ALI) issues restatements of the law that attempt to set forth principles that reflect existing case law on a national basis. Restatements become law when they "restate" principles already recognized in existing cases, or when the principles they recognize are expressly adopted in future decisions. In addressing family dissolution, the ALI decided to promulgate "principles" rather than a restatement, partly because the proposals are addressed to legislatures as well as courts, and partly because "'Principles' seemed the right title for a project that starts with carefully considered assumptions about the best interests of children, fairness to divorcing wives and husbands, and the legitimate economic claims of unmarried partners." ALI Principles of the Law of Family Dissolution (Director's Foreword).

The UPAA is set forth first with detailed questions that take you through the interaction of its various provisions. The ALI Principles that address premarital agreements follow, with problems at the end of this section that will help you to recognize the differences. In examining these provisions, consider whether they reflect *Simeone*'s embrace of freedom of contract in marital bargaining, or some of the criticisms from Professors Brod, Weisbrod, and Bix.

Uniform Premarital Agreements Act

§1. Definitions As used in this Act:

(1) "Premarital agreement" means an agreement between prospective spouses made in contemplation of marriage and to be effective upon marriage.

(2) "Property" means an interest, present or future, legal or equitable, vested or contingent, in real or personal property, including income and earnings. . . .

§2. Formalities A premarital agreement must be in writing and signed by both parties. It is enforceable without consideration.

§3. Content

(a) Parties to a premarital agreement may contract with respect to:

(1) the rights and obligations of each of the parties in any of the property of either or both of them whenever and wherever acquired or located;

(2) the right to buy, sell, use, transfer, exchange, abandon, lease, consume, expend, assign, create a security interest in, mortgage, encumber, dispose of, or otherwise manage and control property;

(3) the disposition of property upon separation, marital dissolution, death, or the occurrence or nonoccurrence of any other event;

(4) the modification or elimination of spousal support;

(5) the making of a will, trust, or other arrangement to carry out the provisions of the agreement;

(6) the ownership rights in and disposition of the death benefit from a life insurance policy;

(7) the choice of law governing the construction of the agreement; and

(8) any other matter, including their personal rights and obligations, not in violation of public policy or a statute imposing a criminal penalty.

(b) The right of a child to support may not be adversely affected by a premarital agreement. . . .

§5. Amendment, Revocation After marriage, a premarital agreement may be amended or revoked only by a written agreement signed by the parties. The amended agreement or the revocation is enforceable without consideration.

§6. Enforcement

(a) A premarital agreement is not enforceable if the party against whom enforcement is sought proves that:

(1) that party did not execute the agreement voluntarily; or

(2) the agreement was unconscionable when it was executed and, before execution of the agreement, that party:

(i) was not provided a fair and reasonable disclosure of the property or financial obligations of the other party;

(ii) did not voluntarily and expressly waive, in writing, any right to disclosure of the property or financial obligations of the other party beyond the disclosure provided; and

(iii) did not have, or reasonably could not have had, an adequate knowledge of the property or financial obligations of the other party.

(b) If a provision of a premarital agreement modifies or eliminates spousal support and that modification or elimination causes one party to the agreement to be eligible for support under a program of public assistance at the time of separation or marital dissolution, a court, notwithstanding the terms of the agreement, may require the other party to provide support to the extent necessary to avoid that eligibility.

(c) An issue of unconscionability of a premarital agreement shall be decided by the court as a matter of law.

NOTES AND QUESTIONS

1. Under the UPAA, what is the relationship between disclosure (or the lack thereof) and the fairness of the terms? How does this differ, if it does, from traditional law? From the approach adopted in *Simeone*? Under the UPAA, what is the relationship between voluntariness and disclosure? *See* Penhallow v. Penhallow, 649 A.2d 1016 (R.I. 1994) (a finding of unconscionability by itself would not render a premarital agreement unenforceable because the UPAA requires proof of both involuntary execution and nondisclosure and/or waivers in addition to unconscionability).

2. What is the test for voluntariness under the UPAA? Most interpretations of the UPAA reject any requirement of independent counsel. *See, e.g.,* Penhallow v. Penhallow, 649 A.2d 1016 (R.I. 1994). It is possible, however, to adopt the UPAA and then change individual provisions to address this and other issues. California, for example, amended its version of the UPAA in response to the *Bonds* ruling that independent counsel was not required.

3. The UPAA, like a number of recent cases, provides that under certain circumstances an agreement is unenforceable if it is "unconscionable." This term is borrowed from the commercial context. Both the Uniform Commercial Code (UCC) and the Restatement of the Law of Contracts 2d provide that unconscionable

contracts are not enforceable.[2] The UCC uses the term without defining it. *See* Arthur A. Leff, The Emperor's New Clause, 115 U. Pa. L. Rev. 485 (1967). What does it mean? Consider Melvin A. Eisenberg, The Bargain Principle and Its Limits, 95 Harv. L. Rev. 741, 752 (1982):

> When the concept of unconscionability was first made explicit by the Uniform Commercial Code, the initial effort was to reconcile it with the bargain principle. A major step in this direction was a distinction, drawn in 1967 by Arthur Leff, between "procedural" and "substantive" unconscionability. Leff defined procedural unconscionability as fault or unfairness in the bargaining *process*; substantive unconscionability as fault or unfairness in the bargaining *outcome* — that is, unfairness of terms. The effect (if not the purpose) of this distinction, which influenced much of the later analysis, was to domesticate unconscionability by accepting the concept insofar as it could be made harmonious with the bargain principle (that is, insofar as it was "procedural"), while rejecting its wider implication that in appropriate cases the courts might review bargains for fairness of terms. Correspondingly, much of the scholarly literature and case law concerning unconscionability has emphasized the element of unfair surprise, in which a major underpinning of the bargain principle — knowing assent — is absent by hypothesis.
>
> Over the last fifteen years, however, there have been strong indications that the principle of unconscionability authorizes a review of elements well beyond unfair surprise, including, in appropriate cases, fairness of terms. For example, comment c to section 208 of the Restatement (Second) of Contracts states that "[t]heoretically it is possible for a contract to be oppressive taken as a whole, even though there is no weakness in the bargaining process." Similarly, section 5.108(4)(c) of the Uniform Consumer Credit Code lists as a factor to be considered in determining whether a transaction is unconscionable "gross disparity between the price of the property or services . . . [and their value] measured by the price at which similar property or services are readily obtainable in credit transactions by like consumers." And a number of cases have held or indicated that the principle of unconscionability permits enforcement of a promise to be limited on the basis of unfair price alone.

2. UCC §2-302. Unconscionable Contract or Clause

(1) If the court as a matter of law finds the contract or any clause of the contract to have been unconscionable at the time it was made, the court may refuse to enforce the contract, or it may enforce the remainder of the contract without the unconscionable clause, or it may so limit the application of any unconscionable clause as to avoid any unconscionable result.

(2) When it is claimed or appears to the court that the contract or any clause thereof may be unconscionable the parties shall be afforded a reasonable opportunity to present evidence as to its commercial setting, purpose and effect to aid the court in making the determination.

Restatement of the Law of Contracts 2d §208, Unconscionable Contract or Term

If a contract or term thereof is unconscionable at the time the contract is made, a court may refuse to enforce the contract, or may enforce the remainder of the contract without the unconscionable term, or may so limit the application of any unconscionable term as to avoid any unconscionable result.

As these phenomena have accumulated, it has become clear that they constitute anomalies under the bargain principle, and can be explained only on the basis of an expanded, paradigmatic concept of unconscionability that is not limited to procedural elements such as unfair surprise. This new paradigm does not replace the bargain principle, which is based on sound sense and continues to govern the normal case. Rather, the new paradigm creates a theoretical framework that explains most of the limits that have been or should be placed upon that principal, based on the quality of the bargain. What lies ahead is to articulate and extend the unconscionability paradigm through the development of specific norms, other than unfair surprise, that can guide the resolution of specific cases. [Four such norms are] exploitation of distress, transactional incapacity, susceptibility to unfair persuasion, and price-ignorance.

4. Section 3(a)(4) of the UPAA expressly sanctions provisions addressing "the modification or elimination of spousal support." How would you interpret the intent of a legislature that otherwise passed the UPAA but deleted Section 3(a)(4)? *See* In re Marriage of Pendleton & Fireman, 5 P.3d 839 (Cal. 2000) (concluding that the intent of the California legislature was to leave pre-UPAA precedents intact, rather than to indicate approval or disapproval of waivers of spousal support). The California legislature responded to the ruling by making waivers and other modifications of spousal support unenforceable "if the party against whom enforcement of the spousal support provision is sought was not represented by independent counsel at the time the agreement containing the provision was signed, or if the provision regarding spousal support is unconscionable at the time of enforcement." Cal. Fam. Code §1612(c) (2004).

5. What does §3(b) of the UPAA, pertaining to child support, mean? What latitude for bargaining does it give the parties? Traditionally, parties' agreements regarding arrangements for children have not been enforceable, on the theory that the court must always have authority to act in the best interests of children. What does this principle suppose about the way parents negotiate agreements? About the capacity of courts?

6. Suppose a prenuptial agreement provided that if the parties disagreed about where to live, the dispute would be decided by a coin toss. Does §3(a)(8) make this agreement enforceable? Would it make enforceable an agreement that one spouse was to be a homemaker and the other would pay a personal allowance of $300 a week? As you answer this question, reconsider the material in Chapter 4, Section C.

7. For commentary on the UPAA, *see* J. Thomas Oldham, Premarital Contracts Are Now Enforceable, Unless . . . , 21 Hous. L. Rev. 757 (1984); Judith T. Younger, Perspectives on Antenuptial Agreements: An Update, 8 J. Am. Acad. Matrimonial L. 1 (1992); Barbara A. Atwood, Ten Years Later: Lingering Concerns About the Uniform Premarital Agreement Act, 19 J. Legis. 127 (1993); Gail F. Brod, Premarital Agreements and Gender Justice, 6 Yale J.L. & Feminism 229, 234-252 (1994). *See more generally* Brian Bix, Bargaining in the Shadow of Love: The Enforcement of Premarital Agreements and How We Think About Marriage, 40 Wm. & Mary L. Rev. 145 (1998); Katharine B. Silbaugh, Marriage Contracts and the Family Economy, 93 Nw. U. L. Rev. 65 (1998); Judith T. Younger, A Minnesota Comparative Family Law Symposium: Antenuptial Agreements, 28 Wm. Mitchell L. Rev. 697, 716-720 (2001).

Principles of the Law of Family Dissolution
§7.04 Procedural Requirements

(1) An agreement is not enforceable if it is not set forth in a writing signed by both parties.

(2) A party seeking to enforce an agreement must show that the other party's consent to it was informed and not obtained under duress.

(3) A premarital agreement is rebuttably presumed to satisfy the requirements of Paragraph (2) when the party seeking to enforce the agreement shows that

(a) it was executed at least 30 days before the parties' marriage;

(b) both parties were advised to obtain independent legal counsel, and had reasonable opportunity to do so, before the agreement's execution; and

(c) in the case of agreements concluded without the assistance of independent legal counsel for each party, the agreement states, in language easily understandable by an adult of ordinary intelligence with no legal training,

(i) the nature of any rights or claims otherwise arising at dissolution that are altered by the contract, and the nature of that alteration, and

(ii) that the interests of the spouses with respect to the agreement may be adverse.

§7.05 When Enforcement Would Work a Substantial Injustice

(1) A court should not enforce a term in an agreement if, pursuant to Paragraphs (2) and (3) of this section,

(a) the circumstances require it to consider whether enforcement would work a substantial injustice; and

(b) the court finds that enforcement would work a substantial injustice.

(2) A court should consider whether enforcement of an agreement would work a substantial injustice if, and only if, the party resisting its enforcement shows that one or more of the following have occurred since the time of the agreement's execution:

(a) more than a fixed number of years have passed, that number being set in a rule of statewide application;

(b) a child was born to, or adopted by, the parties, who at the time of execution had no children in common;

(c) there has been a change in circumstances that has a substantial impact on the parties or their children, but when they executed the agreement the parties probably did not anticipate either the change, or its impact.

(3) The party claiming that enforcement of an agreement would work a substantial injustice has the burden of proof on that question. In deciding whether the agreement's application to the parties' circumstances at dissolution would work a substantial injustice, a court should consider all of the following:

(a) the magnitude of the disparity between the outcome under the agreement and the outcome under otherwise prevailing legal principles;

(b) for those marriages of limited duration in which it is practical to ascertain, the difference between the circumstances of the objecting party if the agreement is enforced, and that party's likely circumstances had the marriage never taken place;

(c) whether the purpose of the agreement was to benefit or protect the interests of third parties (such as children from a prior relationship), whether that purpose is still relevant, and whether the agreement's terms were reasonably designed to serve it;

(d) the impact of the agreement's enforcement upon the children of the parties.

JUDITH T. YOUNGER, *A MINNESOTA COMPARATIVE FAMILY LAW SYMPOSIUM: ANTENUPTIAL AGREEMENTS*

28 Wm. Mitchell L. Rev. 697, 716-720 (2001)

III. THE UNIFORM PREMARITAL AGREEMENT ACT AND THE AMERICAN LAW INSTITUTE PRINCIPLES OF FAMILY DISSOLUTION

California was the first state to adopt the Uniform Premarital Agreement Act, although it, like a number of other jurisdictions, modified it to conform more closely to its own prior law. Since California's adoption in 1985, twenty-five states followed suit. The Act is now law in whole or part in some twenty-six states. The last adoptions were Texas and Indiana in 1997. As the California Supreme Court pointed out in the *Bonds* case, the Act was intended to enhance the enforceability of antenuptial agreements. To that end, it specifically included spousal support as a permissible subject for antenuptial agreement and attempted to circumscribe courts in their reviews of these agreements for procedural and substantive fairness. Under it, a spouse could avoid enforcement of an antenuptial agreement only by proving that at the time of execution (1) it was not voluntary, or (2) that it was unconscionable, there was no reasonable financial disclosure, the right to disclosure was not waived and the challenger did not have independent knowledge of the other party's finances. The Act also limited the review at enforcement to provisions waiving or modifying spousal support rights which, if enforced, would result in making a spouse eligible for public assistance. It has been roundly criticized, of course, and whether it has accomplished its goals in the adopting jurisdictions is hard to determine. As one reads through the cases one is still struck by the uncertainty of enforcement of these agreements and the lack of uniformity in result, not only from jurisdiction to jurisdiction, but among trial and appellate courts ruling on the same facts in the same case and in the same state.

Enter then, the American Law Institute, with its new Principles of Family Dissolution. The Principles provide procedural requirements for antenuptial agreements of the sort already required by most, if not all, states. These requirements are a signed writing, financial disclosure and a showing of informed consent not obtained under duress. The latter is the rough equivalent of the common law and Uniform Act requirements of voluntariness. The Reporters justify the new language by stating their desire to focus the courts' attention on the tactics of the proponent of the agreement rather than on the state of mind of the challenger; however, the change seems little more than a misguided example of "elegant variation." The Principles raise a presumption of informed consent and the absence of duress if the agreement was executed at least thirty days before the parties' marriage, both parties were advised to obtain legal counsel and had opportunity to do so. In an important departure from existing law, the Principles put the burden of proving the lack of duress and the presence of consent on the party who is trying to enforce the agreement. The Reporters hope that this change in the usual contract rule will "caution the stronger party against overreaching tactics that would make this burden of proof more difficult to meet." . . . In cases where one party did not have independent counsel, for the presumption to arise, the agreement must contain understandable language explaining the significance of its terms and the fact that the parties' interests may be adverse with respect to them.

It is on the subject of substantive fairness that the Principles are most remarkable. They depart from the Uniform Act and the common law by omitting any requirement of substantive fairness at the time of execution of an antenuptial agreement. If contained in a signed writing and entered with disclosure, without duress and with informed consent, the agreement satisfies the test at execution no matter how one-sided or unfair its terms. At enforcement, however, the Principles call for a wider substantive review of these agreements than called for by the Uniform Act. . . . The Principles would prohibit enforcement of antenuptial agreements whenever enforcement would "work a substantial injustice." Here, again, the Principles opt for new language abandoning the old standard of unconscionableness at enforcement. They lay out guidelines to help courts in applying the new language. Before making any inquiry into the effects of enforcement, under the Principles, one of three prerequisites must be present: the passage of a certain number of years after execution; or the birth or adoption of a child to parties who had no children at execution; or a significant, unexpected change in circumstances since execution. If one of these events has occurred the court can consider whether the enforcement of the agreement would work a substantial injustice. Again, in an attempt to help courts with the inquiry, the Principles lay out a number of factors which courts already consider: the disparity of outcome under the agreement and under the marital property regime; the likely circumstances of the party challenging the agreement had the marriage never taken place; whether the agreement was designed to benefit or protect the interests of third parties; and the impact of its enforcement on post-execution children. Overall, the Principles are to be applauded for incorporating the best practices of the courts and trying to tread a middle ground between those who would refuse to enforce antenuptial agreements altogether and those who would enforce them as ordinary business contracts.

NOTES AND QUESTIONS

1. Many attorneys are wary of drafting premarital agreements because of potential liability for malpractice in the event that the agreements are found to be unenforceable. Would adoption of the ALI Principles make such attorneys more or less willing to draft premarital agreements?

2. Contract law and the UPAA determine unconscionability at the time the agreement is signed. The ALI Principles and a number of non-UPAA state court

rulings determine validity at the time of enforcement. Which approach makes more sense?

3. Professor Younger emphasizes the ALI Principles' emphasis on procedural requirements such as "a signed writing, financial disclosure and a showing of informed consent not obtained under duress" that she describes as already required by a number of states. Is the approach of the ALI on financial disclosure and a showing of informed consent similar to or different from the UPAA's?

4. Professor Younger also emphasizes the limited review of the substance of the agreement at the time it is signed and the far more extensive review contemplated at the time of enforcement. What does this mean for the validity of a one-sided agreement? Is it possible for it to be valid when signed, but not enforceable 20 years later?

PROBLEMS

1. On the day of Hank and Wanda's wedding they signed a premarital agreement providing that if they divorced, Hank would give Wanda a house and $500,000 or half his assets, whichever value was greater. Hank and Wanda divorced eight months later. Hank has attacked the agreement as violating public policy because it encourages divorce. How should the court rule and why?

2. When Carl and Jill were married, Jill was 18, pregnant, and unemployed. Carl, who was 25, had graduated from college and worked on his family's farm. Their premarital agreement, drafted by Carl's family attorney, provided that if the parties divorced, neither would be entitled to the property of the other, and neither would be entitled to spousal or child support. Carl told Jill that if she would not sign the agreement, he would not marry her. She agreed, reluctantly. Their baby was born six months after the wedding, and ten months later Carl moved out of the house. Jill filed for divorce and sought spousal and child support. Carl responded with the premarital agreement. In a jurisdiction that has adopted the UPAA, what arguments should Jill's attorney make in support of her position that the agreement is not enforceable? How should Carl's attorney respond? How would the analysis change if the parties live in a jurisdiction that follows traditional legal principles about the enforceability of premarital agreements? In a jurisdiction that followed the ALI Principles?

3. Harold and Wynona were married 14 years ago. Each had previously been married and has children from the former marriage. At the time of their wedding, Harry, then 32 years old, was part owner of his family's successful business. Wynona, who was 27, worked as a secretary in the business. When they married, Wynona owned property worth $5,000, and Harold's interest in the family business was worth $550,000. After fully disclosing their assets and income to each other, they signed a premarital agreement, which provided that all of the property Harold owned before marriage, along with increases in value and income from it, would remain his separate property. The agreement also limited Wynona's claim to spousal support to $200 per month for 10 years. During their marriage Harold and Wynona had another child. Wynona did not work outside the home, and

Harold continued to work in the family business, which grew rapidly. At the time of divorce Harold's interest in the business was worth $8 million, and his income was $250,000 per year. Wynona's property had tripled in value, and she had no income and only 14-year-old skills as a secretary. Under traditional rules, would the agreement be enforceable? Under *Simeone*? Under the UPAA? Under the ALI Principles?

4. Susan was 50 and John was 78 when they married four years ago. Susan, who was divorced and had two children and three grandchildren, owned her own home and worked as a real estate agent. John lived on his 30-acre farm. He had never married before and had no children or living siblings. On the day of their wedding they signed a premarital agreement drafted by Susan's attorney. The agreement did not include a written disclosure of their assets, but the attorney explained the agreement in detail to both parties and asked if they had any questions. Neither did, and both affirmed that they wanted to sign the agreement. The agreement provided that all Susan's property would remain her separate property, that John would transfer all his real property into tenancy by the entireties, and that he would transfer all his cash and personal property into joint tenancy with Susan. The agreement also said that if Susan initiated a divorce, she would have to return to John all property she had acquired under the agreement, but that if he initiated a divorce, Susan would retain the property she had acquired. After the wedding the couple lived on John's farm.

Three months ago Susan filed a domestic violence complaint against John and obtained a restraining order requiring him to move out and to stay away from her. He went to stay with neighbors, who filed a complaint with the local senior services agency alleging that Susan was abusing and financially exploiting John. A state social worker investigated the complaint and made a written report that it was "founded," but no further action was taken.

John has now filed a petition for divorce, which requests that the premarital agreement be invalidated. Under the traditional law would the agreement be enforceable? Under *Simeone*? Under the UPAA? Under the ALI Principles?

5. George was 55 and Martha was 50 when they married four years ago. Martha had a teenage daughter from a prior marriage, for whom she received child support, and George had no children. Before the wedding, George and Martha signed a premarital agreement providing that "neither one shall have or acquire any right, title or claim to the property of the other" and that "neither party, in the case of a divorce, shall have a right to division of property or support from the other." Neither was represented by an attorney, but both knew the nature and extent of the other's property. At the time of the wedding, George owned little property, had taken early retirement, and received pension income of $1,247 per month. Martha owned a home worth $60,000 and other assets worth $5,500. Martha was employed and earned $30,000 per year, but during the marriage she became very disabled and had to quit her job. She cannot work and has no source of income, though she may be eligible for Social Security disability benefits. She still owns the home, which together with her other assets is now worth $70,000. George has petitioned for divorce and asked the court to enforce the premarital agreement. Should the agreement be enforced under the UPAA?

C.   SEPARATION AGREEMENTS

In contrast to the relative rarity of premarital agreements, separation agreements are the norm. The great majority of divorce cases are uncontested, and a high percentage of these are settled against the background provided by statutes and case law, with the settlement expressed in a separation agreement. Robert H. Mnookin & Lewis Kornhauser, Bargaining in the Shadow of the Law: The Case of Divorce, 88 Yale L.J. 950, 951 n.3 (1979) (probably less than 10 percent of divorce cases are resolved by litigation); Homer C. Clark, Jr., The Law of Domestic Relations in the United States 755 (2d ed. 1988) (90 percent of all divorces are uncontested and well over 50 percent settled by separation agreement).

Separation agreements must satisfy basic contract law requirements to be enforceable. They sometimes raise issues under the statute of frauds because they concern real property or their terms cannot be performed within one year, although judicial approaches limit the significance of the stationary requirement of a writing. *See* E. Allan Farnsworth, Contracts 286 (1995); Stewart Macauley et al., Contracts 265 (1995).

1.   *The Permissible Scope of the Agreement*

Just as the law of premarital agreements has moved in the last 20 or so years from a position that officially limited the parties' ability to determine by contract the legal consequences of marriage, the law of separation agreements has also moved toward a contractual freedom model. Agreements routinely address issues of spousal and child support and child custody and visitation. However, traditionally, and still officially in some states, parties may not enter into binding contracts with regard to support, custody, and visitation that tie the hands of the court.

SALLY B. SHARP, *FAIRNESS STANDARDS AND SEPARATION AGREEMENTS: A WORD OF CAUTION ON CONTRACTUAL FREEDOM*

132 U. Pa. L. Rev. 1399, 1399-1403 (1984)

At one point in the not so distant past, . . . a wife's legal identity was "merged" into that of her husband, so that issues involving the enforceability of contracts executed between spouses never arose. By the turn of the century, however, restrictions on the nature, scope, and content of marital contracts had largely replaced the expedient of denying the wife the capacity to contract. Thus, husbands and wives were allowed to contract with one another so long as their agreements did not attempt to alter the "essential" incidents of marriage, such as the wife's right to rely on her husband for support, or "promote" or "encourage" divorce. Courts were particularly zealous in voiding any attempts by a husband to abrogate his duty of support.

The public policies sought to be furthered by these restrictions on marital contracts in general and on settlement agreements in particular were somewhat varied: they included the state interest in protecting the essential nature of marriage, the necessity to safeguard economically and politically disadvantaged wives from presumptively dominant husbands, and the desirability of preserving the home as a haven from the marketplace mentality. In essence, however, restrictions centered on the state's interest in maintaining the status quo of marriage, and thereby the hierarchical relationship of the parties to marriage, with the result that limitations on interspousal freedom to contract became identified with perpetuation of inequality between the sexes. It therefore followed that the movement toward greater equality between the sexes was accompanied by demands for decreased state intervention in the regulation of marriage and divorce and in the parties' freedom to contract regarding either.

Partly in response to such demands, and partly in response to greater changes in society and marriage, most states began to limit application of the traditional public policy restrictions on settlement agreements. Indeed, by the 1950s such restrictions had become largely meaningless. States, however, did not forsake their roles as "third parties" to marriage and divorce; rather, they again reaccommodated their own interests, and those of private parties, in controlling the consequences of dissolution.

In general the principle developed that spouses could contract regarding support, or any other incident of marriage, virtually without regard to whether or not such agreements tended to promote divorce, if the contracts were "fair, just and reasonable in view of all the circumstances." The circumstances were apt to include the possibility that the parties were involved in a confidential relationship, moreover, which imposed duties of good faith on the dominant spouse. The combination of this general fairness standard with the confidential relationship concept also presumed some degree of special judicial review not demanded by other types of contracts.

Within the past two decades, however, there has been an even greater demand for a minimizing of such state intervention and for a more unfettered application of simple contract principles to marital agreements. In fairness, it should be noted that most of this scholarship has focussed on antenuptial agreements. Separation agreements, unfortunately, have tended to be swept into both the argument and the conclusion that marital contracts should, in general, be accorded the same judicial treatment as any other contract. The "any other contract" advocates, moreover, would also appear to assume that broad changes in society, in equality between the sexes, and in the substantive law of contracts have rendered the traditional protective system both obsolete and offensive. In particular, these scholars tend to regard judicial review as an unnecessary vestige of a paternalistic legal system that simultaneously creates undue opportunities for excessive subjectivity in the exercise of judicial discretion and undermines the reasonable expectations of the parties in the finality of their agreements.

Uniform Marriage and Divorce Act §306

(a) To promote amicable settlement of disputes between parties to a marriage attendant upon their separation or the dissolution of their marriage, the parties may enter into a written separation agreement containing provisions for disposition of any property owned by either of them, maintenance of either of them, and support, custody, and visitation of their children.

(b) In a proceeding for dissolution of marriage or for legal separation, the terms of the separation agreement, except those providing for the support, custody, and visitation of children, are binding upon the court unless it finds, after considering the economic circumstances of the parties and any other relevant evidence produced by the parties, on their own motion or on request of the court, that the separation agreement is unconscionable.

(c) If the court finds the separation agreement unconscionable, it may request the parties to submit a revised separation agreement or may make orders for the disposition of property, maintenance, and support.

ALI Principles of the Law of Family Dissolution § 7.09

(2) Except as provided in the last sentence of this Paragraph, the terms of a separation agreement providing for the disposition of property or for compensatory payments are unenforceable if they substantially limit or augment property rights or compensatory payments otherwise due under law, and enforcement of those terms would substantially impair the economic well-being of a party who has or will have

(a) primary or dual residential responsibility for a child or

(b) substantially fewer economic resources than the other party.

Nevertheless, the court may enforce such terms if it finds, under the particular circumstances of the case, that enforcement of the terms would not work an injustice.

ROBERT H. MNOOKIN & LEWIS KORNHAUSER, *BARGAINING IN THE SHADOW OF THE LAW: THE CASE OF DIVORCE*

88 Yale L.J. 950, 954-956 (1979)

In families with minor children, existing law imposes substantial doctrinal constraints. For those allocational decisions that directly affect children — that is, child support, custody, and visitation — parents lack the formal power to make their own law. Judges, exercising the state's parens patriae power, are said to have responsibility to determine who should have custody and on what conditions. Private agreements concerning these matters are possible and common, but agreements cannot bind the court, which, as a matter of official dogma, is said to have an independent responsibility for determining what arrangement best serves the child's welfare. Thus, the court has the power to reject a parental agreement and order some other level of child support or some other custodial arrangement it believes to be more desirable. Moreover, even if the parties' initial agreement is accepted by the court, it lacks finality. A court may at any time during the child's minority reopen and modify the initial decree in light of any subsequent change in circumstances. The parties entirely lack the power to deprive the court of this jurisdiction.

On the other hand, available evidence on how the legal system processes undisputed divorce cases involving minor children suggest that parents actually have broad powers to make their own deals. Typically, separation agreements are rubber stamped even in cases involving children. A study of custody in England suggests, for example, that courts rarely set aside an arrangement acceptable to the parents. Anecdotal evidence in America suggests that the same is true here.

The parents' broad discretion is not surprising for several reasons. First, getting information is difficult when there is no dispute. The state usually has very limited resources for a thorough and independent investigation of the family's circumstances. Furthermore, parents may be unwilling to provide damaging information that may upset their agreed arrangements. Second, the applicable legal standards are extremely vague and give judges very little guidance as to what circumstances justify overriding a parental decision. Finally, there are obvious limitations on a court's practical power to control the parents once they leave the courtroom. For all these reasons, it is not surprising that most courts behave as if their function in the divorce process is dispute settlement, not child protection. When there is no dispute, busy judges or registrars are typically quite willing to rubber stamp a private agreement, in order to conserve resources for disputed cases.

NOTES AND QUESTIONS

1. If the parties have agreed to no spousal support or to spousal support for a limited term, should a court have authority to order support beyond that provided for in the agreement if the dependent spouse will otherwise become a "public charge"? *See, e.g.,* O'Brien v. O'Brien, 623 N.E.2d 485 (1993). *Compare* the UMDA *with* the ALI Principles.

2. Should the parties be able to agree to child support below the presumptive amount calculated under the child support guidelines and agree to a correspondingly greater amount of spousal support? Why might the parties desire this agreement? What problems can you see with it? The ALI Principles provide that terms of a separation agreement altering child support or custodial responsibilities are not enforceable, but allow such agreements if approved and adopted by the court. *Compare* §7.09(5) *with* §§3.13 and 2.06.

3. Courts generally hold that the parties may agree to take on more extensive obligations than a court could impose on them. For example, in a jurisdiction that does not allow courts to order parents to support their children after the age of majority, an agreement to support an adult child attending school is usually enforceable. *E.g.,* Solomon v. Findley, 808 P.2d 294 (Ariz. 1991), *aff'g* 796 P.2d 477 (Ariz. 1990).

4. In most jurisdictions, if a court does not award spousal support at the time of the decree, it does not have jurisdiction to award it later. Therefore, in some jurisdictions parties may agree that a separation agreement that would not otherwise provide for spousal support will include a requirement that one spouse pay the other $1 per year. The idea is that if spousal support is needed later, the court can "modify" this provision. In other states, though, this tactic is not permitted.

2. Post-Decree Attacks on Agreements and Decrees Based on Them

Courts often do not scrutinize the terms of separation agreements closely at the time of divorce. Some time after the divorce decree has been entered, however, one of the parties may find fault with the agreement and the negotiating process that produced it. A successful attack at this point requires setting aside not only the agreement but also the decree.

HRESKO V. HRESKO

574 A.2d 24 (Md. App. 1990)

ALPERT, J. . . . . During the spring or early summer of 1985, James and Marie Hresko decided to terminate their 24-year marriage. The parties agreed to and signed a separation and property settlement agreement on July 10, 1985. According to terms of the settlement agreement, James (appellant) agreed to pay $400 per month in child support, to pay the total costs of the minor child's college education, and to assume payment of certain family consumer debts. The agreement further provided that Marie (appellee) had the option of buying out appellant's interest in the family home three years from the date of the settlement agreement.

On August 4, 1987, appellee filed a Complaint for Absolute Divorce against appellant in the Circuit Court for Anne Arundel County. On October 5, 1987, appellant filed an answer to the complaint which did not contest the divorce. A hearing before Master Malcolm M. Smith was held on December 7, 1987, with only appellee and her counsel present. Based on the master's findings, the Honorable James A. Cawood, Jr. entered an order of divorce a vinculo matrimonii on December 23, 1987. A voluntary separation agreement that the parties had executed two years earlier was incorporated but not merged into the order.

In the summer of 1988, appellee exercised her option to buy out appellant's interest in the family home and on the day of settlement, August 4, 1988, paid appellant $30,000 in cash for his one-half interest. Appellant had assumed that appellee would require a mortgage to purchase his interest in the house and claimed that he was "stunned" when she fulfilled her obligation with cash. He then became convinced that a fraud had been perpetrated against him during the 1985 negotiations that led to the property settlement. This alleged fraud involved the concealment, by appellee, of at least $30,000 in cash at the time of the agreement. As a result of this belief, appellant filed a Motion to Revise Judgment and to Rescind Separation and Property Settlement Agreement, together with a memorandum of law and an affidavit. Appellee responded by filing a motion to dismiss appellant's motion. Judge Cawood held a hearing on appellee's motion on June 7, 1989. After briefly holding the matter sub curia, the judge issued a written opinion on June 13, 1989, granting appellee's motion to dismiss appellant's motion to revise judgment. . . .

In an action to set aside an enrolled judgment or decree, the moving party must initially produce evidence sufficient to show that the judgment in question was the product of fraud, mistake or irregularity. Furthermore, it has long been black letter law in Maryland that the type of fraud which is required to authorize the reopening of an enrolled judgment is extrinsic fraud and not fraud which is intrinsic to the trial itself.

Appellant contends that appellee concealed from him an unknown, but apparently sizable, sum of money at the time the two parties were negotiating the subject separation and property settlement agreement. In an affidavit accompanying his motion, appellant alleges that during negotiations between the parties prior to the agreement, appellee represented and constantly reiterated to him that she had no money in any account or investment except for a small reserve account used for her expenses during the summer when she was not working or receiving a salary from her public school teaching job. . . . Appellant claims that, based on these incidents and appellee's frequent assertions that she was not hiding money, he entered into the subject agreement.

Assuming without deciding that appellant has produced facts and circumstances sufficient to establish fraud, we will address whether this alleged fraud is extrinsic or intrinsic to the trial itself. We hold, based on appellant's claims and verified statements, that appellee's alleged concealment of funds is an example of, at most, intrinsic fraud.

Intrinsic fraud is defined as "[t]hat which pertains to issues involved in the original action or where acts constituting fraud were, or could have been, litigated therein." Black's Law Dictionary (5th ed. 1979). Extrinsic fraud, on the other hand, is "[f]raud which is collateral to the issues tried in the case where the judgment is rendered." Id.

Fraud is extrinsic when it actually prevents an adversarial trial. Fleisher, 483 A.2d 1312. In determining whether or not extrinsic fraud exists, the question is not whether the fraud operated to cause the trier of fact to reach an unjust conclusion, but whether the fraud prevented the actual dispute from being submitted to the fact finder at all. Id. In Schwartz v. Merchants Mortgage Co., 322 A.2d 544 (1974), the Court of Appeals, quoting from United States v. Throckmorton, 98 U.S. 61 (1878), provided examples of what would be considered extrinsic fraud:

> Where the unsuccessful party has been prevented from exhibiting fully his case, by fraud or deception practiced on him by his opponent, as by keeping him away from court, a false promise of a compromise; or where the defendant never had knowledge of the suit, being kept in ignorance by the acts of the plaintiff; or where an attorney fraudulently or without authority assumes to represent a party and connives at his defeat; . . . or where the attorney regularly employed corruptly sells out his client's interest in the other side — these, and similar cases which show that there has never been a real contest in the trial or hearing of the case, are reasons for which a new suit may be sustained to set aside and annul the former judgment or decree, and open the case for a new and a fair hearing.

Schwartz, 322 A.2d 544.

Appellant contends that appellee's alleged fraudulent representations were extrinsic to the subsequent divorce action because they took place over two years before its inception and served to prevent appellant from taking advantage of his right to an adversarial proceeding. He argues that appellee's concealment is a "fraud or deception practiced upon the unsuccessful party by his opponent as by keeping him away from court or making a false promise of a compromise."

As stated above, the issue of whether appellee's alleged fraudulent conceal-ment of assets during pre-separation agreement negotiations is intrinsic or extrinsic to the divorce litigation is one of first impression in Maryland courts. Upon looking to other jurisdictions for guidance, we find conflict among our sis-ter states.

California courts have uniformly recognized that the failure of one spouse to disclose the existence of community property assets constitutes extrinsic fraud. In Re Marriage of Modnick, 663 P.2d 187 (Cal. 1983). The principle underlying these cases is that each spouse has an obligation to inform the other spouse of the existence of community property assets. This duty stems in part from the confidential nature of the marital relationship and from the fiduciary relationship that exists between spouses with respect to the control of commu-nity property. . . .

Other courts have found extrinsic fraud holding, as appellant would have us do, that a spouse's concealment or misrepresentation of assets can be classified as an intentional act by which the one spouse has prevented the other spouse from having a fair submission of the controversy and thus amounts to extrinsic fraud. Pilati v. Pilati, 592 P.2d 1374, 1380 (Mont. 1979).

Other jurisdictions have reached the opposite result, determining that the fraudulent concealment of assets by one spouse during a property settlement agreement is intrinsic to the divorce litigation. Recently, in Altman v. Altman, 150 A.D.2d 304, 542 N.Y.S.2d 7, 9 (1989), the New York Supreme Court, Appellate Division, held that alleged fraud in the negotiations of the separation agreement involves the issue in controversy and is not a deprivation of the opportunity to make a full and fair defense. The court reasoned that the alleged misrepresenta-tions of financial status are in essence no different from any other type of perjury committed in the course of litigation and thus constitute intrinsic fraud.

Similarly, in Chapman v. Chapman, 591 S.W.2d 574, 577 (Tex. Civ. App. 1979), the Texas court refused to overturn on the basis of fraud a property settle-ment agreement incorporated into a divorce decree. The court stated that the fraud alleged at most related to untruths which misled the wife into acquiescence and approval of an unjust division of property. Because these misrepresentations bore only on issues in the trial (or which could have been at issue in the trial), they, therefore, amounted to no more than intrinsic fraud. . . .

We are persuaded that these latter cases are the better reasoned ones. Misrepresentations or concealment of assets made in negotiations leading to a voluntary separation and property settlement agreement later incorporated into a divorce decree represent matters intrinsic to the trial itself. In fact, a determina-tion of each party's respective assets, far from being a collateral issue, would seem to be a central issue in a property settlement agreement. . . .

No "extrinsic fraud" prevented appellant from seeking trial and this court will not, therefore, reopen the decree in the present case. To rule otherwise would be to subject every enrolled divorce decree that includes a property settlement to revision upon discovery of alleged fraud in the inducement of the settlement. Public policy of this state demands an end to litigation once the parties have had an opportunity to present in court a matter for determination, the decision has been rendered, and the litigants afforded every opportunity for review.

NOTES AND QUESTIONS

1. For purposes of attacks made on an agreement after the parties have signed it, what difference does it make that the agreement has been the basis for a divorce decree? Should it make a difference? Why or why not? Should a decree that was based on a separation agreement be given the same amount of protection from collateral attack that a decree entered at the close of a trial has? Why or why not?

2. As a matter of contract law, would Mrs. Hresko's concealment of assets (assuming for these purposes that she did hide them) be a basis for setting aside the agreement? On what ground?

3. Are parties in the process of negotiating a divorce in a confidential relationship so that they have a duty of full disclosure to each other? Is this situation distinguishable from that of engaged people negotiating a premarital agreement? If each party is represented by counsel, are they in a confidential relationship? What duties of disclosure do the parties have then? How can a lawyer ensure that the other spouse is not hiding assets? Must the value of property be disclosed? Would you as a lawyer rely on the opposing party's representations about value? *See, e.g.*, In the Matter of the Marriage of Elzroth, 679 P.2d 1369 (Ore. App. 1984); In the Matter of the Marriage of Auble, 866 P.2d 1239 (Ore. App. 1993); Avriett v. Avriett, 363 S.E.2d 875 (N.C. App. 1988); Southers v. Southers 1999 Tenn. App. LEXIS 332, May 27, 1999, Filed.

PROBLEMS

1. Jack and Marian separated five years ago, and they have lived in different cities since then. During their marriage Jack had purchased a business, and their original plan was that Marian and their two children would join him once the business was well established. However, Jack always reported that the business was struggling, and Marian and the children never made the move. When Jack moved away, Marian went back to work, since the children were in school, and she has been self-supporting since Jack left. Jack has sent Marian $400 per month as support for the children. Last year Jack and Marian agreed to divorce, and they negotiated a separation agreement by themselves without a lawyer. Jack told Marian that his business was nearly bankrupt and that he could not afford to pay spousal support but would continue to pay the same amount of child support. He offered to let Marian take the house (and its mortgage payments) and told her there was not much else to share. Jack then took the agreement to a lawyer, who drafted a petition for divorce. Marian consented to entry of a decree consistent with the terms of the agreement. After the time for appeal had passed, Marian learned that in fact Jack's business has been very successful and that he has become a wealthy man. Under the approach of *Hresko*, can Marian successfully reopen the divorce on the grounds of fraud? In a jurisdiction that presumes that married people are in a confidential relationship, will Marian have greater success? Why or why not?

2. Hal and Wilma live in a state in which the appreciation in value of premarital property is marital property unless the increase is attributable purely to market factors or inflation. Wilma had purchased a house before marriage, and

she never added Hal's name to the title to the house during the marriage. During the marriage they made mortgage payments on the house, paying an additional $3,500 in principal. They also did some remodeling, at a cost of $4,500, which increased the house's value by $11,000. During the marriage the housing market was generally rising as well. At the end of the marriage the fair market value of the house was $24,000 greater than it had been at the beginning of the marriage. Wilma was the family bookkeeper, and only she knew this information during the marriage. If Hal and Wilma live in a jurisdiction that imposes a duty of disclosure on spouses who are negotiating a separation agreement without attorneys, how much of the information about the house must Wilma disclose and why?

3. Modification of Agreements

Courts often discuss the enforceability of agreements that purport to limit their authority to revise terms that are ordinarily modifiable. Judicial analysis typically turns on whether the agreement has been "merged" into the decree, merely "approved" or "ratified" by the court, or "incorporated" into the decree. If an agreement is merged into a decree, it has no continuing legal effect. At the other extreme, a court may approve an agreement but not order its terms performed; the agreement is said to be ratified or approved. If an agreement is incorporated, its terms are part of the divorce decree, but it also continues to have independent vitality as a contract. All courts will merge agreements, but some courts are reluctant merely to ratify agreements, and a number will not incorporate them without merging them.

IN RE ESTATE OF HEREFORD

250 S.E.2d 45 (W. Va. 1978)

NEELY, J. We granted this appeal to reexamine the law concerning property settlement agreements and alimony decrees which up to this time has been far from clear.

In the case before us the Circuit Court of Kanawha County upheld the claim of Quinta Beall Couch Hereford, appellee, for alimony against the estate of her ex-husband, Frank Morton Hereford. Appellant, Maxine W. Hereford, executrix of the estate of Frank Morton Hereford, contends that the property settlement agreement between appellee and the deceased was merged into the alimony decree entered upon their divorce, and that, since the decree did not specifically provide for the continuance of alimony payments beyond the death of the payor, the right to alimony ceased at Frank Morton Hereford's death. The lower court found that regardless of whether the agreement merged into the decree, the language used in both the settlement agreement and decree clearly provided for alimony beyond the death of the payor. After examining the equitable considerations in this case we agree with the lower court and affirm its holding.

Quinta Beall Couch Hereford, appellee, and Frank Morton Hereford, deceased, were divorced on June 12, 1957. Before their divorce, they entered into an agreement on February 1, 1957 which provided, in part:

> Frank M. Hereford agrees and promises to pay unto Quinta Beall Couch Hereford, on the first day of each and every month beginning on the date hereof, the sum of two hundred fifty dollars ($250.00) as alimony for her maintenance and support, which monthly payments shall continue so long as said Quinta Beall Couch Hereford is living and has not remarried; upon the remarriage of said Quinta Beall Couch Hereford, or in the event of the death of Quinta Beall Couch Hereford, then and in either of which events, said monthly alimony payments shall cease and terminate. The amounts herein provided to be paid may be set forth in any decree granting a divorce between the parties as the amount of alimony payable by the party of the second part to the party of the first part.

The subsequent divorce decree provided, in part:

> It is further ordered and decreed that defendant, Frank M. Hereford, do pay unto the plaintiff, Quinta Beall Couch Hereford, until the further order of this court, the monthly sum of $250.00 as alimony to said plaintiff, so long as she lives or until she remarries. . . .
>
> And, it appearing to the court that plaintiff and defendant have entered into a property settlement agreement, in writing, bearing date the 1st day of February, 1957, a copy of which was introduced in evidence, and that said agreement is in all respects fair and equitable, it is, therefore, accordingly adjudged, ordered and decreed that said agreement be and the same is hereby ratified, approved and confirmed, insofar as same is not in conflict with the provisions of this decree.

The equitable considerations in this case have a significant bearing on the result. Our law is replete with interesting rules which can be manipulated in such a way as to permit a court to arrive at any desired result in a case of this nature. We suspect that previous cases have manipulated these rules in such a way as to arrive at equitable results in those cases; however, the effect of that manipulation process has been untoward with regard to the degree of certainty with which our law can be predicted. Consequently, we wish to point out that the facts of the case before us have a significant impact on the result, and as domestic relations are governed by the traditions of equity, the pathetic facts before us are a perfectly proper consideration for both the lower court and ourselves. It is uncontested that Frank M. Hereford made all payments during his life and that appellee is now 71 years old, in ill health, and a resident of the Mountain State Nursing Home, where she seems destined to die. Her prognosis indicates that she will never be able to work again and is unable to care for herself.

I.

A great deal of incomprehensible domestic relations law in the State of West Virginia hinges upon the technicality of whether a property settlement has been "ratified and confirmed" by a court, in which case the parties are left to contract remedies for the enforcement of the settlement or, alternatively, whether provisions of a property settlement are "merged" into the divorce decree. If the provisions are "merged" they become subject to the continuing jurisdiction of the court which may extinguish or enlarge rights to periodic payments (alimony) initially provided by the property settlement agreement.

We have held that where a property settlement agreement is merely "ratified and confirmed" the property settlement agreement does not become part of the decree and any periodic payments (alimony) provided for in such property settlement agreement can be neither enlarged or diminished by the circuit court. Where, however, a property settlement agreement providing for alimony or periodic payments is merged or made a part of the decree, we have held that the circuit court may increase or decrease the amount of payments in subsequent proceedings in the same way that it could if it had awarded alimony after a contest without any property settlement agreement.

In answering the question presented by the case before us any one of numerous results could be justified by relying upon our prior precedent. Appellee argues strenuously that when the parties and the court used the words of art ". . . the sum of two hundred fifty dollars ($250.00) as alimony for her maintenance and support, which monthly payments shall continue so long as said Quinta Beall Couch Hereford is living and has not remarried . . . ." and the words of art in the divorce decree ". . . the monthly sum of $250.00 as alimony to said plaintiff, so long as she lives or until she remarries . . ." they intended that the alimony award be chargeable against the husband's estate if the appellee survived him, because it was specifically contemplated that appellee be supported during her entire life notwithstanding her former husband's possible early death.

The appellant, on the other hand, urges two rules: first, that as a general principle alimony does not survive the husband's death; and, second that by ordering and decreeing that Frank M. Hereford pay the plaintiff the monthly sum of $250.00 as "alimony," the court merged the property settlement agreement with regard to periodic payments into the divorce decree and in so doing extinguished all contract rights arising under the settlement agreement. Therefore, according to appellant, even if the appellee would have been entitled to a contract action against the estate based on the language of the property settlement agreement alone, the court converted the consensual agreement for periodic payments into judicially decreed alimony, and thereby extinguished the contract right. . . .

II.

We dream today of inaugurating a system of domestic relations law in this State which is not dependent upon the use of words of art. Any experienced lawyer knows that as often as not so-called "words of art" are used without intending or implying any particular legal consequences, only later to have those consequences imposed upon unsuspecting parties by courts. The Court suspects that this is what happened with regard to the so-called words of art used in both the property settlement agreement and the divorce decree in the case before us, as both parties to this appeal rely upon conflicting words of art. It does not appear to the Court that the lawyers contemplated any deep meaning for the expression "so long as said Quinta Beall Couch Hereford is living" nor did the lawyers drafting the divorce decree speculate at great length upon whether the property settlement agreement was ratified and confirmed or, to the contrary, merged into the decree.

In order to disengage ourselves from the mire of words of art we hold today that in all future cases in which the final order is entered after 1 February 1979 . . . the parties may do anything which they wish by their property settlement agreement as long as it is approved by the circuit court. The parties may specifically agree that the amount of periodic payments or alimony set forth in the property settlement agreement may not ever be increased or decreased by the court; they may specifically contract out of any continuing judicial supervision of their relationship by the circuit court; they may agree that the periodic payments or alimony called for in the property settlement agreement shall be judicially awarded and for the purposes of enforcement may be enforced by the contempt power (if the payor is able to pay), but that the court shall never have jurisdiction either to increase or decrease the amount regardless of change of circumstances; they may agree that a lump sum settlement in lieu of periodic payments shall constitute the final settlement of the rights of the parties; and, they may agree to any other terms and conditions they wish and which appear at the time the decree is entered to be fair and reasonable to the court. If it appears to the court that the terms are fair and reasonable he may approve them, ratify them or merge them, and by whatever words he uses they shall become part of the decree and binding on everyone including the court. However, in the absence of a specific provision to the contrary in a property settlement agreement appended to, made a part of, or incorporated by reference into the court order, which provision specifically and unambiguously denies the court jurisdiction in one or more of the regards just discussed, it shall be presumed that regardless of the language used, whether it be "ratified and confirmed," "merged," or any other language of like import, that a periodic payment to which reference is made in a divorce decree is judicially decreed alimony or alimony and child support and is subject to the continuing jurisdiction of the circuit court. . . .

. . . The question of whether a court shall have continuing supervision over the amount of an alimony award, whether the alimony award shall be enforceable by the contempt remedy, or whether alimony at all shall be awarded as opposed to a lump sum settlement are all fit subjects for negotiation between the parties subject to the overall supervision of the court. Mature adults with the help of the court and counsel should be permitted to negotiate terms and thereby bind themselves. Child support, of course, is always subject to continuing judicial modification. In the case before us we find that there was sufficient language in the property settlement agreement and the divorce decree itself to permit us to infer that the parties contemplated that the appellee receive support until her death, rather than the death of her former husband. While a forthright analysis of our prior case law requires a confession that this is not the only possible result which could be inferred from our body of law; nevertheless, it is a legitimate, permissible result from the law and in this case it is a just and equitable result which is as good a reason for arriving at that holding as any other.

Affirmed.

NOTES AND QUESTIONS

1. Other courts would have interpreted the agreement and decree in this case in light of the usual background rule that spousal support terminates on the death of the payor and would have required far more explicit drafting to take the case out of that rule. Why do you suppose this court interpreted the documents strictly so that the woman had a claim against her former husband's estate?

2. Did the *Hereford* court succeed in clarifying the extent of the parties' freedom to determine what terms are modifiable? Under this case, how would you draft an agreement that allows the parties themselves to modify its terms but does not allow judicial modification? For a review of the aftermath of *Hereford* and of the abundant and confusing case law in this area, *see* Doris Del Tosto Brogan, Divorce Settlement Agreements: The Problem of Merger or Incorporation and the Status of the Agreement in Relation to the Decree, 67 Neb. L. Rev. 235 (1988). *See also* Sally B. Sharp, Semantics as Jurisprudence: The Elevation of Form over Substance in the Treatment of Separation Agreements in North Carolina, 69 N.C. L. Rev. 319 (1991).

3. If the court ratifies but does not incorporate the separation agreement into the divorce decree, may either party be held in contempt for failing to comply with the terms of the agreement? Why or why not?

4. States vary substantially in their treatment of a court's ability to modify an order based on a separation agreement. For example, in Rockwell v. Rockwell, 681 A.2d 1017 (Del. 1996), the court rejected the distinction between incorporation and merger and concluded that the underlying agreement retains its nature as a contract, and, therefore, that a court cannot modify an agreement regarding support according to the standard normally used for court-ordered support. In contrast, in Massachusetts even if the agreement survives the decree as an independently enforceable contract, the court has power to modify the spousal support terms in the decree, though in deciding whether to do so a court is to consider the parties' expressed desire that the support terms not be modifiable. Bercume v. Bercume, 704 N.E.2d 177 (Mass. 1998). In Idaho, if the agreement is merged into the decree, support terms may be modified without consent of the parties unless the court finds that the agreement is integrated. This means that the parties agreed that the property division and support terms were "reciprocal consideration" and thus that the support provisions are "necessarily part and parcel of a division of property." Keeler v. Keeler, 958 P.2d 599 (Idaho App. 1998).

5. The distinction between a contract and a decree may affect the power of the court to grant relief. In Alabama, for example, the court does not have the authority to order alimony payments to a party who remarries. The couple, however, may agree contractually to provide for such payments. In Ex parte Murphy, — So. 2d — (Ala. 2003), the Supreme Court of Alabama accordingly held that when the parties petitioned the court to incorporate an alimony agreement into the decree in light of one of the parties' remarriage, the court lost the authority to order continuing alimony payments. *See* ALI Principles of Family Dissolution §7.10, which provides that contract terms unenforceable as terms of a decree survive as independent contracts even if the rest of the agreement is incorporated into the decree.

6. If a court incorporates a separation agreement into a divorce decree and the agreement and decree allow for modification of spousal support upon the happening of certain events, if the parties agree to reduce support but do not move the court to modify the decree, is the payor obligated to pay the amount in the decree or the amount in the modified agreement? Could the payor be held in contempt for failing to pay the full amount required by the decree? Why or why not? Could the breaching party be ordered to pay damages? Why or why not?

7. Uniform Marriage and Divorce Act (UMDA) §306 deals with the relationship between the agreement and the decree in the following way:

(d) If the court finds that the separation agreement is not unconscionable as to disposition of property or maintenance, and not unsatisfactory as to support:

(1) unless the separation agreement provides to the contrary, its terms shall be set forth in the decree of dissolution or legal separation and the parties shall be ordered to perform them, or

(2) if the separation agreement provides that its terms shall not be set forth in the decree, the decree shall identify the separation agreement and state that the court has found the terms not unconscionable.

(e) Terms of the agreement set forth in the decree are enforceable by all remedies available for enforcement of a judgment, including contempt, and are enforceable as contract terms.

(f) Except for terms concerning the support, custody, or visitation of children, the decree may expressly preclude or limit modification of terms set forth in the decree if the separation agreement so provides. Otherwise, terms of a separation agreement set forth in the decree are automatically modified by modification of the decree.

PROBLEM

When Judy and Richard were divorced in 1985, Richard was a surgeon earning $100,000 per year, and he had unearned income of $15,000 per year and property worth $600,000. Judy was a homemaker who received property worth $400,000, consisting mostly of the marital home. Their separation agreement provides that Richard will pay Judy one-third of his annual gross earned income until his death, her death, or her remarriage. The agreement also provided that the parties intended it to survive entry of a divorce decree and that it would not be modifiable "even though future events might occur that would alter the position of either party as it exists [at the time of the divorce]." Richard, who is now 55 years old, has recently retired. He has no earned income and is living on unearned income of $50,000, and his property has increased in value to $1 million. Judy, who is 57, earns $97 per week as a museum tour guide, and she has unearned income of $104 per month. Richard has stopped paying Judy spousal support, saying that he no longer has any earned income. Judy has filed a petition to modify the decree, seeking one-third of Richard's gross unearned income, notwithstanding the separation agreement. What arguments should each side make? How should the court rule and why?

Jurisdiction

11

A. INTRODUCTION

John and Harriet Haddock were married in New York in the summer of 1868. The marriage was never consummated, however, because John — feeling that he had been tricked into the marriage — left New York the same day. Harriet remained in New York, while John drifted about the country, finally settling in Connecticut nine years later. Thirteen years after the wedding, in 1881, John sought a divorce from Harriet, mailing notice to her last known address in New York and publishing in the local Connecticut newspaper. John obtained his divorce and remarried.

In 1891, 23 years after the wedding and ten years after the divorce action, John inherited considerable property from his father. Harriet, from whom John had not heard since their wedding day, sued John for a legal separation in New York. She received a default separation decree and an award of alimony but could not recover because of lack of personal service on John. Five years later, John returned to New York. Harriet obtained personal service in New York and refiled her suit for legal separation and alimony.

John's defense to Harriet's suit, of course, was his prior Connecticut divorce. The New York court refused to recognize the sister-state decree because Harriet had not been subject to the jurisdiction of the Connecticut court when the decree was rendered. Holding that, as far as New York courts were concerned, John and Harriet were still married, the court awarded Harriet her legal separation and $780 a year in maintenance.[1]

Variations of this story provide the basis for a vexing set of jurisdictional problems peculiar to matrimonial issues. The case itself arises out of desertion, in this case, the husband's, which was the primary ground for divorce in nineteenth-century America. Norma Basch, The Victorian Compromise: Divorce in New

---

1. These are the facts of Haddock v. Haddock, 201 U.S. 562 (1906).

York City, 1787-1870, at 20 (unpublished paper delivered at the 1985 Annual Meeting of the Organization of American Historians), quoted in Neal R. Feigenson, Extraterritorial Recognition of Divorce Decrees in the Nineteenth Century, 34 Am. J. Legal Hist. 119, 123 (1990). Because desertion was the most common basis for divorce, most nineteenth-century suits, like John Haddock's Connecticut action, were uncontested (although it would have been more usual for the deserted spouse to prosecute the suit). As a practical matter, service of process did not notify the defendant of the pending divorce because his or her whereabouts were usually unknown at the time of the suit. And a decree issued by one state, even though relied on by the plaintiff, was often refused recognition by a sister state.

The questions presented by this situation were many. Could Harriet, had she wished, have sought a divorce from John in New York? Was John's Connecticut divorce valid? If the Connecticut divorce was invalid, was John a bigamist? If either Harriet or John could secure a divorce without the presence of the other, would that mean that the defendant could be required to pay or lose any entitlement to property or support she might have claimed had she participated?

The answers to these questions depend on whether a court in one state would, or would be required to, recognize a divorce decree issued in another state. And the answer to that question, in turn, depends on when and to what extent a state court has jurisdiction to enter a decree of divorce. The next section of this chapter discusses this question. The following two sections look at jurisdiction to award support and to divide property and interjurisdictional enforcement of these orders. The fifth section considers jurisdiction over child custody disputes, and the chapter concludes with materials on federal court jurisdiction over domestic relations litigation.

B.   DIVORCE JURISDICTION

A principal benefit of absolute divorce is the possibility of remarriage, and a party seeking a divorce wants assurance that any future alliance will be immune from attack on the ground that it is invalid because of a prior subsisting marriage. Jurisdiction is the key to any such assurance.

The basis for saying so lies in two principles: *res judicata* and full faith and credit. *Res judicata* provides that a matter that has been, or could have been, litigated in an action brought before a court and decided on the merits cannot be relitigated in a subsequent action, at least between the same parties. This is obviously a rule seeking finality of judgments, designed to establish stable relations by denying endless opportunities for harassment and to protect courts from repeated litigation of the same matter. However, a court that lacks jurisdiction over a defendant cannot issue a decision that binds her. Absent jurisdiction, she would be free to ignore the decision and, if need be, could litigate the issues in a second case if the plaintiff were to bring another action. In short, there can be no *res judicata* if there was no jurisdiction.

Full faith and credit becomes important when two or more states deal with issues related to a divorce. Suppose, for example, that Arthur sues Bernice in Florida for breach of contract, and both are present at the time of the suit. Bernice loses and then moves to New York. Arthur writes Bernice asking her to pay up, and Bernice replies, "Nuts" (or words to that effect). Arthur sues Bernice in New York based on the judgment entered in Florida. Bernice says in the New York court, "I shouldn't have to pay this. I have a good defense, and the Florida judge was wrong and silly." Bernice's claim will not be heard, however, because the Florida judgment, which would be *res judicata* in that state, is entitled to recognition in New York under the Full Faith and Credit Clause of Article IV, §1 of the federal Constitution. This clause states

> Full Faith and Credit shall be given in each state to the public acts, Records, and judicial Proceedings of every other State.

By virtue of the Full Faith and Credit Clause, the New York court must say something like this:

> Arthur has a valid final judgment against Bernice rendered by Florida, which is, of course, a sister state. The Full Faith and Credit Clause requires that we accept this judgment as if it were our own. Thus, Arthur is entitled to recover on the basis of the Florida judgment, without retrying the case here.

Matters would be different if Florida did not have jurisdiction over Bernice. Full faith and credit must be given only to orders that the court had power to enter. Thus, the court in New York could refuse to recognize the Florida order. Indeed, New York *cannot* enforce the Florida order. To do so would violate Bernice's right to due process because she did not participate voluntarily, and Florida had no authority to require her participation.

Thus far, we have been talking about jurisdiction in actions to determine personal liability. But jurisdiction is not the same in all actions. Actions to determine personal liability are called "transitory" precisely because jurisdiction depends on the location of the parties rather than on any other fact. There are some cases, however, where it is not enough that the parties are before the court. When land, for example, is involved, a different jurisdictional requirement appears.

Suppose Arthur sues Bernice over title to a piece of land located in New York. The suit is brought in Florida, where Arthur has served Bernice with process during one of her business trips to that state. Presumably, the Florida court would decline jurisdiction. Although service of process on Bernice creates personal jurisdiction over her as the defendant, the court does not have jurisdiction over the subject matter of this action, the land. And because the court does not have jurisdiction over the subject matter, it cannot enter an order touching the land. Jurisdiction over land depends not on the location of the parties but on the location of the land. This power over land, as you will recall, is called *in rem* jurisdiction — jurisdiction over things. An *in rem* order speaks not simply to the relationships between the parties, but to the world at large.

The question then becomes, what is jurisdiction for purposes of divorce? Courts sometimes talk of marriage as a "civil contract," and if it were only that, the answer would be simple. Personal jurisdiction over the parties would be both necessary and sufficient. It would be necessary in the sense that, generally speaking, a court cannot make a binding determination without jurisdiction over the person of the defendant. It would be sufficient in that, if both parties were actually before the court, that circumstance alone would allow the court to render a binding decision concerning the marriage. In practice, this would mean that divorces could be rendered wherever both parties are present. If Arthur wished to sue Bernice, he would have to find her and sue her there. Similarly, if Bernice had moved from the state where Arthur lived and wished to get a divorce, she would have to go back to the state of Arthur's residence, or to any state where Arthur might be found, and bring the divorce action there. (Long-arm statutes can, of course, change this scheme.)

Here, as elsewhere, however, marriage is not viewed as a simple matter of contract. The relationship is the concern not solely of the two parties but, so it is said, of the world at large. The *status* aspect of marriage (or better, the public aspect) is important, and courts sometimes seem to take the same view concerning marriage as they do regarding land — that is, they tend to view it as an *in rem* action. Accordingly, one looks for a forum that has some interest in the marriage relationship, not simply for a court that happens to have power over the litigants. This is done by reifying the marital status into a fictional situs. What is such a situs? In many cases, the answer is simple. If the parties have always lived in state X, were married there, raised their children in X, and seek to get divorced there, surely state X is the forum with an interest in determining whether the marriage should come to an end. Moreover, it is the only state with such an interest and therefore with jurisdiction to end the marriage. No other state may take jurisdiction to divorce the parties. If another state purports to do so, its decree is not entitled to recognition under the Full Faith and Credit Clause.

To this point, determining the jurisdiction with authority over the "res" — the marital status — has been easy enough. Suppose, however, that Albert is physically abusive to his wife, Donna. Donna leaves Albert to live with her mother, a resident of the neighboring state. She intends to remain in that state and wishes to be relieved of her vows to Albert. Can she bring a divorce action in her new residence?

The answer depends on whether the domicile of one spouse (but not the other) is sufficient to give that state jurisdiction over that spouse's marital status. (Recall from Chapter 2 that a married woman can acquire a separate domicile "whenever it is necessary or proper that she should do so." *E.g.*, Cheever v. Wilson, 76 U.S. (9 Wall.) 108, 124 (1869). *See also* Barber v. Barber, 62 U.S. (21 How.) 582, 599-600 (1858). To say that the wife can establish her own domicile, however, does not answer the question of whether the domicile of only one spouse provides jurisdiction to terminate a marital relationship. This issue was much disputed during the nineteenth century but was resolved for some time in Haddock v. Haddock, 201 U.S. 562 (1906), the facts of which are described above. Although some courts had taken the view that, where the parties were domiciled in different jurisdictions, each state had sufficient interest in the subject matter of the relationship to issue a divorce, *Haddock* decided otherwise. An ex parte divorce (that is, one in which only one spouse participates) could be obtained only in the state of the "matrimonial domicile," meaning the last state in which both parties were domiciled as husband and wife. Accordingly, John Haddock's Connecticut decree, which we know was obtained ex parte with service by mail and publication, was not entitled to recognition in New York.

In 1942, however, the Supreme Court reconsidered and overruled *Haddock* in Williams v. North Carolina, 317 U.S. 287 (1942) (*Williams I*). After some 20 years of marriage to their respective spouses in North Carolina, Mr. Williams and Mrs. Hendrix decamped together to Las Vegas, Nevada, where they each obtained a divorce and then married each other. The North Carolina spouses received notice of the divorce proceedings but were not served with process in Nevada, nor did they appear in the divorce proceedings. Upon their return from Nevada, the newlyweds were prosecuted for bigamy. They were convicted on the basis that their Nevada divorces were not entitled to recognition in North Carolina.

Although this conclusion would follow from *Haddock*, the Supreme Court held that every state has a "rightful and legitimate concern" in the marital status of persons domiciled in that state, which is sufficient to justify termination of the marital status even though the other spouse is not present. Moreover, such an assertion of jurisdiction is entitled to full faith and credit by other states. Thus, if Nevada were the domicile of Mr. Williams and Mrs. Hendrix, North Carolina must recognize their divorces. North Carolina's interest in the integrity of its divorce laws, of such concern in *Haddock*, was now dismissed as "part of the price of our federal system." 317 U.S. at 302. In recent cases left-at-home spouses have argued, without success, that permitting a state to grant a divorce or legal separation based on the domicile of the spouse who left violates procedural due process, relying on the minimum contacts test of International Shoe Co. v. Washington, 326 U.S. 310 (1945). *See, e.g.,* Henderson v. Henderson, 818 A.2d 669 (R.I. 2003).

Williams I held that Nevada could exercise divorce jurisdiction *over its domiciliaries.* In the first prosecution, there seemed to be no need for challenging the domicile of Mr. Williams and Mrs. Hendrix. The persistent North Carolina prosecutor retried the defendants for bigamy, claiming that they had never intended to reside indefinitely in Nevada and therefore had never been domiciliaries of that state. The defendants were again convicted and again appealed to the Supreme Court. This time the Court upheld the conviction, holding that, under the Full Faith and Credit Clause, the Nevada finding of the jurisdictional fact of domicile incorporated in the original divorce decree did not bind North Carolina (which did not participate in the Nevada proceeding). That finding, therefore, was subject to reexamination by the North Carolina court. Williams v. North Carolina, 325 U.S. 226 (1945) (*Williams II*).

One of the implications of *Williams II* is that domicile is not only a sufficient, but a necessary condition for full faith and credit recognition of divorce decrees. Another is that Mrs. Williams, the left-at-home spouse, could also have challenged the ex parte divorce decree for lack of jurisdiction. If she had never appeared in the foreign divorce action, she did not have the opportunity to be heard on the jurisdictional issue and thus was not precluded from challenging that jurisdictional basis at a later time. But that is all that she could challenge. If a second court determines that the court issuing the divorce decree did have jurisdiction because the plaintiff was a domiciliary of the forum state at the time the decree was entered, the left-at-home spouse cannot then litigate the existence of adequate grounds for the divorce. And while that spouse can attack the jurisdictional finding if she did not participate, she will carry the burden of proving the absence of domicile. *See* Homer H. Clark, Jr., Domestic Relations 718-719 (2d ed. 1987). Of course, if she prevails on the jurisdictional issue, then the divorce is invalid and has no effect. The following case considers the consequences if both spouses participate in the divorce action.

SHERRER V. SHERRER

334 U.S. 343 (1948)

VINSON, C.J. [Mr. and Mrs. Sherrer lived in Massachusetts during their marriage. In April 1944 Mrs. Sherrer went to Florida, ostensibly for vacation. In July she filed for divorce on the ground of extreme cruelty, alleging that she was domiciled in Florida. Mr. Sherrer was notified by mail of the proceedings and appeared generally through counsel. He denied his wife's jurisdictional allegations and the grounds for divorce, but the Florida court granted Mrs. Sherrer a divorce, specifically finding that she was domiciled there. Mr. Sherrer did not appeal. In December Mrs. Sherrer married Mr. Phelps. They lived together in Florida for two months and then returned to Massachusetts. In June 1945 Mr. Sherrer filed an action in Massachusetts predicated on the claim that he was still married to (the former) Mrs. Sherrer. She defended on the grounds that the Florida divorce was valid and that the parties were no longer married. The Massachusetts court reexamined the Florida court's basis for asserting jurisdiction, found that Mrs. Sherrer had not been domiciled there, and granted Mr. Sherrer the relief he sought.]

At the outset, it should be observed that the proceedings in the Florida court prior to the entry of the decree of divorce were in no way inconsistent with the requirements of procedural due process. We do not understand the respondent to urge the contrary. . . . It is clear that respondent was afforded his day in court with respect to every issue involved in the litigation, including the jurisdictional issue of petitioner's domicile. Under such circumstances, there is nothing in the concept of due process which demands that a defendant be afforded a second opportunity to litigate the existence of jurisdictional facts. . . .

That the jurisdiction of the Florida court to enter a valid decree of divorce was dependent upon petitioner's domicile in that State is not disputed. . . . But whether or not petitioner was domiciled in Florida at the time the divorce was granted was a matter to be resolved by judicial determination. Here, unlike the situation presented in Williams v. North Carolina, 325 U.S. 226 (1945), the finding of the requisite jurisdictional facts was made in proceedings in which the defendant appeared and participated. The question with which we are confronted, therefore, is whether such a finding . . . may be subjected to collateral attack in the courts of a sister State. . . .

The question of what effect is to be given to an adjudication by a court that it possesses requisite jurisdiction in a case, where the judgment of that court is subsequently subjected to collateral attack on jurisdictional grounds has been given frequent consideration by this Court over a period of many years. Insofar as cases originating in the federal courts are concerned, the rule has evolved that the doctrine of *res judicata* applies to adjudications relating either to jurisdiction of the person or of the subject matter where such adjudications have been made in proceedings in which those questions were in issue and in which the parties were given full opportunity to litigate. . . .

Full faith and credit

This Court has also held that the doctrine of *res judicata* must be applied to questions of jurisdiction arising in state courts involving the application of the Full Faith and Credit Clause where, under the law of the state in which the original judgment was rendered, such adjudications are not susceptible to collateral attack. . . .

Applying these principles to this case, we hold that the Massachusetts courts erred in permitting the Florida divorce decree to be subjected to attack on the ground that petitioner was not domiciled in Florida at the time the decree was entered. . . . It has not been contended that respondent was given less than a full opportunity to contest the issue of petitioner's domicile or any other issue relevant to the litigation. There is nothing to indicate that the Florida court would not have evaluated fairly and in good faith all relevant evidence submitted to it. . . . If respondent failed to take advantage of the opportunities afforded him, the responsibility is his own. . . .

It is urged . . . however, that because we are dealing with litigation involving the dissolution of the marital relation, a different result is demanded from that which might properly be reached if this case were concerned with other types of litigation. It is pointed out that under the Constitution the regulation and control of marital and family relationships are reserved to the States. . . .

But the recognition of the importance of a State's power to determine the incidents of basic social relationships into which its domiciliaries enter does not resolve the issues of this case. This is not a situation in which a State has merely sought to exert such power over a domiciliary. This is, rather, a case involving inconsistent assertions of power by courts of two States in the Federal Union and thus presents considerations which go beyond the interests of local policy, however vital. In resolving the issues here presented, we do not conceive it to be a part of our function to weigh the relative merits of the policies of Florida and Massachusetts with respect to divorce and related matters. . . .

It is one thing to recognize as permissible the judicial reexamination of findings of jurisdictional facts where such findings have been made by a court of a sister State which has entered a divorce decree in ex parte proceedings. It is quite another thing to hold that the vital rights and interests involved in divorce litigation may be held in suspense pending the scrutiny by courts of sister States of findings of jurisdictional fact made by a competent court in proceedings conducted in a manner consistent with the highest requirements of due process and in which the defendant has participated. . . . That vital interests are involved in divorce litigation indicates to us that it is a matter of greater rather than lesser importance that there should be a place to end such a litigation. And where a decree of divorce is rendered by a competent court under the circumstances of this case, the obligation of full faith and credit requires that such litigation should end in the courts of the State in which the judgment was rendered.

NOTES AND QUESTIONS

1. The practical effect of *Sherrer* is that a bilateral divorce — one in which both parties appear — cannot be attacked collaterally. Justice Frankfurter dissented vigorously, arguing that the Court's decision largely vitiates the domicile requirement, since it prevents attack on the decree where the defendant appeared and the court makes a finding of domicile, even though subsequent events plainly establish that the finding was erroneous. Is this problem more severe in divorce than in other kinds of litigation?

2. The Court emphasizes that principles of *res judicata* and full faith and credit require that sister states give a decree as much finality as the forum state provides. It follows that no state is required to give greater finality to a decree than does the rendering state and that challenges that would be available to the jurisdictional finding in the forum might be available in a collateral attack brought in a sister state. The requirement of full faith and credit thus depends on the rules of *res judicata* and collateral attack of the state granting the divorce.

This approach provides part of the answer to one of the questions left open by *Sherrer*: the position of third parties who might wish to challenge the validity of the divorce. Suppose that Mr. and Mrs. Lear marry in New York and have two children. The husband receives an ex parte Nevada divorce. He then marries a second wife, who is also a divorcee with three children and a great deal of money. The second wife dies intestate. Can the children of the second Mrs. Lear attack the validity of their stepfather's divorce on the grounds that he was not domiciled in Nevada, and argue therefore that his marriage to their mother was invalid because he was still married? In Johnson v. Muelberger, 340 U.S. 581 (1951), the Court held that where the law of the forum did not permit a child to collaterally attack her parent's divorce decree, the Full Faith and Credit Clause prevented such an attack in any other state. To the same effect is Cook v. Cook, 342 U.S. 126 (1951) (second husband cannot attack wife's divorce from her first husband). *See* Note, Stranger Attacks on Sister-State Decrees of Divorce, 24 U. Chi. L. Rev. 376 (1957).

3. When restrictive divorce laws were prevalent in the United States, some foreign countries — most notably Mexico — conducted a substantial business in matrimonial dissolutions. "Mail-order" Mexican divorces, which could be obtained without the presence of either party in Mexico at any time, were among the most notorious strategies, particularly favored in New York at one time. The validity of foreign divorces is not governed by the Full Faith and Credit Clause, which speaks only to the judicial acts of sister states. Rather, recognition is a matter of comity. Although there is no constitutional obligation to grant comity recognition to a foreign decree, it is regarded as a matter of international duty that should be discharged as long as the foreign court had jurisdiction of the subject matter and acceptance of that judgment will not offend domestic public policy. *See, e.g.*, Kugler v. Haitian Tours, Inc., 293 A.2d 706, 709 (N.J. Super. 1972).

Mexican mail-order divorces were never recognized by U.S. courts because of the complete absence of domiciliary connection. *E.g.*, State v. De Meo 118 A.2d 1 (N.J. 1955). However, in many cases one or both parties visited the foreign country for some time, secured a divorce, and returned shortly afterwards. The *Kugler* case, indeed, deals with an enterprising New Jersey corporation, Haitian Tours, Inc., which sold a travel package including three parts: transportation to and from Haiti, lodging and meals for one or two days at a hotel, and preparations for securing a Haitian divorce. The trips and divorces were for either one or two people; the cost of a unilateral divorce package was $1,125, while a package including a bilateral divorce cost an additional $150.

What issues are relevant to determining whether an American jurisdiction should recognize a unilateral foreign divorce? A bilateral divorce? *Compare* Rosenstiel v. Rosenstiel, 209 N.E.2d 709 (N.Y. 1965), *cert. denied*, 384 U.S. 971 (1966), *and* Hyde v. Hyde, 562 S.W.2d 194 (Tenn. 1978) (recognizing bilateral Dominican Republic divorce), *with* Warrender v. Warrender, 190 A.2d 684 (N.J. App. 1963) (bilateral Mexico divorce "absolutely void on its face"), *and* Everett v. Everett, 345 So. 2d 586 (La. App. 1977), *and* Cason v. Cason, 2001 WL 1830006 (Va. Cir. Ct. 2001) (Dominican divorce invalid because of lack of domicile).

The United States has not signed the United Nations treaty on the recognition of divorce and legal separation promulgated in 1975. 978 United Nations Treaty Series 400 (1975). Though the treaty is not binding in this country, its provisions may influence the granting of comity to foreign decrees. Jurisdiction under the treaty may be based on (1) habitual residence of the respondent, (2) habitual residence of the petitioner (a) for at least one year prior to filing or (b) if the forum is the last joint habitual residence of the spouses, (3) nationality of both spouses, (4) nationality of petitioner if (a) petitioner habitually resided in the jurisdiction or resided there for one year or (b) petitioner was a national of the country and petitioner was present at date of institution of proceedings and spouses last habitually resided together in a state whose law did not provide for divorce. *See* Stephen C. Glassman, Recognition and Enforcement: The Tangled International Divorce Web at Home, 9 Fam. Advoc. 4, 8 (Spring 1987); Adair Dyer, Abroad, 9 Fam. Advoc. 5, 11 (Spring 1987).

4. The doctrine of equitable estoppel may prevent attack on divorces that would otherwise be subject to collateral challenge. This doctrine prevents a party from challenging a decree that one has obtained or has led another to rely on. The most obvious case of estoppel arises when the party who obtained the divorce later claims that it is invalid. The defendant may also be estopped if he or she participated collusively in securing the divorce, perhaps through Haitian Tours, or if he or she acquiesces for a long time in the divorce, knowing of its jurisdictional defect. Acceptance of benefits associated with the divorce may have the same result. Third parties may also be subject to estoppel if they actively participate in securing a defective divorce for another. Analysis and rationalization of estoppel in this setting is one of the many contributions of Professor Clark's treatise on Domestic Relations. *See* 1 Homer H. Clark, Jr., Domestic Relations § 13.3, at 732-755 (2d ed. 1987).

5. In today's increasingly mobile society, does it make sense to base divorce jurisdiction on the domicile of one of the parties? Would you support instead a requirement that the court have *in personam* jurisdiction over both parties to grant a divorce? *See* Rhonda Wasserman, Divorce and Domicile: Time to Sever the Knot, 39 Wm. & Mary L. Rev. 1 (1997).

PROBLEMS

1. Harold and Wendy were domiciled in State A. Harold went to State B on vacation. While there he sought and was granted a divorce. The State B court erroneously found that he was domiciled there. Wendy in no way participated in the State B proceedings. Harold then returned to State A. Wendy collaterally attacked the State B divorce in a State A court. Harold claimed that State A must give the State B decree full faith and credit. Must it?

2. Hiram and Wilma were domiciled in State A. Hiram moved to State B to go to college. Six months later Hiram sued Wilma for a divorce in State B, relying on a State B statute that says that State B has jurisdiction to grant a divorce if either spouse has been resident there for six months. Wilma, who remained in State A, was served by mail, but she did not appear or participate in any way in the State B action. The State B court granted the divorce. Wilma collaterally attacked the decree in State A. Hiram claimed that State A must give the State B decree full faith and credit. Must it?

3. Hank and Willa were domiciled in State A. Hank went to State B and sued Willa for divorce, serving her in State B. Willa entered an appearance by her attorney, but the divorce was granted. Willa collaterally attacked the State B divorce in State A, claiming that State B lacked jurisdiction to grant the divorce since neither she nor Hank was domiciled there. What should Hank argue in response? What if Willa was personally served in State B but elected not to appear?

4. Hinkley and Wren were domiciled in State A. Hinkley went to Mexico and sued Wren for divorce, serving her in State A. Wren did not appear or participate in any way in the Mexican proceedings, but the divorce was granted anyway. Hinkley returned to State A. Wren, who remained in State A, remarried. Her new husband died, and Wren claimed the rights of a surviving spouse in his estate. Her new husband's executor rejected her claim on the basis that her divorce from Hinkley was not valid and that therefore she was not the surviving spouse of her "new husband." What are the arguments of Wren and the executor? If instead Wren claimed rights as Hinkley's surviving spouse, what arguments should the executor of Hinkley's estate make in opposition to Wren's claim?

C. DIVISIBLE DIVORCE

We have seen that jurisdiction to grant a divorce or legal separation is viewed, after *Williams I* and *Williams II*, as an *in rem* matter. The *res* is the marriage relationship itself, embodied in the domicile of one of the parties to the marriage. Accordingly, the state in which one of the parties is domiciled has jurisdiction to adjudicate the divorce action.

The *Williams* cases hold not only that the state of domicile of one party may adjudicate the marital status of its domiciliary but that the state's judgment, even if ex parte, is entitled to extraterritorial effect through the Full Faith and Credit Clause. However, the Supreme Court expressly reserved judgment regarding the extraterritorial effect of ex parte orders about the parties' financial interests. This matter was addressed in Estin v. Estin, 334 U.S. 541 (1948), and in the next case.

VANDERBILT V. VANDERBILT

354 U.S. 416 (1957)

BLACK, J. Cornelius Vanderbilt, Jr., petitioner, and Patricia Vanderbilt, respondent, were married in 1948. They separated in 1952 while living in California. The wife moved to New York, where she has resided since February 1953. In March of that year the husband filed suit for divorce in Nevada. This proceeding culminated, in June 1953, with a decree of final divorce which provided that both husband and wife were "freed and released from the bonds of matrimony and all the duties and obligations thereof. . . ."[2] The wife was not served with process in Nevada and did not appear before the divorce court.

In April 1954, Mrs. Vanderbilt instituted an action in a New York court praying for separation from petitioner and for alimony. The New York court did not have personal jurisdiction over him, but in order to satisfy his obligations, if any, to Mrs. Vanderbilt, it sequestered his property within the State. He appeared specially and, among other defenses to the action, contended that the Full Faith and Credit Clause of the United States Constitution compelled the New York court to treat the Nevada divorce as having ended the marriage and as having destroyed any duty of support which he owed the respondent. While the New York court found the Nevada decree valid and held that it had effectively dissolved the marriage, it nevertheless entered an order, under Section 1170-b of the New York Civil Practice Act, directing petitioner to make designated support payments to respondent. The New York Court of Appeals upheld the support order. Petitioner then applied to this Court for certiorari contending that Section 1170-b, as applied, is unconstitutional because it contravenes the Full Faith and Credit Clause.

In Estin v. Estin, 334 U.S. 541, this Court decided that a Nevada divorce court, which had no personal jurisdiction over the wife, had no power to terminate a husband's obligation to provide her support as required in a pre-existing New York separation decree. . . . Since the wife was not subject to its jurisdiction, the Nevada divorce court had no power to extinguish any right which she had under the law of New York to financial support from her husband. It has long been the constitutional rule that a court cannot adjudicate a personal claim or obligation unless it has jurisdiction over the person of the defendant. Here, the Nevada divorce court was as powerless to cut off the wife's support right as it would have been to order the husband to pay alimony if the wife had brought the divorce action and he had not been subject to the divorce court's jurisdiction. Therefore, the Nevada decree, to the extent it purported to affect the wife's right

---

2. It seems clear that in Nevada the effect of this decree was to put an end to the husband's duty to support the wife — provided, of course, that the Nevada courts had power to do this. Sweeney v. Sweeney, 42 Nev. 431, 438-439, 179 P. 638, 639-640; Herrick v. Herrick, 55 Nev. 59, 68, 25 P.2d 378, 380. See Estin v. Estin, 334 U.S. 541, 547.

to support, was void and the Full Faith and Credit Clause did not obligate New York to give it recognition. . . .

Affirmed.

(The dissenting opinion of Justice Frankfurter is omitted.)

NOTES AND QUESTIONS

1. Is the majority's primary concern the rights of the states or the due process interests of the parties?

2. Suppose New York law did *not* allow the wife to prosecute a suit for support if her marital status had been validly terminated. Would this mean that the wife could not pursue a right to spousal maintenance following a valid ex parte divorce in Nevada? Would such a rule be constitutional?

A Louisiana appellate court recently affirmed that divorce does not require minimum-contacts personal jurisdiction, even if it is possible that the decree will adversely affect the economic rights of the left-at-home spouse in another state, relying on the *Williams* line of cases. Watkins v. Watkins, 862 So. 2d 464 (La. App. 2003).

3. In Simons v. Miami Beach First National Bank, 381 U.S. 81 (1965), the Court indicated that there is at least one situation in which a spouse's economic interests can be affected by an ex parte divorce. The husband, who had lived with his wife in New York, went to Florida and secured an ex parte Florida divorce with constructive service. He continued to pay support to her under a New York judicial separation order until his death. After he died, his "widow" appeared in probate proceedings in Florida, claiming dower rights under Florida law. The respondent bank opposed the dower claim. The petitioner brought an action to set aside the divorce decree and to obtain a declaration that the divorce, even if valid with regard to her marital status, did not affect her claim to dower. The Florida courts dismissed her action. The Supreme Court affirmed, rejecting her argument that Florida could not extinguish her dower right without personal jurisdiction:

> Insofar as petitioner argues that since she was not subject to the jurisdiction of the Florida divorce court its decree could not extinguish any dower right existing under Florida law, Vanderbilt v. Vanderbilt, 354 U.S. 416, 418, the answer is that under Florida law no dower right survived the decree. The Supreme Court of Florida has said that dower rights in Florida property, being inchoate, are extinguished by a divorce decree predicated upon substituted or constructive service.
>
> It follows that the Florida courts transgressed no constitutional bounds in denying petitioner dower in her ex-husband's Florida estate.

The majority assumed that its decision is consistent with *Estin* and *Vanderbilt*. Is this because dower rights are in some way different from the kinds of rights the Court had previously protected? If dower is inchoate, why does that matter? For a consideration of this explanation, *see* Note, Divorce ex Parte Style, 33 U. Chi. L. Rev. 837 (1966).

If *Simons* is consistent with prior decisions, is it because the property interest asserted here arose under the law of the divorcing state rather than the nonparticipating spouse's domicile? What if New York law eliminated dower interests upon divorce?

Suppose that Florida had replaced dower with a forced spousal share upon death. Would that be extinguished as well by an ex parte divorce? If a forced share can be thus terminated, what about the wife's interest in property that she might receive through an "equitable distribution"? If the parties originally lived in and the wife still resides in a community property state, what about community property interests? What about Social Security benefits tied to marriage? Workers' compensation benefits?

4. The principle underlying *Estin* and *Vanderbilt*, that there are different jurisdictional bases for divorce and for support orders, is commonly called "divisible divorce." As you will see in the remainder of the chapter, the principle goes even further, as still different criteria are used to establish jurisdiction to decide property division and custody.

NOTE: PROPERTY DIVISION — JURISDICTION AND FULL FAITH AND CREDIT

As discussed earlier, only a court in the state in which real property is located has *in rem* jurisdiction to determine its ownership and thus to enter property division orders. The Supreme Court applied this principle in Fall v. Eastin, 215 U.S. 1 (1909), holding that a Washington divorce decree awarding real property in Nebraska to a wife was not entitled to full faith and credit. However, many courts today will recognize property division orders from courts in states in which the property is not located if the court validly asserted *in personam* jurisdiction over the parties. *E.g.*, Ivey v. Ivey, 439 A.2d 425 (Conn. 1981); Weesner v. Weesner, 95 N.W.2d 682 (Neb. 1959); McElreath v. McElreath, 345 S.W.2d 722 (Tex. 1961); Kane v. Kane, 577 P.2d 172 (1978), *aff'd*, 616 P.2d 780 (Wyo. 1980); Russo v. Russo, 714 A.2d 466 (Pa. Super. 1998).

A concomitant of the traditional rule is that a court in a state in which real property is located may constitutionally assert jurisdiction to divide the property even though the defendant has no other contact with the state. Homer H. Clark, Jr., Domestic Relations § 13.4 at 763-764, discussing Shaffer v. Heitner, 433 U.S. 186, 207-208 (1977); In re Ramsey's Marriage, 526 P.2d 319 (Colo. App. 1974); Harrod v. Harrod, 526 P.2d 666 (Colo. App. 1974); Hodge v. Hodge, 422 A.2d 280 (Conn. 1979); Gelkop v. Gelkop, 384 So. 2d 195 (Fla. App. 1980).

PROBLEMS

1. Hank and Winifred were domiciled in State A. Winifred moved to State B and established a domicile. She sued Hank for divorce in State B, serving him in State A. Hank did not appear or in any way participate in the State B proceedings. The State B court granted Winifred a divorce, ordered Hank to pay her $200 per month in spousal support, and found that Hank was not entitled to spousal support from Winifred. Winifred took the decree to State A and asked the State A court to enforce the order to Hank to pay her support. Hank cross-claimed for spousal support from Winifred. Winifred argued that the State A court must give full faith

and credit to the State B decree. What should Hank argue in response? Who wins and why?

2. Homer and Wanda were domiciled in State A. Homer moved to State B and established his domicile there. He sued Wanda for divorce in State B, serving her in State A. Wanda did not appear or in any way participate in the State B proceedings. The State B court granted Homer a divorce. The decree was silent on the issue of spousal support. Homer returned to State A, and Wanda sued him in State A for spousal support, serving him personally in State A. Under the law of State A, if a divorce decree makes no provision for spousal support, a court cannot later grant it. How should the court rule on Wanda's motion for support?

3. Holden and Wilma were divorced in State A, where they are both domiciled. The State A court awarded their vacation home, located in State B, to Wilma. After the order was entered, Holden did nothing to comply with the decree, and the State B title continued to show that Holden and Wilma owned the vacation home as joint tenants with right of survivorship. Wilma died. The executor of her estate claimed that Wilma owned the State B vacation home, relying on the divorce decree. Holden claimed that it is his because he is the surviving joint tenant. If this dispute were litigated in State B, would the State B court have to give full faith and credit to the State A order?

D. JURISDICTION AND FULL FAITH AND CREDIT FOR SUPPORT DUTIES

Estin and *Vanderbilt* confirm that *in personam* jurisdiction is required for orders that establish parties' rights and duties regarding spousal and child support. In other words, jurisdiction to decide these rights must satisfy the minimum-contacts test of International Shoe Co. v. Washington, 326 U.S. 310, 316 (1945), and its successors. In Burnham v. Superior Court, 495 U.S. 604 (1990), the Supreme Court addressed the constitutional sufficiency of "tag jurisdiction" — that is, jurisdiction asserted over a defendant who is served while physically present in the state but has no other substantial connection to the state. Burnham, a New Jersey resident, was served with process in a suit for divorce and determination of support and property issues while he was in California to take care of business and visit his children. The Court unanimously agreed that the defendant was subject to California's jurisdiction, although the justices differed significantly as to the theory supporting jurisdiction. For analyses of *Burnham* and its theoretical aspects, *see* The Future of Personal Jurisdiction: A Symposium on Burnham v. Superior Court, 22 Rutgers L.J. No. 3 (1991). The next case considers the extent to which long-arm statutes may constitutionally be used to assert jurisdiction over obligors or obligees who are not physically present in the jurisdiction.

Estin and *Vanderbilt* were, of course, cases concerning interstate enforceability of support orders under the Full Faith and Credit Clause, but since the lower courts' assertion of jurisdiction violated due process, the cases do not actually address when courts must recognize and enforce support orders from other jurisdictions. The second part of this section addresses these issues.

1. Long-Arm Jurisdiction in Support Cases

KULKO V. SUPERIOR COURT

436 U.S. 84 (1978)

[Ezra and Sharon Kulko, then both New York domiciliaries, were married in 1959 in California during Ezra's three-day stopover while he was en route to overseas military duty. After the wedding, Sharon returned to New York, as did Ezra following his tour of duty. In 1961 and 1962 a son and daughter were born in New York. The family lived together in New York until March 1972, when Ezra and Sharon separated. Sharon moved to California. The spouses entered into a separation agreement in New York, which provided that the children would live with Ezra during the school year and visit Sharon in California during specified vacations. Ezra agreed to pay Sharon $3,000 per year in child support for the periods when the children were with her. Sharon obtained a divorce in Haiti, which incorporated the terms of the separation agreement, and returned to California. In December 1973 the daughter asked to move to California to live with her mother. Ezra consented. Without Ezra's consent Sharon arranged for the son to join her in California about two years later. Sharon then sued Ezra in California to establish the Haitian divorce decree as a California judgment, to modify the judgment to award her full custody of the children, and to increase Ezra's child support obligation. Ezra, resisting the claim for increased support, appeared specially, claiming that he lacked sufficient "minimum contacts" with California under International Shoe Co. v. Washington, 326 U.S. 310, 316 (1945), to warrant the state's assertion of personal jurisdiction over him. The California Supreme Court upheld lower-court determinations adverse to Ezra.]

MARSHALL, J. The issue before us is whether, in this action for child support, the California state courts may exercise *in personam* jurisdiction over a nonresident, nondomiciliary parent of minor children domiciled within the State. For reasons set forth below, we hold that the exercise of such jurisdiction would violate the Due Process Clause of the Fourteenth Amendment. . . .

The Due Process Clause of the Fourteenth Amendment operates as a limitation on the jurisdiction of state courts to enter judgments affecting rights or interests of nonresident defendants. *See* Shaffer v. Heitner, 433 U.S. 186, 198-200 (1977). It has long been the rule that a valid judgment imposing a personal obligation or duty in favor of the plaintiff may be entered only by a court having jurisdiction over the person of the defendant. Pennoyer v. Neff, 95 U.S. 714, 732-733 (1878); International Shoe Co. v. Washington, 326 U.S., at 316. The existence of personal jurisdiction, in turn, depends upon the presence of reasonable notice to the defendant that an action has been brought, Mullane v. Central Hanover Trust Co., 339 U.S. 306, 313-314 (1950), and a sufficient connection between the defendant and the forum State to make it fair to require defense of the action in the forum. In this case, appellant does not dispute the adequacy of the notice that he received, but contends that his connection with the State of California is too attenuated, under the standards implicit in the Due Process Clause of the Constitution, to justify imposing upon him the burden and inconvenience of defense in California.

The parties are in agreement that the constitutional standard for determining whether the State may enter a binding judgment against appellant here is that set forth in this Court's opinion in International Shoe Co. v. Washington, supra: that a defendant "have certain minimum contacts with [the forum State] such that the maintenance of the suit does not offend 'traditional notions of fair play and substantial justice.'" . . . [A]n essential criterion in all cases is whether the "quality and nature" of the defendant's activity is such that it is "reasonable" and "fair" to require him to conduct his defense in that State. . . .

In reaching its result, the California Supreme Court did not rely on appellant's glancing presence in the State some 13 years before the events that led to this controversy, nor could it have. . . . To hold such temporary visits to a State a basis for the assertion of *in personam* jurisdiction over unrelated actions arising in the future would make a mockery of the limitations on state jurisdiction imposed by the Fourteenth Amendment. Nor did the California court rely on the fact that appellant was actually married in California on one of his two brief visits. We agree that where two New York domiciliaries, for reasons of convenience, marry in the State of California and thereafter spend their entire married life in New York, the fact of their California marriage by itself cannot support a California court's exercise of jurisdiction over a spouse who remains a New York resident in an action relating to child support.

Finally, in holding that personal jurisdiction existed, the court below carefully disclaimed reliance on the fact that appellant had agreed at the time of separation to allow his children to live with their mother three months a year and that he had sent them to California each year pursuant to this agreement. . . . [T]o find personal jurisdiction in a State on this basis, merely because the mother was residing there, would discourage parents from entering into reasonable visitation agreements. Moreover, it could arbitrarily subject one parent to suit in any State of the Union where the other parent chose to spend time while having custody of their offspring pursuant to a separation agreement. As we have emphasized: "The unilateral activity of those who claim some relationship with a nonresident defendant cannot satisfy the requirement of contact with the forum State. . . . [It] is essential in each case that there be some act by which the defendant purposefully avails [him]self of the privilege of conducting activities within the forum State. . . ." Hanson v. Denckla.

The "purposeful act" that the California Supreme Court believed did warrant the exercise of personal jurisdiction over appellant in California was his "actively and fully [consenting] to Ilsa living in California for the school year . . . and . . . [sending] her to California for that purpose." We cannot accept the proposition that appellant's acquiescence in Ilsa's desire to live with her mother conferred jurisdiction over appellant in the California courts in this action. A father who agrees, in the interests of family harmony and his children's preferences, to allow them to spend more time in California than was required under a separation agreement can hardly be said to have "purposefully availed himself" of the "benefits and protections" of California's laws.

Nor can we agree with the assertion of the court below that the exercise of *in personam* jurisdiction here was warranted by the financial benefit appellant derived from his daughter's presence in California for nine months of the year. This argument rests on the premise that, while appellant's liability for support payments remained unchanged, his yearly expenses for supporting the child in New York decreased. But this circumstance, even if true, does not support California's assertion of jurisdiction here. Any diminution in appellant's household costs resulted, not from the child's presence in California, but rather from her absence from appellant's home. . . .

The circumstances in this case clearly render "unreasonable" California's assertion of personal jurisdiction. . . . The cause of action herein asserted arises, not from the defendant's commercial transactions in interstate commerce, but rather from his personal, domestic relations. It thus cannot be said that appellant has sought a commercial benefit from solicitation of business from a resident of California that could reasonably render him liable to suit in state court; appellant's activities cannot fairly be analogized to an insurer's sending an insurance contract and premium notices into the State to an insured resident of the State. Furthermore, the controversy between the parties arises from a separation that occurred in the State of New York; appellee Horn seeks modification of a contract that was negotiated in New York and that she flew to New York to sign. As in Hanson v. Denckla, the instant action involves an agreement that was entered into with virtually no connection with the forum State.

Finally, basic considerations of fairness point decisively in favor of appellant's State of domicile as the proper forum for adjudication of this case, whatever the merits of appellee's underlying claim. It is appellant who has remained in the State of the marital domicile, whereas it is appellee who has moved across the continent. . . . Appellant has at all times resided in New York State, and, until the separation and appellee's move to California, his entire family resided there as well. As noted above, appellant did no more than acquiesce in the stated preference of one of his children to live with her mother in California. This single act is surely not one that a reasonable parent would expect to result in the substantial financial burden and personal strain of litigating a child-support suit in a forum 3,000 miles away, and we therefore see no basis on which it can be said that appellant could reasonably have anticipated being "haled before a [California] court." To make jurisdiction in a case such as this turn on whether appellant bought his daughter her ticket or instead unsuccessfully sought to prevent her departure would impose an unreasonable burden on family relations, and one wholly unjustified by the "quality and nature" of appellant's activities in or relating to the State of California.

In seeking to justify the burden that would be imposed on appellant were the exercise of *in personam* jurisdiction in California sustained, appellee argues that California has substantial interests in protecting the welfare of its minor residents and in promoting to the fullest extent possible a healthy and supportive family environment in which the children of the State are to be raised. These interests are unquestionably important. . . .

California's legitimate interest in ensuring the support of children resident in California without unduly disrupting the children's lives, moreover, is already being served by the State's participation in the Revised Uniform Reciprocal

Enforcement of Support Act of 1968. This statute provides a mechanism for communication between court systems in different States, in order to facilitate the procurement and enforcement of child-support decrees where the dependent children reside in a State that cannot obtain personal jurisdiction over the defendant. California's version of the Act essentially permits a California resident claiming support from a nonresident to file a petition in California and have its merits adjudicated in the State of the alleged obligor's residence, without either party's having to leave his or her own State. New York State is a signatory to a similar Act. Thus, not only may plaintiff-appellee here vindicate her claimed right to additional child support from her former husband in a New York court . . . but also the Uniform Acts will facilitate both her prosecution of a claim for additional support and collection of any support payments found to be owed by appellant. . . .

Reversed.

NOTES AND QUESTIONS

1. One standard for determining the permissible extent of state court jurisdiction asks whether the defendant purposely availed himself or herself of the protection and benefits of California law. Didn't the defendant in *Kulko* do so? The Court seems to distinguish between commercial undertakings (for example, where an insurance company sends a policy to a California insured) and the father's sending his daughter to California. Doesn't that distinction mean that commercial agreements will be more easily enforced than child support obligations?

2. The Court also addresses the question of whether it is fair to require Kulko to participate in a California adjudication. Is fairness a categorical question? For example, is asking a defendant to participate in a proceeding in another state with which he or she has minimal contacts always unfair? Suppose in *Kulko* that the wife and children were living in New Jersey. What factors influence the meaning of "fairness" and "inconvenience"? *See* Terry S. Kogan, Geography and Due Process: The Social Meaning of Adjudicative Jurisdiction, 22 Rutgers L.J. 627 (1991).

3. The Uniform Interstate Family Support Act (UIFSA),[3] which all states have adopted, deals with all aspects of interstate support orders, including personal jurisdiction. Section 201 is a long-arm statute providing that a court may exercise personal jurisdiction over a nonresident to establish, enforce, or modify a support order or to determine parentage if

   (1) the individual is personally served with [citation, summons, notice] within this State;

   (2) the individual submits to the jurisdiction of this State by consent, by entering a general appearance, or by filing a responsive document having the effect of waiving any contest to personal jurisdiction;

---

3. The UIFSA, with unofficial annotations by one of the reporters, John J. Sampson, is printed at 27 Fam. L.Q. 93 et seq. For a history and full analysis of the act *see* John J. Sampson & Paul M. Kurtz, UIFSA: An Interstate Support Act for the 21st Century, 27 Fam. L.Q. 85 (1993).

(3) the individual resided with the child in this State;

(4) the individual resided in this State and provided prenatal expenses or support for the child;

(5) the child resides in this State as a result of the acts or directives of the individual;

(6) the individual engaged in sexual intercourse in this State and the child may have been conceived by that act of intercourse;

(7) the individual asserted parentage in the [putative father registry] maintained in this State by the [appropriate agency]; or

(8) there is any other basis consistent with the constitutions of this State and the United States for the exercise of personal jurisdiction.

Is this statute constitutional under *Kulko*? UIFSA also creates special procedures that a court may use to invoke the assistance of courts in other states to obtain evidence and discovery in the other states. UIFSA §§ 316, 318.

4. Statutes and case law in many states provide that a court that validly asserts personal jurisdiction to determine a person's support duties has continuing jurisdiction for purposes of modification, even after the person has moved from the state. *See* Annot., E. H. Schopler, Necessity of Personal Service Within State upon Nonresident Spouse as Prerequisite of Court's Power to Modify Its Decree as to Alimony or Child Support in Matrimonial Action, 62 A.L.R.2d 544, 546. What are the outer constitutional limits on such an assertion of jurisdiction? A number of courts have upheld claims of continuing jurisdiction even after *both* parties have moved away. *Compare* the continuing-jurisdiction provisions of UIFSA, which are discussed in the next section.

PROBLEMS

1. Harley and Wendy were married in New York, and their children were born there. After 15 years of marriage, they separated, and Harley moved to California. Wendy brought a divorce action 18 months later, seeking child support. Would New York have jurisdiction to order child support under UIFSA? Would it be constitutional for New York to assert this jurisdiction? What if it were five years later?

2. Hudson and Wanda were married and had two children in California. Ten years later they moved to New York, where they lived for three months before moving overseas. They lived in Mali for three years, and then Wanda returned to California with the children. Could California assert jurisdiction under UIFSA to determine Hudson's child support obligation? If Wanda and the children returned to New York instead, would New York have jurisdiction under UIFSA over Hudson to decide child support?

2. Interstate Modification and Enforcement of Support

Sharon Horn could have pursued her action for child support against Ezra Kulko by traveling to New York and filing suit there. For many people, though, the costs of such a suit would be prohibitive. Further, even if a New York court had ordered Ezra to pay child support, if he refused to pay, Sharon might have had to return to New York or at least retain New York counsel to enforce the order.

If Ezra moved to a third state and refused to pay, Sharon would have had still more difficulties. Besides the practical ones, under traditional legal principles the third state might not have recognized her New York order because states did not have to give full faith and credit to modifiable support orders. Sistare v. Sistare, 218 U.S. 1 (1910); Barber v. Barber, 62 U.S. (21 How.) 582 (1858). While other states might have enforced nonfinal orders as a matter of comity, the practical difficulties of interstate enforcement of support remained. Worthley v. Worthley, 283 P.2d 19 (Cal. 1955); Restatement 2d of Conflicts § 109 (1971). Moreover, due process requires that obligors be given an opportunity to present defenses and arguments for modification in such cases. Griffin v. Griffin, 327 U.S. 220 (1946). The Uniform Reciprocal Enforcement of Support Act (URESA), referred to in *Kulko*, was intended to solve the practical and legal problems of interstate support enforcement. Most American jurisdictions adopted one version or another of the Act, but state law was never uniform because of inconsistencies in the versions adopted by the various states.

To provide a truly uniform set of laws and to resolve ambiguities created by URESA, the Commissioners on Uniform State Laws in 1992 proposed a replacement, the Uniform Interstate Family Support Act (UIFSA). Congress has required that all states enact UIFSA with all subsequent amendments and without modifications. 42 U.S.C. § 666(f). The text of the UIFSA with the 2001 amendments is available online at *http://www.law.upenn.edu/bll/ulc/ulc_frame.htm*. The 1996 version of UIFSA has been adopted in every state, the District of Columbia, Puerto Rico and the U.S. Virgin Islands. The 2001 amendments have been enacted in California, Colorado, Illinois, Maine, Mississippi, Nebraska, Oklahoma, Texas, Utah, Washington, and West Virginia. In 2004 it was introduced into the legislatures of Arizona and Kansas. A Few Facts About the Uniform Interstate Family Support Act (2001), *http://www.nccusl.org/Update/uniformact_factsheets/uniformacts-fs-uifsa.asp* (last visited July 29, 2004).

To complement UIFSA, Congress enacted the Full Faith and Credit for Child Support Orders Act (FFCCSOA), 28 U.S.C. § 1738B, which implements the Full Faith and Credit Clause and requires states to recognize, enforce, and not modify child support orders from other states. Its principles track those of UIFSA.

UIFSA applies to orders to establish, modify, or enforce child or spousal support, including income withholding, and to proceedings to determine parentage. UIFSA § 301. Its fundamental concept is simple: Only one state at a time may exercise jurisdiction to determine the amount of support owed, and all other states must enforce without modifying a support order that was issued by the state exercising jurisdiction consistent with the act. UIFSA §§ 205, 603. Under UIFSA a support order issued in one state may be enforced in other states through state agency administrative processes, which obligees can invoke personally without having to go through their home state agencies. Interstate judicial enforcement is also governed by the act and is initiated by registering a support order from one state in the state where enforcement is sought. UIFSA §§ 601-608. Procedures for contesting the validity or enforceability of a registered order are provided in UIFSA §§ 605-607. A registered order continues to be the order of the issuing state but can be enforced in the same way that an order from a court in the registering state would be enforced. A party seeking to modify an order from one state in the court of another must register it and petition to modify it, but the court in the second state may assert jurisdiction to modify only if the conditions of UIFSA §611 are satisfied. UIFSA §§ 609, 610. If these conditions are not satisfied, the court does not have jurisdiction to modify and may only enforce the order. The next case discusses these UIFSA sections and considers one potentially complex issue, the difference between orders that modify prior support orders and orders that enforce such prior orders.

PHILIPP V. STAHL

781 A.2d 1065 (N.J. Super. A.D. 2001)

LESEMANN, J.A.D. The parties in this Family Part case were married in 1975, divorced in Georgia on April 23, 1993, and seem to have spent much of their time since the divorce battling each other, first in the courts of Georgia and thereafter in the courts of New Jersey. The present appeal stems from an application of the plaintiff wife to require her ex-husband to contribute to their daughter's college expenses at Princeton and for additional miscellaneous relief. The trial court held that the Uniform Interstate Family Support Act (UIFSA), N.J.S.A. 2A:4-30.65 to -30.123, placed "exclusive jurisdiction" in the courts of the state that had issued the original support order (Georgia), and thus this state had no jurisdiction to act. . . .

* * *

The jurisdictional provisions of UIFSA which govern this case are set out in four subsections of N.J.S.A. 2A:4-30.72. Subsection a provides that, unless all parties agree otherwise, if a court of this state has issued "a support order," then that court has "continuing, exclusive jurisdiction over a child support order" so long as either the obligor or obligee under the order, or "the child for whose benefit the support order is issued" continues to reside in this state. Subsection b, however, provides that a court of this state which has issued a child support order "may not exercise its continuing jurisdiction to modify the order if the order has been modified by a tribunal of another state pursuant to this act or a law substantially similar to this act."

Subsection c seems to be essentially a restatement of subsection b. It says that if a "child support order" issued by this state is "modified by a tribunal of another state pursuant to this act or a law substantially similar to this act," the New Jersey court "loses its continuing, exclusive jurisdiction with regard to prospective enforcement of the order issued in this State. . . ." Finally, subsection d directs that a court of this state "shall recognize the continuing, exclusive jurisdiction of a tribunal of another state which has [already] issued a child support order pursuant to this act. . . ."

The anomaly in the statute, and the seeming self-contradiction in its terminology, stems from its direction that so long as a support order issued by one state is in effect, a second state shall not also issue a support order in that same case. However, the statute then contains a description of what is to happen if such a second state does issue a support order: the order of the second state replaces that of the first, and it is the second state not the first which retains "exclusive jurisdiction."

If the New Jersey court has issued one or more orders that "modified" the original Georgia "support order" (embodied in its judgment of divorce), then Georgia lost the "continuing, exclusive jurisdiction" which it once had regarding support matters, and that "continuing, exclusive jurisdiction" is now vested in New Jersey. Plaintiff claims there have been at least three such New Jersey orders and that jurisdiction to decide the support issue she now raises rests here. We agree.

The facts of the case, as they relate to the jurisdictional issue on appeal, are not in dispute. The Georgia divorce decree was issued on April 23, 1993. . . . Less than six months after entry of the divorce judgment, the plaintiff wife decided to move, with the children, to New Jersey. . . .

In March 1994, plaintiff moved in the Family Part of the New Jersey Superior Court for an order modifying visitation. . . . The order . . . changed a portion of the support provisions in the Georgia judgment. It modified the requirement that called on the husband to pay for all visitation costs (which had been entered while the wife still lived in Georgia), and provided instead that the defendant was to pay sixty percent and the plaintiff forty percent of those expenses. The order further stated that, except as thereby changed, all provisions of the divorce judgment were to remain in full force and effect. However, it then included another significant provision, specifying that "[a]ny modifications, supplementations, or enforcement of this Order or of the 1992 judgment shall go forward before this court."

On April 25, 1995, the New Jersey Family Part entered a second order which had a significant effect on support payments. In addition to enforcement provisions, directives respecting reimbursement for past due amounts, and a provision for wage garnishment in the future, the court changed the prior order which had called for payment of $500 per month for each of the two children, to provide for one unallocated payment of $1,000 per month for the two children. That modification was not simply a change in verbiage. As plaintiff correctly argues, while on its face the Georgia judgment would terminate payments for the older child when she became emancipated, and thus defendant's total child support payments would be reduced to $500 per month, the New Jersey child support guidelines provide otherwise. Application of those guidelines would mean that when the older child became emancipated, defendant's payments would be reduced to $688 per month rather than to $500 per month. In addition, this order contained a provision comparable to that quoted above from the March 1999 order, stating that "the Chancery Division of this court shall retain jurisdiction over the subject matters addressed herein."

The third New Jersey order which affected support payments was entered on August 18, 1999. That order, entered by consent of the parties, provided that custody of Eric would pass to defendant in Georgia. However, it also provided that defendant would maintain health insurance for Eric and would be "responsible for all [his] uninsured health care expenses, including but not limited to dental expenses. . . ." It thus relieved plaintiff of the obligation to pay one-half of

Eric's un-reimbursed medical expenses and also relieved her of the obligation to maintain dental insurance for Eric. The order further provided that, except as related to the medical expense and insurance issue, all provisions of the 1992 judgment remained in effect, and it contained a provision similar to that set out in the two other New Jersey orders described above. It said that "Any modifications, supplementation, or enforcement of any [prior order] or of this Order shall go forward before this Court."

. . . [T]he three orders just discussed do, clearly and unequivocally, modify prior support obligations. In the face of those orders, we are satisfied that the UIFSA provisions quoted above not only justify, but indeed require, that further such applications be handled in this state.

Further, it seems clear that the parties at least impliedly understood and acknowledged that all further proceedings in this case — concerning support as well as custody and visitation — would be held in New Jersey. The provisions in the three quoted orders all so state. . . . .

* * *

Reversed and remanded for further proceedings consistent with this opinion. We do not retain jurisdiction.

WECKER, J.A.D., concurring in part, dissenting in part. . . . I disagree with the majority's interpretation and application of the Uniform Interstate Family Support Act (UIFSA or "the Act"), which leads my colleagues to conclude that the New Jersey Family Part has jurisdiction over plaintiff's application for an order requiring defendant to contribute to college costs for their oldest child, Julia, and to determine child support for their younger child, Eric. I therefore dissent from Part I of the majority's opinion and would affirm the Family Part order dismissing plaintiff's application for lack of subject matter jurisdiction.

* * *

I will examine the operative provisions of the New Jersey UIFSA concerning continuing, exclusive jurisdiction over modification of child support orders, which are virtually identical in the New Jersey and Georgia enactments. Each state's statute thus mirrors that of the other. The concept of "continuing, exclusive jurisdiction" to avoid or resolve jurisdictional disputes appears to have been drawn directly from the FFCCSOA,[4] first enacted in 1994. To understand

---

4. The FFCCSOA provides, much like N.J.S.A. 2A:4-30.72a(2) and b, the conditions under which a state court retains its continuing, exclusive jurisdiction:

A court of a State that has made a child support order consistently with this section has continuing, exclusive jurisdiction over the order if the State is the child's State or the residence of any individual contestant unless the court of another State, acting in accordance with subsections (e) and (f), has made a modification of the order.

UIFSA's use of the concept of continuing exclusive jurisdiction, I look first to N.J.S.A. 2A:4-30.72a and O.C.G.A. § 19-11-114a, which provide:

> A tribunal [of this State] issuing a support order consistent with the law of [this State] has continuing, exclusive jurisdiction over a child support order:
>
> (1) as long as [this State] remains the residence of the obligor, the individual obligee, or the child for whose benefit the support order is issued; or
>
> (2) until all of the parties who are individuals have filed written consents with the tribunal of [this State] for a tribunal of another state to modify the order and assume continuing, exclusive jurisdiction.

Next I look to N.J.S.A. 2A:4-30.72d and O.C.G.A. § 19-11-114d, which require that:

> A tribunal [of this State] shall recognize the continuing, exclusive jurisdiction of a tribunal of another state which has issued a child support order pursuant to this [act] or a law substantially similar to this [act].

Thus under the two states' similar provisions, Georgia has continuing exclusive jurisdiction over its child support order because defendant remains a Georgia resident and because the parties have not filed written consents for the New Jersey court to assume jurisdiction. New Jersey is bound to recognize Georgia's jurisdiction. The motion judge obviously based his decision upon these two provisions of UIFSA.

But we must also look at the limitations UIFSA places upon a state's continuing, exclusive jurisdiction, as set forth in N.J.S.A. 2A:4-30.72b and O.C.G.A. § 19-11-114b and relied upon by the majority:

> A tribunal [of this State] issuing a child support order consistent with the law [of this State] may not exercise its continuing jurisdiction to modify the order if the order has been modified by a tribunal of another state pursuant to this [act] or a law substantially similar to this [act].

Thus Georgia, as a state with continuing, exclusive jurisdiction, can lose its power to "exercise its continuing jurisdiction to modify" its child support order if the New Jersey tribunal issues an order modifying child support pursuant to UIFSA or a "substantially similar" law. The majority concludes that the New Jersey tribunal has done just that. I disagree.

---

28 U.S.C.A. § 1738B(d).

Subsection (e) of the federal law conditions the authority of a state court to "modify a child support order issued by a court of another State" upon either (A) both parties and the child having left the original state, or (B) both parties filing their written consent to the second state's assumption of continuing, exclusive jurisdiction over modification. Subsection (f) is virtually identical to N.J.S.A. 2A:4-30.74 in setting forth rules for determining which of multiple child support orders is to be recognized for purposes of establishing continuing, exclusive jurisdiction.

The questions presented by this appeal are whether a New Jersey court has issued an order modifying child support, and if so, whether it has done so consistent with UIFSA or a similar law, such as the FFCCSOA or the now repealed RURESA. . . .

* * *

The majority cites three subsequent New Jersey orders as support orders[5] which purportedly modify the child support provisions of the Georgia divorce judgment, thereby depriving Georgia of the power to exercise its own continuing jurisdiction and establishing "continuing, exclusive jurisdiction over a child support order" in New Jersey. But none of those three New Jersey orders actually modifies the original child support provisions incorporated in the Georgia judgment; each enforces the Georgia judgment, as can be seen by close examination of the orders.

The first order cited by the majority was entered on April 21, 1994, in response to plaintiff's motion to set visitation, and over defendant's objection to New Jersey's jurisdiction. . . . The order concludes by allocating the cost of air travel between New Jersey and Georgia for the children's visits with their father, a necessary corollary to New Jersey's custody and visitation jurisdiction under the Uniform Child Custody Jurisdiction Act. The final operative provision of that order, paragraph 11, says:

> Except as otherwise expressly set forth herein, the 1992 [Georgia] Judgment remains in full force and effect. Any modifications, supplementations, or enforcement of this Order or of the 1992 Judgment shall go forward before this Court.

The second order cited by the majority was entered by the same judge on April 25, 1995, in response to defendant's motion for visitation and plaintiff's cross-motion for arrears and future support. The divorce judgment incorporated the parties' agreement for defendant to pay $500 per month for each of their two children, a total of $1,000 per month as child support. The April 1995 order continued that support

> in the full amount of $1,000 per month payable by a wage execution through the Department of Probation of the State of New Jersey, which shall contact the appropriate department in Georgia to secure the full and speedy effectuation of this provision.

I do not read that provision, continuing the same "full amount" of child support, but adding the interstate collection mechanism then available under RURESA (and now under UIFSA), as a modification of the prior support order. Providing for collection and payment through the New Jersey Probation

_____

5. UIFSA, enacted in New Jersey in 1998, defines a "support order" to include an order "which provides for monetary support, health care coverage, arrearages, or reimbursement, and may include related costs and fees, interest, income withholding, attorney's fees, and other relief."

Department was obviously incidental to enforcement of the Georgia child support order and consistent with the Georgia order allowing plaintiff to move with the children to New Jersey.

The April 1995 order also enforces the existing child support provision of the Georgia judgment, providing for various past due payments owing between the parties, including private school expenses, and requiring a Qualified Medical Child Support Order to be entered pursuant to ERISA. Such an order was entered the same day. The final operative paragraph of the April 1995 order provides: "[T]he Chancery Division of this Court shall retain jurisdiction over the subject matters addressed herein." The "subject matters addressed herein" are the various existing child support provisions enforced or effectuated by the order.

In my view, the majority engages in unwarranted and unsupported speculation by adopting plaintiff's theoretical argument that the April 1995 order should be deemed to modify the Georgia judgment because after the older child is emancipated, child support for the younger child under the New Jersey Child Support Guidelines would be more than the $500 per child provided by the original Georgia order. The assumption that New Jersey law and jurisdiction would then apply assumes the very conclusion that is disputed in this appeal, that is, that New Jersey will exercise jurisdiction and apply New Jersey law to modify the Georgia order. Moreover, in light of the younger child's 1999 return to the physical custody of his father in Georgia, and defendant's representation that he does not seek child support from plaintiff in New Jersey, such speculation has no basis in fact.

The third order cited by the majority is the consent order entered on August 18, 1999, by which the parties agreed that physical custody of Eric would be transferred from plaintiff in New Jersey to defendant in Georgia. Four and one-half pages of that five and one-half page order provide in great detail for plaintiff's visitation with Eric, both in New Jersey and Georgia, including plaintiff's access to Eric's school and extracurricular activities in Georgia, the child's access to a therapist in New Jersey, and for the child's religious observances to be supported by defendant. The only modification to any aspect of the Georgia child support provisions may be found in paragraph 12 of the August 1999 order, which provides for defendant to pay all unreimbursed medical and dental expenses for Eric instead of sharing such expenses equally with plaintiff as originally provided. Significantly, the order then continues:

> Except as set forth in paragraph 12, this order is not intended to address any financial issue, and both parties reserve all rights and arguments regarding any financial issue relating to either of the children's expenses which shall be retroactive to the applicable date, e.g., the date the expense was incurred.

The 1999 order expressly preserves both the 1992 Georgia judgment and the subsequent Georgia and New Jersey custody and visitation orders and then provides that "[a]ny modifications, supplementation, or enforcement of any of these Orders or of this Order shall go forward before this Court."

The majority concludes that these "three orders, . . . clearly and unequivocally, modify prior support obligations." It is neither clear nor unequivocal that they do so. As the motion judge who dismissed plaintiff's application to modify child support for lack of subject matter jurisdiction concluded, the Georgia support order has "never been changed, altered or challenged" — the only minor modification having been in the 1999 order for defendant to pay all rather than half of the children's unreimbursed medical expenses.

* * *

With respect to a second state's authority to modify a child support order, . . . [t]he FFCCSOA expressly requires, as a condition of any state court's authority to modify a child support order issued by a court of another state, that either both parties and the child have left the first state, or that both parties have filed a written consent to the second state's jurisdiction. 28 U.S.C.A. § 1738B(e)(2). Neither condition is satisfied in this case.

If UIFSA does not provide an unambiguous resolution of jurisdiction to modify the Georgia child support order in this case, the FFCCSOA should control. And if the concluding paragraphs of the 1994, 1995, or 1999 New Jersey orders are deemed to declare New Jersey's jurisdiction to modify child support, such declarations would have been beyond the court's limited modification jurisdiction under the FFCCSOA or UIFSA. Commentators have interpreted both UIFSA and FFCCSOA as providing very limited jurisdiction for one state to modify a child support order issued by another state. *E.g.*, Patricia W. Hatamyar, Interstate Establishment, Enforcement, and Modification of Child Support Orders, 25 Okla. City U. L. Rev. 511, 515-16 (2000); Angela R. Arkin, Jurisdiction and the Interstate Child: How to Avoid the Avoidable Complications, 26 Colo. Law. 75, 76 (1997); Joel R. Brandes & Carole L. Weidman, Full Faith and Credit to Child Support Orders, 214 N.Y. L.J. 36 (1995). I therefore read the concluding paragraphs of the 1994, 1995, and 1999 orders more narrowly, consistent with both statutes, to hold that the New Jersey court will continue to enforce the Georgia judgment and to address custody and visitation issues, including the costs associated with interstate visitation.

* * *

. . . Thus the Georgia court has not lost the power to exercise its continuing, exclusive jurisdiction over child support. . . . There being no question that the Georgia divorce judgment included the first child support order, thereby establishing Georgia's continuing, exclusive jurisdiction, the New Jersey tribunal must recognize Georgia's jurisdiction.

Moreover, there is no evidence in the record that plaintiff has ever sought to register the Georgia judgment in New Jersey in accordance with N.J.S.A. 2A:4-30.112,[6] which appears to require registration as a pre-requisite to seeking

---

6. N.J.S.A. 2A:4-30.112 provides:

A party or support enforcement agency seeking to modify, or to modify and enforce, a child support order issued in another state *shall register* that order in this State in the same manner provided in sections 40 through 43 of this act if the order has not been registered. A complaint, petition or comparable pleading for modification may be filed at the same time as a request for registration, or later. The pleading must specify the grounds for modification. (Emphasis added.)

modification, but not enforcement, of a child support order. *Compare* N.J.S.A. 2A:4-30.104.[7] Neither party addresses those provisions of UIFSA concerning registration of a foreign judgment, and I do not rest my decision on that ground. But the difference between the permissive language of N.J.S.A. 2A:4-30.104 and the mandatory language of N.J.S.A. 2A:4-30.112 is a further indication that the uniform law intends to set a very different standard for jurisdiction to modify than for jurisdiction to enforce a child support order.

* * *

A custodial parent in New Jersey, such as plaintiff, is not without a mechanism for modifying child support ordered by another state's court. Plaintiff retains the right under UIFSA to file a claim in New Jersey as the "initiating tribunal," N.J.S.A. 2A:4-30.73(a), asking that it forward her request to modify the original support order to Georgia as the "responding" tribunal, N.J.S.A. 2A:4-30.80(a)(1). I recognize that this procedure is likely to prove futile to plaintiff's claim for contribution to Julia's college expenses, because Georgia substantive law applies to a proceeding in which it is the "responding tribunal," and under Georgia law it appears that a court may not order a parent to contribute to the college education of a child who has reached the age of majority.

PHILIPP V. STAHL

798 A.2d 83 (N.J. 2002)

PER CURIAM. The judgment of the Appellate Division is reversed, substantially for the reasons expressed in Judge Wecker's dissenting opinion.

NOTES AND QUESTIONS

1. As a practical matter, why do you suppose the father in Georgia pressed his claim that New Jersey could not assert jurisdiction over the motion to modify, which was the subject of this appeal, when he had not objected or at least appealed earlier assertions of jurisdiction by the New Jersey court?

UIFSA § 303 provides that the tribunal ordinarily will use forum law rather than the law of another jurisdiction. Important exceptions are set out in § 604, which provides that if a support order from one state is registered in another, the law of the issuing state governs the nature, extent, amount, and duration of current payments, and other obligations of support and the payment of arrearages for so long as the issuing state remains the residence of the obligor, the obligee, or the child for whose benefit the support is ordered. However, the applicable statute of limitations is that of the statute providing the longer time period.

---

7. N.J.S.A. 2A:4-30.104 provides: "A support order or an income-withholding order issued by a tribunal of another state *may be registered* in the State *for enforcement*" (emphasis added).

2. The majority and the dissent in the Appellate Division in *Philipp* disagree about whether the prior New Jersey orders modified the Georgia order or simply enforced it. What distinguishes a modifying order from an enforcing order? What arguments support labeling the prior orders as modifications? As orders of enforcement?

The UIFSA and the FFCCSOA *forbid* a state court to modify a support order from another state if the issuing state has continuing, exclusive jurisdiction. Did Georgia have continuing, exclusive jurisdiction under the UIFSA? If so, it would have been erroneous for the court in the earlier New Jersey actions to modify the Georgia order. How does the majority deal with this apparent contradiction?

On the other hand, the UIFSA and the FFCCSOA *require* a state court that has personal jurisdiction over a defendant to enforce a support order from another state, if the state asserted jurisdiction consistently with those acts and even if the issuing state no longer has jurisdiction to modify. Thus, regardless of whether Georgia had continuing jurisdiction, New Jersey was obliged to enforce the Georgia order (assuming that Georgia properly asserted jurisdiction in the first place) unless and until the order was properly modified.

UIFSA provides for registration of a support order as a means of obtaining enforcement in another state. The obligee can come to the obligor's state in person to register the order, or, as the dissenting judge indicates, the obligee can initiate an enforcement action in his or her home state court, which will forward the case to the appropriate court in the obligor's home state, in much the same way that cases were handled under URESA.

3. If the state that issued a child support order no longer has continuing, exclusive jurisdiction to modify, another state may acquire jurisdiction to modify the order under the provisions of Section 611 or 613.

Section 611. Modification of Child-Support Order of Another State

(a) After a child-support order issued in another state has been registered in this State, the responding tribunal of this State may modify that order only if Section 613 does not apply and after notice and hearing, it finds that:

(1) the following requirements are met:

(i) the child, the individual obligee, and the obligor do not reside in the issuing state;

(ii) a [petitioner] who is a nonresident of this State seeks modification; and

(iii) the [respondent] is subject to the personal jurisdiction of the tribunal of this State; or

(2) the child, or a party who is an individual, is subject to the personal jurisdiction of the tribunal of this State and all of the parties who are individuals have filed written consents in the issuing tribunal for a tribunal of this State to modify the support order and assume continuing, exclusive jurisdiction over the order. However, if the issuing State is a foreign jurisdiction that has not enacted a law or established procedures substantially similar to the procedures under this [Act], the consent otherwise required of an individual residing in this State is not required for the tribunal to assume jurisdiction to modify the child-support order.

* * *

Section 613. Jurisdiction to Modify Child-Support Order of Another State When Individual Parties Reside in This State

(a) If all of the parties who are individuals reside in this State and the child does not reside in the issuing State, a tribunal of this State has jurisdiction to enforce and to modify the issuing state's child-support order in a proceeding to register that order.

* * *

Could New Jersey properly have asserted jurisdiction over the mother's motion to modify under either of these provisions?

4. The UIFSA provides that the state that issued a spousal support order has "continuing, exclusive jurisdiction over a spousal-support order *throughout the existence of the support obligation.*" UIFSA § 205(f). That section further provides, "A tribunal of this State may not modify a spousal-support order issued by a tribunal of another State having continuing, exclusive jurisdiction over that order under the law of that State." This provision is complemented by Section 206(c), which says, "A tribunal of this State which lacks continuing, exclusive jurisdiction over a spousal-support order may not serve as a responding tribunal to modify a spousal-support order of another State." The commentary explains this difference in treatment on the basis that state law regarding spousal support orders varies from state to state much more than does the law regarding child support.

5. UIFSA § 204 governs simultaneous proceedings in two states and provides that if either state is the home state, i.e., the state in which the child has resided for at least six months, the action in its court should proceed and the action in the other court should be stayed. If neither state is the home state, the first action filed should proceed, and the other court should stay its proceeding. The purpose of this rule is to ensure that conflicting orders will not be issued, and the rule requires courts to seek information to determine whether support actions have been filed in other states and to cooperate with each other in determining which action has priority. Section 311 imposes pleading and related requirements so that courts will have the necessary information.

6. UIFSA § 207 establishes an order of priority for enforcing support orders when there are conflicting orders from different states. Its purpose is to resolve conflicts between orders issued under URESA and UIFSA during the transition period between the two acts. However, this section does not apply to spousal support orders. See note 4 above. The possibility exists, then, that during the transition period between URESA and UIFSA an obligor will be subject to inconsistent spousal support orders from more than one state, since this is possible under URESA and RURESA. *See, e.g.,* Lundahl v. Telford, 9 Cal. Rptr. 3d 902 (Cal. App. 2004). This problem does not arise for cases that are commenced after UIFSA was enacted because UIFSA provides that the issuing state has continuing, exclusive jurisdiction to modify spousal support orders. UIFSA § 205(f). See note 4 above.

7. UIFSA § 305(a) provides that visitation interference cannot be raised as a defense to child support enforcement. This resolves an ambiguity under some versions of URESA.

8. Each state and the federal government have parent locator services to facilitate interstate support enforcement. 42 U.S.C. §§ 653, 654(8). The federal Parent Locator Service also maintains a national directory of new hires and a registry of child support orders, which will contain an abstract of every child support order that is part of the IV-D system. The goal of these provisions is to enable the federal Parent Locator Service to match orders in the registry with information in the new hires directory to track down parents quickly.

PROBLEMS

1. Harry and Winifred were domiciled in and divorced in State A. Their divorce decree provides that Harry must pay Winifred $250 per month in child support and $150 per month in spousal support. Harry moved to State B and stopped paying. Winifred registered the State A decree in State B and asked the State B court to order Harry to pay the past-due amounts and to enforce the decree without modifying as to future payments. Harry asked the State B court to modify downward both the past-due amounts and the future award on the grounds that his income has decreased. States A and B have enacted UIFSA. May the State B court take jurisdiction to modify the State A order?

2. In addition to the facts in Problem 1, assume that Winifred and the children moved from State A to State C and that Harry again quit paying support. Winifred registered the State A decree in State C and asked the court to enforce the overdue amounts and to modify the decree to increase the amount of child and spousal support Harry owes in the future. State C has also enacted UIFSA. May the State C court take jurisdiction to modify the State A order?

3. Mary and Fred were divorced in State A; the divorce decree provided that Fred would pay Mary child support of $750 per month. Mary and the children moved to State B, and Fred moved to State C. Mary registered the support order in State C and asked the court to modify the amount of child support upward, alleging changed circumstances under the law of State C. Fred responded that the court should use the law of the issuing state, State A, to determine the amount of child support. Should the court use the law of State A or State C? Why?

NOTE: INTERNATIONAL SUPPORT ENFORCEMENT

Though several international treaties drafted between 1950 and 1975 deal with support enforcement, the United States has not adhered to any of them and probably will not do so because some of the jurisdictional bases allowed in the treaties are inconsistent with American federal constitutional principles and because of substantial procedural differences. UIFSA can apply to international cases, however, and a number of states have individual agreements regarding support enforcement with other countries, called Parallel Unilateral Policy Declarations. The Secretary of State may declare reciprocity between the United States and other countries for purposes of child support enforcement and establishment. 42 U.S.C. 659(a). Only a few countries, however, have been declared foreign reciprocating countries. The result is that most agreements and arrangements continue to be made at the state level. Office of Child Support v. Sholan, 782 A.2d 1199 (Vt. 2001), holds that a state court may also enforce a support order from another country as a matter of comity, even though the country has not been declared a foreign recipro-cating country and if the state does not have an agreement with the country. In *Sholan* the German father unsuccessfully argued that the remedies allowed under the federal legislation were exclusive, based on federal control over relations with other countries. However, the court found that Congress did not intend to preempt the field. The court continued,

> . . . [W]e next examine whether the family court properly applied the principles of comity in recognizing and enforcing the foreign support order. As a general matter, under principles of comity, final judgments of courts of foreign nations which con-cern recovery of sums of money, the status of a person, or determine interests in property, are conclusive between the parties to the action and are entitled to recog-nition in United States courts. Restatement (Third) of Foreign Relations Law of the United States § 481 (1987). The Restatement further refines the principle of comity, providing that "[a] foreign judgment is generally entitled to recognition by courts in the United States to the same extent as a judgment of a court of one State in the courts of another State." *Id.* cmt. c. Reciprocity between the foreign state which issued the order and the domestic state which seeks to recognize and enforce it is unnecessary for the order to be recognized or enforced in the domestic state. *Id.; see also id.* reporter's note 1 (discussing judicial movement in majority of jurisdictions away from requiring reciprocity). For a court to recognize and give effect to a foreign order, the judgment must have been rendered under a judicial system which provides impartial tribunals and procedures compatible with due process of law, and the issu-ing court must have had jurisdiction over the defendant sufficient to support render-ing such a decision in the state in which the order is sought to be enforced. *Id.* § 482(1). If these prerequisites have been met, the state court may still decline to rec-ognize the foreign order, if the issuing court lacked subject matter jurisdiction over the action; the defendant was not accorded adequate notice of the proceeding; the judgment was obtained by fraud; the original action or judgment is in conflict with state or federal public policy; the judgment conflicts with another judgment entitled to recognition; or the foreign proceeding was contrary to an agreement by the par-ties to submit the controversy to another forum for resolution. *Id.* § 482(2).

782 A.2d at 1203-1204. Applying this test to the facts of the case, the court held that comity should be given to the German order because German laws regard-ing child support are similar to those of Vermont and are compatible with due process and the German court properly asserted jurisdiction over the parties. *See also* Country of Luxembourg ex rel. Ribeiro v. Cauderas, 768 A.2d 283 (N.J. Super. 2000), finding that UIFSA permits registration of a foreign order from a country that is not a foreign reciprocating country and with which the state did not have a formal agreement, but refusing to recognize the order as a matter of comity because the Luxembourg court's assertion of personal jurisdiction over the father was inconsistent with due process. For additional information *see* Robert G. Spector, Toward an Accommodation of Divergent Jurisdictional Standards for the Determination of Maintenance Obligations in Private International Law, 36 Fam. L.Q. 273 (2003); Helen Stalford, Old Problems,

New Solutions? — EU Regulation of Cross-National Child Maintenance, 15 Child & Fam. L.Q. 269 (2003).

E. CHILD CUSTODY JURISDICTION

Determining which state may decide a custody dispute is perhaps the most difficult jurisdictional issue of all. The traditional view was that only the state where the child was domiciled had jurisdiction to grant a custody order. Restatement, Conflict of Laws § 117 (1934). Custody was regarded as a status, and only the state of domicile had sufficient interest to regulate that status. *Id.* at §§ 119, 144. The benefit of that approach is simplicity: Only one state can have custody jurisdiction at any given time. However, the rule was sharply criticized on the ground that it was too simple, because it failed to recognize that states other than that of domicile may have substantial interests in the child's care and welfare and may be in a better position than the state of domicile to determine what action would serve the child's welfare. *See, e.g.,* Albert Ehrenzweig, Interstate Recognition of Custody Decrees, 51 Mich. L. Rev. 345 (1953); Leonard Ratner, Child Custody in a Federal System, 62 Mich. L. Rev. 795 (1964); Sampsell v. Superior Court, 197 P.2d 739 (Cal. 1948) (Traynor, J.). Over time, the rigidity of the Restatement view was replaced by a more flexible approach, recognizing that several states may have significant interests in determining the child's custody. In the only Supreme Court case that addresses constitutional limits on custody jurisdiction, May v. Anderson, 345 U.S. 528 (1953), the Court held that Ohio did not have to give full faith and credit to a Wisconsin order granting custody to the father that was issued ex parte by a court that did not have personal jurisdiction over the mother, who lived in Ohio. The Court said,

> . . . [W]e have before us the elemental question whether a court of a state, where a mother is neither domiciled, resident nor present, may cut off her immediate right to the care, custody, management and companionship of her minor children without having jurisdiction over her *in personam*. Rights far more precious to appellant than property rights will be cut off if she is to be bound by the Wisconsin award of custody. "It is now too well settled to be open to further dispute that the 'full faith and credit' clause and the act of Congress passed pursuant to it do not entitle a judgment *in personam* to extra-territorial effect if it be made to appear that it was rendered without jurisdiction over the person sought to be bound." Baker v. Baker, Eccles & Co., 242 U.S. 394.

Justice Jackson dissented, reading the majority as holding that "the Federal Constitution prohibits Ohio from recognizing the validity of this Wisconsin divorce decree insofar as it settles custody of the couple's children." He argued that Wisconsin could validly assert jurisdiction, even though it lacked personal jurisdiction over the mother, because it was the domicile of the children and their father. Justice Frankfurter concurred in the judgment, interpreting the lead opinion as not requiring Ohio to recognize the decree but also as not holding that Wisconsin's assertion of jurisdiction to decide custody violated due process.

At the time May v. Anderson was decided, custody disputes between parents living in different states were comparatively rare. By the mid-1960s, however, the number of cases had increased significantly and continued to grow through the 1970s. Brigitte Bodenheimer, Progress Under the Uniform Child Custody Jurisdiction Act and Remaining Problems: Punitive Decrees, Joint Custody, and Excessive Modifications, 65 Cal. L. Rev. 978 (1977). Parents dissatisfied with unfavorable custody decisions were sorely tempted to take their children and run to other states to seek modification of the decrees. The flexible law of child custody jurisdiction combined with other factors to facilitate interstate child snatching. Once states other than that of a child's domicile could claim an interest in regulating custody, the only substantial obstacle to awards favoring the petitioning (and often snatching) parent was the obligation to give full faith and credit to a prior custody decree. However, as we have seen, courts of one state are required to give judgments of another state only such finality as the rendering forum grants. Child custody orders, as we know, are routinely considered modifiable on a showing of changed circumstances and thus were not traditionally considered to be entitled to full faith and credit. Cf. Kovacs v. Brewer, 356 U.S. 604 (1958); Halvey v. Halvey, 330 U.S. 610 (1947). In addition, as Professor Clark has pointed out, influential psychological literature emphasizing the importance to child development of stability in parenting relationships encouraged state courts to prefer leaving children with a parent with recent custody, despite a contrary judicial order. See 1 Homer C. Clark, Jr., The Law of Domestic Relations in the United States 776-777 (2d ed. 1987).

By the mid-1960s the indeterminacy of child custody jurisdiction law was perceived as intolerable. In 1968 the National Conference of Commissioners on Uniform State Laws approved the Uniform Child Custody Jurisdiction Act (UCCJA), which was adopted, sometimes with modifications, by all 50 states and the District of Columbia. The National Conference recommended replacement of the UCCJA with the Uniform Child Custody Jurisdiction and Enforcement Act (UCCJEA) in 1997. The UCCJEA is available at http://www.law.upenn.edu/bll/ulc/ulc_frame.htm. As of summer 2004, the UCCJEA had been enacted in 37 states and the District of Columbia, and legislation to adopt it had been introduced in seven more states and the Virgin Islands. A Few Facts About the Uniform Child Custody Jurisdiction and Enforcement Act, http://www.nccusl.org/Update/uniformact_factsheets/uniformacts-fs-uccjea.asp, last visited July 29, 2004. The UCCJEA, which applies to a broad range of custody proceedings, including actions regarding visitation, see UCCJEA § 102(3) and (4), prescribes when a state may take jurisdiction in the first instance to decide a custody dispute, when a state must enforce custody orders from other states, and when a state may and may not take jurisdiction to modify a custody order from another state. Under the UCCJEA, only one state at a time has jurisdiction to decide custody disputes, and once a state obtains jurisdiction, it retains exclusive jurisdiction to modify until statutory conditions for losing that jurisdiction occur.

Just as the UIFSA is complemented by the federal FFCCSOA, the UCCJEA is complemented by the federal Parental Kidnapping Prevention Act (PKPA), which was enacted in 1980. The PKPA implements the Full Faith and Credit Clause and prescribes when states must recognize (enforce) custody and visitation decrees from other states and when they must refuse to modify such decrees. Most courts correctly hold that the PKPA does not itself grant jurisdiction; instead state law (the UCCJEA or the UCCJA in states that have not made the switch) does that.

The first part of this section deals with subject matter jurisdiction to make an initial custody order, and the second considers interstate enforcement and modification. The third part addresses jurisdiction in adoption cases, and the last part deals with international custody disputes.

1. *Initial Jurisdiction*

IN RE MCCOY

52 S.W.3d 297 (Tex. App. 2001)

DORSEY, Justice. . . .

Relator [Michelle Sharlene McCoy] and real party in interest [Michael William McCoy] are former spouses who have two minor children. They are United States citizens who lived most of their married life in Texas, but in 1996, moved to the foreign state of Qatar to accommodate Michael's job as a petroleum engineer. Qatar is a Persian Gulf country located off the coast of Saudi Arabia. The family lived there together until October 1999, when relator took the children and moved to Arkansas where her parents were living.

Shortly after moving to Arkansas with the children, relator filed suit in an Arkansas court seeking divorce, maintenance and child support. Michael traveled to Arkansas shortly after the suit was filed, and was personally served with citation in that suit while there. While Michael has continually disputed its jurisdiction, the Arkansas court has issued temporary orders concerning the children and has affirmatively asserted its personal and subject matter jurisdiction over the suit. . . .

The same month that relator filed suit in Arkansas, Michael filed suit in Qatar. Almost a year later, in October 2000, the Qatari court entered a decree that granted the parties a divorce but deferred ruling on the child custody matters on grounds that Texas was a more appropriate forum for that. Then, in February 2001, Michael filed suit in Hidalgo County seeking custody of the children. . .

Relator moved the Hidalgo County court . . . to dismiss on the basis that it lacked jurisdiction. The court denied her motion. . . .

Relator requests this Court to issue a writ of mandamus compelling the Hidalgo County court to . . . dismiss the case for lack of jurisdiction. . . .

* * *

This conflict is governed by the Texas version of the Uniform Child Custody and Jurisdiction and Enforcement Act ("UCCJEA"). The UCCJEA is the successor statute to the Uniform Child Custody Jurisdiction Act ("UCCJA"), The UCCJEA was designed to remedy complaints in the original Act, but the general objectives are the same. The UCCJA was designed to address problems associated with the growing number of custody disputes between geographically separated parents. Its primary concern was the refusal of many courts to accord finality to custody decrees issued by other states, resulting in frequent relitigation of custody judgments, often to the child's detriment. Some of the stated purposes of the UCCJA were to:

(1)   avoid jurisdictional competition and conflict with courts of other states in matters of child custody;

(2)   promote cooperation with the courts of other states so that a custody decree is rendered in that state which can best decide the case in the interest of the child;

(3)   assure that litigation concerning the custody of a child take place ordinarily in the state with which the child and his family have the closest connection and where significant evidence concerning his care, protection, training, and personal relationships is most readily available, and that courts of this state decline the exercise of jurisdiction when the child and his family have a closer connection with another state;

(4)   discourage continuing controversies over child custody;

(5)   deter abductions and other unilateral removals of children undertaken to obtain custody awards.

UNIF. CHILD CUST. JURIS. ACT. § 2.01 (1968). . . .

* * *

Under Texas's version of the UCCJEA, Texas has jurisdiction to make an "initial child custody determination"[8] *only* if:

(1) this state is the home state of the child on the date of the commencement of the proceeding, or was the home state of the child within six months before the commencement of the proceeding and the child is absent from this state but a parent or person acting as a parent continues to live in this state;

(2) a court of another state does not have jurisdiction under Subdivision (1), or a court of the home state of the child has declined to exercise jurisdiction on the ground that this state is the more appropriate forum . . . and:

(A) the child and the child's parents, or the child and at least one parent or a person acting as a parent, have a significant connection with this state other than mere physical presence; and

(B) substantial evidence is available in this state concerning the child's care, protection, training, and personal relationships;

(3) all courts having jurisdiction under Subdivision (1) or (2) have declined to exercise jurisdiction on the ground that a court of this state is the more appropriate forum to determine the custody of the child . . . ; or

(4) no court of any other state would have jurisdiction under the criteria specified in Subdivision (1), (2), or (3).

---

8. "Initial determination" means the first child custody determination concerning a particular child. Tex. Fam. Code Ann. § 152.102(8) (Vernon Supp. 2001). . . .

Tex. Fam. Code Ann. § 152.201(a) (emphasis added) (Vernon Supp. 2001) [This is UCCJEA § 201 — Ed.] Section 152.201(a) is the exclusive means by which a Texas court has jurisdiction over an initial child custody determination.

The first issue we must resolve is whether Texas has jurisdiction under section 152.201(a). We hold it does not. To make that determination, we address each subdivision of 152.201(a), in turn, to see if any provision confers jurisdiction on the Texas court.

Under the first part of subdivision (1), Texas may exercise jurisdiction if Texas is the home state of the child on the date of the commencement of the proceeding. Texas does not have jurisdiction under this section. Texas clearly was not the home state of the children in February of 2001, when Michael filed suit in Texas. "Home state" is defined to mean the state in which a child lived with a parent or a person acting as a parent for at least six consecutive months immediately before the commencement of a child custody proceeding. § 152.102(7). In February of 2001, the children had been living in Arkansas with their mother for well over a year. Thus, Texas was not the home state at that time; Arkansas was.

The second part of subdivision (1) also fails to confer jurisdiction upon Texas. Under that provision, Texas would have jurisdiction if it had been the home state within six months before the commencement of the proceeding and the child is absent from Texas but a parent or person acting as a parent continues to live in Texas. Texas was not the children's home state at any time during the six months prior to February 2001, when Michael filed his suit. Moreover, neither parent continued to live in Texas. Thus, the second part of subdivision (1) did not confer jurisdiction on the Texas court.

Next, Texas did not have jurisdiction under subdivision (a)(2). Under that subdivision, Texas would have jurisdiction if a court of no other state had "home state" jurisdiction, or if a court of the home state of the child had declined to exercise jurisdiction on the ground that Texas is the more appropriate forum, along with certain other requirements. At first blush, this subdivision would seem to confer jurisdiction on the Texas court because the Qatari court, which was the home state when both the Qatari suit and the Arkansas suit were filed, declined to exercise jurisdiction on the ground that Texas was the more appropriate forum.

However, the operative date for determining whether Texas has jurisdiction is not the date that the Qatari suit was filed. Nor is it the date that the Arkansas suit was filed. Rather, the operative date for determining whether *Texas* has jurisdiction is the date the suit was filed *in Texas*. Suit was not filed in Texas until February of 2001, over a year after the children moved to Arkansas with relator. In February of 2001, Arkansas had become the home state because the children had lived there for the preceding six months with their mother.

Finally, the Texas court does not have jurisdiction under the remaining two subdivisions of section 152.201(a). Under subdivision (3), Texas would have jurisdiction only if all courts having jurisdiction had declined to exercise jurisdiction on the ground that a Texas court was the more appropriate forum to determine the custody of the child. The courts exercising jurisdiction were the Arkansas and the Qatari courts. The statute requires that both of those courts declined jurisdiction in favor of Texas in order to confer jurisdiction on the Texas court. While the Qatari court did, in fact, decline jurisdiction in favor of Texas, the Arkansas court had affirmatively asserted jurisdiction at the time Michael filed his suit in Hidalgo County. Thus, that subdivision does not confer jurisdiction on the Texas court because one of the courts that was exercising jurisdiction over the matter did not decline to exercise jurisdiction on grounds that Texas was the appropriate forum.

Similarly, under section 152.201(a)(4), Texas would have jurisdiction only if no court of any other state would have jurisdiction under any section of 152.201(a). As we have discussed, Arkansas had "home state" jurisdiction under section 152.201(a)(1) when Michael filed his suit in Texas. Thus, (a)(4) did not confer jurisdiction on a Texas court.

* * *

The trial court seems also to have relied on family code section 152.206 to confer jurisdiction on the Texas court. Section 152.206 states that Texas may not exercise jurisdiction if, at the time of the commencement of the proceeding, a proceeding concerning the custody of the child has been commenced in a court of another state having jurisdiction substantially in conformity with this chapter. The trial court reasoned that because Arkansas was not exercising jurisdiction "in substantial conformity" with the Texas UCCJA provisions, it was not required to defer to the Arkansas court. That reasoning is flawed. By its plain language, that provision speaks to situations where a Texas court may *not* exercise jurisdiction; it does not *confer* jurisdiction. Rather, section 152.206 only may apply when Texas already has subject matter jurisdiction under section 152.201(a). As its title implies, the purpose of that statute is to deal with situations where a Texas court and a court of another state are both legitimately exercising jurisdiction at the same time.[9]

* * *

Finally, the trial court also seems to have given weight to its finding that the Qatar court deferred jurisdiction to Texas under Tex. Fam. Code § 152.207(a) (Vernon Supp. 2001). However, the Qatari court did not have the power to confer jurisdiction on the Texas court because that "deferral of jurisdiction" was made *after* the Arkansas court gained home state status. . . .

We agree the Qatari court could defer jurisdiction as described in section 152.207. The Texas UCCJA requires that the Qatari court is treated as if it were a court of a state of the United States. However, the deferral of the Qatari court could only confer superior jurisdiction on a Texas court if . . . it was done prior to the time that Arkansas became the home state.

* * *

Texas simply no longer had superior jurisdiction to Arkansas at the time Michael filed his suit in Texas. If Michael had filed suit in Texas while Qatar still

---

9. The section is entitled "Simultaneous Proceedings."

maintained its status as "home state," Qatar's deferral to the Texas court would have made Texas the state with a superior right to jurisdiction. At that time, Arkansas had not become the home state, and Qatar was clearly the home state. However, because Michael waited to file suit in Texas until the children had lived in Arkansas for well over six months, Arkansas achieved "home state" status during his delay.

* * *

We conditionally grant relator's petition for writ of mandamus. Writ will issue only if the trial court fails, within ten days of this opinion, to (1) dismiss the action filed by Michael seeking an initial child custody determination, and (2) specifically vacate any and all orders entered in this matter pertaining to the custody and/or visitation of the children.

NOTES AND QUESTIONS

1. The mother filed suit for a divorce and support in Arkansas "shortly after" she arrived there from Qatar. At that time could Arkansas have taken jurisdiction to decide custody under UCCJEA § 201, set out in *McCoy* above? At the time that Qatar granted the husband a divorce, could it have asserted jurisdiction over custody under the principles of the UCCJEA?

How did the father argue that Texas had jurisdiction under the UCCJEA, even though it was not the children's home state at the time the suit was filed? Why did this argument fail?

The predecessor to the UCCJEA, the UCCJA provides for four bases for jurisdiction (home state, significant connection with substantial evidence, emergency, and default when no other state has jurisdiction) but does rank them or give priority to one over the other. UCCJA § 3. Thus, under the UCCJA it is entirely possible for three states to claim initial jurisdiction simultaneously. Over time, the states' interpretations of how the UCCJA initial jurisdiction provisions should be interpreted varied, leading to inconsistent treatment of similar cases and the continued possibility that dissatisfied claimants would engage in forum shopping. To solve this problem, UCCJEA § 201 provides that a court located in a child's home state has exclusive initial jurisdiction. A court located in another state can take jurisdiction only if there is no home state or if the court in the child's home state declines to exercise jurisdiction. UCCJEA § 201(a). A child's home state is "the State in which a child lived with a parent or a person acting as a parent for at least six consecutive months immediately before the commencement of a child-custody proceeding. . . . A period of temporary absence of any of the mentioned persons is part of the period." UCCJEA § 102(7). In addition, as will be explained below, the orders of courts that assert jurisdiction consistently with the UCCJEA are entitled to interstate enforcement under the PKPA, while some orders that were made under the UCCJA were not.

Under the UCCJEA, if the child has no home state or the home state declines to exercise jurisdiction, the next state that may claim jurisdiction is one with which "the child and the child's parents, or the child and at least one parent or a person acting as a parent, have a significant connection . . . other than mere physical presence" and in which "substantial evidence is available concerning the child's care, protection, training, and personal relationships." UCCJEA § 201(a)(2). If courts in the states with jurisdiction under either of these provisions decline to exercise jurisdiction in favor of a third state, that state may exercise jurisdiction. UCCJEA § 201(a)(3). In the rare case where no state satisfies any of the first three criteria, another state may take jurisdiction. UCCJEA § 201(a)(4).

2. The UCCJEA takes emergency jurisdiction out of the section on initial jurisdiction and instead provides in § 204 that a court may take emergency jurisdiction if the child has been abandoned in the state or if action is necessary to protect the child or the child's sibling or parent from mistreatment or abuse, regardless of whether a prior custody order exists or not. The section also makes explicit that the orders of a court acting on this jurisdictional basis last only until a court with jurisdiction under other provisions of the UCCJEA takes charge. *See, e.g.,* In re Brode, 566 S.E.2d 858 (N.C. App. 2002). The emergency jurisdiction provision of UCCJA § 3 has generally been interpreted narrowly and as allowing a court to enter temporary custody orders only to protect the child until a court with jurisdiction under another provision of the statute can step in.

3. The commentary to UCCJA § 13 indicates that the act's drafters assumed that Frankfurter's concurrence in May v. Anderson, above, states the true rule about when a state may assert personal jurisdiction over an absent parent or other person claiming rights to custody. Thus, both the UCCJA and the UCCJEA do not require that the state have minimum-contacts jurisdiction over all the parties, though notice "reasonably calculated to give actual notice" is required. UCCJEA § 108; UCCJA § 4. Any person who claims a right to the child's custody must be given notice. UCCJEA § 205; UCCJA § 10. Participation in a custody suit does not in and of itself give a court jurisdiction over a person with regard to other matters. UCCJEA § 109. Professor Russell Coombs has argued that in some extreme circumstances, a state's assertion of jurisdiction to determine the custody rights of a person with no contacts with the state would violate due process. Russell M. Coombs, Interstate Child Custody: Jurisdiction, Recognition and Enforcement, 66 Minn. L. Rev. 711 (1982).

The UCCJEA and UCCJA apply to termination of parental rights proceedings, and in several cases parents have argued minimum-contacts jurisdiction is necessary for these proceedings, with mixed results. Cases that require minimum contacts include In Interest of M.A.C., 261 S.E.2d 590, 596 (Ga. 1979); In Interest of Doe, 926 P.2d 1290, 1296 (Haw. 1996); Matter of Laurie R., 760 P.2d 1295, 1297 (N.M. App. 1988); In re Trueman, 99 S.E.2d 569, 570 (N.C. App. 1990). Other courts have found that the "status exception" based on May v. Anderson, above, applies to terminations. Matter of Interest of M.L.K., 768 P.2d 316, 319 (Kan. App. 1989); In re Williams, 563 S.E.2d 202, 205 (N.C. App. 2002); In re Adoption of Copeland, 43 S.W.3d 483, 487 (Tenn. App. 2000); In Interest of M.S.B., 611 S.W.2d 704, 706 (Tex. App. 1980); State ex rel. W.A., 63 P.3d 100 (Utah 2002); Div. Youth & Fam. Serv. v. M.Y.J.P. 823 A.2d 817 (N.J. Super. A.D. 2003); In re Termination of Parental Rights to Thomas J.R., 663 N.W.2d 734 (Wis. 2003); S.B. v. Dep't Health & Soc. Serv., 61 P.3d 6 (Ala. 2002).

4. The drafters of the UIFSA borrowed major substantive principles from the UCCJA. The purpose, according to the drafters, was to consolidate jurisdiction over support and custody issues in the same state. Unofficial Annotation to UIFSA § 207; John J. Sampson, Unofficial Comment to § 801, Uniform Interstate Family Support Act, reprinted at 27 Fam. L.Q. 93, 123 (1993). The jurisdictional provisions of the UCCJEA in many cases enhance the chances that the same state will have jurisdiction over both custody and child support. However, jurisdiction under the UIFSA and the UCCJEA is not always consolidated. For example, under the UCCJEA, a court in a state that is the child's home state has exclusive jurisdiction to determine custody, but it may not have jurisdiction to award child support if the defendant parent does not have sufficient contacts with the state to satisfy due process, as interpreted in *Kulko. See, e.g.,* Coleman v. Coleman, 864 So. 2d 371 (Ala. Civ. App. 2003).

2.   *Interstate Enforcement and Modification Jurisdiction*

The UCCJEA and PKPA both provide that a court must enforce a custody order from another state if the first state exercised jurisdiction in substantial conformity with the act or under factual circumstances meeting the jurisdictional standards of the act. UCCJEA § 303, PKPA 28 U.S.C. § 1738A(a); *see also* UCCJA § 13. A custody order is made consistently with the PKPA or the UCCJA if the court issuing the order had jurisdiction under its own state laws. 28 U.S.C. § 1738A(c)(1). In addition, one of five conditions enumerated in § 1738A(c)(2) must be met. They are:

> (A) such State (i) is the home State of the child on the date of the commencement of the proceeding, or (ii) had been the child's home State within six months before the date of the commencement of the proceeding and the child is absent from such State because of his removal or retention by a contestant or for other reasons, and a contestant continues to live in such State;
>
> (B) (i) it appears that no other State would have jurisdiction under subparagraph (A), and (ii) it is in the best interest of the child that a court of such State assume jurisdiction because (I) the child and his parents, or the child and at least one contestant, have a significant connection with such State other than mere physical presence in such State, and (II) there is available in such State substantial evidence concerning the child's present or future care, protection, training, and personal relationships;
>
> (C) the child is physically present in such State and (i) the child has been abandoned, or (ii) it is necessary in an emergency to protect the child because he has been subjected to or threatened with mistreatment or abuse;
>
> (D) (i) it appears that no other State would have jurisdiction under subparagraph (A), (B), (C), or (E), or another State has declined to exercise jurisdiction on the ground that the State whose jurisdiction is in issue is the more appropriate forum to determine the custody of the child, and (ii) it is in the best interest of the child that such court assume jurisdiction; or
>
> (E) the court has continuing jurisdiction pursuant to subsection (d) of this section.

The UCCJEA provides that the mechanism for obtaining enforcement of a custody order from another state is by registration. A court receiving an order for registration must give notice to the parties, give them an opportunity to contest on the basis that the court lacked jurisdiction or that the order has been modified, or that the person contesting did not receive notice. If the registration is not contested or if objections are overruled, the order is to be enforced to the same extent as custody orders issued by courts in the state. UCCJEA § 305.

The UCCJEA and the PKPA strictly limit the jurisdiction of a court to modify a custody order from another state. The statutory provisions are, for the most part, quite unambiguous. UCCJEA § 202 provides that a court that has validly asserted jurisdiction has exclusive, continuing jurisdiction until a court in that state "determines that neither the child, the child and one parent, nor the child and a person acting as a parent have a significant connection with this State and that substantial evidence is no longer available in this State concerning the child's care, protection, training and personal relationships," or until "the child, the child's parents, and any person acting as a parent do not presently reside in this State." Section 203 complements this section, providing that a court may not modify a child custody determination made by a court of another State unless the court in the state determines it no longer has exclusive, continuing jurisdiction or that a court of this State would be a more convenient forum or any court rules that the child, the child's parents, and any person acting as parent do not presently reside in the other state. *See also* 28 U.S.C. § 1738A(d), (f).

Under these provisions, a court may take jurisdiction to modify a custody order from another state where the child, a parent, or a person acting as parent still resides if a court in the issuing state finds that it no longer has continuing jurisdiction because it no longer has a significant connection with the state and because substantial evidence is no longer available in the state. The next case considers criteria for applying this provision.

IN RE FORLENZA

140 S.W.3d 373 (Tex. 2004)

Justice O'NEILL delivered the opinion of the Court. . . .

Ann Marie and Robert Joseph Forlenza were divorced in Collin County, Texas, on March 1, 1996. On July 23, 1997, the trial court signed an agreed modification order, modifying the original divorce decree, that granted Robert primary custody of their two children, now ten and fourteen years old, and the exclusive right to establish their primary physical residence. That same month, the children moved with Robert to Issaquah, Washington. Over the next five years, Robert moved with the children three more times — on August 30, 1998, they moved to Ohio, on February 19, 1999, they moved to Virginia, and on August 27, 2002, they moved to Colorado, where they now reside.

The current dispute arose in 2001 when Robert lost his job in Virginia and was offered a two-year contract job in Taipei, Taiwan. Claiming that she had experienced difficulty in exercising her possession rights, Ann filed this suit on September 10, 2001, seeking to modify the prior agreed possession order. She also requested a restraining order prohibiting Robert from relocating the children outside the United States, which the trial court granted. . . .

During a pretrial conference seven days before the scheduled trial date, Robert filed a second motion to dismiss alleging that the court did not have exclusive continuing jurisdiction under Texas Family Code section 152.202(a) to modify its previous child-custody order. The trial court conducted another evidentiary hearing and denied the motion. The court of appeals, however, concluded that the trial court had abused its discretion and granted Robert's petition for writ of mandamus. . . . We granted Ann's petition to determine whether the trial court retained exclusive continuing jurisdiction under the Uniform Child Custody Jurisdiction Enforcement Act (UCCJEA).

II

Effective September 1, 1999, Texas adopted the UCCJEA, replacing the previous Uniform Child Custody Jurisdiction Act (UCCJA). The UCCJEA was designed, in large part, to clarify and to unify the standards for courts' continuing and modification jurisdiction in interstate child-custody matters. The Act that the UCCJEA replaced, the UCCJA, was drafted in 1968 as a model act designed to prevent repeated custody litigation. But even though all fifty states adopted the UCCJA, some did so with significant departure from the original text. As a result, states often interpreted the Act inconsistently and child-custody determinations made in one state were often not accorded full faith and credit in another.

To address some of these problems, in 1980 Congress enacted the Parental Kidnaping Prevention Act (PKPA), which requires states to accord full faith and credit to custody decrees issued by sister states that substantially comply with the PKPA. 28 U.S.C. § 1738A (2000). The PKPA authorizes exclusive continuing jurisdiction in the state that issued the original decree as long as one parent or child remains there and that state has exclusive continuing jurisdiction under its own law. Id. § 1738A(d). The UCCJA, though, which the states had adopted, does not clearly articulate when a decree-granting state retains exclusive continuing jurisdiction. As states adopted different interpretations of continuing jurisdiction and reached conflicting conclusions about the circumstances under which it endures, the law's uniformity diminished, often resulting in simultaneous proceedings and conflicting custody decrees. See generally Linda K. Girdner & Patricia M. Hoff, Obstacles to the Recovery and Return of Parentally Abducted Children: Research Summary (1994). The UCCJEA was designed to eliminate inconsistent state interpretations of the UCCJA's jurisdictional aspects and to harmonize the UCCJA with the PKPA. See id.

Article 2 of the UCCJEA specifically grants exclusive continuing jurisdiction over child-custody disputes to the state that made the initial custody determination and provides specific rules on how long this jurisdiction continues. See Unif. Child Custody Jur. & Enf. Act § 202, 9 U.L.A. 673-74 (Supp. 2004). Rules that prevent another state from modifying a child-custody determination while exclusive continuing jurisdiction remains in the original-decree state complement these provisions. Texas adopted Article 2 without substantial variation from the UCCJEA.

Robert's challenge involves the proper interpretation of [UCCJEA § 202(a)], which governs the duration of the decree-granting state's exclusive continuing jurisdiction. That section provides that a court of this state that has made an initial child-custody determination consistent with [UCCJEA § 201 or 203] has exclusive continuing jurisdiction over the determination until

(1)   a court of this state determines that *neither the child, nor the child and one parent*, nor the child and a person acting as a parent, *have a significant connection with this state and* that *substantial evidence is no longer available in this state* concerning the child's care, protection, training, and personal relationships; or

(2)   a court of this state or a court of another state determines that the child, the child's parents, and any person acting as a parent do not presently reside in this state.

Robert does not challenge the prior child-custody order's compliance with section [UCCJEA § 201]. And [UCCJEA § 202(a)(2)] does not apply because Ann continues to reside in Texas. Therefore, we must decide whether the trial court properly applied [UCCJEA § 202(a)(1)] in deciding that it had exclusive continuing jurisdiction over these modification proceedings. Statutory construction is a question of law that we review de novo.

Robert's jurisdictional plea contends that Ann failed to establish that a significant connection with Texas exists and that substantial evidence is available here concerning the children's care, protection, training, and personal relationships. . . . [W]e disagree with Robert's contention. . . . As a general matter, the pleader must allege facts that affirmatively demonstrate the court's jurisdiction to hear the case. Under the statute, a court acquires exclusive continuing jurisdiction by virtue of a prior child-custody determination. By alleging that the court's prior orders conferred exclusive continuing jurisdiction, Ann satisfied her initial statutory burden. The statute specifically provides that a court *retains* exclusive continuing jurisdiction *until* it determines that the significant-connection and substantial-evidence requirements are no longer met. Robert may challenge whether the statutory elements are satisfied, or the court may consider them sua sponte, but Ann has satisfied her initial jurisdictional burden under the statute.

Robert contends that the children no longer have a significant connection with Texas because (1) the children visited here only five times in the four-year period preceding this action, and (2) Ann's residence in Texas is not sufficient, as the commentary to [UCCJEA § 202] specifically notes that the presence of one parent remaining in the state is not determinative. But Ann does not rely on her mere presence in Texas to establish a significant connection under the statute. Contrary to Robert's briefing, the record indicates that the children actually visited Texas six times in the relevant period. On four of these occasions the children lived with Ann for considerable periods, each lasting approximately one month during the summer. Moreover, we presume that the trial court accepted as true Ann's testimony that more visitation would have occurred in Texas but for Robert's actions and the fact that the children were not allowed to fly to Texas.

Other courts commonly consider visitation within the state as evidence of a significant connection. *See, e.g.*, [Fish v. Fish, 596 S.E.2d 654, 656 (Ga. Ct. App. 2004); Ruth v. Ruth, 83 P.3d 1248, 1254 (Kan. Ct. App. 2004)]; In the Interest of

P.H.B.S., A.W.L.S., & M.G.S., — S.W.3d ——, at —— (Tex. App. Fort Worth 2003, no pet.); Olson v. Olson, No. C7-02-344, 2002 WL 31056935, at *3 (Minn. Ct. App. Sept. 10, 2002) (not designated for publication). In addition, numerous relatives, including Ann's mother and sister and Robert's sister and sister-in-law, live in Texas and maintain a relationship with the children. *See* In the Interest of P.H.B.S., — S.W.3d ——, at ——; *cf.* In the Matter of M.B. II v. M.B., 756 N.Y.S.2d 710, 712-13 (N.Y. Fam. Ct. 2002) (finding that child's relatives could not constitute a significant connection to the state in the absence of a relationship between the child and the relatives).

Moreover, the evidence in this case clearly indicates that Ann maintained a significant relationship with her children. *See* Unif. Child Custody Jur. & Enf. Act § 202 cmt. 1, 2, 9 U.L.A. 674 ("If the relationship between the child and the person remaining in the State with exclusive, continuing jurisdiction becomes so attenuated that the court could no longer find significant connections and substantial evidence, jurisdiction would no longer exist. . . . The significant connection to the original decree State must relate to the child, the child and a parent, or the child and a person acting as a parent."). To accommodate the children's schedule over the years, Ann repeatedly flew to Washington, Ohio, and Virginia to see them. Robert admits that Ann made at least fifteen such trips in the four-year period under review. Because the record establishes that the children visited Texas on a number of occasions and maintained a close relationship with their mother and other relatives residing in Texas, all important considerations under the UCCJEA, we hold that the children have a significant connection with Texas sufficient to support the trial court's exclusive continuing jurisdiction over the modification proceedings.

* * *

. . . Robert claims that no other court has exercised exclusive continuing jurisdiction over children who have resided out of state for more than five years. We disagree. In *Fish*, the Georgia Court of Appeals determined that the trial court had exclusive continuing jurisdiction pursuant to a prior divorce decree even though the mother and the children had lived in Florida for seven years. Similarly, in *Ruth*, the Kansas Court of Appeals determined that the trial court had jurisdiction pursuant to a prior divorce decree after the mother and children had lived in Missouri for approximately six years. And in Heath v. Heath, a Connecticut court exercised exclusive continuing jurisdiction even though the children had lived in California for eight years. No. FA910117282S, 2000 WL 1838932, at *2 (Conn. Super. Ct. Nov. 21, 2000) (not designated for publication). Moreover, contrary to Robert's argument, the UCCJEA does not premise the exclusive continuing jurisdiction determination on which state has the *most* significant connection with the child. This relative type of inquiry is appropriate under section [UCCJEA § 7], which allows a court with exclusive continuing jurisdiction to decline it in favor of a more convenient forum, but it does not affect the initial [Section 202] jurisdictional analysis. Importantly, the only issue before us is whether the Texas court retained jurisdiction; the court could still decline to exercise that jurisdiction if another forum was more convenient. In this case, though, the children's almost continual change of residence supports the trial court's conclusion that the children had a significant connection with Texas based on their visits here and their personal relationships maintained in this state.

Finally, Robert argues that substantial evidence does not exist in Texas regarding the children's care, protection, training, and personal relationships, and [Section 202(a)(1)] requires the trial court to find *both* a significant connection with Texas *and* that substantial evidence exists here before it can exercise exclusive continuing jurisdiction. . . . Because section 201, which governs the initial custody determination, requires both a significant connection and substantial evidence, Robert concludes that section 202 must as well. We disagree.

Robert's strained construction of the statutory scheme ignores [Section 202(a)(1)'s] plain language. That section specifically states that jurisdiction continues until the court determines that there is not a significant connection with Texas *and* that substantial evidence concerning the children's care, protection, training, and personal relationships is no longer available here. Clearly, exclusive jurisdiction continues in the decree-granting state as long as a significant connection exists *or* substantial evidence is present.[10] . . . Because we conclude that the trial court did not err in concluding that the children had a substantial connection with Texas on September 10, 2001, we need not address whether substantial evidence existed here as well.

III

For the foregoing reasons, we hold that the trial court had exclusive continuing jurisdiction over this modification proceeding and that mandamus relief is justified. . . .

* * *

NOTES AND QUESTIONS

1. The fundamental question with which *Forlenza* deals is whether a court should interpret the statutory provision regarding its state's continuing jurisdiction

---

10. We note that our interpretation comports with that of other jurisdictions. *See* Fish v. Fish, 596 S.E.2d 654, 656 (Ga. Ct. App. 2004) (stating that for exclusive continuing jurisdiction to be lost "two findings [no significant connection and no substantial evidence] must be made"); Ruth v. Ruth, 83 P.3d 1248, 1254 (Kan. Ct. App. 2004) (affirming trial court's exercise of jurisdiction after determining the children have a significant connection with Kansas); Benson v. Benson, 667 N.W.2d 582, 585 (N.D. 2003) ("Because [the father] still resides in the state, North Dakota retains exclusive, continuing jurisdiction until a court of this state determines [the child] no longer has a significant connection with the state and the state no longer has substantial evidence concerning [the child]"); Lord v. Lord, No. FA970348367S, 2001 WL 1202614, at *3 (Conn. Super. Ct. Sept. 14, 2001) (determining that exclusive continuing jurisdiction exists in Connecticut because the child's relationship with the resident parent is significant, even though the court found that substantial evidence is no longer available). *But see* In re Marriage of David Medill, 40 P.3d 1087, 1093 (Or. Ct. App. 2001) (finding that the trial court would only have continuing exclusive jurisdiction if both requirements were satisfied).

broadly or narrowly. *Forlenza* opts for a broad interpretation, which favors retention of jurisdiction in the issuing state. What policies support such an interpretation? What policies would support a more conservative approach to this issue?

Under the UCCJA a similar question arises. UCCJA § 14 provides that if the court that entered the initial decree has continuing jurisdiction, a court in another state may not take jurisdiction to modify, and the test for whether the originating court has continuing jurisdiction is whether the state in which the court is located continues to have a significant connection with the child and a parent or the child and at least one claimant, and whether there is substantial evidence in the original state. However, the UCCJA provides that the court in the second state (rather than the originating court, as under the UCCJEA) makes the significant-connection/substantial-evidence determination. In Grubs v. Ross, 630 P.2d 353 (Or. en banc 1981), the court concluded that "we should construe the Act in favor of decree state jurisdiction for a reasonable period of time following the abduction of the child." The court explained that this approach best served the goals of deterring encouraging stability in custody decrees and discouraging forum shopping. *See also* Kumar v. Superior Court, 186 Cal. Rptr. 772 (Cal. 1982) (en banc).

What is the significance of the UCCJEA having changed which court makes the significant-connection/substantial-evidence determination?

2. A court that validly asserts initial jurisdiction or jurisdiction to modify has discretion to decline to exercise it on the ground that a court in another state would be a more convenient forum. UCCJEA § 207; UCCJA § 7. UCCJEA § 207 provides that in deciding whether to grant a motion to decline jurisdiction on the basis of forum *non conveniens*, the court should consider

(a)   Whether domestic violence has occurred and is likely to continue in the future and which state could best protect the parties and the child;

(b)   The length of time that the child has resided outside this state;

(c)   The distance between the court in this state and the court in the state that would assume jurisdiction;

(d)   The relative financial circumstances of the parties;

(e)   Any agreement of the parties as to which state should assume jurisdiction;

(f)   The nature and location of the evidence required to resolve the pending litigation, including testimony of the child;

(g)   The ability of the court of each state to decide the issue expeditiously and the procedures necessary to present the evidence; and

(h)   The familiarity of the court of each state with the facts and issues in the pending litigation.

The forum *non conveniens* provision of the UCCJA, in comparison, said that a court was to make a decision "in the interest of the child" considering a nonexclusive list of factors. UCCJA § 7(c). At least one court has observed that the UCCJEA does not include the "interest of the child" language and has held that it is, therefore, error for a court to base a forum *non conveniens* decision on "the interests of the child." In re Marriage of Fontenot, 77 P.3d 206 (Mont. 2003).

In Gestl v. Frederick, 754 A.2d 1087 (Md. App. 2000), the court considered how differences in the visitation laws of two states should affect a forum *non conveniens* analysis. Frederick and Gestl, who were same-sex partners, and Frederick's biological child lived together in Maryland. The women broke up when the child was five years old, and Frederick moved with the child to Tennessee. Then Gestl sued Frederick in Maryland, seeking joint legal custody and visitation. Frederick moved to dismiss on several grounds, including that Maryland was an inconvenient forum. The Maryland judge held that Maryland had jurisdiction under the UCCJA but would not exercise it because Tennessee was a more convenient forum, since most of the information concerning the child was there. Gestl argued on appeal that Tennessee was not in fact a more convenient forum because under Tennessee law she would not have standing to seek custody or visitation. The Maryland appellate court held that even if the weight of evidence suggests that another state is a more convenient forum, the trial court should not have dismissed if in fact Tennessee would not provide an alternative forum for a claim that would be recognized in Maryland. Because Gestl, a nonparent, could argue in Maryland but not in Tennessee that exceptional circumstances justified an award of custody to her or that the child's best interests justified an award of visitation, the Maryland court held that the trial judge erred in dismissing the case on inconvenient-forum grounds. Other cases reaching similar results include Priscilla S. v. Albert B., 424 N.Y.S.2d 613 (1980); Barnae v. Barnae, 943 P.2d 1036 (N.M. App. 1997).

3. UCCJEA § 208 says that a court with initial or modifying jurisdiction shall decline to exercise that authority on the basis that the petitioner "has engaged in unjustifiable conduct" unless the parties agree to the court's exercise of jurisdiction, the court with jurisdiction determines that the state is a more appropriate forum, or no other state has jurisdiction. UCCJA § 8 is similar, though the commentary to the UCCJEA section notes,

> The "Clean Hands" section of the UCCJA has been truncated in this Act. Since there is no longer a multiplicity of jurisdictions which could take cognizance of a child-custody proceeding, there is less of a concern that one parent will take the child to another jurisdiction in an attempt to find a more favorable forum. Most of the jurisdictional problems generated by abducting parents should be solved by the prioritization of home State in Section 201; the exclusive, continuing jurisdiction provisions of Section 202; and the ban on modification in Section 203. . . . Nonetheless, there are still a number of cases where parents, or their surrogates, act in a reprehensible manner, such as removing, secreting, retaining, or restraining the child. This section ensures that abducting parents will not receive an advantage for their unjustifiable conduct. If the conduct that creates the jurisdiction is unjustified, courts must decline to exercise jurisdiction that is inappropriately invoked by one of the parties.

4. If a court learns that another custody proceeding regarding the child is ongoing, UCCJEA § 206 provides that the court may not exercise its jurisdiction if the other court's assumption of jurisdiction is "substantially in conformity with this Act, unless the proceedings has been terminated or is stayed by the court or the other State because a court of this State is a more convenient forum under Section 207."

5. Several sections of the UCCJEA provide that a court may find that it lacks jurisdiction or that it will not exercise jurisdiction on the assumption that a court in another state will have and will take jurisdiction. The sections presuppose a high degree of cooperation among courts in the various states, and the Act includes several sections that facilitate this cooperation. First, the parties must state under oath in its first pleading "the child's present address or whereabouts, the places where the child has lived during the last five years, and the names and present addresses of the persons with whom the child has lived during that period." Each party must also provide information about prior custody proceedings affecting the child and whether anyone not already named has physical custody of the child or claims rights to legal custody of the child. UCCJEA § 209(a); *see also* UCCJA § 9. Failure to satisfy this pleading requirement may deprive the court of subject matter jurisdiction. *See* Ruble v. Ruble, 884 So. 2d 150 (Fla. App. 2004). Courts may communicate with each other and ask that courts in other states take testimony and hold hearings, forward the records to the state in which litigation is occurring, order custody evaluations, and forward records. UCCJEA §§ 110-112; UCCJA §§ 18-21. Judges from different states are encouraged to confer with each other before deciding whether to accept jurisdiction in particular cases.

In Atchison v. Atchison, 664 N.W.2d 249 (Mich. App. 2003), a court in Ontario, Canada, issued an initial custody decree, and Ontario remained the home of the mother and one child. The other child moved to Michigan to live with the father, and after two years the father tried to obtain a change-of-custody decree in Michigan. The Michigan court declined, however, because the Ontario court had not found that it lacked continuing jurisdiction or that it was an inconvenient forum. The father argued that the provisions of the UCCJEA regarding communication and cooperation between courts required that the Michigan court ask the Ontario court whether it would decline jurisdiction. The appellate court concluded, however, that "Review of the plain language of the statute reveals that it does not impose communication requirements upon the courts of this state. Furthermore, there is no minimal evidentiary burden of proof set forth in the plain language of the statute that would mandate communication between the courts. Accordingly, the trial court did not err in denying plaintiff's petition for change of custody on the basis of a lack of jurisdiction." What steps should the father have taken to permit the Michigan court to assert jurisdiction?

6. As *McCoy* observes, custody orders from foreign countries are to be treated like orders from other states if they were made "under factual circumstances in substantial conformity with the jurisdictional standards of the Act." UCCJEA § 105. UCCJEA § 104 is a similar provision that applies to custody determinations made by Native American tribal courts. The UCCJA did not contain such a provision, and courts reached different conclusions about the applicability of the UCCJA to custody orders from other countries and from tribal courts.

The Indian Child Welfare Act (ICWA) provides for tribal court jurisdiction in child welfare and adoption cases and requires state recognition of tribal decrees. However, it does not apply to custody disputes at divorce. 25 U.S.C. §§ 1903, 1911(d). The ICWA is considered in Chapter 13. For a detailed discussion of these and related issues, *see* Barbara A. Atwood, Identity and Assimilation: Changing Definitions of Tribal Power over Children, 83 Minn. L. Rev. 927 (1999).

7. The same legislation that created the PKPA provides that the federal Parent Locator Service, established to facilitate interstate child support enforcement, may also be used to search for people who have taken children in violation of custody decrees in some circumstances. 42 U.S.C. §663. The PKPA also amended the Federal Fugitive Felony Act, 18 U.S.C. §1073, to allow its use in cases of parent child snatching. The act had previously been interpreted to exclude these cases. The effect is to allow FBI involvement in cases of interstate child snatching if a state statute makes parental kidnapping a felony.

NOTE: DOMESTIC VIOLENCE CASES AND THE UCCJEA

A number of interstate custody cases involve claims that a custodial parent, almost always a mother, left the state in which she, the father and the children were living to escape domestic violence. This asserted circumstance may affect determinations under the UCCJEA at a number of points.

In Stoneman v. Drollinger, 64 P.3d 997 (Mont. 2003), the mother obtained several domestic abuse restraining orders against the father in Montana, but he repeatedly violated them. The parties were divorced in Montana in 1998, and the mother then moved to Washington. The Montana trial court ordered her to return the children to Montana every other weekend for unsupervised visits with their father, despite the recommendations of a GAL that unsupervised visits not be allowed; the Montana Supreme Court reversed, holding that it was an abuse of discretion to order unsupervised visitation. The mother then moved the Montana court to decline to exercise its continuing jurisdiction over custody on the basis that Washington was a more convenient forum. The trial court denied her motion, and the Montana Supreme Court again reversed. It explained,

> The UCCJEA places domestic violence at the top of the list of factors that courts are required to evaluate when determining whether to decline jurisdiction as an inconvenient forum for child custody proceedings. Since domestic violence was not raised by the now-repealed UCCJA as a factor for court consideration, the NCCUSL, which drafted the UCCJEA, offered the following guidance to assist courts in applying this factor:
>
>> For this purpose, the court should determine whether the parties are located in different States because one party is a victim of domestic violence or child abuse. If domestic violence or child abuse has occurred, this factor authorizes the court to consider which State can best protect the victim from further violence or abuse.
>
> 9 U.L.A. 683. The NCCUSL explicitly recognized that past abuse or a continuing threat of violence might compel a battered spouse or parent of an abused child to relocate to another state. The NCCUSL further directed courts to proceed with an evaluation of which forum can provide the greater safety whenever domestic violence or child abuse has occurred.

* * *

> Given the high propensity for recidivism in domestic violence, we hold that when a court finds intimate partner violence or abuse of a child has occurred or that

a party has fled Montana to avoid further violence or abuse, the court is authorized to consider whether the party and the child might be better protected if further custody proceedings were held in another state. While this factor alone is not dispositive under §40-7-108, MCA, we urge district courts to give priority to the safety of victims of domestic violence when considering jurisdictional issues under the UCCJEA.

The court held that the trial court abused its discretion when it failed to consider which forum could better protect the mother and children, given the well-documented history of domestic violence in the case.

In McNabb ex rel. Foshee v. McNabb, 65 P.3d 1068 (Kan. App. 2003), the mother alleging abuse left Virginia and went to Kansas with the children. The father filed a custody action in Virginia, the children's home state, and a few months later the mother filed a competing action in Kansas. The Virginia judge originally decided to decline to exercise initial, home-state jurisdiction on the basis that Kansas was a more convenient forum. However, upon learning of allegations that the father was violent toward the mother, the Virginia trial judge vacated the ruling and reclaimed jurisdiction. The Kansas trial court, not knowing of this action, asserted jurisdiction over the custody matter as well. The father appealed, and the Kansas appellate court held that Kansas did not have jurisdiction because Virginia was the home state and observed that the Virginia judge properly took into account the abuse allegations and the availability of evidence to support or refute the domestic violence allegations in deciding the forum *non conveniens* issue.

See also Campbell v. Martin, 802 A.2d 395 (Me. 2002), holding that a state to which a mother alleging domestic violence fled could take temporary emergency jurisdiction to enter a custody order incident to an order of protection, but that it could not hear the mother's paternity suit, which also sought custody and child support. The court also upheld the trial court's determination that the custody order should last only until the date of a hearing in the child's home state on the father's petition regarding paternity and custody.

PROBLEMS

1. Mona and Frank, an unmarried couple, had a child, Cynthia, while they were living in state X. When Cynthia was three months old, Mona left Frank and moved to state Y, where Mona's mother lived. After she left him, Mona refused to let Frank visit Cynthia. Frank sued Mona in state X, seeking custody or visitation. Mona moved to dismiss, alleging that state X lacked jurisdiction under the UCCJEA. How should the court rule and why?

2. Mary and Fred lived with their two children in state A. They were divorced three years ago and were awarded joint physical and legal custody. Two years ago Mary took the children and left the state without telling Fred. She moved to state B and obtained an order granting her full legal and physical custody of the children. To obtain the order she falsely said that she did not know where Fred was, and he was served only by publication in a small newspaper in state B. Eight months ago Mary and the children moved to state C. Fred recently found Mary and the children in state C, and he has brought the state A custody order to a state C court, asking the state C court to recognize the state A order

and modify it to give him full custody. Mary has asked the state C court to enforce the state B order and argues that state C does not have jurisdiction to hear the motion to modify. Fred continues to live in state A. Under the UCCJEA, must the court in state C enforce either of the prior orders? May it take jurisdiction to decide the motion to modify custody?

3. Harold and Wanda lived in state A with their daughter, Connie. When Connie was two years old, a court in state A granted Wanda a divorce and awarded her custody of Connie. Harold moved to state B shortly after the divorce, where he still lives. Wanda and Connie moved to state C four months ago. Wanda sent Connie to visit Harold in state B for two weeks, and he has refused to return her. Wanda went to state B and registered the custody order, asking state B to enforce it. Harold counterclaimed, asking the state B court to modify the order to give him custody. Wanda moved the court to dismiss the counterclaim, alleging that state B lacks jurisdiction to modify the order. How should the court rule and why?

4. Travis and Rachel were divorced in state A; the divorce decree awarded custody to Travis, with visitation to Rachel. Shortly thereafter, Travis, the children, and Travis's mother Dorothy, who lived with them, moved to state B. Four years later Dorothy, believing that Travis was abusing the children, left home with the children over his objection and moved across town. Dorothy then filed a motion in state B, seeking sole custody of the children. Rachel was served but did not enter an appearance. Travis moved to dismiss, arguing that under the UCCJEA state B does not have jurisdiction. How should the court rule and why?

If instead Dorothy had returned to state A and asked the court to find that it had no jurisdiction or that it should decline to exercise its jurisdiction, what arguments should she make? How should the court rule? (Assume again that Rachel is served but does not appear.)

3. Adoption Jurisdiction

The UCCJEA applies to cases of neglect, abuse, dependency, wardship, guardianship, termination of parental rights, and protection from domestic violence. UCCJEA § 102(4). It does not apply to adoption cases but instead defers to the Uniform Adoption Act (UAA). UCCJEA § 103. The jurisdictional provisions of the UAA are fundamentally consistent with those of the UCCJEA and the PKPA, but they are modified to fit the adoption context. UAA § 3-101(a)(1) includes "prospective adoptive parents" among those people whose relationship with a child may give rise to a basis for jurisdiction. The following alternative criteria for asserting jurisdiction over an adoption matter are provided by §§ 3-101(a)(1)-(c)(2):

(1) immediately before commencement of the proceeding, the minor lived in this State with a parent, a guardian, a prospective adoptive parent, or another person acting as parent, for at least six consecutive months, excluding periods of temporary absence, or, in the case of a minor under six months of age, lived in this State from soon after birth with any of those individuals and there is available in this State substantial evidence concerning the minor's present or future care;

(2) immediately before commencement of the proceeding, the prospective adoptive parent lived in this State for at least six consecutive months, excluding periods of temporary absence, and there is available in this State substantial evidence concerning the minor's present or future care;

(3) the agency that placed the minor for adoption is located in this State and it is in the best interest of the minor that a court of this State assume jurisdiction because:

(i) the minor and the minor's parents, or the minor and the prospective adoptive parent, have a significant connection with this State; and

(ii) there is available in this State substantial evidence concerning the minor's present or future care;

(4) the minor and the prospective adoptive parent are physically present in this State and the minor has been abandoned or it is necessary in an emergency to protect the minor because the minor has been subjected to or threatened with mistreatment or abuse or is otherwise neglected; or

(5) it appears that no other State would have jurisdiction under prerequisites substantially in accordance with paragraphs (1) through (4), or another State has declined to exercise jurisdiction on the ground that this State is the more appropriate forum to hear a petition for adoption of the minor, and it is in the best interest of the minor that a court of this State assume jurisdiction.

(b) A court of this State may not exercise jurisdiction over a proceeding for adoption of a minor if at the time the petition for adoption is filed a proceeding concerning the custody or adoption of the minor is pending in a court of another State exercising jurisdiction substantially in conformity with [the UCCJA] or this [act] unless the proceeding is stayed by the court of the other State.

(c) If a court of another State has issued a decree or order concerning the custody of a minor who may be the subject of a proceeding for adoption in this State, a court of this State may not exercise jurisdiction over a proceeding for adoption of the minor unless:

(1) the court of this State finds that the court of the State which issued the decree or order:

(i) does not have continuing jurisdiction to modify the decree or order under jurisdictional prerequisites substantially in accordance with [the Uniform Child Custody Jurisdiction Act] or has declined to assume jurisdiction to modify the decree or order; or

(ii) does not have jurisdiction over a proceeding for adoption substantially in conformity with subsection (a)(1) through (4) or has declined to assume jurisdiction over a proceeding for adoption; and

(2) the court of this State has jurisdiction over the proceeding.

Most courts have held that the UCCJA and PKPA apply to adoption and termination of parental rights proceedings. *E.g.*, Souza v. Superior Court, 193 Cal. App. 3d 1304, 238 Cal. Rptr. 892 (1987); Gainey v. Olivo, 373 S.E.2d 4 (Ga. 1988); In re L. C., 857 P.2d 1375 (Kan. App. 1993); In re Baby Girl Clausen, 502 N.W.2d 649 (Mich. 1993); Foster v. Stein, 454 N.W.2d 244 (Mich. App. 1990); E. E. B. v. D. A., 446 A.2d 871 (N.J. 1982); In re Adoption of Child by T. W. C., 636 A.2d 1083 (N.J. Super. 1994); State ex rel. Torres v. Mason, 848 P.2d 592 (Or. 1993);

Clark v. Gordon, 437 S.E.2d 144 (S.C. 1993); In re Termination of Parental Rights over M. C. S., 504 N.W.2d 322 (S.D. 1993); In re A. E. H., 468 N.W.2d 190 (Wis. 1991). *Contra* State in Interest of R. N. J., 908 P.2d 345 (Utah App. 1995).

In addition, under some circumstances interstate adoptions are subject to the requirements of the Interstate Compact on the Placement of Children, which has been adopted in all U.S. jurisdictions except New Jersey, the District of Columbia, and Puerto Rico. The compact applies to interstate placements of children for foster care or "preliminary to a possible adoption" except for placements of children made by their parents, stepparents, grandparents, adult brothers, sisters, uncles, aunts, or guardians. Interstate Compact Art. III, VIII(a). The Compact requires that interstate placements be coordinated through public authorities. For the full text of the Compact and commentary on its operation, *see* Bernadette W. Hartfield, The Role of the Interstate Compact on the Placement of Children in Interstate Adoption, 68 Neb. L. Rev. 292 (1989). In re Adoption of A.M.M., 949 P.2d 1155 (Kan. App. 1997), held that an adoption petition should be dismissed when the would-be adoptive parents brought children into the state without complying with the Interstate Compact. The court rejected the view of other states that an adoption should be allowed in the best interests of the child despite failure to comply with the compact.

4. *International Enforcement of Custodial Rights*

Child abduction is an international problem as well. The Hague Convention on the Civil Aspects of International Child Abduction is an international treaty intended to solve these problems. As of mid-2004, the Hague Convention was in effect in 80 countries. A current listing is available at *http://www.hcch.net/e/status/abdshte.html*. The Convention does not grant or withhold jurisdiction to determine custody disputes. Jurisdiction continues to be determined by state law, therefore. However, the Convention limits the application of state law because it requires that children wrongfully removed from the country of their "habitual residence" be returned to that country. If the Convention applies, the responding country is supposed to order return of the child without addressing the merits of the custody dispute and without making value judgments about the culture of and conditions in the child's country of habitual residence. The following case considers the meaning of some of the core provisions of the Convention.

FRIEDRICH V. FRIEDRICH

983 F.2d 1396 (6th Cir. 1993)

BOGGS, C.J. . . . In December 1989, Emanuel Friedrich married Jeana Friedrich in the Federal Republic of Germany. Mrs. Friedrich, a citizen of the United States, was a member of the United States Army stationed in Bad Aibling, Germany. Mr. Friedrich, a citizen of Germany, was employed on the military base as a bartender and club manager.

On December 29, 1989, the Friedrichs' only child, Thomas David Friedrich, was born in Bad Aibling. During 1990 and early 1991, Thomas lived with both of his parents in Bad Aibling off the military base. The Friedrichs' marriage was a rocky one from the start. . . .

On the evening of July 27, 1991, the Friedrichs had a heated argument at their apartment. During the argument, Mr. Friedrich ordered Mrs. Friedrich to leave the apartment with Thomas and put most of their belongings in the hallway, including some of Thomas's toys. . . .

. . . In the late evening of August 1, 1991, without Mr. Friedrich's permission, consent or knowledge, Mrs. Friedrich left Bad Aibling en route to the United States with Thomas. . . .

Mr. Friedrich discovered that Thomas had been removed to the United States on August 3, 1991. . . .

Mr. Friedrich filed this action on September 23, 1991, alleging that Mrs. Friedrich had wrongfully removed Thomas from Germany in violation of the Hague Convention on Civil Aspects of International Child Abduction. On January 10, 1992, the district court denied Mr. Friedrich's claim.

II

The Convention on Civil Aspects of International Child Abduction was adopted by the signatory nations in order "to protect children internationally from the harmful effects of their wrongful removal or retention and to establish procedures to ensure their prompt return to the State of their habitual residence, as well as to secure protection for rights of access." Hague Convention, Preamble. The United States ratified the Convention on April 29, 1988. Germany is also a signatory nation to the Convention. Pursuant to Article 19 of the Convention and section 2(b)(4) of the Act, a United States district court has the authority to determine the merits of an abduction claim, but not the merits of the underlying custody claim. It is important to understand that "wrongful removal" is a legal term strictly defined in the Convention. It does not require an ad hoc determination or a balancing of the equities. Such action by a court would be contrary to a primary purpose of the Convention: to preserve the status quo and to deter parents from crossing international boundaries in search of a more sympathetic court.

Under the Convention, the removal of a child from one country to another is wrongful when:

> a) it is in breach of rights of custody attributed to a person, an institution or any other body, either jointly or alone, under the law of the State in which the child was habitually resident immediately before the removal or retention; and b) at the time of removal or retention those rights were actually exercised, either jointly or alone, or would have been so exercised but for the removal or retention. . . .

Under the [International Child Abduction Remedies Act, which implements the Convention], Mr. Friedrich has the burden of showing by a preponderance of the evidence that the removal was wrongful. 42 U.S.C. § 11603(e)(1). If Mr. Friedrich meets his burden, the burden shifts to Mrs. Friedrich to show 1) by clear and convincing evidence that there is a grave risk that the return of the child would expose the child to physical or psychological harm; Hague Convention, Article 13b, 42 U.S.C. §11603(e)(2)(A); 2) by clear and convincing evidence that the return of the child "would not be permitted by the fundamental principles of the requested State relating to the protection of human rights and fundamental freedoms"; Hague Convention, Article 20, 42 U.S.C. §11603(e)(2)(A); 3) by a preponderance of the evidence that the proceeding was commenced more than one year after the abduction and the child has become settled in its new environment; Hague Convention, Article 12, 42 U.S.C. §11603(e)(2)(B); or 4) by a preponderance of the evidence that Mr. Friedrich was not actually exercising the custody right at the time of removal or retention, or had consented to or subsequently acquiesced in the removal or retention; Hague Convention, Article 13a, 42 U.S.C. §11603(e)(2)(B).

Therefore, as a threshold matter, Mr. Friedrich must prove by a preponderance of the evidence that 1) Mrs. Friedrich removed Thomas from his "habitual residence," and 2) Mr. Friedrich was exercising his parental custody rights over Thomas at the time of removal, or that he would have exercised his rights but for the removal, under the law of the state of Thomas's habitual residence. If Mr. Friedrich meets this burden, Mrs. Friedrich may fall back on one of the four affirmative defenses. . . .

The Convention does not define "habitual residence." Little case law exists on the Convention in general; no United States case provides guidance on the construction of "habitual residence." . . . We agree that habitual residence must not be confused with domicile. To determine the habitual residence, the court must focus on the child, not the parents, and examine past experience, not future intentions.

Thomas was born in Germany to a German father and an American mother and lived exclusively in Germany except for a few short vacations before Mrs. Friedrich removed him to the United States. Mrs. Friedrich argues that despite the fact that Thomas's ordinary residence was always in Germany, Thomas was actually a habitual resident of the United States because: 1) he had United States citizenship; 2) his permanent address for the purpose of the United States documentation was listed as Ironton, Ohio; and 3) Mrs. Friedrich intended to return to the United States with Thomas when she was discharged from the military. Although these ties may be strong enough to establish legal residence in the United States, they do not establish habitual residence.

A person can have only one habitual residence. On its face, habitual residence pertains to customary residence prior to the removal. The court must look back in time, not forward. All of the factors listed by Mrs. Friedrich pertain to the future. Moreover, they reflect the intentions of Mrs. Friedrich; it is the habitual residence of the child that must be determined. Mrs. Friedrich undoubtedly established ties between Thomas and the United States and may well have intended for Thomas to move to the United States at some time in the future. But before Mrs. Friedrich removed Thomas to the United States without the knowledge or consent of Mr. Friedrich, Thomas had resided exclusively in Germany. Any future plans that Mrs. Friedrich had for Thomas to reside in the United States are irrelevant to our inquiry.

The district court appears to agree that before the argument of July 27, 1991, Thomas was a habitual resident of Germany. The district court, however, found that Thomas's habitual residence was "altered" from Germany to the United States when Mr. Friedrich forced Mrs. Friedrich and Thomas to leave the family apartment.

Habitual residence cannot be so easily altered. Even if we accept the district court's finding that Mr. Friedrich forced Mrs. Friedrich to leave the family apartment, no evidence supports a finding that Mr. Friedrich forced Mrs. Friedrich to remove Thomas from Germany; Mr. Friedrich was not even aware of the removal until after the fact. . . .

More fundamentally, Thomas's habitual residence in Germany is not predicated on the care or protection provided by his German father nor does it shift to the United States when his American mother assumes the role of primary caretaker. Thomas's habitual residence can be "altered" only by a change in geography and the passage of time, not by changes in parental affection and responsibility. The change in geography must occur before the questionable removal; here, the removal precipitated the change in geography. If we were to determine that by removing Thomas from his habitual residence without Mr. Friedrich's knowledge or consent Mrs. Friedrich "altered" Thomas's habitual residence, we would render the Convention meaningless. It would be an open invitation for all parents who abduct their children to characterize their wrongful removals as alterations of habitual residence. . . .

The district court also found that Mr. Friedrich "terminated his actual exercise of his parental custody rights" when he "unilaterally" expelled Mrs. Friedrich and Thomas from his residence. We are doubtful that the evidence supports a finding that Mr. Friedrich unilaterally expelled Mrs. Friedrich and Thomas from the family apartment. . . .

Even if we accept the district court's finding that Mrs. Friedrich removed Thomas from Mr. Friedrich's residence only because she was forced to do so by Mr. Friedrich, we doubt that Mr. Friedrich terminated his custody rights. Mr. Friedrich continued to have contact with both Mrs. Friedrich and his child. Mr. Friedrich assisted Mrs. Friedrich in establishing quarters on the base and helped her move Thomas's crib on to the base. On July 29, 1991, Mr. Friedrich visited his child for four hours. On August 1, 1991, Mr. Friedrich met with Mrs. Friedrich to discuss the future of their relationship and the custody of Thomas. Although they gave conflicting accounts of the meeting, both stated that plans were made for Mr. Friedrich to visit Thomas within the next week.

Under the Convention, whether a parent was exercising lawful custody rights over a child at the time of removal must be determined under the law of the child's habitual residence. Hague Convention, Article 3. We have determined that Thomas was a habitual resident of Germany when Mrs. Friedrich removed him to the United States. Neither the district court, nor either party on appeal, applied German custody law to the above facts. . . . [W]e remand to the district court with instructions to make a specific inquiry as to whether, under German law, Mr. Friedrich was exercising his custody rights at the time of Thomas's removal.

NOTES AND QUESTIONS

1. Neither the Hague Convention nor the implementing federal legislation defines "habitual residence," even though this is a key term in applying the treaty. A leading British case defines "habitual residence":

> [T]here must be a degree of settled purpose. The purpose may be one or there may be several. It may be specific or general. All that the law requires is that there is a settled purpose. That is not to say that the propositus intends to stay where he is indefinitely. Indeed his purpose while settled may be for a limited period. Education, business or profession, employment, health, family or merely love of the place spring to mind as common reasons for a choice of regular abode, and there may well be many others. All that is necessary is that the purpose of living where one does has a sufficient degree of continuity to be properly described as settled.

In re Bates, No. CA 122.2-89, High Court of Justice, Family Division Court, Royal Court of Justice, United Kingdom, 1989, as quoted in Slagenweit v. Slagenweit, 841 F. Supp. 264, 268-269 (N.D. Iowa 1993). Courts in the United States differ about the appellate standard of review for findings regarding habitual residence, with some courts regarding this as a purely factual question and others as a mixed question of law and fact. *See* Silverman v. Silverman, 338 F.3d 886 (8th Cir. 2003) and cases cited therein.

Could a child acquire a habitual residence in a country to which he or she was wrongfully removed in the first place? Why or why not? Meredith v. Meredith, 759 F. Supp. 1432 (D. Ariz. 1991), in which a mother left the United States to visit France with the father's consent but then went into hiding, suggests that the answer should be no. However, in Slagenweit v. Slagenweit, above, the court held that a child had become a habitual resident of Iowa even though her father refused to return her to Germany, in violation of an agreement with her mother.

Where is the habitual residence of a very young infant? In Delvoye v. Lee, 329 F.3d 330 (3d Cir. 2003), a father argued that his baby, who was born in Belgium, was habitually resident in Belgium. The appellate court ruled for the mother, saying,

> Where a matrimonial home exists, i.e., where both parents share a settled intent to reside, determining the habitual residence of an infant presents no particular problem, it simply calls for application of the analysis under the Convention with which courts have become familiar. Where the parents' relationship has broken down, however, as in this case, the character of the problem changes. Of course, the mere fact that conflict has developed between the parents does not *ipso facto* disestablish a child's habitual residence, once it has come into existence. But where the conflict is contemporaneous with the birth of the child, no habitual residence may ever come into existence.
>
> That is not to say that the infant's habitual residence automatically becomes that of his mother. . . .
>
> . . . Here, . . . the district court found that respondent, at petitioner's urging, had traveled to Belgium to avoid the cost of the birth of the child and intended to live there only temporarily. She retained her ties to New York, not having taken her non-maternity clothes, holding only a three-month visa and living out of the two

suitcases she brought with her. Thus, there is lacking the requisite "degree of common purpose" to habitually reside in Belgium. . . .

Because petitioner and respondent lacked the "shared intentions regarding their child's presence [in Belgium]," Baby S did not become an habitual resident there. Even if petitioner intended that he become an habitual resident, respondent evidenced no such intention. Addressing the status of a newborn child, one Scottish commentator said:

> [A] newborn child born in the country where his . . . parents have their habitual residence could normally be regarded as habitually resident in that country. Where a child is born while his . . . mother is temporarily present in a country other than that of her habitual residence it does seem, however, that the child will normally have no habitual residence until living in a country on a footing of some stability.

Dr. E.M. Clive, "The Concept of Habitual Residence," *The Juridical Review part 3,* 138, 146 (1997).

329 F.3d at 333-334. For commentary, *see* Stephen E. Schwartz, The Myth of Habitual Residence: Why American Courts Should Adopt the *Delvoye* Standard for Habitual Residence Under the Hague Convention on the Civil Aspects of International Child Abduction, 10 Cardozo Women's L.J. 691, 693-694 (2004).

2. On remand in *Friedrich* the trial court found that Thomas Friedrich's father was actually exercising custodial rights at the time his mother removed him from Germany to Ohio, so that her removal was "wrongful" under the Hague Convention. The court ruled that the law of the child's habitual residence should be used to determine what constitutes actual exercise of custodial rights. The court declined to create a common law definition of "exercising custody rights" that would be distinct from having legal custody rights for three reasons: (1) American courts are ill suited to determine the consequences of parental behavior under the law of other countries while they can determine if parents have legal custody rights, (2) for American courts to determine on the facts whether a parent had actually exercised custody rights would come too close to hearing the merits of the custody dispute, and (3) "the confusing dynamics of quarrels and informal separations make it difficult to assess adequately the acts and motivations of a parent." 78 F.3d at 1065. The court concluded, "We therefore hold that, if a person has valid custody rights to a child under the law of the country of the child's habitual residence, that person cannot fail to 'exercise' those custody rights under the Hague Convention short of acts that constitute clear and unequivocal abandonment of the child." 78 F.3d at 1066. The Sixth Circuit affirmed in Friedrich v. Friedrich, 78 F.3d 1060 (6th Cir. 1996). *See also* Miller v. Miller, 240 F.3d 392 (4th Cir. 2000); Zuker v. Andrews, 2 F. Supp. 2d 134 (D. Mass. 1998); Toren v. Toren, 26 F. Supp. 2d 240 (D. Mass. 1998).

3. Under the Hague Convention, a parent who does not have custody but who has visitation rights is not entitled to the remedy of return of the child to redress violation of the visitation rights, but the convention protects those rights without specifying a particular remedy. Hague Convention arts. 12 and 21. In Viragh v. Foldes, 415 Mass. 96, 612 N.E.2d 241 (1993), the Massachusetts Supreme Judicial Court approved an order requiring the custodial mother to pay the airfare for the father's twice-yearly visits from Hungary.

Sometimes a court couples an order granting custody and visitation with an order prohibiting the parents from leaving the jurisdiction; the latter provision is called a *ne exeat* clause in international law. According to Professor Weiner, most foreign courts have held that a right to visitation ("access") protected by a *ne exeat* clause is a custody right under the Hague Convention. Merle Weiner, Navigating the Road Between Uniformity and Progress: The Need for Purposive Analysis of the Hague Convention on the Civil Aspects of International Child Abduction, 33 Colum. Human Rights L. Rev. 275 (2002). American courts are divided on the question. *Compare* Croll v. Croll, 229 F.3d 133 (2d Cir. 2000); Gonzales v. Gutierrez, 311 F.3d 942 (9th Cir. 2002) (visitation with a *ne exeat* clause is not a custody right) *with* Furnes v. Reeves, 362 F.3d 702 (11th Cir. 2004) (contra). *See also* Lalo v. Malca, 318 F. Supp. 2d 1152 (S.D. Fla. 2004) (visitation rights with *ne exeat* clause and patria postestas rights amount to a custody right). Weiner criticizes *Croll*, saying that the court reached the correct outcome but used an analysis that was not sufficiently deferential to foreign case law. She argues that as more and more cases arise under the Hague Convention, problems of consistency of interpretation are becoming more apparent. She develops a method of analysis to solve this problem, applying general principles of international law and the underlying goals of the Hague Convention. *Id.*

4. As *Friedrich* indicates, Articles 12, 13, and 20 of the Convention provide exceptions to the requirement that a wrongfully removed or retained child be returned. In Tahan v. Duquette, 259 N.J. Super. 328, 613 A.2d 486 (App. Div. 1992), a father argued that Article 13(b), which provides that a child should not be returned if there is a grave risk of harm to the child, authorized the court to address the merits of the case and offered several witnesses to prove that the child would suffer psychological harm from being uprooted from the father's home. The court rejected his argument, saying,

> We agree with the trial judge that the Article 13b inquiry was not intended to deal with issues or factual questions which are appropriate for consideration in a plenary custody proceeding. Psychological profiles, detailed evaluations of parental fitness, evidence concerning lifestyle and the nature and quality of relationships all bear upon the ultimate issue. The Convention reserves these considerations to the appropriate tribunal in the place of habitual residence, here Canada, specifically Quebec. . . .
>
> Nevertheless, it is clear that Article 13b requires more than a cursory evaluation of the home jurisdiction's civil stability and the availability there of a tribunal to hear the custody complaint. If that were all that were required, the drafters of the Convention could have found a clear, more direct way of saying so. . . .
>
> To hold, as the trial court did, that the proper scope of inquiry precludes any focus on the people involved is, in our view, too narrow and mechanical. Without engaging in an exploration of psychological make-ups, ultimate determinations of parenting qualities, or the impact of life experiences, a court in the petitioned jurisdiction, in order to determine whether a realistic basis exists for apprehensions concerning the child's physical safety or mental well-being, must be empowered to evaluate the surroundings to which the child is to be sent and the basic personal qualities of those located there. . . . Here, however, the plaintiff indicated no intention to address the surroundings and those located there in his proofs. Every element of his proffer went to issues which, under the Convention, may only be addressed in a plenary custody proceeding in Quebec.

259 N.J. Super. at 334-335. Then what is the proper scope of an Article 13 inquiry? *See* Friedrich v. Friedrich, 78 F.3d 1060 (6th Cir. 1996); Walsh v. Walsh, 221 F.3d 204 (1st Cir. 2000).

Several recent cases have addressed under what circumstances domestic violence directed toward the abducting parent may constitute a grave risk of physical or psychological injury to the children so that return is not required. The leading case is Walsh v. Walsh, 221 F.3d 204 (1st Cir. 2000). The father, an Irish citizen, petitioned for return of his children after his wife took them to Massachusetts. It was undisputed that the children's habitual residence was Ireland and that the mother had wrongfully removed them. She argued that the father's extreme violence toward her and others and his chronic violation of court orders created a grave risk of injury to the children. The trial court rejected the argument, finding that the Irish authorities could act to protect the children and ordered specific undertakings from the father as a condition to the children's return. On appeal the First Circuit held that the trial court had erroneously insisted that the risk be "immediate," which is not required by the language of the convention, though it must be "grave." It then said that even a potentially grave risk does not justify refusal to return children if the court can be assured that the child can be protected in the country of return. However, the court held that on the facts of the case the child should not be returned. "Courts, when confronted with a grave risk of physical harm, have allowed the return of a child to the country of habitual residence, provided sufficient protection was afforded. Such an approach has little chance of working here. John's past acts clearly show that he thinks little of court orders. He has violated the orders of the courts of Massachusetts, and he has violated the orders of the courts of Ireland. There is every reason to believe that he will violate the undertakings he made to the district court in this case and any barring orders from the Irish courts." 221 F.3d at 221.

The court in Blondin v. Dubois, 238 F.3d 153 (2d Cir. 2001), extended this reasoning to more ambiguous facts. The mother took the children to the United States from France in violation of the father's custody rights. He petitioned for their return, and the mother raised the grave-risk-of-injury defense. Initially the trial court found that the children were at risk because of their father's violence and refused to return them, but the Second Circuit reversed and remanded for a determination of whether conditions could be imposed that would make return safe. Blondin v. Dubois, 189 F.3d 240 (2d Cir. 1999). On remand the trial court heard testimony about French law and practice in domestic violence cases and testimony from Dr. Albert Solnit to the effect that the children suffered post-traumatic stress disorder that would likely be triggered by a return to France, and that no conditions that the court might impose could alleviate the danger. The trial court again found that the children faced a grave risk from which they could not be protected, and the Second Circuit affirmed. Merle Weiner, in the article cited above, strongly criticizes the Second Circuit's analysis as being inconsistent with the decisions of most other courts about when consideration of grave danger crosses the line to become a consideration of the merits of the custody dispute. Weiner, supra, at 344-353. *See also* Linda Silberman & Karin Wolfe, The Importance of Private International Law for Family Issues in an Era of Globalization: Two Case Studies — International Child Abduction and Same-Sex Unions, 32 Hofstra L. Rev. 233 (2003).

5. Studies show that, contrary to some expectations, many, perhaps most, international abductors of children are mothers and that many of the relationships that these mothers left were marked by domestic violence. Geoffrey L. Freig & Rebecca L. Hega, When Parents Kidnap 18-19 (1993); Lord Chancellor's Dept., Child Abduction Unit, Report on the Third Meeting of the Special Commission to Discuss the Operation of the Hague Convention on the Civil Aspects of International Child Abduction, Apr. 8, 1997, at 1. Professor Weiner argues that the Hague Convention is not structured to allow flight from domestic violence as a defense and suggests options to assist domestic violence victims, ranging from courts requiring undertakings to guarantee the safety of fleeing mothers to making domestic violence a defense to return of the child. Merle Weiner, International Child Abduction and the Escape from Domestic Violence, 69 Fordham L. Rev. 593 (2000). *See also* Merle Weiner, The Potential and Challenges of Transnational Litigation for Feminists Concerned About Domestic Violence Here and Abroad, 11 Am. U. J. Gender Soc., Pol'y & L. 749 (2003).

More recently, Professor Weiner has argued that Article 20 of the Hague Convention, which provides that return of a child may be refused "if this would not be permitted by the fundamental principles of the requested State relating to the protection of human rights and international freedoms," should be interpreted to preclude ordering the return of a child whose mother is a domestic violence victim who cannot be protected in the child's habitual residence. Strengthening Article 20, in Les Enlévements d'Enfants á Travers les Frontières (Bruylant forthcoming 2004) (published in English); revised and reprinted as Strengthening Article 20, 38 U.S.F. L. Rev. 1 (2004); Using Article 20, 38 Fam. L.Q. — (2004).

6. If a Hague claim is raised in state court litigation regarding the child's custody, a federal court is expressly barred from relitigating the issue. 42 U.S.C. § 11603(g). What, though, if the Hague claim is not raised in the state court? Should a parent be barred by principles of *res judicata* or principles of abstention from later seeking return of the child in federal court? In Holder v. Holder, 305 F.3d 854 (9th Cir. 2002), the Ninth Circuit held that *res judicata* should not be applied to bar the federal court litigation, saying that to apply preclusion would undermine the purposes of the Hague Convention. The court continued, "It would undermine the very scheme created by the Hague Convention and ICARA to hold that a Hague Convention claim is barred by a state court *custody* determination, simply because a petitioner did not raise his Hague Convention claim in the initial custody proceeding. The *Hague Convention* provides that children are not automatically removed from its protections by virtue of a judicial decision awarding custody to the alleged abductor." 305 F.3d at 865 (emphasis in original). The court also held that the federal district court should not have stayed its Hague proceedings pending the outcome of state court custody litigation because the district court litigation was unlikely to resolve the issues in the Hague petition. Essential to the *Holder* decision is the conclusion that the issues in the Hague petition were not substantially similar to the issues in the state custody litigation, even though there might be some overlap between the Hague "habitual residence" and the state court "home state" issues. *See also* Mozes v. Mozes, 239 F.3d 1067 (9th Cir. 2001) and Silverman v. Silverman, 338 F.3d 886 (8th Cir. 2003).

7. Removing a child from the United States or retaining a child who has been in the United States outside the United States with intent to obstruct the lawful exercise of parental rights is a federal felony punishable by up to three years in prison. 18 U.S.C. § 1204, enacted as Pub. L. 103-173 § 2(a), Dec. 2, 1993. The statute creates three affirmative defenses: (1) the defendant had been granted custody or visitation by a court acting pursuant to the UCCJA, (2) the defendant was fleeing from an incident or pattern of domestic violence, and (3) the defendant had physical custody consistent with a custody order and failed to return the child because of circumstances beyond the defendant's control, provided that the defendant made reasonable attempts to notify the other parent or lawful custodian within 24 hours after the visitation period had expired. *Id.*

8. For further discussion, *see* Linda Silberman, Hague Convention on International Child Abduction: A Brief Overview and Case Law Analysis, 28 Fam. L.Q. 9 (1994); Richard Crouch, Resolving International Custody Disputes in the United States, 13 J. Am. Acad. Matrimonial Law. 229 (1996); Jan R. McMillan, Getting Them Back: The Disappointing Reality of Return Orders Under the Hague Convention on the Civil Aspects of International Child Abduction, 14 J. Am. Acad. Matrimonial Law. 99 (1997); Glen Skoler, A Psychological Critique of International Child Custody and Abduction Law, 32 Fam. L.Q. 557 (1998); Marilyn Freeman, The Effects and Consequences of International Child Abduction, 32 Fam. L.Q. 603 (1998).

F.   FEDERAL COURT JURISDICTION OVER DOMESTIC RELATIONS

ANKENBRANDT V. RICHARDS

504 U.S. 689 (1992)

WHITE, J. . . . Petitioner Carol Ankenbrandt, a citizen of Missouri, brought this lawsuit on September 26, 1989, on behalf of her daughters L. R. and S. R. against respondents Jon A. Richards and Debra Kesler, citizens of Louisiana, in the United States District Court for the Eastern District of Louisiana. Alleging federal jurisdiction based on the diversity of citizenship provision of § 1332, Ankenbrandt's complaint sought monetary damages for alleged sexual and physical abuse of the children committed by Richards and Kesler. Richards is the divorced father of the children and Kesler his female companion. On December 10, 1990, the District Court granted respondents' motion to dismiss this lawsuit. Citing In re Burrus, 136 U.S. 586, 593-594 (1890), for the proposition that "[t]he whole subject of the domestic relations of husband and wife, parent and child, belongs to the laws of the States and not to the laws of the United States," the court concluded that this case fell within what has become known as the "domestic relations" exception to diversity jurisdiction, and that it lacked jurisdiction over the case. . . .

We granted certiorari limited to the following questions: (1) Is there a domestic relations exception to federal jurisdiction? (2) If so, does it permit a district court to abstain from exercising diversity jurisdiction over a tort action for damages? . . .

The domestic relations exception upon which the courts below relied to decline jurisdiction has been invoked often by the lower federal courts. The seeming authority for doing so originally stemmed from the announcement in Barber v. Barber, 21 How. 582 (1859), that the federal courts have no jurisdiction over suits for divorce or the allowance of alimony. In that case, the Court heard a suit in equity brought by a wife (by her next friend) in federal district court pursuant to diversity jurisdiction against her former husband. She sought to enforce a decree from a New York state court, which had granted a divorce and awarded her alimony. The former husband thereupon moved to Wisconsin to place himself beyond the New York courts' jurisdiction so that the divorce decree there could not be enforced against him; he then sued for divorce in a Wisconsin court, representing to that court that his wife had abandoned him and failing to disclose the existence of the New York decree. In a suit brought by the former wife in Wisconsin Federal District Court, the former husband alleged that the court lacked jurisdiction. The court accepted jurisdiction and gave judgment for the divorced wife.

On appeal, it was argued that the District Court lacked jurisdiction on two grounds: first, that there was no diversity of citizenship because although divorced, the wife's citizenship necessarily remained that of her former husband; and second, that the whole subject of divorce and alimony, including a suit to enforce an alimony decree, was exclusively ecclesiastical at the time of the adoption of the Constitution and that the Constitution therefore placed the whole subject of divorce and alimony beyond the jurisdiction of the United States courts. Over the dissent of three Justices, the Court rejected both arguments. After an exhaustive survey of the authorities, the Court concluded that a divorced wife could acquire a citizenship separate from that of her former husband and that a suit to enforce an alimony decree rested within the federal courts' equity jurisdiction. . . . [T]he Court also announced the following limitation on federal jurisdiction:

> Our first remark is — and we wish it to be remembered — that this is not a suit asking the court for the allowance of alimony. That has been done by a court of competent jurisdiction. The court in Wisconsin was asked to interfere to prevent that decree from being defeated by fraud.
>
> We disclaim altogether any jurisdiction in the courts of the United States upon the subject of divorce, or for the allowance of alimony, either as an original proceeding in chancery or as an incident to divorce a vinculo, or to one from bed and board. . . .

The statements disclaiming jurisdiction over divorce and alimony decree suits, though technically dicta, formed the basis for excluding "domestic relations" cases from the jurisdiction of the lower federal courts, a jurisdictional limitation those courts have recognized ever since. . . .

Counsel argued in *Barber* that the Constitution prohibited federal courts from exercising jurisdiction over domestic relations cases. An examination of Article III, *Barber* itself, and our cases since *Barber* makes clear that the Constitution does not exclude domestic relations cases from the jurisdiction otherwise granted by statute to the federal courts. . . .

Subsequent decisions confirm that *Barber* was not relying on constitutional limits in justifying the exception. . . .

The Judiciary Act of 1789 provided that "the circuit courts shall have original cognizance, concurrent with the courts of the several States, of *all suits of a civil nature at common law or in equity, where the matter in dispute exceeds*, exclusive of costs, the sum or value of *five hundred dollars*, and . . . an alien is a party, or the suit is *between a citizen of the State where the suit is brought, and a citizen of another State*." Act of Sept. 24, 1789, § 11, 1 Stat. 73, 78. (Emphasis added.) The defining phrase, "all suits of a civil nature at common law or in equity," remained a key element of statutory provisions demarcating the terms of diversity jurisdiction until 1948, when Congress amended the diversity jurisdiction provision to eliminate this phrase and replace in its stead the term "all civil actions."

The *Barber* majority itself did not expressly refer to the diversity statute's use of the limitation on "suits of a civil nature at common law or in equity." The dissenters in *Barber*, however, implicitly made such a reference, for they suggested that the federal courts had no power over certain domestic relations actions because the court of chancery lacked authority to issue divorce and alimony decrees. . . .

We have no occasion here to join the historical debate over whether the English court of chancery had jurisdiction to handle certain domestic relations matters. . . . We thus are content to rest our conclusion that a domestic relations exception exists as a matter of statutory construction not on the accuracy of the historical justifications on which it was seemingly based, but rather on Congress's apparent acceptance of this construction of the diversity jurisdiction provisions in the years prior to 1948, when the statute limited jurisdiction to "suits of a civil nature at common law or in equity." . . . Considerations of *stare decisis* have particular strength in this context, where "the legislative power is implicated, and Congress remains free to alter what we have done." . . .

In the more than 100 years since this Court laid the seeds for the development of the domestic relations exception, the lower federal courts have applied it in a variety of circumstances. Many of these applications go well beyond the circumscribed situations posed by *Barber* and its progeny. *Barber* itself disclaimed federal jurisdiction over a narrow range of domestic relations issues involving the granting of a divorce and a decree of alimony, and stated the limits on federal-court power to intervene prior to the rendering of such orders:

> It is, that when a court of competent jurisdiction over the subject-matter and the parties decrees a divorce, and alimony to the wife as its incident, and is unable of itself to enforce the decree summarily upon the husband, that courts of equity will interfere to prevent the decree from being defeated by fraud. The interference, however, is limited to cases in which alimony has been decreed; then only to the extent of what is due, and always to cases in which no appeal is pending from the decree for the divorce or for alimony. Id., at 591.

The *Barber* Court thus did not intend to strip the federal courts of authority to hear cases arising from the domestic relations of persons unless they seek the granting or modification of a divorce or alimony decree. The holding of the case itself sanctioned the exercise of federal jurisdiction over the enforcement of an alimony decree that had been properly obtained in a state court of competent jurisdiction. . . .

Subsequently, this Court expanded the domestic relations exception to include decrees in child custody cases. . . .

Not only is our conclusion rooted in respect for this long-held understanding, it is also supported by sound policy considerations. Issuance of decrees of this type not infrequently involves retention of jurisdiction by the court and deployment of social workers to monitor compliance. As a matter of judicial economy, state courts are more eminently suited to work of this type than are federal courts, which lack the close association with state and local government organizations dedicated to handling issues that arise out of conflicts over divorce, alimony, and child custody decrees. Moreover, as a matter of judicial expertise, it makes far more sense to retain the rule that federal courts lack power to issue these types of decrees because of the special proficiency developed by state tribunals over the past century and a half in handling issues that arise in the granting of such decrees.

By concluding, as we do, that the domestic relations exception encompasses only cases involving the issuance of a divorce, alimony, or child custody decree, we necessarily find that the Court of Appeals erred by affirming the District Court's invocation of this exception. This lawsuit in no way seeks such a decree; rather, it alleges that respondents Richards and Kesler committed torts against L. R. and S. R., Ankenbrandt's children by Richards. Federal subject-matter jurisdiction pursuant to § 1332 thus is proper in this case. . . .

JUDITH RESNIK, *"NATURALLY" WITHOUT GENDER: WOMEN, JURISDICTION, AND THE FEDERAL COURTS*

66 N.Y.U. L. Rev. 1682, 1742-1744, 1750-1757 (1991)

The assumption of lack of federal judicial power over personal relations has been eroded by litigation over the course of this century about reproduction and federal benefits, both of which structure relations "among different members of private families in their domestic intercourse." Further, that assertion ignored nineteenth century federal efforts to control polygamy and sexual relations, which in turn affect family relations, albeit nontraditional ones. In 1862, 1882, and 1887, Congress outlawed polygamy. Fragments of these laws still remain. While this legislation was directed at federal governance of the territories and was implemented by the federal courts in their capacity as "territorial courts" (thus acting as "state courts" for these purposes), other federal legislation did bring the federal courts into the governance of multiple marriages in the states. The "Mann Act"—involving federal regulation of sexual activity—was used in prosecutions of individuals who transported women in "interstate commerce." In one of the cases prosecuted under the Mann Act, the Court expressly endorsed Congress's authority to "defeat what are deemed to be immoral practices; the fact that the means used may have the 'quality of police regulations' is not consequential." Despite a claim of noninvolvement in interpersonal relations (some of which might bear the title "family"), federal law and federal courts have, on selected occasions, taken on these issues. . . .

Pointing out links between federal law and families raises a question, traditional for federal courts scholars. While not discussed by federal courts jurisprudence, a complex mosaic of federal regulation of economic and social relations now overlays state laws on divorce, alimony, and child support. What is to be made of this fact of joint governance of the field? Because I hope scholars of federal courts will take seriously the topic of federal family law, it is appropriate to consider how doctrinal developments — shaped by different images of what is on the national agenda that federal courts implement and adjudicate — might take federal courts' authority over family life into account. The central question is what "business is the federal business," and it is time to answer this question by recognizing that there already is joint federal and state governance of an array of issues, from land use and torts to families. Once understood as a joint endeavor, the next issue is how to allocate authority.

A first possibility is that federal court involvement in family life is bad, per se, at a structural level. This claim takes seriously the arguments made in the many cases espousing (slight pun intended) state control over family life and fearing that the federal courts would become hopelessly "enmeshed" in family disputes. Under this vision, the states (and Indian tribes) as smaller units of government are closer to "the people" and thus a more appropriate level of government to determine matters affecting intimate life.

Possible justifications for this view exist. Contemporary invocations of the domestic relations exception discard arguments based on ecclesiastical authority, the alleged lack of jurisdictional diversity between married couples, and the claim that divorces lack monetary value — all in favor of a "modern view that state courts have historically decided these matters and have developed both a well-known expertise in these cases and a strong interest in disposing of them." . . . Holding aside the ever-present question of boundaries, doctrine might shift in a variety of ways when ideological claims about the relationship between federal courts and family are revised.

First, one could insist that, despite recognition of federal laws of the family, the claim of deference to state governance remains strong and, as a matter of doctrine, complete abstention (a form of reverse preemption) is desirable. To the extent recent federal law in bankruptcy, pensions, and benefits law points in the other direction, that erosion should be stopped — by legislation or judicial interpretation. But were one to really press this claim — that states are specially situated and should be controlling family life — one would not seek only to cabin the federal courts. This position would also require urging Congress and agencies to avoid defining families by rewriting statutes and regulations to incorporate state law, so as to permit state governance of interpersonal relations. An array of federal statutes would have to incorporate state definitions of families, and what would be lost in uniformity and national norms would be gained in recognition of the special relationship of states in defining family life. . . .

Yet a problem remains. The current hierarchy stipulates the federal courts as most powerful; the supremacy clause confirms that sense of authority. Further, federal courts theorists might affirmatively argue that federal courts are needed in this area — either because of their special capacity to protect the politically disfavored or because federal sovereign and administrative interests are at stake. While neither the appeal to the community envisioned by the claim of closeness of the state to the family nor the concern about attitudes and knowledge of federal judges should be discounted, the "inevitability of federal involvement" in family life remains, as does a sense that the rejection of that role by federal courts reconfirms the marginalization of women and families from national life.

Federal involvement emerges here, as it does in torts, land use, health regulation, criminal law, and other areas, because of the wealth of interactions that make the imagined coherence of the very categories "federal" and "state" themselves problematic. Whether looking at the problem from the top down, and seeing "joint governance" or considering the issue from the perspective of individuals and speaking of "membership in multiple communities," the point is the same: an interlocking, enmeshed regulatory structure covers the host of human activity in the United States. There is no a priori line one can invoke to separate legal regulation into two bounded boxes "state" and "federal." Uniform state laws demonstrate the limits of state court borders and the need for regulatory structures that bridge them. State and federal court interpretations of "family" are unavoidable.

NOTES AND QUESTIONS

1. As *Barber* and *Ankenbrandt* both make clear, and as Professor Resnik also emphasizes, the domestic relations exception does not preclude federal courts from hearing all cases arising from matrimonial matters. For example, the courts have held that tort suits based on interference with custody and visitation are not within the exception. *See*, e.g., Drewes v. Ilnicki, 863 F.2d 469 (6th Cir. 1988); MacIntyre v. MacIntyre, 771 F.2d 1316 (9th Cir. 1985); Bennett v. Bennett, 682 F.2d 1039 (D.C. Cir. 1982). In Lannan v. Maul, 979 F.2d 627 (8th Cir. 1992), the court held that a child's suit to enforce a separation agreement term for her benefit was not within the exception either. In *Ankenbrandt* the Court said that state courts are "eminently more suited" to handle suits requiring the involvement of state social workers. Why? How would you create the line between federal and non-federal jurisdiction? Or should the domestic relations exception simply be abandoned? In addition to Professor Resnik's analysis, *see* Naomi R. Cahn, Family Law, Federalism, and the Federal Courts, 79 Iowa L. Rev. 1073 (1994).

2. If the domestic relations exception is difficult to justify on a purely historical basis, why is it retained in *Ankenbrandt*? Is there any inconsistency between the result in *Ankenbrandt* and the arguably increased constitutional review of restrictions on marriage and the adoption of federal legislation governing child support and child custody awards?

3. In Thompson v. Thompson, 484 U.S. 174 (1988), the Supreme Court held that Congress did not intend to create an implied federal cause of action when it enacted the PKPA. Had the court ruled to the contrary, the effect would have been to open the federal courts to litigation over the validity of conflicting custody orders from different states. In California v. Superior Court, 482 U.S. 400 (1987), Louisiana asked California to extradite a father and grandfather who were charged with kidnapping. The men took the father's children from Louisiana in violation of a Louisiana custody order. They argued, in effect, that Louisiana had not charged them with a crime because the Louisiana order violated the PKPA. The Supreme Court held, however, that in an extradition proceeding California could not inquire into the merits of a jurisdictional dispute.

CHILDREN, PARENTS, AND THE STATE

III

CHILDREN, PARENTS,
AND THE STATE

Determining Legal Parenthood: Marriage, Biology, and Function

12

A. INTRODUCTION

It is tempting to take the meaning of "family" or "parenthood" for granted. In the paradigm case, children live with their birth parents, who married before the children were conceived and born. No question arises about whether this group constitutes a family, about who is considered a parent, or about the status of the children. In addition, the lines of family decision-making authority and financial responsibility are clearly drawn; in the Anglo-American tradition, the nuclear family assumes responsibility for its offspring and receives a large measure of deference from the state.

However, many households do not take this form, and millions of children in the United States do not live in such households. In 1998 approximately 28 percent of all children under 18 lived with only one parent. Most of these (84 percent) lived with their mothers, and about four in ten of these single mothers had never been married. Of the single fathers living with their children, about one-third had never been married. The majority of children living with a single parent were white, but black and Hispanic children were much more likely to live with a single parent than were white children. Census Bureau, Marital Status and Living Arrangements: March 1998 (Update) (Current Population Reports P20-514).

Several social phenomena account for the extent to which family structure departs from the traditional model. In addition to premature death of a parent, high rates of divorce and of childbirth to unmarried mothers have combined to make single-parent, especially mother-headed, families common in this country. The following charts show major trends.

CHILDREN UNDER 18 LIVING IN
ONE-PARENT HOUSEHOLDS
(IN THOUSANDS)

	2003	1990	1980	1970
Child lives with mother who is:				
Never married	7,006	4,365	1,745	527
Married, spouse absent	3,346	3,416	3,610	3,234
Divorced	5,756	5,118	4,766	2,296
Widowed	663	975	1,286	1,395
Child lives with father who is:				
Never married	1,172	488	75	30
Married, spouse absent	550	351	288	287
Divorced	1,429	1,004	515	177
Widowed	173	150	183	254

Source: U.S. Bureau of the Census, Living Arrangements of Children Under 18 Years Old: 1960 to Present, Ch-1 through Ch-5 (2004). Internet release date: September 15, 2004.

The comparable figures for African-American and Latino children are even more dramatic. While significantly more than half of African-American children lived with both parents in 1970, by 2003, that proportion had fallen below 40 percent, with the majority of black children living only with their mothers. A majority of Latino children continue to live with both parents, but in 2003 more than one-third lived in single-parent families.

The labels "single parent" or "mother only" do not tell the full story, however. Researchers from the Urban Institute reported that "[d]uring the late 1990s, the share of children living in single-mother families declined significantly. Rather than a concomitant rise in the share of children living with married parents, however, the data show an increase in cohabitation. This is a source of concern for policymakers and analysts because previous research demonstrates that living with cohabitors is not as beneficial to children as living with married parents and, in some cases, no better than living with a single parent." Gregory Acs & Sandi Nelson, The Kids Are Alright? Children's Well-Being and the Rise in Cohabitation (No. B-48 in series New Federalism: National Survey of America's Families, July 31, 2002), *available at* the institute's web site, *http://www.urban.org/*.

These observations raise the increasingly complex issue of which adults should receive legal recognition in children's lives. Marriage once provided a clear way to distinguish between those biological parents who would be legally bound to their children and those who would not, and which of the mother's partners — who might or might not be biologically related to the child — would receive legal recognition and which would not. Today's family arrangements, however, create several categories of potential parents outside marriage: the biological father who may never have lived with the child, the mother's partner who may have cared for the child from birth, adoptive parents, grandparents, gestational mothers, and a variety of "functional parents" to whom the child may be deeply attached.

This chapter will first examine the constitutional rights of those designated as legal parents in relationship to others who might play a parental role. The rest of the chapter will then explore the legal designation of parenthood, examining its relationship to marriage, biological ties, stepparent status, and same-sex partnership. Chapter 13 considers alternative means of establishing parental status, including adoption and assisted reproduction.

1. The Constitutional Rights of Parents

One way of approaching the definition of family is to ask what difference the definition makes. The issue in the following case is what degree of deference the Constitution guarantees for parental decision making. In reading the following case, consider how the Supreme Court's decision might affect the importance of who fits the definition of a legal parent and who does not in other cases. Consider as well how the definition of "parent" may affect the extent of constitutional protection afforded to "families."

TROXEL V. GRANVILLE

530 U.S. 57 (2000)

Justice O'CONNOR announced the judgment of the Court and delivered an opinion, in which THE CHIEF JUSTICE, Justice GINSBURG, and Justice BREYER join.

* * *

Tommie Granville and Brad Troxel shared a relationship that ended in June 1991. The two never married, but they had two daughters, Isabelle and Natalie. Jenifer and Gary Troxel are Brad's parents, and thus the paternal grandparents of Isabelle and Natalie. After Tommie and Brad separated in 1991, Brad lived with his parents and regularly brought his daughters to his parents' home for weekend visitation. Brad committed suicide in May 1993. Although the Troxels at first continued to see Isabelle and Natalie on a regular basis after their son's death, Tommie Granville informed the Troxels in October 1993 that she wished to limit their visitation with her daughters to one short visit per month.

In December 1993, the Troxels . . . [petitioned for visitation under Washington law.] Section 26.10.160(3) [of the Wash. Rev. Code] provides: "Any person may petition the court for visitation rights at any time including, but not limited to, custody proceedings. The court may order visitation rights for any person when visitation may serve the best interest of the child whether or not there has been any change of circumstances." . . . In 1995, the Superior Court issued an oral ruling and entered a visitation decree ordering visitation one weekend per month, one week during the summer, and four hours on both of the petitioning grandparents' birthdays.

Granville appealed, during which time she married Kelly Wynn. Before addressing the merits of Granville's appeal, the Washington Court of Appeals remanded the case to the Superior Court for entry of written findings of fact and conclusions of law. On remand, the Superior Court found that visitation was in Isabelle and Natalie's best interests.

* * *

The Washington Supreme Court granted the Troxels' petition for review and, after consolidating their case with two other visitation cases, affirmed. . . . We granted certiorari, . . . and now affirm the judgment.

II

The demographic changes of the past century make it difficult to speak of an average American family. The composition of families varies greatly from household to household. While many children may have two married parents and grandparents who visit regularly, many other children are raised in single-parent households. In 1996, children living with only one parent accounted for 28 percent of all children under age 18 in the United States. . . . Understandably, in these single-parent households, persons outside the nuclear family are called upon with increasing frequency to assist in the everyday tasks of child rearing. In many cases, grandparents play an important role. For example, in 1998, approximately 4 million children—or 5.6 percent of all children under age 18—lived in the household of their grandparents.

The nationwide enactment of nonparental visitation statutes is assuredly due, in some part, to the States' recognition of these changing realities of the American family. Because grandparents and other relatives undertake duties of a parental nature in many households, States have sought to ensure the welfare of the children therein by protecting the relationships those children form with such third parties. The States' nonparental visitation statutes are further supported by a recognition, which varies from State to State, that children should have the opportunity to benefit from relationships with statutorily specified persons—for example, their grandparents. The extension of statutory rights in this area to persons other than a child's parents, however, comes with an obvious cost. For example, the State's recognition of an independent third-party interest in a child can place a substantial burden on the traditional parent-child relationship. Contrary to Justice STEVENS' accusation, our description of state nonparental visitation statutes in these terms, of course, is not meant to suggest that "children are so much chattel." Rather, our terminology is intended to highlight the fact that these statutes can present questions of constitutional import.

* * *

The liberty interest at issue in this case—the interest of parents in the care, custody, and control of their children—is perhaps the oldest of the fundamental liberty interests recognized by this Court. More than 75 years ago, in Meyer v. Nebraska, we held that the "liberty" protected by the Due Process Clause includes the right of parents to "establish a home and bring up children" and "to control the education of their own." Two years later, in Pierce v. Society of Sisters, we again held that the "liberty of parents and guardians" includes the right "to direct the upbringing and education of children under their control." We explained in Pierce that "[t]he child is not the mere creature of the State; those who nurture him and direct his destiny have the right, coupled with the high duty, to recognize and prepare him for additional obligations." We returned to the subject in Prince v. Massachusetts, and again confirmed that there is a constitutional dimension to the right of parents to direct the upbringing of their children. "It is cardinal with us that the custody, care and nurture of the child reside first in the parents, whose primary function and freedom include preparation for obligations the state can neither supply nor hinder."

Section 26.10.160(3), as applied to Granville and her family in this case, unconstitutionally infringes on that fundamental parental right. The Washington nonparental visitation statute is breathtakingly broad. According to the statute's text, "[a]ny person may petition the court for visitation rights *at any time*," and the court may grant such visitation rights whenever "visitation may serve *the best interest of the child*." § 26.10.160(3) (emphases added). That language effectively permits any third party seeking visitation to subject any decision by a parent concerning visitation of the parent's children to state-court review. Once the visitation petition has been filed in court and the matter is placed before a judge, a parent's decision that visitation would not be in the child's best interest is accorded no deference. Section 26.10.160(3) contains no requirement that a court accord the parent's decision any presumption of validity or any weight whatsoever. Instead, the Washington statute places the best-interest determination solely in the hands of the judge. Should the judge disagree with the parent's estimation of the child's best interests, the judge's view necessarily prevails. Thus, in practical effect, in the State of Washington a court can disregard and overturn any decision by a fit custodial parent concerning visitation whenever a third party affected by the decision files a visitation petition, based solely on the judge's determination of the child's best interests. The Washington Supreme Court had the opportunity to give § 26.10.160(3) a narrower reading, but it declined to do so. . . .

Turning to the facts of this case, the record reveals that the Superior Court's order was based on precisely the type of mere disagreement we have just described and nothing more. The Superior Court's order was not founded on any special factors that might justify the State's interference with Granville's fundamental right to make decisions concerning the rearing of her two daughters. To be sure, this case involves a visitation petition filed by grandparents soon after the death of their son — the father of Isabelle and Natalie — but the combination of several factors here compels our conclusion that § 26.10.160(3), as applied, exceeded the bounds of the Due Process Clause.

First, the Troxels did not allege, and no court has found, that Granville was an unfit parent. That aspect of the case is important, for there is a presumption that fit parents act in the best interests of their children. . . .

Accordingly, so long as a parent adequately cares for his or her children (i.e., is fit), there will normally be no reason for the State to inject itself into the private realm of the family to further question the ability of that parent to make the best decisions concerning the rearing of that parent's children.

The problem here is not that the Washington Superior Court intervened, but that when it did so, it gave no special weight at all to Granville's determination of her daughters' best interests. More importantly, it appears that the Superior Court applied exactly the opposite presumption. In reciting its oral ruling after the conclusion of closing arguments, the Superior Court judge explained:

"The burden is to show that it is in the best interest of the children to have some visitation and some quality time with their grandparents. I think in most situations a commonsensical approach [is that] it is normally in the best interest of the children to spend quality time with the grandparent, unless the grandparent, [sic] there are some issues or problems involved wherein the grandparents, their lifestyles are going to impact adversely upon the children. That certainly isn't the case here from what I can tell."

The judge's comments suggest that he presumed the grandparents' request should be granted unless the children would be "impact[ed] adversely." In effect, the judge placed on Granville, the fit custodial parent, the burden of disproving that visitation would be in the best interest of her daughters. The judge reiterated moments later: "I think [visitation with the Troxels] would be in the best interest of the children and I haven't been shown it is not in [the] best interest of the children."

The decisional framework employed by the Superior Court directly contravened the traditional presumption that a fit parent will act in the best interest of his or her child. In that respect, the court's presumption failed to provide any protection for Granville's fundamental constitutional right to make decisions concerning the rearing of her own daughters. . . . In an ideal world, parents might always seek to cultivate the bonds between grandparents and their grandchildren. Needless to say, however, our world is far from perfect, and in it the decision whether such an intergenerational relationship would be beneficial in any specific case is for the parent to make in the first instance. And, if a fit parent's decision of the kind at issue here becomes subject to judicial review, the court must accord at least some special weight to the parent's own determination.

Finally, we note that there is no allegation that Granville ever sought to cut off visitation entirely. Rather, the present dispute originated when Granville informed the Troxels that she would prefer to restrict their visitation with Isabelle and Natalie to one short visit per month and special holidays. In the Superior Court proceedings Granville did not oppose visitation but instead asked that the duration of any visitation order be shorter than that requested by the Troxels. . . .

Considered together with the Superior Court's reasons for awarding visitation to the Troxels, the combination of these factors demonstrates that the visitation order in this case was an unconstitutional infringement on Granville's fundamental right to make decisions concerning the care, custody, and control of her two daughters. The Washington Superior Court failed to accord the determination of Granville, a fit custodial parent, any material weight. . . . As we have explained, the Due Process Clause does not permit a State to infringe on the fundamental right of parents to make childrearing decisions simply because a state judge believes a "better" decision could be made. Neither the Washington nonparental visitation statute generally—which places no limits on either the persons who may petition for visitation or the circumstances in which such a petition may be granted—nor the Superior Court in this specific case required anything more. Accordingly, we hold that § 26.10.160(3), as applied in this case, is unconstitutional. . . .

* * *

Justice SOUTER, concurring in the judgment.

I concur in the judgment affirming the decision of the Supreme Court of Washington, whose facial invalidation of its own state statute is consistent with this Court's prior cases addressing the substantive interests at stake. I would say no more. The issues that might well be presented by reviewing a decision addressing the specific application of the state statute by the trial court, are not before us and do not call for turning any fresh furrows in the "treacherous field" of substantive due process.

* * *

Justice THOMAS, concurring in the judgment.

. . . I agree with the plurality that this Court's recognition of a fundamental right of parents to direct the upbringing of their children resolves this case. . . . I would apply strict scrutiny to infringements of fundamental rights. Here, the State of Washington lacks even a legitimate governmental interest—to say nothing of a compelling one—in second-guessing a fit parent's decision regarding visitation with third parties. On this basis, I would affirm the judgment below.

Justice STEVENS, dissenting.

The Court today wisely declines to endorse either the holding or the reasoning of the Supreme Court of Washington. In my opinion, the Court would have been even wiser to deny certiorari. Given the problematic character of the trial court's decision and the uniqueness of the Washington statute, there was no pressing need to review a State Supreme Court decision that merely requires the state legislature to draft a better statute.

* * *

In response to Tommie Granville's federal constitutional challenge, the State Supreme Court broadly held that Wash. Rev. Code § 26.10.160(3) (Supp.1996) was invalid on its face under the Federal Constitution. Despite the nature of this judgment, Justice O'CONNOR would hold that the Washington visitation statute violated the Due Process Clause of the Fourteenth Amendment only as applied. I agree with Justice SOUTER that this approach is untenable.

* * *

We are . . . presented with the unconstrued terms of a state statute and a State Supreme Court opinion that, in my view, significantly misstates the effect of the Federal Constitution upon any construction of that statute. Given that posture, I believe the Court should identify and correct the two flaws in the reasoning of the state court's majority opinion, and remand for further review of the trial court's disposition of this specific case.

II

In my view, the State Supreme Court erred in its federal constitutional analysis because neither the provision granting "any person" the right to petition the court for visitation, nor the absence of a provision requiring a "threshold . . . finding of harm to the child," provides a sufficient basis for holding that the statute is invalid in all its applications. I believe that a facial challenge should fail whenever a statute has "a 'plainly legitimate sweep.'" Under the Washington statute, there are plainly any number of cases—indeed, one suspects, the most common to arise—in which the "person" among "any" seeking visitation is a once-custodial caregiver, an intimate relation, or even a genetic parent. Even the Court would seem to agree that in many circumstances, it would be constitutionally permissible for a court to award some visitation of a child to a parent or previous caregiver in cases of parental separation or divorce, cases of disputed custody, cases involving temporary foster care or guardianship, and so forth. As the statute plainly sweeps in a great deal of the permissible, the State Supreme Court majority incorrectly concluded that a statute authorizing "any person" to file a petition seeking visitation privileges would invariably run afoul of the Fourteenth Amendment.

The second key aspect of the Washington Supreme Court's holding—that the Federal Constitution requires a showing of actual or potential "harm" to the child before a court may order visitation continued over a parent's objections—finds no support in this Court's case law. While, as the Court recognizes, the Federal Constitution certainly protects the parent-child relationship from arbitrary impairment by the State, we have never held that the parent's liberty interest in this relationship is so inflexible as to establish a rigid constitutional shield, protecting every arbitrary parental decision from any challenge absent a threshold finding of harm. The presumption that parental decisions generally serve the best interests of their children is sound, and clearly in the normal case the parent's interest is paramount. But even a fit parent is capable of treating a child like a mere possession.

Cases like this do not present a bipolar struggle between the parents and the State over who has final authority to determine what is in a child's best interests. There is at a minimum a third individual, whose interests are implicated in every case to which the statute applies—the child.

* * *

. . . A parent's rights with respect to her child have thus never been regarded as absolute, but rather are limited by the existence of an actual, developed relationship with a child, and are tied to the presence or absence of some embodiment of family. These limitations have arisen, not simply out of the definition of parenthood itself, but because of this Court's assumption that a parent's interests in a child must be balanced against the State's long-recognized interests as parens patriae, and, critically, the child's own complementary interest in preserving relationships that serve her welfare and protection.

* * *

. . . [P]resumptions notwithstanding, we should recognize that there may be circumstances in which a child has a stronger interest at stake than mere protection from serious harm caused by the termination of visitation by a "person" other than a parent. The almost infinite variety of family relationships that pervade our ever-changing society strongly counsel against the creation by this Court of a constitutional rule that treats a biological parent's liberty interest in the care and supervision of her child as an isolated right that may be exercised arbitrarily. . . . It seems clear to me that the Due Process Clause of the Fourteenth Amendment leaves room for States to consider the impact on a child of possibly arbitrary parental decisions that neither serve nor are motivated by the best interests of the child.

Accordingly, I respectfully dissent.

Justice SCALIA, dissenting.

In my view, a right of parents to direct the upbringing of their children is among the "unalienable Rights" with which the Declaration of Independence proclaims "all Men . . . are endowed by their Creator." And in my view that right is also among the "othe[r] [rights] retained by the people" which the Ninth Amendment says the Constitution's enumeration of rights "shall not be construed to deny or disparage." The Declaration of Independence, however, is not a legal prescription conferring powers upon the courts; and the Constitution's refusal to "deny or disparage" other rights is far removed from affirming any one of them, and even farther removed from authorizing judges to identify what they might be, and to enforce the judges' list against laws duly enacted by the people. Consequently, while I would think it entirely compatible with the commitment to representative democracy set forth in the founding documents to argue, in legislative chambers or in electoral campaigns, that the state has no power to interfere with parents' authority over the rearing of their children, I do not believe that the power which the Constitution confers upon me as a judge entitles me to deny legal effect to laws that (in my view) infringe upon what is (in my view) that unenumerated right.

* * *

Judicial vindication of "parental rights" under a Constitution that does not even mention them requires (as Justice KENNEDY's opinion rightly points out) not only a judicially crafted definition of parents, but also — unless, as no one believes, the parental rights are to be absolute — judicially approved assessments of "harm to the child" and judicially defined gradations of other persons (grandparents, extended family, adoptive family in an adoption later found to be invalid, long-term guardians, etc.) who may have some claim against the wishes of the parents. If we embrace this unenumerated right, I think it obvious — whether we affirm or reverse the judgment here . . . — that we will be ushering in a new regime of judicially prescribed, and federally prescribed, family law. . . .

Justice KENNEDY, dissenting.

* * *

The first flaw the State Supreme Court found in the statute is that it allows an award of visitation to a non-parent without a finding that harm to the child would result if visitation were withheld; and the second is that the statute allows any person to seek visitation at any time. In my view the first theory is too broad to be correct, as it appears to contemplate that the best interests of the child standard may not be applied in any visitation case. I acknowledge the distinct possibility that visitation cases may arise where, considering the absence of other protection for the parent under state laws and procedures, the best interests of the child standard would give insufficient protection to the parent's constitutional right to raise the child without undue intervention by the state; but it is quite a different matter to say, as I understand the Supreme Court of Washington to have said, that a harm to the child standard is required in every instance.

Given the error I see in the State Supreme Court's central conclusion that the best interests of the child standard is never appropriate in third-party visitation cases, that court should have the first opportunity to reconsider this case. I would remand the case to the state court for further proceedings. . . .

My principal concern is that the holding seems to proceed from the assumption that the parent or parents who resist visitation have always been the child's primary caregivers and that the third parties who seek visitation have no legitimate and established relationship with the child. That idea, in turn, appears influenced by the concept that the conventional nuclear family ought to establish the visitation standard for every domestic relations case. . . . As we all know, this is simply not the structure or prevailing condition in many households. For many boys and girls a traditional family with two or even one permanent and caring parent is simply not the reality of their childhood. This may be so whether their childhood has been marked by tragedy or filled with considerable happiness and fulfillment. . . .

NOTES AND QUESTIONS

1. Troxel v. Granville produced a fractured decision with a plurality opinion by Justice O'Connor in which three other justices joined. What differences do you see among the justices? Are there any principles that can be said to command a majority of the Court?

2. At the time that *Troxel* was decided, all 50 states had statutes that permitted grandparent visitation in at least some circumstances. The *Troxel* decision generated a wave of litigation, with some cases upholding and other cases invalidating the state statutes. Professor Solangel Maldonado provides a current survey of state court responses to *Troxel*. Solangel Maldonado, When Father (or Mother) Doesn't Know Best: Quasi-Parents and Parental Deference After Troxel v. Granville, 88 Iowa L. Rev. 865 (2003). She summarizes her findings:

As many courts have recognized, *Troxel* does not signify the end of third party visitation. *Troxel* was a narrow plurality opinion that held only that, as applied, Washington's third party visitation statute violated a fit parent's constitutional right to make decisions concerning her children. Thus, depending on how they are applied, third party visitation statutes and visitation awards could survive constitutional challenges. *Troxel* does require, however, that courts give "at least some special weight" to fit parents' decisions restricting or denying third parties visitation with their children. Although the plurality never defined "special weight," most courts have agreed that a parent's decision concerning visitation is entitled to a presumption that the parent was acting in the child's best interests when denying the third party visitation. Although courts disagree as to what constitutes sufficient reason to override a parent's decision, the majority of courts have held that evidence that the visitation with the third party is in the child's best interests — that the parent's decision to withhold visitation is wrong — does not rebut the presumption. Indeed, many courts have held that trial courts may not even consider evidence of a child's best interests until the third party rebuts the presumption that the parent was acting in the child's best interest in denying visitation. Thus, whereas before *Troxel*, a third party who established standing generally obtained visitation if it was in the child's best interests, since *Troxel*, many third parties never get the opportunity to show that visitation is in the child's best interests. This is unfortunate.

Id. at 870.

Although a majority of the justices in *Troxel* declined to hold that the Constitution required a finding of harm to the child before the judgment of a fit parent could be overruled, a number of states, including California, Connecticut, and Kentucky, have held that only "clear and convincing evidence that harm to the child will result from a deprivation of visitation" will rebut the presumption that the parent was acting in the child's best interest. Maldonado, *id.* at 885. Other states, including Arkansas and Iowa, have ruled that grandparents must make a threshold showing of parental unfitness before the court can proceed to the issue of whether visitation would be in the child's best interest. *Id.* at 884-885. The majority of courts have held at a minimum that "the best way" to satisfy *Troxel*'s special weight requirement "is to apply a presumption that the parent's decision to decline visitation is in the best interest of the child . . . and to place the burden on the non-parent seeking visitation to rebut that presumption." *Id.* at 883-884. The courts, however, have split on the issue of whether a showing of a substantial bond between grandparent and child together with a determination that continuation of the relationship is in the child's best interest is sufficient to overcome the presumption in favor of the parent's decision. *Id.* at 889-892.

Which standard do you believe best advances children's interests?

If third parties requesting visitation must overcome a presumption that the parent's decision is in the child's best interest, what kind of showing would they need to make? What kind of evidence would you advise the grandparents to develop in *Troxel*?

3. The *Troxel* decision potentially affects not just the issue of grandparent visitation, but the question of whether the courts can recognize the interests of any nonparent over the parent's objection. *See* David D. Meyer, What Constitutional Law Can Learn from the ALI Principles of Family Dissolution 2001 BYU L. Rev. 1075.

PROBLEMS

1. Consider the facts of Painter v. Bannister on page 623. On the facts of that case, would the ruling pass constitutional muster under *Troxel*? Why or why not?

2. Kira and Terry, who have never married, have a daughter, Dakota. Kira and Terry broke up after Terry was arrested and sent to prison while Dakota was still less than a year old. Terry's mother, Brenda, helped take care of Dakota during the period immediately after Dakota's birth when Kira was suffering from post-partum depression, and she has remained close to Dakota ever since. Dakota is now two. After one of her visits to Brenda's home, Dakota broke out in hives. Kira believes that Brenda was not sufficiently attentive to Dakota's lactose intolerance, and refuses to permit Dakota to stay at her grandmother's house, though she permits Brenda to visit Dakota at her house. Brenda, who states that Dakota did not receive milk products during the visit in which she broke out in hives, seeks a court order requiring visitation. She introduces evidence that she has had a close relationship with Dakota since her birth, that Kira's new husband has encouraged Kira to cut off visitation, and that numerous complaints have been filed with Social Services. What would be the result in a state that requires a showing of detriment to the child to award grandparent visitation? Parental unfitness? Extraordinary circumstances?

2.   *The Relationship Between Parenthood and Marriage*

The definition of parenthood is a matter of state law. In some states, the definition of parenthood comes from legislation such as the Uniform Parentage Act. In other states, common law precedent continues to govern the determination of parentage. All states, however, have had to revisit their regulation of legal parenthood in light of changing times, new methods of reproduction, and (as we have seen) the evolving boundaries of constitutional protection. A major issue has been the extent to which parentage constitutionally can or should continue be tied to marriage.

The common law rules of parentage were based on a family consisting of children living with their married, biological parents. Marriage was the sine qua non for legal recognition of parenthood, even though then, as now, some children were born to biological parents who were not married to each other, and some lived with other than their biological parents. Writing about the time of the American Revolution, Blackstone described the legal position of children born to unmarried parents.

1 WILLIAM BLACKSTONE, COMMENTARIES ON THE LAWS OF ENGLAND

*454-459

We are next to consider the case of illegitimate children, or bastards; with regard to whom let us inquire, 1. Who are bastards. 2. The legal duties of the parents towards a bastard child. 3. The rights and incapacities attending such bastard children.

A bastard, by our English laws, is one that is not only begotten, but born, out of lawful matrimony. The civil and canon laws do not allow a child to remain a bastard, if the parents afterwards intermarry: and herein they differ most materially from our law; which, though not so strict as to require that the child shall be *begotten*, yet makes it an indispensable condition that it shall be *born*, after lawful wedlock. . . . The main end and design of marriage, therefore, being to ascertain and fix upon some certain person, to whom the care, the protection, the maintenance, and the education of the children should belong. . . .

Let us next see the duty of parents to their bastard children, by our law; which is principally that of maintenance. For, though bastards are not looked upon as children to any civil purposes, yet the ties of nature, of which maintenance is one, are not so easily dissolved: and they hold indeed as to many other intentions; as, particularly, that a man shall not marry his bastard sister or daughter. The civil law, therefore, when it denied maintenance to bastards begotten under certain atrocious circumstances, was neither consonant to nature, nor reason; however profligate and wicked parents might justly be esteemed. . . .

The incapacity of a bastard consists principally in this, that he cannot be heir to anyone, neither can he have heirs, but of his own body; for, being *nullius filius*, he is therefore of kin to nobody, and has no ancestor from whom any inheritable blood can be derived. . . .

bastard cannot be an heir

This description of the nonmarital child's rights, while accurate, is incomplete. The ecclesiastical courts enforced fathers' duties to support their children, whether the children were born in wedlock or not. *See generally* R. H. Helmholz, Support Orders, Church Courts, and the Rule of *Filius Nullius*: A Reassessment of the Common Law, 63 Va. L. Rev. 431 (1977). Actions could be brought by the mother on behalf of the child, or incident to prosecutions for adultery or fornication. *Id.* at 437. In addition, while English law did not recognize the child as the heir of either parent, American law from colonial times recognized the child as a member of the mother's family.

At common law, in addition to having no or only a limited support duty, an unmarried father had no custodial rights at all. Walter C. Tiffany, Persons and Domestic Relations § 114 (1921). Under modern rules, children born to unmarried parents are no longer legal nonentities, but the marital status of a child's parents continues to be important in determining who is the child's father for legal purposes. The next case introduces the major criteria now commonly proposed for defining "legal parenthood"—biological parenthood, being married to a person who already has parental status, intending to become a parent, and functioning as a parent. As you read this case and others in this chapter, consider which bases for parenthood claims are at issue and what values would be promoted by preferring one or another.

children are no longer nonentities

MICHAEL H. V. GERALD D.

491 U.S. 110 (1989)

SCALIA, J., announced the judgment of the Court and delivered an opinion, in which the Chief Justice joins, and in all but note 6[1] of which Justice O'CONNOR and Justice KENNEDY join. . . .

The facts of this case are, we must hope, extraordinary. On May 9, 1976, in Las Vegas, Nevada, Carole D., an international model, and Gerald D., a top executive in a French oil company, were married. The couple established a home in Playa del Rey, California in which they resided as husband and wife when one or the other was not out of the country on business. In the summer of 1978, Carole became involved in an adulterous affair with a neighbor, Michael H. In September 1980, she conceived a child, Victoria D., who was born on May 11, 1981. Gerald was listed as father on the birth certificate and has always held Victoria out to the world as his daughter. Soon after delivery of the child, however, Carole informed Michael that she believed he might be the father.

In the first three years of her life, Victoria remained always with Carole, but found herself within a variety of quasi-family units. In October 1981, Gerald moved to New York City to pursue his business interests, but Carole chose to remain in California. The end of that month, Carole and Michael had blood tests of themselves and Victoria, which showed a 98.07% probability that Michael was Victoria's father. In January 1982, Carole visited Michael in St. Thomas, where his primary business interests were based. There Michael held Victoria out as his child. In March, however, Carole left Michael and returned to California, where she took up residence with yet another man, Scott K. Later that spring, and again in the summer, Carole and Victoria spent time with Gerald in New York City, as well as on vacation in Europe. In the fall, they returned to Scott in California.

In November 1982, rebuffed in his attempts to visit Victoria, Michael filed a filiation action in California Superior Court to establish his paternity and right to visitation. In March 1983, the court appointed an attorney and guardian ad litem to represent Victoria's interests. Victoria then filed a cross-complaint asserting that if she had more than one psychological or de facto father, she was entitled to maintain her filial relationship, with all of the attendant rights, duties, and obligations, with both. In May 1983, Carole filed a motion for summary judgment. During this period, from March through July of 1983, Carole was again living with Gerald in New York. In August, however, she returned to California, became involved once again with Michael, and instructed her attorneys to remove the summary judgment motion from the calendar.

For the ensuing eight months, when Michael was not in St. Thomas he lived with Carole and Victoria in Carole's apartment in Los Angeles, and held Victoria out as his daughter. In April 1984, Carole and Michael signed a stipulation that

---

1. Note 6 addresses the broad question of how to identify what liberty interests are protected by Due Process. This note and the portions of the other opinions on this issue are omitted. — Ed.

Michael was Victoria's natural father. Carole left Michael the next month, however, and instructed her attorneys not to file the stipulation. In June 1984, Carole reconciled with Gerald and joined him in New York, where they now live with Victoria and two other children since born into the marriage.

In May 1984, Michael and Victoria, through her guardian ad litem, sought visitation rights for Michael pendente lite. . . .

On October 19, 1984, Gerald, who had intervened in the action, moved for summary judgment on the ground that under Cal. Evid. Code §621 there were no triable issues of fact as to Victoria's paternity. This law provides that "the issue of a wife cohabiting with her husband, who is not impotent or sterile, is conclusively presumed to be a child of the marriage." Cal. Evid. Code Ann. §621(a) (Supp. 1989). The presumption may be rebutted by blood tests, but only if a motion for such tests is made, within two years from the date of the child's birth, either by the husband or, if the natural father has filed an affidavit acknowledging paternity, by the wife. §§ 621(c) and (d).

On January 28, 1985, having found that affidavits submitted by Carole and Gerald sufficed to demonstrate that the two were cohabiting at conception and birth and that Gerald was neither sterile nor impotent, the Superior Court granted Gerald's motion for summary judgment, rejecting Michael's and Victoria's challenges to the constitutionality of §621. The court also denied their motions for continued visitation pending the appeal under Cal. Civ. Code §4601, which provides that a court may, in its discretion, grant "reasonable visitation rights . . . to any . . . person having an interest in the welfare of the child." . . .

We address first the claims of Michael. At the outset, it is necessary to clarify what he sought and what he was denied. California law, like nature itself, makes no provision for dual fatherhood. Michael was seeking to be declared the father of Victoria. The immediate benefit he evidently sought to obtain from that status was visitation rights. *See* Cal. Civ. Code Ann. §4601 (West 1983) (parent has statutory right to visitation "unless it is shown that such visitation would be detrimental to the best interests of the child"). . . . All parental rights, including visitation, were automatically denied by denying Michael status as the father. While Cal. Civ. Code Ann. §4601 places it within the discretionary power of a court to award visitation rights to a nonparent, the Superior Court here, affirmed by the Court of Appeal, held that California law denies visitation, against the wishes of the mother, to a putative father who has been prevented by §621 from establishing his paternity.

Michael raises two related challenges to the constitutionality of §621. First, he asserts that requirements of procedural due process prevent the State from terminating his liberty interest in his relationship with his child without affording him an opportunity to demonstrate his paternity in an evidentiary hearing. We believe this claim derives from a fundamental misconception of the nature of the California statute. While §621 is phrased in terms of a presumption, that rule of evidence is the implementation of a substantive rule of law. California declares it to be, except in limited circumstances, irrelevant for paternity purposes whether a child conceived during and born into an existing marriage was begotten by someone other than the husband and had a prior relationship with him. . . .

This Court has struck down as illegitimate certain "irrebuttable presumptions." *See*, e.g., Stanley v. Illinois, 405 U.S. 645 (1972); Vlandis v. Kline, 412 U.S.

441 (1973); Cleveland Board of Education v. LaFleur, 414 U.S. 632 (1974). Those holdings did not, however, rest upon procedural due process. A conclusive presumption does, of course, foreclose the person against whom it is invoked from demonstrating, in a particularized proceeding, that applying the presumption to him will in fact not further the lawful governmental policy the presumption is designed to effectuate. But the same can be said of any legal rule that establishes general classifications, whether framed in terms of a presumption or not. In this respect there is no difference between a rule which says that the marital husband shall be irrebuttably presumed to be the father, and a rule which says that the adulterous natural father shall not be recognized as the legal father. Both rules deny someone in Michael's situation a hearing on whether, in the particular circumstances of his case, California's policies would best be served by giving him parental rights. . . . We therefore reject Michael's procedural due process challenge and proceed to his substantive claim.

Michael contends as a matter of substantive due process that because he has established a parental relationship with Victoria, protection of Gerald's and Carole's marital union is an insufficient state interest to support termination of that relationship. This argument is, of course, predicated on the assertion that Michael has a constitutionally protected liberty interest in his relationship with Victoria. . . . In an attempt to limit and guide interpretation of the [Due Process] Clause, we have insisted not merely that the interest denominated as a "liberty" be "fundamental" (a concept that, in isolation, is hard to objectify), but also that it be an interest traditionally protected by our society. As we have put it, the Due Process Clause affords only those protections "so rooted in the traditions and conscience of our people as to be ranked as fundamental." . . .

This insistence that the asserted liberty interest be rooted in history and tradition is evident, as elsewhere, in our cases according constitutional protection to certain parental rights. Michael reads the landmark case of Stanley v. Illinois, 405 U.S. 645 (1972), and the subsequent cases of Quilloin v. Walcott, 434 U.S. 246 (1978), Caban v. Mohammed, 441 U.S. 380 (1979), and Lehr v. Robertson, 463 U.S. 248 (1983), as establishing that a liberty interest is created by biological fatherhood plus an established parental relationship—factors that exist in the present case as well. We think that distorts the rationale of those cases. As we view them, they rest not upon such isolated factors but upon the historic respect—indeed, sanctity would not be too strong a term—traditionally accorded to the relationships that develop within the unitary family. . . .

Thus, the legal issue in the present case reduces to whether the relationship between persons in the situation of Michael and Victoria has been treated as a protected family unit under the historic practices of our society, or whether on any other basis it has been accorded special protection. We think it impossible to find that it has. In fact, quite to the contrary, our traditions have protected the marital family (Gerald, Carole, and the child they acknowledge to be theirs) against the sort of claim Michael asserts. . . .

We have found nothing in the older sources, nor in the older cases, addressing specifically the power of the natural father to assert parental rights over a child born into a woman's existing marriage with another man. Since it is Michael's burden to establish that such a power (at least where the natural father has established a relationship with the child) is so deeply embedded within our traditions as to be a fundamental right, the lack of evidence alone might defeat his case. But the evidence shows that even in modern times—when, as we have noted, the rigid protection of the marital family has in other respects been relaxed—the ability of a person in Michael's position to claim paternity has not been generally acknowledged. . . .

Moreover, even if it were clear that one in Michael's position generally possesses, and has generally always possessed, standing to challenge the marital child's legitimacy, that would still not establish Michael's case. . . . What Michael asserts here is a right to have himself declared the natural father and thereby to obtain parental prerogatives. . . . What counts is whether the States in fact award substantive parental rights to the natural father of a child conceived within and born into an extant marital union that wishes to embrace the child. We are not aware of a single case, old or new, that has done so. This is not the stuff of which fundamental rights qualifying as liberty interests are made.

In Lehr v. Robertson, a case involving a natural father's attempt to block his child's adoption by the unwed mother's new husband, we observed that "[t]he significance of the biological connection is that it offers the natural father an opportunity that no other male possesses to develop a relationship with his offspring," 463 U.S., at 262, and we assumed that the Constitution might require some protection of that opportunity, id., at 262-265. Where, however, the child is born into an extant marital family, the natural father's unique opportunity conflicts with the similarly unique opportunity of the husband of the marriage; and it is not unconstitutional for the State to give categorical preference to the latter. . . . In accord with our traditions, a limit is also imposed by the circumstance that the mother is, at the time of the child's conception and birth, married to and cohabitating with another man, both of whom wish to raise the child as the offspring of their union.[2] . . .

We do not accept Justice Brennan's criticism that this result "squashes" the liberty that consists of "the freedom not to conform." It seems to us that reflects the erroneous view that there is only one side to this controversy—that one disposition can expand a "liberty" of sorts without contracting an equivalent "liberty" on the other side. Such a happy choice is rarely available. Here, to provide protection to an adulterous natural father is to deny protection to a marital father, and vice versa. If Michael has a "freedom not to conform" (whatever that means), Gerald must equivalently have a "freedom to conform." One of them will pay a price for asserting that "freedom"—Michael by being unable to act as father of the child he has adulterously begotten, or Gerald by being unable to preserve the integrity of the traditional family unit he and Victoria have established. Our disposition does not choose between these two "freedoms," but leaves that to the people of California. Justice Brennan's approach chooses one of them as the constitutional imperative, on no apparent basis except that the unconventional is to be preferred.

---

2. . . . We limit our pronouncement to the relevant facts of this case because it is at least possible that our traditions lead to a different conclusion with regard to adulterous fathering of a child whom the marital parents do not wish to raise as their own. . . .

IV

We have never had occasion to decide whether a child has a liberty interest, symmetrical with that of her parent, in maintaining her filial relationship. We need not do so here because, even assuming that such a right exists, Victoria's claim must fail. Victoria's due process challenge is, if anything, weaker than Michael's. Her basic claim is not that California has erred in preventing her from establishing that Michael, not Gerald, should stand as her legal father. Rather, she claims a due process right to maintain filial relationships with both Michael and Gerald. This assertion merits little discussion, for, whatever the merits of the guardian ad litem's belief that such an arrangement can be of great psychological benefit to a child, the claim that a State must recognize multiple fatherhood has no support in the history or traditions of this country. Moreover, even if we were to construe Victoria's argument as forwarding the lesser proposition that, whatever her status vis-à-vis Gerald, she has a liberty interest in maintaining a filial relationship with her natural father, Michael, we find that, at best, her claim is the obverse of Michael's and fails for the same reasons. . . .

The judgment of the California Court of Appeal is affirmed.

STEVENS, J., concurring in the judgment. . . . [D]oes the California statute deny appellants a fair opportunity to prove that Victoria's best interests would be served by granting Michael visitation rights? . . .

. . . I do not agree with Justice Scalia's analysis. He seems to reject the possibility that a natural father might ever have a constitutionally protected interest in his relationship with a child whose mother was married to and cohabiting with another man at the time of the child's conception and birth. I think cases like Stanley v. Illinois, 405 U.S. 645 (1972), and Caban v. Mohammed, 441 U.S. 380 (1979), demonstrate that enduring "family" relationships may develop in unconventional settings. I therefore would not foreclose the possibility that a constitutionally protected relationship between a natural father and his child might exist in a case like this. Indeed, I am willing to assume for the purpose of deciding this case that Michael's relationship with Victoria is strong enough to give him a constitutional right to try to convince a trial judge that Victoria's best interest would be served by granting him visitation rights. I am satisfied, however, that the California statute, as applied in this case, gave him that opportunity.

Section 4601 of the California Civil Code Annotated (West Supp. 1989) provides:

> [R]easonable visitation rights [shall be awarded] to a parent unless it is shown that the visitation would be detrimental to the best interests of the child. In the discretion of the court, reasonable visitation rights may be granted to any other person having an interest in the welfare of the child.

The presumption established by §621 denied Michael the benefit of the first sentence of §4601 because, as a matter of law, he is not a "parent." It does not, however, prevent him from proving that he is an "other person having an interest in the welfare of the child." On its face, therefore, the statute plainly gave the trial judge the authority to grant Michael "reasonable visitation rights."

I recognize that my colleagues have interpreted § 621 as creating an absolute bar that would prevent a California trial judge from regarding the natural father as either a "parent" within the meaning of the first sentence of § 4601 or as "any other person" within the meaning of the second sentence. That is not only an unnatural reading of the statute's plain language, but it is also not consistent with the California courts' reading of the statute. Thus, in Vincent B. v. Joan R., 126 Cal. App. 3d 619, 179 Cal. Rptr. 9 (1981), the California Court of Appeal, after deciding that the § 621 presumption barred a natural father from proving paternity, went on to consider the separate question whether it would be proper to allow visitation pursuant to the second sentence of § 4601 [which gives discretion to grant visitation rights to "any other person having an interest in the welfare of the child."] . . .

Similarly, in this case, the trial judge . . . considered the effect of § 4601 and expressly found "that, at the present time, it is not in the best interests of the child that the Plaintiff have visitation. The Court believes that the existence of two (2) 'fathers' as male authority figures will confuse the child and be counter-productive to her best interests." . . .

. . . In the circumstances of this case, I find nothing fundamentally unfair about the exercise of a judge's discretion that, in the end, allows the mother to decide whether her child's best interest would be served by allowing the natural father visitation privileges. Because I am convinced that the trial judge had the authority under state law both to hear Michael's plea for visitation rights and to grant him such rights if Victoria's best interests so warranted, I am satisfied that the California statutory scheme is consistent with the Due Process Clause of the Fourteenth Amendment.

I therefore concur in the Court's judgment of affirmance.

BRENNAN, J., with whom MARSHALL, J., and BLACKMUN, J., join, dissenting. In a case that has yielded so many opinions as has this one, it is fruitful to begin by emphasizing the common ground shared by a majority of this Court. Five Members of the Court refuse to foreclose "the possibility that a natural father might ever have a constitutionally protected interest in his relationship with a child whose mother was married to and cohabiting with another man at the time of the child's conception and birth." Five Justices agree that the flaw inhering in a conclusive presumption that terminates a constitutionally protected interest without any hearing whatsoever is a procedural one. Four Members of the Court agree that Michael H. has a liberty interest in his relationship with Victoria, and one assumes for purposes of this case that he does. . . .

On four prior occasions, we have considered whether unwed fathers have a constitutionally protected interest in their relationships with their children. See Stanley v. Illinois, supra; Quilloin v. Walcott, 434 U.S. 246 (1978); Caban v. Mohammed, 441 U.S. 380 (1979); and Lehr v. Robertson, 463 U.S. 248 (1983). Though different in factual and legal circumstances, these cases have produced a unifying theme: although an unwed father's biological link to his child does not, in and of itself, guarantee him a constitutional stake in his relationship with that child, such a link combined with a substantial parent-child relationship will do so. . . . This commitment is why Mr. Stanley and Mr. Caban won; why Mr. Quilloin and

Mr. Lehr lost; and why Michael H. should prevail today. Michael H. is almost certainly Victoria D.'s natural father, has lived with her as her father, has contributed to her support, and has from the beginning sought to strengthen and maintain his relationship with her.

Claiming that the intent of these cases was to protect the "unitary family," the plurality waves *Stanley*, *Quilloin*, *Caban*, and *Lehr* aside. In evaluating the plurality's dismissal of these precedents, it is essential to identify its conception of the "unitary family." If, by acknowledging that *Stanley*, et al., sought to protect "the relationships that develop within the unitary family," the plurality meant only to describe the kinds of relationships that develop when parents and children live together (formally or informally) as a family, then the plurality's vision of these cases would be correct. But that is not the plurality's message. Though it pays lip service to the idea that marriage is not the crucial fact in denying constitutional protection to the relationship between Michael and Victoria, the plurality cannot mean what it says.

The evidence is undisputed that Michael, Victoria, and Carole did live together as a family; that is, they shared the same household, Victoria called Michael "Daddy," Michael contributed to Victoria's support, and he is eager to continue his relationship with her. Yet they are not, in the plurality's view, a "unitary family," whereas Gerald, Carole, and Victoria do compose such a family. The only difference between these two sets of relationships, however, is the fact of marriage. The plurality, indeed, expressly recognizes that marriage is the critical fact in denying Michael a constitutionally protected stake in his relationship with Victoria: no fewer than six times, the plurality refers to Michael as the "adulterous natural father." . . . However, the very premise of *Stanley* and the cases following it is that marriage is not decisive in answering the question whether the Constitution protects the parental relationship under consideration. These cases are, after all, important precisely because they involve the rights of unwed fathers. It is important to remember, moreover, that in *Quilloin*, *Caban*, and *Lehr*, the putative father's demands would have disrupted a "unitary family" as the plurality defines it; in each case, the husband of the child's mother sought to adopt the child over the objections of the natural father. . . .

Because the plurality decides that Michael and Victoria have no liberty interest in their relationship with each other, it need consider neither the effect of §621 on their relationship nor the State's interest in bringing about that effect. . . .

We must first understand the nature of the challenged statute: it is a law that stubbornly insists that Gerald is Victoria's father, in the face of evidence showing a 98 percent probability that her father is Michael. What Michael wants is a chance to show that he is Victoria's father. By depriving him of this opportunity, California prevents Michael from taking advantage of the best-interest standard embodied in §4601 of California's Civil Code, which directs that parents be given visitation rights unless "the visitation would be detrimental to the best interests of the child." . . . When, as a result of §621, a putative father may not establish his paternity, neither may he obtain discretionary visitation rights as a "nonparent" under §4601. Justice Stevens' assertion to the contrary . . . is mere wishful thinking. . . .

The purported state interests here . . . stem primarily from the State's antagonism to Michael and Victoria's constitutionally protected interest in their relationship with each other and not from any desire to streamline procedures. Gerald

D. explains that § 621 promotes marriage, maintains the relationship between the child and presumed father, and protects the integrity and privacy of the matrimonial family. It is not, however, § 621, but the best-interest principle, that protects a stable marital relationship and maintains the relationship between the child and presumed father. These interests are implicated by the determination of who gets parental rights, not by the determination of who is the father; in the hearing that Michael seeks, parental rights are not the issue. Of the objectives that Gerald stresses, therefore, only the preservation of family privacy is promoted by the refusal to hold a hearing itself. Yet § 621 furthers even this objective only partially.

. . . Admittedly, § 621 does not foreclose inquiry into the husband's fertility or virility—matters that are ordinarily thought of as the couple's private business. In this day and age, however, proving paternity by asking intimate and detailed questions about a couple's relationship would be decidedly anachronistic. Who on earth would choose this method of establishing fatherhood when blood tests prove it with far more certainty and far less fuss? The State's purported interest in protecting matrimonial privacy thus does not measure up to Michael and Victoria's interest in maintaining their relationship with each other.

Make no mistake: to say that the State must provide Michael with a hearing to prove his paternity is not to express any opinion of the ultimate state of affairs between Michael and Victoria and Carole and Gerald. In order to change the current situation among these people, Michael first must convince a court that he is Victoria's father, and even if he is able to do this, he will be denied visitation rights if that would be in Victoria's best interests. *See* Cal. Civ. Code Ann. § 4601 (West Supp. 1989). It is elementary that a determination that a State must afford procedures before it terminates a given right is not a prediction about the end result of those procedures.[3] . . .

WHITE, J., with whom BRENNAN, J., joins, dissenting. . . . Like Justices Brennan, Marshall, Blackmun and Stevens, I do not agree with the plurality opinion's conclusion that a natural father can never "have a constitutionally protected interest in his relationship with a child whose mother was married to and cohabiting with another man at the time of the child's conception and birth." . . .

---

3. The plurality's failure to see this point causes it to misstate Michael's claim in the following way: "Michael contends as a matter of substantive due process that because he has established a parental relationship with Victoria, protection of Gerald's and Carole's marital union is an insufficient state interest to support termination of that relationship." Michael does not claim that the State may not, under any circumstance, terminate his relationship with Victoria; instead, he simply claims that the State may not do so without affording him a hearing on the issue—paternity—that it deems vital to the question whether their relationship may be discontinued. The plurality makes Michael's claim easier to knock down by turning it into such a big target. The plurality's misunderstanding of Michael's claim also leads to its assertion that "to provide protection to an adulterous natural father is to deny protection to a marital father." To allow Michael a chance to prove his paternity, however, in no way guarantees that Gerald's relationship with Victoria will be changed.

In the case now before us, Michael H. is not a father unwilling to assume his responsibilities as a parent. To the contrary, he is a father who has asserted his interests in raising and providing for his child since the very time of the child's birth. . . . "When an unwed father demonstrates a full commitment to the responsibilities of parenthood by 'com[ing] forward to participate in the rearing of his child,' *Caban*, 441 U.S., at 392, his interest in personal contact with his child acquires substantial protection under the Due Process Clause." *Lehr*, supra, 463 U.S., at 261. The facts in this case satisfy the Lehr criteria, which focused on the relationship between father and child, not on the relationship between father and mother. Under *Lehr* a "mere biological relationship" is not enough, but in light of Carole's vicissitudes, what more could Michael H. have done? It is clear enough that Michael H. more than meets the mark in establishing the constitutionally protected liberty interest discussed in *Lehr* and recognized in Stanley v. Illinois, supra, and Caban v. Mohammed, supra. He therefore has a liberty interest entitled to protection under the Due Process Clause of the Fourteenth Amendment.

II

California plainly denies Michael this protection, by refusing him the opportunity to rebut the State's presumption that the mother's husband is the father of the child. California law not only deprives Michael H. of a legal parent-child relationship with his daughter Victoria but even denies him the opportunity to introduce blood-test evidence to rebut the demonstrable fiction that Gerald is Victoria's father. . . . The Court gives its blessing to §621 by relying on the State's asserted interests in the integrity of the family (defined as Carole and Gerald) and in protecting Victoria from the stigma of illegitimacy and by balancing away Michael's interest in establishing that he is the father of the child.

The interest in protecting a child from the social stigma of illegitimacy lacks any real connection to the facts of a case where a father is seeking to establish, rather than repudiate, paternity. . . . It may be true that a child conceived in an extra-marital relationship would be considered a "bastard" in the literal sense of the word, but whatever stigma remains in today's society is far less compelling in the context of a child of a married mother, especially when there is a father asserting paternity and seeking a relationship with his child. It is hardly rare in this world of divorce and remarriage for a child to live with the "father" to whom her mother is married, and still have a relationship with her biological father.

The State's professed interest in the preservation of the existing marital unit is a more significant concern. To be sure, the intrusion of an outsider asserting that he is the father of a child whom the husband believes to be his own would be disruptive to say the least. On the facts of this case, however, Gerald was well aware of the liaison between Carole and Michael. The conclusive presumption of evidentiary rule §621 virtually eliminates the putative father's chances of succeeding in his effort to establish paternity, but it by no means prevents him from asserting the claim. It may serve as a deterrent to such claims but does not eliminate the threat. Further, the argument that the conclusive presumption preserved the sanctity of the marital unit had more sway in a time when the husband was similarly prevented from challenging paternity. . . .

[Concurring opinion of Justice O'Connor omitted.]

NOTES AND QUESTIONS

1. In *Michael H.*, blood tests established a high probability that Michael was Victoria's biological father and he had established a relationship with her. Is Gerald Victoria's legal father? Is the presumption that a married woman's husband is the father of her child an inference of biological fact? Does it express other policies?

At common law a married woman's husband was presumed to be the father of her children, and the presumption could be rebutted only by showing that the husband had been out of the kingdom of England for more than nine months. Lord Mansfield's Rule, first articulated in Goodright v. Moss, 2 Cowp. 291, 98 Eng. Rep. 1257 (1777), prohibited either spouse from giving testimony in court that cast doubt on whether the husband was the child's father. In an era before fertility and blood testing, these rules effectively operated to define the husband as father of his wife's children, regardless of biological paternity, in almost all circumstances.

Today all states, by statute or common law, continue to recognize at least a rebuttable presumption that a married woman's husband is the father of her children. With blood and DNA tests making it easier to determine biological paternity with certainty, however, the states have varied enormously in how, when, and whether they permit such tests to be used to establish legal parenthood. Until 1980 the section of the California Code establishing the presumption that a husband is the father of his wife's children was conclusive as against all the world if the spouses were cohabiting and the husband was not impotent or sterile. In that year, as *Michael H.* indicates, the legislature amended the statute to permit the husband to introduce blood test evidence to rebut the presumption within two years of the child's birth, and in 1981 amended it to give the mother the same opportunity, provided that the biological father files an affidavit acknowledging paternity. These rules are now codified at Cal. Fam. Code §§ 7540 and 7541.

2. Michael's claim was founded on his biological paternity of Victoria. Why does biological parenthood support a claim to legal parenthood? Michael also argued that in fact he had taken on responsibilities as Victoria's father, and that she regarded him as her father. Of what significance are these facts to determining legal parenthood?

3. If Michael had been permitted to rebut the presumption that Gerald was Victoria's father and establish his own paternity, what would the legal consequences for Gerald, Michael, and Victoria have been? The plurality and dissent disagree sharply about this. Who is right?

4. Justice Scalia begins by saying, "California law, like nature itself, makes no provision for dual fatherhood." Yet Michael was Victoria's natural father, and his status was left unprotected by this decision. What, then, did Justice Scalia mean by this?

5. Parents' custodial rights traditionally include the legal authority to determine who will visit a child, including the authority to cut off visitation. Why? The

Troxel decision protects parents from judicial second-guessing about visitation over the parent's objection. Compare how the various opinions in *Michael H.* interpret the role of visitation. Would the California statute, then Cal. Civ. Code § 4601 (now codified at Cal. Fam. Code § 3100(a)), which allowed visitation in the best interests of the child, be constitutional under *Troxel?* Would it matter that the best-interest test would be applied to a biological (but not legal) father rather than a grandparent?

6. Was Victoria's legal claim the same as Michael's? Was she seeking the same relief? If the Court had recognized her interest in maintaining a relationship with Michael, what would the consequences have been?

7. Does the time of the decision affect the outcome of this case? June Carbone and Naomi Cahn observe,

> . . . We believe that, from a child-centered perspective, *Michael H.* presents a particularly difficult case on its facts. At the time Michael first legally asserted his paternal interest in Victoria, that is, in May 1984, at the point where his relationship with Carole ended, Victoria was three years old, Michael had been living with her and her mother for the preceding eight months, he had bonded with her, blood tests established that he was the likely father, and Carole had what appears to be at best a strained relationship with Gerald. At this point, we believe the appropriate outcome would have been to recognize Michael as a father (if not the father). Victoria viewed Michael as her father, Michael presented himself to the world as Victoria's father, and even Carole appears to have treated Michael as the father. . . .
>
> By the time the case reached the Supreme Court five years later, however, the situation had changed significantly. Victoria was living in New York with Gerald and Carole, two new children had been born into the marriage, and Gerald had legally and practically assumed the responsibilities of fatherhood. The lower court's refusal to recognize Michael's parental status in 1984 cut off Victoria from an established relationship with the man she regarded as her "Daddy." Reestablishing the relationship in 1989, however, would have disrupted an otherwise "unitary family." Gerald and Carole had made a commitment to each other and to Victoria. Michael's involvement would occur over their objections; it might have interfered with the relationship among the siblings, and it might have been difficult to manage as Michael and Victoria lived on different coasts.

June Carbone and Naomi Cahn, Which Ties Bind? Redefining the Parent-Child Relationship in an Age of Genetic Certainty, 11 Wm. & Mary Bill Rts. J. 1011, 1044 (2003).

8. In a subsequent California case with facts similar to *Michael H.*, the California Court of Appeal held that where the biological father's name appeared on the birth certificate and he, not the mother's husband, established a family relationship with the child immediately after birth, the biological father's relationship with the child was entitled to constitutional protection notwithstanding the mother's later reconciliation with her husband. The court distinguished *Michael H.* on the facts, concluding that the child in *Brian C.* was not born into "an extant marital family" and that the mother's later reconciliation with her husband was legally irrelevant. Brian C. v. Ginger K., 92 Cal. Rptr. 2d 294 (Cal. App. 4th Dist. 2000). Do you find the distinction convincing?

9. If Carole and Gerald had been divorced, should Michael have been entitled to establish his paternity? How important to the holding is it that Carole and Gerald wanted to raise Victoria together? Should this affect Michael's rights? *Cf.* In re Melissa G., 261 Cal. Rptr. 894 (Cal. App. 1989) (where mother and husband were divorced and husband had no relationship to child, conclusive presumption cannot be applied constitutionally).

10. In most states, the marital presumption is rebuttable, particularly in the context of divorce. In many divorces, it is the husband who wishes to rebut the presumption of paternity, often to avoid child support. Alternatively, the mother may seek to rebut the presumption in order to defeat her ex-husband's claims for custody or visitation. However, even if the presumption is rebuttable, some courts have held that it cannot be overcome if a finding of nonpaternity would be contrary to the child's best interests. *See* Department of Health & Rehab. Serv. v. Privette, 617 So. 2d 305 (Fla. 1993) (applying best-interest test when putative father asserts marital presumption in a paternity and child support suit); In re Marriage of Ross, 783 P.2d 331 (Kan. 1990) (applying child's best interest when mother sought to establish paternity of man not her husband to facilitate child's adoption by new husband); State in Interest of J. W. F., 799 P.2d 710 (Utah 1990) (allowing child's guardian ad litem to challenge the presumption where child had no relationship to husband); Michael K. T. v. Tina L. T., 387 S.E.2d 866 (W. Va. 1989) (applying best-interest test to determine whether husband may attempt to rebut the presumption of paternity during divorce proceedings); Matter of Adoption of R. S. C., 837 P.2d 1089 (Wyo. 1992) (same as *Ross*).

Other courts have reached similar results by holding that parties may be estopped to deny that a woman's husband is the father of her child under certain circumstances. *See, e.g.*, In re Marriage of K. E. V., 883 P.2d 1246 (Mont. 1994); Pettinato v. Pettinato, 582 A.2d 909 (R.I. 1990); Randy A. J. v. Norma I. J., 677 N.W.2d 630 (Wis. 2004); In re Adoption of R. S. C., 837 P.2d 1089 (Wyo. 1992). *See also* M. H. B. v. H. T. B., 498 A.2d 775 (N.J. 1985), and accompanying notes, below.

11. At least two state supreme courts have held that their state constitutions, unlike the federal constitution as interpreted in *Michael H.*, may protect an unwed father's interest in establishing paternity even though the child's mother is married to another. In the Interest of J. W. T., 872 S.W.2d 189 (Tex. 1994); Callender v. Skiles, 591 N.W.2d 182 (Iowa 1999) (finding denial of standing to biological father unconstitutional).

In C. C. v. A. B., 550 N.E.2d 365 (Mass. 1990), the Massachusetts Supreme Judicial Court avoided the constitutional issue, holding that on facts like those in *Michael H.*, the presumption that the husband is the father no longer exists as a matter of common law, leaving the way open for the putative father to bring a paternity suit.

12. Federal law requires that as a condition of participating in the state-federal welfare program, states must have "procedures ensuring that the putative father has a reasonable opportunity to initiate a paternity action." 42 U.S.C. §666(a)(5)(L). Does application of the best-interest rule and estoppel principles described above violate this requirement?

For a review of the marital presumption, *see* Theresa Glennon, *Somebody's Child: Evaluating the Erosion of the Marital Presumption of Paternity*, 102 W. Va. L. Rev. 547 (2000).

3. Children's Emotional Needs

A critical issue that runs through this chapter is how much weight should be given to the needs and interests of the affected child or children. As in many cases, the focus in *Troxel* and *Michael H.* is on parents' interests, but parents' and children's interests often are not sharply distinct. And in some cases courts expressly emphasize children's interests. However, even when this perspective is taken, the questions of which of the child's interests are to be considered, and how, remain. The argument of the child's guardian ad litem in *Michael H.* implicitly assumed that the child's most important interest was in maintaining a personal relationship with both men. This orientation to children's needs, which emphasizes their emotional and psychological well-being, was brought to the forefront of child custody law by the publication in 1973 of *Beyond the Best Interests of the Child* by Joseph Goldstein, Anna Freud, and Albert Solnit. The fundamental concept of the book is the child's "psychological parent," an adult who "through interaction, companionship, interplay and mutuality, fulfills the child's psychological . . . as well as physical needs." *Id.* at 98. The authors urged, with great success, that courts protect such relationships at all costs and in preference to all other relationships. Since 1973 much writing has addressed children's emotional and psychological needs — refining, qualifying, and sometimes even challenging the claim that protection of the psychological parent-child relationship is essential in all circumstances. The following summarizes some of this work.

KATHARINE BARTLETT, *RETHINKING PARENTHOOD AS AN EXCLUSIVE STATUS: THE NEED FOR LEGAL ALTERNATIVES WHEN THE PREMISE OF THE NUCLEAR FAMILY HAS FAILED*

70 U. Va. L. Rev. 879, 904-905 (1984)

. . . [A] child's needs for continuity change as he passes through the various developmental stages. The infant's need for continuity is most often described as the need for attachment, which can be fulfilled only in a close and selective relationship between a child and caregiver. Children who do not form primary attachments in infancy are likely to suffer damage in many aspects of their development and will be hampered in their ability to form intimate relationships later in life. Although experts disagree as to the minimum requirements for successful attachment during infancy,[4] there seems to be a consensus that the greater the number

---

4. [1 J. Bowlby, Attachment and Loss 177 (1969).] Bowlby and Winnicott, for example, stress the crucial importance of having a single mother. J. Bowlby, Child Care and the Growth of Love 13 (1965); D. Winnicott, The Child, the Family, and the Outside World 85-92 (1964). Michael Rutter, on the other hand, suggests that if the mothering is of high

of separations from a caregiver, the more likely that the child's ability to form lasting attachments will be impaired. . . .

The child's continuity requirement in the pre-school and latency periods takes the form of a need for permanence. Permanence can be achieved when children feel that they belong to a group, most often a family, whose members share a commitment to one another. As the child experiences new impulses and new associations with peers and with adults outside the family, a stable family serves as a dependable reference point. An absence of permanency in a child's pre-school and latency years may cause him to have difficulty learning self-control and absorbing a value system.

The adolescent child's need for continuity is usually expressed through his need to develop a sense of his role in society. As he tries to establish an independent adult identity, he may revolt against parental authority. Psychologists consider it important that the adolescent, as part of his effort to master his environment, control the assertion of his own independence. When the process of breaking the parental attachment is involuntary, compelled by court intervention or by the parents' divorce, the child's identity formation may be thrown off course. Adolescents also need a sense of their own heritage. Those unaware of their biological and cultural pasts may find it difficult to develop satisfying self-concepts. . . . It would seem, then, that while the law may serve infants best by emphasizing stability in their present and future attachments, at the expense of past relationships if necessary, older children are likely to benefit from maintaining ties with their former caretakers. . . .

Psychological perspectives on children's needs are also considered in the discussion of child custody at divorce in Chapter 9.

Case law and statutes in a number of states say that protecting children's emotional bonds can justify limiting parental rights in one way or another. *Troxel* called the constitutionality of such statutes into question, and a number have been amended to take *Troxel* into account. For example, the Oregon legislature provides in Oregon Revised Statutes § 109.119 that "[a]ny person, including but not limited to a related or nonrelated foster parent, stepparent, grandparent or relative by blood or marriage, who has established emotional ties creating a child-parent relationship or an ongoing personal relationship with a child may petition or file a motion for intervention with the court having jurisdiction over the custody, placement, guardianship or wardship of that child, or if no such proceedings are pending, may petition the court for the county in which the child resides, for an order. . . ." A section added in 2001 in response to *Troxel*, however, further states that "[i]n any proceeding under this section, there is a presumption that the legal parent acts in the best interest of the child." § 109.119(2)(a).

---

quality and is provided by persons who remain constant during the child's early life, the child's exposure to four or five mother figures need cause no adverse effects. M. Rutter, Maternal Deprivation Reassessed 27 (1981); *see also* M. Ainsworth, The Development of Infant-Mother Attachment, in 3 Rev. Child Dev. Res. 1, 81 (1973).

4.   The Possibility of Multiple Parenthood

The law ordinarily assumes that a child has one and only one mother and one and only one father. *Michael H.*, for example, may have been decided quite differently if the lower court had had the option of recognizing both Michael and Gerald as Victoria's fathers, and then deciding what role each would play on the basis of a best-interest determination. The insistence on limiting the number of legal parents might be justified either because it will maximize the well-being of children or because it is "in the natural order of things." However, as we will see throughout this chapter and the next, in a variety of circumstances courts and legislatures give some measure of legal protection to the relationship between children and more than one adult of the same sex in ways that can be understood as partial recognition of multiple parenthood. Courts are most willing to do this when all the adults agree; in several cases courts have allocated custody and visitation rights among more than two parents when the parents have agreed. *E.g.,* Weinschel v. Strople, 56 Md. App. 252, 466 A.2d 1301 (1983) (upholding agreement to permit parent whose rights were terminated by adoption to visit the child if in the child's best interests); Beckman v. Boggs, 655 A.2d 901 (Md. Ct. Appeals 1995) (accord); In re Adoption of Children by F, 170 N.J. Super. 419, 406 A.2d 986 (Ch. Div. 1979) (adoption decree provides for visitation by child's biological father). *But see* In re Adoption of a child by W.P and M.P., 748 A.2d 515 (2000) ("Even arrangements that are entered into with mutual consent permitting continued contact between biological relatives and the adopted child, cannot be judicially enforced given the potential for disruption of the child's family life under such arrangements and the fact that under the adoption laws the adoptive parents' rights are paramount.") For more on adoption, see Chapter 13.

Courts in Louisiana have developed a full-blown doctrine of dual paternity where, as in *Michael H.*, the mother conceived a child with a man not her husband while she was married. These cases allow the establishment of biological paternity and give biological fathers legal rights and duties while preserving the child's status as the legal child of the mother's husband. Smith v. Cole, 553 So. 2d 847 (La. 1989); Smith v. Jones, 566 So. 2d 408 (La. App. 1990); Finnerty v. Boyett, 469 So. 2d 287 (La. 1985); Durr v. Blue, 454 So. 2d 315 (La. App. 1984); T. D. v. M. M. M., 730 So. 2d 873 (La. 1999). An unmarried biological father whose paternity is established in Louisiana can be liable for child support, and his child may claim wrongful death benefits or inheritance rights at the father's death.

PROBLEMS

1. Margaret was married to Frank and having an affair with Harry. When she was three months pregnant she divorced Frank, and she and Harry were married a month before her child, Carol, was born. Throughout her marriage to Harry, Margaret told him that he was Carol's biological father. When Carol was six weeks old, blood tests were done to determine whether Harry was the biological father, but they were inconclusive. Harry was a loving father who supported Margaret and Carol and provided much personal care to Carol as well. Margaret

and Carol had nothing to do with Frank after Margaret divorced him. When Carol was five Margaret and Harry divorced.

(a) Seeking to avoid paying child support, Harry offers evidence to rebut the presumption that he is Carol's biological father. In a state that follows the rule that the presumption can be rebutted only if in the child's best interest, should the court allow the presumption to be rebutted? How should the court rule in a state that has adopted the rule that says a person may be estopped from denying paternity?

(b) Margaret seeks to introduce evidence that Harry is not Carol's biological father because she does not want him to have visitation rights. In a state that follows the best-interest rule, should the evidence be admitted? Should it be admitted in a state that has adopted the estoppel doctrine?

(c) Would your answers to (a) or (b) change if Harry and Margaret separated when Carol was five, Harry learned at that time that he was not Carol's biological father, the divorce hearing did not occur until two years later, and by that time Carol was seven and had not seen Harry in the intervening two years?

2. Barbara, an unmarried woman, placed her two-week-old baby for adoption with the Smiths. Six months later she validly revoked her consent to the adoption. The Smiths have petitioned for custody, alleging that because the child has bonded with them, it is in the child's best interests to be in their custody. In a state that has adopted a presumption in favor of parental custody, how should the petition be decided? What decision will result under Oregon Rev. Stat. § 109.119, above?

B. UNMARRIED FATHERS

During the 1800s, statutes and case law softened the harsh common law rule of *nullius filius*, described in the Blackstone excerpt, above, at page 850. By the 1830s, 14 states permitted nonmarital children to inherit from their mothers under some circumstances. The early case of Sleigh v. Strider, 5 Call 439 (Va. 1805), held that a child born to an unmarried woman was legitimated by his parents' marriage and his biological father's acknowledgment of him. During the nineteenth century some states enacted statutes allowing children to be legitimated by their biological fathers' acknowledgment of them. Michael Grossberg, Governing the Hearth ch. 6 (1985). However, the law continued to treat nonmarital children substantially less favorably than children born in wedlock well into the mid-twentieth century.

In a series of cases beginning in 1968 with Levy v. Louisiana, 391 U.S. 68 (1968), the Supreme Court reviewed claims that various forms of discrimination against children born to unmarried parents violated the equal protection clause. At first the level of scrutiny required was uncertain, but in Trimble v. Gordon, 430 U.S. 762 (1977), and in Lalli v. Lalli, 439 U.S. 259 (1978), the Court settled on intermediate scrutiny, requiring that a state regulation burdening nonmarital children be substantially related to an important state interest. The rights at stake in most of these cases were economic, involving children's rights to be supported by or inherit from their fathers, and to take Social Security and other benefits on their fathers' accounts. The first part of this section concerns these issues.

Four years after resolving the first constitutional challenge to laws that discriminated against nonmarital children in the economic realm, the Supreme Court began to review the constitutionality of rules that denied unmarried fathers custodial and visitation rights to their children. The second part of this section begins with the first case in this series and traces the development of constitutional principles to the present.

Some states have eliminated all *legal* differences based on parents' marital status. For example, the Uniform Parentage Act provides, "A child born to parents who are not married to each other has the same rights under the law as a child born to parents who are married to each other."

However, legal distinctions continue to be made for some purposes in some jurisdictions, as you will see. In addition, even in states that have eliminated legal distinctions, marital and nonmarital children are still in significantly different positions as a matter of practicality. As you already know, in all states a child born to a married woman is at least rebuttably presumed to be the child of her husband. Where this presumption is not challenged, nothing more must be done to establish the child's paternity. However, other processes are required to establish the paternity of children born to unmarried women. The last part of this section concerns procedures for establishing biological paternity.

1.   Child Support, Inheritance, and Public Benefits

Legal parenthood is not always a voluntary status. A major impetus in the evolving law of paternity over the last quarter century, particularly as the number and needs of nonmarital children have increased, has been the effort to establish support rights. While today we consider such rights to be the most important claim of a child against parents, the common law did not recognize a generally applicable, legally enforceable support duty for any parents until the nineteenth century. However, the Poor Laws required that parents, including unmarried fathers, support their children, who would otherwise become a burden on the community The modern efforts to enhance the effectiveness of child support enforcement similarly coincided with the expansion of welfare benefits and the desire to protect the public fisc. *See generally* Leslie J. Harris, Dennis Waldrop & Lori R. Waldrop, Making and Breaking Connections Between Parents' Duty to Support and Right to Control Their Children, 60 Or. L. Rev. 691, 692-696 (1990). As recently as 1971 some states still imposed no generally applicable support duty on unmarried fathers. Harry Krause, Illegitmacy: Law and Social Policy 22 (1971). In Gomez v. Perez, 409 U.S. 535 (1973), however, the Supreme Court held that denying a nonmarital child the right to support from the father when marital children had such a right violates the equal protection clause.

Current policy trends contrast sharply with the common law reluctance to enforce parental support duties, including the duties of unmarried fathers. The general rule is that proof of biological parenthood is sufficient for imposing a support duty, and courts and legislatures are extremely reluctant to excuse this duty. Consider whether the case below follows from these principles.

MATTER OF L. PAMELA P. V. FRANK S.

449 N.E.2d 713 (N.Y. 1983)

WACHTLER, J. . . . Following a hearing on the paternity petition, Family Court made an order of filiation, having found by clear and convincing evidence that respondent is the father of petitioner's child. Thereafter respondent endeavored to establish that petitioner, intending to have respondent's child regardless of his wishes, misrepresented to him that she was using contraception. Although petitioner conceded that she was not, at the time of conception, using any form of birth control, she denied that any conversation concerning contraception took place.

Family Court, 110 Misc. 2d 978, 443 N.Y.S.2d 978, found that petitioner had purposely deceived respondent with regard to her use of contraception and that this wrongful conduct should weigh in respondent's favor in determining the parents' respective support obligations. Thus, the Family Court held that the general rule that the apportionment of child support obligations between parents is to be based upon the parents' means would not be applicable to the present case; rather, it held that an order of support would be entered against the father only in the amount by which the mother's means were insufficient to meet the child's needs.

The Appellate Division modified Family Court's order, striking the defense of fraud and deceit and increasing the child support award accordingly. Noting that the only factors to be considered by Family Court in fixing an award of child support are the needs of the child and the means of the parents, the Appellate Division held that the father's allegations concerning the mother's fraud and deceit had no relevance to the determination of his obligation to support the child.

Although at one time the objective of paternity proceedings was merely to prevent a child born out of wedlock from becoming a public charge, it is now well established that the appropriate emphasis must be upon the welfare of the child. The primary purpose of establishing paternity is to ensure that adequate provision will be made for the child's needs, in accordance with the means of the parents. . . .

Respondent argues . . . that petitioner's intentional misrepresentation that she was practicing birth control deprived him of his constitutional right to decide whether to father a child. Recognizing that petitioner herself engaged in no State action by her conduct, respondent urges that imposition of a support obligation upon him under these circumstances constitutes State involvement sufficient to give vitality to his constitutional claim.

Assuming, without deciding, that sufficient State action is present in this case we conclude that respondent's contentions fall short of stating any recognized aspect of the constitutional right of privacy.

Clearly, respondent has a constitutionally protected right to decide for himself whether to father a child. This right is deemed so fundamental that governmental interference in this area of decision-making may be justified only by compelling State. Yet, the interest protected has always been stated in terms of governmental restrictions on the individual's access to contraceptive devices. . . . This aspect of the right of privacy has never been extended so far as to regulate the conduct of private actors as between themselves. Indeed, as the Appellate Division recognized, judicial inquiry into so fundamentally private and intimate conduct as is required to determine the validity of respondent's assertions may itself involve impermissible State interference with the privacy of these individuals.

The interest asserted by the father on this appeal is not, strictly speaking, his freedom to choose to avoid procreation, because the mother's conduct in no way limited his right to use contraception. Rather, he seeks to have his choice regarding procreation fully respected by other individuals and effectuated to the extent that he should be relieved of his obligation to support a child that he did not voluntarily choose to have. But respondent's constitutional entitlement to avoid procreation does not encompass a right to avoid a child support obligation simply because another private person has not fully respected his desires in this regard. However unfairly respondent may have been treated by petitioner's failure to allow him an equal voice in the decision to conceive a child, such a wrong does not rise to the level of a constitutional violation.

Accordingly, the order of the Appellate Division should be affirmed, with costs.

NOTES AND QUESTIONS

1. What rationale for imposing child support duties underlies the *L. Pamela P.* trial court's order? What underlies the approach of the appellate courts?

2. States may not require women to obtain the consent of their husbands (or boyfriends) when they are deciding whether to have an abortion, or even to notify them. Planned Parenthood of Central Missouri v. Danforth, 428 U.S. 52 (1976); Planned Parenthood of Southeastern Pennsylvania v. Casey, 505 U.S. 833 (1992). Nor can biological fathers force women to have abortions. Why, then, can states require men to support their biological children, regardless of whether the men wanted to become fathers?

3. Other appellate courts have reached the same conclusion that the *L. Pamela P.* appellate court did. *See, e.g.,* Erwin L. D. v. Myla Jean L., 847 S.W.2d 45 (Ark. App. 1993); Hughes v. Hutt, 455 A.2d 623 (Pa. 1983). On facts similar to those in *L. Pamela P.,* courts have also rejected claims by men for breach of contract, fraud, and misrepresentation. Stephen K. v. Roni L., 164 Cal. Rptr. 618 (1980); Douglas R. v. Suzanne M., 487 N.Y.S.2d 244 (1985); Linda D. v. Fritz C., 687 P.2d 223 (Wash. 1984); Wallis v. Smith, 22 P.3d 682 (N.M. App.), *cert. denied,* 23 P.3d 929 (N.M. 2001) However, if a man misrepresents to a woman that he is unable to father children and she then becomes pregnant by him, courts have generally held that he is liable to her in tort. *E.g.,* Barbara A. v. John G., 193 Cal. Rptr. 422 (1983) (damages resulting from ectopic pregnancy that left plaintiff sterile); In re Alice D. v. William M., 450 N.Y.S.2d 350 (1982) (damages resulting from abortion). *But see* C.A.M. v. R.A.W., 568 A.2d 556 (N.J. App.Div. 1990) (as a matter of public policy, "courts should not intrude into this manifestly private relationship"). Can these asymmetrical rules be justified? For discussions of these and related issues, *see* Pinhas Shifman, Involuntary Parenthood: Misrepresentation as

to the Use of Contraceptives, 4 Int'l J.L. & Fam. 279 (1990); Donald C. Hubin, Daddy Dilemmas: Untangling the Puzzles of Paternity, 13 Cornell J.L. & Pub. Pol'y 29 (2003).

JUNE CARBONE, *FROM PARTNERS TO PARENTS: THE SECOND REVOLUTION IN FAMILY LAW*

162-163 (2000)

In an earlier era, the "rules" [i.e., understood norms] . . . were designed to persuade the woman to say "no," and failing that, to convince the man to marry her. Marriage was the only way for a father to vindicate his responsibility to the child and, more centrally, to the mother for what was often the understood terms of her consent. In the new era, women may engage in sex for the same reasons as men–with no promise to marry needed or implied. The state, however, still demands a guarantor. The obligation not to impose the consequences of the sexual act on the public fisc is, in these cases, subject only to the father's ability to pay, and the state's ability to make him pay. The mother has no ability to alter the father's obligation except by staying off welfare. The child's right to share in his father's station in life is more of a default rule. One of the reasons child support collection rates in non-marital cases are so low is that many of the mothers never seek support in the first place. Their reasons are varied. They include the father's poverty, his disappearance, fear of his reaction, and the desire to exclude him from a further role in the child's life. They may also include the mother's sense that it is unfair to seek support from the father if he had no role in the decision to forgo contraception, or the one not to seek an abortion. The father's position in these cases, as Frank Serpico can attest, is the same as the woman's in an earlier era who relied on a man's unenforceable promise that he would marry her.

PROBLEMS

1. Francine wanted to have a child, but she did not want to get married. She and Edward signed an agreement, which Francine handwrote, providing that she would not seek support from Edward if she became pregnant by him, and that she would never reveal his identity. They had sexual relations, Francine became pregnant, and she bore a healthy child. Five years later Francine filed a paternity suit against Edward, seeking child support. Edward moved to dismiss, relying on the agreement. What arguments should the parties make?

2. Eighteen-year-old Marie became pregnant by her 15-year-old next-door neighbor, Tom. After her baby is born Marie files a paternity suit against Tom. In this state Marie is guilty of statutory rape because Tom is younger than 16 and she is older than 18. Tom argues that the policy underlying the statutory rape statute also precludes the imposition of a support duty on him. How should the court rule and why?

BENNEMON V. SULLIVAN

914 F.2d 987 (7th Cir. 1990)

Posner, C.J. This is an appeal by a disappointed applicant for child's social security survivor benefits. The child, Tarelle M. Williams, is the illegitimate son of Betty Bennemon, who claims that the father is George Williams, a deceased wage earner covered by social security, and that, as his child, Tarelle is entitled to the benefits that Bennemon is seeking on Tarelle's behalf. In days of yore, the claim would have been laughable from a legal standpoint; illegitimate children had no entitlements to inherit, 1 Blackstone, Commentaries 458 (1765), and social security survivor's benefits are a form of inheritance — inheritance of an entitlement to government benefits. Society wanted to channel all sexual activity into marriage, so far as possible; and one way to discourage extramarital sexual activity, it may have seemed, was to penalize the offspring by stigmatizing them as bastards and denying them the rights that legitimate children enjoy. How effective a deterrent may be questioned. One effect is to reduce a potential cost of children to the father, since, unlike legitimate children, illegitimate ones have no rights in his estate. At all events, in this as in most other countries the channeling policy as we have called it has withered, and the illegitimate birth rate, relative to the legitimate birth rate, has soared; and it has come to seem, to many, that the disabilities attached to bastardy are now pointless and savage.

In a series of decisions illustrated by Weber v. Aetna Casualty & Surety Co., 406 U.S. 164 (1972), and Jimenez v. Weinberger, 417 U.S. 628 (1974), the Supreme Court invalidated, as denials of equal protection, discriminations against illegitimate children that could not be justified other than as efforts to penalize illegitimacy. Yet the Court refused to view other justifications offered for such discriminations as skeptically as the justifications offered for discriminations considered deeply invidious, such as discrimination based on race. . . . In 1965, shortly before the Supreme Court in Levy v. Louisiana, 391 U.S. 68 (1968), and Glona v. American Guarantee & Liability Ins. Co., 391 U.S. 73 (1968), first discovered the constitutional rights of the illegitimate, Congress had broadened the rights (theretofore slight) of illegitimate children under the social security statute, creating the legal structure that we apply today (the 1965 statute, so far as is relevant to this case, has not been amended, notwithstanding the Supreme Court's subsequent recognition of the constitutional rights of illegitimate children).

. . . [T]he provisions of the social security law relating to benefits for the child of a deceased wage earner provide that [i]f the child's biological mother is married to the child's father (the deceased wage earner), then the child is eligible, without more, for the benefits. . . . And for these purposes a common law marriage is good enough. But if the child is illegitimate, he must squeeze himself into one of a limited set of niches, and if he can't, then he gets no benefits even if there is little doubt that the deceased wage earner was the child's biological father, which is the case here. The niches are: eligibility to inherit under the law of the pertinent state (in effect deferring to state policy on the rights of the illegitimate); a written acknowledgment of parenthood by the deceased wage earner or a judicial determination to that effect; or a determination by the Social Security Administration that the deceased was the parent and, at the time of his death, was either living with the child or "contributing to the [child's] support."

George Williams and Betty Bennemon met about a year before his death. They fell in love and entered upon a sexual relationship, exclusive on her side, but they lived apart. Bennemon had a bad credit record, and to enable her to obtain electricity and telephone service Williams . . . subscribed to these services for her in his name. He also paid a couple of utility bills, although the record contains no details. Bennemon became pregnant, and both she and Williams told their friends that he was the father. There is no reason to doubt that they were speaking truthfully. The testimony of friends is that Williams was thrilled by the prospect of becoming the father of a son, as he hoped the fetus would turn out to be. Of course all this evidence may have been hoked up for this proceeding, but there is no indication of that.

[handwritten margin note: Facts the George paid for thing]

Two months after Betty Bennemon became pregnant, George Williams was stabbed to death in a brawl outside a bar. He had never made a written acknowledgment of parentage. He had never been decreed a parent. There is no contention that the law of Wisconsin would have entitled Tarelle to inherit from Williams had he left an estate. There was no marriage, common law or otherwise. And Williams did not live with Bennemon. The only remaining route for establishing Tarelle's eligibility for benefits was to show that Williams had contributed to the child's support during the two months of pregnancy before Williams' unexpected death.

The administrative law judge found . . . that Williams had not contributed to the support of Tarelle (or rather the fetus that was to become Tarelle seven months later) within the meaning of the statute and its implementing regulations. . . .

[handwritten margin note: Administrative law judge said NO]

An initial complication arises from the fact that Williams died early in Bennemon's pregnancy. A father does not provide support directly to his child while it is still in the mother's womb, so if the statute were interpreted literally a child born after his father's death would rarely if ever be able to establish a claim under 42 U.S.C. §416(h)(3)(C)(ii). The Social Security Administration does not read the statute literally. It is satisfied if during the pregnancy the father provides support to the mother.

How much support? The statute does not say, but the Social Security Administration has issued a regulation which requires that it have been "regular and substantial." 20 C.F.R. §404.366(a)(2). In the case of an unemployed or sporadically employed father living at the margin of society, such as the late George Williams, strict application of this test would preclude the award of benefits. It has seemed more civilized to the Sixth Circuit to measure the adequacy of the support by the father's means than automatically to bar the children of the very poor, who, after all, need these modest benefits ($180 a month, we were told at argument) more than other children do. . . . Another line of cases challenging the "regular and substantial" criterion, but limited to cases in which the wage earner died before the child was born, emphasizes the limited needs of a fetus and holds that the statute requires only that "the support by the father for the unborn child [be] commensurate with the needs of the unborn child at the time of the father's death." Adams v. Weinberger, 521 F.2d 656, 660 (2d Cir. 1975). . . . The two lines merge in Doran v. Schweiker, 681 F.2d 605, 609-610 (9th Cir. 1982), where the poverty of the father and the limited needs of the fetal child led the court to hold that help in moving the mother to a new home and repairing the roof satisfied the statutory requirement of support. . . .

The Social Security Administration defends its regulation by reference to what it takes to be the purpose of the program of survivors' benefits—. . . "to pay benefits to replace the support lost by a child when his father" dies. . . . The purpose of the "regular and substantial" regulation is to prevent the child from reaping a windfall by virtue of the death of a father whose contribution to the child's support would not have been as large as that provided by the child's survivor benefits.

This rationale underscores the disparity in treatment between legitimate and illegitimate children. The legitimate child receives survivor's benefits no matter how poor or feckless or absent the father is, provided only that the father had social security coverage, whereas the illegitimate child who cannot fit himself within one of the other provisions of the statute receives benefits only if his father was a responsible father as measured not only by willingness, but also by ability, to contribute regularly and substantially to the support of his child. There are unexplained disparities even within the statute's treatment of illegitimate children, under the view propounded by the Social Security Administration. The child whose father happens to make written acknowledgment of parentage—something that for all we know George Williams would have done had he known his end was so near—is entitled to benefits even if the father had never contributed a nickel to the child's support, and never would.

Maybe all the statute is really after is hard evidence of paternity, and the framers thought that contributing to the child's support was a kind of surrogate acknowledgment of paternity—how likely is one to support a child one does not believe to be one's own? . . . . The Administration has not proposed this interpretation, however, no doubt inhibited by *Jimenez*, where the Supreme Court rejected the evidentiary rationale in striking down another provision of the social security law discriminating against illegitimate children. The Administration takes the safe route by arguing quid pro quo, because that is the argument that persuaded the Court in *Lucas* to uphold the constitutionality of the very provision in issue here, requiring proof that the deceased wage earner contributed to the child's support. The argument fails, it is true, to make sense of the statute as a whole. But not every statute makes sense as a whole. This statute may not be coherent in an intellectual sense, for the framers may have wanted to preserve, and not merely on evidentiary grounds, a distinction between the entitlements of legitimate and illegitimate children. Nor need such a desire be thought merely cruel and ignoble, for the subsidizing of illegitimate births is no favor in the long run to the millions of people mired in the culture of poverty that is associated with rampant illegitimacy. And since the willingness of Congress to fund social programs is distinctly finite, generosity to one class of claimants may spell tightness toward another.

. . . The payment of a couple of utility bills will not do, especially without a clearer idea of frequency and magnitude. And there is no indication that either payment came after Bennemon became pregnant. . . .

The nicest question in the case is whether Williams' lending his name to enable Bennemon to obtain utility services is a form of support that ought to be counted in deciding whether the statute has been satisfied. There is no indication that it cost Williams anything, yet it certainly had financial value to Bennemon and after she became pregnant to their son as well. It was in one sense a mere one-shot deal like the occasional payment of utility bills. But in another and equally valid sense it provided regular and continuous—and substantial—support until the services were cut off, which in the case of the gas and electricity did not occur until Bennemon moved to another apartment, sometime after Williams died. . . .

But although the question is close, we think the administrative law judge's determination that this "support" should not be assigned to the pregnancy period is supported by substantial evidence. . . . Of course sheer poverty may have prevented him from rendering support that for all we know he was desperately eager to render—he seems to have been looking forward with genuine enthusiasm to becoming a father. But the statute requires some support—maybe not so much as the Social Security Administration believes but more than Williams provided— and this regardless of financial capability. If Williams had no financial capabilities or expectations whatsoever, as may well have been the case, the award of benefits to his son would indeed be a windfall; Tarelle would have gotten nothing from Williams if Williams had lived, despite the best will in the world. The statute does award this windfall to the legitimate child, but not to the illegitimate one and the difference was sanctioned by *Lucas*.

So the appeal fails; but is the only consequence to direct the applicant to another forum? Tarelle is entitled to benefits if he can show that he would be entitled to inherit from his father under Wisconsin's law of intestate succession. 42 U.S.C. §416(h)(2)(A). The only possibly applicable provision of that law entitles an illegitimate child to inherit if the father has been determined to be such in a paternity case. Wis. Stat. Ann. §852.05(1). . . . [S]o far as we know there is no bar even at this late date to Tarelle's bringing a paternity proceeding in a Wisconsin state court. George Williams died in 1986, after Wisconsin amended its law to allow posthumous paternity proceedings. And we find no deadline for such proceedings. . . . We mention the matter of paternity proceedings merely to round out the picture of the scheme of entitlements in which the case arose.

Affirmed.

NOTES AND QUESTIONS

1. Should a state be permitted to discourage the birth of children to unmarried parents? Does imposing legal disabilities on nonmarital children discourage out-of-wedlock childbearing?

2. How does a man contribute to the support of his child before the child is born? What is the purpose of this requirement of the Social Security law? Compare the treatment of these issues in the custody cases in the next section.

3. Wolfe v. Sullivan, 988 F.2d 1025 (10th Cir. 1993), rejects the "regular and substantial" test and accepts the more generous "support commensurate with the unborn child's needs" test of Doran v. Schweiker, 681 F.2d 605 (9th Cir. 1982). *See also* Allen v. Callahan, 120 F.3d 86 (7th Cir. 1997). Social Security survivors' benefits, unlike TANF benefits, are not means tested, and the Social Security benefits are generally larger than TANF benefits.

4. Under the Social Security provisions applied in *Bennemon*, certain categories of children are entitled to benefits on the account of a deceased father without the need to prove actual dependency on the father. The categories include children whose parents were married, and nonmarital children entitled to inherit under state intestate succession law, whose fathers' paternity has been judicially established, and whose father has acknowledged them in writing. However, nonmarital children who do not fit into these categories must prove both their biological relationship to the deceased and either that they were living with their father or that he was supporting them at his death. In Mathews v. Lucas, 427 U.S. 495 (1976), nonmarital children whose paternity was not disputed but who did not fit into any of the categories entitling them to Social Security benefits when their father died challenged the constitutionality of the statute requiring that they prove they had been living with or supported by their father at his death. The Supreme Court held that the statute did not violate equal protection, even though the Court agreed that it treated children differently based at least partly on their parents' marital status. The Secretary of Health, Education, and Welfare (HEW) defended the statute on the basis that it was intended to replace support that children lost because of their fathers' death. Even though the statutory classifications were underinclusive and overinclusive, the Court held that they were substantially related to the actual likelihood of dependency.

5. The court in *Bennemon* indicates that Wisconsin law may allow Tarelle to inherit from his father by intestate succession if paternity can be established; if so, he is also entitled to Social Security benefits. See DiBenedetto v. Jaskolski (In re Estate of Thompson), 661 N.W.2d 869 (Wis. Ct. App. 2003) (upholding children's ability to seek a posthumous determination of paternity for purposes of determining right to intestate succession). What is the purpose of this requirement of the Social Security law?

In most states children are intestate heirs of their parents. However, under the 1990 version of the Uniform Probate Code (UPC), children do not inherit from a parent if their other parent also survives, was married to the decedent at the time of death, and had no children from another marriage. UPC § 2-102(1)(ii). Nonmarital children are intestate heirs of their parents, regardless of the parents' marital status. UPC § 2-114(a). Under this provision, would Tarelle have been his father's heir?

As *Bennemon* implies, in some jurisdictions a nonmarital child whose paternity was not established before the father died cannot inherit. The Supreme Court upheld such a statute against an equal protection challenge in Lalli v. Lalli, 439 U.S. 259 (1978), saying that the requirement that paternity be established during the father's lifetime was substantially related to the important state interest of facilitating the administration of decedents' estates. On the other hand, the Court held, in Trimble v. Gordon, 430 U.S. 762 (1977), that an inheritance scheme that did not allow a nonmarital child to inherit when paternity had been established before the father died violated the Constitution. In Haas v. Chater, 79 F.3d 559 (7th Cir. 1996), Judge Posner again found that a posthumous child was not entitled to Social Security benefits after his father's death. Scott Glenn, Sr., died one month after his child was conceived. When the child was one month old, the mother filed a petition in state court to establish paternity. However, the Indiana intestate succession law provides that a paternity suit must be filed within five months of a father's death for a nonmarital child to be entitled to inherit. The Seventh Circuit rejected the argument that the statute should not be strictly applied on the facts of the case and concluded that the statute was not unconstitutional under *Lalli* in part because the statute did not make it impossible for the mother to have filed suit while she was pregnant.

Gillett-Netting v. Barnhart, 371 F.3d 593 (9th Cir. 2004), is one of a series of cases in which children were conceived (by artificial insemination) as well as born after the death of their father and then sought Social Security survivors' benefits. The Ninth Circuit concluded that under Arizona law the children were the legitimate children of the decedent, and it reversed a lower court decision denying benefits because they were not "dependent on their father's earnings" at the time of his death." *See also* Woodward v. Commissioner of Social Security, 760 N.E.2d 257 (Mass. 2002), and In re Estate of Kolacy, 753 A.2d 1257 (N.J. Super. 2000). *Cf.* Findaya W. v. A-T.E.A.M., Co., Inc., 546 N.W.2d 61 (Neb. 1996), holding unconstitutional a statute that required nonmarital children to prove actual dependency on their deceased father to receive worker's compensation benefits but did not impose this burden on marital children. The court concluded that administrative convenience did not justify the disparate treatment. *See generally* Susan N. Gary, The Parent-Child Relationship Under Intestacy Statutes, 32 U. Mem. L. Rev. 643 (2002).

PROBLEMS

1. A state statute regulating private insurance requires that group health insurance offered through employment must cover all children born in marriage to male employees, but children born outside marriage must be covered only if a court has adjudged the employee's paternity. Does this statute violate the equal protection rights of children born outside marriage? Since 1993 employers covered by ERISA cannot deny health insurance coverage to employees' children born outside marriage. 42 U.S.C. § 1396g-1. For more information see Chapter 7.

2. Don and Mary were living together but were not married. Don paid half of Mary's rent, and they shared groceries and utilities. Six months ago they learned that Mary was pregnant, and Don bought gifts of maternity clothes for Mary. Don was recently killed in an automobile accident. Under the test in *Bennemon*, will Don and Mary's child be entitled to Social Security benefits on Don's account?

2. Unmarried Fathers' Custodial Rights

The U.S. Supreme Court extended constitutional protection to unmarried fathers' custodial rights in Stanley v. Illinois (1972). In that case, Illinois law provided that, upon the death of an unmarried mother, her children became wards of the state and the state granted custody to a court-appointed guardian. The father, who had lived intermittently with the mother and children for eighteen years, received no legal recognition. The Court declared the statute, which gave no recognition to any unwed father however devoted to his children, an unconstitutional violation of due process. Chief Justice Burger issued a strong dissent, observing that

. . . I believe that a State is fully justified in concluding, on the basis of common human experience, that the biological role of the mother in carrying and nursing an infant creates stronger bonds between her and the child than the bonds resulting from the male's often casual encounter. This view is reinforced by the observable fact that most unwed mothers exhibit a concern for their offspring either permanently or at least until they are safely placed for adoption, while unwed fathers rarely burden either the mother or the child with their attentions or loyalties. Centuries of human experience buttress this view of the realities of human conditions and suggest that unwed mothers of illegitimate children are generally more dependable protectors of their children than are unwed fathers. While these, like most generalizations, are not without exceptions, they nevertheless provide a sufficient basis to sustain a statutory classification whose objective is not to penalize unwed parents but to further the welfare of illegitimate children in fulfillment of the State's obligations as *parens patriae*.

The *Stanley* majority rejected Burger's approach. Consider, however, how the courts in the next two cases deal with the different positions of mother and father in the birth of a newborn.

LEHR V. ROBERTSON

463 U.S. 248 (1983)

STEVENS, J. . . . Jessica M. was born out of wedlock on November 9, 1976. Her mother, Lorraine Robertson, married Richard Robertson eight months after Jessica's birth. On December 21, 1978, when Jessica was over two years old, the Robertsons filed an adoption petition in the Family Court of Ulster County, New York. The court heard their testimony and received a favorable report from the Ulster County Department of Social Services. On March 7, 1979, the court entered an order of adoption. In this proceeding, appellant contends that the adoption order is invalid because he, Jessica's putative father, was not given advance notice of the adoption proceeding.

The State of New York maintains a "putative father registry." A man who files with that registry demonstrates his intent to claim paternity of a child born out of wedlock and is therefore entitled to receive notice of any proceeding to adopt that child. Before entering Jessica's adoption order, the Ulster County Family Court had the putative father registry examined. Although appellant claims to be Jessica's natural father, he had not entered his name in the registry.

In addition to the persons whose names are listed on the putative father registry, New York law requires that notice of an adoption proceeding be given to several other classes of possible fathers of children born out of wedlock — those who have been adjudicated to be the father, those who have been identified as the father on the child's birth certificate, those who live openly with the child and the child's mother and who hold themselves out to be the father, those who have been identified as the father by the mother in a sworn written statement, and those who were married to the child's mother before the child was six months old. Appellant admittedly was not a member of any of those classes. He had lived with appellee prior to Jessica's birth and visited her in the hospital when Jessica was born, but his name does not appear on Jessica's birth certificate. He did not live with appellee or Jessica after Jessica's birth, he has never provided them with any financial support, and he has never offered to marry appellee. Nevertheless, he contends that the following special circumstances gave him a constitutional right to notice and a hearing before Jessica was adopted.

On January 30, 1979, one month after the adoption proceeding was commenced in Ulster County, appellant filed a "visitation and paternity petition" in the Westchester County Family Court. In that petition, he asked for a determination of paternity, an order of support, and reasonable visitation privileges with Jessica. Notice of that proceeding was served on appellee on February 22, 1979. Four days later appellee's attorney informed the Ulster County Court that appellant had commenced a paternity proceeding in Westchester County; the Ulster County judge then entered an order staying appellant's paternity proceeding until he could rule on a motion to change the venue of that proceeding to Ulster County. On March 3, 1979, appellant received notice of the change of venue motion and, for the first time, learned that an adoption proceeding was pending in Ulster County.

On March 7, 1979, appellant's attorney telephoned the Ulster County judge to inform him that he planned to seek a stay of the adoption proceeding pending the determination of the paternity petition. In that telephone conversation, the judge advised the lawyer that he had already signed the adoption order earlier that day. According to appellant's attorney, the judge stated that he was aware of the pending paternity petition but did not believe he was required to give notice to appellant prior to the entry of the order of adoption.

. . . On June 22, 1979, appellant filed a petition to vacate the order of adoption on the ground that it was obtained by fraud and in violation of his constitutional rights. The Ulster County Family Court . . . denied the petition. . . .

The Appellate Division of the Supreme Court affirmed. . . .

The New York Court of Appeals also affirmed by a divided vote. . . .

THE DUE PROCESS CLAIM

. . . This Court has examined the extent to which a natural father's biological relationship with his illegitimate child receives protection under the Due Process Clause in precisely three cases: Stanley v. Illinois, 405 U.S. 645 (1972), Quilloin v. Walcott, 434 U.S. 246 (1978), and Caban v. Mohammed, 441 U.S. 380 (1979).

Stanley involved the constitutionality of an Illinois statute that conclusively presumed every father of a child born out of wedlock to be an unfit person to have custody of his children. The father in that case had lived with his children all their lives and had lived with their mother for eighteen years. There was nothing in the record to indicate that Stanley had been a neglectful father who had not cared for his children. . . . [T]he Court held that the Due Process Clause was violated by the automatic destruction of the custodial relationship without giving the father any opportunity to present evidence regarding his fitness as a parent.

Quilloin involved the constitutionality of a Georgia statute that authorized the adoption of a child born out of wedlock over the objection of the natural father. The father in that case had never legitimated the child. It was only after the mother had remarried and her new husband had filed an adoption petition that the natural father sought visitation rights and filed a petition for legitimation. The trial court found adoption by the new husband to be in the child's best interests, and we unanimously held that action to be consistent with the Due Process Clause.

Caban involved the conflicting claims of two natural parents who had maintained joint custody of their children from the time of their birth until they were respectively two and four years old. The father challenged the validity of an order authorizing the mother's new husband to adopt the children; he relied on both the Equal Protection Clause and the Due Process Clause. Because this Court upheld his equal protection claim, the majority did not address his due process challenge. The comments on the latter claim by the four dissenting Justices are nevertheless instructive, because they identify the clear distinction between a mere biological relationship and an actual relationship of parental responsibility.

Justice Stewart correctly observed: "Even if it be assumed that each married parent after divorce has some substantive due process right to maintain his or her parental relationship, cf. Smith v. Organization of Foster Families, 431 U.S. 816, 862-863 (opinion concurring in judgment), it by no means follows that each unwed parent has any such right. Parental rights do not spring full-blown from the biological connection between parent and child. They require relationships more enduring." 441 U.S., at 397.[5]

In a similar vein, the other three dissenters in *Caban* were prepared to "assume that, if and when one develops, the relationship between a father and his natural child is entitled to protection against arbitrary state action as a matter of due process." Caban v. Mohammed, 441 U.S. 380, 414.

The difference between the developed parent-child relationship that was implicated in *Stanley* and *Caban*, and the potential relationship involved in *Quilloin* and this case, is both clear and significant. When an unwed father demonstrates a full commitment to the responsibilities of parenthood by "com[ing] forward to participate in the rearing of his child," *Caban*, 441 U.S., at 392, his interest in personal

---

5. In the balance of that paragraph Justice Stewart noted that the relation between a father and his natural child may acquire constitutional protection if the father enters into a traditional marriage with the mother or if "the actual relationship between father and child" is sufficient. The mother carries and bears the child, and in this sense her parental relationship is clear. The validity of the father's parental claims must be gauged by other measures. By tradition, the primary measure has been the legitimate familial relationship he creates with the child by marriage with the mother. By definition, the question before us can arise only when no such marriage has taken place. In some circumstances the actual relationship between father and child may suffice to create in the unwed father parental interests comparable to those of the married father. *Cf.* Stanley v. Illinois, supra. But here we are concerned with the rights the unwed father may have when his wishes and those of the mother are in conflict, and the child's best interests are served by a resolution in favor of the mother. It seems to me that the absence of a legal tie with the mother may in such circumstances appropriately place a limit on whatever substantive constitutional claims might otherwise exist by virtue of the father's actual relationship with the children. Ibid.

contact with his child acquires substantial protection under the due process clause. At that point it may be said that he "act[s] as a father toward his children." Id., at 389, n.7. But the mere existence of a biological link does not merit equivalent constitutional protection. The actions of judges neither create nor sever genetic bonds. "[T]he importance of the familial relationship, to the individuals involved and to the society, stems from the emotional attachments that derive from the intimacy of daily association, and from the role it plays in 'promot[ing] a way of life' through the instruction of children as well as from the fact of blood relationship." Smith v. Organization of Foster Families for Equality and Reform, 431 U.S. 816, 844 (1977) (quoting Wisconsin v. Yoder, 406 U.S. 205, 231-233 (1972)).

The significance of the biological connection is that it offers the natural father an opportunity that no other male possesses to develop a relationship with his offspring. If he grasps that opportunity and accepts some measure of responsibility for the child's future, he may enjoy the blessings of the parent-child relationship and make uniquely valuable contributions to the child's development. If he fails to do so, the Federal Constitution will not automatically compel a state to listen to his opinion of where the child's best interests lie.

In this case, we are not assessing the constitutional adequacy of New York's procedures for terminating a developed relationship. Appellant has never had any significant custodial, personal, or financial relationship with Jessica, and he did not seek to establish a legal tie until after she was two years old.[6] We are concerned only with whether New York has adequately protected his opportunity to form such a relationship. . . .

After this Court's decision in *Stanley*, the New York Legislature appointed a special commission to recommend legislation that would accommodate both the interests of biological fathers in their children and the children's interest in prompt and certain adoption procedures. The commission recommended, and the legislature enacted, a statutory adoption scheme that automatically provides notice to seven categories of putative fathers who are likely to have assumed some responsibility for the care of their natural children. If this scheme were likely to omit many responsible fathers, and if qualification for notice were beyond the control of an interested putative father, it might be thought procedurally inadequate. Yet, as all of the New York courts that reviewed this matter observed, the right to receive notice was completely within appellant's control. By mailing a postcard to the putative father registry, he could have guaranteed that he would

---

6. This case happens to involve an adoption by the husband of the natural mother, but we do not believe the natural father has any greater right to object to such an adoption than to an adoption by two total strangers. If anything, the balance of equities tips the opposite way in a case such as this. In denying the putative father relief in *Quilloin*, we made an observation equally applicable here: "Nor is this a case in which the proposed adoption would place the child with a new set of parents with whom the child had never before lived. Rather, the result of the adoption in this case is to give full recognition to a family unit already in existence, a result desired by all concerned, except appellant. Whatever might be required in other situations, we cannot say that the State was required in this situation to find anything more than that the adoption, and denial of legitimation, were in the 'best interests of the child.'" 434 U.S., at 255.

receive notice of any proceedings to adopt Jessica. The possibility that he may have failed to do so because of his ignorance of the law cannot be a sufficient reason for criticizing the law itself. The New York legislature concluded that a more open-ended notice requirement would merely complicate the adoption process, threaten the privacy interests of unwed mothers, create the risk of unnecessary controversy, and impair the desired finality of adoption decrees. Regardless of whether we would have done likewise if we were legislators instead of judges, we surely cannot characterize the state's conclusion as arbitrary.

Appellant argues, however, that even if the putative father's opportunity to establish a relationship with an illegitimate child is adequately protected by the New York statutory scheme in the normal case, he was nevertheless entitled to special notice because the court and the mother knew that he had filed an affiliation proceeding in another court. This argument amounts to nothing more than an indirect attack on the notice provisions of the New York statute. The legitimate state interests in facilitating the adoption of young children and having the adoption proceeding completed expeditiously that underlie the entire statutory scheme also justify a trial judge's determination to require all interested parties to adhere precisely to the procedural requirements of the statute. The Constitution does not require either a trial judge or a litigant to give special notice to nonparties who are presumptively capable of asserting and protecting their own rights. Since the New York statutes adequately protected appellant's inchoate interest in establishing a relationship with Jessica, we find no merit in the claim that his constitutional rights were offended because the family court strictly complied with the notice provisions of the statute.

THE EQUAL PROTECTION CLAIM

. . . The legislation at issue in this case . . . [is] designed to promote the best interests of the child, protect the rights of interested third parties, and ensure promptness and finality. To serve those ends, the legislation guarantees to certain people the right to veto an adoption and the right to prior notice of any adoption proceeding. The mother of an illegitimate child is always within that favored class, but only certain putative fathers are included. Appellant contends that the gender-based distinction is invidious.

As we noted above, the existence or nonexistence of a substantial relationship between parent and child is a relevant criterion in evaluating both the rights of the parent and the best interests of the child. In Quilloin v. Walcott, supra, we noted that the putative father, like appellant, "ha[d] never shouldered any significant responsibility with respect to the daily supervision, education, protection, or care of the child. Appellant does not complain of his exemption from these responsibilities. . . ." 434 U.S., at 256. We therefore found that a Georgia statute that always required a mother's consent to the adoption of a child born out of wedlock, but required the father's consent only if he had legitimated the child, did not violate the Equal Protection Clause. . . .

We have held that these statutes may not constitutionally be applied in that class of cases where the mother and father are in fact similarly situated with regard to their relationship with the child. In Caban v. Mohammed, 441 U.S. 380 (1979), the Court held that it violated the Equal Protection Clause to grant the mother a veto over the adoption of a four-year-old girl and a six-year-old boy, but not to grant a veto to their father, who had admitted paternity and had participated in the rearing of the children. . . .

Jessica's parents are not like the parents involved in *Caban*. Whereas appellee had a continuous custodial responsibility for Jessica, appellant never established any custodial, personal, or financial relationship with her. If one parent has an established custodial relationship with the child and the other parent has either abandoned or never established a relationship, the Equal Protection Clause does not prevent a state from according the two parents different legal rights.

The judgment of the New York Court of Appeals is affirmed.

WHITE, J., with whom MARSHALL, J., and BLACKMUN, J., join, dissenting. . . . It is axiomatic that "[t]he fundamental requirement of due process is the opportunity to be heard 'at a meaningful time and in a meaningful manner.'" As Jessica's biological father, Lehr either had an interest protected by the Constitution or he did not. If the entry of the adoption order in this case deprived Lehr of a constitutionally protected interest, he is entitled to notice and an opportunity to be heard before the order can be accorded finality.

According to Lehr, he and Jessica's mother met in 1971 and began living together in 1974. The couple cohabited for approximately 2 years, until Jessica's birth in 1976. Throughout the pregnancy and after the birth, Lorraine acknowledged to friends and relatives that Lehr was Jessica's father; Lorraine told Lehr that she had reported to the New York State Department of Social Services that he was the father. Lehr visited Lorraine and Jessica in the hospital every day during Lorraine's confinement. According to Lehr, from the time Lorraine was discharged from the hospital until August, 1978, she concealed her whereabouts from him. During this time Lehr never ceased his efforts to locate Lorraine and Jessica and achieved sporadic success until August, 1977, after which time he was unable to locate them at all. On those occasions when he did determine Lorraine's location, he visited with her and her children to the extent she was willing to permit it. When Lehr, with the aid of a detective agency, located Lorraine and Jessica in August, 1978, Lorraine was already married to Mr. Robertson. Lehr asserts that at this time he offered to provide financial assistance and to set up a trust fund for Jessica, but that Lorraine refused. Lorraine threatened Lehr with arrest unless he stayed away and refused to permit him to see Jessica. Thereafter Lehr retained counsel who wrote to Lorraine in early December, 1978, requesting that she permit Lehr to visit Jessica and threatening legal action on Lehr's behalf. On December 21, 1978, perhaps as a response to Lehr's threatened legal action, appellees commenced the adoption action at issue here. . . .

Lehr's version of the "facts" paints a far different picture than that portrayed by the majority. The majority's recitation, that "[a]ppellant has never had any significant custodial, personal, or financial relationship with Jessica, and he did not seek to establish a legal tie until after she was two years old," obviously does not tell the whole story. Appellant has never been afforded an opportunity to present his case. The legitimation proceeding he instituted was first stayed, and then dismissed, on appellees' motions. Nor could appellant establish his interest during the adoption proceedings, for it is the failure to provide Lehr notice and an opportunity to be heard there that is at issue here. We cannot fairly make a judgment based on the quality or substance of a relationship without a complete and developed factual record. This case requires us to assume that Lehr's allegations are true — that but for the actions of the child's mother there would have been the kind of significant relationship that the majority concedes is entitled to the full panoply of procedural due process protections.

I reject the peculiar notion that the only significance of the biological connection between father and child is that "it offers the natural father an opportunity that no other male possesses to develop a relationship with his offspring." A "mere biological relationship" is not as unimportant in determining the nature of liberty interests as the majority suggests.

"[T]he usual understanding of 'family' implies biological relationships, and most decisions treating the relation between parent and child have stressed this element." Smith v. Organization of Foster Families, supra, 431 U.S., at 843. The "biological connection" is itself a relationship that creates a protected interest. Thus the "nature" of the interest is the parent-child relationship; how well developed that relationship has become goes to its "weight," not its "nature." Whether Lehr's interest is entitled to constitutional protection does not entail a searching inquiry into the quality of the relationship but a simple determination of the fact that the relationship exists — a fact that even the majority agrees must be assumed to be established.

Beyond that, however, because there is no established factual basis on which to proceed, it is quite untenable to conclude that a putative father's interest in his child is lacking in substance, that the father in effect has abandoned the child, or ultimately that the father's interest is not entitled to the same minimum procedural protections as the interests of other putative fathers. Any analysis of the adequacy of the notice in this case must be conducted on the assumption that the interest involved here is as strong as that of any putative father. That is not to say that due process requires actual notice to every putative father or that adoptive parents or the State must conduct an exhaustive search of records or an intensive investigation before a final adoption order may be entered. The procedures adopted by the State, however, must at least represent a reasonable effort to determine the identity of the putative father and to give him adequate notice.

II

In this case, of course, there was no question about either the identity or the location of the putative father. The mother knew exactly who he was and both she and the court entering the order of adoption knew precisely where he was and how to give him actual notice that his parental rights were about to be terminated by an adoption order. Lehr was entitled to due process, and the right to be heard is one of the fundamentals of that right, which "has little reality or worth unless one is informed that the matter is pending and can choose for himself whether to appear or default, acquiesce or contest."

The State concedes this much but insists that Lehr has had all the process that is due to him. . . . I am unpersuaded by the State's position. In the first place, § 111-a defines six categories of unwed fathers to whom notice must be given even though they have not placed their names on file pursuant to the section. Those six categories, however, do not include fathers such as Lehr who have initiated filiation proceedings, even though their identity and interest are as clearly and easily ascertainable as those fathers in the six categories. . . .

The State asserts that any problem in this respect is overcome by the seventh category of putative fathers to whom notice must be given, namely those fathers who have identified themselves in the putative father register maintained by the State. . . . I have difficulty with this position. First, it represents a grudging and crabbed approach to due process. The State is quite willing to give notice and a hearing to putative fathers who have made themselves known by resorting to the putative fathers' register. It makes little sense to me to deny notice and hearing to a father who has not placed his name in the register but who has unmistakably identified himself by filing suit to establish his paternity and has notified the adoption court of his action and his interest. I thus need not question the statutory scheme on its face. Even assuming that Lehr would have been foreclosed if his failure to utilize the register had somehow disadvantaged the State, he effectively made himself known by other means, and it is the sheerest formalism to deny him a hearing because he informed the State in the wrong manner. . . .

The State's undoubted interest in the finality of adoption orders likewise is not well served by a procedure that will deny notice and a hearing to a father whose identity and location are known. As this case well illustrates, denying notice and a hearing to such a father may result in years of additional litigation and threaten the reopening of adoption proceedings and the vacation of the adoption.

NOTES AND QUESTIONS

1. What was Lehr trying to accomplish by attempting to participate in the adoption proceeding? Was it important that this was a stepparent adoption? Should that matter? *See* In re Baby Girl Eason, 358 S.E.2d 459 (Ga. 1987).

2. What test does *Lehr* adopt for determining when an unmarried father has constitutionally protected custodial rights? What is the basis under this test for custodial rights? What interest of the child (if any) does this test protect? What interests (if any) are disserved?

3. Compare the *Lehr* test for custodial rights to the test applied in *Bennemon* for Social Security benefits. Are the tests the same? Should they be?

4. Stanley v. Illinois, on which *Lehr* relies, was the first in a series of Supreme Court cases on the rights of unmarried fathers. *Michael H.* was the last in the line. Are the cases consistent? Could Michael have met the test for asserting parental rights that the Court established in *Lehr*?

5. Under the New York statute considered in *Lehr*, when was an unmarried father entitled to notice of an adoption proceeding and an opportunity to participate in it? Is this statute adequate to identify all biological fathers who are entitled to notice under the *Lehr* criteria?

Does the statute presuppose that the biological father knows about a pregnancy so that a father who does not know might be entitled to notice even without satisfying the statute?

Is the statute intended to discover fathers who have developed a substantial relationship with their children as well as those who have not but might want to? Could there be some fathers who have developed a relationship with their children who would not be entitled to notice under the statute?

Could the father of a newborn satisfy the *Lehr* test for custodial rights? How? Does *Lehr* hold that an unmarried father may have a constitutional right to have an *opportunity* to develop a relationship to his child?

Suppose the mother deliberately hides from the father, successfully preventing him from learning about or participating in the adoption proceeding. If the father learns about the proceeding before the adoption decree becomes final and attacks it, does due process require that the decree be set aside?

On these issues *see, e.g.,* In re Adoption of Reeves, 831 S.W.2d 607 (Ark. 1992); Adoption of Kelsey S, 823 P.2d 1216 (Cal. 1992); Appeal of H. R., 581 A.2d 1141 (D.C. 1990), *on remand*, 630 A.2d 670 (D.C.); In re M. N. M., 605 A.2d 921 (D.C. 1992); In re Baby Girl Eason, 358 S.E.2d 459 (Ga. 1987); In re Application of S. R. S. and M. B. S., 408 N.W.2d 272 (Neb. 1987); Matter of Raquel Marie X, 559 N.E.2d 418 (N.Y. 1990), *appeal following remand*, 570 N.Y.S.2d 604 (A.D. 1991); Robert O. v. Russell K., 604 N.E.2d 99 (N.Y. 1992); Nale v. Robertson, 871 S.W.2d 674 (Tenn. 1994); Kessel v. Leavitt, 511 S.E.2d 720 (W. Va. 1998) (upholding award of millions of dollars in damages for intentional interference with parental relationship where mother placed child for adoption in Canada to defeat father's parental rights); June Carbone, The Missing Piece of the Custody Puzzle: Creating a New Model of Parental Partnership, 39 Santa Clara L. Rev. 1091 (1999).

6. Section 201 of the 2002 Uniform Parentage Act provides that an unmarried man who is rebuttably presumed to be a child's father, who has been adjudicated to be the father, or who has signed a voluntary acknowledgment of paternity with the child's mother is entitled to parental rights. Under §402 of the 2002 Uniform Parentage Act, other putative fathers are not entitled to notice unless they register their claim of paternity with the state. The Act, however, exempts from the registry requirement a man who "commences a proceeding to adjudicate his paternity before the court has terminated his parental rights."

Section 102(3) of the Uniform Parentage Act also provides that if the child is more than a year old, then notice must be provided to every "alleged" father, and the "notice must be given in a manner prescribed for service of process in a civil action." §405(b). An "alleged father" is "a man who alleges himself to be, or is alleged to be, the genetic father or a possible genetic father of a child, but whose paternity has not been determined." §102(3). How would *Lehr* have been decided under the UPA?

7. Under UPA §204 (2002), a man is rebuttably presumed to be the father of a child under the following circumstances:

(1) He and the mother of the child are married to each other and the child is born during the marriage;

(2) He and the mother of the child were married to each other and the child is born within 300 days after the marriage is terminated by death, annulment, declaration of invalidity, or divorce [or after a decree of separation];

(3) Before the birth of the child, he and the mother of the child married each other in apparent compliance with law, even if the attempted marriage is or could be declared invalid, and the child is born during the invalid marriage or within 300 days after its termination by death, annulment, declaration of invalidity, or divorce [or after a decree of separation];

(4) After the birth of the child, he and the mother of the child married each other in apparent compliance with law, whether or not the marriage is or could be declared invalid, and he voluntarily asserted his paternity of the child, and:

    (A) The assertion is in a record filed with [state agency maintaining birth records];

    (B) He agreed to be and is named as the child's father on the child's birth certificate; or

    (C) He promised in a record to support the child as his own; or

(5) For the first two years of the child's life, he resided in the same household with the child and openly held out the child as his own.

If this statute were applied to the facts of *Michael H.*, who would qualify as Victoria's "presumed father"? Could a child have more than one presumed father? *See* In re Jesusa V., 85 P.3d 2 (Cal. 2004). How might this statute affect the outcome of the problems on pages 866–867 above and page 888 below?

8. Statutes of limitation in a number of states provide that an adoption decree may not be collaterally attacked for any reason, including jurisdictional defects, after the statutory period (often one year) expires. If the court applies such statutes of limitation in a case in which the father has not been notified of the adoption, is the result constitutional? *See* In re M. N. M., 605 A.2d 921 (D.C. App. 1992); In re S.L.F., 27 P.3d 583 (Utah App. 2001).

9. In *Caban* and *Lehr* the unmarried father claimed that the statute unconstitutionally discriminated between mothers and fathers. Why did this claim succeed in *Caban* but fail in *Lehr*? On the constitutionality of sex-based classifications in general, see Chapter 2.

Section 309 of the Immigration and Nationality Act, 8 U.S.C. §1409, provides that, subject to residence requirements applicable to parents, a child born to an unmarried citizen mother and an alien father is automatically a citizen, while a child born to an unmarried citizen father and an alien mother is automatically a citizen only if the father has agreed in writing to provide financial support for the child until the child reaches the age of 18, and if one of three conditions is satisfied while the child is less than 18: (1) the child is legitimated under the law of the child's residence or domicile, (2) the father acknowledges paternity in writing under oath, or (3) paternity is established by judicial order.

Tuan Anh Nguyen challenged the statute as sex discrimination in Nguyen v. Immigration and Naturalization Service, 121 S.Ct. 2053 (2001). Nguyen, who had come to the United States at the age of six with his American father, was convicted of two counts of felony sexual assault and subject to deportation. He and his father argued that the statute regarding citizenship of children born outside the United States to American-citizen fathers and mothers who are not citizens violated equal protection. By a 5-4 vote the Supreme Court rejected the challenge. The Court concluded that the biological relationship and the opportunity for a meaningful relationship exist between mother and child because of the birth itself, while the same cannot be said of a father and child. *See* Linda Kelly, Republican Mothers, Bastards' Fathers and Good Victims: Discarding Citizens and Equal Protection Through the Failures of Legal Images, 51 Hastings L.J. 557 (2000).

PROBLEMS

1. Anita and Martin lived together for six years, though they never married. Two children were born to them during this time. Martin supported the children, cared for them, and attended school conferences concerning them. Anita and Martin separated eight months ago, when the children were six months and four years old. Six months ago Anita placed the children for adoption with Tim and Karen. She signed a valid document relinquishing her parental rights and falsely told Tim and Karen that she did not know where the children's father was. Martin learned one week later that Anita had placed the children for adoption. He searched for them unsuccessfully by calling all the adoption agencies in the community. Shortly after a court had entered the order granting Tim and Karen's adoption petition, Martin finally discovered that Anita had placed the children privately. Martin was not personally served, but a notice was published in the local newspaper. Martin has moved to set aside the adoption on the grounds of lack of notice. Under the Uniform Parentage Act, was he entitled to notice? Under *Lehr*, would it be constitutional to terminate his rights to the children without notice?

2. Al, Betty, and Charles live in a jurisdiction that has adopted the Uniform Parentage Act. Betty's daughter Donna was born while she was married to Al. Betty and Al divorced, and Betty and Donna moved in with Charles, with whom she had been having an affair. Betty has told Charles that he is Donna's biological father. Charles has treated Donna as his daughter and has told all his friends and relatives that she was his daughter. Betty was recently killed in an automobile accident. Both Al and Charles would like custody of Donna. Each man claims that he is presumed to be Donna's biological father, relying on the presumptions in the Uniform Parentage Act. Which presumption should prevail and why?

ADOPTION OF MICHAEL H.

898 P.2d 891 (Cal. 1995) (en banc)

MOSK, Justice. In this appeal we further clarify the circumstances (see Adoption of Kelsey S. (1992) 823 P.2d 1216 (hereafter *Kelsey S.*)) in which an unwed biological father has a right under the due process and equal protection clauses of the Fourteenth Amendment to withhold his consent to the biological mother's decision to give their child up at birth for adoption by a third party. . . .

Stephanie H. met Mark K. in December 1988 in Arizona. In February 1990, Mark, then age 20, told Stephanie, then age 15, that he wanted to marry her. She declined to get married until she graduated from high school and until he quit drinking and using drugs. However, they considered themselves engaged at that time. In early July 1990 Stephanie learned she was pregnant with Mark's child. Mark suggested that she have an abortion, but she would not consider it. They also briefly discussed keeping the baby, but finally settled on adoption.

Stephanie came to California with her grandparents in July 1990. While here her aunt introduced her to two friends, John and Margaret S., who were interested in adopting a child. Stephanie told Mark about John and Margaret when she returned to Arizona at the end of July 1990. Around that time Stephanie and Mark were also researching adoption agencies.

In September 1990 Mark and Stephanie began attending birthing classes together, and Mark went to at least one yard sale with Stephanie to buy baby apparel. He also bought a trailer for them to live in together, although they never did. In early October 1990 Mark arranged to have a videotape of Stephanie's ultrasound made.

Mark and Stephanie's relationship started to deteriorate around this time. Stephanie excluded him from the birthing classes. Mark had two violent outbursts involving Stephanie, and after one of these he was arrested on a charge of aggravated assault. Mark quit his job on October 26, 1990. Two days later, on Stephanie's 16th birthday, Mark went into his trailer, which was parked behind Stephanie's mother's house, and attempted to kill himself.

After his suicide attempt, Mark admitted himself into a rehabilitation hospital. While there he decided to stop using drugs, seek stable employment and residence, and continue counseling. He also decided that he did not want to give up his child for adoption and started looking for an attorney to help him obtain custody after the child was born.

Mark and Stephanie had very little contact after his suicide attempt. In January 1991 Stephanie moved from Arizona to San Diego to live with John and Margaret. She gave birth to Michael H. on February 27, 1991. Michael was released from the hospital directly into John and Margaret's custody, where he has remained ever since.

On March 7, 1991, Mark found an attorney who would take his case free of charge. That day his attorney telephoned John and Margaret and learned that Michael had been born. As soon as he found out, Mark asked for custody, sent out some birth announcements, and bought several items, including a car seat, a crib, and some baby clothes.

In April 1991 John and Margaret filed a petition to terminate Mark's legal status as Michael's father. Mark subsequently filed a petition to establish a father-child relationship, and the two proceedings were consolidated. The court concluded that Mark was not a "presumed father" under the statutory definition and that it would be in Michael's best interest to be adopted by John and Margaret. It therefore terminated Mark's parental status and allowed the adoption to proceed.

While Mark's appeal from that judgment was pending we filed our decision in *Kelsey S., supra,* in which a majority held that under certain circumstances unwed fathers have a Fourteenth Amendment right to prevent third parties from adopting their biological children. . . . The Court of Appeal . . . reversed the judgment with directions to the trial court to hold an evidentiary hearing on whether Mark had a constitutional right to veto Michael's adoption under *Kelsey S.* . . .

After holding an evidentiary hearing on remand, the trial court concluded in light of our decision in *Kelsey S.* that Mark had a constitutional right to veto Michael's adoption absent a showing that he would be an unfit parent. John and Margaret noticed an appeal.

The Court of Appeal affirmed the trial court's decision. . . .

Much of the statutory law governing this case is derived from the Uniform Parentage Act of 1973 (UPA), adopted by our Legislature as section 7600 et seq. of the new Family Code. . . .

An unwed father's rights and duties under the UPA substantially depend on whether he is a "presumed father" within the meaning of section 7611. Under section 7611, a man who has neither legally married nor attempted to legally marry the mother of his child cannot become a presumed father unless he both "receives the child into his home and openly holds out the child as his natural child." . . . Therefore, to become a presumed father, a man who has neither married nor attempted to marry his child's biological mother must not only openly and publicly admit paternity, but must also physically bring the child into his home.

If a man is a presumed father, a third party generally cannot adopt his child unless both he and the mother consent. If a man is not a presumed father, however, the situation is quite different. The mother's consent is still required in most cases, but the father's consent is not required unless he successfully petitions to block the adoption and establish his legal status as the child's father. Even if he files such a petition, the adoption will proceed over his objection if either the mother or the party seeking to adopt the child successfully petitions for termination of his parental status.

If the court finds in such a proceeding that "it is in the best interest of the child that the father retain his parental rights," it must enter an order providing that his consent is necessary for an adoption. In making this determination, the court "may consider all relevant evidence, including the efforts made by the father to obtain custody, the age and prior placement of the child, and the effects of a change of placement on the child." If, however, the court finds that it is in the best interest of the child to be adopted by the prospective adoptive parents, it must enter an order stating that the father's consent is not required. This order also "terminates all [the father's] parental rights and responsibilities with respect to the child."

In essence, therefore, our statutory scheme creates three classes of parents: mothers, fathers who are presumed fathers, and fathers who are not presumed fathers. Parents belonging to either the first or second class usually have a statutory right to veto adoption by withholding consent regardless of what the court believes to be the child's best interest. However, a biological father who is not a presumed father has no statutory right to block adoption unless he first proves that it is in the child's best interest that the adoption not proceed. As we noted in *Kelsey S.,* "the trial court's determination is frequently that the child's interests are better served by a third party adoption than by granting custody to the unwed natural father."

Here the trial court determined at the first hearing that Mark is not a presumed father under the statutory definition and that it would be in Michael's best interest to be adopted by John and Margaret. Mark does not contend these conclusions were erroneous. It follows that Mark has no statutory right to withhold consent to Michael's adoption. However, both the trial court and the Court of Appeal concluded that although Mark has no statutory right to block adoption by withholding consent, he has a constitutional right under *Kelsey S.* to prevent Michael's adoption and to establish his legal status as Michael's father unless John and Margaret prove that he would be an unfit parent. The only issue before us is whether that conclusion is correct.

II

We held in *Kelsey S.* that an unwed father who has no statutory right to block a third party adoption by withholding consent may nevertheless have a constitutional right to do so under the due process and equal protection clauses of the Fourteenth Amendment and thereby to preserve his opportunity to develop a parental relationship with his child. Under such circumstances, however, the unwed father's constitutional interest is merely inchoate (Lehr v. Robertson (1983) 463 U.S. 248, 261-263) and does not ripen into a constitutional right that he can assert to prevent adoption unless he proves that he has "promptly come[ ] forward and demonstrate[d] a full commitment to his parental responsibilities. . . ." (*Kelsey S.*, supra). . . .

We must decide whether Mark took sufficient steps to transform his inchoate constitutional interest in his potential parental relationship with Michael into a constitutional right that entitled him to block John and Margaret's efforts to adopt Michael and terminate his status as Michael's father. Our task is made more difficult by the circumstance that here the adoption process began at birth and Michael has been in John and Margaret's custody and care for all of the more than four years of his life. Mark has therefore had little contact with Michael and little opportunity to directly develop a parental relationship with him, and Michael instead experiences only John and Margaret as his parents.

After its hearing devoted to the question whether Mark was entitled to constitutional protection under *Kelsey S.*, the trial court prepared a rather lengthy summary of its findings. In this summary the court declared that during the period between early July 1990, when Mark first learned that Stephanie was pregnant, and October 28, 1990, the day he attempted suicide, "it cannot be said that he was fully committed to his parental responsibilities. While he always acknowledged his paternity, he clearly planned with Stephanie to give the child up. Like many fathers (and mothers) he was initially frightened and eagerly looked for a way out of these responsibilities." During his hospitalization in November 1990, Mark "decided he did not want his child given up for adoption." Despite this decision, however, Mark continued to "speak to Stephanie and even [John and Margaret] as though he still agreed with the adoption" until March 7, 1991, some two weeks after Michael was born, because, according to Mark's testimony, "he did not want to risk the sort of polarization which might totally close the door to further communication."

The trial court found that "After his release from the hospital, and particularly after the birth of his son, Mark's efforts were nothing short of impressive,[7] and "In the two years since his son's birth, Mark has never wavered in expressing his desire to take on the full responsibility of fatherhood." The court also noted that each of Mark's three attorneys testified that Mark "incessantly, relentlessly urged" them to seek visitation rights. In light of these findings, the court concluded that Mark's "struggle before his hospitalization and the subsequent birth of his son does not counterbalance his truly extraordinary efforts and commitment afterward," and that "In the context of all the facts of this case, his efforts sufficiently demonstrate his full commitment to his parental responsibilities" within the meaning of *Kelsey S.* . . .

John and Margaret contend that the trial court and Court of Appeal misinterpreted and misapplied our decision in *Kelsey S.*, supra, and that under the correct standard the trial court's findings do not support its decision that Mark "promptly [came] forward and demonstrate[d] a full commitment to his parental responsibilities" and was therefore entitled to constitutional protection. They focus on that portion of *Kelsey S.* in which we stated that in deciding whether an unwed father is entitled to constitutional protection, "A court should consider all factors relevant to that determination. The father's conduct both before and after the child's birth must be considered. Once the father knows or reasonably should know of the pregnancy, he must promptly attempt to assume his parental responsibilities as fully as the mother will allow and the circumstances permit. In particular, the father must demonstrate 'a willingness himself to assume full custody of the child—not merely to block adoption by others.' A court should also consider the father's public acknowledgment of paternity, payment of pregnancy and birth expenses commensurate with his ability to do so, and prompt legal action to seek custody of the child."

John and Margaret rightly concede that the quoted language does not mean that an unwed father must continually express an unequivocal desire to raise his child from the very moment he learns of the pregnancy or that he can never take a minute to reflect on the importance of his decision and the responsibilities that will come with it. Rather, they contend that although all the unwed father's conduct is relevant and important, he has no constitutional right to withhold his consent to an at-birth, third party adoption under *Kelsey S.* unless he "promptly" demonstrated a "full commitment" to parenthood during pregnancy and within a

---

7. Between November 1990 and March 7, 1991, Mark sought free legal advice, contacted the media, and requested assistance from local political figures. Because he was unable to find an attorney who would take his case free of charge, Mark researched the law himself and filed a custody petition in Arizona in February 1991. He found an attorney who would take his case on March 7, 1991, and the latter contacted John and Margaret to immediately request custody. He also sent out birth announcements and bought things for Michael as soon as he learned of his birth.

short time after he discovered or reasonably should have discovered that the biological mother was pregnant with his child, and that he cannot compensate for his failure to do so by attempting to assume his parental responsibilities many months after learning of the pregnancy.

We agree with John and Margaret's reading of the quoted language. It is difficult to conceive how our statement that "Once the father knows or reasonably should know of the pregnancy, he must promptly attempt to assume his parental responsibilities as fully as the mother will allow and the circumstances permit" could be read in any other way. To construe it as Mark does destroys the mandatory force of the word "must" and makes the word "promptly" meaningless. Such a conclusion is particularly inappropriate in view of the fact that we also stressed the importance of timely action both in the paragraph preceding and in the paragraph following the quoted language. In the former we stated that "[i]f an unwed father promptly comes forward and demonstrates a full commitment to his parental responsibilities—emotional, financial, and otherwise—his federal constitutional right to due process prohibits the termination of his paternal relationship absent a showing of his unfitness as a parent." In the latter paragraph we stated that "[t]he statutory distinction between natural fathers and presumed fathers is constitutionally invalid only to the extent it is applied to an unwed father who has sufficiently and timely demonstrated a full commitment to his parental responsibilities. Our statutes are constitutionally sufficient when applied to a father who has failed to make such a showing." John and Margaret's reading of *Kelsey S.* is not only correct, but virtually inescapable.

John and Margaret also contend their reading of *Kelsey S.* serves several important public policy goals. We find their points persuasive. They first assert that an unwed father should be encouraged to promptly inform the biological mother during pregnancy whether he objects or consents to the child's adoption at birth, and that he should be denied constitutional protection after birth if he concealed his views during pregnancy. They stress that during pregnancy the mother must make many important decisions, most importantly whether to have an abortion, to prepare an adoption plan, or to keep the baby, and that she has only a relatively short time to make and implement her choice. It is therefore important that the father give the mother prompt notice whether he plans to object or consent to adoption so that she can evaluate that and other options on an informed basis.

John and Margaret also point out that the mother may well need emotional, financial, medical, or other assistance during pregnancy, particularly if she, like Stephanie, is a teenager. It can scarcely be disputed that prenatal care is critically important to both the mother and the child. To the extent the mother needs such critical assistance and the unwed father is able to provide it, the father, as one of the two individuals responsible for the pregnancy, should be encouraged to do so early on and should not be granted constitutional protection after birth if he has failed to timely fulfill this responsibility. Indeed, if unwed fathers are not encouraged to provide prenatal assistance when they are able to do so, the burden will often shift to the state and therefore to society generally.

Furthermore, if an unwed father is permitted to ignore his parental role during pregnancy but claim it after birth, it will often be very difficult to know with certainty whether he will be able to successfully contest an adoption until after the child is born. This uncertainty could well dissuade prospective adoptive parents from attempting to adopt the children of unwed mothers who, like Stephanie, have chosen for whatever reason not to keep their child and raise it themselves. And that result would frustrate the state's clear interest in encouraging such adoptions and providing stable homes for children. The state's interest in this matter is particularly important in light of the large number of children born to unwed parents: some 25 percent of all children born in the United States between July 1989 and July 1990—approximately 913,000 out of 3,900,000—were born out of wedlock.

John and Margaret also contend that an adopted child may suffer emotional damage if the unwed father conceals his objection to a third party adoption during pregnancy and the adoptive parents take custody at birth in reliance on the unwed father's apparent consent, but the unwed father then initiates often lengthy legal proceedings after birth in an effort to derail the adoption and remove the child from the adoptive parents' custody. If such an unwed father is allowed to prevail after perhaps years of litigation, during which time the child will likely come to see the adoptive parents as his "true" parents, the resulting disruption in familial relationships and living arrangements can have a very damaging impact on the child's psychological growth and development.

Experts in child development agree with John and Margaret on this point. In the words of one authoritative treatise on the subject, "Continuity of relationships, surroundings, and environmental influence are essential for a child's normal development." (Goldstein et al., Beyond the Best Interests of the Child (1979) p.31.) . . .

Lastly, there can also be little doubt that "the . . . adoptive parents suffer emotionally if the child is separated from them after a prolonged period." It would seem inequitable to give preference to an unwed father who failed to fully grasp his parental obligations in a timely fashion over prospective adoptive parents who have made a significant and continuing effort, both before and after birth, to discharge the responsibilities of parenthood. . . .

Mark contends that John and Margaret's reading of *Kelsey S.* would unfairly discriminate between unwed mothers and unwed fathers. In support of this contention, he notes that all an unwed mother must do to obtain a virtually absolute statutory right to withhold consent to an adoption is to show that she has a biological link with the child by proving that she gave birth to it, and that the mother possesses this statutory right after birth even if she consistently and openly consented to adoption throughout her pregnancy. According to Mark, such disparate treatment would not only conflict with what he asserts is the premise of *Kelsey S.*, i.e., that unwed mothers and unwed fathers are entitled to essentially the same rights in adoption proceedings, but would also violate the equal protection clauses of both the Fourteenth Amendment and article I, section 7, subdivision (a), of the California Constitution. . . .

Although Mark's contention seems plausible at first blush, it has at least two fatal flaws. First, we held in *Kelsey S.* that despite its apparent anomalies our statutory scheme passes constitutional muster except "to the extent it is applied to an unwed father who has sufficiently and timely demonstrated a full commitment to his parental responsibilities." As explained in part III, ante, the words "promptly" and "timely" in *Kelsey S.* mean within a short time after the father knew or reasonably should have known that the mother was pregnant with his child. . . .

Second, the many public policy justifications that John and Margaret have provided and that we have discussed at some length in part III, ante, clearly demonstrate that any disparate treatment resulting from *Kelsey S.* is "substantially related" to a significant number of "important governmental objectives," and therefore does not unconstitutionally discriminate between unwed fathers and unwed mothers on the basis of sex. (Caban v. Mohammed, supra, 441 U.S. 380, 388.)

V

We conclude that an unwed father has no federal constitutional right to withhold consent to an at-birth, third party adoption under our decision in *Kelsey S., supra,* unless he shows that he promptly came forward and demonstrated as full a commitment to his parental responsibilities as the biological mother allowed and the circumstances permitted within a short time after he learned or reasonably should have learned that the biological mother was pregnant with his child.

Here the trial court found that Mark learned that Stephanie was pregnant with his child in early July 1990, that between July 1990 and November 1990, "it cannot be said that he was fully committed to his parental responsibilities . . . [and] he clearly planned with Stephanie to give the child up." The court further found that although Mark decided in November 1990 that "he did not want his child given up for adoption." He "continued to speak to Stephanie and even [John and Margaret] as though he still agreed with the adoption" until March 7, 1991, some two weeks after Michael was born. In light of these findings, we conclude that under *Kelsey S.* Mark has no constitutional right to withhold his consent to Michael's adoption and that the Court of Appeal erred in ruling to the contrary.

We therefore reverse the judgment of the Court of Appeal with directions to remand the case to the superior court for entry of judgment against Mark on his claim he has a constitutional right to veto adoption, against Mark on his petition to declare the existence of a father-child relationship, and in favor of John and Margaret on their petition to terminate Mark's parental rights and adopt Michael.

KENNARD, Justice, concurring and dissenting. Upon learning that his girlfriend, Stephanie H., was pregnant, Mark K. promptly acknowledged paternity; he contributed to the costs of her pregnancy; and he tried to maintain his relationship with Stephanie until she put an end to it. After researching the law himself, Mark filed a petition in propria persona for custody of his son Michael H. Since then, Mark has never wavered in his efforts to attain that goal. The majority terminates Mark's parental rights in Michael solely because in the early stages of Stephanie's pregnancy Mark did not oppose her plan to have the child adopted. The majority's conclusion is at odds with this court's holding in *Adoption of Kelsey S.* that a biological father who "sufficiently and timely demonstrated his full commitment to his parental responsibilities" had the right to veto his child's adoption. In my view, Mark has met the *Kelsey S.* test.

Nevertheless, I would conclude that *Kelsey S.*, supra, should not be applied retroactively, for reasons I shall discuss later. Thus, I agree with the majority, albeit on a different basis, that Michael, who is now four and one-half years old, should remain with the prospective adoptive parents who have provided a home for him since birth. . . .

The majority's decision creates a dilemma for a biological father: If in the early stages of the mother's pregnancy he vigorously opposes the mother's decision to relinquish their child for adoption, he runs the risk of irreparably damaging his relationship with the mother and causing her emotional upset, quite the opposite of the emotional support he must give under *Kelsey S.* If, on the other hand, he initially acquiesces in the mother's decision to place the child for adoption, hoping to change her mind before the child is born, he has, under the majority's holding, forfeited his right to object later in the pregnancy to the child's adoption.

To justify its departure from *Kelsey S.*, the majority states "that during pregnancy the mother must make many important decisions, most importantly whether to have an abortion, to prepare an adoption plan, or to keep the baby, and that she has only a relatively short time to make and implement her choice." Thus, the majority reasons, an unwed father must give the mother "prompt notice whether he plans to object or consent to adoption so that she can evaluate that and other options on an informed basis."

The majority is wrong in asserting that a pregnant woman has "only a relatively short time" to consider the options of keeping her baby or relinquishing it for adoption. Even after agreeing to adoption, the mother can months later legally revoke her consent to the planned adoption. Since the majority acknowledges the mother's right to do so, it is puzzling why the majority insists that the mother has "only a relatively short time" in which to make her decision and that therefore the father must decide in the early stages of the mother's pregnancy whether to object or consent to adoption.[8]

As further justification for its holding, the majority states that a biological father who fails to object to adoption early in the mother's pregnancy should not be allowed to prevail "over prospective adoptive parents who have made a significant and continuing effort, both before and after birth, to discharge the responsibilities of parenthood." In that situation, the majority says, the parental rights of the biological father must give way to "the state's clear interest" in encouraging adoptions. I readily acknowledge that the state's interest in providing for the welfare

---

8. The majority is correct that a pregnant woman who wants to have an abortion is under a time constraint to do so. Generally, an abortion can be performed only within the first two trimesters of a pregnancy (that is, before the seventh month). But the majority never explains why this time constraint on a pregnant woman's decision to choose abortion over carrying a child to full term leads the majority to conclude that the unwed father must decide early in the mother's pregnancy that he does not agree to adoption. In any event, this is an odd case in which to fashion such a rule. Here, Mark's failure to make up his mind about adoption early in Stephanie's pregnancy had no effect on her decision to rule out abortion, which he did in July 1990, during the second month of her pregnancy and before she and Mark had even considered placing their child for adoption.

of children born to unwed parents is a compelling one. Adoption is a means of bringing stability to the lives of these children and securing for them loving homes. But the state's strong interest in adoption arises only when a child's biological mother and father are unfit or unable to care for the child. Therefore, in the case of a "Kelsey S." father (an unwed biological father who comes forward to assume parental responsibility for his child before the child's birth), the state has an interest in the child's adoption only if the father is proven to be an unfit parent.

Unlike the majority, I would uphold the trial court's ruling, affirmed by the Court of Appeal, that Mark is a "Kelsey S." father. Nevertheless, . . . I am of the view that, contrary to this court's directive in *Kelsey S.*, that decision should not be applied retroactively.

NOTES AND QUESTIONS

1. Would Mark K. have been entitled to notice of his baby's adoption under the Uniform Parentage Act, page 886, above? Under *Lehr* would it have been constitutional to allow the baby's adoption without notice to him?

2. After *Michael H.*, if you practiced in California, how would you advise an unmarried man who had just learned that his girlfriend was pregnant and who was unsure of what he wanted?

If you represented would-be adoptive parents in California, under what circumstances would you advise them to proceed with an adoption without first obtaining the consent of an unmarried father?

3. States vary greatly in the extent to which they give unmarried fathers the right to prevent adoption of their children by withholding consent.

A number of states have adopted a test similar to California's. *See, e.g.*, C. V. v. J. M. J., 810 So. 2d 692 (Ala. App. 1999); Matter of Adoption of Doe, 543 So. 2d 741 (Fla. 1989); In the Matter of Raquel Marie X., 559 N.E.2d 418 (N.Y. 1990).

In contrast, in some states, once the fact of the father's paternity is established, his rights are the same as those of the mother. State law in two well-known cases from the mid-1990s took this form, with the result that children who had been placed by their mothers with adoptive parents at birth were eventually returned to their biological fathers after years of litigation. *See* In the Interest of B. G. C, 496 N.W.2d 239 (Iowa 1992) (Baby Jessica case); In re Petition of Kirchner, 649 N.E.2d 324 (Ill. 1995) (Baby Richard case). If you practiced in a state with this rule, how would you advise the unmarried father? The would-be adoptive parents?

David D. Meyer, Family Ties: Solving the Constitutional Dilemma of the Faultless Father, 41 Ariz. L. Rev. 753 (1999), reports that after the Baby Richard and Baby Jessica cases, a number of states amended their laws to head off similar results. Some states made complete elimination of fathers' claims easier, either by expanding the definitions of abandonment and unfitness as grounds for involuntary termination of parental rights or providing that a father who did not take prescribed steps within a certain time lost his right to custody. Other states gave greater protection to the child's existing placement by providing for long-term custody with the would-be adoptive parents and visitation rights for fathers.

4. On unwed fathers' rights generally, *see* Barbara B. Woodhouse, Hatching the Egg: A Child-Centered Perspective on Parents' Rights, 14 Cardozo L. Rev. 1747 (1993); Janet L. Dolgin, The Constitution as Family Arbiter: A Moral in the Mess? 102 Colum. L. Rev. 337 (2002); Laurence C. Nolan, "Unwed Children" and Their Parents Before the United States Supreme Court from Levy to Michael H.: Unlikely Participants in Constitutional Jurisprudence, 28 Cap. U. L. Rev. 1 (1999); Sharon S. Townsend, Fatherhood: A Judicial Perspective: Unmarried Fathers and the Changing Role of the Family Court, 41 Fam. Ct. Rev. 354 (2003).

5. Sahin v. Germany, Sommerfeld v. Germany, Hoffman v. Germany, decided by the European Court of Human Rights, October 11, 2001, holds that aspects of German law concerning the rights of unmarried fathers violated the European Convention for the Protection of Human Rights and Fundamental Freedoms. At the time the cases were brought, German law provided that the mother had the right to custody of a child born outside marriage and to determine whether the father could visit, subject to a court's authority to make a contrary decision in the child's best interests. Fathers could not appeal from the court decision. The Court held that the law violated Articles 14 and 8 of the Convention by unjustifiably failing to protect the relationship of the father and child and by denying the father a right to appeal. The judgments are available from the Court's Web site at *http://www.echr.coe.int/Eng/Judgments.htm*. Effective July 1, 1998, German law has been amended to provide that the father and mother share parental rights and that they have joint custody with regard to children born outside marriage.

PROBLEMS

1. On the facts in the problems above, page 888, if the fathers are given notice of the adoption proceedings and participate in the proceedings, under what circumstances will they be able to veto the adoption of their children under *Adoption of Michael H.?* Under the Uniform Parentage Act?

2. Madelyn and Frank were dating. Madelyn told Frank that she was pregnant, but he seemed indifferent. She told him that she intended to place the baby for adoption, and he was silent. After the baby was born, Frank visited Madelyn and the baby in the hospital once, but he did not provide any financial support to Madelyn or the baby during the pregnancy or after the birth. Madelyn placed the child with an adoption agency, relinquishing her parental rights, when the baby was three days old. Madelyn told the agency that Frank was the father, and a representative of the agency contacted him. He refused to sign a form consenting to the baby's adoption but said that he would not interfere. The agency placed the baby for adoption with the Patrick family. When the baby was seven months old, Frank filed a petition seeking custody or visitation of the baby. The Patricks and the adoption agency responded by filing an adoption petition, alleging that Frank's consent was not required. Under *Michael H.*, is his consent required?

3. While Dawn was separated from her husband, Frank, she began living with Jerry and became pregnant by him. Three months later she moved back in with Frank and in due course gave birth to a son. During this time Jerry took

parenting classes, purchased items for the baby for his house, and did other things to prepare himself for fatherhood. He tried unsuccessfully to see Dawn after she returned to Frank and to persuade Dawn and Frank to let him visit the baby. Jerry has now filed a paternity suit under the Uniform Parentage Act seeking a declaration of paternity and visitation rights. What arguments should Dawn and Frank, who want to keep Jerry out of their lives, make? How should Jerry respond?

3. Establishing Paternity

All states provide a judicial process, usually called a paternity suit or filiation proceeding, for establishing paternity. Until recently, some statutes granted standing to bring suit only to the mother and to public assistance authorities, but not to the putative father. Federal law now requires that states have "procedures ensuring that the putative father has a reasonable opportunity to initiate a paternity action" if they wish to participate in the state-federal welfare program, which all do. 42 U.S.C. §666(a)(5)(L). Some states also grant standing to the child, the child's representative, or a child support enforcement agency. E.g., Uniform Parentage Act §602 (2002).

Traditionally, states imposed short statutes of limitations on paternity suits, often requiring the suit to be brought within a year of the child's birth. Several Supreme Court cases have invalidated short statutes when applied to bar suits by children, on the ground that they violate the equal protection rights of children born outside marriage. The Court invalidated a one-year statute of limitations in Mills v. Habluetzel, 456 U.S. 91 (1982); a two-year statute in Pickett v. Brown, 462 U.S. 1 (1983), and a six-year statute in Clark v. Jeter, 486 U.S. 456 (1988). The federal Child Support Enforcement Amendments of 1984 require that all states participating in the federal child support program permit the establishment of paternity of any child less than 18 years old. 42 U.S.C. §666(a)(5) (1982 ed., Supp. III). In some states a short statute of limitations continues to apply to paternity actions brought by anyone other than the child. See, e.g., Ill. Rev. Stat. ch. 750 §45/8.

In Rivera v. Minnich, 483 U.S. 574 (1987), the Supreme Court held that a statute permitting a private citizen (usually a mother) to establish a man's paternity by a preponderance of the evidence was constitutional. It rejected the father's due process claim that clear and convincing evidence should be required, concluding that the relatively equal interests and positions of the father and the private citizen justify a standard of proof not weighted toward either side.

Federal law provides that states must require the child and all the other parties (unless good cause for an exception is shown) to submit to genetic testing in contested paternity suits upon the request of another party who submits a sworn statement "1) alleging paternity, and setting forth facts establishing a reasonable possibility of the requisite sexual contact between the parties; or 2) denying paternity, and setting forth facts establishing a reasonable possibility of the nonexistence of sexual contact between the parties." 42 U.S.C. §666(a)(5)(B)(i). If a state agency orders testing, the agency must pay for the tests, though the state may elect to require reimbursement from the putative father if paternity is established. 42 U.S.C. §666(a)(5)(B)(ii).

Statutes give courts a number of devices to coerce cooperation with genetic testing, including holding the recalcitrant party in contempt, disclosing the refusal to submit to testing to the factfinder, and permitting counsel to comment on it. In a number of jurisdictions the court may resolve the merits of the suit against a person who refuses to submit to testing. Most courts have rejected Fourth Amendment challenges to statutes requiring submission to blood testing in paternity suits, concluding that, although the test is a search for Fourth Amendment purposes, it is justified by the state interest in determining paternity. *See* In re J. M., 590 So. 2d 565 (La. 1991) (discussing cases).

In the 1950s, state laws typically allowed the admission of blood test evidence that excluded the possibility that a man could be a child's father. *See* Uniform Act on Blood Tests to Determine Paternity, 9 U.L.A. 103-104 (Commissioner's Prefatory Note 2). By the late 1980s, new tests that assess a much larger number of blood factors were widely used, and a decade later, a variety of means of testing DNA became available, increasing the power of genetic testing still more. These tests can exclude more falsely identified men, and they can be analyzed statistically to provide evidence of the probability that a man who is not excluded is the child's father. The next case concerns admission of this kind of statistical evidence.

PLEMEL V. WALTER

735 P.2d 1209 (Or. 1987)

LENT, J. . . . [Dena] Plemel's child was born on June 9, 1983. . . . [S]he initiated filiation proceedings against [Brent] Walter, alleging that he was the father of the child. Subsequently, the state intervened as a petitioner. Walter denied paternity.

Plemel testified that she and Walter had intercourse on one occasion, September 11, 1982. Walter admitted having intercourse with Plemel but testified that it had occurred on the night of August 13-14, 1982. Both Plemel and Walter introduced the testimony of witnesses to corroborate their respective versions of when they had been together. A nurse practitioner who had examined Plemel testified that conception of the child would have been impossible in mid-August; she estimated that conception occurred between September 9 and September 16.

Plemel also called as a witness Dr. E. W. Lovrien, the director of the Oregon Health Sciences University Phenotype Laboratory. The laboratory had conducted blood tests of Plemel, Walter and the child. Lovrien testified that: (1) the tests did not exclude the possibility that Walter was the father; (2) the probability that the tests would have excluded a "falsely accused father" was 97.5 percent; (3) Walter's "paternity index" was 178; (4) Walter's "chance of paternity" was 99.4 percent; (5) Walter's "chance of nonpaternity" was 0.6 percent; and (6) it was "extremely likely" that Walter was the father. The last three statements were essentially equivalent to, and derived from, the paternity index. The "chance of paternity" was the "paternity index" stated as a percentage chance (i.e., odds of

178 to 1 are equal to a 99.4 percent chance); the "chance of nonpaternity" was the "chance of paternity" stated negatively; the expression "extremely likely" was taken from a table developed by a joint committee of the American Medical Association and the American Bar Association to express the significance of any given "chance of paternity."

Walter . . . sought to exclude that portion of Lovrien's testimony related to the paternity index and its equivalents. He argued that the testimony was irrelevant because the "probability of excluding a falsely accused father" provided the jury with all of the information that could be obtained from the blood tests. . . . Walter also argued that the testimony was prejudicial in that the jury would be too confused by it to understand its proper significance. . . .

Because courts have so frequently misinterpreted the meaning and significance of paternity test results, *see*, e.g., McCormick, Evidence §211 (3d ed. 1984) (and cases cited therein); Ellman & Kaye, Probabilities and Proof: Can HLA and Blood Group Testing Prove Paternity?, 54 N.Y.U. L. Rev. 1131 (1979) (and cases cited therein), we believe that some background is appropriate before we analyze Walter's arguments. . . .

Each person has a large number of inherited traits, such as eye color and facial features. Different versions of a particular trait are known as phenotypes. For the inherited trait of eye color, for example, blue eyes are one phenotype, brown eyes are another. The antigens, enzymes and proteins in a person's blood are also inherited traits. One set, or "system," of antigens are the ABO antigens, which have been widely used in the classification of blood. Because no individual possesses every antigen in the ABO system, the ABO antigens that an individual does possess determine that individual's "blood type," or phenotype, for the ABO system. The ABO system can be divided into six phenotypes: O, A1, A2, B, A1B or A2B. *See* Joint AMA-ABA Guidelines: Present Status of Serological Testing in Problems of Disputed Parentage, 10 Fam. L.Q. 247, 263 (1976). If a person has the phenotype A1, this means that a blood test revealed the presence of the A1 antigen. Similarly, if a person has the phenotype A1B, the blood test revealed the presence of both the A1 antigen and the B antigen. If the person's phenotype is O, the blood test was unable to detect the presence of any of the antigens for the ABO system.

The specific set of phenotypes that a person possesses is determined by that person's genes. Genes occur in pairs that contain one gene from each parent. A specific gene pair or a specific group of gene pairs control a particular body trait, and an individual's phenotype for that trait will reflect the nature of the genes that make up the controlling pair or pairs. If a person has the phenotype A1B, that person's ABO gene pair consists of an A1 gene and a B gene. If the phenotype is A1, the pair consists of an A1 gene and either another A1 gene or an O gene. This is because the O gene does not produce a detectable antigen. *See* Reisner & Bolk, A Layman's Guide to the Use of Blood Group Analysis in Paternity Testing, 20 J. Fam. L. 657, 662 (1982). If the phenotype is O, both genes are O.

Information about a person's phenotypes, then, can be used to derive information concerning that person's corresponding gene pairs. Moreover, because each parent contributes one gene to a pair, knowledge of a person's phenotypes can also be used to derive information about that person's parents' or children's phenotypes.

For example, Plemel's phenotype for the ABO system was found to be A1. Thus, she had an A1 gene and either another A1 gene or an O gene. The child's phenotype was found to be A1B, requiring that the child have an A1 gene and a B gene. Because the child received one gene from Plemel and one from its father, and because Plemel did not have a B gene, the child had to have received the A1 gene from Plemel and the B gene from its father. The child's father's phenotype would therefore have to be one of the "B phenotypes": B, A1B or A2B. If Walter's phenotype for this system were O, A1 or A2, he could not have been the father. Because Walter's phenotype was found to be A2B, a phenotype consistent with paternity, the test for this system could not exclude him as a potential father.

In addition to the ABO system, Lovrien's laboratory determined Walter's, Plemel's and the child's phenotypes for 18 other blood systems. Lovrien testified that for each of these systems, Walter's phenotypes were consistent with the accusation of paternity. The "extended red cell enzyme" test did not exclude the possibility that Walter was the father of Plemel's child.

If the frequency with which phenotypes occur in the population of potential fathers is known, more can be said than that the paternity test has failed to exclude the putative father. It is also possible to derive statistics about the ability of the paternity test to exonerate men falsely accused of paternity and the *relative* likelihood that the putative father is the true father.

Probability of Excluding a Falsely Accused Father. This statistic, sometimes termed the "prior probability of exclusion" or, simply, the "probability of exclusion," measures the ability of a paternity test to exclude men falsely accused of paternity. The statistic is calculated as follows: For each mother-child combination of phenotypes, certain phenotypes will be inconsistent with paternity. For example, if the mother is A1 and the child is B, the father cannot be A1. The frequency with which such combinations occur in the population is the probability of excluding a falsely accused father. If there are no such combinations in the population, e.g., if everyone is A1, then the probability of excluding a falsely accused father is zero. A test with this probability would be useless.

As more blood systems are tested, the probability of excluding a falsely accused father can become quite high. The test in this case used 19 systems and had a probability of excluding a falsely accused father of 97.5 percent. Expressed in another way, in 39 instances out of 40 in which a man is falsely accused of being the father of a child, the tests conducted in this case would prove that the man did not father the child.

This statistic frequently is confused with the percentage of men in the population whose phenotypes are inconsistent with paternity, a percentage that is also often called the "probability of exclusion." . . . Although the "extended red cell enzyme" test had a probability of excluding a falsely accused father of 97.5 percent, this does not imply that the proportion of the male population capable of fathering Plemel's child is 2.5 percent. The probability of excluding a falsely accused father is a measure of the ability of the paternity test to exclude falsely accused fathers without reference to the phenotypes of any particular mother-child combination; the probability will be 97.5 percent for everyone tested. The results from the ABO system in this case provide a good illustration of the distinction. Lovrien testified that the ABO system alone will exclude falsely accused

Plemel's child must have a B gene

fathers in about 17 percent of cases. The father of Plemel's child, however, must have a B gene, which, according to Lovrien, occurs in only about 5 percent of the population. Thus, although the ABO system has a probability of excluding a falsely accused father of 17 percent, 95 percent of the male population has been excluded by the ABO system *in this case*.[9]

No statistic on the percentage of the relevant population capable of fathering Plemel's child was presented by Lovrien.

Paternity Index. This statistic, also known as the "likelihood ratio," the "chance of paternity" and the "likelihood of paternity," measures the putative father's likelihood of producing the child's phenotypes against the likelihood of a randomly selected man doing so. Despite the alternative labels, it is *not* the probability that the accused is the father.

Within the group of men genetically capable of fathering a particular child, some will be genetically more likely to have done so than others. For example, we noted above that Walter's phenotype for the ABO system was A2B and that the child's father had to have one of the "B phenotypes." Walter could transmit to his child either his A2 or his B gene. The chance that he would transmit the B gene would be 50 percent. A man who had a B phenotype and two B genes (as opposed to a man with a B phenotype and one B gene and one O gene), however, would have a 100 percent chance of transmitting a B gene. Other things being equal, this man would be more likely to be the father of Plemel's child than would Walter.

The paternity index, which is a ratio that compares the putative father's likelihood of producing the child's phenotypes with the likelihood of a randomly selected man doing so, is not the likelihood of producing the child in question, but the relative likelihood of producing a child with the same phenotypes. The numerator of the ratio is the probability that a man with the phenotypes of the putative father and a woman with the mother's phenotypes would produce an offspring with the child's phenotypes. The denominator is the probability that a randomly selected man and a woman with the mother's phenotypes would produce an offspring with the child's phenotypes.

For example, as we noted above, the father of Plemel's child had to transmit a B gene to the child. We also noted that the chance that someone with Walter's phenotypes would do so was 0.5. This is the numerator of Walter's paternity index for the ABO system. The chance that a randomly selected man would produce an offspring with the child's phenotypes is simply the frequency with which the B gene occurs in the relevant male population, as compared to other genes. In the

---

9. If the testing excluded a total of 99 percent of the population as the potential father, it might be tempting to conclude that the probability that the putative father was the true father was also 99 percent. It is easy to see, though, that this is not the case. If the relevant population were 1,000,000, and if 99 percent were excluded by the testing, then 990,000 would have been excluded, leaving 10,000 as potential fathers. On the basis of the blood tests alone, then, the probability of the putative father's paternity would not be 99 percent, but 1/10,000, or 0.01 percent. *See* 1A Wigmore, Evidence § 165b, 1819-1820 (Tillers rev. 1983); Ellman & Kaye, supra, at 1141; *see also* Tribe, Trial by Mathematics, 84 Harv. L. Rev. 1329, 1355 (1971).

white male population this frequency is approximately 0.0658. (The percentage of white males with B genes will be somewhat less because some men will possess two B genes rather than only one.) This number is the denominator of the paternity index. Dividing the numerator by the denominator yields approximately 7.6, which is Walter's paternity index for the ABO system. Multiplying together his paternity indexes for all 19 serologic systems tested yields his overall paternity index, 178.

From the example above, it can be seen that the denominator of the paternity index will be the same for every putative father. This is because the denominator is the gene frequency in the population. The numerator, however, will vary from putative father to putative father because their phenotypes will vary. In the ABO system, some men will have two B genes, some, such as Walter, will have one B gene, and some will have no B gene. For each combination of genes, there will be a different probability of producing the child's phenotypes. Because the numerator varies from putative father to putative father, the paternity index will also vary. Thus, even though all men not excluded by a paternity test are capable of fathering the child, they will have different paternity indexes and thus different relative likelihoods of having fathered the child.

Because Walter's paternity index was 178, Walter was 178 times more likely than a randomly selected man to have fathered a child with the phenotypes of Plemel's child. Converting this into a percentage resulted in a "chance of paternity" of 99.4 percent and a "chance of nonpaternity" of 0.6 percent. The AMA-ABA "verbal predicate" used to describe a "chance of paternity" of 99.4 percent is "extremely likely." Again, this does not mean that it is "extremely likely" that Walter is the father of Plemel's child, only that, *compared to a randomly selected man*, it is "extremely likely" that Walter is the father of Plemel's child.

Probability of Paternity. In order to convert the paternity index and its equivalents into a probability of paternity, i.e., the actual likelihood that this putative father is the father of the child at issue, some estimate of the strength of the other evidence in the case must be made. If Walter were sterile, he would still have a paternity index of 178 and a "chance of paternity" of 99.4 percent, but obviously his probability of paternity would be zero. Similarly, barring divine intervention, if Walter were the only person to have had intercourse with the mother, his paternity index would be 178 and his "chance of paternity" would be 99.4 percent, but his probability of paternity would be 100 percent. Of course, most cases will fall between these extremes.

The usual method for calculating the probability of paternity is Bayes' formula. This formula demonstrates the effect of a new item of evidence on a previously established probability. In this instance, the new item of evidence is the blood test result (i.e., the paternity index), and the previously established, or prior, probability is the probability of paternity based on the other evidence in the case. The calculation is simplified if the probabilities are expressed as odds. The odds of paternity using Bayes' formula are simply the product of the prior odds and the paternity index. For example, if the other evidence in this case had established that Walter was sterile, his prior odds of paternity would have been zero. His odds of paternity, then, would have been zero times his paternity index of 178, which equals zero. On the other hand, if the other evidence in the case had led one to believe that the odds that Walter was the father were one to one, his odds of paternity would have been one times 178, which equals 178 or a probability of paternity of 99.4 percent. It can be seen, then, that the paternity index will equal the probability of paternity only when the other evidence in the case establishes prior odds of paternity of exactly one. This is because the paternity index's comparison of the putative father with a randomly selected man is mathematically equivalent to the assumption that the prior odds of paternity are one to one, or that the prior probability is 50 percent.

Lovrien did not derive a statistic for probability of paternity, although, as we note below, his testimony frequently referred to the paternity index and its equivalents in language suggestive of a probability of paternity. If the paternity index or its equivalents are presented as the probability of paternity, this amounts to an unstated assumption of a prior probability of 50 percent. . . .

The admissibility of expert testimony is governed by three general constraints. First, expert testimony must be relevant. . . . Second, expert testimony is subject to OEC 702:

> If scientific, technical or other specialized knowledge will assist the trier of fact to understand the evidence or to determine a fact in issue, a witness qualified as an expert may testify thereto in the form of an opinion or otherwise.

Finally, expert testimony must not be unduly prejudicial, confusing or time-consuming. . . .

We conclude that the paternity index and its equivalents are probative. This conclusion, however, does not end our inquiry. We must still assess whether, as asserted by Walter, the probative value is substantially outweighed by any prejudice and confusion engendered by its presentation.

The fundamental problem in the presentation of blood test results is conveying to the trier of fact the need to integrate the blood test results with the other evidence presented in the case. Although there have been many recent advances in paternity testing, leading to very high probabilities of excluding falsely accused fathers, paternity testing alone cannot yet prove paternity. Other evidence must narrow the number of potential fathers so that the test results become meaningful. The presentation to the trier of fact of the putative father's "paternity index," "chance of paternity" or "probability of paternity" creates several difficulties for conveying to the trier of fact the need to integrate these statistics with the other evidence in the case.

First, the expert is unqualified to state that any single figure is the accused's "probability of paternity." As noted above, such a statement requires an estimation of the strength of the other evidence presented in the case (i.e., an estimation of the "prior probability of paternity"), an estimation that the expert is in no better position to make than the trier of fact. If the expert were to make such an estimation, it could not satisfy [the] requirement of assistance to the trier of fact.

Second, the paternity index and its equivalents frequently are confused with the probability of paternity. This case is an example. Lovrien did not calculate a "probability of paternity," but his testimony regarding Walter's paternity index and its equivalents could easily have been confused with a probability of paternity.

Lovrien correctly described the paternity index as the chance that the child received its "genes from this man [Walter] compared with just an average man." Lovrien also testified, however, that the index meant that the odds were "178 times to 1 that he [Walter] is the right father," that a paternity index of 178 meant that "the chance that Brent Walter is the father is extremely likely," that Walter's "chance of paternity" was 99.4 percent, and that the "chance he is not the father based upon these [test results] is 0.6 percent." We doubt that any of the jurors would have made a distinction between the likelihood that Walter, rather than a randomly selected man, was the father (which is what the paternity index and its equivalents measure) and the probability that Walter was in fact the father.

3   Finally, the paternity index's comparison of the putative father with a randomly selected man is only indirectly relevant to the issue the trier of fact must decide. . . . The comparison with a random man is obviously probative, but there is a danger that the trier of fact will accord it too much weight when it comes to decide whether the putative father is the true father. For example, if an individual purchases 178 of a total of 100,000 raffle tickets, and if the average person purchases one ticket, that individual will be 178 times more likely to win the raffle than a randomly selected person. The individual's chances of winning the raffle prize, however, are still minuscule because the proper comparison is not with the number of tickets purchased by a randomly selected person, but with the total tickets purchased by everyone. Similarly, Walter is 178 times more likely to be the father of Plemel's child than a randomly selected man, but this figure standing alone is not particularly meaningful. It is important for the trier of fact to understand that the paternity index must not be taken as practically conclusive evidence of paternity but should be considered in conjunction with other evidence presented in the case. . . .

Evidence of the putative father's paternity index and its equivalents is highly probative but also presents a substantial danger of misleading the trier of fact. For that reason, we conclude that this evidence should be admissible, but only subject to certain conditions. . . .

1   First, the paternity index is admissible so long as the expert explains that the index is not the probability that the defendant is the father, but measures only the chance that the defendant is the father compared to the chance that a randomly selected man is the father. The expert should also not be allowed to use misleading formulations of the paternity index such as "the chance of paternity" and "the chance of nonpaternity" without making this qualification. . . .

2   Second, the expert . . . should never be allowed to present over objection a single figure as "the" probability of paternity. . . . Similarly, the expert should not be allowed to make statements such as "it is extremely likely" or "it is practically proven" that the defendant is the father.

3   Finally, as a corollary to the above conditions, if the expert testifies to the defendant's paternity index or a substantially equivalent statistic, the expert must, if requested, calculate the probability that the defendant is the father by using more than a single assumption about the strength of the other evidence in the case. The expert may also so testify without request or without testifying as to the paternity index. This condition is not at odds with the second condition because this condition requires the expert to use various assumptions about the strength

of the other evidence in the case rather than making a single assumption and presenting the probability calculated from that assumption as "the" probability of paternity. In this way the strength of the blood test results can be demonstrated without overstating the information that can be derived from them. If the expert uses various assumptions and makes these assumptions known, the factfinder's attention will be directed to the other evidence in the case, and it will not be misled into adopting the expert's assumption as the correct weight to be assigned to the other evidence. The expert should present calculations based on assumed prior probabilities of 0, 10, 20, 30, 40, 50, 60, 70, 80, 90 and 100 percent. If the expert is requested to do so and fails to make these calculations, the trier of fact should be instructed to ignore the paternity index and its equivalents. Other statistics, such as the probability of excluding a falsely accused father and the proportion of the relevant population excluded by the blood tests, would still be admissible.

NOTES AND QUESTIONS

1. What was wrong with the expert testimony offered in this case? Why can't an expert testify that the blood tests establish a specific probability that a particular man is the father? In what form can the expert testify about the chances that the man is the father?

2. Assume that on remand the expert testifies consistently with the requirement of this opinion and that Dena Plemel and Brent Walter again give the same conflicting testimony about the timing of their sexual intercourse. If the jury believes Walter, should it find that he is the father? Why or why not? What if the jury believes Plemel? *See* City and County of San Francisco v. Givens, 101 Cal. Rptr. 859 (Cal. App. 2000) (finding that DNA tests establishing a 99.92 percent likelihood of paternity were not enough to overcome credible testimony that established lack of sexual access during the relevant time period).

3. Not all courts have reached the same conclusions that *Plemel* does about the admissibility and presentation of blood test evidence to establish paternity affirmatively. For example, in Commonwealth v. Beausoleil, 490 N.E.2d 788 (Mass. 1986), the Massachusetts Supreme Judicial Court held that such evidence is admissible only under the following conditions:

> [I]nculpatory HLA test results may not be presented to the jury expressed simply . . . as a stated percentage of the population of nonfathers who would have been excluded by the specific array of tests conducted. . . .
>
> [T]he jury may be presented with [the probability of paternity] only where the combined tests administered would exclude at least 90% of the nonfathers tested.
>
> [I]nculpatory blood test evidence shall be admissible only if the probability of the putative father's paternity is 95% or greater.
>
> [T]he judge should instruct the jury . . . that they may not consider HLA test results as evidence of intercourse, and that they may not consider such evidence of paternity unless they have found . . . that sexual intercourse at or about the time of conception had taken place between the mother and the alleged father.

397 Mass. at 217-220; 490 N.E.2d at 795-797. The Utah Supreme Court adopted the same test in Kofford v. Flora, 744 P.2d 1343 (Utah 1987). Professor David Kaye, an authority on statistical evidence, has criticized the *Beausoleil* test and praised the *Plemel* test. David H. Kaye, The Probability of an Ultimate Issue: The Strange Cases of Paternity Testing, 1989 Iowa L. Rev. 75; David H. Kaye, *Plemel* as a Primer for Proving Paternity, 24 Willamette L. Rev. 867 (1988).

4. State law must require admission into evidence of the results of genetic tests to establish paternity if the test is "of a type generally acknowledged as reliable by accreditation bodies designated by the Secretary [of HHS]" and performed by an accredited laboratory. Objections to genetic testing results must be made in writing within a specified number of days. 42 U.S.C. § 666(a)(5)(F). State law must create a rebuttable presumption, or at the option of the state, a conclusive presumption of paternity "upon genetic testing results indicating a threshold probability that the alleged father is the father of the child." 42 U.S.C. § 666(a)(5)(G). Section 505(a) of the Uniform Parentage Act (2002) creates such a rebuttable presumption, providing that a man "is rebuttably identified as the father of a child if the genetic testing . . . results disclose that: (1) the man has at least a 99 percent probability of paternity, using a prior probability of 0.50, as calculated by using the combined paternity index obtained in the testing; and (2) a combined paternity index of at least 100 to 1." The presumption of paternity created by the testing may only be rebutted by "other genetic testing . . . which: (1) excludes the man as a genetic father of the child; or (2) identifies another man as the possible father of the child." § 505(b).

Claims that test results support a finding that a man is the child's father all rely on statistical analyses, since none of the tests provides direct affirmative evidence of paternity. *See* Charles M. Strom, Genetic Justice: A Lawyer's Guide to the Science of DNA Testing, 87 Ill. B.J. 18 (1999). Professor Christopher Blakesley criticizes the federal requirement that statistical evidence be treated as creating a presumption on the basis that it is based on a misunderstanding of the nature of statistical evidence. Christopher L. Blakesley, Scientific Testing and Proof of Paternity: Some Controversy and Key Issues for Family Law Counsel, 57 La. L. Rev. 379 (1997). In State v. Hooper, 1997 WL 83669 (Tenn. App. 1997), the Tennessee Court of Appeals held that a statute that creates a conclusive presumption of paternity from a DNA test showing a 99 percent or greater statistical probability of paternity violates due process. The court applied the balancing test of Mathews v. Eldridge, 424 U.S. 319 (1976):

> The final consideration under Mathews v. Eldridge involves the risk of inaccurately adjudicating someone a father because the conclusive presumption has foreclosed his ability to demonstrate that he is not the father of a particular child. To understand this risk, it is essential to understand what the probability of paternity percentage actually means. With a 9.98% [sic] probability of paternity, which is significantly higher than Defendant's in this case, "in a city with a same-race male population of 500,000, or even 500,001, one hundred other men might theoretically be the father. Taking this to a global scale, if there are 500 million men of the same-race on the planet, 100,000 men might theoretically qualify as putative fathers." E. Donald Shapiro et al., The DNA Paternity Test: Legislating the Future Paternity Action, 7 J.L. & Health, 1, 44 (1992-1993). . . . Although we acknowledge that it is extremely likely that the man named in a paternity action with a 99% or greater probability of

paternity is the true father, "the fact remains that paternity indexes are not mathematically solid." *Id.* In addition, there is the problem of human error in the scientific analyses of the DNA. See Edward J. Imwinkelried, The Debate in the DNA Cases over the Foundation for the Admission of Scientific Evidence: The Importance of Human Error as a Cause of Forensic Misanalysis, 69 Wash U. L.Q. 19, 22 (1991) (indicating that there "is mounting evidence of a significant margin of error in scientific analysis . . . [and] that fifteen percent of all medical laboratory tests are in error.") . . . We therefore find that, in order to have the "meaningful opportunity to be heard" guaranteed by the Due Process Clause, the conclusive presumption cannot stand. We reverse the decision of the trial court and remand the case to the trial court so that this defendant may have an opportunity to rebut the presumption of paternity attached to a 99.71% probability of paternity. . . .

For further exploration of the limitations of statistical analysis, *see* Dep't of Soc. Servs., Support Enforcement Servs. v. Bradley, 779 So. 2d 786 (La. Ct. App. 2000). The scientific testing and the 99.91 probability of paternity in this case were successfully challenged on the basis of "an unwarranted assumption of database homogeneity." The defendant's expert explained that "the database for genetic testing generally mirrors the demographics of the United States as a whole, but that the nationwide data is markedly different from the data for Red River Parish [Louisiana]. Specifically, U.S. census data shows that a substantially higher percentage of Red River Parish residents are black as . . . compared with the percentage nationally. Further, . . . people in Red River Parish tended to stay in that area whereas other areas of the United States tended to have a more mobile population. . . . [T]hese characteristics of the Parish were relevant because relatives of Bradley [the defendant] would share some of Bradley's DNA characteristics and if, as alleged, one or more of Bradley's relatives had intercourse with A.N., genetic tests on the relatives may return results similar to Bradley's." The court concluded that, in part because of the database issue, no presumption of paternity arose in the case.

5. In addition to requiring states to facilitate the use of genetic testing to determine paternity, federal law also requires greater efforts to obtain voluntary acknowledgments of the paternity of nonmarital children. 42 U.S.C. § 666(a)(5)(C) provides that a state must have a simple civil process for parents voluntarily to acknowledge paternity, which must include a hospital-based program "focusing on the period immediately before or after the birth of a child." Before the parents can sign the acknowledgment of paternity, they must be given notice "orally, or through the use of video or audio equipment, and in writing, of the alternatives to, the legal consequences of, and the rights (including, if 1 parent is a minor, any rights afforded due to minority status) and responsibilities that arise from, signing the acknowledgment."

Under these rules, a father's name can be included on the record of a nonmarital child's birth only if both parents have signed a voluntary acknowledgment of paternity, or if a court or an administrative agency of competent jurisdiction has issued an adjudication of paternity. 42 U.S.C. § 666(a)(5)(D)(i). A signed voluntary acknowledgment of paternity must be considered a legal finding of paternity, "subject to the right of any signatory to rescind the acknowledgment within the earlier of 60 days or the date of an administrative or judicial proceeding relating to the child (including a proceeding to establish a support order) in which the signatory is a party." 42 U.S.C. §666(a)(5)(D)(ii). After the 60-day period, a signed voluntary acknowledgment may be challenged in court "only on the basis of fraud, duress, or material mistake of fact, with the burden of proof upon the challenger, and under which the legal responsibilities (including child support obligations) of any signatory arising from the acknowledgment may not be suspended during the challenge, except for good cause shown." 42 U.S.C. §666(a)(5)(D)(iii).

Article 3 of the UPA recognizes voluntary acknowledgments of paternity, which must be signed by the mother and would-be father, in a record, and state that "the child whose paternity is being acknowledged . . . (A) does not have a presumed father, or has a presumed father whose full name is stated; and (B) does not have another acknowledged or adjudicated father." §302(a). The UPA provides that "the acknowledgment is the equivalent of a judicial adjudication of paternity of the child and that a challenge to the acknowledgment is permitted only under limited circumstances and is barred after two years." *Id.*

> In 2002, the Office of Child Support Enforcement reported: "In fiscal year 2000, more than 1.5 million paternities were established and acknowledged, an increase of 46 percent since 1996. Of these, almost 688,000 were in-hospital paternities that were voluntarily acknowledged."

Office of Child Support Enforcement, HHS Role in Child Support Enforcement *http://www.hhs.gov/news/press/2002pres/cse.html* (last visited October 30, 2004).

PROBLEMS

1. Two years after Arthur and Guinevere were married, Guinevere began an affair with Lancelot. A year later, while still married to Arthur, she gave birth to a child, Fred. Blood tests excluded the possibility of Arthur's paternity and showed a paternity index for Lancelot of 178. Guinevere has reconciled with Arthur, and they wish to raise Fred as their child and to have nothing to do with Lancelot. Statutes in this jurisdiction provide (1) that the husband of a married woman is rebuttably presumed to be the father of a child born during the marriage and (2) that a man whose paternity index is 175 or greater is rebuttably presumed to be the father of the child. Lancelot has filed a paternity suit, relying on the second presumption. Arthur, of course, relies on the first. How should the conflicting presumptions be treated, and how should the question of paternity be resolved?

2. Shortly after Christopher's birth, Christopher's mother and Roger, the father of her other children, signed and filed a voluntary declaration of paternity. Christopher tested positive for marijuana at birth, his mother tested positive for cocaine, and because of her problems with substance abuse, Christopher and two of his siblings have been placed in a prospective adoptive home. Albert maintains that he had intercourse with Christopher's mother during the period in which Christopher was conceived and he petitions the court to order DNA tests to establish his paternity. Christopher is ten months old at the time of the petition. What is the likely result under the Uniform Parentage Act (2002)? If Albert is denied an opportunity to establish his paternity, does the result raise constitutional issues under *Lehr* or *Troxel*?

3. J. was born in July 1997. Sheldon, the baby's biological father, had provided no support, and the mother and Leon signed and filed a voluntary declaration of paternity so that the child would have someone to look after her if something happened to her mother. After the birth, blood tests confirmed Sheldon's paternity, and he lived with J. and her mother, providing support until September 2000. In an action against Sheldon for child support, what will be the result?

C.   LEGAL RECOGNITION OF FUNCTIONAL FAMILIES

The marital presumption served not just as a convenient presumption of biological paternity, but as a bright-line rule that locked functional fathers into a parental role. Pregnant women felt the pressure to marry someone, whether or not the biological father, to "give the child a name," and the courts often used estoppel principles to confirm the parental status of a man who held out the child as his own in the face of certain knowledge that he could not have fathered the child. *See, e.g.,* Clevenger v. Clevenger, 189 Cal. App. 2d 658 (1961). Conversely, however, the same courts would almost certainly refuse to recognize the parental status of a man playing the same functional role who neither married the mother nor adopted the child.

Today, dramatically more children live in cohabiting or blended families, and these children often bond with functional parents to whom they may have no biological or legal connection. When should the law recognize the right of these adults to continuing contact with the child, and under what circumstances should such functional parents remain responsible for child support after the adult relationships end? While the majority of states continue to place their primary emphasis on biology, marriage, and adoption in establishing legal parenthood, the states have varied substantially in their responses to functional parents, with some state recognizing "psychological parents," others prescribing special rules of recognition for stepparents married to a legal parent, and still others continuing to reject recognition on the basis of function alone.

1.   *Stepparenthood*

DAVID CHAMBERS, *STEPPARENTS, BIOLOGIC PARENTS, AND THE LAW'S PERCEPTIONS OF "FAMILY" AFTER DIVORCE*

Divorce Reform at the Crossroads 102, 104-108, 118-119 (Stephen D. Sugarman & Herma Hill Kay eds., 1990)

The stepparent relationship, by contrast [to the biologic parent relationship] lacks — and I would argue, cannot possibly obtain — a single paradigm or model of appropriate responsibilities. As a starting point, children acquire two dramatically different and irretrievably "normal" forms of steprelations — the stepparent who is married to a custodial parent and with whom the child lives (a "residential stepparent," if you will) and the stepparent who is married to the noncustodial parent and whom the child sees, if at all, on visits. . . .

Even if we consider residential stepparents only, we still lack a single paradigm for the normal relationship of stepchild and stepparent. . . . The child who begins to live with a stepparent while still an infant is likely to develop a different relationship and bond with the stepparent than the child who begins the relationship as an adolescent.

In cases in which the biologic parents have been divorced (in contrast to cases in which one of the biologic parents has died), the course of the stepparent-child relationship is especially difficult to predict because of the very existence of the nonresidential parent and the variations in the frequency and quality of the visits between the child and the nonresidential parent. Indeed, the range of family compositions in the lives of children one or both of whose parents remarry is vast. . . .

It is thus unsurprising that . . . researchers have confirmed that stepparents and stepchildren come into these relationships uncertain what to expect and what is expected of them. As they begin a stepparent relationship, neither stepparents nor stepchildren have available to them a set of clear norms to guide their behaviors. . . .

To the extent that we do have an image of the stepparent relationship provided to us from our culture, it is a bleak one. . . . As a metaphor, "stepchild" describes a neglected issue or subject. . . . Cinderella's stepmother was wicked. Hamlet's stepfather was evil. . . . How many tales do you know of stepparents who were loving or kind? Some researchers believe that our cultural images of the stepparent increase the awkwardness of the relationship for those who are entering them. . . .

. . . [T]he relationship between many stepparents and stepchildren remains unclear and uncomfortable well beyond the initial stages. In his study of children with a residential stepparent, Furstenberg found that children were much less likely to say they felt "quite close" to their stepparent than to say they felt "quite close" to their custodial parent and much less likely to say that they wanted to grow up to be like their stepparent than to say they wanted to be like their custodial parent. In fact, about a third of children living with a stepparent did not mention that person when asked to name the members of their family. Nearly all named their noncustodial parent, even when they saw him or her erratically.

By much the same token, about half the stepfathers in the Furstenberg study said that their stepchildren did not think of them as a "real" parent, about half said that the children were harder to love than their own children, and about half said that it was easier to think of themselves as a friend than as a parent to the stepchildren. Stepparents had difficulty figuring out their appropriate role in disciplining the child and determining how to show affection for the child. Many stepparents and children remain uninvolved or uncomfortable with each other throughout the years they live together. . . .

Part of the difficulty for stepparents, as Furstenberg's questions themselves may suggest, is that many may believe that they are expected to be seen as a true "parent," an equal at caretaking and counseling, even when they recognize that that role is unlikely to be attainable. To be sure, not all stepparents have difficult relations with their stepchildren. Some—many of those in the other half of Furstenberg's respondents—come to see themselves as a parent and are viewed by children as such. Many others attain a comfortable relationship with the child but not in the role of a parent, establishing themselves over time not as an adult authority figure but as an adult companion and adviser. Those stepparents who prove least comfortable in the stepparent role are often those who find themselves stuck in the role of "other mother" or "other father," seen by themselves and the child as being in a parent role, but competing with and compared unfavorably with the noncustodial parent. . . .

Ultimately, the difficulty for stepparents in our society may be due in part to a want of social imagination, to an incapacity to recognize that, especially in the context of divorce, it will commonly be very hard for a stepparent either to hold a role identical to the biologic parent or, as the partner of the child's biologic parent, to become just a friend. . . . We conceive the stepparent role to be analogous to roles we already know. We expect the stepparent to be "like" someone—and he or she usually falls short.

. . . Perhaps it is impossible to forge coherent or flexible middle views. Perhaps it is psychologically inevitable that children will see a stepparent with whom they live as a person assigned to take the place of the absent parent. The least that can be said is that we as a society do not regard the advent of stepparenthood as we do the arrival of a new baby—as a treat that offers the opportunity for rich relationships.

The awkwardness of the stepparent relationship might be thought to suggest that children would in general be better off if their custodial parents did not remarry and that the law ought in general to discourage the formation of stepfamilies. That is not what the current state of research suggests. Most children living with a custodial mother become much better off economically upon their mother's remarriage. Whether they are typically better or worse off in other respects is uncertain. Research that attempts to measure the developmental effects on children of any life event—a parent's remarriage, parents' divorce, whatever—is fraught with difficulties, and thus research on the developmental effects of a parent's remarriage on children is predictably inconclusive. Clinical studies often find that children living with stepparents have adjustment problems and other difficulties, but so do children living with a single parent; empirical research typically finds few systematic differences between children raised in stepfamilies and children raised in other family configurations. . . .

Almost no information is available about actual patterns of stepparent adoption in this country or about the impact of adoption on the relationships between stepparents and children. . . . What we are able to calculate is that only a small percentage of stepparents actually adopt their stepchildren, despite the fact that the high proportion of children of divorce who never see or receive support from their noncustodial parent suggests that the number of stepparents eligible to adopt, even over the absent biologic parent's objection, must be very large. We know nothing about what distinguishes the families in which adoption occurs from the families in which it does not. . . .

Even though, as Chambers indicates, most stepparents who live with their stepchildren support them, stepparents have no common law child support duty. Only a few states have statutes that impose such a duty, and they generally provide that the duty ends when the marriage between the parent and stepparent ends. See Chapter 8. The next case considers when, if ever, a court may and should order a stepparent to continue to support a child after divorcing the child's parent.

M. H. B. v. H. T. B.

100 N.J. 567, 498 A.2d 775 (1985)

PER CURIAM. The members of the Court being equally divided, the judgment of the Appellate Division is affirmed.

HANDLER, J., concurring. . . . The parties in this case (referred to by their initials or first names in order to protect the child who is the object of the controversy) were married in 1966. The couple settled in New Jersey where, during their first five years together, they conceived two sons, G. B. and M. B. The marriage turned sour during 1975, however, and sometime thereafter the plaintiff-wife, Marilyn, had a brief extra-marital affair. In 1977, while still married to the defendant-husband, Henry, Marilyn gave birth to a daughter, K. B.

Three months later, Henry first learned that he might not be K. B.'s biological father. He discovered a letter, or a diary entry, implicating Marilyn's former paramour as K. B.'s natural father. Henry then confronted Marilyn with this evidence of her infidelity, and moved out of the family residence. Following this separation, the marriage continued for almost three years. After living for six months in the same town as the rest of his family, however, Henry moved twice, first to California and then to Wisconsin, where he continues to live. During this period of separation, Henry maintained close bonds with all of the children, K. B. as well as the two sons, through phone calls, letters, gifts, and visits.

Marilyn also moved several times with the children. Between March and September 1978, she cohabitated with her erstwhile paramour, K. B.'s purported natural father, whom she briefly considered marrying. In December 1978, however, Marilyn brought herself and the children to Henry's home in Wisconsin, and for six months the parties attempted to reconcile their differences. Henry then professed to Marilyn that he would always love K. B., and that he did not want the child's illegitimacy to interfere with the couple's future together.

The reconciliation attempt failed, however, and, in June 1979, the couple signed a separation agreement covering financial support obligations, child custody, and visitation. Marilyn assumed custody of all three children, then ages 2, 7, and 10, and Henry undertook to pay $600 per month as family support, based on his annual income of over $34,000 at a time when Marilyn had no income. Marilyn thereafter moved back to New Jersey with all three children.

It is undisputed that K. B.'s purported father then lived and still lives nearby to the child and her mother. Marilyn testified, however, that she last saw this man in December 1979, six months after returning to New Jersey, and has not seen him since. . . .

In March 1980, the couple obtained a divorce in Wisconsin under terms established by an extensive written settlement agreement. The parties, Henry as well as Marilyn, stipulated that all three children were born of the marriage. They further agreed that Marilyn would have custody of the children during the school year, and that Henry would get custody during the three summer months. Although at this point Henry earned about $51,000 each year while Marilyn still had no income, Henry promised only to continue paying $200 per month per child in Marilyn's custody. . . .

All three minor children remained objects of Henry's affection, attention, and solicitude throughout the post-divorce period. In particular, Henry expressed interest in and concern for K. B. As found by the trial judge, K. B. bears Henry's surname, is registered on all of her records as bearing his surname, knows no other father, and is ignorant of the facts surrounding her paternity. Henry made innumerable representations to K. B. and to the world that he was her father. . . . Thus, Henry treated K. B. exactly as he treated his own son G. B., who was also in Marilyn's custody. Both K. B. and G. B. received Christmas gifts in 1979, 1980, and 1981. Further, Henry willingly provided child support payments on behalf of both children through the end of 1981. Based on all of the evidence, the trial judge concluded that Henry had become K. B.'s "psychological, if not biological parent."

Then, in March of 1981, Henry remarried. The following summer, both K. B. and G. B. visited and remained with Henry. By September 1981, however, Marilyn and Henry's second wife did not get along. The relationship between Marilyn and Henry deteriorated and Henry began withholding child support payments.

In January 1982 Henry petitioned a Wisconsin court to grant him custody of all three children, including K. B. . . . Marilyn filed a separate complaint, in March 1982, in New Jersey, seeking to retain custody of G. B. and K. B., and to obtain an increase in child support. Consistent with the petition he had filed in Wisconsin, Henry filed a counterclaim requesting custody of these children, K. B. as well as G. B. Later, by a pre-trial motion, Henry amended his counterclaim, claiming, in the alternative, that he should be under no duty to provide child support for K. B., and seeking to litigate the issue of the child's paternity. This was the first time that Henry had ever attempted to repudiate his paternal relationship with K. B. Without conceding Henry's right to contest paternity, Marilyn consented to allow the completion of a Human Leucocyte Analysis blood test in December 1982. The results of the test excluded Henry as K. B.'s biological father.

A plenary hearing on the custody and support applications took place over several days in April and May of 1983. . . . [T]he trial judge concluded that the doctrine of equitable estoppel was applicable to preclude Henry from denying the duty to provide child support on behalf of K. B. . . .

II.

The framework for analysis of the issue on this appeal is provided by *Miller v. Miller*, 97 N.J. 154, 478 A.2d 351 (1984). In that case, the Court recognized that the doctrine of equitable estoppel could properly be applied in the context of a matrimonial controversy in which the interests of individual children were at stake. Because we were dealing with responsibilities that may flow from familial relationships that are inherently complicated and subtle, we acknowledged that the application of equitable principles called for great sensitivity, caution, and flexibility.

The *Miller* case involved two girls whose mother remarried after divorcing their father. During the mother's second marriage the defendant, her second husband, assumed sole responsibility for the girls' financial support, as well as other parental privileges and obligations. He also discouraged his wife and stepchildren from maintaining any personal or financial relationship with the children's natural father. The second marriage ended in divorce after seven years, at which time the mother sought to receive continuing child support from the girls' stepfather.

The Court ruled in *Miller* that, before a duty of child support could be imposed based on equitable considerations, it must first be shown that, by a course of conduct, the stepparent affirmatively encouraged the child to rely and depend on the stepparent for parental nurture and financial support. We specifically recognized that such conduct could interfere with the children's relationship to their natural father. Under the facts, we held that the stepfather would be equitably estopped to deny his duty to continue to provide child support on behalf of his stepchildren, if it could be shown that the children would suffer financial harm if the stepparent were permitted to repudiate the parental obligations he had assumed. We further held that the natural father could continue to be legally liable for the support of these children.

Applying the principles set forth in *Miller*, the evidence in this case compels the imposition of equitable estoppel to prevent Henry from denying the duty to provide financial support for K. B. Henry's actions throughout the marriage and following the divorce constituted a continuous course of conduct toward the child that was tantamount to a knowing and affirmative representation that he would support her as would a natural father. By both deed and word, Henry repeatedly and consistently recognized and confirmed the parent-child relationship between himself and K. B. He acted in every way like a father toward his own child. He also stipulated to the child's paternity. At the time of his divorce he promised to pay child support, which obligation was incorporated into the judgment of divorce. . . .

There was clearly reasonable reliance upon Henry's purposeful conduct. The obvious expectations engendered by Henry's conduct were that K. B. fully accepted and reasonably believed Henry to be her father. Significantly, the court found that Henry became K. B.'s psychological father, a finding that imports much more than mere affection. *See generally* Goldstein, Freud & Solnit, Beyond the Best Interests of the Child 9-28 (1973). The strength and durability of a psychological parent-child relationship is perhaps the most relevant consideration in defining a child's best interests. Further, it is not disputed that K. B. never knew any person other then Henry to be her natural father. As found by the trial judge, Henry's absorption of the child's time and affection as her father effectively stultified the development of any other filial relationship between K. B. and anyone else.

In these circumstances, Henry's conduct assuredly engendered material and emotional consequences for K. B. — consequences that would be demonstrably adverse to K. B. if Henry were now permitted to repudiate all his prior actions. . . .

In the present case the trial court found that K. B. would suffer "irreparable harm" if Henry were allowed to repudiate his actions. As so well expressed in Clevenger, 11 Cal. Rptr. at 710, which we quoted in *Miller*, 97 N.J. at 165, 478 A.2d 351,

> [t]here is an innate immorality in the conduct of an adult who for over a decade accepts and proclaims a child as his own, but then, in order to be relieved of the child's support, announces, and relies upon his bastardy. This is a cruel weapon, which works a lasting injury to the child and can bring in its aftermath social harm. The weapon should garner no profit to the wielder; the putative father should earn no premium by the assertion of the illegitimacy of the child.

I am satisfied, as was the trial court, that the evidence in this case establishes that Henry, from the time of K. B.'s birth, engaged in a voluntary and knowing course of conduct with respect to K. B., which constituted in its purpose and effect an affirmative representation that he was her natural father. It is also abundantly clear that the child K. B., as well as her mother Marilyn, relied upon Henry's purposeful conduct and depended upon him for support. Further, it cannot be disputed that the reliance by K. B. was detrimental in the sense of the financial, as well as personal, harm she would suffer if Henry were permitted to disavow his representations, repudiate the expectations he created, and evade the responsibilities he had assumed. Under these circumstances he is equitably estopped from denying a continuing obligation to provide child support on behalf of K. B.

III.

Defendant cites two reasons why he should not be responsible for his stepchild's financial support. He urges that the New Jersey Parentage Act, N.J.S.A. 9:17-38 to -59, requires that if a man is found not to be a child's biological father, then he cannot be held liable to support that child, at least if the biological father may be identified. Defendant also contends that *Miller* stands for the proposition that Marilyn had a duty to bring the purported natural father into court and that, because she did not, we should remand to consider whether that person should be liable for K. B.'s support. Neither argument is persuasive.

POLLOCK, J., concurring in part and dissenting in part. . . . In the eight years that have elapsed since K. B.'s birth, Henry has spent a total of only fourteen months with her. Moreover, Henry has since remarried and begun a new family, one in which the trial court found K. B. is not welcome. Thus, Henry's relationship to K. B., which was always ambivalent, is now in tatters. Consequently, I believe that the present case is a poor vehicle to transport into the law the notion that emotional bonding between a stepparent and a child may terminate a natural parent's support obligation. . . .

Although the concurrence purports to rely on Miller v. Miller, supra, it actually stands the *Miller* opinion on its head. *Miller* recognized "that in appropriate cases, the doctrine of equitable estoppel may be invoked to impose on a stepparent the duty to support a stepchild after a divorce from the child's natural parent." We admonished, however, that the doctrine was to be invoked "cautiously."

Accordingly, we held that a stepparent could be equitably estopped from denying an obligation to support a stepchild on proof of three conditions. First, the stepparent must have made a representation to either the children or the natural parent that he or she would provide support. Second, that representation must have been relied on by either the children or the natural parent. We declined to rely on these two conditions alone to establish estoppel because such a rule would penalize a "stepparent who tried to create a warm family atmosphere with his or her stepchildren." Consistent with that concern, we imposed a third condition, one that required a showing that "the children will suffer future financial detriment as a result of the stepparent's representation or conduct that caused the children to be cut off from their natural parent's financial support." Such financial detriment could be shown if the custodial parent cannot locate or does not know the whereabouts of the natural parent, or cannot obtain legal jurisdiction over the natural parent, and the natural parent's unavailability is attributable to the actions of the stepparent. Thus, a stepparent is responsible for the unavailability of a natural parent only when he or she takes "positive action interfering with the natural parent's support obligation." Accordingly, in *Miller*, we remanded the matter to the trial court to determine whether the stepfather had detrimentally affected his stepchildren's ability to obtain future support by interfering with the children's relationship with the natural father. . . .

I continue to be counselled by *Miller*'s warning not to impose a child-support obligation on a stepfather merely because he developed a close relationship with the stepchildren. Without further proof, I would not alter *Miller*'s requirement that when the natural parent can be located and is financially able, he or she remains principally responsible to pay permanent child support.

The concurring opinion in the present case reflects the understandable desire to spare K. B. the painful knowledge that Henry is not her biological father. As painful as that discovery may be, however, it is inevitable that one day K. B. will learn the facts. For example, Marilyn has already revealed to G. B. and M. B., K. B.'s stepbrothers, the identity of K. B.'s natural father. In addition, Marilyn advises that she intends to inform K. B. at a later date that Henry is not her natural father. As well intentioned as the concurrence may be, it cannot spare K. B. whatever anguish she will feel when she learns the identity of her natural father.

This case stands in stark contrast to *Miller*, where the evidence was that the stepparent actively resisted the natural father's attempt to maintain relations with his children. Here, the whereabouts of the natural father are known; he is in the next town. Most importantly, Henry has not done anything to interfere directly with the natural father's relationship with K. B. On the present record, the absence of financial support from the natural father is as attributable to his insouciance as it is to Henry's conduct.

NOTES AND QUESTIONS

1. Why was Henry not obligated to support K. B. pursuant to the separation agreement (contract) that he and her mother entered into? To what extent should

contracts control who has child support duties? *See* L. v. L., 497 S.W.2d 840 (Mo. Ct. App. 1973); Duffey v. Duffey, 438 S.E.2d 445 (N.C. App. 1994); T. v. T., 224 S.E.2d. 148 (Va. 1976). *Compare* Fuller v. Fuller, 247 A.2d 767 (D.C. App. 1968). *See also* T.F. v. B.L., 813 N.E.2d 1244 (Mass. 2004) (ruling held unenforceable an alleged agreement by a lesbian couple that they would jointly co-parent and support a child conceived through artificial insemination during the relationship); Dunkin v. Boskey, 98 Cal. Rptr. 2d 44 (Cal. App. 2000) (ruling that parenting agreement between unmarried man and biological mother with respect to child conceived by artificial insemination could be enforced only through award of unjust enrichment for support provided where mother refused to grant visitation rights).

2. Should Henry have been barred by *res judicata* from challenging K. B.'s paternity, since he had stipulated that she was born of the marriage? Most courts have held that res judicata applies to stipulated findings of paternity. *See, e.g.,* DeVaux v. DeVaux, 514 N.W.2d 640 (Neb. 1994) (collecting cases). A child's effort to establish paternity in his or her own right, however, may not necessarily be barred by a stipulation between the parents. *See* Annot., Right of Illegitimate Child to Maintain Action to Determine Paternity, 86 A.L.R.5th 637 (2001).

3. Both opinions in *M. H. B.* apply estoppel principles to determine whether K. B.'s stepfather is liable to support her. Under an estoppel theory, what is the justification for imposing a support duty? Do the authors of these opinions reach different conclusions because of different understandings of legal theory? If not, what is the source of their disagreement? What is the relevance of the emotional tie between a stepparent and stepchild to the adult's support duty? Will imposing the duty protect the relationship?

4. The stepfather in *M. H. B.* knew from the outset that he was not K. B.'s biological father. What if he had believed that he was her biological father throughout the time that he was developing a relationship with her and voluntarily supporting her, and repudiated her only upon discovering that she was not his biological child? Would he still be liable under an estoppel theory?

5. What is the support duty of K. B.'s biological father under each of the opinions in *M. H. B.*?

6. A number of other courts have held that estoppel principles may be invoked to require stepparents to continue supporting stepchildren following a divorce. *See, e.g.,* Hubbard v. Hubbard, 44 P.3d 153 (Alaska 2002); L. S. K. v. H. A. N., 813 A.2d 872 (Pa. Super. Ct. 2002) (applying estoppel to hold same-sex partner liable for child support). However, most courts very rarely find that the facts support a finding of estoppel. *See, e.g.,* K. A. T. v. C. A. B., 645 A.2d 570 (D.C. 1994); Portuondo v. Portuondo, 570 So. 2d 1338 (Fla. App. 1990); Markov v. Markov, 758 A.2d 75 (Md. 2000); A. R. v. C. R., 583 N.E.2d 840 (Mass. 1992); Murphy v. Murphy, 714 A.2d 576 (R.I. 1998); E. H. v. M. H., 512 N.W.2d 148 (S.D. 1994); Wiese v. Wiese, 699 P.2d 700 (Utah 1985); Ulrich v. Cornell, 484 N.W.2d 545 (Wis. 1992). Other courts have refused to use estoppel to impose stepparent support duties, regardless of the facts. *E.g.,* In re Marriage of Holcomb, 471 N.W.2d 76 (Iowa App. 1991).

Of those courts that do use estoppel to impose a child support obligation, most regard only financial detriment as sufficient reason. K. B. v. D. B. 639 N.E.2d 725 (Mass. App. 1994). A few courts, however, have accepted the argument that emotional detriment is sufficient. Clevenger v. Clevenger, above; Wright v. Black, 856 P.2d 477 (Alaska 1993). In B. E. B. v. R. L. B., 979 P.2d 514 (Alaska 1999), the Alaska Supreme Court repudiated prior cases and held that emotional detriment alone is no longer a sufficient basis for estoppel, and that financial detriment must be shown.

7. In England, courts have been authorized to order stepparents to pay child support following divorce since 1958, apparently with little objection from the obligated stepparents or the public generally. For discussion, see Sarah H. Ramsey & Judith M. Masson, Stepparent Support of Stepchildren: A Comparative Analysis of Policies and Problems in the American and English Experience, 36 Syracuse L. Rev. 659, 689-698 (1985).

Canadian divorce statutes provide that a stepparent may be required to pay child support if he or she "stands in the place of a parent." Divorce Act, R.S.C., ch. 3 (2d Supp. 1985). In Chartier v. Chartier [1999] 1 S.C.R. 242, the Canadian Supreme Court ruled that once an in loco parentis relationship is established, the stepparent cannot terminate it unilaterally.

8. The ALI Principles of the Law of Family Dissolution do not set out rules that govern the determination of biological parentage or adoption, leaving these issues to other provisions of a state's law. Comment b to § 2.04 However, the Principles create the status of "parent by estoppel," which gives a person who is not a legal parent the rights and duties of a parent in most situations. A "parent by estoppel" is a person who is not a legal parent but 1) who has lived with the child for at least two years and had a reasonable good-faith belief that he was the child's biological father and continued to make reasonable, good-faith efforts to accept parental responsibilities even if the belief no longer existed, or 2) lived with the child since the child's birth or for at least two years and holds out and accepts full and permanent responsibility as a parent as the result of a co-parenting arrangement with the child's legal parent if recognition of the relationship is in the child's best interests, or 3) is liable for child support. ALI Principles § 2.03(1)(b). In turn, § 3.02 provides that one who is not a legal parent may be liable for child support if there was an explicit or implicit agreement or undertaking that he or she would assume a support obligation, the child was born during the cohabitation or marriage between the child's parent and the person to be charged, or the child was conceived as a result of an agreement between that person and the child's parent that they would share responsibility for the child. In determining whether to impose a support obligation, the court is to consider the nature of the relationship between the child and the adult, whether the adult's undertaking supplanted the child's opportunity to develop a relationship with an absent parent, whether the child otherwise has two parents with a support duty, and any other relevant facts.

The ALI Principles of the Law of Family Dissolution also propose a status called de facto parent, defined as a person who is not a legal parent or a parent by estoppel who has lived with a child for at least two years and for reasons primarily other than financial compensation and with the agreement of the child's legal parent or because of the failure of the legal parent to perform caretaking functions, regularly performed a majority of the caretaking functions for the child or at least as much of them as the child's primary parent. ALI Principles § 2.03(1)(c).

For a critique of the ALI approach, *see* Sarah H. Ramsey, Constructing Parenthood for Stepparents: Parents by Estoppel and De Facto Parents Under the American Law Institute's Principles of the Law of Family Dissolution, 8 Duke J. Gender L. & Pol'y 285 (2001).

PROBLEM

When Hank and Wanda were divorced, Hank agreed to pay child support for Bobby, their son born during the marriage, and for Ellie, Wanda's child from a former relationship who had lived with Hank and Wanda throughout their six-year marriage. The agreement was incorporated into Hank and Wanda's divorce decree. During the marriage Hank had signed an affidavit of paternity for Ellie and filed it with the Bureau of Vital Statistics, even though he was not in fact her biological father. He never formally adopted her, though. It is now two years since the divorce. Hank has remarried, and his new wife has just had twins. He has moved to terminate his duty to support Ellie on the basis that she is not his biological child. Ellie's biological father lives in an adjoining state. Wanda has had no contact with him since before Ellie's birth. What arguments should Wanda make? How should Hank respond?

In re Nelson

825 A.2d 501 (N.H. 2003)

DALIANIS, J. . . . The petitioner, Douglas Hoyt Nelson, and the respondent, Sylvia Horsley, began dating in 1992. They have one biological child, Nelson James Robert Horsley, born on June 29, 1993. The parties never married each other.

The parties ended their romantic relationship in November 1994. In December 1994, the respondent adopted a son, Kent Horsley. In December 1995, the parties' romantic relationship resumed, and the petitioner moved in with the respondent. On September 30, 2000, the respondent adopted two children from Ukraine, Emma Horsley and Molly Horsley.

Contrary to the petitioner's assertions, the respondent contends that she assumed all child care duties and was the sole financial support for the children until 1998, at which time the petitioner shared some of the child care responsibilities and allegedly provided minimal financial support for the children. The petitioner refused the respondent's repeated requests that he adopt Kent. In addition, the respondent asserts that although the petitioner traveled to Ukraine to meet Emma and Molly, he stated unequivocally that he would not adopt them.

In July 2001, the respondent asked the petitioner to move out of her residence. He did so in September of that year. Although the petitioner was at first allowed to visit with Kent, the respondent soon terminated the visitation after Kent began to exhibit what the respondent describes as increasing fear and anxiety over his visits with the petitioner.

In October, the petitioner filed a petition for custody and support of the parties' biological child, which he later amended to seek custody and support orders with respect to the respondent's adopted children.

* * *

We address the defendant's State Constitutional claim first, citing federal law only to aid in our analysis. We have recognized that

> the family and the rights of parents over it are natural, essential, and inherent rights within the meaning of the New Hampshire Constitution. Because of their fundamental importance, great judicial deference has been accorded parental rights. They have been found to operate against the State, against third parties, and against the child.

We have long recognized the right to raise and care for one's children as a fundamental liberty interest protected by Part I, Article 2 of the State Constitution, . . . and have extended such protection to both natural and adoptive parents. . . . Similarly, United States Supreme Court precedent recognizes "that the Due Process Clause of the Fourteenth Amendment [to the Federal Constitution] protects the fundamental right of parents to make decisions concerning the care, custody, and control of their children." Troxel v. Granville, 530 U.S. 57, 66, 147 L. Ed. 2d 49, 120 S. Ct. 2054 (2000) (plurality opinion).

As we have explained in the past, the best interests of the child guide all custody matters. . . . There is a presumption, however, that "fit parents act in the best interests of their children." Troxel, 530 U.S. at 68 (plurality opinion). "So long as a parent adequately cares for his or her children (i.e., is fit), there will normally be no reason for the State to inject itself into the private realm of the family to further question the ability of that parent to make the best decisions concerning the rearing of that parent's children." . . .

The State does have "a competing interest in the welfare of children within its jurisdiction, and may, as parens patriae, intervene in the family milieu if a child's welfare is at stake." . . . [T]he petitioner argues that he is entitled to custody of the respondent's adopted children, over her objection, so long as it is in the children's best interests. . . . [A]pplication of the best interests of the child standard in a custody dispute between a natural or adoptive parent and a nonparent would offend due process if the parent's conduct towards the child has not been inconsistent with the parent's constitutionally protected status. . . .

The constitutional rights of the natural or adoptive parent over his or her children are not easily set aside. Only in the most unusual and serious of cases may such fundamental rights be abrogated in favor of an unrelated third person. . . .

The petitioner argues, however, that the status of parent should be extended to cover all persons who have established a parental relationship with a child through the in loco parentis or psychological parent doctrines, affording them the same constitutional protections. We disagree. The common law defines a person in loco parentis as "one who intentionally accepts the rights and duties of natural parenthood with respect to a child not his own." . . . For example, we have held that a couple who stood in loco parentis to a child were "persons . . . legally aggrieved" by a probate court's denial of their petition for continued custody of the child and that the in loco parentis relationship "gave rise to personal rights which entitled them to appeal from the dismissal of their petition." We have also stated that a plaintiff standing in loco parentis was permitted to maintain an action for damages for personal injury suffered by a minor child, and that such a person was "entitled to all the rights of a parent" while the relationship existed. . . . Nevertheless, we have never expressly held that an unrelated third person standing in loco parentis has the same constitutionally protected rights to custody as a natural or adoptive parent, nor are we persuaded to do so here. To do so could elevate the rights of any unrelated third person who has spent considerable time caring for a child over the fundamental liberty interests of natural or adoptive parents.

Because we find the in loco parentis and psychological parent doctrines substantially similar, we will not conduct a separate analysis under the psychological parent doctrine.

Accordingly, we . . . hold that it would violate the fit natural or adoptive parent's State constitutional rights to grant custodial rights to an unrelated third person over the express objection of that parent. We note, however, that this decision does not affect stepparents, who under certain circumstances have been recognized as having the right to seek custody if it is in the best interests of the child. . . .

Remanded.

NADEAU, J. dissenting. Because I believe that the superior court can, under certain circumstances, grant custodial rights to an unrelated third party over the minor children's sole natural or adoptive parent's objection, I respectfully dissent.

The majority contends that "only in the most unusual and serious of cases may [the] fundamental rights [of natural or adoptive parents over their children] be abrogated in favor of an unrelated third person." I believe this is contrary to the tenor of our case law.

* * *

. . . The majority . . . acknowledges that stepparents "under certain circumstances have been recognized as having the right to seek custody if it is in the best interests of the child." The majority offers no rationale, however, for distinguishing stepparents from other nonbiologically related third parties.

The distinction cannot be based upon constitutional rights of the stepparent, as we have never recognized in stepparents the same fundamental interest in the care and custody of their stepchildren as natural or adoptive parents have in their children. . . . Nor does the majority appear to contend that marriage to the natural parent, regardless of its duration or the attendant relationship (or lack thereof) between stepparent and stepchildren, automatically places a stepparent into the category of persons having a right to petition for custody of the children. Rather, the majority asserts that "under certain circumstances" stepparents have the right to seek custody of their stepchildren.

Examination of our case law reveals that the "circumstances" that justify the award of custody to a stepparent are not marriage to the natural parent, but the existence of a "psychological parent-child relationship," or an "in loco parentis" relationship—exactly the kind of relationship the petitioner here asserts. Thus, there is no logical basis in our case law for distinguishing between stepparents and unrelated third parties asserting an in loco parentis relationship with the children over whom they seek custody.

* * *

Rejection of the majority's categorical approach, then, requires consideration of whether an in loco parentis petitioner can, without violating the State or Federal Constitutions, ever be granted custodial rights over the objection of the children's sole natural or adoptive parent.

Let me start by making clear what I consider to be an in loco parentis relationship for these purposes. Under the common law, "a person in loco parentis is one who intentionally accepts the rights and duties of natural parenthood with respect to a child not his own." . . .

The test set forth by the Supreme Court of Wisconsin in Holtzman v. Knott (In re H.S.H-K), 193 Wis. 2d 649, 533 N.W.2d 419, 421 (Wis.), *cert. denied*, 516 U.S. 975 (1995), is sufficiently specific and comprehensive to protect the interests of both children and natural or adoptive parents. See 533 N.W.2d at 436. Accordingly, I would adopt the following Wisconsin test:

> To demonstrate the existence of the petitioner's parent-like relationship with the child, the petitioner must prove four elements: (1) that the biological or adoptive parent consented to, and fostered, the petitioner's formation and establishment of a parent-like relationship with the child; (2) that the petitioner and the child lived together in the same household; (3) that the petitioner assumed obligations of parenthood by taking significant responsibility for the child's care, education and development, including contributing towards the child's support, [although the contribution need not be monetary] without expectation of financial compensation; and (4) that the petitioner has been in a parental role for a length of time sufficient to have established with the child a bonded, dependent relationship parental in nature.

533 N.W.2d at 421 (footnote omitted).

I would also require proof of "a significant triggering event [which] justifies state intervention in the child's relationship with a biological or adoptive parent." Id. In a divorce situation, the triggering event is the dissolution of the relationship. When, as in this case, the parties are not married and the petitioner has not adopted the child, the triggering event occurs when the natural or adoptive parent engages in conduct that the petitioner reasonably believes will significantly impair his or her relationship with the child. Cf. id.

* * *

Accordingly, once an in loco parentis relationship as defined above has been established and a triggering event has occurred, the superior court must then determine whether it would be in the best interests of the child to grant the in loco parentis petitioner custody or visitation. . . . I would require, however, that an in loco parentis petitioner seeking custodial or visitation rights contrary to the wishes of the natural or adoptive parent bear the burden of proving that such custody or visitation is in the best interests of the child because "there is a presumption that fit parents act in the best interests of their children," Troxel, 530 U.S. at 68.

* * *

The test I would adopt also assures that an in loco parentis petitioner will not be able to assert parental rights lightly. It is not possible for the next-door neighbor or the casual romantic partner to meet all the conditions of the test including that the natural or adoptive parent "consent to and foster" the in loco parentis relationship. See V.C. v. M.J.B., 163 N.J. 200, 748 A.2d 539, 551-52 (N.J.), *cert. denied*, 531 U.S. 926 (2000).

The requirement of cooperation by the legal parent is critical because it places control within his or her hands. That parent has the absolute ability to maintain a zone of autonomous privacy for herself and her child. However, if she wishes to maintain that zone of privacy she cannot invite a third party to function as a parent to her child and cannot cede over to that third party parental authority the exercise of which may create a profound bond with the child. . . . A natural or adoptive parent who voluntarily consents to the formation of a relationship between the petitioner and the child is hardly in a position to complain if the natural bounty of that relationship is accorded the child or the petitioner.

* * *

In sum, the two adults in this case have their own reasons for not being married. That fact alone, however, should not prohibit the petitioner from seeking custodial rights based upon the children's best interests. A petitioner who meets the Wisconsin test should not be deprived of the opportunity to obtain custody of or visitation with the child merely because he was not married to the natural parent during the time the relationship was created. The natural parent is protected because the facts necessary to meet the Wisconsin test are subject to evidentiary proof and determination by the superior court.

. . . By denying the petitioner the opportunity to present evidence to the superior court that he has met the Wisconsin test and established a parental relationship with the child, merely because he does not share blood with the child or a marriage certificate with the mother, the majority opinion ignores the realities of the twenty-first century.

For these reasons, respectfully, I dissent.

NOTES AND QUESTIONS

1. As the dissent notes, the courts in some states take the view that they have inherent equitable powers to order visitation "in the best interests of the child." *See, e.g.*, Wills v. Wills, 399 So. 2d 1130 (Fla. App. 1981); Evans v. Evans, 488 A.2d 157 (Md. 1985); Hickenbottom v. Hickenbottom, 477 N.W.2d 8 (Neb. 1991)

(discussing cases). *But see* In re Marriage of Ohr, 97 P.3d 354 (Colo. Ct. App. 2004) (rejecting common law right).

Other courts hold that jurisdiction to make such orders must be granted by statute. However, considering the variety of statutory construction approaches taken in the cases, it is not clear that statutory language is particularly important in this situation. *See* In re Dureno, 854 P.2d 1352 (Colo. App. 1992) (court may award visitation to a stepparent even though the visitation statute speaks only in terms of awards to "parents" because the custody statute allows custody awards to be made to stepparents); Cox v. Williams, 502 N.W.2d 128 (Wis. 1993) (reversing grant of visitation to a former custodial stepmother, very narrowly construing a statute that authorized visitation orders for people who have "maintained a relationship similar to a parent-child relationship with the child" if in the best interests of the child); Weinand v. Weinand, 616 N.W.2d 1 (Neb. 2000).

2. *Troxel* calls into question the constitutionality of all these approaches to the extent that they authorize a court to override a parent's judgment that a stepparent should not have visitation solely on the basis of a best-interest determination. The California Court of Appeal in In re Marriage of W., 114 Cal. App. 4th 68, 7 Cal. Rptr. 3d 461 (2003), held that application of a broadly worded visitation statute that permitted the court to order stepparent visitation without "a presumption that a parent's decision regarding visitation is in the best interest of the child" violated the parent's constitutional rights articulated in *Troxel*. *Compare* Kinnard v. Kinnard, 43 P.3d 150 (Alaska 2002) (upholding order for shared custody between father and stepmother upon showing of harm to child). Does the majority's approach to this issue depend on its interpretation of the constitutional requirement articulated in *Troxel*? If so, how does it justify the distinction between married and functional stepparents? How does the dissent, in advocating the Wisconsin approach, address the constitutional concerns raised by *Troxel*?

3. Sociologist Andrew Cherlin defines stepfamily "as a household in which: 1) two adults are married or cohabiting, and 2) at least one adult has a child present from a previous marriage or relationship." Andrew J. Cherlin, Public and Private Families 404 (2d ed. 1999). Cherlin's definition would accordingly eliminate the distinction between married and unmarried partners. What are the arguments for and against granting visitation to a person who has played the stepparent role without marriage to the legal parent?

4. Is there a constitutional distinction between granting someone who is not a legal parent visitation as opposed to custody? Should stepparents be granted visitation only under the same circumstances in which they would be ordered to pay child support? Why or why not?

5. Many cases limit visitation orders to stepparents who stand "in loco parentis" to the child. What does this term mean? Is it the same as "psychological parent"? Courts typically justify this limitation as necessary to prevent hordes of people from seeking visitation with a child. Is this a realistic concern? Could the term have constitutional significance after *Troxel*?

6. *Nelson* is not unusual in refusing to recognize visitation rights for a parent's unmarried partner. *See* Hughes v. Creighton, 798 P.2d 403 (Ariz. App. 1990); Gayden v. Gayden, 280 Cal. Rptr. 862 (Cal. App. 1991); Temple v. Meyer, 544 A.2d 629 (Conn. 1988); In re Marriage of Freel, 448 N.W.2d 26 (Iowa 1989);

Van v. Zahorik, 575 N.W.2d 566 (Mich. App. 1997); Multari v. Sorrell, 731 N.Y.S.2d 238 (N.Y. App. Div. 2001); Cooper v. Merkel, 470 N.W.2d 253 (S.D. 1991). A few recent decisions take a contrary view, however. *See, e.g.,* Engle v. Kenner, 926 S.W.2d 472 (Mo. App. 1996); Barker v. Briggs, 1996 WL 532468 (Conn. Super. 1996).

PROBLEMS

1. On the facts of the problem above, page 921, would the stepfather be entitled to visit under either the majority or the dissent approach in *Nelson*?

2. Ross and Kathy were married when Kathy's child from her former marriage, Danny, was six months old. Ross knew that he was not Danny's biological father, but he treated him as his son in every way. Kathy died when Danny was seven years old. Until Kathy's death Danny had no contact with his biological father, Greg, who refused to visit. After Kathy's death Greg came forward, claiming the right to Danny's custody. Ross also seeks custody. To whom should the court award custody and why? As between Kathy's mother and Ross, to whom should the court award custody?

2. Second-Parent Adoption?

SHARON S. v. SUPERIOR COURT

73 P.3d 554 (Cal. 2003)

WERDEGAR, J.

. . . Sharon and Annette attended Harvard Business School together and were in a committed relationship from 1989 through mid-2000. In 1996, after being artificially inseminated with sperm from an anonymous donor, Sharon gave birth to Zachary. With Sharon's consent and approval, Annette petitioned to adopt Zachary in a "second parent" adoption, using official forms and procedures that expressly provided that Sharon consented to Zachary's adoption by Annette, but intended to retain her own parental rights.[10] The trial court approved Annette's adoption petition, and Annette has since been one of Zachary's two parents.

Three years later, in 1999, Sharon was inseminated again with sperm from the same anonymous donor and gave birth to Joshua. On August 30 of that year, Sharon signed an Independent Adoption Placement Agreement (Agreement),

---

10. "The phrase 'second-parent adoption' refers to an independent adoption whereby a child born to [or legally adopted by] one partner is adopted by his or her non-biological or non-legal second parent, with the consent of the legal parent, and without changing the latter's rights and responsibilities." (Doskow, The Second Parent Trap (1999) 20 J. Juv. L. 1, 5.) As a result of the adoption, the child has two legal parents who have equal legal status in terms of their relationship with the child.

which begins: "Note to birth parent: This form will become a permanent and irrevocable consent to adoption. Do not sign this form unless you want the adopting parents named below to adopt your child." The Agreement goes on to recite Sharon's "permanent and irrevocable consent to the adoption on the 91st day after I sign" the Agreement.

The Agreement also recites that, upon the court's approval of the Agreement, Sharon will "give up all rights of custody, services, and earnings" with respect to Joshua. However, a written Addendum to Independent Adoption Placement Agreement (Addendum), a form developed by the California Department of Social Services (CDSS), was signed by Sharon and Annette on the same date as they signed the Agreement. The Addendum stated Sharon's intent, as Joshua's birth parent, to retain parental rights and control of Joshua while placing him with Annette for the purpose of independent adoption.[11] These were essentially the same procedures and forms Sharon and Annette had used for Zachary's adoption. . . .

Subsequently, Annette filed a petition to adopt Joshua as a second parent with Sharon. The petition stated that Sharon, as "birth mother of the children [Zachary and Joshua] consents to this adoption and will execute a limited written consent to the child's [Joshua's] adoption in the manner required by law." The petition also stated that Sharon "intends to retain all her rights to custody and control as to said child." In April 2000, the San Diego County Department of Health and Human Services (HHS), acting in its capacity as an agency licensed by CDSS under the Family Code to investigate and report upon proposed independent adoptions, recommended that the court grant Annette's adoption petition.

Annette and Sharon's relationship has been somewhat volatile. Apparently owing to continuing difficulties, Sharon repeatedly requested postponement of the hearing on Annette's adoption petition. In August 2000, Sharon asked Annette to move out of the family residence, which Annette did. Each retained new counsel. In mediation, the parties agreed on a temporary visitation schedule affording Annette time with both boys, but they could not reach an agreement respecting permanent custody or visitation.

On October 23, 2000, Annette filed a motion for an order of adoption respecting Joshua, contending inter alia that Sharon's consent had become irrevocable pursuant to section 8814.5 and that the adoption was in Joshua's best interest.

After a family court mediator recommended that Sharon and Annette share custody and that Annette have specified visitation, Sharon moved for court approval to withdraw her consent to the adoption. She contended there was no legal basis for the adoption, that her consent had been obtained by fraud or duress, and that withdrawal of her consent was in Joshua's best interest. HHS subsequently filed a supplemental report with the court, noting that Sharon had

---

11. Independent adoptions (Fam. Code, § 8800 et seq.) are those in which no agency, state or private, joins in the adoption petition (*id.*, § 8524), although the state does have a role in investigating, evaluating and commenting upon the petition. (See *id.*, § 8807.) Further unlabeled section references are to the Family Code.

moved to withdraw her consent but had not done so within the statutorily specified period for revocation. HHS further reported that Annette had shared in Joshua's medical expenses and in the planning and handling of his daily care since birth, that Annette had a close and loving relationship with Joshua as his second parent, and that Annette's relationship with Joshua was similar to her relationship with Zachary. Finding that adoption continued to be in Joshua's best interest, HHS again recommended that Annette's petition to adopt Joshua be granted.

In late November 2000, the court ordered interim visitation, encouraged the parties to try to agree on an ongoing visitation schedule, and appointed counsel for Joshua. Shortly thereafter, Sharon obtained a domestic violence restraining order against Annette and moved to dismiss the adoption petition. . . .

DISCUSSION

I. SECTION 8617

"The right to adopt a child, and the right of a person to be adopted as the child of another, are wholly statutory." (Estate of Sharon (1918) 179 Cal. 447, 454.) . . .

As noted, in petitioning to adopt Joshua, Annette has proceeded under the independent adoption provisions. Pursuant to the current statutory scheme, birth parents can consent to an independent adoption by entering into an adoption placement agreement with a prospective adoptive parent. (Fam. Code, § 8801.3; see also Cal. Code Regs., tit. 22, § 35108, subd. (b).) The birth parent(s) have 30 days in which to revoke this consent. (Fam. Code, § 8814.5, subd. (a)(1).) If they fail to do so, their consent becomes permanent and irrevocable. (§§ 8801.3, subd. (c)(2), 8814.5, subds. (a)(1), (3), (b), 8815, subd. (a).)

Once the adoption placement agreement has been signed, the prospective adoptive parent may petition for adoption. (§ 8802, subd. (a)(1)(C).) . . .

Subsequently, it is incumbent on CDSS to "investigate the proposed independent adoption" (§ 8807, subd. (a)) and "ascertain whether the child is a proper subject for adoption and whether the proposed home is suitable for the child." (Fam. Code, § 8806; see also Cal. Code Regs., tit. 22, §§ 35079, subd. (b), 35081, 35083, 35087, 35089, 35093.) . . . Although the report is not binding, the court is to accord due weight to CDSS's expertise. (San Diego County Dept. of Pub. Welfare v. Superior Court (1972) 7 Cal.3d 1, 16.) Assuming other statutory prerequisites are met, if the court is "satisfied that the interest of the child will be promoted by the adoption, the court may make and enter an order of adoption of the child by the prospective adoptive parent or parents." (§ 8612, subd. (c).)

Annette argues that these statutes authorize the superior court to finalize her adoption of Joshua, because she has complied with the substantive and procedural prerequisites for an independent adoption. Sharon contends that the adoption is not authorized, because section 8617 mandates full termination of birth parental rights in every independent adoption.

* * *

A. Waiver of statutory rights

In Bickel v. City of Piedmont, *supra*, 16 Cal.4th 1040 (*Bickel*), we held that a party benefited by a statutory provision may waive that benefit if the statute does not prohibit waiver (*id.* at p.1049, fn.4), the statute's "public benefit . . . is merely incidental to [its] primary purpose" (*id.* at p.1049), and "waiver does not seriously compromise any public purpose that [the statute was] intended to serve" (*id.* at p.1050). . . .

Applying these established principles "to determine whether in this case [section 8617] bars application of the waiver doctrine, we must ascertain (1) whether [the statute's provisions] are for the benefit of [the parties to an adoption petition] or are instead for a public purpose, and (2) whether there is any language in [the statute] prohibiting a waiver." (*Bickel*, *supra*, 16 Cal.4th at pp.1048-1049.)

Addressing the latter point first, we immediately observe that section 8617 contains no language prohibiting the parties to an independent adoption from agreeing to waive its provisions. Rather, section 8617 contains a single sentence: "The birth parents of an adopted child are, from the time of the adoption, relieved of all parental duties towards, and all responsibility for, the adopted child, and have no right over the child." Nor need we move beyond the statute's plain language in order to discern its . . . purpose. By its terms, section 8617 exists to "relieve[]" birth parents of "duties towards and all responsibility for, the adopted child" and to assure adoptive parents of exclusive parental control by ending birth parents' "right over the child" from "the time of the adoption." Section 8617 thus affords all the parties to the ordinary adoption an incentive for concluding it. But nothing therein, or in any other statutory provision, prohibits the parties to an independent adoption from waiving the benefits of section 8617 when a birth parent intends and desires to coparent with another adult who has agreed to adopt the child and share parental responsibilities.

Since section 8617's provisions are for the benefit of the parties to an adoption petition and the section contains no language prohibiting a waiver (*Bickel*, *supra*, 16 Cal.4th at pp.1048-1049), we conclude that section 8617 declares a legal consequence of the usual adoption, waivable by the parties thereto, rather than a mandatory prerequisite to every valid adoption. (*Bickel*, *supra*, at p.1048.)[12]

* * *

---

12. In so holding, we do not decide, contrary to what our concurring and dissenting colleagues suggest, whether there exists an overriding legislative policy limiting a child to two parents. This case involves only a second parent adoption, so we have no occasion to address that point. Justice Baxter errs, therefore, in asserting that our decision today frees a family court to assign at will "as many legal parents as the lone judge deems in the child's best interest." While the Family Code contains in several sections language suggesting the Legislature may harbor a two-parent policy (see, e.g., §§ 3003, 3011, 3161, 3624, 4071, 7572, 7822, 7840, 8604), those statutes are not in issue. Section 8617, which is in issue, does not speak to parental numerosity, except incidentally to recognize in its use of the plural, "birth parents," that a child ordinarily has two of these.

persons. Unmarried persons always have been permitted to adopt children. (See 1 Ann. Civ. Code, § 221 (1st ed. 1872, Haymond & Burch, commrs. annotators) [any adult may adopt any eligible child]; Fam. Code, § 8600 [same].) More generally, Justice Brown argues at some length that our decision today "trivializes family bonds." To the contrary, our decision encourages and strengthens family bonds. As Justice Scalia has noted, the "family unit accorded traditional respect in our society . . . includes the household of unmarried parents and their children." (Michael H. v. Gerald D. (1989) 491 U.S. 110, 123, fn.3.)[14]

Justice Brown purports to discern a legislative "insistence that the adopting parent have a legal relationship with the birth parent," but she cites no authority for the existence of such a requirement, and we know of none. Established legislative policy "bases parent and child rights on the existence of a parent and child relationship rather than on the marital status of the parents." (Johnson v. Calvert (1993) 5 Cal. 4th 84, 89 [discussing Uniform Parentage Act]; see also § 7602 ["The parent and child relationship extends equally to every child and to every parent, regardless of the marital status of the parents"].)

* * *

Sharon argues that reversal of the Court of Appeal's decision will permit CDSS to authorize unusual adoptions, e.g., involving multiple parties, far removed from those contemplated by the Legislature. Justice Baxter also expresses concern that our decision will lead to "new and even bizarre family structures," while Justice Brown inexplicably refers to our supposed "irretrievabl[e] commit[ment] to . . . the-more-parents-the-merrier view of parenthood." Nonsense. While CDSS has for some time treated section 8617 as waivable, such scenarios have not materialized. Our explicit recognition in this case of the legal ground for second parent adoptions—a nonmandatory construction of section 8617 that comports with judicial precedent and ratifies administrative interpretation and practice in which the Legislature has acquiesced—obviously cannot be taken as authority for multiple parent or other novel adoption scenarios. Nothing we say in this case can validate an adoption that is not in the child's interest, omits any essential statutory element, or is in violation of a public policy the Legislature may express. CDSS's construction honors the established principle that the beneficiary of a statute may waive it, is consistent both with judicial precedent and discernible legislative intent, and serves the best interests of California's children.

In sum, adherence to the Court of Appeal's construction of section 8617 as precluding second parent adoption would unnecessarily eliminate access to a duly

---

14. Justice Brown states she would find "reasonable any legislative provision requiring that adopting parents share a common residence" (conc. & dis. opn. of Brown, J., citing § 297, subd. (b)(1) [common residence requirement for domestic partner registration]), but she does not claim the adoption statutes contain any such across-the-board requirement. Nor does Justice Brown explain what bearing her remark might have on the legality or utility of second parent adoption. She does not demonstrate that living apart is a greater phenomenon among couples who utilize second parent adoption procedures than it is among couples who utilize other procedures or, indeed, among parents generally.

promulgated, well-tested adoption process that has become "routine in California" (Eskridge & Hunter, Sexuality, Gender and the Law (1997) p.866) and that is fully consistent with the main purpose of the adoption statutes to promote "the welfare of children 'by the legal recognition and regulation of the consummation of the closest conceivable counterpart of the relationship of parent and child'" (Department of Social Welfare v. Superior Court, *supra*, 1 Cal.3d at p. 6).

2. Settled familial expectations. The Court of Appeal's implication that California courts lack jurisdiction to grant second parent adoptions potentially called into question the legitimacy of existing families heretofore created in this state through established administrative and judicial procedures. Such families are of many types.

Although second parent adoptions may involve children conceived, as in this case, by artificial insemination,[15] others involve children placed directly by their birth parents or private agencies with two unmarried adoptive parents.[16] Others involve dependent children, often with special needs because of prior abuse or neglect, who were placed by public agencies with an unmarried "fost-adopt" parent whose partner later became a second adoptive parent. Still others are "kinship" adoptions, in which a grandparent or other relative became a second legal parent of a child whose very young mother was unable to raise the child on her own. Such adoptions also have involved children born in other countries and adopted either in their country of origin or in California by an unmarried adult whose partner later became a second adoptive parent. (1 Hollinger, Adoption Law and Practice, *supra*, pp.3-3 through 3-18.) Established practice in California thus has created settled expectations among many different types of adoptive families. Affirmance would unnecessarily risk disturbing these.

* * *

Sharon errs in asserting that, even if we were to affirm, persons who previously had completed a second parent adoption would have remedies such as compliance with the domestic partner registration provisions (§ 297 et seq.) if they wish to "ratify" the earlier proceeding. Domestic partner registration constitutes no such panacea. With an exception for some seniors, California's domestic partner registry is open only to same-sex couples, and not to heterosexuals.

Registered domestic partners, moreover, must have a common residence (§ 297, subd. (b)(1)), thus excluding qualified adoptive parents who might live apart for reasons having no bearing on whether an adoption is in a particular child's interest. Similarly, blood relatives cannot register, and therefore cannot adopt, as domestic partners (*id.*, subd. (b)(4)), even though many modern adoptions are kinship adoptions. (See 1 Hollinger, Adoption Law and Practice, *supra*, Placing

---

15. Such children otherwise would have only one parent, as in California a mere sperm donor is not a legal parent. (§ 7613, subd. (b).)

16. "Second parent adoptions may occur when a child's heterosexual parents are unable or unwilling to marry and establish paternity or when the parents are lesbian or gay." (Bryant, Second Parent Adoption: A Model Brief (1995) 2 Duke J. Gender L. & Policy 233, 233, . . .).

Children for Adoption, §§ 3.01-3.02, pp.3-3 through 3-18.) And families that have moved out of state, or where one adoptive parent has died, will not be able to seek ratification as domestic partners. Even for parents who are legally qualified to register as domestic partners, undertaking a "re-adoption" would pose financial hardship and painful legal uncertainty.[17] No parent should have to face these kinds of choices, and no child should be placed in this kind of needless jeopardy.

Nothing on the face of the domestic partnership provisions, or in their history as revealed in the record, states or implies a legislative intent to forbid, repeal, or disapprove second parent adoption or CDSS's forms and procedures facilitating such. Thus, contrary to Justice Brown's assertion, the Legislature's conferring on domestic partners "the right . . . to adopt a child of his or her partner *as a stepparent*" (Sen. Rules Com., Off. of Sen. Floor Analyses, 3d reading analysis of Assem. Bill No. 25 (2001-2002 Reg. Sess.) as amended Sept. 7, 2001, pp.1-2, italics added), far from "confirm[ing] its understanding" that second parent adoption was not available, simply streamlines the adoption process for a subset of those who already were accessing second parent procedures, much as occurred in 1931 when the Legislature streamlined stepparent adoption itself. Domestic partner registration does not broadly secure for California's children the benefits of the availability of second parent adoption, nor does it eliminate the uncertainty the Court of Appeal's decision created for existing second parent adoptees and their parents.

II. CONSTITUTIONAL CONSIDERATIONS

Sharon in opposing review specified two additional questions: whether Annette's adoption of Joshua would violate the constitutional doctrine of separation of powers and whether the adoption would violate Sharon's due process rights under the Fourteenth Amendment to the United States Constitution.

* * *

B. Due process

Sharon in her brief on the merits expressly refrains from arguing that Annette's adoption of Joshua would violate her due process rights, but in opposing review she suggested this case presents that question. She cited in support Troxel v. Granville (2000) 530 U.S. 57, 75 (*Troxel*), wherein a plurality of the high court held that a Washington State statute providing that any person may at any time petition for visitation of an unrelated child, and that the court may order such visitation when it is in the child's best interest, violated the birth mother's substantive due process rights.

---

17. Additionally, privacy concerns undermine the utility of domestic partner registration for some qualified adoptive parents who require confidentiality. While records in adoption cases generally are confidential (§ 9200 et seq.), domestic partner registration requires a declaration that the couple shares "an intimate and committed relationship," in a document generally subject to public disclosure. (§ 298.5; 84 Ops. Cal. Atty. Gen. 55 (2001).)

Troxel is readily distinguishable. Most fundamentally, *Troxel* was a visitation case, whereas this case involves an adoption, and in California the statutes and procedures governing adoption are different from those governing visitation. (Compare generally §§ 3100-3103 with §§ 8600-9206.) The Washington statute at issue in *Troxel* provided specifically that "[*a*]*ny person* may petition the court for visitation rights *at any time*" and that courts may award visitation whenever "visitation may serve the best interest of the child" (Wash. Rev. Code, § 26.10.160(3), italics added). Calling this language "breathtakingly broad," the high court noted it "effectively permits any third party seeking visitation to subject any decision by a parent concerning visitation of the parent's children to state-court review." (*Troxel, supra*, 530 U.S. at p.67.) California law provides for no such freestanding visitation proceeding. Nor is Annette just "any person" (Wash. Rev. Code, § 26.10.160(3)); she is a prospective adoptive mother.

The statute at issue in *Troxel* did not require parental consent (or a finding of parental unfitness), and it was that fact, primarily, that led to its invalidation. (*See Troxel, supra*, 530 U.S. at pp.67-70.) While Sharon now wishes to terminate these proceedings, she does not deny that she originally joined Annette in invoking the superior court's adoption jurisdiction (§ 200) or that she failed to revoke her consent within the prescribed statutory period (§ 8814.5, subd. (3)(b)).

* * *

BAXTER, J., concurring and dissenting. The majority's principal holding — which recognizes second parent adoptions as valid in California — is unremarkable. At least 20 other jurisdictions have already done so (Krause & Meyer, What Family for the 21st Century? (2002) 50 Am. J. Comp. L. 101, 114, fn.23), including the highest courts of three sister states. (Adoption of Tammy (Mass. 1993) 619 N.E.2d 315; Matter of Jacob (N.Y. 1995) 660 N.E.2d 397; Adoption of B.L.V.B. (Vt. 1993) 628 A.2d 1271.) I join fully in that holding.

I part company with the majority, however, over its interpretation of Family Code section 8617, which states that from the time of adoption, the birth parent shall "have no right over the child." I would hold that the parties to an adoption may waive section 8617 in the limited circumstance of a second parent adoption. This is sufficient to resolve the case. Unfortunately, the majority does not stop there but makes the additional holding that section 8617 is a nonmandatory consequence of an adoption and can be waived *whenever* the parties agree to do so. Under the majority's approach, section 8617's termination of the birth parents' rights in *any* type of adoption — not merely those that seek to add a second parent — can be waived by mutual agreement, thus permitting a child to have three or more parents.

This makes new law, not only here but nationwide. Other states — even those states that have already validated second parent adoptions — have not taken this step. . . .

I cannot fathom why the majority has deliberately chosen a rationale that is unnecessary to the disposition of this case *and* that has been avoided by other jurisdictions, but I do understand and fear the effect of the majority's additional holding: to put at risk fundamental understandings of family and parentage.

Tomorrow, the question may be: *How many legal parents may a child have in California?* And the answer, according to the majority opinion, will be: *As many parents as a single family court judge, in the exercise of the broadest discretion in our law, deems to be in the child's best interest.*

* * *

I

BROWN, J., concurring and dissenting. This case raises questions concerning the past, present and future of California adoption law. Regarding the past, I agree that we should not disturb settled familial relationships. Regarding the present, Annette may deserve partial custody based on estoppel. The most important question, however, is whether the California Department of Social Services ought to continue authorizing these second parent adoptions in the thousands of cases that will arise in the future. The Legislature has heretofore required a legal relationship between the birth and second parent, and I would defer to this rule and bar second parent adoptions that violate the statutory scheme.

* * *

II. NEITHER MARSHALL NOR WAIVER PRINCIPLES SUPPORT PROSPECTIVE VALIDATION OF SECOND PARENT ADOPTIONS OUTSIDE THE STATUTORY SCHEME

* * *

A. Marshall

The court in *Marshall* retroactively authorized a second parent adoption by the new husband of a widow and held that "a *husband* and *wife* may jointly adopt a child . . . the result of which is to make the child, in law, the child of both spouses." (*Marshall, supra*, 196 Cal. at p.767, italics added.) The majority both disregards the context and finds the italicized language immaterial, concluding instead that the opinion authorizes adoption by any couple wishing to adopt, regardless of marital status. This reads contemporary norms into a 1925 decision, when the prevailing precedents deemed marriage "the most important relation in life, and one in which the state is vitally interested. . . . The well-recognized public policy relating to marriage is to foster and protect it, to make it a permanent and public institution, to encourage the parties to live together, and to prevent separation and illicit unions." (Deyoe v. Superior Court (1903) 140 Cal. 476, 482.)

* * *

The Legislature also recently extended to registered domestic partners the opportunity to follow the stepparent adoption procedure. Unlike the pre-*Marshall* legal landscape, where there was no statutory authorization for a child to live with a birth parent and a second parent, the law currently provides that opportunity to all couples who comply with the statutory prerequisites by formalizing their relationship.

Thus, even if the *Marshall* court lacked any legislative guidance, we do not. The Legislature has twice prescribed the terms by which a child may gain a second parent without losing the first: only where the two parents are related by marriage or domestic partnership. This court has no authority to reject the legislative rule for one it deems preferable.

* * *

B. Waiver

The majority also asserts that the section 8617 transfer of authority from birth parent to adoptive parents is optional, because it amounts to a benefit for the parents themselves. But section 8617 is but one of many rules governing adoption that exist to effect not the preferences of the adults but the welfare of the child, and thus society itself. The majority's reconstruction of section 8617 ignores this imperative.

. . . There would be no point for the Legislature to specify terms if the adoption were nothing more than a mutually self-interested contract between two adults or couples.

But it is not. "The agreement is *for the benefit of the child*, not of the parents or persons making it." (Estate of Grace (1948) 88 Cal.App.2d 956, 966.) We have explained how a complete transfer of duties and rights is necessary to prevent the confusing position of multiple lines of parental authority. We thus announced the general imperative (from which the *Marshall* court and then the Legislature carved exceptions) that "[f]rom the time of adoption, the adopting parent is, so far as concerns all legal rights and duties flowing from the relation of parent and child, the parent of the adopted child. From the same moment, the parent by blood ceases to be, in a legal sense, the parent." (*Jobson, supra,* 164 Cal. at p.317.)

This rule prevents the child from being burdened with a conflict between the birth parent(s) and adoptive parents(s). If the agreement were simply a means for the birth and adopting parents to effect their private preferences, the law could authorize all permutations of divided rights and duties. The Legislature has concluded otherwise, insisting on an unambiguous transfer of authority unless the birth parent and adopting parent have formally joined together to forge a common future.

III. THE MAJORITY TRIVIALIZES FAMILY BONDS

The majority's reliance on a mutual waiver imports the principles of the marketplace into the realm of home and family, which was once thought to represent a "haven in a heartless world" of self-interested interactions. (Lasch, Haven in a Heartless World (1977).) The family is the area where people act not in accordance with specifically contracted agreements but the duties of the heart. Parents are not simply self-interested utility maximizers. Raising a child is, like hope, a task of the spirit. It is so much more than an aggregation of services.

Parenthood instead is the opportunity and responsibility to join the web of human connectedness through which we touch the past, the present, and the future. The relationship of parent and child is the most fundamental bond humans share and the influence of family in determining what kind of people we become is profound. Society has a considerable stake in the health and stability of families, because it is upon the families—what Burke calls "the little platoon—that we rely [on] not only to nurture the young but to provide the seed beds of civic virtue required for citizenship in a self-governing community. [The family teaches us to] care for others, [and] to moderate . . . self-interest. . . ." (Berns, The First Amendment and the Future of American Democracy (1976) p. 222.) All tasks which will be hampered if the family is simply "a collection of individuals united temporarily for their mutual convenience and armed with rights against each other." (Schneider, Moral Discourse and the Transformation of American Family Law (1985) 83 Mich. L.R. 1803, 1859.) The "arduous, long-term educational process [of raising a child] requires not a spirit of contractualist autonomy, but a spirit of adult commitment and . . . sacrifice." (Hafen, Individualism and Autonomy in Family Law: The Waning of Belonging (1991) 1991 BYU L. Rev. 1, 30.)

The majority, irretrievably committed to its the-more-parents-the-merrier view of parenthood, declines to interpret section 8617 to effectively preclude a child from having more than two parents; and at oral argument Annette's counsel asserted no such limit should exist. Such a position is consistent with the stunted view of parenthood as purely ministerial and economic—signing consent slips and providing health insurance. But this is the least part of being a parent, as anyone who has ever seen a newborn resting securely in her father's hand can understand; and anyone who has sat up late at night awaiting the safe return of a newly minted teenage driver knows. The all-encompassing nature of parenthood renders eminently reasonable any legislative provision requiring that adopting parents share a common residence with each other and the adopted child. (See Fam. Code, §297, subd. (b)(1).) Parenthood requires more than a telephone and a checkbook.

The United States Supreme Court has found parental authority constitutes a zero-sum game. (Michael H. v. Gerald D. (1989) 491 U.S. 110, 118.) Parental authority cannot not be divided because it goes beyond ministerial functions; the parent "direct[s] the child's activities; . . . make[s] decisions regarding the control, education, and health of the child; . . . [and exercises] the duty, to prepare the child for additional obligations, which includes the teaching of moral standards, religious beliefs, and elements of good citizenship." (Id. at p.119, quoting 4 Cal. Fam. Law (1987) §60-02[1][b], fns. omitted.) Devolving these responsibilities on a multitude of parties would lead to a variety of conflicts and inconsistencies, as Justice Baxter correctly notes. . . .

The two-person limit is one point on which proponents of Proposition 22 and Assembly Bill No. 25 agree. The Legislature's insistence that the adopting parent have a legal relationship with the birth parent reflects the fact that the adoptive parent's relationship with the child does not exist in a vacuum but is related to the parents' relationship with each other. Justice Thurgood Marshall wrote for a unanimous Supreme Court in holding it was proper to distinguish between formerly married and never-married fathers in granting only the former the right to veto an adoption by the mother's new husband. (Quilloin v. Walcott (1978) 434 U.S. 246, 256.) "[T]he State was not foreclosed from recognizing this difference in the extent of [the] commitment to the welfare of the child." (*Ibid.*) This "commitment enables the courts, as well as those most personally involved, to make certain assumptions — even knowing they will at times be disappointed — about what to expect." (Hafen, The Constitutional Status of Marriage, Kinship, and Sexual Privacy: Balancing the Individual and Social Interests (1983) 81 Mich. L. Rev. 463, 499.)

The law permits single individuals to adopt a child on their own because one parent is better than none. It does not follow, however, that two unrelated parents are better than one. The majority cites the legislative policy that "adoption or guardianship is more suitable to a child's well-being than is foster care," as adoption is a more permanent relationship than foster care. However, if the birth parent has a relationship with a second parent, and then a third, and then a fourth, the child may be worse off than if the birth parent had simply raised the child alone. The choice in second parent adoption cases is not between adoption and foster care. The birth parent in such circumstances is willing and able to continue expressing parental responsibility. If the two adults are uncertain whether the second parent will be a permanent resident of the household, the adoption ought to wait until they are ready for that commitment.

There is a long-standing tension within the law as to whether legal standards should reflect ideal behavior or simply the mean. The majority, however, refuse to impose even a standard of the mean. Couples who raise children together do predominantly have a formal legal relationship with each other. It is not a standard that individuals cannot reach absent heroism, and every Californian adult has access to such a relationship. Today's decision maximizes the self-interest and personal convenience of parents, but poorly serves the state's children who deserve as much stability and security as legal process can provide.

NOTES AND QUESTIONS

1. What is a "second parent" adoption? How is it different from a "stepparent adoption"?

2. The opinions in *Sharon S* mention that California has passed domestic partnership legislation, which took effect on January 1, 2005, that will extend stepparent adoption to registered domestic partners. Cal. Family Code § 9000 et seq. How do the different opinions in *Sharon S* interpret the significance of the legislation for the issue before the court? Would you expect same-sex couples such as Sharon and Annette who would like to raise a child together to prefer the new provisions to second parent adoption?

3. How do the majority, the concurrence, and the dissent differ on the possibility of multiple parents? Under the majority opinion, is it possible that a married stepfather could adopt his wife's child without severing the parental rights of

the biological father? Why does the law provide generally that an adoption can-not take place without the prior termination of the biological parent's rights?

4. What role does the distinction between married and unmarried couples play in Justice Brown's dissent? How does the majority opinion differ?

5. How does the majority opinion define what is at stake in the waiver issue? Is it a private matter between the parties or an issue of public policy? How does the dissent differ on this point? How would you define the public policies that might underlie the issue?

6. The majority in *Nelson* stated that a construction of the state statute in that case that granted custody or visitation rights to an unmarried partner would raise constitutional issues under *Troxel*. Justice Brown's dissent in *Sharon S* sug-gests that the adoption by an unmarried partner may infringe on the biological mother's constitutional rights. How does the majority distinguish *Troxel*? *See* Nancy D. Polikoff, The Impact of Troxel v. Granville on Lesbian and Gay Parents, 32 Rutgers L.J. 825 (2001).

7. As the *Sharon S* opinions note, many states recognize second-parent adop-tion, and most of the states that have addressed the issue of adoption by a same-sex partner have approved it. In addition to the cases cited in the opinion, *see, e.g.,* In re M. M. D. & B. H. M., 662 A.2d 837 (D.C. 1995); In re Petition of K. M., 653 N.E.2d 888 (Ill. App. 1995); In re Adoption of K.S.P., 804 N.E.2d 1253 (Ind. App. 2004). A few states have, however, ruled otherwise. *See, e.g.,* Matter of Adoption of T. K. J., 931 P.2d 488 (Colo. App. 1996); B.P. v. State (In re Luke), 640 N.W.2d 374 (Neb. 2002); In Interest of Angel Lace M., 516 N.W.2d 678 (Wis. 1994). The Connecticut Supreme Court in In re Adoption of Baby Z., 724 A.2d 1035 (Conn. 1998), held that the state's adoption laws did not permit a child with a natural or adoptive legal parent to be adopted by a second person other than that parent's spouse, but the Connecticut legislature quickly reacted to this decision by amending existing adoption statutes to specifically allow for second-parent adoptions. *See* Conn. Gen. Stat. §§ 45a-724(a)(2) and (3); 45a-731(5), (6), and (7). *See also* Vt. Stat Ann. § 1-102(b)(1995). The Pennsylvania Supreme Court in In re: Adoption of R.B.F., 803 A.2d 1195 (Pa. 2002), also concluded that the state statute permitting adoption without severance of birth parents' parental sta-tus applied only to stepparent adoptions, but nonetheless held that the courts had the authority to approve adoptions without complete compliance with statutory requirements upon a showing that the adoption was in the child's best interests. A New Hampshire statute renders every homosexual person and every family unit of which a homosexual person is a member ineligible to adopt a child. N.H. Rev. Stat. Ann. §§ 170-B:4, -F:6 (1994). The Florida statute Fla. Stat. Ann. § 63.042(3) (West 1995) also renders homosexual persons ineligible to adopt a child. *See* Lofton v. Sec'y of the Dep't of Children & Family Servs., 358 F.3d 804 (11th Cir. 2004) (upholding constitutionality of Florida statute).

PROBLEM

Assume that Sharon and Annette had developed the relationship with each other and with their children that is described in *Sharon S*, except that they do not petition for Annette to become the children's adoptive parent. Annette and Sharon then split up, and the children live with Sharon. Initially, Annette visits the children frequently, but as time goes by Sharon and Annette become more estranged. Sharon eventually stops allowing Annette to visit. Annette files suit, seeking visitation under a statute that allows the "parent" of a child to seek visitation. Sharon has moved to dismiss on the ground that Annette lacks standing under the statute. What arguments should the parties make on the basis of the cases in this chapter?

Would the arguments change if the statute allowed "any person who has maintained a relationship similar to a parent-child relationship with the child" to petition for visitation if that is in the child's best interests?

Would the arguments change if Annette and Sharon had entered into a written agreement that they would continue to share parenting rights and duties if they ever stopped living together, and that the partner who did not have custody would be allowed to visit the child?

If instead of Sharon and Annette, the two parties were Sharon and Andy, Sharon's unmarried male partner, would your analysis be different?

Adoption and Alternative Reproductive Technologies

13

In the last chapter we examined basic principles used to determine who the legal parents of a child are — biology, marriage, and functioning in a parental role. We also looked at traditional premises regarding parenthood, such as the proposition that a child has at least but at most one parent of each sex, and challenges to these premises.

The topics of this chapter — adoption and parenthood by means of alternative reproductive technologies — continue our study of these issues and add new ones. The adoption materials, for example, raise fundamental questions about the role of intention in defining parenthood, how society determines when parents can lose their legal status, and what role, if any, larger groups should play in determining how a child will be raised. Alternative reproductive technologies — artificial insemination, embryo transplantation, and others — also raise these issues and even challenge our understanding of what it means to be a biological parent.

Thus, although the issues covered in this chapter do not arise in practice nearly as often as do those in Chapter 12, they are very important for what they reveal about our understanding of legal parent-child relationships.

A. ADOPTION

BURTON Z. SOKOLOFF, *ANTECEDENTS OF AMERICAN ADOPTION*

3(1) The Future of Children 17, 18, 21-22 (Spring 1993)[1]

Reference to adoption may be found in the Bible and in the ancient codes, laws, and writings of Babylonians, Chinese, Egyptians, Hebrews, and Hindus. It

1. This journal, from which much material in this section is taken, is a publication of the Center for the Future of Children, The David and Lucille Packard Foundation.

is believed that this practice was usually employed to provide male heirs to child-less couples, to maintain family lines and estates, or to fulfill the requirements of specific religious practices such as ancestor worship. It is commonly stated that adoption law in the United States is based upon early Roman laws; however, as Presser points out: "In contrast with current adoption law, which has as its pur-pose the 'best interests of the child,' it appears that ancient adoption law . . . was clearly designed to benefit the *adopter*, and any benefits to the adoptee were sec-ondary."[2] . . . Hollinger adds that the adoptees were all male and usually adults, not children, and concludes that the relationship between adoption as known by the Romans and adoption as practiced by Americans "is tenuous at best."[3]

Likewise, English common law cannot be cited as the precedent for American adoption law because the former makes no reference to adoption and because the first general adoption statute was not enacted in England until 1926, some 75 years after passage of the first adoption statute in the United States. Thus, as Hollinger states, American adoption is "purely a creature of the statutes which have been enacted in this country since the mid-nineteenth century."[4] . . .

During the nineteenth century, adoption laws developed in response to the desire both to give legal status to children whose care had been transferred and to encourage more available and better care for dependent children. . . .

The first comprehensive adoption statute was passed in Massachusetts in 1851 and contained the following major provisions: (1) that written consent had to be given by the natural parents of the child to be adopted or by a legal guardian; (2) that the child himself had to consent if he was 14 years of age or older; (3) that the adopter's wife or husband (if he or she was married) had to join in the petition for adoption; (4) that the probate judge to whom the petition for adoption was presented had to be satisfied that the petitioner(s) were "of sufficient ability to bring up the child" and that it was "fit and proper that such adoption should take effect" before he could decree and confirm the adoption; (5) that once the adop-tion had been approved by the probate court, the adopted child would become "to all intents and purposes" the legal child of the petitioner(s); and (6) that the nat-ural parents would be deprived by the decree of adoption of all legal rights and obligations respecting the adopted child.

The Massachusetts statute is particularly notable in that, for the first time, the interests of the child were expressly emphasized and the adoption had to be approved by a judge.

. . . [B]y 1929 all states had enacted some form of adoption legislation. Virtually all statutes emphasized the "best interests of the child" as the basis for adoption. . . .

During the first half of the twentieth century, *secrecy, anonymity*, and the *sealing of records* became statutorily required and standard adoption practice. The Minnesota Act of 1917 is commonly credited with having initiated the secrecy and sealed records aspects of adoption. Actually, as Hollinger points out, these

---

2. Presser, S. B. The historical background of the American law of adoption, Journal of Family Law (1972) 11:446.

3. Hollinger, J. H. Introduction to adoption law and practice. In Adoption Law and Practice. J. H. Hollinger, ed. New York: Matthew Bender & Co., Inc. 1991, p.1-19.

4. *See* [Id.], p.1-18.

practices "were not designed to preserve anonymity between biological parents and adopters, but to shield the adoption proceedings from public scrutiny. These statutes barred all persons from inspecting the files and records on adoption except for the parties to the adoption and their attorneys."[5] Nevertheless, beginning in the 1920s and extending well into the 1940s, states progressively amended their statutes "to provide not only for the sealing of adoption records, but also for denial to everyone of access to these records except upon a judicial finding of 'good cause.'" In these statutes, the identities of the birthparents and the adoptive parents were to remain secret, even from each other. . . .

The movement toward secrecy is said to have been urged by social workers in child-placing agencies with the goal of removing the stigma of illegitimacy from children born out of wedlock. These workers believed that assuring the anonymity of the birth mothers and the privacy of the adoptive family would make the integration of the child into the adoptive family more secure. . . .

In addition to the passage of adoption legislation, the first half of the twentieth century is characterized by a dramatic increase in interest in adoption on the part of childless couples and in the steady trend toward adoption of infants. Prior to the 1920s very few legal adoptions of children actually took place when compared with the numbers of children in institutions, in foster care, or in situations created by informal transfers. . . .

World War I and the influenza epidemic that followed resulted in a sharp drop in the birth rate and an increased interest in infant adoption. . . . Major factors encouraging infant adoption were the development of successful formula feeding and the perception that environment, not heredity, was the major determinant of child development.

Hollinger describes the end of the first half of the twentieth century as follows:

> By the 1950s, a complete transition had occurred from the earlier interest in adopting older children to the present desire for adoptable babies. . . . A 1951 survey of 25 states indicated that nearly 70% of children being placed for adoption were under the age of one. . . . Well over half of the children were born out of wedlock, two-fifths of the mothers being under 18. The remaining children came primarily from "broken homes." . . . Fewer than 10% of the children were placed because both of their parents were dead.

For more on the history of American adoption law, in addition to the sources cited in this excerpt, *see* Jamil S. Zainaldin, The Emergence of a Modern American Family Law: Child Custody, Adoption, and the Courts, 1796-1851, 73 Nw. U. L. Rev. 1038 (1979); Yasuhide Kawashima, Adoption in Early America, 20 J. Fam. L. 677 (1981-1982); Michael Grossberg, Governing the Hearth 268-280 (1985); Naomi Cahn, Birthing Relationships, 17 Wis. Women's L.J. 162 (2002); Naomi Cahn, Perfect Substitutes or the Real Thing? 52 Duke L.J. 1077 (2003). *See also* The Adoption History Project, *http://darkwing.uoregon.edu/~adoption*.

---

5. [Id.], p.13-5.

Most adoptions today are "related adoptions," that is, adoptions by step-parents and relatives. One-fifth are adoptions of foster children, and only 20 to 30 percent are adoptions of infants by adults who are strangers to them. Uniform Adoption Act, Prefatory Note (1994). In 2000, householders reported that 2.1 million adopted children lived with them; of these, 1.6 million were younger than 18. Adopted children made up 2.5 percent of all children living with the householders who responded to the census. Bureau of the Census, Adopted Children and Stepchildren: 2000 at 1, 3 (Oct. 2003), *available at http://www.census.gov/prod/2003pubs/censr-6.pdf* (last visited Nov. 1, 2004). Adopted children were more likely to live with two married parents (78 percent) than were biological children (72 percent). *Id.* at 15.

State law governs adoption, and specific statutory requirements vary significantly from state to state. The relative lack of success of the most recent version of the Uniform Adoption Act, promulgated in 1994, suggests the lack of consensus on how the law should treat specific issues. Only Vermont has changed its law based on the 1994 version, and it did not adopt the Uniform Act verbatim. *See* Vt. Stat. Ann. ch. 15A §§ 1-101 through 7-105. Nevertheless, it is possible generally to describe adoption as a two-stage process. The first stage is the termination of the parent-child relationship between the child and the parent who is going to be "replaced." The second stage is creation of the new parent-child relationship between the adoptive parent and the child, which under most circumstances requires a judicial proceeding.[6] The next two sections consider the adoption process; the third explores the role that a child's membership in a social group plays in determining whether a child will be adopted and, if so, by whom.

1. Terminating the First Parent-Child Relationship

Before a child with a living mother, married or unmarried, may be adopted by another woman, the first mother's relationship to the child must be terminated.

___

6. While some of the older statutes speak of unmarried fathers "adopting" their children by acknowledging them, treating them openly as their children, or receiving them into their homes, these are really devices for legitimating the child and so are not within the process explained here. See Chapter 12, page 886.

In addition, the doctrine of "equitable adoption," which is based on estoppel principles, is recognized in some states. Under this doctrine, the would-be adoptive parents have agreed to adopt a child, but for some reason the adoption is never completed. Upon a showing of detrimental reliance on this agreement to adopt, the adoptive parents (and their successors) are estopped to deny that the child was adopted, and the child has the same rights that he or she would have if the adoption had been completed. Most of the equitable adoption cases arise in the context of probate of the "adoptive" parents' estates, and the effect of finding that a child was equitably adopted is to give the child inheritance rights. For purposes of Social Security survivors' benefits, equitably adopted children are considered a decedent's children. 20 C.F.R. §404.354(a). For a review of the doctrine, *see* James R. Robinson, Comment, Untangling the "Loose Threads": Equitable Adoption, Equitable Legitimation, and Inheritance in Extralegal Family Arrangements, 48 Emory L.J. 943 (1999).

A father's rights must be terminated before his child can be adopted if he is married to the mother or if, as an unmarried father, he is entitled to substantive custodial rights under state law (see Section B of Chapter 12). A parent may voluntarily give up parental rights by consenting to the child's adoption, and all states also have enacted statutes that allow courts to terminate parents' rights without their consent.

Generally, the legal principles for determining when a parent's rights can be terminated are the same for adoptions by both a relative and a stranger, but the most bitterly contested adoptions are probably stepparent and other in-family adoptions. Often such cases are prosecuted on the grounds that the noncustodial biological parent abandoned the child, but the next case considers the validity of a parent's consent to the adoption of a child by a stepparent.

IN RE PETITION OF S. O.

795 P.2d 254 (Colo. 1990) (en banc)

MULLARKEY, J. . . . Appellant D. J. T. began living with T. O. in 1980 and lived with her for about five years. The two were unmarried during their entire relationship. On June 13, 1983, T. O. gave birth to a son, E. E. F., who is the subject of this dispute. T. O. conceded in an affidavit filed in the subsequent adoption action that D. J. T. was E. E. F.'s natural father. Following E. E. F.'s birth, D. J. T. and T. O. continued to live together with their son for about two and one-half years. During that period, D. J. T. exercised at least some of the duties and responsibilities of a father, although the exact extent to which he did so was disputed by the parties. In the Fall of 1985, T. O. ended her relationship with D. J. T. and, together with E. E. F., ceased to live with him. On October 18, 1985, T. O. married S. O., the appellee stepfather. Following T. O.'s marriage to S. O., D. J. T. continued to maintain a relationship with E. E. F., visiting him periodically in T. O. and S. O.'s home. D. J. T. did not contribute significantly to the costs of E. E. F.'s support, and was not asked to do so by T. O.

In the Fall of 1986, T. O. approached D. J. T. to discuss the possibility that her husband S. O. adopt E. E. F. Among other reasons, according to D. J. T., T. O. and S. O. believed it would be better for the child to have S. O.'s last name and be eligible for his medical coverage. The evidence presented at the juvenile court hearing on the appellant's motion to set aside the adoption indicated that the parties understood that D. J. T. would continue to visit E. E. F. after the adoption. The parties dispute, however, whether such visitation was to be as a matter of right for D. J. T. or only so long as T. O. and S. O. consented to such visits. It is undisputed that when T. O. and S. O. obtained a consent form from the juvenile court, they and D. J. T. brought the form to the office of the clerk of the court and asked a clerk whether they could modify the consent form to include a provision recognizing D. J. T.'s right to visit E. E. F. The clerk indicated "there wasn't any way to change the wording." D. J. T. signed the unaltered form.

On October 23, 1986, T. O. and S. O. filed a Petition for Adoption of a Child in Denver Juvenile Court. Included with the petition were D. J. T.'s and T. O.'s separate consents to the adoption. D. J. T.'s consent included a provision under which D. J. T. waived his right to notice of the adoption hearing. D. J. T. received no formal notice of the hearing and D. J. T. testified without contradiction that he was not otherwise informed of the date and time of the hearing. On November 24, 1986, the juvenile court commissioner conducted a hearing on the stepfather's petition to adopt E. E. F., which D. J. T. did not attend. T. O. and S. O. appeared at the hearing without counsel and were questioned by the commissioner on whether they obtained the consent of the child's natural father. They assured the court that the father understood that the adoption decree would terminate his relationship with E. E. F. The commissioner determined that E. E. F. was available for adoption and that it "would serve the best interests of all of the parties" to enter an immediate final decree of adoption.

Following the adoption, D. J. T. continued to visit E. E. F. although over time T. O. became increasingly reluctant to permit the visits. Finally, in May of 1987, the appellees ceased permitting D. J. T. to visit the child and in August of 1987, they obtained a permanent injunction forbidding D. J. T. from contacting E. E. F. About one month after the appellees ceased permitting D. J. T. to visit E. E. F., D. J. T. contacted an attorney and petitioned the juvenile court for a good cause hearing to obtain access to the adoption file. On January 28, 1988, D. J. T. filed in juvenile court what was designated a "Verified Motion to Set Aside Adoption Decree." On October 20, 1988, the court held a hearing on D. J. T.'s motion, receiving testimony from D. J. T., S. O. and T. O., and reviewed the file in the prior adoption action. The court denied the motion to set aside the adoption decree, finding that the father's consent to the adoption was "knowingly and intelligently and voluntarily executed." D. J. T. appealed that decision to the court of appeals, and this case was transferred to this court. . . .

Before specifically addressing D. J. T.'s arguments, it is useful to review the statutory scheme governing stepparent adoptions. . . . The adoption of a child by a stepparent necessarily terminates the parental rights of the noncustodial parent. To commence a proceeding for a stepparent adoption, the stepparent files an adoption petition pursuant to section 19-5-208, 8B C.R.S. (1989 Supp.). The court must decide whether the child is "available for adoption" pursuant to section 19-5-203, 8B C.R.S. (1989 Supp.). Subsection (1) of that section provides in relevant part:

(1) A child may be available for adoption only upon:

(a) Order of the court terminating the parent-child legal relationship in a proceeding brought under article 3 or 5 of this title;

(b) Order of the court decreeing the voluntary relinquishment of the parent-child legal relationship under section 19-5-103 or 19-5-105;

(c) Written and verified consent of the guardian of the person, appointed by the court, of a child whose parents are deceased;

(d)(I) Written and verified consent of the parent in a stepparent adoption where the other parent is deceased or his parent-child legal relationship has been terminated under paragraph (a) or (b) of this subsection (1);

(II) Written and verified consent of the parent in a stepparent adoption where the other parent has abandoned the child for a period of one year or more or where he has failed without cause to provide reasonable support for such child for a period of one year or more. Upon filing of the petition in adoption, the court shall issue a notice directed to the other parent, which notice shall state the nature of the relief sought, the names of the petitioner and the child, and the time and place set for hearing on the petition. If the address of the other parent is known, service of such notice shall be in the manner provided by the Colorado rules of civil procedure for service of process. Upon affidavit by the petitioner that, after diligent search, the address of the other parent remains unknown, the court shall order service upon the other parent by one publication of the notice in a newspaper of general circulation in the county in which the hearing is to be held. The hearing shall not be held sooner than thirty days after service of the notice is complete, and, at such time, the court may enter a final decree of adoption notwithstanding the time limitation in section 19-5-210(2).

(e) Written and verified consent of the parent having only residual parental rights and responsibilities when custody has been awarded to the other parent in a dissolution of marriage proceeding where the spouse of the parent having custody wishes to adopt the child;

(f) Written and verified consent of the parent or parents as defined in section 19-1-103(21) in a stepparent adoption where the child is conceived and born out of wedlock[.]

Here, there was no independent proceeding terminating D. J. T.'s parental rights. Further, . . . the adoption proceeding did not go forward on the basis that D. J. T. had abandoned E. E. F. but rather on the basis that D. J. T. had consented to E. E. F.'s adoption. Thus, the propriety of E. E. F.'s adoption must be considered under section 19-5-203(1)(f), the only subsection by its terms applying to the circumstances of the present case. . . .

. . . D. J. T. claims that although he consented to the adoption of E. E. F, his consent was conditioned upon his retaining the right to visit E. E. F. Because such right is unenforceable, D. J. T. argues, his consent must be invalidated. . . . We disagree. . . .

[handwritten margin note: DJT's claims]

The juvenile court found that D. J. T.'s consent to the adoption of E. E. F. was "knowingly and intelligently and voluntarily" executed. . . . There is sufficient evidence in the record to support the juvenile court's finding that the consent to the adoption . . . was valid. First, we note that the consent/waiver form was written in plain language, clear and unambiguous on its face. D. J. T. consented to the relinquishment of "all my rights and claim to said child," and agreed that the child would "to all legal intents and purposes, be the child of the person or persons so adopting said child." Further, D. J. T. in his testimony conceded that he was told by a court official that the consent form could not be changed to make the adoption conditional so as to grant him visitation rights. Also, T. O. testified that D. J. T. understood completely that his visitation rights would terminate under the agreement and that he would only be permitted to visit E. E. F. with S. O.'s and T. O.'s permission and that such permission would be granted only so long as D. J. T. did not use illegal drugs. Although there was conflicting evidence on this point, the juvenile court was free to reject D. J. T.'s claim that he signed the consent/waiver form only because he did not realize it would terminate his parental rights vis-à-vis E. E. F.

Because D. J. T. validly consented to the adoption of E. E. F. by S. O., there was no basis upon which to grant his motion to set aside the adoption. A parent's change of heart or subsequent regret at having consented to the adoption of his child is not by itself a sufficient reason for setting aside the adoption. Thus, because the juvenile court properly denied D. J. T.'s motion to set aside the adoption, the judgment of that court is affirmed.

QUINN, J., dissents, and ROVIRA, C.J., and ERICKSON, J., join in the dissent. . . . Because a natural parent has a constitutionally protected liberty interest in the parent-child relationship, Stanley v. Illinois, 405 U.S. 645 (1972), a natural parent's consent to an adoption must be knowingly, intelligently, and voluntarily made. A consent is knowing and intelligent when the natural parent is aware of the import and consequences of an adoption decree to which the consent is directed — that is, that the effect of the adoption decree will be to divest the natural parent "of all legal rights and obligations with respect to the child." §19-5-211(2), 8B C.R.S. (1989 Supp.). A consent is voluntary when it is the product of a free and unconstrained choice of the maker. A consent induced by a promise or representation that the natural parent will retain the legal right of visitation after the entry of the adoption decree, when in fact the natural parent will be divested of such right, obviously does not qualify as a voluntary consent. . . .

I would resolve this case by adopting the reasoning of the Pennsylvania Supreme Court in In re Adoption of Singer, 457 Pa. 518, 326 A.2d 275 (1974), a case factually similar to the instant controversy. In *Singer*, the natural father and natural mother, Frederick and Shirley Singer, were divorced in New Jersey, and custody of their minor daughter was awarded to the mother. Upon the mother's remarriage to Thomas Forbes, the natural father executed an agreement modifying the earlier separation agreement to provide that he would consent to the adoption of his daughter by Forbes and that his visitation rights would continue. The Forbes thereafter filed a petition for adoption in Pennsylvania, and the trial court denied the petition because the natural father's consent was not unconditional. The Forbes then obtained the natural father's signature to an unconditional form of consent and, relying upon that document, again petitioned the Pennsylvania court for a decree of adoption, and the trial court entered an adoption decree. Approximately six months later the natural father filed a petition to open the decree on the basis that he had received no notice of the adoption hearing and that his signature had been obtained by deception. At the hearing to open the adoption decree, the natural father testified that Thomas Forbes told him that the judge had been informed of all the conditions that were involved in the adoption and that the new consent form had the same meaning as the one previously executed by the natural father. The trial court concluded that there was a mutual mistake of fact and law between the parties as to the legal effect and consequences of the adoption decree and ordered that the decree be opened. The Pennsylvania Supreme Court affirmed, reasoning as follows:

> A decree of adoption here would terminate forever all relations between [the daughter] and her natural father. For all purposes, legal and practical, she would be dead to [the natural father] and he would lose his right ever to see her again or ever to know of her whereabouts. . . . The [natural] father simply did not consent to such an adoption. The record clearly indicates that from the time that he first agreed to an adoption in the amendment of the New Jersey divorce decree, [the natural father] never intended to give up his parental rights. Although his signature did appear on the unconditional consent form, it was nevertheless conditioned upon the retention of these rights. . . .

The problem is that the preservation of these rights, even through an informal agreement, or on a goodwill basis, conflicts with the incident of complete control and custody of an adopted child by an adopting parent as contemplated by law. We cannot say that a consent conditioned upon the preservation of certain rights with respect to the child is sufficient to effectively establish the statutorily required consent. The severance of natural ties occasioned by adoption is of such obvious finality as to demand clear and unequivocal consent by a natural parent and we believe that [the natural father's] consent here was insufficient.

457 Pa. at 524, 326 A.2d at 278; *see also* McCormick v. State, 218 Neb. 338, 354 N.W.2d 160 (1984) (relinquishment for adoption not voluntary and hence invalid where natural parents were told that they had a chance to see their son through an "open adoption" — an adoption in which the natural parents continue to have contact with the child — if they signed a relinquishment, and natural parents executed their relinquishment on that representation); McLaughlin v. Strickland, 279 S.C. 513, 309 S.E.2d 787 (S.C. App. 1983) (natural father's execution of a consent to adoption was not valid where the consent was qualified by father's intent to retain parental visitation with child).

NOTES AND QUESTIONS

1. What was the stepfather seeking to accomplish by adoption? Absent an adoption, what was his relationship to his stepchildren socially? Legally? How would adoption change these relationships?

2. Some states have special statutes that make it easier for a stepparent than a stranger to adopt without the consent of the biological parent. *See, e.g.,* Colo. Rev. Stat. §19-5-203(1)(d)(II); La. Ch. C. §1245(C); Mich. Comp. Laws Ann. §710.51(6) (West Supp. 1984-1985). What, if anything, justifies this different treatment of stepparent adoptions?

3. Was the biological father's consent involuntary? Uninformed? Conditional? What should be the test for determining when a parent's consent to the adoption of a child is legally sufficient? Why?

The courts are divided on the question of whether a biological parent's consent is invalid or may be rescinded if it was conditioned on the adoptive parents' agreement to allow visitation. Cases ruling in favor of the biological parent or person having the same parental rights as a biological parent include Matter of Adoption of Topel, 571 N.E.2d 1295 (Ind. App. 1991); Dugas v. Adoption of Dugas, 614 So. 2d 228 (La. App. 1993); In re McDevitt, 162 N.Y.S. 1032 (App. Div. 1917).

Cases holding that the consent was valid even though it was conditioned on the biological parent's being able to visit regardless of whether the agreement is breached, include In re Adoption of a Minor, 291 N.E.2d 729 (Mass. 1973); Matter of Adoption of a Child by D. M. H., 641 A.2d 235 (N.J. 1994). *See also* Mont. Code Ann §42-5-30 ("any relinquishment and consent to adopt remains valid whether or not the agreement for contact or communication is later performed. Failure to perform an agreement is not grounds for setting aside an adoption decree.).

4. Section (1)(d)(II) of the adoption statute quoted in *S. O.* allows a court to permit a child to be adopted without parental consent if the parent has "abandoned

the child for a period of one year or more or where he has failed without cause to provide reasonable support for such child for a period of one year or more." If the stepfather in *S. O.* had petitioned to adopt on this ground, would the evidence have been sufficient to support the necessary finding of abandonment or failure to support? Under what circumstances should it be possible for a child to be adopted over the objections of a parent?

5. If the biological father in *S. O.* had sought to enforce the agreement allowing him to visit after the adoption, instead of moving to set the adoption aside, should the court have ruled in his favor? Why or why not? Are there circumstances in which a court should order postadoption visitation by a parent even when that parent and the adoptive parents have not made an agreement?

6. To what extent do and should the answers to these questions depend on the rights of the biological and adoptive parents? To what extent on the interests of the child? Just what are the interests of the child in cases like this?

7. Traditionally parents facing involuntary termination of their parental status through an adoption proceeding had no right to publicly provided legal assistance if they were indigent, but courts in several states have held that due process requires provision of counsel in such cases. *E.g.*, In re K. L. J., 813 P.2d 276 (Alaska 1991); In re Jay R., 197 Cal. Rptr. 672 (Cal. App. 1983); In re Adoption of K. L. P. 763 N.E.2d 741 (Ill. 2002); In re Bauer, 549 N.E.2d 392 (Ind. App. 1990); In re Adoption of K. A. S., 499 N.W.2d 558 (N.D. 1993); Zockert v. Fanning, 800 P.2d 773 (Or. 1990). *See also* Young v. Alongi, 858 P.2d 1339 (Or. App. 1993) (extending *Zockert* to guardianship proceedings).

NOTE: PARENTAL CONSENT TO ADOPTION

All states permit a parent to consent to the adoption of a child, and all require that consent be voluntary. In addition, some statutes provide that a parent may not give legally effective consent to adopt before a child is born, and some say that effective consent cannot be given until several days (typically three to five) after the birth.

If a parent who gave apparent consent changes his or her mind and can show that consent was obtained by duress or fraud or that procedural requirements were not satisfied, the adoption may be invalidated. However, some cases refuse this remedy on theories of estoppel or laches if the parent raises this claim long after the adoptive parents have assumed physical custody.

Even consent validly given may be revocable. In some states consent is revocable for a set period; in others, it is revocable until an adoption decree is entered. In some states consent is revocable until the entry of the final decree for private adoptions; however, if consent is given to an agency, it is irrevocable. Uniform Adoption Act §2-404(a) provides that consent may be revoked within 192 hours (eight days) after the child's birth. If the consent is executed more than eight days after the child's birth, it is generally not revocable. The act also requires that the biological parent have been informed about the meaning and consequences of adoption, the availability of personal and legal counseling, and procedures for release of identifying and nonidentifying information. *Id.* The document of consent must be executed in the presence of a judicial official or attorney. For further information on the revocability of parents' consent to adoption, including a survey of statutes and cases, *see* Karen D. Laverdiere, Content over Form: The Shifting of Adoption Consent Laws, 25 Whittier L. Rev. 599 (2004).

Physical placement of the child with a prospective adoptive family alone does not amount to consent to adoption. In most states, consent must be given to the court. In some states the biological parents must personally appear in court to give their consent, while in other states a written document expressing consent is sufficient. If the adoption is being arranged by an agency, the biological parents relinquish physical custody of the child to the agency and give written consent to termination of their rights to the agency. After the agency has placed the child with the prospective adoptive parents, it gives the necessary consent during the judicial proceedings.

In many states, adoption of an older child requires that the child consent as well. If the adoptee is an adult, only his or her consent may be required; consent of the biological parents is often dispensed with.

NOTE: GROUNDS FOR DISPENSING WITH PARENTAL CONSENT

All states permit adoption without parental consent on proof of statutory grounds, most often some variation of desertion or abandonment and serious neglect.

To establish "abandonment," courts traditionally have required proof that the parent subjectively intended to abandon the relationship; proof of behavior that objectively suggests a fixed loss of interest in the child was not sufficient. *E.g.*, In re Adoption of Walton, 259 P.2d 881 (Utah 1953). In an effort to facilitate adoption when a parent had effectively abandoned a child, even though the parent expressed a wish to maintain a parent-child relationship, some legislatures have adopted alternative grounds. For example, borrowing from modern juvenile court termination-of-parental-rights statutes, many adoption statutes make a parent's failure to provide support or to communicate with the child for some period, often six months or a year, a ground for permitting adoption without that parent's consent. *E.g.*, Uniform Adoption Act § 6(a)(2).

In addition to being a basis for dispensing with parental consent to adopt, some forms of child abandonment are also criminal. In the face of well-publicized stories about panicked mothers abandoning their babies in trash receptacles and other unsafe locations, at least 41 states have enacted safe haven laws, which provide that parents may leave infants at specific locations without providing identifying information and without running the risk that they will be criminally prosecuted for criminal child abandonment. *See* Child Welfare League of America, *http://www.cwla.org/programs/pregprev/flocrittsafehaven.htm* (last visited Nov. 1, 2004).

NOTE: OPEN ADOPTION AND OPEN RECORDS

Open adoption and open adoption records are significant challenges to the traditions of closed, confidential adoption and to the "substitution" theory of adoption, which treats the adoptive relationship as wholly replacing the biological one.

"Open adoption" means different things to different people. Sometimes it means only that the birth mother or parents choose the adoptive family from a pool generated by an adoption agency. Sometimes it connotes contact between the biological and adoptive parents, before the adoption or after it on an ongoing basis. Birth parents' desire for more control over the placement of their children and for information about what happens to them, and the negative experiences of some adults adopted as children in closed (anonymous and confidential) adoptions during the 1940s and 1950s, have provided the impetus for opening adoptions from the outset. In a four- to six-year period during the late 1980s and early 1990s, one study found that the number of adoption agencies offering adoption with contact increased from 35 percent to 77 percent. The primary reason for the change was client demand. Susan M. Henney et al., Changing Agency Practices Toward Openness in Adoption, 1 Adoption Q. 45, 53 (1998), cited in Naomi Cahn, Birthing Relationships, 17 Wis. Women's L.J. 162, 187-188 (2002). In addition, today adoption is more common for older children, often children who have been in foster care for extended periods, and they often remember and may benefit from ongoing contact with their biological parents. *See generally* Annette Baran & Reuben Pannor, Perspectives on Open Adoption, 3(1) The Future of Children 119 (1993); Marianne Berry, Risks and Benefits of Open Adoption, 3(1) The Future of Children 125 (1993).

The law regarding open adoptions has evolved significantly in the last ten years. At least 18 states enacted statutes during the 1990s that allow written and enforceable open adoption agreements in some circumstances. They are Arizona, California, Connecticut, Florida, Indiana, Louisiana, Massachusetts, Minnesota, Montana, Nebraska, New Mexico, New York, Oregon, Rhode Island, South Dakota, Vermont, Washington, and West Virginia. The Connecticut, Nebraska, and New York statutes allow such agreements only with regard to children in foster care. Cooperative Adoptions: Contact Between Adoptive and Birth Families After Finalization (Sept. 2003), *available at http://naic.acf.hhs.gov* (last visited Nov. 1, 2004).

In the absence of a statute, most courts have refused to order that biological parents or other relatives be allowed to visit over the objection of the adopting parents, usually saying that such an arrangement would inevitably be harmful to the child. *E.g.,* In re Adoption of Child by W.P., 748 A.2d 515 (N.J. 2000); In re Gregory B., 542 N.E.2d 1052 (N.Y. 1989); In re Erik Vaughn D., 417 N.Y.S.2d 863 (App. Div. 1979); Catala v. Catala, 395 N.Y.S.2d 453 (App. Div. 1977). *See also* In re M. M., 589 N.E.2d 687 (Ill. App. 1992); State ex rel. Smith v. Abbott, 418 S.E.2d 575 (W.Va. 1992). However, some courts have entered orders permitting visitation by the biological parent after adoption. *See, e.g.,* In re D. G., 795 P.2d 489 (Mont. 1990); Matter of Adoption of Children by F., 406 A.2d 986 (N.J. Super. 1979); In re Adoption of N., 78 Misc. 2d 105, 355 N.Y.S.2d 956 (Sup. Ct. 1974). *See also* Adoption of Gwendolyn, 558 N.E.2d 10 (Mass. App. 1990) (ordering deletion from trial court order terminating parental rights of a clause that precluded biological parents from visiting, leaving matter to the discretion of adoptive parents).

Only a few appellate cases have addressed the enforceability of open adoption (visitation) agreements between biological and adoptive parents. Most have held that the agreements are unenforceable. *See, e.g.,* Custody of Atherton, 438 N.E.2d 513 (Ill. App. 1982); Whetmore v. Fratello, 252 P.2d 1083 (Or. 1953) (en banc). Cases holding that such agreements may be enforceable include Groves v. Clark, 920 P.2d 981 (Mont. 1996); Michaud v. Wawruck, 551 A.2d 738 (Conn. 1988); Weinschel v. Strople, 466 A.2d 1301 (Md. App. 1983). The *Michaud* court wrote:

Traditional models of the nuclear family have come, in recent years to be replaced by various configurations of parents, stepparents, adoptive parents and grandparents. We are not prepared to assume that the welfare of children is best served by a narrow definition of those whom we permit to continue to manifest their deep concern for a child's growth and development. The record [in this case] demonstrates that . . . the "open Adoption and Visitation Agreement" was openly and lovingly negotiated, in good faith, in order to promote the best interest of the child. The attorney for the child reported that the child thought the agreement between her mother and her soon-to-be adoptive parents would be "the best world that she could imagine." This agreement did not violate public policy.

551 A.2d at 742. These courts usually insist, though, that agreements that a court finds not to be in a particular child's best interests are not enforceable. For collected cases on visitation rights of biological parents after adoption, *see* Danny R. Veilleux, Postadoption Visitation by Natural Parent, 78 A.L.R. 4th 218 (2004).

Researchers in Minnesota and Texas have conducted the most extensive studies of open adoption. These researchers have followed 190 adoptive families and 169 birth mothers since the mid-1980s. The adoptions ranged from fully closed through fully disclosed. Among the most significant findings are (1) high percentages of the adoptive parents and adopted children who had ongoing contact with birth mothers were satisfied or very satisfied with the level of openness, (2) over time the level of openness generally remained the same, (3) relationships were dynamic and had to be renegotiated over time, (4) the extent to which adolescents did not have ongoing contact with their birth mothers varied but was not related to how satisfactory their relationships with their parents were, and (5) there was no relationship between the degree of openness and the children's socioemotional adjustment. Harold D. Grotevant & Ruth G. McRoy, Openness in Adoption: Outcomes for Adolescents Within Their Adoptive Kinships Networks (Nov. 2003), chapter to appear in D. Brodzinsky & J. Palacios (eds.), Psychological Issues in Adoption: Theory, Research, and Application (forthcoming). The lead researchers also conclude that no one type of adoption arrangement is best for all families and that the needs and desires of family members may well shift over time. For more information from the project, *see* Minnesota-Texas Adoption Research Project, *http://fsos2.che.umn.edu/mtarp/default.html.*

An early review of published research found that (1) some birth parents are more willing to consider adoption if they can have continued contact with their children; (2) adoptive parents choose open adoption because they think it will be in the best interests of the child; and (3) the more frequent the contact between the birth and adoptive parents, the less the adoptive parents worried about being the child's "real parents" or about feeling entitled to the child. Marianne Berry, at 134. *See also* Empirical Research on Openness in Adoption 1986-1999 from the Evan B. Donaldson Adoption Institute (1999), *available at http://www.adoptioninstitute.org/policy.polopen1.html* (last visited Nov. 1, 2004).

A second challenge to traditional adoption practice is the trend toward open records. While constitutional challenges to closed record laws by adopted children have generally not been successful, *e.g.,* ALMA Soc'y v. Mellon, 601 F.2d 1225 (2d Cir. 1979), most states allow adult adoptees to have access to nonidentifying information, and all but 14 allow birth parents to access nonidentifying information about adoptive families. In most states, identifying information is available through mutual consent registries, and a few states have statutes allowing adult adoptees to gain access to their adoption records even in the absence of consent by the birth parents. In the absence of such a statute, identifying information is available only by court order upon a showing of good cause. State-by-state information on access laws is available at *http://naic.acf.hhs.gov/general/legal/statutes/infoaccessap.cfm* (last visited Nov. 1, 2004). *See generally* Elizabeth J. Samuels, The Idea of Adoption: An Inquiry into the History of Adult Adoptee Access to Birth Records, 53 Rutgers L. Rev. 367, 426-429 (2001); Naomi Cahn & Jana Singer, Adoption, Identity, and the Constitution: The Case for Opening Closed Records, 2 U. Pa. J. Const. L. 113 (1999). For a discussion of international perspectives on these issues *see* D. Marianne Brower Blair, The Impact of Family Paradigms, Domestic Constitutions, and International Conventions on Disclosure of an Adopted Person's Identities and Heritage: A Comparative Examination, 22 Mich. J. Int'l L. 587 (2001).

Article 7 of the United Nations Convention on the Rights of the Child provides for registration of a child at birth and for the protection of the child's rights to name, nationality, and "as far as possible, the right to know and be cared for by his parents." Some commentators argue that this creates a right to know the identities of one's genetic parents and perhaps to have contact with them. Katherine O'Donovan, "Real" Mothers for Abandoned Children, 36 Law & Soc'y Rev. 347, 351 (2002), citing Jane Fortin, Children's Rights: The Developing Law (1998); Michael Freeman, The New Birth Right? 1 Int'l J. Child. Rts. 1 (1996); Judith Masson & Catharine Harrison, Identity: Mapping the Frontiers, in Families Across Frontiers (N. Lowe & G. Douglas eds., 1996).

PROBLEMS

1. Mary was 17 years old, unmarried, and unemployed when her baby was born. She gave the baby to her 26-year-old stepbrother and his wife shortly after birth. Mary visited the child about twice a year and gave her stepbrother small amounts of money irregularly. She is now 23, married, and settled down. She has asked her stepbrother to return custody of her child, but he has refused, and he and his wife have filed an adoption petition alleging that Mary's consent is unnecessary because she has abandoned the child. Mary insists that she wants and has always wanted to raise her child. What arguments should each side make?

2. Anne placed her month-old child with friends of her family, signing a written relinquishment of her parental rights. She told the would-be adoptive parents that she believed the child's father, George, would consent. However, he did not, and under the law in this jurisdiction there are no grounds for allowing the adoption without his consent. Moreover, unless he can be proven unfit, he is entitled to custody as against the would-be adoptive parents. Anne's lawyer has told her that under this state's law it is very unlikely that George will be found unfit. Anne believes that George will be a very bad father and that the child will actually be raised by George's mother and sister, whom Anne dislikes. Anne has therefore moved to withdraw her relinquishment of parental rights on the grounds that it was conditional on her child being adopted. How should the court rule?

3. When Tim and Bonnie were divorced, Bonnie was awarded custody of their two children, and Tim was ordered to pay child support. Tim's visits were always marked by conflict between him and Bonnie, and he paid his child support irregularly. After a year Bonnie told Tim that if he would quit visiting the children, he could quit paying child support. Tim objected, and he continued to send child support irregularly. He also sent the children birthday and Christmas gifts. Bonnie did not cash his support checks and did not give the gifts to the children. Tim quit trying to visit because he did not want to hassle with Bonnie. Eighteen months after the divorce Bonnie remarried, and six months later she and her new husband petitioned to allow him to adopt the children, alleging that Tim's consent was not necessary because he had abandoned the children. How should the court rule?

4. Timmy was born to Margaret and Dave, a married couple. Dave and Margaret were divorced when Timmy was one year old. Margaret was awarded custody, and Dave was granted visitation and ordered to pay child support. For the last two years Dave has irregularly and reluctantly paid child support, and he has rarely visited Timmy. Recently, though, he told Margaret that if he had to pay, he wanted to see Timmy more often and that he might even seek custody. Margaret, who is 23, and her father, who is 50, suggested instead that Dave relinquish his parental rights and consent to Timmy's adoption by Margaret's father. Margaret and Timmy often see Margaret's parents, who live in the same town, although they do not live with them.

Statutes in this jurisdiction provide that ordinarily when a child is adopted, the parental rights of the child's biological parents must be terminated, but provide this exception: "Whenever a parent consents to the adoption of his child by his spouse, the parent-child relationship between him and his child shall remain whether or not he is one of the petitioners in the adoption proceeding." If Margaret and her father file the adoption petition, along with Dave's written consent, is a court likely to grant the adoption? Why or why not?

2. Establishing the New Parent-Child Relationship — Independent vs. Agency Adoption and Adoption of Special-Needs Children

At least six states — Alaska, Delaware, Illinois, Indiana, Ohio, and West Virginia — require that all adoptive placements be made by a state child welfare agency or a private child placement agency licensed by the state. Four more states — Florida, Kentucky, Minnesota, and Rhode Island — require parents to obtain permission from the state child welfare agency or a court before they make a private placement. National Adoption Information Clearinghouse, Parties to an Adoption (2004), *available at http://naic.acf.hhs.gov/general/legal/statutes/parties.cfm* (last visited Nov. 3, 2004). In such states an exception is usually made for stepparent adoptions. Why?

In the other states private adoptions — that is, ones not arranged by an agency — are also permitted. Private adoptions may be arranged directly between the biological parents and adoptive parents or through an intermediary such as a doctor or lawyer. Most states make it a crime for anyone but licensed adoption agencies to accept money to arrange adoptions. In such states private intermediaries such as doctors and lawyers still arrange adoptions, but they are formally paid only for their medical or legal services. Some states also require adoptive parents to disclose fully to the court all their expenses incident to the adoption.

In most states it is a crime to offer or receive money or any valuable consideration for relinquishing or accepting a baby for adoption. However, it is not illegal to pay expenses to the biological parents, including prebirth and birth medical expenses and professional fees of adoption agencies, lawyers, and doctors. Where offering or receiving money for an adoption is not illegal, payment to a mother may render her consent involuntary. Some states recognize an exception where the agreement promotes the child's welfare and the parent is not in a position to furnish proper care for the child.

Because adoptive parents ordinarily must pay an adoption agency or intermediary and often pay expenses of the biological mother, adoption can be expensive. Agency adoptions cost from $5,000 to more than $40,000, and independent adoptions cost from $8,000 to $40,000. Adoptions of children from foster care cost up to $25,000, and international adoptions are comparable in price to agency and independent adoptions. National Adoption Information Clearinghouse, Costs of Adopting: A Factsheet for Families (June 2004).

The functions of adoption agencies include counseling birth parents thinking of adoption, receiving children to be placed for adoption, screening and counseling prospective adoptive parents, placing children with prospective adoptive parents, supervising the adoptive family for an initial probationary period, approving the adoption, giving legal consent in court, and making a report to the court about the desirability of the adoption. In most states the state child welfare agency functions as an adoption agency, and private religiously affiliated and nonsectarian agencies also exist.

In many states agencies still have a role to play in private adoptions, for statutes require that a licensed agency evaluate the adoptive parents' home and make a report to the court recommending for or against adoption. These "home studies" are typically waived in stepparent and relative adoptions. *See, e.g.,* Uniform Adoption Act part 2.

Traditionally, the agency to which the biological parents release a child selects the adoptive parents, and the agency often imposes age limits and infertility and religious requirements. Sometimes single people and previously divorced but currently married parents are excluded. Adoptive parents who pass these screens may still wait years before a child is placed with them. The trend over the last 40 years has been for agencies to arrange a larger and larger portion of unrelated adoptions.

The debate over the relative merits of agency-mediated and independent adoption is often couched in terms of differing views about how best to protect birth and adoptive parents, as well as children, as the following excerpts indicate.

L. JEAN EMERY, *AGENCY VERSUS INDEPENDENT ADOPTION: THE CASE FOR AGENCY ADOPTION,* 3(1) The Future of Children 139, 139-140, 143-144 (1993):

The goal of adoption is to maximize benefits and minimize risks for those children whose parents are unable or unwilling to rear them. Society, through its designated agencies, assumes responsibility for the care and protection of these children. Adoption, therefore, should not be viewed as a private matter. Although the parties to an adoption have a right to make their own decisions, greater society also has an interest in every adoption. . . .

The Child Welfare League of America (CWLA) believes that meeting society's obligation to act in the "best interests" of the child requires some amount of both study and assistance in every adoption, even those by relatives of the child. Every prospective placement should be reviewed to ensure suitability and to avoid obvious hazards to the child's growth and development. Furthermore, many adoptive parents, relative and nonrelative alike, may require and should be able to receive the help that is needed to understand and meet the needs of the adopted child. . . .

Licensed child welfare agencies are essential participants in the adoption process. Birthparents are typically young, vulnerable, stressed, and in need of skilled counseling about their situation and their options. Prospective adoptive parents usually need assessment and preparation for the task ahead because parenting a child who is adopted involves complex dynamics. The child must be included in all phases of the adoptive process to the extent appropriate for his or her age. . . .

Independent adoption appears to be a service primarily structured to help adults in search of a child. Unlike agency adoption, independent adoption agents most often view adults as the primary clients and tend to see their job as simply finding babies for couples.

The lack of objective counseling for the birthparents at a time when they are extremely vulnerable is one of the greatest concerns about independent adoptions. . . .

. . . Dual representation by one independent agent who represents both the adoptive parents and the birthparents may give the appearance of coercion and certainly creates the possibility of a conflict of interest. In addition, nonagency adoption appears to be primarily a service for middle-class or higher-income adults, shutting out parents in a lower income bracket who might also make good adoptive parents. Fees are usually higher than those of agencies, while services are fewer. . . .

Finally, in independent adoptions, the child is frequently placed in an adoptive home before a home study has been completed and before the birthparents have signed consents because of the desire for immediate placement following the birth of the child. Although immediate placement for the child may be important because of permanence and bonding issues, this move may not allow enough post-birth time for the birthparents to consider their final decision and to assure themselves that the prospective adoptive home is a suitable placement for their particular child.

MARK T. MCDERMOTT, *AGENCY VERSUS INDEPENDENT ADOPTION: THE CASE FOR INDEPENDENT ADOPTION,* 3(1) The Future of Children 146, 146-147 (1993):
. . . [M]ore birthparents choose to pursue independent adoption rather than to

Why choose independent adoption

work with agencies. . . . [I]t is not the adoptive parents, but the birthparents, who have the practical ability to make independent adoption exist. If all birthparents were to choose agency adoption, there would be no independent adoption. . . .

While it is difficult to determine why so many birthparents now choose independent adoptions, they do report some reasons consistently. These reasons include (1) a perception by birthparents that agencies are profit oriented and bureaucratic in their treatment of birthparents, (2) a desire by birthparents to play an active role in the selection of the adoptive parents, and (3) a desire on the part of birthparents for the child to go directly into the physical custody of the adoptive parents rather than into temporary foster care.

From the adoptive parents' perspective, the advantages of independent adoption extend beyond the ability to play an active role in the selection of specific birthparents. Other benefits include the possibility of avoiding the long waiting periods that are typical with agency adoptions and the ability to adopt even though the adoptive parents may not meet the often arbitrary standards imposed by agencies. While some of the agency standards relate to concerns about the ability of the prospective adoptive parents to be adequate parents, other agency concerns have no demonstrable relationship to such ability. For example, because of a supply-and-demand imbalance, some agencies employ qualification standards which include age, religious preference, and place of residence.

As a practical matter, most stranger adoptions are arranged by agencies rather than independent intermediaries. "[A]lmost two-fifths (39%) of all unrelated domestic adoptions are handled by public agencies. Independently arranged adoptions and those handled by private agencies account for similar percentages of unrelated domestic adoptions (31% and 29%, respectively)." Kathy S. Stolley, Statistics on Adoption in the United States, 3(1) The Future of Children 31 (1993). However, a large percentage of the agency adoptions involve special-needs children. "Today the agencies are primarily focused on finding homes for the growing number of children with special needs who are in substitute care. The independent adoption intermediaries . . . are committed to helping prospective adoptive couples find healthy, usually same-race infants, preferably newborns." Center for the Future of Children Staff, Adoption: Overview and Major Recommendations, 3(1) The Future of Children 4, 14 (1993).

The movement to find adoptive homes for special-needs children — which include older children; children with physical, mental, or emotional disabilities; children of color; and sibling groups — began in the 1970s. Judith K. McKenzie, Adoption of Children with Special Needs, 3(1) The Future of Children 62 (1993). In practice, placing special-needs children largely means finding adoptive placements in foster care for children whose parents' rights have been terminated. In addition to increased agency emphasis on placing these children, a number of programs facilitate such adoptions. Some state child welfare agencies encourage people to become foster parents with the promise that they will be able to adopt their foster child if she or he becomes free for adoption. With the support of federal funds, parents who adopt children who have been in the child welfare system may receive subsidies for medical and educational expenses up to the amount of foster care payments until the child is 18, under some circumstances. Almost all the people who adopt older foster children — 80 to 90 percent — have been the child's foster parents first. McKenzie, above, at 71. Adoption disruption has increased along with the adoption of special-needs children.

> Taken on balance, [studies of adoption disruption] suggest that the disruption rate may be about 10% to 15% for children placed when older. For younger children with developmental disabilities, the rates are lower. The low percentages overall represent a high level of success, particularly considering that just 20 years ago, adoption would not have been an option for most children with special needs. . . .
>   The sociodemographic factor most powerfully associated with risk for disruption is the child's age at the time of placement. Risk increases with age.

James A. Rosenthal, Outcomes of Adoption of Children with Special Needs, 3(1) The Future of Children 77 (1993).

With increasing frequency adoptive parents are bringing suit to abrogate adoptions. Some discover that the child has a significant physical, mental, or emotional problem, while others are stepparents who are divorcing the child's biological parent. The traditional view is that adoptive parents may not annul an adoption. Kathleen M. Lynch, Adoption: Can Adoptive Parents Change Their Minds? 26 Fam. L.Q. 257, 260 (1992), citing Children's Bureau, HEW, Legislative Guides for the Termination of Parental Rights and Responsibilities and the Adoption of Children 31 (1961). Courts still rarely grant abrogation motions because of the negative effect such an action has on the child. Id. at 260-263, discussing stepparent cases, and 263-269, discussing two-parent cases.

Some courts recognize an alternative remedy — a tort action against an adoption agency where the agency fraudulently induced the adoption. See, e.g., Roe v. Catholic Charities of the Springfield Diocese, 588 N.E.2d 354 (Ill. App. 1992) (collecting cases). Recently some courts have extended this doctrine to allow adoptive parents to recover for an agency's negligent failure to disclose information they are statutorily required to disclose. See, e.g., McKinney v. State, 950 P.2d 461 (Wash. 1998) (en banc). For further discussion see Erica Shultz, Note, Ignoring Distress Signals: Why Courts Should Recognize Emotional Distress Damages in Wrongful Adoption Claims, 52 Fla. L. Rev. 1073 (2000).

3. Child Placement, Race, and Religion

Racial and religious matching of adoptive parents and children was customary and even legally required through the first two-thirds of the twentieth century. Historically, most of the agencies that arranged foster and adoptive placements were religiously affiliated, and they strongly tended to serve only or primarily adults and children who belonged to their sect. In addition, as we have seen, the dominant approach to adoption has until fairly recently been the "complete substitution" theory, in which adoptions are made to mimic biological parent-child relationships as much as possible. Consistent with this approach, a 1954 survey of more than 250 adoption agencies about their placement practices found that the following factors were ranked as the most important matching factors for adoption: intelligence and intellectual potential, religious background, racial background, temperament needs, educational background, and the adoptive parents' physical resemblance to the child. Laura J. Schwartz, Religious Matching for Adoption: Unraveling the Interests Behind the "Best Interests" Standard, 25 Fam. L.Q. 171, 173 (1991).

During the late 1950s and into the 1960s, adoption practice moved away from this approach and toward greater acceptance of transracial adoption, in part because of the general social changes wrought by the civil rights movement. Another important factor was the emergence of international adoption as an important practice following the Korean War, since most international adoptions are also transracial. Arnold R. Silverman, Outcomes of Transracial Adoption, 3(1) The Future of Children 104, 107 (1993). However, transracial adoption became the subject of strong criticism in the 1970s. Objections were particularly vehement to the high incidence of foster care and adoptive placement with white parents of Native American and African-American children. In 1978 Congress enacted the Indian Child Welfare Act (ICWA), 25 U.S.C. §§ 1901-1963, which explicitly requires racial matching in child placement for Native American children. Following enactment of ICWA, adoption of Native American children by white parents dropped dramatically. Silverman, above, at 107.

MISSISSIPPI BAND OF CHOCTAW INDIANS V. HOLYFIELD

490 U.S. 30 (1989)

BRENNAN, J. . . . The Indian Child Welfare Act of 1978 (ICWA), 92 Stat. 3069, 25 U.S.C. §§ 1901-1963, was the product of rising concern in the mid-1970's over the consequences to Indian children, Indian families, and Indian tribes of abusive child welfare practices that resulted in the separation of large numbers of Indian children from their families and tribes through adoption or foster care placement, usually in non-Indian homes. Senate oversight hearings in 1974 yielded numerous examples, statistical data, and expert testimony documenting what one witness called "the wholesale removal of Indian children from their homes, . . . the most tragic aspect of Indian life today." Studies undertaken by the Association on American Indian Affairs in 1969 and 1974, and presented in the Senate hearings, showed that 25 to 35 percent of all Indian children had been separated from their families and placed in adoptive families, foster care, or institutions. Adoptive placements counted significantly in this total: in the State of Minnesota, for example, one in eight Indian children under the age of 18 was in an adoptive home, and during the year 1971-1972 nearly one in every four infants under one year of age was placed for adoption. The adoption rate of Indian children was eight times that of non-Indian children. Approximately 90% of the Indian placements were in non-Indian homes. A number of witnesses also testified to the serious adjustment problems encountered by such children during adolescence, as well as the impact of the adoptions on Indian parents and the tribes themselves.

Further hearings, covering much the same ground, were held during 1977 and 1978 on the bill that became the ICWA. While much of the testimony again focused on the harm to Indian parents and their children who were involuntarily separated by decisions of local welfare authorities, there was also considerable emphasis on the impact on the tribes themselves of the massive removal of their children. For example, Mr. Calvin Isaac, Tribal Chief of the Mississippi Band of Choctaw Indians and representative of the National Tribal Chairmen's Association, testified as follows:

> Culturally, the chances of Indian survival are significantly reduced if our children, the only real means for the transmission of the tribal heritage, are to be raised in non-Indian homes and denied exposure to the ways of their People. Furthermore, these practices seriously undercut the tribes' ability to continue as self-governing communities. Probably in no area is it more important that tribal sovereignty be respected than in an area as socially and culturally determinative as family relationships.

1978 Hearings, at 193. *See also* id., at 62. Chief Isaac also summarized succinctly what numerous witnesses saw as the principal reason for the high rates of removal of Indian children:

> One of the most serious failings of the present system is that Indian children are removed from the custody of their natural parents by nontribal government authorities who have no basis for intelligently evaluating the cultural and social premises underlying Indian home life and childrearing. Many of the individuals who decide the fate of our children are at best ignorant of our cultural values, and at worst contemptful of the Indian way and convinced that removal, usually to a non-Indian household or institution, can only benefit an Indian child.

Id., at 191-192.[7]

The congressional findings that were incorporated into the ICWA reflect these sentiments. The Congress found:

> (3) that there is no resource that is more vital to the continued existence and integrity of Indian tribes than their children . . . ;
>
> (4) that an alarmingly high percentage of Indian families are broken up by the removal, often unwarranted, of their children from them by nontribal public and

---

7. One of the particular points of concern was the failure of non-Indian child welfare workers to understand the role of the extended family in Indian society. The House Report on the ICWA noted: "An Indian child may have scores of, perhaps more than a hundred, relatives who are counted as close, responsible members of the family. Many social workers, untutored in the ways of Indian family life or assuming them to be socially irresponsible, consider leaving the child with persons outside the nuclear family as neglect and thus as grounds for terminating parental rights." House Report, at 10, U.S. Code Cong. & Admin. News 1978, at 7532. At the conclusion of the 1974 Senate hearings, Senator Abourezk noted the role that such extended families played in the care of children: "We've had testimony here that in Indian communities throughout the Nation there is no such thing as an abandoned child because when a child does have a need for parents for one reason or another, a relative or a friend will take that child in. It's the extended family concept." 1974 Hearings 473. See also Wisconsin Potowatomies of Hannahville Indian Community v. Houston, 393 F. Supp. 719 (WD Mich. 1973) (discussing custom of extended family and tribe assuming responsibility for care of orphaned children).

private agencies and that an alarmingly high percentage of such children are placed in non-Indian foster and adoptive homes and institutions; and

(5) that the States, exercising their recognized jurisdiction over Indian child custody proceedings through administrative and judicial bodies, have often failed to recognize the essential tribal relations of Indian people and the cultural and social standards prevailing in Indian communities and families.

25 U.S.C. § 1901.

At the heart of ICWA are its provisions concerning jurisdiction over Indian child custody proceedings. Section 1911 lays out a dual jurisdictional scheme. Section 1911(a) establishes exclusive jurisdiction in the tribal courts for proceedings concerning an Indian child "who resides or is domiciled within the reservation of such tribe," as well as for wards of tribal courts regardless of domicile. Section 1911(b), on the other hand, creates concurrent but presumptively tribal jurisdiction in the case of children not domiciled on the reservation: on petition of either parent or the tribe, state-court proceedings for foster care placement or termination of parental rights are to be transferred to the tribal court, except in cases of "good cause," objection by either parent, or declination of jurisdiction by the tribal court. . . .

This case involves the status of twin babies, known for our purposes as B. B. and G. B., who were born out of wedlock on December 29, 1985. Their mother, J. B., and father, W. J., were both enrolled members of appellant Mississippi Band of Choctaw Indians (Tribe), and were residents and domiciliaries of the Choctaw Reservation in Neshoba County, Mississippi. J. B. gave birth to the twins in Gulfport, Harrison County, Mississippi, some 200 miles from the reservation. On January 10, 1986, J. B. executed a consent-to-adoption form before the Chancery Court of Harrison County. Record 8-10. W. J. signed a similar form. On January 16, appellees Orrey and Vivian Holyfield filed a petition for adoption in the same court, id., at 1-5, and the chancellor issued a Final Decree of Adoption on January 28. Id., at 13-14. Despite the court's apparent awareness of the ICWA, the adoption decree contained no reference to it, nor to the infants' Indian background.

Two months later the Tribe moved in the Chancery Court to vacate the adoption decree on the ground that under the ICWA exclusive jurisdiction was vested in the tribal court. Id., at 15-18. On July 14, 1986, the court overruled the motion, holding that the Tribe "never obtained exclusive jurisdiction over the children involved herein. . . ." The court's one-page opinion relied on two facts in reaching that conclusion. The court noted first that the twins' mother "went to some efforts to see that they were born outside the confines of the Choctaw Indian Reservation" and that the parents had promptly arranged for the adoption by the Holyfields. Second, the court stated: "At no time from the birth of these children to the present date have either of them resided on or physically been on the Choctaw Indian Reservation." Id., at 78.

[The Mississippi Supreme Court affirmed on the basis that, under state law, the children's parents had abandoned them when they relinquished them for adoption and that the domicile of abandoned children is that of adults who stand in loco parentis to them.] . . .

The meaning of "domicile" in the ICWA is, of course, a matter of Congress's intent. The ICWA itself does not define it. The initial question we must confront is whether there is any reason to believe that Congress intended the ICWA definition of "domicile" to be a matter of state law. . . .

First, and most fundamentally, the purpose of the ICWA gives no reason to believe that Congress intended to rely on state law for the definition of a critical term; quite the contrary. It is clear from the very text of the ICWA, not to mention its legislative history and the hearings that led to its enactment, that Congress was concerned with the rights of Indian families and Indian communities vis-à-vis state authorities. More specifically, its purpose was, in part, to make clear that in certain situations the state courts did not have jurisdiction over child custody proceedings. . . . Under these circumstances it is most improbable that Congress would have intended to leave the scope of the statute's key jurisdictional provision subject to definition by state courts as a matter of state law.

Second, Congress could hardly have intended the lack of nationwide uniformity that would result from state-law definitions of domicile. . . .

We therefore think it beyond dispute that Congress intended a uniform federal law of domicile for the ICWA. . . .

That we are dealing with a uniform federal rather than a state definition does not, of course, prevent us from drawing on general state-law principles to determine "the ordinary meaning of the words used." Well-settled state law can inform our understanding of what Congress had in mind when it employed a term it did not define. Accordingly, we find it helpful to borrow established common-law principles of domicile to the extent that they are not inconsistent with the objectives of the congressional scheme.

"Domicile" is, of course, a concept widely used in both federal and state courts for jurisdiction and conflict-of-laws purposes, and its meaning is generally uncontroverted. "Domicile" is not necessarily synonymous with "residence," and one can reside in one place but be domiciled in another. For adults, domicile is established by physical presence in a place in connection with a certain state of mind concerning one's intent to remain there. One acquires a "domicile of origin" at birth, and that domicile continues until a new one (a "domicile of choice") is acquired. Since most minors are legally incapable of forming the requisite intent to establish a domicile, their domicile is determined by that of their parents. In the case of an illegitimate child, that has traditionally meant the domicile of its mother. . . .

It is undisputed in this case that the domicile of the mother (as well as the father) has been, at all relevant times, on the Choctaw Reservation. Thus, it is clear that at their birth the twin babies were also domiciled on the reservation, even though they themselves had never been there. . . .

Nor can the result be any different simply because the twins were "voluntarily surrendered" by their mother. Tribal jurisdiction under § 1911(a) was not meant to be defeated by the actions of individual members of the tribe, for Congress was concerned not solely about the interests of Indian children and families, but also about the impact on the tribes themselves of the large numbers of Indian children adopted by non-Indians. . . .

In addition, it is clear that Congress's concern over the placement of Indian children in non-Indian homes was based in part on evidence of the detrimental impact on the children themselves of such placements outside their culture. Congress determined to subject such placements to the ICWA's jurisdictional and other provisions, even in cases where the parents consented to an adoption, because of concerns going beyond the wishes of individual parents. . . .

These congressional objectives make clear that a rule of domicile that would permit individual Indian parents to defeat the ICWA's jurisdictional scheme is inconsistent with what Congress intended. The appellees in this case argue strenuously that the twins' mother went to great lengths to give birth off the reservation so that her children could be adopted by the Holyfields. But that was precisely part of Congress's concern. Permitting individual members of the tribe to avoid tribal exclusive jurisdiction by the simple expedient of giving birth off the reservation would, to a large extent, nullify the purpose the ICWA was intended to accomplish.

. . . Since, for purposes of the ICWA, the twin babies in this case were domiciled on the reservation when adoption proceedings were begun, the Choctaw tribal court possessed exclusive jurisdiction pursuant to 25 U.S.C. § 1911(a). The Chancery Court of Harrison County was, accordingly, without jurisdiction to enter a decree of adoption; under ICWA § 104, 25 U.S.C. § 1914 its decree of January 28, 1986, must be vacated.

III

We are not unaware that over three years have passed since the twin babies were born and placed in the Holyfield home, and that a court deciding their fate today is not writing on a blank slate in the same way it would have in January 1986. Three years' development of family ties cannot be undone, and a separation at this point would doubtless cause considerable pain.

Whatever feelings we might have as to where the twins should live, however, it is not for us to decide that question. We have been asked to decide the legal question of who should make the custody determination concerning these children — not what the outcome of that determination should be. The law places that decision in the hands of the Choctaw tribal court. Had the mandate of the ICWA been followed in 1986, of course, much potential anguish might have been avoided, and in any case the law cannot be applied so as automatically to "reward those who obtain custody, whether lawfully or otherwise, and maintain it during any ensuing (and protracted) litigation." Halloway, supra, at 972. It is not ours to say whether the trauma that might result from removing these children from their adoptive family should outweigh the interest of the Tribe — and perhaps the children themselves — in having them raised as part of the Choctaw community. Rather, "we must defer to the experience, wisdom, and compassion of the [Choctaw] tribal courts to fashion an appropriate remedy." Ibid.

The judgment of the Supreme Court of Mississippi is reversed and the case remanded for further proceedings not inconsistent with this opinion. It is so ordered.

STEVENS, J., with whom the Chief Justice and KENNEDY, J. join, dissenting. . . .
The [ICWA] gives Indian tribes certain rights, not to restrict the rights of parents

of Indian children, but to complement and help effect them. The Indian tribe may petition to transfer an action in state court to the tribal court, but the Indian parent may veto the transfer. § 1911(b). The Act provides for a tribal right of notice and intervention in involuntary proceedings but not in voluntary ones. §§ 1911(c), 1912(a). Finally, the tribe may petition the court to set aside a parental termination action upon a showing that the provisions of the ICWA that are designed to protect parents and Indian children have been violated. § 1914.

While the Act's substantive and procedural provisions effect a major change in state child custody proceedings, its jurisdictional provision is designed primarily to preserve tribal sovereignty over the domestic relations of tribe members and to confirm a developing line of cases which held that the tribe's exclusive jurisdiction could not be defeated by the temporary presence of an Indian child off the reservation. . . .

Although parents of Indian children are shielded from the exercise of state jurisdiction when they are temporarily off the reservation, the Act also reflects a recognition that allowing the tribe to defeat the parents' deliberate choice of jurisdiction would be conducive neither to the best interests of the child nor to the stability and security of Indian tribes and families. Section 1911(b), providing for the exercise of concurrent jurisdiction by state and tribal courts when the Indian child is not domiciled on the reservation, gives the Indian parents a veto to prevent the transfer of a state court action to tribal court. "By allowing the Indian parents to 'choose' the forum that will decide whether to sever the parent-child relationship, Congress promotes the security of Indian families by allowing the Indian parents to defend in the court system that most reflects the parents' familial standards." Jones, 21 Ariz. L. Rev., at 1141. As Mr. Calvin Isaac, Tribal Chief of the Mississippi Band of Choctaw Indians, stated in testimony to the House Subcommittee on Indian Affairs and Public Lands with respect to a different provision:

> The ultimate responsibility for child welfare rests with the parents and we would not support legislation which interfered with that basic relationship. Hearings on S. 1214 before the Subcommittee on Indian Affairs and Public Lands of the House Committee on Interior and Insular Affairs, 95th Cong., 2d Sess., 62 (1978).[8]

If J. B. and W. J. had established a domicile off the reservation, the state courts would have been required to give effect to their choice of jurisdiction; there should not be a different result when the parents have not changed their own domicile, but have expressed an unequivocal intent to establish a domicile for their children off the reservation. The law of abandonment, as enunciated by the Mississippi Supreme Court in this case, does not defeat, but serves the purposes

---

8. Chief Isaac elsewhere expressed a similar concern for the rights of parents with reference to another provision. *See* Hearing, at 158 (Statement of Calvin Isaac on behalf of National Tribal Chairmen's Association) ("We believe the tribe should receive notice in all such cases but where the child is neither a resident nor domiciliary of the reservation intervention should require the consent of the natural parents or the blood relative in whose custody the child has been left by the natural parents. It seems there is a great potential in the provisions of section 101(c) for infringing parental wishes and rights.").

of the Act. An abandonment occurs when a parent deserts a child and places the child with another with an intent to relinquish all parental rights and obligations. . . . If the child is abandoned by both parents, he takes on the domicile of a person other than the parents who stand in *loco parentis* to him. . . .

. . . [W]hen an Indian child is deliberately abandoned by both parents to a person off the reservation, no purpose of the ICWA is served by closing the state courthouse door to them. The interests of the parents, the Indian child, and the tribe in preventing the unwarranted removal of Indian children from their families and from the reservation are protected by the Act's substantive and procedural provisions. In addition, if both parents have intentionally invoked the jurisdiction of the state court in an action involving a non-Indian, no interest in tribal self-governance is implicated.

The interpretation of domicile adopted by the Court requires the custodian of an Indian child who is off the reservation to haul the child to a potentially distant tribal court unfamiliar with the child's present living conditions and best interests. Moreover, it renders any custody decision made by a state court forever suspect, susceptible to challenge at any time as void for having been entered in the absence of jurisdiction.[9] Finally, it forces parents of Indian children who desire to invoke state court jurisdiction to establish a domicile off the reservation. Only if the custodial parent has the wealth and ability to establish a domicile off the reservation will the parent be able to use the processes of state court. I fail to see how such a requirement serves the paramount congressional purpose of "promot[ing] the stability and security of Indian tribes and families." 25 U.S.C. § 1902.

The Court concludes its opinion with the observation that whatever anguish is suffered by the Indian children, their natural parents, and their adoptive parents because of its decision today is a result of their failure to initially follow the provisions of the ICWA. . . . By holding that parents who are domiciled on the reservation cannot voluntarily avail themselves of the adoption procedures of state court and that all such proceedings will be void for lack of jurisdiction, however, the Court establishes a rule of law that is virtually certain to ensure that similar anguish

---

9. The facts of In re Adoption of Halloway, 732 P.2d 962 (Utah 1986), which the Court cites approvingly, . . . , vividly illustrate the problem. In that case, the mother, a member of an Indian Tribe in New Mexico, voluntarily abandoned an Indian child to the custody of the child's maternal aunt off the reservation with the knowledge that the child would be placed for adoption in Utah. The mother learned of the adoption two weeks after the child left the reservation and did not object and, two months later, she executed a consent to adoption. Nevertheless, some two years after the petition for adoption was filed, the Indian Tribe intervened in the proceeding and set aside the adoption. The Tribe argued successfully that regardless of whether the Indian parent consented to it, the adoption was void because she resided on the reservation and thus the tribal court had exclusive jurisdiction. Although the decision in Halloway, and the Court's approving reference to it, may be colored somewhat by the fact that the mother in that case withdrew her consent (a fact which would entitle her to relief even if there were only concurrent jurisdiction, *see* 25 U.S.C. § 1913(c)), the rule set forth by the majority contains no such limitation. As the Tribe acknowledged at oral argument, any adoption of an Indian child effected through a state court will be susceptible of challenge by the Indian tribe no matter how old the child and how long it has lived with its adoptive parents.

will be suffered by other families in the future. Because that result is not mandated by the language of the ICWA and is contrary to its purposes, I respectfully dissent.

NOTES AND QUESTIONS

1. On what theory did the Mississippi court determine that the children were domiciled off the reservation? What theory of domicile did the Supreme Court adopt? Why? Under what circumstances, if any, would the children have been domiciled off the reservation under the Supreme Court's theory?

2. The majority concludes that individual Indian parents cannot "defeat ICWA's jurisdiction scheme" by placing children for adoption off the reservation. To whom does the Court's opinion give authority to decide about the adoption of a child domiciled on a reservation? What is the justification for this limitation on parental prerogatives?

3. Does ICWA subordinate the child's and the parents' interests to those of the tribe? What theory of the best interests of the child supports the ICWA approach to custody? What alternative view(s) would support greater deference to parental choice?

4. In both *Holyfield* and *Halloway*, discussed in the text and footnotes, an appellate court concluded that the court that had granted the adoption had wrongfully asserted jurisdiction years after the child had been placed with the would-be adoptive parents. In the meantime, of course, the child and the adoptive parents had been living as a family. When an error of this kind is made, what should be the remedy? Does it make sense to ignore all the expectations and relationships that have developed over time? On the other hand, is any other remedy effective? In *Holyfield* the Court holds that the case must be returned to tribal court. What will be the issue before that court?

Barbara Kingsolver's novels *The Bean Trees* (1988) and *Pigs in Heaven* (1993) involve the adoption of an Indian child domiciled on the reservation by a white woman, the efforts of a Native American attorney to assert the tribe's rights, and the ultimate decision by the tribal court. *See also* Christine Metteer, Pigs in Heaven: A Parable of Native American Adoption Under the Indian Child Welfare Act, 28 Ariz. St. L.J. 589 (1996).

5. ICWA applies to foster care and preadoptive placements, adoption, and termination of parental rights of Indian children, but not to custody disputes following divorce. 25 U.S.C. § 1903(1). The courts are divided about its applicability to other intrafamilial custody disputes. *See* Custody of A. K. H., 502 N.W.2d 790 (Minn. App. 1993), for a review of the cases.

6. A critical question for purposes of determining the applicability of the ICWA is whether the child whose custody is at stake is an "Indian child." The statute defines this term to include any unmarried person less than 18 years old who is an enrolled member of an Indian tribe, the biological child of a member of an Indian tribe, or the biological child of a member of an Indian tribe who is also eligible for membership. 25 U.S.C. § 1903(4).

However, courts in at least 11 states, including Alabama, California, Indiana, Kansas, Kentucky, Louisiana, Missouri, Montana, Oklahoma, Tennessee, and

Washington, have crafted an exception to this principle, which provides that ICWA does not govern if the child does not belong to an "existing Indian family," on the theory that in such situations the policies underlying ICWA do not apply. S. A. v. E. J. P., 571 So. 2d 1187 (Ala. Civ. App. 1990); In re Bridget R., 49 Cal. Rptr. 2d 507 (Cal. App. 1996); Matter of Adoption of T. R. M., 525 N.E.2d 298 (Ind. 1988); Matter of Adoption of Baby Boy L., 643 P.2d 168 (Kan. 1982); Rye v. Weasel, 934 S.D.2d 257 (Ky. 1996); Hampton v. J. A. L., 658 So. 2d 331 (La. App. 1995); In the Interest of S. A. M., 703 S.W.2d 603 (Mo. App. 1986); Matter of T. S., 801 P.2d 77 (Mont. 1990); Matter of Adoption of D. M. J., 741 P.2d 1386 (Okla. 1985); In re Morgan, 1997 WL 716880 (Tenn. App. 1997); In re Adoption of Crews, 825 P.2d 305 (Wash. 1992). *But see* S.H. v. Calhoun Ct. Dep't of Human Resources, 748 So.2d 684 (Ala. App. 2001), suggesting rejection of the exception.

In one of the most extensive opinions, *Bridget R.*, the court suggested that if ICWA were not interpreted to include the "existing Indian family exception," it would violate the Fifth, Tenth, and Fourteenth Amendments. Some courts that have adopted this test apply it if neither the child nor a parent has ever lived with a Native American family and has no association with Native American culture. *See, e.g.,* In re Adoption of Crews, above; Hampton v. J.A.L., above. Other courts apply the test if the child has no such ties, regardless of the parent's connections. *See, e.g.,* Matter of Adoption of Baby Boy L., above; In the Interest of S. A. M., above. In response to *Bridget R.*, the California legislature enacted Cal. Welf. & Inst. Code § 360.6, which provides:

(a) The Legislature finds and declares the following:

(1) There is no resource that is more vital to the continued existence and integrity of Indian tribes than their children, and the State of California has an interest in protecting Indian children who are members of, or are eligible for membership in, an Indian tribe.

(2) It is in the interest of an Indian child that the child's membership in the child's Indian tribe and connection to the tribal community be encouraged and protected.

(b) In all Indian child custody proceedings, as defined in the federal Indian Child Welfare Act (25 U.S.C. § 1901 et seq.), the court shall consider all of the findings contained in subdivision (a), strive to promote the stability and security of Indian tribes and families, comply with the federal Indian Child Welfare Act, and seek to protect the best interest of the child.

(c) A determination by an Indian tribe that an unmarried person, who is under the age of 18 years, is either (1) a member of an Indian tribe or (2) eligible for membership in an Indian tribe and a biological child of a member of an Indian tribe shall constitute a significant political affiliation with the tribe and shall require the application of the federal Indian Child Welfare Act to the proceedings.

In re Santos Y., 112 Cal. Rptr. 2d 692 (Cal. App. 2001), concluded that, notwithstanding the statute, the Constitution still limits the applicability of ICWA and specifically held that state interests underlying ICWA were not sufficient to justify depriving a child of his relationship with his foster family where he was a "multiethnic child who has had a minimal relationship with his assimilated parents."

Courts in at least ten states have rejected the existing Indian family doctrine on the basis that the exception is not supported by the statute and that it undermines the primary purposes of the ICWA and undermines tribal sovereignty. These cases include Alaska, Arizona, California, Idaho, Illinois, Michigan, New Jersey, Oregon, South Dakota, and Utah. A. B. M. v. M. H., 651 P.2d 1170 (Alaska 1982); Michael J. v. Michael J., 7 P.3d 960 (Az. App. 2000); In re Alicia S., 76 Cal. Rptr. 2d 121 (Cal. App. 1998); In re Baby Boy Doe, 849 P.2d 925 (Idaho 1993); In re Adoption of S.S., 657 N.E.2d 935 (Ill. 1995); In re Elliott, 554 N.W.2d 32 (Mich. 1996); In re A Child of Indian Heritage, 543 A.2d 925 (N.J. 1988); In re Adoption of Quinn, 845 P.2d 206 (Or. App. 1993), *rev'd on other grounds*, 881 P.2d 795 (Or. 1994); In re Baade, 462 N.W.2d 485 (S.D. 1990); State in Interest of D. A. C., 933 P.2d 993 (Utah 1997).

Does the Supreme Court's opinion in *Holyfield* preclude use of the "existing Indian family" doctrine?

7. ICWA includes other procedural safeguards that make it difficult to remove a Native American child from home. These rules apply only to state court proceedings. The most important are the following:

a. Before a state court may remove a child involuntarily, the court must find that efforts were made to provide services to prevent the breakup of the family and that the efforts were unsuccessful. 25 U.S.C. § 1912.

b. In an involuntary proceeding, the petitioner must prove (by clear and convincing evidence for foster placement and beyond a reasonable doubt for termination of parental rights) that leaving the child in the home is likely to result in serious emotional or physical damage to the child. The petitioner must present testimony from an expert in Indian child rearing and cultural practices to satisfy this burden. 25 U.S.C. § 1912.

c. Voluntary consent to termination of parental rights may be given no earlier than ten days after the birth, and it must be executed in writing and recorded before a judge, who must certify that the terms and consequences of the consent were fully explained and understood. Consent to termination of parental rights or adoption can be withdrawn at any time before a final decree is entered. 25 U.S.C. § 1913. Violation of this section is grounds for setting aside an order. 25 U.S.C. § 1914.

8. ICWA also contains substantive placement preferences that bind state courts. A child removed from home must be placed in the least restrictive setting (one that most approximates a family home) in which the child's special needs can be met. If the child is placed in foster care, a state court must give preference to the child's extended family or to an Indian home. If the child is being placed for adoption, a state court, in the absence of good cause to the contrary, must give preference to a member of the child's extended family, to other members of the Indian child's tribe, or to other Indian families. 25 U.S.C. § 1915. The Bureau of Indian Affairs guidelines on good cause to deviate from the placement preferences can be found at 44 Fed. Reg. 67,584-67,595 (1979).

A number of courts have employed a general "best interests of the child" exception to the placement preferences. *See, e.g.*, In Interest of A. E., 572 N.W.2d 579 (Iowa 1997). Other courts reject the best-interests exception as inconsistent with the fundamental principles of ICWA. Matter of Custody of S. E. G., 521 N.W.2d 357 (Minn. 1994); In re Adoption of Riffle, 922 P.2d 510 (Mont. 1996).

9. For discussions of state courts' interpretations of ICWA, particularly their differing approaches to the "existing Indian family" exception to the applicability of the statute and the "good cause" exception to the statutes' placement preferences, *see* Barbara Ann Atwood, Flashpoints Under the Indian Child Welfare Act: Toward a New Understanding of State Court Resistance, 51 Emory L.J. 587 (2002); Christine Metteer, Hard Cases Making Bad Law: The Need for Revision of the Indian Child Welfare Act, 38 Santa Clara L. Rev. 419 (1998).

NOTE: TRANSRACIAL PLACEMENT

In 1972 the National Association of Black Social Workers (NABSW) adopted a resolution, to which it still adheres, that provides in part:

> [W]e have taken the position that Black children should be placed only with Black families whether in foster care or adoption. Black children belong physically, psychologically and culturally in Black families in order that they receive the total sense of themselves and develop a sound projection of their future. Human beings are products of their environments and develop their sense of values, attitudes and self-concept within their family structures. Black children in White homes are cut off from the healthy development of themselves as Black people.
>
> Our position is based on:
>
> 1. the necessity of self-determination from birth to death of all Black people.
> 2. the need of our young ones to begin at birth to identify with all Black people in a Black community.
> 3. the philosophy that we need our own to build a strong nation.
>
> The socialization process for every child begins at birth. Included in the socialization process is the child's cultural heritage, which is an important segment of the total process. This must begin at the earliest moment; otherwise our children will not have the background and knowledge which is necessary to survive in a racist society. This is impossible if the child is placed with White parents in a White environment. . . .
>
> We the participants of the workshop have committed ourselves to go back to our communities and work to end this particular form of genocide.

Quoted in Rita J. Simon & Howard Altstein, Transracial Adoption 50, 52 (1977). After the NABSW issued its statement, transracial adoption declined sharply. From a peak of 2574 transracial adoptions in 1971, the number fell to 831 in 1975. Elizabeth Bartholet, Where Do Black Children Belong? The Politics of Race Matching in Adoption, 139 U. Pa. L. Rev. 1163, 1180 (1991).

Interest in transracial and international adoption has resurfaced, and racial matching practices are again being challenged. Two trends underlie the increased interest in transracial adoption. The first is emphasis on placing foster children. As the chart below shows, substantially more than half of all children waiting in foster care to be adopted are children of color.

Race and Ethnicity of Children in Public Foster Care Waiting for Adoption and Adopted — FY 2001

	Native American/ Non-Hispanic	Asian/ Non-Hispanic	Black/ Non-Hispanic	Hawaiian/ Pac. Is./ Non-Hispanic	Hispanic	White/ Non-Hispanic	Unknown	Two or More Races/ Non-NH
Children in foster care	2%	1%	38%	2%	17%	37%	3%	2%
Children in foster care waiting to be adopted	2%	0%	45%	0%	12%	34%	4%	2%
Children adopted from foster care	1%	1%	35%	0%	16%	38%	5%	3%

Source: Children's Bureau, The AFCARS Report–Preliminary FY Estimates as of March 2001. *Note:* Using U.S. Bureau of the Census Standards, children in FY 2000, children could receive more than one race designation.

The second trend is continued interest in international adoption as a way of finding infants available for adoption. International adoptions in the United States have increased dramatically in the last two decades. In FY 2003, the U.S. State Department issued 21,616 visas to orphans from other countries, which provides a reasonably reliable measure of adoptions of children from other countries. This number is up from 20,099 in 2002, 19,237 in 2001, and 17,718 in 2000. The number has risen every year since 1992, when 6,472 visas were issued. In each of the years 2003, 2002, and 2001, China sent the most children to the United States, followed by Russia. Guatemala was the third most common country of origin in 2003 and 2002, and the fourth most common in 2001; Korea was the fourth most common in 2003 and 2002, and the third most common in 2001. Immigrant Visas Issued to Orphans Coming to the U.S., Top Countries of Origin, *available at http://travel.state.gov/family/adoption_resources_02.html* (last visited Nov. 1, 2004). Of all foreign-born adopted children in the United States, a little more than one-fifth are from Korea. Bureau of the Census, Adopted Children and Stepchildren: 2000 (Oct. 2003), *available at http://www.census.gov/prod/2003pubs/censr-6.pdf* (last visited Nov. 1, 2004).

The Supreme Court has twice considered the constitutionality of laws that determined family relationships based on race, and both times it applied strict scrutiny and held that the laws violate the equal protection clause. In Loving v. Virginia, 388 U.S. 1 (1967), at page 177, the Court struck down a statute that forbade interracial marriage, and in Palmore v. Sidoti, 466 U.S. 429 (1984) (see Chapter 9, at page 669), it held unconstitutional the use of race to determine custody between parents. Lower courts have stricken statutes that require racial matching in adoption and foster care, but they have consistently upheld statutes that allow race to be a factor considered in determining whether a placement is in a child's best interests. *See, e.g.,* Drummond v. Fulton County Dep't of Family & Children's Services, 563 F.2d 1200 (5th Cir. 1977); McLaughlin v. Pernsley, 693 F. Supp. 318 (E.D. Pa. 1988); Compos v. McKeithen, 341 F. Supp. 264 (E.D. La. 1972); Petition of R. M. G., 454 A.2d 776 (D.C. 1982).

The 1994 Multiethnic Placement Act, as amended in 1996, prohibits discrimination in a child's placement on the basis of the race, national origin, or ethnicity of the child or the prospective foster or adoptive parents. The 1996 amendments deleted language that permitted an agency to "consider" the child's cultural, ethnic, or racial background as a factor in assessing the parents' ability to meet the needs of the child. The Act imposes obligations on agencies to seek out potential adoptive families of the races and ethnicities of the children needing placement. Pub. L. No. 103-382, § 553 (1994), as amended by Pub. L. No. 104-188, § 1808 (1996), codified at 42 U.S.C. § 5115a.

TWILA L. PERRY, *TRANSRACIAL AND INTERNATIONAL ADOPTION: MOTHERS, HIERARCHY, RACE AND FEMINIST LEGAL THEORY*

10 Yale J.L. & Feminism 102, 115-116, 121-122 (1998)

One troubling aspect of both transracial and international adoption is that each often results in the transfer of children from the least advantaged women to the most advantaged. At the same time, such adoptions, per se, do nothing to alleviate the conditions in the societies or communities from which the children come and thus do nothing to change the conditions that place some women in the position of being unable to care for their children themselves. Perhaps for these reasons, at least in part, recent scholarship by women of color on transracial adoption suggests that many of them are less than enthusiastic about the practice. . . .

There are probably many reasons why Black women often appear to be ambivalent or even hostile toward transracial adoption. Some of the reasons certainly involve perceptions about the needs of individual Black children — there is skepticism about whether white women can provide Black children with the skills they need to survive in a racist society. Some Black women may also feel that white women often raise white children with a sense of superiority over Blacks and that they will naturally raise Black transracially adopted children to feel the same way. Some Black women may simply believe that white people cannot love a Black child the same way they would love a white one. They understand that however precious Black children may be to Black people, for many whites seeking to adopt, a Black child is a second, third or last choice, behind children that are white, Asian or Hispanic. Some Black women are quite critical of the mothering skills displayed by white mothers with respect to their own children, and thus view arguments of some advocates of transracial adoption that white families may be able to parent Black children better than Black families with amused contempt. Others may be concerned that white women are interested in adopting Black children to fulfill their own desires to parent, but have no interest in the condition of Black children in general or in conditions that threaten the stability of so many Black families.

I offer two additional explanations for the feelings some Black women may have toward transracial adoption — feelings unrelated to concerns about the competence of white women to raise Black children. I argue that many Black women feel that arguments in favor of transracial adoption that minimize the role of race in parenting devalue an important part of what motherhood means to them — a historical and contemporary struggle to raise Black children successfully in a racist world. In addition, many Black women may also resent transracial adoption because they see it as part of a larger system of racial hierarchy and privilege that advantages white women while it devalues and subordinates women of color. . . .

Because women play a dominant role in caring for children, a subtext in the debate over transracial adoption involves the issue of mothering. Thus, a question underlying the debate about giving Black children "survival skills" is: who is qualified to mother children in a society that even the advocates of transracial adoption admit is racist? It is interesting that there are ways in which this issue is discussed, and ways in which it is not discussed. I argue that society's perception of the competence of women to mother children is intricately tied to the racial hierarchies among women in this society and that these perceptions are reflected in the controversy concerning transracial adoption. All too often, Black women are seen as inadequate to the task of mothering Black children, while white women are seen as competent to raise children of any race.

I view this racial hierarchy among mothers as having a number of troubling ramifications. First, if society values the mothering of some women more than it values of the mothering of others, the separation of the devalued mother from her children is less likely to be a cause of concern. Indeed, children transferred from devalued women to valued women are deemed to have received a lucky break. Second, women who know that they are devalued as mothers are likely to resent a pattern of adoption in which children from their group are always transferred to the women of higher status. Finally, the perception of the more valued group of women as competent to mother all children may deflect other important inquiries. In the context of the controversy over transracial adoption, assumptions about the ability of white women to mother Black children avoids a different inquiry about mothering, race, and racism that deserves attention. . . . I argue for a shift of the debate from the question of who is qualified to raise Black children in a racist society to the question of what it means to raise white children in a racist society. . . .

There are important links to be drawn between the transracial adoption of Black children in the United States and the adoption of children of color from Asia and Latin America. The factors of racism and economic discrimination that result in large numbers of Black children being separated from their biological parents in this country have counterparts in the international context, where a history of colonialism, neocolonialism, cultural imperialism, and economic exploitation often results in mothers being unable to keep the children to whom they have given birth. Thus, both domestically and internationally, transracial and international adoption often result in a pattern in which there is the transfer of children from the least advantaged women to the most advantaged women. Despite the differences between the specific circumstances of Black women in America and some other third world women, there is a connection in terms of a struggle by both to function as mothers under political and economic conditions which severely challenge their ability to adequately parent their own children. Moreover, many transracial adoptions, international adoptions, and adoptions in which racial and ethnic differences are not a factor, also share another connection — a link to the institution of patriarchy.

ELIZABETH BARTHOLET, *INTERNATIONAL ADOPTION: PROPRIETY, PROSPECTS AND PRAGMATICS*

13 J. Am. Acad. Matrimonial L. 181, 196-198 (1996)

The problems that should be seen as central to the international adoption debate are the misery and deprivation that characterize the lives of huge numbers of the children of the world. Millions of children die regularly of malnutrition and of diseases that should not kill. Millions more live in miserably inadequate institutions or on the streets. Their situations vary: some institutions are worse than others; some "street children" maintain a connection with a family while others are entirely on their own. But there can be no doubt that overwhelming numbers of children in the poor countries of the world are living and dying in conditions which involve extreme degrees of deprivation, neglect, exploitation, and abuse. These are the real problems of the children of the world. International adoption should be seen as an opportunity to solve some of these problems for some children. It should be structured to maximize this positive potential by facilitating the placement of children in need of nurturing homes with people in a position to provide those homes.

International adoption can, of course, play only a very limited role in addressing these problems. Solutions lie in reallocating social and economic resources both among countries and within countries, so that more children can be cared for by their birth families. But, given the fact that social reordering on a grand scale is not on the immediate horizon, international adoption clearly can serve the interests of at least those children in need of homes for whom adoptive parents can be found.

A. ADOPTION AND UNDERLYING SOCIAL ILLS

Some have suggested that international adoption programs might conflict with programs designed to improve the lives of the millions of children now in need, or with efforts to accomplish the kind of social reordering that might help the children of the future. . . .

Such efforts, however, are not inconsistent with supporting foreign adoption. Indeed, the opposite is true. Foreign adoption programs are likely to increase awareness in the United States and other receiving countries of the problems of children in the sending countries. Those who adopt have reason to identify, through their children, with the situations of other children not lucky enough to have found homes. Foreign adoption is thus likely to help create a climate more sympathetic to wide-ranging forms of support for children abroad.

Another argument voiced against international adoption is that it might relieve pressure within some sending countries to deal with social problems that need attention. But this argument also collapses upon analysis. Sending children abroad for adoption tends to highlight rather than to hide the fact that there are problems at home. Indeed, it seems likely that a major reason for the hostility exhibited by many sending countries toward foreign adoption relates to their governments' embarrassment at having domestic problems spotlighted by this public confession of their inability to take care of their children.

Although speculative arguments can always be mounted, it is unlikely that adoption of a relatively small number of the world's homeless children will interfere with efforts to assist those other children who remain in their native countries. The nations of the world are in general agreement that "the best interests of the child" should be the paramount principle governing the placement of children outside their biological families. Given the real problems confronting the world's children, it should be clear that this principle requires laws and policies designed to facilitate the international placement of children in need of homes.

See also Randall Kennedy, Interracial Intimacies: Sex, Marriage, Identity and Adoption (2003), arguing that encouraging intimate, familial relationships across racial lines will promote racial justice. Kennedy's position has been criticized as devaluing black families and black identity and failing to protect adequately the interests of adopted children. *See, e.g.*, Annette R. Apell, Book Review: Disposable Mothers, Deployable Children, 9 Mich. J. Race & L. 421 (2003); Margaret F. Brinig, Book Review: The Child's Best Interests: A Neglected Perspective on Interracial Intimacies, 117 Harv. L. Rev. 2120 (2004).

NOTES AND QUESTIONS

1. Does protecting children's interests require that racial matching or at least racial preferences be employed in adoption and foster care, as the National Association of Black Social Workers argues? What are the interests of children in these cases?

Does some form of open adoption, with ongoing contact between an adopted child and his or her family of origin, resolve the problem by allowing the child to form an identity that includes both families and cultures? *See* Gilbert A. Holmes, The Extended Family System in the Black Community: A Child-Centered Model for Adoption Policy, 68 Temp. L. Rev. 1649 (1995); Barbara Bennett Woodhouse, "Are You My Mother?": Conceptualizing Children's Identity Rights in Transracial Adoptions, 2 Duke J. Gender L. & Pol'y 107 (1995).

2. Do matching practices institutionalize racism, as others have argued? *See, e.g.*, Laura J. Schwartz, Religious Matching for Adoption: Unraveling the Interests Behind the "Best Interests" Standard, 25 Fam. L.Q. 171, 176-177 (1991); Joan Mahoney, The Black Baby Doll: Transracial Adoption and Cultural Preservation, 59 U. Mo. Kansas City L. Rev. 487 (1991).

Some have argued that where judges have discretion to consider race in making placements, they are likely to overemphasize it. If so, what laws or policies should be adopted to limit their discretion? *See, e.g.*, Twila L. Perry, Race and Child Placement: The Best Interests Test and the Cost of Discretion, 29 J. Fam. L. 51 (1990); Note, Kim Forde-Mazrui, Black Identity and Child Placement: The Best Interests of Black and Biracial Children, 92 Mich. L. Rev. 925 (1994).

3. Professor Bartholet has also shown that most agencies exercise their discretion in ways that make transracial placements unlikely. She has described the widespread use of several policies that have this effect, including holding African-American children in foster care after they are or could be free for adoption when no same-race adoptive family is available, practicing various race-conscious adoptive family recruitments, administering federal adoptive subsidy programs so that they largely support adoption of children of color by parents of the same race, and using different criteria in screening prospective African-American and white adoptive parents so as to increase the prospects of same-race adoptions. Elizabeth Bartholet, Where Do Black Children Belong? The Politics of Race Matching in Adoption, 139 U. Pa. L. Rev. 1163, 1183-1200 (1991). To what extent are these practices inconsistent with the Multiethnic Placement Act?

4. The NABSW statement also speaks of the interests of the African-American community. What are the interests of this community? Should the interests of the group be considered, as the interests of Native American tribes are protected by the Indian Child Welfare Act?

5. International adoption is complex, because practices and procedures vary so much from country to country. While the great majority of foreign adoptions are legally proper, illegal baby trafficking is also widely acknowledged as a serious problem. *See, e.g.*, Kelly M. Wittner, Comment, Curbing Child-Trafficking in Intercountry Adoptions: Will International Treaties and Adoption Moratoriums Accomplish the Job in Cambodia? 12 Pac. Rim L. & Pol'y J. 595 (2003); Ethan B. Kapstein, The Baby Trade, Foreign Affairs (Nov./Dec. 2003), *http://www.foreignaffairs.org/20031101faessay82611-p20/ethan-b-kapstein/ the-baby-trade.html* (last visited Nov. 1, 2004).

In 1993 the Hague Conference on Private International Law completed its Convention on Intercountry Adoption; the convention attempts to protect all the parties to an adoption, especially the children. The United States signed the convention on March 31, 1994, and Congress enacted implementing legislation in 2000. However, the Act does not come into force until implementing regulations are adopted; the implementation process is in progress. The Convention endorses intercountry adoption to provide permanent families for children but only when in-country adoption is not available. *See* Peter H. Pfund, Intercountry Adoption: The 1993 Hague Convention: Its Purpose, Implementation, and Promise, 28 Fam. L.Q. 53 (1994); Richard R. Carlson, The Emerging Law of Intercountry Adoptions: An Analysis of the Hague Conference on Intercountry Adoption, 30 Tulsa L.J. 243 (1994).

The convention itself is available from the home page of the Hague Conference on Private International Law, *http://hcch.e-vision.nl/index_en.php* (last visited Nov. 1, 2004). Information about the U.S. implementation process is available at *http://travel.state.gov/family/adoption_implementation.html* (last visited Nov. 1, 2004). General information on intercountry adoption from the State Department is available at *http://travel.state.gov/family/adoption.html* (last visited Nov. 1, 2004).

NOTE: RELIGIOUS MATCHING

Legally, religious matching in adoption and foster care, like racial matching, has been transformed from a mandatory rule to a discretionary policy. In the late 1980s one-third of the states had some form of religious matching provision regarding adoption. Note, Gregory A. Horowitz, Accommodations and Neutrality Under the Establishment Clause: The Foster Care Challenge, 98 Yale L.J. 617, 624 (1989). Practices vary significantly from state to state as well. Professor Clark has argued that religious matching rules were created to impose a truce on proselytizing and to avoid conflict among religious groups. He cites as support the New York practice during the 1950s of arbitrarily designating foundling children as one-third each Catholic, Protestant, and Jewish. Homer H. Clark, Jr., Domestic Relations in the United States §20.7 at 917 (2d ed. 1988).

Religious matching is most deeply entrenched in New York, where the child welfare system is "completely intertwined with religion." Martin Guggenheim, State-Supported Foster Care: The Interplay Between the Prohibition of Establishing Religion and the Free Exercise Rights of Parents and Children: *Wilder v. Bernstein*, 56 Brook. L. Rev. 603, 605 (1990). New York State provides public support for children in the care of private agencies, most of which are religious. Religiously affiliated and other private agencies directly or indirectly place and supervise children in foster care. Until the Wilder v. Bernstein litigation described in Professor Guggenheim's article, sectarian agencies gave placement preferences to children from their own religious groups for homes and institutions that they ran. There were more Catholic and Jewish placements than there were children of those faiths but fewer Protestant placements than there were Protestant children, and many of the placements regarded as most desirable were Catholic and Jewish. The result, according to the plaintiffs in *Wilder*, was that the Protestant children, who were predominantly African-American, did not have equal access to the better placements. Eventually the litigation was settled so that foster children are to be placed on a first-come, first-serve basis but with religious matching permitted if it does not allow a child to jump ahead of other children who have been waiting longer.

Most of the litigation in New York and other states after *Wilder* has involved claims by parents that their own free exercise rights require that their children be placed with foster parents of the same religion. These requests are typically honored if possible, and, at least in New York, if a child is placed with foster parents of a different religion, the agency is supposed to provide support and supervision to the foster parent to ensure that the child's religious practices are protected. *See, e.g.*, Bruker v. City of New York, — F. Supp. 2d —, 2004 WL 2189590 (S.D.N.Y. 2004); Whalen v. Allers, 302 F. Supp. 2d 194 (S.D.N.Y. 2003).

On these issues in addition to the articles already cited, *see* Laura J. Schwartz, Religious Matching for Adoption: Unraveling the Interests Behind the "Best Interests" Standard, 25 Fam. L.Q. 171 (1991).

PROBLEM

The juvenile court ordered that 14-year-old Liz be placed in foster care after finding that her mother had physically and emotionally abused her. Liz was placed in the foster home of Susan, a single mother living with two children. Liz thrived in Susan's home. Her grades improved, her depression lifted, and she described herself as happier than she had ever been in her life. After Liz had been in Susan's home for three months, Liz's mother learned that Susan is a Catholic. Liz has been raised to be an observant Jew. Statutes in this jurisdiction provide that

> Whenever a child is committed to an agency, such commitment shall be made, when practicable, to an authorized agency under the control of persons of the same religious faith as that of the child. The placement of any child thus committed must, when practicable, be with or in the custody of a person or persons of the same religious faith or persuasion as that of the child.

Liz was not placed in a Jewish foster home originally because none was available when she was removed from her mother's home. Citing this statute, Liz's mother has asked that Liz be moved from Susan's home to the home of practicing Jewish foster parents. While Liz has resided at Susan's home, she has attended synagogue and observed Jewish holidays. However, prior case law in this jurisdiction provides that the religious matching requirement is not satisfied by placing a child with a person of another faith, even if that person tries to protect the child's faith. Liz vehemently objects to being removed from Susan's home. She believes that her mother's request has nothing to do with religion but is part of her continuing effort to control Liz.

Based on all the materials we have read so far and assuming that the religious-matching statute does not violate the First Amendment, how should the lawyers for Liz's mother argue that Liz must be moved to the first available Jewish foster home? Assuming that Liz is granted party status and that her guardian ad litem agrees with her position, how should Liz's lawyers argue that she should be allowed to remain at Susan's home?

B. ALTERNATIVE REPRODUCTIVE TECHNOLOGIES

1. *Artificial Insemination and In Vitro Fertilization*

The most common, most basic, and simplest "alternative reproductive technology" is artificial insemination, a relatively old, relatively simple process. Artificial insemination by donor (AID) was first used openly by married couples when the husband was infertile. When questions about the child's legal status and the husband's liability for child support and right to visitation arose, the courts originally were divided. Leading cases imposing a parent-child relationship between the husband and child on the theory that he had voluntarily taken on responsibility for the child by assenting to AID include Levin v. Levin, 626 N.E.2d 527 (Ind. 1993); People v. Sorensen, 437 P.2d 495 (Cal. 1968) (en banc); and Strnad v. Strnad, 78 N.Y.S.2d 390 (Sup. Ct. 1948). *But see* Gursky v. Gursky, 242 N.Y.S.2d 406 (Sup. Ct. 1963) (child illegitimate but husband liable for child's support because consent to the insemination implied a promise to support).

To clarify parental status, these techniques have been the subject of a number of uniform acts, most notably the Uniform Parentage Act of 1973, which was adopted by 18 states. The Uniform Parentage Act of 2002 substantially changes the 1973 Act and incorporates many of the features of the intervening uniform Acts. It has been adopted by Texas and Washington, with legislation pending elsewhere.

Uniform Parentage Act (2002)

§702. A donor is not a parent of a child conceived by means of assisted reproduction.

§704(a) Consent by a woman, and a man who intends to be a parent of a child born to the woman by assisted reproduction must be in a record signed by the woman and the man. This requirement does not apply to a donor.

(b) Failure of a man to sign a consent required by subsection (a), before or after birth of the child, does not preclude a finding of paternity if the woman and the man, during the first two years of the child's life resided together in the same household with the child and openly held out the child as their own.

§705(a) Except as otherwise provided in subsection (b), the husband of a wife who gives birth to a child by means of assisted reproduction may not challenge his paternity of the child unless:

(1) within two years after learning of the birth of the child he commences a proceeding to adjudicate his paternity; and

(2) the court finds that he did not consent to the assisted reproduction, before or after birth of the child.

(b) A proceeding to adjudicate paternity may be maintained at any time if the court determines that:

(1) the husband did not provide sperm for, or before or after the birth of the child consent to, assisted reproduction by his wife;

(2) the husband and the mother of the child have not cohabited since the probable time of assisted reproduction; and

(3) the husband never openly held out the child as his own.

(c) The limitation provided in this section applies to a marriage declared invalid after assisted reproduction.

§706(a) If a marriage is dissolved before placement of eggs, sperm, or embryos, the former spouse is not a parent of the resulting child unless the former spouse consented in a record that if assisted reproduction were to occur after a divorce, the former spouse would be a parent of the child.

(b) The consent of a woman or a man to assisted reproduction may be withdrawn by that individual in a record at any time before placement of eggs, sperm, or embryos. An individual who withdraws consent under this section is not a parent of the resulting child.

§707. If an individual who consented in a record to be a parent by assisted reproduction dies before placement of eggs, sperm, or embryos, the deceased individual is not a parent of the resulting child unless the deceased spouse consented in a record that if assisted reproduction were to occur after death, the deceased individual would be a parent of the child.

NOTES AND QUESTIONS

1. The Uniform Parentage Act of 1973 terminated a donor's parental rights only if the donor provided the semen to a licensed physician for insemination. Twenty-one states adopted either the UPA or other statutes referring to the execution of the procedure by a physician. The 1973 Act also limited the termination of the donor's parental status to insemination of married women. Thirteen states have codes that do not specifically mention marital status as a requirement. Sixteen states have no legislation addressing artificial insemination. They employ common law principles, such as estoppel or in loco parentis, that require case-by-case adjudication. *See* Bridget R. Penick, Note, Give the Child a Legal Father: A Plea for Iowa to Adopt a Statute Regulating Artificial Insemination by Anonymous Donor, 83 Iowa L. Rev. 633 (1998); Gaia Bernstein, The Socio-Legal Acceptance of New Technologies: A Close Look at Artificial Insemination, 77 Wash. L. Rev. 1035 (2002). *See more generally* Fred A. Bernstein, This Child Does Have Two Mothers . . . and a Sperm Donor with Visitation, 22 N.Y.U. Rev. L. & Soc.

Change 1 (1996); Marsha Garrison, Law Making for Baby Making: An Interpretative Approach to the Determination of Legal Parenthood, 113 Harv. L. Rev. 835 (2000); Audra Elizabeth Laabs, Lesbian Art, 19 Law & Ineq. 65 (2001).

2. For the first reported case to raise the relationship between the 1973 Act and the 2002 Act in a state that has adopted both, *see* Carvin v. Britain (In re Parentage of L.B.), 89 P.3d 271 (Wash. App. 2004), Filed, Review granted by, Motion to vacate denied by, in part Carvin v. Britain (In re L.B.), 2004 Wash. LEXIS 663 (Wash., Oct. 6, 2004).

PROBLEMS

1. Hank and Wendy went to Dr. Donaldson to discuss artificial insemination of Wendy by a donor. Hank did not consent in writing to the insemination then or at any later time, but Dr. Donaldson artificially inseminated Wendy with semen from an unknown donor three times, and Wendy became pregnant and gave birth to a healthy child. Under the Uniform Parentage Act (2002), who is the child's legal father? In a state with no legislation on the subject?

2. Helen decided to conceive a child by artificial insemination and to raise it jointly with her partner, Victoria. Helen chose Mark as the semen donor. Helen now claims that she made clear to Mark that he was to have no role in the child's life, while Mark says that he and Helen agreed that he would see the child regularly and act as a noncustodial father. Victoria, who is a nurse, performed the artificial inseminations with Mark's semen. After several unsuccessful attempts, Helen became pregnant and gave birth to a baby girl. Mark was listed as the father on the birth certificate. Mark visited Helen in the hospital several times, purchased gifts for the baby, and visited at least monthly until last month, when Helen cut off the visits. The baby is now 18 months old. Victoria and Helen have remained close, and Victoria actively participates in raising the baby. Mark has filed a paternity suit against Helen, seeking a declaration of paternity and visitation rights.

a. How should this suit be resolved under the Uniform Parentage Act (2002)?

b. How would Mark's suit be resolved if he had impregnated Helen through intercourse? Why should artificial insemination change the result? Or should it? Should the law be structured so that there will always be a way to identify some man as a child's legal father?

c. What if Helen and Mark had signed a written agreement that provided that Mark would not petition for paternity and waived all claims to legal parenthood?

3. After having created embryos through in vitro fertilization, a married couple divorced. They could not agree about the disposition of seven frozen embryos stored in a fertility clinic. The mother, Mary Sue, asked for control of the embryos so that she could have them implanted in her uterus and perhaps bear a child. The father, Junior, objected because he was not sure he wanted to become a parent and asked that the embryos remain in cold storage. As the case progressed, both changed their minds: Mary Sue wanted the embryos donated to a childless couple, and Junior wanted them destroyed. Should the embryos be

treated like children and the dispute between Mary Sue and Junior handled like a custody fight? Are the embryos property, subject to equitable division between them? If the parties have entered into an agreement with the fertility clinic about the disposition of the embryos in a situation like this, should the agreement be specifically enforced? Is either party entitled as a matter of constitutional right to control the destiny of the embryos?

4. Robert and Denise, a married couple, arranged with a fertility clinic to use in vitro fertilization to attempt a pregnancy with donated ovum and Robert's sperm. Denise successfully bore a resulting child. During the same time period, Susan, a single woman, arranged with the same clinic to attempt a pregnancy using donated ovum and sperm. She also successfully bore a resulting child, giving birth ten days after Denise. Ten months later, the fertility clinic informed the three parents that the clinic had mistakenly implanted embryos fertilized with Robert's sperm into Susan, and that Robert was the genetic father of the child to whom Susan had given birth. Robert, Denise, and Susan all seek recognition as parents and custody of the child. What is the likely result?

2. *Surrogate Motherhood*

Medically and biologically, "simple" surrogate motherhood and AID are the same; from the point of view of the birth mother, this is AID. To call the practice "surrogate motherhood" signals looking at the situation from the perspective of the sperm donor/biological father who wants to be recognized as the child's legal father. The first surrogacy case to capture national attention involved this type of arrangement. William Stern and Mary Beth Whitehead entered into a contract providing that Whitehead would bear Stern's child, who would also be Mary Beth Whitehead's genetic and gestational child. The New Jersey Supreme Court ruled in that case that, absent adoption, Whitehead was Baby M's legal mother. In re Baby M, 537 A.2d 1227 (N.J. 1988). The *Baby M* decision today seems unremarkable. Most courts would continue to find that Whitehead and other traditional surrogates are the mothers of the children they bear. The more complicated cases involve gestational surrogacy. In these cases, the sperm and an egg from one woman are combined in vitro and implanted in the womb of another woman, the gestational surrogate. In the first of the cases below, the egg donor is the intended mother. In the second case, the egg donor surrenders her parental status, and the sperm donor intends that his unmarried partner will help him care for the child. The courts become involved when the relationships in these cases break down.

JOHNSON V. CALVERT

19 Cal. Rptr. 2d 494, 851 P.2d 776 (1993) (en banc)

PANELLI, J. . . . Mark and Crispina Calvert are a married couple who desired to have a child. Crispina was forced to undergo a hysterectomy in 1984. Her ovaries remained capable of producing eggs, however, and the couple eventually considered surrogacy. In 1989 Anna Johnson heard about Crispina's plight from a coworker and offered to serve as a surrogate for the Calverts.

On January 15, 1990, Mark, Crispina, and Anna signed a contract providing that an embryo created by the sperm of Mark and the egg of Crispina would be implanted in Anna and the child born would be taken into Mark and Crispina's home "as their child." Anna agreed she would relinquish "all parental rights" to the child in favor of Mark and Crispina. In return, Mark and Crispina would pay Anna $10,000 in a series of installments, the last to be paid six weeks after the child's birth. Mark and Crispina were also to pay for a $200,000 life insurance policy on Anna's life.

The zygote was implanted on January 19, 1990. Less than a month later, an ultrasound test confirmed Anna was pregnant.

Unfortunately, relations deteriorated between the two sides. Mark learned that Anna had not disclosed she had suffered several stillbirths and miscarriages. Anna felt Mark and Crispina did not do enough to obtain the required insurance policy. She also felt abandoned during an onset of premature labor in June.

In July 1990, Anna sent Mark and Crispina a letter demanding the balance of the payments due her or else she would refuse to give up the child. The following month, Mark and Crispina responded with a lawsuit, seeking a declaration they were the legal parents of the unborn child. Anna filed her own action to be declared the mother of the child, and the two cases were eventually consolidated. The parties agreed to an independent guardian ad litem for the purposes of the suit.

The child was born on September 19, 1990, and blood samples were obtained from both Anna and the child for analysis. The blood test results excluded Anna as the genetic mother. The parties agreed to a court order providing that the child would remain with Mark and Crispina on a temporary basis with visits by Anna.

At trial in October 1990, the parties stipulated that Mark and Crispina were the child's genetic parents. After hearing evidence and arguments, the trial court ruled that Mark and Crispina were the child's "genetic, biological and natural" father and mother, that Anna had no "parental" rights to the child, and that the surrogacy contract was legal and enforceable against Anna's claims. The court also terminated the order allowing visitation. Anna appealed from the trial court's judgment. The Court of Appeal for the Fourth District, Division Three, affirmed. We granted review. . . .

Civil Code sections 7001 and 7002 replace the distinction between legitimate and illegitimate children with the concept of the "parent and child relationship." The "parent and child relationship" means "the legal relationship existing between a child and his natural or adoptive parents incident to which the law confers or imposes rights, privileges, duties, and obligations. It includes the mother and child relationship and the father and child relationship." (Civ. Code, § 7001.) "The parent and child relationship extends equally to every child and to every parent, regardless of the marital status of the parents." (Civ. Code, § 7002.) The "parent and child relationship" is thus a legal relationship encompassing two kinds of parents, "natural" and "adoptive."

Passage of the Act clearly was not motivated by the need to resolve surrogacy disputes, which were virtually unknown in 1975. Yet it facially applies to *any* parentage determination, including the rare case in which a child's maternity is in issue. We are invited to disregard the Act and decide this case according to other criteria, including constitutional precepts and our sense of the demands of public policy. We feel constrained, however, to decline the invitation. Not uncommonly, courts must construe statutes in factual settings not contemplated by the enacting legislature. . . . [T]he Act offers a mechanism to resolve this dispute, albeit one not specifically tooled for it. We therefore proceed to analyze the parties' contentions within the Act's framework.

These contentions are readily summarized. Anna, of course, predicates her claim of maternity on the fact that she gave birth to the child. The Calverts contend that Crispina's genetic relationship to the child establishes that she is his mother. . . .

. . . Civil Code section 7003 provides, in relevant part, that between a child and the natural mother a parent and child relationship "*may* be established by proof of her having given birth to the child, or under [the Act]." (Civ. Code, § 7003, subd. (1), emphasis added.) Apart from Civil Code section 7003, the Act sets forth no specific means by which a natural mother can establish a parent and child relationship. . . .

Significantly for this case, Evidence Code section 892 provides that blood testing may be ordered in an action when paternity is a relevant fact. When maternity is disputed, genetic evidence derived from blood testing is likewise admissible. The Evidence Code further provides that if the court finds the conclusions of all the experts, as disclosed by the evidence based on the blood tests, are that the alleged father is not the father of the child, the question of paternity is resolved accordingly. By parity of reasoning, blood testing may also be dispositive of the question of maternity. Further, there is a rebuttable presumption of paternity (hence, maternity as well) on the finding of a certain number of genetic markers.

. . . [W]e are left with the undisputed evidence that Anna, not Crispina, gave birth to the child and that Crispina, not Anna, is genetically related to him. Both women thus have adduced evidence of a mother and child relationship as contemplated by the Act. Yet for any child California law recognizes only one natural mother, despite advances in reproductive technology rendering a different outcome biologically possible.[10]

We see no clear legislative preference in Civil Code section 7003 as between blood testing evidence and proof of having given birth. . . .

Because two women each have presented acceptable proof of maternity, we do not believe this case can be decided without enquiring into the parties' intentions as manifested in the surrogacy agreement. Mark and Crispina are a couple

---

10. We decline to accept the contention of amicus curiae the American Civil Liberties Union (ACLU) that we should find the child has two mothers. Even though rising divorce rates have made multiple parent arrangements common in our society, we see no compelling reason to recognize such a situation here. The Calverts are the genetic and intending parents of their son and have provided him, by all accounts, with a stable, intact, and nurturing home. To recognize parental rights in a third party with whom the Calvert family has had little contact since shortly after the child's birth would diminish Crispina's role as mother.

who desired to have a child of their own genetic stock but are physically unable to do so without the help of reproductive technology. They affirmatively intended the birth of the child, and took the steps necessary to effect in vitro fertilization. But for their acted-on intention, the child would not exist. Anna agreed to facilitate the procreation of Mark's and Crispina's child. The parties' aim was to bring Mark's and Crispina's child into the world, not for Mark and Crispina to donate a zygote to Anna. Crispina from the outset intended to be the child's mother. Although the gestative function Anna performed was necessary to bring about the child's birth, it is safe to say that Anna would not have been given the opportunity to gestate or deliver the child had she, prior to implantation of the zygote, manifested her own intent to be the child's mother. No reason appears why Anna's later change of heart should vitiate the determination that Crispina is the child's natural mother.

We conclude that although the Act recognizes both genetic consanguinity and giving birth as means of establishing a mother and child relationship, when the two means do not coincide in one woman, she who intended to procreate the child — that is, she who intended to bring about the birth of a child that she intended to raise as her own — is the natural mother under California law.[11]

Our conclusion finds support in the writings of several legal commentators. (*See* Hill, What Does It Mean to Be a "Parent"? The Claims of Biology as the Basis for Parental Rights, supra, 66 N.Y.U. L. Rev. 353; Shultz, Reproductive Technology and Intent-Based Parenthood: An Opportunity for Gender Neutrality (1990) Wis. L. Rev. 297 [Shultz]; Note, Redefining Mother: A Legal Matrix for New Reproductive Technologies (1986) 96 Yale L.J. 187, 197-202 [note].) . . .

Another commentator has cogently suggested, in connection with reproductive technology, that "[t]he mental concept of the child is a controlling factor of its creation, and the originators of that concept merit full credit as conceivers. The mental concept must be recognized as independently valuable; it creates expectations in the initiating parents of a child, and it creates expectations in society for adequate performance on the part of the initiators as parents of the child." (Note, op. cit. supra, 96 Yale L.J. at p.196.)

---

11. Thus, under our analysis, in a true "egg donation" situation, where a woman gestates and gives birth to a child formed from the egg of another woman with the intent to raise the child as her own, the birth mother is the natural mother under California law.

The dissent would decide parentage based on the best interests of the child. Such an approach raises the repugnant specter of governmental interference in matters implicating our most fundamental notions of privacy, and confuses concepts of parentage and custody. Logically, the determination of parentage must precede, and should not be dictated by, eventual custody decisions. The implicit assumption of the dissent is that a recognition of the genetic intending mother as the natural mother may sometimes harm the child. This assumption overlooks California's dependency laws, which are designed to protect all children irrespective of the manner of birth or conception. Moreover, the best interest standard poorly serves the child in the present situation: it fosters instability during litigation and, if applied to recognize the gestator as natural mother, results in a split of custody between the natural father and the gestator, an outcome not likely to benefit the child. Further, it may be argued that, by voluntarily contracting away any rights to the child, the gestator has, in effect, conceded the best interest of the child is not with her.

Moreover, as Professor Shultz recognizes, the interests of children, particularly at the outset of their lives, are "[un]likely to run contrary to those of adults who choose to bring them into being." (Shultz, op. cit. supra, at p.397.) Thus, "[h]onoring the plans and expectations of adults who will be responsible for a child's welfare is likely to correlate significantly with positive outcomes for parents and children alike." (Ibid.) Under Anna's interpretation of the Act, by contrast, a woman who agreed to gestate a fetus genetically related to the intending parents would, contrary to her expectations, be held to be the child's natural mother, with all the responsibilities that ruling would entail, if the intending mother declined to accept the child after its birth. In what we must hope will be the extremely rare situation in which neither the gestator nor the woman who provided the ovum for fertilization is willing to assume custody of the child after birth, a rule recognizing the intending parents as the child's legal, natural parents should best promote certainty and stability for the child. . . .

Anna urges that surrogacy contracts violate several social policies. Relying on her contention that she is the child's legal, natural mother, she cites the public policy embodied in Penal Code section 273, prohibiting the payment for consent to adoption of a child. She argues further that the policies underlying the adoption laws of this state are violated by the surrogacy contract because it in effect constitutes a prebirth waiver of her parental rights.

We disagree. Gestational surrogacy differs in crucial respects from adoption and so is not subject to the adoption statutes. The parties voluntarily agreed to participate in in vitro fertilization and related medical procedures before the child was conceived; at the time when Anna entered into the contract, therefore, she was not vulnerable to financial inducements to part with her own expected offspring. As discussed above, Anna was not the genetic mother of the child. The payments to Anna under the contract were meant to compensate her for her services in gestating the fetus and undergoing labor, rather than for giving up "parental" rights to the child. Payments were due both during the pregnancy and after the child's birth. We are, accordingly, unpersuaded that the contract used in this case violates the public policies embodied in Penal Code section 273 and the adoption statutes. For the same reasons, we conclude these contracts do not implicate the policies underlying the statutes governing termination of parental rights.

It has been suggested that gestational surrogacy may run afoul of prohibitions on involuntary servitude. (*See* U.S. Const., Amend. XIII; Cal. Const., art. I, § 6; Pen. Code, § 181.) Involuntary servitude has been recognized in cases of criminal punishment for refusal to work. We see no potential for that evil in the contract at issue here, and extrinsic evidence of coercion or duress is utterly lacking. We note that although at one point the contract purports to give Mark and Crispina the sole right to determine whether to abort the pregnancy, at another point it acknowledges: "All parties understand that a pregnant woman has the absolute right to abort or not abort any fetus she is carrying. Any promise to the contrary is unenforceable." We therefore need not determine the validity of a surrogacy contract purporting to deprive the gestator of her freedom to terminate the pregnancy.

Finally, Anna and some commentators have expressed concern that surrogacy contracts tend to exploit or dehumanize women, especially women of lower economic status. Anna's objections center around the psychological harm she asserts may result from the gestator's relinquishing the child to whom she has given birth. Some have also cautioned that the practice of surrogacy may encourage society to view children as commodities, subject to trade at their parents' will.

We are all too aware that the proper forum for resolution of this issue is the Legislature, where empirical data, largely lacking from this record, can be studied and rules of general applicability developed. However, in light of our responsibility to decide this case, we have considered as best we can its possible consequences.

We are unpersuaded that gestational surrogacy arrangements are so likely to cause the untoward results Anna cites as to demand their invalidation on public policy grounds. Although common sense suggests that women of lesser means serve as surrogate mothers more often than do wealthy women, there has been no proof that surrogacy contracts exploit poor women to any greater degree than economic necessity in general exploits them by inducing them to accept lower-paid or otherwise undesirable employment. We are likewise unpersuaded by the claim that surrogacy will foster the attitude that children are mere commodities; no evidence is offered to support it. The limited data available seem to reflect an absence of significant adverse effects of surrogacy on all participants.

The argument that a woman cannot knowingly and intelligently agree to gestate and deliver a baby for intending parents carries overtones of the reasoning that for centuries prevented women from attaining equal economic rights and professional status under the law. To resurrect this view is both to foreclose a personal and economic choice on the part of the surrogate mother, and to deny intending parents what may be their only means of procreating a child of their own genetic stock. Certainly in the present case it cannot seriously be argued that Anna, a licensed vocational nurse who had done well in school and who had previously borne a child, lacked the intellectual wherewithal or life experience necessary to make an informed decision to enter into the surrogacy contract. . . .

Anna argues at length that her right to the continued companionship of the child is protected under the federal Constitution. . . .

These cases do not support recognition of parental rights for a gestational surrogate. Although Anna quotes language stressing the primacy of a developed parent-child relationship in assessing unwed fathers' rights (*see* Lehr v. Robertson, [(1983) 463 U.S. 248] at pp.260-262), certain language in the cases reinforces the importance of genetic parents' rights. (Lehr v. Robertson, supra, 463 U.S. at p.262 ["The significance of the biological connection is that it offers the natural father an opportunity that no other male possesses to develop a relationship with his offspring. If he grasps that opportunity and accepts some measure of responsibility for the child's future, he may enjoy the blessings of the parent-child relationship and make uniquely valuable contributions to the child's development."]. Anna's argument depends on a prior determination that she is indeed the child's mother. Since Crispina is the child's mother under California law because she, not Anna, provided the ovum for the in vitro fertilization procedure, intending to raise the child as her own, it follows that any constitutional interests Anna possesses in this situation are something less than those of a mother. As counsel for the minor points out, the issue in this case is not whether Anna's asserted rights as a natural mother were unconstitutionally violated, but rather whether the determination that she is not the legal natural mother at all is constitutional.

Anna relies principally on the decision of the United States Supreme Court in Michael H. v. Gerald D. (1989) 491 U.S. 110, to support her claim to a constitutionally protected liberty interest in the companionship of the child, based on her status as "birth mother." . . . The reasoning of the plurality in *Michael H.* does not assist Anna. Society has not traditionally protected the right of a woman who gestates and delivers a baby pursuant to an agreement with a couple who supply the zygote from which the baby develops and who intend to raise the child as their own; such arrangements are of too recent an origin to claim the protection of tradition. To the extent that tradition has a bearing on the present case, we believe it supports the claim of the couple who exercise their right to procreate in order to form a family of their own, albeit through novel medical procedures.

Moreover, if we were to conclude that Anna enjoys some sort of liberty interest in the companionship of the child, then the liberty interests of Mark and Crispina, the child's natural parents, in their procreative choices and their relationship with the child would perforce be infringed. Any parental rights Anna might successfully assert could come only at Crispina's expense. As we have seen, Anna has no parental rights to the child under California law, and she fails to persuade us that sufficiently strong policy reasons exist to accord her a protected liberty interest in the companionship of the child when such an interest would necessarily detract from or impair the parental bond enjoyed by Mark and Crispina. . . .

Drawing an analogy to artificial insemination, Anna argues that Mark and Crispina were mere genetic donors who are entitled to no constitutional protection. That characterization of the facts is, however, inaccurate. Mark and Crispina never intended to "donate" genetic material to anyone. Rather, they intended to procreate a child genetically related to them by the only available means. Civil Code section 7005, governing artificial insemination, has no application here. . . .

The judgment of the Court of Appeal is affirmed.

KENNARD, J., dissenting. . . . In my view, the woman who provided the fertilized ovum and the woman who gave birth to the child both have substantial claims to legal motherhood. Pregnancy entails a unique commitment, both psychological and emotional, to an unborn child. No less substantial, however, is the contribution of the woman from whose egg the child developed and without whose desire the child would not exist.

For each child, California law accords the legal rights and responsibilities of parenthood to only one "natural mother." When, as here, the female reproductive role is divided between two women, California law requires courts to make a decision as to which woman is the child's natural mother, but provides no standards by which to make that decision. The majority's resort to "intent" to break the "tie" between the genetic and gestational mothers is unsupported by statute, and in the absence of appropriate protections in the law to guard against abuse of surrogacy arrangements, it is ill-advised. To determine who is the legal mother of a child born of a gestational surrogacy arrangement, I would apply the standard most protective of child welfare — the best interests of the child. . . .

The ethical, moral and legal implications of using gestational surrogacy for human reproduction have engendered substantial debate. . . .

Surrogacy proponents generally contend that gestational surrogacy, like the other reproductive technologies that extend the ability to procreate to persons who might not otherwise be able to have children, enhances "individual freedom, fulfillment and responsibility." (Shultz, Reproductive Technology, supra, 1990 Wis. L. Rev. 297, 303.) Under this view, women capable of bearing children should be allowed to freely agree to be paid to do so by infertile couples desiring to form a family. (Shalev, Birth Power: The Case for Surrogacy, supra, at p.145 [arguing for a "free market in reproduction" in which the "reproducing woman" operates as an "autonomous moral and economic agent"]; see also Posner, Economic Analysis of Law (3d ed. 1986) p.139; Landes & Posner, The Economics of the Baby Shortage (1978) 7 J. Legal Stud. 323 [proposing a "market in babies"].) The "surrogate mother" is expected "to weigh the prospective investment in her birthing labor" before entering into the arrangement, and if her "autonomous reproductive decision" is "voluntary," she should be held responsible for it so as "to fulfill the expectations of the other parties. . . ." (Shalev, Birth Power: The Case for Surrogacy, supra, at p.96.)

One constitutional law scholar argues that the use of techniques such as gestational surrogacy is constitutionally protected and should be restricted only on a showing of a compelling state interest. . . .

Professor Robertson's thesis of broad application of the right of privacy for all procreational techniques has been questioned, however, in light of recent United States Supreme Court jurisprudence. See Medical Technology, supra, 103 Harv. L. Rev. 1519, 1530, citing Michael H. v. Gerald D. (1989) 491 U.S. 110 as evidence of the high court's reluctance "to extend the right of privacy to new relationships and activities" that the court has not perceived to merit "traditional protection."

Surrogacy critics, however, maintain that the payment of money for the gestation and relinquishment of a child threatens the economic exploitation of poor women who may be induced to engage in commercial surrogacy arrangements out of financial need. (Capron & Radin, Choosing Family Law Over Contract Law as a Paradigm for Surrogate Motherhood, in Surrogate Motherhood, supra, p.62.) Some fear the development of a "breeder" class of poor women who will be regularly employed to bear children for the economically advantaged. (See Women and Children Used in Systems of Surrogacy: Position Statement of the Institute on Women and Technology, in Surrogate Motherhood, supra, at p.322; and Corea, Junk Liberty, testimony before Cal. Assem. Judiciary Com., April 5, 1988, in Surrogate Motherhood, supra, at pp.325, 335.) Others suggest that women who enter into surrogacy arrangements may underestimate the psychological impact of relinquishing a child they have nurtured in their bodies for nine months. (See Macklin, Artificial Means of Reproduction and Our Understanding of the Family, supra, 21 Hastings Center Rep. 5, 10.)

Gestational surrogacy is also said to be "dehumanizing" (Capron & Radin, Choosing Family Law Over Contract Law as a Paradigm for Surrogate Motherhood, in Surrogate Motherhood, supra, at p.62) and to "commodify" women and children by treating the female reproductive capacity and the children born of gestational surrogacy arrangements as products that can be bought and sold (Radin, Market-Inalienability (1987) 100 Harv. L. Rev. 1849, 1930-1932). The commodification of women and children, it is feared, will reinforce oppressive gender stereotypes and threaten the well-being of all children. (Medical Technology, supra, 103 Harv. L. Rev. 1519, 1550; Annas, Fairy Tales Surrogate Mothers Tell, in Surrogate Motherhood, supra, p.50.) Some critics foresee promotion of an ever-expanding "business of surrogacy brokerage." (E.g., Goodwin, Determination of Legal Parentage, supra, 26 Fam. L.Q. at p.283.) . . .

Organizations representing diverse viewpoints share many of the concerns highlighted by the legal commentators. For example, the American Medical Association considers the conception of a child for relinquishment after birth to pose grave ethical problems. (Rep. of the Judicial Council, in Surrogate Motherhood, supra, at p.304.) Likewise, the official position of the Catholic Church is that surrogacy arrangements are "contrary to the unity of marriage and to the dignity of the procreation of the human person." (Magisterium of the Catholic Church, Instruction on Respect for Human Life in Its Origin and on the Dignity of Procreation: Replies to Certain Questions of the Day 25 (Feb. 22, 1987), cited in Radin, Market-Inalienability, supra, 100 Harv. L. Rev. 1849, 1928, fn.271.)

The policy statement of the New York State Task Force on Life and the Law sums up the broad range of ethical problems that commercial surrogacy arrangements are viewed to present: "The gestation of children as a service for others in exchange for a fee is a radical departure from the way in which society understands and values pregnancy. It substitutes commercial values for the web of social, affective and moral meanings associated with human reproduction. . . . This transformation has profound implications for childbearing, for women, and for the relationship between parents and the children they bring into the world. . . .

Surrogate parenting allows the genetic, gestational and social components of parenthood to be fragmented, creating unprecedented relationships among people bound together by contractual obligation rather than by the bonds of kinship and caring. . . .

. . . Surrogate parenting alters deep-rooted social and moral assumptions about the relationship between parents and children. . . .

. . . [It] is premised on the ability and willingness of women to abdicate [their parental] responsibility without moral compunction or regret [and] makes the obligations that accompany parenthood alienable and negotiable." (New York State Task Force on Life and the Law, Surrogate Parenting: Analysis and Recommendations for Public Policy (May 1988) in Surrogate Motherhood, supra, at pp.317-318.)

Proponents and critics of gestational surrogacy propose widely differing approaches for deciding who should be the legal mother of a child born of a gestational surrogacy arrangement. Surrogacy advocates propose to enforce preconception contracts in which gestational mothers have agreed to relinquish parental rights, and, thus, would make "bargained-for intentions determinative of legal parenthood." (Shultz, Reproductive Technology, supra, 1990 Wis. L. Rev. at p.323.) Professor Robertson, for instance, contends that "[t]he right to noncoital, collaborative reproduction also includes the right of the parties to agree how they should allocate their obligations and entitlements with respect to the child. Legal presumptions of paternity and maternity would be overridden by this agreement of the parties." (Robertson, Procreative Liberty and the Control of Conception, Pregnancy, and Childbirth, supra, 69 Va. L. Rev. 405, 436; *see also* Shalev, Birth Power: The Case for Surrogacy, supra, at p.141 [arguing for enforcing the parties' legal expectations].)

Surrogacy critics, on the other hand, consider the unique female role in human reproduction as the determinative factor of questions of legal parentage. They reason that although males and females both contribute genetic material for the child, the act of gestating the fetus falls only on the female. (*See* Radin, Market-Inalienability, supra, 100 Harv. L. Rev. 1849, 1932, fn. 285 [pointing out the "asymmetrical" interests of males and females in human reproduction].) Accordingly, in their view, a woman who, as the result of gestational surrogacy, is not genetically related to the child she bears is like any other woman who gives birth to a child. In either situation the woman giving birth is the child's mother. (*See* Capron & Radin, Choosing Family Law Over Contract Law as a Paradigm for Surrogate Motherhood, in Surrogate Motherhood, supra, at pp.64-65.) Under this approach, the laws governing adoption should govern the parental rights to a child born of gestational surrogacy. Upon the birth of the child, the gestational mother can decide whether or not to relinquish her parental rights in favor of the genetic mother. (Ibid.) . . .

Faced with the failure of current statutory law to adequately address the issue of who is a child's natural mother when two women qualify under the UPA, the majority breaks the "tie" by resort to a criterion not found in the UPA — the "intent" of the genetic mother to be the child's mother.

This case presents a difficult issue. The majority's resolution of that issue deserves serious consideration. Ultimately, however, I cannot agree that "intent" is the appropriate test for resolving this case.

The majority offers four arguments in support of its conclusion to rely on the intent of the genetic mother as the exclusive determinant for deciding who is the natural mother of a child born of gestational surrogacy. Careful examination, however, demonstrates that none of the arguments mandates the majority's conclusion.

The first argument that the majority uses in support of its conclusion that the intent of the genetic mother to bear a child should be dispositive of the question of motherhood is "but-for" causation. . . . Neither the "but for" nor the "substantial factor" test of causation provides any basis for preferring the genetic mother's intent as the determinative factor in gestational surrogacy cases: Both the genetic and the gestational mothers are indispensable to the birth of a child in a gestational surrogacy arrangement.

Behind the majority's reliance on "but-for" causation as justification for its intent test is a second, closely related argument. The majority draws its second rationale from a student note: "The mental concept of the child is a controlling factor of its creation, and the originators of that concept merit full credit as conceivers."

* * *

The problem with this argument, of course, is that children are not property. Unlike songs or inventions, rights in children cannot be sold for consideration, or made freely available to the general public. Our most fundamental notions of personhood tell us it is inappropriate to treat children as property. . . . Accordingly, I cannot endorse the majority's "originators of the concept" or intellectual property rationale for employing intent to break the "tie" between the genetic mother and the gestational mother of the child.

Next, the majority offers as its third rationale the notion that bargained-for expectations support its conclusion regarding the dispositive significance of the genetic mother's intent. . . . The unsuitability of applying the notion that, because contract intentions are "voluntarily chosen, deliberate, express and bargained-for," their performance ought to be compelled by the courts is even more clear when the concept of specific performance is used to determine the course of the life of a child. Just as children are not the intellectual property of their parents, neither are they the personal property of anyone, and their delivery cannot be ordered as a contract remedy on the same terms that a court would, for example, order a breaching party to deliver a truckload of nuts and bolts.

Thus, three of the majority's four arguments in support of its exclusive reliance on the intent of the genetic mother as determinative in gestational surrogacy cases cannot withstand analysis. . . . [B]efore turning to the majority's fourth rationale, I shall discuss two additional considerations, not noted by the majority, that in my view also weigh against utilizing the intent of the genetic mother as the sole determinant of the result in this case and others like it.

First, in making the intent of the genetic mother who wants to have a child the dispositive factor, the majority renders a certain result preordained and inflexible in every such case: as between an intending genetic mother and a gestational mother, the genetic mother will, under the majority's analysis, always prevail. The majority recognizes no meaningful contribution by a woman who agrees to carry a fetus to term for the genetic mother beyond that of mere employment to perform a specified biological function.

The majority's approach entirely devalues the substantial claims of motherhood by a gestational mother such as Anna. True, a woman who enters into a surrogacy arrangement intending to raise the child has by her intent manifested an assumption of parental responsibility in addition to her biological contribution of providing the genetic material. But the gestational mother's biological contribution of carrying a child for nine months and giving birth is likewise an assumption of parental responsibility. (See Dolgin, Just a Gene: Judicial Assumptions About Parenthood (1993) 40 UCLA L. Rev. 637, 659.) A pregnant woman's commitment to the unborn child she carries is not just physical; it is psychological and emotional as well. . . . A pregnant woman intending to bring a child into the world is more than a mere container or breeding animal; she is a conscious agent of creation no less than the genetic mother, and her humanity is implicated on a deep level. Her role should not be devalued. . . .

I find the majority's reliance on "intent" unsatisfactory for yet another reason. By making intent determinative of parental rights to a child born of a gestational surrogacy arrangement, the majority would permit enforcement of a gestational surrogacy agreement without requiring any of the protections that would be afforded by the [Uniform Status of Children of Assisted Conception Act]. . . .

In my view, protective requirements such as those set forth in the USCACA are necessary to minimize any possibility in gestational surrogacy arrangements for overreaching or abuse by a party with economic advantage. As the New Jersey Supreme Court recognized, it will be a rare instance when a low income infertile couple can employ an upper income surrogate. (Matter of Baby M., supra, 109 N.J. 396, 537 A.2d 1227, 1249.) The model act's carefully drafted provisions would assure that the surrogacy arrangement is a matter of medical necessity on the part of the intending parents, and not merely the product of a desire to avoid the inconveniences of pregnancy, together with the financial ability to do so. Also, by requiring both pre-conception psychological counseling for all parties and judicial approval, the model act would assure that parties enter into a surrogacy arrangement only if they are legally and psychologically capable of doing so and fully understand all the risks involved, and that the surrogacy arrangement would not be substantially detrimental to the interests of any individual. Moreover, by requiring judicial approval, the model act would significantly discourage the rapid expansion of commercial surrogacy brokerage and the resulting commodification of the products of pregnancy. In contrast, here the majority's grant of parental rights to the intending mother contains no provisions for the procedural protections suggested by the commissioners who drafted the model act. The majority opinion is a sweeping endorsement of unregulated gestational surrogacy.

The majority's final argument in support of using the intent of the genetic mother as the exclusive determinant of the outcome in gestational surrogacy cases is that preferring the intending mother serves the child's interests, which are "[u]nlikely to run contrary to those of adults who choose to bring [the child] into being."

I agree with the majority that the best interests of the child is an important goal. . . . The problem with the majority's rule of intent is that application of this inflexible rule will not serve the child's best interests in every case. . . .

. . . In the absence of legislation that is designed to address the unique problems of gestational surrogacy, this court should look not to tort, property or contract law, but to family law, as the governing paradigm and source of a rule of decision.

The allocation of parental rights and responsibilities necessarily impacts the welfare of a minor child. And in issues of child welfare, the standard that courts frequently apply is the best interests of the child. . . . This "best interests" standard serves to assure that in the judicial resolution of disputes affecting a child's well-being, protection of the minor child is the foremost consideration. Consequently, I would apply "the best interests of the child" standard to determine who can best assume the social and legal responsibilities of motherhood for a child born of a gestational surrogacy arrangement. . . .

. . . I would remand the matter to the trial court to undertake that evaluation.

NOTES AND QUESTIONS

1. The majority concludes that the Parentage Act and provisions of the Evidence Code regarding the admissibility of blood testing are relevant to this

case but that laws regarding adoption and the consequences of artificial insemination are not. Why?

2. Johnson v. Calvert was decided under the Uniform Parentage Act of 1973. § 803 of the Uniform Parentage Act of 2002 provides:

(a) If the requirements of subsection (b) are satisfied, a court may issue an order validating the gestational agreement and declaring that the intended parents will be the parents of a child born during the term of the of the agreement.

(b) The court may issue an order under subsection (a) only on finding that:

(1) the residence requirements of Section 802 have been satisfied and the parties have submitted to the jurisdiction of the court under the jurisdictional standards of this [Act];

(2) unless waived by the court, the [relevant child-welfare agency] has made a home study of the intended parents and the intended parents meet the standards of suitability applicable to adoptive parents;

(3) all parties have voluntarily entered into the agreement and understand its terms;

(4) adequate provision has been made for all reasonable health-care expense associated with the gestational agreement until the birth of the child, including responsibility for those expenses if the agreement is terminated; and

(5) the consideration, if any, paid to the prospective gestational mother is reasonable.

If the parties do not comply with these requirements, the act recognizes the gestational mother as the mother of the child. If California were to adopt these provisions, how would they affect a subsequent case similar to Johnson v. Calvert?

3. For other efforts to regulate surrogacy, see Fla. Stat. ch. 742.15 (1995); N.H. Rev. Stat. Ann. ch. 168-B; Nev. Rev. Stat. § 126.045. Va. Code Ann. 20-160(B) (Michie 2000 & Supp. 2002). If you were going to regulate the practice, what requirements would you impose and why? For discussion, see Cynthia L. Gallee, Comment: Surrogate Mother Contracts: A View of Recent Legislative Approaches, 25 J. Health & Hosp. L. 175 (1992); Weldon E. Havins & James J. Dalessio, Regulating Surrogacy at the Millennium: Proposed Model Legislation Regulating "Non-traditional Gestational Surrogacy Contracts," 31 McGeorge L. Rev. 673 (2000). See also Martha A. Field, Surrogate Motherhood: The Legal and Human Issues (1988) (arguing that surrogacy should be integrated into adoption law and practice).

4. England adopted its Human Fertilisation and Embryology Act in 1990. Section 27 of that act provides that the woman who carries a child is the legal mother. Thus, in a Baby M situation, the genetic and gestational mother is also the legal mother, as is a woman who is given an egg so that she may bear a child. However, under § 30, a court may issue an order recognizing that a child born of a gestational surrogate mother is the legal child of the genetic parents where the original arrangement was that the genetic parents would raise the child. For discussion, see Gillian Douglas, The Human Fertilisation and Embryology Act 1990, March [1991] Fam. Law 330; J. G. Hogg, Surrogacy — Nobody's Child, July [1991] Fam. Law 276.

Most countries do not follow the *Johnson* approach; in a contest between a genetic and a gestational mother the gestational mother prevails as the legal mother. R. Alta Charo, Biological Determinism in Legal Decisionmaking: The Parent Trap, 3 Tex. J. Women & L. 265, 294, citing Office of Technology Assessment, U.S. Congress, Infertility: Medical and Social Choices OTA-BA-358, 329-363 (1988).

PROBLEMS

1. Under the *Johnson* court's analysis, who would be the legal mother of the child in a case involving a surrogate who gave birth to a child genetically hers pursuant to a contract specifying that the father and his wife would have custody?

2. If Mary donated an egg to be fertilized with John's sperm and the fetus were to be gestated by John's wife Wendy, who would be the child's legal mother under Johnson v. Calvert?

3. Alison gestated a fetus conceived from the egg and sperm of anonymous donors, agreeing that the child would be adopted by Barbara and George. Shortly before the child was born, George filed for divorce, alleging that no children were born of the marriage. Barbara responded that she and George expected to adopt the soon-to-be-born child of Alison and sought custody and a child support order against George. After the baby was born, Alison made clear that she did not want custody. The trial judge ruled that the baby had no legal parents. What arguments should Barbara and George make on appeal?

J.F. v. D.B.

66 Pa. D. & C.4th 1 (2004)

CONNELLY, J. This unusual matter comes before the court primarily on the issue of standing for child custody. At the center of the custodial dispute are male triplets A, B and C, born to a surrogate mother not genetically related to them and a biological father whose sperm fertilized the three donor eggs that created them.

* * *

FINDINGS OF FACT

Given the already complicated history of this case, a time line of the relevant facts is necessary. At the end of 2001, D.B., interested in the idea of being a surrogate mother, found and applied online to Surrogate Mothers Inc. (SMI), a private surrogacy agency based in Indiana. . . . SMI matched D.B. with J.F. and E.D., his paramour, to be a gestational surrogate. A gestational surrogate is a woman who carries implanted embryos, created by donor eggs fertilized by the biological father's sperm, in her womb until birth. . . .

In April 2002, D.B. and E.D. met for the first time. J.F. was not present for this meeting. During July and August 2002, J.F., D.B. and her husband, and the egg donor, J.R., signed and notarized a surrogacy contract drawn up by SMI director and attorney, Steven Litz.[12] At the end of 2002 and beginning of 2003, the parties underwent extensive medical and psychological testing.

In April 2003, D.B. was implanted with three embryos in Cleveland, Ohio. J.F. and E.D. were present for this procedure. D.B.'s pregnancy was confirmed in May and shortly thereafter it was discovered that she was carrying triplets, with a tentative due date of December 3, 2003. Hearing testimony revealed this to be a very unusual situation because normally only one embryo may take, not all three.

From May to November 2003, D.B. attended doctor's visits every two weeks in Erie, Pennsylvania. J.F. and E.D. attended the first few visits until D.B.'s doctor asked them to stay in Cleveland. Per doctor's orders in June, D.B. quit her job to go on bed rest. From July to November, D.B. remained on bed rest. During this time, she requested that J.F. and E.D. pay her $1000 per month to cover her expenses, including housekeeping, a babysitter for her three children, and lost wages from quitting her job. J.F. and E.D. agreed and mailed checks of $500 to D.B.'s home address every two weeks. They, in particular E.D., also remained in frequent phone contact with D.B. about her condition.

In September 2003, Hamot Medical Center was informed via letter from SMI, that D.B., a surrogate mother, was choosing to give birth to triplets at their hospital and to make arrangements as needed. Hamot was also told to expect a court order accompanying the intended parents, J.F. and E.D., that would give them legal custody of the triplets after their birth. At that time, according to witness Paul Huckno, head of risk management at Hamot, the hospital had never dealt with a surrogate pregnancy before and had no specific policy in place governing such.

On Wednesday, November 19, 2003, at approximately 10 a.m., D.B. gave birth to triplets by C-section at Hamot. The babies were slightly premature at 35 weeks old and had some minor medical problems typical of their age. They were placed in the neonatal intensive care unit (NICU) under the care of doctors Jonathan and Michelle Kay Chai.

J.F. and E.D. were called at 8 a.m. on November 19 to inform them that D.B. was in labor. They arrived at Hamot that night between 7 and 8 p.m. from Ohio, with no court order. Hamot staff then employed their normal procedure of allowing the birth mother to consent to any and all visitors. From her hospital

---

12. The court does not wish to forcibly include J.R., the egg donor, in this matter, after she has already declined to become involved. As the court views it, an egg donor should be likened to a sperm donor. Because egg donation is a newer medical process than sperm donation, most states have not passed legislation addressing it. However, both donors contribute genetic material to others in exchange for payment, signing away all biological, parental, and other legal rights to their contribution and any child they may help produce. The majority of egg and sperm donations are anonymous proceedings, with neither the donors nor the recipients knowing the other. The donors, by choice and often by contract, choose to be uninvolved in the lives of any children that may result from their donations. For these reasons, the court does not consider J.R. to be a party to this matter. . . . .

bed, D.B. consented to J.F. and E.D. seeing the triplets. At that time, D.B. testified that she fully expected J.F. and E.D. to take care and custody of the triplets and she would return home without them.

The following days, November 20-24, E.D. maintained phone contact with Hamot NICU staff, checking on the triplets' condition and making appointments to visit them again that weekend. J.F. helped her complete legal and medical insurance paperwork and bought a mini-van with three car seats, as well as clothes, toys, and other things for the triplets.

On Saturday, November 22, D.B. was discharged from the hospital. She received a call from E.D. saying they were very "busy." E.D. made an appointment by phone with Dr. Jonathan Chai for November 22 to undergo sleep apnea monitor training for the triplets. The appointment was cancelled the next day because two triplets were put on oxygen by Dr. Michelle Chai. Both Doctors Chai later testified that cancellation of the appointment did not bar J.F. and E.D. from visiting the triplets. Meanwhile, D.B. continued to receive updates on the triplets' progress from her mother, a Hamot employee, who would stop by to check on them.

On Monday, November 24, E.D. called Hamot and scheduled monitor training. E.D. also called D.B. and said she and J.F. visited the triplets that weekend. The next day, D.B. called Hamot NICU to check on the triplets and discovered that E.D. and J.F. never visited the triplets that weekend. D.B. then called SMI concerned about this information.

On Tuesday, November 25, E.D. called Hamot for an update and indicated that she and J.F. would arrive at the hospital that evening. The same day, D.B. returned to Hamot to meet with several staff members, including Dr. Michelle Chai, NICU nurses, and social workers, about the triplets and whether she could take them home herself. She expressed concerns about the lack of visits from the intended parents, the fact that no names had been selected for the triplets, and E.D.'s apparent lie about visiting them. At the conclusion of the meeting, D.B. revoked her consent for J.F. and E.D. to visit the triplets and prepared to take them home with her. According to the testimony at the hearing from various Hamot staff members, no one encouraged or convinced D.B. that she should take the triplets home. Rather, it appears to have been her own idea.

Hamot set up "nesting" with D.B., her husband, and the triplets for that night (November 25). Nesting allows the parents or caretakers to care for their babies overnight, use the apnea sleep monitors, etc. as they would at home, but with hospital staff nearby to assist them with any problems and emergencies. D.B. and her husband also completed monitor training that day. D.B. did not call J.F. and E.D., testifying she assumed SMI would call them about her decision.

That evening, J.F. and E.D. arrived at Hamot and were met by security. They were informed that the triplets had been discharged to D.B. Upon returning home to Ohio, E.D. called D.B. and left a message, asking, "What's going on?" E.D. and J.F. also received a message from SMI Director Steven Litz, informing them of D.B.'s decision. On Thursday, November 27, the triplets were officially discharged to D.B.

From November 27 to December 11, 2003, D.B. received two phone calls from J.F. and E.D., which she did not return because she was "upset" and "angry."

J.F. and E.D. did not attempt to visit the triplets, claiming they did not know where they were until the December 11 court hearing before Judge Trucilla.

According to D.B.'s testimony at the hearing, J.F. and E.D. have only visited the triplets at D.B.'s residence two or three times a week, often at inconvenient times, instead of the allowed five visits per week. J.F. and E.D. testified that D.B. often cuts their visits short. D.B. also testified when J.F. and E.D. take the triplets with them, they often return them in soiled clothing and dirty diapers; E.D. often insists on feeding them, even when they have just been fed; and J.F. often sits silently or watches television, and once even fell asleep. D.B. further testified about increasing tension and conflicts between herself, her husband, and J.F. and E.D. whenever they visit. J.F. and E.D. maintain that they still intend to be parents to the triplets. The matter is now before the court.

CONCLUSIONS OF LAW

* * *

I. SURROGACY LAW IN PENNSYLVANIA

With these terms in mind, the court now turns to the issue at bar — whether a gestational surrogate like D.B. has standing to pursue a custody action against a biological parent like J.F. The only case in Pennsylvania to address a surrogate mother's standing is Huddleston v. Infertility Center of America Inc., 700 A.2d 453 (Pa. Super. 1997), a negligence and wrongful death case, but it is barely on point.

In *Huddleston*, a surrogate mother entered into a surrogate parenting agreement with a biological father, a single man. A month after birth, the child died as a result of the biological father's abuse. The surrogate mother filed suit against the fertility clinic that had arranged the surrogacy, alleging that the clinic's negligence in choosing the biological father caused the wrongful death of the child. The trial court found that the surrogate mother had no standing because she was not the child's legal parent. On appeal, the Superior Court found that the surrogate mother had standing, mostly because no one had challenged her standing to seek letters of administration for the child's estate. Further, the court found that the biological father's abusive actions were foreseeable and that the clinic had a duty of care to screen its surrogacy applicants for potential negative characteristics.

Since no Pennsylvania cases relating to surrogacy existed at that time, the *Huddleston* court relied on a Sixth Circuit case, Stiver v. Parker, 975 F.2d 261 (1992), which held a surrogacy agency liable for allowing surrogate mother to be infected by biological father's untested semen. The court determined that the agency had a "special relationship" with the surrogate mother and a duty of care to reduce harm to her and the child she carried.

However, *Stiver* is no more on point to the case at bar than *Huddleston*. As the trial court in *Huddleston* stated, "The absence of judicial precedence, and . . . legislative offerings, point out that there is no articulated fixed policy on many surrogacy issues in Pennsylvania at this time." Huddleston v. Infertility Center of America Inc., 31 D. & C.4th 128, 144 (1996).

This court is inclined to agree. Its own research has revealed very little stated policy regarding surrogacy in Pennsylvania. The last proposed surrogacy legislation was in 1997, H.B. 527 P.N. 590, a bill introduced in the House. . . . H.B. 527 proposed legalizing surrogate parenting agreements with court review and approval. If the parties did not seek court approval, a fine of up to $20,000 could be imposed and any agreement made would be null and void. The bill also required criminal background checks and extensive medical and psychological testing for all parties involved. Upon birth of the child/children, the surrogate mother's parental rights would terminate immediately and the intended parents would take full legal custody. If, for any reason, prior to the birth the surrogate parenting agreement was terminated, written notice would be given to the court and the surrogate mother would become the legal mother of the child/children. Unfortunately, H.B. 527 succumbed to the fate of several predecessors and died in judiciary committee. . . .

While it is premature to say that the Pennsylvania Legislature intended that a surrogate mother have legal custody in situations where there is no surrogacy contract or where it has been declared void, the possibility has at least been considered by the legislature and the court takes that into minor consideration in issuing its decision. Without an actual surrogacy statute in place, however, the court can only strongly urge the legislature to address the issue as soon as possible to prevent more complicated cases such as the one at bar.

II. SURROGACY LAWS IN OTHER STATES

Since this is a case of first impression in Pennsylvania, the court must look to the decisions rendered in sister states. In general, 31 states have either some type of surrogacy statute or case law setting forth the legality or illegality of surrogate parenting arrangements. Nineteen states, including Pennsylvania, are generally silent about surrogacy or do not have surrogacy laws or cases yet.

Sixteen of those 31 states have made surrogacy itself or surrogacy contracts illegal. Those states that make surrogacy (e.g., paid surrogacy or baby selling) expressly illegal are Delaware, Iowa, Michigan, New Mexico, New York, Oregon, Utah, Washington D.C. and Wisconsin. Surrogacy is exempt from criminal baby selling statutes in Iowa, Alabama and Washington. Those states that ban surrogacy contracts are Arizona, Connecticut, Indiana, Louisiana, New Jersey, North Dakota and Tennessee. Despite the fact that paid surrogacy contracts are illegal in New Jersey, free surrogacy volunteers (usually family members) are permitted. (Citations omitted).

Seven states generally allow surrogacy, with or without a contract, fees, etc. They are Arkansas, California, Hawaii, Illinois, Massachusetts, Ohio and West Virginia. Two of them, Massachusetts and California, require prebirth orders that terminate the surrogate mother's parental rights and give custody to the intended parents. Illinois allows all "parents" to be listed on birth certificate, including the surrogate mother or gestational surrogate, the intended parents, the biological parents, and/or sperm and egg donors.

Florida, New Hampshire, Virginia and Arkansas allow surrogacy contracts and mothers, with the first three states requiring that the intended mother be infertile. New Hampshire and Virginia courts review and approve surrogacy contracts while the Arkansas statute presumes a child born to a surrogate mother to be the child of the intended parents, not the surrogate mother.

California appears to be the state with the most surrogacy procedures, cases, and clinics. . . . It also appears to have some of the most complicated surrogacy case law and statutes. Generally, a surrogacy arrangement requires a contract between the parties prior to any medical procedures being performed. Then the intended parents must obtain a judgment of maternity and paternity prior to the child's birth. This judgment makes the intended parents the legal custodial parents. The surrogate mother, with or without a contract, is not the legal mother in California.

Such contracts are not barred by public policy as held in Johnson v. Calvert, 5 Cal. 4th 84, 851 P.2d 776 . . . (1993). In that case, the court ruled that the genetic parents were determined to be the natural, intended parents of the gestated child. The parties' intentions were foremost in determining who would have legal custody of a child conceived by surrogacy. This "intent test" continues to be followed in California and by other states, including Pennsylvania's neighbor, Ohio. See Belsito v. Clark, 644 N.E.2d 760 (1994), where a common pleas court determined those with genetic ties to a child conceived by surrogacy were the intended parents.

The Connecticut Supreme Court in Doe v. Doe, 244 Conn. 403, 710 A.2d 1297 (1998), granted a custody trial concerning a child conceived by surrogacy and related biologically only to the father/husband. The court decided to treat the wife as a third party with standing (the surrogate mother and egg donor had terminated their rights). Ultimately, the court determined that the best interests of the children would control, no matter the legal standing of the parties.

In Massachusetts, the case of R.R. v. M.H., 426 Mass. 501, 689 N.E.2d 790 (1998), set forth a requirement of three or more days for a surrogate mother to decide whether to terminate her parental rights, a time period similar to the state's adoption process. The Massachusetts Supreme Court found the surrogacy contract to be unenforceable because the surrogate mother received a fee for her services, which was against state public policy. The court expressed a preference for court-approved surrogacy contracts, or at the very least, some type of surrogacy statute passed by the legislature:

"We recognize that there is nothing inherently unlawful in an arrangement by which an informed woman agrees to attempt to conceive artificially and give birth to a child whose father would be the husband of an infertile wife. We suspect that many such arrangements are made and carried out without disagreement. . . . The mother and father may not, however, make a binding best-interests-of-the-child determination by private agreement. Any custody agreement is subject to a judicial determination of custody based on the best interests of the child. . . . A surrogacy agreement judicially approved before conception may be a better procedure. . . . *A Massachusetts statute concerning surrogacy agreements, pro or con, would provide guidance to judges, lawyers, infertile couples interested in surrogate parenthood, and prospective surrogate mothers.*" at 512-13. (emphasis added)

In a Massachusetts case addressing the custody of frozen embryos, the court in A.Z. v. B.Z., 431 Mass. 150, 725 N.E.2d 1051 (2000), remarked:

"We glean from . . . statutes and judicial decisions that prior agreements to enter into familial relationships (marriage or parenthood) should not be enforced against individuals who subsequently reconsider their decisions. This enhances the 'freedom of personal choice in matters of marriage and family life. We derive from existing state laws and judicial precedent a public policy in this Commonwealth that individuals shall not be compelled to enter into intimate family relationships, and that the law shall not be used as a mechanism for forcing such relationships when they are not desired. This policy is grounded in the notion that respect for liberty and privacy requires that individuals be accorded the freedom to decide whether to enter into a family relationship.'" at 162.

A New Jersey case, J.B. v. M.B., 331 N.J. Super. 223, 751 A.2d 613 (2000), similarly decided that a contract to procreate is against state public policy and agreements entering into or terminating family relations should not be enforced against unwilling parties. New Jersey is also home to the infamous In re Baby M, 109 N.J. 396, 537 A.2d 1227 (1988), case, which caused many states to either criminalize or regulate surrogacy. Since the surrogate was genetically related to the child she gave birth to, the *Baby M* case is not on point to the case at bar.

Based on the above cases, it appears to this court that the best way to address this matter is in terms of contract law and public policy.

III. LEGALITY OF THE SURROGACY CONTRACT

While the court is encouraged by several states' approach to surrogacy via contract law regulation, it is keenly aware that there is no Pennsylvania statute in place yet. Still, the court is inclined to look at the surrogacy contract entered into during July and August 2002 that started this entire sequence of events. (Plaintiff's exhibit B.)

The parties to the contract are the plaintiffs, J.F. and his paramour E.D.; the defendant, D.B., and her husband; J.R., the egg donor; SMI and its director/attorney, Steven Litz. The court again notes that J.R. is not considered a party to this action, despite the fact that the contract refers to her together with D.B. The court reviews some of the more interesting sections of the contract as follows:

Section 3 of the contract informs D.B. in capital letters that she is not consenting to termination of her parental rights or adoption at that time, just her intention to do so after the children are born.

Section 9 states biological father's obligations, except those required by law of a biological parent, will cease if the surrogate mother, D.B., refuses to abort or selectively reduce any of the fetuses she carries at J.F.'s request. The section does not state who would then take legal custody of the children once they were born.

Section 15 provides in the event that custody is awarded to surrogate mother, the other parties are indemnified and should be reimbursed any monies paid to the surrogate mother.

Section 20 states that the biological father, J.F., is legally responsible for the children, even if they have abnormalities, unless a paternity test reveals that the children are not J.F.'s. There is no provision providing for a legally responsible mother or other co-parent, especially if the children are not his.

Section 21 is where J.F. names E.D. to be his successor should something happen to him, but the space for a successor to E.D. is left blank. Again, there is no provision for whom takes custody of the children then.

The *Release and hold harmless agreement*, the last pages of the contract, appears to bar D.B. and her husband from seeking custody of the children. (Plaintiff's exhibit B, p. 9, P1.) It reads in relevant part: "Upon the birth of the child, Surrogate and/or E.D. [egg donor] *will surrender any custody rights to the child to the biological father* [biological father] whose identity (unless otherwise agreed upon) I/we may never know." [emphasis added]

These contractual inconsistencies and the failure to name a legal mother for these children greatly trouble the court. Section 3 and the Release and hold harmless agreement contradict each other when D.B. agrees that she *intends* to terminate her rights and then agrees that she *will* surrender her rights. Sections 9 and 20, 20 and 21, 15 and 20, and 9 and 20 are in conflict with each other in that section 20 says J.F. will be legally responsible for the children but the other sections undermine that responsibility by allowing it to "cease" or be "indemnified." At no time does the contract state who the legal mother of the children shall be, particularly if something were to happen to J.F. and E.D., or if they were to decide not to take custody of the children.

Pennsylvania has traditionally recognized that a child has two legal parents, usually a mother and father. According to the aforementioned definition of "parent," it includes anyone entitled to take under a child's estate, natural parents, adoptive parents, illegitimate parents, or any individual or agency acting as a child's guardian. In some circumstances, there may only be one legal parent (i.e., death or abandonment). However, there cannot be three legal parents. See Beltran v. Piersody, 2000 PA Super 66, 748 A.2d 715 (Pa. Super. 2000) . . .

Thus, J.F., E.D. and D.B. cannot all be parents simultaneously. Since E.D. is not actually a plaintiff/party to this action nor is she related to the triplets, the court excludes her from consideration.

Children should be able to identify who their parents are, even if they are not biologically or genetically connected to them. As the court in J.C. v. J.S., 2003 PA Super 172, 826 A.2d 1 (Pa. Super. 2003), recently held:

"Estoppel in paternity actions is merely the *legal determination* that because of a *person's conduct* (e.g., holding out the child as his own, or supporting the child) that person, *regardless of his true biological status, will not be permitted to deny parentage*. . . . The doctrine of estoppel in paternity actions is *aimed at 'achieving fairness as between the parents by holding them, both mother and father, to their prior conduct regarding paternity of the child.'*

"Warfield v. Warfield, 2003 PA Super 16, 815 A.2d 1073, P8 (Pa. Super. 2003) (quoting Fish v. Behers, 559 Pa. 523, 741 A.2d 721, 723 (1999)). Moreover,

"Estoppel is based on the public policy that children should be secure in knowing who their parents are. If a certain person has acted as the parent and bonded with the child, the child should not be required to suffer the potentially damaging trauma that may come from being told that the father he has known all his life is not in fact his father.

"Hamilton v. Hamilton, 2002 PA Super 72, 795 A.2d 403, 405 (Pa. Super. 2002) (quoting Fish, 741 A.2d at 724)." At 3-4 (emphasis added). . . .

There is no maternity by estoppel doctrine nor is there any legal definition of maternity, both of which might be suitable for this case since no legal mother has been named for the triplets. The court theorizes that if the doctrine of paternity by estoppel is based on the public policy that a child should know its father, then a doctrine of maternity by estoppel would be based on the corresponding public policy that a child should know its mother as well.

Moving on, a contract is void if it is used to bargain away rights belonging to children. See Sams v. Sams, 2002 PA Super 300, 808 A.2d 206 (Pa. Super. 2002) (Father/NFL player could not compel his ex-wife/mother to contract away his child support obligation. The court found the agreement to reduce the child support amount was unconscionable, reducing father's obligation from $3,400/month to $1,000/month.), . . . and Ferguson v. McKiernan, 60 D. & C.4th 353 (Dauphin Cty. 2002) (Court voided an oral contract between the parties where biological mother would release biological father from his child support obligation if he secretly volunteered to be her sperm donor.).

The contract in the case at bar did precisely the same as the parties attempted in *Sam*, . . . and *Ferguson*, to sign away the rights of the triplets. The court therefore declares the surrogacy contract entered into by the parties to be void as against public policy because it does not provide for a legal mother for the triplets and it allows the parties to bargain away the children's custody and support rights. . . .

The contract allowed D.B. to sign away her custodial rights without a time period to consider them or a court hearing to address them. That is against Pennsylvania public policy and the contract should not be enforced against her. . . .

* * *

A, B and C did not hatch, they were born. They can only identify their father in the contract as J.F., but they cannot identify their mother so easily. It cannot be J.R., the egg donor, because she is not a party to this action. It cannot be E.D., who is not genetically related to them, nor is she even married to J.F. She has contributed nothing more than her presence and her interest in the triplets. That leaves D.B., who like E.D. is not genetically related to the triplets, but carried them in her womb and then gave birth to them. Her every decision prior to their birth has affected them — health, nutrition, prenatal care, etc. In addition, she has not terminated any parental rights she may have to the triplets. She has instead taken the triplets into her home and cared for them along with her three other children. She is more a mother and a parent by her actions than by genetics. She has assumed "maternity" if there were such a legal definition as there exists for "paternity." Since the contract is void because it does not provide for a legal mother, the court finds D.B. to be the legal mother of the triplets since she carried and bore them and has taken care of them as a natural parent would.

IV. STANDING IN LOCO PARENTIS

Even if this court did not determine that D.B. is the legal mother of the triplets, she would most likely still have third-party standing in loco parentis. Black's Law Dictionary defines in loco parentis to be, literally, "in place of parent." (Citations omitted). It is also a legal doctrine that allows a person who assumes the duties and rights of a natural parent to have temporary standing in parental matters, such as custody and support, in absence of legal proceedings. Given D.B.'s unusual situation as a gestational surrogate with no genetic tie to A, B, and C, and her previous intentions to give them to J.F. and E.D., she does not neatly fit into any particular category of third party that has tried to claim custodial standing in loco parentis.

* * *

Stepparents and same sex parents

D.B. is much more like a stepparent or a same sex parent, taking into account her lack of genetic tie and her voluntary care of the triplets. In Parton v. Parton, 36 D. & C.4th 241 (Monroe Cty. 1996), the court granted a stepfather partial custody in loco parentis based on his good relationship with his stepsons. He met the preponderance of evidence burden of proof by showing that he was doing all the things a parent would do, including feeding, bathing, playing and disciplining his stepsons. In Liebner v. Simcox, 2003 PA Super 377, 834 A.2d 606, 610 (Pa. Super. 2003) another stepfather was granted standing in loco parentis because he provided a "family setting [for the child], irrespective of . . . traditional or nontraditional composition." The nature of the relationship between parents has no legal significance for in loco parentis standing. T.B. v. L.R.M., 567 Pa. 222, 786 A.2d 913 (2001), and children are not to be treated as the offspring of the biological single parent only. J.A.L. v. E.P.H., 453 Pa. Super. 78, 682 A.2d 1314 (1996). Thus, despite the unusualness of a surrogacy arrangement, J.F. cannot claim to be the sole parent of the triplets. D.B., through her actions, has clearly shown that she is "doing all things a parent would do" and as a surrogate mother has and is creating a non-traditional family setting.

The court also notes a "void in the law" for surrogate mother standing. As the court in L. S. K. v. H. A. N., 813 A.2d 872 (Pa. Super. 2002) (emphasis in original), said, "We recognize this is a matter which is better addressed by the legislature rather than the courts. However, in the absence of legislative mandates, the courts must construct a fair, workable and responsible basis for the protection of children, aside from whatever rights the adults may have *vis-a-vis* each other."

D.B. has assumed parental duties when she could have simply taken her surrogacy fee and walked away. She was not legally obligated to provide care or child support, yet she took on those responsibilities willingly and voluntarily. She and her husband went through monitor training and car seat testing and overnight nesting with the triplets. They continue to care for the triplets plus three other children in their home. It does not appear to the court that D.B. was pressured or talked into bringing the triplets home with her or that she is unable to handle the responsibility of being a legal mother to A, B and C.

V. PARENTAL DUTIES AND WISHES

The court disagrees with plaintiff's argument that D.B. acted in defiance of J.F.'s wishes by taking the triplets home with her and thus should not be granted standing in loco parentis because J.F., as biological father, does not approve. See B.A. v. E.E., 559 Pa. 545, 741 A.2d 1227 (1999). The court would point out the unfortunate reality that many custody decisions are made where one party/parent does not approve of the other's actions and decisions, but must acquiesce because a court has allowed it.

Claims of parenthood and parental disagreement are not enough to defeat standing.

* * *

In the case at bar and prior to this court's determination of D.B.'s legal parental status, D.B. is a third party seeking custody against J.F., the biological father of the triplets. As *Cardamone* [Cardamone v. Elshoff, 442 Pa. Super. 263, 659 A.2d 575 (1995)] held, his claim of parenthood alone is not enough to defeat D.B.'s counterclaim for custody. The court may consider the triplets' present well-being as well as their future welfare. (Citations omitted).

The court heard the testimony of D.B. as to her care of the triplets as well as their condition upon their return from visits with J.F. and E.D., and found her to be credible. Even discounting her testimony, the court also heard testimony from various Hamot medical staff and read their reports regarding the lack of visits from the intended parents and their behavior when they did visit (i.e., arriving late or canceling appointments, the delay in monitor training, nursing staff repeatedly telling E.D. to be quiet or calm down in the NICU). This is more than enough to cause the court some concern regarding J.F. and E.D. and the fulfillment of their parental duties.

As in the case In re C.M.S., 2003 PA Super 292, 832 A.2d 457 (Pa. Super. 2003), the biological father argued that since he was not aware of the child's whereabouts, he had no recourse but to wait for the adoption papers. The court determined that the father failed to take any action to overcome the obstacles to assert his parental rights.

* * *

It is obvious from J.F. and E.D.'s testimony that they have an interest in the triplets. J.F. vowed at one hearing to fight for custody "all the way to the United States Supreme Court." But, their testimony and actions, or rather inactions, belie their professed intentions for these children. They have provided financial support and insurance and amenities that children need, but they have not named the children, have not visited them with regular frequency, did not buy and prepare things for the triplets *prior* to their birth nor make insurance arrangements, schedule monitor and car seat training, etc. with Hamot in a timely manner. They have not shown this court that they exerted themselves to maintain a parent-child relationship with the triplets, such as going to court as soon as D.B. took triplets home against their wishes, or exercised reasonable firmness in overcoming obstacles, like locating D.B.'s home to visit the triplets or speak with her in person. Even after they obtained a court order allowing them visitation five days a week, they have not fully utilized it. See also, C.T.D. v. N.E.E., 439 Pa. Super. 58, 653 A.2d 28 (1995) (delay is arguable abandonment and failure to perform parental duties).

* * *

CONCLUSION

It is the finding of this court that D.B. is the legal mother of the triplets, A, B and C, due to the fact that no legal mother was provided for in the surrogacy contract. Because the contract encouraged parties to sign away certain legal rights belonging to the triplets, the court finds it to be unconscionable. Thus, the contract is void as against Pennsylvania public policy.

Aside from the court's determination that D.B. is the legal mother of the triplets and therefore has automatic standing, the court also finds that D.B. has standing in loco parentis to pursue both custody and child support for the triplets. As biological father, J.F. has a legal duty to provide child support even if he disagrees with who has custody of the triplets. The court refers the parties back to custody conciliation with all due haste.

Finally, the court asks that the plaintiff and defendant bear in mind that the best interests of the triplets are most important here. "To say that the child is merely the subject of the proceeding, not a 'party' to it, would be to return to the child-as-chattel mentality." Stapleton v. Dauphin County Child Care Service, 228 Pa. Super. 371, 392, 324 A.2d 562, 573 (1974). (Opinion of Spaeth, J., overruled on other grounds.) It is the hope of this court that a custodial tug-of-war will not begin here. It is additionally the court's hope that the legislature will address surrogacy matters in Pennsylvania to prevent cases like this one from appearing before the courts without statutory guidance.

NOTES AND QUESTIONS

1. What is the basis for the gestational mother's claim to parental status on the facts of this case? Is the reasoning of this decision consistent with or inconsistent with the reasoning of Johnson v. Calvert?

2. Is it critical to the outcome of this case that the surrogacy contract provided for no legal mother? Would the outcome of the case have been different if J.F., the biological intended father, had been married and his wife had been named as the intended legal mother? If his "paramour," E.D., had been named in the contract as the intended legal mother?

3. How important to the outcome of this case is the finding that the gestational mother has standing in loco parentis to pursue custody and child support? Would the outcome of this case have been different if the lawsuit were filed while the child was still in the hospital?

4. As the *J.F.* opinion notes, a number of states reject surrogacy, with some making it a crime, a larger number treating surrogacy contracts as void, and other states distinguishing between paid surrogacy and unpaid surrogacy. As a practical matter, given the technical simplicity of artificial insemination, is it possible to ban surrogacy arrangements altogether? What is the difference between banning them and making agreements for such arrangements unenforceable? How would you expect the result in this case to change surrogacy practice in Pennsylvania?

5. A few states simply have exempted surrogacy agreements from provisions making it a crime to sell babies. *E.g.,* Ala. Code. § 26-10A-34 (1992); Iowa Code

§ 710.11 (1997); W. Va. Code § 48-4-16(e)(3) (1996). An Arkansas statute creates a presumption that a child born to a surrogate mother is the child of the intended parents and not of the surrogate. Ark. Code Ann. § 9-10-201 (Michie 1993).

6. The court states that in California "the intended parents must obtain a judgment of maternity and paternity prior to the child's birth," but, in fact, the status of such judgments is in doubt. These declaratory judgments have been called "UPA declarations," based on the Uniform Parentage Act of 1973 principles that formed the basis for the ruling in Buzzanca v. Buzzanca, 72 Cal. Rptr. 2d 280 (Cal. App. 1998). The *Buzzanca* court reasoned that where the intended parents had engineered the birth of a child under circumstances that severed the involvement of the biological parents and their spouses, the intended parents bore the responsibility for the child. In subsequent cases, intended parents in agreement on the desired outcome have filed before a judge receptive to their request, seeking a determination of parental status effective upon the birth of the child. Over a hundred such declarations have been granted at the trial court level in California. The first appellate test of the UPA declarations occurred in Kristine H. v. Lisa R., 16 Cal. Rptr. 3d 123 (Cal. App. 2004). The court ruled that UPA declarations, like other efforts to establish parenthood by contract, are void. The California Supreme Court, however, has granted review, and as we go to press, a decision had not been issued. *See* Kristine Renee H. v. Lisa Anne R., 97 P.3d 72 (Cal. 2004).

7. If the court were to hold that D.B. had standing on the basis of in loco parentis without also finding that she is a legal mother on the basis of gestation, would such a ruling pose constitutional questions under *Troxel*? The *J.F.* opinion mentions the Connecticut case of Doe v. Doe, 710 A.2d 1297 (Conn. 1998), which used a best-interest test to rebut the presumption in favor of parental custody in order to allow the father's wife standing to seek custody of a child she had helped raise for eight years. After *Troxel*, however, the Connecticut Supreme Court overruled *Doe*. Connecticut now requires that a "third party must allege and prove, by clear and convincing evidence, a relationship with the child that is similar in nature to a parent-child relationship, and that denial of the visitation would cause real and significant harm to the child." In re Joshua S, 796 A.2d 1141, 1156 (2002). How would D.B. fare under the Connecticut standard?

Table of Cases

Principal cases are in italics.

A.A.M., In re Adoption of, 822
Abate, Estate of, 251
Abbott v. Smith, State ex rel., 954
Abitz v. Abitz, 574, 575
A.B.M. v. M.H., 971
Accord Holy Name Hosp. v. Montroy, 28
Adam v. Adam, 666
Adams, In re, 401
Adoption of _____. *See also* name of party
Adoption of a Child by D.M.H., Matter of, 951
Adoption of a Child by W.P., 954
Adoption of a Minor, In re, 951
Adoption of Child by T.W.C., In re, 821
Adoption of Children by F., Matter of, 954
Adoption of Copeland, In re, 808
A.E.H., In re, 822
A.E., In Interest of, 971
Ainsworth and Ainsworth, 574
Ainsworth v. Ainsworth, 566, 571, 572, 573, 574
A.K.H., Custody of, 969
Alford v. Alford, 428
Alibrando v. Alibrando, 562
Alicia S., In re, 971
Alison D. v. Virginia M., 17
Allen v. Farrow, 691, 693, 694
Almario v. Attorney General, 164
ALMA Soc'y v. Mellon, 955
Altman, In re marriage of, 422
Altman v. Altman, 760
A.M.D., In the Interest of, 523
American Healthcare Center v. Randall, 543
Amsellem v. Amsellem, 157
Ankenbrandt v. Richards, 831, 836
Anonymous v. Anonymous, 162
Antolik v. Harvey, 484
Arceneaux, State v., 699
Archina v. People, 163
Arnelle v. Fisher, 174

Arnold v. Arnold, 443
Aronson v. Aronson, 304
Askins v. Askins, 422
Atchison v. Atchison, 817
Atherton, Custody of, 955
Atlanta, City of, v. Morgan, 279
Attorney-General v. _____. *See* name of party
Auble, In the Matter of the Marriage of, 761
Avriett v. Avriett, 761
A.Z. v. B.Z., 1002

Baade, In re, 971
Baby Boy Doe, In re, 971
Baby Boy L., Matter of Adoption of, 970
Baby Girl Clausen, In re, 821
Baby M., In re, 984, 1003
Baby M., Matter of, 995, 996
Backes, In re, 320
Baehr v. Lewin, 207, 223
Baehr v. Miike, 207
Baker v. Baker, 801
Baker v. Vermont, 206, 208
Balfour v. Balfour, 104
Ballesteros v. Jones, 354
Barbara Haven, In re, 215
Barber v. Barber, 772, 788, 832, 836
Barker v. State, 27
Barnae v. Barnae, 816
Bartlett v. Bartlett, 349
Baskerville v. Baskerville, 353
Bass v. Bass, 259
Bates and Bates, 560, 561
Bates, In re, 826
Bates v. Tesar, 706
Battersby v. Battersby, 523
Bauer, In re, 952
Baugh v. Baugh, 307
Baures v. Lewis, 709

B.A. v. E.E., 1006
Bedford v. Bedford, 541
Belsito v. Clark, 1002
Beltran v. Piersody, 1004
Bennett v. Bennett, 836
Benson v. Benson, 814
Bentz v. Bentz, 451
Bercume v. Bercume, 766
Bergen Cty. Bd. of Servs. v. Steinhauer, 533
Berger v. State, 27
Berle v. Berle, 425
Bersani v. Bersani, 712, 714
Bessette v. W.B. Conkey Co., 592
Beverly v. Beverly, 575
Bhaiji v. Chauhan, 321
Bielby v. Bielby, 172
Birt v. Birt, 616
Bishop v. Bishop, 162, 163
Blondin v. Dubois, 829
Boddie v. Connecticut, 316, 351
Boggs v. Boggs, 53, 59, 61, 388
Bolando v. Catalano, 252
Bonds, In re, 738, 739, 746, 750
Booth v. Booth, 401
Borden v. Borden, 351
Borelli v. Brusseau, 98, 112
Borough of Glassboro v. Vallorosi, 25
Boswell v. Boswell, 665
Bottoms v. Bottoms, 668
Bove v. Pinciotti, 163
Bowen v. Bowen, 490
Bowen v. Gilliard, 576, 578
Bowers v. Hardwick, 208, 209
Bowman v. Bowman, 653
Bozzi v. Bozzi, 722
Bracklow v. Bracklow, 449, 450
Braddock v. Braddock, 425
Bradewell v. Illinois, 89
Bradley v. Superior Court, 592
Brandt v. Brandt, 523
Branstetter, In re Marriage of, 476
Braschi v. Stahl Associates Company, 13
Brewer v. Brewer, 556
Bridget R., In re, 970
Brode, In re, 808
Brooks v. Brooks, 100, 101, 102
Browning v. Melton, People ex rel., 572
Brown, In re (21 F. Supp. 935), 614
Brown, In re (136 Cal.App.2d 40), 583, 584
Brown v. Brown, 43, 667
Brozowski v. Brozowski, 659
Bruker v. City of New York, 980
Brunges v. Brunges, 308
Buck v. Bell, 170
Burchard v. Garay, 635, 639, 642, 702, 704, 719
Burgess v. Burgess, 406, 700, 707, 708, 721
Burnham v. Superior Court, 782
Burns v. Burns, 137, 277, 281
Burns v. Stewart, 354
Burrus, In re, 831
Butler v. Butler, 43, 484
Buzzanca v. Buzzanca, 1009

Caldwell v. Caldwell, 549
Calhoun, In re, 617, 618
Califano v. Goldfarb, 92
Califano v. Jobst, 182
Califano v. Webster, 94, 95
California under International Shoe Co. v. Washington, 783
California v. Superior Court, 836
Callahan v. Davis, 720
Cameron v. Baker, 504
Cameron v. Cameron, 401
Campbell v. Campbell, 388, 693
Campbell v. Martin, 819
Canakaris v. Canakaris, 406
Carabetta v. Carabetta, 157
Cardamone v. Elshoff, 1007
Carnes v. Sheldon, 252
Carney, In re Marriage of, 636
Carol v. Lee, 252
Carrieres v. Commission, 606
Carvin v. Britain (In re Parentage of L.B.), 983
Cash v. Catholic Diocese, 21
Cason v. Cason, 777
Casper v. Casper, 440
Catalano v. Catalano, 221
Catala v. Catala, 954
Catli, In re, 615
C.D., People in Interest of, 568
Centazzo v. Centazzo, 422
Central States v. Gray, 244
Chance v. Chance, 483
Chandler v. Chandler, 480
Chapman v. Chapman, 760
Charter Township of Delta v. Dinolfo, 30
Cheever v. Wilson, 772
Cherradi v. LaVoie, 639
Childers v. Childers, 534, 539
A Child of Indian Heritage, In re, 971
Ching v. Ching, 524
Ciganovich, In re Marriage of, 704
Citizens for Equal Protection, Inc. v. Bruning, 278
City of _____. *See* name of city
C.J.L. v. M.W.B., 692
Clark v. Gordon, 822
Clark v. Tabor, 572
Cleaves v. City of Chicago, 279
Cleland v. Cleland, 351
C.M.S., In re, 1007
Coleman v. Coleman, 809
Collins, In re Marriage of, 321
Collins v. Commissioner, 606
Colonna v. Colonna, 528, 531, 532
Combs v. Combs, 562
Comer v. Comer, 590
Commissioner v. Lester, 609
Committee on Professional Ethics & Conduct v. Hill, 365
Compos v. McKeithen, 974
Condon, In re Marriage of, 707
Connally v. General Constr. Co., 632
Connell v. Francisco, 260, 263, 264, 266

Cook v. Cook, 776
Cooper, In re, 354
Cordone v. Cordone, 354
Costello v. Costello, 174
Country of Luxembourg ex rel. Ribeiro v.
  Cauderas, 800
Cox v. Cox, 524
Craig v. Boren, 80, *90*, 94, 95
Crawford v. City of Chicago, 279
C.R.B. v. C.C., 631, 720
Creasman v. Boyle, 261, 263
Crews, In re Adoption of, 970
Crews v. Crews, 560
Crockett v. Crockett, 574
Croll v. Croll, 828
Crouch, In re marriage of, 422
C.T.D. v. N.E.E., 1007
Curtis v. Kline, 539
Custody of _____. *See* name of party

D.A.C, Interest of, 971
Dalip Singh Bir's Estate, In re, 223
Dallenger, In re Custody of, 720
Dallman, In re Estate of, 236
Damiano v. Damiano, 84
Damico v. Damico, 590
Davenport v. Commissioner, 606
Davis v. Davis (16 P.3d478), 321
Davis v. Davis (657 S.W.2d 753), *300*
Davis v. Davis (658 N.Y.S.2d 548 [App.
  Div.1997]), 672
Dawley, In re Marriage of, 105
Debenham v. Debenham, 659
Deegan v. Deegan, *551*, *555*, *556*
Deffenbaugh, 416
DeGrace v. De Grace, 592
Deitz v. Deitz, 422
DeJesus v. DeJesus, 469
Delfino v. Delfino, 162
DeLong v. DeLong, 667
DeLorean v. DeLorean, 738
Delvoye v. Lee, 826
De Meo v. State, 776
Dennis, In re Marriage of, 590
DePasse, Estate of, 157
Desrochers v. Desrochers, 312, 315
DeTevis v. Aragon, 574
Devlin v. Philadelphia, 279
De Vries v. De Vries, 163
D.G., In re, 954
Dilger v. Dilger, 553, 554
DiSandro, In re, 366
Dixon v. Dixon, 451
Dix v. Plank, State ex rel., 572
D.M.J., Matter of Adoption of, 970
Dockins v. Dockins, 665
Doe, In Interest of, 808
Doe v. Doe, 668, 1002, 1009
Donahue v. Donahue, 483
D'Onofrio v. D'Onofrio, 722
Do v. Superior Court (Nguyen), 354
Downing v. Downing, 524

Draper v. Draper, 618
Drewes v. Ilnicki, 836
Drummond v. Fulton County Dep't of Family
  & Children's Services, 974
Dudgeon v. United Kingdom, 208
Duffey v. Duffey, 574
Duffy, In re Marriage of, 380
Dugan v. Dugan, 481
Dugas v. Adoption of Dugas, 951
Duncan, In re Marriage of, 354
Dungan v. Dungan, 318
D.W.W. (R.W. v. D.W.W.), Ex parte, 668
Dwyer, In re Marriage of, *561*, *562*, *563*, *566*

Earle v. Earle, 65, 66
Earls v. Earls, 314, 315
Eastis, In re Marriage of, 428
Eaton v. Johnston, 264
Eder v. Grifka, 79
Edmunds v. Edwards, *165*
Edwards v. California, 706
E.E.B. v. D.A., 821
E.E.C. v. E.J.C., 484
Egelhoff v. Egelhoff, 61, 63
Eggmeyer v. Eggmeyer, 401
Elchinger v. Elchinger, 540
Elliott, In re, 971
Elliot v. Elliot, 592
Elmer, In re Marriage of, 697
Elser, In re Marriage of, 709
Elzroth, In the Matter of the Marriage of,
  761
Employment Division v. Smith, 24
Eriksen, In re Estate of, 252
Erik Vaughn D., In re, 954
Ertel v. Ertel, 169
Eslami v. Eslami, 484
Estate of _____. *See* name of party
Esteb v. Esteb, 535, 536
Estelle, In re Marriage of, 638
Estin v. Estin, 779
Evans v. Evans, 287
Everett v. Everett, 777
Ewell v. State, 82
Ex parte _____. *See* name of party
Ezeonu, People v., 223

Fairclaw v. Forrest, 46
Fall v. Eastin, 781
Falrey v. Liskey, 572
Farmer v. Farmer, 439
Farrey v. Sanderfoot, 614, 615
Featherston v. Steinhoff, 258
Feely v. Birenbaum, 21
Feiock, In re , supra, 588
Fellerman v. Bradley, 713
Feltman v. Feltman, 573
Ferguson, In the Interest of, 631, 720
Ferguson v. Ferguson, 406
Ferguson v. McKiernan, 1005
Finer, Marriage of, 692

Fink, In re Marriage of, 398
Fisher v. Fisher, 469
Fish v. Behers, 1004
Fish v. Fish, 812, 814
Fitzgerald v. Fitzgerald, 618
Fitzpatrick v. Sterling Housing Association, 17
Flaherty v. Flaherty, 376
Flores v. Flores, 319, 351
Fonstein, In re Marriage of, 428
Fontenot, In re Marriage of, 815
Foran, In re Marriage of, 740
Foray v. Bell Atlantic, 279
Ford v. Ford, 481
Foretich v. United States, 699
Forlenza, In re, *810*, 814
Forsdick v. Turgeon, 618
Foster, In re, 481
Foster v. Stein, 821
Fountain v. Fountain, 469
Fourie and Bonthuys v. Minister of Home
    Affairs, 213
Foy, Estate of, 242
Frances B. v. Mark B., 214
Francis, In re, 708, 709
Francis, In re Marriage of, 450
Frase v. Barhart, 707
Frederick, In re, 469
Friedrich v. Friedrich, *822, 827, 829*
Frontiero v. Richardson, 90
Furillio v. Crowther, 504
Furnes v. Reeves, 828

Gainey v. Olivo, 821
Gallaher v. Elam, 572
Gammelgaard v. Gammelgaard, 236
Gant v. Gant, 739
Gardiner, In re Estate of, 214
Gardner v. Perry, 575
Garlinger v. Garlinger, 562
Garska v. McCoy, 641, 666
Geldmeier v. Geldmeier, *425, 428, 429*
Gelkop v. Gelkop, 781
Gestl v. Frederick, 816
Geyer, Estate of, 733, 736
Gilbert, In Marriage of, 532
Gilley v. McCarthy, 572
Gillmore, In re Marriage of, 474
Gimbel Bros., Inc. v. Pinto, 81
Glasscock v. Glasscock, 353
Goesart v. Cleary, *90*
Golden v. Golden, 482
Goldman v. Goldman, 484
Gomprecht, In the Matter of, 84
Gonzalez v. City of Castle Rock, 134
Gonzalez v. Gutierrez, 828
Goodridge v. Department of Public Health, *195*,
    206, 208, 226, 278
Gormley v. Robertson, 264
Gould v. Gould, 380
Graby v. Graby, 556
Gragg v. Gragg, 476
Graham v. State, 300

Green, State v., 187, 239
Gregory B., In re, 954
Griffin v. Griffin, 658, 788
Grishman v. Grishman, 422
Griswold v. Connecticut, 140, 178, 180, 182
Grother, In re Marriage of, 236
Groves v. Clark, 954
Grubs v. Ross, 815
Guardian of _____. *See* name of party
Guardianship of _____. *See* name of party
Gursky v. Gursky, 981
Guzman v. Guzman, 484
Gwendolyn, Adoption of, 955

Haddock v. Haddock, *769, 772, 773*
Hadeen, In re Marriage of, *673*
Hadjimilitis v. Tsavliris, 315
Haguewood, 404
Haley v. Haley, 592
Hall, In re, 572
Hall, In re Marriage of, 481, 486
Halloway, In re Adoption of, 968, 969
Hall v. Dustr, 238
Halloway, In re Adoption (732 P.2d 762),
    968
Halpern et al. v. Canada, 211
Halstead v. Halstead, 472
Halvey v. Halvey, 802
Hamilton v. Hamilton, 1004
Hampton v. J.A.L., 970
Hanks v. Hanks, 592
Hanson v. Denckla, 784
Hanson v. Hanson, 161, 484
Hardesty v. Hardesty, 559
Hard's Case, 504
Harman v. Rogers, 260
Harper v. Virginia State Board of Elections,
    182
Harrell, In re, 617, 618
Harris v. Harris, 592
Harris v. Smith, 720
Harrod v. Harrod, 781
Harvey v. Harvey, 592
Hatch v. Hatch, 401
Hathcock v. Hathcock, 711
Havens v. Henning, 521, 522
Haxton v. Haxton, 540
Haymes v. Haymes, 304
Head, In re Marriage of, 484
Heath v. Heath, 813
Heller v. Heller, 481
Henderson v. City of Simi Valley, 122
Henderson v. Henderson, 773
Hendrickson, State v., 190
Hendricks v. Hendricks, 304, 354
Henry v. Henry, 722
Hereford, In re Estate of, *762*
Herrick v. Herrick, 779
Hewitt v. Hewitt, *10*, *252*
Hicks v. Feiock, 588, 592
Hightower v. Hightower, 318
Hillegass Estate, 733

Hill v. Hill, 138
Hines v. Hines, 574
Hisquierdo v. Hisquierdo, 471
Hoak v. Hoak, 488
Hodge v. Hodge, 781
Hoffman v. Hoffman, 523
Holder v. Holder, 830
Hollis v. Hollis, 303
Holman v. Holman, 476
Holm v. Holm, 559
Holt v. Geter, 533
Homan v. Homan, 167
Hoover v. Hoover, 572
Howell v. Howell, 484
Hresko v. Hresko, 758, 761
Huckfeldt, In re, 612, 613, 614
Huddleston v. Infertility Center of America
    Inc., 1000
Hudson v. Hudson, 592
Huff, In re Marriage of, 481
Huff v. Director, 244
Hughes v. Hughes, 425
Hugo, Adoption of, 653
Humberger v. Humberger, 354
Hunt, In re Marriage of, 467
Huston, In re Marriage of, 469
Hutchinson v. Hutchinson, 555
Hyde v. Hyde, 777

Imel v. United States, 606
In Petition of _____. *See* name
    of party
In re _____. *See* name of party
In the Interest of _____. *See* name of party
In the Matter of _____. *See* name
    of party
International Shoe Co. v. Washington, 773,
    782, 783, 784
Ipscott v. Maryland, 193
Irizarry v. Board of Education of the City of
    Chicago, 279
Isham v. Isham, 569
Ivey v. Ivey, 781

Jacobitti v. Jacobitti, 581
Jacqueline F., Matter of, 715
Jafarian-Kerman v. Jafarian-Kerman, 715
J.A.L. v. E.P.H., 1006
Jarrett v. Jarrett, 665
Jay R., In re, 952
J.B. v. A.B., 666
J.B. v. M.B., 1003
J.E.B. v. Alabama Ex Rel. T.B., 97
Jeffcoat v. Jeffcoat, 409
Jenkins v. Jenkins, 406
Jennings, In re, 583, 584
Jensen-Branch, In re, 678
Jersey Shore Medical Center v. Baum, 82
J.F. v. D.B., 997
J.L.P.(H.) v. D.J.P., 697
Johnson v. Bail, State ex rel., 716

Johnson v. Calvert, 984, 996, 997, 1002, 1008
Johnson v. Johnson (239 Ga. 714, 238 S.E.2d
    437 [1977]), 244
Johnson v. Johnson (329 A.2d 451), 318
Johnson v. Muelberger, 776
Johnsrud, In re Marriage of, 439
Johnston v. Johnston, 175
Johns v. Johns, 678
J.O.L., In the Matter of, 632
Jones v. Jones, 158, 671
Jones v. Williams, 540
Jordan v. Jordan, 722
Jorgensen v. Jorgensen, 574
Joshua S., In re, 1009

Kalinoski v. Kalinoski, 473
Kallas v. Kallas, 722
Kampf v. Kampf, 133
Kane v. Kane, 781
Kantaras v. Kantaras, 214
Kanta v. Kanta, 473
Kapfer v. Kapfer, 469
K.A.S., In re Adoption of, 952
Keeler v. Keeler, 766
Kendall v. Kendall, 677, 682
Kessler, In re Marriage of, 574
Kevin, Attorney-General (Cth) v., 215
Khalil, In re, 157
Khan v. Khan, 698
Kimsey, Ex parte, 355
King v. King, 721
Kirchberg v. Feenstra, 49
Kirkpatrick v. Dist. Ct., 218
Kirsch Holding Co. v. Borough of Manasquan,
    27
Kittredge v. Kittredge, 409
Klein v. Klein, 138
Klemme v. Schoneman, 615
Klemm v. Klemm, 345, 378
Klingberg v. Klingberg, 409
K.L.J., In re, 952
K.L.P., In re Adoption of, 952
Knight v. Knight, 686, 698
Kober v. Kober, 174
Koelsch v. Koelsch, 468
Koidl v. Schreiber, 549
Konzelman v. Konzelman, 564
Koon v. Koon, 315
Kovacs v. Brewer, 802
Kowalesky v. Kowalesky, 481
Kozlowski v. Kozlowski, 255
Kreyling v. Kreyling, 302
Kristine H. v. Lisa R., 1009
Kristine Renee H. v. Lisa Anne R., 1009
Krupa v. Green, State ex. rel., 175
Kucera v. Kucera, 295, 301, 304
Kugler v. Haitian Tours, Inc., 776, 777
Kulko v. Superior Court, 783, 786, 788, 809
Kumar v. Superior Court, 815
Kummer, Matter of, 84
Kunkel, In re Marriage of, 693
Kuppinger, In re Marriage of, 440

Ladely, In re Marriage of, 572
Ladue, City of, v. Horn, 18
Laing v. Laing, 463, 466, 467, 471, 475
Lalo v. Malca, 828
Lalone, In re, 523
LaMusga, In re Marriage of, 707, 721
Langan v. St. Vincent's Hospital of New York, 278
Lang v. Koon, 524
Lannan v. Maul, 836
Larocque, In re the Marriage of, 443, 448, 450, 451, 456
Larroquette v. Larroquette, 697
LaRue v. LaRue, 406
Lasky, In re Marriage of, 650
Laurie R., Matter of, 808
Lawrence v. Texas, 195, 208, 209, 226
L.C., In re, 821
Leathers and Leathers, 408
LeBlanc, In re, 523
Lehr v. Robertson, 989
Lepis v. Lepis, 440, 443, 560
Leseberg v. Taylor, 610
Lesko v. Lesko, 469
Levin v. Levin, 981
Lewis v. Harris, 210
Lewis v. Lewis, 140
Liberta v. People, 114, 117
Liebner v. Simcox, 1006
Lien v. Lien (Lien II), 558
Lindsey, In re Marriage of, 261, 263
Littleton v. Prange, 214
Loll v. Loll, 653
Lombardo v. Lombardo, 657
London v. Handicapped Facilities Board of St. Charles County, 21
Lord v. Lord, 814
Loughmiller, In re, 222
Loving v. Virginia, 177, 178, 180, 198, 207, 670, 974
Lower, In re Marriage of, 722
Lowe v. Broward County, 279
Lozada v. Rivera, 532
L.S.K. v. H.A.N., 1006
Lucas v. Earl, 603
Lundahl v. Telford, 798
Luthen v. Luthen, 307
Lutwak v. United States, 158, 163, 164, 226
Lyons v. Lederle Laboratories, 544

MacGregor v. Unemployment Insurance Appeals Board, 17
M.A.C., In Interest of, 808
MacIntyre v. MacIntyre, 836
Maglica v. Maglica, 259
Mahoney v. Mahoney, 493
Mangone v. Mangone, 422
Manion v. Manion, 319
Mansell v. Mansell, 472
Marquardt v. Marquardt, 557, 558, 559
Marriage of _____. *See* name of party
Marrocco v. Giardino, 532

Marshfield Clinic v. Discher, 87
Marsh v. Marsh, 477
Martin v. Ohio, 587
Martin v. Ohio, supra, 587
Marvin v. Marvin, 249, 258, 264, 266, 406
Masek v. Masek, 638
Mason v. Mason, 222
Matherne v. Matherne, 574
Mathews v. Eldridge, 682, 684
Matter of _____. *See* name of party
Maxwell, Matter of Marriage of, 484
Maxwell v. Maxwell, 43
Maynard v. Hill, 177, 316
May's Estate, In re, 218, 222
May v. Anderson, 801, 808
May v. May, 479, 489
May v. Sessums, 355
M.B. II v. M.B., In the Matter of, 813
Mazique v. Mazique, 50
McAlear v. McAlear, 592
McAlpine v. McAlpine, 732
McCann v. McCann, 646
McCarty v. McCarty, 471
McClary v. Thompson, 468
McCormick v. State, 951
McCoy, In re, 803, 817
McCready v. Hoffius, 24
McDevitt, In re, 951
McDiarmid v. McDiarmid, 484
McElreath v. McElreath, 781
McFarland v. McFarland, 236
McGuire v. McGuire, 33, 63, 67, 68, 73, 81, 98, 139, 503
McKim v. McKim, 321
McKinney v. State, 961
McLaughlin v. Florida, 670
McLaughlin v. Pernsley, 974
McLaughlin v. Strickland, 951
McNabb ex rel. Foshee v. McNabb, 819
Mead v. Batchlor, 593
Medill, David, In re Marriage of, 814
Medlin v. Medlin, 158
Meredith v. Meredith, 826
Merenoff v. Merenoff, 140
Meyers v. Handlon, 352, 353
Meyer v. Nebraska, 177, 180
Micaletti, In re, 523
Michael H. v. Gerald D., 990, 991
Michael J. Michael J., 971
Michael M. v. Superior Court of Sonoma County, 95
Michaud v. Wawruck, 954
Michelson v. Michelson, 398
Miller v. Miller, 541, 827
Milne v. Milne, 541
Minnesota v. French, 24
Miron v. Trudel, 280
Mississippi Band of Choctaw Indians v. Holyfield, 962, 969
Mitchell, In re Marriage of, 315
Mitchell v. Mitchell
Mitchell v. WT Grant, 133
M.J. v. J.T., 214

M.L.K., Matter of Interest of, 808
M.M., In re, 954
Modnick, In re Marriage of, 760
Moe, Matter of, 170
Moge v. Moge, 448, 449
Moll v. Moll, 481
Moncrief's Will, Matter of, 158
Montenegro v. Diaz, 720
Moore v. City of East Cleveland, 20
Moore v. Jacobsen, 559
Moore v. Moore, 581
Moran v. Moran, 476
Moretti v. Moretti, 484
Morgan, In re, 970
Morgan v. Foretich, 695, 698, 699
Morgan v. Morgan, 450
Morone v. Morone, 252
Morrison v. Sadler, 210
Mortimore v. Wright, 501
Moss v. Superior Court, 582, 589
Mozes v. Mozes, 830
Mpirilis v. Hellenic Lines, Ltd., 164
M.S.B., Matter of Interest of, 808
Mullane v. Central Hanover Trust Co., 783
Murdoch v. Murdoch, 40, 259
Murphy, Ex parte, 766

Nail v. Nail, 489
Nash, In re A Marriage License for, 214
Nash v. Mulle, 524
Nehra v. Uhlar, 688
Nemeth v. Nemeth, 304
Newburgh v. Arrigo, 541
Nicholson v. Nicholson, 109
Nielson v. Thompson, 307
Niles v. Niles, 669
N, In re Adoption of, 955
Nixon v. Perry, 504
Norman v. Thomson, 251
Norman v. Unemployment Insurance Appeals
  Board, 17
North Ottowa Community Hospital v. Kieft, 88
Novak v. Novak, 659
Nova Scotia v. Walsh, 281
Nugent v. Nugent, 559
Nuzman, State v., 589

Oakley, State v., 591
O'Brien v. O'Brien (489 N.E.2d 712), 495, 497
O'Brien v. O'Brien (508 S.E.2nd 300), 412, 418,
  419
O'Brien v. O'Brien (623 N.E.2d 485), 757
Office of Child Support v. Sholan, 800
Oliver v. Doga, 354
Olson v. Olson, 813
Open Door Alcoholism Program, Inc. v. Board
  of Adjustment of New Brunswick, 28
Oregon Health Sciences University v. Tanner, 18
Orr v. Orr, 94, 388, 431
Ortiz and Ortiz (310 Or. 644, 801 P.2d 767
  [1990]), 717

Osicka, In re Estate of, 422
Osier v. Osier, 678
Otahuhu Family Court, Attorney-General v.,
  215
Owan v. Owan, 684
Owensby v. Lepper, 692
Owens v. Owens, 301

Pacelli v. Pacelli, 107, 112
Padgett v. James, Steuben County Dept. Soc.
  Serv. ex rel., 572
Painter v. Bannister, 623, 720
Painter v. Painter, 422
Palmore v. Sidoti, 669, 974
Parton v. Parton, 1006
Patetta v. Patetta, 540
Patterson v. New York, 587
Paxton v. Paxton, 540
Pearson v. Pearson, 524
Peerenboom v. Peerenboom, 484, 524
Pendleton & Fireman, In re Marriage of, 748
Penhallow v. Penhallow, 746
Pennington, In re Marriage of, 263
Pennoyer v. Neff, 783
People in Interest of _____. *See* name of
  party
People v. _____. *See* name of party
Pereira v. Pereira, 420, 421
Periquet-Febres v. Febres, 650
Persad v. Balram, 157
Personnel Administrator v. Feeney, 121
Peterson v. Peterson, 519, 522, 523, 526, 557,
  559, 560, 561, 563
Petrowsky v. Krause, 132
Pezas v. Pezas, 82
P.H.B.S., A.W.L.S., & M.G.S., In the Interest
  of, 812
P.H.B.S., In the Interest of, 813
Philipp v. Stahl (781 A.2d 1065), 789
Philipp v. Stahl (798 A.2d 83), 796, 797
Pickens v. Pickens, 264
Pierce v. Society of Sisters, 180
Pierson, In the Matter of the Marriage of, 402,
  405, 406, 407, 408
Pilati v. Pilati, 760
Pimm v. Pimm, 553
Piscopo v. Piscopo, 492
Planned Parenthood of Southeastern Pa. v.
  Casey, 208
Plyler v. Doe, 182
Poe v. Seaborn, 603
Pohlmann v. Pohlmann, 573
Polette and Polette, 451
Pollock v. Pollock, 709
Pontbriand v. Pontbriand, 556
Poore v. Poore, 481, 482
Posey v. Bunney, 721
Posik v. Layton, 252
Posner v. Posner, 732
Postema v. Postema, 497
Potter v. Murray City, 184
Powell v. Powell, 158, 483

Prahinski v. Prahinski, 484
Presbyterian Medical Center v. Budd, 548
Priscilla S. v. Albert B., 816
Pundt, In re Marriage of, 652
Pusey v. Pusey, 639

Quinn, In re Adoption of, 971

Ramos, In re Marriage of, 592
Randall, 545, 547, 548
Randolph v. Randolph, 739, 740
Rann v. Rann, 574
Rathwell v. Rathwell, 42
Realty Assocs. V. Pittman, 16
Roccamonte, In the Matter of the Estate of, 253, 266
Roccamonte II, 255
Roe v. Roe, 667
Rosson, In re Marriage of, 705
Rea v. Rea, 308
Reed v. Reed, 90, 91, 94, 115
Regina v. Gould, 191
Regina v. Tolson, 190
Rehak v. Mathis, 252
Renaud v. Renaud, 574, 687, 691, 694
Reynolds v. Reynolds, 173
Reynolds v. United States, 184, 185, 186, 187, 189, 190
Richardson v. Stuesser, 87
Richmond v. Richmond, 484
Riffle, In re Adoption of, 971
Riggs v. Riggs, 541
Riley v. Riley, 313
Rimkus v. Rimkus, 523
R.M.G., Petition of, 974
R.N.J., Contra State in Interst of, 822
Robinson and Thiel, In re Marriage of, 354
Rock v. Rock, 401
Rockwell v. Rockwell, 766
Rodrigue v. Rodrigue, 60
Roe v. Catholic Charities of the Springfield Diocese, 961
Roe v. Doe, 541
Roe v. Wade, 180, 182
Rolle v. Rolle
Romer v. Evans, 200, 209, 226
Root v. Root, 484
Rosengarten v. Downes, 278
Rosenstiel v. Rosenstiel, 777
Rothman v. Rothman, 401
Roth v. Roth, 484
Rotsker v. Goldberg, 97
Roush v. Director for the Division of Employment Security, 574
R.R. v. M.H., 1002
Ruble v. Ruble, 817
Russenberger v. Russenberger, 708, 709
Russo v. Russo, 781
Rutgers Council of AAUP Chapters v. Rutgers University, 17
Ruth v. Ruth, 812, 814

Ryan v. Ryan, 469
Rye v. Weasel, 970

Saenz v. Roe, 706
Salucco v. Alldredge, 278
Salzman v. Bachrach, 258
S.A.M., In the Interest of, 970
Sampsell v. Superior Court, 801
Sams v. Sams, 1005
Sanders v. Sanders, 728
Santa Barbara, City of, v. Adamson, 30
Santos Y., In re, 970
Sara P. v. Richard T., 709
S.A. v. E.J.P., 970
S.A.V. v. K.G.V., 140
Sawada v. Endo, 45, 46
Schaefer v. City & County of Denver, 279
Schaeffer v. Schaeffer, 174
Schaheen v. Schaheen, 592
Scheiner v. Scheiner, 722
Schibi v. Schibi, 161, 162
Schichtl v. Schichtl, 388
Schieber v. City of Philadelphia, 122
Schlesinger v. Ballard, 88, 90
Schlick v. Schlick, 697
Schober v. Schober, 469
Schriner, In re marriage of, 422
Schwartz v. Merchants Mortgage Co., 759
Schwegmann v. Schwegmann, 252
Schweiker v. Gray Panthers, 84
Scoffield, In re Marriage of, 429
S.E.G., Matter of Custody of, 971
Seiber v. Seiber, 562
Self v. Self, 451
Selzer, In re Marriage of, 705
Sentner v. Sentner, 555
Septuagenarian v. Septuagenarian, 83
Sexton v. Sexton, 355
Shaffer v. Heitner, 781, 783
Shanks v. Kilgore, 353
Shank v. Shank, 574
Shapiro v. Thompson, 182, 706
Sharon H., State v., 191, 194
Sharpe Furniture, Inc. v. Buckstaff, 77, 81
Shelley v. Westbrooke, 673
Shelton v. Springett, 501
Sherrer v. Sherrer, 774, 776
Shirk v. Shirk, 366
Shockley v. Foraker, In re Real Estate of, 259
Short v. Short, 572
Shuraleff v. Donnelly, 264
S.H. v. Calhoun Ct. Dept. of Human Resources, 970
Sifers v. Sifers, 553
Silbaugh v. Silbaugh, 708, 709
Silverman v. Silverman, 826, 830
Simeone v. Simeone, 728, 732, 742, 743, 746, 753
Simmons v. Bull, 504
Simmons v, Simmons, 450
Simons v. Miami Beach First National Bank, 780

Simons v. Simons, 721, 722
Simpson Garment Co. v. Schultz, 79
Simpson v. Simpson (172 A.2d 168 [Pa. 1961]), 259
Simpson v. Simpson (716 S.W.2d 27), 297, 303, 305
Sinaiko v. Sinaiko, 355
Singer, In re Adoption of, 950
Singley v. Singley, 483
Sistare v. Sistare, 788
Skinner v. Oklahoma ex rel. Williamson, 170, 177, 182, 591
Slagenweit v. Slagenweit, 826
Slattery v. City of New York, 279
Smiley, In re (330 N.E.2d 53, 56), 319
Smiley, In re Marriage of (518 N.W.2d 376, 380 [Iowa 1994]), 652
Smith and Smith (606 P.2d 694), 541
Smith, In re, 523
Smith, In re Marriage of (86 Ill. 2d 518), 415
Smith, In re Marriage of (396 N.E.2d 859), 553
Smith v Abbott, State ex rel.(418 S.E.2d575), 954
Smith v. Fair Employment and Housing Commission, 24
Smith v. Immigration and Naturalization Service, 164
Smith v. Lewis, 460
Smith v. Ross, 119
Smith v. Smith (371 A.2d 1), 422
Smith v. Smith (419 A.2d 1035), 553
Smith v. Smith (447 N.W.2d 715), 541
Smith v. Smith (709 S.W.2d 588), 483
Snyder v. Snyder, 575
Sobieski v. Maresco, 353
S.O., *In re Petition of*, 947
Solomon v. Findley, 757
Sommers v. Sommers, 481
Sonnicksen, Estate of, 100, 101, 102
Sorensen, People v., 981
Sorensen v. Sorensen, 484, 489
Southers v. Southers, 761
Souza v. Superior Court, 821
Spearman v. Spearman, 241
Spears v. Spears, 244
Spilovoy v. Spilovoy, 575
Spivey v. Schneider, 574
Srock v. Srock, 429
S.S., In re Adoption of, 971
Stacy v. Stacy, 666
Stallings v. Stallings, 422
Standhardt v. Superior Court ex rel. County of Maricopa, 209
Stanley v. Illinois, 685, 950
Stanton v. Stanton, 91, 94
Stapleton v. Dauphin County Child Care Service, 1008
State in Interest of _____. *See* name of party
State v. _____. *See* name of party
Stern v. Stern, 493
Stevenson v. Stevenson, 302
Stiver v. Parker, 1000
Stoneman v. Drollinger, 818

Stone v. Stidham, 592
Strnad v. Strnad, 981
Stromsted, Estate of, 82
Stuart v. Board of Supervisors of Elections, 175
Stufft, In re Marriage of, 481
Suggs v. Norris, 252
Sullivan, In re, 523
Surratt v. Surratt, 472
Sweeney v. Sweeney, 779
Swoap v. Superior Court, 544, *545*
Sylvester v. Sylvester, *616*, 618

Tacchi v. Tacchi, 174
Tahan v. Duquette, 828
Tankersley v. Tankersley, 488
Tapley v. Tapley, 252
Tatum v. Tatum, 241
Taylor (Mitten) v. Taylor, 722
Taylor v. Taylor (110 S.W.3d 731), 661, 666, 669, 671
Taylor v. Taylor (222 Neb. 721), 484
Taylor v. Taylor (345 Ark.), 665
Taylor v. Taylor (508 A.2d 964), 644, 649, 650
Taylor v. Taylor (508 S.E.2d 50), 354
T.B. v. L.R.M., 1006
Tedford v. Dempsey, 574
Termination of Parental Rights over M.C.S., In re, 822
Thies v. MacDonald, 575
Thomas J.R., In re Termination of Parental Rights to, 808
Thomasian v. Thomasian, 469
Thompson v. Thompson, 484, 836
Thornton, In re Estate of, 259
Thronson v. Thronson, 650
Todd, Ex parte, 583, 584
Tomashefski v. Tomashefski, 318
Topel, Matter of Adoption of, 951
Toren v. Toren, 827
Torres v. Mason, State ex rel., 821
Tortorich v. Tortorich, 484
Township of Pemberton v. State, 28
Township of Washington v. Central Bergen Community Mental Health Center, Inc., 28
Travis v. Travis, 484
Travitsky v. Travitsky, Commonwealth ex rel., 574
T.R.M., Matter of Adoption of, 970
Trombley, In re, 586, 587
Tropea v. Tropea, 708, 709, 721
Troxel v. Granville, 200, 623, 631, 684, 1009
Trueman, In re, 808
T.S., Matter of, 970
Tukker M.L., IN re Paternity of, 524
Turner v. Turner, 440, 450, 451, 523
Tyma v. Montgomery County, 279

United Mine Workers of America v. Bagwell, 592, 593
United States v. Bigford, 591
United States v. Craft, 46

United States v. Davis, 605
United States v. Grigsby, 591
United States v. Hodge & Zweig, 714
United States v. Klinzing, 591
United States v. Lopez, 136
United States v. Morrison, 136
United States v. Throckmorton, 759
United States v. Virginia, 97
University of Alaska v. Tumeo, 18
Ulrich v. State, 82

V.A.E. v. D.A.E., 666
Van Camp v. Van Camp, 420, 421
Vanderbilt v. Vanderbilt, 779, 780
Van Dyke v. Thompson, 574
Van Voorhis v. Brintnall, 219
Vasquez v. Hawthorne, 264
Vaughn, Custody of, 683
Verna v. Verna, 540
Viera v. Viera, 354
Village of Arlington Heights v. Metropolitan
    Housing Development Corp., 120
Village of Belle Terre v. Boraas, 20, 28
Vincent v. State of California, 100
Viragh v. Foldes, 827
Vogel, People v., 191
Voishan v. Palma, 523
Von Tersch v. Von Tersch, 658
Voyles v. Voyles, 558

W.A., State ex rel., 808
Waite v. Waite, 316
Wall, In re Marriage of, 721
Walsh v. Walsh, 829
Walters, In re Marriage of, 590
Walton, In re Adoption of, 953
Walz v. Commissioner, 606
Wang, Marriage of, 692
Warfield v. Warfield, 1004
Warner and Ryan v. Heiden, 78
Warner, In re, 617
Warrender v. Warrender, 777
Warren, People v., 699
Washington v. Davis, 119
Waterworth, In re, 484
Watkins v. Watkins, 780
Watts v. Watts, 252
Watt v. Watt, 706
Wayno v. Wayno, 380
Weesner v. Weesner, 781
Weinberger v. Wiesenfeld, 80, 92
Weinschel v. Strople, 954
Weinstein v. Barnett, 355
Weishaus v. Weishaus, 560

Welby v. Welby, 717, 718
Welch, In re Marriage of, 429
Wendt v. Wendt, 469
Western States Construction, Inc. v. Michoff,
    264
Westinghouse Electric Corp. v. Gulf Oil Corp.,
    351
West v. West, 658
Whalen v. Allers, 980
Whetmore v. Fratello, 954
White v. White, 408, 708
Wiand v. Wiand, 497
Wilcox v. Trautz, 259
Wilder v. Bernstein, 979
Wilkins v. Zelichowski, 222
Williams, In re, 808
Williams I, See Williams v. North Carolina
    (317 U.S. 287)
Williams II, See Williams v. North Carolina
    (325 U.S. 226)
Williams v. Lynch, 259
Williams v. North Carolina (317 U.S. 287),
    342, 773, 774, 778, 780
Williams v. North Carolina (325 U.S. 226),
    342, 773, 774, 778, 780
Williams v. Williams, 245
Winegard, In re Marriage of, 233
Wisconsin Potowatomies of Hannahville Indian
    Community v. Houston, 946
Wisconsin v. Yoder, 185, 676
Wisner v. Wisner, 481
Wolfe v. Wolfe, 171
Woodall v. Woodall, 639
Wood v. Wood, 523
Woronzoff-Daschkoff v. Woronzoff-Daschkoff,
    174
Worthley v. Worthley, 788
Wrenn v. Lewis, 556
Wren v. Commissioner, 606
Wright v. State, 128
Wylie v. Wylie, 523

Yankoskie v. Lenker, 132
Yarbrough v. Celebrezze, 244
Yelin v. Yelin, 174
Yoon v. Yoon, 484
Young v. Alongi, 952
Ysla v. Lopez, 650

Zablocki v. Redhail, 176, 183, 184, 189, 190,
    194, 198, 218, 591, 592
Ziegler v. Ziegler, 706
Zockert v. Fanning, 952
Zuker v. Andrews, 827

Index

Abandonment, 302
Abortion and families, 140-149
Adoption
    abrogating, 961
    agencies and, 957, 958
    agency functions, 958
    agency versus independent, 958-961
    childless couples and, 945
    costs of, 958
    demographics, modern, 946
    English common law and, 944
    first comprehensive adoption statue in U.S.,
        944
    goal of, 959
    grounds for dispensing with parental consent,
        953
    history of, in U.S., 943-946
    homosexuality and, 941
    international, 972, 974-978, 979
    jurisdiction for, 820-822
    modern process, 946
    Native Americans and, 946n6, 969-972
    open adoption and open records, 953-955
    parental consent to, 952-953
    payments and, 958
    private, 957-958
    race and religion and, 961-962
    recognition of second-parent, 941
    religious matching in, 979-980
    Roman law and, 944
    second-parent defined, 927n10
    secrecy and sealing of records of,
        944-945
    special-needs children and, 960-961
    states requiring agency adoptions, 957
    studies of open, 955
    transracial placement, 972-973, 975-976
    trend toward open records, 955-956
    visits by biological parents, 954-955
Adultery and divorce, 301

ALI Principles of the Law of Family
        Dissolution, 264-266, 408, 421, 422,
        451-452, 453-455, 489, 497, 511-514,
        549, 560, 572, 640-642, 655-656, 686,
        711, 720-721, 749-752, 756, 766, 920
Alimony, 431. See also Spousal support
    earning capacities and, 437-438
    history of, 430-432
    and post-divorce conditions, 438-439
    rare issues and, 458-459
    social and psychological effects of, 432-433
    societal interest in, 397-398
    theory of, 437
Alternative reproductive technologies
    artificial insemination, 981-984
    surrogate motherhood and, 984, 995-997,
        1008-1009
    Uniform Parentage Act (2002), 981-982
    in vitro fertilization, 983-984
Annulment, 173, 287
Arbitration and divorce, 374-376
Artificial insemination, 981-984

Bankruptcy
    bad faith, 614
    and children, 611-612
    and defeating claims of former spouse,
        614-616
    and divorce decrees, 612
    and support payments, 616, 618-619
Bigamy, 190-191

Child abduction, 822
Child abuse, false charges of, 692-693
Child custody, 366
    alienation issues and, 691
    ALI principles, 640-641
    basis for order modification, 720-721

Child custody (continued)
  best interests judgments, 632
  child's visitation preferences, 698
  constitution of a custody order, 719-720
  custodial relocation, 706-711
  denial of visitation, 694-698
  dispute resolution and, 693-694
  disqualifying conduct and, 623
  domestic violence issues and, 684, 829-830
  expert witnesses and, 632
  gender conflicts and, 694
  gender issues and, 639-640
  habitual residence and international
      enforcement of, 826-827
  impact of divorce on, 632-634
  in nineteenth century, 621-622
  interference with visitation, 698-699
  international enforcement of, 822
  interstate enforcement and modification
      jurisdiction, 809-810
  joint. See Joint custody
  judging parental fitness, 660-661
  jurisdiction and, 801
  jurisdiction for domestic violence cases, 818
  jurisdiction issues, 807-809
  legal representation for children and, 679
  limits of movement of parents, 828
  mediation and, 379-380
  modification of orders, 719-722
  ne exeat clause, 828
  noncustodial fathers and contact with their
      children, 710-711
  nonparents and, 631-632
  parental extramarital activity and, 665-669
  parental homosexuality and, 668-669
  parental rights (nineteenth century), 622
  parenting plans and, 656
  presumptions favoring parents, 631
  primary caretaker issues, 641-642
  primary caretaker preference, 639, 640
  social expectations and, 639
  social workers and mediators and, 384-385
  split physical custody, 652-653
  spousal abuse and, 681-684
  racial and ethnic issues, 671-672
  religion and, 672
  religion and health care choices, 678-679
  religious issues in, 676-679
  relocation of custodial parent, 721-722
  remarriage of custodial parent, 721
  transition to best interests standard, 622-623
  wishes of the child and, 679
  wrongfully removed or retained children,
      828
Children
  adult disabled, 541
  citizenship rights of, 887-888
  custodial rights of unmarried fathers,
      877-878
  custody of. See Child custody
  and divorce, 330-332, 344-345
  divorce and welfare of children, 335-339
  inheritance rights of nonmarital, 876-877
  judging parental fitness, 660-661
  jurisdiction for adoption, 820-822
  and legal definition of family, 839-841
  legal determination of paternity, 861-864
  naming of, 175-176
  parenthood and emotional needs of, 864-865
  parents' legal duties to, 501-504
  rights of illegitimate, 850-851
  rights of unmarried fathers, 885-888
  social security benefits for, 875-876
  support for. See Child support
  support rights, 868-869
  transracial placement, 978
Child support
  ability to pay and, 589
  access to child and, 590
  for adult disabled children, 541
  ALI principles for, 511-514
  arrears in, 697-600
  challenges to prevailing, 511
  changes of circumstances and, 549-551
  childhood poverty, 600
  children's medical expenses and, 524-525
  child support assurance, 600-602
  compliance with, 578-581
  constitutional challenges to guidelines, 518
  the cost-shares approach, 514-516
  court decisions and college costs, 539-541
  criminal contempt proceedings and, 592-593
  criminal nonsupport statutes and, 591
  death of obligor and, 549-550
  Delaware Melson Formula, 508
  economic units concept and, 578-579
  effectiveness of state-federal enforcement,
      596-600
  enforcement of, 578-582
  equal living standards (ELS) model, 577-578
  expedited processes, 595
  federal intent for, 515-516
  First Family First, 572
  foreseeable changes in circumstances and,
      550-551
  formula appreciation, 517
  goals for, 512-513
  goods and services in lieu of money, 590-591
  health insurance and, 525
  higher education costs and, 537-539
  high income cases, 523-524
  impact of guidelines, 510-511
  incarcerated parents and, 532
  and income of new spouse, 574-575
  income shares formula, 508
  interests of nonresidential parent, 513-514
  interests of the child, 512-513
  international enforcement, 779-801
  interstate modification and enforcement of
      support, 787-789
  issues in applying formulas for, 522-525
  jailing "deadbeat" parents, 582
  locating parents, 596
  loss of employment and, 589-590
  marginal expenditures model, 512
  new families and, 566

nonresidential parent expenditures, 526-528
obligations of low-income parents, 532-533
obligator, income reductions and, 554-556
and obligators marital standard of living, 514
older children and, 533-534
other enforcement devices, 596
postmajority support, 540, 541
prevailing model, 504-505
private enforcement mechanisms, 581
public assistance payments and, 576-577
resistance to paying, 518
Second Family First, 572
setting levels of, 505-508
state-federal enforcement program, 594-600
and subsequent children and stepchildren,
    571-575
voluntary versus involuntary decreases in the
    payor's income and, 551
wage withholding, 595-596
Wisconsin formula, 509-510
Child Support Enforcement Amendments of
    1984, 899
Civil unions
    dissolution of, interstate recognition,
        277-278
    and domestic partnerships, 269-276
Cohabitation
    Australia and New Zealand, 281
    and business relationships, 259-260
    in Canada, 280-281
    children and, 840
    civil unions and domestic partnerships,
        269-276
    common law marriage, 231-233
    domestic partners, 264, 265-266
    economic factors and, 247, 248, 249
    employee benefits and, 279
    enforceable contracts and, 252-253
    family formation and, 248-249
    fiduciary duties and, 259
    legal, recovery following termination,
        258-259
    meretricious relationships and, 263-264
    motivations for, 230-231
    racial and ethnic differences and, 247-248
    rates, 229-230, 246
    recognition of, 246
    same-sex couples and, 247, 248
    South America, 283
    stability of relationships and, 246
    types of, 230
    United Kingdom, 281
    views of, 247-248
    Western Europe, 282-283
Cohabitation without marriage
    arguments about institutionalizing, 4-6
    increase of, 3-4
    mutual property rights and, 11-13
Co-housing groups, 23-24
Collaborative lawyering, 373
Collusion
    and no-fault divorce, 321
    and traditional divorce, 304

Common law marriage
    choice-of-law rule and, 239
    elements of, 237
    history of, 232-233
    previous marriage(s) and, 237-238
    religion and, 232
    under Utah law, 238-239
    versus ceremonial marriage, 239
Common law, property ownership for married
    couples, 44
Common law tradition, marital property under,
    35-39
Communes
    co-housing groups, 23
    contemporary, 23-24
    history of, 23
Community property
    approach under, 47-48
    equalization of authority over, 49
    and gifts of marital property, 50-51
    management power, 49
    Married Women's Property Acts and, 48-49
    Roman-Dutch, 48
    Spanish law, 48n6
    and wealth not earned during the marriage,
        48
Condonation, 303-304
Connivance, 303
Consanguinity statutes, 192-194
Contracts for gestational surrogacy, 984,
    1008-1009
Copyright Act of 1976, 60
Covenant marriage, 332-335
    children and, 343-344
    first states to adopt, 340
    goals of, 341-342
    liberalism and, 343
    problems with, 342-343
    provisions of statutes, 341-343
    religion and, 343
Cruelty and divorce, 301-302
Custodial rights of unmarried fathers,
    877-878
Custody of children. *See* Child custody

Defense of Marriage Act (DOMA), 223
Desertion, 302
Divorce
    abandonment and, 302
    access to council for, 318-319
    access to the court for, 318-319
    the adoption of no-fault, 309-311
    adultery as grounds for, 301
    alimony and, 397-398
    alternative dispute resolution and, 368
    arbitration and, 374-376
    attorney fees and, 352-355
    changing trends in, 288
    children and, 307, 330-332, 335-339,
        344-345
    children's rights and, 332
    collaborative lawyering and, 373-374

Divorce *(continued)*
collusion and, 304-305
collusion under no-fault, 321
condonation, 303-304
connivance and, 303
"cooling off" periods, 308
court congestion and, 366-367
cruelty as grounds for, 301
demographics, 324
desertion and, 302
dividing marital status and property issues,
778-779
economic consequences for women and
children, 394-395
economic orders and no-fault, 389-396
equitable estoppel and, 777
evaluation, 323-329
ex parte and jurisdiction, 780
fault system, 293-294
grounds and defenses, traditional, 293-294
grounds for, 311-312
history of, 287-288
history of economic awards, 388-389
impotence and, 303
insanity and, 303
interlocutory orders, 308
interstate recognition of, 776
jurisdiction and, 770-774
jurisdiction principles, 770-771
lawyer-client relations and, 356-357
lawyers and, 345, 349-352
legal counseling, 358-359
legal representation for children and, 679
legal strategy and, 359-363
Mexican mail-order, 776
negotiation and, 368-374
in nineteenth century, 293
no-fault and rates of, 327-328
poverty and, 394
procedure (nineteenth century), 306-307
proctors and, 305
proof of grounds of, 314-315
property division, 398-402
the public and, 307-308
rate of, 327-328
recent availability of, 288
recognition of foreign, 776-777
recrimination and, 304
reform of, 290-291
religion and, 288-289
rights of states and, 780-781
serial marriage and, 396-397
societal role of, 292
spousal abuse and child custody, 681-684
summary dissolution, 322-323
theory of, 303
third parties and, 307-308
tort suits and, 411
traditional, 293-294
truthfulness in negotiation during,
371-373
Divorce proctors, 305
DNA testing, paternity and, 908-910

Domestic partners
defining, 264, 265
flaw in concept, 265-266
social effects, 266
Domestic partnerships
and civil unions, 269-276
local registration ordinances, 278-279
models, 276-277
Domestic relations, federal court jurisdiction
over, 831, 834-836
Domestic violence
battered women, 126-127
battery, 117-118
child custody and, 681-686
the constitution and, 122
criminal prosecution and, 131-132
criminal sanctions and, 128
cultures and, 124
enforcing protective orders, 134-135
federal legislation and, 136-137
gender differences and, 126
history of reform against, 123-124
legal and social issues, 113-114
Minneapolis Domestic Violence experiment,
128-129
National Family Violence Survey (NFVS),
124-126
police response to, 118-119
protective orders, 132-135
rape, 117
responses to arrests for, 129-131
same-sex co-residents, 132
societal responses to, 124
by women against men, 128
Dower rights and ex parte divorce, 780-781

Employee Retirement Income Security Act of
1974 (ERISA), 53, 58, 466
anti-alienation provision of, 61-62
benefit plans covered by, 62
divorce and beneficiaries of pension plans, 61
state laws and, 61
Employment benefits plans
domestic partners and, 279
same-sex partners and, 279
Enoch Arden statutes, 191
Equal management system, 50
Estoppel principles and support duties, 919-
920

Family. *See also* Family unit
assumption about roles in, 85
autonomy, 33, 70
cohabitation and, 3-6, 248-249
as a community, 71-74
contracts within. *See* Family contracts
and current state of marriage, 324-327
defining, 3, 839-841
defining stepfamily, 926
and divorce, 330-332
divorce reform and, 290

dual paternity, 866
ecology of, 438-439
enforcement of spousal agreements,
    104-106
extended care systems and, 10
federal court jurisdiction over, 834-836
financial support for single-parent, 340
genetic basis for incest restrictions, 193
history of response to violence in,
    123-124
history of women in, 74-76
income and authority in, 75-76
increase of cohabitation, 290
issues in defining, 17-18
legal recognition of functional, 911-914
liability of spouses, 82-85
marriage and, 6-7
medical decision making within, 149-153
minorities and, 10
morals and the law and, 290-293
multiple parenthood, 866-867
nonmarital, 230
notion of family privacy, 68
principal of family autonomy, 68-69
privacy and, 33
reproductive choice within, 140-149
rights of unwed fathers, 863
single-parent, 331, 339, 344-345
social basis for incest restrictions, 193-194
social history of, 68
society and, 9
spouse support issues, 82-85
stepparents, 911-914
support for adult, 542-543
as a system, 71, 73-74
taxation after divorce, 605-610
taxation of ongoing, 602-604
as a unit, 70-71
unmarried fathers, 867-869
value of caregiving in, 458
violence between spouses, 113-114
zoning ordinances and definition of, 22-25
Family contracts defined, 725
Family law
    expressive function of, 328
    forces shaping, 292
    morals and, 291-293
    in nineteenth century, 292-293
Family unit
    autonomy and, 33
    function as, 70, 71
    idea of, 32-33
    privacy and, 33
    roots of concept, 31-32
    and the state, 33
Federal Consumer Credit Protection Act,
    596
Federal Gun Control Act of 1994, 136
Foster care
    religious matching in, 979-980
    transracial placement and, 978
Full Faith and Credit for Child Support Orders
    Act (FFCCSOA), 788

Gestational surrogacy, 984, 1008-1009
Grandparents, rights of, 849

Hague Convention on the Civil Aspects of
    International Child Abduction, 822
Health care power of attorney, 153
Homosexuality and adoption, 941

Immigration and Nationality Act, 887
Impotence and divorce, 303
Insanity, 303
Interspousal tort immunity, 139-140
In vitro fertilization, 983-984

Joint custody, 643
    early use of, 650-651
    growing use of, 649-650
    history of, 648-649
    parental willingness to accept, 650
    parenting plans and, 656
    physical versus legal, 651-652
    professional views on, 653-656
    split physical custody, 652-653
Joint management system, 50
Joint ownership with right of survivorship,
    44
Joint tenancy versus tenancy by the entirety,
    45
Judicial separation
    defined, 287
    history of, 287-288
Jurisdiction
    for adoption, 820-822
    child custody, 801-803, 807-809
    divorce, 770-774
    domestic violence cases and the UCCJEA,
        818
    equitable estoppel and, 777
    and ex-parte divorce, 780
    fairness and out-of-state proceedings, 786
    federal courts and domestic relations,
        834-836
    foreign divorces and, 776
    full faith and credit for support duties and,
        782-783
    international child custody cases, 830
    international support enforcement, 779-801
    and interstate enforcement and modification,
        809-810
    interstate modification and enforcement of
        support, 787-789
    interstate recognition of divorce decrees, 776
    and land, 771
    limits of movement of parents, 828
    marriage and divorce and, 769-770
    modification and changes in, 815
    ne exeat clause, 828
    real property and, 781
    rights of states and, 780-781
    societal mobility and, 777

Jurisdiction (*continued*)
    standard for determining state court, 786
    wrongfully removed or retained children,
        828

Lawyer-client privilege, 714-715
Lawyers
    Australian, 363-364
    counseling and client relations, 356-357
    divorce counseling, 358-359
    divorce practice, 364
    and divorce process, 345, 349-352
    Dutch matrimonial, 363
    family law and women, 364-365
    fees and divorce cases, 352-355
    professional conduct, 714
    and sexual relations with clients, 365-366
    strategy in divorce cases, 359-363
    withdrawing from cases, 364
Living wills, 153

Mann Act, 834
Marital commitment, changing attitudes
        toward, 337
Marital property
    "automatic redesignation" statutes, 60-61
    common law system and, 35
        death of spouse, 36
        gifts between spouses, 43
        gifts of marital property, 50-51
        modifications, 37-39
        personal property, 37
        real property, 36-37
        traditional, 35-36
        women and, 36-39
    community property, 47-49
    community property states, 35n2
    contracts by married women, 103-104
    and contribution of labor or services, 43
    copyrighted works and, 60
    debt liability, 88
    domiciles, 87
    equity versus equitable, 39n5
    home ownership, 44
    homestead statutes, 47
    joint tenancy, 44-45
    liability for necessaries, 87-88
    management of, 76-77
    management systems for, 50
    mid-marriage agreements, 111-112
    necessaries, 82
    new property, 51-53, 82
    nursing home care and, 82-85
    overview of, 34-35
    pension funds, 52-53
    separate estate in equity, 37-39
    spendthrift trust, 62
    spouse support issues, 82-85
    tax debt and, 46
    tenancy by the entirety (or entireties),
        44-46

Marital property laws, equality issues and,
        395-396
Marital unity
    influence of, 32-33
    myth of, 32
Marriage
    age issues and, 216-218
    annulment and, 173-174
    ban against polygamy, 186-191
    bigamy, 190-191
    capacity to agree, 165-171
    ceremonies, 157
    changes in rules about, 871
    changing attitudes toward, 337
    children and divorce, 330-332
    children of invalid, 158
    cohabitation and, 247
    cohabitation rates, 229-230
    cohabitation types, 230
    common law versus ceremonial, 239
    and community, 7-8
    conflict of laws regarding, 218-226
    constitutional framework for, 176-184
    content of the agreement, 158-165
    covenant, 332-335
    decision making within, 67-68
    declining importance of, 289-290
    defining broken, 315-316
    federal court jurisdiction over, 834-836
    fraud and duress and, 171-176
    fraudulent claims of, 164
    fundamental liberties and, 182
    genetic basis for incest restrictions, 193
    and government, 8-9
    interspousal tort immunity, 139-140
    jurisdiction, 769-770
    legal alternatives to marriage, 246-249
    limited purposes, 162-163
    medical decision making within, 149-153
    medical examinations and, 156-157
    mental retardation and, 168-171
    monogamy, 184-191
    mutual consent and, 163
    myth of marital unity, 32-33
    names and, 175-176
    non-marital families, 230
    parental presumption, 863-864
    parenthood and, 850-851
    presumptions about, 243-245
    presumptions of, 232-233
    price of devaluing, 9
    putative spouses, 244-245
    quality of, 324-327
    recognition of same sex marriage, 225-226
    reform of (late 19th century), 233
    relationship restrictions, 191-195
    religion and plural marriage, 186-191
    reproductive choice within, 140-149
    requirements for, 155, 156-157
    same sex couples and, 206-215
    serial monogamy, 190
    social basis for incest restrictions, 193-194
    spousal contracts during, 98-112

termination of. *See* Annulment, Divorce, Judicial separation, Separation
traditional view of fraud and, 173-174
transsexual, 214-215
Uniform Marriage and Divorce Act, 156-157
used as conspiracy to defraud, 161
validity of, 155-156
validity of limited purposes, 163-164
"void" and "voidable," 157-158
Marriage Fraud Amendments of 1986, 164
Married Women's Property Acts, 32, 38-39, 48-49
Mediation
mandatory, 380
questions about, 382-384
standards of professional conduct for, 380-382
women's views of, 384
Medical decisions within families, 149-153
Mental retardation and marriage, 168-171
Meretricious relationships, property distribution and, 236-264
Mid-marriage agreements, 111-112
Minneapolis Domestic Violence experiment, 128-129
Multiethnic Placement Act of 1994 (amended 1996), 974

National Family Violence Survey (NFVS), 124-126
Native Americans and adoption issues, 946n6, 969-972
Necessaries, 82
New property, 51, 82
defined, 459-460, 461-462
and divorce settlements, 460
in marriage, 34
valuing streams of payments, 460-461
No-fault divorce
economic consequences, 394-395
impact on women and children, 390-394
property division under, 389-390
social response to, 338

Office of Child Support Enforcement, 595

Parallel Unilateral Policy Declarations, 799
Parent-child relationship, terminating first, 946-947
Parenthood
alternative reproductive technologies and, 981-984
de facto, 920-921
functional, 911
involuntary, 868
legal determination of paternity, 861-864
legal issues surrounding, 839-841
marriage and, 850-851
and men's claims of infertility, 870-871
parent by estoppel principle, 920

personal rights and, 870
possibility of multiple, 866-867
supporting children, 868-869
Parents
constitutional rights of, 841, 848-849
judging fitness of, 660-661
legal duty to support their children, 501-504
rights of, 926
Parents, support for
asset transfers and, 548
irrevocable trusts and, 547, 548
Medicaid eligibility issues and, 548
reciprocity concept and, 547
special needs trusts, 548
state interest and, 545
trends, 542
voluntary relationship issue, 545
Paternity
blood test evidence and, 907-910
custodial rights of unmarried fathers, 877-878
establishing, 899-900
expert testimony regarding, 907
federal law and, 899-900
genetic tests and, 908-910
legal determination of, 861-864
legal finding of, 909-910
rights of unmarried fathers, 885-888, 898
rules for acknowledgment of, 909-910
unmarried fathers, 867-869
varying laws regarding unwed fathers, 897-898
voluntary acknowledgments of, 910
Pensions and retirement plans
assets in, 52-53
civil service, 472
military retirement benefits, 471-472
social Security and other federal plans, 470-471, 472-473
valuing, 466-470, 473-474
Personal Responsibility and Work Opportunity Reconciliation Act of 1996 (PRWORA)
Polygamy, 186-191
movements to legalize, 189
serial, 190
Power of attorney, health care, 153
Property division at divorce
appreciation of separate, 420-421
businesses and professional organizations, 489-491
changes since 1985, 406-409
characterization of property, 412
choice of law issues, 424-425
date of marriage and, 422-423
debt division, 428-429
degrees and licenses and, 497-500
disability pay and, 476-477
equitable distribution, 399-400, 402
income from marital property, 421-422
marital fault and, 409-410
marital homes, 429-430

Property division at divorce *(continued)*
  need and, 409
  new property and, 459-462
  property acquired during premarital
    cohabitation, 422
  pure equitable distribution, 398-399
  qualified domestic relations orders, 474-476
  separate and marital, 419
  theories of, 405-409
  title-based distribution, 398
  transmutation and, 419-420
  valuing goodwill, 489-490
  valuing pension plans, 466-470
  when wife has greater income, 408
Putative spouses, 244-245

Qualified domestic relations orders, 474

Racial discrimination, 119-120
Reciprocal beneficiary relationships, 267-269
Recrimination, 304
Religion and polygamy, 187-188
Reproductive choice and families, 140-149
Retirement Equity Act (REACT) of 1984, 53,
  466

Same sex couples and family definitions, 17-18
Same-sex marriage, 211
  alternatives to, 267-276
  Canada and, 211-212
  cultural responses to, 277
  Europe and, 212-213
  recognition of, 225-226
  South Africa and, 213-214
  in U.S., 206-215
Second-parent adoption
  defined, 927n10
  recognition of, 941
Separation, early use of, 287
Shared parenting. *See* Joint custody
Single-parents, demographics for, 839-840
Social Security benefits and children, 875-877
Spousal abuse
  desirability of mediation and, 685
  false charges of, 692-693
Spousal support, 430, 431. *See also*
    Alimony
  ALI Family Dissolution Principles, 560
  and breach of contract approach, 453-455
  Canadian trends, 448-450
  changes of circumstances and, 549-551
  changing attitudes toward, 433-434
  children and, 457-458
  cohabitation and, 557
  death of the obligor and, 549-550
  determining the adequacy of, 560
  and employment and gender issues, 435-436
  foreseeable changes in circumstances and,
    550-551
  human capital and, 435-436

international enforcement, 779-801
interstate modification and enforcement of
    support, 787-789
  misconduct and, 453
  modifications and terminations, 562-565
  need and compensatory payments, 451-453
  obligator, income reductions and, 554-556
  public policy issues and, 455
  purpose of initial award and termination, 560
  totality-of-the-circumstances test, 560
  voluntary versus involuntary decreases in the
    payor's income and, 551
Spouses
  battery of, 117-118
  crimes between, 114-118
  rape and, 117
  violence between, 113-114
Stepparenthood, 911-914
  child support and, 919-920
  visitation orders, 926
Summary dissolution, 322
Surrogate motherhood, 984, 995-997,
    1008-1009

Taxation
  after divorce, 605-610
  child support and, 609
  exemption and other tax issues, 610
  of ongoing family, 602-604
  property division and, 605-606
  sale of residence, 607
  spousal support and, 607-609
  transfer of pensions and related assets,
    606-607
Tenancy by the entirety (or entireties),
    44-45
Transsexuals and marriage, 214, 215

Uniform Act on Blood Tests to Determine
    Paternity, 900
Uniform Adoption Act (1994), 946
Uniform Child Custody Jurisdiction Act
    (UICCJA), 802
Uniform Child Custody Jurisdiction and
    Enforcement Act (UCCJEA), 802
Uniform Health Care Decisions Act of 1994,
    153
Uniform Interstate Family Support Act
    (UIFSA), 786, 788
Uniform Marital Property Act, 51
Uniform Marriage and Divorce Act, 156-157,
    311-312, 399-401, 439-440, 550, 720
Uniform Parentage Act (1973), 982
Uniform Parentage Act (2002), 850, 888, 908,
    981-982
Uniform Probate Code (UPC), 876
United Nations Commission on the Status of
    Women, 189
Unmarried couples and housing, 24-25
Unmarried fathers. *See* Paternity
Usufructs, 54

Violence Against Women Act of 1994 (VAWA),
    136

Women
    constitutional decisions regarding role of,
        89-98
    names and marriage, 175-176

polygamy and equal rights for, 189
Working parents, empirical data
        on, 457

Zoning ordinances
    control of population with, 22-23
    definition of family and, 22-25